Oracle Press™

Oracle 24x7 Tips & Techniques

Venkat S. Devraj

Osborne/**McGraw-Hill**

Berkeley New York St. Louis
San Francisco Auckland Bogotá Hamburg London Madrid
Mexico City Milan Montreal New Delhi Panama City
Paris São Paulo Singapore Sydney Tokyo Toronto

Osborne/McGraw-Hill
2600 Tenth Street
Berkeley, California 94710
U.S.A.

For information on translations or book distributors outside the U.S.A., or to arrange bulk purchase discounts for sales promotions, premiums, or fund-raisers, please contact Osborne/**McGraw-Hill** at the above address.

Oracle 24x7 Tips & Techniques

1234567890 AGM AGM 019876543210

ISBN 0-07-211999-3

Publisher
Brandon A. Nordin

Associate Publisher and Editor-in-Chief
Scott Rogers

Acquisitions Editor
Jeremy Judson

Project Editor
Carolyn Welch

Editorial Assistant
Monika Faltiss

Technical Editor
Peter Utzig

Proofreader
Linda Medoff

Indexer
David Heiret

Computer Designers
Jani Beckwith
Gary Corrigan
Roberta Steele

Illustrators
Robert Hansen
Brian Wells
Beth Young

Series Design
Peter Hancik, Jani Beckwith

This book was composed with Corel VENTURA.

This book is for my father, S. Devrajan, my mother, Vatsala Devrajan, and my brother Shiv Devraj. "Without your ceaseless and unselfish love, guidance, sacrifices and support, I wouldn't be standing where I stand today."

Contents at a Glance

PART IV
Database Maintenance

PART V
Troubleshooting

PART VI
High Availability Solutions

PART VII
Building a Real-World Arsenal

PART VIII
New Features

Contents

PART II
Understanding Your Environment

PART III
Database Setup and Configuration

PART IV
Database Maintenance

PART V
Troubleshooting

PART VI
High Availability Solutions

PART VII
Building a Real-World Arsenal

PART VIII
New Features

Foreword

Enterprises are deploying mission critical and complex applications to fulfill business requirements. The ongoing availability of these applications to users across the organization becomes hypercritical. The Oracle database is at the heart of these applications.

The availability equation necessarily involves a number of elements, each of which must function in a symbiotic relationship: the computing platform, peripherals, network, and the database applications. Historically, customers with the aid of systems vendors have emphasized the hardware part of this equation, reasoning that without reliable system performance, application availability is impossible. Similarly, as network infrastructures have become more vital in most organizations' IT implementations, greater attention has been paid to the performance of routers, hubs, and other network-specific elements of availability. But as enterprise implementations have evolved and software applications have become ever more integrated with business processes themselves, a new emphasis has been placed on database availability.

As availability requirements are becoming more stringent, organizations are realizing that adequate attention needs to be paid to designing systems with multiple levels of redundancy – or failure masking mechanisms. Network and system uptime do not by themselves guarantee maximum application availability. Database systems are becoming an increasingly important component of the availability equation. High Availability Architects have begun to look beyond hardware and networks in their efforts to achieve reliability and seek techniques and best practices that are specific to database availability.

There are several key market drivers behind the push for maximum application availability and performance:

- **The Internet** Perhaps no single driver is more powerful than the Internet, which has thrust organizations of all sizes and in all industries into a 24 x 7, 365-day-a-year world of IT dependence. Today, with the e-commerce revolution literally changing business models overnight, customers look to Web-based servers, network devices, and applications to be constantly available. Failures related to downtime—whether occurring on a stock-trading Web site, at an Internet Service Provider (ISP), or on a consumer online service—now become the fodder for national news stories that instantly tarnish the reputation of the affected organization. Downtime on online order entry systems accessed by users around the world can become extremely visible. With tighter integration and dependencies between applications deployed across organizational and geographic boundaries, it is even more important for applications to be available.
- **Increasing integration of business processes with IT** Parallel to the impact of the Internet on availability needs is the continuing integration of business processes with IT, to the level where the process itself is virtually indistinguishable from the application that enables it. For example, the ability of organizations to store and retrieve customer information, once the thing of folders and file cabinets, is now the province of data warehousing and data mining applications that have completely transformed the entire activity. Along with this transformation has come much greater importance placed on these applications, to the level where an inferior implementation can mean the loss of competitive advantages in a particular market.
- **Globalization of markets and businesses** The other key driver behind the push to availability is the rapid globalization of businesses and organizations. Today, if the database on an intranet server located in Sydney becomes unavailable, it can affect a company's operations in London, New York, and Tokyo. This represents far greater impact from downtime than would have been the case only a few years ago, when even most multinational companies implemented applications on a local or regional basis only. Systems deployed for global communities need to be available around the clock. Normal maintenance windows are shrinking rapidly to meet a growing demand for access and reliability.

In order to provide users the option to compete in the global Internet age, Oracle has provided a highly tunable and available database engine. To help customers leverage Oracle's High Availability features and minimize risk of downtime, requires extensive planning and use of best practices. Oracle Consulting's Systems Performance Group helps customers achieve uptime targets by providing services in the areas of High Availability architecture design, System Management Procedures and HA validation. These solutions are geared to minimize the risk of scheduled and unscheduled downtime in mission critical environments.

This book arrives at a very timely juncture, when companies are beginning to realize the importance of availability. The author has presented a very comprehensive approach to managing scheduled and unscheduled downtime. The easy to read and reference "tips and techniques" format makes this a valuable reference for someone looking to deploy Oracle databases. The best practices and real-life examples have never before been compiled in a documented dedicated extensively to this subject. This book will be useful to not only all Oracle DBAs but could also be a valuable resource for System Architects and Application designers responsible for deploying applications for "no surprises" environment. Specific expert methods and techniques to realize high availability will serve as guiding principles for designing and operating any Oracle environment.

The author has done an excellent job of demonstrating that availability is something that needs extensive proactive planning and experience. DBAs looking to deploy high availability solutions can greatly benefit from the experience and tips provided in this book. Most of the information is well supported with facts and examples. When designing high availability solutions there is no tolerance data loss, and this field does not provide opportunities to make incremental improvements based on discovery and learn as you go. It has to be done right the first time around, and costs of downtime can be significant. This book serves as an excellent source for avoiding planned and unplanned outages. It does a good job of providing techniques for outage detection, notification, masking, and recovery, and will be useful to all Oracle professionals looking to achieve varying levels of availability.

This book is definitely a necessary step towards achieving 99.999 percent availability.

Ravi Balwada
Director
System Performance Group
Oracle Services

Acknowledgments

Nothing monumental can ever be attained without the support of others. This book has been monumental from my perspective, to say the very least. It took nearly a year to write and encompasses a decade of experience in the database industry. Typically, experience is judged in man-years in terms of a 40-hour workweek. However, for years at a stretch, I have had the opportunity to work roughly twice that many hours in a week. Accordingly, I can state with high confidence that this book probably summarizes much more than a decade's worth of hardcore experience. I have been very fortunate to work with some very talented people. Those long hours allowed me to soak in their experiences and foresight and avoid many mistakes that I would normally have made. During the time I was writing this book, I was right down there — in the trenches, addressing problems affecting availability and performance on a daily basis, and collectively taking steps to overcome them. This non-dedicated approach to writing definitely delayed the book. However, I'm positive it has also made the book technically that much richer. In places, I have recounted some of my late-night battles with the Oracle server in taking it to the next level: operating in *true* 24x7 mode.

First of all, I wish to thank the Osborne/McGraw-Hill team: Jeremy Judson, Carolyn Welch, Monika Faltiss, Scott Rogers, Robert Campbell, Lee Healy, and the others who were instrumental in ensuring that the book saw the light of day. Jeremy and Scott's zeal absolutely matched my passion for writing this book. Monika's super efficiency and sound advice kept me marching. Carolyn's guidance saw me make it to the finishing line. Thanks to everyone on the team, this book grew from a mere desire, a dream into reality.

I would also like to thank Peter Utzig and Ravi Balwada from Oracle Corporation. Peter was the technical reviewer for the book. His insightful comments and technical contributions are highly appreciated. Figure 9-5 (in Chapter 9) is based on one of his diagrams. Ravi Balwada provided a thought-provoking Foreword for the book. Also, many thanks to Robert Deszell, who technically reviewed a portion of the book. I'm also in gratitude to Oracle Corporation's many technical personnel, especially those in Oracle Development, Oracle Support, and Oracle Services, who have worked on the Oracle server, extended it to its current wondrous state, and written various papers and books on its working. Also, there are several individuals, both from and outside Oracle Corporation, who have made presentations at various Oracle conferences around the world. Over the years, I have avidly read many of their papers and books as I worked with the Oracle software, allowing me to understand the product better. I have listed the names of many of these people in Appendix A at the back of the book.

Thanks to my good friend and colleague Uday Nayak for his assistance with Chapter 20. Uday made any technical question for the book a personal mission and spent a substantial amount of time in research. He either always has the answers or he gets them!

Sincere thanks to my friends and colleagues at Raymond James Consulting, especially Monte Malenke, Charles Livingston, Scott French, Dhiraj Soni, and Manoj Gopalkrishnan for their constant support and good wishes. Also many thanks to all my friends and colleagues at my current and previous client sites and companies, especially Sunil Nair, Harbinder Saini, Ham Pasupuleti, Scott Lockhart, George Elango, Badruddin El Sadiq, Khalid Sattar Khan, Suleiman, Dave Davis, Christine Pimblett, Dave Warner, Chris Heroux, Reg Brown, Mike Martell, and Peter Wenker. I have learned so much from all of you.

I also wish to especially thank a few of my close friends: Anatasia Zaikina, Chandra Honnavalli, Pankaj Soni, Vivek Amin, Trupti Mehta, Anil Gajra, and Deepak Dodani. Their encouragement over the years has enabled me to grow continuously.

I also want to express my gratitude to my mentor Rainier Luistro. I have had the good fortune of knowing Rainier over the last several years and there is still so much to learn from him, both technically and non-technically. Preaching very little and directly practicing much more, Rainier has never hesitated to share his wealth of knowledge with people working with him. In fact, the desire to write this book is, in many ways, a result of my association with him.

Finally, I wish to acknowledge the perpetual love and support from my family: my parents S. Devrajan and Vatsala Devrajan, my brother Shiv Devraj and my uncle V. Balakrishnan. My uncle awakened in me a propensity to work hard and succeed very early in life. The strong family support infrastructure has been vital in helping me embark on the arduous journey of writing such a voluminous tome.

Preface

In this section, I wish to share some of the thoughts that were with me throughout the writing of this book.

The Background and Need for this Book

In October 1994, Mosaic Communications (later, Netscape Communications Corporation) launched beta 0.9 of its browser Netscape. That single event allowed users all over the world to download a magical piece of software absolutely free of charge. Little did anyone imagine at that time that this software would actually open up hundreds of opportunities for businesses around the world. Previously looked upon as a haven for researchers and academicians, the Internet was virtually unlocked to millions of ordinary laymen through the wondrous browser. Netscape's ease-of-use virtually launched a revolution by allowing the neighboring housewife to shop for toys for Christmas on the Internet for her kids while they were asleep or the equally busy sales executive in a far-off mid-town office to trade stock during lunch! In other words, this monumental occasion allowed many existing and new companies to launch a booming e-business with a vast, vast market: the world.

However, this revolution also brought forward a need to have systems and resources to be open and accessible around the clock since literally, the world never sleeps! "The Internet changes everything" — that has been one of Oracle Corporation's war cries in recent times. And it's true. With the rapid growth of electronic commerce and the proliferation of Web-based databases, companies around the world feel a real urgency to have a Web presence. More than a presence, they need to reach out to the market via the Web to remain competitive. And this is possible largely by deploying a Web-enabled database to collect and process the customers' orders. No longer bound by geographical restrictions, these customers are located around the globe. So, while the customer in North America sleeps, the customer in Australia and Asia is placing an order and vice-versa. Even businesses operating only in specific geographical locations (such as only North America) are discovering that their customers are shopping at all hours — day or night— right from the comfort of their homes. Such operations uncompromisingly require the database to be available 24x7. In other words, there is a genuine need felt by businesses to make their data and information available to people all the time. Companies stand to lose millions of dollars with every hour of downtime, not to mention credibility and goodwill. As a result, there is a direct and huge pressure on IS personnel to maintain and manage their systems in a proactive manner to ensure total availability.

High availability used to be a stringent requirement for certain businesses even before the Internet and e-business revolution. However, these businesses had the muscle (think of the airline industry) to afford mainframes and the like, which could provide them high availability. With e-business emerging, even much smaller businesses (think startups) are forced to remain highly available to remain economically viable. Larger businesses are shaken by the collar to join the fray to remain competitive with these young usurps. With such demand being on high availability, it takes no prizes to guess that there are many businesses that can't afford mainframes but need mainframe-like reliability and availability. What do they do? Any outage results in bad press and consequently loss of customers, sales, volume, and revenue. Are mainframes and similar big-iron the only practical answer? No, obviously that is not true. Mid-range and lower-range machines are getting better and better, having the capability to outclass mainframes of a few years ago.

The key is to adopt a holistic approach. Required availability should be correctly determined and uptime needs should be integrated into the technical architecture, application analysis, and design and implementation cycles. Robust standby and failover solutions need to be in place. Maintenance and monitoring should be accomplished with as little impact on availability as possible. In other words, availability needs to encompass the entire system's life cycle from conception to physical implementation. As a flip side to this well-rounded approach, no matter if you are a DBA, an architect, or a developer, you have a specific role to play to ensure high availability. The key to successfully implementing high availability solutions for your organization depends on your familiarity with that role and the specific steps you need to take. This is precisely what this book attempts to illustrate via tips and real-world examples — integrating core high availability goals into your final Oracle-based solution.

The Audience for This Book and Recommended Ways to Read It

You don't need to have absolute *24x7* uptime requirements to take advantage of this book. If at all, you are looking for techniques (beyond what the standard documentation offers) to enhance your current Oracle availability or even, to make your current availability more consistent and reliable, then you are looking at the right book. These tips presume that both availability and performance are the top priorities at any 24x7 site. In fact, it would be hard to name just one of these as the top-most priority. For some clients, a slow database is almost as bad as no database! System manageability and administrative ease are other important driving factors in this book.

Many of the tips are of an advanced nature. They assume that the reader is well versed in basic areas of administration and development. However, even if you are relatively new to Oracle, this book should act as a reference in helping you gain a deeper understanding of specific areas that you might want in-depth information on. Also, most of these tips are directed towards technical personnel (DBAs, developers, and so on). However, at some sites, I have observed non-technical/semi-technical personnel managing highly technical operations and people. Hence, I have provided a handful of tips in certain chapters for such managers and supervisors towards making it easier to manage the hardware, the OS, the network, the database, and of course, the technical people who manage all these, day in and day out. If your boss is non- or semi-technical, please pass on these tips to him or her.

People in different technical roles can read this book in different ways. Ideally, I would insist that it be read from start to finish. However, I also know that would be an unrealistic expectation. I, for one, rarely read a technical book completely from start to finish. I often flip through the pages and settle on a topic that seems interesting or necessary at the time. The "Tips and Techniques" format of this book allows you to do exactly that. As mentioned earlier, you can also use this book for constant easy reference to many Oracle-related topics. However, if you are more inclined to follow a specific sequence, the following table lists the recommended sequence of chapters to readers in specific roles.

Role	Recommended sequence of chapters
Architect	1, 2, 3, 4, 5, 6, 15, 16, 17, 18, 20, any other chapter that seems interesting/useful
DBA	1, 2, 3, 4, 5, 6, 7, 8, 9, 10, 11, 12, 13, 14, 15, 16, 17, 18, 19, 20
Developer	1, 2, 3, 4, 5, 6, 15, 16, 19, 20, any other chapter that seems interesting/useful

Apart from the first 5 to 6 chapters, feel free to skip any and read in any desired sequence. Each chapter is intended to provide a comprehensive set of tips in a specific area. Wherever necessary, appropriate references are made to other chapters.

Why Did I Write This Book (and not just let someone else do the job...)?

Why did I end up writing this book? With the pain and agony I went through writing it, why did I actually do it? I inherently lack the discipline necessary to sit down and work for almost a year on a book. In school, I hated writing. At work, I hate to do the technical documentation (but I still do it). Actually for the first few months, I loved what I was doing and managed to pump out some core chapters, which were close to my heart. However, after a while the going got tough! Caffeine wouldn't work anymore. I needed a vacation badly but couldn't afford the time. Somehow I had gotten myself into a project that required months of dedicated writing. (Did I mention before that I hate writing?) I was passing through a stage where my burn-rate was higher than my productivity. But somehow I passed through this unscathed and mustered the motivation to reach the finishing line.

And what really did it for me was the Internet culture. And here I don't necessarily refer to the e-business boom. Money is the best motivator (for many people, including me). However, this project did not involve money (nothing worth mentioning, at least!). As most technical authors will tell you, unless you are a Stephen King or Michael Crichton, you shouldn't turn to writing to get food on the table. As a technical consultant, I was making enough money to keep the wolves at bay. And the money promised me from the book was nothing to leap about. Honestly, however, sometimes you have to rise higher than what money can fetch — for the common good. And that is precisely what drove me on through the endless late nights and combining writing with a full-time job (very often, much more than "full-time"). The Internet is chock-block with examples of innovative and hard-working people giving away things for free. I used to read about Marc Andreessen and his team at Netscape Communications giving away their "pot of gold" —- their browser for free, similar to Linus Torvalds giving away the Linux source-code for free. I'm no Marc Andreessen or Linus Torvalds. However, the least I could do was to give away some of the knowledge I had amassed over the years for almost free! Believe me, it was for almost free. The money I managed to make writing probably didn't even pay for all the pizza, the coffee, Mountain Dew, and Jolt Colas! All this knowledge I had managed to gather over the years from books, white papers, knowledgeable peers, endless time playing with the software, working my back-side off in production environments, waking up at 2:30 in the morning to that blaring pager — the list is endless. However, knowledge I did gather and realized I needed to give it back. I had to share it with the people around me. The Internet at least fosters that spirit among its denizens — sacrifice a little bit of personal pleasure and gain for the common good. And to drive you on, there is a major sense of responsibility that lies with you when you are writing a book covering an advanced topic — a book of tips and techniques for people already well versed with most basic aspects of the technology, a book that is expected to take them to the next level of knowledge. I hope that you agree (after reading it, of course) that this book did take you there! I know writing it took me even further than where I was before.

I had always felt the need for a book for the real people — the people who always have their hands dirty, the people who do the actual typing — without too much theory. At various client sites, I have seen technical personnel struggle to maintain the desired uptime. Due to lack of information on acquiring 24x7 uptime in public domain, there was this niche in the market for a "working Oracle professional's book on high availability." There are books out there that talk in detail about every Oracle component in theory; however, how many people really need to know or are interested in knowing pure theory? Many of these books do not share anything from the real world. I have seen many DBAs get discouraged with too much theory, so discouraged they avoid reading the documentation and the books, which dwell on such theory. I hoped to get a book out, which won't bore readers to sleep. Instead it will provide them with real-world tips — tips they can use in specific real-world situations. I hope you manage to read this tome of knowledge and gain something from it — anything that will help you understand the Oracle kernel better and tune it to derive maximum availability and performance. Many times I have skipped what I thought was the ordinary, available in most books. Rather than trying to constantly bombard the reader with technical theory, I have intentionally tried to bypass those. Instead I focussed on the little things, which if done properly, will allow you to go the extra mile in tuning. But remember, the little things are to be done in conjunction with the bigger things, the things that are well documented in manuals and other commonly accessible publications. I have, however, provided just sufficient theory to explain the rationale behind a tip. I have explained at length various "behind the scenes" operations. Wherever appropriate, I have pointed to other reference material — additional theory material to be read, as necessary. If I have provided in the following pages enough real-world material to interest you to go out there, grab the theory book and read in detail, if I have kindled within you adequate confidence and familiarity with various high availability measures to try to provide your company with optimal database uptime, I have succeeded in my efforts. Total confidence will come only with experience. However, this book should help in providing some impetus as you gain that experience.

A Final Important Note Prior to Starting

I need to mention this just prior to your launching into the chapters: There are certain previously undocumented Oracle features and functionality (example: underscore *init.ora* parameters, tracing and so on) listed in this book. They are explained purely from an informational perspective just to aid you understand how Oracle operates internally. Please do not change any undocumented features, unless specifically requested to do so by Oracle Support. Some of these features directly affect the way Oracle works. As such, changing them without accurate, in-depth knowledge of their functionality and impact may potentially corrupt your database and render it useless. Also, changing them without Oracle Support's explicit permission violates your Support contract and changes your database into an unsupported one (something every 24x7 site can do without!).

With that, let's leap into Chapter 1. May you achieve the availability and performance you require. Godspeed to you!

Venkat S. Devraj
Denver, Colorado
October 1, 1999

PART I

Introduction

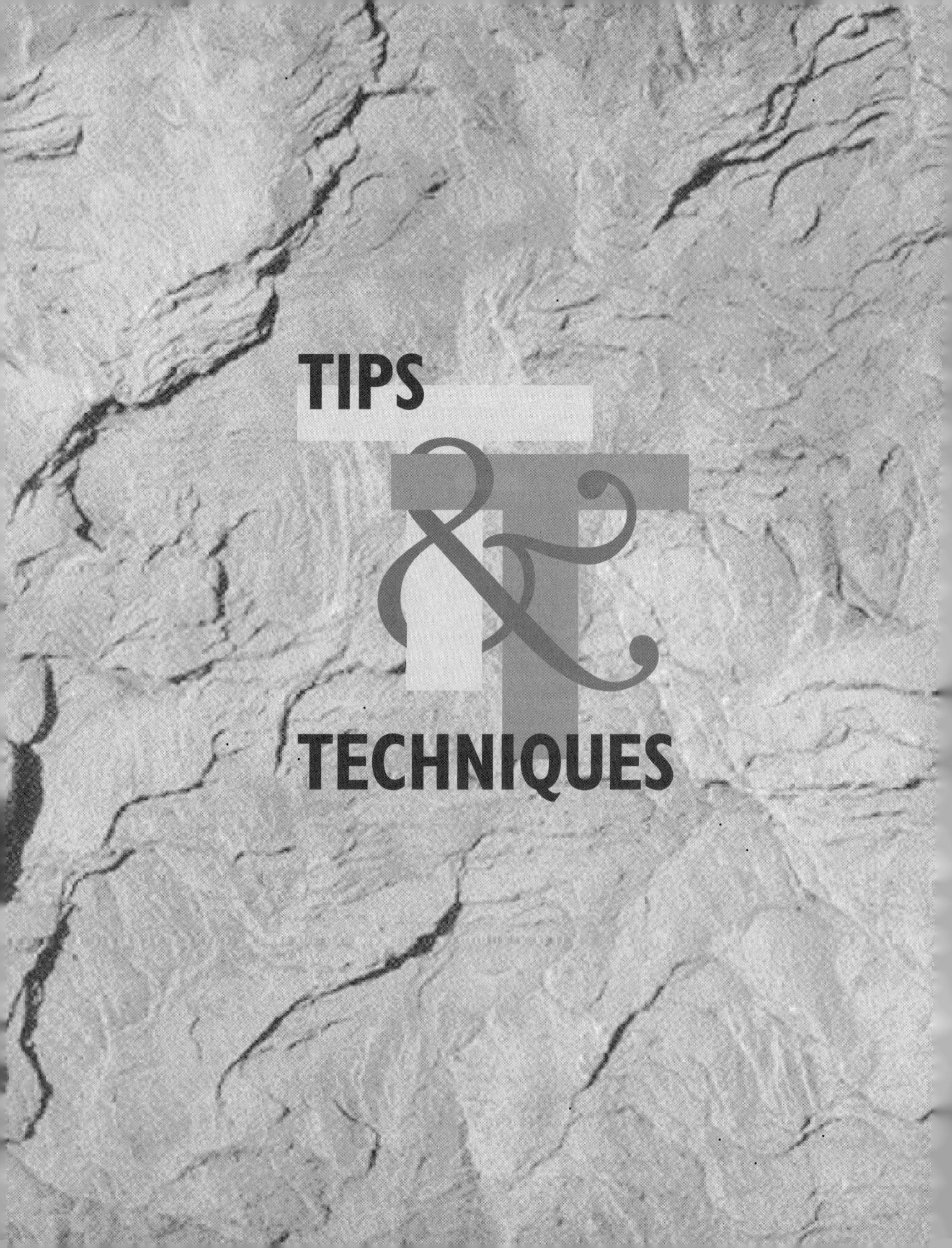
TIPS
&
TECHNIQUES

Identifying Your Uptime Requirements

Imagine this: You are part of an operations team for a company that sells books over the Internet. You have customers all over the world logging onto your database to access your online book catalogs and pay for their selections. During the middle of the night (which is your least busy time), there are at least a hundred users on your database. Any database downtime is not acceptable. Any performance bottleneck is not acceptable. Your database is expected to run—all the time and fast! What do you do? When do you perform your backups? When do you defragment your database? When do you do all those maintenance activities that a database needs?

Welcome to the world of 24×7! This expression, 24×7, is a term frequently used in the Information Technology (IT) arena, especially in systems and database operations, to indicate all-time availability of resources (such as databases and computer systems). In other words, when a database/system is open and available for users 24 hours a day, 7 days a week, it is said to be operating in "24×7 mode."

Most companies require no introduction to the term "24×7." They are no strangers to downtime and understand the importance of high database availability. However, extended uptime comes at a price. Performing even mundane database administration tasks becomes a tall order, requiring extensive prior planning, hard work, and lots of prayers!

Full-fledged 24×7 support has been historically required by operations managers of many companies. Until recently, operations managers would mention that they needed their databases to be up and running in 24×7 mode. The DBAs would wholeheartedly agree with a shrug and a "Sure! Go, use mainframes!" comment. There were just too many things that could go wrong on a midrange machine running a resource-hungry Oracle database.

Today, it's a different story. The operations managers still insist that they would like their databases to be constantly available. And surprisingly, the DBAs don't shrug and walk away anymore. With the release of Oracle8 and Oracle8*i*, the spotlight is on high availability. With the proliferation of e-commerce and large-scale global markets, no longer can the DBA nonchalantly take the database down even for a cold backup.

In a perfect world (with no database corruption, crashes, fragmentation, environmental disasters, and so on), even a solitary Oracle7 or Oracle8 database with no standby (or even backups, for that matter) can provide full 100 percent uptime. In real-world terms, however, operating a solitary database at a 24×7 site without adequate measures for ensuring high availability is not realistic. Being in 24×7 mode requires understanding overall uptime requirements, anticipating different causes of downtime, and preparing for each without compromising the required availability.

Both Oracle7 and Oracle8 support features that realistically allow high availability. Even though it would still take highly expensive globally replicated standby databases to achieve a rock-solid 99.99 percent availability (not to even mention full 100 percent availability), a good 90 percent availability is still within the realm of possibility for most companies running Oracle7 or Oracle8 without incurring any extraordinary measures. However, can you afford to remain just 90 percent available? Being 90 percent available means tolerating a downtime of either 2.4 hours a day, 1 day every 10 days, or 36.5 days a year. Prima facie, these are not very attractive numbers for any company desiring high database uptime. But do you really need higher availability? This opening chapter focuses on identifying your database uptime requirements.

This chapter offers the following tips and techniques:

- Analyze whether your company needs 24×7 uptime
- Understand the components of your "database"
- Analyze what could go wrong and the odds of those happening
- Be familiar with the common goals for engineering a 24x7 system
- Manage expectations via a solid Service Level Agreement
- Being only 90 percent available takes away 90 percent of the cost
- Understand maintenance operations' effect on availability
- 24×7 uptime requires a radical approach to operations management
- Create "24×7 teams" available during key database-access times
- Maintain an escalation-list of individuals to be notified during crises
- Always provide advance notice of outages to your customers/end-users

Understanding What 24×7 Means for Your Organization

This section outlines the common implications of operating in 24x7 mode. Then it goes on to identify the components that are vulnerable to downtime.

Analyze whether your company needs 24×7 uptime

Before escalating your uptime requirements to 24×7, you must assess your organization's availability needs. Let me recount my experiences at two client sites.

Three years ago, I visited a client site in Chicago (let's call them Company_A). They are a major player in the travel and ticketing industry. They have hundreds of travel agents, spread all over North America and Europe, accessing their database. Their main complaint was an acute performance problem in their production database. After spending a few hours running *utlbstat/utlestat* and digging deeply into the database alert-log, I discovered that their database needed major tuning. I made a nice, impressive list outlining the "top 10 things" that could be done to tune their database. That was easy, or so I thought.

Their on-site DBA said he already knew this stuff, as I showed him my "top 10" list. So why wasn't he doing something to rectify the situation, I wondered. I decided to bypass the DBA and made a detailed report of my study and recommendations to the CIO.

Some of my recommendations included the following:

- Change certain *init.ora* parameters and bounce the database.
- While the database is down, also reboot the UNIX box (memory was heavily fragmented).
- Rebuild the DATA and INDEX tablespaces (they were heavily fragmented, as well).
- Drop and recreate four indexes on the main table (containing 16 million rows). All those indexes were "flat," causing large-scale range scans (see Chapter 6 for an explanation on how I figured that out).
- Stop taking hot backups all the time (they were taking hot backups for 14 continuous hours in a day, even during peak production hours).

"Would applying your recommendations require the database to be bounced?" the CIO asked. When I naively answered in the affirmative, I was asked to pack my bags and leave.

So what went wrong? It seems great performance was not their only requirement. Their main requirement was 24×7 database uptime, *in addition* to good performance. Travel agents could access their database anytime day or night to book tickets. They would definitely lose money if they were to go down even for an hour. They really needed 24×7 uptime.

Shortly after, I had the opportunity to visit another client site in Woodridge (let's refer to them as Company_B). The company manufactures cakes and assorted sweetmeats. During my first day on the job, the operations manager mentioned without even cringing that he expected full 24×7 availability, including weekends. Why would a cake-manufacturing company's employees need access to their Oracle database on a Saturday night, I wondered.

Meanwhile, I deployed some lean (minimal-resource-consuming) scripts via the UNIX *cron* command to periodically poll their database and record usage patterns. These scripts ran once every ten minutes for an entire week (including the weekend). Table 1-1 lists the information I managed to gather.

I went back to the operations manager with the report and mentioned that the bulk of his usage was during regular office hours. He didn't really need 24×7 uptime. I lectured that he would lose a lot of database management flexibility by

Hours	Usage Pattern
08:00 to 18:00	Average of 60 concurrent user sessions
18:00 to 20:00	Average of 15 concurrent user sessions
20:00 to 22:00	Average of 6 concurrent user sessions
22:00 to 00:00	Average of 2 concurrent user sessions
00:00 to 04:00	No user logged on (hot backups were in progress)
04:00 to 07:00	No user logged on (backups were completed; absolutely no activity)
07:00 to 08:00	Average of 10 concurrent user sessions

TABLE 1-1. *Usage Patterns at Company_B During Each 24-Hour Period*

trying to operate in 24×7 mode, even though there was no real business need. Needless to add, that consulting assignment didn't go too well either (ever tried telling a senior manager what he or she doesn't want to hear?). I found myself back at the consulting office, waiting for my next assignment.

Looking at these two examples, you have on one hand—Company_A, with a genuine need for 24×7 database uptime. On the other hand, Company_B mistakenly believes it needs to have 24×7 uptime and tries to achieve that. Let's try to evaluate the cost of running in 24×7 mode.

Evaluating the "Cost" of 24×7 Uptime

Typically, the following factors are adversely impacted when operating in 24x7 mode:

ADMINISTRATIVE FLEXIBILITY For starters, tasks one would normally take for granted become almost impossible. A few such tasks are

- Applying patches to the database or the underlying operating system
- Cold backups
- Reorganizing tablespaces and tables
- Creating/rebuilding indexes
- Analyzing tables/indexes with the VALIDATE STRUCTURE option

In fact, just about any task requiring an exclusive lock on an important table, a bounce of the database instance, or a reboot of the machine is not possible. God forbid that the machine should crash during peak production hours (especially since it has not been rebooted for the last seven months). I have observed quite a few sites abusing the machine and the database just on pure whim. They live with various performance problems, when all it would take is a quick reboot to free up the fragmented memory. In other words, the first thing that is compromised by high availability requirements is administrative flexibility.

NOTE
I'm not in any way recommending frequent or whimsical reboots of the machine or the database. In fact, I strongly recommend keeping the machine up for as much time as possible without incurring any major performance degradation. In some situations, however, there are hardware or software (OS, Oracle, or other software) bugs that cause high memory fragmentation or memory leaks (where memory is constantly being gobbled up by a program and not being freed—this may be caused either by malloc() calls without corresponding free() calls or by pointers going awry). It takes a decent amount of analysis and troubleshooting to determine the exact cause of the problem and working with the appropriate vendor (hardware, OS, Oracle Support) or sometimes with multiple vendors simultaneously, to fix the problem. Many times, a fix is not readily available and one needs to wait for the vendor to make a patch available. In such situations, rebooting the machine at pre-determined intervals (say, once every four to six months or so) becomes a necessary evil (to quickly release the wasted or fragmented memory). The decision to reboot needs to be made after careful evaluation of the level of fragmentation.

So is running Oracle in 24×7 mode an absolutely overwhelming task? There is no easy answer to that. If implemented properly with detailed requirements analysis and robust architectural design, there is a very good chance that Oracle will live up to pre-determined availability and performance expectations. However, haphazardly slapping together expensive hardware and trying to meet all organizational expectations is futile. The first thing to die is performance, quickly followed by availability, the core requirement.

PERFORMANCE In real-world terms, performance is often (not always) inversely related to database uptime (Figure 1-1). RAID 0 is a classic example of this inverse relationship. In RAID 0, data is striped across multiple disks/controllers to enhance performance. However, each disk becomes a single point of failure (in the absence of RAID 1 or other mirroring mechanisms). The higher the number of disks involved, the higher the chances of failure. To illustrate an example within the database, reducing database checkpoints (the process of writing modified data block buffers to data-files on disk) enhances performance by reducing physical I/O. However, fewer checkpoints also increase downtime by increasing the time to perform recovery, in the event of a database crash.

Another database example is that creating an index in UNRECOVERABLE or NOLOGGING mode expedites the creation process, helping performance tremendously. However, the same clause would increase database downtime, if the database were to crash right after the index creation. The recovery process would not recover the newly created index and would have to be manually recreated prior to making the database available, thus adding to the downtime (a subsequent paragraph provides detailed explanation of how a UNRECOVERABLE/NOLOGGING operation may cause more downtime). Of course, there are always exceptions to the rule. For example, a faster index build (especially on a table with a million or more rows) makes the table available to all applications sooner (as soon as the exclusive lock put in place by the CREATE INDEX statement is released). So from that perspective, building an index in UNRECOVERABLE or NOLOGGING mode actually enhances availability in such situations (unless there is a database crash immediately after the index creation, as mentioned earlier).

NOTE

Performance and availability are not inversely related by definition. Theoretically, availability is a subset of performance (you have zero throughput, if you have no availability). From a practical perspective, however, performance and availability are two disparate phenomena. Performance is generally related with "how fast or slow is the database," and availability is geared toward "what times do the users need access to the database." From that perspective, I have provided a few examples (UNRECOVERABLE operations and CHECKPOINT operations) to illustrate the inverse nature between the two.

Let's take short detour to see how an UNRECOVERABLE/NOLOGGING operation may cause more downtime. This example is applicable to pre-Oracle8*i* environments. An index creation causes the table to be locked up, preventing concurrent DML (inserts, updates, and deletes). So in versions prior to Oracle8*i*, during the time an index is being built on a highly accessed table, the table is not

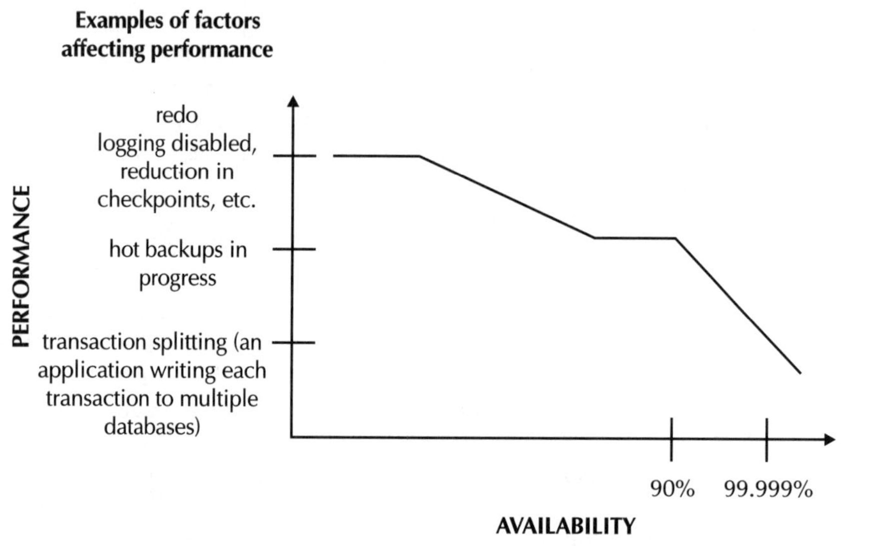

FIGURE 1-1. *Chart depicting the inverse real-world relationship between performance and database availability*

available. If the table is a popular table, then effectively all applications that access that table need to be brought down. And without those applications, the database is not accessible to end-users. Let's look at two scenarios in Table 1-2 and Table 1-3.

Scenario 1

Sequence of Events	Downtime Caused
Index created in UNRECOVERABLE (or NOLOGGING) mode	30 minutes
Database crashes	
Database recovery done from last night's backup	30 minutes
Database open and available	
Newly created index is missing	
Index is re-created	30 minutes
Total downtime	**90 minutes**

TABLE 1-2. *Events During Table-Creation in UNRECOVERABLE/NOLOGGING Mode*

Scenario 2

Sequence of Events	**Downtime Caused**
Index created in RECOVERABLE (or LOGGING) mode	40 minutes
Database crashes	
Database recovery done from last night's backup	30 minutes
Database open and available	
Newly created index is present	
Total downtime	**70 minutes**

TABLE 1-3. *Events During Table-Creation in RECOVERABLE/LOGGING Mode*

The two scenarios just depicted illustrate how UNRECOVERABLE, though it helps performance, may increase downtime, whereas, the second scenario where the index is created in RECOVERABLE mode increases actual index-creation time but decreases overall downtime in the event of a database crash.

But note that even though performance has a tendency to degrade due to 24x7 uptime requirements and lack of the administrative flexibility required to intervene to ensure that performance remains acceptable, the matter does not end there. Rather than half-heartedly accepting (or trying to force users/management into accepting) bad performance due to the database having to be up 24x7 or taking the stand that you cannot make good performance and high availability coexist, it is essential to take steps right from the time of initial installation and configuration to target availability and performance as twin objectives, rather than solely focusing on availability. After all, a badly performing database can only offer limited throughput and response time. In fact, after a certain point of bad performance, it may become so unusable that users may not even consider it to be "available" anymore. The point I'm trying to make is that, in spite of the (frequent) inverse relationship between performance and availability, there are concrete steps you can take—as a DBA, as a systems analyst or data modeler, or as an architect or developer—steps that will allow you to maximize both availability and performance, without compromising one for the another. (Subsequent chapters discuss these steps; as an example, specifying proper STORAGE parameters, after due analysis, reduces rampant segment fragmentation in tablespaces, reducing the need for frequent maintenance and preventing performance from degrading.) Many of these steps need to be proactive, and you need to have a good understanding of diverse areas (internal and external to the database) in order to implement 24x7 for your company successfully. Additionally, reliable "lights-out" monitoring, where automated scripts do the bulk of the monitoring and page the administrative personnel when a potential problem is noticed, is mandatory. (This is advisable even for a company that has a large number of administrative personnel, for immunity against human errors.) Only then will you be able to realistically narrow the gap between availability and performance—rather than seeing a bigger drift between the two to make their relationship even more inverse than it needs to be.

MONETARY COST Finally, besides administrative flexibility and performance, another major factor I allude to in previous paragraphs is cost. Implementing high availability can be monetarily expensive. There is a direct relationship between expense and availability—the higher the availability desired, the bigger the cost (see Figure 1-2). For instance, suppose that you need the database to be available only from 9 A.M. to 5 P.M. (five days a week), and suppose that at certain times it is not available due to a systems or database problem. If your company can still survive without major revenue/productivity loss, then your operations personnel can configure the database on a single machine (that is, no standby machines are required) and perform regular backups to meet your 9–5 availability requirements as much as possible. Once in a while, a database failure may occur in the middle of regular work hours; however, your company could withstand that—so your IT budget need not consider spending on redundant hardware and failover systems/databases, thus saving money. However, if your availability requirements are more stringent—for instance, if you need availability 24x7 or even 8x5 (availability is strongly required eight hours a day, five days a week)—and your company cannot financially tolerate downtime during those mandatory hours, then you will need to consider nonstandard system-building techniques by including provisions for redundant hardware, failover systems, and additional administrative personnel in your IT budget, thus causing the budget to rise. In other words, the higher your availability requirements, the higher the cost for your company, since you will have to invest in additional hardware/software/firmware to meet those requirements.

Evaluating Your Availability Requirements

With this background information regarding the 24x7 "penalty" (in terms of performance, price, and flexibility), let's examine the art of evaluating your availability requirements. Do you really need access to the database 24 hours a day, 7 days a week? Or do you just need access 24 hours a day, 5 days a week? Or is it actually 18 hours a day, 7 days a week? How do you find out for sure? The users are always clamoring for total access all the time. It seems whenever you look, there is always someone doing something in the database.

The best approach is to communicate with the users directly. Sometimes it's amazing how cooperative users can be, especially when they are told that it would take a few million dollars to provide true 24x7 access via multiple database servers

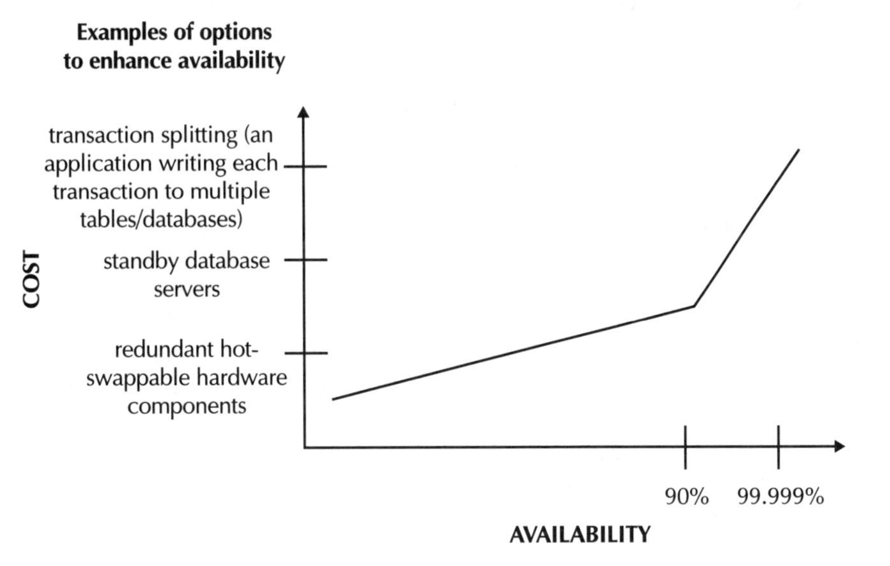

FIGURE 1-2. *The direct relationship between cost and database availability*

at diverse locations and high-speed networks connecting all these servers to provide near-instantaneous replication. (Please note, whenever I mention "replication," I don't necessarily refer to Oracle's Advanced Replication option—note the capital "R" when I refer to Oracle's Advanced Replication option. Rather, I use the term "replication" to refer to diverse replication products/tools, including Oracle's Advanced Replication and other third-party hardware- and/or software-based replication solutions available in the market.)

If your users happen to be a little stubborn, the next best way to evaluate these requirements is to gather statistics on database usage patterns (you might find the scripts I have mentioned to be handy; they are listed in Chapter 19) and present them with those statistics to make your argument more convincing.

Generally, late Saturday nights/early hours of Sunday morning are the best times to schedule maintenance work. Worldwide, there is minimal database traffic (if any at all) during those hours. If only a few users access your database during the wee hours of Sunday morning, it doesn't mean that you cannot schedule maintenance work at that time. Maybe they could be persuaded to do their work some other time. Also, if automated batch jobs are running during those hours, maybe they can be scheduled to run later (after the maintenance work is complete) or maybe they can be run only during weeknights. However, if such work cannot be rescheduled

due to practical commercial or economic reasons, then maybe your site really does need 24×7 uptime.

My objective is not to discourage you from trying to achieve true 24×7 uptime—rather, it is to make you verify that your site indeed needs such high availability and is prepared to pay the price (either by investing the money to buy necessary resources and/or by incurring the performance penalty due to lack of database administrative flexibility). Also, analyzing your uptime requirements really helps in determining your hours and areas of vulnerability.

- During which hours should your database be totally available? What are the peaks and valleys (that is, peak and non-peak hours) of applications accessing your database? Are there any peak weeks/months (such as end-of-year accounting) when more transactions are likely to hit the database than usual?
- What is the potential lost revenue during both peak and non-peak periods?
- Can the database be partially available (that is, can certain applications be down or certain tablespaces be offline during certain hours)? If so, which are those applications and tablespaces?
- What are the functional and physical dependencies between your various database components?
- How should each application react if a specific component is unavailable?
- Can all your applications still continue to function at a slower pace on a less-powerful standby server, while the primary server is undergoing maintenance?
- Is such degraded performance acceptable to your organization?

These are some of the key questions you will need to consider as part of your uptime requirements analysis. The objective of these questions is to understand your organization's tolerance to downtime. The more time you spend in workload characterization, the better understanding you develop in determining throughput/response-time requirements, availability needs, and most important, the money lost when there is no availability. A business case needs to be developed for achieving 24×7 availability (or not). Potential money lost is the single most important driver for any capital expenditure to make a database more available.

Evaluating the "Real Cost" of Not Being Available

Loss of money can be measured against loss in direct revenue and loss in productivity (where the return on investment is not optimal). This can be related to various aspects such as

- Customers/sales opportunities lost during the downtime (accompanied by bad publicity and adverse press coverage).
- Cost of resources being idle during downtime ("hidden" cost).
- Potential additional manpower required during recovery (for instance, calling in experts to recover the database) due to intolerance for extended recovery time. When you have adequately prepared for 24×7 access by investing in redundant hardware/software, tolerance for downtime for a specific (primary) system is generally higher, since a failover (secondary) system is available. Accordingly, in many cases, recovery performed by in-house personnel (even if such recovery takes more time due to the relatively lesser expertise of in-house personnel) is tolerated, since a system (the failover system) is functioning. Thus, availability is still maintained during recovery. However, if you are using regular systems (without adequate failover capabilities), system failure during peak hours may require you to urgently bring in more experienced experts (who specialize in recovery and do it frequently) to expedite recovery, so that revenue loss during peak hours is mitigated.
- In case of certain applications (medical, airline/traffic control, and so on), even loss of life is not a vague notion during downtime.

All such aspects need to be considered prior to computing the "real cost" of downtime to your company. For example, after considering everything, if the loss to your company is measured at $5,000, at worst, during every hour of downtime during peak business hours, is it worth investing $1,000,000 to keep the database constantly available? Also, with the potential for data from multiple applications (Order Entry, Bill of Materials, Accounting, and so forth) to reside on a single database, there is a need to prioritize access to all such applications. Database recovery or failover may be too complicated to cater to all applications with equal priority. It needs to be determined whether "If access to this application is delayed, the business goes under." For example, with Order Entry, if you can't get the sale in on time, you may lose revenue, and more important, lose the customer, as well. Eventually with frequent outages, your company's bottom line may plunge and stock prices may go down. Well, you get the idea. Only with a strong business case and an in-depth understanding of organizational needs and downtime repercussions on revenue and productivity can you venture to custom-design a highly available system for your organization.

The challenge here is, you need to have intimate knowledge of diverse organization and technical components. Lack of knowledge in either area will result in an incorrect solution. As your familiarity with database growth and use patterns increases, it becomes easier to predict and plan for availability and performance. This is the reason why achieving 24×7 uptime is *initially* much harder.

Understand the components of your "database"

So what makes up your "database"? No, no, really. . .what makes up your database? Is it the version? Or is it a combination of the physical files and the memory structures? I love asking this question to DBAs I interview. And you will be amazed at the varied answers I get (don't wanna go there, just yet!). There are multiple answers that could be considered technically correct. However, my own personal view is as follows:

Any database is dependent on multiple layers, each layer as important as the next (Figure 1-3). These layers may be intertwined with each other, even be transparent to the DBA. Nevertheless, they stand out loud and clear:

- Hardware
- Operating system
- Network
- DBMS (Oracle)
- Applications that use the DBMS
- Data managed by the DBMS

One without the other is unthinkable! Even Oracle Corporation's "Raw Iron" initiative has some kind of an operating system flavor (for more details on Raw Iron or the Database Appliance, see Chapter 20 on Oracle8*i*). Should any of these components fail, your database becomes unavailable. So much for trying to operate in 24x7 mode!

If there's one thing you take away from this chapter, let it be the fact that your database is dependent on many factors, each of which has to be configured and tuned separately. Any DBA worth his or her salt can tell you that a vanilla install of Oracle is not the most efficient one. Oracle is complex and requires a lot of prior planning and customization to make the installation optimal for your environment. Many Oracle tools have lately become quite user-friendly (especially on NT), allowing even a relatively new DBA to install Oracle straight out of the box and make it work. However, making it work *well* is a totally different ball game! That's where being cognizant of the preceding factors becomes extremely important because each layer needs to be well oiled to be fluent and really transparent.

Each individual component needs to be addressed separately and treated with the same respect one would give the DBMS. Here's where a little teamwork comes into play.

A "complete" DBA needs to know database administration, network administration, systems administration, application development and of course,

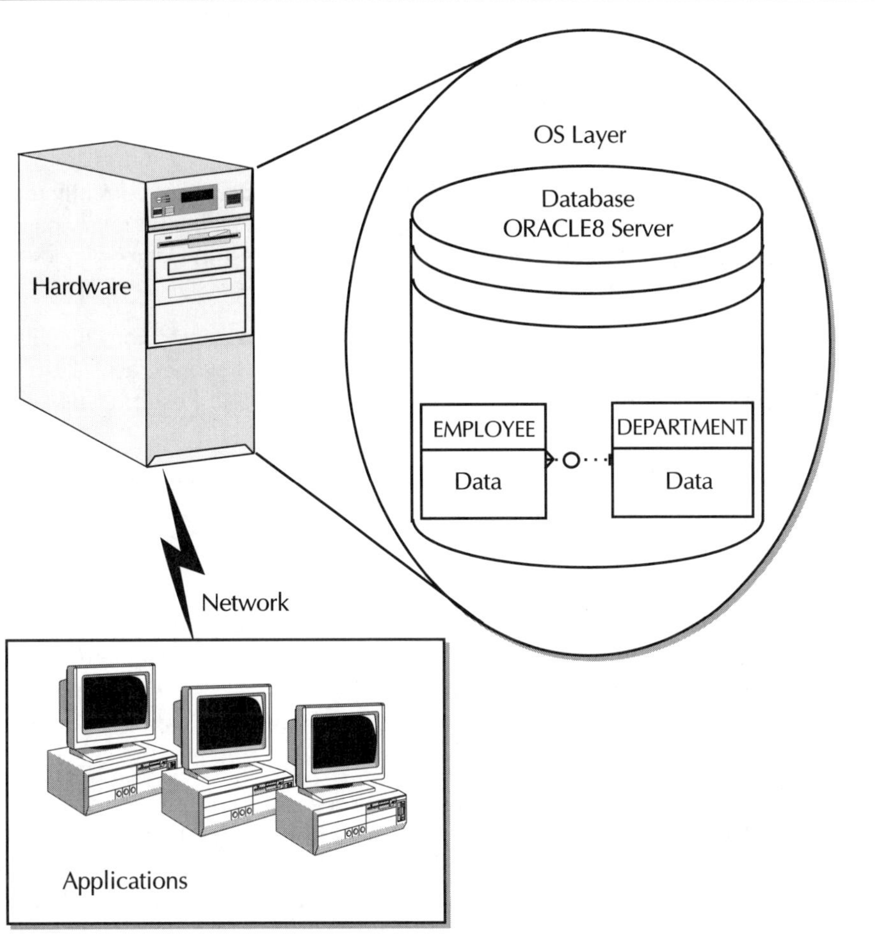

FIGURE 1-3. *"Components" of a database*

data administration. Is that a tall order or what? Going by that yardstick, I wouldn't be able to find a single DBA to work for me. The next best alternative is to team up a DBA with good systems administrators, network administrators, developers, and data administrators. Depending on your environment, you might even have a Webmaster as part of your "24×7 team" (especially if you have deployed e-commerce applications over the Web).

Achieving high availability is a precise science, rather than a vague art. As long as each component is polished and falls in place well, you can certainly achieve

high uptime. Now, let's take a practical look at how each component could demolish your database uptime:

- **Hardware** A disk on which your Oracle data-files exist, crashes. Result: Database goes down and is unavailable.
- **Operating System** Your OS needs more swap space. It has currently reached the maximum available and can't allocate any more. It continuously pages, swaps, page faults, and then, panics and crashes! Result: Database goes down and is unavailable.
- **Network** A mouse (this *really* happened at a data center!) has just finished lunch and snipped through your network cable. Network crashes. No more clients can connect to your database via the network. Result: Database is unavailable.
- **DBMS** You have to rebuild an index due to excessive DML on a popular table. Since the rebuild index process needs an exclusive lock on the table, all applications using that table have to be taken down. Result: Database is unavailable.
- **Applications** A serious bug has crept unnoticed into production, and as a result the application has to be brought down and "repaired." No user can access this application for the next two hours. Result: Database is unavailable to your users, who generally use this application to access the database.
- **Data** You have a data-warehouse composed of 22 tables. The batch job populating the warehouse from an operational source-system goofed up, and the product-dimension (a table holding product details) in your star-schema (a specialized schema-design used predominantly in data-warehousing) now has corrupt data. Result: Your database is unusable.

Achieving 24x7 is not just the art of tuning your DBMS till you achieve "database nirvana." It involves robust understanding and proactive tuning of all the previously mentioned components. It means having to anticipate what could possibly go wrong with each component and how to react to the failure. All single points of failure within each component need to be identified, and there needs to be a "Plan B" to counter every such point of failure—a real, feasible plan that can immediately deployed. For instance, for critical hardware components, the failure of which would result in immediate downtime, you need to have redundant components that, during failure, will either automatically take over or can be swapped in while the system is still up and running (hot-swappable).

All right, end of lecture! Let's move on. There are complete books written on how to configure and tune each of the previously mentioned components. For sake of completeness, however, I have touched upon each area in more detail from an Oracle-centric perspective. Subsequent chapters discuss the issues involved in hardware, OS, network, applications, and data management.

Analyze what could go wrong and the odds of those happening

What could go wrong if the database is forced to operate for months at a stretch without a decent bounce? Simple answer: *plenty!* The following are the broad classifications of things that could break (usually in the middle of the night). These classifications are only examples and are by no means exhaustive (after all, each night, it's something new).

Manual Glitches (User Errors and Administrative Errors)

These errors seem to occur more frequently than any other problem. Manual errors usually fall into either of two categories: user and administrative. User errors are generally a result of an user having one too many privileges and unintentionally misusing those privileges. Ever had a user drop/truncate a table "accidentally?" If so, you know what I mean. On the other hand, administrative glitches are more a direct result of an overworked or overzealous (or underpaid) systems, network, or database administrator having an "accident" in the computer room. Ever seen the CIO scream at the new systems administrator for managing to "trip" on a network cable and causing loss of service? Oops!

Note that this could also apply to a "lack of security" scenario. The new DBA turns out to be lazy, gets fired, and "accidentally" wipes out the database before departing.

Hardware/Software Hiccups and Failures

As mentioned earlier, each component on which the database relies is either software (operating system, database), prone to occasional bugs, or hardware, prone to occasional failures. In either case, each software bug or hardware failure has the potential to crash your entire system. Whenever software bugs are encountered, appropriate patches need to be applied, and inevitably, the machine has to be rebooted. In fact, even if no such specific problems are encountered, most midrange operating systems (namely, UNIX and NT) have regular hiccups such as memory/page faults, core-dumps, heavy swapping, occasional memory leaks, and such. The average systems administrator or DBA learns to live with these quirks and just does a reboot to set things right. In a high-availability environment, however, such an approach is unthinkable.

Hardware needs to be extensively evaluated prior to purchase. At high-availability sites, it's not uncommon to perform benchmarks using real-life data and applications for extended periods of time (depending on the Quality Assurance life cycle) on the new hardware. The technical specification of each product needs to be well understood by the Operations staff. Special attention needs to be paid to each product's theoretical and operational MTBF (mean time between failure; more about MTBF follows in a later paragraph). For example, if the theoretical MTBF of a disk drive (one of the most common causes of hardware failure) is 500,000 hours, it indicates (theoretically) that the disk drive may continuously be used in 24×7 mode for up to 57 years, before it fails and has to be replaced. Also, it is not uncommon to have test platforms that exactly simulate the production environment. Any change (OS patch, release, new development) gets tested in that environment first. Nothing new gets put into a production environment without being fully qualified. The expenditure to maintain such test environments may be part of the capital expenditure to provide high availability.

Environmental Failures

Seen a notice lately from the building management that the power supply will be down on Saturday? (This needs to occur at least once a year to satisfy Mother Nature.) Not to worry, the local utilities company is on the job. Power will be restored *almost* immediately in the next six hours! Apart from electrical power surges and failures, other environmental factors interfering in the smooth functioning of database operations include labor disputes and strikes. A few years ago, while I was working as a full-time DBA contractor for a chemical manufacturing company, a strike was declared by the factory workers, and to avoid mishaps, all contractors were prevented from entering the company premises. As a result, I couldn't even go in to start up the database and had to perform all DBA work remotely. It was unimaginable to consider any operation that required me to be on-site. Even taking database backups was out of the question, since I could not replace the tape in the tape drive.

Natural and Man-Made Disasters

Earthquakes, floods, fires, wars, riots. . .need I say more?

These things are bound to happen at some point in time. The key question to ask yourself is: Are you prepared? What if it happens tomorrow? Do you need to be prepared against all of these, or only against software, hardware, and user errors? These are genuine questions that I ask my clients. Not everybody who needs 24×7 access during normal times needs 24×7 access during a war or an earthquake. This is a fundamental truth. Of course, there are lots of companies with an international presence, especially in the e-commerce space, who need total 24×7 access, even during such times. That's their legitimate business requirement. If you are a smaller-/mid-sized company, however, even though you may need full-fledged protection against such events, you may not be able to afford the potentially multimillion dollar solutions. So what's the best solution for you? Spend adequate time understanding your company's goals and requirements prior to engineering the solution, and craft your solution to cater to them. If the solution revolves around the organizational goals, it has a better chance of being successfully accepted and implemented.

Working Toward an "Ideal" 24×7 System

This section discusses certain desirable characteristics in a 24x7 system and taking concrete steps to attain them. Some of the characteristics may be more pertinent than others for your organization. Your overall solution needs to be designed keeping these characteristics in mind.

Be familiar with the common goals for engineering a 24x7 system

As far as possible, an "ideal" 24×7 system needs to be architected with the following goals in mind:

- **Robustness** The system should accommodate a variety of system and database failures. All single points of failure should be identified, and adequate redundancy should be provided to each such component.
- **Transparent failover** The system should provide as much failover transparency as possible when the primary system crashes, restricting major service disruptions. Note that smooth failover depends on the time taken to detect failure of the primary system and act accordingly. It may require periodic polling to determine stability of the primary system. Setting the poll to occur too frequently may hamper overall system performance, whereas making it occur less often than required may result in a service disruption not being detected till the poll occurs again, potentially causing the disruption to be visible to the end-users. Additionally, once failure is detected, the failover strategy should be robust enough to reroute new database connections, as well as divert (reconnect) existing connections. Keep in mind that existing connections may be active or inactive. Diverting active connections can be a real challenge. The 24×7 solution must enforce having restartability features built into applications (that initiated the active connections). In case that is not possible, then the solution must provide a

wrapper around application-connections to restart as and when necessary, minimizing duplication of work and reissuing the call to the failover instance. A brief service disruption may be evident to users at certain times, as their active connections are broken.

- **Data integrity** The 24×7 should preserve data integrity. There shouldn't be any data loss or violation of inherent data relationships. For instance, while propagating all writes from the primary database to the secondary one, no data loss should be allowed to creep in.
- **Affordability** The cost of engineering the system, and the system itself, ought to be less than the revenue/productivity loss in not attaining 24×7 uptime. The cost of a 24×7 system may be higher in the short run. (Your books of accounts may show relatively astronomical costs for hardware/software for that accounting period). However, such high costs may be mitigated over a period of time, since they represent capital expenditure. It is necessary to consider this fact when comparing the loss from potential downtime with the 24×7 system cost. Always consider system failure during peak hours when computing revenue loss. Doing so allows you to evaluate worst-case scenarios—chances are, system failure may occur during peak hours or may occur during non-peak hours but creep into the peak-hours time frame, if timely recovery is not possible.
- **Optimal resource use** The 24×7 system should attempt to use system resources as optimally as possible, without reaching the ceiling (system saturation), especially during peak hours.
- **Implementation simplicity** Migration to the 24×7 system should be relatively uncomplicated, with downtime and service disruption (to users) being within an acceptable range (this "range" needs to be determined as part of the analysis, prior to crafting the solution). Changes to related components (applications, security policies, and so on) should be feasible.
- **Maintainability** Existing in-house personnel should be able to maintain the new system without having to resort to infeasible means (such as frequent off-site training, complex tools, or regular visits by expert consulting staff)
- **Performance** On a regular day-to-day basis, the new system should not (excessively) impede performance. Note that a certain level of impact may be unavoidable. For instance, if the 24×7 solution requires all application writes to be split across multiple databases (including one at a remote site), the network latency may affect the speed of every write. However, it has to be ensured that such an impact is within an acceptable range.

Your actual solution may not be able to successfully cater to all these goals (especially the *affordability* goal). However, the idea is to accommodate as many goals as possible, starting with the ones most important to your organization. The tips in subsequent chapters may help you in selecting practical, pragmatic solutions, specifically from a database perspective and generally from an overall systems perspective. Chapter 2 especially elaborates on the kind of solutions that are needed in some of the situations outlined previously.

Manage expectations via a solid Service Level Agreement

A Service Level Agreement (SLA) is a document that formally states specific system requirements with regards to availability and performance. Such requirements are generally arrived at after discussions with the end-user community and/or the management. The SLA aids in ensuring that the operations staff and the end-user community are on the same page and that there are no assumptions about the quality of service desired. It clearly states common avenues of systems failure and options available and implemented to recover from such failures. A good SLA also specifies performance versus availability trade-offs and the costs incurred in implementing high availability and performance options. Such an internal SLA also forms the basis of other external SLAs between the company and third-party hardware and software vendors.

Based on my experience, I have seen quite a few companies operate their data centers without a genuine SLA. Even the ones that do have an SLA do not pay a lot of attention to the clauses outlined therein. However, an SLA is absolutely necessary for any company that seeks high database availability. Unless your needs are well known to you (documented), you cannot adequately seek means to satisfy those needs.

The single most important thing that will aid you in determining your database uptime requirements is your end-user expectations. Your organization may support different categories of end-users with varying needs and diverse expectations, such as data-entry operators, mid-level and senior managers, and so on. Certain end-users may be accessing the database for a good eight hours. Other end-users like the VPs and CEO may access it for a few minutes each day. During those few minutes, however, they may be running powerful resource-intensive graphical reports or similar applications. End-user expectations can get pretty vague and fanciful. You need to decide which of these requirements are genuine and which are not. Also keeping those decisions to yourself is not going to help any. They have to be documented in detail in an SLA between you (the Operations Department) and specific end-users. If your end-users are geographically spread out and cannot be easily pinpointed (as in an e-commerce site), the SLA basically needs to outline availability requirements based on

high-level specifications. Such high-level specifications can be derived from initial trial monitoring of database usage patterns, or even generic rules of thumb. For example, a regular financial applications site may start with an universal rule of thumb—the database has to be available between 8:00 A.M. and 6:00 P.M. So an initial SLA may be drawn based on this premise. Later after monitoring (interactive and batch) usage for say, two months, a more specific inference may be drawn and a newer SLA may be created catering to actual usage hours.

Most important, the SLA has to have the following features:

Completeness

A good SLA has to list all key success factors affecting your business. For example, if, for your business to remain viable, the database cannot be down for more than three hours at any given point in time, that fact must be clearly documented. If your database needs to have the ability to accommodate at least 200 concurrent sessions, that must be clearly stated.

Usage of Real-World Numbers

All expectations related to each critical success factor must be documented in real terms. In other words, the SLA must state actual numbers for each expectation. For example, if your system needs to have a standby database located across town, that would cost X number of dollars and is expected to impose a performance strain of Y on the primary production database (due to the replication), that should be mentioned. X and Y may not be real numbers, but may be a percentage, based on educated guesses. It would help to indicate to the user community and the management what kind of tradeoffs they are looking at to achieve high availability. Merely indicating that there would be some performance tradeoff would not help to place their thoughts on the same page as yours. Actual concrete numbers of some kind will validate your expectations and make it real facts, rather than letting it remain just vague assumptions. Again, an SLA is a contract. So rather than just talk about "if we do this, then that happens," it should be clearly specified "if we do this, then that happens; if we do that, then this happens, but the latter option costs twice as much."

Adaptability

An SLA has to be dynamic and up to date. Some organizations create an SLA and conveniently forget all about it after a few months. The primary reason this happens is because an SLA is rigid—so rigid that it is impractical to adopt. A variety of facts, applicable during the time the SLA was created, have been taken into account. As the organization undergoes changes, however, those facts themselves do not remain static. Accordingly, the SLA has to be revamped periodically to accommodate those changes. Especially in the Internet era, where changes (to usage patterns) occur swiftly, your SLA should be flexible enough to expand and accommodate those changes. If it means having to rework your SLA every two months, so be it! For example, in the case of a startup e-commerce site, the customers the site will draw can only be "guesstimated." The initial SLA would be created based on this guesstimate. After a couple of months, however, more concrete figures indicating actual use will be available and can be used to recreate the SLA. The older the SLA is, the more of a gap develops between the concerns it addresses and actual reality. The purchase of new hardware/software using the latest technology might make certain clauses in the SLA redundant. During such times, the SLA has to be updated immediately.

Non-Ambiguity

The SLA should be precise and unambiguous about all points mentioned. There should be sufficient explanation to ensure that there is no two-way interpretation of the same point. For example, merely making a blanket statement like "high availability is required" won't work. The expected hours of uptime should be clearly mentioned. Scheduled maintenance and notification procedures should be outlined. If the same database houses multiple applications, either cumulative information (covering all applications) can be provided, or the information can be broken down by application and then a high-level table can be prepared that consolidates all applications. Additionally, it will help a lot if availability requirements can be broken down by time of day. Table 1-4 provides an example of documenting such uptime requirements. Performance requirements need to be delineated as well. For example, it may be specified that certain small reports should be able to run in 10 minutes or less when there are less than 150 users, but when there are more (as at peak time), then they can run in 30 minutes. Peak versus non-peak performance metrics and critical versus non-critical applications should be documented in the SLA.

Time Interval	Uptime Requirement	Applications Running During Time Interval
08:00 to 18:00	Extremely critical	Materials management, sales, financials, production planning, manufacturing
18:00 to 23:00	Critical	Materials management, manufacturing
23:00 to 04:00	Not in use	
04:00 to 08:00	Critical	Manufacturing, data-warehouse batch jobs

TABLE 1-4. *Uptime Requirements According to Applications in Use*

Drawing on such a specific requirements definition, the operations department can determine when to schedule regular maintenance tasks such as backups and index-rebuilds. Also, listing all applications running during specific time frames helps the DBA to determine what kind of partial availability is acceptable to end-users (which tablespaces can be taken offline during certain times; which need to stay online). Also during recovery operations, such information will help the DBA in determining which application needs to be restored first. (If the data-warehouse batch jobs don't need to be run immediately, there's no point in restoring the warehouse tables first; instead the Sales application tables can be made available on a priority basis.)

Economic and Technical Feasibility

A valid SLA must take into account economic and technological constraints. Any high-availability solution that the SLA lists should not only be technically possible (the technology to implement it should be readily available) but also must be affordable for your organization. Any SLA that violates these clauses would be unfeasible and unfit for implementation. For example, providing real-time replication for ensuring 24×7 availability without the least adverse effect on performance may not be technically possible in your environment. Replicating the entire production database at a different data center across the ocean may be technically possible, but such a solution may be unaffordable and unacceptable to your company. Thus, for an SLA to be successfully implemented, it's vital that representatives from the operations department, senior management and end-user community should take part in the discussions. The end-users should provide the basic requirements, the operations department should come up with possible solutions, and the senior management should keep an eye on economic feasibility. What the operations team may find technically feasible may not be acceptable to the senior management due to the cost involved. If the cost involved in achieving high availability is more than the gains derived from such availability, then the exercise of enhancing availability becomes unnecessary. (If not the entire exercise, at least the part that cost too much becomes unnecessary.) Also, many times, the solution may come from the end-users. If the expense involved in running certain mission-critical batch jobs during the day is too high, then the end-users may opt not to run it every day or even run it late at night. Such a call would have to come from the end-users. Operations personnel generally have little idea as to whether a functional batch job-run can be deferred or not.

Acceptable Mean-Times

A valid SLA has to specify acceptable MTBF and MTTR times for your database either directly or via supporting documents. *MTBF (mean time between failures)* is the average functional time of a system, before it fails. For example, if a database is up and available for use for 600 hours before it crashes due to a disk failure or network failure, its MTBF is said to be 600 hours. Typically, the MTBF of a database is directly dependent on the MTBF of the underlying components.

There are two facets to MTBF: theoretical and operational. *Theoretical* MTBF is the statistics provided by the vendor based on extensive tests within controlled laboratory environments. They do not account for the vagaries of real life (such as manual administrative errors). *Operational* MTBF is the actual life of the component, as experienced in real life.

Let's consider an example to understand MTBF. ABC Corporation has an Oracle8 database running on a Sun Enterprise 4000 with data striped across an EMC 3100 disk-array using RAID-S. Let's say the MTBF of the disk-array is 250,000 hours and the array is composed of 32 disks. That will give us an MTBF average of 7,800 hours (250,000 hours / 32 disks) per disk. This indicates that approximately once every ten months (7,800 hours / 24 hours in a day / 30 days in a month = 10 months), a disk may crash. So in this case, the MTBF of the database will not be more than ten months (since the database relies on those disks to be up and running). In addition, other key components such as network and disparate hardware peripherals (CPU, controllers, and so on) need to be considered before arriving at the net database MTBF. Generally, database MTBF will never be more than the lowest common denominator of all the critical components' MTBF.

MTTR (mean time to recover) is the average time it takes to restore services whenever there is a failure. Let's continue with the preceding example to understand this term better. Let's assume that online database backups are performed on this Oracle8 database every night. The backups start at 2:00 A.M. and end at around 4:00 A.M. Furthermore, the database has four online redo-log files, and an average of two log-switches take place every hour (thereby creating two archived log-files per hour). Let's assume it takes an average of 3 minutes to roll forward each archived log-file during database recovery. So if the database goes down during the peak production hour of 11:00 A.M. due to a disk-controller failure, it will take approximately 8 hours to recover and restore all database operations (Table 1-5). The MTTR in this case will be 8 hours.

A simplistic way of looking at MTBF is the average time your database is up and running. Similarly, MTTR is the average time it's down and unavailable.

As you may see from the preceding discussion, the SLA is the result of some serious studies, evaluations, and benchmarks. It would require major use of critical organizational resources to arrive at the SLA. However, any company that is serious about its database availability needs to invest such resources to produce the SLA. The SLA identifies all weak links in the systems-chain. Only after complete identification of all possible weaknesses can an organization be prepared with viable solutions to meet database uptime requirements.

Task	Time Required
Replace damaged disk-controller	6 hours (this time will depend on your SLA with the disk vendor)
Restore affected data-files from last night's backup onto disk from tape	30 minutes
Perform database recovery (roll forward through 14 archived redo-log files [7 hours since backup ended × 2 archived redo-log files per hour = 14 archived log-files])	42 minutes (3 minutes per archived log)
Perform database recovery (roll back uncommitted transactions)	15 minutes
Reopen database and restart all applications	8 minutes
Buffer time (to accomodate delays in preceeding tasks)	30 minutes
Total time required	**8 hrs (approx.)**

TABLE 1-5. *Tasks Necessary to Recover from a Disk-Controller Failure*

Being only 90 percent available takes away 90 percent of the cost

Something worth really thinking about while determining your uptime requirements is the "90-percent" rule. Being only 90 percent available reduces 90 percent of your expenses. In other words it's the additional 10 percent availability that contributes to 90 percent of the cost of operating in 24×7 mode. It is essential to understand what uptime requirements translate to. Table 1-6 reconciles uptime requirements in percentage with real-world man-hours. As mentioned earlier, being 90 percent available means tolerating a downtime of either 2.4 hours a day, 1 day every 10 days, or 36.5 days a year. Normally, with reasonably adept operations staff and the regular monitoring/proactive maintenance they perform, it is very much possible that your database will be subject to occasional failures. At times, there will be a hardware or software failure, requiring a new component or patch to be applied. At times, there might be environmental disasters like a typhoon or an earthquake. These incidents depend a lot on where your data center is located. If such occurrences are very few and far between, maybe you can incur the risk and just live with them—or maybe, not. You need to evaluate how frequently such things could occur and what could be the extent of damage. What I'm trying to convey here is, you should ask yourself—these failures don't happen every day; should

Uptime Percentage	Downtime per Year
90.0	36 days, 12 hours
99.0	3 days, 15.5 hours
99.9	9 hours
99.99	50 minutes
99.999	5 minutes

TABLE 1-6. *Uptime Statistics in Real-World Numbers*

your company spend a lot of money trying to cover for such failures? Based on my general observation, data centers can run pretty smoothly even with things as simple as a regular backup policy and robust recovery plan in place. In other words, standard system-building techniques are usually adequate to provide around 90 percent availability.

By using the tips in the subsequent chapters, you can implement a relatively cost-effective high-availability plan allowing for component failures and database maintenance tasks. However, such a plan generally will not cover natural or man-made disasters. Being available even during such circumstances requires a lot of money to be invested for replicating your entire data center at a geographically different location. With careful analysis of your business requirements, your environment, and all database components, *you* need to arrive at the right conclusion.

Understand maintenance operations' effect on availability

We keep hearing the word "maintenance" pop up among operations personnel. Why does the database need to be down next weekend night? Why does the system need to be powered off next Saturday at midnight? It's a simple one-word answer: maintenance. All operations managers and administrative personnel realize the importance of systems/database maintenance.

For any system to continue to run smoothly, it needs a touch-up and a tweak every now and then. In the 24×7 context, maintenance tasks can be classified as follows:

- Proactive maintenance
- Reactive maintenance

As the names indicate, *proactive maintenance* is based on both actual database monitoring and certain "good-to-do" age-old wisdom. An example of the former category would be increasing the number of allowable extents on a fast-growing table according to its use to avoid the "MAXEXTENTS reached" error. An example of the latter category would be to place an index segment on a different set of disks, away from its corresponding table segment, to avoid contention between the two, based on OFA (Optimal Flexible Architecture) guidelines from Oracle.

Reactive maintenance is generally based either on last-minute database monitoring or specific errors/problems encountered. An example of the former kind would be adding another data-file to the DATA tablespace in sheer panic, when only 3MB of free space is left in the tablespace and the next extent of a fast-growing table is a huge 5MB chunk. An example of the latter kind would be adding another data-file to the DATA tablespace under the CIO's stern look, after every application user has the message "ORA-1540: Unable to allocate 5242880 bytes in tablespace DATA" on their screen.

Higher availability requirements cause a catch-22 situation by demanding a very high degree of proactive maintenance (and reactive, at times). Many times, such maintenance requires more downtime, which defeats the very purpose of the higher availability requirements. Such situations call for innovative solutions to be implemented that allow proactive maintenance operations to be scheduled at regular intervals without causing an adverse impact on availability. (Chapters 15 to 18 discuss some of these solutions.) Again, it may be wise to note (perhaps as part of the original SLA) that more maintenance is required during the initial life of the database (or any new application), when usage patterns are not as well known.

All necessary maintenance operations have to be identified and listed in the SLA. These maintenance operations need to be understood adequately by all concerned technical parties prior to determining uptime requirements—what are they, why are they necessary, how frequently they need to be performed, and so on. It is absolutely imperative to realize which operations actually cause downtime and why; are there any alternative ways of achieving the same maintenance goals without the accompanying downtime? Table 1-7 lists some sample maintenance operations. You can add to the table according to the specific requirements of your company and make the table a part of your SLA.

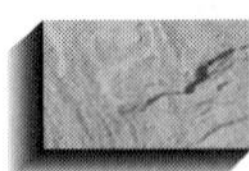

NOTE
The "Frequency" column in Table 1-7 is not meant to serve as a guide on to how often to do things. It merely provides some examples of how often a task could be performed. The required frequency is dependent on a number of factors and may vary from site to site.

Task	Frequency	Downtime Required
Table rebuilds (defragmentation, row-chain repairs)	Once a quarter or after major loads, whichever is sooner	Yes
Index rebuilds (defragmentation)	Once a quarter or after major loads, whichever is sooner	Yes
Analyzing segments for Cost-Based Optimizer	Nightly	No
Analyzing segments for validating structure (checking for database corruption)	Once a quarter (or sooner, if symptoms of corruption are encountered)	Yes
Backups—hot backups	Nightly	No
Backups—export of pre-determined tables/schemas	Weekly	No
Running statistical utilities (utlbstat, utlestat, other home-grown utilities)	Weekly	No
Altering segment characteristics (storage parameters, FREELISTS, INITRANS, PCTUSED, PCTFREE, parallel degree, etc.)	On an as-needed basis	For certain operations
Changing static database initialization parameters (*init.ora* parameters)	On an as-needed basis	Yes
Creating new tablespaces, adding new datafiles to existing tablespaces	As per capacity plan (also on an as-needed basis)	No
Upgrading database to a newer version, applying necessary patches	On an as-needed basis	Yes
Copying specific data to other specialized databases (loading data-warehouses and data-marts from operational data sources)	Nightly	No
Move archived redo-logs to offline media	Nightly	No

TABLE 1-7. *Sample Operational Tasks with Their Frequencies and Downtime Requirements*

Task	Frequency	Downtime Required
Change size of online redo-log files, create more redo-log files	On an as-needed basis	No
Rebuild entire database (change database block size, move database to different machine, defragment entire database [if not too big])	On an as-needed basis	Yes
Copy/apply archived redo-logs to standby database server	On an as-needed basis	No

TABLE 1-7. *Sample Operational Tasks with Their Frequencies and Downtime Requirements* (continued)

Tips for Semi-Technical Managers and Supervisors

The following tips are directed towards semi-technical managers and supervisors.

24×7 uptime requires a radical approach to operations management

Attainment of 24x7 is not just a requirement but is a total philosophy, requiring high levels of proactiveness and commitment from your entire team, including your designers and developers. If high availability is not a concern, then you can afford to be lax. In 24x7 mode, however, laxity may well lead to instant disaster. Your approach makes all the difference between having a well-oiled database providing continuous, peak performance, and having a weak, untuned database continuously crashing down. Every operations task, no matter how simple it sounds, needs to be evaluated: how will it affect the system and the database? Will it acquire an exclusive lock on an important table? Will it render the database unusable? Will it take up too many resources and cause the database to slow down tremendously?

Create "24×7 teams" available during key database-access times

As mentioned before, a single DBA (or even a team of just DBAs) is not enough to handle all problems that could occur. A DBA needs to be paired with adequate support/operations staff. Once your critical times have been identified, it is extremely necessary to have a specific team responsible for each specific time frame.

Ideally, each 24×7 team would be composed of a DBA, a systems administrator, and a network administrator, who would be on-site during that time frame. They need to be aptly supported by a development team and a data administrator, who could be reached immediately in times of crisis. Let's look at an example.

At a company running three large (80GB+) Web-based databases, we have identified the key personnel and the time frames they are accountable for (Table 1-8).

The example in Table 1-8 gives an idea about how an entire day may be broken up into different time frames, based on business done during those hours. Further, Table 1-8 shows a minimum of two DBAs and systems administrators available on-site during all "extremely critical" periods. You may not have two. You may

Time Frame	Importance of Time Frame to Business	Personnel Responsible
07:00 to 15:00	Extremely critical	Primary (on-site): Susan M—DBA Marty G—DBA Joe A—sys admin Michelle P—sys admin Rob F—sys admin Dave S—network admin Brian G—developer Peter H—developer/data admin Secondary (on-call): Sam J—DBA Bill K—sys admin
15:00 to 19:00	Extremely critical	Primary (on-site): Sam J—DBA Lucas S—DBA Thomas A—sys admin Vladimir P—sys admin Bill T—network admin Patti N—developer Secondary (on-call): Susan M—DBA Rob F—sys admin

TABLE 1-8. *A Time-Frame-Based Call-List*

Time Frame	Importance of Time Frame to Business	Personnel Responsible
19:00 to 23:00	Critical	Primary (on-site): Sam J—DBA Lucas S—DBA Thomas A—sys admin Vladimir P—sys admin Patti N—developer/data admin Secondary (on-call) Marty G—DBA Joe A—sys admin
23:00 to 07:00	Non-critical	Primary (on-site): John L – DBA Lisa W – sys admin Secondary (on-call): Lucas S – DBA Vladimir P – sys admin

TABLE 1-8. *A Time-Frame-Based Call-List* (continued)

have more, or even less, people, depending on your organizational requirements and the amount of revenue involved.

One thing to bear in mind though is, throwing people at a potential problem may not prevent it. Presence of these 24x7 teams is not guaranteed to prevent database or system outages. However, having them around helps directly in two ways:

- Proactive monitoring for problems and taking steps to prevent them
- Availability of dedicated resources to quickly resolve problems, when they occur

Another important fact to note here is, you need to be aware of which are the peak periods of database activity and how much revenue is at stake if the database is unavailable during a certain time. If you are bound to lose a significant amount of revenue while the database is unavailable between 19:00 and 21:00 hrs, then it might be worthwhile to ensure that there are at least two DBAs and two sys admins around. However, if you might just lose a paltry sum during those hours, then it might be worth having just one relatively inexpensive operator or maybe just one DBA and/or sys admin watching the systems during that time. If disaster strikes, then that operator may page/call other, more expensive DBAs and/or sys admins.

Another significant fact implicitly depicted in Table 1-8 is, the secondary (on-call) list is a list of people who have already worked for eight hours during their primary shift. Hence it is important to call them in a specific order that least bothers them during their personal time. For example, if Susan M has worked from 07:00 to 15:00 hours, then she's not going to be very happy if she's paged again at 20:00 hours (while she's with her kids). Instead, somebody else should be accountable for that span of time, and Susan should only be reached only in case of an extreme emergency. Such considerations go a long way toward staff retention (which is a major concern in a typical 24×7 environment, where staff tend to get burned out pretty fast).

Also, ensure that members of your key staff never take their vacations simultaneously. I know, this is the holy rule, that every operations manager and CIO is aware of, right? Well, not always! I have heard the following conversation more than once:

> Operations Manager (OM): "Bob, we have a problem. The database seems to have crashed"
> CIO: "So, is Jeff looking at it?"
> OM: "Err...Jeff's on vacation, right now"
> CIO: "Oh! How about Lisa?"
> OM: "Actually, Lisa's away too! She's coming back on the twentieth, though..."
> CIO: "OK...So what are our options now? Can we reach Jeff somehow?"
> OM: "Actually we don't know where Jeff is right now... I paged him a half-hour ago. Joe, the new guy, and I are looking at the system right now. I will call back with more details soon..."

Moral of the story: Make absolutely sure that you have at least one key person in each area, who knows his or her stuff, available at *all* times.

Maintain an escalation-list of individuals to be notified during crises

An *escalation-list* is a list of individuals, who need to be contacted in a specific order of importance during times of disaster. Table 1-9 gives an example of such an escalation-list.

Hours of Downtime	Person to be Contacted	Title of the Person
Immediate	Refer to "Call-list"	Concerned technical administrator(s) [DBA, sys admin, network admin]
0.5	Jeff A	Operations manager
0.5	Christine L	Customer service manager
1.0	Sheila P	CIO
1.0	Greg S	VP—Customer Service
2.0+	Timothy S	VP—Sales
2.0+	Leslie G	CEO

TABLE 1-9. *A Sample Escalation-List*

Such an escalation list will help manage expectations better during downtime. For example, if the database is down or expected to be down for more than two hours, it's a good idea to let the VP of Sales know about it. That way he or she could call up key customers and inform them about the situation personally. It's always better for a senior management person to call up key customers and inform them about your site being down, than letting them figure it out themselves via repeated frustrating attempts at logging on.

Also, it's sometimes amazing how fast things get done when the technical personnel realize that the CEO *knows* that the database is down and that *they* are working on it (provided the CEO is not standing behind their shoulders and watching). Again, it's necessary to attain some balance here. Having an escalation that occurs too quickly is a good way to cast too much pressure on the DBA and have him or her work badly.

Always provide advance notice of outages to your customers/end-users

It's been my experience that end-users and customers get mad at outages primarily, not because of the outage itself, but due to its abruptness, which interrupts the normal functioning of the business. If sufficient advance notice had been given, they could have (in many cases) planned around the outage, so the impact would have been minimal.

A sudden outage comes across as the operations personnel being incompetent and/or careless about the end-user. Especially in e-commerce, where it's very difficult to reach out to the customer, leave alone to maintain a close relationship, giving advance notice is very difficult but, at the same time, highly essential.

The best that one can do during such circumstances is to post a message on the home page of the Web site prominently mentioning the outage. If possible, an e-mail message may also be sent to a specific group of key customers (no spam, please!) informing them about the outage. Ideally, at least 24 to 48 hours notice needs to be provided, depending on the severity of the outage.

Summary

This chapter focused on the primary necessity of a high-availability site: accurately identifying database uptime requirements. Also, the basic 24x7 concepts were explained from both technical and non-technical perspectives. The primary components on which a database is dependent on were listed. Finally, an important weapon in the hands of both end-users and operations personnel was discussed: the Service Level Agreement.

In the next chapter, we consider different emergencies commonly encountered and look at ways of dealing with them.

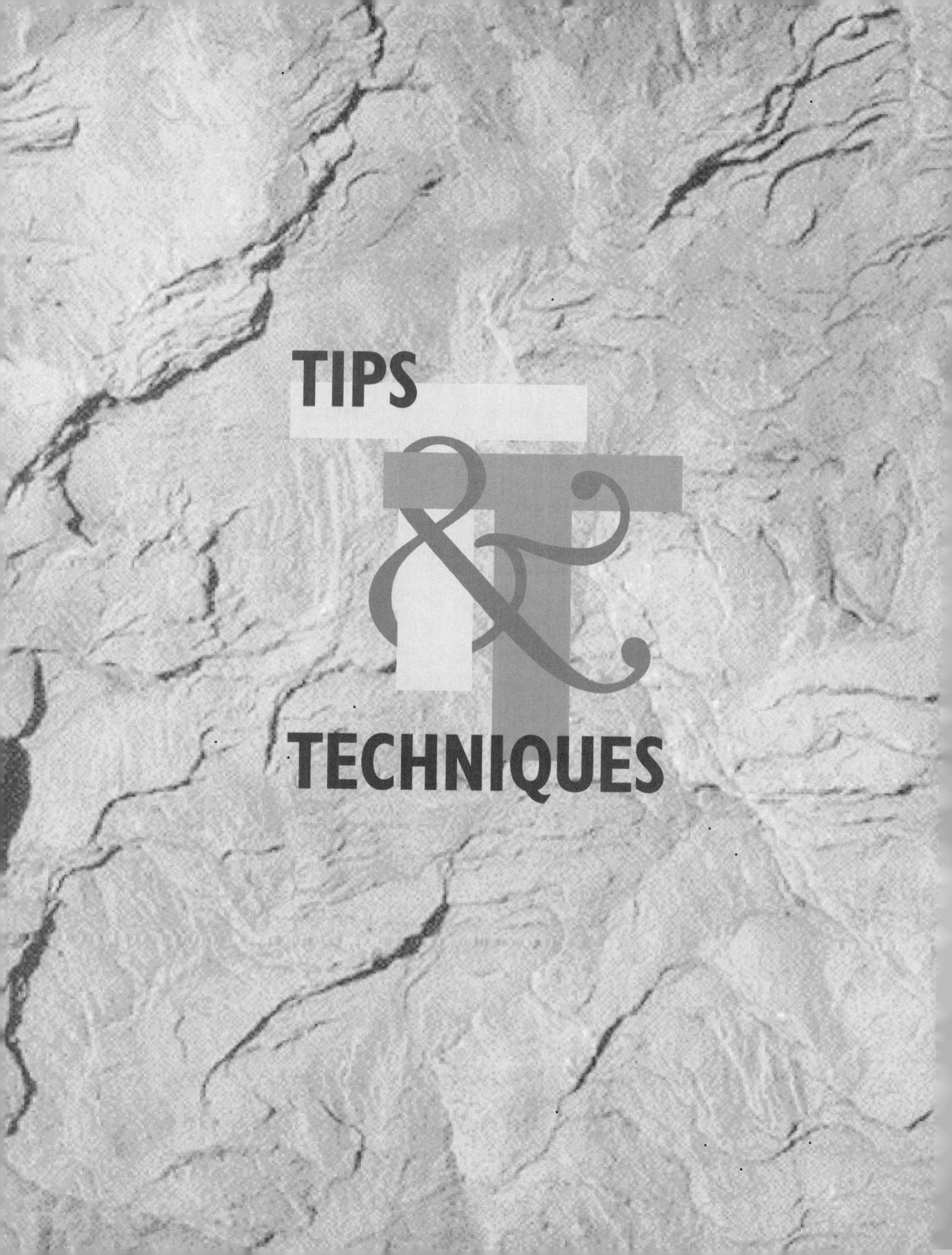
TIPS
&
TECHNIQUES

CHAPTER 2

Understanding and Dealing with Emergencies

Administering a 24×7 site requires a high level of proactiveness. Even then, certain unique, unanticipated emergencies can occur that can tear your uptime statistics to shreds. For instance, you may have managed to achieve 99.9 percent availability (less than nine hours of downtime) throughout the year and it's almost the end of the year (phew!). However, a major outage may occur during the last week of the year and bring your uptime record crashing down. Accordingly, it is necessary to familiarize yourself with the emergencies that can potentially affect your site and come up with robust measures for preventing and combating them. Dealing with emergencies can potentially consume a lot of time and energy of administrative personnel in a 24×7 site.

This chapter offers the following tips and techniques:

- Categorize and List All Emergencies Specific to Your Environment
- Know What to Do in an Emergency

Additionally, the chapter presents a sample format of an emergency list allowing potential service disruptions to be listed in a comprehensive manner. This list can be referenced for restoring normalcy as soon as possible. Finally, the chapter also lists some common emergencies specific to an Oracle environment and ways to overcome them.

What Is an Emergency?

In the 24x7 context, what is an emergency? Any current or impending incident that seriously threatens availability and/or performance in the immediate or short term is termed an emergency. During an emergency, it is essential to analyze

- What has actually happened or is about to happen?
- What are the solutions to recover?
- Which among them is the best? The best solution is one that allows the outage to be prevented, but, if it is inevitable, limits its duration. The solution that would successfully restrict the outage to MTTR specifications within the SLA needs to be chosen.

Though performance-related emergencies generally take a back seat when compared to availability, to many 24x7 customers, a badly performing database may be equivalent to no database at all! A slow database may repel end users, including key customers. To quote a personal example, I have in the past changed Web-based e-mail service providers when I experience excessive and frequent delays in retrieving my e-mail messages with the current provider. Each time that happens, the provider loses customers like me, due to increasing dissatisfaction with the service. Either customers remain dormant and don't use that service for a while or they just switch to another provider. With strong rivals just around the corner, a company cannot remain competitive in its particular market space if it is continuously bogged down by bad performance or frequent outages. And this is especially so in the e-business market space. A new customer could be lost forever in just the few seconds it takes to type in a new URL, if a Web site appears to be very slow or unresponsive. For instance, if www.etrade.com appears to be excessively slow, a new investor could easily switch over to www.charlesschwab.com, or vice versa. Accordingly, any company operating in 24x7 mode needs to take threats to performance almost as seriously as threats to availability. As mentioned in Chapter 1, however, in situations where they clash, availability has to be given priority.

Database complexity greatly influences the frequency of emergencies. Complexity is determined by a variety of factors such as database size, the number of schemas and segments, the relationships among them, the number of concurrent users and/or batch jobs, the number of hardware and software (applications) components involved, the number of tablespaces and data-files, and so on. For instance, if the database size runs into hundreds of gigabytes or even terabytes, it will consist of a large number of components (disks, data-files, tables, and so on), each one susceptible to failure. And given the bulky size, recovery from failure may be tricky. Accordingly, complexity frequently determines the duration of an outage.

Categorize and list all emergencies specific to your environment

In Chapter 1, downtime was broadly classified as occurring due to manual glitches, hardware/software failures, environmental failures, and natural/man-made disasters. Based on this classification, a list of things specific to your environment needs to be prepared. Such a list may initially be prepared from the 24x7 team's (composed of DBAs, system administrators, network administrators, and so on) individual experience. Try to include as many potential failures in the list as you can think of. Besides identifying all possibilities, the list must also include recommended solutions or steps to recover. In some instances, the possible solutions may be many, each more appropriate than the others under specific circumstances. Rather than listing all possible solutions for a single failure scenario at a macro level, list all possible permutations and combinations of each critical failure and the best possible solution to cater to that specific failure. In other words, rather than just provide a broad outline of the recovery scenario and leave the administrative personnel at the scene to figure out which one to use, mention just one best solution for a specific form of failure to eliminate guess work. If such guess work cannot be totally eliminated in your environment, try to eliminate as much as possible. That should be the primary objective of such a list. Guess work is not bad in itself; however, due to the intense pressure on administrative personnel during outages, it is easy to make the wrong decision and potentially increase the outage duration by causing more problems. At times, as I have observed during database crashes, the in-house personnel pick up the manual and attempt recovery without taking sufficient time to analyze the scenario and assess the damage. They perform recovery or make changes without prior backups to revert to, in case their attempt to restore normalcy is not successful. Even senior, highly experienced people are prone to errors, due to the pressure. And it is not always possible to predict who (among the administrative personnel) would be actually around at the time of failure to restore normalcy, what kind of expertise they would have, what kind of damage analysis they would perform, what kind of guesses they would make regarding the cause and effect of the failure, and what steps they would take to restore normalcy. Accordingly, it is highly recommended to include the best possible course of action to take during each failure scenario. If the course of action is too comprehensive to list in the narrow space provided, you may place references to other documents, where detailed instructions are available (the sample emergency list that follows gives examples of listing the actual steps in some cases and references to other in-house documentation and third-party books and manuals for other cases, which may be more complicated).

Know What to Do in an Emergency

Even though specific failures may be many across all categories, the general course of action is more or less the same in each scenario and may be outlined in this way:

1. Proactively take steps to prevent failure. This refers to proactive maintenance tasks such as checking for database corruption, locking conflicts, space issues (whether segments can grow as needed), and so on.
2. Look for signs of potential (imminent) failure. This refers to having extensive monitoring in place and frequently studying the results of such monitoring to detect potential failure.
3. If signs of impending failure are observed, take steps to prevent the failure.
4. If failure occurs regardless of preventive steps taken, switch over/fail over as smoothly as possible to the standby system/database.
5. Ensure that appropriate administrative personnel are immediately notified and other parties (senior management, end users, customers, and so on) are notified, as and when necessary, of the failure.
6. Assess the damage.
7. Think of possible solutions.
8. Select the most appropriate solution.
9. Apply the solution.
10. Restore normalcy. This would involve restarting the database(s), the listener(s), the applications and notifying management, end users, and others that the database services have been restored. If the failover systems are not as capable as the original systems, then you will need to switch back over to the original (after it has been restored/repaired). If the failover systems are as powerful as the original, then they can continue to function as the primary, and the original system can function as a standby until it becomes necessary to switch over once again.
11. Do a postmortem of the failure. Such a postmortem should be a complete analysis of what went wrong, why, and what could have been done to prevent it. Such analysis would help in augmenting preventive policies and procedures currently in place.

The emergency list just outlined will directly aid in steps 6, 7, and 8. Furthermore, such a list should form part of the more comprehensive documentation providing guidelines for each of the preceding steps. Even though some of the preceding steps might strike one as being mere common sense, the concept of common sense becomes very subjective during intense pressure. At times, I have observed, during outage postmortems, what is common sense and what is not being heavily debated. Accordingly, it is advisable to presume that the administrative person responding to the emergency is fairly inexperienced and provide detailed instructions to aid him or her take the appropriate steps.

As you may note, the preceding steps refer to a failover system/database. Thus, comprehensive failover strategies need to be in place, which can be resorted to if necessary. Note that if the time taken to perform the failover is higher than the time to restore/repair the currently malfunctioning system, the failover becomes redundant. The switchover needs to be implemented to occur as smoothly as possible, with the least impact on end users. All client connections need to be switched over gracefully. Chapter 6 elaborates on application/user failover strategies that need to be considered during the switchover operation, and Chapters 15 to 18 cover database failover in more detail.

The Emergency List

A sample emergency list in Table 2-1 gives you an idea of the overall structure and its contents. You do not have to adopt the exact same format. As long as you systematically list and document all emergency scenarios, you may adopt any format, as you feel appropriate. The contents within the sample format provided are not comprehensive in terms of emergencies covered under each category (it would take a whole book to offer a comprehensive listing). Accordingly, prior to adopting this format, you must enhance it to cover scenarios specific to your environment. Another list later in the chapter provides a relatively more comprehensive list of emergencies from an Oracle perspective. The sample emergency list lists all events as scheduled or unscheduled. Just because there is an emergency does not mean that preventive measures (especially if requiring an outage) cannot be scheduled in advance. Rather, many times, it's possible to have advance knowledge (however little it is) of an impending emergency and schedule a maintenance task and/or an outage to respond to it. Also, proactively performing tasks to prevent emergencies can be easily scheduled with sufficient advance notice to end users and customers.

Emergency classification: hardware/software failure

Description	Reason	Recommended steps for recovery	Scheduled (Y/N)	Times occurred in current year	Avg. time taken to recover	Downtime
Hardware components						
Unmirrored disk failure	Hardware problem	Shut down services Replace damaged disk Restore files lost/corrupted Perform database recovery Restart services	N	0	60 mins	60 mins, if failover is not initiated (3 mins if failover is initiated)
Mirrored disk failure	Hardware problem	Replace damaged disk (hot-pluggable) Resilver new disk with mirror	N	0	25 mins	0 mins
RAID 5 Controller failure	Hardware problem	Refer to Document 10112A, Chapter 9, page 214 for detailed instructions	N	0	120 mins	120 mins (3 mins)
CPU failure	Hardware problem	Refer to Document 2012C, Chapter 8, page 158 for detailed instructions	N	0	10 mins	0 mins
Software component		**Operating system (Solaris 7)**				
Heavy swapping	Insufficient memory	Stop all unimportant jobs until swapping subsides Upgrade memory to increase capacity Determine if some applications can use less memory	Y (memory upgrade can be scheduled)	1	Varies	0 mins
Out of swap space	Memory leak	Identify source of memory leak Repair source	N	0	Varies	0 to 15 mins (may require a reboot)

TABLE 2-1. *A Sample Emergency-List Format*

Description	**Reason**	**Recommended steps for recovery**	**Scheduled (Y/N)**	**Times occurred in current year**	**Avg. time taken to recover**	**Downtime**
Software component		**Oracle8 v8.0.5**				
Maxextents reached (ORA-1628 to 1632 and ORA-1656)	Physical storage parameters of segment set improperly	See Chapter 12 of *Oracle 24x7 Tips & Techniques*	N	3	4 mins	4 mins
Unable to allocate next extent (ORA-1650 to 1655)	Insufficient free space in tablespace	See Chapter 12 of *Oracle 24x7 Tips and Techniques*	N	1	15 mins	15 mins (3 mins)
Emergency classification: Manual glitches						
Description	**Reason**	**Recommended steps for recovery**	**Scheduled (Y/N)**	**Times occurred in current year**	**Avg. time taken to recover**	**Downtime**
Data-file deleted or overwritten	Accident	See Document 8012A, page 24	N	0	60 mins	60 mins (for users of that tablespace). If tablespace is critical, failover may be initiated, causing 3 mins. of downtime.
Online redo-log deleted or over-written	Accident	See Document 8012A, page 29	N	0	60 mins	60 mins (3 mins)
Table truncated	Accident	See Document 8012A, page 81	N	2	Varies	Possible, varies
Table dropped	Accident	See Document 8012A, page 79	N	0	Varies	Possible, varies

TABLE 2-1. *A Sample Emergency-List Format* (continued)

Emergency classification: Environmental failures

Description	Reason	Recommended steps for recovery	Scheduled (Y/N)	Times occurred in current year	Avg. time to recover	Downtime
Power failure	Building maintenance heavy rains	Automatic switchover by UPS	Y	2	2 hours	0 hrs.
Workers' strikes		Ensure all necessary components are readily accessible	Y	0	Varies	Possible, would vary
Building construction/ maintenance	Building Maintenance	Administrative personnel to be in standby mode	Y	0	Varies	Possible, varies

Emergency classification: Natural/man-made disaster

Description	Reason	Recommended steps for recovery	Scheduled (Y/N)	Times occurred in current year	Avg. time taken to recover	Downtime
Fires		Initiate failover. See Document 9124A, page 22 for recovery steps	N	0	Varies	3 mins
Floods		Initiate failover. See Document 9124A, page 45	N	0	Varies	3 mins
Tornadoes	Act of nature	Initiate failover. See Document 9124A, page 85	N	0	Varies	3 mins
Earthquakes	Act of nature	Initiate failover. See Document 9124A, page 128	N	0	Varies	3 mins

TABLE 2-1. *A Sample Emergency-List Format* (continued)

NOTE
All references to documents under "Recommended steps for recovery" are just examples and not actual references. While creating the emergency list, you may make actual references to in-house documentation, books, manuals, and so forth.

Under "Downtime," the 3 mins mentioned in parentheses refer to the downtime that will be incurred if failover operations are resorted to. The "3 mins" number used here is just an example and may be more or less (even none at all) depending on the actual failover solution used.

Hardware failures pertain to failures experienced by different components such as disks, controllers, CPUs, memory, routers, gateways, cables, tape drives, fans, and so on. Such failures generally call for the malfunctioning component to be repaired or replaced. Once that's done, regular operations can be restarted. It is important to maintain multiple components for those susceptible to frequent failures. Single points of failure are common causes of high downtime. For instance, twin-tailed disks (connected across two nodes) or mirrored disks allow systems to remain functional even when a node or mirror goes down (in the case of a node going down, there may be a brief disruption, again depending on the failover solution implemented). If just a single component is maintained, during the time it is being repaired/replaced (the repair window), service will be unavailable. Sometimes, the time required to obtain a component can be horrendously long. For example, when we blew a disk controller at a client site, the hardware engineers determined that the component needed to be totally replaced. Alas! It was not available locally and had to be flown in from out of state, taking at least two days to get in and be replaced. Situations like these can cause tremendous downtime. A two-day service interruption may cause a company to go out of business in certain cases. To avoid situations like these, some of my clients have a "component-availability guarantee" clause put in all hardware contracts, wherein the vendor would ensure that specific components prone to failure would be available locally or obtained within an acceptable predetermined time period from specific remote sources for immediate replacement. Identify all critical components and augment them with clones. Additionally, all hardware should be maintained securely inside cabinets to prevent accidental (or intentional) damage. All guidelines from the manufacturer (temperature, proximity to other devices, and so on) should be strictly followed. Cabling should be done as neatly as possible, so as not to get in the way of people walking about. Raised floors in your data centers greatly help in preventing accidents.

Software should be individually classified, prior to preparing an emergency list. Emergencies pertaining to different software components should be covered in detail separately. Instances of different software components include the OS, RDBMS, RAID, and volume management software, media (tape/disk) management software, custom application software, middleware such as TP monitors, and so on. Software need not necessarily fail to cause an emergency. It may need regular maintenance. Such maintenance may result in downtime. Hence, such maintenance operations need to be listed and their impact fully apprehended. Also, certain maintenance tasks help in limiting high downtime in the future. Accordingly, it may be necessary to incur a little downtime to prevent future emergencies. HA (high-availability) solutions (such as Oracle Parallel Server, standby databases, and replication) help tremendously by allowing failover during hardware/software failures.

A valid backup is essential to enable a site to come back to normal after manual glitches. If an important table is dropped by the junior DBA during peak hours, point-in-time recovery or an export dump-file would allow the site to come back up relatively soon. However, for allowing services to be available even as recovery is being performed, either standby databases or the less resource-intensive "standby tables" will help tremendously (Chapter 15 provides more details on standby tables).

Power outages are a common environmental failure experienced by most sites. A good practice is to have an agreement with the facility management to provide sufficient advance notice prior to a major outage. For instance, at a client site, we have an agreement with the building management that provides us with at least 72 hours notice prior to an outage lasting 4 hours or more. However, even such agreements are not totally guaranteed to prevent random power failures. Hence, there's nothing like a UPS (uninterrupted power supply) system with the required capacity to take over during intermittent power failures and prevent disruptions. Any site requiring serious 24×7 database access ought to make the investment in buying robust UPS systems for all their data centers (primary, as well as secondary). Like other hardware, these UPS systems should also be well protected within locked cabinets, with very few people (UPS technicians, for instance) having access to them. The electricity outlets should be out-of-reach of most people. The last thing you want is someone accidentally/intentionally switching off your power and/or UPS systems.

High-availability solutions to withstand natural/man-made disasters can get very expensive. Geographically replicated data centers (hardware and software) via geo-mirrors may ensure database availability during disasters. As mentioned earlier, it is important to evaluate whether availability is still desired during natural/man-made disasters. During a war, for instance, availability may not be required. However, the answer to this question eventually depends on the scope of operations of the company and its market. For instance, if the market for a product or service sold by the company exists beyond the affected geographical area or the company has branch offices in countries not involved in the war or the company supplies key defense equipment, the company may have to remain operational even during a war. This analysis should be done fairly early and integrated into the Service Level Agreement.

An aspect of maintaining such an emergency list is that it records and documents the number of times various emergencies occur. Over a period of time, it highlights which emergencies your site is most prone to. Based on such information, appropriate steps can be taken to resolve and prevent such emergencies from occurring too frequently. The objective of the emergency list is to provide as much information as possible regarding potential failures, so that the element of surprise is removed and the correct preventive measures can be taken well in time, in a relatively pressure-free environment (the higher the pressure, the greater the number of errors made). Even if failure has already occurred, the list helps in keeping downtime to the minimum by systematically listing the steps to be taken to bring the system back up as soon as possible. However, the list would need to be constantly updated by the concerned administrative personnel in order to remain accurate. Table 2-2 provides a list of emergencies that commonly occur in an Oracle environment (again, this is not a comprehensive list). Please keep in mind that it's difficult to prepare a complete list of all possible emergencies. Such a list cannot be created from the ground up; rather, it develops as the life of the database progresses. You might encounter emergencies that you could hardly have anticipated. Such rare emergencies need to be eventually listed, so that you and your team can have an in-depth perspective into the nature of all emergencies your site has encountered or is likely to encounter. Unless such a perspective on emergencies is gained, you cannot effectively be prepared to stop them. This list mentions all events that are known show-stoppers and cause downtime in one way or the other. These events range from bringing the entire database down to bringing down just a solitary table and the applications that use that table. Your database may be up and running, but if the jobs running on it fail constantly, the users are not getting their work done. You need to ask yourself, which are the events that prevent my database from being accessed or that render the data within the database unavailable to my users? List all events that come to mind and devise methods to minimize their occurrence. If they are inevitable, devise ways to ensure that MTTR requirements are comfortably met in each case. The experience of the administrative personnel involved in preparing the emergency list plays a vital role in listing the different kinds of "common" and "uncommon" emergencies.

In the "Steps to recover" column of Table 2-2, a reference to another chapter is often provided, where details may be found. Similarly, when you adapt this list, you may place a reference to your in-house documentation or a book or Oracle manual (including chapter and page number) where more details are readily available. That will prevent this list from getting too cramped or excessively lengthy. All events, both internal (logical) and external (physical) to Oracle, are listed. In the "Avg. time taken to recover" and "Downtime caused" columns, the duration of the entire operation and the actual downtime are respectively mentioned. For specific events, the concept of "average time" gives the wrong picture, since the time to recover/downtime varies significantly during each occurrence. For such events, I just describe the average time taken/downtime as "Varies," rather than risk presenting an incorrect picture.

Emergency classification: hardware/software failure	
Software component	Oracle8 v8.0.5
Scope	Internal to Oracle
Emergency Description	Snapshot too old (ORA-1555)
Reason	Readers blocked by writers
Steps to recover	Chapter 11 covers this topic in detail.
Scheduled (Y/N)	N
Times occurred in current year	7
Avg. time taken to recover	Varies depending on the reason.
Downtime caused	0 mins, if the job runs successfully in a subsequent attempt. If the job constantly fails, the output may not be produced, thus causing the report or data to be unavailable to end users or subsequent jobs.
Emergency Description	Maxextents reached (ORA-1628 to 1632 and ORA-1656)
Reason	Physical storage parameters of segment set improperly
Steps to recover	Alter the segment to increase the value for maxextents or make maxextents UNLIMITED (v7.3 onward) and/or Drop and rebuild the segment to exist within a lesser number of extents (by increasing the INITIAL and NEXT storage parameters appropriately).
Scheduled (Y/N)	The segment rebuild can be scheduled.
Times occurred in current year	4
Avg. time taken to recover	Altering a segment takes a few seconds. However, if one or more sessions hold a lock on that segment, those sessions would need to be terminated prior to altering it, since altering requires a lock on the segment. Also, time to rebuild a segment depends on the segment size.

TABLE 2-2. *List of Emergencies in an Oracle Server Environment*

Downtime caused	Downtime here would be the time that the segment could be populated via DML. Such downtime can vary. If the situation is spotted early, then the segment may be altered quickly and downtime would be very limited. However, if the segment is in this state for a long time, then the downtime for the applications accessing that segment will be high. Also, rebuilding that segment may cause significant downtime for all applications accessing that segment. If the segment in question is a rollback or temporary segment (and not a table or index segment), then downtime will be little, as well. However, for a large table or index, it can be substantial.
Emergency Description	Unable to allocate next extent (ORA-1650 to 1655)
Reason	Insufficient contiguous free space in the tablespace
Steps to recover	Add another data-file to the tablespace or Extend the size of the existing data-file(s) and/or Coalesce available free-space chunks to increase the contiguous free space (via the ALTER TABLESPACE command in v7.3 and above, or set PCTINCREASE for that tablespace to a value greater than zero to allow SMON to do it—I do not recommend the latter choice—see Chapter 12 for details)
Scheduled (Y/N)	N
Times occurred in current year	3
Avg. time taken to recover	The time taken to add another data-file or resize the existing data-files depends on the sizes of the data-files. Coalescing is fairly fast but may not yield any result in terms of producing contiguous free space. Accordingly, the former two options would be more reliable.

TABLE 2-2. *List of Emergencies in an Oracle Server Environment* (continued)

Downtime caused	As in the previous case, the amount of time taken to detect this problem and resolve it would be the time the applications accessing the segment (that could not extend) are down. Also, adding a large data-file may be time-consuming (at times, I have observed a 2GB data-file to take up to 25 minutes to be created. This delay is primarily due to the excessive writes that occur, causing I/O contention). In such situations, consider adding a smaller data-file (like 100MB or so) to temporarily get through the situation very fast and thus reduce the downtime. Later this small data-file may be extended for consistency with other data-files. Ensure that this small data-file is bigger than the next extent that needs to be allocated for the segment currently experiencing trouble.
Emergency Description	Table corruption
Reason	Hardware problems/bugs OS bugs Oracle bugs Application bugs Accidents
Steps to recover	Detect the cause of corruption Rectify the cause of corruption Import the table if an export dump file exists If hot/cold backup exists, restore the table off the backup (via point-in-time recovery on a different machine)
Scheduled (Y/N)	Certain tasks may be scheduled (such as rectifying the cause of corruption)
Times occurred in current year	0
Avg. time taken to recover	Varies (depending on the table size, how recent the backups are, how many archived logs need to be applied, etc.)
Downtime caused	Varies

TABLE 2-2. *List of Emergencies in an Oracle Server Environment* (continued)

Emergency Description	Index corruption
Reason	As mentioned under "Table corruption" (In addition, SQL*Loader's direct path may leave indexes in UNUSABLE state.)
Steps to recover	Detect the cause of corruption Rectify the cause of corruption Drop and re-create the index (do not use the ALTER INDEX REBUILD command). Re-creation can be done in parallel and unrecoverable/nologging modes.
Scheduled (Y/N)	Index re-creation can be scheduled in advance.
Times occurred in current year	0
Avg. time taken to recover	Varies
Downtime caused	Varies
Emergency Description	SYS-owned segment (data-dictionary) corruption
Reason	As mentioned under "Table corruption" (In addition, directly manipulating data-dictionary segments can lead to corruption. For instance, trying to rename columns by manipulating the data-dictionary tables can corrupt the data dictionary, especially if done improperly. Also, incorrectly installing/configuring Oracle may lead to corruption.)
Steps to recover	Detect the cause of corruption Rectify the cause of corruption Restore and recover database from latest backup
Scheduled (Y/N)	N
Times occurred in current year	0
Avg. time taken to recover	Varies, depending on the size of database
Downtime caused	Varies

TABLE 2-2. *List of Emergencies in an Oracle Server Environment* (continued)

Emergency Description	Rollback segment corruption
Reason	As mentioned under "Table corruption"
Steps to recover	Detect the cause of corruption Rectify the cause of corruption Take the corrupt rollback segment offline Drop and re-create the corrupt rollback segment
Scheduled (Y/N)	N
Times occurred in current year	1
Avg. time taken to recover	Varies
Downtime caused	Varies. I have seen cases where applications cannot perform DML due to the corruption, thus resulting in downtime for users of those applications. Also, the steps taken to detect the actual source of corruption may be time consuming (going through the right trace dumps, finding out which dba [data-block address] is corrupt and which segment that DBA belongs to, etc.).
Emergency Description	Table fragmented
Reason	Improper physical storage parameters defined for the table Heavy DML operations performed on the table Heavy contention for space among different segments in the tablespace that the table is present in Long columns/BLOBs present within the table
Steps to recover	Reorganize the table (retain the data either in a different table or in an export dump file, then drop and re-create the table with more appropriate storage parameters and repopulate the data more densely). The newer storage parameters should prevent high fragmentation.

TABLE 2-2. *List of Emergencies in an Oracle Server Environment* (continued)

Scheduled (Y/N)	Y. The reorganization can be scheduled.
Times occurred in current year	2
Avg. time taken to recover	Varies. Depends on the size of the table, physical resources (disks/controllers, etc.) involved, and other factors.
Downtime caused	Varies. Chapter 8 discusses ways to reduce downtime during reorganizations.
Emergency Description	Index fragmented
Reason	Improper physical storage parameters defined for the index Heavy DML operations performed on the index Heavy contention for space among different segments in the tablespace that the index is present in
Steps to recover	Drop and rebuild the index (in parallel and unrecoverable/nologging mode, if the index is large) with appropriate storage parameters Prior to large data loads in DSS environments, the indexes may be dropped and rebuilt as a post-load step
Scheduled (Y/N)	Y. The index rebuild can be scheduled.
Times occurred in current year	11
Avg. time taken to recover	Varies
Downtime caused	Varies
Emergency Description	Excessive row-chaining
Reason	Improper physical storage parameters defined for the table LONG/BLOB columns present in table

TABLE 2-2. *List of Emergencies in an Oracle Server Environment* (continued)

Steps to recover	Row chaining in tables with LONG/BLOB columns may be inevitable. However, if the row chaining is not due to LONG/BLOB columns, then the following steps may be taken to repair the situation. If the table is very large and only a small degree of row chaining exists: Alter the storage parameters on the table to discourage future row-chaining Analyze the table to identify all chained rows (capture their ROWIDs in the CHAINED_ROWS table) Copy those rows to a temporary table Delete those rows off the original table Reinsert those rows into the original table from the temporary table Drop the temporary table Reanalyze the original table to ensure that there are no more chained rows If the table is small/medium-sized or a high degree of row-chaining exists: Copy the data to a temporary table or export the data to a dump file Drop the original table Re-create the original table with appropriate storage parameters Repopulate the table from the temporary table or the export dump file Drop the temporary table, if one is used Analyze the new table to ensure that row-chaining has been eliminated

TABLE 2-2. *List of Emergencies in an Oracle Server Environment* (continued)

Scheduled (Y/N)	Y. The repair tasks can be scheduled.
Times occurred in current year	2
Avg. time taken to recover	Varies
Downtime caused	Varies
Emergency classification: hardware/software failure	
Software component	Oracle8 v8.0.5
Scope	External to Oracle
Emergency Description	Version upgrade
Reason	Regular maintenance To eliminate serious bugs in current version
Steps to recover	Either the Migration Utility provided in the newer version can be utilized or The data can be preserved, the database upgraded (remove the old database, install the new version, create the new database as per newer requirements) and then repopulated with the preserved data
Scheduled (Y/N)	Y
Times occurred in current year	1
Avg. time taken to recover	Varies
Downtime caused	Varies
Emergency Description	Application of patches
Reason	To eliminate serious bugs in the current version

TABLE 2-2. *List of Emergencies in an Oracle Server Environment* (continued)

Steps to recover	Steps are generally specific to the patch being applied. However, they more or less follow this pattern: Take a complete hot backup Stop all access to the database (stop all applications) Do a normal shutdown of the database(s) and listener(s) Copy the necessary files to the appropriate directories Relink the Oracle executables Restart the database(s) and the listener(s) and test the configuration Restart all applications Test everything to ensure normalcy
Scheduled (Y/N)	Y
Times occurred in current year	3
Avg. time taken to recover	25 minutes (incl. testing)
Downtime caused	5 minutes
Emergency Description	Initialization parameter changes
Reason	To enable/disable certain Oracle options To tune options currently enabled To enable events at the instance level for debugging, testing, etc.
Steps to recover	Modify the necessary *init.ora* file to make changes as necessary Do a normal shutdown of the database Restart the database Test the parameter changes to ensure there are no problems

TABLE 2-2. *List of Emergencies in an Oracle Server Environment* (continued)

Scheduled (Y/N)	Y
Times occurred in current year	14
Avg. time taken to recover	3 minutes
Downtime caused	3 minutes. Please note that certain parameters are dynamically changeable (via the ALTER SESSION or ALTER SYSTEM commands) and do not require a database bounce.
Emergency Description	SYSTEM data-file lost/corrupt
Reason	Hardware problems/bugs OS bugs Other software (Volume Managers, RAID, etc.) bugs Accidents
Steps to recover	Detect the cause of corruption Rectify the cause of corruption Restore database from the backups and roll forward using the archived redo-logs
Scheduled (Y/N)	N
Times occurred in current year	0
Avg. time taken to recover	Varies (depending on the database size, how recent the backups are, how many archived logs need to be applied, etc.)
Downtime caused	Varies (entire database would be down, since the SYSTEM tablespace is involved)
Emergency Description	TEMP data-file lost/corrupt
Reason	As mentioned under "SYSTEM data-file lost/corrupt"

TABLE 2-2. *List of Emergencies in an Oracle Server Environment* (continued)

Steps to recover	Detect the cause of corruption Rectify the cause of corruption If there is adequate space for another temporary tablespace: Create an intermediate temporary tablespace Alter all user IDs to use the new temporary tablespace If there is inadequate space for another temporary tablespace: Alter all user IDs to use their default tablespace as the temporary tablespace (note this may fragment their default tablespace) Take offline and drop corrupt temporary tablespace Re-create the temporary tablespace Alter all user IDs to use the re-created temporary tablespace Drop the intermediate temporary tablespace, if one was created
Scheduled (Y/N)	N
Times occurred in current year	1
Avg. time taken to recover	60 mins
Downtime caused	0 mins (if done properly). Even if downtime ensues, it should only be for a few minutes, as all user IDs are altered to point to a different temporary tablespace.
Emergency Description	Application data tablespace data-file lost/corrupt
Reason	As mentioned under "SYSTEM data-file lost/corrupt"

TABLE 2-2. *List of emergencies in an Oracle Server environment* (continued)

Steps to recover	Stop all applications that access that tablespace Restore the data-files (only the corrupt/lost ones) of that tablespace from the latest backups Roll forward using the archived redo-logs. Recovery needs to be done either at data-file or tablespace level (if more than one data-file is corrupt/lost) After recovery is complete, test and ensure normalcy has been restored Restart all applications using that tablespace
Scheduled (Y/N)	N
Times occurred in current year	0
Avg. time taken to recover	As mentioned under "SYSTEM data-file lost/corrupt"
Downtime caused	Varies. However, downtime would only apply to applications/users accessing the corrupt tablespace/data-file.
Emergency Description	Application index tablespace data-file lost/corrupt
Reason	As mentioned under "SYSTEM data-file lost/corrupt"
Steps to recover	As mentioned under "Application data tablespace data-file lost/corrupt." Alternatively, you could drop the (index) tablespace pertaining to that data-file, re-create the tablespace on reliable disks, and rebuild the necessary indexes. The latter method may be accomplished with no downtime (especially if the indexes are not very crucial).
Scheduled (Y/N)	N
Times occurred in current year	0
Avg. time taken to recover	As mentioned under "SYSTEM data-file lost/corrupt"
Downtime caused	As mentioned under "Application data tablespace data-file lost/corrupt." May be 0, depending on recovery method used.

TABLE 2-2. *List of Emergencies in an Oracle Server Environment* (continued)

Emergency Description	RBS data-file lost/corrupt
Reason	As mentioned under "SYSTEM data-file lost/corrupt"
Steps to recover	As mentioned under "SYSTEM data-file lost/corrupt". Additionally, the _CORRUPT_ROLLBACK_SEGMENTS initialization parameter can be set to mark the rollback segments in the RBS tablespace as corrupt and open the database. Once the database is open, the RBS tablespace can be taken offline, dropped, and re-created to accommodate new rollback segments. However logical corruption within the database may be introduced, a database reorganization would be necessary.
Scheduled (Y/N)	N
Times occurred in current year	0
Avg. time taken to recover	Varies
Downtime caused	Varies
Emergency Description	Online current redo-log lost/corrupt
Reason	As mentioned under "SYSTEM data-file lost/corrupt"
Steps to recover	As mentioned under "SYSTEM data-file lost/corrupt"
Scheduled (Y/N)	N
Times occurred in current year	0
Avg. time taken to recover	Varies
Downtime caused	Varies
Emergency Description	Online non-current unarchived redo-log lost/corrupt
Reason	As mentioned under "SYSTEM data-file lost/corrupt"

TABLE 2-2. *List of Emergencies in an Oracle Server Environment* (continued)

Steps to recover	The short route: Perform a SHUTDOWN ABORT (if the instance has not crashed already) Start up the instance and mount the database (STARTUP MOUNT) Alter the database to NOARCHIVELOG mode (this step is required to drop an unarchived online redo-log file. Trying to do so with the database in ARCHIVELOG mode produces the ORA-350 error) Alter the database to drop the lost/corrupt redo-log Restart the database, let instance recovery occur, and then shut down the database in normal mode Start up the instance and mount the database again (STARTUP MOUNT) Alter the database to ARCHIVELOG mode (cannot set to ARCHIVELOG mode immediately after dropping the lost/corrupt redo-log, since instance recovery needs to be performed. Accordingly, it is essential to restart the database, perform instance recovery, shut down normally, and then set to ARCHIVELOG mode, while restarting the database. Otherwise, the ORA-265 error is produced). Open the database Create a new redo-log (same size, same group as the previous one) The long route (needs to be taken when the short route errors out while trying to alter the database): Restore database from latest backup and roll forward
Scheduled (Y/N)	N
Times occurred in current year	1
Avg. time taken to recover	7 mins for the short route (may be less or more depending on time required to perform instance recovery) Varies for the long route (dependent on time to restore from backup, perform recovery, etc.)
Downtime caused	7 mins for the short route (may be less or more depending on time required to perform instance recovery) Varies for the long route

TABLE 2-2. *List of Emergencies in an Oracle Server Environment* (continued)

Emergency Description	Online non-current archived redo-log lost/corrupt
Reason	As mentioned under "SYSTEM data-file lost/corrupt"
Steps to recover	Drop the lost/corrupt redo-log and create a new one in its place (same size, same group, etc.)
Scheduled (Y/N)	N
Times occurred in current year	1
Avg. time taken to recover	3 mins
Downtime caused	0 mins
Emergency Description	Archived redo-log (not yet backed up) lost/corrupt
Reason	As mentioned under "SYSTEM data-file lost/corrupt"
Steps to recover	Take a complete hot backup as soon as possible, else roll-forward will not be possible, if database recovery is required suddenly.
Scheduled (Y/N)	Y. The backup can be scheduled.
Times occurred in current year	3
Avg. time taken to recover	Varies (time required to back up)
Downtime caused	0 mins
Emergency Description	One control-file lost/corrupt
Reason	As mentioned under "SYSTEM data-file lost/corrupt"
Steps to recover	Perform a SHUTDOWN ABORT (if the instance has not crashed already) Either Change the CONTROL_FILES parameter in the *init.ora* file to point to only the valid control-file copies or Overwrite the lost/corrupt control-file with the valid control-file copy and then Restart the database (instance recovery will be performed)

TABLE 2-2. *List of Emergencies in an Oracle Server Environment* (continued)

Scheduled (Y/N)	N
Times occurred in current year	1
Avg. time taken to recover	3 mins
Downtime caused	3 mins
Emergency Description	All control-files lost/corrupt
Reason	As mentioned under "SYSTEM data-file lost/corrupt"
Steps to recover	Perform a SHUTDOWN ABORT (if the instance has not crashed already) Start up the instance (STARTUP NOMOUNT) Use the dump file created during the last backup, containing the control-file creation script (this dump file needs to be created as part of every backup via the ALTER DATABASE BACKUP CONTROLFILE TO TRACE command) to create a new control-file. If the dump file does not exist, then the control-file creation script needs to be manually created (during such times, it helps to have a listing of all current database filenames/paths) Perform recovery Open the database
Scheduled (Y/N)	N
Times occurred in current year	1
Avg. time taken to recover	5 mins (may take more time, if the control-file creation script has to be manually created)
Downtime caused	5 mins
Emergency Description	Standby database corrupt
Reason	As mentioned under "SYSTEM data-file lost/corrupt." In environments where standby databases are maintained, various events at the primary database could affect them. For instance, redo-log corruption in the primary database could render the standby database useless.
Steps to recover	Rebuild standby database from primary database

TABLE 2-2. *List of Emergencies in an Oracle Server Environment* (continued)

Scheduled (Y/N)	Y. The standby rebuild can be scheduled.
Times occurred in current year	2
Avg. time taken to recover	Varies
Downtime caused	Prima facie, there won't be any downtime for the primary database. However, in case something goes wrong with the primary database, there won't be a standby database for failover. That may cause high downtime. Accordingly, it is extremely crucial to get the standby up and running again, as soon as possible.
Emergency classification: manual glitches	
Software component	Oracle8 v8.0.5
Scope	Internal to Oracle
Level	Administrative (DBA) level
Emergency Description	All non-SYSTEM rollback segments dropped
Reason	Accident (ran the wrong script, in the wrong database, etc.)
Steps to recover	Run script to recreate all rollback segments and make them online
Scheduled (Y/N)	N
Times occurred in current year	0
Avg. time taken to recover	5 mins (If the script to re-create the rollback segments is not available, time may be lost in creating it. Accordingly, it is always smart to keep the database DDL [to create tablespaces, users, rollback segments, privilege grants, etc.] on disk.)
Downtime caused	The database will be up and available. However, due to rollback segments being unavailable, applications may be unable to run. Such downtime would be equivalent to the time to re-create the rollback segments.
Emergency Description	Wrong data-file taken offline or offline-dropped
Reason	Accident

TABLE 2-2. *List of Emergencies in an Oracle Server Environment* (continued)

Steps to recover	If database is running in ARCHIVELOG mode (presumably, any 24x7 database should) and the data-file has been taken offline: Make the data-file online (via the ALTER DATABASE command). If the database is running in ARCHIVELOG mode and the data-file has been offline-dropped: Restore data-file from latest (hot) backup and roll forward using the archived redo-logs. If the database is running in NOARCHIVELOG mode (the file cannot be merely taken offline and would have been offline-dropped): Restore data-file from latest (cold) backup. Recovery up to the latest transaction is not possible in this situation.
Scheduled (Y/N)	N
Times occurred in current year	0
Avg. time taken to recover	Varies
Downtime caused	Varies
Emergency Description	Wrong tablespace taken offline or made read-only or dropped
Reason	Accident
Steps to recover	If a tablespace is taken offline or made read-only, the ALTER TABLESPACE command may be used to bring it online or place it in read/write mode again. If a tablespace has been dropped, its data-files need to be restored from the latest backup and tablespace-level recovery needs to be performed using the archived redo-logs.
Scheduled (Y/N)	N
Times occurred in current year	0
Avg. time taken to recover	Varies
Downtime caused	Varies. Applications using that tablespace would have to be taken down for the duration of the operation.

TABLE 2-2. *List of Emergencies in an Oracle Server Environment* (continued)

Emergency classification: manual glitches	
Software component	Oracle8 v8.0.5
Scope	External to Oracle
Level	Administrative (DBA) level
Emergency Description	Data-file accidentally deleted or overwritten
Reason	Accident
Steps to recover	Restore data-file from latest backup and perform recovery using the archived redo-logs.
Scheduled (Y/N)	N
Times occurred in current year	0
Avg. time taken to recover	Varies
Downtime caused	Varies. Application using the tablespace that owns the data-file would need to be taken down for the duration of the operation.
Emergency Description	Online redo-log deleted or overwritten
Reason	Accident
Steps to recover Scheduled (Y/N) Times occurred in current year Avg. time taken to recover Downtime caused	As mentioned under "Online current redo-log lost/corrupt," "Online non-current unarchived redo-log lost/corrupt," and "Online non-current archived redo-log lost/corrupt" (as the case may be) under "Hardware/Software Failure"
Emergency Description	Archived redo-log deleted or overwritten
Reason	Accident
Steps to recover Scheduled (Y/N) Times occurred in current year Avg. time taken to recover Downtime caused	As mentioned under "Archived redo-log (not yet backed up) lost/corrupt" under "Hardware/ Software Failure"

TABLE 2-2. *List of Emergencies in an Oracle Server Environment* (continued)

Emergency classification: manual glitches	
Software component	Oracle8 v8.0.5
Scope	Internal to Oracle
Level	User/developer level
Emergency Description	Table accidentally deleted/truncated
Reason	Accident
Steps to recover	Here are some available options: Import the table using the latest export dump (if one exists). Determine if there are any relational integrity issues, as the export would be from an earlier point in time. Perform point-in-time recovery on a different database/different system, export the table recovered thus, and then import it into the original database. Rebuild the table from the original source of record (flat files, etc.) in a DSS environment. Retrieve the table off the standby database, prior to the delete getting propagated across. A combination of the preceding ways may be required to retrieve the data completely.
Scheduled (Y/N)	N
Times occurred in current year	0
Avg. time taken to recover	Varies (depends on the table size, backups available, how current the backups are, etc.)
Downtime caused	Varies. All applications using that table would need to be taken down.
Emergency Description	Table accidentally dropped
Reason	Accident

TABLE 2-2. *List of Emergencies in an Oracle Server Environment* (continued)

Steps to recover	As mentioned under "Table accidentally deleted/truncated." Additionally, prior to getting the data back in, the table would need to be re-created, privileges granted again to other user IDs, and the appropriate synonyms re-created. Having scripts ready to do this would help greatly in accuracy and speed. Accordingly, all DDL changes need to be maintained in scripts (and version-controlled). They increase productivity tremendously during such situations.
Scheduled (Y/N)	N
Times occurred in current year	0
Avg. time taken to recover	Varies
Downtime caused	Varies
Emergency Description	Index accidentally dropped
Reason	Accident
Steps to recover	Re-create the index (in PARALLEL and UNRECOVERABLE/NOLOGGING mode).
Scheduled (Y/N)	Y
Times occurred in current year	2
Avg. time taken to recover	Varies
Downtime caused	Varies. Just an index being dropped would not cause downtime. However, it could potentially slow down applications badly enough to warrant an immediate re-create. During the re-create, all applications that access the index (and the table it belongs to) would need to be taken down, since a CREATE INDEX statement acquires a lock on the table and concurrent inserts/updates/deletes are not permitted.

TABLE 2-2. *List of Emergencies in an Oracle Server Environment* (continued)

Emergency Description	View accidentally dropped
Reason	Accident
Steps to recover	Re-create (Again, having DDL ready to perform such operations would expedite them.)
Scheduled (Y/N)	N
Times occurred in current year	2
Avg. time taken to recover	2 mins or less
Downtime caused	2 mins or less (if at all). Only the applications dependent on the view would have to be taken down.
Emergency Description	Trigger/stored procedure/function/package accidentally dropped
Reason	Accident
Steps to recover	As mentioned under "View accidentally dropped"
Scheduled (Y/N)	N
Times occurred in current year	0
Avg. time taken to recover	2 mins or less
Downtime caused	As mentioned under "View accidentally dropped"
Emergency Description	Constraint accidentally dropped/disabled
Reason	Accident
Steps to recover	As mentioned under "View accidentally dropped"
Scheduled (Y/N)	N
Times occurred in current year	0
Avg. time taken to recover	Varies. If erroneous data get inside the table during the time the constraint is not present, it may be time-consuming to weed out (especially if the table is large).
Downtime caused	Varies. Only applications dependent on such constraints may have to be taken down to acquire a lock on the table, so that the constraint can be re-created.

TABLE 2-2. *List of Emergencies in an Oracle Server Environment* (continued)

On close examination of the events in the list, it becomes apparent that many of the emergencies described can be averted by regular proactive monitoring. Many proactive monitoring tasks can be implemented in a "lights-out" (without manual intervention) fashion. For instance, scripts can be deployed (via *cron,* DBMS_JOB, or similar means) to periodically check for segments reaching the maximum number of allowable extents, tablespaces running out of space, and such. Proactive monitoring provides advance warning of such emergencies, thus allowing you to act (rather than react) to preventing such emergencies from causing downtime.

Another fact that is evident from the preceding scenarios is the importance of retaining DDL scripts. Whenever tables or other segments are created, altered, or dropped, the scripts used to accomplish the task should be retained, so that they can be reused during emergencies. Ideally, all such scripts ought to be maintained within a source-code control tool with version-control capabilities.

Also, in order to be on top of emergencies requiring database recovery (and to determine the correct and least restrictive level of recovery—database, tablespace, or data-file), all DBAs should be fully oriented in performing recovery *in your environment.* In fact, the "Avg. time taken to recover" and "Downtime caused" categories in Table 2-2 list optimistic times assuming that the administrative personnel involved are well versed in restore/recovery operations. All DBAs should make it a point to practice various database recovery scenarios, so that the confidence level and knowledge are not lacking during an actual emergency.

Summary

The chapter stressed the necessity of being familiar with the types of emergencies that occur, the impact they have on availability and performance, and the importance of proactively watching for any signs of such emergencies. A sample "emergency list" was provided that lists all emergencies, based on the categorizations in Chapter 1. Finally, a list of emergencies specific to an Oracle environment was outlined.

The next section explores the environment, including such factors as hardware, OS, networks, applications, and data, the maintenance of which is very crucial for successfully operating in 24x7 mode.

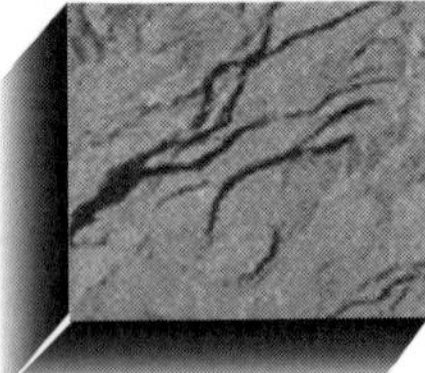

PART II

Understanding Your Environment

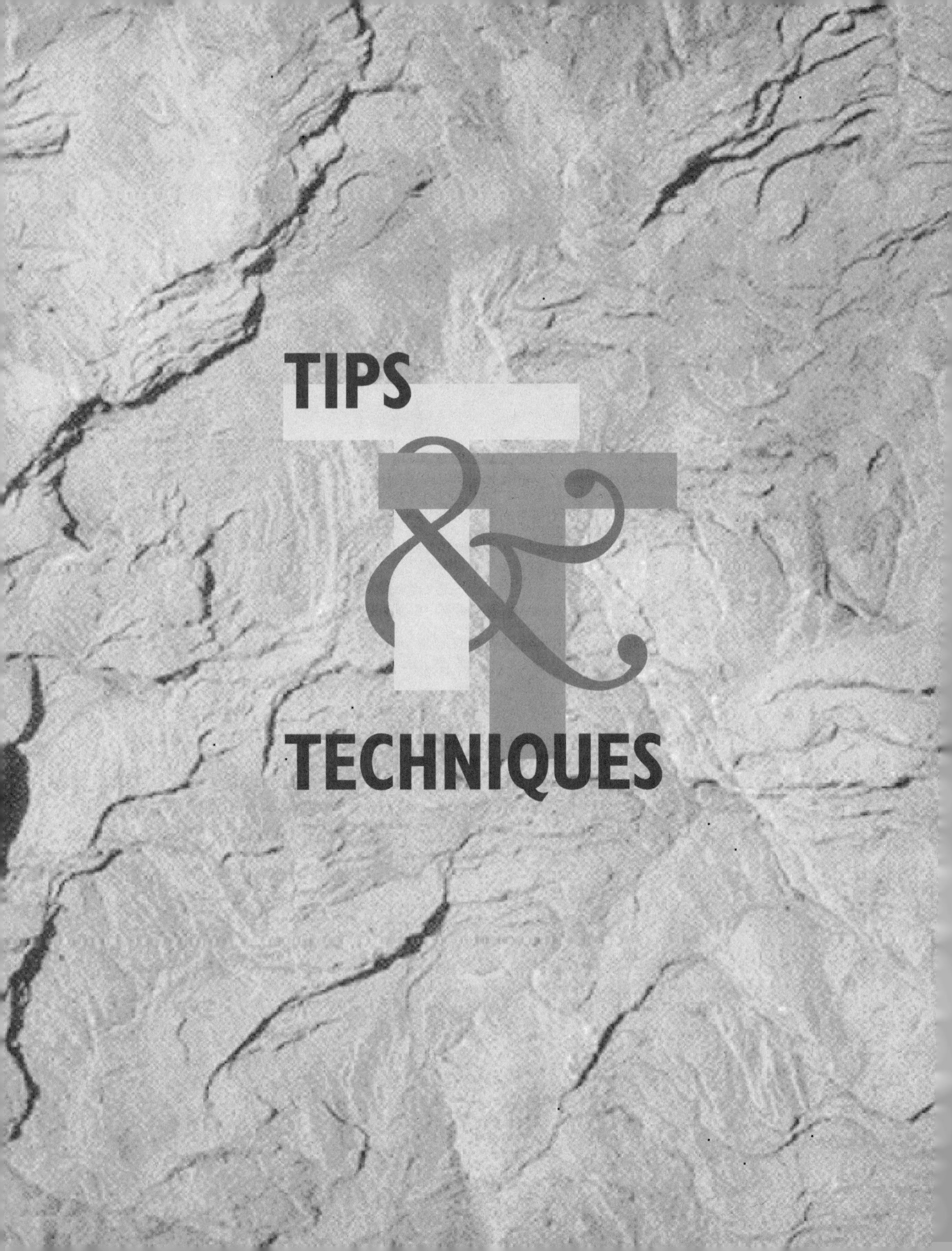
TIPS
&
TECHNIQUES

CHAPTER 3

Hardware Configuration

Understanding your hardware, your operating system (OS), and your network along with their full capabilities is extremely crucial in the context of 24×7 availability. An improper understanding not only impairs your ability to avoid emergencies but also affects your response during such emergencies; at times, it can escalate the emergency into a total catastrophe. For your organization, this catastrophe might be an outage of just 48 hours or less. Your ability to prevent outages and reduce downtime totally depends on how familiar you are with your environment.

In most medium-to-large organizations, specialized operations personnel are in charge of maintaining systems, networks, and databases. In smaller organizations, however, there might be no personnel in charge of specific areas. For example, there might not be a full-time network administrator. The systems administrator might also multitask as a network administrator or vice versa. Almost invariably, organizations realize the importance of retaining a full-time DBA on staff. Usually the DBA is responsible for the welfare of the database only. In organizations with 24×7 database uptime requirements, however, the DBA cannot monitor and prevent just database problems. She has to gain familiarity with all factors, contributing to the smooth working of the database (see Chapter 1). She needs to wear multiple caps ranging from a systems administrator's to a network administrator's, in addition to her regular database administrator's.

The tips in this section apply not to the database itself, but primarily to related layers such as the hardware, the operating system, and the network. During tuning, it is sometimes easy to lose sight of the forest for the trees. With each tip, always consider the overall picture. Try one tip, then document and test the results. If satisfied, plod on ahead. Try all experiments on your development/test machines first (make sure that your test machine closely mirrors the production box, in terms of OS versions, patch levels, and so on). Since many of the following tips affect the hardware configuration and underlying base structure of the OS, please ensure that during tuning, you do not inadvertently lose the ability to undo changes. Ensure that you do not buy better performance at the cost of availability. Having the fastest server is great, but if it is prone to frequent crashes, then it is useless. Always have a good backup before you test any tip. And at times, it's not a bad idea to back up those backups, too!

Please note that I use the term "tuning" to indicate efforts to increase not just system availability and performance, but also total capacity and manageability. Tuning means configuring the system to be faster and more available, in terms of increased uptime and capacity to run more jobs, with lesser strain on specific resources such as the CPU and disk controllers.

At some 24×7 sites, all the production hardware and data are mirrored at another site (see Chapters 15, 17, and 18). In such scenarios, all suggestions made in this chapter would apply to both sites—the source and the target.

This chapter offers the following tips and techniques:

- Be real familiar with what's inside the box
- Choose your disk-array size with caution
- Do not use read-ahead caches for OLTP applications
- Do not rely on write-caches to eliminate I/O hotspots
- Use multi-level RAIDs
- Ensure your stripe-sizes are consistent with your OS and database block-sizes
- Ensure that your disk and tape I/O sizes match
- Figure out which components are "hot-swappable"
- Consider implementing cluster-based solutions
- Unless it's a very large-scale implementation, avoid MPP machines
- Consider NUMA machines as an alternative to MPP machines
- Negotiate with the vendor for a loaner machine

Hardware Configuration

The following tips focus on gaining familiarity with the hardware and using that familiarity to attain higher availability and performance.

Know real well what's inside the box

It is absolutely imperative to know what kind of hardware your organization has invested in, its quirks and strengths, and whether those strengths are being exploited. Information such as the number of disks available, whether they are internal or external, the number of controllers present, whether they are SCSI based, and the number of CPUs is highly valuable. Answers gained from these questions would act as the drivers of any tuning strategy. Let's take a look at some of the most important questions that need to be asked and how the information can be used. These questions would typically be asked by the DBA or database architect during either of two stages:

- During capacity planning (if the DBA is lucky enough to be present during this process)
- Before initiating any major tuning process (especially if the DBA has come into the scene late, after significant hardware has been purchased)

During stage one, the questions would be directed toward the technical representatives of the hardware manufacturer, and during stage two, they would be directed toward the in-house systems personnel, who manage the hardware.

Disk/Controller-Based Questions

The following questions pertain to the I/O channels:

HOW MANY DISKS ARE AVAILABLE? HOW BIG IS EACH DISK? Once you understand your organization's storage needs, both current and future (for the next year at least), you need to ensure that the disks in your system are adequate to hold the desired amount of data. However, if you buy those disks with your eyes closed, you are liable to get disks providing "state-of-the-art" technology from your vendor. Those disks might be great for a variety of applications, but Oracle might have trouble working optimally on them. For example, with disk technology getting better constantly, vendors would like to sell you bigger and bigger disks all the time. In fact, it is not at all uncommon to see organizations buying a cabinet full of huge 9GB disks. As the database grows, so do the individual disk sizes. Vendors are now coming out with massive 18GB disks. However, once data has been effectively striped across those disks, a lot of space would be wasted on each disk. On the other hand, if all that space is used thoroughly, that might result in I/O bottlenecks.

Ideally, for an Oracle application, there should be a large number of small-to-medium-sized disks (1–4GB). Larger number of disks would offer greater flexibility in setting up various RAID (explained later) or JBOD (Just a Bunch of Disks) options, including striping and mirroring. If you buy fewer but bigger disks, then the number of disks available for distributing data is limited. Use larger disks for non-database applications such as creating home directories, NFS drives, file servers, software staging areas, and documentation repositories.

HOW MUCH DISK SPACE IS USABLE? Do not plan out Oracle file sizes based on the vendor's disk-size specifications. After you format the disks, you may find that the size has shrunk. For example, when a 9GB disk is formatted, usable space shrinks to around 8.4GB. You have limited control over this process, as usable space depends on a variety of factors including OS overhead, RAID configurations, damage to disks, and other factors. Hence, understand the average usable size of your disks and plan your file sizes accordingly.

ARE THE DISKS INTERNAL OR EXTERNAL? WHICH ARE FASTER AND BETTER CONFIGURED IN YOUR ENVIRONMENT? Usually the internal disks are the fastest, since the data does not have to travel via a SCSI cable or FDDI link to the external storage device. Internal buses are extremely fast and provide the best disk access times. You might want to ensure that your most popular files (redo-logs and data-files pertaining to tables and indexes) are placed on your fastest disks. In an OLTP environment, for example, there is a tremendous amount of sequential redo activity. Since internal disks are usually smaller in size, it is a good idea to place the relatively small redo-logs on the internal disks. Similarly, swap files are good candidates for internal disks.

At certain client sites, however, I have observed that the internal disks are sometimes older and slower, without any kind of optimization such as striping. In such scenarios, internal disks would be more of a liability than better-configured external disks. Also, disk-access times eventually depend on the number of disks and controllers available. For these reasons, ensure that your internal disks are indeed better before placing important files there.

HOW MANY CONTROLLERS ARE PRESENT? WHAT'S THE DISKS-PER-CONTROLLER RATIO? ARE CERTAIN CONTROLLERS BOUND TO CERTAIN DISKS, OR CAN ANY DISK BE ACCESSED BY ANY CONTROLLER? ARE THE CONTROLLERS SCSI-BASED? Many disk vendors allow multiple disks to be daisy-chained to one controller. Thus, although you might have eight physical disks, there might be only two controllers. That won't buy you much. Ideally, there should be a one-to-one correspondence between a disk and a controller (unless the controller throughput is substantially higher than the throughput of a single disk, in which case the controller throughput ought to match the sum of the maximum potential throughput for all disks daisy-chained to it). However, as the databases get bigger and bigger and the number of disks grows exponentially, an organization will find it difficult to invest in an equivalent number of controllers. Accordingly, you should understand how many controllers are present and how many disks are daisy-chained to each controller.

It helps to be familiar with the conventions that vendors use to indicate disk/controller relationships. For example, EMC and Sun storage arrays use the CnTnDn convention, where Cn refers to controller # n, Tn refers to target # n, and Dn refers to disk # n. (Furthermore, unlike most vendors, Sun refers to a partition as a "slice." So a Sun disk slice may have an "address" of CnTnDnSn, where Sn refers to slice # n.) Usually, once the configuration has been set up, certain disks map to certain controllers only. So prior to the actual setup, any disk may potentially be accessed by any controller. After setup, however, once a disk slice c0t1d4s3 has been created, it may be accessed only by controller 0 (c0). So if controller 0 is busy working on c0t1d2s1 and controllers 5 and 6 are free waiting for an I/O request, they still cannot speed things up by accessing c0t1d4s3. Accordingly, tasks for controller 0 will have to be serialized. Keep such facts in mind while distributing data across different disks/controllers.

Find out what kind of channel the vendor has used between the host computer and the external disks. Is it Fast/Wide SCSI, UltraSCSI, or FDDI? Also, be familiar with the kinds of controllers being provided by the vendor. Are they based upon newer SCSI standards, or are they based upon the older SMD-E or ESDI interfaces?

Know what standards are available in the market and which of these standards have the support of mainstream vendors. If you are still in the vendor-selection stage, select the one who offers the fastest and the best medium (if price is a restraining factor, analyze the price versus performance/availability ratio). This area is really critical; you will spend a lot of time in the future tuning I/O and related aspects. So a little bit of homework toward this end will not hurt. If your organization has already purchased the hardware, any time spent in familiarizing yourself with the components will be time well spent.

WHAT ARE THE ACCESS TIMES FOR THESE DISKS? WHAT ARE THE SEEK TIMES, ROTATIONAL SPEEDS, TRANSFER RATES, AND LATENCIES? These questions are best asked at the end. Most vendors have this information prominently displayed on their brochures. No doubt, this information is important. However, it is far more important to understand the overall build of the I/O subsystem and make sure all the components are well balanced and complementary to each other.

Definitions

SCSI stands for Small Computer Systems Interface. *FDDI* stands for Fiber Distributed Data Interface. A discussion of different SCSI options and FDDI is outside the scope of this book.

Seek time is the time spent in moving the disk drive head from one data track to another. Seek time is highly random, since the head has to move from the current track and position itself toward the new track. Hence, look at the average seek time for the right picture. Seek times are getting smaller and smaller, with technology reducing the gap between subsequent tracks with each generation of disks.

Rotational speed refers to the speed at which the disk spins to position itself beneath the disk drive's head. Usually the speeds vary from 3,600 rpm to 10,000 rpm (in disks used for practical business applications).

Transfer rate is the speed at which data is read from or written to a disk. It is a measure of the raw speed at which bits come from or are sent to the disk drive for reading or writing. It does not account for seek times.

Latency is the overall time it takes to position the proper sector of the disk under the read/write heads. It consists of the delay caused by seek times and rotational times.

For instance, even if you have the fastest disks that technology and money can provide, if those disks happen to be daisy-chained to an older, slower SCSI controller, then your I/O subsystem is not well balanced. No matter how efficient those disks may be, a lot of system time will be spent in managing the controller. In other words, ensure that all the different I/O components such as your controller, disks, and channels match each other's throughput. Your performance will be only as good as the lowest common denominator of all these components.

Having considered the importance of fast controllers, look at the nodes of the tree: the disks. Most 24×7 implementations deal with large databases. The sizes may not necessarily be in the terabyte range, but they are usually hundreds of gigabytes. Hence such sites find that the internal disks provided by the vendor are not adequate. There are a plethora of external disk storage array vendors. Take a hard look at what your current vendor provides. For example, Sun provides the *SPARC Storage Arrays*, and HP provides the *HP High Availability Storage Systems*. Most vendors are competitive in this area. If you are spending "x" number of dollars for your storage arrays, chances are the seek times, rotational speeds, and latencies are highly proportionate among competing vendors. In other words, latency is something that all vendors are furiously trying to reduce. Nevertheless, make a comparative study and ensure that maximum seek times are less than 20 ms, rotational speeds are at least 7200 rpm, transfer rates are between 8 and 10MB per second (especially for reads; write rates may be less), and average latency is less than 4.5 ms for your business applications.

Also, for configuring OLTP databases, look at seek times more closely than transfer rates. For batch and data-warehousing applications, examine transfer rates more closely. This is because OLTP applications involve random reads and writes, where the amount of time required to locate the data is much more than to actually read or write it, whereas in batch and data-warehousing applications, it's the other way around.

WHAT IS THE DISK MTBF (MEAN TIME BETWEEN FAILURES)? No matter what kind of administration you perform, hardware is prone to failure. Keeping user errors (ever seen a few disks conk out "mysteriously" immediately after the disk cabinet is moved?) aside, an administrator for a 24×7 site has to take every precaution possible to ensure product reliability. Operational MTBF is a good measure of product reliability. Dividing the total number of observed operating hours by the total number of failures derives operational MTBF (Chapter 1).

MTBF claims from vendors are theoretical and are based on analysis of relatively short-term statistics in controlled environments. As such, they only lend an idea as to the estimated life of the disk. Considering that most problems are experienced sooner rather than later, a disk is most likely to fail when you first start using it. Any disk that has lived through its first month should be relatively reliable over the rest

of its design life, after which the probability of failure increases again. What is this design life? Check with the technical personnel working for the vendor (not the salesperson!) for exact numbers. Typically, it is around three to five years. Also, these technical personnel tend to have a better idea of operational MTBF based on the disks sold versus returns/repairs ratio each vendor maintains.

ARE THE DISKS HOT-PLUGGABLE? This is definitely a big concern for any 24×7 site. Once the disks have been bought, there's very little that can be done. However, if you are still in the vendor-selection stage, ensure that the disks are hot-pluggable/swappable. This means that in case a disk fails, it can be plugged out and a new one can be plugged in, *while the system is still up and running* (unless, of course, a non-mirrored disk holding critical Oracle data-files dies on you). It can be quite a life saver, since it reduces the number of times a box has to be rebooted. Fortunately, quite a few vendors seem to provide this feature. A subsequent section covers hot-plugging/swapping in more detail.

HOW MANY DISKS CAN THE CABINET HOLD? Usually the disk cabinet (where the disks reside) has a certain size and capacity. It can hold a specific number of disks. Ensure that your current and medium-term storage requirements fall within the capacity of the cabinet. Cabinets might appear to be a very petty issue, but they can assume a lot of importance—especially since they tend to be quite restrictive in nature.

I have been in a situation at a client site where there was a sudden growth in data and more disks were required over the next two months. Our vendor informed us that those disks were available, but there was no space in our cabinet to hold them! We asked them to get us another cabinet, a bigger one this time. Alas, we soon discovered that our computer room wasn't big enough to hold another cabinet. Finally, we had to swap out our old cabinet and move in the newer, bigger one—a process that caused significant downtime. Such an experience can be quite an eye-opener, when hitherto small issues assume magnified proportions. The 24×7 technical architect needs to be cognizant of such issues and to focus on them right in the initial planning stages.

IS THE DISK SOLUTION OPEN? Steer away from vendors selling closed, proprietary disk solutions. They will adversely affect your flexibility. If you need to switch off journaling and your vendor does not allow that, you will incur the penalty of dual writes for every write initiated by your application. The disk solution you choose should give you the ability to configure disks to your unique requirements. Furthermore, proprietary systems will affect your ability to migrate to newer technologies, and you will be at the mercy of the vendor to provide quality service, reasonable prices, and timely upgrades.

CPU-Based Questions

The following questions pertain to the processors:

HOW MANY CPUS ARE PRESENT WITHIN THE SYSTEM? The CPU is one of the most sought-after components within the system. Many programs run simultaneously (user programs and system utilities), and each of them requires a certain number of CPU cycles to get executed. The OS kernel usually allocates the CPU based on the priority of each process. Most production boxes in a 24×7 shop have more than one CPU. With Oracle's Parallel Query Option (PQO), one can exploit the existence of multiple CPUs in a powerful manner. In order to use PQO effectively, it is essential to know how many CPUs are present and how data is spread across multiple disks/controllers (Chapter 6).

It is a smart idea to grow familiar with the current CPU usage via OS tools—how much time does the CPU spend idle and what are the current load averages? It is sensible to measure load averages during peak as well as nonpeak hours. Once you understand the characteristics of your CPU usage, you can decide whether you need more to add more CPUs. I have generally observed that in eight cases out of ten, the CPU is hardly the culprit in most performance problems. It's usually either disk I/O bottlenecks or lack of memory. In fact, the existing CPUs are often underutilized, due to lack of awareness of PQO at many sites. Sometimes, however, with CPU-intensive applications competing for existing processors or high values being specified for the initialization parameter SPIN_COUNT (Chapter 7), CPU usage can shoot up. In such situations, it's a good idea to schedule certain non-primary CPU-intensive applications to run during off-peak hours (late nights) or to set the SPIN_COUNT value lower. If all CPU-intensive applications are primary and cannot be rescheduled, then other options need to be evaluated, such as shifting some of the applications to a different box or adding more CPUs to the current box.

Additionally, ensure that all the CPUs in the box are enabled and being used (at times, CPUs are intentionally disabled during testing to simulate performance on a box with lesser resources, and occasionally people forget to reenable them).

Another important point is that, many times, untuned or badly written application code may result in high CPU usage. Having a large number of CPUs does not resolve this problem. As a case in point, a client was experiencing performance problems. The system was mostly CPU-bound. Statistics always showed the system to be 100 percent busy with processes perpetually waiting to run. The client approached the hardware vendor and invested in a larger system. The result: exactly the same. The system was still experiencing CPU bottlenecks, and throughput was still unacceptable. Finally, the client spent time in fixing bad SQL in the application source code. Suddenly, the CPU usage went down. In fact, the client could go back to the original machine with quite a bit of CPU room to spare. Thus, the $20,000 spent on fixing the bad SQL code proved more effective

than the $500,000+ spent on buying new hardware. It is mandatory to ensure that all SQL code is efficiently tuned prior to increasing CPU capacity.

HOW MANY MORE CPUS CAN BE ADDED? Once you know how many CPUs are currently present, the next question to ask is, has the box reached maximum capacity or can more CPUs be added? This is a critical scalability question. Certain configurations can handle only 8 or 12 CPUs maximum. Also, some OSs place a hard limit on the number of CPUs that can be utilized. For example, the standard edition of Windows NT Server 4.0 can only handle up to 4 CPUs, whereas Windows NT Server Enterprise Edition 4.0 can handle up to 8 CPUs, even though the machines on which they run might have the capacity to support more.

Also, before investing in more CPUs, confirm that the CPUs are indeed the bottleneck. If your existing CPUs are idle most of the time, then buying additional or faster CPUs will only increase their idle time. The CPUs will be very quick at not doing any work. Load averages may not always indicate how many more or how much faster your new CPUs need to be. For intelligent interpretation, such averages need to be analyzed along with your current and future load requirements. Chapter 4 lists a few handy commands to detect whether the CPUs are overloaded.

Overall scalability is also a concern here. CPU scalability is non-linear in nature. For instance, a box may be capable of holding 16 CPUs. However, doubling the number of CPUs from 8 to 16 may not necessarily double the processing speed.

HOW FAST ARE THE EXISTING CPUS? CPU speed in terms of Mhz or SPECint helps in determining the speed at which CPUs can perform various blocking and non-blocking operations. In a uniprocessor environment, CPU speed is very critical, since there's just one CPU and the completion time for each task depends on the execution speed of all the CPU cycles required for that task. In a multi-processor environment, multiple system resources are shared between CPUs. Higher CPU speeds mean a CPU finishes its task and abdicates a certain resource to another CPU sooner. CPUs are getting faster and faster with each passing year.

With higher CPU speeds, you might need to increase the SPIN_COUNT value. SPIN_COUNT has a default value of 2000 on most OSs. When a latch is unavailable to an Oracle process that's willing to wait for the latch, it continues to spin based on the SPIN_COUNT value. Given a faster CPU, the CPU cycles for this process tend to execute faster. This results in the process using up all its CPU cycles much sooner, and it has no choice but to sleep, if the latch is still unavailable. Since more sleeps affect performance adversely, you might need to increase SPIN_COUNT to prevent rampant sleeps. (Note that tuning latch contention may require a variety of steps to be taken besides adjusting SPIN_COUNT. Depending on the type of latch, the shared pool, the database buffer cache size, or the redo buffer size may need to be changed, or, as mentioned earlier, the SQL code may need to be further tuned.)

WHAT'S THE CACHE SIZE OF THE EXISTING CPUS? Every CPU has a small memory cache associated with it. This cache is used to store rapidly needed instructions and local data. This cache is referred to as the Level-1 or L1 CPU cache. It functions very much like any memory cache, such as the UNIX file-systems buffers or the Oracle SGA. If the local data a CPU needs is available in the cache, this fact results in a "cache hit" and allows the CPU to execute much faster. The absence of such data in the cache results in a "cache miss," and the data has to be fetched from secondary caches or main memory. Main memory fetches are always slower than CPU cache hits due to higher latencies involved in travel via the system bus to access the main memory. Apart from the time SMP systems spend in cache coherence (synchronizing the multiple CPU caches), cache usage increases CPU throughput tremendously. Accordingly, for machines running high-traffic database and network applications with stiff response-time and throughput requirements, bigger CPU caches can be a real boost.

Achieving a higher CPU cache hit ratio is the primary reason for setting up processor affinity, where a specific process is bound to a certain CPU to lock and reuse the local data for that process (and prevent other processes from displacing that data from the cache). Though ideal for some applications, it's not a good idea for Oracle-based applications. Chapter 4 explains processor affinity in greater detail.

Cache size can increase significantly with each leap in processor speeds. For example, Intel's 450 Mhz Xeon chip offers a 2MB Level-2 (L2) cache size, which is twice the size of the L2 cache offered by the previous 400 Mhz Xeon chip. Historically, most SMP (symmetric multiprocessor) systems have prevented CPUs of varying speeds and cache sizes from coexisting. However, some of the newer SMP models do not make such restrictions.

Memory-Based Questions

The following questions pertain to RAM:

HOW MUCH PHYSICAL MEMORY DOES THE BOX HAVE? Lack of adequate memory can easily give rise to memory contention. When memory requirements of active processes exceed the physical memory available on the system, the system starts *paging,* that is, moving portions of active processes to disk in order to reclaim physical memory. At this point, performance starts degrading. Gradually, available memory continues to decrease, and in order to handle the shortage without eliminating processes or crashing, the system starts *swapping,* that is, moving *entire* processes to disk to reclaim the memory used by them. Nominal paging is not usually an effective indication of memory bottlenecks. With some OSs, some paging is inevitable (since they page in and out of free memory to dynamically accommodate the UNIX file system buffers). Also, swapping during certain OS housekeeping operations is normal. When paging and swapping seem excessive,

however, then there is certainly a memory bottleneck. Ideally, paging should be reduced to the minimum and there should be very little or no swapping.

Also, much depends on user perception. Paging doesn't present a problem as long as the OS kernel does a good job of selecting infrequently used pages to move to disk. An entire program doesn't need to be in memory while it runs; only parts of the program that are in use need to be there. Most programs spend most of their time (up to 70 percent) running a small portion (15–20 percent) of the code. Accordingly, paging often takes place without being noticeable to users. Performance slightly deteriorates as paging begins. However, this deterioration may be barely noticeable. Yet, as the demand on memory increases, the degradation gets bigger and bigger and performance starts taking a nosedive.

Regular swapping as a part of the OS's normal housekeeping does not impede performance too much. Certain processes that are inactive for more than a specific amount of time (this time is OS-dependent) may be swapped out to conserve memory. However, swapping done by the OS on an emergency basis to overcome extreme lack of memory affects performance adversely almost instantaneously. This is because entire active processes are written out to disk, usually resulting in heavy I/O bottlenecks. Such swapping is referred to as *urgent* or *desperation* swapping. Desperation swapping tries to start off with inactive processes and moves to the active ones as the last resort. But, unfortunately, the processes that are prone to be inactive are also the interactive ones that you fire off from the command line, such as shell scripts and other programs. For example, have you ever logged onto SQL*Plus and kept the screen dormant for a while (as you went to grab a drink . . .) and then typed in a command at the SQL*Plus prompt without seeing any sign of the characters typed in? After a few seconds, the characters are echoed back on the screen. Chances are, SQL*Plus was swapped out by your OS and had to travel back to memory from disk, due to the demand placed on the OS by your typing. And since swapping, in turn, causes disk I/O loads to shoot up, this travel becomes even slower.

In order to reduce paging and prevent swapping, you need to either curtail the number of active concurrent processes or add more memory. Chapter 4 provides some tips on reducing the file-system buffers and changing OS kernel tables to reduce runtime memory allocation and conserve memory. Additionally, you need to ensure that your programmers write code to use memory optimally. In many situations, however, adding additional memory is the more realistic route to follow.

DO YOU HAVE ANY MEMORY-BASED DISKS (SOLID-STATE DISKS [SSDS], PRESTOSERVE, OR THE LIKE)? Memory-based disks or Solid-State Disks (SSDs) are based on the concept of RAM disks. However, they are relatively more stable. An SSD is very similar to a standard disk drive and, for most practical purposes, behaves like one. To the host system, an SSD *is* a disk drive. But an SSD does not store data on magnetic disk media. Instead, it stores data on high-density arrays of high-speed DRAM memory chips. This eliminates the inherent mechanical delays that come with the need to spin a hard disk and position the read/write heads to execute an I/O request. By eliminating such latencies, SSDs achieve access times much faster than conventional disk drives (up to 500 times faster). With most vendors, SSD performance is fast and reliable. An SSD has an integral battery-powered hard-disk drive and associated software continuously backing up its contents. At any moment, typically 80 percent of the data on the SSD is backed up to the hard disk. During power failures, batteries maintain power long enough to back up the rest of the data. In some implementations, backing up the contents onto disk is handled at the hardware level, enhancing performance and reliability further.

For database applications, SSDs provide a viable option for enhancing performance by eliminating variable seek times without compromising availability. Most vendors implement custom versions of the SSD concept. For example, Sun Microsystems has PrestoServe, a high-speed static memory–based storage medium, that is backed up by lithium-powered batteries. In typical Oracle implementations, small but heavily accessed files, such as online redo logs, can be placed on SSDs.

Most implementations of SSDs incorporate highly resilient fault monitoring during regular operations, which includes continuous header checking and data-retention system monitoring. However, have a chat with your vendor's technical personnel and ensure that such checks are indeed *continuous* in your case. Also, have an arrangement with your vendor so that their technical personnel can visit your site and perform data-integrity checks at regular intervals (at least every three months). If possible, purchase tools from the vendor to conduct such tests in house, more often if necessary.

RAID Questions

The following questions relate to disk redundancy via RAID options:

KNOW WHAT RAID OPTIONS YOUR VENDOR SUPPORTS AND WHAT TYPE OF RAID IS CURRENTLY IMPLEMENTED AT YOUR SITE The RAID (redundant array of inexpensive disks) concept was first introduced in 1987 in a University of California white-paper. The paper mentioned innovative ways of organizing multiple physical disks (called an "array") to appear as one logical disk to increase availability and performance. The paper described five different levels of RAID implementation.

RAID relies on redundancy or parity information to reconstruct and retrieve data from failed disk drives. RAID has historically been implemented at the software level. In recent years, however, hardware-based RAID or a combination of hardware- and software-based RAID solutions have been offered by major vendors.

Depending on your core application characteristics, certain RAID levels have no practical utility. Although theoretically there are nine primary RAID levels (0, 1, 2, 3, 4, 5, 6, 7, S), only RAID levels 0, 1, 5, 7, and S (and variations thereof, such as

0+1, 0+S, and so on) are being commercially implemented at most Oracle sites. When selecting a vendor, it is essential to know what levels of RAID they support. Some vendors do not support RAID 0 by itself. All vendors have their own proprietary RAID implementations. However, most vendors ensure adherence to the ANSI- and ISO-standard SCSI protocols. Let's understand RAID and its options better.

- **RAID 0** RAID 0 offers pure disk striping. The striping allows a large file to be spread across multiple disks/controllers, providing concurrent access to data because all the controllers are working in parallel (see Figure 3-1). It does not provide either data redundancy or parity protection. In fact, RAID 0 is the only RAID level focusing solely on performance. Some vendors, such as EMC Corporation, do not consider level 0 as true RAID and do not offer solutions based on it. Pure RAID 0 significantly lowers MTBF, since it is highly prone to downtime. If *any* disk in the array (across which Oracle files are striped) fails, the database goes down.
- **RAID 1** With RAID 1, all data is written onto two independent disks (a "disk pair") for complete data protection and redundancy (see Figure 3-2). RAID 1 is also referred to as *disk mirroring* or *disk shadowing.* Data is written simultaneously to both disks to ensure that writes are *almost* as fast

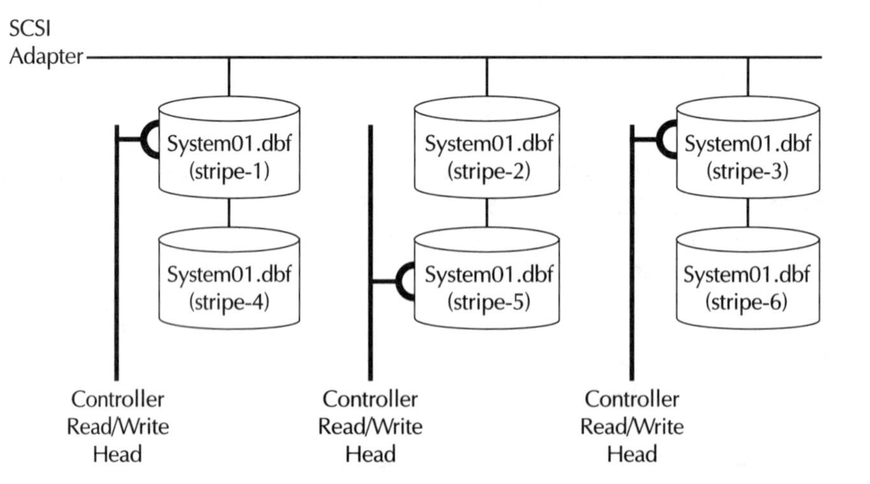

FIGURE 3-1. *The System01.dbf data-file is striped across six disks and three controllers in RAID 0; it is accessed concurrently by all three controllers*

as to a single disk. During reads, the disk that is the least busy is utilized. RAID 1 is the most secure and reliable of all levels due to full 100 percent redundancy. However, the main disadvantage from a performance perspective is that every write has to be duplicated. Nevertheless, read performance is enhanced, as the read can come from either disk. RAID 1 demands a significant monetary investment to duplicate each disk; however, it provides a very high MTBF. Combining RAID levels 0 and 1 (RAID 0+1) allows data to be striped across an array, in addition to mirroring each disk in the array.

- **RAID 5** Instead of total disk mirroring, RAID 5 computes and writes parity for every write operation (see Figure 3-3). The parity disks avoid the cost of full duplication of the disk drives of RAID 1. If a disk fails, parity is used to reconstruct data without system loss. Both data and parity are spread across all the disks in the array, thus reducing disk bottleneck problems. Read performance is improved, but every write has to incur the additional overhead of reading old parity, computing new parity, writing new parity, and then writing the actual data, with the last two operations happening while two disk drives are simultaneously locked. This overhead is notorious as the RAID 5 *write penalty.* This write penalty can make writes significantly slower. Also, if a disk fails in a RAID 5 configuration, the I/O

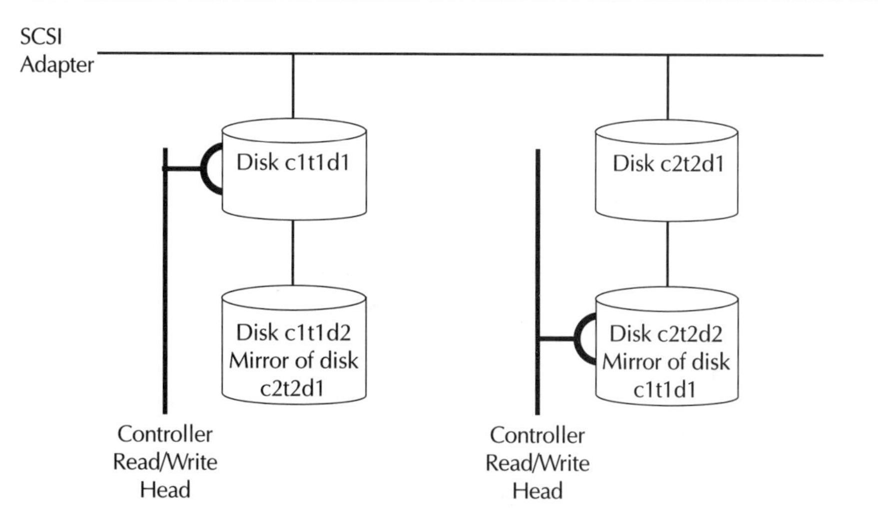

FIGURE 3-2. *Two arrays of two disks each illustrating RAID 1 (note simultaneous access of each mirror by multiple controllers)*

penalty incurred during the disk rebuild is extremely high. Read-intensive applications (DSS, data warehousing) can use RAID 5 without major real-time performance degradation (the write penalty would still be incurred during batch load operations in DSS applications). In terms of storage, however, parity constitutes a mere 20 percent overhead, compared to the 100 percent overhead in RAID 1 and 0+1.

Initially, when RAID 5 technology was introduced, it was labeled as the cost-effective panacea for combining high availability and performance. Gradually, users realized the truth, and until about a couple of years ago, RAID 5 was being regarded the villain in most OLTP shops. Many sites contemplated getting rid of RAID 5 and started looking at alternative solutions. RAID 0+1 gained prominence as the best OLTP solution for people who could afford it. Over the last two years, RAID 5 is making a comeback either as hardware-based RAID 5 or as enhanced RAID 7 or RAID S implementations. However, RAID 5 evokes bad memories for too many OLTP database architects.

- **RAID S** RAID S is EMC Corporation's implementation of RAID 5. However, it differs from pure RAID 5 in two main aspects: (1) It stripes the parity, but it *does not* stripe the data. (2) It incorporates an asynchronous hardware environment with a *write cache.* This cache is primarily a

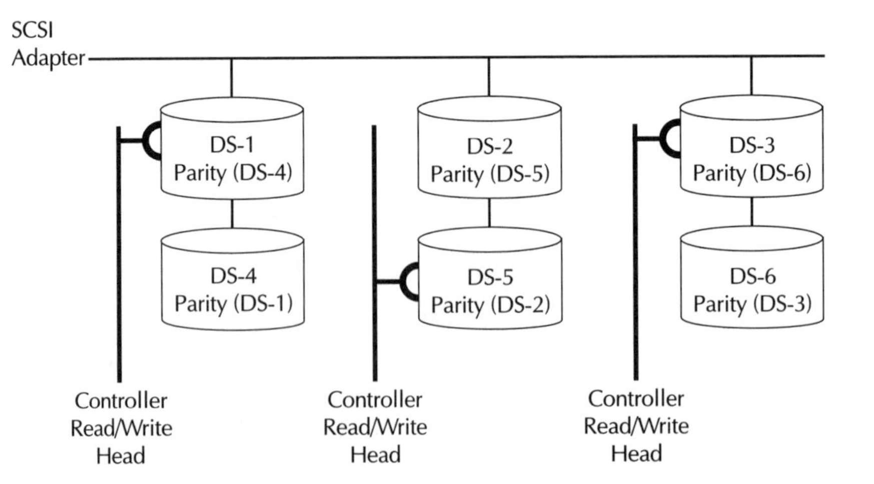

FIGURE 3-3. *Data and parity striped across three disk-arrays of two disks each in RAID 5 ("DS* n*" indicates data stripe* n*, and "Parity (DS* n*)" indicates parity for data stripe* n*)*

mechanism to defer writes, so that the overhead of calculating and writing parity information can be done by the system, while it is relatively less busy (and less likely to exasperate the user!).

Many users of RAID S imagine that since RAID S is supposedly an enhanced version of RAID 5, data striping is automatic. They often wonder how they are experiencing I/O bottlenecks, in spite of all that striping. It is vital to remember that in RAID S, striping of data is *not* automatic and has to be done manually via third-party disk-management software.

- **RAID 7** RAID 7 also implements a cache, controlled by a sophisticated built-in real-time operating system. Here, however, data is striped and parity is not. Instead, parity is held on one or more dedicated drives. RAID 7 is a patented architecture of Storage Computer Corporation.

RAID 5, S, and 7 come at a lower cost than RAID 1 or 0+1, since there is a 100 percent overhead in the case of the latter. However, the investment in this overhead provides insurance against a variety of disk-drive failures. RAID 1 and 0+1 offer protection against multiple points of failure in a disk-array (except when both mirrors fail simultaneously). In RAID 5/S/7, there is uninterrupted service only in the case of a single point of failure in a disk-array. In other words, RAID 5/S/7 will not continue to function when more than one disk crashes at the same time. Also, with RAID 5/S/7, performance degrades substantially even with a single disk failure, in addition to increased exposure to a full-fledged outage.

To drive home the point, let me quote the RAID rule: "RAID 5/S/7 can be used without much performance degradation for read-intensive applications such as DSS. For write-intensive OLTP applications, however, they often are the poor man's choice. RAID 0+1 is the optimal configuration from both availability and performance perspectives, for most Oracle applications (OLTP and DSS). Use it if you have the money."

Choose your disk-array size with caution

The term "disk-array size" refers to the number of physical disks in an array. Two primary factors seem to influence disk-array sizes at most customer sites:

- Hardware budget
- Performance

That one's hardware budget must guide disk-array purchase needs no explanation. First of all, if the budget is small, the RAID-1 and 0+1 options are generally out of the question, since procurement costs are doubled.

Generally, the cost of purchasing a RAID 5/S/7 subsystem increases with each additional disk in the array. However, the rate of increase becomes substantially lower because of certain fixed overheads in the procurement costs of each array (for example, specialized "RAID 5/S/7 aware" controllers). Once the fixed costs are covered, the variable cost (for each additional disk) becomes progressively lower. This characteristic of RAID 5/S/7 tempts a company to buy more disks in an array. Additionally, the greater the number of disks in an array, the better the ability to parallelize I/O calls across more disks, resulting in better performance. Thus, both the budget and the tilt toward performance lead one to purchase an array with more disks.

For a 24×7 site, however, this introduces new worries. The MTBF for each disk-array becomes lower with each new disk. In other words, the greater the number of disks, the higher the chances of a disk failure. In the case of RAID 1 or 0+1, this is not a major problem. Due to total mirroring of each disk, the fault resilience of such arrays is very high. With RAID 5/S/7, however, fault resilience is limited to an individual disk failure in the array. A RAID 5/S/7 implementation can survive one disk crash. Since the parity data for a particular disk is written to other disks in the array, such parity data can be used to reconstruct the data in the failed disk. However, as the number of disks increases, the likelihood of more than one disk being impacted also rises. In RAID 5/S/7, media recovery is required to restore and recover from multiple disk crashes, and this entails downtime.

Do not get lured by vendor promises of bigger discounts on larger arrays—have only as many disks in each array as is required to handle your throughput requirements, without compromising the MTBF and MTTR times in your service agreements.

Do Not Use Read-Ahead Caches for OLTP Applications

Many disk-management software and hardware vendors provide a buffer cache. This cache can be anywhere from 512MB to 4GB. Most of the time, these caches have a specific purpose in life. Vendors call them write or write-back caches, read-ahead caches, or read/write caches. Read-ahead caches may be provided independent of any RAID configuration and are similar in nature to the UNIX file buffers. In read-intensive DSS applications, they perform a valuable role: pre-reading. During sequential reads (such as full-table scans and full-index scans), they pre-read the data and store it in the buffer cache. This causes subsequent requests for data to be satisfied via a logical read from memory and enhances performance by reducing the number of total physical disk reads. However, they are not desirable for OLTP applications, where the reads are small and random in nature. Most pre-reading amounts to a waste of CPU time. In such applications, a little sequential read (an index scan, for example) would induce cache read-aheads.

Since the reads are mostly random, the next read would read another disk or another cylinder of the same disk, thereby wasting the pre-read data in the cache. Accordingly, it is better not to rely on such read-ahead caches for OLTP applications, but to disable the read-ahead algorithm, whenever possible.

NOTE
If your database uses UNIX file systems, reading multiple OS blocks can also trigger a read-ahead, where the file-system buffers are populated with pre-read data. This is especially important if your DB_BLOCK_SIZE is a multiple of the OS block size. For example, if your OS block size is 512 bytes and your DB_BLOCK_SIZE is 8KB, then each database block retrieved will always cause read-aheads, since one database block corresponds to multiple OS blocks. Even a simple SELECT based on a unique index would cause at least one I/O to the table (unless the index itself satisfies the query) and two or more I/Os to the index (depending on the index depth). In this case, the index root node fetch may cause (say, on a Sequent) a 64KB I/O, followed by another 64KB I/O for the index leaf node, followed by another 64KB I/O for the table block. This can be a genuine irritant for OLTP databases, since in addition to causing extra I/O, it is also cleaning out the UNIX buffer cache of "hot" data. The easiest way to limit such occurrences is to ensure that the OS block size matches the database block size.

Do Not Rely on Write Caches to Eliminate I/O Hotspots

In RAID S, RAID 7, and some implementations of RAID 5, a write cache is provided. The primary objective of this cache is to expedite writes. When data is written, it is initially written to the write cache. Later when the system is less active or when the buffer is full, the cache writes the data to the physical disk. This helps in deferring writes in a RAID environment, where penalties are incurred during every write due to parity. Writing to the cache directly is supposed to enhance performance, by making users oblivious to the deferred RAID write penalties. In an extensively used OLTP application, however, the cache tends to fill up rather quickly and the physical disk writes have to inevitably follow, thus defeating its purpose. Additionally, many cache algorithms encourage pre-reading in addition to

writing, as read activity is generally much higher in any database. For OLTP applications, in addition to wasteful pre-reading (as discussed in the previous tip), there is another danger: a false sense of confidence among systems administrators.

At a client site, a little while ago, we implemented EMC's disk-array, complete with RAID S and a 1.5GB write cache. We went from SPARC internal disks to the new disk-array. Our systems administrators, who were not very familiar with the nature of OLTP applications, believed that the presence of the cache would greatly speed up writes as well as reads, thereby achieving optimal performance. They completely rejected suggestions for disk striping (RAID 0). No matter how much I tried to convince them, they felt it would involve additional administration and the additional work and costs were not really needed. Well, time is the best teacher. After three months, with many users breathing down our throats and severe I/O bottlenecks causing performance to be at an all-time low, we had to undertake a series of outages over a period of two months to completely stripe all disks using *Veritas Volume Manager™*. The sad part was, extensive downtime was not available for any full-fledged striping operation. We had lost the opportunity to tune an unused system. All subsequent striping exercises had to be undertaken in bits and pieces, as and when fragments of downtime were allowed by management.

The moral of this story is: Do not rely on write or read/write caches to eliminate disk I/O bottlenecks. Proactive striping for database applications is always a good idea. Write caches primarily aid in deferring the RAID 5/S/7 write penalty. They are not intended, in any case, to guarantee optimal I/O, since I/O is driven by the nature of your applications (OLTP or DSS).

Use multi-level RAIDs

Hardware-based RAID 0+1 is ideal for most OLTP and data-warehousing applications. Since duplicate writes are handled at the hardware level by high-speed controllers, performance impact is negligible. Additionally, uptime dramatically increases. Outages due to most disk crashes can be avoided. In fact, certain sites use software such as Veritas Volume Manager™ to create a third *deferred* mirror. In such three-way mirrored environments, all writes to the third disk can be deferred by a quarter hour to half an hour, so that user errors (such as dropping a table or an index) will not be propagated to all three mirrors immediately. Also, since such deferral is usually done at the software level, it also helps performance by avoiding the overhead of an immediate third write (Chapter 15 discusses three-way mirroring strategies in detail). However, due to the exorbitant costs involved in providing two-way or three-way mirroring, especially in VLDB environments where massive amounts of data are involved, many sites find it unfeasible to invest in RAID 0+1. Many of them instead use RAID 0+1 for certain critical data and use RAID levels 5/S/7 for the rest of the data, in an attempt to provide better overall application performance on the host system.

This approach is highly pragmatic and can combine performance benefits with cost effectiveness. Let's face it—not every chunk of data deserves to be duplicated. With careful analysis and planning, the best of both worlds can be attained. However, there's a little caveat here: A multi-level RAID implementation raises administrative complexity and, if done haphazardly, creates the possibility of large performance and cost penalties. Data optimized and stored in one RAID level may need to be relocated to a different RAID level when the capacity of a given disk-array is exceeded. Don't try this out by yourself, without having experts around. If you don't know what you are doing, you could indeed foul things up. Make sure you involve experienced database architects in the entire process, right from the capacity planning stage. And, most important, have the vendor's technical personnel always involved. They usually are the most knowledgeable about their products and bring in valuable experience from similar implementations at other companies.

Ensure Your Stripe-Sizes Are in Line with Your OS and Database Block-Sizes

When you are implementing RAID 0, RAID 5, or software-based striping, deciding upon the optimal stripe-size is usually a matter of great concern. Usually there are three factors to consider in any striping initiative:

- The nature of your primary application: OLTP or DSS
- OS and database block sizes
- The number of members (disks) in the striped volume (the disk-array)

Almost every DBA book refers to the importance of the database block size being a multiple of the OS block size (I refer to it, too, in Chapter 7). So I will assume that you are well-read and your OS and database block sizes are compatible. The same rule applies to the stripe-size for all stripe sets: The stripe-size has to be a multiple of the OS block size. If you are using raw devices, only the physical OS block size need be considered. The physical block size on UNIX is usually 512 bytes. When using Logical Volume Managers (LVMs), the logical OS block size overrides the physical OS block size. LVMs usually default the logical block size to 8KB. Usually this is not a problem, since both 512 bytes and 8KB easily fit into most commonly used stripe-sizes (64KB, 128KB, 256KB, 512KB, and so on). So it's hard to go wrong there. The third area is where most people need help.

Striping can either be horizontal (across controllers) or vertical (across a set of disks). Since striping is usually done to make use of multiple controllers and attain parallel data access, it is necessary to consider the number of controllers available and the members in each stripe set. Let's assume that four controllers are available

and that there are four members per stripe set (it is generally not a good idea to have more members in a stripe set than the number of available controllers, as it defeats the purpose of striping—to spread data onto multiple available resources to ensure concurrent access). Given OS and database block sizes of 8KB each, the system would have to read and write a minimum of 32KB (8KB × 4 controllers) each time to even attempt parallel access of all four stripe sets. Again, it is assumed that this is the only transaction currently in process, which is not a good assumption in any multi-user environment. However, this simple illustration shows that a minimum stripe-size of 32KB would be required to even trigger attempts by the system to parallelize access in such an environment. Requests for smaller information would definitely not result in optimal access. Usually in OLTP environments, access requests are small in size (seldom above 32KB). In DSS applications, access requests are usually bigger and thereby warrant a bigger stripe-size. Refer to Table 3-1 for a list of commonly observed database block sizes and optimal stripe-sizes based on number of disks per stripe set. Here, I have assumed that four controllers are available and the members per stripe set are four.

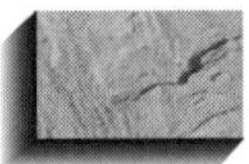

NOTE
Horizontal striping may add some overhead to the I/O, since the OS has to deal with a larger code access path (separating I/Os across disks and collating the results). The trick is in understanding whether the benefits derived from horizontal striping outweigh the overhead. In DSS applications, due to the need for heavy data access quickly, the overhead is usually negligible. For both OLTP and DSS, horizontal striping may be necessary to overcome I/O hot-spots.

From a detailed look at Table 3-1, it can generally be summarized that either a 32KB or 64KB stripe-size is effective for most OLTP applications. I would not recommend 16KB, unless the application is *purely* OLTP in nature. Most applications involve some kind of sequential access (either late-night batch jobs or critical managerial reports) and hence are better off using either a 32KB or 64KB stripe-size. A size of 16KB would be too granular for such applications. For DSS applications, I would recommend either 64KB or 128KB, or at times even 256KB or 512KB stripe-sizes. Everything is relative and eventually depends upon the total size of the database. If your database is a VLDB running into terabytes, it could potentially span hundreds of disk volumes, and very granular stripe-sizes would be difficult to manage. Table 3-1 serves as an excellent "rule of thumb" for most applications. It has served me rather well over the years, providing accurate and practical numbers for diverse environments and applications. Note that [× *n*] in the last column indicates optional multiplication by *n* (where *n* = 1, 2, 3, . . .). This

Nature of Application	Database Block Size (a)	# of Controllers	# of Disks per Stripe-Size (b)	Stripe-Size (a × b)[× *n*]
OLTP	4KB	4	4	16KB or 32KB
OLTP	8KB	4	4	32KB or 64KB
DSS	8KB	4	4	64KB, 128KB, or higher
DSS	16KB	4	4	128KB, 256KB, or higher
Mixture of OLTP & DSS	4KB	4	4	16KB, 32KB, or higher
Mixture of OLTP & DSS	8KB	4	4	32KB, 64KB, or higher
Mixture of OLTP & DSS	16KB	4	4	64KB or 128KB

TABLE 3-1. *Cheat-Sheet for Calculating Optimal Stripe-Size*

optional multiplication by "*n*" ([× *n*]) allows the stripe-size to be offset against variable factors such as application characteristics (OLTP, DSS) and the overall database size. Determine and use it with discretion after analysis of application characteristics and database size.

NOTE
If performance is a major issue, you can establish different stripe-sizes for different disk volumes (ideally, two or three standard stripe-sizes across all volumes). Though multiple stripe-sizes increase administrative complexities, they allow a great deal of flexibility in enhancing I/O. Different Oracle files can be placed on volumes with different stripe-sizes according to their access characteristics. For example, the SYSTEM tablespace, INDEX tablespaces holding unique-key indexes, and tablespaces holding rollback segments in OLTP systems are candidates for a smaller stripe-size equivalent to the DB_BLOCK_SIZE. Even redo-logs (especially if they are placed on dedicated disk-arrays) can be striped with a smaller size. The temporary tablespace should be striped as a factor of SORT_AREA_SIZE. Tablespaces holding table data and non-unique indexes may be placed on volumes with larger stripe-sizes.

Tape-Drive Questions

The following questions are specific to tape drives:

HOW MANY TAPE DRIVES DO YOU HAVE? As mentioned earlier, most databases running in 24×7 mode are in the hundreds of gigabytes size range. Every time they are backed up, performance is affected, since the database blocks have to be read and written to output media such as tape. This is a resource-intensive operation. Furthermore, unless the Oracle8 RMAN is configured for backup sets or image copies, tablespaces have to be explicitly put into online backup mode during hot backups (RMAN also supports the latter option). This results in additional redo getting generated. Accordingly, writes to online redo-logs and archived logs are increased, resulting in heavy I/O activity. However, reliable database backups are extremely critical, allowing no compromise. In order to ensure that the backups are performed with minimal effect on performance, it is essential to have smaller backup windows, preferably during non-peak hours.

If you are backing up your database to tape, consider parallelizing the entire operation. Both Oracle7 Enterprise Backup Utility (EBU) and Oracle8 Recovery Manager (RMAN), as well as third-party backup management tools such as *DataTools Inc.'s SQL*BackTrack*, have interfaces to tape management software such as *Legato Networker* and *IBM ADSM* allowing multiple tape drives to be used for fast parallel backups. Hence, know how many tape drives your site has, in order to create multiple backup streams.

Besides performance, multiple tape drives also provide redundancy to allow backup and recovery operations to occur even when one or more tape drives have failed and are unavailable.

HOW MANY TAPE DRIVES ARE AVAILABLE FOR DATABASE BACKUPS? This might seem like an absurd question. Since the database is the most critical software component, it is logical that all available tape drives would be utilized for database backups, right? Nope. To the typical systems administrator, the database files are no more important than any other file residing on that disk. If any file is not backed up and gets lost, there will be hell to catch! So, inevitably, the database backups share the available tape drives with the other, non-database files.

Find out what else needs to be/is being backed up simultaneously with your database backups (for tips on planning and enhancing online backups, refer to Chapter 9). Use this information to parallelize the database backups by creating an adequate number of streams. Each stream will communicate with a tape drive. Remember, if more streams are defined than available tape drives, then there is a good chance that there will be contention among multiple streams for a tape drive, delaying the backups further. Hence, knowing the number of *available* tape drives is important.

Ensure that your disk and tape I/O sizes match

Most sites use the default for the disk and tape I/O sizes. Unfortunately, the default sizes for tape and disk are not the same in most tools. For example, in Oracle EBU, the default size for disk I/O (the DISK_IO_SIZE parameter) is 16 database blocks (each database block = DB_BLOCK_SIZE); whereas the tape I/O size (the TAPE_IO_SIZE parameter) is 32 database blocks. This discrepancy causes incompatibility between the disk reads and tape writes. The disk reads do not match the tape drive's capacity, resulting in slower backups. Ensure that I/O sizes of both are the same and are in multiples of the volume stripe-size (if striping is used). I have seen backup times cut in half by using equal disk and tape I/O sizes. At a client site, with a disk I/O size of 64KB (DISK_IO_SIZE = 16; DB_BLOCK_SIZE = 4KB) and a tape I/O size of 128KB (DISK_IO_SIZE = 32), a full 80GB database backup would take four hours using four dedicated tape drives via Oracle EBU/Legato Networker. We tried to do everything we could to further reduce this time. We did not get much success initially. However, by just increasing the disk I/O size to 128KB (DISK_IO_SIZE = 32) to match the tape I/O size, we could complete the backups in just under two hours.

Chapter 11 discusses some high-availability backup strategies using tape drives and triple mirrors.

Architectural Alternatives for System Redundancy and Performance

Historically there's been a great deal of dependence on system redundancy to enhance availability. Redundancy allows multiple copies of a similar component to be maintained. During failures, when the primary component is unavailable, the copy can be utilized to provide uninterrupted service. In an earlier section, we examined disk redundancy in mirroring and multiple tape drives used concurrently during backup and recovery operations. The same principle can be extended to other hardware components (such as multiple CPUs and memory boards) in a typical SMP- or NUMA-based system or even to entire systems as a whole, in a cluster- or MPP-based architecture. SMP, NUMA, clusters, and MPP solutions offer highly varied architectures and are explained from both redundancy and performance perspectives in the text that follows.

Figure out which components are "hot-swappable"

In 24×7 environments, hot-swappable hardware components are a real boon. "Hot-swappable" refers to the capability of a component to be plugged into the

system or unplugged from a system dynamically at run time, without causing any outage. Different vendors allow different components to be hot-swapped. They range from power supplies to CPUs and many things in between, such as memory boards, I/O boards, and disk drives. Hot-swapping allows potentially defective components to be removed from the system and replaced with newer functional ones. Also, such a feature allows system capacity to be upgraded without enduring any downtime.

In data centers where planned downtime seems inevitable for upgrade/repair operations, hot-swappable components inject new hope. Most high-end vendors offering enterprise-level storage offer hot-swappable components. For example, models in the Sun Enterprise series such as the 6500 and the 10000 (Starfire™) allow even the CPUs to be hot-swapped. If you are in the hardware evaluation stage, ensure that your vendor offers matching capabilities. For production hardware already in-house, keep track of which components can be hot-swapped. At all times, try to ensure that at least your disk drives, which are heavily prone to failure, are hot-swappable.

Hot-swappability may not save your skin if an unmirrored disk containing critical Oracle data crashes on you. However, if an unmirrored disk containing non-critical data goes down, it won't take the entire system with it. Additionally, critical or not, if the disk is mirrored, your system is left intact in the event of its crash. Hot-swappability can go a long way toward preventing outages due to accidents and also avoiding the need for downtime during certain maintenance operations.

Also, some vendors provide systems with built-in redundancy (system buses, memory boards, SCSI channels) that allows switchover during component failures. These components are not considered to be *hot-swappable.* Though these typically require a reboot of the machine for the failover to successfully take place, they do provide an additional layer of insulation from total failure and higher downtime.

Consider implementing cluster-based solutions

Any company that is serious about high availability needs to evaluate cluster-based hardware solutions. A *cluster* is composed of multiple computer systems connected together to appear as one. Each system that is part of a cluster is called a *node.* Each node is generally a full-fledged SMP (symmetric multi-processing) machine, where system resources such as disks, controllers, and memory are shared by all CPUs existing within each node under a single OS, resulting in a tightly coupled "share everything" architecture (see Figure 3-4). Prior to the popularity of SMP systems, clusters were composed of uniprocessor (single-CPU) machines. Currently, most Oracle shops stay away from uniprocessor machines. Recently, clusters composed of NUMA systems (more about NUMA later) have also emerged in the market.

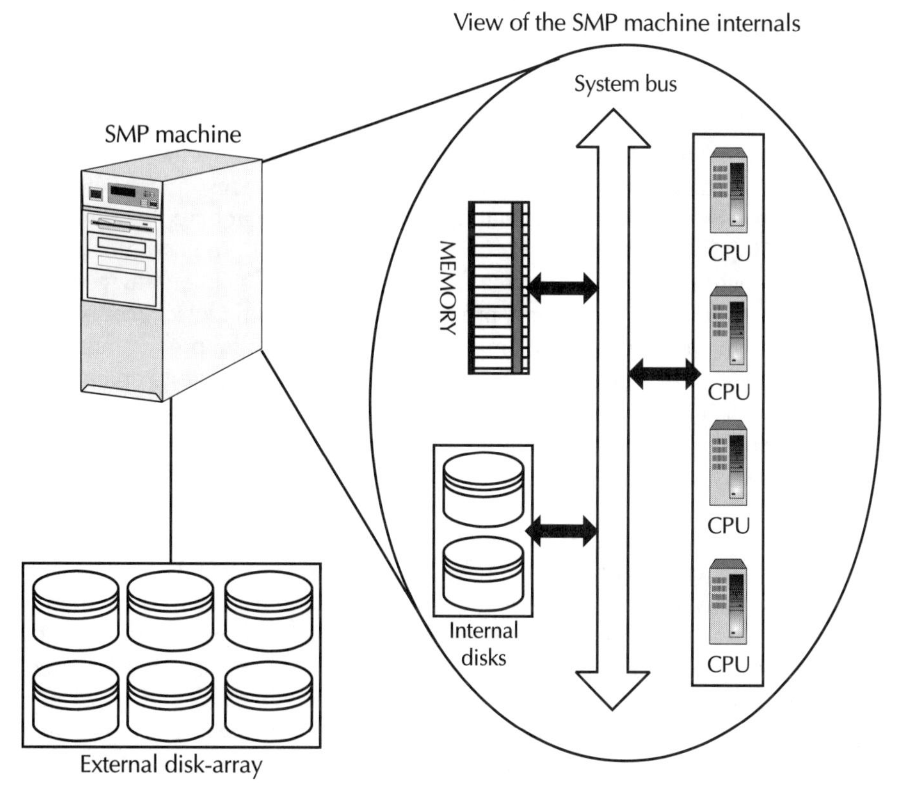

FIGURE 3-4. *A view of the SMP machine internals*

Clusters reduce the chances of unexpected downtime. Each hardware and software component is made redundant across all nodes of the cluster. Such redundancy eliminates most single points of failure. For example, if one node crashes due to a hardware or software problem, another node can take over *almost* seamlessly (usually within a few minutes, depending on the time taken for the secondary node to detect the failure, gain control of the external disks, and restart the database after instance recovery) and continue to provide access to the database.

From an Oracle perspective, the main disadvantage of clusters is that they do not provide comprehensive standby database solutions. This is because nodes in a cluster are present usually very close to each other (generally within the same data center), so replication of databases across geographically disparate locations is not possible. That rules out availability during environmental failures and natural and man-made disasters. However, clusters provide very cost-effective failover solutions during many manual glitches and hardware/software failures.

Besides high availability, clusters boost performance by providing more horsepower (multiple nodes working simultaneously) and better load balancing. Partitioning specific applications (OLTP, DSS, batch) to use a specific node enables performance to be highly enhanced by segregating dissimilar resource usage. Thus, OLTP applications would not tread on the feet of DSS and batch applications, and, theoretically, all can coexist without too much interference from each other. Also, clusters allow decent scalability, since another node could easily be plugged into the cluster to handle additional loads, provided the maximum cluster size is not reached. Generally, a cluster, unlike an MPP (massively parallel processing) machine, has a very finite upper limit on the number of nodes that it can handle. Usually this upper limit varies from four to sixteen nodes.

Two different kinds of high-availability solutions can be implemented across clusters:

- **Oracle Parallel Server (OPS)** OPS is a specific high-availability Oracle option that exploits clusters and MPP architectures. OPS allows multiple database instances to share a single physical database. Each participating node has an instance (Oracle memory structures and processes) that mounts a common database, laid across the shared external disks. Each instance is simultaneously available, and in the event of one instance crashing, the database is still available for access via the other instances. OPS is available for most major OSs, including Windows NT. Prior to implementing OPS, make sure that you evaluate it thoroughly for your environment, especially in light of all the OPS limitations, such as additional I/O caused by false pinging. Chapter 16 discusses OPS in more detail.
- **Standby instances** Standby instances are usually implemented across two cluster nodes. The main difference between a standby instance configuration and OPS is that there is only one database instance in the former and there are multiple instances in the latter. IBM's *HACMP/6000*, NCR's *LifeKeeper*, and Sun's *Sun Clusters* are popular examples of cluster offerings from mainstream vendors that can be configured to provide standby instances. Many vendors providing cluster solutions have an "Oracle configuration pack" that pre-configures a standby instance on a non-primary node to take over during disasters. For Windows NT, Oracle provides Fail Safe® that can be implemented on *Microsoft® Cluster Server* (formerly code-named *Wolfpack*). Additionally, third-party software such as *Veritas FirstWatch®* is available for monitoring and managing failover (Chapter 18).

Standby instances can be configured in either of two ways (depending on the vendor/platform):

- **Primary/secondary nodes** Here, there is a primary (active) node whose instance mounts the database, and there is a secondary node that periodically polls the primary node to ensure its availability. All SQL*Net or Net8 requests go to the primary node specifically (by IP address or node name (DNS) in the *tnsnames.ora* file). During a disaster, when the primary node crashes, there is a brief service interruption as the second node takes over and performs instance recovery. Once the second node is up, any database request from any client is routed to the new node via a transparent IP-address takeover, where the new node assumes the IP addresses of both nodes. This results in almost continuous database availability with very little service interruption.
- **Direct cluster access** Here, the cluster has a unique name/IP address, in addition to each node having its own name/IP address. All SQL*Net or Net8 requests go explicitly to the cluster and not to any specific node, and they are in turn routed to the primary node. When the primary node crashes, there is a brief outage as the secondary node comes up and mounts the file systems and disks of the primary node. Database instance recovery is then performed. All requests are then automatically routed to this newly active node.

In both cases, fault detection occurs via a "heartbeat" message exchanged by the two nodes (as shown in Figure 3-5) at pre-defined intervals (usually a minute, by default). Also, once the secondary node becomes active, the first node can be repaired and made the secondary node (that is, it will send heartbeat messages to ensure that the other node is up and running). Chapter 15 discusses both OPS and standby instances in more detail.

Unless it's a very large-scale implementation, avoid MPP machines

Unlike a cluster where only a few nodes are interconnected, MPP (massively parallel processing) systems allow a large number of nodes to be interconnected. There are MPP systems with more than one thousand nodes. Each of these nodes is a separate system having its own CPU, disks, controllers, memory, and internal system buses to form a "loosely coupled," "share-nothing" architecture (certain MPP systems such as the *Siemens Reliant® RM1000* combine the MPP and SMP architectures to form a large MPP machine composed of multiple SMP nodes). All of these nodes are connected via a high-speed, high-bandwidth interconnect. Each

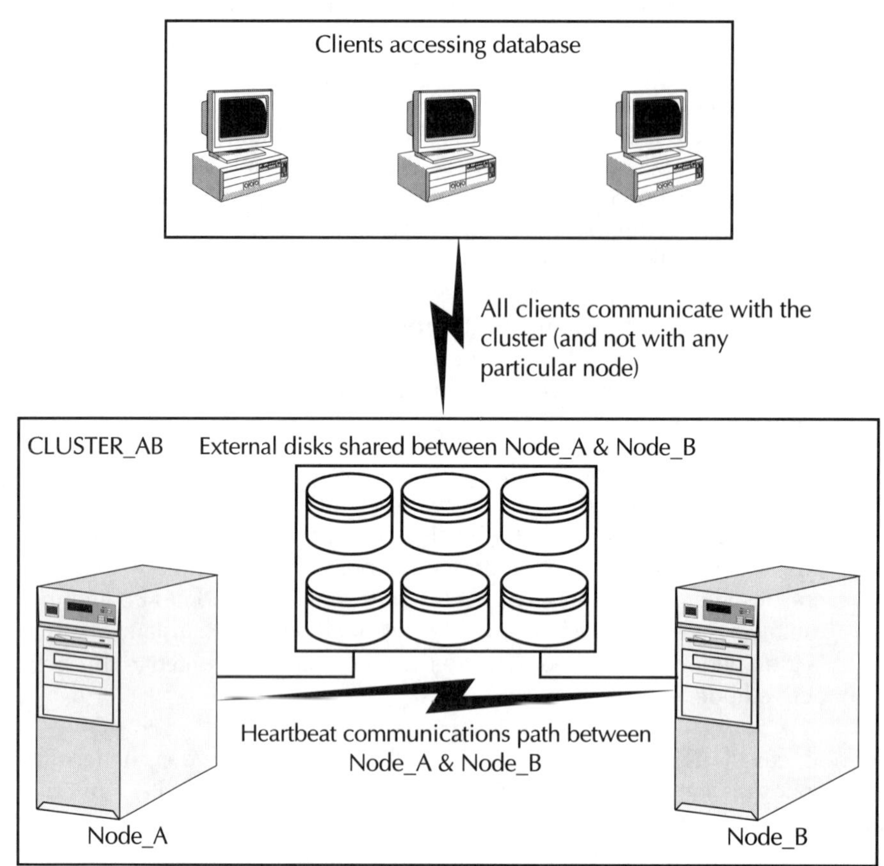

FIGURE 3-5. *A cluster CLUSTER_AB with two nodes, Node_A and Node_B (here option B is depicted, where clients communicate directly with the cluster and not with a node)*

node has a separate copy of the OS. In an MPP architecture, Oracle is installed in OPS mode. Each Oracle instance on each node is responsible for all resources it holds, has a view of the entire database, and can find out which node holds a lock on any part of the database. If it needs something that is locked by another node, it will require an inter-instance ping, where the other instance would have to write to disk all the changes it has made (after they are made) and those would be reread by the current instance (with Oracle8*i* Cache Fusion™, the need for inter-instance pings has reduced; refer to Chapter 16 for more details). A typical database query would go against one node; data would be picked up from the memory and/or disks of any appropriate node and travel via the interconnect to return the data to the requesting node. Each node controls its own set of disks and can take over control of another set if a node fails. Thus, all the nodes may be configured to be primary or a combination of primary and secondary. The database files are placed on the primary nodes, whereas the secondary nodes provide the necessary redundancy to take over and replace the primary nodes, in case the latter fail.

The biggest disadvantage in MPP architectures is not the architecture itself, but application design flaws that exist in a typical implementation. Most application designers are well versed in implementing applications on SMP machines. However, MPP architectures require a total paradigm shift in terms of analyzing which data needs to be placed on which node to reduce "data sharing" (inter-instance pings) across nodes. Since each node is highly independent in a "share-nothing" architecture, any situation that causes nodes to trade large-scale resources (due to data sharing) results in high traffic across the interconnect.

In a typical SMP architecture, as long as extensive physical I/O is avoided and data is cached in memory, performance is relatively optimized, since most of the data needs to travel just from memory to CPU and back via the internal system bus. The closer CPUs and physical memory are placed together, the less the latency and the faster the performance, since internal system bus traffic is thus kept at a minimum (in a typical SMP system, the average latency is around 4 microseconds due to the proximity of the CPUs and memory; whereas in a typical MPP system such as the *IBM SP*, average latency is in the region of 40 microseconds). In an MPP architecture, however, besides excessive physical I/O, there is an additional worry. If proper application partitioning is not done, data may reside in the memory or disk of any node. Thus, the calling node needs to talk to the target node via the interconnect and the data has to travel via the interconnect to the calling node to satisfy a SQL statement. In a high-transaction environment, this can choke the interconnect. The interconnect bandwidth may prove inadequate for handling extremely large traffic volumes, thereby serializing the traffic and causing slow response times. This is the biggest reason for performance disappointments that result from an improper MPP implementation. Additionally, inter-node data movement occurs in "hops" (movement of data from one node to a neighboring node is termed a "hop"). The more the number of hops required to satisfy a SQL statement, the higher the degradation in performance. For example, in Figure 3-6, data movement between nodes N1 and N2 would take less time than movement between nodes N1 and N64 (presume that N64 is another distant node) due to the larger number of hops required for data to travel between N1 and N64. Inter-node hops occur for two primary reasons:

- To obtain data in the memory of another node
- To obtain data in the disks of another node

Deploy MPP only for Large-Scale Use

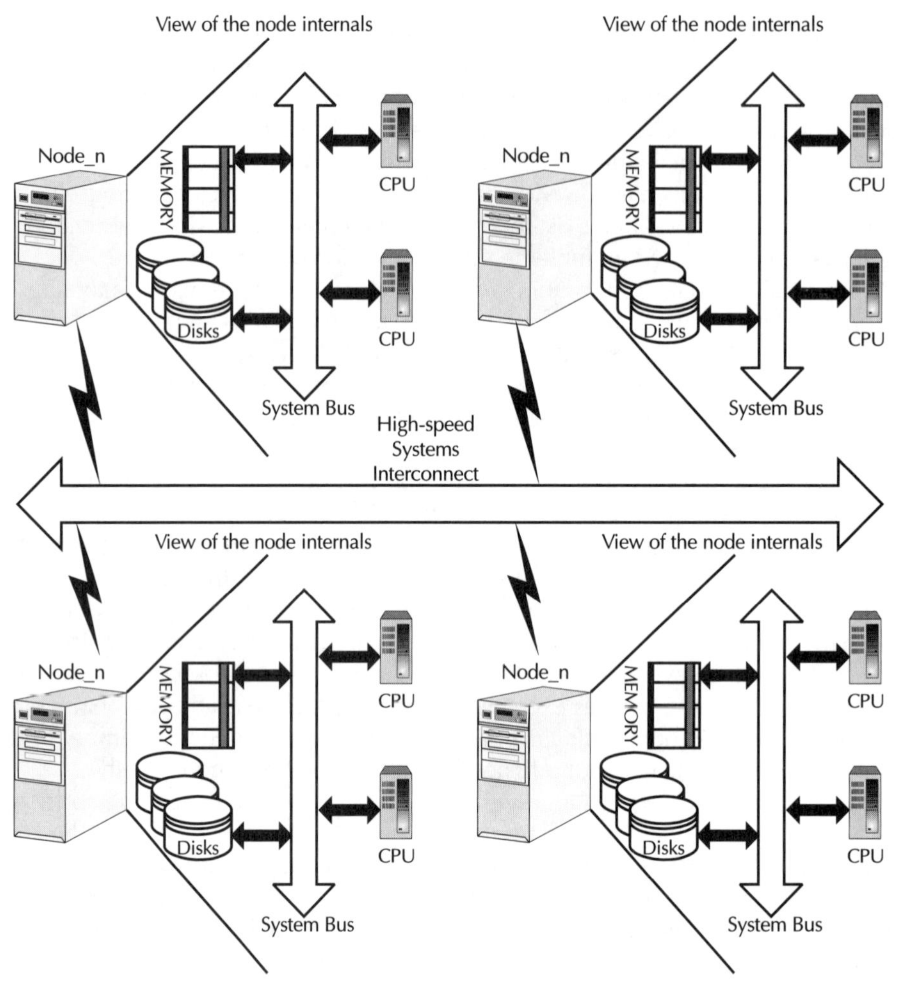

FIGURE 3-6. *MPP architecture*

Both cases require data to travel via the interconnect. However, obtaining data from the disks of another node causes even more performance delays, since the target node needs to perform physical I/O and then the data retrieved needs to hop back to the source node via the interconnect.

In order to fully grasp the significance of the overhead involved in the inter-node hops, consider the following example: Node 1 needs a specific data-block. Node 3 currently holds that block. Node 2 is positioned between the two and controls the I/O for where the block resides. Node 1 requests Node 3 to give the block, once it is done. Node 3 asks Node 2 to write the block (since Node 2 controls the I/O to that data-block). Node 3 communicates back to Node 1 that the block is now available. Now, Node 1 requests Node 2 to get the block. Node 2 reads the block and gives it to Node 1. All this inter-node communication occurs via the interconnect for just one block request. Imagine the interconnect traffic generated in a high-transaction OLTP environment.

MPPs traditionally have offered the power of a large number of CPUs. In many cases, however, due to the latency involved in inter-node hops, the CPUs may be sitting idle. Thus, application usage, overall access methodology, and data-file placement require a lot of analysis to ensure that inter-node hops are reduced.

MPP vendors have been working hard to optimize the MPP architecture and increase interconnect bandwidth and speed. Also, in Oracle7 v7.3 and Oracle8, the Oracle Parallel Server option (OPS) is highly optimized to take advantage of the MPP architecture. A large number of operations are parallelized via a disk-affinity algorithm, where the request for data is routed to the node that holds the requested data in its local disks, thereby reducing the need for interconnect travel. Even then, an improper physical design and implementation can restrict disk affinity and force interconnect travel. As mentioned earlier, Cache Fusion™ in Oracle8*i* offers some enhancements where read data does not have to travel to disk first, only changed data has to be written to disk prior to being accessed by another node. As Cache Fusion™ technology matures, there may be further enhancements.

Also, MPP systems are very expensive. Such high prices are primarily a result of the high-speed interconnect that links all the nodes. Systems offer various types of interconnects, such as crossbar, hypercube, spanning-tree, toroidal meshes, fat-tree, 2D meshes, and 3D meshes. Each interconnect type attempts to minimize the distance between subsequent nodes, thus reducing the distance traveled during each hop. For example, the IBM SP currently uses the crossbar technology, which is also one of the most advanced. However, the crossbar technology scales very little in terms of price and does not accommodate lower prices for fewer nodes. Variable costs escalate with each additional node. However, the fixed costs remain the same—whether it's a 4-node system or a 256-node system.

Due to the sheer number of components involved in an MPP system, it's harder to maintain. Since an MPP architecture inherently shares nothing, it needs to be explicitly designed to provide redundancy. For example, each MPP node has its own set of disks. If one node goes down, its disks become unavailable, unless they are dual-ported, such that another node takes over the disks during a node failure. Each MPP node designates a single point of failure. Unless the MPP machine has been configured to have the disks shared between nodes, such that one node can be the primary node and another can be the secondary, backup node, node unavailability may result in major downtime. Hence, unless your site has outgrown a single-node SMP machine or even a multinode cluster, it's advisable to avoid MPP. Ideally, MPP should be deployed if your site has a VLDB or a series of complex interrelated applications and really needs the power and scalability of several (tens and hundreds of) nodes working in tandem to handle total transaction throughput with experienced systems administrators available at all times. Large read-intensive applications such as data-warehouses, data-marts, and similar DSS-type reporting systems tend to perform better (than OLTP applications) on MPP, since the movement of data across disks of different nodes is reduced. Even then, ensure that you analyze usage patterns and distribute data effectively across appropriate nodes, prior to deployment to minimize interconnect traffic.

Consider NUMA machines as an alternative to MPP machines

Sometimes, sites hit the upper limit on their SMP machines and are forced to invest in MPP hardware to attain scalability. One of the most realistic limits to the SMP architecture is the number of CPUs that can be added. In an SMP server, multiple CPUs have their own local caches and also share and communicate with the I/O subsystem and main memory (RAM) via a high-speed bus, resulting in a *uniform memory access* (UMA) arrangement (see earlier Figure 3-4). In such an arrangement, a CPU first tries to locate local data and instructions in the cache associated with it (called a Level-1 or L1 cache). When the required data is unavailable, it checks in a larger (usually 512KB to 2MB) Level-2 or L2 cache a little further away. Due to the limited size of both the L1 and L2 caches, most data is stored in main memory, which has to be accessed for transferring the data to the cache. Each CPU accesses main memory via the bus. A higher number of CPUs in the SMP machine results in higher traffic in the limited bandwidth of the bus, thus saturating the bus. Once the server reaches 12 to 16 CPUs, it reaches the upper limit, where adding any more CPUs doesn't result in any performance improvement. And this is largely a direct result of the bottleneck caused at the bus. Thus, most SMP machines limit the CPU capacity to 12 or 16 CPUs. Traditionally, sites whose response time and throughput requirements cannot be met by an SMP machine resort to an MPP alternative.

Even though MPP machines scale very well and have been used by vendors to achieve high throughput in the industry benchmarks (TPC-D, for instance), they have their own share of drawbacks (as mentioned in the previous tip). Rather than going all the way to the MPP architecture, there is a newer, less-expensive alternative emerging: NUMA.

NUMA (Non-Uniform Memory Access), though very similar to SMP, addresses some of the limitations outlined previously and provides much higher CPU scalability. Instead of having main memory available uniformly to all CPUs, NUMA is composed of multiple groups, each group consisting of one or more CPUs, memory, and I/O subsystem(s). Figure 3-7 illustrates the NUMA architecture. Thus, all available memory is broken up and made local to each group. Each NUMA group can be thought of as a node in a cluster or MPP environment. Within each group, all the components (CPUs, memory, I/O subsystem) are tightly coupled in a similar fashion as SMP. Communication between each component in a group occurs via a shared local bus. All groups are connected via a high-speed interconnect, which maintains its own cache (referred to as the Level-3 or L3 cache) per group to provide cache coherence between all the interconnected groups. The data-access algorithm in NUMA is roughly as follows: A CPU first checks its L1 cache for data availability. If it is unsuccessful, then the larger L2 cache is checked. If it is unsuccessful once again, the memory local to the group is checked. When the required data is not available locally, then a remote access is made to check the memory of another group. NUMA uses "snooping" agents to locate the right group. Once the data is obtained, it is copied to the L3 cache for access. Note that local access is almost invariably not enough. For example, certain models of Sequent NUMA stripe their memory in a 4KB stripe. If you have an 8KB or bigger database block, any access will cause a non-local memory get. So far, however, I haven't found such scenarios to be an issue, since they are handled quite well.

The success of a NUMA implementation depends primarily on three factors:

- **Proximity of data to each group** If most data requests result in remote memory accesses of other groups, they will generate a lot of interconnect traffic and be subject to the same performance problems of a saturated SMP machine. Ideally, most requests need to be satisfied locally without resort to any remote access. All NUMA vendors are trying to implement sophisticated process affinity algorithms, where requests for data would be routed to those groups that hold it.
- **Interconnect bandwidth** During high inter-group travel, if the interconnect does not provide sufficient bandwidth, then performance would deteriorate. Based on the SCI (Scalable Coherent Interface) technology in use in most NUMA machines available today, interconnect bandwidths can be as high as one gigabit per second.
- **Application characteristics** A purely OLTP application consists of highly random reads. Since it is very difficult to implement any kind of reliable process affinity for random operations, OLTP applications are not very well suited for NUMA. However, there are quite a few sites (among them are some of Oracle's largest customers) that are using NUMA for OLTP applications. As long as the limit of the high-speed interconnect is not reached, it can be used even with OLTP applications. As a general rule, with the current maturity of NUMA systems in the market, they are more suited for batch or DSS applications such as data-warehouses and data-marts, where parallel bulk reads and writes (during data loads) can

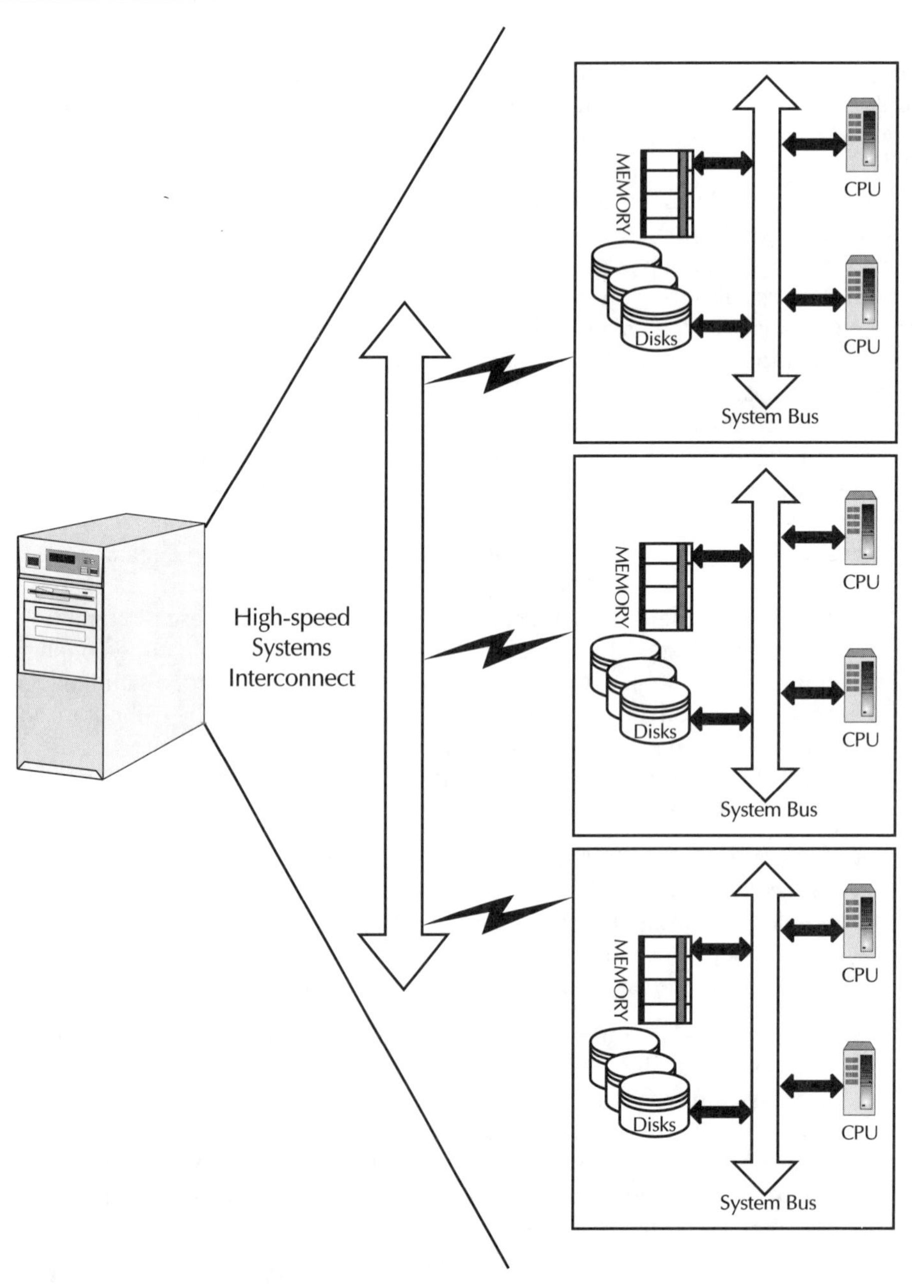

FIGURE 3-7. *NUMA architecture*

occur locally in several NUMA groups. Also, another caveat is, Oracle is not currently optimized to run on NUMA. Accordingly, the SGA may be broken up across the local memories of multiple groups. It will require rigorous benchmarking to ensure that this does not result in high interconnect traffic and, even if so, the resultant latency does not kill performance.

Though NUMA does not yet offer the scalability of a typical MPP machine, it allows much higher scalability than a comparable SMP machine. Typically, a NUMA group consists of up to four CPUs on a single motherboard connected to a disk I/O subsystem and main memory between 512MB and 4GB. Most NUMA machines available today can supposedly scale up to 256 groups (practically, going beyond 8 NUMA groups involves much greater administrative complexities). NUMA runs a single OS across all groups and supports Oracle in non-OPS (single instance per database) mode. NUMA is a viable alternative for companies who have reached the ceiling with the regular SMP architecture and desire higher capacity, albeit not as high or expensive as an MPP box.

From an availability perspective, NUMA is more complicated and composed of more components than a comparable SMP system (see Figure 3-7). Typically, the higher the number of components, the lower the MTBF (since overall system MTBF would revert to the lowest MTBF of all components). NUMA is fairly new and has been embraced mostly by companies for DSS applications, with a few notable exceptions. Hence there has been no real pressure on NUMA to prove itself as a high-availability platform, since DSS application uptime requirements are generally not as rigorous as those for OLTP applications. For that reason, for sites with high uptime requirements, it is advisable to set up NUMA machines in a cluster arrangement (with a secondary standby machine/database).

Negotiate with the vendor for a loaner machine

The preceding pages have included quite a few hardware tips. How are you going to test these tips prior to implementation? The standard test machine at your site cannot be used for such tests, since it may already be in use for testing database and application versions. Many of these tips require specific hardware to be added or removed and the OS to be reinstalled more than once. Possible sources of new test environments are loaners.

Frequently, vendors (if you ask them!) provide you with loaners, so that you can evaluate their hardware before you buy. Especially for a decent-sized contract, they are willing to participate in a "proof of concept" by replicating your environment and demonstrating the high availability of their products. Do not hesitate to test alternative approaches discussed here, on these machines. Make sure the loaner environments closely mirror your production needs and throughput requirements.

Use load/stress creating software (such as *LoadRunner* from *Mercury Interactive*) to simulate production loads and monitor performance. Come up with alternative strategies to crash the hardware and/or corrupt the data. See whether you can recover within the MTTR (mean time to recover) times specified in your service agreement. Remember, achieving high uptime and good performance is highly iterative and requires many repetitions on the loaner or other test machines to get it right.

Summary

This chapter examined some common hardware architecture and configuration issues. Several important hardware components prone to frequent failure, such as CPUs, disk drives, tape drives, I/O subsystems, disk controllers, and physical memory, were highlighted. The importance of high MTBF and hot-swappability for all critical hardware components was emphasized. Commercial RAID levels were explained in detail. Various hardware architectural alternatives such as SMP, NUMA, clusters, and MPP were presented from both availability and performance perspectives.

Though hardware forms the foundation of the entire 24×7 topology, it is only the first key piece in the overall puzzle. The following chapter discusses the next piece: operating systems.

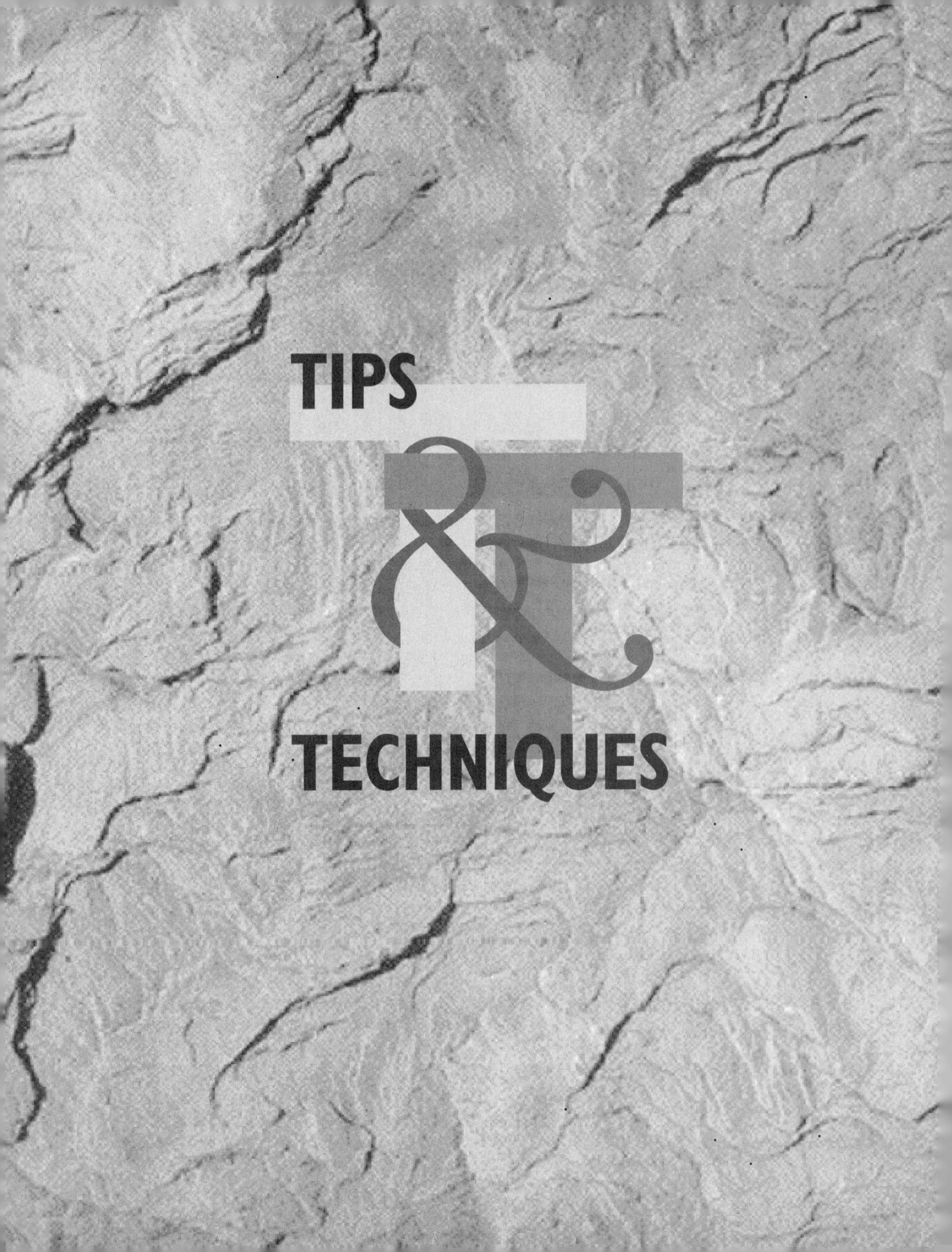
TIPS
&
TECHNIQUES

CHAPTER 4

Operating Systems

The operating system (OS) is one of the most complex pieces of software that runs on your machine. Since it operates in close interaction with the hardware, it is a key component in maintaining system availability. All applications, including databases, are highly dependent on the services provided by the OS. A sick OS is capable of crashing any system. Any effort to attain high availability would be grossly incomplete without addressing OS configuration.

This chapter offers the following tips and techniques:

- Learn to customize your kernel
- Know your OS logical and physical block sizes
- Pre-create abundant raw partitions
- Choose multiple standard sizes for raw partitions
- If using raw devices, definitely place online redo-logs on them
- Do not use cylinder 0 of the disk for creating raw partitions
- Create symbolic links for all raw-devices
- Be aware of other file-system options
- Proactively ensure that system capacity is not reached at *any* time
- Distribute all resource-intensive applications onto multiple servers
- Set up limits on *non-database* servers with limited CPUs / memory
- Do not set priority levels for Oracle-related processes
- Do not use processor-affinity on the database server
- Discourage non-production jobs during peak production hours
- Avoid resource-intensive commands that compete with Oracle processes
- Frequently check for memory leaks
- Set swap space between two and four times the physical memory
- Distribute swap area across your fastest disks
- Know whether your OS can address more than 2GB of RAM
- If possible, lock your shared memory area in physical memory
- Understand logical and physical drive mappings
- Enable file-system journaling on all production boxes

- Check disk free-space availability on a regular basis
- Keep your file-systems and directories slim
- Maintain a spare root file-system
- If available, turn on large file support
- Look at important OS logs at regular intervals
- Invest in automated tools to monitor system bottlenecks

Oracle runs on umpteen platforms, ranging from big-iron behemoths to handheld devices, and each platform has its own OS variation. It would be difficult to cover every platform here. Rather than attempting to do so, I have taken shelter behind the sheer magnitude of numbers. Based on my experience, UNIX seems to be the OS of choice at most 24x7 sites running midrange computers. As such, I focus primarily on the UNIX operating system in this chapter. However, I do refer to Windows NT 4.0 occasionally to illustrate certain scenarios under different operating systems. Hence, before proceeding any further, let me list some core differences between the Oracle Server architecture on UNIX and that on Windows NT 4.0.

Oracle on UNIX Versus Oracle on Windows NT

The basic differences between an Oracle system running under UNIX and an Oracle system running under Windows NT are as follows:

- **Process structure** An Oracle instance on UNIX constitutes multiple background and foreground processes, whereas an Oracle instance on Windows NT is a single process composed of multiple threads. Thus, on Windows NT, DBWR, LGWR, ARCH, and so on are all internal threads of the *oracle7x* or *oracle8x* process (where *7x* and *8x* refer to the Oracle version) and are not visible from the NT Task Manager. Under NT, the dynamic view *v$bgprocess* has to be queried to verify the existence of each background process, whereas in UNIX, the *ps* command lists all background processes.

  Furthermore, in spite of Oracle's intrinsic multithreaded architecture on NT, the MTS (Multi-Threaded Server) option is not supported. Hence, multiple dispatchers and shared servers cannot be configured in Oracle on NT. Each user session is dedicated and spawns a separate thread within the main

process. For very large, heavily accessed OLTP databtases, scalability becomes an issue on NT, since total memory address space for any process is restricted to 2GB. This means that the Oracle kernel and all connected user sessions are confined to that size. In UNIX, that's not an issue, since each process is separate and has its own distinct process space.

- **File system options** Under NT, there are only two viable file system options: raw and NTFS. (FAT cannot be implemented on most production boxes due to inadequate security.) Under UNIX, there are relatively more options available, such as raw, UFS, VxFS, xFS, and so on.
- **Database block size** Under Windows NT 4.0, the maximum value for the initialization parameter DB_BLOCK_SIZE is 8KB, whereas on most flavors of UNIX, it's significantly higher. This limitation of NT may cause genuine performance setbacks for DSS applications.
- **Hot backups** Windows NT 4.0 commands such as *ntbackup* prevent open database files from being copied. Hence, the Oracle utility *ocopy* needs to be used to perform hot backups. However, *ocopy* does not provide for direct backups to tape. All files first need to be copied to disk and then transferred via NT commands to tape. For VLDB sites, this may cause a serious administrative impediment, since sufficient disk space may not be available for the online backup of certain large tablespaces (which also rules out backing up the entire database at one stretch).

Kernel and Block Size

The tips in this section apply to most flavors of UNIX. If a tip applies to only a specific implementation of UNIX, such as Solaris or HP-UX, I have indicated this.

Learn to customize your kernel

In most database environments, it's tough to conduct tuning efforts without somehow needing to tune the UNIX kernel. The database instance uses shared memory and semaphores, which need to be adjusted at the kernel level to have a decent-sized instance.

The kernel is at the core of the UNIX operating system. It performs all of the base tasks, such as memory, process, and I/O management, that keep the system operational. It is the skeletal framework over which all other external layers exist.

The kernel has some unique characteristics. Most kernels are perpetually bound to physical memory. In other words, they cannot be swapped or paged out. As such, the kernel should be configured to be as condensed as possible.

Due to inherent installation complexities, many systems administrators install UNIX in its default form, with all of its bells and whistles. This translates to a big, fat kernel, requiring a good portion of the physical memory. It's desirable to remove all unwanted features, making the kernel tables as compact as possible. Especially at sites where memory is a diminishing resource, this is a not a bad skill to have.

The flip side of the coin also presents an interesting picture. If you have a VLDB, chances are that you support a large number of users and programs. As such, the default kernel, with all of its limitations, might obstruct smooth operations. (Remember the error "maximum users reached"?) So if you want to support more users and processes or have more files open, you will have to modify the kernel at one time or another.

Another issue is that many sites use raw devices rather than file systems. (Raw devices are discussed in detail later in this chapter.) One of the most important tasks, which quite a few sites forget to do, is to reduce the size of the default file system buffer after converting to raw devices. Once you are on raw devices, the file system buffer usage is minimal. The buffer can be trimmed down to a quarter of its original size without affecting performance. Such trimming also requires kernel customization.

The challenge for most Oracle sites is to remove all unwanted OS options while increasing all database-related resources. Most kernels come generously equipped with support for a large number of device drivers and have huge kernel tables. You can easily measure the total physical memory your kernel uses, either by checking with your hardware vendor or by looking at the messages on your screen when your system boots. Look for messages indicating real memory (total RAM) and available memory. The difference between the two is approximately the size of your kernel. If the difference seems too high, the kernel needs to be curtailed at the next opportunity.

Most production boxes at 24x7 sites cannot be rebooted. In such instances, look at the system's log files (for example, */var/adm/messages* on Sun Solaris). These files capture a variety of bootstrap information, including real and available memory sizes. Any kernel customization requires a reboot. Hence, such tasks need to be performed only during initial configuration or later during scheduled outages with a standby server active. Making all kernel changes prior to deployment is preferable.

Most flavors of UNIX have a menu-driven kernel configuration tool (SAM on HP-UX and SMIT on IBM AIX) that make such editing easier. Some of the kernel parameters that you might find interesting from a database perspective are listed in Table 4-1. Many of them are explained in detail in the tips that follow. Most kernel parameters are specified in configuration files as a sequence of single-line entries in the following format:

```
kernel-parameter-name                          value
```

These kernel configuration filenames and locations vary, based on the UNIX flavor. For example, in Sun Solaris, the kernel file is */etc/system*.

Before changing any kernel parameter, make sure that you have a reliable backup of a working version of the kernel. By working version, I mean the current version of the operating system plus all of the patches necessary to eliminate show-stopping kinks and bugs. Ensure that you can easily get back to the pre-change scenario before saving any changes. If possible, test out all changes on a non-production system with the same configuration. After changes are made, check that the system comes back up without any error or warning messages after rebooting and that there are no unwanted side effects. Needless to say, a version of the kernel that works inefficiently but reliably is more desirable than a more efficient albeit unreliable one.

Kernel Classification	Generic Parameter Name	Description
Core parameters	NPROC	Maximum number of concurrent processes that a user can run.
For 24x7 systems supporting a large user community, ensure that these parameters have high values. Since such systems cannot be rebooted often, estimate and set the value to the maximum that you are likely to need.	MAXUSERS	Estimated maximum number of users in your system. This is usually a soft limit.

TABLE 4-1. *Some Important UNIX Kernel Parameters, from an Oracle Perspective*

Kernel Classification	Generic Parameter Name	Description
	NFILE	Maximum number of concurrent open files.
	NINODE	Maximum number of inodes (all open files, pipes, etc., require an inode). This should be greater than NFILE.
	ULIMIT	Maximum file size for users in physical OS blocks (512 bytes). Consider your biggest Oracle export dump sizes when specifying this.
File system buffer parameters Decrease the values for these parameters if you are using raw devices. If using pure file systems, consider increasing them, depending on the number of data files and application characteristics. Generally, the file system buffer size is 10 to 20 percent of physical memory for most file system–based Oracle installations. In some UNIX releases (such as SVR4), the size of the file system buffer is managed dynamically. However, these parameters influence the buffer-management algorithm.	BUFPAGES NBUF	Number of pages to be added to the file system buffer. The size of each page is usually 1K. In System V release 3, this specifies the total number of buffers that can exist. In release 4, it indicates the number of buffer headers allocated in each batch. A new batch is allocated when the system runs out of buffer headers (until BUFHWM is reached). Unused buffer headers cannot be returned to memory. Low values for NBUF force the system to allocate more batches of buffers, decreasing efficiency. Very high values run the risk of increasing unused buffer headers, wasting memory.

TABLE 4-1. *Some Important UNIX Kernel Parameters, from an Oracle Perspective* (continued)

Kernel Classification	Generic Parameter Name	Description
	BUFHWM	Maximum physical memory (buffer high-water mark) that can be used by the buffers. Specified in K. Limits the number of buffers that can exist. If the system does a lot of paging, try reducing this value. However when running DSS applications, good hit ratios are obtained by increasing this value, if more physical memory is available.
	SYSPTSIZE	Size of the system page table. If you increase the buffer cache, increase this value too. If the page table is too small to map the entire buffer cache, the system will reduce the size of the cache at startup. Some systems will not let you change this value, and you are stuck with the upper limit imposed by it.
Swapping and paging parameters If you need to prevent swapping, try increasing LOTSFREE. This increases paging but reduces the chances of free memory dipping below DESFREE. If you cannot tolerate much paging either, decrease LOTSFREE. If you have sufficient physical memory to usually avoid swapping, this may be the way to go. However, remember this "hit me less now rather than more later" rule: The later paging begins, the greater the chance that the system will resort to swapping. Another danger is that memory will dip below MINFREE, at which point the system might be virtually unusable and eventually go into panic mode.	LOTSFREE	The threshold at which paging begins. Paging starts when the free memory dips below LOTSFREE.
	DESFREE	The threshold at which desperation swapping begins. It is usually a lot lower than LOTSFREE.
	MINFREE	The threshold at which the system considers itself completely out of memory. Systems have to be configured not to reach this level. At this level, the system will refuse to allocate more memory until it has managed to free some memory.
	MAXSLP	The number of seconds that a process must be idle before it becomes a candidate for swapping.

TABLE 4-1. *Some Important UNIX Kernel Parameters, from an Oracle Perspective* (continued)

Kernel Classification	Generic Parameter Name	Description
Semaphore parameters Semaphores are counters used to facilitate interprocess communication. When a process takes up a resource, the counter is increased. As the resource is freed, the counter is decreased. Semaphores can be looked at as "pseudo-locks."If your Oracle site uses post-wait drivers instead of semaphores, this part is less critical. (Chapter 7 describes post-waite drivers in more detail.)	SEMMNI	Maximum number of semaphore sets (each set consists of SEMMSL semaphores).
	SEMMSL	Maximum number of semaphores per set.
	SEMMAP	Number of semaphores allocated.
	SEMMNS	Maximum number of semaphores for all sets.
	SEMMNU	Maximum number of undo entries per process.
Shared-memory parameters Shared memory is a special part of memory (usually physical) that facilitates interprocess communication. It allows multiple processes to share the same memory without requiring memory contents to be passed from process to process. Oracle's entire SGA has to fit into the shared memory. If you are setting up a large SGA, ensure that you specify high values for these parameters.	SHMMAX	Maximum size of a shared-memory segment (in bytes). Make this bigger than the SGA of your biggest Oracle instance. Note that it is not strictly necessary to fit the entire SGA into one shared memory segment. However, it helps performance, since IPC (interprocess communication) overhead is reduced. Also, if the SGA cannot be allocated onto a single shared memory segment, multiple segments will automatically be used.
	SHMMIN	Minimum size of a shared-memory segment.
	SHMMNI	Maximum number of shared-memory segments.
	SHMSEG	Maximum number of shared-memory segments per process.
	SHMALL	Maximum number of concurrent shared-memory segments.

TABLE 4-1. *Some Important UNIX Kernel Parameters, from an Oracle Perspective* (continued)

Know your OS logical and physical block sizes

I often go on short assignments to customer sites, mainly to tune a database that is providing horrendous performance. While examining the Oracle initialization parameters, I encounter diverse database block sizes ranging from 2K to 16K. When asked about the corresponding OS block size, the DBA responds with a shrug and a plaintive "Do we care?" look.

Many parameters in the Oracle initialization file depend on the database block size (DB_BLOCK_SIZE), which in turn implicitly depends on the OS block size. DBAs who accept the Oracle installer's default setting (2KB) or explicitly set the DB_BLOCK_SIZE without regard for the OS block size risk a significant performance loss and wastage of resources. Always be aware of your OS block size. If you didn't have this information while creating the database, there's a chance that your database block size is not set optimally.

During creation of the database, the block size is one of the most important settings, since this parameter is virtually unchangeable during the lifetime of the database. Ensure that you are armed with the OS block size before you embark on this one-way journey. Make the database block size at least equivalent to the OS block size, if not some multiple thereof. If your site uses raw devices, consider the physical OS block size, which is almost always 512 bytes. When using a regular file system, consider the logical OS block size, which can vary at the discretion of the systems administrator. By default, most Logical Volume Managers (LVMs) set the logical OS block size to 8K. So if your site uses an LVM, chances are that it is set to the default size of 8K. In such cases, it is advisable to set the database block size to at least 8K.

If you manage an OLTP application and want to set a more granular database block size, like 4K, you should rebuild your file system with the new OS block size of 4K (manually via the *mkfs* command or using a menu-driven system administration tool). This is similar to having to rebuild the database in order to change the database block size. All this might seem like a lot of administrative overhead. However, for ensuring database speed and availability, there is no sacrifice too great.

Also, as was mentioned in Chapter 3, setting the DB_BLOCK_SIZE to a multiple of the OS block size may induce pre-reading, since reading even a single database block causes multiple OS blocks to be read. In OLTP environments where read-ahead is not desired, set the DB_BLOCK_SIZE to be equivalent to the OS block size (not a multiple of the OS block size).

Raw Devices

This section discusses use of raw devices (or raw partitions) in a mission-critical environment.

Know what raw devices are and what they can do for you

A raw device or raw disk is an unformatted disk partition. Raw devices do not have a file system mounted on them, and they are written to and read from character device drivers. Due to the absence of a regular file system such as UFS, VxFS, or NTFS, such partitions are considered to be raw or "uncooked." When a regular file system is used, the file system manages all I/O requests, each of which passes through the file system buffers. In other words, data is written to the file system buffers and then synchronized with the physical disks. When an Oracle file (such as a data-file, online redo-log, or control-file) is created on a raw disk, Oracle takes responsibility for reading from and writing to that disk, since the file system is absent.

Figure 4-1 illustrates raw and cooked disks under UNIX and Windows NT.

In UNIX, files are usually of the following five types:

- Regular files
- Device files (block and character)
- Links (hard links and symbolic links)
- Named pipes
- Domain socket files

A discussion of most of these file types is beyond the scope of this book. (Some of the types, such as links and named pipes, are explained in later sections or chapters.) However, you need to know about regular files and device files to be able to understand the concept of a raw disk in UNIX.

UNIX uses device files to communicate with hardware components such as disk drives and tape drives. Each disk drive has a corresponding entry in the */dev* directory. A cooked disk may have both a block device file and a character device file associated with it. However, a raw disk has only a character device file. A character device file uses its own device drivers to read from and write to a disk and performs I/O operations in variable sizes. A block device file is dependent on file system buffers for performing I/O operations, and it reads from and writes to a disk in a fixed-length size (generally in physical block-sized units or some multiple thereof).

A regular file basically contains binary data as you and I know it—words, numbers, images, and so on. An Oracle database is composed of such regular files (data-files, redo-logs, control-files). Each regular file needs to exist on some portion of the disk partition. In the case of cooked disks, multiple regular files can coexist on one disk partition, either in one large directory or in specific subdirectories.

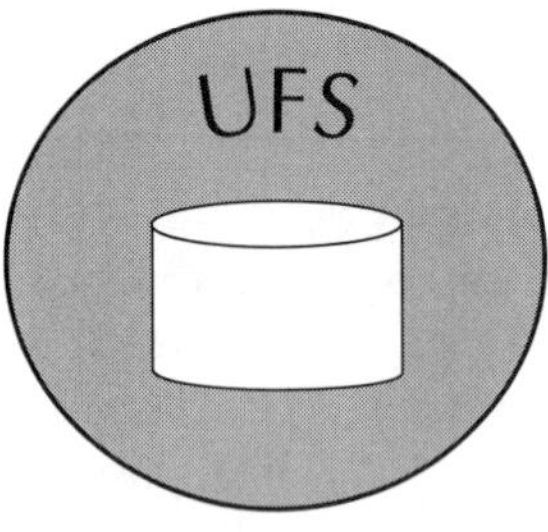

Cooked disk on UNIX File System (UFS)

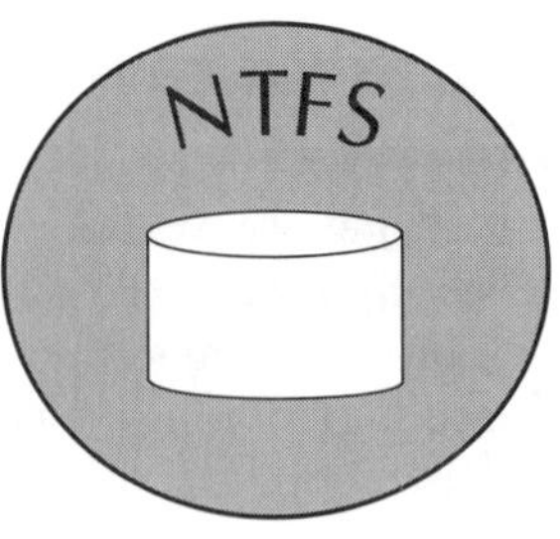

Cooked disk on Windows NT File System (NTFS)

Cooked disk on regular Windows NT or DOS (FAT)

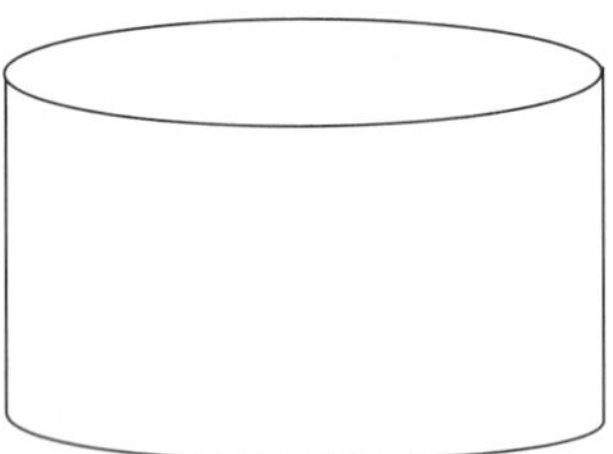

Raw-disk on Unix or Windows NT

FIGURE 4-1. *The difference between raw disks and cooked disks under UNIX and Windows NT (a file system is mounted on each cooked disk)*

However, in the case of an uncooked disk, each raw partition can accommodate only one regular file (as far as Oracle is concerned). In other words, there has to be a one-to-one correspondence between a raw partition and an Oracle file. The raw device on which the Oracle file exists needs to be owned by the user ID under which the Oracle software has been installed (usually "oracle").

At many client sites where raw disks are used in a non-OPS (Oracle Parallel Server) environment (under OPS, raw disks are mandatory), I've seen a common pattern: During design and configuration, the operations personnel excitedly discuss the pros and cons of raw devices. Though agreeing that raw disks are very difficult to maintain, they decide to take the plunge and use raw devices to reap the performance benefits. After a few months, however, they find that they have not seen spectacular performance gains. Instead, they discover that what they have really bought is inflexibility, uncertainty, and more downtime. Some texts blandly claim that a 10 to 20 percent performance improvement can be expected with raw devices. However, in talking with numerous veteran DBAs, I have come up with no concrete evidence, in terms of real, hard numbers, that raw devices improve performance. The best I have managed to get so far is, "Yeah, there seems to be a little improvement." That's hardly enough reason to recommend that you "go raw."

I have heard of Oracle's technical teams using raw devices during OLTP industry benchmark stress tests such as the TPC-C to come up with great numbers that prove Oracle's speed and robustness. (These are the numbers you see in the magazine ads.) However, many members of these very same technical teams would probably shrink away from using raw devices in real-life scenarios, when high availability is of prime importance.

Raw devices help performance, but only if disk I/O is a major bottleneck. Oracle's sophisticated memory architecture uses data-block buffers to store and manage data reasonably well and minimize disk I/O. I have found that most I/O bottlenecks would not have been avoided if raw devices had been used. Instead, the bottlenecks occur because far too few disks or controllers were available for optimal data placement or even because the data files were not optimally spread across all available disks and controllers. Raw devices are not a panacea to prevent I/O bottlenecks. Whether you use raw devices or file systems, an optimal file placement strategy is the right approach to avoid I/O bottlenecks.

Another important cause of I/O bottlenecks is untuned SQL statements. Many times, untuned SQL statements cause rampant full index and table scans, resulting in a lot of unnecessary I/O. Such I/O may cause disk bottlenecks, even in an optimally configured environment, leading the administrators to believe that migrating to raw devices may be the solution. In fact, however, tuning the SQL statements and preventing unnecessary I/O on large tables may very well solve the problem.

I recently worked at a site that had just gone raw. All of the DBAs were jubilant that they had solved their performance problems by taking the right step. Needless to say, their jubilation was short-lived. Within the next six months, when additional data files were needed, they found that they had created a nightmare. The initial performance improvement resulted from the actual move to raw devices and not from the raw devices themselves. During the move, the entire old database was exported in chunks (large tables separately, small tables together) and reimported into the new database built on the raw devices. All of the major indexes were rebuilt. This caused an entirely unintended, albeit effective, defragmentation to occur: rows in tables were bundled together, row chaining was eliminated, indexes were re-created more tersely—all because of the move. As a result, performance improved. Disk I/O had never been the problem. Within a few months, the database became fragmented again and the familiar strain on performance was back. Only this time, the flexibility in managing data files was missing. Needless to say, we had the same performance gain when we made the move back to UFS, defragmenting the database en route (intentionally this time).

This example illustrates that utilizing raw devices without understanding the possible effects can actually impede many DBA tasks—tasks that most sites not using raw devices take for granted. Such impediments can easily cascade deeper to affect availability adversely. Even simple tasks such as moving a raw device can prove to be quite challenging.

Let's take a short detour and analyze the pros and cons of raw devices.

Advantages offered by raw devices

Following are the advantages of using raw devices:

- **Better performance due to direct reads and writes because file system buffers are bypassed** Directly writing to or reading from disk eliminates the work of synchronizing the disks with the file system buffers and vice versa. This is very good for a pure OLTP system, in which the reads and writes are so random that once data is written or read it won't be needed for a while. Besides OLTP, raw devices also help DSS applications in the following ways:
    - **Sorting** For the large sorts prevalent in DSS environments, the direct writes offered by raw devices are very beneficial, since writes to the temporary tablespace can be faster. This is true even with the SORT_DIRECT_WRITES initialization parameter enabled, since any write to disk benefits (whether bypassing the SGA or not).
    - **Sequential access** Raw devices are optimal for sequential I/O. As such, the sequential I/O (full table/index scans) that is commonplace in DSS makes raw devices apt for such applications.

  Many times, the improvements due to direct reads and writes are minuscule (since buffer I/O is very fast) and are generally not very apparent to the end user, except in cases in which there are heavy disk I/O bottlenecks. Again, with the direct I/O capabilities of regular file systems in many flavors of UNIX, raw devices are not the only way to achieve direct reads and writes. (Note, however, that "pure" direct I/O can be achieved only by using raw devices; direct writes offered by file systems have some level of involvement with file system buffers.)
- **Availability of more memory for Oracle** In regular file systems, precious memory is taken up by the file system buffers. These days, however, most major production machines have at least a gigabyte of memory, meaning that the allocation of some memory for the file system buffers does not cause a major strain. Also, some preplanning and intelligent configuration

of the Oracle memory structures can result in better memory usage. If you do use raw devices but you don't shrink the file system buffers, you will miss out on this advantage.

Disadvantages of raw devices

The disadvantages of using raw devices are quite prominent—prominent enough to discourage most sites from going raw.

- **Greater maintenance difficulty** Most of the data-file management flexibility offered by Oracle cannot be exploited with raw devices. Any site whose performance has been affected by an I/O bottleneck understands the importance of the flexibility in moving data files around. If a disk is found to be busy (in excess of 90 percent) most of the time (such disks are referred to as "hot disks"), certain data files on that disk can be transferred to another disk that is not so busy.

  With a regular file system, this task is relatively easy, provided that sufficient space is available on the target disk. However, raw devices introduce new considerations and complexities. Since each file is stored in a separate raw partition, a free raw partition that can accommodate the data file has to be available on the target disk. For example, if the data file on the hot disk is 1GB, and the raw partition on which it is present is 1GB plus 1MB (the additional 1MB is for the raw partition overhead), a raw partition of the same size or bigger needs to be available on the target disk. This sounds easy enough; but, considering the disparity in the sizes of various Oracle tablespaces, maintaining free raw partitions catering to the data files of each tablespace can be a daunting task—especially for larger databases. Capacity planning becomes extremely tedious, since raw partitions of the same size or larger have to be made available for database expansion and I/O balancing without wasting disk space.

  Further, many standard, easy to use and remember commands, such as *cp*, *mv*, *rm*, and so on, do not work with raw devices, introducing the need for relatively complicated commands and tools to administer the database.

- **Absence of file system buffers** Ironically, the feature that gives raw devices their claim to fame can also hamper performance. In applications (both OLTP and DSS) in which data that is read or written may be required again shortly, raw devices require another disk read to obtain the data if the data is not available in the SGA. File system buffers may help in such scenarios, since data is held in the buffers for a little while, until the buffer space is reused for something else. If the required data is already in the file system buffers, an additional disk read or write can be avoided because the OS will retrieve the data from the buffers.

As you can see, before deciding to use raw devices you must carefully evaluate your environment and requirements. Other than OPS environments, in which raw devices are mandatory, applications rarely call for the inflexibility of raw devices. And both Oracle7 and Oracle8 support direct I/O. The availability of direct I/O features in the OS makes raw devices almost redundant.

As was mentioned earlier, however, if the transaction rates of an application are so high that they are expected to cause or are causing I/O bottlenecks, raw device usage might be worthwhile. This can be established by pre-production benchmarking. Using automated tools, you can simulate production-level transaction loads and determine whether I/O bottlenecks are occurring in spite of the best physical data file placement possible. You should also take into account that high transaction volumes may be caused by the SQL statements in use. Tuning the SQL statements may reduce transaction loads.

If you are a real "raw" enthusiast and remain convinced that you need to use raw devices, or if you are already past the point of easy return in using them, you might find the following tips helpful, especially while managing critical production environments.

Pre-create abundant raw partitions

According to Oracle's Optimal Flexible Architecture (OFA) recommendations, you need to separate your tables from your indexes, temporary segments, and rollback segments. To achieve this, you need at least as many raw partitions as you have tablespaces (DATA, INDEX, SYSTEM, TEMPORARY, and so on). The alternative of putting all of your segments into one large tablespace (SYSTEM) is unthinkable for any site, let alone a 24x7 site. Therefore, the higher the number of tablespaces, the more raw partitions you will need. Pre-created raw partitions allow the timely expansion of required tablespaces (so that you don't find yourself desperately hunting for more raw partitions just prior to getting the "Unable to allocate next extent" error message). In addition, abundantly available raw partitions provide the flexibility to spread data onto as many tablespaces and data files as required for higher performance.

Choose multiple standard sizes for raw partitions

It might seem at first that if you're going to pre-create abundant raw partitions, you should identify a standard size to use for all partitions. After all, making all raw partitions the same standard size allows maximum flexibility in handling Oracle data files. It also allows optimal usage of Oracle's intrinsic file-management features, such as renaming or moving data files, dropping and re-creating data files, and so on. And having diverse section sizes usually increases the complexity of moving a data file from one disk to another.

Let's look at the flip side of the coin, however: If you use one standard size universally, you cannot avoid overallocating space to smaller tablespaces. In other words, you may be setting yourself up for large-scale wastage of space. For example, if the SYSTEM tablespace takes up 80MB and needs to be moved to a disk that has only a few 300MB raw partitions free, this move would waste 220MB of disk space. In such a situation, it would be tempting to use up that 220MB for storing non-SYSTEM data (that is, non-data-dictionary data), such as regular application tables or indexes. However, indiscriminately mixing segments within a common tablespace (especially by putting non-dictionary segments in SYSTEM) can prove much more expensive than just wasting disk space.

In addition, when all of the pre-created raw partitions were eventually used up due to regular database growth and additional space wastage, the DBA could be forced to add a data file from space already available in the file system rather than invest in new disks immediately. This complicates matters even more, since then all maintenance operations, including backup and recovery strategies, need to be flexible enough to handle raw devices as well as file systems.

Thus, determining a "standard size" requires a lot of analysis because a lot is at stake. You have to ensure that the size is not too small—that it can accommodate large tablespaces. For example, if a 10GB tablespace uses small 200MB raw disk partitions, a total of 50 data files would be required for that tablespace alone. Such a small standard size restricts total database size because Oracle enforces both soft and hard limits on the number of data files available to an instance. Increasing the soft limit involves parameter changes and a database bounce. Increasing the hard limit means re-creating the control file, and once the maximum hard limit is reached it cannot be increased. This is a real fear in Oracle7, where the maximum value for the hard limit is between 1022 and 4000 files. Oracle8 has rectified this by increasing the maximum value for the hard limit to between 64 and 256 million files. In any case, bouncing the database instance and re-creating the control file require downtime, which is a scarce commodity in 24×7 environments.

NOTE

In addition to the MAXDATAFILES parameter of the CREATE DATABASE command and the OPEN_FILES initialization parameter, the maximum number of Oracle data files also depends on certain OS kernel parameters (for example, NFILE and NINODE) and on individual session limits on open files (LIMIT) set for the Oracle software owner. Also, in Oracle7 the DB_BLOCK_SIZE plays a role in the total number of files that can be held open by an Oracle instance (for example, a DB_BLOCK_SIZE of 8K can support up to 502 files).

At the same time, you also have to ensure that the standard size is not overly large, resulting in extensive wastage of space in the case of small tablespaces.

To have the best of both worlds, you must compromise. Rather than trying to choose one standard size, it is better to have three—small, medium, and large (see Table 4-2). Control files (remember that in Oracle8 control files have grown in size) and other smaller data files (such as SYSTEM) can be in the "small" raw sections. Online redo logs and other mid-sized tablespaces (such as TEMPORARY) can be in the "medium" raw sections. Finally, data files of huge tablespaces can reside in the "large" raw sections. If yours is a VLDB site, you could also have a "very large" section size.

If using raw devices, definitely place online redo logs on them

Although data file I/O can be asynchronous (provided that the OS supports asynchronous I/O), redo and control file I/O is always synchronous. Raw devices are highly effective for synchronous or sequential I/O operations. If you are using raw devices at all at your site, do use them for the online redo logs. Redo logs are written sequentially by the LGWR and are read sequentially by the ARCH. In addition, redo logs are usually I/O intensive. As such, they are good candidates for being placed in raw sections.

If you are using OPS, you *have* to place online redo logs on raw devices. Remember, however, that you cannot place archived logs on raw devices. They must be placed on regular file systems. Since Oracle requires that only one Oracle file be placed in a single raw partition, you cannot have multiple archived logs in a single large raw partition. Current versions of Oracle also do not allow a specific number of raw partitions to be pre-configured for creating archived logs. As such, a file system has to be designated on each participating node for the archived logs. This is more of a hardware issue. In a clustered/MPP environment (in which OPS is

Size Classification	**Size (in MB)**
Small	101
Medium	501
Large	1001
Very large	2001

TABLE 4-2. *Generic Raw Disk Section Sizes (Each Size Includes an Additional 1MB for Raw Disk Overhead)*

used), one node cannot be aware of another node's file systems (because of the potential high overhead incurred by the different file system buffer caches, locking, and so on). However, the nodes can be aware of one another's raw partitions and can assume that an application (such as Oracle) is taking care of all concurrency issues.

Do not use cylinder 0 of the disk for creating raw partitions

No matter how much I stress it, I cannot overemphasize the importance of this tip. In fact, it is not even a tip; it is well documented in OPS manuals. However, if you are not using OPS, chances are that you have not read the OPS documentation. The non-OPS documentation covers this point in a rather sketchy fashion, in bits and pieces. (If you yawn as often as I do while reading manuals, you will certainly miss it!) And none of the documentation emphasizes and illustrates this fact adequately. If I had any say in the matter, this piece of advice would be printed in huge 24-point bold type. It is a wicked show-stopper.

A while ago, total lack of knowledge in this area made me stay up for more than 56 hours straight in order to finish an Oracle installation for a client. Since the client was running in 24×7 mode, we had scheduled a planned outage to migrate to a newer version of Oracle. We also planned to migrate simultaneously to a different, more powerful system. And this time we decided to "go raw." We were expected to finish most of the upgrade tasks, such as creating the raw devices and setting up the new database on the new machine prior to the data migration, during the outage, which was supposed to be relatively short.

Well, the actual outage *was* short. But the amount of pre-work stretched into continuous days and nights. It turned out that the systems administrator had inadvertently created all of the raw partitions on cylinder 0 of each disk. Having done that, he handed everything over to me and asked me to do my DBA stuff. I went ahead and created the database. We tried some practice loads and everything went smoothly. Then we bounced the system. But when we came back up, the disks were completely useless. All of the data we had loaded was gone. After a few more iterations, we finally uncovered the elusive problem: creating the raw disk on cylinder 0 had overwritten valuable disk partition information.

Cylinder 0 is used to maintain key disk-specific information, such as partition and logical volume control maps. When you are using a file system, cylinder 0 is automatically protected by UNIX. However, when you use raw devices, UNIX leaves the application totally in charge. As such, you have to manually ensure that you do not create raw partitions on cylinder 0. Newer versions of UNIX are said to prevent this problem, as they have more sophisticated disk-management routines. However, since that incident, I have somehow lost the inclination to experiment with this particular aspect of disk management. I just steer clear of cylinder 0.

Another point worth mentioning (depicted in Table 4-2) is that when creating a data file on a raw device, always specify the data file size to be smaller than the raw partition size—*at least* two Oracle block sizes smaller. It's also good practice to make the raw partitions 1MB larger than the data files. For example, if your Oracle data file size is 500MB, specify the raw partition size to be 501MB. In other words, plan on having your standard sizes be a little bigger than the actual data files that will reside on them.

Before I move on, let me remind you again to reduce the UNIX file system buffer size when using raw devices. Allocate all freed buffers to the Oracle SGA instead. Failure to do so will result in wastage of memory by the file system buffers.

Create symbolic links for all raw devices

When using raw devices, it's a smart idea to create UNIX symbolic links for each raw partition and to use these symbolic link names in all Oracle commands (CREATE DATABASE, CREATE/ALTER TABLESPACE, and so on), rather than referring to the raw partitions directly. This will give you additional administrative flexibility. For example, if you ever need to move the raw devices around (to combat disk I/O bottlenecks), you can shut down the database (see how raw partitions affect availability?), re-create the necessary symbolic link (with the same name) pointing to the newly moved partition, and just restart the database. The symbolic links add a helpful layer between the physical raw devices and the filenames within Oracle.

Symbolic links also help in using *dbv* against raw devices. (*dbv* is an Oracle utility used for verifying data file integrity.) If the name and path of a raw device is given as a parameter for *dbv*, it produces an error ("DEV-00100: Specified file (*filename*) not accessible"). The workaround is to create a symbolic link for the raw device and provide the link name as a parameter to *dbv*.

Also, while using *dbv* against raw devices in certain versions of Oracle 7.3, you need to specify the end-block parameter value explicitly to avoid misleading messages about data file corruption. To understand this better, look at the following representation of the physical structure of a data file on a raw device:

H-D-D-D-D-D-F-F-F-R

(where *H* = data file header, *D* = data-blocks, *F* = free space, and *R* = raw device overhead)

Since the raw device is bigger than the actual data file, the data file is read incorrectly by *dbv*, which has no idea how much overhead the raw device has been allotted (it has to be a minimum of two Oracle blocks). For example, let's assume that a 500MB data file is created on a 501MB raw device partition. When *dbv* reads the 501MB file, it reports data corruption.

To overcome this situation, follow these steps:

1. Determine the database block size (DB_BLOCK_SIZE) via the following query:

```
SQL> SELECT name, value FROM v$parameter WHERE name =
'db_block_size';
```

2. Ascertain the size of the data file via another query:

```
SQL> SELECT bytes/1024/1024 "Size in MB" FROM v$datafile WHERE
name = '&actual_file_name';
```

The query reports 500MB (and not 501MB), since Oracle believes that's the correct size of the data file.

3. Determine the total number of database blocks (#_db_blocks) occupied by the file (500MB / DB_BLOCK_SIZE).

4. Run *dbv* again. This time, however, specify the END parameter value as the total number of database blocks held by the data file minus 1 (since, by convention, the block offset begins at 0).

```
$ dbv FILE=<actual_file_name> END=<#_db_blocks-1>
```

With the END block value specified, *dbv* understands where the data file actually begins and ends within the raw device and reads the data file accordingly by skipping the blocks devoted to raw disk overhead.

Be aware of other file system options

The clash between the UNIX file system (UFS) and raw devices does not have to be a holy war. In reality, there are quite a few other acceptable options. Evaluate alternative and newer file systems such as Veritas's VxFS, Ciprico's xFS, and IBM's Vesta Parallel File-system. At the time of this writing, xFS and Vesta Parallel File-System are still evolving. However, VxFS is in full-fledged commercial use. VxFS is a robust file system providing various high-availability options and decent performance. It provides transaction-based journaling; fast recovery options; custom I/O sizes using extent-based allocation; direct I/O; and online administrative operations such as backups, resizing, and defragmentation of the file system. The online resizing and defragmentation options are highly useful in a 24x7 environment. The direct I/O option provides raw device–like throughput. Furthermore, it allows direct I/O to coexist with buffered I/O.

In other words, be aware of third-party file systems that combine the performance of raw devices with the ease of administration of file systems. Perform benchmarks on in-house test machines, and talk to systems administrators *and* users at other organizations using these file systems. You have more options than just raw devices and UFS.

There is an excellent paper from Oracle Corporation entitled "Making the Decision to Use UNIX Raw Devices," authored by Cary Millsap. It provides an in-depth discussion of many of the points mentioned here concerning raw devices. This paper can be obtained from Oracle Support.

System Capacity and Bottlenecks

This section discusses determining whether system capacity has been or is about to be reached. It examines various potential bottlenecks.

Proactively ensure that system capacity is not reached at any time

Reaching system capacity at any time directly results in performance and availability bottlenecks. Initially, as system resources get depleted, throughput and response times are adversely affected. As the situation gradually worsens, the system spends more and more time trying to combat resource shortages, and finally it shuts down by going into panic mode. So much for high availability!

Always practice proactive monitoring to ensure that system capacity is not being reached. If you or a colleague cannot be around physically to monitor capacity, use system schedulers such as *cron* and *at* to run specific scripts to capture snapshots of system capacity at random hours. Make sure that sufficient RAM is available and that there is little paging and no swapping. Ensure that adequate swap space is available, so that there is enough room for the system to swap, if necessary. When a system reaches maximum capacity too soon, it is an indication that your initial capacity planning was not correct. The truth is, however, that no matter how much you plan, your system will reach maximum capacity at some point. The trick is to anticipate it, watch for it, and be ready to act when it happens.

Many times, proactive monitoring will warn you of potential problems. For example, when you run *top* or *ps*, you can see the size of each process. If a process appears to be too big, it might be an indication that it is constantly taking up memory and not releasing it (memory leaks). Investigating such scenarios will allow you to get to the bottom of uncertainties before they explode into full-fledged problems.

Types of System Problems

A sick OS provides several indications of a problem. Subsequent tips in this chapter talk about watching out for and recognizing such signs. Please keep in mind that these tips only scratch the surface. They illustrate common techniques employed by

24×7 sites to spot potential system breakdown. You may observe different problems at your site. A good understanding of these core issues will help you in building your 24×7 script arsenal (see Chapter 19) to effectively combat problems before they arise.

From a high-level perspective, when the system appears to be unusually slow, it is usually the result of any or all of the following three factors:

- Heavy system loads caused by overloaded CPUs
- Swapping, paging, and page faults due to inadequate memory
- I/O bottlenecks due to inappropriate disk drive management

If left unchecked, each of these performance killers has the ability to escalate, gradually causing the system to be virtually unusable and at times to totally collapse. Further, the problem underlying each of these factors may not be obvious at first. For example, overloaded CPUs may be the result of bad SQL code, too many processes, or very high values set for the SPIN_COUNT initialization parameter. Memory problems can be a result of very high values set for the SORT_AREA_SIZE parameter, too many processes, or too large an SGA. I/O bottlenecks can result from a bad configuration or bad SQL code. Let's take a detailed look at each of these factors in turn.

Note that I make numerous references to several UNIX commands (SVR4 and BSD) in the following text. I have not explained the usage and syntax of most standard commands such as *ps* and *cron*, since that is outside the scope of this book. The UNIX *man* pages explain these commands in detail. However, I have briefly explained certain useful non-standard UNIX commands, such as *top* and *sar*.

System Load Levels

System load levels are determined by all of the processes sharing the kernel run queue. If there are not enough CPU cycles to handle the workload of all such processes efficiently, chances are that the processes have to get in line, waiting for the CPU to become available. The *uptime* command gives you a good picture of the system load averages. You can get good insight into typical usage patterns by periodically observing the output of *uptime*. Such insight can point out potential problems, thus helping you confront them before they cause severe performance degradation or downtime.

Your system's tolerance for heavy loads relies upon a number of configurable areas, such as CPUs, memory, and the I/O subsystem. If a system is prone to high load averages without any adverse impact on performance, then perhaps a high load average is normal for that system. In other words, know what is normal for your system by monitoring it when performance is good. Unless you have an understanding of what the load averages look like during good performance, you won't be able to judge whether the current load averages are bad. If performance is largely bad during high averages and reasonably good during low averages, that is a indication of consistent system load problems, and you should probably take steps to distribute CPU, memory, and I/O loads more evenly.

The first thing to do is to look at the big picture. Analyze what the system is doing, during both high and low load levels. Using brute force and implementing stopgap solutions such as adding more hardware or simply reducing the number of jobs might help in the short run. However, a thorough analysis of the entire situation is absolutely required to fully understand the problem and implement the right solution. For example, you may notice that the system performance of your OLTP application is good most of the time, except for those three hours when that late evening batch job populating the data warehouse runs. Once you have made this observation, you can then start thinking about solutions. Maybe that batch job can be moved to the wee hours of the morning, when not too many users are around and it won't coincide with the hot backups. Or maybe tuning the SQL statements in the job would allow the job to run without causing system loads to shoot up. Or maybe the design of that data warehouse ought to be revamped, so that in certain cases it uses a pull method to get populated, rather than a batch-oriented push method—that might even eliminate the need for the batch job. Or if the batch job is a non-Oracle process, maybe its priority level can be changed (via *nice*) to make it less of a nuisance. See what I mean? Various options present themselves once you have a good understanding of the problem.

TECHNIQUES FOR UNDERSTANDING AND INTERPRETING SYSTEM LOAD LEVELS The *uptime* command provides three load averages: over the last minute, over the last 5 minutes, and over the last 15 minutes. The output of the command is as follows:

```
$ uptime
joker up 162 days, 11:38    load average : 5.34, 6.28, 5.48
```

The output tells you the system's name (joker) and how long it has been running (162 days, 11 hours, and 38 minutes). The three load averages reported are 5.34, 6.28, and 5.48. It is essential to note whether the load average is diminishing or escalating. In this example, a minute ago the load average was 5.34; 5 minutes ago it was 6.28; and 15 minutes ago it was 5.48. Hence, it appears to be quite stable.

If you observe some big averages or find that the load averages are gradually growing, find out which processes are running (via *ps*). If possible, take snapshots of all of the processes at each 10-minute interval, along with the *uptime* output. When you compare the snapshots, a picture will emerge as to which processes are causing the load averages to shoot up. Test your theory during a period of 48 hours by waiting for the load averages to go up again. You can set up a *cron* job to randomly poll the system for *uptime* results (every hour or so). If the averages seem high, the system can probably page you or another administrator. You can then immediately verify whether the same or similar jobs are running during these peak load averages. This is one method by which the culprit processes can be traced. (Refer to chapter 19 for an example of such a shell script to be called via *cron*.)

Running the *top* command can also give you information necessary to narrow down the culprits. (*top* is actually a third-party utility that ships with certain UNIX flavors; a version of *top* can be downloaded from various UNIX utility Web sites.) Be aware that *top* is not highly accurate; however, it provides a good picture of the load averages, as well as other useful information, such as which processes are on CPU and which are sleeping, the memory taken up by each process, information about zombie processes, swap space usage, and so on. The following is a sample of the output of the *top* command:

```
$ top

last pid: 11579;  load averages:  2.69,  2.77,  2.91    12:44:41
307 processes: 299 sleeping, 2 running, 4 zombie, 2 on cpu

Memory: 147M swap, 63M free swap

  PID USERNAME PRI NICE  SIZE   RES STATE   TIME   WCPU    CPU COMMAND
 9111 zisadm   -22    0   31M   13M cpu    10:31  63.0% 24.61% oracle
12149 oracle   -22    0   30M  824K run    44.9H  41.0% 16.02% oracle
11579 devrajve   6    0  796K  764K cpu     0:00  24.0%  9.38% top
 6276 root      53    0  440K  220K sleep 419:11   6.0%  2.34% sys_mon
 9104 zisadm    53    0 2228K  700K sleep   0:23   4.0%  1.56% plpqinweekly
 9447 muckdw    51    0   20M 9092K sleep   2:12   3.0%  1.17% oracle
11578 root      51    0  816K  656K sleep   0:00   3.0%  1.17% ping
29131 desaipq   53    0 3060K  760K sleep   0:29   2.0%  0.78% motifterm
 6614 desaipq   51    0  924K  536K sleep   0:12   2.0%  0.78% vi
11494 devrajve  49    0  448K  428K sleep   0:00   2.0%  0.78% ksh
    1 root      40    0  124K   88K sleep 479:08   1.0%  0.39% init
29132 desaipq   53    0  748K  332K run     0:14   1.0%  0.39% rlogin
 5271 root      51    0 3880K  500K sleep 281:20   0.0%  0.00% event_demon
 5346 root      51    0    0K    0K sleep 210:36   0.0%  0.00% nfsd
 5332 root      51    0    0K    0K sleep 205:55   0.0%  0.00% nfsd
```

The top three lines of the output show extremely useful information, such as load information, process information, memory usage, and swap statistics. The detail lines show information such as the percentage of CPU and memory used by each process and its current state (sleeping or on CPU). By default, *top* displays the top 15 resource users, sorted by CPU usage levels. The very first line of *top*'s output is very similar to the *uptime* command's output.

Some systems administrators prefer not to run *top*, since it is quite resource-intensive. In fact, it shows itself as one of the top CPU users in its output (it's number 3 in the sample output), which is refreshed every second, adding to

the resource usage. Some versions of *top* allow the output to be refreshed less frequently. Even then, it scans and reads a number of kernel tables to get its information, and that invariably results in extensive resource consumption. Other useful commands to capture system load levels include *sar* and *vmstat*.

REDUCING SYSTEM BOTTLENECKS Once you have determined that there is indeed CPU contention on your system, you might want to explore ways to reduce the contention. Realistically, the last resort might be investing in additional CPUs. However, if you have already reached maximum capacity for CPUs in your system or if your budget won't currently permit additional investments in hardware, some of the following tips in reducing CPU bottlenecks might interest you.

Distribute all resource-intensive applications among multiple servers

Find out what else besides the Oracle Server is running on your database server machine. Determine the CPU requirements for those applications (using the commands just described). If they seem high, look into running them on some other existing server. Ideally, the database server should be dedicated to the database. Especially with Oracle's NCA architecture, it is easy and tempting to overload the database server machine with middle-tier applications such as the Developer Server, Oracle (Web) Application Server, and even Oracle8's multiple cartridges. This results in a lopsided two-tier implementation, violating everything that NCA stands for. Distribute these applications onto their own servers. Compared to the Oracle server, they probably need far fewer resources. Hence, you can run them on less-powerful servers that may already be available in-house and reduce the overall load on the database server.

Set up limits on CPU and memory use by non-database *servers*

The *limit* command sets limits on the amount of resources (CPU time or memory) that a process can consume. You can set both soft and hard limits. A hard limit is stricter than a soft limit. When a soft limit is reached, the offending process is given the chance to increase its own soft limit just before it is killed. When a hard limit is reached, the process is killed immediately without a second chance.

Do not set limits for any Oracle-related process in your database server. The Oracle database engine is very sophisticated in its resource management, and such limits will result only in miscarriages. You can limit non-critical resources such as idle time for connections. For example, if idle time is limited to 10 minutes, any user remaining idle beyond that time would be forcibly disconnected. Also, limits on critical CPU time and memory can be applied to the middle-tier/subordinate servers, on which a number of processes run, resulting in a large number of database requests. On such servers, an inadequately tested "rogue" program can potentially monopolize all memory and/or CPU time.

Here is an example of the type of problem that hard limits can prevent: At a client site running an e-commerce application, a number of Web servers were used for load balancing of Web requests. A number of Pro*C-based CGIs were running on each Web server, making continuous calls to the database. New features were frequently deployed to enhance the client's Web site. This meant that a number of new CGI routines would be deployed on each Web server. Occasionally, due to the urgency of deployment, some of these CGI programs would escape too fast through the quality control channels, resulting in some severe run-time bugs. Some of them would go into uncontrolled loops while processing large amounts of data, resulting in a program using up all available CPU time. Performance on the Web site would subsequently begin to crawl. Setting up hard limits on all of the Web servers prevented future occurrences of such situations. Before setting limits, consider all factors that might be affected.

The limit command is used in the following manner:

```
$ limit cputime 60m
```

This command would limit a process to 60 minutes of CPU time. Using the *-h* switch sets a hard limit:

```
$ limit -h cputime 60m
```

A word of caution: Do not depend on these limits being active all the time. Limits are available only on the C shell (*csh*), and it's possible that not all users and programmers will be using the C shell at your site. Since the limits are set within the initialization files (*.cshrc*) of specific users/programmers, the ones who are aware of them might easily undo the limits by commenting out the commands prior to running their programs. As such, limits can usually be set only with the total cooperation of the development and user community, working toward the common end of achieving optimal usage of existing resources and preventing unwanted "accidents" such as having a program spin out of control.

Do not set priority levels for Oracle-related processes

Let me start by explaining a couple of OS-specific terms: scheduling and preemption. Let's assume that the box we are talking about has only one CPU. Every process that starts up is scheduled to run at a certain time — generally immediately. However, this schedule is ultimately based on priority level. The higher the priority level, the more attention the process gets from the CPU. If two processes are

scheduled to run at the same time, the one with higher priority would run and, as soon as it completes or reaches a wait state (where the CPU has to wait for some resource to become available for that process to continue), the CPU's attention turns to the second process. While that second process is running, if yet another process is scheduled to kick off, and this third process also has a higher priority level than the second, the second process is preempted and made to wait while the CPU executes the third process. Thus, the CPU's time can be spent primarily in servicing processes of equal priority levels until one of the following occurs:

- The process being serviced reaches a wait state.
- Another process with a higher priority level starts up.
- The process being serviced completes.

When a process reaches a wait state or completes, the process with the next-highest priority is given attention. Thus, scheduling is the act of setting up a process to run at a specific time, and preemption is the usurping of a process's schedule by another process with a higher priority.

As you can see, the priority level of a process determines its schedule and preemption. For example, low-level system processes have a higher priority than user-level processes. So if a user-level process is using the CPU and a system-level process starts up, the user-level process will have to relinquish the CPU and sleep. Once the system-level process exits, the user-level process can start using the CPU again. Generally, given the fact that system-level processes are performing basic critical tasks, they should indeed be given preference so that the system continues to function smoothly.

However, in the case of multiple user-level processes, higher priority levels provide a distinct advantage and should be used as a tool only when there are lots of processes usually running and a select handful have a genuine priority. In other words, each user-level process should be analyzed and allocated a specific priority level based on functionality and urgency. Performance can be adversely affected in cases where multiple user-level processes with different priorities constantly compete against one another, because a lot of time is spent getting the CPU to relinquish a process and latch on to another. Also, users who manipulate scheduling priorities can force the CPU to spend most of its time working on specific processes to the point that it almost ignores others, causing frustration for the users who own the latter processes. As such, priority levels should be explicitly set in only a few deserving cases.

Any Oracle-related process should be left alone. Its priority level should not be tinkered with. The Oracle Server is a complex piece of software with built-in scheduling functions. It presumes that the operating system environment gives equal priority to all user processes and that the Oracle processes will behave according to their built-in functionality. So setting certain Oracle processes at a higher or lower priority impedes the smooth functioning of the Oracle Server.

UNIX provides a *nice* command for setting priority levels for user processes. This command sets the "niceness" of a process. The lower the niceness, the more aggressive the process gets in terms of monopolizing CPU. If your users are performing non-Oracle, CPU-intensive functions on your database server, thereby inadvertently slowing down the database, you could increase the niceness of those processes, so that all Oracle-related processes get maximum CPU attention. Also, many flavors of UNIX support the *renice* command, which allows you to change the priority levels of processes that are already running. Thus, if you find that the database performance is bad because of a user process taking up extensive CPU resources, you could *renice* it to make it more passive.

Be sure that you are not accidentally changing the priority levels of "hidden" Oracle processes. For example, at a customer site, the systems administrators lowered the priority of all non-Oracle processes, including those owned by the BACKUP user ID. The BACKUP user ID had been set up to run all backup jobs, including Oracle hot backups. This resulted in hot backups running continuously for more than eight hours and still not completing. In fact, the backup window extended into peak morning production hours, causing database performance to reach new levels of deterioration. It took me quite a while to figure out *why* the hot backups were taking so long to complete—usually they would be done in three hours flat.

My advice to lower the priorities of non-Oracle processes presumes that on a production database server the database processes are getting the highest resource priority. Changing the *nice* and *renice* levels of non-Oracle processes is justified toward that end. However, this is a short-term solution. Ultimately, the reason and logic behind users running resource-intensive non-database processes on a production database server have to be evaluated.

Do not use processor affinity on the database server

Cache affinity or processor affinity is the binding of a process to a specific CPU. Historically, the presumption has been that since a certain CPU is running a process, there is a good chance that the process will benefit if it is run on the same CPU next time (see Chapter 3). Specifically, it is assumed that the process might be able to reuse the data in the CPU Level-1 (L1) cache, thus avoiding having to read physical memory. For most modern Oracle applications, however, this is rarely true. That's because the CPU L1 cache is too small to store anything of real value. Also, any performance benefit (a few nanoseconds) derived would be negligible. Newer uniprocessor and SMP machines are implementing shorter buses linking the CPU to physical memory. Hence, access to physical memory is blazingly fast nowadays.

However, technical gurus at some sites insist on using processor affinity to enhance performance. What they end up getting in return is increased administrative overhead and performance degradation. Since processor binding forces a certain process to use only a certain CPU, the process will have to wait (sleep) if that CPU happens to be busy running another process. Even if other CPUs are available at the time, the process cannot be run by them. Such scenarios are extremely common at sites running both OLTP and DSS applications.

In trying to decrease system load levels, do not resort to methods that may instead impede performance and bar optimal usage of resources.

Discourage non-production jobs during peak production hours

At various times, we all encounter users who tend to run huge queries during peak production hours (and they often are the first to complain about performance). This is more prevalent in companies having DSS systems such as data-warehouses and data-marts. Somehow, the job that was meant to run late at night to populate the warehouse ends up running during peak morning or early afternoon hours. How? Why? Nobody ever seems to know. Make sure that you detect and prevent such non-production or non-mission critical tasks from taking up valuable resources on the production boxes. Even if you cannot achieve 100 percent watertight prevention, you can at least make it a standard and announce that all non-production and non-mission critical jobs need to be approved by the DBA prior to being run during peak hours. Bullheaded users may still try to sneak past you, but the majority of users will try and follow that commandment.

Avoid resource-intensive commands that compete with Oracle processes

In addition to preventing users from running non-Oracle processes such as C programs or Perl scripts, also avoid using resource-intensive UNIX commands. At more than one customer site, I have seen systems administrators and DBAs lay down strict production standards and etiquette for developers and end-users and then turn around and punch up a resource-intensive UNIX command on the production database server without pausing to think about the repercussions. Certain UNIX commands can be as offensive as a bulky C program.

Any production etiquette document has to include standards for systems administrators and DBAs in addition to developers and end-users. Commands have to be categorized, and usage of resource hogs during peak hours has to be minimized if not eliminated altogether. For example, some systems administrators use *ps –ef* quite frequently to see whether any processes are using too much CPU resources. The *ps –ef* command does a complete scan of the process table and is quite resource-intensive itself. Also, on some large sites, I have noticed a whole bunch of DBAs and systems administrators using various monitoring tools continuously during peak hours, all at the same time. Unlike *sar*, these tools run independently and consume a lot of CPU resources.

Look for innovative alternatives that achieve the same results. For example, a full-fledged *find* command run from the root file system during peak production hours can have a cruel effect on system usage and performance. A workaround would be to issue the *ls –lR* command from the root file system via *cron* during the wee hours of every morning and save the output of the command in a predefined file. Then, when a file needs to be located, instead of using *find*, the user can issue a relatively small *grep* against the file storing the *ls –lR* output. Since the *grep* is issued against a single file, the act of locating a file becomes a lot faster and less resource-intensive. This method can be used to find the location of any file that existed prior to the time that *ls –lR* was run.

Memory Loads

Memory becomes a performance bottleneck when it is insufficient to handle all active processes—Oracle and non-Oracle. To offset the inadequacy, the OS uses the disk as a seamless extension of physical memory and starts copying memory pages to and from specific portions of the disk. This overflow of memory onto disk is called *virtual memory,* and it allows processes to continue running in spite of memory shortages. However, each time virtual memory is accessed, performance starts deteriorating, since physical disk I/O is involved. Access to memory happens at electronic speeds—in nanoseconds—whereas access to disk occurs at mechanical speeds measured in milliseconds. Add to that the contention between different processes to access the same disk, and this delay of a few milliseconds escalates to seconds and becomes highly noticeable by end users.

The space in memory that is freed up by transferring the contents to disk is reused by other processes or different portions of the same process. Memory is transferred back and forth in page units. Each page is generally 4K in size. The memory pages that are moved from memory to disk are called *page-outs,* the pages moved back from disk to memory are called *page-ins,* and the entire process is referred to as *paging.*

Page-ins are inevitable in many operating systems, especially if the system supports demand paging. In demand paging, an entire program need not be physically preloaded into memory to run. A call to a portion (page) of a program not present in physical memory causes that portion to be loaded into memory at run time from disk. This reference to a page not present in physical memory is called a page fault. Since demand paging is used by many operating systems to start processes, a page fault and subsequent page-in merely indicates that a new process is starting. It does not mean that there is a memory problem. However, a large

number of page-outs does indicate inadequate memory. Also, during genuine memory problems, there are excessive page-ins, page-outs, and page faults. In other words, you should evaluate page-ins and page faults in combination with page-outs to arrive at any conclusion regarding memory-related bottlenecks.

Another factor to consider regarding page faults is that a page fault may not necessarily involve physical disk I/O. Generally, the kernel maintains a list of pages that can be paged out, known as a *free list.* As in the Oracle SGA, an LRU algorithm determines when a page can be sent back to the free list. As pages remain inactive, they are moved toward the end of the LRU list and finally onto the free list. At times, however, after a page has been moved to the free list, it is requested for access by its owning process before it is actually paged out to disk. The subsequent page fault is known as a soft or minor page fault because it does not need a physical disk read to regenerate the page. The page is simply placed into the front of the LRU list from the free list. However, if the page has already been phased out to disk, a physical disk read is required; this is known as a hard or major page fault. During extreme memory shortages, the LRU algorithm is not very effective at pushing inactive pages onto the free list, since many more pages are active than can be held in physical memory. As such, pages that are less active than others have to be pushed to the free list (almost at random) and are immediately written to disk. Hence, any page fault will translate to a hard fault during extreme memory shortages.

Generally, when excessive paging occurs and performance seems to be dipping, some remedial action is called for. If the heavy paging continues unchecked and the memory demands of active processes continue to increase, the system begins *swapping*. Swapping occurs when an entire process is moved to disk to reclaim space in physical memory. A previous section elaborated on different levels of swapping, such as normal swapping—that is, swapping done during routine OS housekeeping tasks—and urgent or desperation swapping, which is used as a last resort by the OS to urgently provide memory to active processes. Similar to paging, swapping involves swap-outs, in which processes are written out to disk from memory, and swap-ins, in which processes are read in from disk. Again, with some operating systems, swap-ins are inevitable. However, they are usually minimal. It is indeed cause for alarm if the number of swap-ins and swap-outs appears to be high. Performance almost always suffers during such times. As a rule of thumb, minimal swap-ins and absolutely no swap-outs are signs of a healthy system with sufficient memory.

TECHNIQUES FOR MONITORING MEMORY LOADS How can you detect whether page-outs and swap-outs are high on your production boxes? This section mentions some handy UNIX commands that could be used to monitor paging and swapping. While looking at the command outputs, remember to keep an eye open for excessive occurrences of swap-outs, page-outs, swap-ins, page-ins, and page faults (in that order). You need to examine all five of these together to analyze and interpret performance surges. To get the true picture, you first have to look at swap-outs and page-outs and then swap-ins, page-ins, and page faults. If the former are high, there is a good chance that the latter will be high as well, indicating a genuine memory shortage.

UNIX commands such as *vmstat* and *sar* provide the primary information about paging and swapping. Other commands, such as *ps* and *top,* can provide additional insight by showing the memory usage patterns of different processes. Here's an example of the use of *vmstat*:

```
$ vmstat 5 5

procs     memory            page                       disk          faults       cpu
 r b w    swap   free   re  mf pi po fr de sr s0 s1 s1 s1   in    sy    cs us sy id
 0 0 0    1000   3284    0 244  6  2  2  0  0  0  0  0  0   28   624    92  5  8 87
 0 0 0 148632   1064    0   2  0  0  0  0  0  0  0  0  0    6    14    16  0  1 99
 0 0 0 148632   1072    0   0  0  1  1  0  0  0  0  0  0   16  1363    66 23 10 67
 0 0 0 148632   1076    0   0  0  0  0  0  0  0  0  0  0   19  4082    71 31 12 57
 0 0 0 148632   1076    0   0  0  0  0  0  0  0  0  0  0   18    91    47  1  1 97
```

This sample shows *vmstat* output polled five times in intervals of five seconds. It is usually a good idea to set the interval to at least five seconds, lest the results become skewed due to the running of the command itself. While using *vmstat,* always ignore the first row of values, since they are unreliable averages accumulated since the time the system was booted.

The *-S* switch can be used to display detailed swap information:

```
$ vmstat -S 5 5

procs     memory            page                       disk          faults       cpu
 r b w    swap   free   si  so pi po fr de sr s0 s1 s1 s1   in    sy    cs us sy id
 0 0 0    1004   3284    0   0  6  2  2  0  0  0  0  0  0   28   624    92  5  8 87
 0 0 0 148628   1132    0   0  0  1  1  0  0  2  1  0  1   30    14    20  0  2 98
 0 0 0 148628   1140    0   0  0  0  0  0  0  0  0  0  0   17    54    37  0  2 98
 0 0 0 148628   1140    0   0  0  0  0  0  0  0  0  0  0   19  2706    41 19  7 74
 0 0 0 148628   1140    0   0  0  0  0  0  0  0  0  0  0   12  2355    26  2  2 96
```

The sixth and seventh columns in this listing show "si" (swap-ins) and "so" (swap-outs), which are missing in the first listing. If swapping is occurring on your system, the values for "si" and "so" will be greater than zero. Run this command at random intervals (either manually or via *cron*) to determine whether excessive paging or swapping is occurring.

REDUCING MEMORY BOTTLENECKS Most of the tips mentioned previously for reducing system loads also help conserve memory. However, the most effective (not to mention realistic) solution in many cases is to buy more memory and reconfigure the memory settings, including the SGA size. That provides the maximum bang for the buck. If you have already deflated your hardware budget or have already reached the maximum physical memory that your OS can address, you should consider the tips mentioned earlier for using memory more prudently. A few additional tips specific to memory conservation and management follow.

Check frequently for memory leaks

Some programs, especially new versions of software, have bugs that induce memory leaks. These programs absorb memory at an exponential rate and keep growing. They do not release the memory they take up. This problem may be caused by reasons as simple as a programmer forgetting to follow up a *malloc()* call with a subsequent call to *free()* in a loop within a daemon.

Monitor memory usage by processes at frequent intervals, using *ps* or *top*. When you see a process that is unusually large, it might be an indication of a memory leak. Watch the process over the next 12 to 24 hours, and if it does not die normally or the size does not appear to diminish, you might need to kill it manually. Sometimes killing a process doesn't release the memory, and the system has to be rebooted (yikes!). Memory leaks used to be a major problem with the Multi-Threaded Server (MTS) configuration in certain versions of Oracle7. Before installing a newer version of Oracle, it's a good idea to search for bug reports referring to any memory leaks in the newer version in the Oracle Support *MetaLink* repository.

Set swap space between two and four times larger than physical memory

Swap space is used heavily during paging and swapping. During such times, it is essential that sufficient swap space be configured on disk. If the system cannot find sufficient swap space, it could go into panic mode and crash. At times, a system low on swap space will prevent any new logons, including root. This will prevent you from taking the logical step of logging on as root to kill the program stealing all your swap space.

At the risk of sounding old-fashioned, I want to emphasize that *in high-availability sites, it is of utmost importance that you have swap space that is between two and four times the size of your physical memory.* I have seen sites supporting systems with huge physical memories (2GB or more) allocate swap space of the same size as physical memory (sometimes even less). That is fine, as long as you don't need more. If you do need more in the future, it might be too late, because the space necessary to extend the swap area may no longer be available.

Configure swap space when space is abundant—when you are installing the OS and setting up your disks.

In the case of small and medium memory boxes (1GB or less), it's a smart move to allocate swap space equivalent to four times your RAM. For boxes with large amounts of RAM (2GB or more), allocate at least twice the amount of RAM.

In specific versions of Solaris, a feature called a "virtual swap file system" is available, which allows you to operate without allocating any swap space on physical disks. If your RAM is large enough, it allows applications to treat the RAM as a physical swap file on disk and permits them to run unfettered. Hence the term *virtual* swap file system. However, Oracle would have problems running on such systems (in which no swap space is allocated on disk). This is because Oracle uses large amounts of shared memory (due to the SGA being mapped to shared memory segments), and its virtual address space requirements (the memory required for mapping data, text, stack, and heap areas) are quite high, sometimes higher than the physical RAM available. In such cases, Oracle would not be able to operate purely on the virtual swap file system; it needs at least an equivalent amount on disk so that it can, if needed, use up all RAM without running out of (virtual) swap space.

Distribute swap area across your fastest disks

If you create your swap area as one large swap file on a single disk, you could potentially have a severe disk I/O problem on your hands. Optionally, you could create multiple swap files across multiple disks and controllers. In such a scenario, swap space is allocated serially across all available swap files to ensure that the load is balanced across all available partitions. However, if each partition was located on a single disk, a substantially large swap-out could cause major problems. Even in the absence of swap-outs, small writes to the swap area could potentially conflict with regular application data access on that disk. As it is, performance degrades considerably during heavy swapping. The last thing you want on your hands during such situations is a stinging I/O bottleneck, too.

Striping usually provides the best answer. Ensure that you stripe your swap area across multiple disks and controllers. If the host system's internal disks are the fastest, keep the swap files there. If not, place them on the external disk array. If possible, try to avoid placing swap areas on RAID 5, RAID S, or RAID 7 partitions, so that the write penalty can be avoided. Ideally, you should place them on just RAID 0 (striped) volumes, so that the dual-write penalty of RAID 1 can be avoided as well. However, if the RAID 1 is controller based rather than software based, it can be just as effective to place the swap area on RAID 0+1 (since the dual writes occur in parallel).

Another thing worth noting as you plan your swap-file placement is that on some UNIX flavors there is an upper limit of 2GB on each individual swap file. So you would need to ensure that as you stripe your swap files across multiple disks you do not accidentally create a swap-file partition greater than 2GB. Unfortunately, in some OS versions, you won't even get an error message alerting you—the excess space would just get wasted.

Know whether your OS can address more than 2GB of RAM

Sometimes, the best method of resolving memory problems appears to be investing in more memory. However, merely buying more without proper evaluation of the need and capacity may result in total wastage. For example, at one customer site, we made a significant investment in 10GB of RAM in an all-out effort toward increasing performance. We were using a Sun Enterprise 4000 attached to an EMC disk array running Sun Solaris 2.5. Everyone was highly enthusiastic that this was going to end our performance problems. The DBA team (including yours truly) went ahead and made plans about how effective the new, bigger SGA was going to be and how each individual component was going to be sized. To make a long story short, we learned that Solaris 2.5 on the Enterprise 4000 cannot address more than 2GB of RAM. So much for adding 10GB! Furthermore, we learned that even the soon-to-be-released Solaris 2.6 would not handle 10GB of RAM. We would have to wait for the 64-bit Solaris 2.7 (or Solaris 7 as the version is now known) to be released.

Learn from our lesson: Know the memory capabilities of your operating system before you invest in memory beyond 2GB. And if you do manage to talk your management into parting with the money for such massive amounts of physical memory, ensure that you have the disk space to create a large enough swap space, too.

If possible, lock your shared-memory area in physical memory

Certain flavors of UNIX support locking of the shared-memory area in RAM. The main prerequisite is sufficient available RAM; otherwise, the whole purpose is lost. When your shared-memory area is locked, as multiple processes access the shared memory concurrently, interprocess communication overhead is substantially reduced. In other words, this will result in the entire Oracle SGA being locked into main memory, preventing it from getting paged or swapped out.

I/O Loads

While running Oracle-based applications (or any I/O-intensive application, for that matter), always follow the "spread 'em out" rule. Spread the data files and redo logs evenly across as many disks and controllers as possible. If you are using external disk arrays, ensure that all disks in the array have uniform sizes and access speeds. This will ensure optimal configuration flexibility. Improper configuration can literally kill performance. I/O bottlenecks are one of the first things to look for in a slow-performing Oracle server. Lack of memory is branded as a big performance choker, but I/O bottlenecks have equivalent power, if not more, to convert a reasonably well-tuned application into a slow-moving slug.

TECHNIQUES FOR MONITORING I/O LOADS The question is, how do you proactively monitor I/O loads to ensure that you do not run into bottlenecks? The trick is to have the right high-water mark indicating the danger level. This danger level should be iteratively determined by looking at current I/O loads during periods of low performance as well as high performance.

UNIX provides some excellent commands for checking I/O load. As was mentioned earlier in this chapter, you can also deploy GUI-based third-party software to do this. Whatever method you choose, ensure that you understand how to use these commands and tools optimally. UNIX commands to check I/O loads include *iostat* and *sar*.

The following listings show some sample output of the *iostat* command:

```
$ iostat 5 5
      tty          sd0           sd1           sd15          sd16          cpu
 tin tout Kps tps serv  Kps tps serv  Kps tps serv  Kps tps serv  us sy wt id
   1    1   3   0  104    1   0   18    2   0   40    2   0   68   5  8  1 86
   0   16   0   0    0    0   0    0    0   0    0    0   0    0   0  1  0 99
   0   16  14   2  111    0   0    0    2   0   12    2   0   10   8  3  0 89
   0   16   0   0    0    0   0    0    0   0    0    1   0   13   1  1  0 98
   0   16   0   0    0    0   0    0    0   0    0    0   0    0   0  1  0 99

$ iostat -x 5 2
                             extended disk statistics
disk      r/s  w/s   Kr/s   Kw/s wait actv  svc_t  %w  %b
sd0       0.2  0.2    1.1    1.9  0.0  0.0  104.4   0   1
sd1       0.0  0.1    0.7    0.5  0.0  0.0   17.8   0   0
sd15      0.1  0.2    1.0    1.4  0.0  0.0   39.5   0   0
sd16      0.1  0.1    1.0    0.5  0.0  0.0   67.5   0   0
sd17      0.1  0.2    2.0    0.8  0.0  0.0   15.2   0   0
sd18      0.0  0.0    0.0    0.0  0.0  0.0    0.0   0   0
sd19      0.0  0.1    0.2    0.3  0.0  0.0   13.9   0   0
sd2       0.1  0.1    1.0    0.5  0.0  0.0   99.7   0   0
sd3       0.0  0.0    0.0    0.0  0.0  0.0    0.0   0   0
sd30      0.1  0.1    1.9    1.2  0.0  0.0   73.2   0   0
sd31      0.0  0.0    0.0    0.0  0.0  0.0    0.0   0   0
sd32      0.0  0.0    0.3    0.0  0.0  0.0   62.2   0   0
sd33      0.0  0.0    0.0    0.0  0.0  0.0    0.0   0   0
sd34      0.0  0.0    0.0    0.0  0.0  0.0    0.0   0   0
```

```
                              extended disk statistics
disk       r/s  w/s   Kr/s   Kw/s wait actv  svc_t  %w  %b
sd0        0.0  0.0    0.0    0.0  0.0  0.0    0.0   0   0
sd1        0.0  0.0    0.0    0.0  0.0  0.0    0.0   0   0
sd15       0.0  0.0    0.0    0.0  0.0  0.0    0.0   0   0
sd16       0.0  0.0    0.0    0.0  0.0  0.0    0.0   0   0
sd17       0.0  0.0    0.0    0.0  0.0  0.0    0.0   0   0
sd18       0.0  0.0    0.0    0.0  0.0  0.0    0.0   0   0
sd19       0.0  0.0    0.0    0.0  0.0  0.0    0.0   0   0
sd2        0.0  0.0    0.0    0.0  0.0  0.0    0.0   0   0
sd3        0.0  0.0    0.0    0.0  0.0  0.0    0.0   0   0
sd30       0.0  0.0    0.0    0.0  0.0  0.0    0.0   0   0
sd31       0.0  0.0    0.0    0.0  0.0  0.0    0.0   0   0
sd32       0.0  0.0    0.0    0.0  0.0  0.0    0.0   0   0
sd33       0.0  0.0    0.0    0.0  0.0  0.0    0.0   0   0
sd34       0.0  0.0    0.0    0.0  0.0  0.0    0.0   0   0
```

The first listing displays *iostat* output polled in five intervals, every five seconds. The second listing shows extended disk statistics via usage of the *-x* switch, polled twice at an interval of five seconds. The *-x* switch displays information such as reads per second (r/s), writes per second (w/s), and percentage of time spent waiting (wait) due to I/O bottlenecks. When wait seems high and performance is bad, it is a good indication of disk hot spots that need to be resolved.

On systems in which *iostat* is not available (such as System V releases 3 and 4), *sar* can be used to obtain the same results. The following listing shows the output of the *sar* command, invoked with the *-d* (for disk information) switch:

```
$ sar -d 5 5

shark 4.0 3.0 3435    06/25/98

12:46:09              device  %busy   avque   r+w/s  blks/s  avwait  avserv
12:46:14 /dev/rdsk/c0t4d0s0       0     1.0       0       4     0.0    20.0
         /dev/rdsk/c0t6d0s0      10     1.0       9      68     0.3    11.4
         /dev/rdsk/c1t3d0s0       5     1.0       3      23     0.0    15.8
         /dev/rdsk/c11t1d0s0      1     1.3       1      10     2.0     6.0
         /dev/rdsk/c11t4d0s0      1     1.0       0       4     0.0    15.0
         /dev/rdsk/c21t3d0s0      1     1.0       1       8     0.0    10.0
12:46:19 /dev/rdsk/c0t4d0s0       1     2.0       1       5    13.3    13.3
         /dev/rdsk/c0t6d0s0       0     2.0       0       3    10.0    10.0
         /dev/rdsk/c1t3d0s0       1     1.0       0       3     0.0    20.0
         /dev/rdsk/c11t1d0s0      1     1.0       0       3     0.0    15.0
12:46:24 /dev/rdsk/c0t4d0s0       1     1.2       0       6     5.0    25.0
         /dev/rdsk/c1t3d0s0       4     1.1       3      21     0.8    14.6
         /dev/rdsk/c11t1d0s0      1     1.0       1      11     0.0     8.6
         /dev/rdsk/c11t4d0s0      1     1.0       0       3     0.0    20.0
         /dev/rdsk/c21t3d0s0      0     1.0       0       3     0.0     5.0
```

```
12:46:29 /dev/rdsk/c0t4d0s0       0      1.0       0        3     0.0    20.0
         /dev/rdsk/c0t6d0s0      16      1.0      14      116     0.1    11.3
         /dev/rdsk/c1t3d0s0       2      1.1       1        7     1.4    14.3
         /dev/rdsk/c11t1d0s0      1      1.0       0        3     0.0    15.0
         /dev/rdsk/c11t4d0s0      2      1.0       2       19     0.0    10.0
         /dev/rdsk/c21t3d0s0      0      1.0       0        3     0.0     5.0
12:46:34 /dev/rdsk/c0t4d0s0       0      1.0       0        2     0.0    10.0
         /dev/rdsk/c0t6d0s0      32      1.0      33      264     0.1     9.8
         /dev/rdsk/c1t3d0s0      11      1.0       9       50     0.2    12.4
         /dev/rdsk/c1t5d0s0       0      1.0       0        2     0.0    20.0
         /dev/rdsk/c11t1d0s0      2      1.0       2       16     0.0     9.0
         /dev/rdsk/c11t4d0s0      5      1.1       9       74     0.5     5.8
         /dev/rdsk/c21t3d0s0      1      1.0       1        8     0.0     8.0
Average  /dev/rdsk/c0t4d0s0       1    1.357       0        4     6.2    17.5
         /dev/rdsk/c0t6d0s0      12    1.021      11       91     0.2    10.4
         /dev/rdsk/c1t3d0s0       5    1.028       3       21     0.4    13.6
         /dev/rdsk/c1t5d0s0       0    1.000       0        0     0.0    20.0
         /dev/rdsk/c11t1d0s0      1    1.042       1        9     0.4     9.2
         /dev/rdsk/c11t4d0s0      2    1.049       2       20     0.4     7.3
         /dev/rdsk/c21t3d0s0      0    1.000       1        4     0.0     7.7
```

This listing shows *sar* output taken five times at five-second intervals. Critical columns include reads and writes per second (r+w/s) and %busy. If the %busy figure appears high and performance seems bad, it is again a good indication of disk hot spots.

REDUCING I/O BOTTLENECKS Methods such as disk striping or altogether moving "hot" files to less active disks are usually the only solutions that effectively eliminate disk bottlenecks. If the disks concerned are already striped, selecting a more granular stripe size and subsequently restriping the disks might help. It might also help to reanalyze the current striping configuration. If your system does not provide hardware-based striping, use LVMs (Logical Volume Managers) rather than manual Oracle striping. (Oracle striping is not even real striping per se. It involves pre-allocating potentially "hot" table and index extents onto different disks and controllers. It requires a lot of manual intervention, and in a volatile environment with high database growth, can be an administrative nightmare.)

Lots of disk-management software on the market, such as *Veritas Volume Manager,* performs excellent striping. Also, some flavors of UNIX bundle LVMs that can be used without additional cost to do the striping. Hardware striping is ideal. However, software-based striping (using LVMs) is better than no striping at all or mere Oracle striping. Striping methods were discussed in detail in Chapter 3.

In the case of I/O load balancing, pre-configuration planning is extremely important. You do get a second chance to rectify things, in case the first attempt at laying out data files is unsuccessful and hot spots begin to appear. However, the

second and every subsequent chance usually comes with a major price tag—downtime. There is nothing as effective as exhaustive analysis and planning and getting it right the first time.

Before using OS-related commands and tools, you might also take a look at *v$datafile* and *v$filestat* statistics within the database to determine which tablespaces and data files are "hot." This may help you narrow down your search to the external logical and physical disks and disk stripes that are causing the problem.

Additional tips for managing I/O loads and disk space are presented below.

Understand logical and physical drive mappings

When setting up the disks, you would have referred to them in physical notation, such as *c4t2d5s2,* indicating the controller, target, disk, and slice (partition) numbers, respectively. However, *iostat* refers to disks using its own notation—for example, *sdnn,* where *nn* stands for the disk number. In order to interpret this output and understand which disks are actually being referred to, it is necessary to understand the relationship between *sdnn* and the physical disk notation *c0t1d3s4.* Resolve this notation accurately with either the systems administrator or the disk vendor. Remember, trying to correct hot spots based on an incorrect interpretation of *iostat* might result in additional disk bottlenecks. Refer to Chapter 19 for a sample C shell script that accepts *sdnn* as input and produces the correct *CnTnDnSn* value.

Enable file system journaling on all production boxes

Many mainstream operating systems support journaling (in addition to RAID), which is very similar to the mechanism used in Oracle redo logs. Every write to the system is recorded in a journal file prior to being applied to the file system. During a file system crash, the journal is used to roll forward and roll backward, as necessary, all changes to that file system, to recover in a very short time (*fsck* times are highly reduced). Journals maintain relatively high integrity by preventing file system inconsistencies and minimizing corruption. Machine reboot times are also lowered because file system verification tests are faster due to the journals. (Fast reboots are very significant—ask any 24×7 site personnel.)

Journaling does not take up a lot of space. (Solaris 7 requires just 1MB of journal space for a 1GB file system, with an upper-limit of 64MB.) Usually, journal space is allocated from free blocks on a file system. It can be configured to use a different disk partition, if necessary.

Although journaling is configured to write only during periods of low activity, it does tend to have an adverse effect on performance due to the additional I/O involved. But with a reasonably good I/O configuration, the impact can be made minuscule. Overall, given the advantages journaling brings to mission-critical environments, it's worth the additional pain.

Check the availability of free disk space on a regular basis

In addition to checking for I/O bottlenecks, proactive monitoring for availability of free space is also mandatory. In a 24×7 environment, lack of free space is instant death. Adding more disks to an external disk array is usually a relatively easy task, especially with hot-pluggable configurations, in which new disks can be plugged in while the system is online. However, availability of the required disks might be a problem. I have been in situations in which we have had to wait for more than five weeks for the right 4.2GB 7200 rpm disks to become available and be shipped to us. Or the disks might be available but you might have reached the maximum capacity of either the disk cabinet or the external disk array. Such a situation usually requires a major hardware purchase.

Given such external environments in which we have limited control, the best we can do is to implement full-fledged proactive monitoring for free space. When required free space is in danger of being used up, or when maximum hardware capacity is about to be reached, give advance warning to your higher-ups to ensure timely availability of resources.

Keep your file systems and directories slim

Keeping your file systems and directories, including the root directory, slim helps prevent cluttering of the file system, thus helping administration. This also enhances performance, since the file system does not have to deal with the overhead of managing a large number of unwieldy partitions. Directory lookups are relatively slow, and their speed is in many ways directly proportional to directory size. Hence, keep your directories as small as possible. Directory sizes are usually based on 512 bytes in most UNIX systems. You can check the directory sizes via the *ls –l* command. When you start seeing multiples of 512 bytes (4096, 8192), it's time to start cleaning up.

Truncate all old log files. If left unattended, Oracle's trace and other logs, such as alert.log, listener.log, and so on, can grow very large, taking up a lot of file system space. For tips on managing Oracle log files, refer to Chapter 7. Chapter 19 contains a sample C shell script to trim all Oracle-related logs at periodic intervals. Similarly, purge all core dumps, temporary files, and error logs generated by your applications. Remove very old backups (export dumps), e-mails, and so forth from disk and, if necessary, archive them to tape.

Many times, even after a good cleanup, directory entries do not reduce in size. Dropping and re-creating the directory can rectify such a situation. However, if multiple subdirectories are involved, this can be quite cumbersome. Large directory entries are not problems in themselves. They are only reminders that we need to clean up, remove all unnecessary files, and keep directories compact.

Maintain a spare root file system

The root file system literally forms the roots of any system. As such, it is essential to take extra precautions to protect it from injury. A non-root file system crash may result in an application being unavailable, but other applications on the system can usually still function without interruption. If the root file system crashes, however, the entire system goes down. Although keeping a copy of the root file system takes up additional disk space, it is one of the best practices a 24×7 site can implement. Many sites remain content to mirror the entire root file system onto a different disk. Since such mirroring is usually real time, disasters such as block corruption in the root file system are propagated to the mirror immediately. However, if a static copy of the root file system is preserved online on another disk, it can be used for quick recovery to prevent such disasters from turning into a total calamity.

If available, turn on large file support

Any file greater than 2GB is referred to as a large file. Most 32-bit versions of UNIX can accommodate a maximum file size of only 2GB (unless they have specific additional support for large files, in which the file offset is stored as 64 bits [referred to as a "64on32" implementation], allowing file sizes greater than 2GB). The newer 64-bit operating systems do not have this restriction, since they provide native support for file sizes up to 1 terabyte. However, most of these 64-bit operating systems also have the capability to operate in 32-bit mode. Know whether your current OS has such support for large files, and if so, have strategies and scripts ready to tackle such situations.

In most 24×7 Oracle environments, it is usually essential to have some kind of export backup (rarely the entire database, usually just a few critical tables) complementing the hot backups. If the database or specific tables are very large, the export file could be bigger than 2GB. Even if the export files are compressed, they could still potentially be larger than 2GB, in which case OS support for large files would help tremendously. In the absence of large file support, turn to Chapter 19 for a script that can be used to slice such compressed files into smaller files, each less than 2GB.

Look at important OS logs at regular intervals

On high-availability systems, it is essential to ensure that the I/O subsystem and all disks are fully functional, without block corruption. Such hardware/OS–level corruption can very easily escalate and cause database corruption. All flavors of

UNIX support OS-level logging, where important events are written to key log files (such as */var/adm/messages* on Sun Solaris). These OS logs need to be checked without fail on a regular basis. If possible, systems administrators should have a dedicated process tailing the file (*tail –f /var/adm/messages*) on one of the windows on their console. This will help them be aware of all system-level problems well before they adversely affect system availability.

Invest in automated tools to monitor system bottlenecks

There is a plethora of third-party software tools out there that provide system-level monitoring. For example, the Patrol suite of tools from BMC Corporation is well suited for such tasks. Most disk array vendors, such as EMC, also sell their own versions of such tools. Most of these tools are quite expensive, but in many cases, it is money well spent. Especially if you are managing a highly available site with a large number of users, it is in your interest to invest in these tools. You cannot always depend on a home-grown shell or Perl script to provide industrial-strength systems monitoring.

Many of these third-party tools can be closely integrated with the specific hardware and OS flavor you are using. Most of them are GUI based and allow you to set up certain levels of resource usage, such as warning level, error level, and fatal level, for a wide variety of events and devices. When usage of a resource gets to a specific level, these tools can either change the color of certain widgets (for example, the disk widget can become red from green or yellow if the percentage used goes above 25) or e-mail or page you. These tools are "aware" of a wide variety of variable and fixed system factors, and they use that information for optimal monitoring. Rather than spending considerable time and energy reinventing the wheel, it would be a wise decision to buy one.

One important fact to note here is that usage periods for all monitoring tools need to be planned carefully because the tools have their own overhead. They need to be used in moderation at appropriate sampling intervals, with as little impact as possible on the actual production loads being monitored.

Summary

This chapter discussed at length various possible OS bottlenecks, ways to detect them, and means to prevent them. Bottlenecks occur due to unavailability of adequate system resources, primarily CPU, memory, and I/O capacity. Kernel customization for a large Oracle site was also discussed, and monitoring techniques necessary for a 24×7 site were explored.

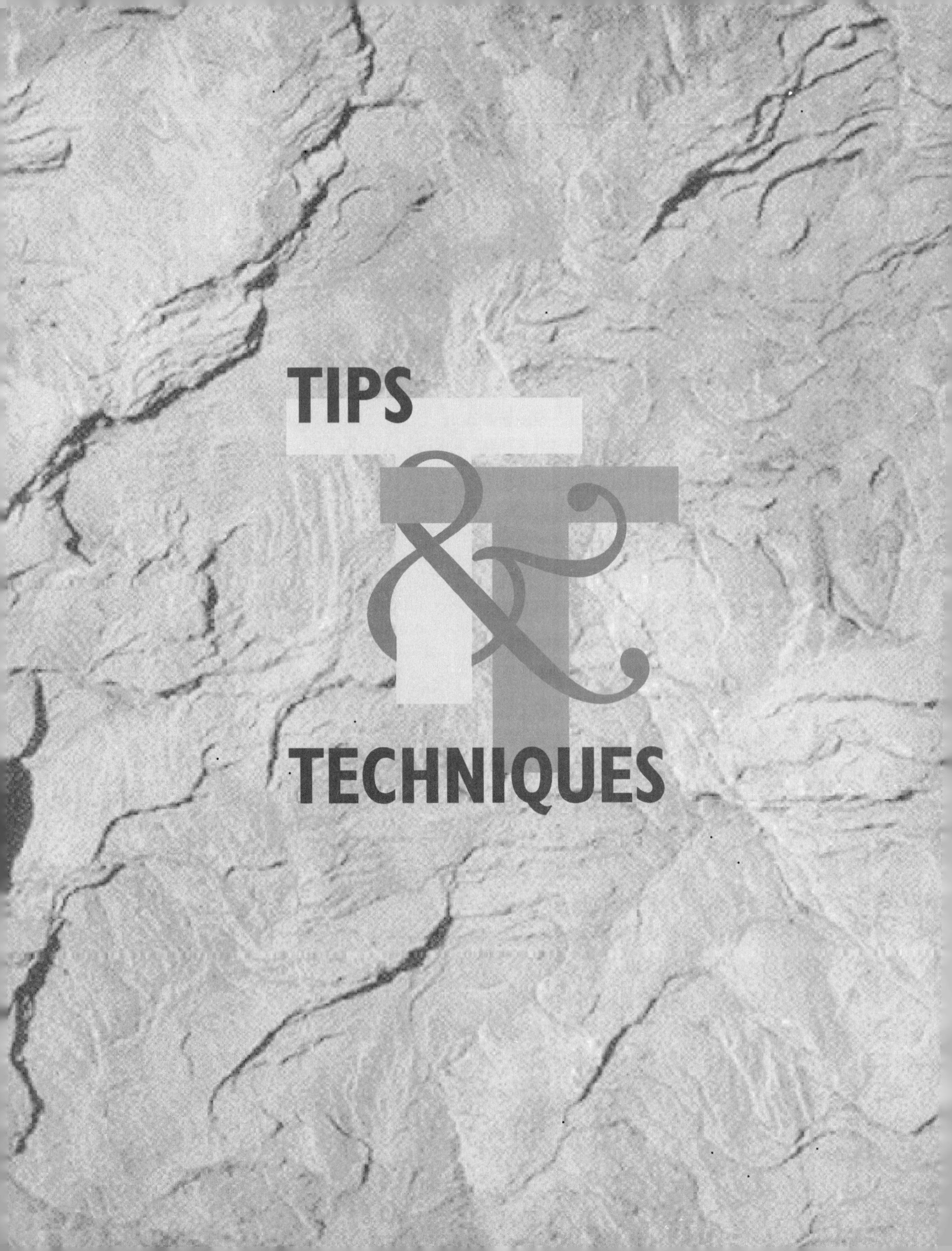
TIPS
&
TECHNIQUES

CHAPTER 5

Networks

Most companies I visit are still highly dependent on the client/server architecture. The advent of client/server introduced a new piece in the database puzzle: the network. Over the past few years, networks have become omnipresent. Instead of using a dumb terminal to work directly on the server, users have come to rely on the multi-functional client PC. Many site administrators spend countless hours configuring and tuning the back-end database server and the client applications but conveniently forgetting the network. However, the network can easily become at least as big a bottleneck in system performance.

Network performance is easy to overlook. There are usually few alarming indications of problems in a network. And since the database server and client applications usually have very high visibility, technical personnel spend most of their time dealing with these two components. Furthermore, problems with networks are usually more complicated than other types of problems, since a network deals with multiple systems, not just one.

Network problems are primarily of two types:

- Inability to transfer data accurately
- Inability to transfer data within an acceptable time frame

The first problem results in a lack of data integrity. It is generally a hardware issue, requiring replacement of a faulty network card, cable, connector, or router. Devices are available to isolate and detect the faulty equipment.

The second problem is usually either due to inadequate bandwidth or to improper configuration and tuning. Inadequate bandwidth or network capacity generally indicates a failure on the part of the network architect (if there is one) to sufficiently analyze and estimate a network's load. Improper network configuration and tuning usually results from insufficient or incorrect attempts by technical personnel to tune the network. This chapter focuses on preventing this second type of problem.

This chapter offers the following tips and techniques:

- Ensure that your network is not being overloaded
- Ping critical hosts at frequent intervals
- Invest in network cable analyzers
- Do not create Oracle data-files on NFS mounted partitions
- Do not use your database server as an NFS server
- Configure your network to use sub-netting effectively
- Increase the network QUEUESIZE
- Disable NAGLE algorithm
- Set the SQL*Net/Net8 packet-size optimally to match the protocol MTU
- Deploy homogenous servers throughout your enterprise

Managing Your Network

Network problems can seriously impair database availability and performance. The tips in this section describe optimal network management from an Oracle database perspective.

Ensure that your network is not being overloaded

Most flavors of UNIX support the *netstat* command to check the network load. This command displays important information such as the number of packets transmitted, collisions, input errors, and output errors. Here is a sample *netstat* output:

```
$ netstat
Active Internet connections
Proto Recv-Q Send-Q  Local Address        Foreign Address        (state)
tcp        0      0  tiger-2.netbios-     sys105.1424        ESTABLISHED
tcp        0      0  tiger-2.netbios-     tempsrvr.1043      ESTABLISHED
tcp        0      1  tiger-2.login        odin-2.1023        ESTABLISHED
tcp        0      0  tiger-2.4615         sys90.xserver0     ESTABLISHED
tcp        0      0  tiger-2.shell        *.*                     CLOSED
tcp        0      0  tiger-2.login        tiger-2.1002       ESTABLISHED
tcp        0      0  tiger-2.4376         204.209.64.244     ESTABLISHED
tcp        0      0  tiger-2.exec         *.*                     CLOSED
tcp        0      0  tiger-2.netbios-     sys214.2159          TIME_WAIT
```

The output displays the protocol used to transmit packets across the network—TCP (transmission control protocol) in this case. It shows the local address of the system sending the packets, as well as the foreign address of the system to which the packets are sent. It also displays the number of entries currently in the "send" and "receive" queues (packets being sent or received). Finally, it displays the status of each active network connection, such as already established (ESTABLISHED), closed (CLOSED), or currently waiting (TIME_WAIT).

One specific status to watch out for is FIN_WAIT_2. Having a lot of connections in this status can crash the kernel. When the target system (server) closes a TCP connection, it sends a packet with the FIN (finish or close of active connection indicator) to the source system (the client), which then responds with a packet containing the ACK (acknowledgment). The client, in return, sends a packet containing the FIN to the server, which then responds with an ACK, and the connection is effectively closed. The state that the connection is in during the period between when the server gets the ACK from the client and when the server gets the FIN from the client is known as FIN_WAIT_2. Sometimes the connection between the client and the server appears to remain in this state for a long time. More connections reach this state as they attempt to finish. No timeout parameter is

defined for this state in the TCP/IP specifications, although many flavors of UNIX define their own timeout values. A large number of connections remaining in FIN_WAIT_2 state usually happens due to a bug on the client system OS, and it can be rectified in most cases with a patch from the vendor. It is sometimes necessary to increase the default timeout defined by the OS. These timeouts are defined with a LAN (local area network) in mind, where the distance between a client and server is limited, leading to faster acknowledgments. However a WAN (wide area network) is composed of clients and servers that have a much greater distance between them, causing delays in the delivery of the acknowledgments. Assuming that there are no OS bugs, when the timeout is reached and no ACK has been received, another FIN packet is sent out. This keeps occurring until an ACK is received or the connection is severed. Increasing the timeout value in such a scenario tells the server to wait longer for the ACK, thus reducing network traffic.

Note that *netstat* displays a point-in-time snapshot of network activity. Thus, by the time you read the output, the entries in the queues may have reached their respective destinations and the status may have changed.

The *–i* switch of the *netstat* command produces another set of useful information. A sample output is provided here:

```
$ netstat -i
   input      (en1)        output                input    (Total)      output
packets    errs  packets    errs   colls    packets    errs  packets    errs   colls
28505446 446553 38249682 4969026      0   289934644 446553 421252192 4969026     0
       7      0        1       0      0          85      0        67       0     0
       4      0        0       0      0         157      0       146       0     0
       5      0        0       0      0         386      0       522       0     0
       4      0        0       0      0         192      0       228       0     0
       2      0        0       0      0         140      0       154       0     0
       6      0        5       0      0         218      0       304       0     0
       4      0        0       0      0          81      0        64       0     0
       3      0        0       0      0         568      0       615       0     0
```

Used with the *-i* switch, *netstat* gives information on the number of input errors, output errors, and collisions (colls). Input errors occur while receiving packets from the network. This usually results from faulty hardware. Output errors occur while sending packets to other systems. Such errors indicate problems in the local network interface. Collisions occur when multiple systems try to send packets at the same time. When a collision occurs, the system usually waits and retries. A high number of collisions usually means that the network is extremely busy and can indicate an overloaded network. Often the only solution is to reconfigure the network to reduce workloads. This means increasing the network bandwidth, cutting down on processes that use the network, or even implementing processes that make fewer network round-trips (via explicit cursors, stored procedures, and so on).

Analysis of input and output errors can reveal data corruption. When a system receives a bad packet via the network, it detects the error and asks the sender to transmit another packet. This is referred to as *packet dropping.* Data integrity is usually not compromised, since the packets are requested again. However, these errors can result in significant performance problems. For each network packet that becomes corrupted, a retransmission has to be requested, and a subsequent wait then ensues for the retransmitted packet to arrive. Also, retransmissions increase the number of packets traveling across the network, which in turn increases the probability of more collisions and subsequently even more errors. This vicious circle can quickly bring a network to its knees during peak hours.

In older operating systems, another performance killer is the fact that if a certain packet in a multi-packet batch transmission incurs errors, that packet and all subsequent packets in the batch need to be retransmitted, thus adding to network traffic. However, newer OS versions support a feature called selective acknowledgment, wherein only the erroneous packets need to be retransmitted. All of the valid packets before and after the erroneous packet are accepted without any need for retransmission. For example, if packets 3 and 8 in a 9-packet batch incur errors, only those packets (3 and 8) need to be retransmitted. In OSs not supporting selective acknowledgment, all packets between 3 and 9 (both inclusive) would have to be retransmitted.

Proactive use of the *netstat* command and other commands will help you determine and prevent network overloads based on early warning signs.

Ping critical hosts at frequent intervals

Since a network interconnects multiple systems, the well-being of the network depends on the well-being of all of the systems it connects. To ensure that all critical systems are up and running smoothly, it is a good idea to ping each one of them at frequent intervals. The *ping* utility is a simple network utility existing on most UNIX systems and Windows NT. It sends packets to a specified host and requests a response. Based on the response, it prints statistics regarding transmission times. Using *ping* regularly can alert you whenever a remote system is down. It can be run via *cron,* and the administrator can be e-mailed or paged whenever a critical remote system does not respond.

Pinging is also useful when a performance problem is reported. A ping will help determine whether the performance problem is due to the network. Additionally, when an application has been reported to have a problem, running the application locally will help isolate the problem, allowing you to determine whether the bottleneck is due to the network or the database (or even the application itself).

The following is an example of pinging a database server from a Windows 95 client:

```
C:\WINDOWS\DESKTOP> ping 248.12.24.82
Pinging 248.12.24.82 with 32 bytes of data:
```

```
Reply from 248.12.24.82: bytes=32  time=38ms  TTL=128
Reply from 248.12.24.82: bytes=32  time=<10ms  TTL=128
Reply from 248.12.24.82: bytes=32  time=<10ms  TTL=128
Reply from 248.12.24.82: bytes=32  time=<10ms  TTL=128
```

Invest in network cable analyzers

Obstructions on the network cable can cause choke-ups in the network. Because of the obstruction, the signal traveling via the cable is reflected, leading to packet corruption. Such obstructions are usually due to sudden bends in the cable or faulty cable material. The ideal way to track down and correct such problems is to use a network cable analyzer. The analyzer sends signals down the network and waits for them to echo back. The results can be used to determine where potential problems lie. Such analyzers help detect physical network problems as quickly as possible. Manual methods take a lot more time and are not very reliable. Network cable analyzer equipment is a must for all high-availability sites.

Do not create Oracle data-files on NFS mounted partitions

An NFS (Network File System) appears to be part of the local file system. However, it is actually a file system on a remote system, mounted over the network. NFS volumes are generally large in size. They tend to be very useful in a variety of situations in which volumes need to be shared among systems. It can be very tempting to create an Oracle data-file on an NFS, especially when there is a shortage of space on the local disk-array. Doing so, however, is highly dangerous. The well-being of an NFS depends on too many variables, such as smooth functioning of the remote host, well-configured networks, and trouble-free running of *nfsd* daemons on the local system. NFSs are well-known sources of various performance and reliability problems. Intensive, high-bandwidth operations, such as copying large files across to a remote system, frequently timeout when done via NFS. (To some extent, this is also a sign of improper NFS configuration.) However, NFS can be used for relatively non-critical purposes, such as to contain users' home directories, software staging areas, archived files, and so on. Any task requiring near-realtime responses should not be carried out via NFS.

Do not use your database server as an NFS server

This might appear obvious, yet the number of client sites that violate this unwritten rule constantly amazes me. Ideally, the database server should, as the name suggests, be dedicated to the database. Except for NFS, even running mid-tier or secondary Oracle-based applications such as Web Application Server or Oracle

Developer Server on the database server is tantamount to stealing valuable resources from the database. NFS, as I mentioned previously, is not very reliable and is prone to many performance problems. Making the database server marry NFS is bound to result in unpleasant results sooner or later. NFS is highly popular and makes certain operations very convenient. However, you should have a non-critical, non-database server act as the NFS server. Ideally, you should set up a dedicated NFS server.

Configure your network to use sub-networking effectively

If your site uses PCs or NCs (Network Computers) within Oracle's Network Computing Architecture framework, set up the NCs/PCs to be on the same sub-network as their application server. For example, when setting up the Oracle Developer Server (formerly Oracle Developer/2000 Server) as your mid-tier application server, configure your network so that you have all NC users of the Developer Server *and* the Developer Server itself on the same sub-network. If you have different instances of the Developer Server for different applications, and each application is used by different departments, set up the folks in each department and the Developer Server that they use in their own sub-network. Systems accessed by multiple users should be on the same sub-network as the users, themselves. Such sub-netting helps conserve memory and network bandwidth because movement of packets across different sub-networks is minimized.

In your environment a different configuration may be best. For instance, if there is more traffic between the application server and the database server than between the application server and the clients, the application server should be on the same sub-network as the database server. In certain cases, there may be a lot more network traffic between the application server and the database server than between a front-end client and the application server, due to very high SQL traffic (parses, executions, fetches, and so on). If there is high traffic across all three tiers, consider placing all three tiers on the same sub-network. Also, if the executables for front-end forms and reports are held on a file server, that file server should be on the same sub-network as the actual front-end machine. In addition, if the NFS traffic between certain systems is high, those systems should be placed on the same sub-network.

Customizing SQL*Net and Net8 for Your Network Configuration

SQL*Net/Net8 is Oracle's connectivity software. The following tips discuss tuning SQL*Net/Net8 from a physical network perspective.

Increase the network queue size

The performance of the SQL*Net (or Net8) listener is highly dependent on your system's network settings. For a high-volume OLTP system, it is very important to increase the listener queue size. Queue size is essentially the bandwidth available to the listener daemon to process requests coming in via a specific port. In other words, it determines the approximate number of concurrent connections that can occur over the network.

The listener queue size depends on the network queue size set via operating system utilities. (For example, on Sun Solaris, *ndd* is used to set network TCP/IP settings.) The network queue size is determined by the protocol adapter and is valid for the entire protocol stack (not just for SQL*Net or Net8). In TCP/IP, the protocol stack sets up a *pending connection queue,* which has an upper limit equal to the maximum number of connections specified in the queue size setting. When this limit is reached, subsequent connections are rejected from the current queue at the protocol level and are placed in the next queue. Such requests must wait for the current queue to be processed. If the listener cannot handle all incoming connections in a timely fashion, the connections may appear to hang. Increasing the queue size minimizes rejected client connections and problems with hung connections when a large number of clients try to connect at the same time (for example, over the Web).

By default, the queue size is set to 32 on most flavors of UNIX. This limits the queue size of the SQL*Net listener to a maximum of 32 concurrent requests. Starting with SQL*Net version 2.1, the default TCP/IP queue size can be increased for both the TCP/IP and DECNET protocols (the maximum size is 1024 for most OSs). In addition, the *listener.ora* file can be changed to make the listener use the new queue size (via the QUEUESIZE listener parameter).

For example, on Solaris the following command would be run as *root* in order to increase the TCP/IP queue size:

```
# ndd -set /dev/tcp tcp_conn_req_max 1024
```

However, when the system is rebooted, *tcp_conn_req_max* would revert to the original value of 32. To make the change permanent, include the same command in the necessary boot files (for example, */etc/rc2.d* on Solaris).

Once you've changed the OS setting, you need to configure the listener to use the new queue size. A sample listing of the *listener.ora* file follows:

```
LISTENER =
   (ADDRESS_LIST =
        (ADDRESS=
            (COMMUNITY= TCP.world)
            (HOST= tiger)
```

```
        (PROTOCOL= TCP)
        (Port= 1521)
        (QUEUESIZE= 1024)
      )
  )
STARTUP_WAIT_TIME_LISTENER = 0
CONNECT_TIMEOUT_LISTENER = 10
TRACE_LEVEL_LISTENER = ADMIN
SID_LIST_LISTENER =
  (SID_LIST =
    (SID_DESC =
      (SID_NAME = DEV1)
      (ORACLE_HOME = /opt/apps/oracle/product/8.0.4)
    )
  )
PASSWORDS_LISTENER = (2good2btrue)
```

Disable the NAGLE algorithm

The NAGLE algorithm is a timing option that determines when a packet should be transmitted. It is enabled by default and causes a delay of 200 milliseconds per packet on most UNIX systems, including all SQL*Net configurations. Disabling the NAGLE algorithm provides performance improvements of up to 200 milliseconds *per packet transfer*. If a substantial number of your database transactions occur over the network, this can result in a large savings, especially when you consider the fact that every transaction is broken up into multiple packets and every packet sent across the network has to receive an acknowledgment packet back (the original packet and the acknowledgment packet together are known as *packet pairs*). Most operating systems discourage the disabling of the NAGLE algorithm at the OS level to avoid affecting overall network throughput. Instead, they recommend disabling it at the application level. In Oracle, it can be disabled by setting *tcp.no_delay = true* in the *protocol.ora* file. (This file is used to store protocol-specific configuration parameters.) Since the *protocol.ora* file is optional in both SQL*Net and Net8, your site may not have it. You can, however, create this file and include in it just this one command.

Set the SQL*Net or Net8 packet size to match the protocol MTU

Let's first go over some network basics. In the Open Systems Interconnection (OSI) model, each network protocol is composed of multiple layers, such as the network layer, the transport layer, the data-link layer, the physical layer, and so on. Each layer is at a different level and uses services provided by the other layers. Figure 5-1 shows the different layers in a Fast Ethernet implementation. The upper layers, such as session and transport (TCP, UDP), are encapsulated from the underlying physical implementations such as Ethernet, Token Ring, X.25, and so on. This is depicted in Figure 5-2. This abstraction is independent of all physical network attributes such as maximum transmission unit (MTU), maximum transmission rate, address size, and so on.

For the purpose of our discussion, the MTU specifies the maximum datagram size that can travel on the physical network. The MTU size varies for different networks. For example, it is 1518 bytes (including header) for an Ethernet network, 4440 bytes for a 4 Mbps Token Ring network, and between 64 bytes and 4KB for an X.25 network. Usually in an internet (note the small "i") composed of diverse smaller networks, such as a WAN, the MTU should be the least common denominator of all networks through which the datagram passes (except in cases in which the MTU can be increased by negotiation), since the network layer (the IP layer) combines all of these physical networks into one logical IP network, devoid of physical differences.

One fact to keep in the back of your mind is that even though the MTU for a specific protocol is low, it may be increased via negotiation with your Public Data Network (PDN) (depending on your agreement with your PDN and the technology adopted by them). It can sometimes be highly beneficial to purchase the flexibility to increase the protocol MTU from your PDN, since doing so enhances the bandwidth between the routers. For example, if two Ethernet-based networks (with an MTU of 1518 bytes) are connected by an X.25 network (supporting MTU sizes of up to 4096 bytes but with a default MTU size of 256 bytes), a datagram would need to be broken into 6 packets to accommodate the transition from Ethernet to X.25. In such a case, investing in a larger X.25 MTU to match the Ethernet MTU would reduce network traffic and help performance. (Of course, you would need to evaluate response time and throughput requirements before taking this step.)

Additionally, due to the abstract nature of the upper protocol layers, each datagram is treated independently, and successive datagrams may be routed along different paths and reach their destinations at different times. This may cause delays because not all paths are optimal. It is generally a good idea to configure a specific more reliable, low-traffic path for mission-critical applications and set the bridge/router up to use that path. Such specialized networks reduce packet dropping and transmission errors and thus help performance greatly. To avoid a single point of failure, it is also advisable to set up a backup path. A backup path may be configured on the bridge/router as a protocol characteristic with a higher *cost of service*. Due to the higher cost of service, the backup path would be used only if the hard-wired primary path became unavailable.

Because each datagram is independent, it needs to store various parameters, such as source address, destination address, status (usually a CRC [Cyclic

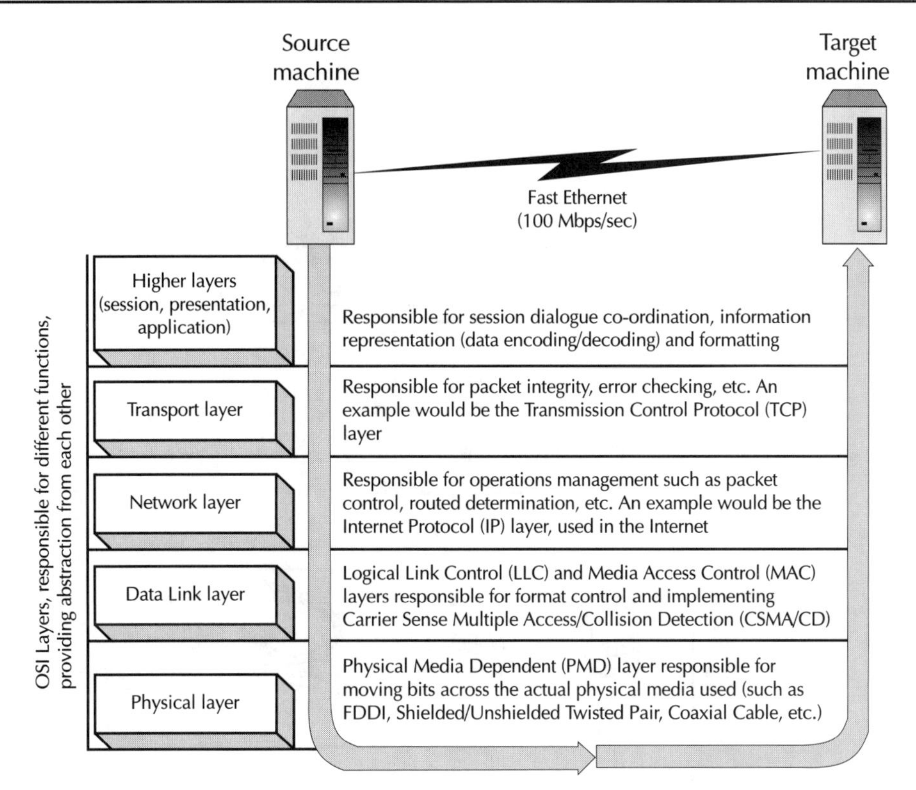
Source machine
Target machine
Fast Ethernet
(100 Mbps/sec)
OSI Layers, responsible for different functions, providing abstraction from each other
Higher layers (session, presentation, application)
Responsible for session dialogue co-ordination, information representation (data encoding/decoding) and formatting
Transport layer
Responsible for packet integrity, error checking, etc. An example would be the Transmission Control Protocol (TCP) layer
Network layer
Responsible for operations management such as packet control, routed determination, etc. An example would be the Internet Protocol (IP) layer, used in the Internet
Data Link layer
Logical Link Control (LLC) and Media Access Control (MAC) layers responsible for format control and implementing Carrier Sense Multiple Access/Collision Detection (CSMA/CD)
Physical layer
Physical Media Dependent (PMD) layer responsible for moving bits across the actual physical media used (such as FDDI, Shielded/Unshielded Twisted Pair, Coaxial Cable, etc.)

FIGURE 5-1. *Different layers in a Fast Ethernet (IEEE 802.3) implementation*

Redundancy Check] checksum), and so on (see Figure 5-3). Due to the fixed size of the MTU, a datagram that does not fit within the MTU size may be broken up into multiple packets prior to being sent across the network (see Figure 5-4). In such cases, additional parameters such as the start delimiter, end delimiter, and frame sequence must be stored in the header of each packet. All such information forms the overhead in each packet. Each fragmented datagram is reassembled by the destination host.

To size each Net8 packet optimally and reduce overall network traffic, you need to set the Net8 buffer sizes to be compatible with the network MTU size. Beginning with SQL*Net version 2.3, you can set the service layer (SDU or Session Data Unit) and transport layer (TDU or Transport Data Unit) buffer sizes. Both the SDU and the TDU revert to 2KB. If a different size has to be specified for your network, the values for both need to be set explicitly in the *listener.ora* and *tnsnames.ora* configuration files.

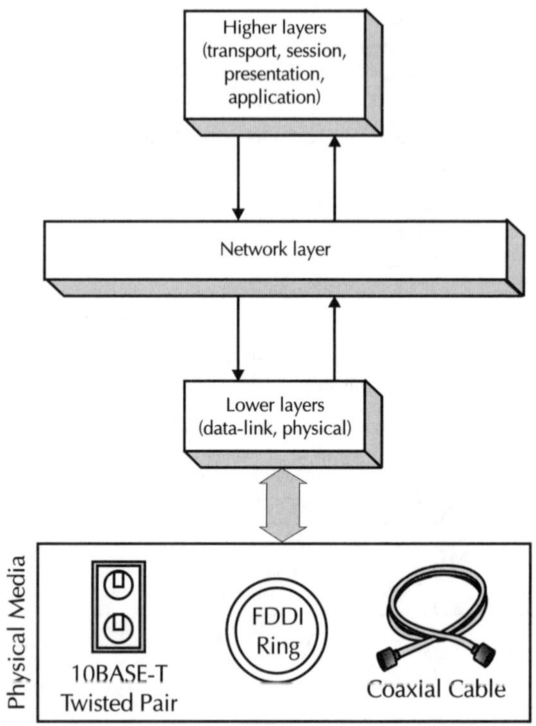

FIGURE 5-2. *Network abstraction (the network (IP) layer serves to abstract the upper layers from the physical implementation)*

The default 2KB size is generally optimal. However, if your network MTU allows a larger size, going up to 8KB for network-intensive applications may

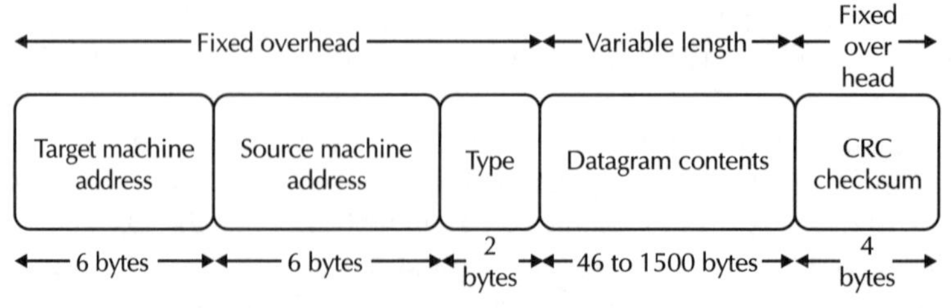

FIGURE 5-3. *Packet composition for Fast Ethernet in an Ethernet II frame*

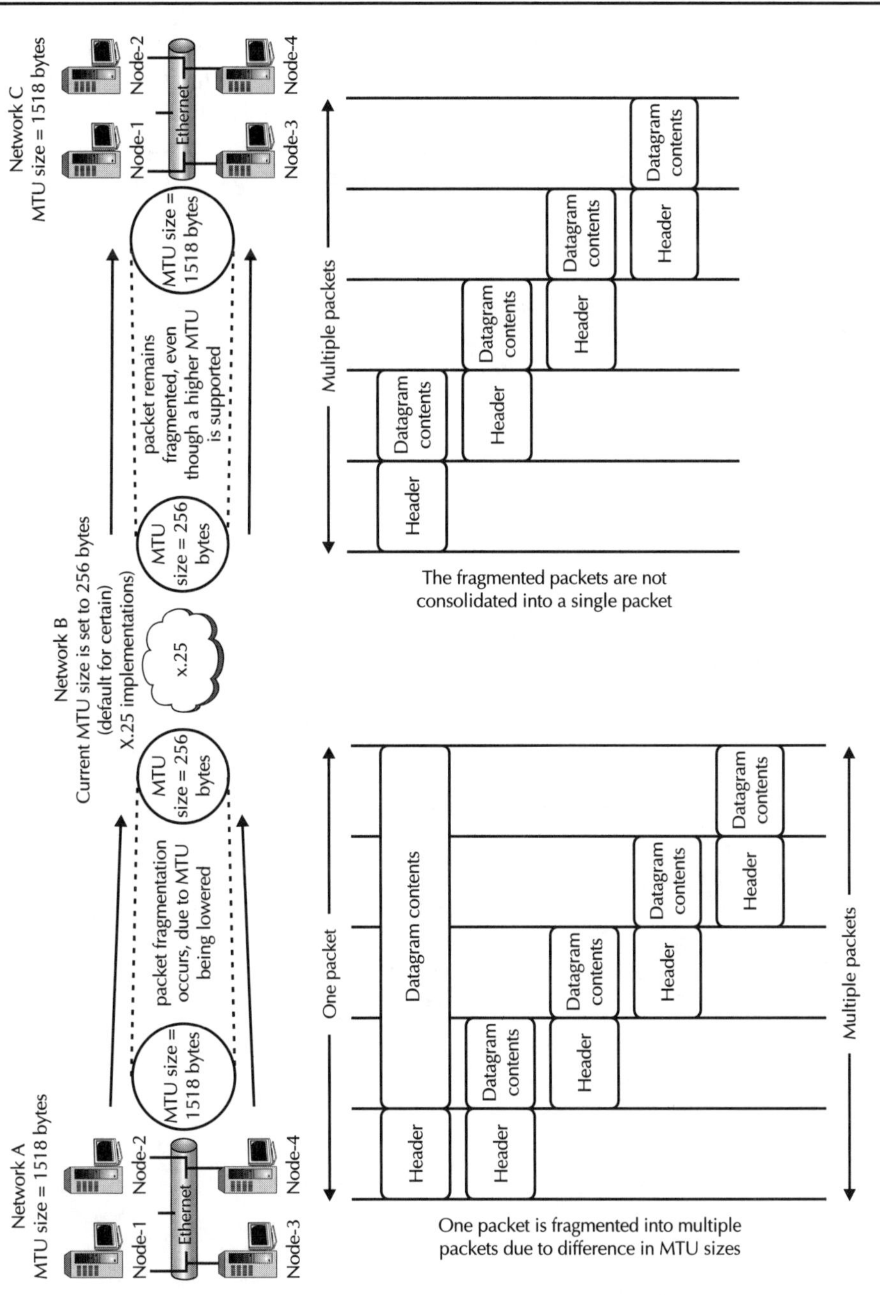

FIGURE 5-4. *Different machines on a network with different MTU sizes cause fragmentation*

improve performance by up to 5 percent. The larger SDU size allows SQL*Net or Net8 to pack data more effectively within each packet before sending it across the network. More data per packet translates to fewer packets per transaction and thus less network traffic. Sizes bigger than 8KB generally bring diminishing returns, because the overhead involved in bigger packets outweighs their potential benefits. Always evaluate the amount of data being transferred across the network prior to increasing the packet sizes.

NOTE
The 5 percent performance improvement was obtained by setting SDU and TDU to 8KB in combination with setting tcp.no_delay = true in the protocol.ora *file.*

The following is a sample listing of *listener.ora* with TDU and SDU settings of 8KB) :

```
LISTENER =
  (ADDRESS_LIST =
     (ADDRESS=
           (COMMUNITY= TCP.world)
           (HOST= tiger)
           (PROTOCOL= TCP)
           (Port= 1521)
           (QUEUESIZE= 1024)
      )
  )
STARTUP_WAIT_TIME_LISTENER = 0
CONNECT_TIMEOUT_LISTENER = 10
TRACE_LEVEL_LISTENER = ADMIN
SID_LIST_LISTENER =
  (SID_LIST =
    (SID_DESC =
      (SDU = 8192)
      (TDU = 8192)
      (SID_NAME = DEV1)
      (ORACLE_HOME = /opt/apps/oracle/product/8.0.4)
    )
  )
```

Here is a sample listing of *tnsnames.ora* with TDU and SDU settings of 8KB:

```
DEV1.world =
  (DESCRIPTION =
    (SDU = 8192)
    (TDU = 8192)
```

```
   (ADDRESS_LIST =
       (ADDRESS =
         (COMMUNITY = tcp.world)
         (PROTOCOL = TCP)
         (Host = tiger)
         (Port = 1521)
       )
    )
   (CONNECT_DATA = (SID = ORC8)
   )
)
```

If the MTU and SQL*Net or Net8 packet sizes are different, datagram fragmentation may result (see Figure 5-4). For example, if the SQL*Net or Net8 packet size is 8KB and the TCP/IP packet size is 2KB, the SQL*Net or Net8 packets would have to be broken down to match the underlying TCP/IP packet size. This would cause network throughput to be degraded, since more time and resources would be needed to fragment the packets prior to sending them and to defragment the packets after receiving them. Additionally, as was mentioned earlier, each packet has a header involving some fixed overhead. Thus, reducing the total number of packets reduces the total fixed overhead (since fewer packets means fewer bytes occupied by the headers).

Even with a small MTU size of 1518 bytes (1500 bytes for the datagram and an additional 18 bytes for the packet header) in an Ethernet implementation, a bigger SDU/TDU may prove beneficial in some cases. This is because a larger SDU/TDU size (such as 8KB) helps reduce interlayer communication, since communication between different protocol layers (such as the session, network, and transport layers) would then occur in bigger chunks.

If possible, use a protocol analyzer (a sniffer) to find out whether the Net8 packets are getting fragmented. If so, change the SDU/TDU size. Once it has been changed, check the fragmentation again. An iterative approach is generally necessary to hit upon the size that works best for you.

Finally, let me mention that the maximum benefit to your network will not be derived by tuning only datagram sizes. Rather, it will be achieved by addressing the root cause of heavy network traffic: the application. Any application that runs across the network needs to be designed to send only the barest minimum of data. The application designer needs to use a variety of techniques, such as setting the correct array sizes at runtime in all tools (Forms, SQL*Plus, and so on), stored procedures, and explicit cursors, to reduce network traffic. For example, rather than directly running a query on a large table and returning a half-million rows across a database link, one could call a stored procedure on the remote database to query the rows, process them, and return the required atomic value (perhaps a status code or the cumulative result).

Furthermore, all SQL (especially SQL code involving distributed transactions) needs to be tuned to the hilt. For example, a SQL statement joining multiple tables with too few qualifiers may result in large-scale Cartesian products, thus increasing the number of rows retrieved. When using an Oracle Transparent Gateway to a non-Oracle source, avoid Oracle-specific SQL extensions and qualifiers. If the non-Oracle source cannot interpret the qualifiers, it will return all rows across the network to Oracle. Once the data is available locally, the qualifiers will then be applied again. If only a few rows satisfy the conditions, returning all of the rows is a major waste of network resources. Net8 is only a messenger service. If the application asks for a million bytes, Net8 works with the underlying protocol to break the data up into SDU-size fragments and deliver them to the destination machine.

This brings up a variety of interesting scenarios:

- If the Net8 SDU/TDU size is 4096 bytes, the data to be transferred is 4097 bytes, and the MTU size for the Ethernet across which the datagram is expected to travel is 1518 bytes, the datagram would be broken into three packets. The first packet would be 1518 bytes (1500 bytes of data and 18 bytes of header), the second packet would also be 1518 bytes, and the third packet would be 1115 bytes (1097 bytes of data and 18 bytes of header). This shows that the application determines how much data will travel across the network and the MTU size determines the number and size of packets that actually travel. The DBA is responsible for setting the SDU and TDU sizes. However, the effectiveness of these parameters is limited. This is an important reason why the DBA needs to work hand-in-glove with the developers/designers and the systems administrators.

- Most tools allow an array-size to be set for the retrieval of rows from a table. For example, in SQL*Plus, running the command *SET ARRAYSIZE 1000* and querying a large table across the network would allow 1000 rows to be buffered and retrieved across the network. If the average row size is 150 bytes, a total of 150,000 bytes would be retrieved in each pass across the network (in other words, each datagram would comprise 1000 rows or 150,000 bytes). Given an MTU size of 1518 and an SDU/TDU size of 2KB, and assuming that there are no collisions or transmission errors, this would require a total of 100 packets per datagram. If the query returned a total of 1000 rows, it would take 1 datagram fragmented into 100 packets to retrieve all of the rows. If the array-size were set to 10, Net8 would generate 10 rows per pass (that is, each datagram would comprise 10 rows, or 1500 bytes). This means that it would require a total of 100 datagrams to retrieve all 1000 rows. Since each datagram already comprises 1,500 bytes, it need not be fragmented any further. Thus, even though the total number of packets that physically move across the network is the same (100 in each case), the overhead of datagram fragmentation at the source and re-assembly at the destination is avoided by setting the right array-size in the application tool.

- Let's look at another alternative. Suppose that the array-size is 1, the SDU/TDU size is 500 bytes, the size of each row is 450 bytes, and 3 rows are being retrieved by the query. This would cause 3 datagrams to be created, each 468 bytes (450 bytes for data and 18 bytes for the header) in size. There would be no datagram fragmentation, but 3 packets would need to travel across the network to satisfy the query. If the array-size is set to 3 instead of 1, there would still be 3 datagrams created, the first 2 consisting of 518 bytes (500 bytes allowed by the SDU/TDU size plus 18 bytes for the header) and the last comprising 368 bytes. Thus, three packets (each corresponding to one datagram) would also traverse the network in the latter scenario. If the default SDU/TDU size (2KB) was used, or if it was increased to 4KB or 8KB, only one datagram would be created, since the larger SDU/TDU buffer can accommodate all three rows and deliver them as one unit to the network protocol. This scenario shows the importance of setting the SDU and TDU to be higher than the protocol MTU size. In addition, it illustrates the importance of setting the correct array-size. Ideally, the following need to be taken into consideration when setting the array-size:

- Approximate number of rows returned
- Average row size
- Protocol MTU size
- Net8 SDU/TDU size

Deploy homogeneous servers throughout your enterprise

As was mentioned earlier, a network connects multiple systems. If those systems are from disparate vendors, supporting different OSs and protocols, an additional software layer is needed that translates all communication between the different machines, so that all can correspond via the common protocol. Such inter-protocol interchange can result in a significant performance overhead for both small and large transactions that flow across the network. Hence, deploying similar systems (at least using the same protocol, if not the same vendor, make and model, and OS) helps reduce such overhead.

Tips for Semi-Technical Managers and Supervisors

- Document all current system, network, hardware, and software configurations. Place such change-documentation on a separate system (not on the system being documented, since if it crashes the documentation becomes unavailable, defeating the entire purpose). Specifically, create the following two logs on a daily basis (or as needed):
  - A *change log* for logging all hardware/software/network changes
  - A *repair log* for logging all problems encountered and their resolutions
- Instruct all administrators responsible for managing the systems to keep a copy of such documentation at home. (You never know when they are going to get the next call about a system crash . . . .) This will make it convenient for them to perform recovery and reconstruction work from home if their physical presence on-site is not required.
- Encourage your DBAs to participate in the hardware evaluation process. Make sure that they have sufficient training so that they know what to look for and what to ask for (make this book *mandatory* reading for all of them . . . just kidding!).
- Avoid implementing general "rule-of-thumb" configurations. Rules of thumb are for generic systems, not ones that have to be groomed constantly to provide continuous 24x7 service.
- Make a habit of segregating work queues for different classes of users. You don't really want ten users to start different heavy-hitting jobs at exactly 4:00 in the evening. Create schedules for individual users or groups of users. Workload management worked very effectively in the past, when it was necessary to manage time-slots for monolithic mainframes. Similar principles work just as well today for achieving high availability and performance.
- Have SLAs (Service Level Agreements) with vendors to provide support during emergencies. Make sure that their service personnel are aware of changes in passwords and codes, not only for pertinent systems but also for the doors to your data-centers. This is necessary because remote support doesn't work all the time. When physical intervention is required (for example, when a disk-array has to be examined), the service personnel would need to rush to your site. During such times, you need to ensure that they have complete access to every necessary resource.

- Install heat-monitors and emergency air-conditioners in your data-centers. The heat-monitors provide advance warning when temperatures become dangerously high. If the systems start failing due to high heat-levels, you can use the emergency air-conditioners. I usually see these gadgets only in the data-centers of big organizations. However, if you have a mission-critical application requiring 24x7 uptime, you should invest in them, even if you are a small startup. They are not overly expensive, and they will spare you from having to hold a heavy fan for two hours while the systems administrators furiously try to rectify the problem (this literally happened at a client site).
- Don't allow operational resources (hardware/OS/network/database) to be changed on Friday afternoons (or on Thursday afternoons in those parts of the world where Friday is the weekend), unless it's an emergency. If something breaks over the weekend, your best staff members may not be around to fix them.
- Issue cell phones (not numeric pagers) to all technical staff responsible for managing mission-critical systems. When systems crash or networks go down, it's the technical personnel who get paged, and if a public phone is not available or they have no change to make a phone call, there is an inevitable delay in getting things back to normal. Make the investment to protect your investment—arm your best technical personnel adequately with reliable and high-quality modes of communication, such as cell phones, laptops, and frame-relay connections at home, if possible, so that they can be highly productive wherever they are—at work or at home.
- This may sound real basic. However, I do come across sites that violate it. Never allow food or drinks inside the server room. An accidental spill may cause damage to machinery (especially to exposed tape drives, console keyboards, and so on) and, in addition, may attract mice and other pests (and that's *real* havoc!).

Summary

This chapter has described ways to understand and interpret the idiosyncrasies of another critical database component: your network. It has looked at some network basics such as protocol layers, datagram formation, and packet fragmentation. Additionally, it has examined some network hardware issues and commands used to monitor and tune the network. Finally, we took a peek at the interplay between Net8/SQL*Plus and the physical aspects of the network. The next chapter discusses installing and configuring your database environment, based on the tips given here.

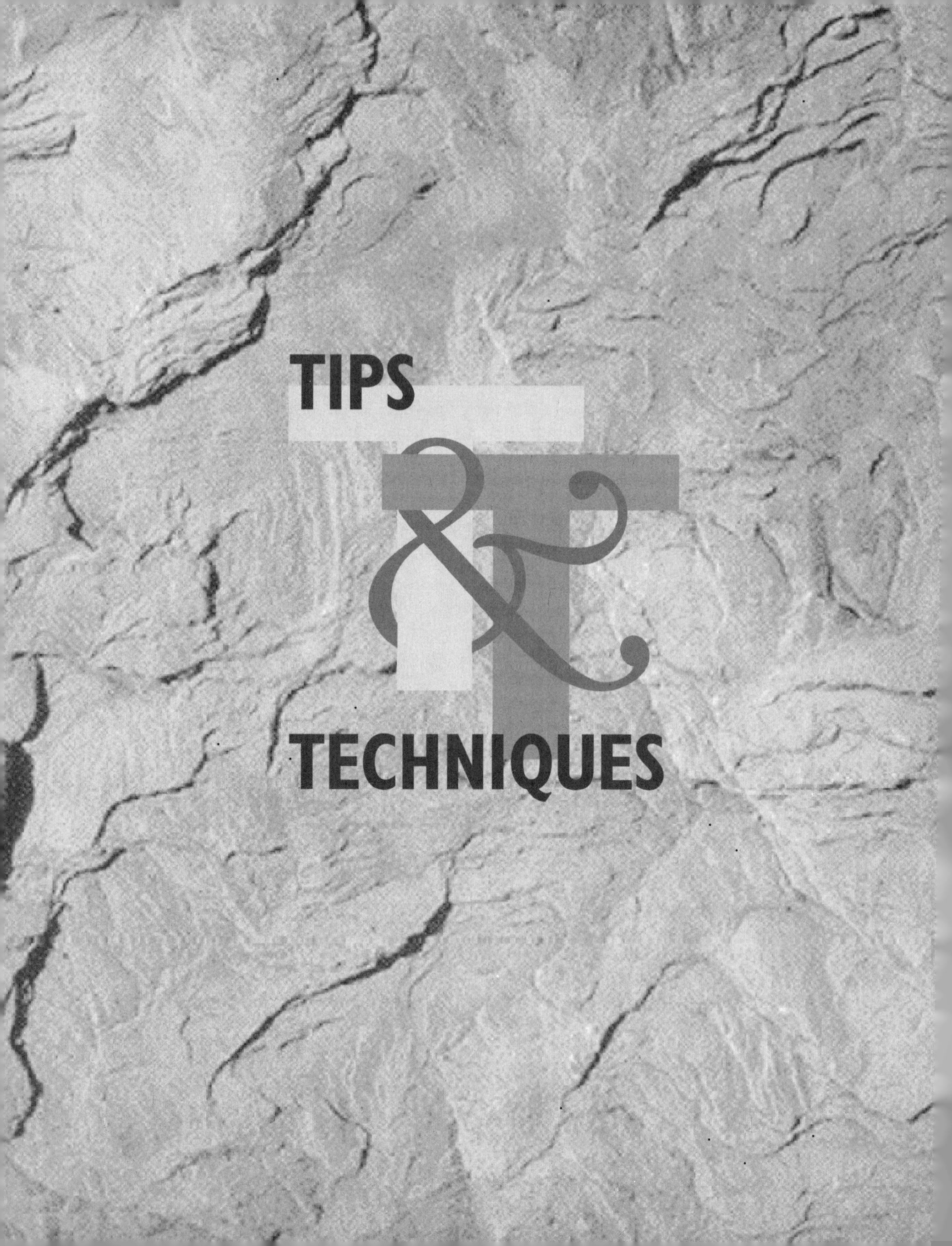
TIPS
&
TECHNIQUES

Applications and Data

In this chapter, we look at the last two components that compose your database environment—applications and data.

The following tips and techniques are discussed:

- Familiarize Yourself with Your Applications
- Categorize Your Applications
- Tune Your Code
- Make Application Code Independent of Future Schematic Changes
- Evaluate Using Transaction Splitting to Clone Data
- Evaluate Using Pro*C or OCI for All Mission-Critical Applications
- Implement Failover Capabilities Within All Mission-Critical Applications
- Be Familiar with Various Automatic Failover Options
- Have MAXEXTENTS Unlimited for all Volatile Application Segments
- Expedite Your Data Loads
- Version Control Your Application Source Code
- Manage Your Indexes Efficiently
- Use Threads, Rather Than Processes, in Your Applications
- Use Shared Libraries in Your Applications
- Invest Time in Physical Database Design
- Take Time to Understand the Schema Model
- Categorize Your Data

Applications

Applications often are an end user's only access to the database. Only through an application can the end user peek into the database. In other words, the application offers database visibility to the end user. If the applications are up and running, the database is available. If not, as far as the end user is concerned, the *database* is down and unavailable. Similarly, if the applications are poorly written or untuned and appear slow, then as far as the end user is concerned, the *database* is slow. Again, if the reports or ad hoc queries cannot run within the allotted time, then it is the same as the database being unavailable. No matter how hard your DBA works to keep the database fast, all his or her efforts are futile if the application is slow or prone to constant failure. I have observed countless situations at end-user sites where the database and the poor DBA take the blame for a slow-moving slug of an application.

Accordingly, it is highly necessary to architect applications appropriately right from the stage of inception. While designing and developing the application, the designers and developers have to keep availability and performance foremost in their minds. Just rolling out applications mindlessly with a single-dimensional objective of meeting the functional requirements is never the correct approach. Unfortunately, it is the most resorted-to option in real life. As long as an application rolls out on time and meets all functional requirements, end users, management, and the development team themselves are happy. That is a very short-sighted view, however, which more often than not leads to unhappiness very soon. It starts with the end user being unhappy, escalates to the management being unhappy, and goes up and then down the chain, until the database and the DBA are pointed to as the source of the unhappiness. After all, what could possibly be wrong with the application, right? It's a simple one that merely does some inserts and deletes, right? On the other hand, the application may be acknowledged to be highly complex—so complex that it is thought to be futile to try to mess with it. It may be thought of as a

black box, and tuning it may take months and may not provide the necessary gratification in terms of enhanced speed and/or availability. As for the database—tuning it may appear to be much faster and easier and provide more "bang for the buck." People live with all kinds of fallacies. The preceding statements may not necessarily be fallacies in all situations. More often than not, however, they are. It requires quite a bit of analysis to determine what is appropriate and what is not. The following tips do not help you perform such analysis, since each situation may be unique to your environment. However, they provide some insight to help you determine what are some of the primary things to look for while analyzing the application and what to do to enhance availability and performance.

Familiarize yourself with your applications

It's extremely crucial to thoroughly familiarize yourself with the applications that are using your database. This rule applies not only to the development DBAs, but also to the production DBAs. Merely administering the database without intimate knowledge of your applications is a recipe for quick failure. Your applications may have come into your company from varied sources—custom-made, off-the-shelf,or developed in-house or by a consulting company. However, it is essential to list them all down and learn the following about each and all of them:

- Their functionality (that is, what they do)
- Their nature (that is, whether they are OLTP or DSS, whether they are batch-oriented or interactive, and so on)
- When they run (that is, hours of operation) and what are their peak and non-peak hours; besides daily peak hours, are there any peak periods (such as end-of-quarter processing, end-of-year processing, and so on)
- Who they cater to (that is, who are the users—senior management, accountants, payroll personnel, direct customers, and so on)
- What tables they access within the database and whether they access more than one database (for instance, whether they partake in distributed transactions)
- Transactions per minute generated by the application during both peak and non-peak hours
- The components of the application (data-entry screens, reports, and so on) and which components are already known to be expensive in terms of resources consumed, time taken to complete, and so on (candidates for tuning)
- Whether there is any interplay across applications (for instance, whether certain tables are shared among multiple applications)

Each of these questions is extremely important to ask. They should be asked at an early stage—ideally, before the applications are deployed. Due to application complexity, you many not have all accurate answers at this stage. However, at least a basic idea will get you started. The important part here is, you need to get as many answers as you can, prior to deployment. The answers to these questions will help you decide how to deploy each application. Especially if your organization is big and has various applications, deployment needs to be studied in detail. Randomly choosing a system (the "least busy" one) and building a new database on the system or using an existing one to go with it does not constitute appropriate deployment. Due analysis needs to be done to determine which system/database the application has to be placed on, after understanding the nature of the application and the current traffic handled by the existing systems/databases. Each system/database's peak capacity has to be understood and reconciled with the current traffic. If current traffic is close to the peak capacity, then obviously new applications may not be deployed against such systems/databases. Doing so would only cause bad performance, not only to the new application being deployed, but also to the existing applications currently using the system/database. Similarly, if an application shares tables already used by other existing or new applications, all such applications may or may not be run on the same box, depending on the nature of the applications sharing the tables. For instance, a reporting database and an operational OLTP database may be sharing the same tables; however, due to their highly varied nature (primarily read-only versus read/write), they may not coexist peacefully on the same system/database. Conversely, even if two OLTP applications are sharing just a couple of master tables, it doesn't mean that they need to reside on the same system/database. Especially if both are high-volume applications, they may exceed the capacity of the given system/database. Accordingly, they may have to be placed on separate systems/databases, and separate copies of the shared tables may have to be independently maintained or stored in master/slave fashion, wherein one application may own them and the other application merely reads from them via a database link or via a snapshot. The tables may even have to be stored in a master/master fashion, where both applications may own the tables and the copies must be synchronized via replication. Again, if two applications share a lot of data, you may have to place both on the same system/database and ensure that the hardware and software architecture is robust enough to handle both without reaching peak capacity. Similarly, if two applications do not share anything at all but are tiny enough to be placed on the same system/database without overloading system resources, they may be placed together. Application deployment does not merely mean assigning a database to one or more applications and just tuning and tweaking the database. It requires a detailed understanding of the previously mentioned issues to make the right decisions. In a mission-critical environment, it may be prudent to avail yourself of the services of a skilled physical architect to perform an in-depth analysis, suggest available alternatives for application placement, and recommend the best ones, allowing you to choose the correct solution. Again, these steps have to be taken prior to deployment. I have been in countless situations where such analysis has not been performed, disparate applications have been haphazardly deployed on the same system/database, and bad performance is caused as a result. Re-deploying applications to correct the situation may not always be simple (especially where applications share data) and may involve high downtime. In fact, the older and more widely used the application, the higher the potential downtime. Frequently, it is irritating to see even the most basic physical architecture tenets violated. An example is using a single system/database to house OLTP transactions and also DSS-type applications, where untuned ad hoc queries may be run along with the tuned OLTP queries. It is enough for a single untuned statement to degrade the performance of the entire database. A full-table scan of a large table may potentially displace useful data in the buffer cache and replace it with data that would only be used once, thus causing the useful data to have to be read in again from disk, thereby hurting performance. These facts have to be kept in mind when assigning systems resources/databases to applications. Only then can you live up to the clauses in your service-level agreement.

It is necessary to know the scope of each application, such as which tables are used; how big each table is; where tables get their data from; and whether the data can be easily re-obtained in case the table is lost, and, correspondingly, whether backing up the table is necessary or not. This will help you determine the correct mode of recovery after a database crash, especially if a standby database is not available. If certain tables are not crucial or will not be required immediately, immediate attention can be paid to more important tables and the latter can be recovered first, so that mission-critical applications can be restarted as soon as possible.

It is important to know the hours of operation, so that you can easily schedule maintenance operations to occur during off-peak hours (hours of low use or nonuse). Also, it is very essential to know who the potential users of the application are. Knowing your end-user community is important because this determines the degree of visibility commanded by the applications. If they are used directly by customers (for instance, in a Web-based application) or senior management, obviously revenue is tied to their smooth functioning and they are very important in nature. Any disruption in their smooth running has to be paid immediate attention. Sometimes, your end users may consist of different levels of people, such as data-entry clerks and senior executives. In such cases, you need to know the composition of the end-user community. For instance, if your users are surgeons or nuclear physicists, they may have more urgent requirements. If an application is deployed on the Web, people from different walks of life may access it. In such situations, understanding the composition may not be viable or easily accomplished. In such situations, it may be necessary to consider all users equally important, and knowing the hours of use would be more useful and practical.

Tables 6-1 and 6-2 outline charts that help me in documenting each application. They are tools for putting application-related facts in perspective and act as a handy reference. The development DBA (if you have one) responsible for the application should aid in preparing these charts. Also, the chart needs to be updated as and when functionality/usage-patterns change, to keep it current and useful. The reason for Table 6-2 is that it provides details about all modules in an application. When it comes to recovering certain tables that are lost, corrupt, and so on, it allows you to make a right decision regarding which table needs to be recovered first, based on the hours of use, recovery priority, and so on.

Application Name	**Fund Management**
Functionality	Repository of funds, allows fund tracking—funds bought and sold
Type	OLTP
Hours of daily use Daily peak hours	0700 to 1900 hrs 0800 to 1100 hrs and 1300 to 1600 hrs
Peak periods	Last two weeks of each quarter
Transactions per minute Avg. Daily peak hours End-of-quarter peak hours	 50 200 250
# of named users Average concurrent users Daily peak concurrent users End-of-quarter peak concurrent users	250 50 150 200
User composition	Fund accounting personnel (incl. managers)
Tables accessed	FD_ACCT_MST, FD_SHRHLDRS_MST, FD_FUNDS_MST, FD_FUND_TYPES, FD_SHRHLDRS_FUNDS
Other databases involved	N/A
Application composition	22 data-entry screens 60 reports 12 batch jobs
Shares data with	Accounts payable and accounts receivable
Recovery priority	Very high

TABLE 6-1. *Sample Application Summary Chart*

Application Name	**Fund Management**
Module name	Fund Master Maintenance
Functionality	To insert/update/delete FD_FUNDS_MST table
Module type	Data-entry screen
Hours of use Peak	0800 to 1700 hrs 0800 to 1200 hrs and 1400 to 1700 hrs
Transactions per minute Avg. Peak	 2 5
# of users	22
User composition	Data-entry operators
Tables accessed	FD_FUNDS_MST, FD_FUND_TYPES
Other databases involved	NA
Recovery priority	Low

TABLE 6-2. *Sample Application Detail (Modules) Chart*

Note that Table 6-1 highlights daily peak hours and peak periods. Furthermore, it distinguishes between named users, average number of concurrent users, concurrent users during daily peak hours, and concurrent users during peak periods. These are important pieces of information that allow you to specifically document usage patterns. Note that the details allow you to specifically tie peak usage periods with application functionality (example: order entry generally occurs before quarter end, whereas accounting occurs after).

Categorize your applications

As the last portion of the previous tip alludes, it is useful to categorize your applications. Seldom do all applications running in your organization have the same utility, and so applications should be assigned priority levels according to their utility. For instance, all "bread and butter" OLTP applications should have the highest priority. Such information proves priceless during database failures. In case a standby database is not maintained by your company or if it's unavailable due to corruption, time to recovery becomes very critical. It may not be possible to recover and make available all databases/applications. Accordingly, it may be necessary to use your discretion with regard to the documented priority levels, in deciding which applications to restore and make available first. If multiple applications share high priority, then you may need to look at "Hours of daily use" and "Daily peak hours" (Table 6-1) and focus on recovering those applications that are currently in peak hours or are about to reach peak hours.

Tune your code

In my experience, many performance problems are caused by bad SQL. Make it a point to integrate tuning into your application development life cycle. Tuning your code is necessary at least at two distinct stages: during and after a program unit is developed, and during the final integration, prior to deployment.

During and After a Program Unit Is Developed

During development, the developer writes the code in a manner he or she presumes is functionally correct. As long as the code looks and feels right, and as long as it retrieves/inserts/updates/deletes the correct number of rows, it is acceptable. Few developers make the extra effort to really perform any kind of performance check. And even fewer make the effort to analyze whether the code is prone to breakage and failure and whether any steps can be taken to prevent, detect, and repair problems in code. Repairing code breakdown at runtime requires a detailed understanding of the environment in which it will be run, so that anticipated and unanticipated runtime errors can be repaired ad hoc in a manner that prevents or minimizes downtime. If the development efforts are targeted toward a custom application for a specific environment, it is always easier to take into account possible areas of failure specific to that environment and try to deal with them. However, developing a generic application that would run at many sites, some of which may require 24×7 access, is always more difficult. Even then, the best efforts need to be taken to determine as many areas of failure as possible along with ways of circumnavigating them. Integrating such preventive actions into the code development process may increase the time taken to develop each module. While developing for a 24×7 shop, however, it is generally well worth the extra time in the medium-to-long run.

Tuning of individual program units can be accomplished by using Oracle utilities like EXPLAIN PLAN and SQL_TRACE/TKPROF. It is generally better to have a peer review of code where someone other than the original programmer (a colleague, for instance) is designated to be the reviewer. Too often when programmers are asked to review their own code they don't, as they are too busy or they "know" they write good code.

During the Final Integration, Prior to Deployment

Every single program-unit may be tuned and run reasonably fast. When all the modules are integrated, however, a few unpleasant surprises may be revealed in terms of shoddy performance of the application as a whole. This is frequently the result of enthusiastically deploying the application and then tuning the application only if the performance is unacceptable. Why fix something if it is not broken, huh? This maxim is the main reason given by such "optimistic" deployers. They feel rather than make the development and deployment process more complicated or time-consuming, it is easier to just deploy and run. Unfortunately, however, things seldom are that easy in a 24x7 shop. Tuning the application after deployment may, in turn, increase the complexity and downtime; and, at times, it may not even be possible (due to users actually using the application, the chunks of downtime required to tune and repair it may not be available). In other words, trying to fix the problem after the pain is felt may be too late. A proactive approach is almost mandatory to anticipate, understand, and resolve performance and availability issues. Accordingly, a pre-deployment integrated tuning approach is always recommended.

Test databases populated with real data are essential for successful integration testing. Again, the use of tuning utilities such as TKPROF is recommended with the initialization parameters SQL_TRACE and TIMED_STATISTICS set to true.

As may be apparent from the preceding discussion, tuning of all application code needs to happen in two phases (see Figure 6-1):

- As a single, stand-alone unit
- Along with other related units in a globally integrated fashion

Now, what are the steps mentioned previously to enhance availability and performance that need to be taken into account during the development stage? Several good books address specific performance-related areas and recommend proactive actions to take. The reference section mentions some of them. As far as availability is concerned, a detailed chart has to be made that takes into account all database and non-database (hardware, OS, TP monitor, and so on) failures specific to your environment and accommodate ways to counteract them. Chapter 2 provides a sample list of such potential failures. Also, the tips in this chapter provide ways to tackle failures via your application code.

Additionally, it is very important to ensure that tuning is conducted in an environment that closely mirrors your production environment. Development usually occurs in a separate development database, which might be on a different system than the production database. Also, the development database may be a lot smaller than the production database, which means that the number of rows held in each relevant table may be a fraction of what is held in tables in the production

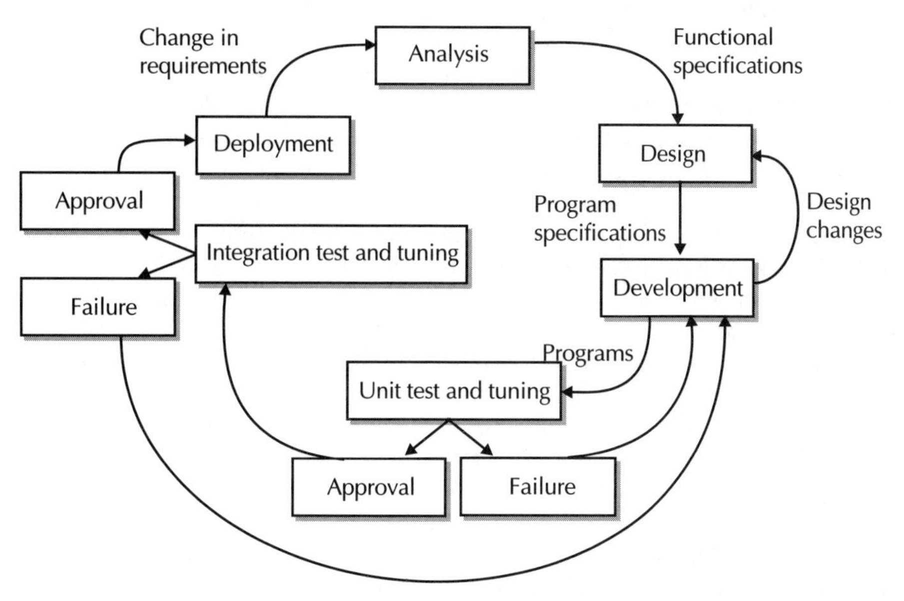

FIGURE 6-1. *The inception of tuning in the overall application development life cycle*

database. Due to the small number of rows involved, application code may appear to be blazingly fast in the development instance. Amazingly, many developers are puzzled that the same code runs slowly in the production instance (it's the same program after all, right?). As the database size scales, performance may potentially deteriorate, unless steps are taken to study the degree of deterioration and ways are implemented to avoid large-scale or noticeable performance degradation. A full-table scan on a table with a dozen rows would be a lot faster than a full-table scan on the same table with half a million rows, instead. Accordingly, the right index may have to be created and the table accessed via that index, rather than directly via a full-table scan.

Always maintain a test instance that closely mirrors production, ready for full-fledged tuning and testing. As soon as a module is developed, run it on the test instance to evaluate the results. Also, perform a benchmark on all modules in an integrated fashion to ensure that they provide acceptable response time and throughput. When performing such integration testing/tuning, run all modules in the correct sequence to simulate a full-fledged production run. Even though the development, test, and production instances may vary in terms of size, ensure that both development and test are structurally up-to-date and consistent with

production (in terms of tables, indexes, views, and so on). This is very important while checking the execution path of DML statements. As mentioned earlier, the execution path is checked via the EXPLAIN PLAN command or the SQL_TRACE/TKPROF utility with the EXPLAIN_PLAN option. If development and test/production instances are structurally different from production, then tuning exercises performed on development/test may have no bearing or relevance whatsoever to what is actually running on production. For instance, a large query running on production may take an execution path totally different from what was observed during tuning in the test instance or while developing in the development instance. It is necessary to set the exact same optimizer mode across all three environments. For instance, if the production instance is set to use cost-based optimization and development/test instances are set to use rule-based optimization, then the execution paths won't be consistent across all three environments. It is also advisable to name all schema objects the same across all three environments. This is highly essential if you are using hints in your tuned SQL statements. For instance, if you have an INDEX hint in a SELECT statement to use an index named NAMES_IDX in the development instance, the same columns need to be indexed in the test and production instances as well, and the name of that index in the test and production instances has to match the index name in the development instance. If the index name happens to be NAME_IDX in production, instead of NAMES_IDX, then the hint will be ignored by Oracle and the resultant execution path on production may be different from what is implied by putting in the hint.

Last, remember that tuning is iterative. Tuning may encompass multiple practice runs (test, tune, retest), until performance and availability expectations are met. Accordingly, always allocate sufficient time to tune and reconfigure your environment, prior to deployment.

Make application code independent of future schematic changes

Due to changes in application vision/scope and user requirements during the lifetime of an application, the tables used by it may require schematic enhancements such as removal of an existing column, addition of new columns, alteration of existing columns, and so on). After such changes have been made to a table, application code may have to be changed to accommodate the changes to the table(s). The amount of time required to roll out these schematic changes directly depends on the extent of application code to be changed. The bigger the impact of these changes on the application code, the more code needs to be rewritten, tested, tuned, and deployed. The actual schematic change may be accomplished very quickly via a few DDL statements to alter the table(s). However, each of these steps may significantly increase the time to implement the changes.

Accordingly, code needs to be written in such a fashion as to minimize the impact. What follows are some tips to achieve the same.

Use "Wrapper" Views in All Application SQL to Camouflage Changes to Underlying Tables

For instance, instead of directly referencing all tables (table names, column names, and so on) in application code, create a view on top of each table and reference the view in the application code. This will reduce direct reliance on the table structure. The following example illustrates how:

```
SQL> DESC names
  Name                                    Null?    Type
  ------------------------------          -------- ----
  ID                                      NOT NULL NUMBER(5)
  NAME                                    NOT NULL VARCHAR2(255)
  AGE                                              NUMBER(3)
  DATE_OF_BIRTH                                    DATE
  DATE_OF_JOINING                                  DATE
```

The application code may be using the following piece of code to retrieve rows from the NAMES table:

```
DECLARE
    CURSOR c_names(pID names.ID%TYPE) IS
     SELECT * FROM names WHERE id = pID;

    user_specified_id name.id%TYPE;
    nID names.id%TYPE;
    vName names.name%TYPE;
    nAge names.age%TYPE;
    dDate_of_Birth names.date_of_birth%TYPE;
    dDate_of_Joining names.date_of_joining%TYPE;
BEGIN
     -- other lines of code --
    OPEN c_name(user_specified_id);
    FETCH c_name INTO nID, vName, nAge, dDate_of_Birth, dDate_of_Joining;
    CLOSE c_name;
    -- other lines of code --
END;
/
```

When a new column is added to the table, the application code would fail (since "SELECT *" is used to populate a predefined number of variables). Alternatively, having a view on top of the NAMES table to keep the number of selected columns static would help.

```
SQL> CREATE OR REPLACE VIEW v_names AS
     SELECT id, name, age, date_of_birth, date_of_joining FROM names;
```

The application code would be written to use the view, rather than the table directly. The new code would be as follows:

```
DECLARE
     CURSOR c_names(pID names.ID%TYPE) IS
      SELECT * FROM v_names WHERE id = pID;

    user_specified_id name.id%TYPE;
    nID names.id%TYPE;
    vName names.name%TYPE;
    nAge names.age%TYPE;
    dDate_of_Birth names.date_of_birth%TYPE;
    dDate_of_Joining names.date_of_joining%TYPE;
BEGIN
     -- other lines of code --
    OPEN c_name(user_specified_id);
    FETCH c_name INTO nID, vName, nAge, dDate_of_Birth, dDate_of_Joining;
    CLOSE c_name;
    -- other lines of code --
END;
/
```

Thus, even though the structure of the base table has changed, the view definition has not, and so the application code can still be used without any changes whatsoever. The application would only be changed as appropriate, to use the new columns introduced in the table. Other portions of code, referencing the view, can remain untouched, thus resulting in faster deployment.

Note that when using this approach, you would need to tune the application code extensively to ensure that the view acting as a "middle layer" does not result in a sub-optimal execution path. Also, if you are introducing the views at a later stage (when the application is already running in production mode), you need to ensure that the execution plan does not deteriorate, causing you and your users very unpleasant surprises ("It was running fine before—until you came along and messed things up!"). Oracle's optimizers may come up with a different execution plan when views are involved than when the base tables are accessed directly. Accordingly, this approach requires detailed tuning until the desired execution plan is attained and you are sure that the plan has not changed (for the worse) in any way.

Use Relative Variable-Type Definitions, Rather Than Hard-Coding Their Data Types

Variables may be defined in two ways in PL/SQL—by relative referencing or by absolute referencing. By relative referencing, I refer to the feature in PL/SQL where a variable may be defined based on an existing table/column. For instance, the following definition uses relative referencing:

```
nID v_names.id%TYPE;
```

Whereas the following definition uses absolute referencing:

```
nID NUMBER(5);
```

When relative referencing is used, changes to code are not necessary if the column data type in the table changes. For instance, if NAMES.ID is changed from NUMBER(5) to NUMBER(10) or even VARCHAR2(10), no application-code changes would be necessary, since relative referencing changes the data type of the variable at runtime. Alternatively, absolute referencing helps performance a little bit by hard-coding data type and length (since a runtime lookup to determine the referenced table/column data type is avoided), but it increases application-code maintenance and time to deploy, in case the column data-type changes. The application code would manually need to be changed to accommodate the new data type/length, thus increasing the impact.

Use Record Variables in PL/SQL Code

PL/SQL record variables tremendously help in making application code independent of schematic changes. Record variables can be defined in two ways: by relative referencing (via the %ROWTYPE clause) or via the TYPE RECORD command. For instance, let's take the preceding example to illustrate the usefulness of record variables.

```
DECLARE
    CURSOR c_names(pID names.ID%TYPE) IS
     SELECT * FROM names WHERE id = pID;

    -- instead of distinct variables such as nID, nAge, etc.,
    -- use a record-variable
    r_names c_names%ROWTYPE;
BEGIN
    -- other lines of code --
    OPEN c_name(user_specified_id);

    -- fetch into the record-variable, instead of into distinct variables --
    FETCH c_name INTO r_name;
    CLOSE c_name;
    -- now r_name can be used, wherever necessary --
    -- other lines of code --
END;
/
```

Thus, if the structure of the NAMES table changes (new columns are added, existing column data types/sizes are changed), no application code changes are required. Since "SELECT *" is being used to retrieve the rows into a record variable, both "SELECT *" and the record variable will accommodate the schematic changes without any further changes to application code.

Record variables prove useful, even if no wrapper views are being used in the application. However, wrapper views in conjunction with record variables provide even higher encapsulation of code and a greater degree of security from schematic changes. Using wrapper views in conjunction with record variables guarantees that the application code wouldn't be exposed to any new column. The extent of exposure would only be the columns defined by the view.

Use Table-Driven Application Logic

If a program undergoes or is expected to undergo constant changes, it may be necessary to table-drive the logic and use dynamic SQL to parse and execute the DML statements (if possible, parse once, execute multiple times by placing the parse statement prior to a loop and placing the execute statement within the loop). If the situation demands that program logic be changed frequently, high maintenance may be required to keep the program up-to-date, potentially causing downtime for the application users each time a new version of the program is rolled out. At one of my client sites, we have an application that tracks product dealers throughout the country. We identify each dealer via a distinct code (which is also the primary key in the DEALERS table). At times, certain dealers come up with promotional offers that affect a specific program's logic (business rules need to be changed for those dealers). Since such promotional offers are periodic, the change in logic remains in effect for a short while and then has to be removed or changed to something else. Initially, the client had written a lengthy program to process data for each dealer. As promotional offers came and went, the program would need to be updated constantly. Moreover, to make matters worse, as months passed, the program went from developer to developer and gradually the program turned into a mess of hard-coded, dealer-specific logic, which no developer wanted to handle anymore. Finally (based on an idea that the software development manager at the client site had), we placed all dealer-specific logic in a table. Each row would have the necessary "IF DEALER_CODE = 'AA01' THEN calc_revenue_from_promo_offer; END IF;" dealer-specific code. When the promotional offer expired, we just deleted the row off the table, so that it would not be processed anymore. The program was turned into a terse piece of code that merely read from the table and used dynamic SQL to parse and execute the logic. Thus, inserting and deleting rows in the table was the only maintenance that was required. Such maintenance was very fast, requiring no downtime at all. Using table-driven application logic deteriorates performance (up to five percent in my tests), but it significantly reduces maintenance overhead and downtime.

Please note that even after using some of the measures outlined previously, a detailed check of all applications is still recommended after any schematic changes to ensure that there is no other hitherto unforeseen impact.

Evaluate using transaction splitting to clone data

A copy of all critical data needs to be maintained either as standby tables within the same database or as separate standby databases. Standby tables are maintained by retaining a copy of certain core, mission-critical tables within the same database. During problems with the original tables such as block corruption, user errors/accidents, and so on (where only one or more specific tables are affected), the standby tables can be made primary and database activity can continue with very little interruption. With such standby options, an easy way to clone the data would be to split the transaction directly at the application level to write to multiple copies of each target table. For instance, if the NAMES table is being written to, two tables can be maintained with the same database NAMES_1 and NAMES_2, each a mirror of the other. Each application routine that writes to the NAMES table writes to both NAMES_1 and NAMES_2. One of the tables acts as the primary NAMES table and is referred to via a synonym or a view (CREATE VIEW names AS SELECT * FROM NAMES_1). Reads can then occur via the synonym/view, thus, in turn, selecting from the current primary table. When NAMES_1 becomes unavailable, then the synonym/view can be re-created to point to NAMES_2 and the application can still continue unabated. However, the application needs to be written in such a fashion that if one of the two tables is unavailable (due to the problems mentioned previously), then the transaction can still continue, as long as the primary table is accessible and has been written to. Thus, when NAMES_1 is unavailable, NAMES_2 becomes the primary table. The synonym/view is re-created to refer to NAMES_2, instead of NAMES_1. The application still tries to write to both NAMES_1 and NAMES_2. However, if the standby table (NAMES_1) is unavailable, then transactions can still continue as long as at least NAMES_2 has been written to. The transactions will fail if the primary table (NAMES_2) or both the primary and the standby become unavailable.

The same example can scale to allow a standby database that is separately maintained via custom methods (that is, not via the standby database functionality of Oracle 7.3 and above) and is open all the time, allowing reporting, ad hoc queries, and so on, to be run by end users. Thus, the applications can be written to split each transaction to write to both the primary and the standby database concurrently (via parallel threads of execution). Transaction splitting is highly effective in being prepared to face different types of failure and reacting to such failure in a fast and efficient manner.

While constructing a transaction-splitting strategy, consider post-failover scenarios as well. For instance, when the primary table becomes unavailable, you would have a short outage as the applications fail and you immediately switch over to the secondary table. Now the secondary would be functioning as the primary, while the original primary needs to be repaired and, subsequently, made the standby

table. You need to have an effective way in place to make the original primary table catch up with the current primary, so that it can function as a true standby (that is, not have it lag behind too much after the repair, because if there is another failure and the current primary becomes unavailable, you won't have a standby to switch over to, since both tables are out of action). You need to devise a robust strategy to repair/rebuild/restore the original primary table and get it back as an operational standby. Subsequent chapters on maintenance and troubleshooting discuss ways to evaluate problems and quickly repair them. Chapter 15 outlines a complete standby table and custom standby database strategy that provides insight on keeping the primary and secondary tables in sync with each other before and after failures.

Evaluate using pro*C or OCI for all mission-critical applications

Evaluate coding applications dealing extensively with the database (for instance, large batch jobs processing a large number of rows) in Pro*C or OCI, rather than PL/SQL. OCI especially has a more direct path to the kernel and is significantly faster than Pro*C (and, of course, PL/SQL). Additionally, it is a lot easier to code explicit failover to a standby instance/database in Pro*C and OCI than in PL/SQL since, in the latter case, the database connection is acquired external to the PL/SQL routine (for instance, via the shell script that invokes the PL/SQL block through SQL*Plus or via the Oracle Forms module that calls the PL/SQL stored procedure), making reconnections within the PL/SQL code block difficult to achieve. (Nevertheless, failover is essential to achieve within PL/SQL, given the language's sheer popularity. A subsequent paragraph elaborates on this point, and a shell script in Chapter 19 illustrates explicit failover with PL/SQL scripts.) In Pro*C and OCI, it is relatively straightforward to check for specific errors that indicate lost connections and to try to reconnect to the same instance or to a standby database/instance within the same program, without the end user realizing that there has been a failure and that failover has occurred (in most cases). Furthermore, in Oracle8/8*i*, OCI implements transparent application failover (TAF), which allows automatic failover to occur in the case of "failover-aware" applications. TAF is explained in detail in the Oracle8*i* documentation. Also, a subsequent tip expounds further on TAF. OCI is relatively more complex to learn, deploy, and maintain. However, its TAF capabilities often make the "pain" worthwhile.

Implement failover capabilities within all mission-critical applications

You may have applications written in various languages/tools such as Pro*C, OCI, PL/SQL, Java, Oracle Developer (Forms, Reports, and so on) or third-party front-ends/tools such as PowerBuilder, Visual Basic, PERL, and so on. Failover capabilities provided by each of these tools may vary. In some cases, there may not be any automatic failover capability built into the tool. Accordingly, you may have to resort to manual means to allow application failover to occur successfully and as transparently as possible. Following are some issues to deal with when writing code to achieve failover during system/database failures.

Designate a Standby/Parallel Database/Instance

Ensure that you designate a standby or parallel database/instance to switch over to. In the case of OPS, another instance should be readily available, whereas in the case of a regular Oracle standby database implementation, a standby database may not be immediately available (since the standby database has to be explicitly brought up and made available for the switchover to commence). Accordingly, in the latter case, the application may have to "spin" for a while and retry connecting to the designated standby database until the connection attempt is successful. Certain custom standby databases (using custom methods or Advanced Replication or third-party tools) allow the standby database to remain open and readily available. With such an option, the application does not have to spin and can immediately connect to the open standby and continue its work.

Immediate Versus Deferred Connection to the Standby

Evaluate whether you want to retry connecting to the same instance or to a standby/parallel instance, when failure occurs. Sometimes, certain intermittent errors (within the application itself or at the middle layer, such as at the Web server or a TP Monitor or even at the database server) may force process disconnection. Immediately attempting to reconnect may resolve the issue and allow the application to go ahead and rerun the transaction. At times, however, there may be a critical error and retrying would only cause another failure, forcing you to connect instead to the standby. You need to decide which approach is appropriate for your environment. For instance, if you have a regular standby database implementation, then the standby database would not be available for switchover immediately. Accordingly, rather than merely spinning and waiting for it to come up, it's more prudent to retry connecting to the original instance (where the failure occurred) for a pre-determined number of times (say, three retry attempts), before deciding that the original instance is truly unavailable and then trying to switch over to the standby. On the other hand, if you use OPS, then another instance may be readily available; and, rather than wasting time with the original instance, it may be more beneficial to immediately reconnect to another active instance.

Client Process Termination

In certain cases, the instance and the database may be just fine. However, the application process on the client may have been disrupted (say, killed accidentally or "hung"). Automatic failover is generally not possible during such times (since the application that usually is responsible for initiating the connection has itself died) and manual reconnection needs to be explicitly done by the end user or the application wrapper (the parent process) that invoked the original application (the one that died). Adequate training needs to be provided to end users to recognize symptoms of such failure and take steps to reconnect. Similarly, failover capabilities need to be built into the application wrapper itself to check for abrupt failures of all child processes it invokes and take steps to reconnect.

Middle-Tier Failure

Similarly, in a three-tier application, a middle tier is involved between the client (that runs the application) and the database server. For instance, Web application servers (such as Oracle Application Server or the Apache Web server) or Transaction Processing (TP) Monitors (such as *BEA Systems' Tuxedo*) form the middle tier. Generally, all applications are routed to the middle tier, which, based on built-in load balancing and availability algorithms, routes the application processes to the appropriate database server(s). Typically, TP Monitors and Web application servers have built-in failure-detection mechanisms and rerouting capabilities when failures on the back end are detected. However, when the middle tier itself fails, your applications may not be able to access the database anymore (since they are built to use a middle tier). There are two options to overcome such middle-tier failures:

- Use multiple middle tiers to prevent any single point of failure and allow applications to be routed via a different one than the one that failed.

and/or

- Build more intelligence into the applications to connect directly to the database when the middle tier returns a failure.

Implementing one or both of the preceding options is necessary when using a middle tier. Also, most TP Monitors have special built-in mechanisms for load sharing and addressing single points of failure. Accordingly, you need to utilize those features and configure them such that failed TP Monitors are ejected automatically from the current configuration and the applications continue with the remaining ones.

Session-State Information

When an application fails (for any reason—database failure or client process failure or middle-tier failure), its session state is lost. Session state is the environment established by the application within the database immediately after connecting the first time. This session state allows the application to configure an environment conducive to running. Such a session state is generally created by running one or more ALTER SESSION commands. For instance, an application may connect and change the default date format to something it prefers by issuing the following ALTER SESSION command:

```
ALTER SESSION SET NLS_DATE_FORMAT = 'MM/DD/YYYY HH24:MI:SS';
```

Note that session state does not have to be explicitly set or changed by an application. An example of session state where the application does not have to issue any explicit command is the package state. When an application uses a package, it initializes the package and its contents (the cursors, global/static/private variable values, and so on). When there is a failure and, subsequently, switchover occurs, the session state must be re-created if the application needs to start exactly from where it left off the previous time (just prior to the failure). It is not always possible to do that (unless you are using an OCI program that uses Oracle8/8*i*-transparent application failover capabilities). Certain commands (such as the ALTER SESSION commands) can be rerun after connecting to the standby instance/database. However, package states, variable states, and so on, cannot be automatically reestablished. The only way to do that generally is to repeat the call to the package or rerun the specific transaction from the start.

Data Integrity Violation

Even though the session state information may have been lost, the transaction may have already completed part of its work. For instance, it may have inserted a bunch of new rows, issued a COMMIT, and then inserted a few more rows just before the failure. In this case, the rows inserted the second time would be lost, since a COMMIT was not issued. They would be automatically rolled back due to the failure. This is acceptable in most cases, especially when the transaction will be restarted and, hopefully, constraints will be in place to prevent the rows already inserted and committed from being reinserted and the application can start with inserting the second batch of rows. At times, however, constraints may not be present in the database (example: a DSS-type environment) and duplicate rows could get in. Alternatively, even with certain constraints (say, the primary-key constraint) enabled, the same rows could still be assigned a new primary-key value (say, from a sequence) and reinserted without violating any of the constraints. Again, if adequate referential integrity is not defined, then the application may delete the parent rows and, before it can delete the corresponding children (in

another table), the application may fail. After switchover, it may check for the existence of the parent rows. When they are not found, it may assume that both the parents and the children for that specific criterion have been deleted and continue with the next criterion.

What I'm trying to convey here via these examples (if you haven't guessed already) is that data integrity is a basic component for consideration during application failover. You need to design and code your applications and database such that such basic violations do not occur. For instance, when performing a DELETE in an environment where referential integrity is not explicitly defined (within the database), the application needs to ensure that no orphans are inadvertently left due to an abrupt failure. It needs to apply the delete criteria to both the parent and child tables and verify existence of any rows matching the criteria in all tables concerned. Similarly, all mission-critical applications would need to check for the existence of a logical key value prior to inserting one. Rather than using just a physical key value (such as a plain number from a sequence), they need to know and use logical keys. An example of a logical key in an EMPLOYEE table would be the EMPLOYEE_NAME, DEPARTMENT_NUMBER, and ADDRESS_LINE_1, whereas the physical key would be the EMPLOYEE_ID. Note that these additional checks may involve higher overhead and affect performance adversely. Once they are tuned effectively, however, the overhead ought to be minimal. In any case, given the choice between guaranteed data integrity and higher performance, any rational analyst/designer of a mission-critical application (actually, any application) should and would adopt the former course.

With these issues in mind, ensure that you check for specific disconnection errors and take steps to reconnect to a designated standby or parallel instance/database. The following sample pseudo-code (independent of any specific language/tool) illustrates switchover when the primary instance/database has failed. Drawing on this illustration, you can construct your own strategies for checking disconnection errors from all two or three tiers (as the case may be) and conduct switchover accordingly. The pseudo-code checks for specific error codes indicating both connection failures and abrupt disconnection from the current instance. If these errors do occur, the pseudo-code illustrates switchover to the designated standby or parallel database/instance. The database error codes it explicitly checks for are listed here (you may add additional error codes based on your specific environment and the Oracle version you are using).

Errors encountered during attempts to connect (unsuccessful connections):

- ORA-1033: ORACLE initialization or shutdown in progress
- ORA-1034: ORACLE not available
- ORA-1089: immediate shutdown in progress—no operations are permitted
- ORA-9352: Windows 32-bit Two-Task driver unable to spawn new ORACLE task (Windows NT only)

Session-disconnection errors encountered as transactions are run (abrupt disconnections):

- ORA-1092: ORACLE instance terminated. Disconnection forced
- ORA-3113: end of file on communication channel (note that this error can also occur immediately after a connection attempt. However, that does not indicate that the connection attempt failed. Rather, it indicates that the previous connection was abruptly terminated, typically due to the database crashing/going down (while the session was still connected). The current attempt to connect may very well have succeeded.)
- ORA-3114: not connected to ORACLE

The preceding error codes are the most common ones an application will encounter during connection failures or as the current session is disconnected during failure of the primary database/instance. The following pseudo-code performs checks for failures at various places (after connection attempt, after every transaction is run, and so on). Since very frequent failure checks may affect performance adversely, in your actual implementation, you will need to balance the failure checks within the code with your overall availability and performance requirements and place such checks only at certain critical junctures (as is appropriate for your environment).

```
DECLARE return_status NUMBER;
DECLARE loop_Ctr NUMBER;

BEGIN;
SET loop_Ctr TO 0;

WHILE loop_Ctr < 100000
LOOP
   SET return_status TO 0;
   SET loop_Ctr TO loop_Ctr + 1;

   CONNECT TO username/password@primary_db;
   SET return_status TO CONNECTION_RETURN_STATUS;

   COMMENT : In Pro*C, you would use SQLCA.SQLCODE,
   COMMENT : in lieu of CONNECTION_RETURN_STATUS

   IF return_status IS ANY("ORA-1033", "ORA-1034", "ORA-1089", "ORA-9352")
   THEN
      COMMENT : Connection attempt to primary_db failed!
      COMMENT : Being a 24x7 database, any of these errors
      COMMENT : can only mean that primary-db is currently down.
      COMMENT : Try connecting to standby (parallel) instance
```

```
      CONNECT TO username/password@standby_db;
      SET return_status TO CONNECTION_RETURN_STATUS;

     IF return_status IS ANY("ORA-1033", "ORA-1034", "ORA-1089", "ORA-9352")
      THEN
         COMMENT : Connection attempt to standby instance failed!
         COMMENT : Continue looping for 100,000 times and re-trying
         COMMENT : If connection still can't be made, then raise
         COMMENT : error-message and abort

         IF loop_Ctr < 100000 THEN
            COMMENT : go to beginning of loop
            LOOP TO BEGINNING;
         ELSE
            ERROR 'Error during connection. Cannot connect to database';
            ERROR 'Please contact 1800-888-8888 for Support Personnel';
            ABORT WITH RETURN-CODE 1 INDICATING FAILURE;
         END-IF;
      ELSE
         COMMENT : connection attempt to standby_db succeeded. Can exit.
         SET loop_Ctr TO 100000;
         EXIT FROM LOOP;
      END-IF;

   ELSE
      COMMENT : connection attempt to primary_db succeeded. Can exit.
      SET loop_Ctr TO 100000;
      EXIT FROM LOOP;
   END-IF;
END-LOOP;

COMMENT : Run database commands to set specific session-state
EXEC SET DATE_FORMAT = 'MM/DD/YYYY';

COMMENT : Start transactions
EXEC INSERT INTO orders_table;
SET return_status TO CONNECTION_RETURN_STATUS;

COMMENT : Check for abrupt disconnection during transaction
IF return_status IS ANY("ORA-1092", "ORA-3113", "ORA-3114")
THEN
  COMMENT : Current session disconnected. Re-connect to standby.
  SET loop_Ctr TO 0;

  WHILE loop_Ctr < 100000
  LOOP
    SET loop_Ctr TO loop_Ctr + 1;
```

```
    CONNECT TO username/password@standby_db;
    SET return_status TO CONNECTION_RETURN_STATUS;

    IF return_status IS ANY("ORA-1033", "ORA-1034", "ORA-1089", "ORA-9352")
    THEN
      COMMENT : Connection attempt to standby instance failed!
       COMMENT : Continue looping and re-try
       IF loop_Ctr < 100000 THEN
          COMMENT : go to beginning of (second) loop
          LOOP TO BEGINNING;
       ELSE
          ERROR 'Error during transaction. Cannot re-connect';
          ERROR 'Please contact 1800-888-8888 for Support Personnel';
       END-IF;
     ELSE
       COMMENT : connection attempt to standby_db succeeded. Can exit.
       COMMENT : Re-set session-state and re-run failed transaction(s)
       COMMENT : prior to exiting

       EXEC SET DATE_FORMAT = 'MM/DD/YYYY';
       EXEC INSERT INTO orders_table;
       SET return_status TO CONNECTION_RETURN_STATUS;

       IF return_status IS ANY("ORA-1092", "ORA-3113", "ORA-3114")
       THEN
          ERROR 'Error during re-running of transaction in standby';
          ERROR 'Please contact 1800-888-8888 for Support Personnel';
          ABORT WITH RETURN-CODE 1 INDICATING FAILURE;
       END IF;
       SET loop_Ctr TO 100000;
       EXIT FROM LOOP;
     END-IF;
   END-LOOP;
END-IF;

COMMENT : safe to continue with other transactions
COMMENT : either connection to primary or standby is intact
COMMENT : at this point

END;
/* EOF() */
```

In PL/SQL, direct reconnection cannot be obtained within a code block (as illustrated in the pseudo-code just shown). Accordingly, you would need to plug in the failover features within the external calling routines (that call the code block). Sample code for achieving this is provided in Chapter 19, where a PL/SQL script is called via a *Korn* shell script. So the failover code is embedded within the shell script.

Be familiar with various automatic failover options

In the previous tip, we examined failover methods explicitly coded within critical applications. However, this failover can also be automated (to an extent) with certain architectural configurations and product features. Such automation is imperative because this allows even ordinary applications, where no explicit steps have been taken, to failover successfully with the end user having little or no knowledge about the process. Let's face it: it is not realistic to explicitly code all applications to have failover capabilities. Each application may have different levels of complexity, and trying to understand this complexity and incorporate failover features would be highly difficult, especially considering that various well-functioning applications are already written (sometimes, years ago) and many others are (off-the-shelf) third-party applications, where you have little or no access to the source code. However, these very same applications may be mission-critical as well, requiring failover. So, rather than trying to address all failover issues with just one weapon—explicit coding, it is essential to combine explicit coding with automated application failover. Due analysis is needed to determine which approach makes better sense among the various applications within your environment. At the very least, automated failover can be a backup in case the explicit coding proves inadequate under certain circumstances (say, you have not anticipated a certain failure scenario and coded for it).

Automatic Application Failover

Why is client failover so important that all these explicit (extra) precautions and steps during configuration and coding need to be taken? These extra steps take up more time and resources, delaying application rollout (in the eyes of the management). By properly justifying these tasks beforehand and incorporating them in the overall plan/schedule, this perception of delay can be eliminate altogether. Reliable 24×7 operation cannot be achieved merely by providing redundancy at the database level. The clients need to be configured to switch over and use the redundant resources in a timely fashion when the primary resources fail. During a failure, client sessions normally lose transactions that remain uncommitted and are also subjected to wastage of time, as they realize that their database session has failed and they have to manually reconnect to a secondary database resource. Especially if the transaction/query is a long one and has been running for several hours before the failure, restarting it from scratch can prove very costly, in terms of time and money. In order to avoid wastage of time and inconvenience to end users, it is essential to take a comprehensive two-pronged approach: Provide adequate redundancy and configure all clients to automatically switch over to the redundant resources. The two main objectives of such switchover should be:

- Switchover should be transparent, without the client having to manually reconnect.

- The transactions current at the time of failure should be transferred to the secondary database resource with as little loss as possible. Wherever appropriate, the current state of the transactions should be determined and only the leftover portions should have to be run on the secondary database resource.

Of these objectives, the second is quite difficult to satisfy in its entirety. Certain portions of transactions can be rerun. However, exactly determining where the transaction failed and switching only the remaining portion over is a daunting task and requires the solution to be highly sophisticated. Currently available solutions help to transfer only SELECT statements over. All uncommitted writes tend to get lost and need to be rerun.

In this context, failover needs to be considered at two stages: during connection and during transaction processing. In other words, connect-time failover and runtime failover are the two failover aspects that need to be considered. Drawing on this overall guideline, we can classify all database connections as

- Active connections
- Inactive connections
- (New) connections initiated, but not yet established

In the first category, the client has already connected to the database and is currently running certain transactions. In the second category, the client is connected to the database but is not running any transactions currently. In both of the preceding scenarios, the client has already initiated a specific state within the database. In other words, packages, cursors, and variables have been initiated, certain ALTER SESSION commands may have been run, and so on. This may not be relevant in the second case, since such connections may have completed all required transactions and may be ready to disconnect from the database. For failover purposes, however, it is safer to assume that these connections still have incomplete work left to do within the database. It is necessary for any failover strategy to explore ways to retain as much state as possible, and, if this is not possible, to re-create as much state as possible. If the complete state cannot be re-created, then the end user/application has to be notified so that the state and remaining transactions can be rerun in the current or standby/parallel instance. Such a scenario would require a combination of automated failover configuration and explicit failover coding within the application (where the previous tip would help). It is to be remembered here that the end user is used to dealing only with the application and not the database. If, in certain cases, the database connection was initiated directly by end users and not via a formal application (due to ad hoc database access being prevalent, such as in a DSS environment), adequate end-user training is necessary to recognize failover symptoms and resubmit necessary commands to reestablish the state (necessary ALTER SESSION commands) and the commands to complete the transaction (DML commands) in the current or failed-over instance/database. The first category is often the toughest to fail over intact. Generally, the current transactions are aborted. Finally, the third category is the easiest to fail over to a designated standby. (Note that I'm using the terms "standby" and "parallel" interchangeably. I'm using the terms "database" and "instance" in a similar fashion. These just indicate the secondary resources for the applications to be failed over to, when the current resources experience failure. For instance, in a standby database configuration, a "standby database" would be designated as the secondary resource for the failover, whereas in an OPS environment, a "parallel instance" may be designated as the secondary. Certain robust configurations may even combine the two and use a parallel instance as the first failover option; if that fails also due to the entire primary database having failed, then the failover can be escalated to a separate standby database configuration).

There are a few automated failover options. Let's take a look at them and the type of connections they help to fail over:

- Static failover via Net8 (this addresses connect-time failures only)
- Transparent application failover via OCI8 combined with Net8 failover features (this option addresses both connect-time and runtime failover)
- Failover via middle-tier components such as TP Monitors and Application Servers (again, this option provides both connect-time and runtime failover)

Finally, all the preceding options can be combined with explicit failover coded within the applications that the clients run. Also, implementation differs for each of the preceding options, depending on the technology used to maintain secondary database resources. For instance, in the case of OPS, a parallel instance is readily available and failover can be immediately attempted; whereas in the case of a regular standby database, it may not be open/ready to accept transactions. Accordingly, it may need to be opened in an appropriate manner, and until then, failover cannot be commenced. Accordingly, the end user would need to be notified of the attempt to fail over and requested to wait via a message on the client screen. Alternatively, if the standby database is a custom one or maintained via Advanced Replication or certain third-party tools, then it may be open and ready for use. In such a circumstance, failover can be attempted immediately.

STATIC FAILOVER VIA NET8 Net8 allows service names to be set up to refer to more than one database/instance. Under this method, the same service name (say, HADB.world) is mapped to the primary and the secondary databases. All incoming requests go to the database resource referred to by the first service name description.

When the first one is unavailable, however, all requests are routed to the secondary database. Let's understand how it works.

When a client needs to access a database, it refers (via Net8 on the client) to the configuration information maintained in the *tnsnames.ora* file to scan for the appropriate service name and the corresponding description of the host name, listener port number, SID, and so on. Net8 allows multiple instances to be described as part of the same service name. Once the relevant connection information is obtained, it attempts to connect to the database pointed to by the first description. Now, if the attempt to connect fails (the target database, the listener, or even the system is down), then it looks at the next description associated with the service name and attempts to connect there. Thus, the primary database instance can be listed in the first description and the standby database instance can be referred in the second to allow automatic connect-time failover. Since this failover is achieved via static configuration information maintained in the *tnsnames.ora* file (or in a Names Server), this method is also referred to as static failover (see Figure 6-2).

Let's look at an example:

```
HADB.world =                    (the service-name)
  (DESCRIPTION_LIST =                  (this describes the various databases/instances)
   (DESCRIPTION =               (the primary resource description begins here)
     (ADDRESS =
       (PROTOCOL = TCP)
       (HOST = attic)                  (the primary server)
       (PORT = 1526)
     )
     (CONNECT_DATA = (SID = HADB1))    (SID of the primary instance)
   )
   (DESCRIPTION =               (the secondary resource description begins here)
       (ADDRESS =
         (PROTOCOL = TCP)
         (HOST = loft)          (the secondary server)
         (PORT = 1526)
       )
       (CONNECT_DATA = (SID = HADB2))  (SID of the secondary instance)
   )
  )
```

The preceding sample listing of the *tnsnames.ora* makes the configuration quite clear. If Oracle Names is enabled, however, the client refers to the Names Server repository for the appropriate connection information. The client knows that Oracle Names is enabled based on the existence of the following setting in *sqlnet.ora:*

```
NAMES.DIRECTORY_PATH = (ONAMES)
```

If the Names Server is down due to a reason, the client access will fail. However, if the entry within *sqlnet.ora* is as below, then the *tnsnames.ora* file is used instead. This, in fact, is a good way to overcome Names Server failures by maintaining a current copy of the *tnsnames.ora* file on all the clients and allowing it to be used as a fallback option, whenever the Names Server is unavailable:

```
NAMES.DIRECTORY_PATH = (ONAMES, TNSNAMES)
```

Once the client determines that Oracle Names is enabled, it contacts the Names Server based on the *sdns.ora* file. If the required Names Server entry is missing in the *sdns.ora* file, then the client attempts to contact a host with the name ORANAMESRV0. Thus, ORANAMESRV0 is the default "well-known" name used by Net8 clients for the Names Server host.

Once the Names Server is contacted, the client presents the desired service name and gets the appropriate connection description back. Again, in Net8, a single service name may correspond to multiple connection descriptions. Net8 will provide the first one in the list and, if that connection attempt fails, subsequent descriptions are used, thus allowing the connection to the secondary database to be used when the primary database is unavailable.

TRANSPARENT APPLICATION FAILOVER VIA OCI8 AND NET8

Starting with v8, OCI allows automatic runtime failover (see Figure 6-3). This feature is commonly referred to as transparent application failover (TAF). Any application developed in OCI8 (using the OCI8 libraries) is made aware of transaction/statement failures. Given this notification, the application can use specific OCI calls to fail over to a secondary database/instance. The actual failover is conducted by Net8 (which needs to be configured accordingly beforehand). TAF is available for programs written in OCI8. Such programs are called "failover-aware" applications. This includes both Oracle tools/utilities and custom programs (that are developed in-house). At the time of writing, only SQL*Plus v8.0 and above are failover-aware. Oracle Corporation has indicated that other critical Oracle applications, tools, and utilities such as Oracle Developer and Oracle Application Server will be made "failover-aware" in subsequent releases.

OCI8 allows client-session information to be maintained separately from database server information via separate *handles* (a handle is an opaque pointer to refer to specific structures that maintain information on connections, contexts, and other data used internally). Each handle is maintained via the OCI8 libraries (rather than by the application itself). When the current database server fails and the connection is severed, the failure is registered and appropriate failover can be initiated via a *failover callback* (routines to react to the failover). Such failover can occur at either of two levels:

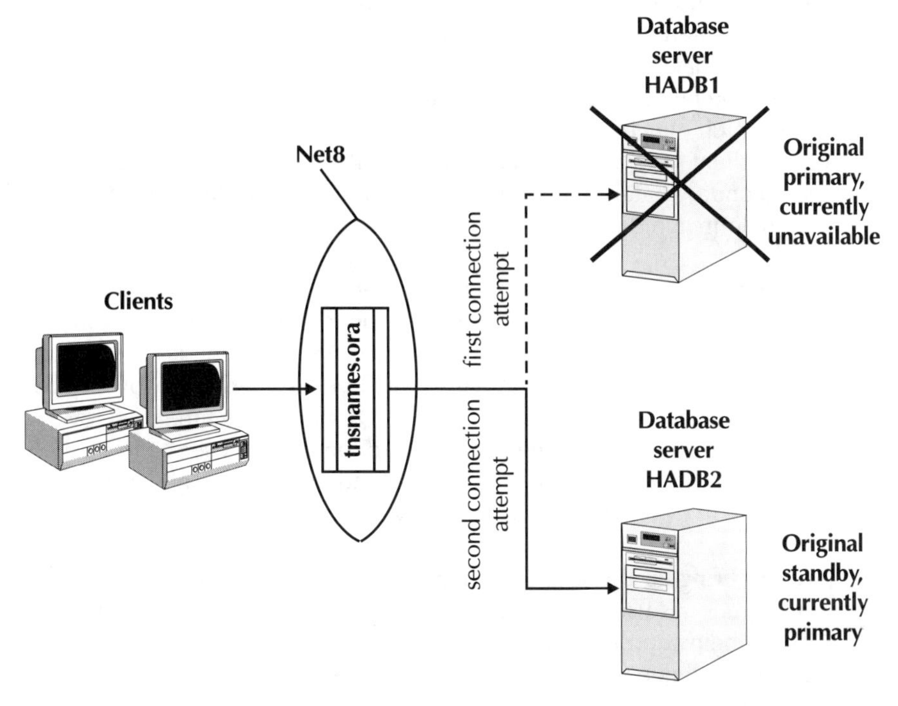

FIGURE 6-2. *Static (connect-time) failover via Net8*

- **Via static Net8 failover capabilities** This is already discussed in the previous section (prior to this section on TAF via OCI8). When failover is experienced on the primary database server, the *tnsnames.ora* or the Names Server is referred to in order to acquire the connection description of the next database/instance mapped to the service name and an attempt is made to connect there. Some additional information needs to be recorded in *tnsnames.ora* (or the Names Server) to allow Net8 to decide which TYPE of failover needs to occur and which METHOD to use to accomplish this (failover TYPE and METHOD are discussed later).
- **Via explicit OCI8 coding** Here, the failover callback is utilized within the application to decide which of the standby databases/instances to connect to and to take necessary steps to re-create the required session state (such as running specific ALTER SESSION commands, restoring certain cursors and

variables, and so on). This approach is quite sophisticated and allows the application to be literally transferred in a transparent fashion to the secondary database. Obviously, it requires additional coding to define and register the failover callback. Also, this approach may require additional time, which may become apparent to the end user. Accordingly, a message on the client such as "The database has failed. Connection is being made to the secondary database to continue your transaction. Please stand by . . ." may help in avoiding user frustrations.

With either of the preceding approaches, the end user does not have to do anything manually. Only if the approaches fail (due to the secondary database not being accessible), then he or she may have to manually intervene (to call support personnel, retry later, or take some similar step). Time required to fail over depends on the configuration and overall system loads/user traffic at the time of failover. Obviously, if a large number of users are involved (peak-hour user traffic), it will take more time to switch them all over to the secondary. Additionally, the following factors play a role in determining time to fail over:

- **Time to bring up the secondary database** If a regular standby configuration is used, obviously it will be in mounted mode (as the redo logs are being applied). Recovery will need to stop and the standby database will need to be opened before failover can succeed.
- **Time to reconnect to the standby** If the listener on the standby server gets saturated with a large number of simultaneous requests (if a large number of users are being failed over), then having multiple listeners will help, since they can share the overall load (on a round-robin basis). Also, whether the standby database is configured to use MTS or dedicated connections also makes a difference. Typically, MTS is faster, since the dispatchers are already available; whereas under dedicated mode, the shadow process will need to be spawned at runtime to allow the client process to connect. If you are using dedicated mode, pre-spawning a few dedicated server processes will expedite the failover. Chapter 7 discusses pre-spawning of dedicated server processes.

  Another very effective method to reduce connection time is to have pre-connected sessions. When the client session connects to the primary database, it can also pre-connect to the standby database/instance (provided they are up and running). So, during failover, the connection to the standby is already present and does not take up additional time. OCI8 automates such pre-connection (via the PRECONNECT METHOD) and is discussed further later in the text.
- **Time to fail over the statement** Under OCI8's current TAF capabilities, statements other than SELECTs cannot be failed over. So, if a lengthy

INSERT/UPDATE/DELETE was active at the time of failure, the transaction will have to be resubmitted to the secondary database. All the changes that were committed will survive. However, the uncommitted ones will be rolled back. Transaction resubmission is another factor that will have to be handled by the failover callback. With SELECTs, however, the OCI8 library keeps track of the number of rows that were already retrieved. When the SELECT is rerun, an equivalent number of rows are ignored (since they were already fetched earlier) and the SELECT continues with the rest of the rows. This may save a little time (since the rows already retrieved earlier will not have to be processed). In most cases, however, this definitely adds to overall failover time, since the same statement has to be rerun until the exact point where it aborted (in the primary database) is reached. This can be difficult to achieve, especially if the statement is highly complex. So some duplicate processing is imminent. Also, failover slows the overall throughput. A SELECT, which normally would take an hour to complete, now may take an hour and a half (I'm just using random numbers to illustrate my point) after failover.

As mentioned earlier, Net8 needs to be configured with information (within the *tnsnames.ora* or the Names Server) on the required TYPE and METHOD to use during failover. TYPE specifies the type of action to take during failover: whether failover needs to occur in the first place and, if so, whether to fail over SELECT statements or not. TYPE supports the following options:

- **NONE** This is the default TYPE. When this is used, the OCI8 application will need to explicitly handle the failover (via the failover callback) without help from Net8.
- **SESSION** Here, no statements/transactions are failed over by Net8. Only the session is failed over to the secondary database/instance (specified via the static DESCRIPTION_LIST). All statements are reissued via the failover callback in the OCI8 application.
- **SELECT** With this option, SELECT statements are failed over along with the session. Note that other DML statements are not failed over.

METHOD determines when the connection to the secondary database/instance is acquired. It supports the following options:

- **BASIC** Here, an attempt is made to acquire the connection to the secondary database/instance only during failover (after the primary database/instance has failed).

- **PRECONNECT** Here, the connection to the secondary is acquired at the same time as the primary. This ensures that failover time is kept to a minimum because during failover a new connection to the standby does not have to be initiated—a connection was already acquired earlier. Accordingly, all that needs to happen now is that necessary statements will need to be rerun. This option is suitable only for applications with the most stringent availability requirements, since it takes up resources on the secondary even when there is no failure. This approach assumes that failure might occur anytime and always remains prepared. Besides higher resource utilization, there is also an impact on performance with this approach (another example of the inherent inverse relationship between availability and performance). If the secondary database/instance is used to cater to another sub-set of users/clients, then there will be lesser resources available for them. Additionally, network traffic may increase due to the periodic pinging across client and the secondary database/instance (to keep the connection alive). In most environments, failures are pretty rare. Accordingly, the PRECONNECT option may be overkill in such environments. On the positive side, however, it does help in reducing failover time, which is critical for certain mission- critical applications. Also note that the secondary database/instance has to be open/available in order to use this option (that rules out a regular standby database configuration).

The following sample entry in *tnsnames.ora* illustrates usage of these options:

```
HADB.world =
  (DESCRIPTION_LIST =
    (DESCRIPTION =
      (ADDRESS =
        (PROTOCOL = TCP)
        (HOST = attic)
        (PORT = 1526)
      )
      (CONNECT_DATA = (SID = HADB1)
        (FAILOVER_MODE =
           (TYPE = SELECT)
           (METHOD = BASIC)
        )
      )
    )
     (DESCRIPTION =
        (ADDRESS =
          (PROTOCOL = TCP)
          (HOST = loft)
          (PORT = 1526)
```

```
      )
      (CONNECT_DATA = (SID = HADB2)
        (FAILOVER_MODE =
          (TYPE = SESSION)
          (METHOD = BASIC)
        )
      )
    )
  )
```

Note that TAF will not occur via any of the preceding methods if failure is caused by the client application process being terminated (say, the client PC crashes or the end user explicitly kills it). It will occur only when the database session experiences a failure. Besides an actual database failure, another way to force TAF to occur is by issuing the ALTER SYSTEM DISCONNECT SESSION command. The utility of this command is explained in a subsequent paragraph.

TAF can occur under either MTS or dedicated server architecture. However, MTS is recommended when using TAF functionality. The Oracle8*i* documentation explains how to configure TAF. One important thing to note is that when using TAF, *listener.ora*

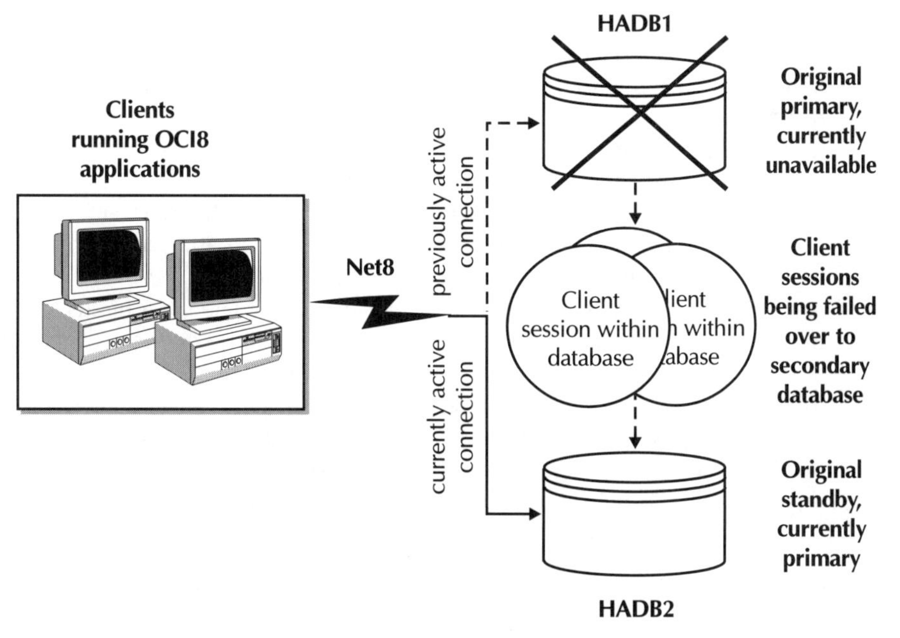

FIGURE 6-3. *Transparent application failover via OCI8/Net8 features*

should not list the SIDs of the primary/secondary instances. Instead, each instance needs to register itself with the listener via the LOCAL_LISTENER database initialization parameter to activate a primary-secondary relationship. When using dedicated server architecture, both the primary and secondary databases should have separate listeners, unless both are maintained on the same machine (having both on the same machine actually defeats a major purpose of a standby database: avoiding a single point of system failure).

DBAs at my client sites ask whether TAF can be configured and failover can be set to occur merely by appropriately configuring the *tnsnames.ora* and *listener.ora* files (by setting the TYPE, METHOD, and so on). No, unfortunately, only a "failover-aware" application written using OCI8's libraries can utilize the Net8 configuration to achieve failover. This is because the OCI8's libraries intimate the application when failures occur and the primary database connection gets broken. This intimation is the key to failover. Ordinary applications do not receive this intimation automatically. In the case of ordinary applications, however, you can code failure recognition and subsequent failover explicitly (as an earlier tip illustrated). A detailed discussion of OCI8 is beyond the scope of this book. Please refer to the Oracle8/8*i* documentation for details on OCI and implementing TAF via OCI8.

Besides regular application failover, the TAF features also allow certain other advantages, such as these:

- **Load balancing** Using TAF, the DBA can evaluate the total load incurred by a single database/instance during peak hours and, if necessary, redirect the load to a different database/instance by disconnecting certain users and forcing the session to transparently connect to the secondary database/instance (without the end user having to manually reconnect). Manual disconnection can be performed via the ALTER SYSTEM DISCONNECT SESSION command. Use of this command will terminate the database session on the primary database/instance and, via TAF features, automatically reconnect to the secondary. The DBA needs to be very careful about which users he disconnects. If he chooses users that are running write-intensive transactions, then their transactions may have to be resubmitted from the start (especially if the application does not intermittently commit the writes). Only users running SELECT statements (for instance, end users sneaking in large reports/queries on the OLTP database) should be redirected. For this to successfully work, failover TYPE needs to be set to SELECT.

  Also, on certain Oracle ports (such as on the IBM SP), automatic load balancing can be set to occur by configuring instance groups consisting of multiple instances via the INSTANCE_GROUPS initialization parameter.

Then this instance group can be specified in the *tnsnames.ora* (or the Names Server) via the SIDGRP clause. Thus, an entire instance group can be used instead of a single SID. Net8 then performs load balancing across the instances composing the group, alleviating the load on each individual instance. The following sample entries in the *tnsnames.ora* file illustrate the configuration for such load balancing (*ins_grp1* is the name of the instance group comprising the HADB1 and HADB2 instances and is referenced in the SID of the HADB.world service-name description):

```
ins_grp1 =
  (SIDGRP =
    (SID = HADB1)
    (SID = HABD2)
   )

HADB.world =
  (DESCRIPTION_LIST =
    (DESCRIPTION =
      (ADDRESS =
        (PROTOCOL = TCP)
        (HOST = attic)
        (PORT = 1526)
      )
      (CONNECT_DATA = (SID = ins_grp1)
        (FAILOVER_MODE =
            (TYPE = SELECT)
            (METHOD = BASIC)
         )
      )
     )
     (DESCRIPTION =
        (ADDRESS =
          (PROTOCOL = TCP)
          (HOST = loft)
          (PORT = 1526)
         )
        (CONNECT_DATA = (SID = ins_grp1)
          (FAILOVER_MODE =
            (TYPE = SESSION)
            (METHOD = BASIC)
           )
         )
      )
   )
```

Chapter 7 outlines some strategies for load balancing using SQL*Net v2.3.x and/or Net8.

- **Periodic pre-scheduled shutdowns** In a 24×7 environment, the primary database cannot be normally shut down. However, periodically it may need to be shut down (for, say, certain maintenance activities, such as applying an OS patch or changing an initialization parameter or, even, to workaround an OS memory bug). Prior to shutting it down, the secondary database needs to be available so that all users can continue to use the secondary database. The SHUTDOWN TRANSACTIONAL command can be utilized during the shutdown. The TRANSACTIONAL option waits for all current transactions to complete. Any new client sessions are disconnected, causing them to be failed over to the secondary database/instance (automatically, without manual intervention). Once all the current transactions complete, they are disconnected as well, causing them to switch over to the secondary database/instance. Then the current instance is shut down in IMMEDIATE mode.

FAILOVER VIA MIDDLE-TIER COMPONENTS Certain middle-tier components such as TP Monitors are utilized (in an n-tier architecture, as shown in Figure 6-4) for a variety of reasons such as accommodating large user populations; performing load balancing; coordinating client access to multiple databases/systems; insulating client applications from business logic; and, not the least, affording higher availability. In the case of Web databases, typically there is a Web server that functions at the middle tier. Also, application servers such as the Oracle Application Server (OAS), Oracle Developer Server, and so on, are utilized in a similar fashion. Note that all middle-tier components do not have similar capabilities. Some are more powerful and focused toward specific solutions, whereas others are less powerful in those areas. In our discussion on enhancing application availability via certain middle-tier components, we look specifically at TP Monitors, unless otherwise specified (we later take a peek at the Oracle Application Server). Also, the functionality of certain TP Monitors available in the market may vary from what is listed here. Please check the documentation provided by the specific TP Monitor vendor prior to configuring/using them.

One of the features of TP Monitors oriented toward high availability is that all database services are registered with them for routing purposes. In other words, the TP Monitor is aware of which database services are available and which are not. Given this information, it accepts and routes client connections to the database services that are available (primary and/or secondary). It tracks this information by periodically polling the various database services and maintains it within a custom repository (such as the Bulletin Board used by BEA Systems' Tuxedo). Services that are deemed to be unavailable are marked, and subsequent client connections are

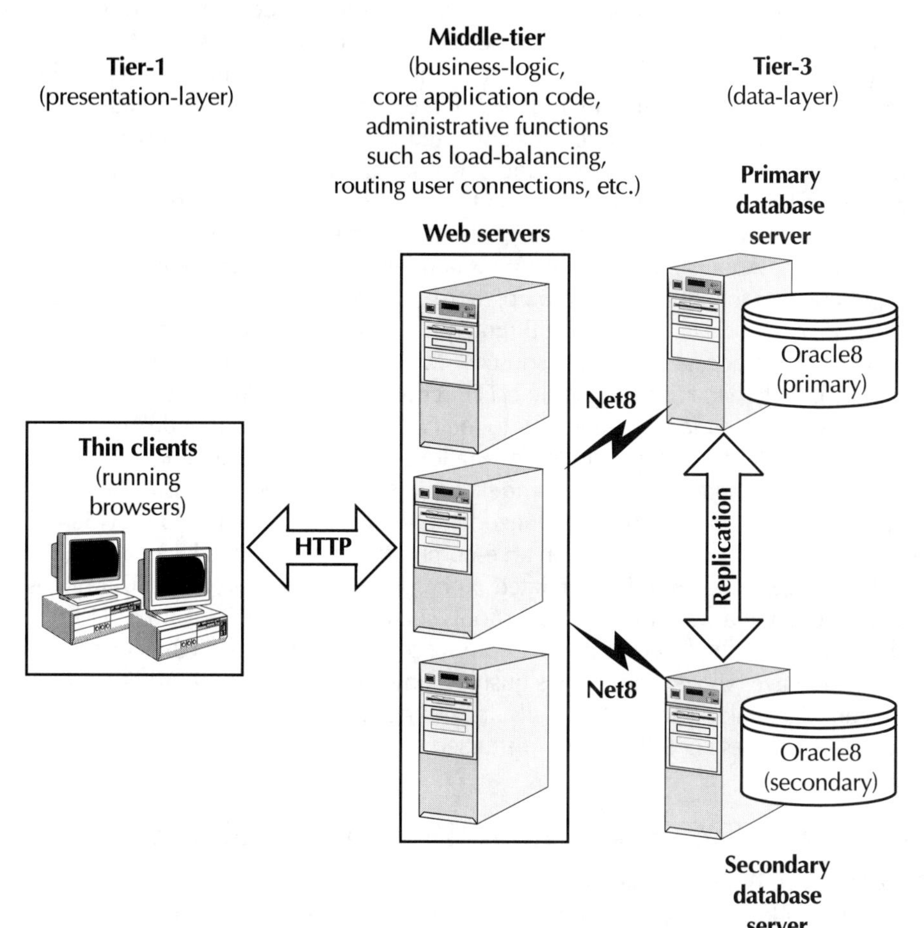

FIGURE 6-4. *N-tier architecture*

routed to other databases, thus avoiding connect-time failure. In case an application experiences a connect-time failure in spite of such coordination (say, the primary database crashes during the interval between the TP Monitor routing the connection there and the connection actually being acquired), the application submits an error back and is subsequently rerouted to secondary database resources.

TP Monitors also allow the returned error code to be trapped by the application, which can take action accordingly. For instance, if the primary database fails, the error code will inform the application of this failure and code can be written within the application to either retry the connection, return control to the TP Monitor and let the TP Monitor deal with it (by rerouting the application to the next available database service), or specifically request for a different (secondary) database connection. Once the application is connected to an appropriate database service, it will need to resubmit the current and subsequent transactions itself. Generally, the TP Monitor will not/cannot resubmit the transaction, since it operates at a higher level. In any case, the rerouting allows runtime failover to occur.

The Oracle Application Server (OAS) is another example of a middle-tier component. It functions as a common platform for both CORBA (Common Object Request Broker Architecture)– and EJB (Enterprise Java Beans)–compliant objects to be deployed and access database resources. OAS allows each transaction within an application to encompass multiple HTTP requests, maintaining the application state across these requests. Please refer to the OAS documentation for details on its architecture. OAS by itself is not currently failover-aware. However, it implements both ready-made and custom (user-made) cartridges. Cartridges are basically specialized code modules that are plugged into the OAS architecture to provide certain functionality. For instance, in an e-commerce application, a Java cartridge may be plugged in to provide tax-related processing (of customer orders). Cartridges may be written in a variety of languages/tools such as Java, Pro*C, C++, or PERL. Since they can be totally custom-written from scratch, you can explicitly code for the cartridge to have failover capabilities (just like any other application). Additionally, if the cartridge makes use of OCI8 calls, it can implement connect-time and runtime failover capabilities via TAF features discussed earlier.

Have MAXEXTENTS unlimited for all volatile application segments

One of the most common causes of application failure is the inability of a segment to grow. This inability to grow may result from lack of space in the tablespace to accommodate growth or be due to MAXEXTENTS being reached. Lack of space is a maintenance issue and can be prevented by proactively monitoring for lack of space and adding data-files as and when necessary (this topic is covered in more detail in Chapters 2 and 12). However, the other reason (MAXEXTENTS reached) is a sheer waste of time and does not really deserve the attention it ends up getting. It is a simple task to proactively set the MAXEXTENTS to as high a number as possible. In versions prior to Oracle7 v7.3, the limitation on the setting for MAXEXTENTS was dependent on the DB_BLOCK_SIZE initialization parameter (since the maximum number of extents for each segment was limited to the space map that could be held within one database block). Thus, for example, with a DB_BLOCK_SIZE of 2K, the maximum size for MAXEXTENTS was 121, since the space map for only 121 extents could be held within a 2KB database block. However, starting with v7.3, MAXEXTENTS' dependency on

DB_BLOCK_SIZE has been eliminated. Accordingly, MAXEXTENTS can be set as high as necessary. It can even be set to UNLIMITED (when UNLIMITED is used, Oracle automatically sets it to 249,000,000). Setting it to UNLIMITED will prevent a segment from ever reaching the maximum number of extents and causing applications to fail due to the segment not being able to accept any additional data. Accordingly, proactively setting the MAXEXTENTS for all application segments to UNLIMITED will greatly help in reducing downtime. Also, if possible, set the default storage parameters for all tablespaces holding application segments to use MAXEXTENTS UNLIMITED, so that segments that are created without explicit storage parameters can also acquire an unlimited number of extents, if necessary, without failing and causing downtime.

As a side note, do not set MAXEXTENTS UNLIMITED for rollback segments, tablespaces containing rollback segments, and temporary tablespaces. It's good to set a finite number of maximum allowable extents for such objects. This will help in stopping runaway jobs more easily. Allowing an unlimited number of maximum extents will allow the temporary or rollback segment to grow as needed to an extraordinarily large size by consuming large amounts of space, causing space problems and even bringing the entire database down. Conversely, setting the maximum number of allowable extents to a finite number such as 121 will help contain and manage such abrupt and unwanted growth. A runaway process should always be stopped. However, if the DBA is not aware that a process has run away and is consuming large amounts of space, he or she won't be able to stop it (explicitly) on time. Accordingly, if the process (implicitly) fails due to a temporary/rollback segment not being able to grow, it would prevent an emergency.

Expedite your data loads

Availability for DSS applications such as data-warehouses and data-marts depends on the time taken to populate them. Only after they are populated fully and the data has been checked for errors can the data be made available to end users for querying and so on. Accordingly, it is necessary to take steps to expedite your data loads as much as possible. The following text describes some methods for achieving this end.

Keep Indexes to a Minimum

It's a common notion that DSS applications have a lot of indexes. It's true that, generally, DSS applications have more indexes than OLTP applications. However, it's easy to go overboard and over-index the tables. Indexes can slow down performance of data loads (especially bulk-insert operations). Accordingly, it is necessary to keep them to a minimum, no matter what the application type is. Also, the greater the number of indexes, the more time is required to create them. Also, DML (inserts/updates/deletes) cannot run concurrently while an index is being built (in versions 8.0.x and below), and this fact adds to post-load downtime. If usage patterns dictate that a large number of indexes be built, try to reduce the number of columns in each index. Fewer indexed columns reduces the overall index size. It's a common practice to index all columns that are present in the WHERE clause of the DML statements. In fact, I have observed at certain client sites that different indexes are created based on the sequence of columns within the index. For instance, there may be one index on (FUND_ID, FUND_TYPE_ID, FUND_NAME) and there may be another on (FUND_TYPE_ID, FUND_ID) and yet another on just FUND_NAME. Certain situations may genuinely call for the existence of such indexes. More often than not, however, analysis and tweaking of the execution paths taken by the highly used DML statements may result in some of those indexes being made redundant, and those may be safely dropped without affecting performance adversely. For instance, when two or more tables are being joined, an index on all join-columns may not always be necessary. If an index exists merely on the "primary columns," that statement should provide comparable performance to having all columns in the WHERE clause indexed. Such "primary columns" are the columns that cause the result set to be the smallest. In other words, such columns will filter out all rows that don't match the primary (or most obvious) query criteria and return just the rows that need to be joined subsequently. Let's look at an example to understand this better:

Two tables FD_FUNDS_MST and FD_FUND_PRICES are involved in a join. The result set of this join is used to bulk-load data into another table. FD_FUNDS_MST has over 80,000 rows and FD_FUND_PRICES has over 1.5 million rows. Here is the original statement:

```
SQL> SELECT m.fund_name, p.fund_price
       FROM fd_funds_mst m, fd_fund_prices p
        WHERE m.fund_id = p.fund_id
        AND p.price_period = TO_DATE('05/01/1999', 'MM/DD/YYYY');
```

To aid the preceding statement, indexes were created by the developer as follows:

FD_FUNDS_MST	FD_FUNDS_MST_PK on Fund_ID (primary-key index)
FD_FUND_PRICES	FD_FUND_PRICES_UNQ01 on Fund_ID and Price_Period (a unique index was created for this particular query, in addition to the primary-key index, which was on Fund_ID, Fund_Type, Price_Period).

The statement was tuned as follows:

```
SQL> SELECT /*+ INDEX(m FD_FUNDS_MST_PK )
                INDEX(p FD_FUND_PRICES_UNQ01) */
            m.fund_name, p.fund_price FROM fd_funds_mst m, fd_fund_prices p
      WHERE m.fund_id = p.fund_id
        AND p.price_period = TO_DATE('05/01/1999', 'MM/DD/YYYY');
```

The resultant execution path was as follows for the query:

```
SELECT STATEMENT
   NESTED LOOPS
      TABLE ACCESS BY INDEX ROWID FD_FUND_PRICES
         INDEX RANGE SCAN FD_FUND_PRICES_UNQ01
      TABLE ACCESS BY INDEX ROWID FD_FUNDS_MST
         INDEX FULL SCAN FD_FUNDS_MST_PK
```

This execution path resulted in the query being done in three hours. Even though it was better than the original query, the performance was still not acceptable. Finally, the following things were done to speed up the query:

- Since all rows from FD_FUNDS_MST were being retrieved, it was converted to a full-table scan, instead of the full-index scan/table-access combination that was being performed earlier. A parallel degree of four was used to perform the full-table scan.
- The FD_FUND_PRICES_UNQ01 index on FD_FUND_PRICES (FUND_ID, PRICE_PERIOD) was dropped and instead, a bitmap index on PRICE_PERIOD was created (a bitmap index was necessary, since the cardinality/degree of uniqueness of the PRICE_PERIOD column was low).
- A hash join was used to join the two tables together

  The new query resembled the following:

```
SQL> SELECT /*+ FULL(m) PARALLEL(m, 4)
                INDEX(p FD_FUND_PRICES_BTMP01) USE_HASH(m) */
           m.fund_name, p.fund_price
      FROM fd_funds_mst m, fd_fund_prices p
     WHERE m.fund_id = p.fund_id
       AND p.price_period = TO_DATE('05/01/1999', 'MM/DD/YYYY');
```

The following execution path was derived:

```
SELECT STATEMENT
   HASH JOIN
      TABLE ACCESS BY INDEX ROWID FD_FUNDS_MST
         BITMAP CONVERSION TO ROWIDS
            BITMAP INDEX SCAN FD_FUND_PRICES_BTMP01
      TABLE ACCESS FULL FD_FUNDS_MST
```

The resultant query took less than ten minutes to complete. Though a number of other things were done besides just reducing the use of indexes, for the purpose of our discussion, let's understand how reducing the indexes helped performance:

- An index scan was unnecessary in the case of FD_FUNDS_MST. Since a full-index/table scan was being performed, the index-scan only helped to add more overhead, rather than reducing it. It's a good "rule of thumb" to remember that if more than 15 percent of the rows in the table are being retrieved, it's desirable to perform a full-table scan, rather than an index-scan/table-access combination. One exception to this rule (that comes to mind) is when all the necessary columns are held in the index itself, thus making it a pure full-index scan. A table will not be accessed if the index itself contains all the necessary columns.

NOTE
Keep in mind here that the "rule of thumb" I refer to is not universally applicable. There are times an index will be helpful even when more than 15 percent of the rows in a table are accessed. Conversely, there are also times when an index-based lookup can potentially delay the results even when much less than 15 percent of the rows in a table are accessed. In other words, being familiar with the 15 percent "rule of thumb" is good; however, don't treat that as the only "holy rule" and be misled. Make the final decision only after comparing the number of I/Os required to perform a full-table scan versus the I/Os required to perform an index-based lookup. A guiding factor here is the number of database blocks that would be read by the two approaches if the number of blocks under a certain approach is higher. (For instance, 40 percent of rows in a table being read off an index constitute 350 blocks [including the index blocks], whereas the entire table constitutes 750 blocks. So, chances are, the index-based lookup may be better even though 40 percent of the rows are being read. Again, these factors are further complicated by diverse parameters such as fragmentation, concurrent access by other users, and various different activities currently happening on the system on which the database resides.) You can find the truth by actually running the query during different parallel periods (so that the results from the earlier query do not cause higher logical hits for the next one and cause the latter to complete sooner with a

lesser number of physical I/Os) with SQL_TRACE and TIMED_STATISTICS enabled and then running TKPROF on the resultant trace-files. This approach would reveal the correct number of I/O calls required by the full-table scan and the index-based lookup.

- The index on the FD_FUND_PRICES table was restricted to a single column PRICE_PERIOD, rather than (FUND_ID, PRICE_PERIOD). This is because FD_FUND_PRICES is the driving table (since it is supposed to retrieve the least number of rows) and the column PRICE_PERIOD is the "primary column" for this query, since it applies the condition "p.price_period = TO_DATE('05/01/1999', 'MM/DD/YYYY')" to the driving table and returns only the rows that match that primary condition, after filtering out the ones that do not meet the criteria. Once the rows meeting the primary condition are returned, they are then joined with the rows from the FD_FUNDS_MST table via a hash join, wherein FD_FUNDS_MST is accessed via a full-table scan (since all the rows in FD_FUNDS_MST need to be joined with the current result set from FD_FUND_PRICES).

Besides restricting the number of columns in the existing indexes, it may be necessary to monitor which indexes are actually being used (do an EXPLAIN_PLAN on statements that access that table) and gradually drop off the ones that are not being used, so that your bulk insert operations are subjected to as little impact as possible.

Disable Expensive Constraints During the Loads

Certain constraints may be very expensive in terms of resources consumed to enforce them. For instance, populating a fact table with foreign keys enabled to half a dozen dimension tables will cause high resource consumption to occur, especially if the dimension tables are fairly big, in terms of rows they contain. Furthermore, if the fact tables and the dimension tables share the same physical resources (disks/controllers, SCSI channels, and so on), they could cause heavy physical bottlenecks. All constraints may not be expensive. For instance, a check constraint to enforce NOT NULL (NOT NULL constraints are enforced as CHECK constraints) values may not be as expensive. It's a good idea to leave inexpensive constraints enabled. The reason is, when they are finally enabled at the end of the load, they may take a long time to get enabled, thus potentially delaying availability to the end users. The reason for even simple constraints taking a long time to get enabled after a large load is the cumulative time required to enforce the constraint for all the rows in the table. Accordingly, it may be easier to leave inexpensive constraints alone. Since certain constraints are so easy to check for, keeping them enabled simply means a few more CPU cycles and context switches, rather than any additional physical I/O (since they are already present in the buffer cache). Inversely, keeping such simple constraints disabled and enabling them after the load will mean reading in the rows into the buffer cache once again (assuming that the table is too big to be retained in the cache) to check whether each row satisfies the constraint; it will thus cause extra I/O, in addition to the extra CPU cycles and context switches (which need to occur, anyway). However, complex constraints (such as foreign keys) usually incur extra physical I/O in either case. Accordingly, it is better to disable them and let the loads occur uninterrupted. Another option is to use the Oracle8 deferred constraints feature and not perform the check for constraint violation among the existing rows but merely keep expensive constraints enabled for future rows that might come in. In any case, a policy decision has to be made regarding the constraints in any DSS environment: whether they need to be even created and, if so, whether they need to be kept enabled and, if so, whether they need to remain enabled even during the data loads. Such a policy may have to cater to each table on a case-by-case basis, after considering table functionality, criticality, physical size in terms of number of rows, and so on. As much as possible, create the constraints, but keep them disabled during the loads. If your confidence level in the data just loaded is high, then you may want to keep constraints disabled always (before, during, and after the loads). This will allow you to perform the loads faster and make the database available to end users faster. You may be wondering, if the constraints are to remain disabled, why bother creating them in the first place? Well, this serves two purposes:

- The disabled constraints document the schema and the interrelationships between the tables.
- Some of the end-user ad hoc query tools use the constraints to understand the schema relationship and formulate effective queries. In the absence of the constraints, the queries generated may not be as effective.

Use a Procedural Language

Use a procedural language (such as PL/SQL, Java, or Pro*C) to gain more control over the sequence of joined tables (that is, the join order). This is especially useful when joining a relatively large number of tables, and if, for some reason, you can't get them to join in the right order. In such situations, define explicit cursors to apply each table's individual conditions to retrieve the requisite rows off that table. Now loop through each cursor in the desired order to simulate a join in the correct sequence. For instance, the following query lists the tables to be joined:

```
SQL> SELECT t.fund_type_desc, m.fund_name, p.fund_price
       FROM fd_fund_prices p, fd_funds_mst m, fd_fund_types t
```

```
    WHERE t.fund_type = m.fund_type
      AND p.fund_id = m.fund_id
      AND p.price_period = TO_DATE('05/01/1999', 'MM/DD/YYYY');
```

In the preceding query, the desired join order is the following:

1. FD_FUND_TYPES
2. FD_FUNDS_MST
3. FD_FUND_PRICES

However, if the join occurs in some other order and for some reason, you can't get it to occur in the preceding order (even with the USE_NL, USE_MERGE, or USE_HASH hints), you can use PL/SQL code similar to the following to achieve the same:

```
DECLARE
  CURSOR c_types IS
  SELECT /*+ FULL(t) */ fund_type_desc
    FROM fd_fund_types t;

  CURSOR c_funds(typ fd_funds_mst.fund_type%TYPE) IS
  SELECT fund_id, fund_name
    FROM fd_funds_mst
   WHERE fund_type = typ;

  CURSOR c_prices(fnd fd_fund_prices.fund_id%TYPE,
                  pr_period fund_prices.price_period%TYPE) IS
  SELECT fund_id, fund_price
    FROM fd_fund_prices
   WHERE fund_id = fnd
     AND price_period = pr_period;

  r_types c_types%ROWTYPE;
  r_funds c_funds%ROWTYPE;
  r_prices c_prices%ROWTYPE;
BEGIN
  FOR r_types IN c_types LOOP
    FOR r_funds IN c_funds(r_types.fund_type) LOOP
      FOR r_prices IN c_prices(r_funds.fund_id,
                               TO_DATE('05/01/1999', 'MM/DD/YYYY')) LOOP
-- now, do whatever processing is necessary with r_prices.fund_id
-- and r_prices.fund_price columns
      END LOOP;
    END LOOP;
  END LOOP;
END;
/
```

The preceding piece of code successfully joins the tables in the right order. It is to be borne in mind that such procedure language–based processing may incur higher CPU overhead. Accordingly, ensure that you have sufficient CPU horsepower to achieve the right join order using this method.

When using third-party tools to generate SQL statements, you may have limited control over the SQL statements generated. They may not be well tuned or may not be as effective as you would like them to be. There are some steps you can take to ensure that the SQL statements generated are executed effectively:

- If you are using Oracle7 v7.3 or above, use the cost-based optimizer (CBO). It helps in generating good execution plans for even fairly ugly queries. This may not apply in all circumstances. However, I have seen CBO actually generate some very good execution plans, especially in Oracle8. Rule-based optimization tends to under-perform in such situations, where you do not have any control over the query generation process. One caveat to bear in mind with CBO is that the statistics need to be kept fairly current for effective execution plans to be generated. Ideally, regenerate the statistics after every major data-load operation. In fact, not regenerating the statistics or not generating them accurately enough (either not computing the statistics or not estimating with a good enough percentage) accounts for the most failures and disappointments in using CBO at my client sites.
- Periodically take a dump of the SQL statements present in the shared-pool library cache. The following queries will help you achieve that:
  - To do a straight dump of all user statements:

```
SQL> SELECT sql_text FROM v$sqltext_with_newlines
      WHERE (hash_value, address) IN
    (SELECT sql_hash_value, sql_address
       FROM v$session
      WHERE username NOT IN ('SYS', 'SYSTEM'));
```

  - To do a dump of all statements belonging to a specific user (this user would be the Oracle user ID that the third-party tools connect as):

```
SQL> SELECT sql_text FROM v$sqltext_with_newlines
        WHERE (address, hash_value) IN
       (SELECT sql_address, sql_hash_value
          FROM v$session
        WHERE Username='&username')
          ORDER BY address, piece;
```

  Once the SQL statements in the shared pool have been retrieved, run an EXPLAIN PLAN (or use SQL_TRACE/TKPROF on these statements or SET AUTOTRACE ON TRACEONLY at the SQL*Plus prompt) to get the execution path used by Oracle for these statements. Find out whether the current execution paths are appropriate. If not, try to make them more effective. For instance, if an index scan is occurring on a very small table, you may want to drop the index (unless it's used to enforce a primary/unique key). Or, if an index is not being used because its columns are in a different order than desired by the SQL statement, you may want to drop and re-create the index, so that the columns are in the desired order (unless some other statement is using that index). These are problems commonly encountered when using RBO. Using CBO should alleviate some of these issues. In any case, the point I'm trying to get across is that you should try to make your environment match what is expected by the statements generated by the query tool.

Certain query tools allow manual intervention (such as putting in SQL hints, changing the join order, and so on) to override or enhance what is generated by the tool. Find out whether the query tools used by your end users allow such manual fine-tuning.

Take a Detailed Look at What Jobs Are Running Concurrently

Find out whether these jobs are using the same resources (that is, accessing the same table, using the same disks/controllers, using a high degree of parallelism simultaneously and taxing the CPUs, and so on) and potentially stepping on each other. You might want to schedule such jobs to occur in a serial fashion. Try to parallelize only those jobs that you know are not contending for each other's resources. Else they may cause severe performance degradation due to system bottlenecks. Ideally, all jobs that run in your environment need to be categorized and analyzed, and their scheduling should be determined on the basis of the results. That will allow you to anticipate and prevent failures, an ability that is very crucial in ensuring successful timely completion of the jobs. The higher the number of failures, the more often jobs will need to be restarted. Such conditions can cause heavy delays, and, at times, jobs may not even complete successfully, preventing the results from being made available to the end users. Tables 6-3, 6-4, 6-5, 6-6, and 6-7 provide a format for performing such analysis.

#	Job_Name	Functionality	Tablespaces Accessed
1	B_INIT_CNTRLS	Load job-control file	BL_DATA
2	B_INIT_MSTRS	Load master tables	BL_DATA, BL_INDX, GL_DATA, GL_INDX, TEMP

TABLE 6-3. *Chart Providing Information on Batch Jobs*

#	Job_Name
Jobs accessing BL_DATA	
1	B_INIT_CNTRLS
2	B_INIT_MSTRS
Jobs accessing GL_DATA	
6	B_FUND_PRICES
12	B_FUND_SMMRY

TABLE 6-4. *Chart Categorizing Jobs According to I/O Resources (Disks/Controllers/ SCSI Channels) Shared*

Small jobs, although they may share I/O resources, may be run concurrently, since there will be little impact, if any. Jobs that are functionally dependent on each other need to be serialized. For instance, if Job_B is dependent on the results attained by Job_A, then Job_B can be scheduled to run only after Job_A is complete. So, even though both Job_A and Job_B may be small, inexpensive jobs, they still cannot be parallelized due to functionality requirements. Conversely, even if Job_C and Job_D are not related to each other, but both are expensive heavy-hitting jobs (in terms of physical resources consumed), then they cannot be run concurrently and need to be serialized. Ideally, small or medium jobs that

#	Job_Name
Heavy jobs	
2	B_INIT_MSTRS
12	B_FUND_SMMRY
Medium jobs	
6	B_FUND_PRICES
Small jobs	
1	B_INIT_CNTRLS

TABLE 6-5. *Chart Categorizing Jobs According to Resource-Intensiveness (in Terms of System Resources Such As CPU, Memory, and I/O)*

Required_Job_Sequence	#	Job_Name
1	1	B_INIT_CNTRLS
2	2	B_INIT_MSTRS
2	6	B_FUND_PRICES

TABLE 6-6. *Chart Listing Jobs According to Functionally Required Order of Execution*

share few or no resources are ideal candidates for concurrent execution. Ultimately, everything depends on the overall system resources available. If sufficient memory, CPUs, and I/O bandwidth are available to support concurrent heavy jobs, then such jobs may still be made to run in parallel. Accordingly, knowing the capacity of the system is crucial before populating Table 6-7. Finally, knowing functional requirements is also key in scheduling the jobs. For instance, if the entire batch load needs to occur within six hours, then appropriate steps needs to be taken while determining the job schedule. Merely serializing all jobs may not yield the required throughput. Accordingly, one needs to tune each job to use fewer resources and execute faster with as few errors as possible. Evaluate how many jobs may be run in parallel without reaching system capacity and causing performance bottlenecks and, more important, without causing the jobs to fail due to inadequate resources.

#	Job_Name	Start_Time	Estimated_end_time
1	B_INIT_CNTRLS	2300 hrs	2315 hrs
2	B_INIT_MSTRS	2315 hrs	0100 hrs
3	B_SH_RECS	0100 hrs	0200 hrs
4	B_SH_SMMRY	0100 hrs	0200 hrs
6	B_FUND_PRICES	0100 hrs	0200 hrs
12	B_FUND_SMMRY	0200 hrs	0400 hrs

TABLE 6-7. *Chart listing Order/Timing of Execution (Determining What Can Be Run Concurrently)*

Parts of the preceding discussions refer to SQL tuning. SQL tuning is a vast area and deserves more detailed coverage. However, the topic of this book is not SQL tuning. There are good performance tuning books, which cover the topic in more detail. The reference section lists some of these books.

Version control your application source code

Source code version control seems quite prevalent in large organizations. Accordingly, this tip is geared toward small- and medium-sized organizations, where source code is not being version-controlled. Developers in many smaller companies I work at think of source code versioning as unnecessary overhead. Ironically, many of these smaller companies are Internet startup companies, requiring high availability to remain economically viable. The importance of version-controlling source code in a 24×7 environment cannot be overstated. Imagine a situation as follows: You just rolled out a critical application. Six developers were involved in writing the code. Each developer wrote approximately a dozen programs. Each developer has the source code in his or her directory. After a couple of weeks, the end users request enhancements and a couple of programs need to be changed to accommodate the new requirements. The developer who worked on them is sick and is absent from work. Instead, another developer takes a copy of the source code, makes the changes, and puts it into production (after adequate testing and so on). Again, after a couple of weeks, the end users request a few more additions to the two programs. However, now the original developer who worked on these programs is back at work. He just got in today, hears about the new requirements, promptly fishes out the old source code in his local directory, makes the changes as he thinks appropriate, submits them for testing, and pushes them into production. Fast work, huh? Well, in the scenario just outlined, the changes done by the other developer (in the original developer's absence) were lost! Version-controlling the source code will prevent scenarios like this, where multiple copies and versions of a program float around, causing confusion and potentially substantial downtime, as valuable time is spent in identifying and rectifying errors. A million scenarios like the preceding one come to mind. To keep it short, the moral of the story is this: ensure that all production source code is version-controlled and that all versions are funneled through in the correct sequence, without one overriding the other. Version control allows you to maintain a back-out plan before introducing any new code. If the new code has serious bugs (that have slipped through your QA cycles), your back-out plan will allow you to downgrade and get back to the earlier version.

Manage your indexes efficiently

In most applications, OLTP or DSS, indexes are one of the most ardently used objects. In spite of this, they are highly underestimated. Creating an index is considered to be a simple and precise science. In my experience, I have noted quite a few sites creating indexes with great vigor and finally ending up with one too many and not knowing which ones deserve to stay and which ones can be eliminated without an adverse impact on queries. And, of course, other sites tend to seriously under-exploit them, worrying about the possible detrimental impact on inserts and deletes. Furthermore, the rich and varied indexing options offered by Oracle8 add fuel to the fire. Be it new full-fledged index types or new index-access paths, indexing is emerging as an art, demanding a rock-solid understanding of both concepts and implementation from developers and DBAs. The objective of this tip is twofold:

- To introduce the various index types and access paths available in Oracle8 and shed more technical light on them
- To present specific examples of index use at my client sites to foster better understanding

Hopefully, this will help the reader in determining specifically what type of index to create in a given situation; when an index should be rebuilt; and what kind of access path should be determined for major DML statements, using those indexes.

Oracle8 offers the following *major* index types:

- B*Tree indexes
- Bitmapped indexes

In addition, there are the following variations of the B*Tree index (sub-types):

- Partitioned indexes
- Reverse-key indexes
- Index-organized tables (IOTs)
- Cluster indexes

Furthermore, Oracle8 and 8*i* introduce the following index-related terms:

- Local and global indexes
- Prefixed and non-prefixed indexes

- Abstract data-type indexes
- Function-based indexes (Oracle8*i* only)
- Application domain indexes (Oracle8*i* only)

And the following index access paths are provided:

- **Regular index/table lookups** Use the ROWID from the index to locate a row in the table.
- **Index-only lookups** If all the necessary columns are available in the index itself, the table lookup is avoided.
- **Index range scans** A range of index keys are scanned to locate the desired key value.
- **Fast full index scans (FFIs)** FFIs allow reading of multiple index blocks to expedite full index scans. Since an index is usually smaller than a table, an index full-scan is a much faster alternative to a full table scan, if the index includes all required columns. The initialization parameter DB_FILE_MULTIBLOCK_READ_COUNT determines the number of index blocks read in one I/O operation (remember, many OSs have a 64K upper limit on I/O).
- **Parallel Query Option (PQO) "enriched" paths** In Oracle8, PQO is available for all the preceding access paths.

This tip assumes prior knowledge of certain key concepts. Before we start, let's take a quick peek at those concepts:

- **Constraints and index creation** Declaring primary-key and unique constraints automatically creates an index on the concerned columns. The USING INDEX clause of the CREATE and ALTER TABLE commands allows more control over this index-creation process. Also, declaring a foreign key does not automatically create an index. As a quick note, starting with Oracle8*i*, an index is not mandatory to enforce a primary or unique key. However, it may not be practical in all situations not to have an index to perform the enforcement, especially on large tables.
- **Rule- and cost-based optimization** RBO is supported in all versions of Oracle7 and Oracle8. RULE, COST, or CHOOSE can be used as a value for the OPTIMIZER_MODE initialization parameter. This setting is of paramount importance in the way Oracle8 uses indexes. For example, RBO merges non-unique indexes only when equality predicates are being

applied in the WHERE clause. This is to avoid the additional processing that would be required to process range predicates with multiple non-unique indexes. Such additional processing would impede performance more than the indexes would help. Under CBO, such merging of indexes would not necessarily happen if the cost of doing the merge were higher than the cost of using multiple non-unique indexes. There are various such intricate differences between how RBO handles indexes and how CBO handles them. In addition, certain newer index types and access paths are available only while using CBO, including bitmapped indexes, partitioned indexes, and fast full index scans (FFIS).

With changes in CBO in almost every new release, never assume that your DML statements are using a certain index. Always run an EXPLAIN PLAN on every important DML statement to ensure use of the right indexes.

- **Analysis of tables and indexes** CBO requires all tables and indexes to be analyzed periodically, especially after periods of high DML activity. These statistics are used by CBO to evaluate the "cost" of all available access paths; the path with the lowest cost is selected.
- **Use of hints to force index selection** Under both RBO and CBO, certain hints may be provided to DML statements to specifically select a certain index. This functionality is provided to override the optimizer, in case the access path selected by it is sub-optimal. Syntax for hints is very similar to that for comments, except for the addition of a plus (+) symbol. If a hint is provided incorrectly, the optimizer ignores the hint. This is an example of a hint:

```
SELECT /*+ INDEX(table_a, index_a) */ id, name FROM table_a;
```

- Index-related hints supported by Oracle8 include INDEX/INDEX_ASC, INDEX_DESC, INDEX_COMBINE, INDEX_FFS, and PARALLEL_INDEX for retrieving rows from indexes in an ascending order, retrieving them in a descending order, combining bitmapped indexes using Boolean logic, prompting the optimizer to use the fast full index scan in lieu of a full-table scan, and inducing a parallel scan of an index (using PQO), respectively.

B*Tree Indexes: Everybody's Favorite Index

This is one of the earliest indexing options available in Oracle. The Oracle documentation assumes that all the readers are absolutely familiar with this index type. But my experience at various client sites indicates the contrary. Not many developers and DBAs understand or remember a B*Tree structure. Good use of these "basic" indexes requires a good understanding of how B*Tree indexes

operate. Implementations of B*Trees are a little unique in every application in terms of their height and order. However, the basic behavior is the same. Let's take a quick practical look at how B*Trees indexes have been implemented in Oracle.

B*Trees are an excellent way of looking up pointers to large information with a minimal number of disk reads. In a B*Tree, all information is either a branch/root node or a leaf node. The final information (ROWIDs and keys) is always stored in a leaf (node). Up to 16 columns can compose the key in Oracle7.*x*; whereas in Oracle8, the limit is 32 columns. Furthermore, a key cannot be greater than one-third the size of the database block (violating this restriction would result in the ORA-01450 error). A leaf may contain multiple physical rows. The leaves are always present only at the last "level." A B*Tree is a "balanced tree" because every leaf is equidistant from the root node. It takes the same time to access any row in any given leaf. Figure 6-5 is a picture of a basic B*Tree implementation. It clearly indicates the root, the branches, and the leaves. Every tree has a certain order and height. The order is the number of "branches" for every node of the tree. The height is the number of levels the tree contains. Ideally, the height has to be minimal, since the number of reads required to get information is proportionate to the height of the tree. In Figure 6-5, for example, in order to locate "R," two reads are required ("M" at the root node and "S" at the second-level node). Thus, here, a minimum of three reads would be required to locate a key (two reads at the root/branch level and the third at the leaf-node level). It is to be borne in mind that each read may be a logical read or a physical read, depending on how the index is laid out. If a single read operation places the required number of blocks in memory, subsequent reads will be performed from memory; otherwise, they will need to go to disk. The height is inversely proportionate to the order. The higher the order, the lower the height (termed as a "flat" tree). An important objective in any B*Tree implementation is to increase the branches and reduce the height, thereby ensuring speedy access to the leaves.

A major challenge with a B*Tree implementation occurs during INSERTs, DELETEs, and UPDATEs. During every INSERT, the key has to be inserted appropriately within the right leaf. Every key has one and only one place within the tree. If the leaf is already full and cannot accommodate any additional keys, then the leaf has to be split into two. Here, there are two options available:

- If the new key value is the biggest (of all the keys existing in the old leaf block), then the total keys are split in a 99:1 ratio, wherein only the new key is placed in the new leaf block, and the rest of the (old) keys are retained within the old leaf block (including all deleted keys).
- If the new key value is not the biggest, then the total keys are split in a 50:50 ratio, wherein each of the leaf blocks (old and new) will absorb half the keys of the original leaf.

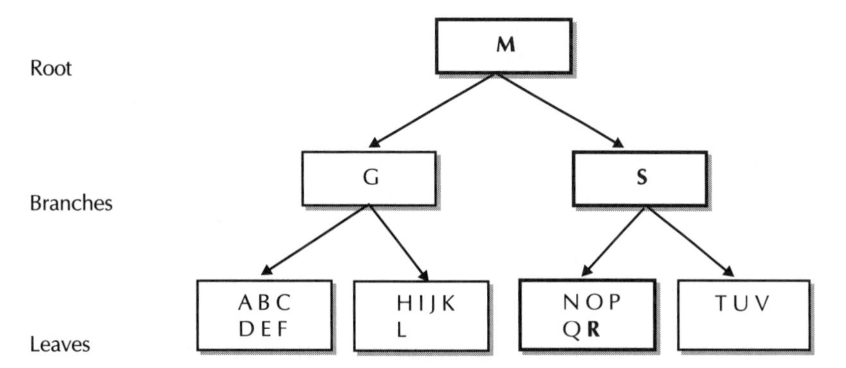

FIGURE 6-5. *A simplistic B*Tree implementation (height: 2 and order: 2) (Nodes read to locate R are displayed in bold)*

This split has to be propagated upward to the parent node by means of a new entry to point to the new leaves. If the parent node happens to be full, then the node has to be split into two and its parent has to be notified of the split. God forbid, if that parent is full, as well! Thus, a split may be propagated all the way up to the root node itself. Remember, each split is costly, involving physical disk I/O. Additionally, prior to splitting, Oracle has to seek and find an empty block to accommodate the split. The following steps are taken to do so:

1. Seek in the index free-list for a free block. More than one free-list can be defined for an index (via the CREATE/ALTER INDEX commands). Free-lists for indexes do not aid Oracle in finding an available block for accommodating the new key value being inserted. This is because a key value cannot be randomly placed in the first "free" leaf block that's available within the index. The value has to be placed within a specific leaf block after appropriate sorting. Free-lists in indexes are used only during block splitting. Each free-list comprises a linked list of "empty" blocks. When more than one free-list is defined for an index, the free-list allotted to the process is initially scanned for a free block. If none are found, the master free-list is checked.
2. If no free blocks are found, Oracle tries to allocate another extent. If there is no free space in the tablespace, Oracle gives an error (ORA-01654).
3. If a free block is found via either of the preceding steps, the high-watermark for the index is increased.
4. The free block found is used to perform the split.

Part of the challenge in creating B*Tree indexes is to avoid splits at runtime, or rather, to induce splits during index creation ("pre-splitting") and take the performance hit at that point in time, and not during runtime inserts. These splits may not be restricted merely to inserts; they may occur during updates, as well.

Let's take a look at what goes on within Oracle during an indexed-key UPDATE. Index updates differ vastly from table updates. In a table update, data is changed within the data block (assuming there is sufficient space in the block for this change to take place). In an index, however, when a key is changed, its position within the tree has to change. Remember, a key has one and only one position within a B*Tree. So when it changes, *the old entry has to be deleted and a new one has to be created at a new leaf.* Chances are, the old entry may never be reused. This is because Oracle will reuse a key-entry slot only during very specific situations, such as when the newly inserted key is exactly the same as an old (deleted) one, including data type, length, and case. And what are the chances of that happening? Many applications at my client sites use a *sequence* to generate NUMBER keys (especially primary keys). Unless they are using the RECYCLE option, the sequences do not generate the same number twice. Thus, the deleted space within the index remains unused. This is the reason that during large-scale deletes and updates, the table size shrinks or at least remains constant, whereas the indexes *grow* continuously.

From the preceding explanation of B*Trees, the following do's and don'ts emerge:

- Avoid indexing columns that are subject to high updates.
- Avoid indexing multiple columns in tables that are subject to high deletes. If possible, only index the primary key and/or column(s) determining the deletes on such tables. If indexing multiple columns is unavoidable, then consider partitioning the tables according to those columns and do a TRUNCATE on each such partition (instead of a DELETE). TRUNCATE simulates a drop and re-create of the table *and* index by resetting the high-water mark, when used with the DROP STORAGE clause.
- Avoid creating B*Tree indexes for columns with low cardinality (less uniqueness). Such low selectivity leads to dense leaf blocks, causing large-scale index scans due to the indexes being "flat." The higher the uniqueness, the better the performance, since range scans will be reduced, and maybe even be replaced, with a unique scan.
- Null values are never stored in single-column indexes. In the case of compound indexes, the value is stored only if one of the columns is not null. Bear this in mind while constructing IS NULL or IS NOT NULL clauses for DML statements. An IS NULL will not induce an index scan, whereas an unrestrained IS NOT NULL may cause a *full* index scan.

You have heard this advice before, but now the precise logic behind these words of wisdom is apparent.

The Importance of PCTFREE

For a B*Tree index, PCTFREE determines the extent of a leaf split. In other words, PCTFREE indicates the amount of free space within a block for "future updates." However, in the case of an index (unlike a table), these *updates* do not make sense, since an update forces a delete and subsequent insert anyway.

In the case of indexes, PCTFREE plays a role mostly at the time of index creation. A non-zero value specifies the block-splitting ratio. If PCTFREE is set to 20 during index creation, up to 80 percent of the leaf may contain key information. However, the remaining 20 percent should be available for future inserts of key information into that leaf block. This ensures minimal overhead during runtime inserts in terms of incurring leaf-block splits. Even though a higher PCTFREE may cause index-creation time to increase, it prevents the performance hit from being deferred to actual use time. So the end user who is waiting for a row to be inserted does not incur the performance penalty associated with a leaf-block split.

Based on this information, the following points emerge:

- PCTFREE for an index is used primarily during creation. It is ignored during actual use.
- Specify a higher PCTFREE for OLTP applications if the table is a popular one, incurring a lot of DML changes (via interactive user screens);
- Specify a lower PCTFREE if the index-creation time is critical. This will pack in more rows per leaf block, thereby avoiding the need for further splitting at creation time. This is of significance to 24×7 shops. Index creation in most cases requires considerable downtime (especially if the table is a multi-million row table). The shorter the index-creation time, the smaller can be the maintenance window. I have seen this tiny, often unnoticed parameter save around 20 percent of index-creation time. At a high-availability site, an index on a table containing around 11 million rows took me about 80 minutes to build using a PCTFREE value of 30 and a parallel degree of 4. The same index on the same table, with 13.5 million rows took me around 90 minutes to create with a PCTFREE of 0 (without any hardware/software enhancements). NOLOGGING (minimal redo) was on during both creations. As a side note, Oracle8*i* allows concurrent DML while an index is being built, thus greatly reducing downtime.
- For any column where the values are constantly increasing, it is probably a good idea to set a very low PCTFREE (even zero). This is because only the rightmost leaf block will always be inserted into. This will make the tree

grow toward the right. The leftmost leaves will remain static. So there is no sense in leaving any part of those blocks empty with a non-zero PCTFREE.

Partitioned Indexes

Partitioned indexes are indexes that have been horizontally sub-divided according to a specific range of key values. Partitioning allows logically dependent structures to be physically independent. This allows maintenance operations to be performed on a specific partition while the others are still available for access. Thus, a specific partition may be offline and unavailable, while the other partitions are online and available for access. With a "rolling-window" scheme (where data for a pre-determined period may be stored in partitions so that the older partitions can be easily truncated [after archiving the old data, if necessary] to keep the data relevant to the selected period), data management becomes very simple and non-resource intensive. An index partition may be rebuilt or recovered with minimal effect on applications. Each index partition may have different storage characteristics and may be created in different tablespaces. Partitioned indexes may be created even for non-partitioned tables.

The text that follows offers some partitioned index–related concepts.

GLOBAL AND LOCAL INDEXES When an index is partitioned in a similar fashion as the table, in terms of ranges of partition keys, then it is referred to as a local index. In other words, the local index shares the key ranges with the parent table. It will store the keys of only its corresponding table partition. A global index does not have a one-to-one correspondence with any table partition in terms of partition-key ranges. A global index will store rows from multiple table partitions. A local index is also referred to as an equipartitioned index, whereas a global index is also referred to as a non-equipartitioned index.

For example, a table may be partitioned into 52 segments based on the week of year. However, the index may be partitioned into 12 segments based on month of year. Such an index would be termed a global index. If the index were partitioned into 52 segments, it would be referred to as a local index.

A bitmapped index on a partitioned table has to be a local index.

PREFIXED AND NON-PREFIXED INDEXES When an index of a partitioned table contains the partition key as the leading column, it is termed as a prefixed index. A non-prefixed index does not have partition-key columns as the leading keys.

Local prefixed indexes should be created whenever possible. Since they have a one-to-one correspondence with the partitioned table, administration is easier. Global prefixed indexes theoretically may have a slight performance edge at times, since the overhead of accessing a large number of indexes is avoided. However, *partition pruning* (where the partition-key value specified in the WHERE clause helps Oracle in determining which partition might contain the required results and accesses only that partition) helps in super-charging local partition access. Even in situations where partition pruning is not possible, parallel access of multiple local indexes via PQO may provide higher performance. It is generally more expensive to scan a non-prefixed index than to a prefixed index since, as mentioned earlier, in the case of a prefixed index, the optimizer can use the partition-key value to scan just the necessary index partitions (rather than all) for a predicate referring to the indexed columns.

Oracle8 (as of v8.0.*x*) does not support global non-prefixed indexes, since they do not have any practical utility. A global index may be split into local indexes, or multiple local indexes may be merged into a global one.

Considering Partitioned Indexes

Let me illustrate this "partitioning scenario" with an example. One of my clients is a company providing free e-mail via the Web. Their users receive a lot of e-mail. When a user deletes a message, the mail entry is "deleted" from the main-messages table and moved to a *garbage bin*. This is achieved by setting the garbage-flag to '1' for that row in the main table. Only when the user specifically deletes it from his garbage bin is the mail permanently deleted. Many users set up their account such that once a week, their garbage bin is automatically purged. So, every weekend, this huge batch job was run to delete all rows from the main table where the garbage-flag = '1'. Since the garbage-flag column was being used in the WHERE clause of the DELETE, it was part of a regular B*Tree index (a bitmapped index was not used even though the cardinality was low, because the column was subject to high updates and another key column was being used as the index prefix). However, every time it was updated to '1', its index entry would be deleted and a new one would be created. Furthermore, when the record would finally be deleted, the index entry would continue to take up space. Thus the table would not significantly grow in size (due to e-mail being deleted and inserted all the time). However, the index was growing at an incredible rate, taking up large amounts of tablespace area. Finally, this problem was solved by replacing the design with a "partition-aware" design.

Consider partitioning indexes for

- Intense OLTP applications, dealing with a large number of rows. The flexibility in administering relatively small segments is a great boon.
- High-availability (24x7) environments, where the downtime associated with an index rebuild cannot be tolerated.
- Better overall performance. Whenever possible, Oracle8 parallelizes scans of partitioned indexes. Also, partition pruning or *partition elimination* allows specific partitions to be eliminated from searches based on the key ranges. This vastly expedites index scans. Finally, partitioning allows an index to be spread out over multiple physical tablespaces/data-files, thereby reducing the occurrence of I/O hot spots.

Do not partition indexes on key values prone to constant updates, especially if such updates may cause partition migration, where a row has to be moved from one partition to another. Such migration is not allowed.

Last, one question that pops up frequently at client sites is, how canmany partitions be realistically created without any performance degradation? Theory apart (where thousands and thousands of partitions can be created), the answer to this question depends on various factors such as system resources (CPUs, memory, I/O channels across which the partitions are created, and so on) and varies from site to site. A lot also depends on applications and data. If the data lends itself to a "clean" partitioning structure, based on a popular (frequently used in most queries) key column(s), then partitioning across a large number of partitions would be more effective, since partition pruning is possible in most situations. If such a popular key column is not available, however, then utilizing a large number of partitions may cause performance degradation, since multiple partitions would need to be frequently visited to retrieve the required values. Accordingly, it is always essential to ensure that you select a popular key column as the partitioning key. If such a column does not currently exist, evaluate introducing it explicitly (for instance, by denormalizing the table). Additionally, always ensure that there is sufficient scope for parallelizing partitioned operations (multiple CPUs, data spread across multiple disks/controllers, and so on). I have found partitioning to be very effective in certain situations, when the number of partitions does not exceed a few hundred. After that, the law of diminishing returns comes into play, as system resources get saturated and performance begins to stink.

Reverse-Key Indexes

A reverse-key index is primarily a B*Tree index, where the bytes of key values are stored in a reverse order. By reversing the keys, index entries are spread more evenly throughout the B*Tree. This is very useful in an OPS (Oracle Parallel Server) environment, where contention for the same leaf blocks might cause inter-instance "pinging" to occur, thereby affecting performance adversely due to excessive disk I/O. Thus, contention for leaf blocks or uneven density in leaf blocks primarily calls for reverse-key indexes.

Examples of a reversed key are as follows:

```
PEACOCK        KCOCAEP
1558           8551
```

Dates in a reverse-key index are stored by reversing the seven bytes contained in a DATE data type.

Considering Reverse-Key Indexes

At a client site in late 1996, our team was implementing a Custodial Services system. We faced a major performance impediment with the *share-certificates* table, especially when the clients would acquire a large number of share certificates with sequential numbering. We had created the right index on the table and had ensured that the index was indeed being used. However, even a pure index access would take unusually long: at least 15 seconds more than what we expected (based on our experiments with other, similar tables). Finally, we figured out that storing those sequential certificate numbers caused the index to be lopsided. In other words, some of the leaves would be dense (heavily populated), whereas some of them would be sparse, based on the series of share certificates we obtained. Most DML activity would focus on these dense leaves, thereby creating "hot spots" on the index. By hot spots, I mean index activity would be much more for these few leaf blocks, compared to the others. Since there would usually be only one disk controller accessing those blocks, all activity would have to be serialized, thereby adversely affecting response time and throughput.

In such a situation, reverse-key indexes would have been a boon. However, we were using Oracle7 v7.3 at that time, where the feature was still not available. We lived with the situation for a while. Finally, we circumvented the situation by reversing the values within the application. We had two columns in the table—a column that would store the share-certificate number as it was and a primary-key column that would store the same share certificate in a reversed order. We wrote a stored function that would accept the actual share certificate as an input parameter and return the reversed number, which would subsequently be inserted in the table as the primary key. This gave us a relatively "well-balanced" index.

The same concept applies to any value that increases in spurts: sequential numbers, date and time columns, and so on. Increasing in spurts indicates a scenario where the value monotonously increases; then there is not much activity for a while, thereby creating "gaps" in the values; and then the value constantly increases again. Such columns would be prime candidates for using the Oracle8 reverse-key indexes. Also, in fast-growing tables where indexes are built on sequential values (such as a primary-key index) and large-scale deletes frequently occur, the index may begin to "slide." A sliding index is one that continuously grows toward the right (newer rows being inserted), while the left portion is constantly being deleted (older rows being purged). The left portions of the tree consist of nulls or empty leaf nodes, whereas the tree is expanding to the right, thus appearing to "slide." Reversing the index may halt the right-oriented growth (due to constantly increasing key values) and make the growth more balanced by placing the reversed key values in all directions (left and right). Additionally, partitioning the index (on a "rolling window" scheme) and truncating older partitions (rather than deleting) would help in eliminating the large number of empty leaf blocks.

One question might come to your mind: How did we manage to figure out that our index was indeed lopsided? We used the "ALTER SESSION SET EVENTS . . . TREEDUMP . . . " command to understand the index structure better. This command may even be used to figure out whether an index is "flat" (as in columns with low cardinality, wherein there will be a large number of key values within a leaf node, thus causing heavy range-scans). This command is mentioned in detail in Chapter 12.

Some caveats to bear in mind while using reverse-key indexes:

- Reverse-key indexes are not effective when used in range scans.
- Reverse-key indexes are prone to all the restrictions of regular B*Tree indexes, such as avoiding excessive DML activity, periodic rebuilding, and so on (since they are merely a variation of B*Trees).

Index-Organized Tables (IOTs)

Index-organized tables are tables where the rows are stored in a B*Tree structure, based on the primary-key value. A primary-key definition is mandatory for an IOT. In Oracle8 v8.0.x, IOTs do not have ROWIDs. An index entry is expected to be terse to remain effective. Since a full-fledged row may be too big to retain index-effectiveness, Oracle8 provides the PCTTHRESHOLD clause to indicate a percentage of the total block size. All non-primary-key columns that cause a row to grow beyond the size of this percentage are moved to an "overflow" tablespace.

Considering Index-Organized Tables

A short while ago, I was part of a team building a large data-warehouse for a major investment company. In the data-warehouse, we have a bunch of code tables, acting as dimension tables. In the first iteration of the physical design, we built all those code tables as regular tables with two columns: the code ID and the description. We had a primary-key index on the code ID. We also cached some of these tables and their indexes in the SGA.

Later, with more familiarity with Oracle8, we observed that these code tables were prime candidates for using the index-organized table feature. Since there was only one index on each of these tables, we could use the primary key to structure the rows in these tables in a B*Tree format. In the second iteration of the physical design, we redefined most of our code tables as index-organized tables. It did not bring about any noticeable performance benefit. However, it brought us space savings to the tune of 35 percent. From around 800MB for both regular tables and the primary-key indexes, the space consumption has dropped to approximately 520MB for the index-organized tables. These space savings affect not only disk space consumption but also memory consumption (since many of the tables were cached). That is *true* space savings for us, since memory is always at a premium! This allows more data to be cached within the SGA, without having to expand it.

Needless to add, this space saving is obtained due to absence of the ROWIDs and any indexes on the index-organized tables. This example illustrates that tables such as code tables or certain master tables not prone to frequent changes are ideal for using the index-organized feature of Oracle8, provided additional indexes are not needed. Also, the best candidates for creating as an IOT or converting to an IOT will be tables with smaller-sized rows, where the rows do not reach the threshold specified. That may cause an effect similar to row chaining, since multiple I/Os may be required to read the entire row, thus degrading performance. This useful option brings substantial space savings to the table, especially when going from a regular table with an index comprised of most of the columns in the table (built that way to exploit the "index-only lookup" access path) to an index-organized table.

Some caveats with IOTs in v8.0.*x*:

- The table structure cannot be altered.
- The primary-key is mandatory.
- Non-primary-key indexes cannot be created.
- Absence of ROWIDs might cause problems while migrating Oracle7 applications to Oracle8, if the application DML explicitly depends on ROWIDs.
- Row-chaining is inevitable with large-sized rows.

Bitmapped Indexes

The biggest difference between a B*Tree index and a bitmapped index is that the former encourages indexing on columns with high selectivity, whereas the latter encourages low selectivity. This is primarily due to inherent structural differences. A bitmapped index creates a binary bitmap stream, consisting of 1's and 0's for every distinct key value. Due to application of bit-level binary arithmetic, large numbers of rows can be processed at high speeds. Also, if a table has multiple low-cardinality columns, then bitmap indexes may be created on each of those columns. Multiple indexes in turn can be merged using bit-level Boolean logic resulting in very fast index-access times. In the case of compound indexes, a bitmapped index can have up

to a maximum of 14 columns in Oracle7.*x* and up to 30 columns in Oracle8 v8.0.*x* (always 2 less than B*Tree indexes). Bitmapped indexes are available only with CBO.

Bitmapped indexes are stored in compressed form, thereby causing huge space savings. Oracle uses a proprietary compression algorithm, capable of handling even high-cardinality columns (this is useful in scenarios such as a star schema, where the dimension tables have very high cardinality). On a data-warehouse at a client site, a B*tree index on a column with two distinct values on a table with 12 million rows took up around 184MB, whereas a bitmapped index on the same column took up a mere 3MB—a direct saving of more than 98 percent disk space!

The new *star-transformation* access path in Oracle8 uses bitmapped indexes to merge results from multiple-dimension tables with a large fact table to produce extremely fast query results, without having to perform an expensive Cartesian product as in a regular *star* query.

A good example of a candidate for a bitmapped index would be the "salaried status" column in the employee table in a data-mart for the personnel department. Let's say the "salaried status" column has a domain consisting of the following values: "Salaried" (employee), "Hourly" (consultant/contractor), "1099" (consultant/contractor). A logical view of the bitmapped index created on this column is represented in Table 6-8.

From a physical standpoint, each bitmap stream consists of a header portion and a body, wherein the header comprises the key value and the beginning and ending rowids for a range of rows having that key value. The body comprises the actual bitmap stream for the same range of rows. The size of the body is guaranteed to be 50 percent or less of the initialization parameter DB_BLOCK_SIZE. Thus, a bitmap may be stored as smaller pieces to adhere to this rule. The physical structure is depicted in Figure 6-6.

Domain Value	**Salaried**	**Hourly**	**1099**	**Bitmap Pattern**
Employee last name				
Smith	1	0	0	100
White	0	0	1	001
Brown	0	1	0	010

TABLE 6-8. *A "Logical View" of a Bitmapped Index. Column "Bitmap Pattern" Provides the Index-Key Pattern (a Bit May Be Either On [1] or Off [0])*

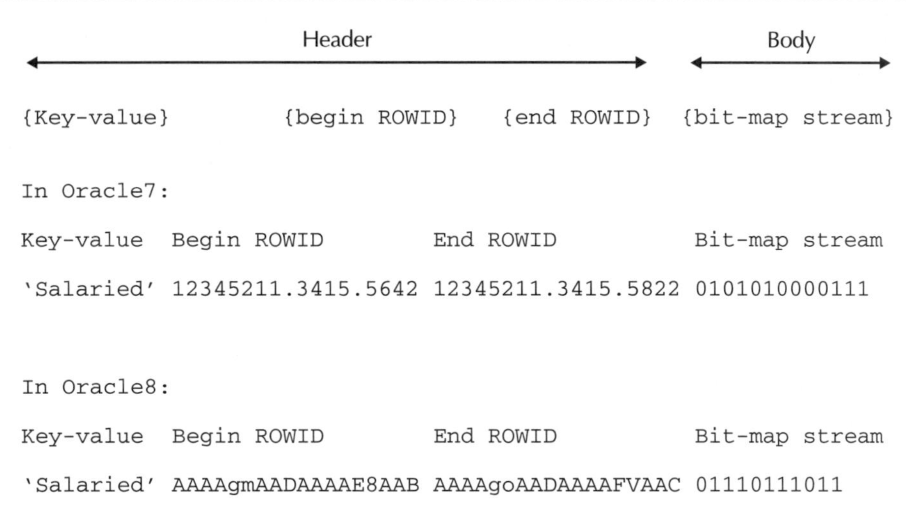

FIGURE 6-6. *A "physical view" of a bitmapped index*

B*Tree structures are used even within a bitmapped index. The leaf nodes of the B*Tree store the bitmaps corresponding to each key value. The begin-rowid and end-rowid specify the range of the table that is covered by the given bitmap. The rowid is an internal structure used by Oracle to uniquely identify each row. Externally, it consists of 18 bytes, whereas internal it is 6 bytes in Oracle7 and 10 bytes in Oracle8. It holds physical storage information such as the object ID, data-file number, block number within the data-file, and a row-serial number within the block. Based on the rowid and the table/column structure, the maximum number of rows with a specific key value that can be accommodated within a single bitmap stream is determined. The downside to using the table/column structure to determine the bitmap stream is that the bitmapped index may be invalidated due to certain changes to the table structure. The key columns' data types and sizes provide insight on the space required to hold each key value. Key columns declared as NOT NULL (for instance, mandatory foreign keys) will cause Oracle to create more condensed bitmap patterns, since bit-masking with OFF bits is reduced. (OFF bits are used to act as a "buffer" in case optional columns have values. With mandatory columns, such buffering is not required, since every column will definitely have some value.) Accordingly, it is recommended to explicitly declare mandatory columns on which bitmapped indexes would be created, as NOT NULL.

Bitmapped indexes can withstand a decent amount of DML. However, it's recommended to drop and re-create them during very large data loads. Certain tools, such as SQL*Loader in Oracle8, automatically re-create the bitmapped indexes during

large loads (unless the SINGLEROW option is specified) by sorting the data loaded and updating the existing bitmap steams. By default, Oracle keeps bitmapped indexes current during DML operations via a "delayed maintenance" algorithm. Here, index maintenance is performed at the statement level, rather than at the row level. All DML changes are logged as the statement is being executed, and Oracle waits for the statement to complete. Once it is complete, the following steps are taken:

- The DML changes are sorted.
- The index is read in from disk.
- The index is uncompressed.
- The changes are integrated with the existing bitmap patterns in the index.
- The index is compressed.
- The index is written back to disk.

This delayed maintenance algorithm results in high throughput. When loads are performed on partitioned tables, parallelism is used to speed up bitmap maintenance. At times, it may even be faster than changes to B*Tree indexes (as explained earlier, changing a B*Tree may involve a lot of work).

Bitmapped indexes can provide very high throughput in specific situations where B*Tree indexes cannot be used effectively, due to low cardinality or inability of multiple B*Tree indexes to be merged as efficiently as bitmapped indexes (bitmapped indexes use bit-level set operations such as minus, union, intersection, and so on, to merge with each other to satisfy diverse WHERE clauses). Accordingly, a full-table scan is often the only feasible alternative to a bitmapped index. Full-table scans can be very expensive for large tables due to the heavy I/O processing involved. Bitmapped indexes, on the other hand, are lean and can be read with a substantially lesser number of I/O operations, since they are stored in a compressed form. Uncompressing the bitmap generally does not require I/O (unless the system is low on memory). It may involve additional context switches. However, even that will be a lot faster than I/O processing.

Here are a few things to consider prior to creating a bitmap index:

- Is the table often queried by this column? If not, is an index really needed on the column?
- How many rows are present in the table? A small table (a few thousand rows) does not warrant a bitmapped index. A full-table scan will generally be much faster in such situations.
- What is the cardinality of the column? At client sites, developers and DBAs often get confused about whether a bitmapped index will be appropriate on

a high-cardinality column. The reason for this confusion is that various publications often recommend bitmapped indexes for low cardinality columns and B*Tree indexes for high-cardinality columns. However, there are situations where bitmapped indexes become necessary even for high-cardinality columns. For instance, in order to make use of the new *star transformation* path in Oracle8, bitmapped indexes need to be created on the foreign-key columns of the fact table. However, if the dimension table has a large number of rows, then the cardinality of the foreign key will be high. Accordingly, it is easy to be confused regarding whether to create the bitmapped index and use *star transformation* or not to create the bitmapped index and use an alternative path. As may be apparent from the preceding paragraphs, bitmapped indexes are capable of handling even high cardinality. Accordingly, they ought to be created in the situation outlined previously. In situations where the cardinality appears very high, however, the creation of bitmapped indexes will have to be properly evaluated against other criteria.

There are times when client personnel ask me whether a bitmapped index on a column with a couple of thousand distinct values would be effective. Rather than looking only at the number of unique values, a better way of measuring whether a bitmapped index would be effective or not would be to examine the degree of uniqueness (that is, number of unique values / total number of rows in the table × 100). For instance, if there are a few million rows in the table, a few thousand unique values would not matter. However, if the degree of uniqueness is very high (for instance, if in a ten thousand–row table there are six thousand distinct values), then a bitmapped index may not be appropriate—rather a B*Tree index would be. The degree of uniqueness would also affect the capability of the index to be compressed. A low degree of uniqueness would produce higher compression and vice versa. Always look at the big picture (total number of rows *and* the cardinality) prior to deciding.

- Is the column prone to frequent heavy-duty DML operations? Is a tool being used to perform the DML? If so, does the tool maintain bitmapped indexes automatically? If not, can the bitmap index be dropped prior to the load and re-created after the load?
- Are there multiple columns in the table that are good candidates for bitmapped indexes? If so, will such columns be frequently referred to in the WHERE clause of queries? If so, there are high chances of the bitmapped indexes on these columns being merged by CBO to provide high query throughput.

- Is the data in the table subject to frequent changes simultaneously by multiple users? If so, a bitmapped index may not be convenient. Bitmapped indexes restrict concurrency, due to the entire bitmap being locked during a single DML operation affecting any row in the range of rows represented by the bitmap. This could potentially cause hundreds of rows to be locked by a single DML statement intended to affect a single row. This is not an issue during parallel DML operations affecting partitioned tables, since index maintenance during parallel DML occurs at the partition level. Accordingly, a single index partition is not subjected to parallelism, thus leading to concurrency problems.

Abstract Data Types and Their Indexes

Peek into your abstract data types with a magnifying glass to identify the scalar data types, which need indexing. Once the abstract type has been broken down into scalars, all the previously mentioned indexing rules apply to them. Whenever possible, ensure that all your DML specifies the absolute path to these scalar types (else the optimizer may not use the right index). By absolute path, I mean "person.name.last_name" and not just "person" or even "person.name."

Function-Based Indexing

This new feature introduced in Oracle8*i* allows functions to be indexed and used in SQL statements. Earlier Oracle releases expressly disabled index use when functions were utilized on the key column. Now, however, SQL or user-defined functions can be indexed. For instance, a query such as the following will benefit tremendously from function-based indexes:

```
SQL> SELECT * FROM names WHERE INITCAP(name) LIKE 'Joy%';
```

An index can be created on a function as follows:

```
SQL> CREATE INDEX upper_nm_idx03 ON names(INITCAP(name))
     TABLESPACE <some_tblspc> STORAGE(<some_storage>);
```

Now, applications can issue case-insensitive queries such as the following:

```
SQL> SELECT * FROM name WHERE name LIKE 'Joy%';
```

Function-based indexes are also physically stored in a B*Tree structure. Refer to the Oracle8*i* documentation set (*Oracle8i Concepts*) for a further explanation of function-based indexing. Also, an article entitled *Digging-in to Function-Based Indexes* by Tom Kyte (part of the *Digging-in to Oracle8i* series) provides excellent information on the subject. This article can be found online at http://technet.oracle.com or http://www.oracle.com/ideveloper (*Internet Developer* magazine).

Application Domain Indexes

Application domain indexes are "extended" indexes specific to a certain application domain. These are indexes created on non-conventional data types (domains), such as spatial data, and multimedia data types, such as images and audio/video streams, spreadsheets and documents, and so on. Here, an encapsulated set of code routines referred to as an *indextype* defines the index access and implementation rules for efficient and speedy retrieval of complex domains. A data cartridge is custom built (via the *Oracle8i Data-Cartridge Interface*) to define the application that controls the domain and also defines the inherent structure of the domain index. In other words, all operations performed on the index, such as range scans and equality checks, need to be explicitly defined. The index can be stored inside the database as an index-organized table or externally as a file. As of Oracle8*i* v8.1.5, a domain index can have only a single column. This column can be a regular scalar data type or a user-defined attribute of an object or a LOB. Information on domain indexes (meta-data) cannot be found in conventional index-related views such as DBA_INDEXES and USER_INDEXES. The data cartridge needs to utilize a specific index meta-data management strategy and nominate a predefined table to hold the meta-data on domain indexes of a certain *indextype*. Furthermore, wrapper views can be created on top of the meta-data table, if necessary, for additional encapsulation.

The Oracle8*i* documentation set (*Oracle8i Data Cartridge Developer's Guide*) discusses application domain indexes in detail.

As you may see, Oracle8 and 8*i* have vastly increased the number of indexing options available. However, regular B*Tree indexes continue to offer the best solution in most cases. As long as they are well maintained, they provide acceptable performance under diverse conditions. However, certain situations, explained previously, prove to be ideal for deviating from the B*Tree approach and instead using another index type, such as bitmapped, or even variations of the B*Tree, such as reverse-key, partitioned, or index-organized tables. With the versatile index offerings of Oracle8/8*i*, there has never been a better time to put on that new thinking cap and look at the process of indexing as an art, not a science!

Use threads, rather than processes, in your applications

Threads are multiple simultaneous sequences of execution emanating from a single process. Threads can be used to increase parallelism without incurring high overhead. Prior to threads, parallelism was achieved by invoking the same process multiple times. However, each process has its separate stack and data segments, resulting in high overhead. Threads share the same process space as the original process from which they are created. This drastically reduces CPU and memory requirements. Creating a thread is substantially quicker than creating a process,

since the base process already exists. A cost of using threads is the inter-thread communication that must be achieved in order to coordinate the work done by individual threads. However, this is almost negligible compared to inter-process communication overheads while using multiple processes in lieu of threads. Since threads share the same address space, overhead is extremely low.

If your platform supports thread-safe applications, do encourage your programmers to use threads while developing new applications. Also, if possible, ensure that third-party applications that you purchase and deploy are multi-threaded. Many sites are reevaluating and creating threaded versions of existing applications. The Oracle Server itself is multi-threaded, and its development tools, such as Pro*C/C++ (version 2.2 onward), include new thread-enabled libraries and commands that allow creation of multi-threaded applications. As mentioned earlier, on Windows NT, the entire Oracle Server architecture is thread-based.

Certain platforms support multiple thread standards (example, Sun Solaris supports Solaris threads, as well as POSIX threads). Encourage use of POSIX threads, wherever possible, to create more portable applications.

Use shared libraries in your applications

In your C, Pro*C/C++, or other precompiler applications, encourage use of shared libraries whenever possible. Shared libraries help conserve memory. Before addressing the memory advantage, let's understand in detail how shared libraries differ from their more conventional cousins— static libraries.

Any application (written in a language such as C or C++) is a collection of source-code files, consisting of a lot of custom code and calls to predefined library routines. The custom code will handle the business logic specific to your company, and the library routines will handle specific common functions, including conversion to uppercase, error-condition checks, and so on. Library functions help prevent reinventing the wheel for miniscule reusable tasks. Each source file will be compiled; the source code will be checked for errors and then converted to an intermediate object file. Each object file consists of relatively error-free code and a number of links to specific library routines, which remain unresolved. Then all the object files and necessary library files are linked together to resolve all these tangled-up calls. Now here's where we come to the main part of the story. There are two ways to resolve all the library calls: either by statically embedding each library call used into the actual code or by putting in "jump-links" to each library routine. The former method is referred to as "static" linking, and the latter method is called "dynamic" linking. A typical Windows user can relate to this concept by thinking of OLE (Object Linking and Embedding).

Static linking uses libraries in a static manner, since the library routines are sewn into the code; dynamic linking allows the libraries to be shared between different program files, and thus remain independent of the code. Links to shared libraries are resolved at runtime by locating the appropriate library link via the inserted "jump-link" and dynamically loading the routines in memory.

From a memory perspective, the shared libraries allow an application to use a lot less memory than static libraries, because the reference to each library routine is loaded in only once and not duplicated with every call to the routine. (While using static libraries, repeated calls to the same library routine will result in that routine being embedded multiple times in the code, resulting in "fatter" code that will take up more memory to load.) Additionally, each individual program file will be smaller, taking up less disk space, since the library code is not embedded. In fact, most major applications, including Oracle on UNIX, use shared libraries. At times, however, static libraries may provide superior performance, since there is no need to seek and load the library routines at runtime. However, this runtime delay will generally be incurred only the first time the program is run. Every subsequent call should be a lot faster, since the routine has already been loaded into memory.

Invest time in physical database design

Most companies are typically in a hurry when it comes to deploying an application. Teams tend to spend quite a bit of time in analysis, design, and coding. However, the design mostly consists of conceptual/logical and some physical design. The physical design aspect is often sorely incomplete and misses the database design stage altogether. With teams spending substantial time in other areas that are thought to be more "necessary" and, generally, overstepping their budgets and deadlines, they try to race for the finish line with little time to spare. Along the way, all unimportant or not-as-important steps are skipped in their haste. And part of this is due to lack of sufficient knowledge about database design. Many teams are not aware of what Oracle physical design fully involves. As a result, no strong business case can be made for not skipping it or not spending substantial time in that area.

When the application is ready to be deployed, the DBA is asked to look at everything and make sure there is no obvious problem. Instructions are provided on what kind of database environment is desired, and the DBA hastens to create a database of the required size (the required size is determined after some quick calculations, mainly involving average row size of each table times the number of rows in that table plus some buffer space). Then the application is formally "live." Then come the end users, frequently followed by performance and availability problems. Time out! Database physical design is absolutely required to avoid many post-deployment problems. The topic of physical database design is a vast one and entire books are written on the subject. Accordingly, I won't dwell too much on the basics. The point I'm trying to make is this: don't skip physical database design. The rest of the tip focuses on providing some tools to help you perform the task thoroughly and some obvious areas (in the form of a "Top 20 Checklist") you don't want to cut corners on.

Identify Segments That Need to Be Considered in the Design

The following forms allow you to list all segments and relevant characteristics. Once they are listed, you can easily drill down to each area and ensure that all physical requirements are met in terms of current and future disk-space consumption; backup and recovery; periodic maintenance; performance aspects; and, last but not least, availability aspects. These forms list areas that I find are relevant to most of my clients. You may need to edit the forms to add additional areas that may apply to you or delete some that don't. Based on the results of evaluating these forms, you can arrive at appropriate numbers and sizes of other physical objects, such as rollback segments, temporary segments, redo-logs, and even overall database size. Ensure that you consider all applications likely to use the database before you configure the database.

Form: PD-1 **Table details**	
Table name	
# of columns	
# of constraints	
# of triggers	
# of LOBs	
Source of record	
Partitioned	
# of partitions	
Partition range	
# of records in initial data load	
Frequency of data loads	
# of records in each subsequent load	
Parent tables	
Child tables	
Other tables accessed with this table	
Full-table scans (%)	
Indexed lookups (%)	

Form: PD-1 **Table details**	
Table name	
For indexed lookups, would all columns be used (SELECT *, WHERE . . . , GROUP BY . . . , ORDER BY . . .)	
Purge frequency	
Archival to offline storage necessary before purge (Y/N)	
Archival retention period	
Tolerable downtime	
Time required to re-create table from source of record	
Heavy access periods	
# of concurrent transactions during heavy access periods	
Non-access periods	
Average # of concurrent transactions	
Average transaction size	
Transaction % that can select a rollback segment	
Table format (Index-Only/Regular)	

Form: PD-2 **Column details**	
Table name	
Column name	
Data type	
Length	
Scale	

Form: PD-2 **Column details**	
Table name	
Column name	
Null value allowed	
Source-of-record formulae	
Average size	
Access frequency	
(U)nique/(N)on-unique	
Density	
# of constraints	

Form: PD-3 **Constraint details**	
Table name	
Column name	
Constraint name	
Constraint type	
Constraint columns (in proper sequence)	
Referenced table name	
Referenced columns (in proper sequence)	
Constraint condition	
Permanent status	
"During load" status	
Deferrable	

Form: PD-4 **Index details**	
Table name	
Index name	
Index type (Bitmap/B*Tree/Reversed)	
(U)nique/(N)on-unique	
Columns in index (in proper sequence)	
Data already sorted (Y/N)	
Partitioned (Y/N)	
# of partitions	
Partition range	

Form: PD-5 **Trigger details**	
Table name	
Trigger name	
Trigger event	
(E)vent/(R)ow level	
WHEN condition	
Trigger body	

Form: PD-6 **LOB details**	
Table name	
LOB column name	
LOB type	
LOB content type	
Average LOB size	

The "Top 20 Physical Database Design" Checklist

The following may be used as a checklist of powerful database features/characteristics that merit being considered during the physical database design stage:

PARALLEL QUERY OPTION (PQO) Set appropriate degree for all large segments. Use PQO to enhance application performance and reduce application downtime, while performing various maintenance operations on application segments (creating/defragmenting tables, rebuilding indexes, and so on). This is particularly relevant to versions prior to Oracle8*i*. Also, ensure that tables/processes that are accessed/run simultaneously do not compete with each other, in terms of CPU, disks/controllers, and memory, and saturate system resources. Severe bottlenecks due to such competition may virtually bring the system to a halt!

COST-BASED OPTIMIZER (CBO) Unless CBO is turned on and statistics are analyzed after every major load, many newer Oracle features cannot be used. Regular analyzing only places a Shared-Exclusive row lock (SX-R) on the table. Accordingly, it can be run during any time of the day or night. Since it is resource-intensive, however, it is advisable to run it during times of low use. Ensure that adequate temporary space is available during an analyze. Analyzes sometimes take up temporary space up to four times the segment size. If possible, always do a COMPUTE STATISTICS, rather than an ESTIMATE. While using indexes on columns with skewed values (example: 500,000 => Females, 10,000 => Males), consider creating histograms for the columns.

MULTIPLE POOLS Based on the segment grouping discussed previously, place each segment group in a specific pool in the buffer cache. Identify all large tables needing full-table scans. Place such tables in the RECYCLE pool, separate from the smaller tables, which need to be placed in the KEEP pool. This will allow the smaller-table blocks to be retained in the buffer cache for a longer time. Configuring separate pools will minimize occurrences of smaller tables being phased out of the buffer cache. In Oracle7, the buffer cache is not explicitly segregated. In such cases, however, CACHE extremely small code and reference tables/indexes in the buffer cache. Usually, segments with less than 5,000 rows are good candidates for caching. Cached segments are placed at the MRU end of the buffer cache (so that it takes awhile before these segments are phased out via the LRU algorithm).

PARTITIONED SEGMENTS Create multiple partitions for large segments. Place popular partitions on separate tablespaces, across multiple disks/controllers. This will reduce contention during bulk loads and enhance parallel performance (whenever possible, Oracle8 implicitly tries the PQO path while accessing partitions). Also, placing different partitions on separate tablespaces allows specific (older) partitions to be taken offline during routine maintenance and emergencies, while other (newer) partitions are still online and available for user access. Such features of partitioning enhance availability. Also, devising a robust partitioning strategy is the most effective way to allow periodic purging of (old) data. With partitioning, for instance, it is relatively easy to implement a "rolling window" scheme where data prior to the desired window of time (say older than five years) can be truncated (after being archived, if necessary). Wherever possible, create local partition-key indexes to allow table partitions and their corresponding local indexes to be taken offline/online simultaneously as a single unit.

FAST FULL INDEX SCANS (FFIS) Enable and use FFIS—especially for large indexes, consisting of all required columns (if Oracle finds the necessary columns in the index, it will skip the table access).

BITMAPPED INDEXES FOR LOW-SELECTIVITY COLUMNS Create bitmapped indexes for all columns with low degree of uniqueness. Bitmapped indexes help read performance drastically. In addition, bitmapped indexes take just a fraction of the space of a regular B-Tree index. Also, the new STAR_TRANSFORMATION access path is possible only if bitmapped indexes exist across the fact/dimension set.

REVERSE-KEY INDEXES FOR LOPSIDED B-TREE INDEXES For columns with high selectivity, B-Tree indexes are often the best solution. Consider reversing the indexes if they are (expected to be) lopsided (where the number of rows per leaf block varies drastically).

INDEX-ORGANIZED TABLES (IOT) All code and reference tables with only one index (on the primary key) may be created as an IOT. The entire row in an IOT is stored in a B-Tree format (similar to an index). Performance improves drastically during an access of a cached IOT.

FULL TABLE/INDEX SCANS This is of importance only if your application performs full-segment scans. Full table scans and fast full index scans (FFIS) in Oracle are governed by the parameter DB_FILE_MULTIBLOCK_READ_COUNT. Ensure that the product of this parameter and DB_BLOCK_SIZE equals (at least) 64K. 64K is the OS upper limit on I/O operations in many OSs. This will allow more blocks of a table/index to be read in a single I/O operation.

NOLOGGING/UNRECOVERABLE For very large loads on DSS-type databases, set NOLOGGING at the segment level. This will reduce redo generation and, subsequently, reduce log switches. In versions prior to Oracle8, UNRECOVERABLE was the only option to reduce redo generation. However, UNRECOVERABLE was set at the operation level. Accordingly, if a third-party tool was used to perform the loads and if the DBA had no control over the tool to perform large loads in

UNRECOVERABLE mode, there was no way of reducing redo (unless the database was altered to NOARCHIVELOG mode, which would mean a database bounce and downtime). The Oracle8 NOLOGGING attribute is set at the segment level. Accordingly, no matter what tool is used to perform the loading, redo can still be restricted for certain operations. If NOLOGGING cannot be set prior to huge loads (due to versions prior to Oracle8 being used or if performing non-direct SQL operations), you might have to change to NOARCHIVELOG mode. This will prevent the online redo-logs from being archived, reducing I/O operations. Also, this will prevent the archive-log destination directory from quickly filling up and freezing the database. However, ensure that the new data written is backed up as soon as possible after all NOLOGGING operations or after the database is placed back in ARCHIVELOG mode. Enable database archiving only on the production instance. Note that here I assume that since the availability requirements of DSS applications are not generally as stringent as those for OLTP applications, you will be able to change ARCHIVELOG modes as a pre- and post-data load step (change to NOARCHIVELOG mode prior to the load and revert back to ARCHIVELOG mode after the load)—since data loads are run on DSS databases when no end users are accessing the data.

For huge bulk inserts, in addition to NOLOGGING/UNRECOVERABLE, use the APPEND hint in the INSERT statement to perform direct-path inserts and avoid the overhead of additional scans for free space in blocks below the segment high-watermark.

NEWER JOIN AND SUB-QUERY EXECUTION PATHS Enable HASH_JOINS, SEMI_JOINS, and ANTI_JOINS to enhance execution paths of joins and queries with the EXISTS and NOT IN clauses, respectively.

CONSTRAINTS Declare all constraints. Careful analysis is needed to determine whether they can be disabled without violating basic referential and domain integrity. If possible, keep most of them disabled, so that they don't hamper performance. So why create such (disabled) constraints in the first place? Another tip in this chapter provides more details.

Determine whether all enabled constraints can be deferred. If so, defer them for the duration of the entire load. If the load is very large, then check whether the load can be broken up into pieces, parallelized, and inserted with the constraints deferred.

FREELISTS, FREELIST GROUPS, AND INITRANS When multiple insert operations are concurrently expected to occur on a single segment (table and index), set the FREELISTs of such segments equivalent to the number of concurrent insert operations. That will prevent latch contention for the FREELIST in the segment header. Similarly, when using OPS, set FREELIST GROUPS to be adequate for each segment in addition to the FREELISTs to spread out the FREELISTs GROUPS onto multiple database blocks, and thus prevent inter-instance contention for the

FREELIST. Set the FREELIST GROUPS according to the number of concurrent insert operations across instances. Set the FREELISTs according to the maximum number of concurrent insert operations within each instance. Finally, set INITRANS to be at least equivalent to FREELISTs. If additional UPDATEs/DELETEs are expected to occur on the segment, then increase INITRANS accordingly. Chapter 12 elaborates on these options.

ROLLBACK SEGMENTS Create medium- and large-sized rollback segments. However, keep the large ones disabled. Do not reference them in the ROLLBACK_SEGMENTS initialization parameter (so that they remain disabled even after an instance bounce). Enable them only when specific jobs that need large rollbacks segments are run. Alternatively, you may keep a couple of large ones enabled at all times (along with the medium-sized ones) and have large jobs specifically refer to them by name (so that the large jobs are not inadvertently assigned smaller rollback segments). Additionally, if your site has some excessively large loads, create at least one mammoth rollback segment (for instance, with an INITIAL/NEXT of 100MB or 500MB). Keep this big segment disabled also. Just prior to a huge data load, disable all other rollback segments (except the SYSTEM, of course) and enable the big one. This way, with just one non-SYSTEM rollback segment enabled, the large load is bound to use it and chances of the load failing are minimized. Ensure that you have sufficient free space in the rollback segment tablespace, prior to attempting these operations. The free space should be adequate for the big rollback segment to extend even further, if necessary (examining the job and estimating the undo information it is likely to generate will greatly help in proactively preventing failure).

CLUSTERS Oracle clusters allow pre-joining of related tables according to an indexed cluster key or a hash algorithm. The main disadvantage with clusters is their lack of flexibility. This flexibility is more pronounced for OLTP applications. However, a DSS application could benefit substantially from a cluster. Much manual denormalization can be avoided by using clusters. Consider index and hash clusters for medium-sized tables. However, small and large tables are best left alone. The reason is this: small tables are really insignificant, as far as storage is concerned. By placing them in a cluster with a large table, a significant amount of disk space could potentially be wasted (due to constant repetition of a small number of values). In the case of large tables, a lot of flexibility is required for organization and maintenance before and after large data loads. This flexibility will be lost due to clusters. The best candidates for clusters are medium-sized tables that are related to one another and are almost always accessed together.

DENORMALIZATION OF FACT TABLES In the case of DSS applications, do not denormalize fact tables extensively (that is, carry a number of dimension columns within the fact). This defeats the purpose of a star join (since the smaller dimension table is used to reduce the number of rows accessed), since for many queries, fact tables alone may suffice without the need to do a join. Besides hampering performance, extensive denormalization of fact tables also results in extensive wastage of space. Joins are not always bad. In fact, under certain conditions, they can indeed be faster (if the right driving table is selected).

LARGE TABLES AND INDEXING Do not index large tables extensively. This piece of advice applies even to DSS applications. Analyze *potential* usage patterns carefully and prepare a list of candidate columns in each large table requiring indexes. With OLTP applications, it is fairly easy to analyze potential usage—one just needs to look at the code. For DSS applications, however, there will be a lot of ad hoc queries. Accordingly, during the initial deployment, index all columns that are likely to be widely used (seek the designer/developer's input). Once the warehouse is deployed, monitor it for *actual* usage patterns. The index list needs to be revisited at that point, and all redundant indexes need to be removed and new ones added as necessary.

Extensive indexing can be a nightmare for both DBAs and end users due to the additional maintenance requirements. If an index is not well maintained, it can easily degrade performance. Data loads on tables with a large number of indexes can be very slow, compared to a table with a few or no indexes. Sometimes, in order to enable large data loads to complete on time, it is essential to drop the indexes prior to the load and re-create them later. If the table is very large, index re-creation can take a lot of time, sometimes more time than the load itself! Indexes for a table cannot be created in parallel, since each index creation statement requires a table-level lock (in Oracle8*i*, this is no longer the case—you can run concurrent DML during an index build).

EQUALITY PREDICATES AND USAGE OF NEWER INDEX TYPES ON DATE COLUMNS On date columns, if the time portion is not absolutely necessary, store only the DD-MON-YYYY portion (in other words, store the time portion as zeros). When indexed, this will allow equality searches (WHERE date_col = <value>) to be used more often, helping performance (allowing you to use bitmapped and reversed key indexes on date columns more efficiently). In case the time part needs to be retained, consider denormalizing the table by introducing a second column to store only the DD-MON-YYYY (in addition to the original column that stores the data and time). This second column may be indexed to enhance equality searches (the probability of using an equality search reduces drastically if the time is also stored).

LONG DATA TYPES In Oracle8 and above, do not use LONG and LONG RAW data types in your physical model. Use VARCHAR2s for storage of characters up to 4,000 bytes. For greater storage capacity, use BLOBs or other LOBs.

MATERIALIZED VIEWS During various situations, end users are forced to run massive queries that summarize large amounts of data and compute certain values based on such summaries. Generally, these kinds of queries are prevalent in databases supporting DSS-type applications. Occasionally, however, even OLTP databases see these ugly queries being run, thus affecting regular OLTP performance adversely. Oracle8*i* introduces a new feature called *materialized views* where the requisite data may already be stored in a pre-summarized fashion, thus allowing applications to directly access and use them without having to perform any real-time/ad hoc summarization of the data. The summarized result sets are made available for single-row retrieval, just as with retrieval from a regular table. Materialized views work on the concept of "summarize the data once and use many times," thus saving repetitive data aggregations by end users.

Materialized views are schema objects (like tables, indexes, and so on) that allow data from a base table to be maintained in a different form within the same database or in the same or different form within a different database. Snapshots (used for replication) fall under this broad category, as well. Materialized views in the form of snapshots are maintained purely for data replication (across distributed databases). However, one of the prominent reasons for introducing materialized views in your physical design is to allow applications ready-made access to summarized data. However, detailed analysis is required prior to creating a materialized view to determine which are the necessary base tables/columns to be included in the view, what kind of summarizations and aggregations do users typically perform on this data, and the best way to present it to them in a ready-to-use format.

Materialized views are quite similar to indexes in concept, since they will need to be maintained as the data in the base tables change (thus potentially causing overhead during writes). In order to prevent materialized views from delaying bulk data loads to the base tables, you may drop/disable them prior to the load and re-create/reenable them after the load. Additionally, they tend to consume space. This space consumption may be substantial, if the views are built on large tables; however, they save a correspondingly large amount of work. Materialized views can be refreshed completely each time or on an incremental basis. A materialized view log (similar in concept to a snapshot log) is used by Oracle to allow incremental refreshes.

Materialized views use a table internally (again, just like the snapshots you are so familiar with). You can treat this table just like any other table. In other words,

you can create an index on it, you can partition it, and so on (you can also create a materialized view on a partitioned table). Materialized views require the cost-based optimizer (CBO). Materialized views can be used explicitly or implicitly by end users, who can directly query the views (if they are aware of their existence). In case the application is an existing one and the users are long accustomed to using the base tables directly, they do not have to be retrained in any way. They can still continue using the base tables in their queries and CBO will automatically rewrite their queries to use the materialized views whenever possible/appropriate.

Big queries are prone to frequent failure. Think about how often your end users have ended up getting an error after hours of work ("Snapshot too old" messages, not being able to perform large sorts due to inadequate space in the temporary tablespace, and so on). Also if your site lacks a full-fledged reporting instance, a certain class of users are prone to issue large DSS-type queries directly to your OLTP database. Think of the times you had to stop them to prevent regular OLTP transactions from slowing down, thus depriving them of the database availability they need. Materialized views enhance availability by allowing the required summary data to be readily available in a pre-formatted fashion. Thus, the end user does not have to perform any complicated computations of data, and critical reports are guaranteed to run in time without any major impact on system resources. The required data is there, whenever they need to access it. These features of materialized views make them almost mandatory in any environment.

Some quick application-related tips

Here are a few more application-related tips:

- Design and enforce proper application standards throughout the application development life cycle.
- Monitor resource-intensive SQL in production environments via *v$sqlarea* and *v$sqltext.*
- Note that small SQL statements badly written may be more important to tune than big bad ones in a batch job, as the batch job may only run once a day, but the small statements may run hundreds or thousands of times a day. For instance, in an ORDER ENTRY application, a statement to check inventory of items available may be run a few hundred times a day by operators accepting/processing the order (over the phone, the Web, and so on). If the statement takes four seconds or so to run each time, it may not be considered too bad. However, cumulatively it constitutes slow runtime. If the same statement can be tuned to run in a few milliseconds, it will greatly speed up the overall order processing procedure. By contrast, a batch job may be running for four hours. Making it run in half an hour will not be very beneficial

(generally) because it is run only once at night. Thus, enhancing response time of miniscule but important statements that individually seem to have no performance problems may be much more beneficial than enhancing the throughput of statements that appear slow but are not run as often.

- Check for potential deadlocks in applications to prevent application failures (refer to the *Oracle8 Server Concepts* for a discussion of application-induced deadlocks). Oracle's default lock-management algorithms are very sophisticated and generally prevent deadlocks from occurring. However, certain approaches to application programming and server configuration (such as allowing locks to cascade, issuing manual table locks, and allowing the same set of rows to be locked concurrently by different users in different sequences) are prone to deadlocks. Deadlocks may also result due to Oracle bugs and also under the MTS (multi-threaded server) architecture. It's highly essential to monitor for different locking problems (Chapter 11 outlines some methods to do this), including deadlocks. Let's take a close look at deadlocks caused under MTS (this is actually the least known of all deadlock-causing situations).
- Usually under MTS, a specific number of shared servers are allocated during startup and this number is allowed to grow during peak hours up to MTS_MAX_SERVERS. In other words, MTS_MAX_SERVERS specifies the upper limit for the shared servers. At times, this may lead to a deadlock-like situation (referred to as an "artificial deadlock") due to all shared servers being tied to specific dispatchers and none being available to resolve the issue that caused this effect. Let's take an example: Say, transaction_A locks a large number of rows (via a server process) by issuing a SELECT FOR UPDATE statement (or an explicit LOCK TABLE command). Once the statement finishes, the shared server process is released. Now when other server processes need to access some of the locked rows, they will have to wait for transaction_A to release the locks. In the meantime, transaction_A may be busy with other processing. Due to the large number of rows locked, potentially all available shared server processes may be forced to wait on transaction_A to release the locks. Thus, when transaction_A is finally ready to release the locks, no free shared server processes are available to service that request, since they are all tied up with the other waiting processes, thereby causing a deadlock-like situation. At this point, Oracle cannot allocate a new shared server process, since the MTS_MAX_SERVERS has already been reached.
- Whenever deadlocks occur, the DBA will need to watch for and manually resolve them by killing the offending session (in this case, the one that locked the rows: the session performing transaction_A). During integration

testing, deadlocks should be one thing that the QA personnel should explicitly look for. Production user/application activity should be simulated; batch jobs should be run to see whether deadlocks ensue. Frequently during deadlocks, trace-files and alert-log entries are dumped out by Oracle in the USER_DUMP_DEST and BACKGROUND_DUMP_DEST directories. The DBA needs to periodically monitor these directories.

- Do not use *discrete transactions* in any mission-critical application. Discrete transactions impose various restrictions (refer to the Oracle documentation set for an explanation of discrete transactions and the restrictions they impose), which are rarely met in complex mission-critical applications. Also, they may be met currently; but, as user requirements and data size and structures change/increase, those restrictions may not be met anymore. For instance, a discrete transaction may currently be changing data held within a block only once. As more rows are involved over time, however, the same transaction may have to change data within a block multiple times, thus violating a discrete transaction restriction. Thus, applications that were functioning previously would begin to fail, causing downtime. In any case, the performance advantages of discrete transactions are not as attractive, when compared to the cost of the restrictions they impose.
- Partition your applications effectively when using OPS across different nodes of your system to try to provide data affinity. Chapter 16 discusses application partitioning in more detail.

Data

In most environments, data is highly underestimated. Most DBAs consider data to be outside their domain. In a 24×7 shop, however, that is never the correct approach. Any data-related problem will be a more serious show-stopper than, for instance, a mere hardware problem such as a disk going bad. This is largely because, in many environments, there is a huge amount of data. Any kind of logical corruption will involve lots and lots of time to detect the problem, determine the cause, eliminate the cause, repair the corruption, and restore services. Other threats to availability, such as hardware and software problems, are fairly easy to detect. However, problems in a group of tables with millions of rows may present a daunting task. In other words, data problems could potentially cause very high downtime and, even more important, you could lose the faith of the customers with bad data. It is essential for any DBA to take the time and effort to understand what the data actually consists of, what the source-of-record is, how data is spread across physical system resources, which applications access them, who the end users are for the data, how frequently the data is accessed by such end users, whether the data is valid without any corruption, whether any checks can be built in to alert one when any logical or physical corruption creeps in, and so on.

Take time to understand the schema model

Understanding the schema model is the first step toward understanding data. Figure out which are the master tables, which are the transaction tables, and so on, and figure out which segments are absolutely necessary for applications to function smoothly and which segments should get priority during recovery. Apart from recovery, such information is of unlimited utility during application SQL tuning. The major reason for an application tuning exercise failing is lack of sufficient information about the data. For instance, determining the proper "driving" table in a multi-table join is of paramount importance in speeding up the query and making it use less resources. The table that is bound to retrieve the least number of rows ought to be selected as the driving table. Without proper knowledge of data, however, it's not possible to figure out which table will return the least number of rows (is it the table that contains the least number of rows or the table that will return the least given the condition being applied in the WHERE clause?). Similarly, in order to determine whether a full-table scan will be faster or an indexed lookup, again, one has to understand the data. There are many such instances where intimate knowledge of data will prove tremendously useful.

There are various ways to understand the schema. Current ERD diagrams, analysis/design and program documents, and even the Oracle data dictionary are useful sources of information. It is essential to ensure that you are looking at current information. Due to constantly changing user requirements, applications are highly dynamic. Frequently, designers and developers skip channels and avoid updating the ERD diagrams and the systems documentation with the latest enhancements. This is a universal problem at many companies. When using powerful tool sets such as Oracle Designer, the repository needs to be updated to contain the latest schema definitions. Once the repository is kept up-to-date, current ERD diagrams can be easily generated and printed. In case current information regarding data is not available, much of it (such as the primary key/unique keys, cardinality, and master/detail relationships) can be retrieved from the Oracle data dictionary (views such as USER_TABLES, USER_TAB_COLUMNS, USER_CONSTRAINTS, and USER_CONS_COLUMNS help provide such information). Chapter 19 provides scripts to accomplish these ends.

Categorize your data

Generally, recoverability of data is the primary driver for almost any application. This may not necessarily be true for a DSS application, such as a data-warehouse, due to the following reasons:

- All the data in the warehouse is derived from existing operational systems. Hence, in a worst-case scenario, they can be completely re-created, using the programs built in. Accordingly, all data-load modules ought to be designed and developed from a "reusability" standpoint.
- Data-warehouses are generally not mission-critical. They help businesses tremendously. However, they are generally not the "bread and butter" operational applications. Accordingly, relatively more downtime is tolerated.
- Data-warehouses tend to be extremely large in size. Accordingly, MTTR (mean time to recover) is proportionately large. On many occasions, urgently required data can be *re-created* within the same time frames by reloading from the operational sources. Such reloading will save time required to back up the warehouse and spare resources such as disk space, tape drives, backup hardware, and software. A prudent approach would be to evaluate the warehouse, classify all data segments (tables and indexes) into different backup groups, and frame backup and recovery strategies accordingly.

Segment Groupings

All segments need to be grouped according to specific criteria and treated accordingly.

BACKUP REQUIREMENTS As mentioned previously, all segments belonging to a specific backup type need to be physically stored in a similar fashion. That will help backup and recovery operations considerably, as Table 6-9 shows.

Different backup strategies could be adopted for different segment types. For example, ARAT and ARPT segments could be backed up just as zealously as regular operational segments (every night). RMT and WGMT segments may be backed up during predefined intervals (say, every month). CER segments may not even be backed up (they can be easily re-created in case they are lost).

Usually in most applications, a handful of segments dominate the database. Such segments will usually form the ARAT segments. Examples of such segments are the fact tables in a data-warehouse/data-mart or the transaction-detail tables in an OLTP application.

Backup Classification	(Sample) Backup Strategy
Absolutely required all the time (ARAT)	Every night including weekends
Absolutely required during predefined times (ARPT)	Every night including weekends
Required most of the time (RMT)	Weekly
Would be good to have most of the time (WGMT)	Monthly
Can be easily re-created (CER)	No backups required

TABLE 6-9. *A Segment Classification Based on Backup Frequency*

SEGMENT SIZES With size as a criterion, all data segments may be analyzed and grouped into the types shown in Table 6-10.

Segments need to be stored according to their classification. Similar segments can be stored in the same tablespace. If they are accessed together, however, they need to be separated to allow concurrent access by the disk controllers. Also, storing segments with similar size and growth characteristics together controls fragmentation effectively (since free data blocks can be reused). Chapter 12 discusses physical storage in more detail.

	Possible Classification Criteria		
Size Classification	**# Rows**	**Size**	**Examples**
Very large	> 5 million	> 1GB	Fact tables, transaction-detail tables
Large	Between 1 million and 5 million	> 512MB and <= 1GB	Summary tables, transaction-master tables
Medium	Between 10,000 and 1 million	> 100MB and <= 512MB	Dimension tables, temporary data staging tables, master tables
Small	< 10,000	<= 100MB	Reference, lookup, and domain tables

TABLE 6-10. *A Segment Classification Based on Size*

GROWTH Certain segments may be currently small or medium-sized. However, they may have the potential to grow at an extremely fast rate. For such segments, a small initial extent (an Oracle segment grows in *extents*) is usually adequate. However, the next extent size needs to be large. Similarly, when partitioning a large segment, the first partition may be the only one to get populated immediately. The other partitions may only be populated in the forthcoming years. Accordingly, rather than wasting space by allocating a large initial extent to these dormant partitions, it's prudent to allocate a very small initial extent (a very small multiple of the DB_BLOCK_SIZE) and a very large next extent to them. That way, they won't use up a large chunk of disk space, waiting for data to be inserted. That disk space may be better used elsewhere, to manage more urgent disk space requirements. Data segments need to be classified according to their growth. Very large segments that are expected to grow extremely fast (at a pace different from other large segments) need to be placed in separate tablespaces. The STORAGE clause for such segments needs to be determined from their current growth and future growth potential.

Some of the important considerations for setting storage parameters are

- INITIAL and NEXT extents should be multiples of the DB_BLOCK_SIZE. There should be a predefined number of standard INITIAL and NEXT segment sizes for all segments. Table 6-11 lists some sample sizes that I use at my client sites. A tool such as Oracle Designer may be used to create, assign, and track such diverse storage classifications more easily. (Storage clauses may be assigned names such as VERY_LARGE and LARGE within Oracle Designer and assigned to segments. When a storage clause is changed, all segments to which that storage clause has been assigned change to reflect the current sizes.)

  Ideally, all the data should be filled into the first extent (in which case the INITIAL extent will be a lot bigger than the next extent). However, in case database striping is required, then multiple extents may be pre-allocated (via the ALTER TABLE/INDEX ALLOCATE commands) onto separate disks/controllers.

- PCTINCREASE should be set to 0 as far as possible, to minimize fragmentation. In some specific (rare) cases, it may be set to 100 on application segments if the segment growth patterns are currently unknown but are suspected to grow very fast. Setting it to 100 allows the segments to grow at an exponential rate with limited impact on fragmentation. Any value for PCTINCREASE other than 0 or 100 is bound to cause higher fragmentation. Also, PCTINCREASE for temporary segments always ought to be set to zero.

Size Classification	Initial Extent	Next Extent	Comments
SUPER_LARGE	100MB	100MB	
PART_SUPER_LARGE	8KB	100MB	For partitioned segments, where the non-initial partitions are expected to remain empty for a while
VERY_LARGE	10MB	10MB	If the index of a SUPER_LARGE table has very few columns, it could potentially be assigned a VERY_LARGE initial/next extent, rather than a SUPER_LARGE one, to avoid space wastage
PART_VERY_LARGE	8KB	10MB	
LARGE	5MB	5MB	
PART_LARGE	8KB	5MB	
MEDIUM	1MB	1MB	Having a PART_MEDIUM may not be worthwhile (since the unit is just 1MB [not very large])
SMALL	8KB	8KB	Assuming that DB_BLOCK_SIZE is set to 8KB

TABLE 6-11. *A Sample STORAGE Classification*

- PCTFREE may be set very low (say, 5) for segments that are prone to few updates, if any at all. Conversely, it needs to be high for segments prone to frequent updates. For B*Tree indexes, PCTFREE may be set to zero, even for populated tables, if block pre-splitting is not desired. This is because, in B*Tree indexes, available excess space is not used during updates (since an UPDATE results in a DELETE and a re-INSERT). If pre-splitting is desired at creation time, however, then PCTFREE may be set high for B*Tree indexes. PCTFREE for indexes on empty tables may be set to zero, since pre-splitting blocks becomes irrelevant. If tables are prone to high deletion, PCTUSED needs to be set high to reuse the freed space.
- Set INITTRANS and FREELISTS to the same value (higher than the default of 1). Ideally, they should be set to the maximum number of concurrent transactions on the table. For bulk parallel loads, determine the degree of parallelism and set them accordingly.

Summary

This chapter provided tips in managing the last two environmental components: applications and data. Stressing the importance of having robust standards in place throughout the application development life cycle, we looked at various performance- and availability-enhancing and maintenance-reducing tips. Furthermore, the importance of conducting detailed physical database design to reduce post-deployment problems was discussed.

The next chapter provides guidelines for installing and configuring the database.

PART III

Database Setup and Configuration

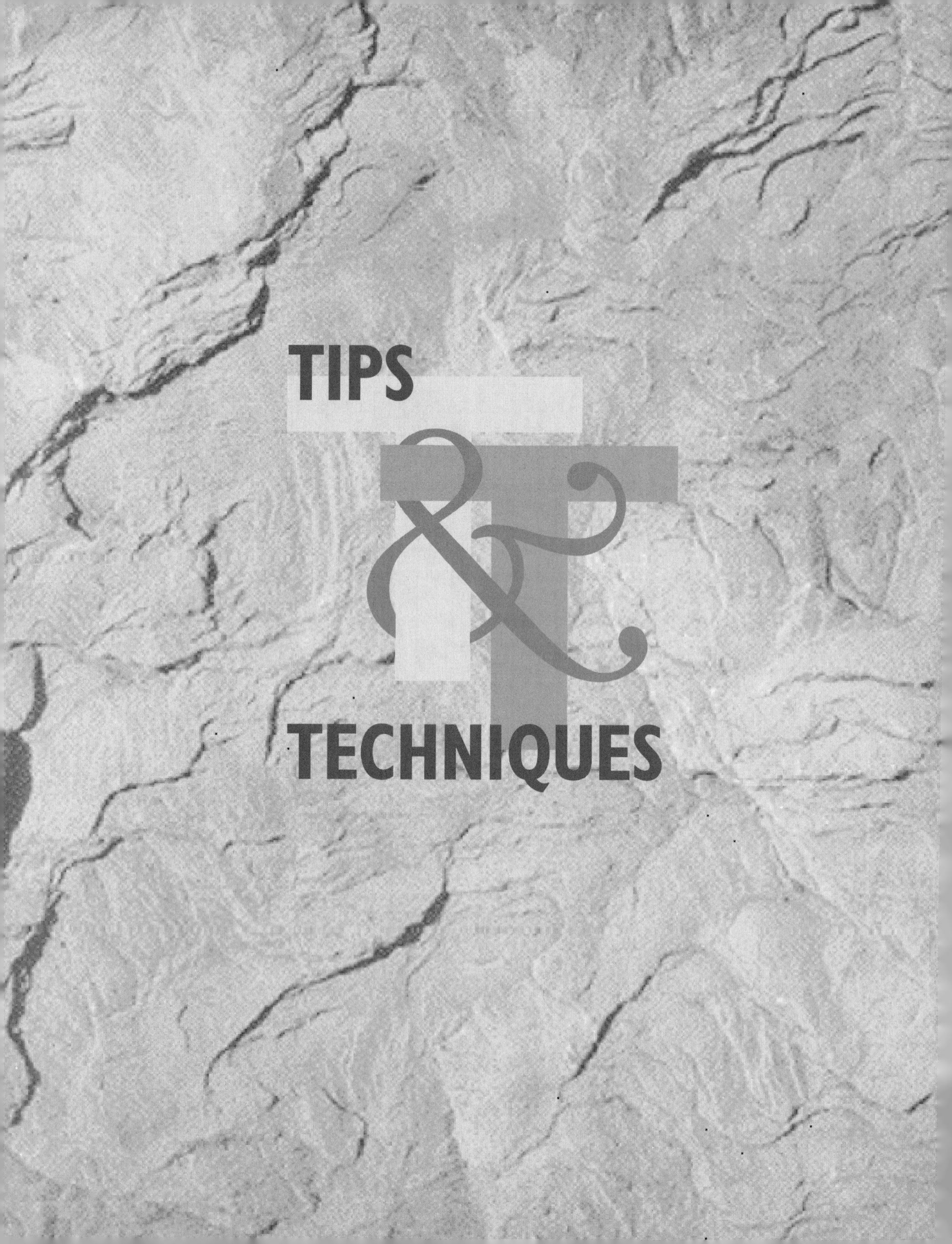
TIPS
&
TECHNIQUES

CHAPTER 7

Installing, Configuring, and Customizing Your Database Environment

Oracle installation and configuration introduces a number of challenges. If it's a brand new installation, some of these challenges, such as estimating disk space, laying out the data-files, deciding on the OS and database block sizes, and determining the maximum number of data-files, require making decisions about parameters that are appropriate for your environment—even before you have had a chance to use your database and find out their appropriateness. The seriousness of making the right decisions intensifies with high availability requirements, where the impact of an improper decision is much more severe because these decisions impose themselves throughout the life of the database. Correcting an improper decision involves downtime—which is seldom tolerated. Installation and configuration are highly critical from a 24×7 perspective, since they form the foundation upon which all other routine tuning and maintenance tasks operate.

At most 24×7 sites, performance relatively takes a back seat to availability, recoverability, and maintainability. In their enthusiasm to configure a highly available and maintainable site, however, DBAs sometimes make the database virtually unusable from a performance perspective. This causes major performance audits and corrective actions to take place, resulting in downtime and defeating the entire purpose of ignoring performance goals during installation and initial configuration. Rather than focusing solely on availability and causing downtime due to such short-sightedness during initial configuration, it's always better to look at performance as an equally important objective, at par with recoverability and maintainability. In specific cases where performance objectives directly clash with availability, it's advisable to let the latter prevail.

So how do DBAs tend to do things right the first time? How can they ever manage to get everything installed and working right "out of the box"? The bad news is, they can't! 24×7 uptime cannot be achieved merely by doing a vanilla install. It can only be attained by following a combination of good recommendations from Oracle and enhancing those practices based on the DBA's experience in similar environments. This chapter provides some recommendations based on my own experience. I have tried to be fairly OS-generic. In cases where specific examples are needed, however, I have leaned toward UNIX (and Windows NT, quite a few times) to provide those examples.

This chapter provides the following tips and techniques:

- Follow the OFA standard
- Always use a *config.ora* file
- Use the *crdb_SID.sql* and *crdb2_SID.sql* creation scripts
- Retain at least two weeks' worth of trace-files and alert-log

- Consider OS block size and application characteristics when setting DB_BLOCK_SIZE
- Ensure that contiguous blocks per write are set high
- For a large number of data-files in Oracle7.*x*, enable CKPT
- Ensure instance-recovery times specified in your SLA are met
- Create more than three mirrored online redo-log groups
- Place redo-logs to avoid ARCH and LGWR contention
- Configure adequate redo latches to minimize contention
- Ensure that DBWR can keep up with database loads
- Partition your buffer cache based on segment-usage patterns
- Use process slaves to alleviate I/O bottlenecks
- Enable vector posting
- Set up dedicated temporary tablespaces
- Set up sort areas efficiently
- Use direct writes for sorts
- Use profiles to prevent runaway processes from hogging all resources
- Evaluate using vectorized reads for cooked file-systems
- Enable direct I/O when using cooked file-systems
- Use intimate shared memory (ISM) for high concurrent user access
- Use post-wait drivers for high IPC throughput
- Pre-page and "lock" the SGA in main memory
- Whenever possible, set COMPATIBLE to current database version
- Always install SQL*Plus Help
- Use Oracle Names when dealing with a large number of clients
- Use out-of-band breaks with SQL*Net/Net8 or set poll-frequency high
- Keep dead-connection detection to the minimum
- Manage large user populations effectively
- Pre-spawn dedicated server processes

Server Configuration

This section discusses ways to optimize the Oracle Server configuration.

Follow the OFA standard

Yes, I had to start with this one. Pick up any book on Oracle database administration and chances are, you will see the term "OFA" mentioned. The Oracle documentation refers to it in detail. In fact, the Oracle installer program (*orainst*) on certain operating systems does an OFA-compliant installation by default. OFA greatly eases the administration and maintenance of many sites with 24×7 uptime requirements.

OFA (Optimal Flexible Architecture) is a set of installation and configuration guidelines from Oracle Corporation. OFA allows you to install, set up, and configure your database and operating system environments without having to reinvent the wheel by cooking up your own new standard. It allows you to reuse the Oracle knowledge bank of "do's and don'ts" derived from real-life experience at many client sites. It lets you implement some of the best practices followed by Oracle customers worldwide.

The original OFA consists of 13 basic system requirements and 11 full-fledged recommendations in naming UNIX mount points, managing raw-devices, segregating Oracle software and data-files, creating a minimum number of tablespaces, and observing data-file and tablespace naming conventions for both regular (single-instance) and OPS installations. Figure 7-1 provides an example of an OFA-compliant directory structure under UNIX. A typical Oracle installation deals with a number of different file types (data-files for data, indexes, temporary and rollback segments, redo-logs, archived logs, control-files, and so on), many of which have the potential to create I/O bottlenecks if laid out together.

With all the advantages OFA brings to the table, there are still many sites that choose not to use OFA. While using *orainst* to install Oracle software, it is possible to bypass the default installation mode and skip OFA. Such a decision may not necessarily be bad, if some other standard is used in lieu of OFA. However, total lack of standards and haphazard configuration techniques lock you into a specific version of Oracle without an easy way to undo or upgrade without significant downtime. Following a specific standard allows easy maintenance. For instance, OFA recommends that you do not create any data-files on the same mount point as the Oracle software. Doing so may cause problems potentially leading to downtime when you create another database on the same machine, upgrade the current version, or even apply a simple patch. Thus, following OFA allows you to minimize downtime in ways not easily anticipated during a first-time install.

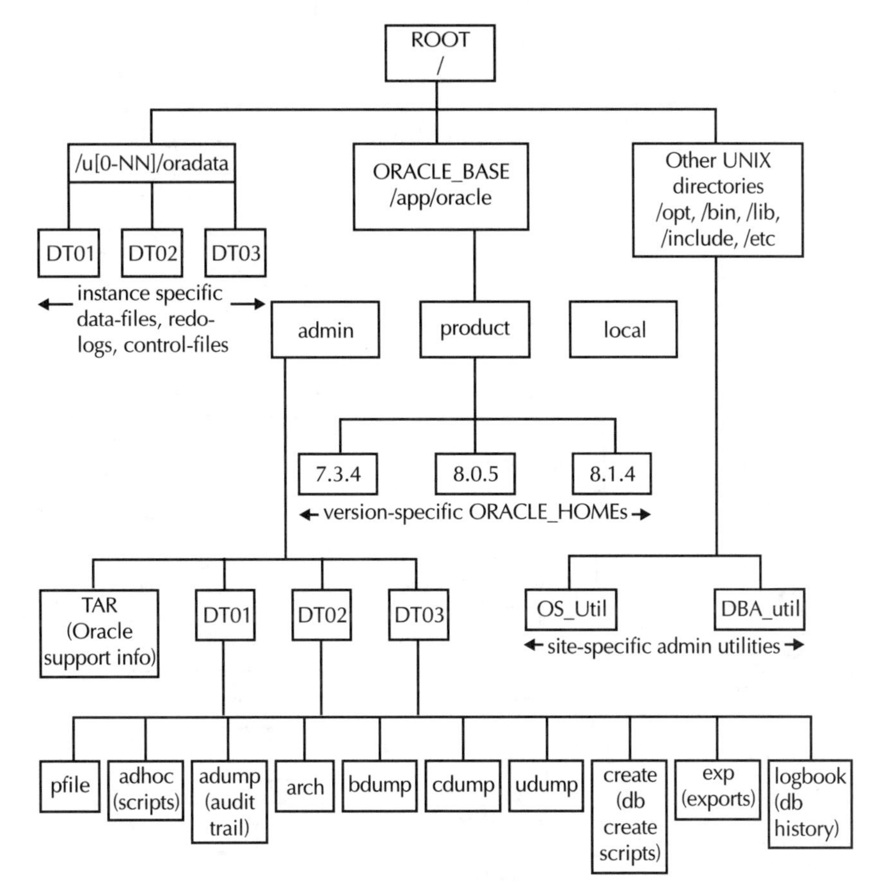

FIGURE 7-1. *An OFA-compliant directory structure under UNIX (here, three instances, DT01, DT02, and DT03, are depicted)*

OFA allows you to build on the existing standards with your own. In fact, at some of my client sites, we use a customized version of OFA, modifying it with standards as dictated by our unique requirements. Figure 7-2 provides an example of a customized OFA-compliant directory structure that may be used on a production UNIX box. With some changes, any site using a non-UNIX operating

system can adopt the very same OFA rules. Figure 7-3 shows an example of a customized OFA-compliant setup under Windows NT (the installer program for Oracle8*i* on Windows NT does an OFA-compliant installation by default).

The *DBA Handbook* from Oracle Press/Osborne provides a detailed discussion of customizing your setup by going beyond vanilla OFA. In Chapter 4, the book

ROOT /
/u[0-NN]/oradata
DT01
DT02
DT03
usr_dbf
application tablespace data-files
sys_dbf
SYSTEM, RBS, TEMP data-files
ORAKRNL
control-files, redo-logs
ORACLE_BASE /app/oracle
admin
product
local
7.3.4
8.0.5
8.1.4
version-specific ORACLE_HOMEs
OS_Util
DBA_util
site-specific admin utilities
Other UNIX directories /opt, /bin, /lib, /include, /etc
/var/opt/oracle
tnsnames.ora, listener.ora, sqlnet.ora, oratab
/uMM/oracle/arch
DT01
DT02
DT03
TAR (oracle support info)
DT01
DT02
DT03
pfile
scripts
adump (audit-trail)
bdump
cdump
udump
backs (online backups)
exp (exports)
logbook (db history)
ORAKRNL
copies of control-files, redo-logs
SCHEMA (File on schema details, such as schema-names, passwords, applications they belong to, etc.)

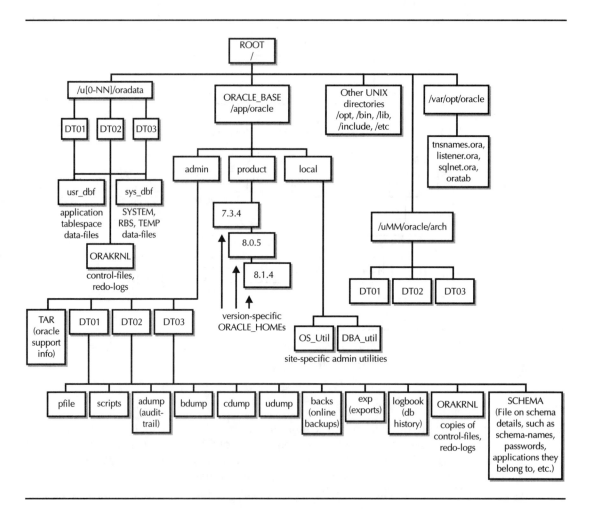

FIGURE 7-2. *A customized OFA-compliant directory structure under UNIX*

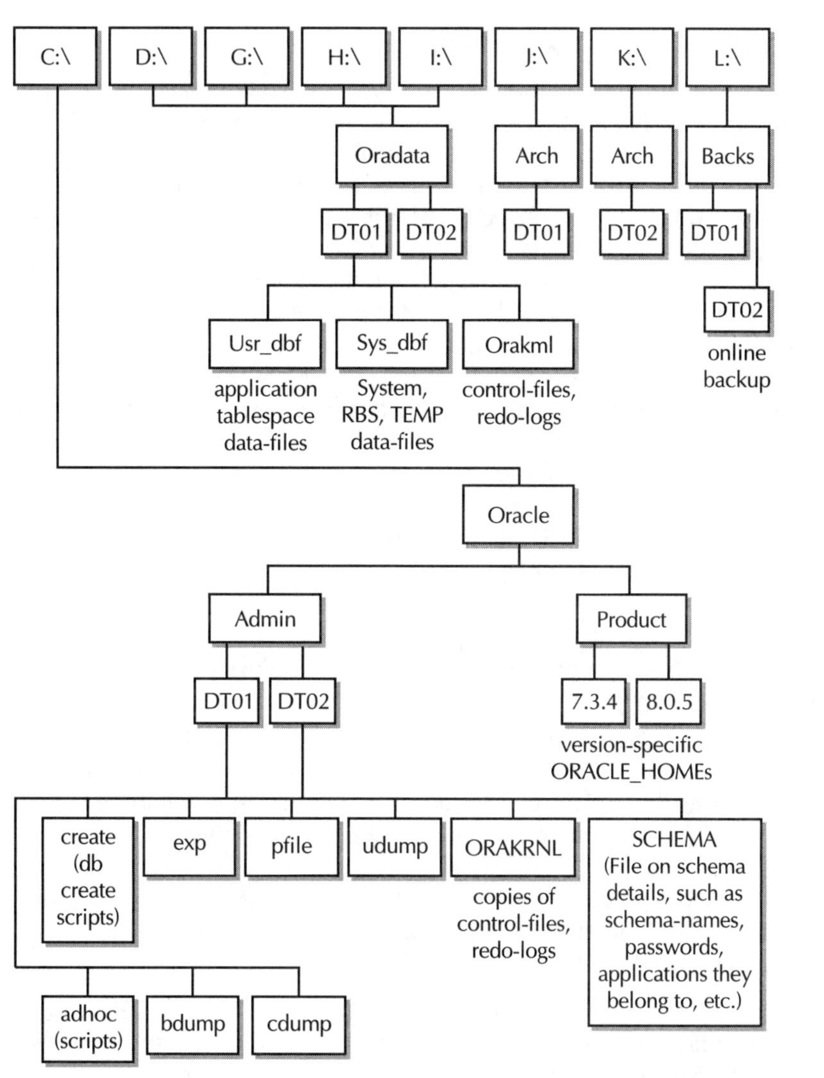

FIGURE 7-3. *A customized OFA-compliant directory structure under Windows NT*

outlines an interesting weight-based approach for distributing data-files by allocating I/O weights to each tablespace and separating them based on such weights to proactively avoid I/O contention.

Always use a *config.ora* file

A *config.ora* file contains all the "permanent" initialization parameters (such as DB_BLOCK_SIZE, DB_NAME, and BACKGROUND_DUMP_DEST). It is used during database startup via the IFILE parameter in the *init.ora* file (IFILE supports nesting of initialization parameter files up to three levels deep). On many operating systems, a *config.ora* file is created by default during installation. Some DBAs prefer not to use it, but setting up and using the *config.ora* is advisable. It separates all the changeable and non-changeable database initialization parameters into different files. In some cases, such "non-changeable" parameters are physically changeable but may not be changed under certain circumstances without causing database corruption (such as when the DB_BLOCK_SIZE, DB_NAME, CONTROL_FILES, or COMPATIBLE parameters are accidentally changed immediately after a *shutdown abort* or prior to a *startup force*). Alternatively, installations supporting multiple instances (OPS or multiple physical databases on the same machine) may find it advantageous to place all common initialization parameters (such as DB_BLOCK_SIZE and CORE_DUMP_DEST) in one common *config.ora* file, which can then be referenced via different *init.ora* files.

Use the *crdb_SID.sql* and *crdb2_SID.sql* creation scripts

Generally, the installation media on most operating systems have a file *crdb* in the *orainst* directory (for example */cdrom/orainst/crdb,* where */cdrom* is the mount point for the CD-ROM drive). This file contains the statements for database creation (the CREATE DATABASE command). This file helps directly in two ways:

- It provides an easy checklist of all critical values to be provided during database creation, such as database name, MAXDATAFILES, MAXLOGFILES, and MAXLOGHISTORY.
- It provides documentation on all critical values actually set during database creation. Such documentation is invaluable whenever the database is down and unavailable (for example, during control-file re-creation when the control-file is accidentally overwritten and the database crashes).

The *crdb* file should be renamed to *crdb_SID.sql* (where *_SID* is the value defined by the ORACLE_SID environment variable) and customized with necessary values for all database creation parameters prior to usage. Another file called *crdb2_SID.sql* needs to be created. This second file would contain the following:

- Non-SYSTEM tablespace creation commands

- Rollback segment creation commands
- Running of *catalog.sql, catproc.sql,* and *catdbsyn.sql*
- Changing of SYS and SYSTEM passwords
- Database user, role, and profile creation commands
- Running of *pupbld.sql* (to create the PRODUCT_USER_PROFILE table and get rid of the irritating message "User profile information not loaded" whenever a user other than SYSTEM logs on—in Oracle8, this doesn't seem to happen anymore.)
- Any ALTER DATABASE or ALTER SYSTEM commands

Both files need to be backed up along with the first database backup (hot or cold). When using these files as documentation to understand what values were provided during database creation, it's imperative to remember that some database creation values are alterable (such as ARCHIVELOG mode). For this reason, these files may not necessarily reflect the current database values. Hence, it's a good idea to follow the standard of updating the *crdb2_SID.sql* file with the appropriate values whenever the database is altered.

Both files spool their output to log files. These log files should be examined for any runtime errors. This is a very important step—ensure that no creation errors escape your attention. If undetected, they might spring a few unpleasant surprises down the road—PL/SQL may not work properly, database links may be unable to be created, or the like. Additionally, they need to be backed up along with the original files. They come in extremely handy during database audits and also when database behavior appears strange after creation (those "surprises" I mentioned earlier).

Ensure sufficient disk space for at least two weeks' worth of trace files and alert-log

Most sites spend a lot of time configuring and planning for the archive-log destination directory (and rightfully so). However, the background, core, and user dump destination directories are conveniently forgotten. These directories refer to the targets for trace files, generated by Oracle background processes, core dumps, and user trace files respectively. It's not surprising to find that the default settings for these initialization parameters remain unchanged—which is not too bad but for the fact that, by default, these directories are usually set up on the same drive as the Oracle software. This may potentially cause performance problems due to the contention between reads of the Oracle software and writes done on these log directories. Also, the Oracle software drive is best suited to store relatively non-volatile executable files. Usually sites tend to choose a 2GB or smaller

(sometimes bigger if multiple Oracle versions are maintained) disk-slice to hold the entire Oracle software. A typical Oracle7 or Oracle8 installation (with a few bells and whistles) takes up around half a gig, thus leaving little room for growth. Usually, a database constantly spits out informational and error messages and warnings, causing the alert-log and other trace files to swell up until the respective directories are 100 percent full within a short period after the installation.

As OFA recommends, it's a good practice to keep the background, core, and user dump destinations away from the Oracle software directory. However, what OFA doesn't recommend is how big these destinations need to be. Typically, if you follow a good alert-log and trace files archival policy, then you will back up all these files to tape (these tapes could be recycled) on a periodic basis and purge these directories to free up the space. It is quite important to keep the alert-log reasonably slim, since it would be opened up and examined quite often—in fact, several times in a day (if you have tried opening up a 300MB file with *vi* or *wordpad,* you know what I mean). However, purging these directories too frequently also poses a problem, since you would lose convenient access to useful audit information (such information would need to be accessed off tape). The best approach usually is to hold at least two weeks' worth of trace files and alert-log information. Ensure that you place the background, core, and user dump destinations on non-Oracle software drives to prevent such drives from getting 100 percent full. Furthermore, ensure that whichever drives your standards make you designate for those destinations have the capacity to support a solid two weeks' growth with 25 percent extra room for sudden spurts. Chapter 13 discusses the alert-log and trace files in more detail.

Consider OS block size and application characteristics when setting the database block size

At the risk of flogging a dead horse (no offense meant to animal lovers), I need to emphasize that the database block size needs to be equivalent to or multiples of the OS block size. If raw devices are being used, the physical OS block size needs to be considered (usually 512 bytes). If a Logical Volume Manager (LVM) or RAID is being used, however, then the logical OS block size plays a dominant role and should be the criterion for the database block size.

Since most LVMs revert the logical block size to 8K, they leave the DBA with little choice but to make the database block size equivalent to at least 8K. If the application is purely OLTP in nature, with very small and random reads and writes, it may become necessary to reconfigure the OS with a smaller logical block size (usually 2K or 4K). In any case, ensure that you know what that logical block size is and that you consider it and overall application characteristics in forming the database block size. For instance, a DSS application that encourages full-segment scans such as data-warehouses and data-marts ought to have a larger database block size, whereas applications driven by small transactions and indexed segment accesses should use a smaller block size. The reason for selecting a larger block size for DSS environments is that such environments require a large number of rows to be read for sorting, grouping/summarizing, and so on, and for this reason, it's efficient to pack in as many rows as possible within every block read. Table 7-1 provides a high-level view of the I/O required to read 25,000 rows via an index (table access via an index lookup for each row) in a table with 11 million rows with three different block sizes: 2K, 4K, and 8K. The statistics were obtained on three Sun Enterprise 4000 machines attached to an EMC 3200 disk-array using RAID 1. To perform the tests, we configured three different databases on the three machines with different block sizes. The data in Table 7-1 was derived using a combination of EMC's disk performance monitoring tools and the *utlbstat/utlestat* utility in Oracle. The comparison provides an overall indication of the effectiveness of a larger block size (it is to be borne in mind that such effectiveness may not be obvious in all cases and is largely dependent on a variety of factors such as the access mode (indexed or full-segment scan, joins done via hash/sort-merge/nested-loop methods, and so forth), the number of blocks read per I/O operation, the RAID subsystem utilized, specific Oracle settings (DB_FILE_MULTIBLOCK_READ_COUNT, CCF_IO_SIZE), overall system and database activity at the time of measurement, and so on.

The reason for selecting a smaller block size for OLTP environments is that the transactions usually are smaller and affect very few rows, compared to a DSS environment. Accordingly, the idea is to read only as much data as is required and not waste valuable buffer cache space with unnecessary data (displacing rows already present in the buffer cache to make room for the unnecessary data). Also, in OLTP environments, a large number of writes are performed. Database concurrency is affected (due to latch and physical resource [such as I/O channel] contention) when such writes affect the rows within a single block. The larger the database block, the greater number of rows present within each block and, thus, the higher

DB_BLOCK_SIZE	2K	4K	8K
Statistics for 25,000 rows (avg. row length = 980 bytes)			
# of I/Os required to read all blocks	15,000	8,000	4,500
Avg. I/O time per block	16 ms	20 ms	23 ms
Cumulative read time for the entire operation	4 mins	2 mins, 40 secs	1 min, 43.5 secs

TABLE 7-1. *I/O Statistics for 2K, 4K, and 8K Database Block Sizes*

the chances of rows within a single block being affected by concurrent operations. A large block size may frequently serialize and slow down such concurrent operations (depending on the striping mechanism used, disks/controllers available, and specific Oracle storage settings such as FREELISTS and INITRANS). Accordingly, a smaller database block size is recommended in such environments. In case a larger block size has been already used, ensure that you specify a higher PCTFREE for tables to reduce the number of rows per block. Also, specifying a larger number of FREELISTS and INITRANS for tables will expedite inserts by reducing block contention and the overhead of allocating additional transaction slots at runtime, respectively. A larger block size may cause higher wastage of redo-log space. When transactions are insufficient to fill up complete blocks within the redo-log, partially empty blocks may be written to the log, causing space to be wasted. Accordingly, when using a larger database block size, it may be necessary to increase the size of the online redo-logs to prevent redo-log wastage from causing log switches too frequently and thus hurting performance (due to the additional I/O caused by the checkpoint involved with every log switch).

Certain environments may have a combination of both DSS/batch and OLTP characteristics. Also, some applications have tables with large row sizes (especially in DSS environments due to a higher degree of denormalization; but this may occur even in OLTP applications, where LONG/LONG RAW or BLOB/CLOB/NCLOB data types are used). Such applications may need to use a larger database block size to avoid rampant row-chaining in these tables, especially if these tables happen to be heavily used within the application. Accordingly, application characteristics have to be thoroughly analyzed before the "ideal" block size can be determined.

Evaluate the criteria for setting the database block size as early as possible. The database block size is one of the earliest decisions to make during the database creation process. Unfortunately, however, the setting doesn't easily pardon wrong decisions, because the database block size, once determined, remains constant throughout the life of the database and a wrong decision surfaces time and again in the form of bad performance, manifesting through sub-optimal I/O and cache usage, segment fragmentation, and possibly row chaining. Repairing the wrong decision and changing the database block size requires a database rebuild and consequently substantial downtime.

Ensure that contiguous blocks per write are set high

If you are dealing with a very large database, the actual database creation time can be highly critical. On certain operating systems (example: HP-UX), Oracle supports an initialization parameter called CCF_IO_SIZE, which determines the number of contiguous blocks per write during database creation. Generally, a higher number allows Oracle to use as many contiguous blocks as possible. The valid range for CCF_IO_SIZE is usually between 1 and 131,072. Oracle proactively sets this value to the highest possible. Since the database has not been created yet, however, you cannot check the *v$parameter* dynamic view to ensure that this value is indeed set high for your OS. You can manually set it to 131,072 in the *init.ora* file. Prior to doing so, check your platform-specific Oracle documentation to ensure that CCF_IO_SIZE is supported and that the default setting is sub-optimal.

For a large number of data-files in Oracle7.*x*, enable CKPT

Before I proceed further, let me explain what is meant by a checkpoint (see Figure 7-4). Due to typical DML/DDL activity, data gets changed within the data-block buffer cache. These changes are periodically written to disk to ensure that the data-files are synchronized with the data block buffers. This synchronization is termed a *checkpoint*. Once a checkpoint occurs, all the redo information generated thus far becomes redundant and is used only when media recovery is required. A checkpoint is generally caused by any of the following events:

- By unavailability of any free data block buffers (all the data block buffers scanned are either dirty or pinned), thus triggering off DBWR to write some of the dirty buffers to disk and freeing them for reuse
- Explicitly by issue of the ALTER SYSTEM CHECKPOINT command
- Implicitly by a command performing tablespace or data-file operations such as ALTER TABLESPACE BEGIN BACKUP or ALTER TABLESPACE OFFLINE
- Implicitly during a redo-log switch (either caused when the current online redo-log is full or via the ALTER SYSTEM SWITCH LOGFILE command)
- Explicitly by time elapsed as set by the LOG_CHECKPOINT_TIMEOUT or OS blocks written as set by the LOG_CHECKPOINT_INTERVAL initialization parameters
- During database shutdown (except during *shutdown abort*)

Generally, the DBWR process performs the bulk of the work during a checkpoint. During a checkpoint, DBWR is signaled by LGWR. DBWR examines the LRUW list (discussed later) of dirty buffer headers and writes them to disk in units of _DB_BLOCK_CHECKPOINT_BATCH. Checkpoints may be either fast or slow. During fast checkpoints, DBWR writes frantically without pausing to clear off the LRUW list. Additionally, DBWR may also scan the LRU list for dirty buffers and flush them to disk. Fast checkpointing reduces the amount of time that server processes wait on DBWR. Once the buffers are flushed, they are not removed from the LRU list. Instead, they are retained so that they may be readily available in

memory in case server processes need them. Occasionally a server process may need to read a buffer as it is being written to disk by DBWR during the checkpoint. During such times, the server process would need to undergo a "write complete wait" until the time DBWR completes writing that particular buffer to disk (prior to version 7.2, the server process would need to wait until the entire batch of buffers were written). After the buffers are flushed, LGWR (in addition to its regular task of writing data from the redo-log buffers to the online redo-log files) updates the control-files and data-file headers with the checkpoint information (information such as the checkpoint SCN [System Change Number], date/time stamp, and redo thread information).

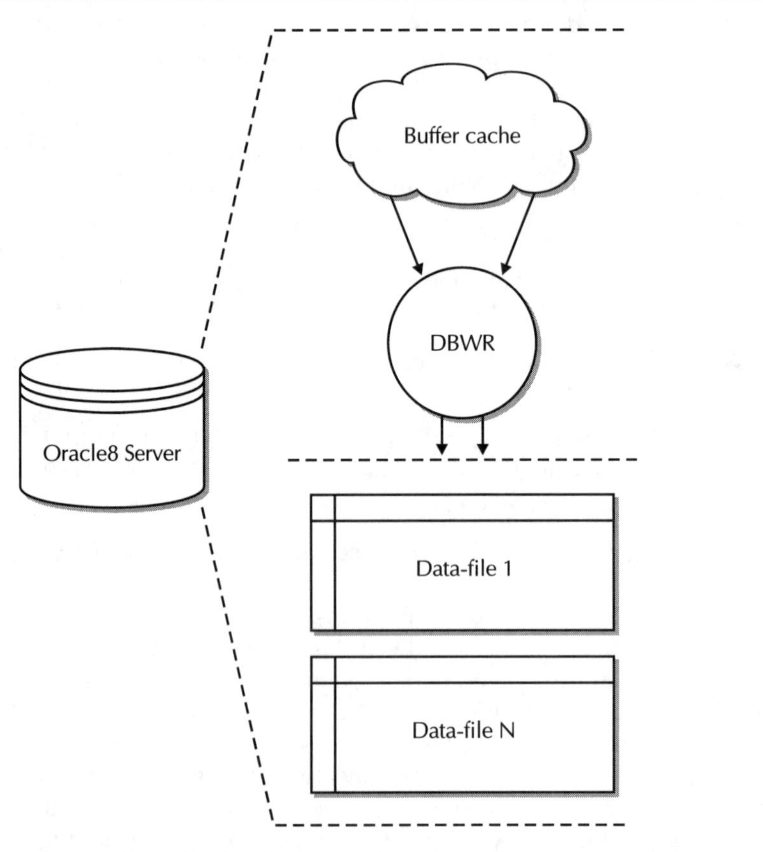

FIGURE 7-4. *The checkpoint process*

This arrangement is fine, except in cases where the database is highly volatile with a large number of writes taking place or when the database is pretty voluminous with a large number of data-files. During such times, the LGWR is merrily trying to keep pace with its regular task of synchronizing the online redo logs with the contents of the log buffers. When it is called upon to carry out the additional task of updating the control-files and the data-file headers with checkpoint information, it tends to fall behind and cause *real* problems, such as checkpoint delays and interference with log switches (potentially causing the message in the alert-log—"cannot allocate new log—checkpoint not complete"). During such times, a companion process called the checkpoint process (CKPT) is available to help LGWR. CKPT takes over the task of updating the control-files and data-file headers with checkpoint information, thus allowing LGWR to focus on what it does best—writing the online redo-logs.

Typically, most 24×7 sites have a fairly immense database with a large number of data-files. Also, 24×7 sites tend to support mission-critical, write-intensive OLTP applications more often than DSS applications or data-warehouses (which are not as mission-critical), causing large-scale writes to the redo-log files. Thus, LGWR would be under heavy strain at such sites. In such scenarios, turning CKPT on would help reduce LGWR's load.

Also, since recovery timing is a major issue at all 24×7 sites, checkpoints would need to occur more frequently than at a site that does not require 24×7 access and fast recovery timings (see next tip). Hence, in order to prevent such frequent checkpoints from degrading the overall database performance in general and the LGWR throughput in particular, it's a good idea to turn CKPT on.

Please note that in Oracle8, CKPT is enabled at all times, whereas in version 7.*x*, CKPT would be enabled only by setting the initialization parameter CHECKPOINT_PROCESS to true. When enabling CKPT, adjust all your calculations dependent on the number of processes to accommodate the additional CKPT process. For instance, increase the PROCESSES parameter by one, and explicitly increase all other parameters whose default values are dependent on PROCESSES (such as SESSIONS), if you use non-default values for those parameters.

Use LOG_CHECKPOINT_TIMEOUT and/or LOG_CHECKPOINT_INTERVAL to ensure instance-recovery times specified in your SLA are met

As explained earlier, checkpoints involve physical disk I/O and tend to affect performance adversely. Many DBAs are tempted to reduce checkpoints as much as possible (by disabling LOG_CHECKPOINT_TIMEOUT and LOG_CHECKPOINT_INTERVAL by setting the former to zero and the latter to a very high value), thereby

causing checkpoints to occur only during a log switch. If the online redo-log files are large (say, 20MB or more), then they tend to hold a lot of information that has never made it to the data-files (due to lack of interim checkpoints). This helps performance greatly, since disk I/O is reduced. However, if the database were to crash without a checkpoint occurring, then instance-recovery time would increase greatly (since the entire 20MB or more of the current online redo-log would need to be applied). Also, if all existing copies of the current online redo-log file were to be overwritten or destroyed somehow, then a significant portion of data might potentially be lost (up to the total size of the online redo-log). A small test may be required (a *shutdown abort* issued on a similar-sized test database followed by a *startup*) to figure out the time it takes to perform the entire instance recovery with 20MB redo-log files. If the time taken is not acceptable to you (preferably, as per your SLA), then you may need to force checkpoints to occur more frequently than just at a log switch.

You can set LOG_CHECKPOINT_INTERVAL to the total number of OS blocks, the writing of which should trigger a checkpoint. I have seen many sites set this to half the size of the online redo-log file, so that at any given point in time, redo of only up to half the size of the online redo-log file would need to be rolled forward during instance recovery, thus cutting total instance recovery time by almost 50 percent. You can also set LOG_CHECKPOINT_TIMEOUT to the number of seconds after which a checkpoint should mandatorily occur. This parameter is especially useful in read-intensive databases, where writes (to OS/database blocks) may be insufficient to trigger a checkpoint, thereby creating the need for a time-based checkpoint (for any few writes that may have occurred).

Also, you don't need to worry about the checkpoints caused by these parameters interfering with the checkpoints occurring due to a regular log switch (or other events). These parameters cause a passive checkpoint—which is overridden by the checkpoint caused by a log switch. Thus, the log switch checkpoint cancels the checkpoint caused by these parameters and takes over in their stead. Due to this "overriding" characteristic, checkpoints seldom step on each other's toes and cause the resultant I/O activity to shoot up.

As a general rule of thumb for high-availability sites, it's a good idea to ensure that checkpoints occur at least once during writes of every 5MB of data or every 20 minutes, whichever is appropriate in terms of reducing I/O. (This rule of thumb needs to be reconciled with the amount of redo being generated in your environment. For instance, if an environment with very high transaction throughput generates, say, more than 1GB of redo in an hour, causing a checkpoint to occur once every 5MB of data would obviously be very expensive. Accordingly, in such environments, checkpoints should be configured to occur every 20 minutes, rather than be based on the size of data. Alternatively, in a primarily read-only environment, there is no real advantage in having a checkpoint occur every 20 minutes. In such an environment, it is beneficial to apply the "5MB data" rule.)

Create more than three mirrored online redo-log groups for high-activity databases

The utility of mirroring redo-logs is discussed in a variety of Oracle books. Since the redo-logs are the only Oracle files that cannot be recovered in case they are lost (unlike the control-file that can be re-created or the data-files that can be rolled forward), it's extremely important to mirror them, preferably by creating multiple redo-log files (at least two) within each group. In addition, all redo-logs may be mirrored via RAID 1 or other OS features.

An advantage in having multiple log-file members per group is revealed during archiving. The ARCH process switches back and forth between all the members in a group on a round-robin basis, so that the bottleneck in reading just one redo-log file is avoided. If there is just one log file per group, it might potentially cause an I/O bottleneck. Carefully spreading all redo-log files in a group onto different disks/controllers helps prevent this problem.

There is quite a bit of confusion about which is better—mirroring a redo-log via OS utilities (volume managers, software RAID 1, and so on) or via Oracle functionality (creating multiple log-file members within each group). Let me share my experience with you. I used to think that either way, it's not a major issue as long as the redo-logs *are* mirrored and protected from a single point of failure. However, an experience at a customer site revealed otherwise. We were using *IBM AIX*'s Volume Manager to mirror the three online redo-log groups (one member per group). Everything was fine, except I used to see this message quite frequently in the alert-log—"online redo-log not available for archiving." On contacting Oracle Support, I was advised that this problem seemed to be occurring because of too few redo-log groups. So we added two more groups to the already existing three, hoping that we had seen the last of that message. No such luck! They just continued. I started monitoring the redo-log activity and the frequency of these messages to see some kind of a pattern. Fortunately, I didn't have to wait too long.

Every time there was a log switch, the message occurred almost instantaneously. What seemed to be happening was this: LGWR would fill up a log and it would switch to the next group. ARCH would then try to read the filled redo-log file for archiving. At the same time, AIX's Volume Manager software was already reading that file to write to its mirror (the mirror writes seemed either to be occurring synchronously or to be delayed). And the ARCH process, seeing that the file was in use, would immediately complain that the redo-log was unavailable for archiving. Once AIX was done with the file, ARCH could finish its task without interruptions.

In order to prove this theory and solve the problem, I created two redo-log files per group (that is, I made Oracle mirror the redo-logs) in addition to the AIX mirroring, and I placed the second redo-log file from each redo-log group in a non-mirrored volume. Bingo, that did it! ARCH complained no more. After a log

switch, ARCH tried to read from one redo-log member. If that file was in use by the AIX Volume Manager software, ARCH just tried the other member and could read it without problems. It could finish the job without hiccups.

It's a good idea to have Oracle mirror the online redo-logs. Even if you mirror the redo-logs, it's good to place one member from each group on a non-mirrored volume. This will protect the redo-logs against hardware/software mirroring problems and bugs.

In addition to mirroring, create more than three redo-log groups, if the database workload is fairly high. Oracle needs a minimum of two redo-log groups to be functional—so that it can switch back and forth between the two (however, installations on most platforms create three redo-log groups by default). Prior to moving to the next redo-log group, Oracle performs a checkpoint on the first. Only after this checkpoint is complete can the next redo-log group be written to. The majority of the work in a checkpoint is performed by DBWR. Sometimes DBWR is already under heavy stress and may not keep current with its workload (a subsequent tip addresses this). Unless a checkpoint is fully complete for a redo-log group, it cannot be overwritten. Sometimes, LGWR gets well ahead of DBWR, finishes writing to the next log file, and is ready to switch back to the previous one. Since the checkpoint for the previous one is not yet complete, however, its contents cannot be overwritten, and so it cannot be allocated as the next log group in the current redo thread. Oracle highlights this situation generally via a message in the alert-log. The following lines from the alert-log of a sample database illustrate a situation where LGWR cannot switch to the next redo-log, due to a checkpoint not being complete. This situation is explained further in Chapter 13.

```
Sat Oct  3 13:47:20 1998
Thread 1 advanced to log sequence 13522
  Current log# 1 seq# 13522 mem# 0: /opt/apps/oracle/ORAKRNL/PD01/log01PD01.log
  Current log# 1 seq# 13522 mem# 1: /opt/apps/oracle/odata1/PD01/ORAKRNL/log01PD01.log
Sat Oct  3 13:47:39 1998
Thread 1 cannot allocate new log, sequence 13523
Checkpoint not complete
  Current log# 1 seq# 13522 mem# 0: /opt/apps/oracle/ORAKRNL/PD01/log01PD01.log
  Current log# 1 seq# 13522 mem# 1: /opt/apps/oracle/odata1/PD01/ORAKRNL/log01PD01.log
Thread 1 advanced to log sequence 13523
  Current log# 2 seq# 13523 mem# 0: /opt/apps/oracle/odata2/PD01/ORAKRNL/log02PD01.log
  Current log# 2 seq# 13523 mem# 1: /opt/apps/oracle/odata3/PD01/ORAKRNL/log02PD01.log
Similarly, soon as a log switch occurs, ARCH starts reading the previous redo-log for
archiving. Sometimes during heavy writes, the LGWR finishes writing the next log file and
needs to switch back, even before ARCH is done. Thus, LGWR can get way ahead of ARCH, as
well. Unless the previous redo-log file is archived, Oracle cannot write to it (to avoid
overwriting the original, unarchived contents).
```

In both the preceding scenarios where LGWR is faster than DBWR and ARCH, if there are other groups that LGWR can switch to, then database performance is not affected. Otherwise, if there are only the two or three groups created by default,

LGWR will need to wait for DBWR and ARCH to get done. Thus, creating more than three redo-log groups gives a chance for a slow DBWR or a slow ARCH to wrap up its stuff without affecting overall database activity. For a fair-sized database (50GB and up) with large write activity (concurrent OLTP writes, heavy batch operations), it's a good idea to have at least four redo-log groups to prevent the preceding scenarios from occurring. (Again, four is just a generic "rule of thumb" number for most mid-sized environments. If your database is a VDLD generating mammoth redo [say, 1GB per hour], then you will definitely need a lot more than four redo-log groups.)

NOTE

Mirroring control-files is also extremely important. Control-files can be mirrored via the CONTROL_FILES initialization parameter (usually placed in the configSID.ora *file). The reason I don't mention this as a tip is due to its basic criticality. In other words, it's not a tip, rather it's almost a mandatory instruction for any 24×7 site. Mirroring control-files helps protect them against a wide variety of failures (hardware, software corruption, accidents, and so on). Ideally, at least three copies of the control-file need to be maintained on different disks/controllers. Even if your environment does not allow this (for example, if all data is striped across all available disks in a RAID 5 environment), still preserve at least three copies, to protect against non-hardware related failures such as administrative accidents. Control-files are relatively very small (compared to the data-files and redo-logs) and take up little space. Also, they impose a very tiny read/write performance penalty (if any, at all). One point to note is, if Oracle cannot write to even one copy of the control-file, it signals a fatal error and the database crashes (unlike multiplexed online redo logs, where Oracle continues to function even if a redo-log member within a group is unavailable). During such times, it would be necessary to overwrite the unavailable/corrupt control-file copy with the valid one (the valid control-file copy may be determined from the most recent OS data/time stamp) and restart the database. Crash recovery is performed as the database comes up.*

Place redo-logs such that ARCH and LGWR do not contend with each other

Typically, as soon as a log switch occurs and LGWR starts writing to the next redo-log group, ARCH springs into action and starts reading from the previous redo-log group to create the archived redo-logs. Thus, LGWR is writing and ARCH is reading concurrently. Obviously, it is essential to ensure that the ARCHIVE_LOG_DEST directory is maintained on separate disks/controllers than the online redo-logs to prevent contention between LGWR and ARCH as they (concurrently) write to the online and archived redo-logs, respectively. Additionally, it helps to place redo-log groups onto different disks/controllers in such a fashion that LGWR and ARCH do not contend with each other at any given point in time. For example, Figure 7-5 shows a redo-log file placement scenario using four redo-log groups and one member per group. The scenario depicts five points in time (T1 through T5) in the redo-log life cycle (a life cycle spans log switches across all redo-log groups). In such a scenario, contention between LGWR and ARCH is inevitable during times T2 and T4, since they would share the same controller during those times. A better alternative for redo-log file placement is depicted in Figure 7-6, where LGWR and ARCH do not (generally) contend with each other, even with the very same hardware resources. In both figures, I have just displayed four controllers and four disks (one-to-one correspondence between the disk and controller) and just one log-file member per group to keep things visually simple. You may have more or less hardware resources in your environment, and you will most definitely have more than one redo-log member per group (if you have followed the advice in the preceding pages). However, the figures demonstrate that by avoiding carelessness and with a bit of ingenuity, you can ensure that LGWR and ARCH stay out of each other's hair—in your specific environment.

As you determine the optimal placement scenario for the redo logs in your environment, it is imperative to remember that ARCH is a slower process than LGWR. During peak hours, when there are bursts of write activity, ARCH may tend to fall very much behind LGWR. Thus, LGWR may complete multiple log switches (provided enough redo-log groups are available), whereas ARCH may still be working on an earlier redo-log. For example, in Figure 7-6, during timeline T2, ARCH may still be working on redo-log group #1 on disk c1d1, while LGWR has already reached redo-log group #3 on disk c1d2 (after a quick log switch from group #2 on disk c2d2) and is forced to share the same controller C1 with ARCH, causing contention. Similarly, during timeline T3, LGWR may switch over to group #4 on disk c2d1, even as ARCH (slowly) makes its way to group #2 on disk c2d2, thus causing both to be sharing controller C2. Even the best possible configuration is not guaranteed to prevent LGWR from traversing all redo-log groups and bumping into its own "tail," while ARCH is still working on the "tail" (the "tail" would be the oldest redo-log group unarchived/currently being archived). Total database activity needs to be kept in mind prior to deciding upon the number of redo-log groups to

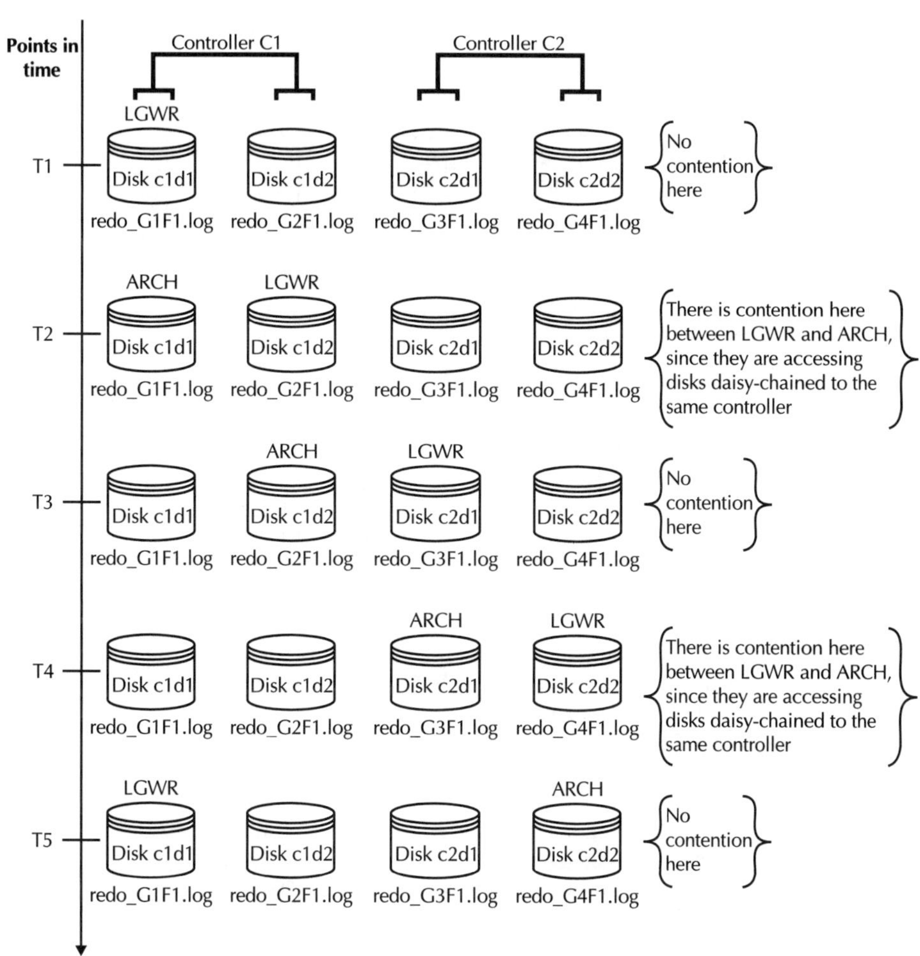

FIGURE 7-5. *A redo-log placement scenario causing LGWR and ARCH contention*

have and the number of disks/controllers to spread them across. The main idea is to alternate consecutive redo-log groups across different disks/controllers, so that contention is minimized in most cases. The greater the write activity in the database, the greater the number of redo-log groups to introduce, and the greater the number of disks/controllers to alternate them across.

Figures 7-5 and 7-6 assume that all online redo-logs are placed on disks containing files, requiring low to medium I/O. In other words, additional I/O contention is not caused by non-redo log files. If the redo-logs are placed on disks containing files that require heavy I/O, then the whole purpose of

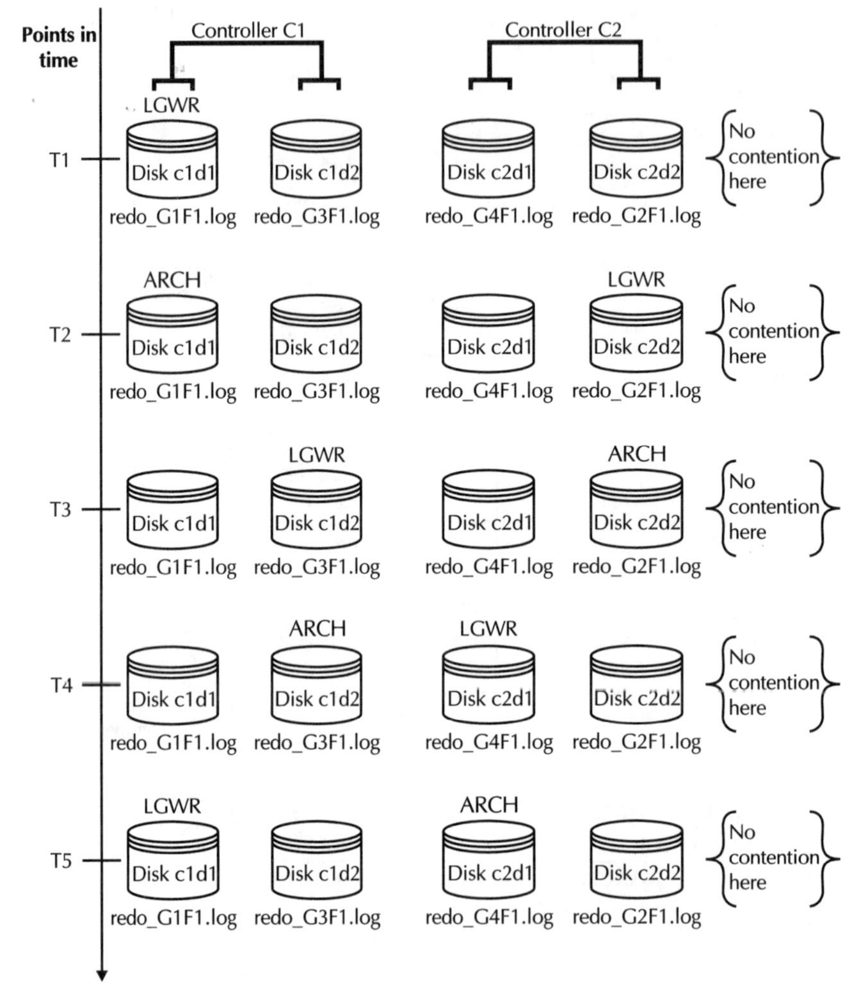

FIGURE 7-6. *A redo-log placement scenario eliminating LGWR and ARCH contention*

trying to separate ARCH and LGWR becomes less important. I say "less important" and not "wasted" because, in such situations, where other files cause I/O contention for, say, 40 percent of the time, then at least 60 percent of the time, segregating ARCH and LGWR improves throughput. In other words, setting aside I/O from all other sources, contention between ARCH and LGWR is still eliminated (which is the actual purpose), thus keeping overall contention low.

Finally, to drive the point home, Figures 7-7 and 7-8 provide another example, where the number of redo-log groups is higher than the number of disks/controllers

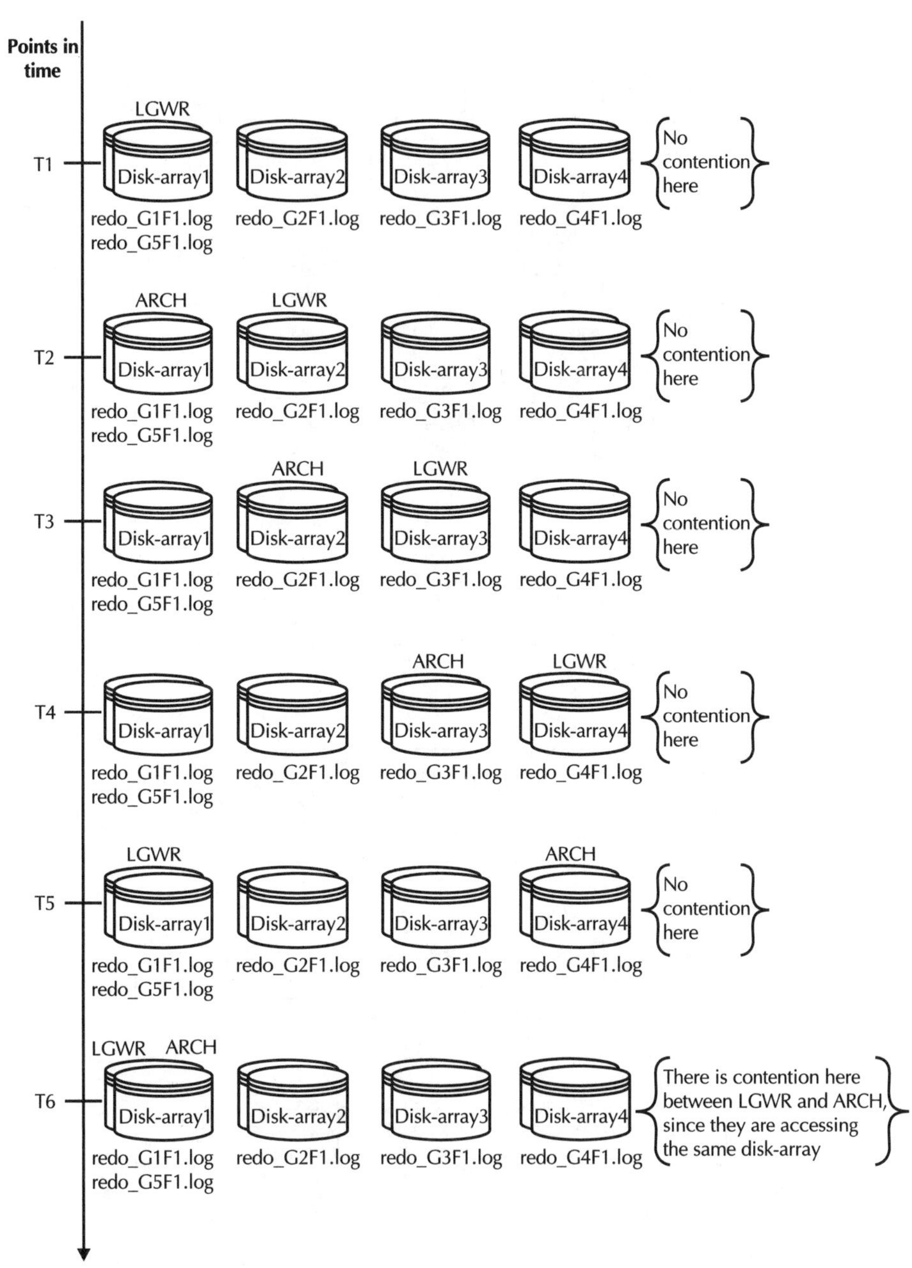

FIGURE 7-7. *Keeping the first and last redo-log groups on the same disk-array may cause LGWR/ARCH contention*

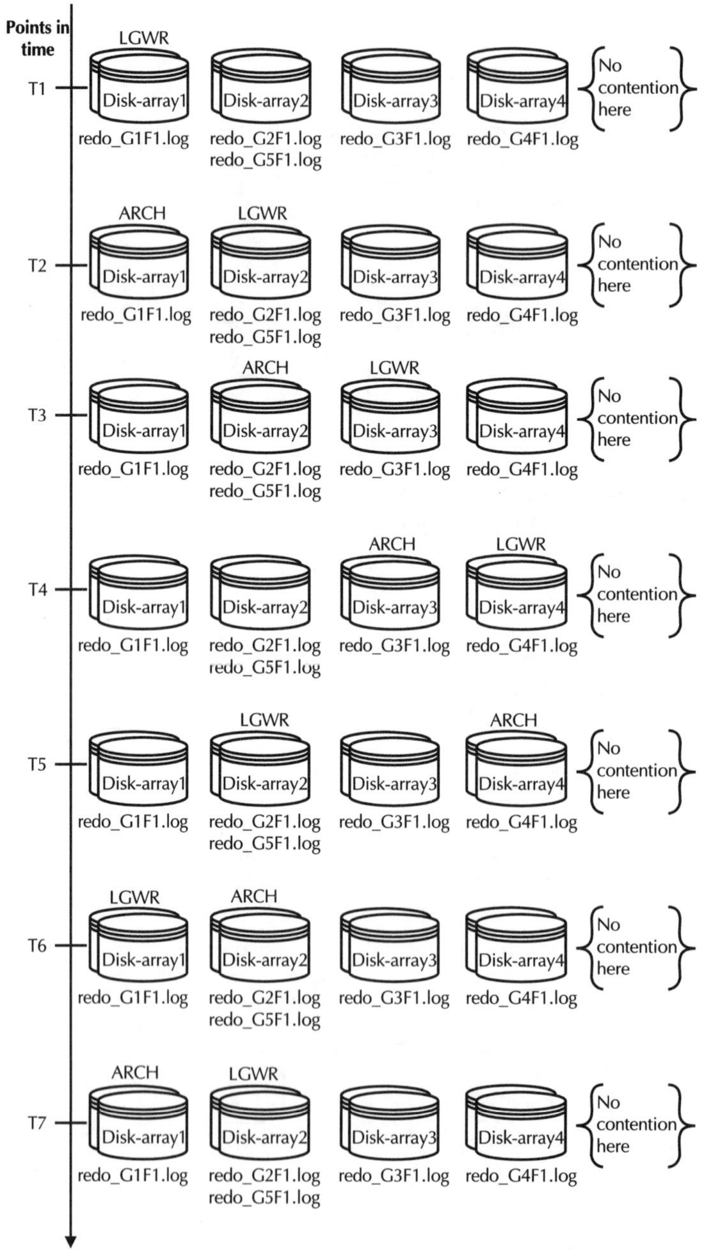

Points in time

T1 — LGWR: Disk-array1 (redo_G1F1.log); Disk-array2 (redo_G2F1.log, redo_G5F1.log); Disk-array3 (redo_G3F1.log); Disk-array4 (redo_G4F1.log) — No contention here

T2 — ARCH: Disk-array1 (redo_G1F1.log); LGWR: Disk-array2 (redo_G2F1.log, redo_G5F1.log); Disk-array3 (redo_G3F1.log); Disk-array4 (redo_G4F1.log) — No contention here

T3 — Disk-array1 (redo_G1F1.log); ARCH: Disk-array2 (redo_G2F1.log, redo_G5F1.log); LGWR: Disk-array3 (redo_G3F1.log); Disk-array4 (redo_G4F1.log) — No contention here

T4 — Disk-array1 (redo_G1F1.log); Disk-array2 (redo_G2F1.log, redo_G5F1.log); ARCH: Disk-array3 (redo_G3F1.log); LGWR: Disk-array4 (redo_G4F1.log) — No contention here

T5 — Disk-array1 (redo_G1F1.log); LGWR: Disk-array2 (redo_G2F1.log, redo_G5F1.log); Disk-array3 (redo_G3F1.log); ARCH: Disk-array4 (redo_G4F1.log) — No contention here

T6 — LGWR: Disk-array1 (redo_G1F1.log); ARCH: Disk-array2 (redo_G2F1.log, redo_G5F1.log); Disk-array3 (redo_G3F1.log); Disk-array4 (redo_G4F1.log) — No contention here

T7 — ARCH: Disk-array1 (redo_G1F1.log); LGWR: Disk-array2 (redo_G2F1.log, redo_G5F1.log); Disk-array3 (redo_G3F1.log); Disk-array4 (redo_G4F1.log) — No contention here

FIGURE 7-8. *The contention illustrated in Figure 7-7 is eliminated via this configuration*

actually used/available. Let's say you have four disk-arrays (with each array having its own set of one or more controllers) and five redo-log groups (again, one member per group to keep the example simple). Figure 7-7 illustrates how a careless configuration may induce contention during timeline T6. Since the first and last redo-log groups are placed on the same disk-array (disk-array1), LGWR and ARCH share that array during timeline T6. The configuration illustrated in Figure 7-8 alleviates this contention by placing the last redo-log group (#5, in this case) to a different disk-array (disk-array2) than the one on which the first redo-log group is placed.

Configure adequate redo latches to minimize contention

As server processes change data, redo information is generated and gets written to the log buffer in the SGA. Prior to writing redo information to the log buffer, a latch needs to be obtained, so that no other server process can concurrently write to the same portion of the log buffer (thus overwriting the first process's redo). The following three types of latches are available for writing to the redo log buffer:

- The redo allocation latch
- The redo copy latch(es)
- The redo writing latch

Any installation of Oracle always has one (and only one) redo allocation latch. The redo allocation latch is primarily responsible for allocating space in the log buffer. Once the space is allocated, if the redo to be written is equivalent to or greater than the value of the initialization parameter LOG_SMALL_ENTRY_MAX_SIZE (specified in bytes), then the redo allocation latch is released by the server process and a redo copy latch is used to perform the actual task of copying the redo information to the log buffer. If the redo to be written is smaller than LOG_SMALL_ENTRY_MAX_SIZE, however, then the allocation latch continues to be held by the server process until the redo is copied over to the allotted space in the log buffer. In other words, the LOG_SMALL_ENTRY_MAX_SIZE parameter provides the threshold value, below which the redo allocation latch is held for both log buffer space allocation and log buffer writes. Otherwise, it is held only for log buffer space allocation. The redo writing latch has been introduced in Oracle8. It allows the online redo logs to be written and also facilitates the waits between subsequent writes.

Generally, the default value for LOG_SMALL_ENTRY_MAX_SIZE is 80 (this parameter has been done away with in Oracle8*i* v8.1.4, where redo latch allocation is performed dynamically by Oracle). The number of redo copy latches depends on the initialization parameter LOG_SIMULTANEOUS_COPIES. The value for this parameter varies from system to system and depends on the number of CPUs available (based on the initialization parameter CPU_COUNT; the value for this parameter is set automatically by Oracle and should not be changed). Oracle installed on machines with a single CPU only has a single allocation latch. The number of redo copy latches is set to zero in such cases. (LOG_SIMULTANEOUS_COPIES has been changed to an underscore parameter in Oracle8*i* v8.1.4, and the value for this parameter is automatically set to CPU_COUNT × 2. So even on a uniprocessor machine, the value defaults to 2.) LOG_SIMULTANEOUS_COPIES needs to be zero on a uniprocessor machine, since redo copy latches cannot be effective used with just one CPU (the existing CPU would be used up by the server process with the allocation latch). So, rather than switch latches, the server process continues to hold the allocation latch. Even if the latch switch occurred, the allocation latch would need to remain passive (since there is just one CPU present). However, generally on machines supporting 24×7 databases, there is more than one CPU, so this is not an issue.

If the database is subjected to high activity, the values of both LOG_SMALL_ENTRY_MAX_SIZE and LOG_SIMULTANEOUS_COPIES assume a lot of importance. Prior to changing the values for these parameters, check the amount of redo generated in *v$sysstat* (statistic: "redo size", expressed in bytes) and the number of redo entries generated by server processes (statistic: "redo entries"). If it's a new installation, it's good to determine these statistics on a test database. If that's not possible, estimate the traffic to be handled by the database. If the statistics appear high, then the contention for the redo latches needs to be monitored. If there is high contention, these initialization parameters need to be set appropriately. On a multiprocessor machine, the number of redo copy latches should be set to at least the number of CPUs (or twice the number of CPUs, if an excessively large number of redo entries are generated). The value for LOG_SMALL_ENTRY_MAX_SIZE should be reduced incrementally to lower values, until contention becomes negligible (ideally, zero contention). If there is high contention for the copy latches but much less contention for the allocation latch, it may be necessary to increase the value for this parameter. Usually, there is higher contention for the allocation latch. It may be necessary to set LOG_SMALL_ENTRY_MAX_SIZE to zero, if the contention on the allocation latch is high or is persistent. This will cause all requests to use the allocation latch very frugally, only for the purpose of log buffer space allocation. Once the space is allotted, the allocation latch is released and a copy latch is obtained. Thus, multiple copy latches are available for sharing among the server processes and are less prone to contention. This leaves the solitary allocation latch free to go around allocating log buffer space, thus reducing allocation latch contention. Furthermore, in Oracle7, the initialization parameter LOG_ENTRY_PREBUILD_THRESHOLD may be set to a value greater than zero to specify that redo information would be prebuilt by server processes, prior to acquiring the redo latches. This would further reduce the time that the latch is held by a server process. Starting with Oracle7 7.3.*x*, however, this parameter has been converted into an underscore parameter. Also, in Oracle8*i* v8.1.4, it has been eliminated altogether. (I think one of the main reasons for this parameter being removed is the amount of confusion it causes—mainly among senior DBAs, most junior DBAs don't even know about these parameters—regarding the value to be specified. It requires careful monitoring of the redo statistics to determine an appropriate value.)

Also in Oracle8, shared latches have been implemented on certain platforms, allowing different latches, including the redo latches, to be shared concurrently among multiple server processes. This makes it possible for other server processes to obtain read access to a resource that has been locked by another process. This further reduces redo latch contention, since it mitigates the need for server processes waiting on the redo allocation and copy latches.

Contention for the redo latches can be monitored via the following query:

```
SQL> SELECT SUBSTR(name, 1, 16) "NAME", gets, misses,
  2         immediate_gets "I_GETS", immediate_misses "I_MISSES", sleeps
  3    FROM v$latch
  4   WHERE name LIKE 'redo%';

NAME                  GETS    MISSES    I_GETS  I_MISSES    SLEEPS
---------------- --------- --------- --------- --------- ---------
redo allocation    1245355       233         0         0        21
redo copy              345        12  23456675      5627       678
redo writing      67878431         0         0         0         0
```

Contention for log buffer space can be monitored via the following query:

```
SQL> SELECT SUBSTR(name, 1, 25) "NAME", value
  2    FROM v$sysstat
    WHERE name LIKE '%redo log space%'
       OR name LIKE '%redo log space wait time%'
       OR name LIKE '%redo buffer allocation retries%';

NAME                          VALUE
------------------------- ---------
redo log space requests           0
redo log space wait time          0
redo buffer allocation retries    0
```

High values for the preceding statistics are usually indications that the log buffer is too small. The "redo log space requests" event occurs when there is not sufficient space in the log buffer to accommodate all requests for space. When the buffer gets full or when COMMITs in the application occur, the contents of the log buffer are flushed to disk by LGWR. If server processes request space while LGWR is performing the write, however, the former would need to wait until the write is complete and the log buffer has the space for the allocations. Thus, the "redo log space requests" statistic indicates the times that server processes had to wait due to the log buffer being full (while the LGWR write was in progress). The other statistics are supplementary to the first. The "redo log space wait time" statistic indicates the total time, in hundredths of a second, that the server processes had to spend waiting, and "redo buffer allocation retries" indicates the number of times server processes tried to have space allocated in the log buffer via the allocation latch.

Ensure that dbwr can keep up with database loads

In the preceding paragraphs, we saw how LGWR can easily get ahead of DBWR, especially if the latter is overburdened. DBWR performs various data buffer management functions, such as flushing the buffers to disk during checkpoints and also cleaning up dirty buffers when a sufficient number of clean buffers are not available for server processes to write to. If DBWR is excessively bogged down during one of these tasks, it adversely impacts the other. For example, if DBWR is busy writing the buffer contents to disk to satisfy a request for space from a foreground server process or is aiding in an index-build by writing data to the temporary tablespace, it may not be able to keep up with the required checkpointing, thus leading to slower checkpoints (another reason for the "cannot allocate new log—checkpoint not complete" warning in the alert-log). Sufficient throughput needs to be derived from DBWR to match total database loads and prevent DBWR from being a bottleneck. Prior to evaluating DBWR throughput, let us understand the internal working of the DBWR.

DBWR is one of the primary background processes and starts up right after PMON (even before SMON). It usually is listed in the dynamic view *v$process* with a process ID (pid) of 3. DBWR is primarily responsible for transferring the contents of changed data-block buffers (also referred to as "dirty" buffers) in the buffer cache to the data-files. Oracle utilizes an LRU (least recently used) based buffer cache–management algorithm to manage the data-block buffer cache. Thus, DBWR operates within the purview of the LRU algorithm. The LRU algorithm depends on three core structures, which are an intrinsic part of the data-block buffer cache (in addition to the actual buffered data blocks):

- LRU list
- LRUW list
- Hash-bucket chain list

The first structure, that is, the LRU list, is a linked list of data-block headers with the headers of "hot" or most recently used buffers placed at the beginning of the list. The "heat" tapers as the list progresses and the tail end of the list typically holds headers of buffers that are free or ready for reuse (unless there has been heavy write activity in the database, as a result of which all buffers are "dirty" and need to be written to disk by the DBWR prior to being reused). Thus, the buffers in the LRU list can be in any of the following conditions:

- **Free** These are typically found toward the tail end of the LRU list (unless the database is inactive, in which case almost all the buffers are free). The ones at the tail end are considered to be "cold" (that is, they have less chances of them being reread by a server process) by Oracle and may be overwritten by a server process with fresh data from disk. When such new data is written to a free buffer, it generally moves up the food chain to the beginning of the LRU list (the MRU or most recently used end).
- **Dirty** These are buffers that have been written to by server processes. However, they are not currently being used and are ready to be written to disk by DBWR during the next checkpoint. These buffers typically get moved to the LRUW list by DBWR, after the server process releases the latch on them.
- **Pinned dirty** These are buffers in "busy" mode and are currently being written to by server processes; they cannot be flushed to disk by DBWR.
- **Pinned clean** These buffers are also in "busy" mode, and a server process holds a latch on them. However, they are not being written to and hence are referred to as being "clean." Both the pinned dirty and pinned clean buffers may have other server processes (waiters) waiting to access them.

The second structure, that is, the LRUW list, is a linked list of dirty data-block headers. After the latch on a pinned dirty buffer is released by the server process performing the write, it is marked as dirty in the LRU list. It is moved to the LRUW list by DBWR. Sometimes, however, DBWR may be too busy to perform this move. And a server process may encounter the dirty buffers in the LRU list during a scan for free buffers and perform the move itself. During the move, the headers of the dirty data-block buffers are taken off the LRU list and transferred to the LRUW list. During subsequent checkpoints, DBWR can write the data-block buffers in the LRUW list to disk (in units smaller than or equivalent to the size specified by the initialization parameter _DB_BLOCK_WRITE_BATCH). If the LRUW is "full" (as determined by the initialization parameter _DB_LARGE_DIRTY_QUEUE), the server processes cannot write to the LRU and LRUW lists until DBWR has cleaned the dirty buffers. DBWR usually times out once every three seconds and wakes up to scan for dirty buffers to clean. In order to minimize the wait time experienced by the server processes, however, DBWR responds in an urgent fashion to clean the dirty buffers when the LRUW list is determined to be full. While handling such compelling requirements, DBWR usually writes in fully packed units of _DB_BLOCK_WRITE_BATCH. Starting with v7.2, this parameter is initialized to zero and the value is determined dynamically by Oracle. The current value for _DB_BLOCK_WRITE_BATCH can be determined via the following query:

In Oracle8:

```
SQL> SELECT kviidsc, kviival
  2    FROM x$kvii
  3   WHERE kviidsc LIKE '%DBWR write%';

KVIIDSC                                                           KVIIVAL
---------------------------------------------------------------- ---------
DBWR write chunk                                                        82
```

In Oracle7 (v7.3.4):

```
SQL> SELECT kviidsc, kviival
  2    FROM x$kvii
  3   WHERE kviidsc LIKE '%IO clump%';

KVIIDSC                                                           KVIIVAL
---------------------------------------------------------------- ---------
DB writer IO clump                                                      64
```

From the preceding discussion it is apparent that the LRU and LRUW lists are mutually exclusive. In other words, a data-block buffer header can exist in only one list at a point in time.

The third structure, that is, the hash-bucket chain list, acts as a map of the data-block buffer cache (see Figure 7-9). Each of these hash buckets maintains a doubly linked list consisting of a range of data-block headers ordered by how recently they were accessed (that is, by the LRU algorithm). Each data-block header is placed within a hash bucket as the result of a hash function applied to the dba (data-block address). Oracle accesses a data block in memory by applying the hash algorithm to the dba, and the resultant hash value is used to determine which hash bucket would contain the data-block header. Once that is known, a *cache buffers chain* latch is obtained on the hash bucket and a range scan is performed to detect the right data-block header (the latch prevents the hash bucket from changing during the scan). The data-block header maintains a pointer to the actual buffered data block. If the data-block header is present within a hash bucket, it results in a logical hit and the data block may be accessed directly in memory; otherwise, it has to be read in from disk and the appropriate hash bucket needs to be updated with the header of the new block. Free buffers are sought by server processes in the LRU list so that they can be populated with the blocks read from disk. A server process obtains a *cache buffers lru chain* latch on the LRU list and performs a seek for free buffers starting from the tail end of the LRU list (as there are better chances of finding free buffers there), rather than the front (MRU) end of the LRU list. Also, a

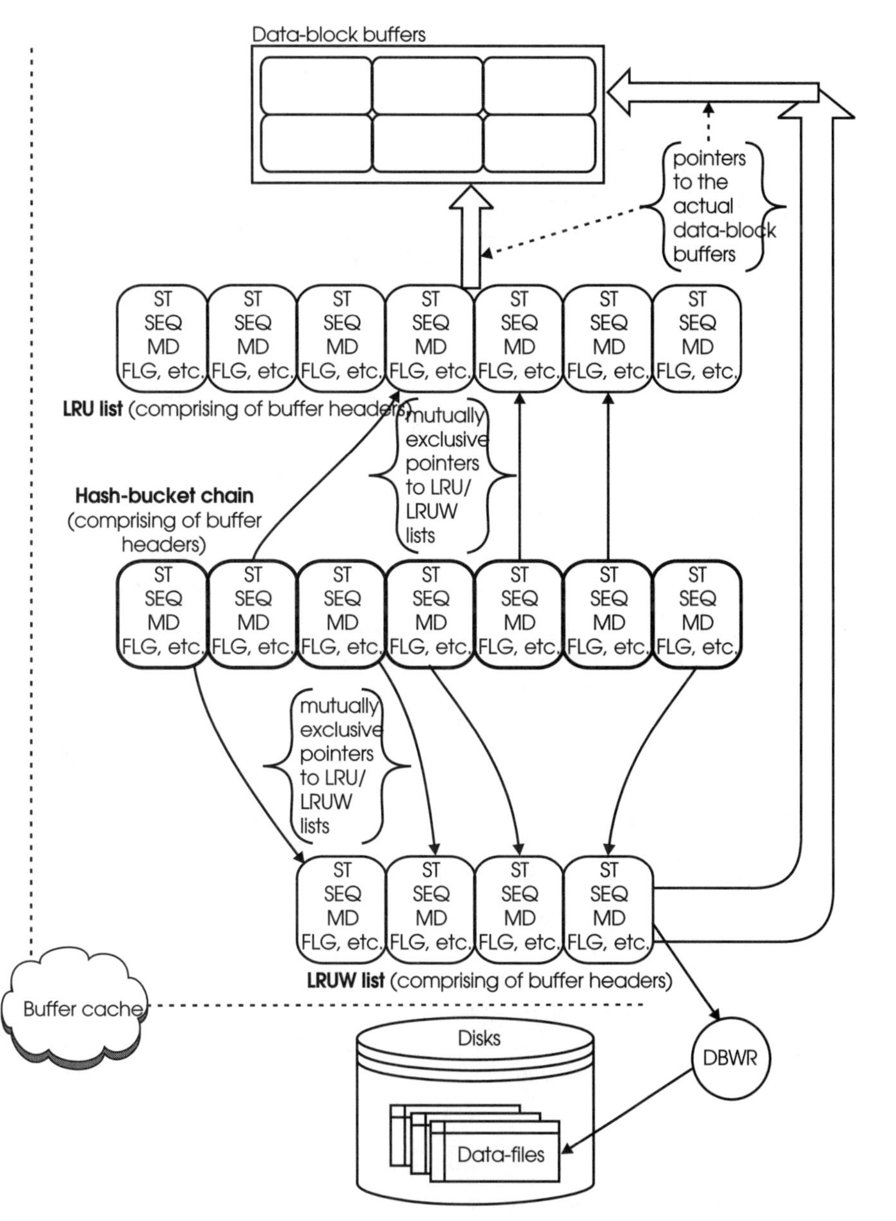

FIGURE 7-9. *Hash-bucket chain and LRU and LRUW lists in the buffer cache*

higher chance exists of a server process reusing (rereading) the buffers at the front end of the LRU list, since those buffers are relatively more "hot." Accordingly, it is a good practice not to overwrite them. During the scan, the statistics "free buffers found" and "dirty buffers found" are updated (query *v$sysstat* for the current count of these statistics). The scan depth (number of buffers to scan) adopted by these server processes is determined by the initialization parameter _DB_BLOCK_MAX_SCAN_COUNT. If no free buffers could be found in the scans performed, DBWR is signaled to write out dirty buffers to disk, while the server processes wait (query *v$waitstat* for the "free buffer waits" event to see the frequency of these waits).

NOTE
Starting with Oracle7 v7.2, the wait endured by the server processes is reduced, due to a dirty buffer being marked free and placed on the tail end of the LRU list, as soon as DBWR writes it to disk. Earlier, a dirty buffer would not gain free status until DBWR completed the entire batch write.

In order to ensure that free buffers are not extinguished totally, Oracle keeps track of the current number of free buffers. This count diminishes as server processes use up the free buffers, and the number increases as DBWR scans and cleans them. (The DBWR scan depth or number of buffers scanned is set via the initialization parameter _DB_WRITER_SCAN_DEPTH, which is determined dynamically depending on the number of dirty buffers toward the end of the LRU list; the statistic "DBWR summed scan depth" is updated with each individual scan depth.) As soon as this number gets beyond a certain limit, DBWR is signaled to clean up. However, if it is determined that DBWR is way too far behind (if the free buffers count is below 50 percent of _DB_WRITER_SCAN_DEPTH), then _DB_WRITER_SCAN_DEPTH is incremented by _DB_WRITER_SCAN_DEPTH_INCREMENT. Also, if there is no heavy backlog of dirty buffers (if the free buffers count is greater than 75 percent of _DB_WRITER_SCAN_DEPTH), then to prevent DBWR from working as hard, _DB_WRITER_SCAN_DEPTH is decreased by _DB_WRITER_SCAN_DEPTH_DECREMENT. Values for both _DB_WRITER_SCAN_DEPTH_INCREMENT and _DB_WRITER_SCAN_DEPTH_DECREMENT are determined dynamically, too, based on the dirty buffer backlog.

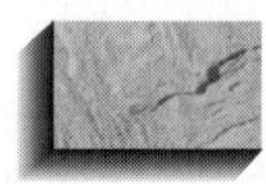

NOTE
DBWR does not write out dirty buffers resulting from temporary operations (such as blocks from sort-area segments in the temporary tablespace).

The number of hash buckets is equivalent to the prime number derived by calculating DB_BLOCK_BUFFERS / 4 (the next available prime number is selected, if DB_BLOCK_BUFFERS / 4 is not a prime number). The number can be explicitly changed by specifying a value for the initialization parameter _DB_BLOCK_HASH_BUCKETS. However, it is not recommended to change this parameter without the explicit permission of Oracle Support. (Very few circumstances warrant changing this parameter; they may include when data-block headers are sub-optimally spread across the hash buckets; a subsequent paragraph specifies how to detect imbalances in the data-block header distribution across hash buckets.) The number of hash buckets maintained in the current instance can be derived via the following query:

In Oracle7:

```
SQL> SELECT kviidsc, kviival
  2    FROM x$kvii
  3   WHERE kviidsc LIKE '%number of hash queue%';

KVIIDSC                                                            KVIIVAL
---------------------------------------------------------------- ---------
number of hash queue latch structures                                   43
```

In Oracle8:

```
SQL> SELECT kviidsc, kviival
  2    FROM x$kvii
  3   WHERE kviidsc LIKE '%number of current%';

KVIIDSC                                                            KVIIVAL
---------------------------------------------------------------- ----------
number of current  buckets                                               61
```

Each data-block header present in the hash-bucket chain contains information such as buffer status or "st" (whether a buffer is being read or dirtied); buffer change version/sequence number or "seq"; the pointer to the data-block header in the LRU or LRUW list; the pointer to the actual buffered data block or "ba"; the latch/lock mode or "md" (indicating whether a latch is being held on a buffer); flags ("flg") indicating ongoing operations on the buffer; and current foreground waiters on the block. This information can be verified by performing a block-header dump via the following command:

```
SQL> ALTER SESSION SET EVENTS 'IMMEDIATE TRACE NAME BUFFERS LEVEL 10';
```

The preceding command takes a little while (it takes me a full minute on an Oracle8 database on NT) to execute and produces a dump file in the user-dump destination directory. Figure 7-10 lists portions of the data-block header dump highlighting the information mentioned previously.

For any new database, potential activity (transaction rates per minute, amount/concurrency of batch loads, and so on) needs to be analyzed prior to configuring DBWR. Ideally, a test instance ought to be created and production-level operations need to be performed to fully grasp the impact on DBWR. For such a test

```
Dump file C:\ORANT\rdbms80\trace\ORA00220.TRC
Sun Apr 04 18:07:32 1999
ORACLE V8.0.3.0.0 - Production vsnsta=0
Windows NT V4.0, OS V5.101, CPU type 586
Oracle8 Enterprise Edition Release 8.0.3.0.0
With the Partitioning and Objects options
PL/SQL Release 8.0.3.0.0 - Production
Windows NT V4.0, OS V5.101, CPU type 586
Instance name: orc8
Redo thread mounted by this instance: 1
Oracle process number: 8
Sun Apr 04 18:07:32 1999
*** SESSION ID:(7.6) 1999.04.04.18.07.32.161
Dump of buffer cache at level 10
CHAIN: 0 LOC: 0x23247a0 HEAD: [23414bc,234aa8c]
BH #360 file#: 1 rdba: 0x00400058 (1/88) class 1 ba: 0x21e4000
  Hash: [23340c4,23247a0],  lru: [2348110,23413e4]
  Ckptq: [NULL] Fileq: [NULL]
  St: XCURRENT, md: NULL, rsop: 0x0, temp: 762
  Cr:[[scn: 0xffff.ffffffff],[xid: 0x0000.000.00000000],
      [uba: 0x00000000.0000.00], sfl: 0x0]
Buffer tsn: 0 rdba: 0x00400058 (1/88)
scn:0x0000.00000399 seq:0x01 flg:0x00 tail:0x03990601
frmt:0x02 chkval:0x0000 type:0x06=trans data
Block header dump: rdba: 0x00400058
 Object id on Block? Y
 seg/obj: 0x2  csc: 0x00.38f  itc: 2  flg: -  typ: 1 - DATA
```

FIGURE 7-10. *A sample portion of a data-block header dump on an Oracle8 database*

instance (or any existing database for that matter), you can look at the following statistics in *v$sysstat* or the *utlbstat/utlestat* output to detect whether DBWR is failing to keep up with the total workload:

- Free buffers requested
- Free buffers inspected
- Dirty buffers inspected
- DBWR make free requests
- DBWR free buffers found
- DBWR timeouts

- DBWR summed scan depth
- DBWR buffers scanned
- DBWR LRU scans
- DBWR checkpoints
- Summed dirty queue length
- Physical writes
- Write requests

The preceding listed statistics are explained in Chapter 9 (as part of a more comprehensive list, from a recovery perspective). The *v$sysstat* statistic numbers are not mentioned in the preceding list, since they are not guaranteed to remain consistent across versions. Sometimes, values for these statistics may appear to be very small or even negative, indicating that the values have rolled over (when the values grow too big for the data type holding them, they roll over, starting from the lowest possible value for that data type [which may be negative] and keep getting incremented until they reach the highest value possible; whereupon they roll over again).

The result of *summed dirty queue length / write requests* reveals the average length of the dirty buffer write queue. As per the *utlbstat/utlestat* report output, it should be less than (DB_FILES × DB_FILE_SIMULTANEOUS_WRITES) / 2 or one-fourth the size of DB_BLOCK_BUFFERS, whichever is smaller. Additionally, it should be close to _DB_BLOCK_WRITE_BATCH. That is an indication of DBWR keeping up with the volume of dirty buffers being generated by server processes. Also, *dbwr make free requests / dbwr free buffers found* should be low (single-digit numbers). If so, it indicates that free buffers are adequate.

Additionally, the dynamic views *v$waitstat, v$system_event, v$session_event, v$session_wait,* and *v$buffer_pool_statistics* (created explicitly in Oracle8 via the *catperf.sql* script) can be queried for the following statistics to check whether server processes are waiting on DBWR (for individual sessions, as well as the entire database).

Maintain DBWR Pace

Free Buffer Waits

This is the number of times server processes were forced to wait on DBWR to obtain the requisite free buffers. This may happen when DBWR hits the "free buffers inspected" boundary.

Buffer Busy Waits

This is the number of times buffers were not available for server processes due to the buffers being in the busy state. This may happen due to other server processes using the buffers (reading from them or writing to them) and holding latches on them. The result of (buffer busy waits / (consistent gets + db blocks gets)) × 100 should be less than five percent.

Write Complete Waits

This is the number of times server processes needed to read a block that was being written to disk by DBWR during a checkpoint.

DB File Sequential Read, DB File Single Write, DB File Scattered Read, DB File Parallel Write

These events indicate the I/O caused by DBWR writing the data buffers to the data-files. For instance, the "db file sequential read" event indicates the number of times server processes were waiting on DBWR before they could complete a sequential read operation. High wait occurrences recorded against these events might be an indication of I/O bottlenecks, which may substantially reduce DBWR throughput. One thing to bear in mind while observing these events is that a small portion of these constitute CKPT/LGWR activity caused by data-file header writes incurred during checkpoints (in Oracle7, LGWR updates the data-file headers in the absence of CKPT; whereas in Oracle8, CKPT is mandatory and updates data-file headers during checkpoints).

Also, the dynamic view *v$latch* can be monitored to record latch activity against the data-block buffers. The columns *gets, misses, immediate_gets, immediate_misses,* and *sleeps* need to be monitored to figure out the latch hit ratio. Additionally, in Oracle8*i*, the column *waits_holding_latch* needs to be checked (this tells us how many foreground processes that are currently waiting for resources such as a row-exclusive lock, are holding a particular latch).

Cache Buffer Handles

Prior to dirtying a data-block buffer, a server process needs to obtain a *cache buffer handle* latch on that data-block buffer. However, if the buffer is already dirtied by another process and DBWR has not yet written it to disk, a wait ensues until DBWR cleans the buffer and makes the latch available. (This is assuming that DBWR has already decided to write the buffer to disk. Oracle does not force a dirty buffer to be written to disk every time it has changed or if another server process wants to write to it. Redo generation takes care of issues to do with crashes. Naturally, checkpoints are exceptions, as is Oracle Parallel Server, when a different instance wants that block.) This wait may occur either because

- DBWR throughput is inadequate to clean the buffers in a timely fashion

  or because

- Large transactions are occurring within the database that hold the latches on the data-block buffers and do not allow DBWR to clean up due to the buffers being *busy*. (This isn't *always* an issue, as a transaction in progress will not stop a dirty block from being freed. DBWR can potentially write dirty blocks independent of whether the transaction has completed or not. This is one of the reasons for *delayed block cleanout* [explained in Chapter 11].)

Cache Buffer Chains

Requests from different server processes for changing various different data-block buffers may revert to the same latch, since the dbas of the concerned data-block buffers may be part of the same hash bucket. Accordingly, Oracle may allocate a *cache buffer chain* latch against all the data-block buffers within a hash bucket. High waits on this latch may indicate the following:

- DBWR throughput may be inadequate to clean up the buffers (as already mentioned).
- Large transactions may be occurring (again, as already mentioned).
- There may be a large number of dbas within each hash bucket in the data-block buffer cache. The large number of dbas within each hash bucket is an indication of sub-optimal buffer cache hash-bucket management and may require manual intervention from Oracle Support (via a change to the initialization parameter _DB_BLOCK_HASH_ BUCKETS). The following query may be used to check whether a hash bucket is over-populated:

  In Oracle8:

  ```
  SELECT dbarfil "File", dbablk "Block", COUNT(*) FROM x$bh
    GROUP BY dbarfil, dbablk
  HAVING COUNT(*) > 1;
  ```

  In Oracle7:

  ```
  SELECT dbafil "File", dbablk "Block", COUNT(*) FROM x$bh
    GROUP BY dbafil, dbablk
  HAVING COUNT(*) > 1;
  ```

Cache Buffer LRU Chain

This latch is used in aging out old data-block buffers in the LRU list. High waits for this latch may be indicative of heavy database activity. They may also mean that DBWR is working in sub-optimal units to clean up dirty buffers, thereby causing frequent shifts in the LRU list. In such a case, value for the initialization parameter _DB_WRITER_MAX_SCAN_CNT may have to be reduced, or the value for the parameter _DB_BLOCK_WRITE_BATCH may need to be increased (ensure that you solicit Oracle Support's help prior to changing them).

If the numbers against these statistics seem inappropriately high (interpret them keeping your overall database activity in mind; generally four-digit numbers or bigger are considered inappropriately high), this might indicate failure of the DBWR to keep up in a timely fashion. Following are some of the possible solutions to increase DBWR throughput. (Note that these solutions assume that the SQL is well tuned. If this assumption is incorrect, one of the first areas to tune is the SQL.)

Enable Asynchronous I/O

Asynchronous I/O (AIO) allows DBWR to issue non-blocking read and write calls, in lieu of sequential calls. When DBWR uses regular synchronous I/O system calls, it follows the sequential pattern of "issue system call, wait for issued call to complete and return, issue next call." Instead, when using AIO, the pattern can be envisaged to be "issue system call, wait for issued call to return, issue next call." In other words, AIO system calls return immediately without waiting for the call to complete. This allows the I/O operations and processing to proceed in parallel, rather than sequentially, thereby increasing process throughput. In other words, a lesser wait is involved for server processes ("free buffer waits," "write complete waits," and so on) waiting on DBWR to flush dirty buffers to disk. It is to be borne in mind, however, that AIO would provide maximum benefit when the destination disks are not already subject to hot spots. In other words, disk contention should not be present, since that would cause subsequent I/O calls to wait on the disk controller as the former calls are being processed, and each call would anyway be serialized at the hardware level. To alleviate the preceding scenario, DBWR issues an AIO call and then performs other non-I/O related tasks, rather than issuing another AIO call that would require I/O. Subsequent AIO calls are issued after the previous ones are polled (via the *poll()* system call) to ensure there are no errors, prior to proceeding.

AIO may be enabled via one or more initialization parameters, depending on the platform. Oracle on certain platforms uses just one initialization parameter (example: USE_ASYNC_IO in Oracle7 on HP-UX) to enable and use AIO, whereas on certain other platforms, different initialization parameters are used for enabling asynchronous reads and writes (example: ASYNC_READ and ASYNC_WRITE in Oracle7 on Solaris). When multiple parameters are used, ensure that both are set to the same Boolean value (either TRUE or FALSE, thus enabling or disabling both asynchronous reads and writes). Also, the parameter names have changed between Oracle7 and Oracle8. Oracle8 has standardized the initialization parameter names for AIO under different platforms to just one. Thus, in Oracle8, the single parameter DISK_ASYNCH_IO is used under diverse platforms such as Sun Solaris, HP-UX, NCR UNIX, Sequent, and so on, to enable or disable AIO.

One thing to note prior to enabling AIO is that certain OSs do not support AIO (they only support the regular *read()* and *write()* calls and, in some cases, the newer *pread()* and *pwrite()* calls, which combine *lseek()* and the subsequent *read()*/*write()* calls, thus reducing overall system call overhead); and some others provide AIO only for raw devices (examples: Sequent and HP-UX). On certain OSs, such as Sun Solaris, AIO is enabled and available by default; whereas on other OSs, such as HP-UX, the AIO driver needs to be explicitly configured and the kernel needs to be rebuilt (requiring a machine reboot). On platforms that support AIO, a distinct set of thread-based read/write calls are available to perform non-blocking, parallel reads and writes. In addition to proprietary AIO calls, most of the OSs that support AIO also provide for POSIX-compliant AIO calls. For example, Solaris 7 supports both Solaris proprietary AIO calls *aioread()* and *aiowrite(),* in addition to the POSIX-compliant AIO calls *aio_read()* and *aio_write()*. It is desirable to use the POSIX AIO calls wherever possible to enhance portability. As of version 8.0.*x*, Oracle uses proprietary AIO calls on most platforms.

An additional AIO feature in Solaris that enhances performance on raw devices is kernelized AIO (KAIO). When KAIO is used (it is enabled by default), the AIO system calls are run directly from the OS kernel itself, rather than the shared user space, used by regular AIO calls. This reduces the communication overhead and the need for context switching between the shared user space and the kernel. KAIO utilizes additional buffers to hold data pertinent to the I/O operation within the kernel. Accordingly, KAIO requires adequate memory to be present on the box, without which the KAIO requests would result in failure. Additionally, if the KAIO call is explicitly issued by an application against a cooked file system, it would result in failure and instead a non-kernelized AIO call would be used to perform the same operation.

List I/O

Another alternative to increasing DBWR throughput is to utilize list I/O. When list I/O is utilized, the OS accepts all I/O requests, groups together a bunch of such requests to form a list, and then processes the list asynchronously as a single collective unit. This reduces the overhead involved in regular I/O processing, where each read or write is treated individually, thus involving high resource costs in terms of CPU cycles and memory required to process each individual system call. Certain platforms support both AIO and list I/O (examples: HP-UX, NCR UNIX, and Solaris 7). However, certain platforms support list I/O only when raw devices are used (example: HP-UX). Oracle supports list I/O via an initialization parameter. (The name of this parameter differs on various platforms. For example, on NCR UNIX, it is USE_LIST_IO_EXTENSION.)

Multiple DBWR Slaves in Oracle7 and Oracle8

On platforms where AIO is not supported, multiple DBWR slaves may be enabled to simulate AIO. Here, the DBWR process constitutes a master process and multiple slaves. The number of slaves is dependent on an initialization parameter. In Oracle7, this parameter is termed DB_WRITERS, and in Oracle8, it is called DBWR_IO_SLAVES. The main difference between Oracle7 and Oracle8 in enabling multiple slave DBWR processes is the capability to handle AIO. In Oracle7, each slave process is capable of performing only synchronous I/O (this is the reason why DBWR slaves were considered as alternatives to AIO, as multiple synchronous slaves could work in tandem to simulate AIO), whereas in Oracle8 each slave process is "AIO aware" and can perform AIO, if the OS supports it. Furthermore, the DBWR slaves are made part of the Oracle8 kernel, thus avoiding too much dependence on the OS. Thus, the DBWR slave code is capable of and ready to perform asynchronous writes and reads, if the OS underneath doesn't shy away. In other words, enabling AIO within Oracle and creating multiple DBWR slaves are mutually exclusive (either one or the other can be used, but not both) in both Oracle7 and Oracle8. However, even with AIO disabled within Oracle, if the OS supports it, Oracle8's DBWR slaves can utilize it, whereas Oracle7's DBWR slaves cannot.

All DBWR slave processes are created at the time the database is opened. The master DBWR process is listed as "ora_dbw0_SID" (where SID is the ORACLE_SID), and the slaves are listed as "ora_iKnn_SID" (where "i" refers to the process being a slave, "K" refers to the disk adapter sequence, and "nn" refers to the DBWR slave process sequence).

Multiple DBWR Processes in Oracle8

As of Oracle8 v8.0.4, multiple DBWR processes can be created to increase overall DBWR throughput. This requires an initialization parameter called DB_WRITER_PROCESSES to be set to the number of DBWR processes required. This process does not break up a single DBWR process into one master and multiple slaves. Instead, it creates multiple DBWR processes, with each process being a sibling of the other. Multiple DBWR processes may be created even with AIO enabled within Oracle. Thus, this is an ideal option for environments (especially OLTP VLDBs) requiring very high DBWR throughput. With the OS underneath supporting AIO, multiple DBWR processes, each capable of AIO, may very well provide optimal DBWR throughput.

Here, since each DBWR process is independent, unless more LRU latches are provided, the DBWR processes would choke while trying to share the single LRU latch. Accordingly, it is necessary to increase the number of LRU latches to match the number of DBWR processes. This change may be accomplished via the initialization parameter DB_LRU_LATCHES. Ideally, set DB_LRU_LATCHES and DB_WRITER_PROCESSES equivalent to the number of CPUs on the box. By enforcing LRU latches to be at least equal to the DBWR processes, Oracle ensures that each DBWR process will have access to an LRU latch, thus allowing it access to a distinct portion of the LRUW list. Thus, all DBWR processes can independently coexist without treading on each other's toes or waiting on each other. Each DBWR process is listed as "ora_dbwN_SID" (where "N" is the DBWR process sequence and SID refers to ORACLE_SID).

Having multiple DBWR processes and enabling multiple DBWR slaves are mutually exclusive. So which option is better? Typically, the answer depends on the resources available on the box and the overall database activity. For most environments, if AIO is supported on the box, then it's advisable to enable AIO and retain just one DBWR process. For databases with high activity, however, if better DBWR throughput is desired (based on statistics discussed previously), then one may enable multiple DBWR processes. If AIO is not supported, however, then it's advisable to utilize multiple DBWR slaves, instead. Also, if the box contains a decent number of CPUs (eight or more), it's a good idea to have multiple DBWR processes. If the box has fewer CPUs, however, then it's advisable to configure multiple DBWR slaves, instead. On the other hand, if your box is really low on CPUs (two or less) or memory, it's a good idea to refrain from configuring either multiple DBWR slaves or processes, since these options require additional buffers for storing intermediate data and additional CPU cycles for handling interthread/interprocess communication overhead.

Increase DB_BLOCK_CHECKPOINT_BATCH

DB_BLOCK_CHECKPOINT_BATCH sets the maximum number of database blocks that DBWR will write in one batch during a checkpoint. By default, DB_BLOCK_CHECKPOINT_BATCH is set to 8. Setting it to a higher value increases DBWR throughput during checkpoints and allows checkpoints to complete faster. However, setting DB_BLOCK_CHECKPOINT_BATCH high on a machine where memory is not abundant causes DBWR to pay high attention to checkpoints, to the point of ignoring other modified blocks that need to be written to disk to accommodate requests for free space from foreground processes (thus lagging behind in that area). As a generic rule of thumb, set DB_BLOCK_CHECKPOINT_BATCH to a value that allows the checkpoint to complete between redo-log switches. If a redo-log switch occurs every twenty minutes, then this parameter should be set to the number of database blocks that would allow the checkpoint to complete within twenty minutes. In order to use the default value (8), do not set DB_BLOCK_CHECKPOINT_BATCH in the *init.ora* or set it to zero. Specifying a very high value does not necessarily indicate that DBWR is using that value. Only the maximum possible will be used by DBWR in each batch.

Increase DB_FILE_MULTIBLOCK_READ_COUNT

This increases the number of database blocks that foreground server processes read in a single sequential I/O operation (such as during full table scans and fast-full index scans). DB_FILE_MULTIBLOCK_READ_COUNT sets the maximum number of

database blocks that can be packed in a single read operation. The default value varies depending on the OS and is set based on the DB_BLOCK_SIZE, DB_BLOCK_BUFFERS, and PROCESSES parameters. Set the value of DB_FILE_MULTIBLOCK_READ_COUNT such that DBWR manages to grab 32K to 64K of data per read (of more than one block). This greatly increases DBWR throughput during full table scans and is helpful in DSS applications where pre-reading of data blocks is very useful. Most OSs have a specific upper limit on the total size per I/O operation (many UNIX flavors have an upper limit of 64K). Setting DB_FILE_MULTIBLOCK_READ_COUNT to a value higher than the OS limit is permissible; however, it doesn't help any, since more than the OS upper limit cannot be read (a physical limitation). Also, DB_FILE_MULTIBLOCK_READ_COUNT cannot be set to a value higher than a quarter portion of the total DB_BLOCK_BUFFERS. For example, if the DB_BLOCK_BUFFERS is 10000, then DB_FILE_MULTIBLOCK_READ_COUNT needs to be less than 2500. Additionally, if the DB_BLOCK_SIZE is 4K, then setting DB_FILE_MULTIBLOCK_READ_COUNT to 2500 will not cause DBWR to read (2500 × 4K) 10MB each time. In such situations, it will revert to the OS upper limit (64K).

Increase DB_FILE_SIMULTANEOUS_WRITES

Wherever possible, DBWR writes to each data-file in a series of simultaneous writes (termed a "group write" or a "batch"). DB_FILE_SIMULTANEOUS_WRITES sets the maximum number of simultaneous writes per data-file. This is useful under the following circumstances:

- If the data-file has been striped across multiple physical disks/controllers
- In the absence of the preceding condition, if the OS can consolidate simultaneous writes to one physical write operation, rather than serializing them

If either of these cases apply, then DBWR throughput may be drastically increased. If the data-file has been striped, then DB_FILE_SIMULTANEOUS_WRITES should be set to the highest number of disk volumes involved in a stripe set. By default, DB_FILE_SIMULTANEOUS_WRITES is set to 4. If both the preceding cases are not applicable, then the value for DB_FILE_SIMULTANEOUS_WRITES should be set to 1. Setting it any higher would have no utility and may even cause DBWR writes to become uneven across data-files, leading to I/O contention. Also, Oracle recommends that it be set to a value lower than 24, since there's no utility to doing otherwise.

As a quick reference, Table 7-2 lists some of the important parameters that affect DBWR throughput (note that some of the parameters may be unavailable or their names may vary depending on the Oracle version and platform).

Initialization Parameter Name	Description
DB_FILE_SIMULTANEOUS_WRITES	The maximum number of simultaneous writes per data-file.
DB_BLOCK_CHECKPOINT_BATCH	The maximum number of dirty buffers written out by DBWR in one I/O operation during (both fast and slow) checkpoints.
DB_FILE_MULTIBLOCK_READ_COUNT	The maximum number of database blocks that can be packed in a single sequential read operation (such as during a full-table scan). This operation usually populates the tail end of the LRU list (exceptions to this rule are listed in a subsequent tip).
_DB_BLOCK_WRITE_BATCH	Determines the upper limit for the number of dirty blocks that DBWR should write to disk in a single I/O operation.
_DB_WRITER_SCAN_DEPTH	The number of buffers that DBWR will scan in the LRU list when looking for dirty buffers. This parameter is influenced by _DB_ BLOCK_WRITE_BATCH.
_DB_WRITER_SCAN_DEPTH_INCREMENT	The number of additional buffers to scan when DBWR is lagging behind. This parameter increases the DBWR scan depth.
_DB_WRITER_SCAN_DEPTH_DECREMENT	The number of buffers by which to reduce the DBWR scan depth, if DBWR is keeping up with the dirty buffers in the LRU list and the LRUW list is empty.
_DB_BLOCK_MAX_SCAN_CNT	The maximum number of buffers that a server process can inspect, starting from the tail end of the LRU list, when looking for free buffers.
_DB_WRITER_MAX_WRITES	The maximum number of DBWR write operations (I/Os) that are outstanding. The value is set dynamically. In Oracle8, the current outstanding DBWR write operations can be noted via the following query:

```
SQL> SELECT kviidsc, kviival
2    FROM x$kvii WHERE kviidsc LIKE '%DBWR max outstanding%'

KVIIDSC                                                        KVIIVAL
-------------------------------------------------------------- ----------
DBWR max outstanding writes                                          2048
```

TABLE 7-2. *Initialization Parameters Influencing DBWR*

Initialization Parameter Name	Description
_DB_LARGE_DIRTY_QUEUE	The number of buffers in the LRUW list, which signals DBWR to clean the dirty queue.
_DB_WRITER_CHUNK_WRITES	The number of writes that DBWR should try to group into one batch I/O operation.
_DB_BLOCK_MED_PRIORITY_BATCH_SIZE	The size of write batches with medium priority (regular writes).
_DB_BLOCK_HI_PRIORITY_BATCH_SIZE	The size of write batches with high priority (urgent writes, as that evidenced when the LURW list is full or the number of free buffers in the LRU list falls below the limit).
_DBWR_ASYNC_IO	Whether asynchronous writes for DBWR are to be turned on. Turned on by default, if ASYNC_IO is on.
DB_BLOCK_MAX_DIRTY_TARGET	The upper limit on dirty buffers.

TABLE 7-2. *Initialization Parameters Influencing DBWR* (continued)

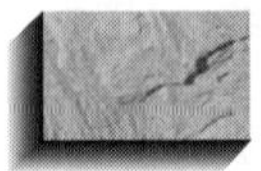

NOTE

All the underscore parameters listed in Table 7-2 are explained purely from an informational perspective—just to help you understand how Oracle operates internally. Please do not change any undocumented initialization parameters, unless specifically requested to do so by Oracle Support. These parameters are core parameters, directly affecting the way Oracle works. Accordingly, changing them without accurate, in-depth knowledge of their functionality and impact may potentially corrupt your database and render it useless. Also, changing them without Oracle Support's explicit permission violates your Support contract and changes your database into an unsupported one (something every 24×7 site can do without!).

Partition your buffer cache into multiple buffer pools according to segment usage patterns

In both Oracle7 and Oracle8, the data-block buffer cache (or simply, the "buffer cache") is broken up into different sub-caches. In Oracle8, it is explicit, whereas in Oracle7, it is managed internally via a specific algorithm. However, the utility of algorithmic management of the cache is limited, since cache isolation is dependent on certain rules imposed by the algorithm. Any algorithm can only assume certain scenarios and apply rules accordingly. It can never anticipate and provide for every possible scenario. In Oracle7, the breakup of the data-block buffer cache into different sub-caches was implemented as follows:

- In Oracle7 v7.3.*x*, more than one LRU latch can be enabled on multi-CPU machines via the initialization parameter DB_BLOCK_LRU_LATCHES. LRU latches are acquired by the DBWR and server processes for scanning the data-block buffer cache. Such latches are necessary to prevent buffers from being dirtied and changed by other processes, thus causing a scan to return inconsistent results. Also, if no latch was placed, a process scanning for a free buffer may find one, only to have that stolen immediately by another process. Each LRU latch needs a minimum of 50 data-block buffers, which it "guards." All buffers are allocated to a specific LRU latch by Oracle based on a hashing algorithm of their DBAs. Prior to v7.3.*x*, only one LRU latch was available, potentially causing contention during heavy database activity. The contention would be higher on multi-CPU machines, where multiple server processes may queue up to try to acquire the single LRU latch.
- The blocks retrieved due to a full-segment (table or index) scan are placed at the tail end of the LRU list (Figure 7-11). The blocks are fetched in units specified by the initialization parameter DB_FILE_MULTIBLOCK_READ_COUNT. Thus, full segment scans never interfere with and displace the non-full scan blocks (for instance, blocks obtained via an indexed lookup) held in the cache by default. There are some exceptions to this rule. One of them is, if the segment has the cache option enabled (via the CREATE TABLE|INDEX CACHE or ALTER TABLE|INDEX CACHE commands). An important side note here is that caching is not permanent or meant to guarantee that the segment would remain in the cache indefinitely. All the cache option does is move the data blocks accessed via the full-segment scan to the beginning of the LRU list (the most recently used or MRU area). That way, the blocks of the "cached" segment would remain in cache for a longer time, until they got phased out of the cache due to regular database activity. Figure 7-12 provides an illustration of the way cached segments are treated when a full-segment scan is performed on them. Also, on specific platforms, Oracle uses the CACHE_SIZE_THRESHOLD initialization parameter to determine the maximum number of blocks of a single segment that can be placed on the MRU end. So if you decide (especially in a DSS environment) to cache some of your critical code/reference/dimension tables, you would need to set CACHE_SIZE_THRESHOLD to the number of blocks occupied by the largest such table. The default value is usually ten percent of the DB_BLOCK_BUFFERS value.

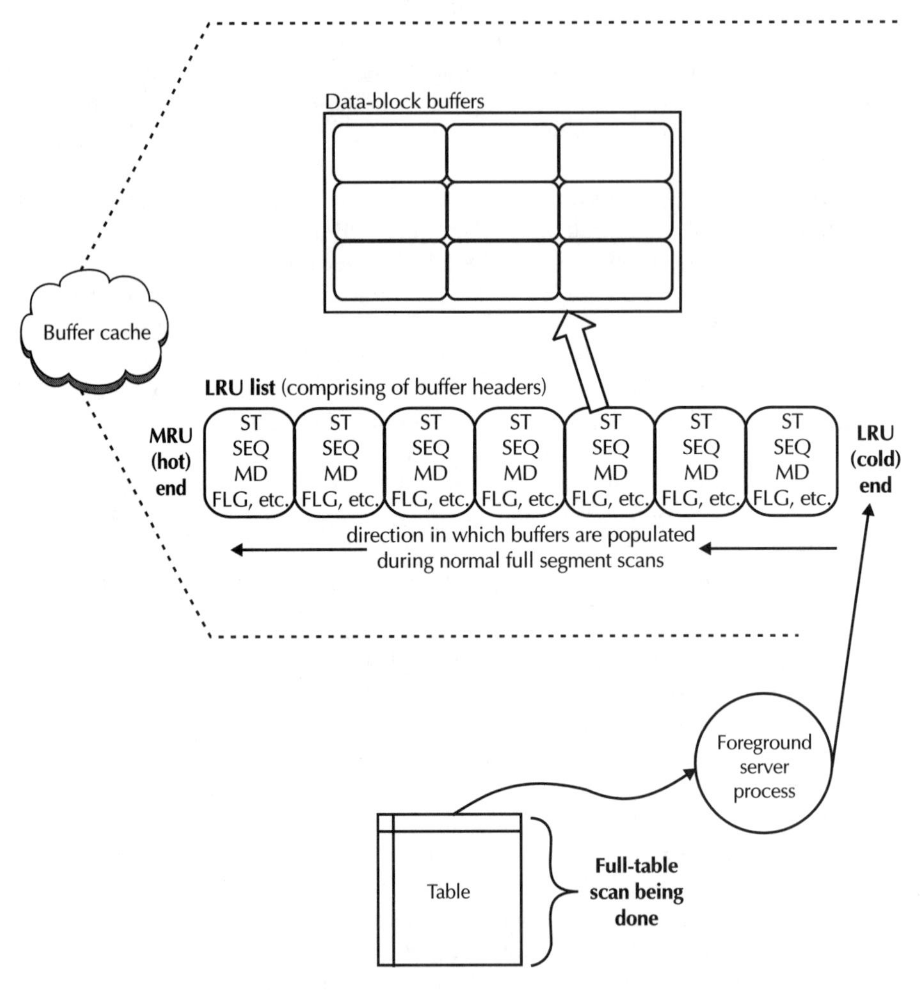

FIGURE 7-11. *Blocks read via full-segment scans are placed at the tail of the LRU list*

Another exception to the rule of placing blocks retrieved via full-table scans at the tail end of the LRU list is if the table is determined to be a "small" table. Blocks of a small table are also placed at the MRU end of the LRU list. A table is considered to be a small table if it is contained within four Oracle blocks or less. Also, prior to version 7.3, the initialization parameter SMALL_TABLE_THRESHOLD was used to decide whether a table is small or not. This parameter defaults to two percent of DB_BLOCK_BUFFERS or

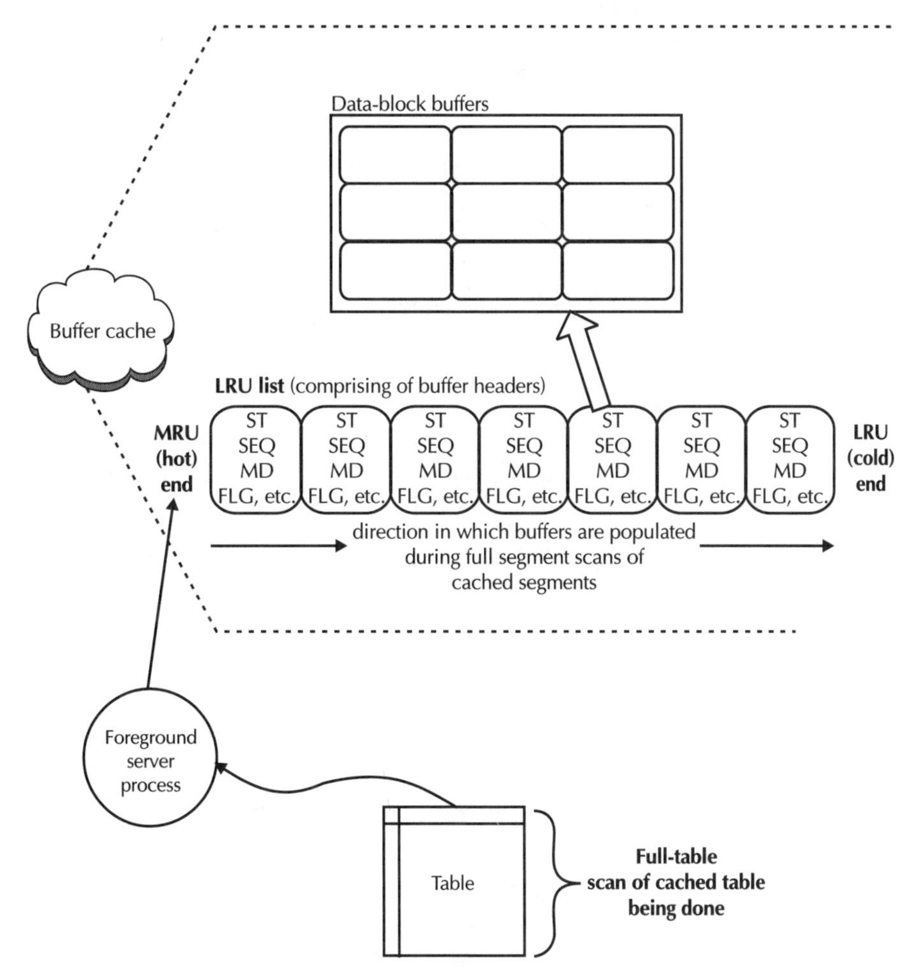

FIGURE 7-12. *Blocks of* cached *segments read as a result of a full-segment scan are placed at the head (MRU-end) of the LRU list*

four Oracle blocks, whichever is higher. Thus, a table would be considered small if the number of Oracle blocks it occupies is equivalent to or less than two percent of the total data-block buffers (assuming that two percent of the DB_BLOCK_BUFFERS value would almost always exceed four Oracle blocks in a production environment).

Even with such sophisticated buffer management, however, isolation of data blocks with different specific usage spans is not highly reliable in Oracle7.

Frequently, blocks that should be pinned in the cache are swept out and the ones that would probably be referenced only once are retained for longer periods. Oracle8 allows a finer degree of control over block isolation by explicitly partitioning the buffer cache into three sub-caches: the *keep, recycle,* and *default* pools. The keep pool should be used to hold blocks of segments, which would be referenced time and again. The recycle pool ought to be used to hold blocks of segments, which would probably be referenced only once. The remaining data-block buffer cache forms the default pool, which is subject to the cache-management algorithm outlined previously. If the keep and recycle pools are not defined by the DBA, the entire data-block buffer cache forms the default pool. The keep pool may be defined via the BUFFER_POOL_KEEP initialization parameter. An example of declaring the keep pool follows:

```
BUFFER_POOL_KEEP = ("buffers:500","lru_latches:4")
```

The recycle pool may be defined via the BUFFER_POOL_RECYCLE initialization parameter. An example of declaring the recycle pool follows:

```
BUFFER_POOL_RECYCLE = ("buffers=100","lru_latches:1")
```

The buffers specified in both examples are part of those specified via the DB_ BLOCK_BUFFERS initialization parameter. As such, each of them is of the size DB_BLOCK_SIZE. To verify that different buffer pools have indeed been configured, use the following query:

```
SQL> COLUMN NAME FORMAT a10
SQL> SELECT id, name, set_count "# LRU Latches", buffers, lo_bnum, hi_bnum
  2    FROM v$buffer_pool;

       ID NAME       # LRU Latches   BUFFERS   LO_BNUM   HI_BNUM
--------- ---------- ------------- --------- --------- ---------
        0                        0         0         0         0
        1 KEEP                   4       500         0       499
        2 RECYCLE                1       100       500       599
        3 DEFAULT                3      4400       600      4999
```

The columns *lo_bnum* and *hi_bnum* indicate the lower and upper buffer number ranges assigned to each pool. The column *set_count* refers to the number of LRU latch sets available to each pool. The default pool has LRU latches equivalent to DB_BLOCK_LRU_LATCHES (the number of LRU latches for the keep pool + number of LRU latches for the recycle pool). If the DB_BLOCK_LRU_LATCHES parameter is not set explicitly (or if it is set too high), it would revert to two percent of the DB_BLOCK_BUFFERS or twice the number of CPUs, whichever is less. On most single-CPU systems, it defaults to 1.

Once the different buffer pools are set up, segments need to be allocated to each one based on known usage patterns. Such usage patterns may be derived via pre-implementation analysis (part of the physical design process; for more details, refer to Chapter 6) or after monitoring of actual usage during the initial weeks of implementation. Segments may be assigned to different buffer pools via the new BUFFER_POOL KEEP|RECYCLE clause of the CREATE TABLE|INDEX or ALTER TABLE|INDEX commands. If no segments are allocated to the keep/recycle pool, then they are accessed via the default pool and the space allocated to the keep/recycle pools tends to be wasted. The effectiveness of the different pools can be evaluated via the dynamic view *v$buffer_pool_statistics* (created via the *catperf.sql* script located in the *$ORACLE_HOME/rdbms/admin* directory on UNIX and *%ORACLE_HOME%\rdbms80\admin* directory on Windows NT). The *v$buffer_pool_statistics* view provides a comprehensive report on the physical reads and writes, logical reads (consistent gets, db block gets), and other useful waits or events such as "buffer busy waits," "free buffer waits," "write complete waits," "free buffers inspected," and "dirty buffers inspected" as separate columns for each buffer pool.

Use process slaves to alleviate I/O bottlenecks during high database activity

Databases subject to high transactional rates can utilize multiple I/O slaves to alleviate the loads. (That is, provided the underscore parameter _IO_SLAVES_DISABLED is set to FALSE. If this parameter is set to TRUE by default for your platform, prior to changing it to FALSE, verify with Oracle Support that no bugs would be introduced by changing the value of this parameter.) Oracle8 allows certain background processes to be broken up into master/slave processes to parallelize the I/O operations and increase process throughput. These slaves are allocated at runtime, as and when necessary (up to the maximum limit specified by the initialization parameters). Let's take a peek in Table 7-3 at some of the processes whose throughput can be increased via multiple slaves.

Generally, if asynchronous I/O (AIO) is not supported by the OS, starting up additional slave processes greatly helps in simulating AIO (in many cases, additional slave processes can be started even if the OS supports AIO). The decision whether to implement slave processes or not needs to be made on the basis of the observation whether a single background process (LGWR, DBWR, and so on) is able to handle the current database workload (a previous tip mentioned ways to detect

Background Process / Procedure	Initialization Parameter	Description
DBWR	DBWR_IO_SLAVES DB_WRITER_PROCESSES	Discussed in a previous tip
LGWR	LGWR_IO_SLAVES	The number of I/O slaves to be started up for assisting the LGWR background process (aid in writing contents of the log buffer within the SGA to the online redo log files.
ARCH	ARCH_IO_SLAVES	The number of I/O slaves to be configured for aiding the ARCH background process (aid in writing out copies of the online redo log files to the archive log destination[s])
Backup to disk	BACKUP_DISK_IO_SLAVES	The number of I/O slaves that aid in backing up to disk
Backup to tape	BACKUP_TAPE_IO_SLAVES	The number of I/O slaves that aid in backing up to tape

TABLE 7-3. *A Listing of Oracle8 Initialization Parameters to Increase I/O Slaves*

whether DBWR is lagging behind). From a generic process-independent perspective, the *utlbstat/utlestat* report output or the following views can be queried for determining whether server processes are waiting on the background processes (column names to be observed are mentioned within parentheses):

- At the entire database level:
  - *v$waitstat* (count, time)
  - *v$system_event* (total_waits, total_timeouts, time_waited, average_wait)
- At the individual session level:
  - *v$session_wait* (wait_time, seconds_in_wait, state)
  - *v$session_event* (total_waits, total_timeouts, time_waited, average_wait, max_wait)

Wait events at the database level and individual session levels can be matched against each other to get the big picture and then narrow down to the session level. For example, the *event* column in *v$system_event* can be matched against the *event* column in the *v$session_event* and *v$session_wait* views for the purpose of drilling down. The following events may be monitored (please refer to Chapter 11 for an explanation of these events):

- DB file sequential read
- DB file scattered read
- DB file single write
- DB file parallel write
- Free buffer waits
- Buffer busy waits
- Write complete waits
- Log file sequential read
- Log file single write
- Log file parallel write
- Log file space/switch
- Log file sync
- Control file sequential read
- Control file parallel write

Enabling the initialization parameter TIMED_STATISTICS prior to monitoring these events provides the total time (in seconds) spent by server processes waiting on these events being performed by the background processes, in addition to the number of times the waits occurred. For example, the events "log file sequential read," "log file single write," and "log file parallel write" refer to the times server processes were waiting on LGWR to finish performing I/O against the online redo-log files. If there are a high number of waits and the waits run into several hundreds and thousands of seconds, it is an indication that the throughput of the background processes may be inadequate and they may need to be parallelized.

It is to be noted that enabling these slave processes only helps to alleviate and distribute the database workload across multiple processes, rather than overloading a single one (as in Oracle7). However, at no point in time should these slave processes be considered the silver bullet to make all the waits disappear. In fact, if the database is not configured appropriately, these additional processes could very well cause newer bottlenecks by treading on each other (examples: a single-process ARCH failing to keep up with the multiple slaves of LGWR, different LGWR slaves contending among themselves for writing via the same I/O channel, different ARCH slaves contending with the different LGWR slaves for writing via the same I/O channel, and so on). Prior to enabling multiple slave processes, ensure that data is well spread out across multiple disks/controllers. Also, memory should be adequate to support the extra shared-memory requirements of the additional process slaves. And the machine should have the adequate processor horsepower to support all these different processes and the additional interprocess communication (IPC) overhead. Otherwise, you could inadvertently cause contention for system resources among the different slave processes. For instance, if the I/O distribution across data-files appears skewed (based on *v$filestat, v$datafile, v$sess_io,* and so on), there is a probability that the data-files are not spread across multiple disks/spindles efficiently. Both the OS and the database should be periodically monitored for indications of I/O, memory, and CPU bottlenecks. I/O hot spots at the OS level can be perceived from statistics obtained via commands/utilities such as *iostat* and *sar* in UNIX, Performance Monitor with *diskperf* enabled on Windows NT, and so on (Chapter 4 lists additional commands to monitor the system resources). Statistics within the database can be derived from various dynamic views such as *v$sysstat* and *v$sesstat*. For example, if the values for statistics such as "physical reads," "logical reads," and "physical writes" in *v$sysstat* seem high, this is an indication of high I/O occurring.

Enable vector posting

Interprocess communication is at times referred to as occurring in "posts." For instance, DBWR may be posted by LGWR to write dirty buffers to disk during a checkpoint. Similarly, server processes may be posted after DBWR cleans up the dirty buffers. These posts may occur via separate calls to each process. In Oracle8, it is possible to combine multiple posts into one post call, thus reducing the total number of system calls issued. Thus, posts may be delivered to a group of processes as a single vector. For example, as soon as DBWR has cleaned up the dirty buffers, all the waiting foreground processes may be signaled via a single vector post.

Vector posting is currently enabled via an underscore parameter, _USE_VECTOR_POST. A Boolean value of TRUE or FALSE may be specified as the value for this parameter. Depending on the OS flavor and the Oracle version, this parameter may be enabled or disabled by default. You can check the current value for this parameter (or any underscore parameter, for that matter—just substitute "vector_post" with the name of the parameter whose value you want to check in the query that follows) via the following query:

```
SQL> SELECT ksppinm, ksppstvl FROM x$ksppi i, x$ksppcv v
  2   WHERE v.indx = i.indx
  3     AND ksppinm like '%vector_post%';

KSPPINM                    KSPPSTVL
-------------------------- ---------------------------------------------
_use_vector_post           FALSE
```

If vector posting is disabled by default (it was explicitly disabled in versions prior to 8.0.4), check with Oracle Support prior to enabling it to ensure that there are no bugs associated with this parameter for your platform.

Set up dedicated temporary tablespaces

Temporary tablespaces are used by Oracle for creating temporary segments and holding intermediate result sets (which may be later merged to form the final result set). For instance, temporary tablespaces may be used to store the sorted pieces derived by an index creation or the ORDER BY clause of SQL statements operating on a large table, prior to merging them and returning the fully sorted final results. Typically, all temporary segments are created in the current user's temporary tablespace (defined via the CREATE USER or ALTER USER commands). All temporary segments are owned by the SYS user ID. Temporary segments are written to in units determined by the initialization parameter SORT_AREA_SIZE. (The size of the actual extents allocated in the temporary tablespace are based on the default INITIAL/NEXT setting for the tablespace; thus, each extent may accommodate multiple SORT_AREA_SIZE units.) A tablespace may be marked as permanent (by default) or temporary. The latter option would prevent all users from creating any permanent segments (tables, indexes, rollback segments, and so on) there. Oracle would make use of it internally (via the SYS user ID). A tablespace may be marked as temporary via the CREATE TABLESPACE or ALTER TABLESPACE command. An example of each command is provided here:

```
SQL> CREATE TABLESPACE temp DATAFILE 'file-name'
  2  DEFAULT STORAGE (INITIAL 1M NEXT 1M PCTINCREASE 0 MAXEXTENTS 248)
  3  TEMPORARY;
SQL> ALTER TABLESPACE temp TEMPORARY;
```

When a permanent tablespace is used for storing temporary segments, each transaction requiring temporary space would need to create a temporary segment and drop it after its use. Thus, the overhead of segment creation, lock allocation, and subsequent segment dropping is incurred each time. If the tablespace is marked as temporary, then a temporary segment is created there the first time a transaction needs to use it. Once the subsequent transaction is complete, it does not drop the temporary segment. Instead the segment is reused by all subsequent transactions requiring temporary space. Thus, the constant overhead of segment creation and dropping is avoided. Furthermore, dedicated temporary tablespaces help in reducing data-block buffer overhead, since, as mentioned earlier, DBWR does not write out dirty buffers resulting from operations on dedicated temporary tablespaces.

Set up sort areas efficiently

For applications with large sorting requirements (DSS systems such as data-warehouses), it's very important to size all sort-related parameters appropriately, since sorting directly affects performance. SORT_AREA_SIZE is the initialization parameter that sets the maximum size for a sort within the PGA (Program Global Area). The sort area is allocated in the SGA if the MTS (multi-threaded server) architecture is used. Once the sorting is done and the output rows are placed in the queue for fetching, the memory is whittled down to the size specified by another initialization parameter, SORT_AREA_RETAINED_SIZE. Once the output rows are fetched out, all memory is released back to the PGA/SGA. SORT_AREA_SIZE needs to be at least equivalent to two database blocks and defaults to 64K on most OSs. Each sort operation would allocate its own SORT_AREA_SIZE within the PGA/SGA. As such, SQL statements causing concurrent sorts to occur may end up allocating multiple SORT_AREA_SIZE units. During large sorting operations, the (default) SORT_AREA_SIZE may prove inadequate. Hence Oracle needs to resort to virtual memory (temporary tablespace) to complete the operation. Oracle continues the sort by resorting to space in the temporary tablespace in units of SORT_AREA_SIZE (again, the size of the actual extents allocated in the temporary tablespace are based on its default INITIAL/NEXT setting). Accordingly, setting SORT_AREA_SIZE to be multiples of the DB_BLOCK_SIZE helps in controlling fragmentation within the temporary tablespace (within each allocated extent). Each individual unit is treated separately; the rows within each unit are sorted first, and then the result of each individual sort is merged with the others to form the final result set.

Increasing SORT_AREA_SIZE vastly improves the efficiency of large sorts by performing everything in memory and avoiding the need to use the temporary tablespace on disk. Ensure that you have adequate physical memory on your machine before increasing SORT_AREA_SIZE; otherwise, OS swapping may be induced. Remember, SORT_AREA_SIZE affects *all* user processes equally (in Oracle7 and by default in Oracle8). Starting with Oracle8, you can selectively set different SORT_AREA_SIZEs for different database sessions (via the ALTER SYSTEM or ALTER SESSION commands).

NOTE

*Changing SORT_AREA_SIZE dynamically offers great advantages to 24x7 environments. Now, in order to increase SORT_AREA_SIZE prior to running an exceptionally large batch job/report or even to create/rebuild an index, you don't have to bounce the instance. For instance, in Oracle7, prior to building a large index, you might have had to increase the SORT_AREA_SIZE in the initialization parameter file, bounce the instance, create the index, reset the SORT_AREA_SIZE in the initialization parameter file, and then bounce the instance once again (a total of two bounces). This caused quite a bit of downtime. Alternatively, if SORT_AREA_SIZE was not changed prior to the index build, then the creation process could potentially take up a long time, during which all applications accessing that table had to be taken down (due to a table-level lock issued by the index-creation statement), resulting in high downtime for those applications. With Oracle8, the SORT_AREA_SIZE can be changed dynamically prior to issuing the index-creation command, thus avoiding the need to bounce the instance. Furthermore, with Oracle8*i*, even applications accessing that table need not be brought down, since concurrent DML is supported during an index build. These options offer great flexibility to 24x7 environments.*

CAUTION
The flexibility of SORT_AREA_SIZE being dynamic in Oracle8 comes with a warning. This flexibility can also cause severe performance problems due to a single session using up most or all of the system resources. For instance, a developer or a power-user can easily change this parameter dynamically to a very large value and drag the system/database performance down. In an Oracle8 environment, the DBA needs to watch out to prevent such situations from happening (by monitoring, setting up database profiles for individual developers/users, and so on). There needs to be a good deal of knowledge of available system resources and current database loads (each developer/user needs to asks himself or herself, how much of the resources are my jobs using up and how much are my neighbors' jobs using up?), prior to changing the SORT_AREA_SIZE at the session-level.

Also, when using the PQO or Oracle Parallel Query Option (parallel sorts), total sort area requirements may increase, since each query server may allocate units of SORT_AREA_SIZE (which would later be merged by the master query server). Also, setting SORT_AREA_SIZE to be too high (example: 5MB or more) may not necessarily increase the sort throughput, since the law of diminishing returns would come into play. However, if the mammoth SORT_AREA_SIZE serves to prevent the temporary tablespace (causing disk I/O) from being used, then sort throughput would definitely be increased. In such situations, one may observe the sort-area and temporary-segment usage in a test instance, prior to setting the SORT_AREA_SIZE on the production instance (the *v$sort_segment, dba_segments,* and *v$sort_usage* [Oracle8 only] views may be monitored to record sorting activity).

As far as possible, set SORT_AREA_RETAINED_SIZE to be equal to SORT_AREA_SIZE, especially in situations where the sorted data is expected to be referenced more than once (multiple passes of the sorted data in SQL statements can be revealed via the EXPLAIN PLAN output). As mentioned earlier, SORT_AREA_RETAINED_SIZE determines how much memory is to be retained and how much memory is to be released back to the PGA/SGA after the sorting operation. It can range from zero to the full SORT_AREA_SIZE. Usually, it defaults to zero on most operating systems. Setting SORT_AREA_RETAINED_SIZE to equal SORT_AREA_SIZE prevents the overhead of constant dynamic memory allocation and deallocation, especially for processes with multiple serial sorting requirements (sorts for different non-concurrent operations in a process).

Often during database upgrades and migrations, installation of new applications, and other procedures involving high sorting activity such as index builds, it is common to temporarily set very high values for SORT_AREA_SIZE and SORT_AREA_RETAINED_SIZE. If only one user is expected to be using the database for performing operations involving high sorting, it is advisable to set SORT_AREA_SIZE to a high value (such that the entire operation may be done in memory). Once the operation is complete, SORT_AREA_SIZE can revert to its original, smaller value (in Oracle8, the ALTER SYSTEM command may be used to achieve this). In Oracle7, SORT_AREA_SIZE cannot be set dynamically (while the database is open). It requires a database bounce. For this reason, set it wisely to avoid frequent bounces in the future. Prior to setting this value, you need to analyze overall concurrent database activity during all times and estimate the average and maximum sort-area requirements. If the maximum and average sizes do not deviate from each other too much, then the size may be set to the maximum. If they deviate, however, and allocations of sort area beyond the average are few and far between, then it's advisable to stay close to the average size.

Another parameter that plays an important role in large sorts is SORT_READ_FAC. This parameter determines the number of blocks that are read essentially during large sorts/merges. During a mammoth sort operation (if it cannot be held in memory), Oracle breaks up the total data to be sorted into multiple pieces. Each piece is then sorted individually via multiple passes (either parallel or serial). Once the pieces are all sorted, they need to be merged together. The number of pieces that need to be merged constitutes the merge-width. Again, there may not be adequate memory to merge them in a single pass. Hence, multiple sort blocks from a few pieces are read and merged and the list of pieces is systematically narrowed down until only a few large pieces remain, which are then merged to form the final result set. The number of blocks to be read and merged in a single I/O operation is determined by the multi-block sort-read factor (SORT_READ_FAC). Oracle sets it automatically during intermediate sort passes based on the time taken to read a single database block divided by the transfer rate for a single block. The default value varies with the platform. Setting it explicitly requires a good understanding of the I/O throughput in your environment (transfer time, seek time, and latency) and may be set according to the following formula: (Average Latency + Average Seek Time + Block Transfer Time) / Block Transfer Time.

During sorts carried out in an MTS configuration, the initialization parameter SORT_MTS_BUFFER_FOR_FETCH_SIZE determines the size of the memory buffer allocated in the SGA for fetches. This may be increased in versions prior to 7.2.2. Starting with version 7.2.2, this parameter has been replaced with an underscore parameter, _SHARED_SESSION_SORT_FETCH_BUFFER. Accordingly, it is not recommended to change it.

Once you are sure that a certain sort operation, such as building a large index, would definitely involve temporary tablespace usage (if it's too big to fit within

SORT_AREA_SIZE in memory), it's a good idea to ensure that the initialization parameter SORT_SPACEMAP_SIZE is set to at least (*total_bytes_to_be_sorted* / SORT_AREA_SIZE), where *total_bytes_to_be_sorted* is the sum of the sizes of all columns involved in the sort operation. Examples include those forming the index key during index creation (add 6 bytes in Oracle7 and 10 bytes in Oracle8 per row for the ROWID to be stored as part of the index) or the columns that are part of the SELECT DISTINCT, ORDER BY, GROUP BY list multiplied by the number of rows involved in the sort operation ([Size_of_Col_1 + Size_of_Col_2 + . . . Size_of_Col_n] × number_rows). SORT_SPACEMAP_SIZE sets the size of the memory map for sorting within the PGA. Usually, sort-space allocation on disk happens on an as-needed basis in a haphazard manner at runtime. Setting SORT_SPACEMAP_SIZE appropriately reduces such frequent unorganized disk allocations.

Use direct writes for sorts

Generally, sorts that write to disk (temporary tablespace) pass through the buffer cache. This additional step of writing to the buffer cache, which is then flushed to disk, is redundant and only helps to displace genuine (potentially "hot") data blocks that might be reused in the buffer cache. In case the displaced data blocks are needed shortly after, they would need to be read in again from disk via physical disk I/O, thus affecting performance. Starting with Oracle7 v7.2, *direct writes for sorts* are supported. Direct writes for sorts write directly to disk via private process memory called direct-sort buffers, bypassing the data-block buffer cache (as opposed to a *conventional read/write,* which involves the buffer cache) and the DBWR. When direct writes for sorts are explicitly enabled, additional buffers for each sort operation are allocated in memory to write directly to disk. This reduces the need to tune the DBWR (for sorting operations) and also helps DBWR performance, since eliminating sort-related I/O reduces the burden on DBWR. Also, bypassing the buffer cache reduces the number of system calls issued and the resultant context switches.

Direct writes for sorts can be enabled via the initialization parameter SORT_DIRECT_WRITES. It is automatically enabled in Oracle8. This parameter supports a value of TRUE, FALSE, or AUTO (AUTO is supported starting with v7.3) and is set to AUTO by default (again, in v7.3 and higher; in prior versions, SORT_DIRECT_WRITES is set to FALSE), during which the number and size of the direct-sort buffers are managed automatically by Oracle (set to the minimum values of SORT_WRITE_BUFFERS = 2 and SORT_WRITE_BUFFER_SIZE = 32KB, thus providing a direct-sort buffer size of [32KB × 2] = 64KB). When SORT_DIRECT_WRITES is explicitly set to TRUE, the DBA needs to set the values for the number and size of the direct-sort buffers manually via the SORT_WRITE_BUFFERS and SORT_WRITE_BUFFER_SIZE initialization parameters, respectively. If you are setting them explicitly, it is advisable to set the values for these parameters such that the total direct-sort buffers are less than one-tenth the size of the current total sort-area size (derived by SORT_AREA_SIZE × n [where "n" is the highest number of concurrent sorts occurring in units of SORT_AREA_SIZE]). Also, manually setting them leads to allocation of sort space (direct sort buffers) in addition to the non-direct sort-area size. When AUTO is used, Oracle utilizes direct sorts only when the direct-sort buffer size is less than one-tenth the size of the current total sort-area size and the space for the direct-sort buffers is allocated from the sort area (non-direct sort area), thus conserving memory.

Use profiles to prevent runaway processes from hogging all resources

At times, it is possible that a process may consume the bulk of available system resources, leaving very little for other processes. In fact, a runaway process grabbing large amounts of memory and CPU cycles can bring a reasonably well-configured system to its knees within minutes. To prevent such scenarios, Oracle allows limits to be set on resources that are available to a process via a mechanism called *profiles.* A profile is a set of specific resource limits that can be assigned to users.

During initial configuration, the DBA in conjunction with application developers/designers needs to identify and categorize all users according to resource usage. Such categories would form the basis for creating profiles and assigning an appropriate profile to each database user. Profiles can be set up on a per-call (SQL calls) or a per-session (database session) basis. Profiles can be set up to control consumption of many system resources, such as

- Memory
- CPU usage
- I/O
- Session idle time (how long a session can remain dormant)
- Connect time (how long a user can remain connected to the database)
- Number of open sessions (how many sessions a user can have)

Such resource limits set by profiles can be enabled or disabled at the database level via an initialization parameter called RESOURCE_LIMIT. For any high-availability site, profiles are very useful, since they prevent uncontrolled use of all available system resources by specific processes.

Evaluate using vectorized reads for cooked file systems

On certain OSs, Oracle supports vectorized reads, which avoid the use of memory-to-memory copying from file-system buffers to application (Oracle) buffers during sequential read operations. Wherever possible (during sequential reads), the *readv()* system call is used, instead of a regular *read()* or *pread()*. The *readv()* system call copies the data read directly into Oracle buffers and bypasses the file-system buffers. This reduces the file-system buffer overhead and results in better performance due to decreased strain on the CPUs. This performance enhancement is evident on cooked file systems during multi-block reads, occurring during sequential I/O.

In the case of raw devices, however, I/O does not involve the use of file-system buffers. In this case, the overhead of the file-system buffers is absent anyway. In such cases, issuing a regular *read()* or *pread()* system call instead of a *readv()* does not result in any specific advantage.

Depending on your environment and application characteristics, you many find it beneficial to enable *readv()*. For instance, if you have a non-OPS environment (in OPS, raw disks are mandatory) set up on cooked file systems and are running DSS applications such as a data-warehouse or data-mart, where sequential segment accesses are fairly commonplace, *readv()* may improve database throughput by three to five percent. On OSs that support it, *readv()* may be enabled within the Oracle kernel via the USE_READV initialization parameter, which accepts a Boolean value of TRUE or FALSE.

Enable direct I/O when using cooked file systems

In Chapter 4, we examined the administrative inflexibility introduced by raw devices. With direct I/O for file systems, it is possible, to a certain extent, to bring in the performance advantages of raw devices, while keeping the administrative overheads at bay. Direct I/O, a distinctive hallmark of raw devices, is the I/O mechanism where data is directly written from the application (Oracle) buffers into the data-files without being copied into the intervening file-system buffers. Similarly, direct I/O allows data to be read directly into the application buffers from the data-files without being copied into the file-system buffers. Certain OSs (examples: Solaris 7 and Sequent) allow direct I/O to be utilized against file systems.

Oracle8 allows direct I/O to be utilized for certain database operations, such as sequential segment reads via PQO (Parallel Query Option), large sorts, backups, and restores. Oracle uses special buffers to store the data involved in the direct I/O operations. Operations that use direct I/O employ these buffers to hold the data to be written to disk and also read the data into these buffers from disk. The size of the buffers is determined via the initialization parameter DB_FILE_DIRECT_IO_COUNT, which specifies the number of buffers, each of the size DB_BLOCK_SIZE. Set the value for DB_FILE_DIRECT_IO_COUNT after evaluating the potential for direct I/O in your environment. Generally, DSS applications afford more opportunities for utilizing direct I/O (since occurrences of sequential segment access, large-scale sorting, and so forth are higher). As such, they may require a larger buffer to be set up. In any case, ensure that DB_FILE_DIRECT_IO_COUNT × DB_BLOCK_SIZE is at least equivalent to the maximum I/O size on your OS (64K on many UNIX flavors). This will allow direct I/O to occur in the biggest I/O unit possible for your OS, greatly enhancing direct I/O throughput. If you set up a direct buffer area bigger than the I/O limit, then any single read/write will be restricted to the maximum I/O limit. Also, the buffer size ought to be a multiple of the OS logical block size (if you have ensured that your DB_BLOCK_SIZE is equivalent to or a multiple of the OS block size, you should be fine). If your data-files are laid out on striped disk volumes, make the buffer size a multiple of the volume stripe size. If different disk volumes use different stripe sizes, then use the largest stripe size used by all volumes as the criterion for determining direct-buffer size.

Use intimate shared memory (ISM) for databases with high concurrent user access

The Oracle SGA is attached to shared memory. As the name indicates, shared memory facilitates interprocess communication by allowing multiple physically distinct processes to share a common pool of memory. Each process has access to the same memory contents, without having to create and maintain a local copy, resulting in gigantic memory consumption. Ordinarily, however, each process needs to maintain a local copy of the page table that allows it to interpret and selectively access the various pages that constitute the SGA. In a system with a large number of users concurrently accessing the database, there would be a corresponding large number of foreground server processes. Thus, with each process maintaining a local copy of the page table, memory consumption can shoot up.

Certain OSs (example: Solaris) provide an option called the intimate shared memory (ISM), which allows different (server) processes to share the entries of a single page table. ISM takes the shared memory model a step further. ISM generally needs to be configured in the OS explicitly via a kernel rebuild. Once it is configured at the OS level, it can be enabled within Oracle via the initialization parameter USE_ISM. The parameter takes a Boolean value of TRUE or FALSE. This parameter has been converted into an underscore parameter in Oracle8i v8.1.4 and is set to TRUE by default.

Use post-wait drivers for high IPC throughput

Semaphores are the guardians of the shared memory resources. When multiple processes concurrently access the shared memory area (the Oracle SGA), they need a mechanism for preventing them from overwriting each other's work. Semaphores precisely provide for such interprocess communication (IPC) and coordination. Semaphores are implemented as pseudo-locks in the form of counters. Each process takes up a semaphore. When a process needs to access a structure within shared memory, the counter is incremented. This prevents other processes from gaining control of the memory structure and causes them to wait until the resource is released. Once the original process has completed its work and released the structure, the semaphore is decremented, and the waiters are posted to intimate to them that the resource is available now. The efficiency of the semaphore model varies with the implementation in different OSs. For example, Solaris provides for high-speed semaphores that afford very high performance and scalability. In other OSs, however, semaphores may be a potential bottleneck during high concurrent usage (for example, large OLTP databases) due to the constant switching between user mode and kernel mode to detect whether a resource has been released, post the waiters, and increment or decrement the semaphores. Committees representing UNIX vendors from various parts of the world are addressing the issues of performance and scalability offered by the semaphore model.

One potential solution offered by certain UNIX vendors to increase IPC throughput is to use post-wait drivers (also referred to as "sleeper" drivers) to coordinate the waiting and posting, instead of semaphores. On such platforms, Oracle allows post-wait drivers to be configured via two initialization parameters, the names of which vary depending on the platform. For example, in NCR UNIX, they are called USE_POST_WAIT_DRIVER and POST_WAIT_DEVICE. The former parameter takes a Boolean value of TRUE or FALSE, and the latter requires the name and path of the post-wait driver supported by the OS (please refer to your platform-specific documentation for more details).

If your database supports a very large user community and your OS supports post-wait drivers, you may want to configure them to enhance IPC scalability. As per tests conducted by system vendors, the performance increase afforded by post-wait drivers for RDBMS installations varies from three percent to five percent. To ensure that they are necessary for your environment, use OS commands (*sar, vmstat,* and such) to monitor the system calls issued in user and kernel (system) mode. If calls seem excessive, switch to post-wait drivers, ensure that semaphores are not being used anymore (via *ipcs*), and then check the system calls again to verify whether the system calls have gone down. These tests should be conducted on a test machine to prevent actual production operations from being disrupted.

Pre-page and "lock" the SGA in main memory

Oracle uses a paging algorithm, very similar to the one deployed by operating systems, to gradually build up all the memory pages within the SGA. This expedites instance startup, since not all required pages need to be fetched off disk during startup. Whenever a process refers to a page not physically present in memory, however, it generates a page fault, as the page has to be read in from disk. Thus, the performance hit caused by page faults is tolerated on an incremental (as necessary) basis at runtime.

An alternative model for enhancing performance would be to induce pre-paging, wherein the entire SGA is built during startup and reduces the number of page faults subsequently. This prevents server processes from being exposed to the performance hit caused by rampant page faults and readies the instance for maximum performance immediately after startup. Oracle allows this to occur or not depending on an initialization parameter, PRE_PAGE_SGA. This parameter specifies a Boolean value (TRUE or FALSE); by default, it is set to FALSE. When it is set to TRUE, Oracle touches all the pages that form the SGA, thus bringing them into main memory immediately.

One side effect of pre-paging is that all the pages are "hot" when they are brought in, thus allowing them to remain in memory for a while (until they get cold). This virtually "locks" the SGA in main memory, preventing it from being paged/swapped out, thus enhancing performance significantly. This is a very powerful performance-enhancing option for systems with abundant memory (adequate to hold the entire SGA in RAM, without paging portions of it out to disk or affecting other processes adversely). However, this option does not guarantee that the entire SGA will remain in memory at all times. As portions of the SGA remain unaccessed, they get "cold" and gradually become victims of paging. However, certain OSs can be set up to lock all of shared memory in RAM, preventing paging/swapping (examples: Solaris, Sequent, NCR UNIX). The latter is a more foolproof method of locking the SGA in memory.

Also, in Oracle8, a new parameter has been introduced to explicitly allow locking the SGA in physical memory: LOCK_SGA (this parameter existed under different names for certain OSs that supported this feature in Oracle7). LOCK_SGA is set to FALSE by default; enabling it, however, will prevent the SGA from being swapped out of RAM. Another parameter, LOCK_SGA_AREAS, allows specific areas of the SGA to be locked in physical memory (it has been changed to an underscore parameter in some versions of Oracle8*i*). LOCK_SGA_AREAS accepts a numeric value indicating the SGA components to be locked. The numeric value is derived from the dynamic view *v$sga*.

```
SQL> SELECT * FROM v$sga;
NAME                    VALUE
-------------------- --------
Fixed Size              64380
Variable Size        54648832
Database Buffers      8388608
Redo Buffers            73728
```

Based on the contents of *v$sga,* the numeric values shown in Table 7-4 are allotted to the LOCK_SGA_AREAS parameter.

Thus, if the database buffers need to be locked in memory, LOCK_SGA_AREAS should be set to 4. If both database buffers and the log buffers need to be locked, then LOCK_SGA_AREAS ought to be set to 12 (4 + 8).

Whenever possible, set COMPATIBLE to the current database version

Every major release from Oracle introduces various new features that didn't exist in the previous version. The COMPATIBLE initialization parameter sets the backward compatibility of the current instance. For instance, if the COMPATIBLE parameter in an Oracle8 v8.0.4 database is set to 7.3.4, it would only allow features that are allowable in v7.3.4 to be utilized. This allows an instance to be downgraded or migrated to an earlier instance, if necessary. For instance, if you are a software development company developing an application that may be deployed by customers on any Oracle7 or Oracle8 version starting with Oracle 7.1, you would set COMPATIBLE to 7.1.0. Another situation to set a lower value for COMPATIBLE would be when going to a newer version of Oracle, which has not been fully evaluated for bugs in your environment. In such a case, COMPATIBLE may be set to a release level you are comfortable with (one that is tried and tested in your environment). However, setting this parameter to a lower value doesn't really bring in any benefit for companies that are using a relatively stable version of Oracle and are not planning to downgrade. Instead, a lower value only restricts the features that the current version offers. For example, if COMPATIBLE is set to 7.3.4 in an Oracle8 database, you cannot use the multitude of Oracle8 features such as partitioning and parallel DML. By default, COMPATIBLE may not necessarily be set to the current version. Changing it to the current version requires a database bounce, since it's a static parameter. So it helps to proactively set this to the current version during the initial configuration itself, thus preventing downtime in the future.

SGA Component	Numeric Value Assigned
Fixed size	1
Variable size	2
Database buffers	4
Redo buffers	8

TABLE 7-4. *Values for LOCK_SGA_AREAS Initialization Parameter*

NOTE
When bouncing the database to change the value for COMPATIBLE, always perform a normal/immediate shutdown. Doing a SHUTDOWN ABORT just prior to changing it or STARTUP FORCE after changing it corrupts the online redo logs (it's a bug in certain Oracle versions).

Always install SQL*Plus help

Has this ever happened to you: After wrangling for a mere one hour of downtime from the operations manager, you try to run an index creation command within SQL*Plus at midnight and for some reason, the #$#% command errors out? (This happens to all those veteran DBAs who still can't live without good old SQL*Plus). More frustrating than not remembering the syntax is seeing the message "Help not installed" when you type in "help create index" at the SQL prompt! Rather than spend time searching for the syntax within those huge documentation tomes, always install SQL*Plus Help to have all the syntax handy. And this is no small matter either. Oracle sometimes changes the syntax of very commonly used commands between releases (remember the differences in the simple CREATE TABLE ... ADD CONSTRAINT... command between versions 7.2 and 7.3?). Accordingly, whenever you upgrade to a newer version, always remember to install SQL*Plus Help. There's nothing more handy than having the entire SQL syntax literally at your fingertips.

In UNIX, one of the reasons newer DBAs don't install SQL*Plus Help is because the process requires an additional step (unlike Windows NT, where it is part of the installation) and is not very well documented. In earlier releases, the entire process was clearly explained. The Help takes up less than 2MB in the SYSTEM user's default tablespace (generally, TOOLS) and is well worth the extra step.

SQL*Plus Help under UNIX may be installed as follows:

1. Log on as the Oracle software owner.
2. Set up an environment variable called SYSTEM_PASS with the SYSTEM username and password via the following command:

   under Korn shell:

   ```
   export SYSTEM_PASS=SYSTEM/MANAGER
   ```

   under C shell:

   ```
   setenv SYSTEM_PASS SYSTEM/MANAGER
   ```

3. Type in "helpins" at the UNIX prompt.
4. Unset the SYSTEM_PASS environment variable (if possible, immediately change the SYSTEM password).

5. Ensure Help is properly installed (no errors) by typing in "Help" at the SQL*Prompt.

Step 3 kicks off a SQL*Loader process that loads the SYSTEM.HELP table with all the SQL*Plus help records.

Other Self-Explanatory (Well, Almost!) Server Configuration Tips

- Always leave ample free space in SYSTEM tablespace. As a general rule of thumb, it's best to ensure that all tablespaces have adequate room for future growth. If any tablespace has to run out of room, however, one can only pray that it's not the SYSTEM tablespace. Since the SYSTEM tablespace is so intrinsic to the database, most failures there can have severe consequences, involving potentially high downtime. So always ensure at least 40 percent free space in SYSTEM. This is especially important if your applications are highly reliant on server-stored code (such as stored procedures, functions, packages, and triggers). Sometimes, it is amazing how fast SYSTEM gets used up. Just installing certain tools can use up all the free space you previously thought was adequate. Oracle Designer is a good example of a tool that uses up quite a bit of SYSTEM space. Other examples would be Oracle and third-party applications such as Oracle Financials and SAP. Some DBAs change the location of the SYS-owned tables where the initial rollback segment (also called SYSTEM), stored procedures, packages, and so on, are created and stored (from SYSTEM to some other tablespace) by editing the *$ORACLE_HOME/rdbms/admin/sql.bsq* and other data-dictionary catalog script files, hoping that this would reduce fragmentation and usage of the SYSTEM tablespace. However, if this is done improperly or the slightest error is introduced, it can have dangerous repercussions and potentially cause database corruption. Accordingly, it is best to size the SYSTEM tablespace appropriately (Chapter 12 outlines tips on managing space in the SYSTEM tablespace), rather than try and limit its usage to even genuine data-dictionary segments. Of course, SYSTEM's usage should be restricted only to data-dictionary segments. Application, temporary, or non-SYSTEM rollback segments should never be created there.
- Ensure that there is sufficient free space on each disk volume where the Oracle data-files are stored to allow growth. This can be quite difficult to achieve, especially when dealing with a large database. However, this step is very critical to prevent lack of disk space from causing downtime. If a segment cannot grow due to inadequate space in the tablespace, then no

more rows can be inserted, thus causing an application to fail. Imagine a situation where your sales people are talking to customers and taking orders over the phone and the application won't allow them to record the sale due to a segment not having the room to grow. For all practical purposes, even though the database is still open, the application cannot function and is *unavailable*. Accordingly, ensure that at all times there is free disk space—at least ten percent free space even on disks that hold static tablespaces. Sometimes with changing application requirements, even static tablespaces grow (when you least expect them to). Once free disk space is ensured, set AUTOEXTEND on for all data-files belonging to application tablespaces (note that this is recommended only on cooked file systems and not on raw devices). This will allow the tablespaces and segments within them to grow as needed. In addition, have scripts page you if it is anticipated that a segment would not be able to allocate another extent (see Chapter 19 for the scripts).

- Make a list of static initialization parameters (those requiring a database bounce) that you would need to enable or disable in the short or medium term and enable or disable them accordingly during the initial configuration itself. This list doesn't have to be totally comprehensive. However, the more parameters you cover, the less are the chances of a database bounce in the near future. For instance, even though you might not be using any distributed transactions (those involving a remote database) currently, you might want to proactively set the initialization parameter DISTRIBUTED_TRANSACTIONS to a value greater than zero. That way, if at a later stage (short to medium term) your application needs to conduct remote transactions, you won't need to bounce an operational database. This proactively allows downtime to be kept to a minimum.

NOTE

Setting DISTRIBUTED_TRANSACTIONS to a value greater than zero enables the RECO process to start up during database startup. The RECO process periodically checks for pending (in-doubt) transactions in the local pending queue (the SYS.DBA_2PC_PENDING view displays all in-doubt transactions in the local pending queue) and tries to resolve them by connecting to the remote database. If they cannot be resolved due to the remote site being unavailable, RECO retries the connection after an interval. This interval keeps growing after each subsequent attempt. Once the transaction is resolved by RECO, it removes the in-doubt transaction entry from the local queue.

- Do not set any specific events within the database (via the EVENTS initialization parameter) unless Oracle Support explicitly requests for it. Also, make sure that previously set events are disabled at the next available opportunity (during the next scheduled bounce), once the problem for which the event was enabled is resolved. Sometimes, the events continue to remain enabled long after the specific problems are resolved. It's acceptable if the event does not impact performance. If database performance is not optimal, however, these unneeded events need to be disabled (especially expensive events such as data-block or index-block verification). It's best not to wait until performance becomes unacceptable but to proactively disable them at the next possible opportunity. Once performance becomes bad, these events may need to be disabled immediately, thus causing database downtime (since a database bounce is required to disable them). One more thing to keep in mind is that many of these events can be set at the session/system level via the ALTER SESSION or ALTER SYSTEM command without requiring a database bounce. So even if Oracle Support requests an event to be set, inquire whether the same event can be set at the session/system level, rather than at the instance level (via the EVENTS initialization parameter). Also, application code can often be changed without too many hassles to include an ALTER SESSION command prior to a specific operation (that is suspected to cause the problem). Though this will require multiple changes to be made to an application (initially to include the ALTER SESSION command and later to disable the command), it will avoid a database bounce.

- As part of the installation and initial configuration, ensure that all unneeded options are disabled. Include all options that you are not likely to use in the short to medium term. Depending on the version being used, certain options may be enabled by default. Spend time reading the installation manual and the latest release notes to make a list of all such options and disable them. They may later be reenabled when needed. Discovering at a later point in time (when the database is already operational) that certain options are enabled and disabling them may incur downtime. For example, in some versions of Oracle7 v7.3.*x*, Oracle Trace is enabled by default. Oracle Trace allows various event-based database statistics to be captured for later analysis and tuning. However, capturing statistics can be resource intensive and expensive—especially when those statistics are not being used. Even simple events such as logging onto the database could be time consuming. Disabling Oracle Trace requires the existing trace files (*regid.dat* and *process.dat* in *$ORACLE_HOME/otrace/admin*) to be deleted and for the EPC_DISABLED environment variable to be set to TRUE for the Oracle software owner (generally, the *oracle* user ID)—preferably, in the

OS startup file (*.profile, .kshrc,* or what have you) and also in the *listener.ora* file. The following listing of the *listener.ora* file provides an example for setting the EPC_DISABLED variable:

```
################
# Filename......: listener.ora
# Name..........: db01.world
# Date..........: 04-NOV-98 13:23:39
################
LISTENER=
  (ADDRESS_LIST =
        (ADDRESS =
          (PROTOCOL=IPC)
          (KEY=db01.world)
        )
        (ADDRESS =
          (COMMUNITY = orasqlnet.world)
          (PROTOCOL = TCP)
          (HOST=db01-fast)
          (PORT=1521)
          (QUEUESIZE=256)
        )
  )

STARTUP_WAIT_TIME_LISTENER = 0
CONNECT_TIMEOUT_LISTENER = 0
log_DIRECTORY_LISTENER = /oracle/trace_logs/db01
TRACE_LEVEL_LISTENER = OFF
SID_LIST_LISTENER=
 (SID_LIST=
  (SID_DESC=
   (SID_NAME=db01)
   (ORACLE_HOME=/oracle/8.0.4)
(ENVS='EPC_DISABLED=TRUE')
)
 )
```

Once these tasks are done, both the database and the listener need to be bounced for these changes to take effect. This is obviously not very easily achieved in a 24×7 environment. So users would need to live with the performance hit for a while until an opportunity is found to perform these changes and bounce the database. Thus, taking time to identify these glitches and rectify them should ideally be done as part of the initial configuration itself.

- Ensure that you have a high-priority 24x7 (gold or silver) support contract with Oracle Support. In addition, you may want to negotiate either with Oracle Support or a third party for remote DBA support, where someone can log on and help out during critical junctures or just provide a second pair of eyes for monitoring and such at pre-determined intervals (example: 10 hours a week).

Chapter 11 explains configuration of some other server structures and components such as the shared pool, various latches and enqueues, and so on, from a general maintenance perspective.

SQL*Net/Net8 Configuration

SQL*Net/Net8 is the component that links the Oracle Server and clients, or even multiple servers, together. This section discusses certain optimal ways to configure SQL*Net/Net8.

Use Oracle names when dealing with a large number of clients

When a large number of clients are involved, using the file-based approach to storing and managing service names can be difficult. With each new server that comes in, the *tnsnames.ora* file would potentially get updated with a new service name. Propagating this addition across to the client PCs owned by the entire user community in a large company requires detailed tracking of all the clients. As the number of clients grows large, the task of reconciling and maintaining up-to-date information in the *tnsnames.ora* file on every client PC can escalate from being merely difficult to being a full-fledged nightmare. Certain customer sites I have worked for deal with this issue in a variety of innovative ways. One site uses the operating system *CacheFS** feature to store a "master copy" of the *tnsnames.ora* file (which is always "up to date" in terms of all service names), and that version is made available to all workstations (their clients are Sun SPARC 10 and SPARC 20 workstations). Another site stores the "master" *tnsnames.ora* file on a LAN file server, which is visible to all the client PCs. When client PCs are rebooted (typically at the beginning of the day), a script is executed that overwrites the local copy of *tnsnames.ora* with the master copy. Though such solutions typically work, they are not foolproof and have their weaknesses. For instance, *CacheFS* may not be available on your platform, or it may not be convenient for you to NFS-mount the directory that holds the *tnsnames.ora* file across all clients. Similarly, the second approach may not work if a user (or a group of users) does not reboot his or her PC. Such users would not be using the latest version of the *tnsnames.ora* file.

NOTE
CacheFS or cached file system allows a specific directory path, usually NFS-mounted, to be cached in memory. Typically smaller, popular, read-only or read-mostly files are placed in CacheFS. When such files on NFS-mounted partitions are cached, network traffic is reduced (since the files are already available in cache, no traffic across the network is required to access them). To ensure that the cached files are kept up-to-date with the files on disk (since the cached files may become unsynchronized with the ones on disk due to writes performed on the files), CacheFS periodically checks for consistency according to a user-configurable timer.

To counter such problems, Oracle offers Oracle Names. With Oracle Names, rather than maintaining server addresses and services names across multiple clients, a more consolidated approach is adopted. The entire service name information is maintained in a central location, consisting of one or more names servers. Multiple names servers synchronize information among themselves via continuous replication. When a new service name is registered or an existing one is changed, this information is propagated across to all the names servers. This repository of service-name information can optionally be maintained in an Oracle database, thus further easing administration of the service names. Additionally, for very large sites, multiple names servers can be functionally grouped to form one or more administrative "regions." All the names servers in an administrative region keep themselves up-to-date either by continuous replicating service-name information or by accessing the Oracle database (if one is maintained). All administrative regions can be configured to use the same database. All clients that need to access the database would route their requests to a names server (rather than accessing a *tnsnames.ora* file), which would then resolve the service name and return the necessary connect information back to the clients.

When using Oracle Names in a 24×7 environment, there are two things to keep in mind:

- Since Oracle Names consolidates service-name information, it is essential to provide failover capabilities. If the centralized repository experiences a failure, without an alternative source for the service-name information, the entire system would be crippled. Redundancy may be provided by maintaining multiple names servers in each administrative region. Since all names servers in a region continually replicate themselves, they can be utilized for failover. Another method for providing failover is to maintain a

redundant copy of the *tnsnames.ora* file on each client. Each copy of the *tnsnames.ora* file ought to be kept fairly up-to-date by methods discussed previously (refreshing them during reboots or via CacheFS). Thus, ideally, such methods ought to form a secondary layer of protection, with Oracle Names (with multiple names servers within each region) acting as the primary layer for service-name resolution.

- When a database is used to hold the service-name repository, it needs to be subjected to the same robust backup routines as the production databases. In addition, a standby configuration for this database may be examined (if the production database(s) use a standby configuration).

Use out-of-band breaks with SQL*Net/Net8 or set poll frequency high when out-of-band breaks are unavailable

As a DML statement executes, the Oracle server checks periodically for interrupts from the client (that ran the statement via SQL*Net/Net8). Such checking becomes important, especially when the DML statement involves a large number of rows (like an ad hoc query fetching a thousand or so rows). Looking at the large number of rows being processed, the person issuing the query may change his or her mind and press the cancel (CTRL-C) key, so that the statement would be aborted. Two modes are supported in SQL*Net/Net8 for checking for such interrupts: in-band breaks and out-of-band (or "urgent") breaks.

When in-band breaks are used, the Oracle server frequently polls the client to see whether an interrupt (such as the CTRL-C key combination) has been issued. Depending on the frequency at which these polls are issued, they can contribute to high traffic on the network. Accordingly, it is desirable to reduce the polls. The poll frequency can be controlled via a parameter in the *sqlnet.ora* file: BREAK_POLL_SKIP. This parameter sets the interval between subsequent polls. On clients that do not issue ad hoc queries, the poll interval needs to be set very high, so that fewer polls (if any, at all) are issued by the Oracle Server. However, on clients where ad hoc queries are relatively common (example: DSS clients), the interval should be set such that genuine interrupt requests from clients are not ignored. Thus, depending on your application environment and ad hoc DML usage, it's prudent to evaluate different high values (such as 100000000, 10000000, 1000000, 100000, and so on). The following listing of the *sqlnet.ora* file provides an example of the parameter setting:

```
##
## File : $ORACLE_HOME/net80/admin/sqlnet.ora
## Created on : 06/24/98
```

```
##
trace_level_client = off
names.directory_path = (TNSNAMES)
names.default_domain = world
name.default_zone = world # not applicable for Net8
break_poll_skip = 1000000
```

As a rule of thumb, out-of-band breaks are beneficial from a performance perspective. When out-of-band breaks are used, the client process asynchronously alerts the Oracle server that an interrupt has been issued from the client. This occurs when the interrupt is actually issued, thus resulting in very little traffic, compared to in-band breaks, where the polls occur regardless of whether any interrupts have actually been issued. Overall, out-of-band breaks increase DML statement throughput tremendously. On the negative side, they may waste some space within the packets traversing the network, since the out-of-band break information needs to be maintained within the packet (in the case of TCP/IP, out-of-band information is maintained in the variable portion of the IP packet header). However, this wastage is miniscule and not does result in any significant increase in the number of packets.

Depending on the protocol used on a platform, either method may be set as the default (in most cases, if available, out-of-band breaks are set as the default in both SQL*Net v2.*x* and Net8). Check whether your network protocol stack supports out-of-band breaks. Sometimes, even when the core protocol stack supports them, specific products (example: a SQL*Net Interchange) may disable out-of-band breaks. If out-of-band breaks are supported, ensure that they have been set as the default mode in SQL*Net/Net8 (refer to your protocol-specific sections in the SQL*Net/Net8 documentation to check whether out-of-band breaks are set as default or not). If not, set DISABLE_OOB=OFF in the *sqlnet.ora* file to enable out-of-band breaks. Conversely, if out-of-band breaks are not supported by your protocol stack or usage of specific product layers disallow them, set DISABLE_OOB=ON and keep the poll frequency high via the BREAK_POLL_SKIP parameter in the *sqlnet.ora* file.

Keep dead-connection detection to a minimum

Similar to in-band breaks that may generate high network traffic if polling is conducted frequently, dead-connection detection (DCD), which also uses a similar polling mechanism, may also contribute to high traffic. DCD is a timer-induced probe available in SQL*Net (starting with v2.1) and Net8 that allows periodic checking for disconnected client connections. Sometimes, an end-user may reboot his or her PC, thinking that it is not responding, whereas it is right in the middle of a database transaction. This would cause the client session to terminate. Depending on when the break occurred, however, the shadow process involved in the database transaction may still remain connected to the database, wasting valuable server

resources. DCD allows periodic probing for such "dead" database connections, and if any are found, they are terminated and the server resources are freed.

DCD involves a probe in the form of a small packet sent from the server to the client periodically. This period is determined by a parameter in the *sqlnet.ora* file (on the client): SQLNET.EXPIRE_TIME. This parameter determines the number of minutes between successive probes. If the probe returns an error, then the sessions from that client are determined to be abnormally terminated and a cleanup operation is initiated, wherein the locks/latches held by the sessions are released, all uncommitted transactions are rolled back, and the sessions are terminated. Though the intention is good, the frequency at which these operations are carried out may hurt performance. If the probes are conducted too frequently, they may contribute to excessive network traffic (especially during peak hours). As a rule of thumb, it's not advisable to set the probes to occur more than once every ten minutes. In high-traffic OLTP environments, it may be judicious to set the probe to occur once every half hour.

The following listing of the *sqlnet.ora* file shows an example of setting the SQLNET.EXPIRE_TIME parameter:

```
##
## File : $ORACLE_HOME/net80/admin/sqlnet.ora
## Created on : 06/24/98
##
trace_level_client = off
names.default_domain = world
sqlnet.expire_time = 30  # DCD set to 30 minutes
```

Manage large user populations effectively via SQL*Net and Net8 features

With large user populations generating a high volume of concurrent database connections, it becomes necessary to take additional steps to enable SQL*Net/Net8 to scale to accommodate the volume. Besides increasing connection bandwidth, steps also need to be taken to provide redundancy for failover, in case the solitary service goes down. Following are some of the features provided by Net8 and SQL*Net v2.*x* to aid in these areas.

Multi-Threaded Server Architecture

Starting with SQL*Net v2.*x*, the multi-threaded server (MTS) architecture is supported for large user communities. Figure 7-13 illustrates the MTS architecture. In situations where memory is constrained or heavy context-switching is occurring due to the database accepting a very high volume of concurrent sessions, with each session remaining connected for short periods of time (such as in an OLTP

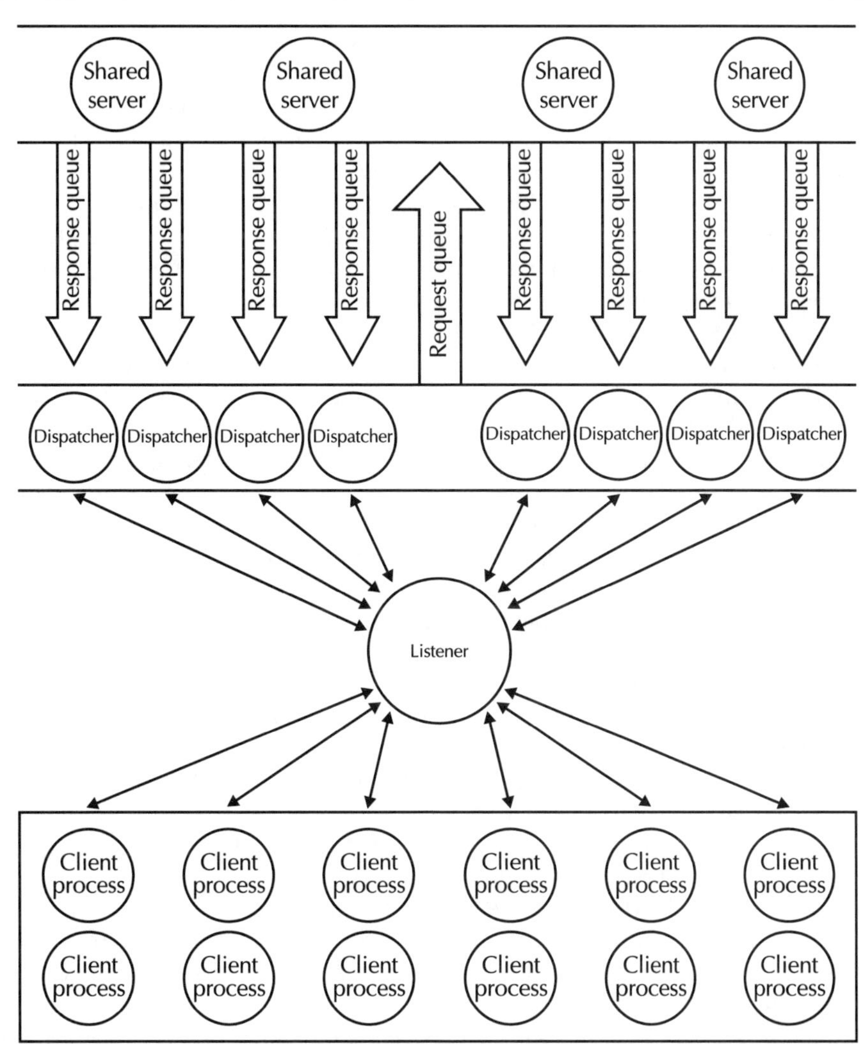

FIGURE 7-13. *MTS configuration*

environment), the Oracle MTS architecture may be effectively utilized. MTS allows a pool with a pre-determined upper limit of dispatchers and shared servers to be configured. In dedicated environments, an additional server process needs to start up and remain dedicated to every user session, thus causing the total number of processes and memory requirements to shoot up when dealing with a large number of users. In an MTS environment, however, a small group of server processes (the shared servers) are shared across multiple sessions, thus effectively limiting the overall number of processes. This also allows cumulatively less memory to be utilized by all processes, thus allowing a larger number of concurrent users to exist. In lieu of a dedicated server catering to each session, the listener provides the address of a dispatcher process to each incoming user connection (unless a dedicated server process is explicitly requested), which then communicates with the shared server on an as-needed basis—only to fulfill the actual database requests. Once the request is fulfilled and the results are placed in the *response queue* of the dispatcher, the shared server moves on to cater to the next request queued up in the *request queue* (Oracle dynamically starts up and stops shared server processes based on the request queue length; additional shared servers can be started up provided the current number is less than the value specified by the initialization parameter MTS_MAX_SERVERS).

When using MTS, ensure that besides the regular MTS-related initialization parameters, you also increase the SHARED_POOL_SIZE by at least 1KB for each concurrent session that is expected to access the database via MTS. Additional space in the shared pool is required to store session-specific data for all sessions, so that any shared server may access them. In this case, the PGA of each connected session only contains the stack space required to hold session-specific variables, arrays, and so on. All other session-specific information (such as private SQL areas) is held in the shared pool.

Refrain from using MTS for sessions that need to remain continuously connected to the database for long periods of time, such as sessions in a batch application or sessions executing a series of stored procedures. During such long-winded database-intensive transactions, there is little reprieve for the server process (that is, little or no idle time). In such cases, it's advisable to connect via a dedicated server, since using a shared server does not bring any benefit but only hampers performance due to the overhead involved in the shared server periodically checking the request queue (during whatever little idle time it gets) and servicing a different session, while the current batch session has to place its subsequent requests in the request queue and wait for the same or another shared server to service those requests. In case your database handles a combination of batch and OLTP transactions (ideally, at different times of the day), you can configure two different service names for the same database. One service name would be configured to request dedicated servers, and the other would be configured to request dispatchers/shared servers. This configuration can be achieved by setting SRVR=DEDICATED for the service name requesting dedicated servers in the *tnsnames.ora* file. If you are using Oracle Names, then dedicated servers can be used by setting USE_DEDICATED_SERVER=ON in the *sqlnet.ora* file. All batch sessions can then explicitly use the service name corresponding to a dedicated server to connect to the database, while OLTP sessions can use the other service name corresponding to dispatchers/shared servers. Also, for core DBA tasks such as starting or stopping the database and performing recovery, it's required to connect using a dedicated server.

Based either on your estimation or observation (of an active instance), pre-spawn as many dispatchers as required to handle peak volume (the number of database connections occurring during peak hours). This will ensure that dispatchers are readily available for each user connection request and that no wait arises from Oracle having to spawn additional dispatchers at runtime. This configuration can be achieved by setting MTS_DISPATCHERS equivalent to CEIL(maximum number of concurrent sessions during peak hours / n), where "n" refers to the number of connections that a dispatcher can service (refer to your platform-specific documentation for the value of "n," since it is OS-dependent). Always set MTS_MAX_DISPATCHERS to a high value to ensure that more dispatchers can be spawned by Oracle, if necessary. Similarly, the number of shared servers needs to be set after adequate analysis of the amount and nature of database activity during peak hours. The ALTER SYSTEM command can be used to spawn additional dispatchers and shared servers dynamically without requiring a database bounce. However, take care that you do not proactively start too many dispatchers and shared servers (more than will ever be used). This will incur high process overhead and negate the benefits derived from using MTS. The dynamic views *vmts, vdispatcher, v$shared_server, v$circuit,* and *v$queue* should be periodically monitored to check for contention occurring in your configuration. Refer to your Oracle documentation for more details on setting up the appropriate number of shared servers and dispatchers.

Connection Pooling for DSS Applications with Large User Populations

Typically in the case of DSS applications, an end-user connects to the database, runs one or more large queries, and spends time analyzing the results. During such analyzing, the end-user's database session is idle, whereas other sessions (either new or existing) may be issuing other queries to the database. If the DSS user population is large, there may not be enough resources to handle all the concurrent sessions. During such times, it's advisable to use connection pooling to maximize usage of the available resources.

Connection pooling is a feature introduced in Net8. Connection pooling works on top on MTS by allowing physical connections (transports) to be shared among different sessions. If a certain user session is idle beyond a (configurable) timeout parameter, connection pooling allows a logical connection to be maintained with this session, while the transport used by this session's dispatcher is taken away (borrowed) and used for processing another active session's requests. When the

client becomes active again, the transport resources are returned. This allows fewer physical resources to be shared among a large number of connected sessions. Figure 7-14 illustrates connection pooling.

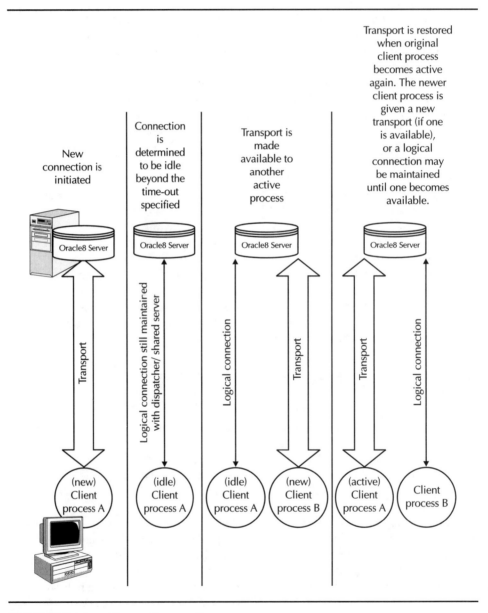

FIGURE 7-14. *Connection pooling*

Connection pooling is enabled via the MTS_DISPATCHERS initialization parameter:

```
MTS_DISPATCHERS = "(PROTOCOL=TCP) (DISPATCHERS=8) (POOL=ON) (IN=50) (OUT=50) (TICKS=1)"
```

The pool option specifies whether connection pooling is enabled or disabled. The IN/OUT strings specified with POOL determine whether connection pooling is to be used only for incoming (IN) network connections or outgoing (OUT) network connections, or both. The numeric values specified with the IN/OUT strings indicate the timeout values, beyond which if a connection is idle, its resources are utilized for processing active connections. The timeout values are in "ticks," the duration of which may be defined in seconds via the TICKS option.

Connection Concentration with Net8 Connection Manager

Apart from connection pooling (which is primarily useful for DSS applications), another feature introduced in Net8 is *connection concentration* via the Connection Manager utility. Connection concentration is a very useful option for databases with a large number of simultaneous sessions, with each session continuously interacting with the database (having little or no idle time). Especially in large OLTP applications, where a multitude of sessions quickly connect to the database, execute one or more DML statements, and disconnect, it may be useful to achieve higher connection bandwidth by utilizing connection concentration, in addition to MTS. Connection concentration allows different database requests to be multiplexed or funneled through the same physical transport to a shared server. In other words, multiple concurrent connections are consolidated to occur via the same physical port. This greatly increases the number of active sessions that may concurrently exist by maximizing the "per port" throughput. Using connection concentration, a database may scale to thousands of concurrent users. Figure 7-15 illustrates connection concentration.

The difference between connection pooling and connection concentration is that in the case of the former, the physical transport is taken away from an idle session and given to an active one, whereas in the case of the latter, multiple sessions are allotted the same physical transport and they all retain the allotted transport. Connection concentration may be set up by configuring Connection Manager and via the MULTIPLEX option of the MTS_DISPATCHERS initialization parameter.

```
MTS_DISPATCHERS = "(PROTOCOL=TCP) (DISPATCHERS=8) (MULTIPLEX=ON)"
```

Multiple Listeners for Listener Failover and Load Balancing

With a large number of concurrent client connections, a single listener can get saturated (even with a large queue size, as specified in Chapter 5). Accordingly, it

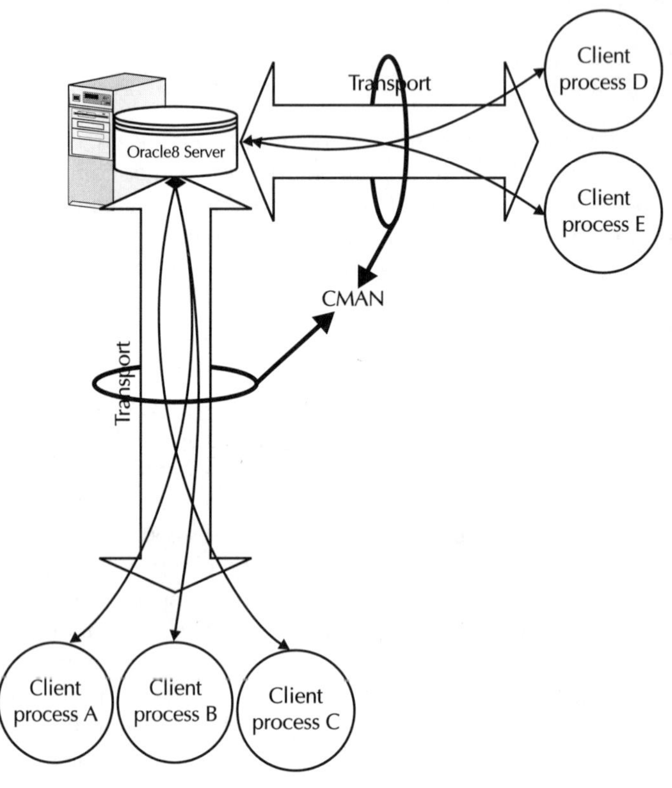

FIGURE 7-15. *Connection concentration*

may be necessary to balance the load across multiple listeners. Multiple listeners can be configured to listen for requests to connect to the same database across different ports. Each listener is registered with a service handler, which maintains load information. Depending on how busy each listener is, incoming requests are routed to the least-busy service handler. Each listener may be configured on the same server (as the database) or on different servers. All listeners on the same server as the database (local listeners) may be specified via the LOCAL_LISTENER initialization parameter. All requests to connect to a dedicated server are routed to a local listener. However, a session may connect to an MTS dispatcher via listeners on remote servers.

The following listing of the *listener.ora* file configures two listeners (LISTENER and DB01LSNR) for the same database instance (DB01). Note the enhanced listener queue size for both listeners:

```
################
# Filename......: listener.ora
# Name..........: db01.world
# Date..........: 04-NOV-98 13:23:39
################
LISTENER=
  (ADDRESS_LIST =
        (ADDRESS =
          (PROTOCOL=IPC)
          (KEY=db01.world)
        )
  (ADDRESS =
          (COMMUNITY = orasqlnet.world)
          (PROTOCOL = TCP)
          (HOST=db01-fast)
          (PORT=1521)
          (QUEUESIZE=256)
        )
  )

STARTUP_WAIT_TIME_LISTENER = 0
CONNECT_TIMEOUT_LISTENER = 0
log_DIRECTORY_LISTENER = /oracle/trace_logs/db01
TRACE_LEVEL_LISTENER = OFF
SID_LIST_LISTENER=
 (SID_LIST=
  (SID_DESC=
   (SID_NAME=db01)
   (ORACLE_HOME=/oracle/8.0.4)
  )
 )

DB01LSNR=
  (ADDRESS_LIST =
       (ADDRESS =
          (COMMUNITY = orasqlnet.world)
          (PROTOCOL = TCP)
          (HOST=db01-fast)
          (PORT=1525)
          (QUEUESIZE=256)
```

```
      )
  )

STARTUP_WAIT_TIME_DB01LSNR = 0
CONNECT_TIMEOUT_DB01LSNR = 0
log_DIRECTORY_DB01LSNR = /oracle/trace_logs/db01
TRACE_LEVEL_DB01LSNR = OFF
SID_LIST_DB01LSNR=
 (SID_LIST=
  (SID_DESC=
   (SID_NAME=db01)
   (ORACLE_HOME=/oracle/8.0.4)
  )
 )
```

When multiple listeners are configured, it is possible to randomize client connections over the different listeners, such that the incoming load is shared across all available listeners. It is possible to achieve this in one of two ways:

- **Automatic randomization** Starting with SQL*Net v2.3, it is possible to automatically randomize client connections by creating multiple service entries in the *tnsnames.ora* file corresponding to the same name service. A TNS round-robin algorithm was used by SQL*Net v2.3.*x* to route incoming connections to the appropriate listener. In Net8, depending on the service handler statistics, new connections are routed to the least busy listener. The following listing provides an example of such duplicate service entries via the ADDRESS clause:

```
db01.world =
  (DESCRIPTION =
    (ADDRESS_LIST =
        (ADDRESS =
          (COMMUNITY = tcp.world)
          (PROTOCOL = TCP)
          (Host = db01-fast)
          (Port = 1521)
        )
       (ADDRESS =
         (COMMUNITY = tcp.world)
         (PROTOCOL = TCP)
```

```
            (Host = db01-fast)
            (Port = 1526)
          )
        )
      (CONNECT_DATA = (SID = DB01)
      )
    )
```

If Oracle Names is being used (instead of a local *tnsnames.ora* file), the different listening addresses for each service name may be specified in the names server.

- **Manual randomization** Versions of SQL*Net prior to v2.3 required manual intervention to "randomize" the client connections across multiple listeners. Different service entries pointing to the ports (used by the different listeners) would be set up in the *tnsnames.ora* file (such as DB01_LSNR1.world, DB01_LSNR2.world, and so on). Then each service name would be either hard-coded within the application or set outside the application via the TWO_TASK environment variable (on UNIX clients). This method provided information about the current and estimated number of clients and the database activity generated via each client. According to such information, each client would be configured to use a certain listener port. For instance, if there were 16 clients generating more or less equal amounts of traffic, then eight of them would be configured to connect via the DB01_LSNR1 service name and the rest would be configured to connect via the DB01_LSNR2 service name.

Obviously, the first method is the preferred method, since it is easier to set up (automatic) and requires less administration and no application-code/OS-variable changes. Furthermore, if the listener used by the service name hard-coded in the application goes down, it could potentially cause downtime. In the automatic method, since no application hard-coding is involved, the service names pointing to different listeners are the same and are independent of the various listener statuses. So, even if one listener goes down, the others would still be available and allow seamless and uninterrupted access to all clients.

It must be apparent that Net8 introduces a variety of new load-balancing/connection bandwidth–increasing features. Accordingly, it's advisable to migrate to Net8 if possible, to take advantage of these enhancements. Furthermore, wherever

possible, Net8 allows packets to be transmitted without application (Net8) headers (referred to as Net8 TNS raw). This reduces overall packet size and thus results in lesser network traffic, since more data can be packed into each packet.

Additional load-balancing features have been introduced in Net8 with Oracle8*i* (with the automatic *database instance registration to listeners* option) such as connect-time failover and client/connection load balancing. These are discussed in Chapter 6.

Pre-spawn dedicated server processes

When you are connecting to dedicated server processes using a single listener, performance can be increased by pre-spawning as many dedicated server processes as peak-hour operations would require. The number of processes to pre-spawn may either already be known (if it is known beforehand that a certain number of batch processes would be running), estimated, on the basis of user requirements, or observed during prior times (on the production database, if it is already live or, alternatively, on a test database). Such pre-spawning needs to occur prior to the peak hours, such as just before the workday, when users come in and log on. By default, dedicated server processes are not pre-spawned. Rather, whenever the listener detects an incoming dedicated user connection on the port it is registered for, it spawns a dedicated server process (at runtime) and allows the user connection request to connect to the newly spawned server process to access the database. By pre-spawning dedicated server processes, the time taken by the listener to spawn a new process at runtime can be avoided. Pre-spawned dedicated server processes cannot take advantage of automatic listener load balancing (client randomization), since a pre-spawned dedicated server process can only connect to the database via the listener that spawned it.

Dedicated server processes may be pre-spawned by setting the following parameters in the *listener.ora* file:

- **PRESPAWN_MAX** This is the maximum number of dedicated server processes to be pre-spawned across all protocols (TCP/IP, SPX/IPX, and so on).
- **PRESPAWN_LIST** This consists of a list of descriptions of the pre-spawned server processes (PRESPAWN_DESC). Each entry in the list specifies the protocol (PROTOCOL), the number of dedicated server processes to pre-spawn for that protocol (POOL_SIZE) (the sum total of POOL_SIZE across all protocols has to be less than the PRESPAWN_MAX), and the timeout in minutes (TIME_OUT), beyond which an inactive pre-spawned dedicated server process is terminated by Oracle. All pre-spawned processes need to have catered to a connection already before they can be

terminated (that is, virgin pre-spawned processes, which have never handled a user connection, continue to wait past the timeout value).

The following listing of the *listener.ora* file provides an example of how these values can be set:

```
################
# Filename......: listener.ora
# Name..........: db01.world
# Date..........: 04-NOV-98 13:23:39
################
LISTENER=
  (ADDRESS_LIST =
        (ADDRESS =
          (PROTOCOL=IPC)
          (KEY=db01.world)
        )
        (ADDRESS =
          (PROTOCOL=IPC)
          (KEY=db01)
        )
        (ADDRESS =
          (COMMUNITY = orasqlnet.world)
          (PROTOCOL = TCP)
          (HOST=db01-fast)
          (PORT=1521)
          (QUEUESIZE=256)
        )
  )

STARTUP_WAIT_TIME_LISTENER = 0
CONNECT_TIMEOUT_LISTENER = 0
log_DIRECTORY_LISTENER = /oracle/trace_logs/db01
TRACE_LEVEL_LISTENER = OFF
SID_LIST_LISTENER=
 (SID_LIST=
  (SID_DESC=
   (SID_NAME=db01)
   (ORACLE_HOME=/oracle/8.0.4)
   (prespawn_max = 40)
   (prespawn_list=
      (prespawn_desc=(protocol=tcp)(pool_size=40)(timeout=10))
   )
  )
 )
```

Summary

This chapter offered tips on installation and customization. It emphasized ease of future administration/management and moved on to performance, all with higher availability as the final objective. Starting off with OFA, we looked at configuring different initialization parameters relating to the SGA and background processes, as well as at multiplexing the control-file and the online and archived redo-logs. Finally, we ended with some tips on SQL*Net/Net8 configuration.

The next chapter takes us to another core issue: upgrading. No matter which Oracle version we install, at some point in time, we always need to move on to the newer and better version. Accordingly, the next chapter provides some tips on upgrading the Oracle software and the database while incurring as little downtime as possible.

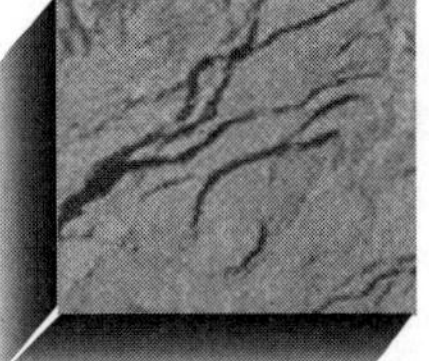

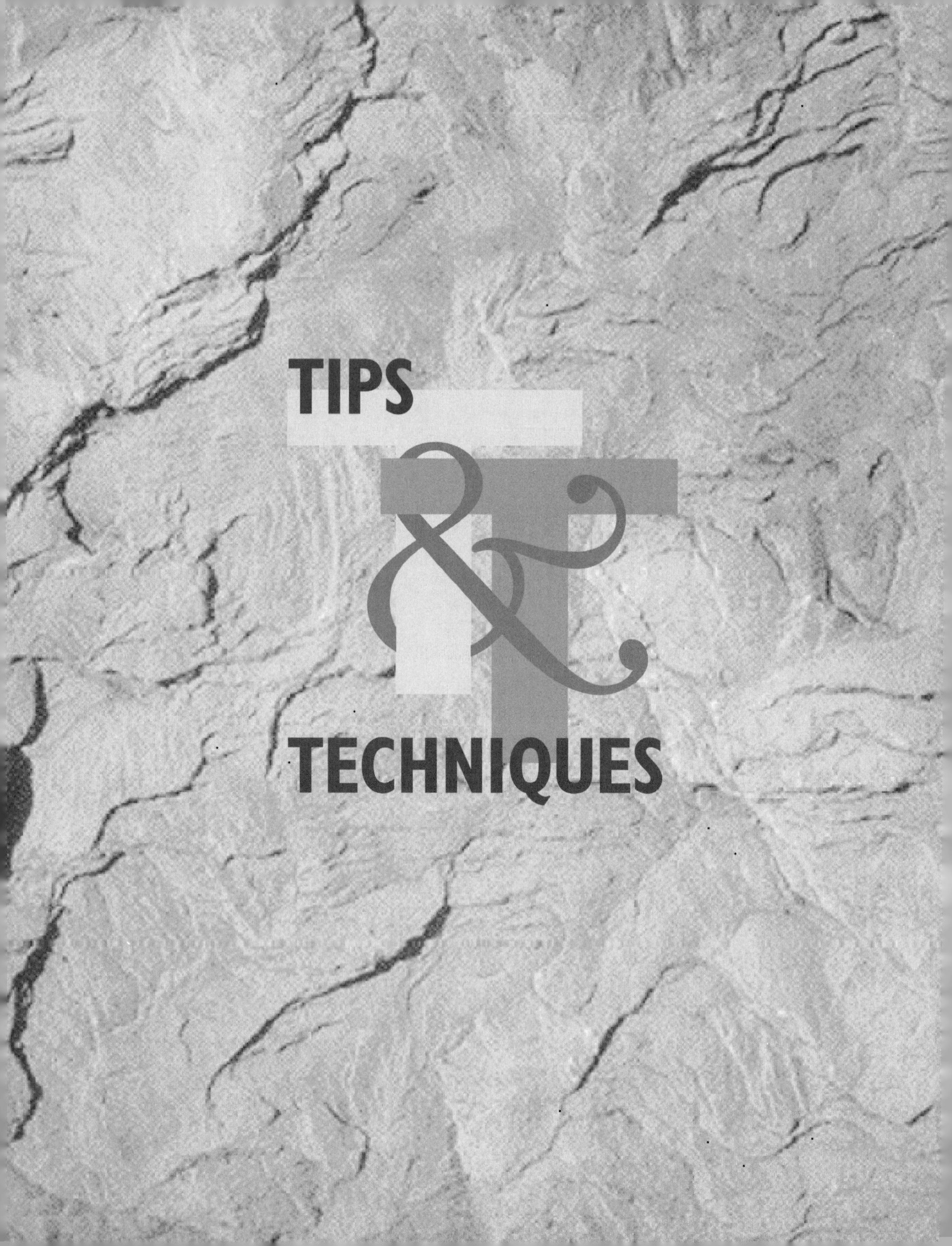
TIPS
&
TECHNIQUES

CHAPTER 8

Database Upgrades, Downgrades, Reorganizations, and Migrations

In the previous chapter we looked at various installation and initial configuration scenarios. Many steps in this "initial" configuration may need to be repeated more than once during the lifetime of a database, such as during upgrades, downgrades, reorganizations and migrations. Accordingly, many tips in the previous chapter also apply here. Each of the strategies discussed in this chapter—upgrades, downgrades, reorganizations, and migrations—may potentially require downtime.

This chapter contains the following tips and techniques:

- Always practice the migration on a test environment
- Analyze each step and construct strategies to expedite it
- Watch for gotchas while migrating to Oracle8/8*i* from Oracle7

It concludes with a real-life case study that summarizes the preceding tips.

Prior to continuing any further, I would like to pause a moment and explain the usage of terms mentioned earlier, as I use them often in this chapter. Generally, these terms may have various meanings depending on the context in which they are used. However, I would like to explain how I use them to ensure that we are on the same page.

Upgrades

An *upgrade* is the process of moving from an older database version to a newer database version, for instance, moving from v7.3.4 to v8.0.5. An upgrade may be performed due to reasons such as these:

- To take advantage of the newer features available in the newer release.
- To get rid of bugs that may exist in the previous version.
- To ensure compliance with Oracle Support. (For instance, migrating from Oracle7 v7.1 to Oracle7 7.3.4 may be necessary to stick to a supported release, since v7.1 is not supported.)
- To get away from versions that are not Y2K complaint. (Oracle Support has a white paper that specifically mentions versions that are Y2K compliant.)

Downgrades

A *downgrade* is the process of moving from a newer version to an older version. Although they are relatively rare, downgrades may sometimes be necessary due to reasons such as these:

- When major show-stopping bugs are encountered in the newer release. For instance, a few years ago at one of my client sites, a bug in Oracle7 v7.3.3 (a bug that used to frequently produce the "ORA-6502" error without any rhyme or reason, causing the application to fail) forced us to downgrade to v7.2 (which was still supported at the time). The workaround to this bug in v7.3.3 was to issue the ALTER SYSTEM FLUSH SHARED_POOL command. This would eliminate the errors for a while; however, they would soon re-appear. Furthermore, each time the shared-pool was flushed, performance would hurt, since the shared-pool would have to be repopulated again (causing additional physical I/O and CPU calls). This workaround was not acceptable to the client, thus forcing us to perform a downgrade.
- When applications fail to function due to the use of older version-specific features, which are no longer supported in the newer version (or are buggy in the newer version). This is more of a problem with third-party applications, where one does not have access to source code, and eliminating those version-specific features is not very easy. In fact, one of my clients still uses Oracle6 due to a third-party ERP package they are using not being certified against Oracle7 or Oracle8 (the manufacturer of that package shut down shop a while ago).

Reorganizations

A *reorganization* is the process of moving data within the database to attain better performance or to manage space more efficiently. For instance, in non-striped (OS or hardware) environments, data may need to be striped manually by spreading it across multiple disks/controllers via pre-allocated extents. So if a large table already exists within one large extent on a single disk, the data in the table may need to be copied over to a different table (usually the old table is renamed and the new table is given the old name) with a pre-determined number of extents spread across data-files over multiple disks/controllers. Alternatively, a table may be highly fragmented and may need to be rebuilt with better physical storage characteristics (with the data being copied over via the import/export utilities or the PARALLEL CREATE TABLE AS SELECT command) to pack the data more efficiently across a smaller number of database blocks. Also, a total database reorganization may be required to rebuild the database from scratch after certain recovery situations (such as when incomplete recovery is done, causing logical corruption within the database or when active rollback segments are marked as corrupt via the _CORRUPT_ROLLBACK_SEGMENTS initialization parameter). Such reorganization is generally done within a single system (assuming there is sufficient space to perform such reorganizations). Also, while migrating to a different system, such reorganization may be performed along the way as part of the migration process. This chapter does not provide an in-depth outline of the various maintenance tasks that would fall under the broad category of reorganization (there are far too many to mention them all; Chapters 11 and 12 provide more details). Rather, this chapter concentrates on methods to achieve faster reorganization in situations where large-scale data transfer is involved.

Migrations

I use the term *migration* in a generic fashion to refer to both database and non-database moves, such as database or system upgrades and downgrades or data-transfers required during database reorganizations. Thus, I describe migrations as encompassing upgrades, downgrades, and data-transfers during database reorganizations. Instances of system migration include cases where the database is moved from a smaller box to a more powerful system (for example, from a *Sun E3000* to a *Sun Starfire™ E10000*) or from one OS to another (for example, from Windows NT to Linux or vice versa) or from an older version of the OS to a newer version (for example, from Solaris 2.51 to Solaris 7).

When to Upgrade

This is a burning question asked by many IT personnel. Unfortunately, there is no single answer that would uniformly apply to all scenarios. With different versions of Oracle running on multiple hardware and software platforms, and a plethora of applications running against these databases, different situations may call for different responses in real life. Upgrading too soon, without adequate benchmarking and testing, may result in severe bugs remaining undetected, and the buggy higher release may need to be subsequently downgraded (causing further downtime) due to patches not being available on time. Conversely, taking too long to upgrade may prevent your site from making use of the performance and availability enhancements that the newer release offers.

For these reasons, I won't even attempt to advise you on when to specifically upgrade. However, I do attempt to provide the following broad guidelines that will help you determine when to do so.

- **Scalability** When you have outgrown system and/or database capacity, you may need to migrate to a higher database version or a better hardware/software platform. Following are some instances of such migrations:
    - **Migrate to a different hardware platform** An example is migrating from a four-CPU machine to an eight-CPU machine with capacity for an additional four CPUs for the increased scalability to handle higher

end-user traffic or to accommodate higher response-time and throughput requirements. Another is migrating from a single SMP machine to a multiple-node cluster to meet availability requirements outlined in the SLA.

- **Migrate to a different OS** An example is migrating from Windows NT to Linux or vice versa.
- **Migrate to a newer Oracle release** For instance, you might migrate from Oracle7 v7.3.4 to Oracle8 v8.0.5 to make use of features such as connection concentration and multiplexing to allow thousands of concurrent connections, if your site has outgrown the normal support from MTS (multi-threaded server) for large user communities.

  Ensure that you accurately understand and document the maximum capacity level of each critical systems and database component (see Chapter 2 for more details). As soon as that level is reached, you would need to upgrade that component to prevent performance and/or availability from suffering.

- **Peer knowledge-base** Check with reliable sources (for instance, Oracle Support, or your peers in the local and international Oracle User Groups) about their experiences with the newer release prior to deciding to upgrade. Also, search for bug reports in the Oracle MetaLink site specific to the newer version. Especially, check for bugs that might be relevant to your environment.
- **Compliance with Oracle Support** Always upgrade to ensure compliance with Oracle Support requirements. Upgrade sufficiently in time, so that you never get behind on the minimum supported Oracle version.
- **Testing** Of course, the newer release needs to be tested as thoroughly as possible on a test platform (closely mirroring the production environment), running the same production applications, prior to deciding to upgrade the production environment. A subsequent tip elaborates further.

As a rule of thumb for any 24×7 environment, I do not recommend upgrading prior to at least six months after the release date. Of course, patches (database and OS) may be required on a more urgent basis. Normally, patches do not call for migration (nevertheless, some downtime may be required, during which the standby database, if present, may be used; Chapter 11 discusses applying patches in more detail). In other words, I always try to migrate to the newer version of Oracle at least after six months after the date of release of a major version. Generally, at least six months are required for Oracle to iron out the bugs and kinks encountered in the initial production releases. At the same time, do not delay excessively in upgrading. Ensure that the upgrades are done in reasonable time—at least within a year of release (if no show-stopping problems have been encountered in the newer release during testing). This is because (as mentioned earlier) with every new release, Oracle introduces powerful and useful new features, which enhance availability and performance (note that these features may entail increased licensing costs). Accordingly, it may be worthwhile to take a small hit (this "hit" would be caused by the downtime endured during the upgrade; and, if a standby database on a less powerful machine is used, there would also be a performance degradation), perform the upgrade, and then take advantage of the new performance and availability enhancing features on a daily basis. Again, at the risk of repeating myself, I would recommend that a 24×7 site upgrade to the new version between six to twelve months of its release—definitely not any less and preferably not too much more.

Speed is very much of the essence during a migration. And this statement applies more to environments where there isn't a standby database or the standby database is running on a slow machine. Speed determines the duration of downtime during the upgrade window. It is prudent to schedule the downtime well in advance, migrate, and make the system available again as quickly as possible. Advance planning is very important to ensure that the entire operation goes smoothly without unanticipated events occurring and to keep the disruption caused by the upgrade to the minimum. Major migrations can take hours to complete. It is highly recommended in such scenarios to maintain a standby database; switch over to the standby database to prevent major service disruptions and ensure compliance with uptime requirements outlined in the SLA. Also, having a standby database substantially relieves the administrative personnel who are performing the migration, and it reduces chances of manual errors during the intense task of migrating. Conversely, not having a standby database increases the pressure on the personnel (since the production database is being migrated and is unavailable), who have to work within a very finite deadline, leaving little margin for errors or unanticipated events. Note that a regular standby database may not be useful during all migration situations, such as when upgrading (from an earlier release to a newer release), since the redo-log formats are different and cannot be directly applied. However, you could design and implement a custom standby database (CSDs) to provide the desired availability even during upgrades. Chapter 15 discusses CSDs in detail.

The following tips focus on enhancing migration speed and safety. The real-life case study provided at the end of the chapter outlines the steps taken by us (a team at a client site, comprising some very bright individuals) to accomplish a migration of 80GB of data to a new system with as little downtime as possible. The case study uses many of the tips outlined in the text that follows to place them in perspective.

Practice the migration on a test environment

Prior to conducting the migration on the actual production box, conduct a few practice runs on a test environment. For a 24×7 environment, this is of prime importance. This test environment should mirror the production environment, as closely as possible. During each run, note down the sequence of operations, with an emphasis on unanticipated events (read, unpleasant surprises) occurring. Prior to the subsequent run, accommodate all such events within the plan. Practicing such migration operations help directly in two ways:

- **It allows you to predict the time taken to migrate with reasonable accuracy** Based on such predictions, appropriate downtime can be scheduled for the primary database. Select a good interval of time when the downtime is least likely to affect the business. End users can be notified well in advance (this is very important to avoid disrupting their work).
- **It removes the element of surprise during the live run and makes the overall operation smoother** As any experienced operations personnel can tell you, the migration's success depends on the degree of advance knowledge that you can gather. When I say "success," I don't only refer to the outcome of the migration. Rather, I refer to the migration occurring within the pre-determined interval of time. The fewer the number of unanticipated events, the smoother the migration occurs and, most important, the more likely it is to complete on time. Finally, such practice runs increase the confidence level of administrative personnel performing the migration.

Once the migration is complete, ensure that the new production environment is again thoroughly tested to ensure that nothing has been forgotten. Again, practice runs help in determining what to look for after the migration is complete (based on things left undone during the earlier practice runs).

Analyze each step and construct strategies to expedite it

Every migration process consists of multiple steps. The steps may be broadly classified as follows:

Determine the Unit of Migration

In other words, figure out what needs to be migrated: either the physical objects (such as the Oracle software, data-files, redo-logs, and control-files), logical structures (such as tables and indexes), and data, or only the logical structures and data. Both cases may be possible under different scenarios. For instance, if the current physical database layout is acceptable, the current configuration may merely be copied over to the new system. If the current version needs to be upgraded to a newer one without any schematic/structural changes or reorganizations, evaluate using the migration utility that ships with the newer Oracle release. These tools save a lot of time in upgrading, since the data does not have to be unloaded (prior to the upgrade) and reloaded (after the upgrade and after the database is re-created under the new version). For instance, when migrating from Oracle7 to Oracle8, the Oracle8 Migration Utility may be used. When using such a migration tool, ensure that the current configuration is fully backed up (in case you need to revert if the upgrade does not succeed) and all pre-requisites are well understood and complied with (such as space requirements for migration). However, if the current configuration is a problem (does not scale, provides bad performance, crashes frequently, and so on), then the problematic physical structure may have to be left behind, only the data and the logical structures that are contained within being copied over to a newly designed physical layout. Additionally, if the logical structures are faulty (bad design or do not scale to accommodate new user requirements, for instance), then the data needs to be transformed to a new format, prior to being moved over to the new structures. Such situations may call for utilities that read the data only and write it out for subsequent loading into the new database (utilities such as import/export and SQL*Loader). One more thing to consider is that, during the migration of very large databases (VLDBs) from one system to another, it may be prudent to move the entire physical database or units thereof (such as data-files). This is because the import/export utilities used to migrate logical structures and data do not scale very well to accommodate large amounts of data. Subsequent tips provide more details.

Unload Data from Source Database

This involves retrieving source data and having it ready either for transformation (if necessary) and/or for loading into the target database. In order to keep downtime to a minimum, this may have to be accomplished in multiple passes (at least two passes). In the first pass, data prior to a specific delta (a date, a primary-key sequence, and so on) can be retrieved from the source. Ideally, all tables should be kept current with respect to each other during the movement to prevent logical corruption. However, if that is not feasible (if different deltas are chosen for different large tables), then after the final installment of data is moved across, extensive tests should be performed to ensure data-consistency across tables. This may be achieved by enabling referential integrity only after the last pass. All passes except the last (the last pass would migrate the post-delta rows) should occur prior to the outage caused during the migration. The post-delta rows cannot be migrated without an outage because the cutover from the source to the target system cannot be accomplished while the source database is still up and running. If the amount of data to be migrated is large (as in the case of VLDBs), there could be several intermediate passes (between the first and last pass—these intermediate passes may consist of pre-delta and post-delta data; however, post-delta passes would occur during the outage, whereas pre-delta data passes should occur prior to the outage) to avoid migrating a major amount of data in just one or two trips and causing a large strain on the database server resources. Thus, the data would be moved across in multiple installments or passes to mitigate high downtime and heavy resource consumption. Only the last pass, comprising post-delta data, should be loaded during the actual outage. Thus, the outage is restricted to moving across only the last installment of data. Write out as much data as possible from the source database, prior to the outage. For instance, if your mode of migration is export and a subsequent import, then you need to export as much data as possible.

To illustrate the preceding points, let me provide an example: Let's say a database consisting of two (just to keep things simple) very large tables has to be migrated over to a new system. Each table has over 20 million rows.

SCENARIO I Both the tables have a CREATE_DATE column that is populated with the SYSDATE during inserts. (Again, to keep the example simple, I only mention inserts, no updates or deletes. The case study provided at the end describes a method that handles updates and deletes, as well.) If the migration is scheduled to occur on December 1, then the delta would be November 30. So a statement similar to the following may be issued on both tables to retrieve all data prior to November 30. Please note that these statements ought to be issued during periods of low activity (on the source database).

```
SQL> CREATE TABLE temp_migration_schema.table_A
     TABLESPACE <some_tblspc_with_adequate_free_space>
     STORAGE(<required_storage_clause>)
     NOLOGGING
     PARALLEL(DEGREE <appropriate_degree>)
     AS SELECT * FROM actual_schema.table_A
        WHERE create_date < TO_DATE('11/30/1999', 'MM/DD/YYYY);
```

Now, "temp_migration_schema.table_A" would contain all the pre-delta rows. The rows in this table can be copied over to the target database (on the new system) with the tool of choice (such as export/import via named pipes, SQL*Loader after writing the records out to a flat-file, database links if the number of rows is not too great and the underlying network has sufficient capacity and bandwidth, third-party data-movement tool-sets such as *Informatica PowerMart*, and so on) even as the source database is still running. Thus, a major portion of the data can be moved over without any downtime. If a lot of rows are involved (such as the 20 million mentioned previously), it may be prudent to issue multiple statements (for instance, the first statement would write all rows for the year 1997 to table t1_table_A; a second statement could write all rows for the year 1998 to table t2_table_A; and, finally, a third statement could write all rows up to November 30, 1999, to table t3_table_A). The number of statements to issue would eventually depend on the number of rows involved. The objective is to break up the workload into smaller units and then migrate these smaller units instead of one or two large units. This entire exercise can be done well before the actual migration (like a week or so before). This will allow reasonable time for checking the validity of data migrated. Again, it is recommended that you run these statements during periods of low load in order to minimize any adverse impact on the database on the source system. These statements could be serialized (that is, not run concurrently) to further minimize impact on the source system. If there is very little activity going on in the source system, however, you could run these statements in parallel to achieve higher throughput. Thus, the decision regarding into how many units the pre-delta data needs to be broken up and whether those statements can be run simultaneously or not depends on the following:

- Number of rows involved.
- Physical resources available on the source machine (number of CPUs, disks/controllers, memory, and so forth). Ensure that if each of the statements uses PQO (as in the preceding example), you tune the degree of parallelism prior to running the statements concurrently to prevent system resource contention.
- Overall database activity at the time of running these statements (both interactive and batch).

During the outage on December 1, statements similar to the following can be used to retrieve the post-delta data and complete the migration:

```
SQL> DROP TABLE temp_migration_schema.table_A;
SQL> CREATE TABLE temp_migration_schema.table_A
     TABLESPACE <some_tblspc_with_adequate_free_space>
     STORAGE(<required_storage_clause>)
     NOLOGGING
     PARALLEL(DEGREE <appropriate_degree>)
     AS SELECT * FROM actual_schema.table_A
        WHERE create_date >= TO_DATE('11/30/1999', 'MM/DD/YYYY);
```

SCENARIO 2 One of the tables (TABLE_A) has a CREATE_DATE column that could be used to determine the delta. The other table (TABLE_B) has no such column. However, TABLE_B uses a sequential number as the primary-key. In such scenarios, where a consistent delta may not be available, it may be necessary to select different deltas (for different tables), disable referential integrity (since different deltas are selected, referential integrity across tables may not be maintained, as the tables are not consistent to a point in time, and the migration may fail due to the referential integrity not being maintained temporarily) on the target database, and load as much pre-delta data as possible for each table. For instance, you could migrate all TABLE_A data, prior to November 30 (as in the preceding scenario). You would need a different approach to migrate TABLE_B's data. You could find out the current maximum value of the primary-key. If the current value is, say, 19,000,052, then you could make 19,000,000 the delta for TABLE_B. So TABLE_B's pre-delta data would be written out to a temporary table (which would be migrated across) via a statement similar to the following:

```
SQL> CREATE TABLE temp_migration_schema.table_B
     TABLESPACE <some_tblspc_with_adequate_free_space>
     STORAGE(<required_storage_clause>)
     NOLOGGING
     PARALLEL(DEGREE <appropriate_degree>)
     AS SELECT * FROM actual_schema.table_B
         WHERE table_B_id <= 19000000;
```

Once all the rows (pre-delta and post-delta) have been loaded, referential integrity should be enabled as a check to ensure that all the parent/child relationships have been resolved and there is no logical corruption within the database. This additional checking for data integrity may potentially increase the duration of the outage (since, in most situations, the database cannot be brought back up until the data is guaranteed to be accurate). For this reason, whenever possible, ensure that your units of migration are consistent to a specific point in time. This will allow integrity checks to be made for each unit on an incremental basis, rather than across the entire database at the end of the migration (which may, depending on the size of the database, take up a lot of time). Furthermore, this incremental method of ensuring referential integrity will require a relatively smaller number of rows (only the post-delta rows) to be validated during the outage at the end of the migration, thus keeping the outage time to a minimum.

Transform Data, If Necessary, at Source, Target, or Both

Data transformation may be necessary if the source data structures do not match the target data structures. An instance of source and target structures not matching would be when going from a poorly designed source database to a target database with an enhanced design. This transformation may be done:

- At the time of retrieving the data from the source database
- After retrieving the data, but prior to loading the data in the target database
- At the time of writing the data out to the target database

One of these choices or a combination may be selected based on the specific environment and requirements. For instance, if the source system is a very busy system with ongoing activity during both days and nights, you would want to cause as little an impact as possible to the source system. For this reason, you might want to retrieve data on an "as-is" basis and then format the data on the target system, prior to or at the time of loading it into the target database. Alternatively, if the fastest throughput is achieved by performing the data transformation at the source, then you need to figure out the least disruptive windows of time on the source database for such transformations and schedule them accordingly.

Copy Data from Source System to Target System

In situations where the source and target databases are on different systems (during a system migration) and the data has been retrieved onto the source system, it needs to be copied (always try to make it a "copy," instead of a direct "move," so that the fallback position is not compromised) over to the target system. The method for copying over will vary based on the mode of retrieval. The speed of the operation is highly dependent on the network (available bandwidth, capacity, and so on). Table 8-1 provides some examples of copying data from the source to the target.

Multiple iterations of such copying may need to occur depending on the number of pre-delta and post-delta units. Again, try to pre-load as much data as possible. Create deltas via change-capture columns and bitmap indexes with Y/N column values. These Boolean columns may be newly introduced to identify rows that have already been migrated. For instance, rows with 'N' or NULL values for these columns for not-yet-loaded data can be retrieved very fast (remember, bitmapped indexes hold NULLs, as well) to capture the rest of the data (the non-migrated portion) and migrate that, as well. This allows the final outage to remain small—limited to the time it takes to unload, transform, and load the final delta-set.

Load Data into Target Database

This should be treated as a separate step in situations where the copying merely consists of transferring data from the source system to the target system (such as an FTP or remote copy). In cases where the copying and loading occurs in one step (such as via database links or the SQL*Plus COPY command), this step may be considered part of the previous one. Again, ways to achieve high throughput in loading data should be considered, such as parallelizing the loads (based on the number of dump files to import, flat-files to be loaded via SQL*Loader, and so on). During parallelization, adequate thought should be given to the available physical resources, such as the number of CPUs, and disks/controllers, so that resource contention is not inadvertently caused. Another potential way of increasing throughput is to perform the loads in direct-path mode (such as with SQL*Loader or

Retrieval Mode	Possible Method for Copying Data Over to Target
Direct-mode exports (table, schema, or database level)	Perform an FTP or a remote copy (*rcp*) and import the dump file(s) (more than one dump file may be utilized to perform the imports in parallel; also, the export and import may be done concurrently via named pipes, significantly expediting the operation). The entire table on the source may be exported, or portions of it (pre-delta and post-delta data sets).
Database links	Perform a parallel CREATE TABLE AS SELECT on the target database to pull the data over from the source.
SQL*Plus COPY command (allows retrieval in array-sized chunks)	Use the COPY on the source or target to push or pull the data, respectively.
Write out data to flat-files	Perform an FTP or a remote copy of the flat-files and load via SQL*Loader in direct-path mode on the target.
Replication and direct PDML	Use the refresh mechanism of snapshots to copy data over to the snapshot tables. The data can be transferred over to the target tables via direct PDML, once the snapshots have been refreshed (completely and/or on an incremental basis). This method can be effectively used to copy both pre- and post-delta data sets on small and medium-sized tables.
Copy entire portions of the database (data-files)	Use FTP or a remote-copy to copy the data-files over to the target system, as per the location specified by the control-file used for the process.

TABLE 8-1. *An Outline of Possible Copy/Load Methods*

parallel direct-path INSERTs via the PARALLEL and APPEND hints in Oracle8). Again, wherever possible, perform the loads in UNRECOVERABLE/NOLOGGING mode to minimize the amount of redo generated. Once the loads are complete, a complete backup may be taken.

Post-Migration Validation and Testing for Consistency and Accuracy

Last, but not least, comprehensive testing needs to be done after each pre- and post-delta unit of data has been migrated. A combination of different test criteria may be adopted, such as complete checks of smaller core tables (master tables, dimension tables, and so on) and random sampling of rows in larger tables (transaction tables, fact tables, and the like). Each time errors are encountered, the problem(s) needs to be determined and fixed at every stage and the fixes need to be propagated to the subsequent unload/transform/load cycles. These steps in database migration are summed up in Figure 8-1.

Again, I cannot overemphasize the importance of performing all possible tasks in advance (before the actual outage). Doing most of the tasks in advance reduces the duration of the outage. Have scripts ready and available to handle tasks that cannot be done in advance. This will ensure that you do not waste valuable time coding/preparing scripts during the outage. Additionally, analyze tasks that can be parallelized and create scripts accordingly to minimize contention of both database and system resources. Again, keep overall systems resources (such as CPU and

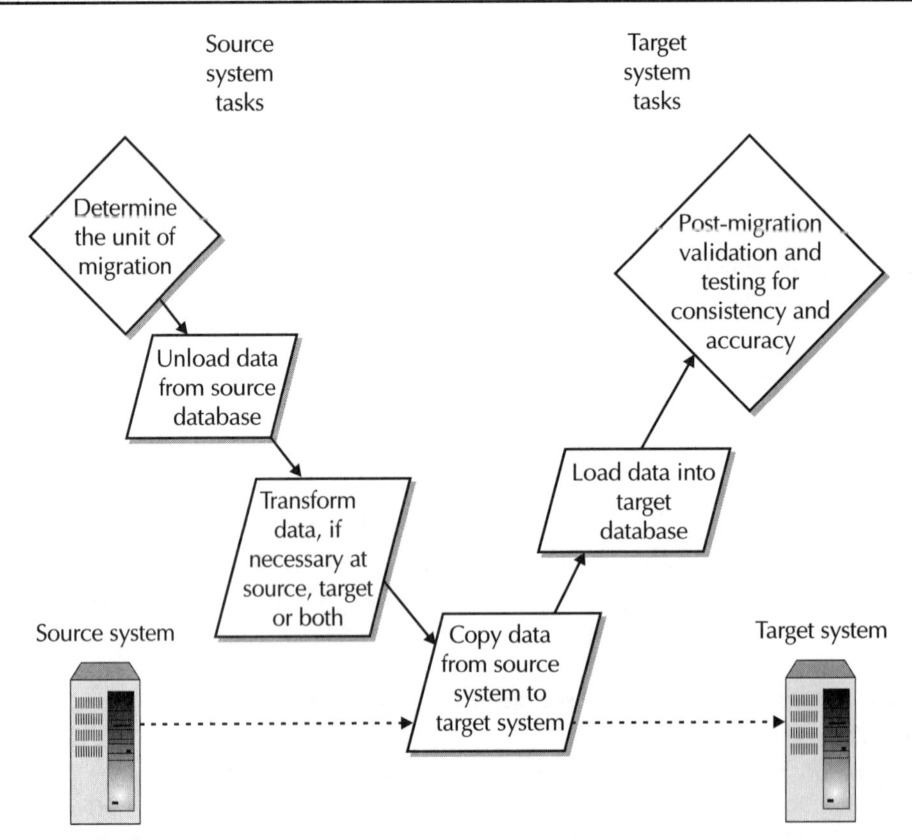

FIGURE 8-1. *Steps in database migration*

memory) in mind while creating the scripts to be run in parallel (this is an area that is generally ignored, thus causing disk I/O bottlenecks during the unload/transform/load cycle). Practice runs should indicate contention, if any, and scripts can be changed accordingly. Parallelize as many tasks as much as possible to optimize resource use, without causing contention. Also, it is essential to ensure that sufficient disk space is available to carry out all the tasks. The last thing you need is for the load process to fail due to lack of space. Time spent in analyzing space requirements for the entire migration is time well spent. In the absence of sufficient disk space, secondary storage space (such as tapes, optical disks) may have to be used, which will affect the overall migration speed.

Gotchas to watch for while upgrading from Oracle7 to Oracle8/8*i*

Using the migration utilities that come with Oracle8 and Oracle8*i* (such as the Oracle8 Migration Utility) allows you to save on upgrade time. However, these tools assume and enforce certain factors during the migration. Not being familiar with these assumptions or omitting to address them would cause the process to fail and have to be restarted. Obviously, the greater the number of failures, the more time it will take to convert. With a high number of failures and false starts, the total time to upgrade may even exceed the time taken by an upgrade strategy utilizing regular export/import and moving large amounts of data from the old v7 database to the v8 database. There is a "point of no-return" during the conversion (when the ALTER DATABASE CONVERT command is issued), and if the conversion effort fails during or after that stage, you would need to restore from the previous backups and reinitiate the entire process, thus causing heavy downtime. Also, no matter what procedure you decide to use during the upgrade, actual conversion would still be time consuming. Accordingly, I recommend using custom standby databases (Chapter 15) to prevent high downtime. Being forewarned is being forearmed, and here's a list of things to watch out for during the conversion. Hopefully, it will help in minimizing downtime in your case.

Prior to the Upgrade

The following tasks should be included in your pre-upgrade checklist:

- Acquire from Oracle Support a bug checklist pertaining to the migration tool you are using. Go through the list with a magnifying glass to ensure that you are proactively implementing workarounds wherever necessary to avoid hitting any bugs (such as setting specific events in the *init.ora* file to overcome certain bugs).
- Always perform a complete (hot or cold, if possible) backup prior to the upgrade.

- Ensure that you do not have any database user or role called MIGRATE in the Oracle7 database (source database).
- Ensure that the SYSTEM rollback segment is not about to hit MAXEXTENTS and that it is adequately sized. Migration tools typically use the SYSTEM rollback segment for certain DML activity. Do not set the OPTIMAL clause for the SYSTEM rollback segment.
- Ensure that Advanced Replication features (if you are using them) are disabled.
- Ensure that there are no pending distributed transactions (in DBA_2PC_PENDING, PENDING_TRANS$, PENDING_SESSIONS$, PENDING_SUB_SESSIONS$). If there are, manually resolve them prior to the upgrade via a COMMIT or a ROLLBACK FORCE. Also, ensure that there are no uncommitted local transactions pending. Transactions could remain uncommitted if tablespaces that are needed for the COMMIT are offline. Such uncommitted transactions are retained in the form of *save undo* within the database. You can check for the existence of save undo via the following query:

  ```
  SQL> SELECT name FROM SYS.ts$
               WHERE ts# IN (SELECT kttvstnm FROM x$kttvs);
  ```

  If any non-SYSTEM tablespaces are listed with this query, then, chances are, those tablespaces are currently in OFFLINE mode. If so, make them ONLINE again and after a little while (half an hour or so), the save undo should be resolved and removed by SMON. Alternatively, if the tablespaces listed by the preceding query are not in OFFLINE mode, you may want to get help from Oracle Support in resolving the issue (it may be a bug).
- Ensure that there is adequate free space in the SYSTEM tablespace. Note that Oracle8's and Oracle8*i*'s data dictionary is larger than Oracle7's (approximately 1.5 times the size in Oracle7) and, accordingly, the space requirement is higher.
- Ensure that there is adequate free space in the directory where control-files are maintained. Note that control-files in Oracle8/8*i* are larger.
- Ensure that the new Oracle8/8*i* home will have adequate free space. Note that the homes for these newer versions require more space than in Oracle7.
- Delete parameters from the *init.ora* file that are not needed in Oracle8/8*i*, such as CHECKPOINT_PROCESS, INIT_SQL_FILES, SERIALIZABLE, DB_WRITERS, PARALLEL_DEFAULT_SCAN_SIZE, PARALLEL_DEFAULT_

MAX_SCANS, SESSION_CACHED_CURSORS, USE_ASYNC_IO / ASYNC_READ / ASYNC_WRITE, and so on. The migration utility documentation would list all obsolete and changed parameters.

- Make a list of all important tables that are heavily accessed by end users and applications (the reason is explained later).
- Also make a list of all applications that rely on the ROWID (that use the ROWID in SELECTs, and so on)
- Last, just prior to the upgrade, make all tablespaces (including all application tablespaces holding tables and indexes) OFFLINE, except for the SYSTEM tablespace and any tablespace holding active rollback segments. This will save you restore time, in case the upgrade fails and you need to revert (especially after the point of no return). In case failures do occur, all you need to restore are the SYSTEM tablespace and the rollback segment tablespace(s). All tablespaces previously made offline need not be restored during recovery. Ensure that the STATUS of all data-files in *v$database* are either OFFLINE or ONLINE. Any other status (such as RECOVERY) would need to be addressed and rectified prior to the upgrade (since such data-files cannot be opened after the upgrade).

During the Upgrade

The following caveats pertaining to the actual upgrade process should be noted:

- If using a character-set other than US7ASCII (in different non-English speaking parts of the world, 8-bit character-sets are prevalent), use the command-line version of the Migration Utility. When invoked via the GUI-mode Oracle Installer, the Migration Utility defaults to US7ASCII for some reason, causing more headaches than the original migration effort set out to resolve in the first place.
- When running SQL scripts during the upgrade, always spool the output to a log-file (if they are not already built to do so). And make sure that you check these log-files for possible errors. Syntax errors (bugs) in some of the scripts will cause them to fail. Accordingly, you may need to manually figure out which part failed by looking at the log-file and rerun that and subsequent portions. Without a log-file, this task would be very difficult. With a log-file, you can easily *grep* for errors (such as by scanning for "ORA-").
- Do not attempt to access the database while the migration utility is running (ensure that no users attempt to access the database either). Doing so could potentially lead to corruption or abort the migration process.

After the Upgrade

The following points pertain to the post-upgrade process:

- Remember to make all tablespaces ONLINE again. These would be the tablespaces that you made OFFLINE prior to the upgrade. When you make these tablespaces ONLINE, their file-headers get converted to the new version format. If some of these tablespaces need to remain OFFLINE, then you can temporarily make them ONLINE and then make them OFFLINE immediately after.
- Search for any invalid constraints. You can search DBA_CONSTRAINTS for constraints with STATUS = 'INVALID'. Alternatively, run the *$ORACLE_HOME/rdbms/admin/utlconst.sql* script, which will list all invalid constraints. If any invalid constraints are found, they need to be dropped and re-created.
- Search for any invalid stored procedures, functions, packages, views, and triggers (these objects are typically invalidated after a migration). You may need to manually recompile them via the ALTER <object-type> <object-name> COMPILE command. Do not use DBMS_UTILITY.COMPILE_SCHEMA in this situation because all object dependencies may not have been successfully resolved during the upgrade. You can easily compile all invalid objects as follows:

```
SQL> SELECT 'ALTER ' || object_type || ' ' || object_name || ' COMPILE;'
       FROM dba_objects
      WHERE status = 'INVALID';
SQL> SPOOL compile_all.sql
SQL> /
SQL> SPOOL OFF
SQL> @compile_all
```

- Recompute all statistics when using the cost-based optimizer (since the existing statistics will have been destroyed).
- Check for indexes with status = UNUSABLE in DBA_INDEXES. Bitmapped indexes may have been marked UNUSABLE during the upgrade. Re-create all such indexes.
- The ROWIDs of the tables will still be in a state of flux because they need to be converted to the extended format. The migration utilities do not actually perform the ROWID conversion. Any subsequent DML statement (during actual use) that accesses a row would perform the conversion, thus affecting real-time performance. If you do not want the cost of conversion to be borne by the users (running the DML statement), then you need to

perform full-table scans to induce automatic conversion prior to opening the database for regular use. At the very least, you can induce full-table scans on all tables identified earlier (when you were asked to make a list of all important tables). Make all read-only tablespaces read/write prior to having the ROWID format changed (you can make them read-only again after the ROWID format has changed). An easy way to induce full-table scans on all tables in the database would be to perform a full database export and write out the output to */dev/null* as follows:

```
$ exp userid=USERID file=/dev/null full=y
```

- Wherever necessary, change application code to either eliminate references to the ROWID within the application-code (use the primary-key instead, if possible) or alter the code to use the ROWIDs via the DBMS_ROWID package in Oracle8/8*i*.
- Bounce the database to clear the buffers. Do not use the *shutdown abort* option. Always shut down in NORMAL or IMMEDIATE mode after an upgrade.
- Finally, test the new version completely for unwanted side effects prior to releasing it to end users and applications. Ensure that the applications are not using any new reserved words (which were not reserved in the earlier release) and that reliance on ROWIDs is not causing problems. Ensure that your failover/switchover plans still function properly under the new version.

Quick tips to enhance load/unload performance

The following tips enhance the performance of load/unload operations during the migration:

- Perform bulk-loads without indexes and with constraints disabled (especially CHECK and FOREIGN KEY constraints). Indexes can be built as part of the post-load operations. This will prevent the indexes from slowing up the bulk loads and also prevent them from getting highly fragmented during the loads. Also, if the data loaded is in sorted form, the indexes can be built using the NOSORT option. This will avoid the need for explicit sorting during index creation and significantly speed up the process. If the index creation process finds that the keys are not actually sorted, then it will perform the sorting explicitly. So there is no harm in trying to pre-sort the data and using the NOSORT option. Also, indexes may be built concurrently on different tables. That will allow the process to parallelized (to a certain degree). Furthermore, each index may be built in UNRECOVERABLE/NOLOGGING mode (to

avoid redo generation) and also use the PARALLEL clause to expedite creation using multiple parallel slaves.

- When using export/import to migrate under UNIX, utilize named pipes. When named pipes are used, the import process matches the speed of the export process. Especially when done over a fast network, it results in very high throughput. The case study provided in a subsequent paragraph illustrates their effectiveness. The following steps may be taken to perform exports/imports over named pipes (note that the sequence of steps is important):

  1. Create the named pipes on both the source machine and the target machine. Note the actual command to create the named pipes may vary depending on your OS flavor. Also, the named pipe could have any name. In this example, the export and import pipes are called *p_exp* and *p_imp*, respectively.

     On the source machine (let's call it SRC), where the export will occur:

```
$ mknod /dev/p_exp p
```

     On the target machine (let's call it TRGT), where the import will occur:

```
$ mknod /dev/p_imp p
```

     Ensure that both pipes have been created via the *ls* command on the corresponding machines.

  2. Copy the "export pipe" (on SRC) onto the "import pipe" (on TRGT). Basically, any command that allows remote copying (such as *rcp*) may be used. This example uses *dd* via *rsh*.

     On TRGT:

```
$ rsh SRC dd if=/dev/p_exp > /dev/p_imp
```

  3. Start the export process.

     On SRC:

```
$ exp userid=USERNAME file=/dev/p_exp full=y direct=y log=LOGFILE
```

  4. Start the import process.

     On TRGT:

```
$ imp userid=USERNAME file=/dev/p_imp buffer=1024000 full=y log=LOGFILE
```

     Now, both the export and import processes should be concurrently working.

- Another option to increase export/import throughput is to use a single-task version of the export and import utilities. By default on UNIX, both utilities are linked in two-task mode (in other words a shadow process is spawned to cleanly separate Oracle kernel code and export/import code). Using single-task export/import can increase overall throughput in the region of 0–20 percent. However, utilities linked in single-task mode may consume more memory, since the Oracle executable is no longer shared across all foreground and background processes. The names of the single-task executables are the same as for the regular two-task ones, except that the former have an "st" suffix (so single-task *exp* becomes *expst* and single-task *imp* becomes *impst*). Single-task versions of the utilities need to be explicitly linked in via the following commands:

```
$ cd $ORACLE_HOME/rdbms/lib
$ make -f ins_rdbms.mk expst
$ make -f ins_rdbms.mk impst
```

  You may need to use the *oracle.mk* make-file, instead of *ins_rdbms.mk,* depending on the version of Oracle you are using. It is advisable to solicit Oracle Support's help prior to using single-tasking, to ensure that no corruption is inadvertently caused.

- Use OCI routines to write out data to flat-files and use the SQL*Loader direct-path option to load the data into the target database. Since OCI routines directly allow low-level functions to be used in accessing the database, they can result in substantial throughput improvements due to a straight reduction in overall context switching and system calls issued. Also, the performance improvements afforded by SQL*Loader's direct-path option are well known (and well documented) and need little elaboration.
- Parallelize both unload and load jobs by using PQO and by starting parallel instances of unload/load processes (export/import, SQL*Loader, pCTAS, and so on). The objective is to transfer all data within the time it takes to get the largest table across. For example, in order to achieve this, all large tables would be exported to different dump files, whereas all smaller and medium-sized tables would be exported to a single dump file (which would be different from the dump files for large tables). All the imports may be run in parallel, thus loading multiple tables at the same time. Thus, by the time the largest table is imported, all other tables would already be imported. During such parallelization, ensure that the tables being imported concurrently are spread across different disks/controllers. Otherwise, such parallelization may cause I/O contention, potentially delaying the migration, rather than expediting it.

- pCTAS (parallel CREATE TABLE AS SELECT) may be performed in UNRECOVERABLE/NOLOGGING mode either to create temporary tables containing the pre- and post-delta data-sets (which can then be exported and moved over to the target) or to pull the data over directly from the target database. Using pCTAS in UNRECOVERABLE/NOLOGGING mode provides high throughput by avoiding undo (rollback information) and redo generation. You can also use the PDML and direct-insert options in Oracle8. If the tables are already captured (via export, pCTAS, or the like) from the source database in an "as-is" format, but certain complex transformations need to occur at the target prior to loading the final target tables, you can initially import the tables as they are (if export has been used). Then a script may be written to transform the data and perform bulk inserts into the target tables in parallel/direct mode (via the PARALLEL and APPEND hints). If you have a reasonably fast network and the number of rows involved is not too high, you could even use a database link to pull the data over and perform the bulk inserts in parallel/direct mode.
- Oracle's (simple) replication features can be very effective in certain situations. For instance, you may use snapshots to get the data across. Ideal candidates for such an implementation would be large tables with small incremental changes. Thus, the bulk of the data can be brought across initially (in the first phase) and then on a regular basis, only the incremental rows needing to be copied over via snapshot logs.
- Avoid using additional layers (ODBC, SQL*Net, Net8, and so on) while trying to move large amounts of data across. For instance, pCTAS or the SQL*Plus COPY command may involve SQL*Net intervention, especially when run from a client PC. Similarly, when you are trying to use certain third-party tools to perform data transformation and loading, ODBC may be involved, thus potentially causing a delay. As a rule of thumb, the fewer the number of layers involved, the better the performance. Accordingly, it may be necessary to provide for adequate disk space and retain the source files (export dump files, flat-files, and so on) on the target system (copied over via FTP or *rcp* or through NFS) and directly load the data. If adequate disk space is unavailable, consider performing the export/import via named pipes.
- When dealing with large databases, you may want to consider copying data-files from the source directly over to the target system. This strategy is very useful, especially when the physical structure at the source is quite acceptable (for instance, it has a decent physical design/layout and there is little or no fragmentation) and thus there is no need for any defragmentation or any other kind of reorganization during the migration. This strategy avoids

the need for manually moving raw data and for various related tasks such as resolving inter-table relationships, rebuilding indexes, granting privileges, creating synonyms across schemas, and so on; it greatly reduces migration time. Just the time taken to actually move/copy the entire database (or necessary units thereof) would form the bulk of the time taken for the migration to complete. The following steps may be taken to achieve this end:

- Configure the target database to have the same directory structure as the source (that is, the same ORACLE_HOME directory, data-file paths, and so on). If the target system is already configured in a different fashion, either reconfigure it or use soft links (on UNIX) on the target system to simulate the source database path-names.
- Configure the same Oracle-specific environment variables on the target as the source (ORACLE_BASE, ORACLE_SID, ORACLE_HOME, and so on).
- Using the latest (hot) backup from the source database, copy the data-files onto the target in the exact same location as on the source system. Also, copy the initialization files (*init<SID>.ora, config<SID>.ora*) to the target.
- Write a script to create a new control-file for this "new" database on the target system, referring to each of the data-files copied over. Also, make references to the online redo-log groups within the script in the directory where you want them (ideally, this should also match the source system, although it is not mandatory). Also, ensure that the ARCHIVELOG mode is enabled for the new database.
- On the target system, take the following steps to bring the "new" database into existence:

1. Edit the initialization files on the target as necessary (for instance, ensure that the CONTROL_FILES parameter is properly defined to refer to the right locations).
2. Start up the instance in NOMOUNT mode.
3. Run the script to create the control-file. Once successfully run, the database would be in mounted mode.
4. Open the database via the command:

   ```
   SQL> ALTER DATABASE OPEN RESETLOGS;
   ```

   The RESETLOGS option needs to be used to explicitly create the redo-logs (since they do not yet exist prior to this point).

- Now that the database is in existence, take a complete backup (hot or cold) of the new database at this point.
- Shut down the database and restart it in mounted mode.
- Copy over the archived redo-logs from the source that have been generated since its latest backup (remember, the latest backup of the source was used to create the new database) and apply them to the target database to make it as current as possible. Note that it will still be behind the source database, since the source database is currently processing transactions and writing them to the online redo-logs.
- Take a small outage (for say, 15 minutes), stop all applications, archive all unarchived redo-logs on the source database, and shut down the source database. Now copy all the latest archived redo-logs to the target system and apply them to the target database to make it completely current. This outage can be scheduled during low-usage hours. If an outage is not acceptable to your company, however, then use a custom standby database (CSD) to remain up and available (Chapter 15 discusses CSDs in detail).
- Now, open the target database. Reroute all applications to use the new target database instead of the original source database, and start up the applications (Chapter 6 discusses application rerouting methods). The migration to the new target system is complete.

- If your objective is to merely upgrade the system (without any Oracle version upgrade) and you have a triple-mirrored configuration, you can use the third mirror to move data over to the target system. Here it's assumed that the target system is compatible with the disks that the source system uses (not an unrealistic assumption, since most target systems have the same or better configurations compared to the source during migrations). Here's how the strategy would work:
  - Take a small outage to perform the reconfiguration. This outage shouldn't take more than a few minutes. Stop all applications and close the database. If necessary, revert to a standby database during the upgrade, if the downtime is not acceptable.
  - Break the third mirror. At that point, the source database would be left with just two mirrors. So in case a primary disk fails on the source during the reconfiguration, there is still one other mirror to revert to and function without disruption.
  - Plug the third mirror into the target system.

- Re-silver the target system's original (primary) disks with the mirror just plugged in, thus making the mirror the master disk(s). The original (primary) disks on the target system would function as the mirrors henceforth. Time to re-silver may vary depending on the overall disk size and I/O capacity.
- Once disks are re-silvered, bring up the target database as the primary database.
- If you used a standby database to prevent disruption during this operation, then you would need to sync the database (the new database on the upgraded target system) with the standby (that is, to apply the online redo logs or play back the writes, depending on the standby strategy in use at your site).
- Reroute all applications to use the target system/database henceforth (and not the source) and start up all the applications. Chapter 6 discusses methods to perform client failover and rerouting.

Now, your site is operational on the upgraded system. You can continue to employ the original (source) system as a standby or make another use of it, as appropriate (if you already have a standby). This strategy is especially effective when working with VLDBs, where time to unload/reload data can be horrendously long.

Real-Life Migration Case Study

The following case study serves to summarize all the preceding points and place them in perspective.

- **Objective** To migrate an OLTP database from a *Sun ULTRA Enterprise 3000* to a *Sun ULTRA Enterprise 6000* with less than four hours of downtime (on a Saturday night/Sunday morning) for a client running an e-commerce application on the Web. Along with the migration, it was necessary to defragment the data and indexes in the four large tables listed in Table 8-2 (these tables had a high percentage of row chaining, in addition to large-scale bubble fragments).
- **Source system** Sun ULTRA Enterprise 3000 with 8 CPUs, 1GB RAM, and the database spread across four RAID 5 (software-based) disk volumes.
- **Target system** Sun ULTRA Enterprise 6000 with 12 CPUs, 2GB RAM, and the database to be spread across sixteen RAID S (hardware-based) and two RAID 1 disk volumes. The RAID S volumes were on an *EMC 3200* and were striped using a stripe-size of 64KB using *Veritas Volume Manager.*

Table Name	# of Rows (Approx.)	# of Indexes
Customers	16 million	2
Customer_Profiles	160 million	2
Orders_Booked	60 million	2
Items_Ordered	120 million	3

TABLE 8-2. *Large Tables to Be Defragmented During the Migration*

- **Database** The client had a 120GB database (with 80GB data), running on Oracle7 v7.3.4. Even though the database had a total of fifty-six tables dedicated to the e-commerce application, only four tables (the ones mentioned previously) were large in size. All the other tables had less than 100,000 rows.
- **The team** We mainly had a database administrator, a technical architect (yours truly), a network administrator, and two systems administrators dedicated to the task (of course, with the CIO calling us up constantly on a round-robin basis).
- **Strategy followed** There were two main tasks (specified in the order of importance):
    1. Migrate the database from the E3000 to the E6000.
    2. Defragment four large tables and rebuild their indexes.

We decided to perform as many tasks as we could, prior to the outage. During the outage we decided to perform only tasks that could not be done in advance. The broad strategy we took was as follows:

- Enhance the network connection between the source and target systems to ensure high throughput during the data transfer.
- Create the new database on the new system prior to the outage with well-estimated storage parameters to reduce fragmentation in the future. However, no indexes (including primary-key and unique-key indexes) were to be built. No constraints were to be created prior to the migration (since the constraints would have heavily slowed down the data transfer).

- Put a logical barrier (a "delta") within the database to distinguish between existing data and the new data that comes in (after a certain point in time) for the four large tables. A small outage would have to be taken to implement this logical barrier. The logical barrier, in our case, was a new audit column to track all new inserts and updates, a new table to log all deletes, and triggers to populate these new columns and the new table.
- Migrate the existing data in these four large tables prior to the outage in a manner that would eliminate the current fragmentation in the tables (we selected the export/import utilities for this purpose—in our environment, they provided high throughput when performed via named pipes over a fast network; the export/import utilities were linked in single-task mode). Then create and enable all the constraints, except referential integrity constraints (foreign keys) on the tables. Furthermore, rebuild the indexes after this initial migration. The initial migration would get the bulk of the data. Thus, the bulk of the data could be obtained prior to the actual outage itself. The remainder of the data (that is, data that was being currently written) would be brought in during the actual outage.
- Conduct the actual outage by disabling all application access.
- Migrate the new data during the outage based on the audit columns and the new table introduced. The indexes could still be present on the target tables during this migration, since only a relatively small number of rows (the "delta changes") would be brought in. Enable referential integrity after the complete migration.
- Test and ensure that all the data has been migrated without errors. Develop scripts to automate such testing. Examples of these tests included finding out row counts in all critical tables (large and small) and random sampling of data to ensure data validity (to ensure that no important columns have NULLs in them, and so on).
- Restart the applications and restore access to the database.

We took the following steps to implement the strategy:

Prior to the Outage

The following steps were taken prior to any service disruption:

- Upgraded the network connection between the two (source and target) machines to a 100 Mbps FDDI interlink.
- Created the database on the target system as per our capacity plan for the new system (120GB striped across 18 disk volumes). Based on previous

usage patterns, we placed the data-files involving the most intensive writes on the RAID 1 disk volumes (to avoid the parity write-penalty). We also placed some of the online redo logs on the RAID 1 disk volumes. All the appropriate tablespaces and user IDs (schemas) were created.

- Created the scripts to create all the tables (without indexes) with the appropriate storage parameters (especially PCTFREE and PCTUSED to reduce future fragmentation) and ran them on the new database. Now the table structures were present in the new database. We did not create any constraints (including the primary keys) other than the NOT NULL constraints on the table columns. Once the tables were created, all application roles and profiles were created and necessary privileges were granted across all schemas, similar to the old database.
- Wrote the code for adding a new column (WRITE_DATE) to the four tables, so that any writes (INSERTs and UPDATEs) could be logged in the column. We also wrote the code for row-level triggers to populate this column in each table. For DELETEs, we wrote row-level triggers to write the old record (complete record with the ROWID) to another (log) table.
- On an early Sunday morning (at 2:00 A.M.), a week prior to the actual migration, we took a five-minute outage to run the code (in the old database) to add the new column to the four tables and also to add the necessary triggers to capture all writes that occurred to those four tables. The small outage was necessary to disable all applications and run the code to alter the tables (with the applications running, this wouldn't have been possible, since ALTER TABLE and CREATE TRIGGER statements acquire table-level locks). The delta to distinguish between "old/existing" and "new" data was enforced during this small outage. Now we were ready to capture and migrate all the old/existing data, prior to the actual cutover. By the way, this five-minute outage was announced a week earlier on the client's Web-site.
- The old data was migrated via the following steps:
  - We copied the old data in the four large tables to temporary tables via a series of pCTAS (parallel CREATE TABLE AS SELECT) commands in UNRECOVERABLE mode. All these temporary tables had the same names as the original tables but were present in a different (temporary) schema called MOVETAB. For instance, commands similar to the following were issued:

```
SQL> CREATE TABLE movetab.customers
     TABLESPACE appl_data
     STORAGE(INITIAL 100M NEXT 100M PCTINCREASE 0 MAXEXTENTS UNLIMITED)
     PARALLEL(DEGREE 6)
     UNRECOVERABLE
     AS
     SELECT * FROM sales.customers
      WHERE write_date < TO_DATE('19970324 01:01:00','YYYYMMDD HH24:MI:SS');
     /* where 19970324 01:01:00 was the time of the initial outage taken to
        implement the new audit column WRITE_DATE
     */
```

- Then we started up exports (of the data in these new temporary tables) to named pipes on the source machine and imports from named pipes on the target machine, performed a remote copy of the named pipes from source to target, and let the speedy network do the rest. The export and import zoomed by and completed in less than six hours.
- After the exports, the temporary tables were dropped.
- Then we created indexes on the four large tables in the target database with the necessary storage parameters (with a PCTFREE of 40 for non-sequential indexes [non-sequential indexes have keys whose values are not sequential] to induce high pre-splitting of index branch and leaf blocks; see Chapter 6 for a detailed discussion of pre-splitting index blocks). All other constraints (except foreign keys) were created and enabled.

- Scripts to capture the rest of the data (after the delta) were written. Each script consisted of the following code skeleton:

```
DROP TABLE movetab.customers;

CREATE TABLE movetab.customers
  TABLESPACE appl_data
  STORAGE(INITIAL 10M NEXT 10M PCTINCREASE 0 MAXEXTENTS UNLIMITED)
  PARALLEL(DEGREE 6)
  UNRECOVERABLE
  AS
  SELECT * FROM sales.customers
   WHERE write_date >= TO_DATE('19970324 01:01:00','YYYYMMDD HH24:MI:SS');
/* where 19970324 01:01:00 was the time of the initial outage taken to
   implement the new audit column WRITE_DATE
*/

/* Now delete all rows in the temporary MOVETAB.CUSTOMERS table that
```

```
** were logged in DELETE_CUSTOMER_LOG table (to repeat all
** deletes made in the actual SALES.CUSTOMERS since the delta)
*/
DELETE FROM movetab.customers tc
 WHERE EXISTS
(SELECT customer_id FROM movetab.delete_customer_log dcl
  WHERE dcl.customer_id = tc.customer_id);

COMMIT;
```

- Scripts to perform the import (with the IGNORE flag set to Y) were written for each of the four tables (to parallelize the imports across the four large tables). The import commands utilized the FROMUSER and TOUSER clauses to write the data out from the MOVETAB schema on the source to the actual schemas (such as SALES) on the target. Another script was written to import the rest of the fifty-two tables (this last import command did not use the FROMUSER/TOUSER clauses, since the source and target schemas both were the actual schemas). Thus, we had a total of five export and five import scripts that needed to run concurrently on the source and target machines, respectively. Each of the export scripts created a named pipe on the source system and started the export. Each of the import scripts created a named pipe on the target system and started the import. All the export processes were scripted to run in DIRECT mode.
- Scripts to create indexes on the remaining fifty-two tables were written. All indexes were scripted to be created in UNRECOVERABLE mode. Furthermore, index-creation statements on fairly large (medium-sized) tables were placed in separate scripts, so that they could be run independently and concurrently (to create indexes in parallel on all medium-sized tables). Multiple indexes on the same table had to be created sequentially (since in v7.3, the CREATE INDEX statement places a lock on the table, preventing another index-creation statement from accessing the same table). The overall intention was to create all indexes on all tables within the time it takes to create the biggest index. Since index-creation scripts were being run concurrently, we had to spend a lot of time analyzing the appropriate degree of parallelism to set on each CREATE INDEX statement (too high a degree on each statement would cause resource contention and performance bottlenecks).
- Scripts to create and enable all foreign keys were written.
- Finally, the appropriate changes to the *tnsnames.ora* entries on all servers, clients, and application-tiers were noted and ready to be made manually as the last step, prior to the final test (the client used *cacheFS* to maintain the *tnsnames.ora* file, and so there were just a handful of places that needed the change).

During the Outage

Database access was disabled during the following steps:

- The subsequent Saturday night (at 23:55 hours), we took another outage (this one was also announced two weeks previously, along with the announcement for the earlier outage, done a week earlier). We took all the applications (that accessed the database) down. A polite notice was put up on our home page informing customers who had missed our advance notice that we were down for scheduled maintenance for the next four hours.
- We ran the scripts to populate the temporary tables with the delta rows in the four large tables. The four scripts were run concurrently.
- Then the five export scripts and five import scripts were fired on the source and target machines, respectively, to export and import the deltas for the four large tables and all the remaining tables. All five scripts were run concurrently on both the source and target machines. The fifth set of scripts performed a complete (non-delta) export and import of the remaining fifty-two tables. No delta was placed for them, because they were fairly small tables and exporting/importing them hardly consumed time during our initial tests. In fact, the export/import of the CUSTOMER_PROFILES delta-table took longer than the export/import of the entire set of fifty-two complete (non-delta) tables (see Table 8-3). Because we had parallelized the entire operation, all five scripts were running concurrently. And they all completed within the time it took for the largest table (CUSTOMER_PROFILES) to be imported. So the time it took for the largest table to be exported/imported comprised a major portion of the total downtime. Even with a high bandwidth, there was quite a bit of congestion on the network (the network was the bottleneck). The timings we observed are documented in Table 8-3.
- The scripts to create indexes on the remaining fifty-two tables were run.
- The scripts to create and enable all foreign keys were run on the target database. Indexes on all the foreign keys were already created either after the first migration (of the "old" data in the four large tables) or during the previous step.
- A complete final test was performed to ensure that all structures (tables, indexes, views, synonyms, and so on) were present, that the privileges necessary to access them had been granted to all other schemas, and that there weren't any objects with INVALID status.
- The *tnsnames.ora* files were manually updated to reflect the migration.
- Then, finally, the applications were restarted.

Table Name	# of Rows Exported (Approx.)	Time to Complete	Migration Type (Complete/Delta)
Customers	80,000	10 mins	Delta
Customer_Profiles	800,000	90 mins	Delta
Orders_Booked	300,000	40 mins	Delta
Items_Ordered	600,000	75 mins	Delta
Remaining 52 tables	< 700,000	80 mins	Complete

TABLE 8-3. *Migration Statistics on Export/Import via Named Pipes*

After the Outage

The following steps were taken after the services were restored and all users and application processes could access the database:

- After the applications were restarted, another thorough test was performed to ensure that everybody could still access the Web-site (from inside or outside a firewall, with different browser versions, and so on). In addition to Web-site functionality and data-validation checks, performance was also benchmarked to ensure that we had not inadvertently caused a performance bottleneck somewhere. These tests were repeated once every 5 to 10 hours over the next 48 hours (during different times of the day and night).
- A complete backup of the new database was taken.

Notes and Comments

The preceding strategy was tested out using a Sun SPARC 1000 as the source system with a copy of the entire production database (from a recent hot backup). We performed about three successful tests before the final run. The result? Successful, of course! The entire outage lasted for less than two hours—complete within 50 percent of the scheduled time.

In the preceding case study, up to four hours of downtime on a Saturday night/Sunday morning was acceptable to the client, provided their customers were notified in advance of the outage and stringent SLA clauses were not violated (that is, the four hours didn't stretch into more). As you may note, practice and planning made the key difference, allowing us to successfully complete the entire migration within less than the estimated time. For certain organizations, however, even four hours of downtime may be unacceptable. For such organizations, downtime needs to be averted somehow during all maintenance operations, migrations, and emergencies. Certain innovative (and expensive) solutions such as custom standby databases (CSDs) can be implemented that would allow the database to be available even during such migrations. Chapter 15 discusses CSDs in detail.

Summary

This chapter took a look at issues encountered during database upgrades, downgrades, reorganizations, and migrations. We looked at some ways to expedite the process and keep downtime to a minimum. We examined some gotchas during conversion from Oracle7 to Oracle8/8*i*. Finally, a case study was discussed to provide a real-world view of migration. The next chapter examines backup and recovery policies and procedures.

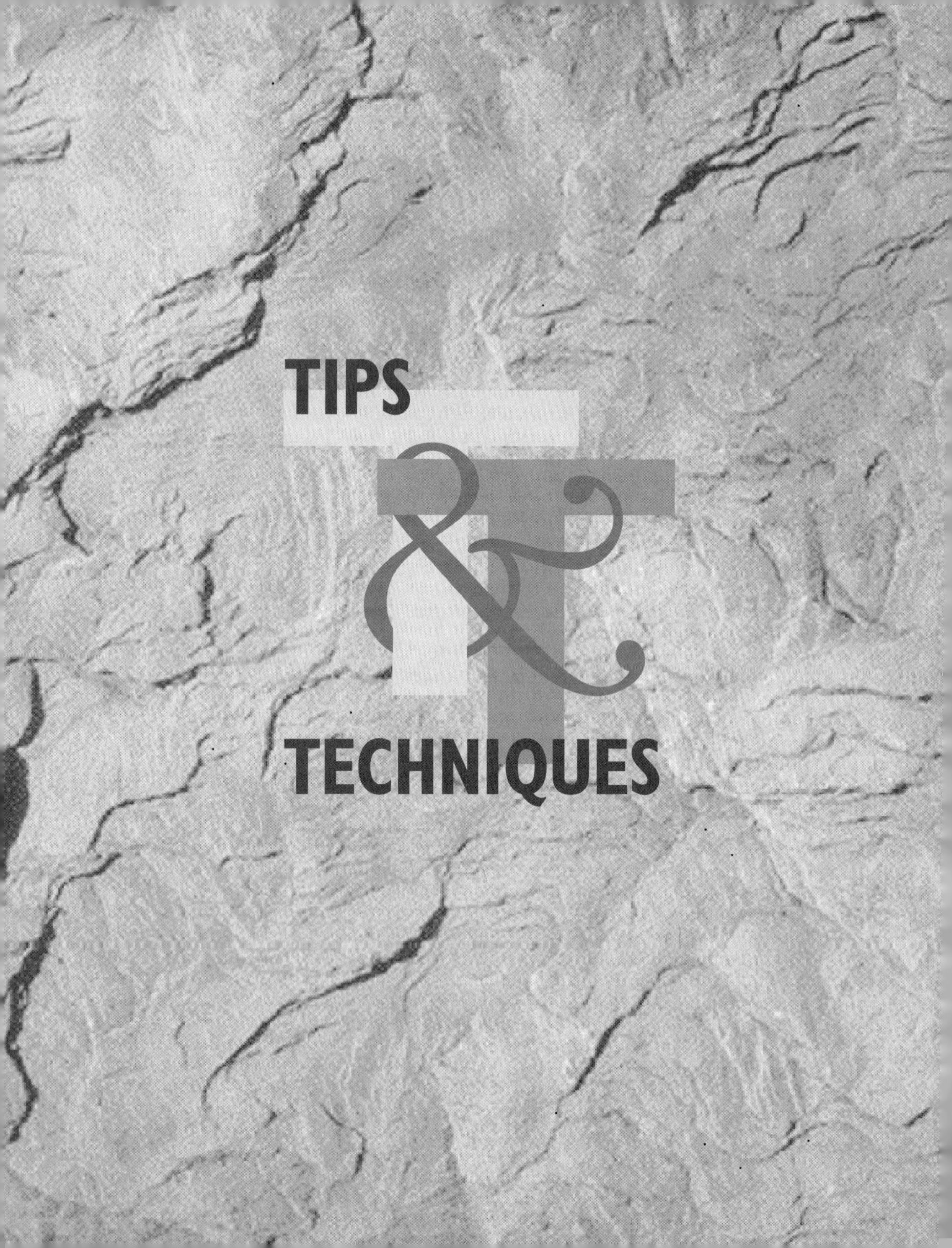
TIPS
&
TECHNIQUES

CHAPTER 9

Backup, Recovery, and Archiving Policies and Procedures

Backup operations constitute some of the most important maintenance tasks that an administrator performs for a 24×7 database. Backups are key for any database. In a 24×7 scenario, however, they assume even more importance because during an outage, a robust backup strategy allows fast and safe recovery. In the absence of a standby database/instance, a valid backup and the DBA's familiarity with recovery procedures determine the amount of downtime incurred. Both Oracle7 and Oracle8 offer a number of backup options. Similarly, there are a plethora of recovery options that need to be well understood in order to react correctly to a database crash. The intention of this chapter is not to talk about the available options for backup and recovery, but to provide some tips to make the procedures simpler and faster and to help you develop and implement robust backup and recovery policies.

We start off with backups and then move on to a key feature in Oracle that allows complete recovery: archiving. Then, finally, we wrap up with some tips on recovery operations.

This chapter offers the following tips and techniques:

- Select at least two backup methods after adequate analysis
- Perform hot backups during periods of low DML activity
- Do not place all tablespaces in hot backup mode simultaneously
- If possible, back up to disk first and then to tape
- Do not back up online redo-logs during OS hot backups
- Evaluate the use of triple mirrors
- Make sure that hot backup commands are executed synchronously
- Check the backup log files regularly
- Avoid performing backups manually
- Ensure that security is not compromised when using backup tools
- With RMAN, periodically resynchronize the recovery catalog
- Ensure that your backup strategy accounts for all Oracle file-types
- Back up the control-file immediately after all database changes
- Address export-related concerns before you start performing exports
- Form "export-groups" for inter-segment consistency
- Plan sufficient space for export dumps
- Perform exports using direct path, rather than conventional path

- Ensure compatibility and usability of all backed-up export-dumps
- Perform a backup immediately after any system clock changes
- Check for database corruption during and after backups
- Set optimal I/O size during backups
- Make use of incremental backups available in Oracle8
- Evaluate whether ARCHIVELOG is necessary for your environment
- Implement automatic archival as the primary archival mode
- Allocate adequate space for ARCHIVE_LOG_DEST
- Use "ALTER DATABASE ARCHIVELOG" for enabling archiving
- Take a complete backup as soon as ARCHIVELOG mode is enabled
- Use ARCHIVE LOG CURRENT rather than a variation
- Do not create holes in the archived log sequence
- If possible, keep dual copies of archived logs on disk
- Create more online redo-log groups when archiving to offline media
- Be aware of special archiving considerations, when using OPS
- Understand the need for recovery and take proactive steps to avoid failure
- Understand factors affecting recovery time
- Ensure recovery timings are consistent with your SLA MTTR specifications
- Consider alternate backup/recovery approaches for point-in-time recovery
- Ensure checkpoints occur at sufficient intervals and redo-logs are sized appropriately to prevent recovery delays
- Always consider the lowest unit of recovery
- Always examine *v$datafile* prior to recovery
- Maintain a special *init.ora* file for recovery operations
- Always use RESETLOGS as the last resort
- Evaluate all UNRECOVERABLE and NOLOGGING operations
- Categorize all segments and tablespaces for recovery
- Keep tablespaces without write activity READONLY to expedite backup and recovery

- Set AUTORECOVERY on during recovery
- Always test your backups to ensure valid recovery
- Ensure that relevant DBA staff are fully trained in recovery operations
- Create a "database recovery team"
- Document all database structural changes

Backups

This section discusses various backup-related issues with an overall aim of enhancing backup throughput with little or no impact on regular database availability.

Select at least two backup methods after adequate analysis

Due to the multitude of backup options available in Oracle, the appropriate one(s) for your site needs to be selected after careful reconciliation of your organizational requirements with each option's capabilities. Backup methods may be selected according to various criteria, including

- Whether the specific method allows 24×7 access (that is, whether the database has to be shut down while taking backups)
- Whether the method allows backups to complete within the predetermined window of time (via parallel backup steams, and so on)
- Whether the method allows restore and recovery within times specified in the SLA (via parallel restore/recovery streams, and so on)
- What kind of recovery flexibility the method allows in a variety of situations including
  - Recovery to the last committed transaction (whether the method causes any data to be lost)
  - Recovery to a past point in time
  - Recovery from loss of a physical object (visible from outside the database) such as a data-file, control-file, or redo-log
  - Recovery from loss of a logical object (not visible from outside the database) such as a table or an index

- Whether the method allows different types of file-systems (UFS, VxFS, raw, NTFS, and so on) to be directly backed up to diverse media (disk, tape, NFS, Zip drive, and so on) and whether the method allows hardware/software already available in-house to be used (if not, whether the new hardware/software required by the method is affordable to the organization at that point in time)
- Whether the method allows manual customization (for compression, error checking, and so on) and whether the backups can be automated (for "lights-out" backups)
- Whether the method allows user-defined extensions via easy-to-use, industry-standard APIs (for interfacing with Oracle's Enterprise Manager and/or third-party media managers and SNMP-MIBs [Small Network Management Protocol—Management Information Bases], and so on)
- Whether the method supports easy scheduling or allows external scheduling tools and utilities to be utilized
- Whether the backups created by the method are portable across different machines/platforms
- Whether the tool is easy to understand and use
- Whether the tool provides good reporting functionality (canned reports, as well as ad hoc query support) to detect potential backup/recovery errors

Considering all the preceding criteria, it is very difficult to select any one backup method. Though many of Oracle's backup options cater to a variety of situations, it is still not realistic to expect one backup strategy to cater to all recovery scenarios. For example, a hot backup may be highly desirable for quick recovery from a data-file loss; however, it may not be the fastest way to recover from an accidental truncation of a table. Hence, at least two methods need to be part of the overall backup strategy at any 24×7 site.

Backup methods supported by Oracle are

- Backup sets (Oracle8/RMAN only)
- Data-file copies (Oracle8/RMAN only)
- OS hot or online backups
- OS cold or offline backups
- Logical backups or database exports

Generally for a 24×7 site, method 1, 2, or 3 may form the primary method, and database exports form the secondary one. For databases not requiring 24×7 access, method 4 may form the primary method.

Perform hot backups during periods of low DML activity

Backups, though critical, use up a lot of system resources due to reading of the data-files, redo-logs, and control-files and writing to the backup media. This high consumption of critical system resources leaves very little for other concurrent operations, including all database activity. And especially if the backup hardware/software is not configured properly, the impact on performance is even greater. If the backup hardware/software does not have the necessary capacity to provide adequate throughput, it could affect the database in two ways:

- The backups cannot complete within the desired window of time and subsequently clash with regular database use.
- The backup processes gobble up most of the available system resources (I/O, CPU, memory) and leave very little margin for the database to function optimally.

In fact, both these symptoms may result in a vicious "catch-22" situation by being the cause and effect of each other. If it's a cold backup, it's usually not a very major issue, since the performance impact is not felt by users, with the database being down. It becomes a major issue only when it's time to open up the database for the users and the cold backups are still running. Most of the backup-related struggles I have had with hardware/software at client sites have been to expedite hot backups, to somehow use the available resources to minimize the window of time to perform a hot backup. At a 24×7 client site, either users are logged on during backups (imagine the customer's reaction in an e-commerce application where the database is crawling due to the ongoing backups, and customers are slowly being prompted for credit-card numbers) or critical batch jobs are running, or both. In addition to the I/O during backups, hot backups impose an additional performance penalty: excessive redo being written. Excessive redo is generated during hot backups while the tablespaces are in backup mode (via the ALTER TABLESPACE … BEGIN BACKUP command). This additional redo-generation is primarily caused by entire block-images (potentially composed of multiple OS blocks) being written to the redo-logs during hot backups (due to the _LOG_BLOCKS_DURING_BACKUP initialization parameter being set to

TRUE by default to overcome *split* or *fractured blocks*). Additionally, the same block is logged (as redo) more than once if it is changed and flushed to disk and subsequently read into the SGA and changed again.

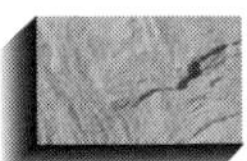

NOTE
It is not advisable to change the value of the _LOG_BLOCKS_DURING_BACKUP initialization parameter. This affects the default functionality of Oracle and needs to be set to TRUE to make online backups possible on certain OSs. Performing backups with this parameter set to FALSE without any specific reasons could result in invalid backups. Furthermore, doing so without the knowledge of Oracle Support would be a violation of your Support contract.

NOTE
Split or fractured blocks may be caused when the Oracle DB_BLOCK_SIZE is a multiple of the OS block size. During a hot backup, it is possible for different OS blocks (which are part of the same Oracle block) to be written at different times, thus causing different portions of the Oracle block to be inconsistent with each other. Thus, if the front portion (physically, a different OS block) of the Oracle block is written at a different time than the back portion (another OS block, different from the first), it would induce the block to "split" (Figure 9-1). Oracle resolves split blocks by logging entire Oracle blocks during hot backups. During recovery, the block consistency is determined by comparing the version numbers at the beginning and end of the block. If they are different, the block has been split and the before image of the block is written to disk from the redo before applying any redo changes to derive a consistent version of the block.

In order to minimize the amount of redo generated, to reduce the adverse impact on performance, and to increase overall logical consistency (where all internal database objects are relatively current, with respect to each other's SCN),

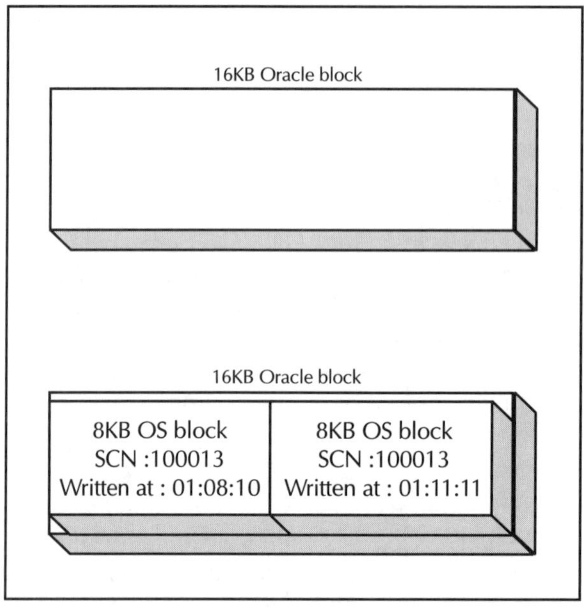

FIGURE 9-1. *Block splits caused during OS hot backups*

backups need to be scheduled during relatively low periods of DML activity. Such low periods of activity may occur at night or day, depending on database use patterns. Both interactive access by end-users and access by batch jobs needs to be considered while evaluating use patterns.

NOTE
SCN (System Change Number) is the unique key provided by Oracle to every committed transaction. For example, when an update is committed, it may be assigned an SCN of 10000, and as a subsequent delete is committed, it would be assigned a higher SCN such as 10028 (Figure 9-2). SCNs are assigned in an ascending order and are guaranteed to be unique across transactions. SCNs are written to block headers, data-file headers, control-files, and redo-logs. They are used during recovery to construct read-consistent snapshots of the database.

User transaction

At 10:40 a.m.

```
......................
......................
UPDATE names
    SET name = 'VSD'
WHERE id = 1
COMMIT;
......................
......................
```

SCN = 10000 assigned

Internal Oracle house-keeping transactions

At 10:41 a.m.

```
......................
......................
INSERT INTO FET$
    .............;
COMMIT;
......................
......................
```

SCNs 10001 to 10027 assigned

User transaction

At 10:42 a.m.

```
......................
......................
DELETE sales
WHERE sale_id = 66
COMMIT;
......................
......................
```

SCN = 10028 assigned

Oracle data-block

Header | Data | SCN

Data-file: SCN | Header | Data

Control-file

Redo logs

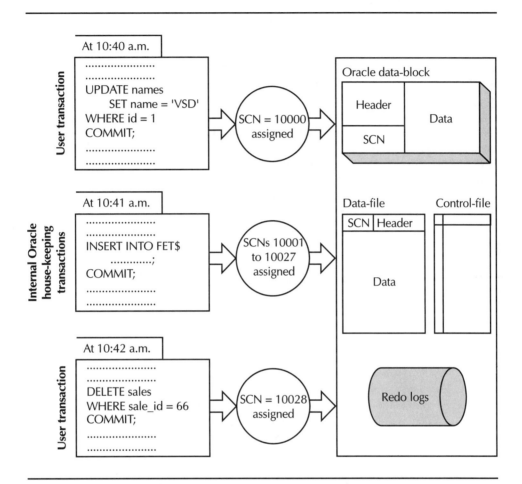

FIGURE 9-2. *SCNs being assigned as transactions are committed*

Do not place all tablespaces in hot backup mode simultaneously

When a tablespace is placed in hot-backup mode, Oracle performs a *fast checkpoint* on all data-files belonging to that tablespace, thus flushing all dirty buffers belonging to that tablespace to disk. The SCN that was current when the ALTER TABLESPACE … BEGIN BACKUP command was issued is written to the data-file header as the *checkpoint SCN.* The checkpoint SCN is used during recovery to determine what changes need to be applied to the data-file from the

redo-logs (at least the redo-logs that were created *during* the backup need to be applied for the recovery to be valid). Once the checkpoint SCN is written, the data-file header will not be updated with subsequent checkpoints until the ALTER TABLESPACE ... END BACKUP command is issued. For each tablespace in hot-backup mode, additional redo is generated due to entire block images being logged. To reduce the impact on performance due to excessive redo, hot backups should be performed sequentially on each tablespace. Thus, one tablespace may be placed in hot-backup mode, the data-files pertaining to that tablespace may be backed up via OS commands, and then the hot-backup mode for that tablespace needs to be ended, prior to placing another tablespace in hot-backup mode. In other words, each tablespace should be kept in hot-backup mode individually for as little time as possible. The more tablespaces are concurrently placed in hot-backup mode, the higher the amount of redo generated.

NOTE

During a "fast" checkpoint, DBWR continuously scans for dirty buffers and writes them to disk, as opposed to during a regular checkpoint, where DBWR stops scanning if the number of buffers scanned is equivalent to the DB_CHECKPOINT_WRITE_BATCH initialization parameter or more than a thousand buffers are scanned and none among those are dirty. A regular checkpoint allows better balance among all Oracle processes in sharing system resources (such as CPU cycles). A fast checkpoint allows checkpointing to be carried out on an urgent basis (necessary during emergency situations such as when a tablespace is being put into backup mode or being taken offline or when the database is being shut down). Query v$sysstat to monitor checkpoint activity or, alternatively, the initialization parameter LOG_CHECKPOINTS_TO_ALERT may be set to TRUE to log all checkpoints to the database alert-log.

It is fairly easy to write scripts that perform hot backups in the sequential manner described previously. However, when using certain Oracle or third-party tools to perform hot backups, one may not have the desired flexibility to place each tablespace in hot-backup mode individually. For example, when configured to use parallel backup streams, Oracle EBU (Enterprise Backup Utility) places all tablespaces in hot-backup mode simultaneously and fires off the multiple backup streams. It is a good idea to explore whether a specific tool can be configured to perform sequential tablespace backups prior to deploying it. Rather than using parallel backup streams against different tablespaces, verify whether the multiple streams can be configured against different data-files of the same tablespace or even against different blocks of the same data-file. That way the higher throughput offered by parallel backup streams is achieved without incurring the cost of very high redo generation. Especially if the online and archived redo-logs are not configured and spread out onto separate disks/controllers (see Chapter 7), excessive redo generation can wreak havoc on database performance.

A few years ago, I, along with a database "SWAT" team, visited a VLDB site running a major, predominantly OLTP application. Primarily their database was being accessed by end-users via custom-built PowerBuilder screens during the day and via Pro*C and PL/SQL batch jobs during the night. Downtime during weekdays and weeknights was not acceptable. Their main complaint was that due to severe I/O bottlenecks, most of their batch applications running at night were not completing within their specific windows of time and were stretching on to peak daytime hours, causing intolerable response time. They needed help in determining the optimal file-layout to eliminate the I/O hot spots and move the data-files with as little downtime as possible. The prominent I/O hot spots seemed to be more of a symptom than a cause. After examining the overall database activity during the night, we discovered that they were using a home-grown UNIX shell-script to perform hot backups. During the day, due to high interactive access volumes, taking backups was unthinkable. During the night, there was high batch access, but interactive access was limited. So they chose to perform hot backups during the night, when the performance degradation would be less noticeable to end-users. Using home-grown scripts in a VLDB environment may not particularly be an ugly idea, except in this case, the script was putting all tablespaces in hot-backup mode simultaneously and using the *dd* command to copy all data-files off to tape. When I requested to meet with the creator of that script to suggest appropriate modifications, their DBA informed me that his predecessor had lifted the script off a UNIX magazine!

Placing all tablespaces in hot-backup mode and performing a backup of the entire (250GB+) database in a single stream was definitely a very slow process taking up more than 15 hours. In addition, due to all the tablespaces being in hot-backup mode with concurrent batch and some interactive access volumes at night, the excessive redo generation was impeding performance severely, thus delaying the batch jobs and causing them to overlap with the primary interactive end-user traffic during peak morning hours. This scenario had resulted in the I/O bottlenecks we saw.

Our team took a three-fold approach to deal with the problem:

1. We tuned the SQL in the batch applications to fix potentially bad code that resulted in unnecessary I/O.

2. We spread out the online redo-logs, archived redo-logs and data-files onto separate disks/controllers to eliminate as much I/O contention as possible.

3. We threw out the shell-script and selected EBU (Oracle8/RMAN wasn't available yet) as our backup tool. They already had *Legato Networker* in-house. In order to achieve fast backup rates, we configured four parallel backup streams to write to four tape drives simultaneously. This allowed the backups to complete in less than 6 hours.

This improved the situation significantly. However, the batch jobs that were running during the backups were still providing unacceptable throughput. Even though no batch job was currently overlapping with peak morning traffic, the situation was still shaky due to the near-future batch-job/interactive-access overlap potential caused by the steady database growth. While digging deeper, we noticed that EBU was also placing all tablespaces in hot-backup mode concurrently and each parallel stream was reading a different data-file from a different tablespace. No matter what we tried, we couldn't get EBU to back up one tablespace at a time. Even all our calls to Oracle Support seemed futile.

Finally, we implemented a "round-robin" backup approach that did the trick! Table 9-1 outlines this strategy. We classified all tablespaces based on their sizes and growth characteristics. The smaller tablespaces were all grouped together as one unit (Group A) and backed up on one night, and all the bigger tablespaces were grouped separately and backed up sequentially on different nights of the week. This

Group #	Day Backed Up	Time	Component Tablespaces
A	Monday	10:00 P.M.	SYSTEM, USERS TEMP,RBS
B	Tuesday	10:00 P.M.	LARGE_TBLSPC_1
C	Tuesday	12:00 P.M.	LARGE_TBLSPC_2
D	Wednesday	10:00 P.M.	LARGE_TBLSPC_3
E	Wednesday	12:00 P.M.	LARGE_TBLSPC_4
F	Thursday	10:00 P.M.	SUPER_LARGE_TBLSPC_1
G	Friday	10:00 P.M.	SUPER_LARGE_TBLSPC_2
H	Sunday	01:00 A.M.	Cold backup of entire database
A	Monday	10:00 P.M.	SYSTEM, USERS, TEMP, RBS

TABLE 9-1. *Backup Strategy at a Client Site, Forcing EBU to Back Up All Large Tablespaces Individually*

allowed the four parallel EBU streams to operate on a single large tablespace on any given night, without contention from other tablespaces. Additionally, this helped the backup strategy scale without delaying the backups because even with the constant database growth, the strategy ensured that the backups wouldn't take more than the time to back up a single backup group on any given night (it was recommended that each group's components be reviewed and revised annually or after periods of significant growth). Each night we were able to complete the tablespace backups in less than four hours. Also, on weekends, a cold backup was implemented (since downtime during weekends was acceptable).

The preceding strategy allowed the client to achieve acceptable backup and batch-job throughput without affecting response time during peak-hour interactive access. However, this strategy required the client to allocate a separate, larger archived log destination to hold all log files for the entire week. Accordingly, it may not be feasible for sites that do not have the capacity to dedicate a large amount of space for archived redo-logs.

Another perspective on this strategy is the backup time in a 24-hour period and total recovery time. When only one tablespace (or a few select tablespaces) are backed up in a 24-hour period, it takes less time for the backup during that period as opposed to backing up the entire database. So, even though cumulatively the time taken to back up is no lesser than a complete database backup, there is a lesser impact on performance during a 24-hour period. As a consequence, however, more archived redo-logs need to be stored (at least spanning the entire backup) and this directly affects roll-forward times during recovery (since there are more logs to roll forward). Accordingly, a decision about implementing such a strategy needs to be made after considering various factors such as

- Outage recovery timings (total time required to restore the backups, including the archived logs, and then apply recovery)
- Total tolerable downtime (based on business requirements)
- Backup timings (Is the time taken to back up the entire database tolerable?)
- Capacity available for storing backups (Can the archived logs for an entire week be held?)

In other words, if the entire database can be backed up as a single unit (each tablespace sequentially), within acceptable time frames, with the effect on performance during that period being acceptable and disk space for storing archived logs being scarce, then perform complete database backups in a 24-hour period. Else break up the backups on a tablespace basis based on the previously mentioned or other similar strategy. Again, acceptability needs to be determined after sufficient testing and benchmarking. The bottom line is this: availability and performance are the key drivers, with the former usually taking precedence in any 24×7 environment.

Availability during crashes depends on recovery times. Recovery is fastest when the entire database is backed up as a single unit, due to less time to roll forward. However, depending on the database size and desired transaction throughput, performance may be totally unacceptable during the longer time it takes to back up the entire database. Accordingly, a compromise between availability and performance may be required that spreads out the entire database backup on a tablespace basis over multiple days. Prior to deployment, it should be verified that this compromise solution does not cause recovery times to exceed SLA specifications. One should be able to recover from different crash scenarios using the data-files and archived logs backed up, within acceptable downtime windows.

If possible, back up to disk first and then to tape

It's essential to take every step possible to expedite backups in order to reduce the effect on performance. From this perspective, depending on the backup hardware/software being used, backing up to disk may be faster or backing up directly to other offline media (such as tape or writeable optical disks) may be faster. It's a common misconception that backing up to disk is always faster. With tape technology getting better and better, it's not uncommon to see mammoth databases of several hundred gigabytes in size getting backed up in parallel streams (referred to as "multi-streaming") to multiple tape drives in just a few hours. In fact, some tape configurations can provide a throughput of 12MB/sec or higher in controlled environments. If that throughput can be matched in real-world environments, backing up directly to tape may prove much faster than backing up to disk. In fact, backups to tape are often constrained by disk-drive throughput, which seldom rises above 8–10MB/sec for most database activity (since data to tape drives can only be written as fast as data is read from disk). Again, I have observed this 8–10MB/sec in environments where the disk sub-system uses newer technology (for instance, fiber channels connected to FastSCSI controllers) and is laid out extremely well. Quite a few OLTP environments, where I/O channels are scarce (that is, backups have to contend with regular database operations) and reads/writes are highly random, are restricted to disk-drive throughput of merely 3–5MB/sec.

However, this might not be true for your environment. Depending on various factors such as the kind of offline backup media you are using, whether such devices are locally attached or remotely connected (networked) to the production machine, the number of parallel backups streams they can handle, each stream's throughput, the disk drive throughput, whether you have dedicated I/O channels for backups (such as in specific triple-mirrored implementations), and so on, backups either to disk or backups directly to tape may prove faster for you. If you are writing in a single stream to a networked tape device, chances are, backups to disk may provide much higher throughput. In any case (not discounting the importance of fast backups), backup speed is not the main reason for this tip. Rather, recovery speed is.

Once the files are readily available on disk, in the event of a database crash, they do not have to be restored off offline storage media, thus reducing MTTR (mean time to recover). Most of the delay during recovery occurs not during the actual act itself, but during restore of the necessary files from the offline backup media. If the files pertaining to the most current backup are already on disk, such delays due to high restore time can be avoided. This is a strong reason for any 24x7 site to maintain the most recent online backups (on disk).

While backing up to disk, it's essential to ensure the following:

- It's necessary to estimate the total size of the backup files that would get created and ensure that sufficient space is available on the target disks. Many sites do this the first time the backups are configured. However, every time a new tablespace is created or a data-file is resized or added to an existing tablespace, this process needs to be redone. It's easy to remain oblivious to changes in sizes and get a jolt the next morning after the backups have already failed and can't be restarted until the next night (God forbid that there be a database mishap that day, because the backups from two nights ago would need to be restored and it would be necessary to roll forward through two day's worth of archived logs). If the target disks do not have adequate space, the source files may need to be compressed via an OS utility.
- The backups are being written to disks/controllers different from the original disks/controllers where the Oracle files are held. In other words, the source and target disks/controllers for backups need to be different. This will restrict the I/O strain on the source disks/controllers to the reading of the Oracle files (writing will be handled by different disks/controllers) and the source disks/controllers are free to deal with the ongoing database activity. Also, later while copying the backups off the disk to offline media, the disks/controllers on which the database is placed are not unduly affected.
- The backups are written to a logical disk-volume that is well-striped across multiple physical disks/controllers. This will prevent potential I/O hot spots. I have observed backups of medium-sized databases (50GB to 100GB) being written to a dedicated non-striped disk and causing heavy I/O contention, thus delaying backups tremendously (losing the very advantage of backing up to disk first).
- It's essential to ensure that backups have been copied to an offline medium prior to overwriting or deleting them. It's best to keep backups around on disk for as much time as possible. In the event of a database crash, having the most recent backups already available on disk will eliminate the need for restoring those backups from offline media. If you have the disk space, it's best to rename the previous day's backup files (or write to a different

target area) prior to starting the new backup. That way, if the current backup process terminates with errors, the previous day's backups are still valid and available on disk.

There are certain exceptions to backing up to disk directly:

- If sufficient disk space is not available to accommodate the files to be backed up, then it becomes necessary to back up to offline media directly. Usually this is a common problem at sites with fairly large databases. Alternatively, if the database is very small, it may be reasonable to back up the database to offline media directly, since restore/recovery times may be insignificant.
- If the backup throughput offered by the disk drives is inadequate to complete the backups within the predetermined backup window of time. If the performance degradation is totally unacceptable during backups to disk, somehow the organization would need to invest in faster backup media, which might very well mean multi-streaming directly to a bunch of tape drives and bypassing disk storage.

In any case, the utility of backing up to offline media cannot be disputed. If it's necessary to get back to the previous week or month, it is not possible to depend on backups stored on disk. Also, offline storage provides higher storage flexibility. A tape potentially containing the entire database backup can be kept in a secure off-site location to be preserved during fires, floods, and so on. Accordingly, backing up to offline media is mandatory. However, ensuring the disk drive is one of the primary media, such that a copy of the current backup is maintained online on disk, is very useful during recovery.

Once the files are backed up to disk, they can be moved to other offline media such as tape (backing up to offline media is *mandatory*). Additionally, during hot backups, it is necessary to configure backups such that the Oracle files (data-files, control-files, archived redo-logs) are subjected to backup-related I/O for as little time as possible. The delay in writing to offline devices is felt by the Oracle files because they remain in backup mode longer, thus generating more redo and affecting performance adversely for a larger span of time. Backing up directly to disk helps to reduce the time the tablespaces are in backup mode.

Do not back up online redo-logs during OS hot backups

Even though it's not necessary, some sites still continue to back up online redo-logs during OS hot backups. This basically results from the DBA's paranoia that the online redo-logs, which are key to the database, have to be backed up as a safety precaution. The problem here is, online redo-logs are used by Oracle only during instance recovery (that is, the *current* online redo-log group). They cannot be restored and used during media recovery since they contain the "end of redo-thread" marker (due to the ALTER TABLESPACE END BACKUP command issued) and may cause corruption if used during media recovery. Additional redo may have been generated in the thread, due to ongoing transactions occurring during the hot backup. In other words, redo is being written to the current online redo-log, even during the hot backup. However, if during recovery the current online redo-log is used (along with the archived redo-logs) to roll forward, the recovery process will incorrectly detect that the redo-thread has ended and abort prematurely, possibly causing database corruption. Hence, in order to prevent mishaps, it's advisable not to back up online redo-logs during hot backups, but if they have been backed up, it's crucial to ensure that they are not applied during media recovery.

So how do the transactions contained in the online redo-logs get backed up during hot backups? Remember, an ARCHIVE LOG CURRENT (or a variation such as ARCHIVE LOG ALL or ALTER SYSTEM SWITCH LOGFILE) command is issued as one of the final steps in a hot backup. As a result of this command, all non-archived online redo-logs (requiring archival) are archived. Thus, all transactions present in the online redo-logs are written to those archived logs. As long as these newly created archived logs are backed up safely along with the others, recovery up to the last committed transaction is not a problem. And how do the online redo-logs get re-created after a restore and recovery if they are not backed up? When the database is reopened after recovery, the online redo-logs are re-created via the RESETLOGS option. (In such situations, when recovering using a hot backup, it's necessary to use the RESETLOGS option to re-create the online redo-logs. Just remember to take a backup immediately after the database is opened. Again, this is not an exceptional price to pay, since a backup is highly recommended after any media recovery effort anyway.)

In environments where the backup strategy consists of hot and cold backups, there's another potential danger to watch out for in restoring online redo-logs. Restoring the online redo-logs may cause multiple parallel redo-log timelines. Let me illustrate this via a real-life incident. At a customer site using Oracle8 v8.0.4, we have a backup strategy consisting of hot backups six nights a week from Sunday to Friday and a cold backup performed on Saturday night. The database is fairly small—24GB with around 21GB of data. Generally, there is no database use over the weekend. Sometimes during year-end, however, end-users work during day hours on Saturday and Sunday. A few months ago, a database crash occurred on early Monday morning at around 4:00 A.M. (prior to any user/job accessing the database). The on-site DBA was called in. He had two options to recover. The first choice was to restore the hot backups taken the previous night (Sunday night) and

roll forward (which shouldn't have taken much time, since, as per the DBA, there was no database activity since the backup) using the archived redo-logs. Here, however, the RESETLOGS option would need to be used to reopen the database (as mentioned earlier, the RESETLOGS option would be required to re-create the online redo-logs). Another option was to use the cold backups performed the previous Saturday night and restore the database without any roll-forward at all, since (again, as per the DBA) there was no database access over the weekend. Since it was Monday morning and almost time for end-users to get in and start their work, he was in an extreme hurry to reopen the database. Accordingly, he chose the latter option, to restore from the cold backup and not perform any recovery, since he could save time by not rolling forward and also he wouldn't have to use the RESETLOGS option (he remembered that the RESETLOGS option is to be avoided to prevent a new incarnation of the database from being created), since the online redo-logs are a part of the cold backup. The only problem here was that some folks from the Financial Department had come in on Sunday and spent time working on the database. Hence reopening the database for use after restoring the online redo-logs off the cold backup generated log sequence numbers that were already previously generated by the database (during the weekend when the users were working on the database) as end-users started coming in and working on Monday morning. Later, at around 10:00 A.M., the users who had come in over the weekend informed the DBA that their "critical" work performed over the weekend was missing and it was needed by them urgently. The DBA, in a state of panic, hurriedly announced emergency downtime that evening, backed up the current state of the database (that really saved his neck later), and tried to revert and use the hot backups done on Sunday night to recover using the archived redo-logs generated over the weekend. He managed to recover all the work done over the weekend; however, the work done on Monday was lost. Oracle could not apply the archived logs generated on Monday, since the log sequence numbers were duplicated (the archived logs generated over the weekend matched those generated on Monday), and Oracle could not figure out which log sequence numbers were the correct ones to apply. (The reason for this confusion is not just the duplicate log sequence numbers; rather, it is due to the fact that different database events occurred in two different, albeit parallel time lines—different changes were made to potentially the same database blocks, as depicted in Figure 9-3. Simply put, the work done on Monday was done on a different database incarnation than the one on Sunday.) All efforts to apply Monday's first archived redo-log resulted in a flurry of ORA-00310 (archived log contains sequence <n>; sequence <n> required), ORA-00314 (log name of thread <n>; expected sequence # <n> does not match <n>), ORA-00355 (change numbers out of order), and ORA-00283 (recovery session canceled due to errors) errors.

The end result was that the *entirety* of Monday's transactions were lost (as you might have guessed, using the backups taken by the DBA prior to restoring the hot

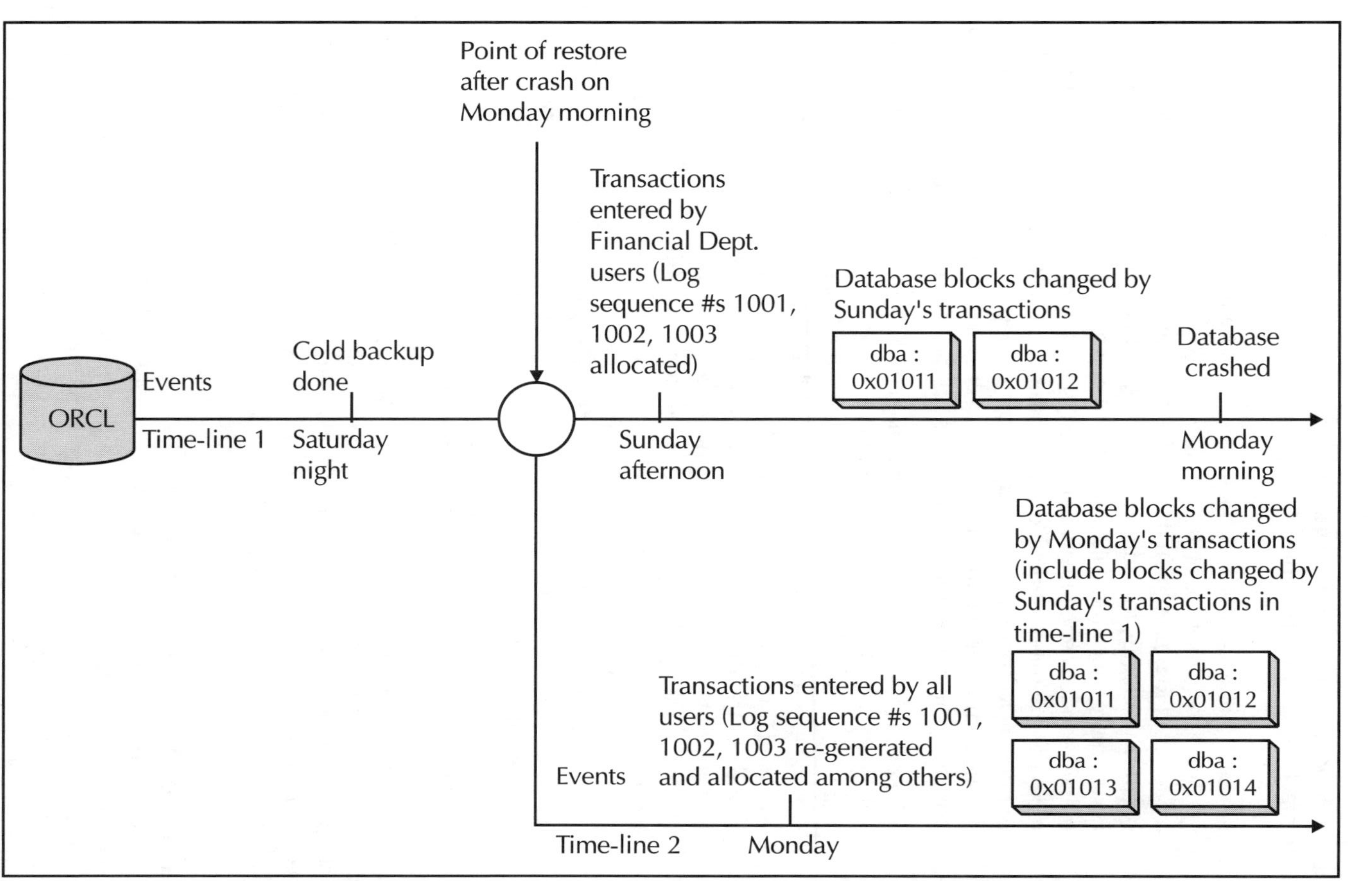

FIGURE 9-3. *Different changes made to database blocks across parallel time lines*

Leave Out Online Redo-logs During Hot Backups

backups, Monday's transactions were recovered later by restoring them on a separate machine). In this example:

- If the DBA had used the hot backups the first time (when the database crashed at 4:00 A.M.), that would have allowed him to roll forward through all archived logs present in the archive destination (including those created over the weekend), in addition to holding all of Monday's transactions. Furthermore, since the database would have been opened by resetting the online redo-logs (the only way to open the database when the online redo-logs are not present) after roll-forward, that would have prevented him from trying to apply archived logs from an older backup and force Oracle to reconcile multiple parallel redo-log timelines, since only redo-logs created from the point of resetting the online redo-logs can be applied henceforth.
- If he had restored the hot backups taken on Sunday night onto a separate machine instead of restoring them directly onto the production box, he would have two databases on two machines. The production database would have had all transactions, except the ones performed over the weekend. The other database would have all transactions, except for Monday's transactions. At this point, it would have been fairly easy to use SQL to copy the work done over the weekend to the production database. However, the DBA didn't do this because he was fairly confident that even though he had restored off a cold backup, he could still apply all the logs that were generated over the weekend and also the logs that were generated by Monday's transactions. He didn't envisage that Oracle would generate the same redo-log sequences and that reconciliation between the two sets of archived redo-logs would be a show-stopper.

As a moral of the story, do not back up online redo-logs when performing hot backups (even for a combination of hot and cold backups). If you do, do not restore them, and if you do, do not use them during recovery. In fact, to make things simpler, even Oracle's tools such as EBU and RMAN do not back up online redo-logs when performing hot backups. And remember, the RESETLOGS option is not such a great villain, when used in conjunction with hot backups and a newer backup is taken immediately after its use.

Evaluate the use of triple mirrors

Using triple mirrors, as the name suggests, involves mirroring each primary disk to two other disks. Generally, the entire disk-array holding the database files is mirrored onto two separate disk-arrays. Triple-mirror solutions can be implemented either at the hardware level or using a combination of hardware and software. Triple mirrors prevent the database performance from being too adversely affected during backups (provided the mirrored disks are daisy-chained to controllers separate from the primary disks/controllers). In a triple-mirrored environment, backups are performed as follows:

1. All tablespaces are placed in hot-backup mode simultaneously (via the ALTER TABLESPACE BEGIN BACKUP command). Note that, usually, it is recommended that multiple tablespaces not be simultaneously placed in hot-backup mode. Each tablespace should be backed up individually to avoid redo-generation from being too high. However, triple-mirrored environments are an exception to this rule. Placing all tablespaces in hot-backup mode may take a few minutes, depending on the database workload at that time.
2. The third mirror is broken.
3. All tablespaces are taken out of hot-backup mode (via the ALTER TABLESPACE END BACKUP command).
4. The third mirror is used as a source to back up the database to offline media, such as tape.
5. Once the backups are complete, the third mirror needs to be resynchronized (resilvered) with the others.

During backups, the database continues to function unaffected, since the third mirror is broken and the database continues to function independent of the third mirror. The additional redo generated while the tablespaces are in hot-backup mode persists only for a few minutes (during the time taken to break the third mirror). Thus, performance is not impacted during the backups. However, performance may be affected during the resilvering of the third mirror. Generally, hardware-based triple mirrors do not impose as much of a performance penalty on the machine during the resilvering. However, software-based approaches may cause a 5 to 15 percent strain on performance, depending on the database activity prevalent at the time of resilvering. The performance impact can be higher if the third mirror is not properly configured (to use separate controllers, SCSI channels, and so on).

The major disadvantage of triple mirrors is the high acquisition cost. Triple mirrors require a substantial investment from companies. Ironically, the sites that need them the most, such as VLDB sites, also incur the maximum cost. However, the benefits that triple mirrors bring to the table are manifold, including

- Allowing backups to be performed while the database is open and available to end-users without having to incur the performance cost.
- Retaining the second mirror for redundancy to ensure that there is very little exposure to disk failure while the third mirror is broken to perform the backups.

- A highly versatile form of mirroring that can provide recoverability in a variety of situations. For example, the third mirror can be configured to lag behind the other two by half an hour, so that user errors such as accidental table deletions, and so on, will not be propagated immediately to the third mirror and the third mirror can be used to recover the table. Thus, the third mirror can act as a backup by itself (prior to even being copied to an offline backup medium) to provide protection during situations when the other two mirrors become unusable simultaneously (the chances of this occurring are slim—even if it does, it's more likely to be a bug in the mirroring mechanism or the propagation of invalid DML/DDL across both mirrors, making them both useless, than to be a simultaneous physical crash). Also, when the third mirror lags behind the other two, point-in-time recovery is much easier with less impact on the production database. For recovering from user errors (such as an accidental table deletion), the third mirror can be broken up and files can be copied off the third mirror to a different machine to perform point-in-time recovery. In certain configurations, even copying the files off the third mirror is not necessary. The disks composing the third mirror can just be plugged directly into the same or a different but compatible system. If a logical volume manager is used, there may be a disk-configuration file (such as */etc/vstab*) pointing to the volumes, consisting of entries such as the following:

```
/r1/rvol12
        /r1/d1/stripe1/rvol12     active
        /r1/d2/stripe1/rvol12     active
        /raw/d3/stripe1/rvol12    inactive
```

The control-file for the new database may use the physical volumes underlying the logical volumes that are part of the third mirror. Hence, an entry like */r1/d2/stripe1/rvol12* could be the first data-file. A different ORACLE_SID could be given to the new database (if the same system is being used to house the new database). Once the new database is brought up, the necessary tables can be retrieved (via *export* or other utilities) and placed into the original database. Please note that not all hardware/OS configurations may support using the third mirror to create a new database on the same system. In such cases, a separate but compatible system may have to be used to achieve this.

Prior to deploying triple mirrors, test extensively to ensure that the mirroring mechanism does not diverge from the Oracle internal OS dependency code. Figure 9-4 illustrates backups using triple mirrors.

From both an availability and performance standpoint, triple mirrors provide a robust and highly versatile backup solution. One thing to note while using triple mirrors is that during the course of the mirroring (that is, resilvering) you have no

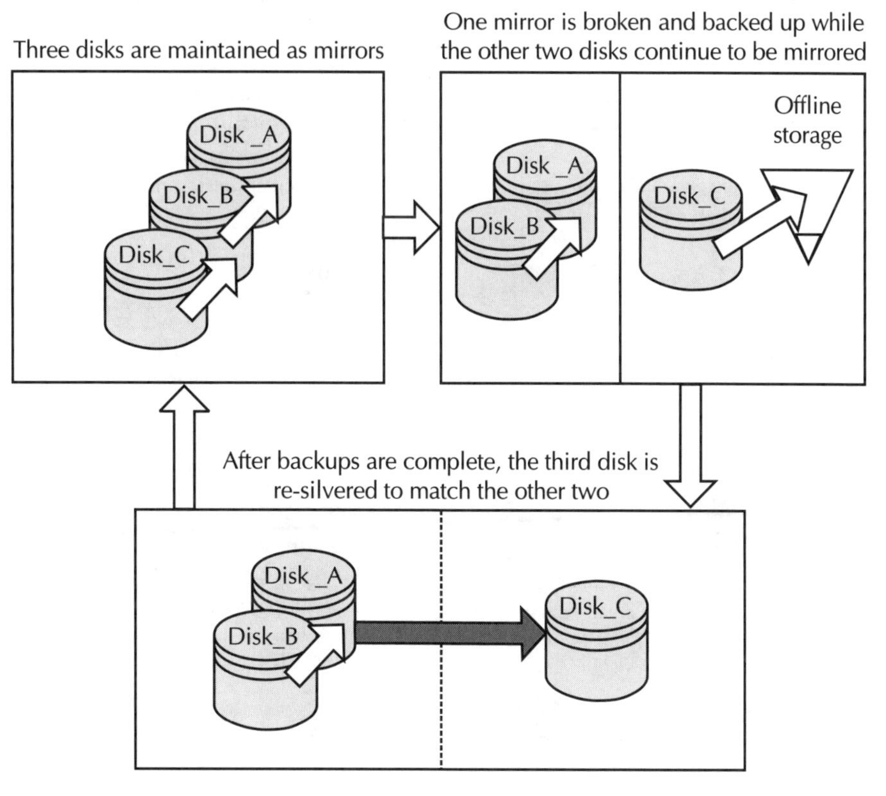
Three disks are maintained as mirrors
One mirror is broken and backed up while the other two disks continue to be mirrored
Offline storage
Disk_A
Disk_B
Disk_C
After backups are complete, the third disk is re-silvered to match the other two

FIGURE 9-4. *Backups using triple mirrors*

online backup. To overcome this, some sites have another set of mirrored disks (a fourth set). Even though this stretches the cost even higher, if the exposure to risk (of not having an online backup during the resilvering) is too great, then a genuine business case may be made for the fourth set. So you would always have two online backups during normal times and at least one during resilvering of the third mirror. For example, one mirrored set could be 0–12 hours old, and the other set could be 12–24 hours old. Obviously, this example implies that you mirror every 12 hours. Figure 9-5 illustrates maintaining four sets of mirrors, where two sets lag behind by a few hours. Four-way mirroring is ideal for small- to medium-sized mission-critical databases. Sites with large databases may find it difficult to take advantage of such mirroring, due to the enormous capital investment required.

Here, a possible 4-mirror environment is depicted. The primary disk and it's current mirror are indicated via the color black. The 0-12 hour mirrors (online backups) are indicated via the color gray. The 12-24 hour online backups are indicated via the color white. This strategy performs load-balancing between the third and fourth mirrors. Also, note that if backups to offline media are only necessary once every 24 hours in your environment (and not every 12 hours, as in this example), then you may change this strategy to have 0-24 hour and 24-48 hour backups.

Stage 1 : The first and third columns show the primary and current mirror. The second is the third mirror, and the fourth is the 0-12 hour old backup. This is a triple mirrored environment with an online backup.

Stage 2 : After 12 hours, the third mirror is broken to perform an offline backup. Thus, the third mirror becomes the 0-12 hour online backup (as it is being copied to offline media). The original 0-12 hour backup becomes the 12-24 hour backup.

Stage 3 : Now, that the third mirror is acting as a 0-12 hour backup, the fourth mirror can be re-silvered with the primary disks to re-create the triple mirrored environment. After the offline backup with the third mirror is complete, it will continue to act as the 0-12 hour backup, until the next 12-hour period is reached.

Stage 4 : When the next 12-hour period is reached, the fourth mirror is broken to perform an offline backup. Thus, the fourth mirror becomes the 0-12 hour backup, whereas the third mirror becomes the 12-24 hour backup.

Stage 5 : Now, that the fourth mirror is acting as a 0-12 hour backup, the third mirror can be re-silvered with the primary disks to re-create the triple mirrored environment. This goes back a full-cycle to stage 1. This cycle is an example of having an online backup (0-12 hour backup) during the re-silvering of the broken mirror. This example can be expanded to perform complete load-balancing between all four mirrors.

FIGURE 9-5. *A strategy for maintaining four mirrors (one set acts as a redundant set [to protect against physical disk failures that the primary set may experience], the third set aids in backups, and the fourth set retains online backups while the third set is being resilvered)*

Make sure that hot backup commands are executed synchronously

Many sites use a command file consisting of various backup-related commands to perform the backup. For instance, to perform a hot backup, commands such as those to place each tablespace in hot-backup mode, the OS commands to back up the corresponding files to disk or offline media, and the commands to end the hot-backup mode for that tablespace may be listed one below the other in a sequential fashion. Each of these command files is submitted to the OS (usually via *cron* or a similar scheduling utility) and expected to run in a sequential manner. What I mean by "sequential" is that the commands have to be executed synchronously. In other words, a subsequent command should not be executed prior to the previous one being complete. For instance, you wouldn't want the hot-backup mode to be ended before the OS copy command is done. Violating this condition can result in "fuzzy backups" because the data-files are in a state of flux as they are being backed up, while the tablespace is no longer in hot-backup mode. The files are constantly being written to as the backup is running (as opposed to a normal backup state where only the file-headers are updated, when the ALTER TABLESPACE BEGIN BACKUP command is issued and only redo is generated from that point onward, until the ALTER TABLESPACE END BACKUP command is issued). Restoring such fuzzy files would not allow successful recovery to be done (if recovery becomes necessary).

On many OSs, all the commands in a command file are executed synchronously. However, certain OSs or certain tools cause the commands to be executed asynchronously, resulting in invalid backups. An example of asynchronous execution would be execution of command-scripts in the Novell NetWare environment. It is essential to monitor your backup scripts to detect whether they are being executed asynchronously; if so, the issue needs to be addressed, so that all interdependent commands are not being concurrently fired off. Certain tools have flags to indicate that synchronous execution is desired, whereas you may need to put in manual timers (sleeps and so on) for others to regulate every individual command within the job. Fuzzy backups are certainly a major caveat to watch for while testing your backups (by attempting recovery on a similarly configured test machine).

Check the backup log files regularly

One of the most common mistakes that DBAs make is to not look at the log-file created by the backup process. If the backups are done nightly, then it's necessary to examine the backup logs every morning for errors. Log-files can be created either directly by a command parameter (such as the LOG=<file-name> parameter of the *export* command) or by redirecting the output of the backup command to a log-file. Many DBAs have the log-file e-mailed to them at the end of backup, or even parse

the log-file for errors (via *grep,* and so on) and if any are found, have themselves paged/e-mailed. Whatever method you deploy, it's essential to ensure that you spend the time to study the backup results and tune/repair any erroneous conditions before they escalate into total disasters. It's the worse thing that can happen to a DBA to discover during restoration after a database crash that the backup files are corrupt or one of the archived redo-logs is missing, thus preventing recovery. Periodic review of the backup log and validating the contents of the offline media (for instance, verifying tape contents) can prevent such situations.

Avoid performing backups manually

When performing backups manually, various subjective factors come into play, such as the mood and memory of the DBA, that may cause errors leading to an invalid backup. Always use a script or an automated tool. When using home-grown scripts, once those scripts are tested and deployed, they prevent manual errors from creeping in. Ensure that all such scripts are updated after all schema/structural changes (new tablespaces, datafiles being added/dropped). Use some kind of mechanism for impact analysis after all schema/structural changes to ensure that no errors are introduced in these scripts. In fact, rather than hard-coding the names of all files to be backed up, it is advisable to read that information off the data-dictionary catalog (*v$datafile, dba_data_files,* and so on). That way, the script is sure to get the most current information. For sites dealing with large databases or concerned with backup throughput, it's advisable to configure an automated tool such as EBU or RMAN. From a backup and recovery throughput standpoint, it's essential to choose the right backup tools. It's essential to ensure that such tools do not hog all available resources, such as CPU time and memory. In other words, the backup tools should not be the bottleneck (unfortunately, CPU saturation is caused by the *actual* backup and recovery process, rather than the procedure adopted by the tools, especially when the files are being compressed). Certain media management software vendors provide "Oracle-compliant" tools that perform backups of Oracle databases to the predetermined media. It's essential to benchmark such tools on a test environment prior to deploying them in production. Test them against a variety of factors, specific to your environment. For instance, if you use or plan to use raw devices, ensure that these tools can handle raw devices, in terms of backing up and recovering to raw devices (certain products have problems recovering to raw devices); find out whether a raw device of a specific size can be restored on to a different-sized (bigger) raw device (without overwriting critical OS information on cylinder 0), in case in a real-life recovery scenario, you are forced to do so, due to unavailability of a raw device of the same size as the one backed up.

Both RMAN and EBU are proved to be lean (read, minimal resource–consuming) and powerful tools for backing up Oracle databases. Both RMAN and EBU provide an open interface and work with a variety of backup media-management software (such as IBM ADSM, Legato Networker, and CA Cheyenne ARCserve). Once they are configured, both backup and recovery operations can be totally automated. Additionally, a recovery catalog is provided that preserves details of backups taken and recovery to be applied. When using RMAN, EBU, or some other tool that uses such a backup/recovery catalog, ensure that the catalog is set up on a different database on a different machine to prohibit machine/database crashes from preventing recovery. Additionally, provide adequate failover capacity for the machine hosting the recovery catalog (such as a high-availability standby instance).

Ensure that security is not compromised when using backup tools

A variety of tools are available in the market for automating Oracle backup and recovery. Many of these tools perform OS hot backups by logging onto the database, placing each tablespace in hot-backup mode, and then actually conducting the backup by issuing OS commands. Some of these tools use a preconfigured Oracle user ID to log onto the database and issue the necessary commands. This preconfigured user ID is generally an administrative account and rich in privileges. The problem here is, usually this preconfigured user ID has a preconfigured password, which may be hard-coded in many of the tool's scripts. For example, when using the Oracle Agent option of Computer Associates' Cheyenne ARCserve Enterprise Edition v2, by default, the INTERNAL (SYS) account is used to perform backups of databases (including *remote* databases), thus potentially exposing the database to a serious security breach. However, a different, newer Oracle user ID can be created to perform the backups. This new user ID should not be as rich as the INTERNAL account in terms of database privileges and just have the necessary privileges to perform the backups. Additionally, this new user ID should be named something obvious, such as BACKUP_MGR, to indicate its nature. No passwords should be hard-coded in any of the backup/recovery scripts.

With RMAN, periodically resynchronize the recovery catalog

When using RMAN, the recovery catalog is automatically synchronized with information on the backups taken. This synchronization is done when any of the COPY, BACKUP, SWITCH, or RESTORE commands are run. However, this synchronization may not always include information on the redo-log switches and the archived redo-logs created. It is advisable to periodically update the recovery catalog with information on the redo-logs. The interval for resynchronizing may

vary depending upon the frequency of your backups. I would recommend updating the recovery catalog as one of the last steps in performing the backups. If you perform complete database backups every day and your archived logs get backed up every day as part of this backup, the recovery catalog should also be updated daily (via the RESYNC command). That way, the recovery catalog is always kept fairly up-to-date and does not lag behind the backups.

Ensure that your backup strategy accounts for all Oracle file-types

Oracle is composed of different types of files: data-files, online redo-logs, control-files, archived redo-logs, initialization parameter files, necessary trace-files, and the software itself. Ensure that you account for all these files in your backup strategy. Not all these files need to be backed up at the same frequency. For instance, the software only needs to be backed up after the installation and subsequently, after any patches and so on are applied. Hence, a robust backup strategy should not only make a valid backup of all necessary files, it should also provide guidelines for backing up various file-types at different points in time. The data-files, redo-logs, and control-files forming the tablespaces need to be backed up with a regular frequency, such as every night or every weekend. This frequency would depend on your database size, total transactions in the database, time required to back up, and the available maintenance time-windows. You may back up one tablespace per night or all tablespaces every night. Especially in VLDB sites, all file-types cannot be treated in a similar fashion and be subjected to the same backup frequency. Total backup times may exceed 24 hours, and the database backups would dominate the machine, leaving very little system resources for database use. Accordingly, each file-type needs to be segregated and placed in different backup queues to be backed up at different times.

Tablespaces/Data-Files

Tablespaces have no physical representation and are backed up as data-files. Each data-file logically belongs to a specific tablespace. All data-files belonging to a tablespace ought to backed up as a single unit. Only if a tablespace comprises a single data-file, that data-file may be backed up individually. Each tablespace has varying importance. Accordingly, the backup plan for each tablespace may vary according to its relevance. For instance, the SYSTEM tablespace forms the core of the database, since it contains critical data-dictionary information, without which the database cannot function. And also, generally, the SYSTEM tablespace is pretty small. Accordingly, it is relatively easy to back it up every night. Also, preferably the SYSTEM tablespace should be placed on a mirrored volume. Due to the small size of the SYSTEM tablespace, placing it on a striped volume may not introduce any performance advantages. (Again, this is a general view. Eventually, it depends on the nature of your application—how frequently the SYSTEM tablespace is accessed. For instance, a DSS application may access it heavily for space management such as temporary segment allocation, and so on. Such applications requiring intensive access of SYSTEM may benefit from SYSTEM being placed on a striped volume.) Moreover, striping without mirroring would increase the database points of failure due to multiple disks being used to store the SYSTEM tablespace. (This is true for any tablespace. However, this applies more to SYSTEM, due to its ultra-critical nature. A database can still be brought back up fairly easily with certain other tablespaces being inaccessible. With SYSTEM being inaccessible, however, the database cannot be brought up at all.)

Online Redo-Logs

Online redo-logs are key during instance (thread) recovery and in certain situations, during media recovery. The online redo-logs contain the redo records to roll the database forward. The redo records include undo or rollback information for transactions in the database. This rollback information will be used to roll back uncommitted transactions at the end of the recovery event. Prior to Oracle7, each of the online redo-log files is used to represent a single point of failure. The loss of an online redo-log results in an outage. To prevent that, it is necessary to multiplex the redo-log files, such that each online redo-log group comprises multiple members (at least two). All the members of a specific group are copies of each other and are completely maintained by Oracle. Each member of a redo group should be on separate disks/controllers. Striping them across multiple disks is not very advantageous from a performance perspective, since redo writes are sequential. (Note that not striping the redo-logs is not a guarantee of being able to write sequentially to them, since the read/write head may still have to move back and forth to perform I/O on other files resident on the same disk/controller. However, it certainly increases the chances of sequential writes, and thus higher throughput. Also, note that certain systems can parallelize even sequential writes, under specific situations. In such cases, striping the redo-logs may achieve the same throughput.) However, striping may alleviate disk hot spots if they are observed due to heavy writes being done to the online redo-logs in certain environments. But again, as mentioned earlier, striping without mirroring would spread each online redo-log across multiple disks, thus increasing the points of failure. Multiplexing of the online redo-logs within Oracle is preferred to hardware/software mirroring (in case both cannot be utilized). With multiplexing, Oracle continues to run even if just one member in each online redo-log group is available and the rest are corrupt. In the case of hardware/software mirroring, however, Oracle would stop running if the primary file becomes corrupt (even with the mirror still valid). Additionally, Oracle multiplexing protects from administrative accidents such as a systems administrator accidentally removing a file, whereas hardware/software mirroring may not.

Before, during, and after backups, periodically monitoring the online redo-logs is advisable to watch for any logs acquiring the STALE or INVALID status. An online redo-log can become STALE if writes to that log are pending due to the log being temporarily unavailable, such as when a SHUTDOWN ABORT is issued just prior to a write. A redo-log may become INVALID if there is any file corruption due to hardware errors, and so on. Both situations can be monitored via the STATUS column in the dynamic view *v$logfile*. Additionally, when a redo-log becomes INVALID, it is logged in the database alert-log.

Control-File

The control-file contains physical database structural information and is crucial during recovery. It needs to be backed up during all complete or partial backups and also immediately after any database structural changes. Both a binary copy of the control-file and an ASCII one that reflect the current database status need to be present on both online and offline media. Besides backups, ensure that at least three control-file copies are present on separate disks/controllers. If possible, place them on mirrored volumes (in addition to multiplexing them within Oracle). Placing a control-file on a striped disk-volume does not present any performance advantages due to the small size of the file. If anything, a striped volume only increases the points of failure by distributing a control-file across more than one disk (the database would go down if even one control-file is unavailable). A subsequent tip covers control-file backups in more detail.

Archived Redo-Logs

All applicable archived redo-logs need to be backed up at periodic intervals. If your archive-log destination is limited in size, then you need to ensure that you back them up and delete them, prior to the archive-log destination getting filled. For instance, the archived log files may continuously be backed up once every four hours to tape and deleted from disk via an OS scheduling utility (like the *cron* command in UNIX). If you compress the archived logs prior to backing them up, ensure that the compression utility you are using is well tested in your environment and that it does not cause corruption of any kind (especially due to usage of any special switches). Also note that it is a good idea to retain some amount of archived redo-logs online. Ideally (disk-space permitting), this amount should be equivalent to the archived redo generated since the last hot backup, so that recovery (if needed) can be faster due to the files being present on disk and the need for restoring them from offline media being averted.

Initialization and Configuration Files

Initialization files, such as *init.ora* and *config.ora,* contain parameters that Oracle reads while starting up and as such are important. Even though they are relatively easy to re-create, in some cases, they may contain information specific to your site (such as special events set for capturing certain bug information), and it is advisable to ensure that they get backed up as changes are made to them. Current copies of all configuration files, such as *listener.ora, tnsnames.ora, protocol.ora,* and *snmp.ora* also need to be backed up.

Alert-Log and Relevant Trace-Files

The alert-log contains information about various events inside the database, right from the time the database is created. Since the file can grow to a large size over a period of time, it is necessary to slice up the file and archive the earlier portions (after renaming them with the date/time stamp) to offline media. Whenever necessary, the history of the database can be understood by examining such archives. At any given point in time, however, it is advisable to retain at least the most recent two weeks' history within the alert-log on disk (provided it does not cause the alert-log to bloat excessively). Similar treatment needs to be given to all important trace-files generated by Oracle. Irrelevant trace dumps produced may be discarded. However, trace-files containing important information about abnormal process terminations, database crashes, internal errors (ORA-600s), and so on, need to be saved. Such information may be required by Oracle Support for debugging purposes at a later point in time.

Oracle Software

Last but not least, the Oracle software directory needs to be backed up immediately after installation and after any subsequent upgrades, patch-installs, and so on. If possible, the Oracle software directory needs to be mounted on a disk/controller separate from the data-files and redo-logs to avoid contention.

Table 9-2 provides an example of setting different backup queues based on the file-type. In the example, the site performs OS hot backups every night and performs a cold backup once a week on Saturday night. The backup queues have been set up accordingly. File-types sharing backup queues would be backed up together as a single unit (albeit, in a sequential order—for example, during a cold backup, data-files would be backed up first, followed by the online redo-logs, finally followed by the control-file).

Back up the control-file immediately after all database changes

Whenever any structural changes (new tablespaces/data-files are added/dropped) are made to the database, it is advisable to take an immediate backup. However, it is not always practical or feasible to do so. For example, if your site takes an OS hot backup every night and you add a data-file during the afternoon to make space for an urgent requirement, you cannot usually perform a backup immediately. You would need to wait until the nightly backup begins. During such situations, it is advisable to back up at least the control-file.

File-Type	Backup Queue	Backup Frequency	Comments
Data-files	BQ_HOT_01	Nightly	6 nights a week, excluding Saturday nights.
Data-files	BQ_COLD_01	Once a week	Saturday night.
Online redo-logs	BQ_COLD_01	Once a week	These are not backed up as part of the hot backups.
Control-file	BQ_HOT_01	Nightly	Via the ALTER DATABASE BACKUP CONTROLFILE command.
Control-file	BQ_COLD_01	Once a week	Via a direct OS copy.
Control-file	BQ_SCHEMA_01	As needed	After any database structural change.
Archived redo-logs	BQ_ARCH_01	Every 4 hours	On all days, except Sunday.
Oracle software files	BQ_FLSYSTM_00	Nightly	Here, Oracle software files are being backed up as part of regular OS file-system backups (which excludes Oracle data-files, redo-logs and control-files). They may also be placed in a separate backup queue and backed up less frequently (only after initial installation, upgrades, and patches).
Initialization parameter files (*init.ora* and *config.ora*), password files, and other configuration files such as *listener.ora* and *tnsnames.ora*	BQ_FLSYSTM_00	Nightly	These files may also be placed in a separate backup queue and backed up only the first time they are created and after any changes are made to them.
Alert-log and important trace-files	BQ_FLSYSTM_00	Nightly	Again, these files could be placed in a separate backup queue and backed up less frequently (weekly or fortnightly).

TABLE 9-2. *Sample Backup Frequencies Set for Different Oracle File-Types*

When a new tablespace/data-file is added or an existing tablespace/data-file is dropped, or whenever the control-file is re-created (to increase MAXDATAFILES, MAXLOGFILES, and so on), ensure that you immediately take a backup of the control-file via the ALTER DATABASE BACKUP CONTROLFILE TO TRACE command. This command can be run while the database is open. All it does is dump out a trace-file containing the CREATE CONTROLFILE command for the database, so that the control-file can be re-created whenever necessary. Create trace-files with and without the RESETLOGS option so that both can be immediately available whenever required for recovery. Rename the trace-files generated to include the date/time stamp and also back them up onto offline media. In the event of a database crash, the trace-file containing the CREATE CONTROLFILE command helps in two ways:

- Maintains a record of the tablespaces/data-files currently existing in the database (so no error-prone manual recollection is required). Especially during a database crash, when everybody is shaky, it's not a good idea to try to recollect which tablespaces/data-files were present in the database.
- Allows the control-file to be re-created by directly running the command in Server Manager.

In fact, it is advisable to take a control-file backup every morning/evening. In my opinion, this ranks as one of the best practices at any 24×7 site. This practice has saved my skin more than once in the past. Let me recount one such experience. At a site with high availability requirements, we were creating a new secondary database (the standby database) on a different machine. The DBA performing this task had multiple windows open on his PC screen. One window had a Telnet session to the production machine and another had a Telnet session to the machine, that would host the secondary database. Instead of running the CREATE DATABASE command on the latter window, the DBA accidentally ran it on the former window. At first, he was blissfully unaware of his error and continued staring at his screen until he heard the operator's screams about the database being down, after which he went berserk with the CTRL-C keys. However, the damage had already been done—the control-files of the production database had been overwritten due to the CREATE DATABASE command. Luckily, I had a backup of the control-file taken just that morning. We used that backup to re-create the control-file and reopen the database in less than 10 minutes.

Additionally, a binary image of the control-file can be created via a variation of the ALTER DATABASE BACKUP CONTROLFILE command (ALTER DATABASE BACKUP CONTROLFILE TO <filename>). It is advisable to run this command to take a binary backup of the control-file in addition to generating the CREATE CONTROLFILE command. A situation where a binary backup of the control-file is invaluable is when a database structural change is made (example: a new data-file

is added) and the database crashes prior to the next backup. In order to recover, the previous backup will be restored. However, it does not contain the newly added data-file. Accordingly, roll-forward won't be successful due to the absence of the new data-file. In such a situation, using a backup of the control-file that has the entry for the new data-file would allow a new data-file to be created (via the ALTER DATABASE CREATE DATAFILE command), and the roll-forward process can be successfully performed.

Besides structural changes, it is also recommended to back up the control-file every time a tablespace is switched from read-only mode to read/write mode and vice versa or from online mode to offline mode and vice versa. If recovery is required, and if during recovery a data-file/tablespace (all data-files for that tablespace) changes from offline to online or from read-only to read/write or vice versa, the current control-file needs to be used to perform the recovery. If the current control-file is not available, a new control-file needs to be made available using the CREATE CONTROLFILE command or a backup control-file that marks the data-files in read/write or online mode needs to be used. If a tablespace/data-file is in read-only mode, then it should be taken offline during recovery (otherwise, when incomplete recovery is performed or a backup control-file is used, the RESETLOGS option would have to *write* to the read-only files). Thus, the current control-file or a backup control-file that marks those data-files as offline needs to be utilized during recovery. Hence, the control-file needs to be backed up after any such structural change, and this backup needs to be preserved until the next valid backup.

NOTE

Recovery with a backup control-file should be done as the last resort, since that would involve opening the database with the RESETLOGS option (another tip in this chapter discusses the ramifications of opening the database with the RESETLOGS option). Ideally, the current control-file should be used during recovery. If that is not available, consider re-creating the control-file (via the CREATE CONTROLFILE command generated via the ALTER DATABASE BACKUP CONTROLFILE TO TRACE operation) rather than using an older backup control-file. Only if the CREATE CONTROLFILE command is not readily available or is not current (is not synchronized with the files inside the database) and the DBA doesn't have an up-to-date record of all files composing the database, the backup control-file may be used during recovery. Once the database is opened using RESETLOGS, ensure that a backup is taken as soon as possible.

Address export-related concerns before you start performing exports

An important point to keep in mind is that, prior to performing exports, you must be sure that you understand the inter-table dependencies in all relevant schemas. Unless you have a good understanding of the referential integrity in place, it may be easy to cause logical corruption within the database if you ever have to import the data exported. For instance, if the SALES table is lost, then you may decide to use the latest export dump-file to re-create the table via import. Users may have to reenter the last few sales transactions (if they can) to make the table current. There may be processes that read new rows in the SALES table and populate other tables. Various business processes may be dependent on the data in these subsidiary tables—sales projection and forecasting, invoicing, trial balance preparation, and so on, may be done by processes that read these tables. Prior to the SALES table being imported and certain sales transactions being reentered, these business processes may already have been run for the day. The people in the Finance Department may see these new rows and run the business processes again (the same day or the next), causing duplication of information or, even worse, causing important business decisions to be taken based on inaccurate information within the database. For instance, the sales projections may look better than they really are or customers may be billed twice or Cash-in-Bank may be credited twice . . . Scary! The moral of the story is, ensure that you understand the place of each key table in the overall schema and the effect of reimporting the data in these key tables, if they are lost. Do not blindly export key tables and reimport them, in case object recovery is needed, without understanding the effect of such an action. The bigger and more complex the schema, the higher the damage that may potentially be caused—imagine an ERP application with hundreds and hundreds of interrelated tables. Each of the tables exported have to be reimported back, such that the point-in-time consistency is not lost. It's very alluring in a heavy OLTP environment to perform a read-inconsistent export (CONSISTENT=N), since no rollback segment is large enough to perform a fully read-consistent export. (In a typical OLTP environment, all online rollback segments would be configured to handle smaller transactions. Accordingly, a long-running export job may not succeed with rollback segments not equipped to handle them.) Trying to do so may result in ORA-1555 ("Snapshot too old") errors. However, at the same time, from a business perspective, you may not be able to afford a point-in-time inconsistent export either. Imagine you perform an inconsistent export of certain parent tables. Somehow due to an administrative goof-up, these tables get lost or get corrupted, and object (segment) recovery is needed. You may resort to using the export dump-files to reimport these parent tables. However, these parent tables now contain "old" data—they are not consistent with their child tables. In other words, merely reimporting the parent tables may result in the child tables having rows that don't exist in the parents—causing logical corruption within the database. So what's the solution in such situations? Maybe exports are not the solution in situations where there are complex schemas, consisting of a large number of interdependent objects subject to continuous high OLTP activity. Exports could still aid in some of these situations, in exporting static data—key master or reference tables that do not change frequently. However, performing an inconsistent export of highly dynamic tables in such circumstances may not be very useful. Alternatively, if you still need to export certain dynamic tables, and if they are not very large in size, maybe your rollback segments could still accommodate them to allow a read-consistent export to be taken.

Form "export-groups" for inter-segment consistency

As mentioned earlier, exports almost seem unrealistic in many OLTP and/or VLDB environments. Ideally, exports are suited for small or mid-sized tables only in such environments. Alternatively, larger tables may be exported in relatively static environments. You may be able to export large tables even in a dynamic environment—however, reimporting the data would be a challenge. Besides referential integrity and point-in-time consistency, your rollback segments may not accommodate the reimport of these large tables. However, I find that the usefulness of exports make them necessary in many environments, including OLTP and/or VLDB environments. If your segments to export are chosen with caution, exports can be a powerful tool against a variety of segment failures. Exports are the easiest way to recover from table corruptions or situations where a user/developer/DBA accidentally drops a table (provided the reimported table is consistent with other dependent tables). However, the following steps need to be taken to perform reliable exports in dynamic OLTP/VLDB environments:

- Identify all your key tables. (By "key tables", I refer to core master/reference tables that your application totally depends on. In other words, your application cannot function at all without these key tables. For instance, the CUSTOMERS and PRODUCTS tables would be considered key tables in a SALES application, whereas transaction tables such as ORDERS and ORDER_DETAILS may not be key tables. To elucidate, an order from a customer cannot be processed if the PRODUCTS table has been accidentally deleted, preventing the customer from selecting the products. However, new orders can be accepted even if the ORDERS table has been deleted, thus allowing certain core areas of the application to function without too much disruption.)
- Identify the interdependency between each of these key tables and other tables in the same or different schemas.
- Form different "export-groups," based on such key tables. Place each key table at the center and place other dependent tables around it. All

dependent tables should be included in the same export-group as the key-table they are dependent on. Sometimes, multiple key tables may be dependent on each other. All such key tables should be placed in the same export-group.

- Each export-group would be the mandatory unit for each export process. In other words, every time you export a key table, all the tables are included in that export-group would also be exported. Each export should be performed with the CONSISTENT flag set to Y, so that all tables in each export-group are consistent with each other in terms of a specific point in time. Consistency is key when you try to reimport the data. Figure 9-6 illustrates exports occurring by export-groups.
- Always perform the exports during periods of low DML activity (late Saturday nights, for instance). Also, ensure that your rollback segments are sufficiently big to accommodate read-consistent export to occur. Low DML will also help in reducing the chances of the read-consistent view of the

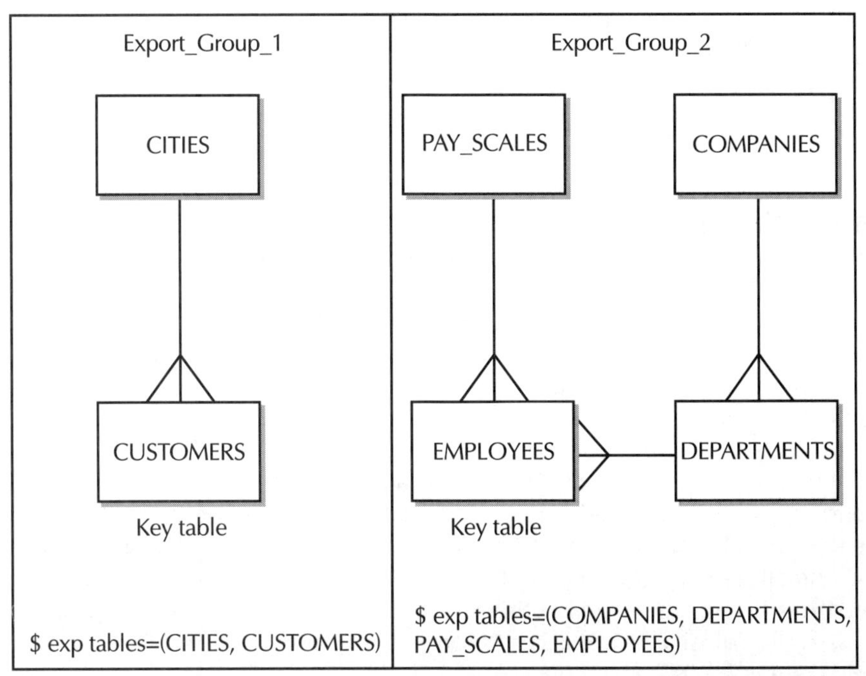

FIGURE 9-6. *Each export process comprises all tables in a specific export-group*

export process from being blocked by a writer process (such as another insert/update/delete process). If there are fewer or no writer processes running at the same time as the export process, no rows will be changed, thus forcing the export process to look at the rollback segment blocks, rather than the actual table blocks, to construct a read-consistent view. Also, with fewer or no writer processes, chances that the read-consistent view maintained in the rollback segments will be overwritten are slim.

- When it is necessary to reimport data (to recovery certain segments), ensure that you reimport the entire export-group. In other words, all tables in the export-group have to be reimported as a single unit—not just the one that has become corrupt or lost. If necessary, truncate all tables that you are about to reimport. This will prevent duplicate records from being introduced (especially if you have the database constraints disabled). You could create more than one export dump-file for each export-group. This will allow you to perform the imports in parallel (each dump-file can be imported simultaneously), thus reducing load-times.
- Also while reimporting data, you may have to disable smaller rollback segments and enable a different set of bigger rollback segments, one that will allow the imports to proceed without failures or interruptions. Accordingly, maintaining a special group of large rollback segments to aid in large imports would be useful. Such large rollback segments could also be utilized during other large operations such as cumulative data-loads.

Plan sufficient space for export dumps

It's a good idea to ensure that a valid copy of the latest export-file is always kept on disk. Smaller tables may always be exported directly to disk. If sufficient disk-space is available, larger tables may also be exported directly to disk. At times, it may be necessary to compress large-table export-files via a pipe to occupy less space (see Chapter 19 for a sample script that does this). If the compress process hogs way too much CPU, more than your environment can afford, then an (uncompressed) export to tape via a named-pipe should be considered.

Try to ensure that sufficient disk-space is allotted for the export dumps. Usually, exports need to be performed during periods of low database activity. Also, it is necessary to make exports as speedily as possible to ensure that they get completed within the allotted window of time. Usually, directly exporting to disk affords the fastest export time, whereas exporting to tape takes longer (subsequent tips in this section outline other ways for faster exports). It may also be advisable to plan for keeping multiple versions or copies of an export-file on disk. For example, at some of my client sites, the data and time stamp is part of the filename when multiple export versions are kept. If only one export file (of a few select tables) is kept on disk, then the filename may be reused (rather than including the date/time stamp in the filename). If the filename is being reused, prior to taking the export, it is advisable to rename the existing export file (to "*.old*" or something). This will prevent the existing file from being overwritten. This is especially important, since if the export process fails, at least both export-files won't be lost (the older export file will have been overwritten, and the current export will fail and creates an invalid export-file—so both files are lost).

Perform exports using direct path, rather than conventional path

To reduce the performance impact caused by database exports to the production database, it is essential to speed it up as much as possible. Starting with Oracle7 v7.3, a new export path is available: the *direct path* (not to be confused with the newer *direct reads* database option; direct reads database access is explained in Chapter 7). Direct path exports are up to 70 percent faster than conventional-path exports (note that this percentage may vary according to resources available for the export process and the existing table formats). Let's take a quick look at the export internal operations to find out the exact reason for the difference in speed (Figure 9-7).

When the conventional path is used, data has to undergo multiple courses of conversion, prior to being written out in an export file. Columns are physically stored in a data-file in a distinct order. For example, columns with LONG data-types are always stored at the end of the row, and newer column types such as BFILE may be represented as just a pointer to the data, which may be actually stored out of line on a separate disk. Also, a single row may be physically broken up across different OS blocks (due to row chaining). However, pointers are maintained to ensure that each row is treated atomically. During a conventional export, a row-special format is derived from a data-block as it is copied into the data-block buffer cache. At a later stage, it is reconverted into a column-special format, essential for the different stages of SQL processing. Finally, it is converted into a row-special format again, just prior to being transferred to the export buffer for writing out to the export file.

When the direct path is utilized, the data in the data-blocks is converted to row-special format (via a single SQL statement: *SELECT * FROM <table_name>*) and the result-set is directly written to the export file. Thus, two additional data conversions are avoided, saving heavily on CPU use (otherwise required to perform the conversions) and memory (otherwise required to store the different converted row copies). Thus direct exports seem to be much faster due to the miniscule code-path involved in the reduced processing.

Chapter 8 discusses other "database upgrade"–related export/import tips including using named pipes, single-task export/import processes, and so on.

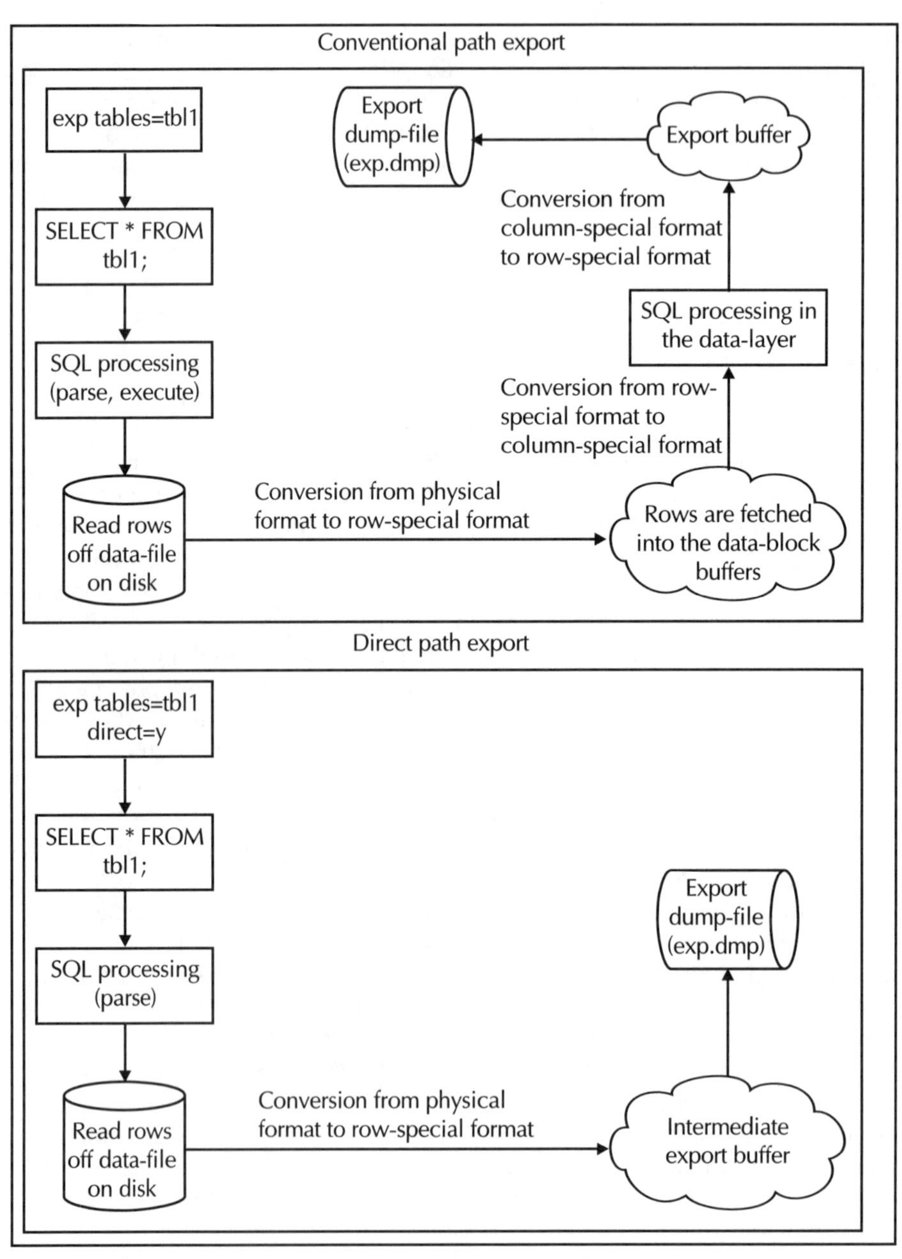

FIGURE 9-7. *Conventional export path versus direct export path*

Ensure compatibility and usability of all backed-up export-dumps

When dealing with multiple database versions, export file compatibility becomes an issue. Exports may be used to upgrade the database to a newer version. Export-dumps are upward compatible. Accordingly, a newer version of the export utility can create export-files off an older database or read export-files already created using an earlier version. However, export-files may not be backward compatible. In other words, an older import-utility may not be able to read an export-file created by a newer version of export. For example, if a version7.3–compliant export-file has been created using the direct-path option, a pre-7.3 version import cannot read and interpret the export-dump, since the direct-path option didn't exist prior to version7.3. Also, an older version of export may not automatically be able to read a newer version of the database to create export-dumps, unless a specialized script provided by Oracle is run in the newer version of the database. For example, a script called *catexp7.sql* needs to be run in an Oracle8 database to create version7-specific export-views so that the version7 export utility can read an Oracle8 database and create export-dumps. Ensure that all backed-up export-dumps are compatible and usable with the current version of the database.

Upgrading a database version is not generally a problem. Sometimes, however, sites are forced to downgrade to escape a major bug in the newer Oracle version or to deploy third-party software, which is supported only against an earlier Oracle version. During such situations, export-dumps created with the newer Oracle version may not be usable with the current older version. All such export-dumps need to be identified, re-created, and backed up to offline media as soon as possible.

Perform a backup immediately after any system clock changes

While conducting Year-2000 testing or during daylight saving changes, it's fairly common for the system clock on machines to change time. It is essential to back up the database immediately after any system clock changes made on the database server so that point-in-time (database and tablespace) recovery can be successfully done. If backups are not taken, database changes made just prior to the change in time may be lost. Let's take an example to understand this better.

Let's imagine a production database named PROD hosted on a machine called ALPHA. Also, the same company has a development database called DEVL on a different box called BETA. As depicted in Figure 9-8, the following (imaginary) events have taken place on October 25, 1998:

1. A hot backup of the PROD completes at 01:30 A.M.

2. A batch process performs a bulk-insertion of 10,000 rows from a flat-file to a table (let's name it TRANSACTION_DETAILS) at 01:45 A.M.
3. Another batch process kicks off and inserts a number of rows into another table (let's call it SALES_SUMMARY) at 02:30 A.M.
4. Another nightly process starts up and updates a different table (let's call this table SHARE_QUOTAS) at 03:00 A.M.
5. At 3:01 A.M., to activate daylight saving, the system clock gets pushed back an hour to 02:01 A.M.
6. At 02:15 A.M., a sleepy developer working on DEVL accidentally runs a TRUNCATE command on the SHARE_QUOTAS table on a different window connected to PROD, thinking it's DEVL (believe it or not, sometimes developers do have access to production!).
7. The developer pages the DBA and politely requests that the table be restored off the backup and be recovered to just prior to the truncation.

Analyzing this situation, the DBA can recover all transactions up to 02:14 A.M. and, subsequently, batch jobs mentioned in steps 3 and 4 would need to be rerun, since those transactions would never be recovered via the point-in-time recovery

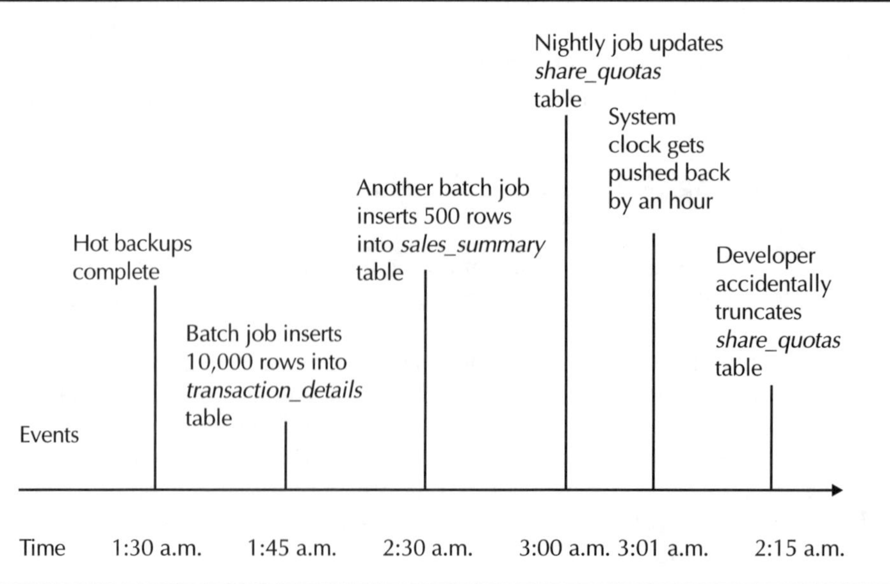

FIGURE 9-8. *Chart outlining database changes occurring at various times*

performed until 02:14 A.M. Recovery is based on the SCN associated with every transaction. However, the date/time stamp associated with every SCN would be used by Oracle to perform the point-in-time recovery. The DBA would run the following command in Server Manager to recover the database:

```
SVRMGR> RECOVER DATABASE UNTIL TIME '1998-10-25:02:14:00';
```

This would roll forward and recover all transactions until step 2 in the preceding series. Thus, all transactions performed in steps 3 and 4 are lost. If there was a backup taken immediately after step 5, that backup could be used to recover completely just prior to the table truncation in step 6. Recovery could be accomplished by restoring the backup taken after the system clock change and applying any archived redo-logs to roll forward up to the necessary point in time. Thus, it's always advisable to perform a backup immediately after any system clock changes.

When using Oracle Parallel Server, it is important to keep all participating nodes in sync timewise. Problems can arise with point-in-time recovery if the nodes are too far apart in time.

For more information on recovery after system-clock changes, refer to the *Oracle8 Backup and Recovery Handbook* from Oracle Press/Osborne. It provides complete case studies of time-based recovery during such situations.

Check for database corruption during and after backups

One of the key areas where backups are useful (besides recovery, if necessary) is to detect database corruption. Some backup options just ignore corruption, whereas other options highlight corruption, when found. Depending on the backup method deployed, it is necessary to check for database corruption either while the backups are being performed or after they are done, or, if possible, during both times. For example, when performing OS hot backups, database corruption is not immediately highlighted. So corruption, if any, would get propagated to the backup media as well. However, if RMAN is configured to perform database backups via backup sets or image copies, it populates two dynamic views with information on database corruption. Depending on whether backup sets or image copies are used, RMAN populates *v$backup_corruption* or *v$copy_corruption,* respectively. These views are populated when RMAN spots corruption, and if the allowable corruptions (MAXCORRUPT) setting is a value greater than zero. By default, MAXCORRUPT is set to zero, and hence RMAN gives an error and fails without populating these views.

As mentioned earlier, when performing OS hot backups or cold backups, database corruption cannot be detected immediately. The db_verify (*dbv*) utility needs to be used to check for corruptions. Db_verify can be used either directly against the online data-files or against the backed-up copies. It's advisable to make it a practice to use db_verify against all backed-up data-files at least once a week or even more frequently if any corruption is suspected.

As database exports perform full-table scans, they are also very efficient in detecting corruption. If using exports as a secondary source of backup, examine the logs where the export output is written (the output log-files can be created via the *log=<file_name>* export parameter or by redirecting the export output to a log file via OS commands).

The backup job needs to be configured such that when corruption is detected, the script or tool notifies the DBA via a page. Most automated tools, including *Oracle Enterprise Manager,* allow that. If home-grown scripts are being utilized, the notification needs to be explicitly coded (Chapter 19 provides an example of a UNIX Korn-shell script that notifies the DBA).

Chapter 14 discusses detecting and repairing database corruption in more detail.

Set optimal I/O size during backups

The I/O size used for backups primarily determines backup throughput. Backup tools use a default I/O size, which may be sub-optimal for your environment. Most backup tools allow this I/O size to be changed. For example, with Oracle EBU (Enterprise Backup Utility), I/O size can be set via the DISK_IO_SIZE and TAPE_IO_SIZE parameters in the EBU configuration file. On UNIX platforms, EBU works with the media management software (such as Legato Networker) to internally issue a series of *dd* commands to perform backups of both UNIX files and raw devices. The I/O size used by *dd* is set by EBU set via the *bs* (block-size) parameter according to the values specified for DISK_IO_SIZE and TAPE_IO_SIZE. If you use scripts to perform backups directly using *dd,* then you would need to configure the I/O size by explicitly setting *bs* to a higher size. This higher value should ideally be a multiple of the DB_BLOCK_SIZE. In case the I/O size specified is higher than what the OS supports, then it would automatically be trimmed down to what the OS is capable of. In any case, that would allow the OS to use the maximum size possible. Since the backup tool cannot guarantee that each Oracle block would be read entirely as an atomic unit (most backup tools cannot guarantee this because it depends on how the OS actually performs the read; if the DB_BLOCK_SIZE is a multiple of the OS block size, an OS read may not constitute the entire Oracle block), it may cause split blocks during hot backups (as discussed earlier). Accordingly, the initialization parameter _LOG_BLOCKS_DURING_ BACKUP needs to be set to TRUE (the default on UNIX platforms) to resolve split blocks during recovery.

Make use of incremental backups available in Oracle8

Oracle8 introduces incremental backups via RMAN, wherein only new or changed database blocks are backed up. This is a very powerful backup enhancement, invaluable especially for 24x7 and VLDB sites, aimed at reducing the window of time required to perform the backups.

Incremental backups can be performed by configuring *backup sets* within RMAN. A backup set comprises a group of similar Oracle files to be backed up as a single unit. For instance, a backup set may consist of data-files or archived redo-logs (but not both). Control-files can be backed up as part of any backup set. A whole database backup consists of all data-files within the database and all control-files, and backs up all used and unused database blocks. For sites requiring high availability, backup sets can be used to perform an online backup. As with earlier versions, Oracle needs to be in ARCHIVELOG mode to conduct an online backup. Backup sets can be used to perform a full or incremental backup. A full backup of a backup set consists of all the blocks of a specific set of data-files forming that backup set, whereas an incremental backup consists of only blocks that are new or have changed since the last time the backup set was backed up. A full backup is different from a whole database backup, in terms of the components of the backup set: A whole database backup always consists of all data-files, whereas a full backup may refer to only a few data-files within a backup set. Furthermore, a full backup only backs up all *used* database blocks, whereas a whole database backup backs up all database blocks, including static ones.

Incremental backups may be configured to occur at different levels. Each level is an integer forming a logical point that determines whether used database blocks are to be backed up or not beyond that point. For instance, a level 0 backup may be done on Monday. On Tuesday, a level 5 backup may be done. This level 5 backup will back up only blocks that have changed since the last level 5 or lower backup was done. In this case, the level 5 backup would back up all blocks that have changed since the level 0 backup done on Monday. On Wednesday, a level 2 backup may be done. This would only back up blocks that have changed since the last level 2 or lower backup. So this wouldn't back up blocks that level 5 backed up. In other words, the level 2 backup would consolidate and back up blocks that changed since Monday. Thus, the backup file produced by the level 5 backup can be discarded. The backup file produced by the level 2 backup now contains all the changes that were present in the level 5 backup. This reduces the number of files to be restored during recovery and thus expedites recovery.

Besides the level, another factor influencing incremental backups is whether they are being performed cumulatively or non-cumulatively. Cumulative backups back up all database blocks changed since the last lower-level backup. Non-cumulative backups only back up database blocks changed since the previous (most recent) same- or lower-level backup. The preceding example depicted an incremental backup being done cumulatively.

If configured and used correctly (with a well-analyzed backup strategy), incremental backups can be very effective in expediting backups without compromising overall recovery times. The backup strategy should be aimed at capturing all changed database blocks over a short period (say, a week), without producing too many incremental files. Accordingly, a combination of different

incremental levels should be used to effectively balance backup time and time to restore/recover.

Archiving

This section focuses on using and optimizing the archiving procedure within Oracle.

Evaluate whether ARCHIVELOG is necessary for your environment

I know, you are thinking—"What's this tip doing in a 24×7 book?" Most DBA texts refer to the absolute necessity of running the database in ARCHIVELOG mode. And I totally agree with that: in any 24×7 environment, it is absolutely necessary. Rationally, however, when true 24×7 uptime is not an absolute must, there are certain situations where the validity of enabling archiving needs to be questioned. However, before questioning the necessity of archiving for any environment, let's understand the advantages and disadvantages of ARCHIVELOG mode:

Advantages of ARCHIVELOG mode

Following are the advantages of running the database in ARCHIVELOG mode:

- Complete media recovery is possible. During crashes, the database can be recovered up to the last committed transaction (this is possible with NOARCHIVELOG only if all the redo entries to be applied have not been overwritten and are still contained in the online redo-logs).
- The database can be backed up while it's open and running.
- ARCHIVELOG mode allows inconsistent backups, where the database can be backed up in smaller units (like one tablespace per day, which causes the various tablespaces to be inconsistent with each other; however, the necessary archived redo-logs are also backed up, applying which allows the database to become consistent during media recovery).
- ARCHIVELOG mode allows distributed recovery if all databases involved in the distributed relationship are running in ARCHIVELOG mode.
- ARCHIVELOG mode allows non-SYSTEM tablespaces to be taken offline in IMMEDIATE mode.

Disadvantages of ARCHIVELOG mode

Following are the disadvantages of ARCHIVELOG mode:

- It is quite administration intensive. The DBA has to ensure that archiving is turned on, running normally, and keeping up with the other background processes such as LGWR (in other words, it's not hanging, and so on). He or she has to ensure that all archived files are being backed up to tape without losing any of them. The entire archival implementation process has to be well tested prior to deployment. Also, archiving, if done manually, increases administrative complexity.
- Additional storage space is required to preserve the archived logs. Offline media such as tape drives can be used as the archive-log destination. However, if supported by the OS, writing directly to disk is recommended to ensure smoother/faster archiving. Especially in a VLDB environment, directly archiving to offline media is not advisable. Additionally, it is necessary to use offline media to store older versions of archived logs in case it becomes necessary to go back in time during recovery. One fact to keep in mind is that Oracle uses a physiological logging mechanism (physiological logging combines features of physical and logical logging to track the physical after-image of the changed blocks and the logical transactions that made the changes to the blocks; please refer to *Transaction Processing: Concepts and Techniques* by Gray and Reuter and published by *Morgan Kaufmann* for a detailed explanation of physiological logging) to guarantee that all database changes are written to the redo-logs. Changes are recorded to redo-logs via *change vectors,* which basically describe an atomic change made to a single database block. Change vectors are created prior to any blocks being actually changed. A change vector consists of the data-block address (dba) being changed, the data-block class (identifying whether it's a data-block [that is, block class 1 or KCBCDATA] or a temporary segment/sort block [that is, block class 2 or KCBCSORT], and so on), the operation (op) changing it, the sequence (seq) of the operation, and the SCN that is generated for that transaction. A group of change vectors typically make up a *redo record.* All redo records in the redo-logs are then archived and made available during media recovery. Accordingly, if space on the archive-log destination fills up, the database freezes (since none of the online, unarchived redo-logs can be overwritten) until more space is made available to resume the archival process. This is the single most important reason that enabling ARCHIVELOG mode needs to be evaluated in situations where disk-space is at a premium. The DBA needs to implement monitoring processes to ensure that this never happens. Thus, this ensures that in ARCHIVELOG mode, even though LGWR can get ahead of ARCH, it can never run circles around ARCH (not more than one). ARCH can archive a redo-log that's not been checkpointed yet. Thus, ARCH can move ahead of DBWR. However, a redo-log that's not been

check-pointed cannot be overwritten by LGWR. (This brings up the question—how many online redo-logs are required? This question is answered in Chapter 7. However, as a generic rule of thumb, make certain that you have enough so that during the period of heaviest write activity, LGWR is never stopped by having to wait for ARCH.)

- Additional overhead is involved in archiving and keeping track of all archived logs. Oracle tracks the status of each online redo-log group via information written to the control-files. Archive log history is also maintained in the control-files. The extent of this information is dependent on the database parameter MAXLOGHISTORY (set at the time of database creation) and is available via the dynamic view *v$log_history*. Oracle maintains an *archive link-list* in the control-file to track the inactive redo-log groups that need to be archived.

Additionally, the ARCH process needs to be up and running to perform the archival (Figure 9-9), thus adding to the IPC (interprocess communication) overhead. ARCH has to be posted (the process of signaling ARCH to perform some work is called posting) periodically to check for inactive redo-logs that need to be archived. ARCH may be posted to perform archiving via any of the following methods:

- Log-switches
- Time-out intervals (300 seconds)
- Archiving being started (via the ALTER SYSTEM or ARCHIVE LOG commands)
- Database being opened (if the initialization parameter LOG_ARCHIVE_START is set to TRUE; except when instance recovery needs to be performed, in which case, ARCH is posted *not* to perform any archiving)
- Self-posting (ARCH posts itself, if it is already awake, has finished with archiving a log, and notices that another log needs archiving.)
- Posting via LGWR (LGWR may signal ARCH to stop archiving a certain redo-log and archive another instead, if LGWR needs to overwrite the latter redo-log. Once ARCH has archived the other log, it returns to the original log to finish the archiving process. Such escalation avoids users' processes from having to wait excessively on LGWR.)

Such overhead (especially if archiving is improperly configured by the DBA) may result in performance being impacted. The extent of such impact would depend on how archiving is configured (whether the archive-log destination uses separate disks/controllers from the online redo-logs, whether multiple archive-log

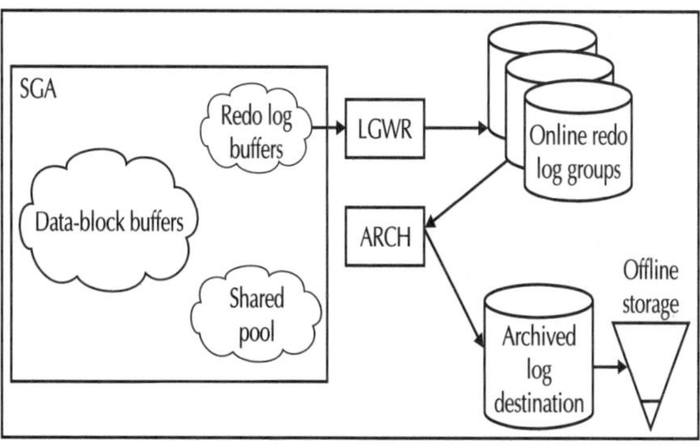

FIGURE 9-9. *The archiving process*

destinations are set up, and so on) and the physical resources available. (For instance, in a CPU- and memory-rich environment, where there is no I/O contention, there may not be any noticeable impact; whereas in an environment with limited memory, CPU, and I/O capacity, the impact may be highly noticeable.) When the ARCHIVELOG mode is not enabled, only information pertaining to which online redo-log group is current is maintained. An archive link-list is not kept, nor are any checks made to determine whether an online redo-log group was archived prior to being overwritten.

The advantages of archiving generally make it necessary for almost any environment. However, in certain environments it becomes more of a source of overhead than a facility. It's always necessary to evaluate the amount of data loss that is "tolerable" to the end-users. (Prima facie, absolutely no data loss is "tolerable" to the end-users. However, with some patience and persistence, you may find that some data loss may be acceptable, after all. For instance, if the end-users are more interested in data for the last three years, loss of older data may be tolerable, until the time it is needed again.) Even when no data loss is tolerable, if the time required to repopulate the database is less than the time required to recover it, then archiving becomes redundant. For example in a data-mart, a cold backup (if the database is not being operated in ARCHIVELOG mode, a hot backup is not possible) and/or a logical backup (if the data-mart is not overly large) may be taken every night. The data-mart may be loaded via nightly batch processes following the backup. If there is a database crash any time during the day and a data-file is lost, then the database may be restored using the previous night's backup. Then the batch processes that populated it may be rerun to restore it to its pre-crash state. If this "restoring and repopulating" occurs faster than "restoring and applying recovery," then archiving may not be necessary for such an environment. Also, another factor that aids the decision is the availability of disk-space for archiving. I have observed that, at some of my client sites, a smaller machine is dedicated for each data-mart. And these smaller machines do not always have access to the necessary disk-space for archiving. If space is a major concern (due to lack of funds and so on) and repopulating the database occurs at the same pace or faster than recovery, then I'm generally inclined to tilt toward not having archiving turned on. However, it has to be borne in mind that besides recovery up to the last transaction, you would be missing some other significant advantages (as mentioned previously) by disabling archiving. The point here is, after evaluating availability requirements, if 24×5 or 22×7 is what is required rather than 24×7, you may still be able to configure a satisfactory environment (one that satisfies all SLA clauses) without archiving being turned on. In the few hours of downtime that's available, you still may be able to perform backups, restores, and rebuilds, rather than backups, restores, and recovery.

If disk-space is scarce and archiving is highly necessary, then archiving to other offline media such as a tape drive needs to be considered. As long as the administrators ensure that the tapes are changed frequently to prevent them from filling up and freezing the database, this should be a workable, albeit slower and even more administration-intensive, alternative. Also I have observed some sites enabling ARCHIVELOG mode only so that online backups can be performed. In such cases, restoring the online backups, applying the archived redo-logs created during the backups, and rerunning certain batch jobs would also allow recovery up to the last committed transaction. In such situations, the archived logs created after the backups may be deleted off disk (via a periodic *cron* job) without even backing them up. As long as the archived logs created during the online backups are retained, recovery should not be a problem. Such an approach is useful during high disk-space scarcity. In any case, ensure that you understand all availability requirements either directly from the end-users or from the SLA, prior to disabling ARCHIVELOG mode or deleting archived redo-logs (I repeat, only the ones generated *after* the backup is complete, else the backup would be invalid). If requirements change later and the database in question needs to be made available absolutely 24×7, then ARCHIVELOG mode can be enabled at this stage without too much ado.

Implement automatic archival as the primary archival mode

In a 24×7 environment, the word "manual" (as in working manually, not the documentation text) implies introducing errors and possible failure. Manual archiving is performed when the database is running in ARCHIVELOG mode and the initialization parameter LOG_ARCHIVE_START is set to FALSE (or the ARCH process has suspended due to errors or has been stopped explicitly via the ALTER SYSTEM ARCHIVE STOP command). For any 24×7 environment, it's almost a rule of thumb to enable automatic archiving because the administrator does not have to watch for a group to become inactive and available for archiving. Furthermore, as mentioned earlier, if automatic archiving is disabled and manual archiving is not performed soon enough, the database can freeze and suspend all database operations whenever LGWR is forced to wait for an inactive redo-log group to become available for reuse. The manual archiving option is provided by Oracle so that the DBA can

- Archive all redo-log groups that need archiving, when automatic archiving has been stopped because of a problem. (Example: the disk drive specified as the archive-log destination has been filled up or crashed.)
- Archive all online redo-log groups that were active during a hot backup at the end of the backup.
- Archive a certain redo-log group in a different manner than the others. (Example: archiving the next few redo-log groups to tape to prevent disk-space from totally filling up and to buy some more time and prevent the database from freezing until more disk-space is made available.)
- Rearchive a redo-log group if, for some reason, the original archived log is lost or corrupt.
- Issue manual archiving commands to start up extra processes for expediting archival.

Automatic archiving is performed by the ARCH background process, whereas when archiving is done manually, the user process issuing the command to archive a redo-log group actually performs the task of archiving the group. Even if ARCH is currently running, it does not perform manual archiving.

In a 24×7 environment, it is highly necessary to ensure that automatic archiving does not fail, thereby impeding database availability. Accordingly, it is essential to put in place monitoring processes to detect potential failure and take appropriate action. One of the actions may be to supplement automatic archiving with manual archiving as and when necessary (example: when the archive-log destination is about to fill up). However, at no point in time should a DBA rely purely on manual archiving, since it tends to be an administrative ordeal. The only manual archiving that is of any value is that performed in conjunction with automatic archiving.

Allocate adequate space for ARCHIVE_LOG_DEST

As mentioned previously, Oracle uses a physiological mechanism to guarantee that all committed transactions are written to online redo-logs and archived, prior to being overwritten. If there is insufficient space in the archive-log destination, that would cause the database to freeze. So how big should the archive-log destination be? If the archive-log destination is an offline device, available space depends on the device capacity. For example, if the capacity of an 8mm DAT is 5GB, you cannot hold data beyond that at a specific point in time. If your archive-log destination is disk, as a general rule of thumb, it should be big enough to accommodate at least two consecutive backup cycles. For example, if you perform a hot backup once in 24 hours, then the archive-log destination should be able to hold the archived redo-logs generated over 48 hours. This aids in two ways:

- It allows the archived logs pertaining to the most current backups to be held on disk for immediate recovery.
- It tolerates failures from the current backup process. If there is space on the archive-log destination to hold only archived logs generated since the last backup (24 hours in this case), it cannot tolerate any backup failures. The archived logs pertaining to the last backup would be deleted prior to starting up a new backup process to ensure that sufficient space is available for the archived logs generated by the new backup process. If the new backup process fails, the archived logs pertaining to the last backup would already have been deleted from disk. In case of a sudden database failure, a restore of those archived logs from offline media to disk would be necessary to perform recovery thus increasing MTTR. Thus, sizing the archive-log destination to accommodate archived logs pertaining to at least two backup cycles (the last successful backup and the current backup) would eliminate such problems.

Use "ALTER DATABASE ARCHIVELOG" for enabling archiving

Archiving may be turned on via two different methods:

- During database creation (via the CREATE DATABASE...ARCHIVELOG... command)
- After database creation (via the ALTER DATABASE...ARCHIVELOG... command)

Generally, creating the database takes up a lot of time. Especially if each tablespace is quite large, creating the entire database can take hours. So my tendency is to take whatever steps I can to reduce the overall time taken. One of the useful things is to create the database with ARCHIVELOG mode disabled. Creating the database with ARCHIVELOG mode enabled takes up more time. For example, here are the results of a test I performed on a 40GB database with 16 tablespaces on a Sun Enterprise 4000 with 1.5GB of RAM, connected to an EMC disk-array using RAID S. It took me a total of eight hours to create the entire database with ARCHIVELOG turned on. And, in effect, this large amount of time was caused by the "hot spots" caused by the CREATE DATABASE and CREATE TABLESPACE commands (and the RAID S parity write-penalty). Each concerned disk showed busy times exceeding 80 percent. However, I could create another 40GB database on a different box with the exact same configuration in just 6.45 hours in NOARCHIVELOG mode, resulting in a time saving of 14 percent or 1.15 hours. Even though the same disk bottlenecks were observed this time as well, the overall database creation took less time (due to lesser I/O generated by NOARCHIVELOG).

After the database is created, the ALTER DATABASE ARCHIVELOG command may be used to enable archiving. This command usually takes a few seconds to run. Thus, creating the database in NOARCHIVELOG mode (and later enabling it) may save a significant amount of time.

Also, for newly created databases, ensure that archiving is indeed being done. Quite often, I have seen pleas for help in the Oracle newsgroups by relatively inexperienced DBAs saying that the ARCH process seems to be running, but that no archived logs are being created in spite of multiple log-switches by Oracle. Some DBAs merely check whether the ARCH process is running or not at the OS level (via the *ps –ef* command in UNIX). However, ensure that the database is in ARCHIVELOG mode. ARCH may run (if the LOG_ARCHIVE_START initialization parameter is set to TRUE), but if the database is not in ARCHIVELOG mode, the redo-logs are not being archived. You can ensure that the database is in ARCHIVELOG mode by running the following command in Server Manager:

```
SVRMGR> ARCHIVE LOG LIST;
Database log mode              ARCHIVELOG
Automatic archival             ENABLED
Archive destination            /odata6/oracle/product/8.0.4/dbs/arch
Oldest online log sequence     68
Next log sequence to archive   71
Current log sequence           71
```

Take a complete backup as soon as ARCHIVELOG mode is enabled

Accordingly, at some sites running DSS applications, prior to huge batch loads, ARCHIVELOG mode is disabled to prevent a large number of archived logs from being created and quickly filling up the archive-log destination, and causing the

database to freeze. Once the loads are complete, ARCHIVELOG mode is reenabled. The following steps are taken to achieve this:

1. The database is shut down (this is not a major problem for most databases supporting DSS applications, since DSS application availability requirements are generally not as critical as OLTP applications).
2. The database is mounted, but not opened.
3. ARCHIVELOG mode is disabled (via the ALTER DATABASE NOARCHIVELOG command).
4. The database is opened (via the ALTER DATABASE OPEN command).
5. The batch loads occur, populating all necessary DSS tables.
6. The database is shut down again.
7. The Database is mounted.
8. ARCHIVELOG mode is reenabled (via the ALTER DATABASE ARCHIVELOG command).
9. The database is opened.

So what exactly happens when the ARCHIVELOG mode is reset that makes an immediate backup so necessary? Disabling the ARCHIVELOG mode causes all information about the archived logs, including the high and low SCN numbers corresponding to each archived log, to be zeroed out from the control-files. The archive link-list is deleted and no longer maintained. Oracle stops tracking whether the online redo-logs have been archived prior to overwriting them. When ARCHIVELOG mode is subsequently enabled, the opposite occurs. Oracle once again archives the online redo-logs prior to overwriting them and maintains the archive link-list and the high and low SCN numbers for each archived log to apply during recovery. Thus, resetting the ARCHIVELOG mode marks an inherent split in the sequential availability of archived logs. During the time the ARCHIVELOG mode is disabled, a "hole" in the archive-log sequence is created, thus making complete recovery impossible (as explained in a previous tip). By using a backup prior to the ARCHIVELOG mode being reset, recovery is possible only until the point of time that ARCHIVELOG mode was disabled. Roll-forward would fail beyond that and recovery would be incomplete, thus causing the DBA to open the database with the RESETLOGS option. Any data entered after the ARCHIVELOG mode is reset would be lost.

Thus, in order to maintain complete database recoverability, it is highly necessary to take a complete backup (hot or cold) as soon as ARCHIVELOG mode is reenabled. Once a valid backup has been taken after an ARCHIVELOG mode has been reenabled, that backup can be used to ensure complete recovery. In a DSS environment, if an immediate backup is not possible, it is necessary to keep track of which batch loads are occurring after the ARCHIVELOG mode has been reset, so that such jobs could be rerun in case there is a database failure. If your site maintains a standby database, another repercussion of disabling and reenabling ARCHIVELOG is that the standby database will have to be rebuilt, since the steady sequence of archived redo-logs to be applied to the standby database is broken.

Why ARCHIVELOG Should Be Reenabled

You may wonder why should ARCHIVELOG mode be even reenabled in a DSS environment? After the loads take place in a DSS environment, the data should basically be read-only and there shouldn't be any insert/update/delete occurring. Accordingly, what benefit would reenabling ARCHIVELOG mode bring? After a batch load completes, there may be errors typically (due to various reasons such as erroneous source-data, new bugs in the loading routines, administrative accidents, and so on). Thus, miscellaneous DML (updates, inserts, deletes) may occur incrementally after a major load is complete to correct such errors or merely to perform referential integrity checks and report discrepancies, and so on. Theoretically, all such activities ought to occur as part of the load. Practically, however, these tasks occur at whatever point the developers/designers implement them. Some sites prefer to implement such audit checks separately after all loads are complete and the database has been placed in ARCHIVELOG mode.

On a related note, you may also be wondering—most of the loads and subsequent index-builds would be done in UNRECOVERABLE/NOLOGGING mode in a DSS environment, so minimal redo is generated. So what's the point of placing the database in NOARCHIVELOG mode in the first place? Again, the assumption that most loads and index-builds would be done in UNRECOVERABLE/NOLOGGING mode may not necessarily be true. In cases where the site has the option of performing unrecoverable operations, that would be a better option than manually changing the ARCHIVELOG mode. However, certain situations exist where there is no choice. Let me give two examples of such situations:

- In a data-warehouse, you have a fairly large table (with say, 25 million rows). The site maintains three year's worth of data in that table. Each year an additional 25 million rows get written via a batch job, transferring data from the operational data-sources. This translates to roughly 95,000 incremental rows (updates and inserts, no deletes) every day (discounting weekends and holidays). The table can be re-created (with the UNRECOVERABLE option) during the first few months (since the number of rows is fairly less). Once it reaches 10 million or so rows, it cannot be dropped and re-created each time, considering the table-creation delay (unrecoverable or not). As the table keeps growing, only DML can be applied to the existing table. In Oracle8, certain DML operations can be parallelized and made "direct" (PDML with the APPEND hint). However, not all DML operations can be made direct. In cases where they cannot be made direct, they would still continue to generate redo and thus cause a large number of archived redo-logs to be created, unless archiving is disabled explicitly. Here I have mentioned just one table. However, if you scale this example to a warehouse with half a dozen such tables, you get into a no-choice situation, where the direct operations available (as of 8.0.x) may not be adequate and one may have to resort to disabling ARCHIVELOG mode explicitly.

- When using an automated tool (such as Prism Warehouse Executive or Platinum Decision Base or Informatica PowerMart/PowerCenter), the tool generates most of the DML for batch inserts/updates, and so on, leaving little scope for putting in hints to parallelize the DML or make the operations direct. In many cases, these tools do not allow re-creation of a segment with the UNRECOVERABLE/NOLOGGING option (for instance, a parallel CREATE TABLE UNRECOVERABLE AS SELECT operation cannot be performed via most of these tools). Only regular vanilla DML is supported. Due to the popularity of these tool sets, in many cases, many DSS sites are forced to perform regular "recoverable" loads due to practical constraints that their tool enforces on them. If such tools perform loads in a regular, non-direct fashion without using the UNRECOVERABLE/NOLOGGING features, such loads will continue to generate high volumes of redo, making it necessary to place the database in NOARCHIVELOG mode to escape the overhead of archiving.

Use ARCHIVE LOG CURRENT rather than a variation

Manual archiving is done generally via the ALTER SYSTEM command with any of the three options (note that these options can be run directly in Server Manager without the ALTER SYSTEM prefix):

- ARCHIVE LOG ALL
- ARCHIVE LOG NEXT
- ARCHIVE LOG CURRENT

The first variation archives all inactive redo-log groups that haven't been archived yet (all except the *current* one). The second variation archives the next redo-log group that needs to be archived (this may be the group that was last *current* and has just been switched). The third variation archives all inactive redo-log groups, including the one that is currently being written to. Issuing any of these commands starts up additional user processes that concurrently work with ARCH (if it is enabled and running) to archive inactive or active redo-log groups. This is a very useful feature that allows higher archiving throughput, especially during peak hours when ARCH cannot keep pace with LGWR due to very high transaction volumes.

The last option is the most versatile and most useful of the three because it archives all unarchived online redo-log groups, including the current one (which is still being written to). The other two options tend to underachieve. The first option does not archive the current redo-log group. Normally, archiving the current redo-log group may not be beneficial if it contains only a small amount of redo (if LGWR has just begun writing to it). During hot backups, however, it's necessary to ensure that *all* redo-log groups that were ever current during the backups (including the one that's current at the end) are archived and backed up to ensure a valid backup that can be used to reproduce a consistent database. The second option tries to archive only the next redo-log group that needs to be archived. If the next online redo-log group has already been archived, the command fails without checking whether the subsequent group needs archiving. Thus, you should make it a practice to use ARCHIVE LOG CURRENT rather than the variations, at all times, especially during hot backups.

Do not create holes in the archived log sequence

As mentioned earlier, when the archive-log destination is filled up, the ARCH process cannot archive any more online redo-logs (that is, it gets "stuck") and that suspends all database operations, since all the online redo-logs need to be archived and cannot be overwritten while the database is in ARCHIVELOG mode. During such database freezes, the first reaction of most DBAs is to delete some of the older archived redo-logs (some DBAs do not pause to even consider the age of the archived logs) in the archive-log destination to make space, so that archiving can continue and all database operations may resume.

The first, foremost and correct reaction when this occurs is—do not panic! Inadvertently deleting archived redo-logs prior to their being backed up to offline media creates "holes" in the archived log sequence. Remember, during recovery, roll-forward will occur only through the last sequential archived redo-log. Oracle will not jump across archived redo-logs during recovery to ensure the logical consistency of the recovered database. An online backup is performed during ongoing database activity, and so all tablespaces backed up are inconsistent with respect to each other. Applying the archived redo-logs is what makes the recovered database consistent and valid. Once a gap is created in the sequence of archived redo-logs to be applied (due to a missing archived log file), recovery will fail and the database will need to be opened with the RESETLOGS option (due to the incomplete recovery operation). If you absolutely need to delete some of the archived redo-logs due to the urgency of the situation, move off those archived logs to another directory (*/tmp*), rather than deleting them (just don't reboot after moving critical files to */tmp*). Also, if you (or another DBA) end up deleting them, take an immediate database backup to ensure the archived log sequence is uninterrupted once again without any holes.

Rather than just deleting some of the archived redo-logs, you actually have several options to try when the archiver is stuck, such as redirecting ARCH to a different archive-destination, moving already archived logs to a different directory, and selectively deleting the oldest archived logs. Let's look at these options in more detail.

Redirect ARCH to a Different Destination

Always have a spare archive-log destination that has free space available at all times. If you do not maintain a pre-designated space archive-log destination, perform a quick check to see which other disk-drive (assuming you are archiving to disk) has the required free space (space enough to hold at least half a dozen or so archived redo-logs). Once such a space destination is located, ensure that the new directory has the requisite write-privileges for Oracle to create the archived redo-logs there. You can then redirect ARCH to write to the newer destination by issuing the following command:

```
SVRMGR> ALTER SYSTEM ARCHIVE LOG TO '<new-destination-path>';
```

Substitute <new-destination-path> with the name of the actual destination (example: '/oraback/space_arch/ARCH_'). ARCH will then start archiving the online redo-logs to this newer destination, providing an opportunity to the DBA to back up the archived logs in the primary destination and to make some free space available there by deleting all archived logs backed up already. Once free space is created there or when this newer destination seems to get filled up, the archive-log destination may be switched back to the primary destination again, thus averting the need to delete archived logs not backed up. Ideally, a proactive approach would be to always maintain two archive-log destinations: a primary and a secondary destination. Scripts can be deployed via *cron* (or any other scheduling utility) to periodically check the primary destination for free space. Once the primary destination gets 85 percent full, an automatic switchover to the secondary destination can be performed, after which the archived logs in the primary destination can be backed up and subsequently purged from disk. Then the secondary destination's free space can be constantly monitored and, if that gets 85 percent filled up, the same treatment can be provided to the secondary destination.

Move Already Archived Logs to a Different Directory

As mentioned earlier, move some of the already archived logs to a different directory (*/tmp* for instance), thus freeing up space. (Again, just don't reboot after moving critical files to */tmp*.) Then Oracle can continue writing to the same destination. In the meantime, you can immediately back up some/all of the archived redo-logs (including those you moved to another directory) and then delete them, thus making more space available. In situations where you have just one archive-log destination (rather than primary and secondary destinations), it's advisable to deploy scripts to periodically (at least once every four log-switches) back up all archived logs created and then delete them off disk. This will ensure that the ARCH process does not get stuck. One important fact to note here is that most databases switch logs at a different pace during different levels of database activity. Thus during peak hours, archived logs are created at a much faster pace than during non-peak hours. Deploying the scripts to always account for peak-hour traffic will ensure that the archive-log destination never gets full—either during peak or non-peak hours. Either the dynamic view *v$log* can be queried for a list of redo-logs with the column ARCHIVED = 'YES' that can be backed up and deleted or free space in the archive-log destination needs to be monitored. Chapter 19 provides an example of a script that backs up and deletes archived log files, starting with the oldest in the archive-log destination.

Selectively Delete Oldest Archived Logs

If no directory is available for temporarily changing the archive-log destination due to inadequate space or privileges, then selectively deleting some of the archived logs may be necessary to allow database operations to resume. However, this should be the last resort. Also, when doing this, run a directory listing such that the oldest archived logs show up first (*ls –ltr* on UNIX). Highlight the oldest among those and delete them first. If some of the oldest archived logs have already been backed up (and not deleted off disk for some reason), manually deleting only those will prevent holes from occurring in the archived redo-log sequence. If even the oldest archived redo-logs on disk haven't been backed up and manually deleting

them is necessary, immediately take another database backup as soon as the database starts working again. Once you a have a valid backup, that backup can be used to ensure complete recovery, since all archived redo-logs necessary for roll-forward would be available again. Also, immediately after a backup, deploy a script that will periodically back up archived logs and delete them off disk, as discussed previously.

If possible, keep dual copies of archived logs on disk

An earlier tip mentioned the utility of having two archive-log destinations: a primary one and a secondary one. In addition or as an alternative, starting with Oracle8 v8.0.*x*, you can also maintain two concurrent archive-log destinations. In other words, it is possible to simultaneously archive two copies of an online redo-log group. This helps in two ways:

- If one of the archive-log destinations is bigger than the other, the bigger one will still allow Oracle to continue unabated (without freezing), in case the smaller one gets full (provided the value for the initialization parameter LOG_ARCHIVE_MIN_SUCCEED_DEST is set appropriately). Also, it will provide the DBA some buffer time to back up older archive logs and delete them so that none of the archive-log destinations is full.
- Another layer of protection for the archived redo-logs is provided. If for some reason, prior to being backed up, the archived logs on one destination are deleted accidentally or become corrupt due to hardware problems, having a copy of those on another disk drive (or other offline storage such as tape) will prevent "holes" in the archived log sequence.

This is extremely useful for a 24x7 site, since it further protects the archived redo-logs against media failure. The second archive-log destination may be set via the initialization parameter LOG_ARCHIVE_DUPLEX_DEST. All online redo-log files will be archived to both LOG_ARCHIVE_DEST and LOG_ARCHIVE_DUPLEX_DEST. If set, another initialization parameter, LOG_ARCHIVE_MIN_SUCCEED_DEST, determines the number of archive log destinations that a redo-log group must be successfully archived to, thus preventing Oracle from freezing in case one of the archive-log destination is full or has a media failure.

NOTE

While archiving to two concurrent archive-log destinations, ensure that the two destinations are configured on separate disks/controllers to avoid I/O contention from affecting database performance.

Create more online redo-log groups when archiving to offline media

Whenever possible, always try to archive to disk. However, if archiving directly to offline media such as tape, create more online redo-log groups (at least four) to provide the database more logs for switching. Writing directly to tape in a sequential fashion (redo is generated sequentially) is usually slower than writing to disk. Also, if the tape-drive is connected remotely via the network, other delays such as network latency may also delay the archiving process. Due to such delays, LGWR may finish using all the available online redo-logs and ARCH may be heavily lagging behind by still trying to archive the first redo-log group. Since no online redo-log group can be overwritten until it's been archived, ARCH may get stuck and freeze all database operations. Having additional online redo-log groups helps mitigate this problem by providing additional buffer time and additional online redo-logs for LGWR to write to, until the time ARCH has finished archiving to tape. That is, it provides additional time for ARCH to catch up.

Also, selecting the right offline media helps to alleviate the delays. If the throughput offered by the offline media matches the disk-drive throughput, then archiving to offline media may not be an issue. For example, for most practical database applications, disk I/O rates occur at 3MB/sec or less (theoretical data transfer rates may be much higher, especially for reads). If a single tape-drive with a maximum throughput of just 512KB/sec is used, obviously archiving throughput is affected. However, if an autoloader or jukebox with a maximum throughput of 20MB/sec is utilized, it prevents saturation of the tape device and allows higher archiving throughput. While archiving directly to tape, try to procure autoloaders with high-volume tape libraries. That will prevent frequent manual tape handling and thus avoid manual errors from disrupting operations or causing unnecessary delays.

OPS Archiving Considerations

Be aware of special archiving considerations, when using OPS

There are some special issues that a DBA needs to be aware of when running a database in ARCHIVELOG mode under an OPS configuration.

- **Back up archived redo from all threads** Under Oracle Parallel Server (OPS) configurations, each instance maintains a distinct thread of redo and as such is responsible for archiving its own thread separately. All threads are retained such that they are relatively current with each other in terms of SCNs generated. Threads of instances are kept current by forcing log-switches and subsequently archiving the logs (also referred to as "kicking an instance"). Thus, even if a specific instance is idle, it still creates small archived redo-logs containing just the header information that is necessary during media recovery. The control-file maintains a *force archive SCN*. The ARCH process scans the archive link-list (also maintained in the control-file), and if the current SCN in the online redo-logs for an instance is too old compared to the force archive SCN, it kicks the instance to archive its online redo-logs. Also, the ARCH process of an active instance may need to switch and archive the logs of an instance with a closed but enabled redo thread if the latter's current SCN is too old with respect to the force archive SCN. Accordingly, do not fail to monitor the archive-log destination of an instance, just because it is not undergoing any activity. Ensure that the archived redo-logs from all threads (pertaining to all instances) are backed up. In order to facilitate this process, configure all instances to share the same archive-log destination.

- **Set up local archive-log destinations** When implementing Oracle Parallel Server (OPS), there are two options to set up the archive-log destination:
  - Shared disks, such that all nodes having an Oracle instance (that is, each "participating" node) can access those disks and write out their archived redo-logs there
  - Local disks, such that each participating node writes out to a local archive-log destination

Most installations choose the former option due to administrative convenience (smaller number of archive-log destinations to back up, a single place to monitor for free-space availability, and so on). In a 24x7 environment, however, ordinarily such a global archive-log destination may result in a single point of failure (unless the destination is mirrored). All instances would be unavailable if the global archive-log destination fills up or crashes. In Oracle8, multiple destinations may be set up via the ARCHIVE_LOG_DUPLEX_DESTINATION initialization parameter to prevent this scenario. However, for 24x7 sites running Oracle7 or sites running Oracle8 but not duplexing their archived logs, it is essential to eliminate all single points of failure. Hence for such sites, the second option, of setting up local disks as the archive-log destination for each participating node, is better. Since the disks are local, the archive-log destination for each node could be named the same.

When setting up local archive-log destinations, it is advisable to ensure that each destination has the space necessary to accommodate archived logs generated by all instances since the previous backup. This proves invaluable for expediting recovery, since it is then possible to restore all archived logs generated by all instances onto the archive-log destination of the instance performing the recovery. If sufficient space is not available, then the archived logs would need to be restored on a partial/incremental basis, thus delaying recovery.

Recovery

This section looks at ways to make recovery a fast and error-free operation.

Understand the need for recovery and take proactive steps to avoid failure

Database recovery is the process of reinstating the database to normal operational mode in the event of a failure. Failure can occur at different levels such as block failure, thread failure, and media failure. Accordingly, recovery is initiated at different levels.

Block Recovery

Block recovery is initiated when a server process terminates abruptly while writing to a data block, thus corrupting the block. The PMON (process monitor) background process periodically wakes up and automatically performs block recovery by rolling back any uncommitted changes and releasing any latches/locks that may have been held by a terminated process. Prima facie, there is no manual intervention by the DBA required to resolve block-level failure. However, if the DBA understands scenarios where a server process can prematurely terminate, he or she can also take steps to prevent some of those from happening. Let's take a peek at some of these scenarios, which may require block recovery:

HARDWARE/OS READ/WRITE ERRORS A process may end with errors if it cannot continue writing due to unexpected hardware/OS errors such as a disk/controller failure, a network failure, or a sudden change in privileges.

MANUAL TERMINATION When a user process is killed at the OS level (the *kill* command in UNIX), or within Oracle (via the ALTER SYSTEM KILL SESSION command), it may require block recovery. Sometimes, however, PMON fails to detect this situation, especially if the shadow process is still running. During such times, manual intervention may be required to kill the shadow process and tell PMON that the resources held by that process need to be released. Sometimes, even when all related processes are killed, PMON still refrains from releasing the resources. Gradually after a while, PMON does release them. I have noticed cases where it has taken more than 48 hours for locks to be released after a process has died. In such an event, the only way of quickly releasing all resources is to perform a database shutdown (which is hardly possible in a 24×7 environment). Also in the cases of user processes coming in via SQL*Net, starting with version 2.1, it's possible to use a feature called *dead connection detection* to detect a terminated user process and clean up the related OS processes. This increases the chances of

PMON being able to tell that a process has died and its resources need to be cleaned up.

STATEMENT FAILURES When a DML statement fails due to a fatal error, it may leave the data blocks changed by that statement in a state of flux and may need recovery. Some such scenarios include operations exceeding tablespace quotas, unavailability of free space in a tablespace, inadequate privileges on a table, integrity constraint violations, hitting the maximum extents allowable (if MAXEXTENTS is not set to UNLIMITED), and logical application errors that cause deadlocks.

DISTRIBUTED LOCK MANAGER (DLM) FAILURES In Oracle Parallel Server (OPS) configurations, DLM failures may require block recovery.

Thread Recovery

When an instance crashes without gracefully closing the current thread of redo, thread or crash recovery is initiated by Oracle the next time the instance is started up. An instance may crash and need thread recovery in a variety of situations such as after a sudden power outage (if UPS systems are not used), due to an accident where someone kills a background process, when the SHUTDOWN ABORT command is used, and so on. Thread recovery is performed by the SMON (system monitor) background process. During thread recovery, the online redo-logs are used to roll forward all transactions (committed and uncommitted), and then the rollback segments are used to determine and rollback all uncommitted transactions.

Under OPS environments, an open instance would have to perform crash recovery on an instance that has crashed but still remains unopened. Such crash recovery is performed by the SMON process of an open instance, which periodically wakes up and checks on the status of the other instances. Such crash recovery may also be performed by forcibly waking the SMON when the crashed instance holds a lock that an open instance needs.

Media Recovery

Media recovery is necessary when a data-file is lost or damaged such that Oracle cannot access it anymore, or recovery to a past point in time is needed. Such loss or damage may occur due to a variety of reason, including hardware/OS problems (disk crash, physical corruption, and so on) and administrative errors (someone accidentally deleting or overwriting the file). Media recovery, unlike block and thread recovery, requires manual intervention by the DBA. During media recovery, a valid version of the file needs to be restored from a backup. All data may be safely recovered if the database is running in ARCHIVELOG mode and all required archived redo-logs are available to roll forward.

It is mandatory for a production DBA to evaluate potential points of failure and take steps to reduce the areas and times of vulnerability via robust policies and procedures.

Understand factors affecting recovery time

Prior to developing any kind of recovery plan, you should understand the factors affecting recovery time. Let's take a short tour of the recovery process to understand the operations involved and which among those are prone to delay.

Prior to recovery, all necessary data-files and archived redo-logs need to be restored onto disk, if they are not already present on disk. Restoring from offline media is, no doubt, a very I/O-intensive operation, causing the majority of the delay involved in recovery. Once restore is complete, the actual recovery process would constitute other I/O operations such as these:

- The archived redo-logs are read by the dedicated server process performing the recovery.
- The data-file blocks to which changes need to be applied are read by the DBWR.
- Once the changes are applied in memory (the data-block buffer cache within the SGA), the changed blocks are written back to disk by the DBWR.

All I/O operations are restricted by the I/O sub-system capacity and configuration. Also, the application of redo data to the data blocks is a CPU-intensive procedure and is constrained by the bandwidth of available CPUs and memory. Talking about memory use, a "recovery buffer" is allocated within the PGA of the user process performing the recovery. Redo is read in from the archived redo-logs into this buffer. The redo is interpreted to form a linked-list of data-block addresses (dbas) that the redo needs to be applied to. Once the redo is applied to these blocks, the space taken up by the earlier redo and the dba-list can be overwritten by new redo, read in from the archived redo-logs.

For Oracle Parallel Server (OPS) configurations, there would be a different recovery buffer for each enabled redo thread. Also in the case of OPS, there is an additional overhead: merging redo from different threads prior to rolling forward. The process of rolling forward is inherently sequential in nature (since the redo-logs that are being read have been written to sequentially). The redo is generated sequentially even with the existence of multiple instances, since the data-files are shared between

all the instances. However, the basic reading of redo could be parallelized by using multiple CPUs and placing the archived redo-logs on a striped disk partition (across multiple controllers). The redo from each thread would need to be merged in the right pattern, prior to being applied to the data-files. There is a high overhead in reading one redo thread, switching the context to other threads (based on the number of active instances), and then finally merging the results together. Though parallelism would help in such circumstances by causing different threads to be read concurrently, there would still be some overhead due to the inter-thread communication (ITC) involved. However, if the degree of parallelism is set properly, such ITC overhead should be less than the overhead of context switching, since in the case of the former, each thread could gain high throughput by sequentially reading redo, without having to scan for the correct context between different threads, thus minimizing disk seek times and rotational latency.

Parallelizing recovery is theoretically helpful even in the case of single instances (non-OPS configurations), since the data-files can be segregated into different groups, with each group having its own recovery slave process. All slave processes may then read redo from the archived logs simultaneously and apply the redo to their respective groups. In such cases, however, such parallel reading of the archived redo-logs during recovery would offer limited help and at times may even delay recovery, since there is only one redo thread to be read. Once that thread has been read, the dba-list needs to be created and the changes need to be applied to the data-blocks in the list. Thus all operations are sequential, and parallelizing single-threaded recovery would only unnecessarily introduce inter-thread communication between the master and slave threads. Furthermore, another area of contention would be the finite number of latches for the data-block buffer cache such as *LRU latches* and *hash-bucket chain latches*. (Hash-bucket chains are explained in the next paragraph; please refer to Chapter 7 for an explanation of the LRU latches and a listing of the hash-bucket chain latches such as *cache buffer handles, cache buffer chains,* and *cache buffer lru chain*.) An alternative way of increasing recovery throughput in such a scenario would be to enable asynchronous I/O (if the OS supports it) and utilize just one recovery server process (without any parallelization). Using asynchronous I/O prevents the server process from being delayed from having to wait on every system call.

Once the dba linked-list is formed, the appropriate data-blocks are read into the data-block buffer cache for applying the redo changes. As mentioned in Chapter 7, in addition to the LRU and LRUW lists and the actual buffered blocks, the data-block buffers comprise a number of hash-buckets to which the data-block headers are chained. Oracle has a map of the data-block headers attached to the hash buckets based on a linked-list, ordered by how recently they were accessed (that is, the least recently used (LRU) algorithm). Oracle accesses a data-block in memory by applying a hash algorithm to the dba, and the resultant hash value is used to determine which hash-bucket would contain the data-block header. Once the correct hash-bucket is known, a range scan is performed to detect the right data-block header. The data-block header maintains a pointer to the actual buffered data-block. Depending on the dba hash value, the data-block either is already present in memory (a logical hit) or has to be read in from disk (a logical miss). If the data-block buffer cache is full, each logical miss would cause an old (old meaning, one that was accessed last of all) data-block, present at the end of the linked-list to be removed, as the newly required block is read into the front of the list (see Figure 9-10). If the block at the end of the list is "dirty" (that is, changed), the DBWR would have to write it back to disk. The number of reads/writes performed by DBWR depends on the size of the data block buffer. This process essentially tells us the following:

Size of the Buffer Cache

If a block that needs to have redo records applied to it is already present in one of the data-block buffer hash-buckets, then a physical read at runtime can be avoided. Thus the server process applying the redo records does not have to wait for an old data-block to be popped off the linked-list, and for the new data-block to be scanned for and read from disk into one of the hash-buckets in the data-block buffer cache. Thus, if the required data-blocks can be pre-read into the SGA, that would increase the hit ratio tremendously. Initially when recovery is just started, none of the data-blocks would be found in memory and would have to be page-faulted in. However, once a number of pages (or blocks) have been read in and the data-block buffer cache is full, the LRU algorithm kicks in and keeps shuffling all the data-blocks in a circular manner. If a data-block that has been removed from the linked-list is required a few seconds later, it would have to be page-faulted in once again, thus causing the recovery process to wait. If the data-block buffer cache can be made bigger (as big as possible, without inducing excessive paging and/or swapping at the OS level due to the SGA exceeding available RAM) to accommodate a larger number of data-blocks, it would reduce the occurrences of page-faulting and thus reduce physical I/O.

DBWR Throughput

The throughput of the DBWR is extremely important. It needs to match the speed of the server process performing recovery. During such recovery, a *media recovery checkpoint* occurs, thus requiring the DBWR to burst into writes again. If the DBWR lags behind, the server process would wait on it to make the necessary free space in the data-block buffer cache available for newer data-blocks and also to apply the redo records to the newer data-blocks. The DBWR would be faced with a situation where the number of data-blocks to be written out or read in increases linearly, and it would either need to increase the number of trips to and from disk (to write and fetch more data-blocks) or it would need to make fewer trips but carry a higher number of data-blocks during each trip. Depending on the Oracle version and the OS flavor, there are various documented and undocumented initialization parameters to affect the behavior of the DBWR. A subsequent tip in this section outlines some of them. Also, Chapter 7 outlines tips to increase DBWR throughput. While analyzing post-recovery scenarios, DBWR throughput can be observed by querying *v$sysstat* for the following statistics (note that the statistic numbers are not being provided, since those numbers could change with the Oracle version; rather, the statistic names are being listed):

FREE BUFFERS REQUESTED The number of times that a free data-block buffer was requested by a server process for writing out data. This statistic shows how frequently DBWR was kicked into working by a server process.

FREE BUFFERS INSPECTED The number of data-block buffers that were skipped by server processes in the LRU list, when looking for a free buffer. Data-block buffers are generally skipped when they are "busy" or pinned (that is, there is a latch on them) due to another server process accessing them or DBWR writing them out to disk or populating them from a disk read. This statistic shows how busy the DBWR has been. The number of buffers scanned is dependent on the initialization parameter _DB_BLOCK_MAX_SCAN_CNT.

DIRTY BUFFERS INSPECTED The number of dirty data-block buffers that were skipped in the LRU list by server processes when looking for a free buffer. This statistic should be very low if DBWR is keeping up with the transaction load generated by the server processes. When dirty buffers are encountered in the LRU list, the server process moves them to the LRUW list.

DBWR MAKE FREE REQUESTS The number of times DBWR is requested to make buffers free by writing them out to disk, so that they can be reused by server processes. These requests may either be signaled by server processes or triggered by DBWR itself, when it finds dirty buffers during its routine scans.

DBWR FREE BUFFERS FOUND The number of free buffers found by DBWR in the LRU list, when scanning for free buffers as requested by a server process.

DBWR TIMEOUTS DBWR times out after three seconds of inactivity. When timed-out, it is awakened to scan for dirty buffers to write to disk. This statistic indicates the number of occasions that DBWR timed out.

DBWR SUMMED SCAN DEPTH The cumulative depth of all scans made by DBWR for dirty buffers to write to disk. Each time DBWR performs a scan, this statistic is incremented with the depth of the scan. The depth of the scan depends on the number of dirty buffers found. If the number of dirty buffers is enough to execute a batch write (the number of buffers in a batch write is based on the initialization parameter _DB_BLOCK_WRITE_BATCH), the scan is ended. Otherwise, the scans continue until the number of buffers scanned equals the initialization parameter _DB_WRITER_SCAN_DEPTH.

DBWR BUFFERS SCANNED The number of buffers scanned by the DBWR while detecting dirty buffers. As mentioned previously, each scan may result in a write, if the number of dirty buffers found is equivalent to _DB_BLOCK_WRITE_BATCH.

DBWR LRU SCANS The number of times DBWR scans the data-block buffers for dirty buffers to write to disk.

SUMMED DIRTY QUEUE LENGTH The cumulative sum of the number of dirty buffers (in other words, the length of the "dirty buffer queue") at the end of every successful batch write by the DBWR.

DBWR CHECKPOINTS The number of times DBWR was called upon to do a checkpoint (via log-switches, initialization parameters [LOG_CHECKPOINT_INTERVAL, LOG_CHECKPOINT_TIMEOUT], tablespaces/data-files being taken offline, tablespaces being placed in hot-backup mode, and so on). However, this does not reflect the number of checkpoints completed successfully.

PHYSICAL WRITES The number of blocks written out by DBWR as a result of cleaning up dirty buffers.

WRITE REQUESTS The number of times DBWR was requested to write out blocks by server processes and itself.

RECOVERY BLOCKS READ The number of blocks read during recovery.

RECOVERY ARRAY READS The number of reads incurred in pre-reading and populating the array used for recovery.

RECOVERY ARRAY READ TIME The time incurred in the pre-reads to populate the array used for recovery.

NOTE

The statistics "dbwr free buffers found" and "dbwr make free requests" may be used to derive the average number of reusable buffers available, based on the formula: dbwr make free requests/dbwr free buffers found = avg. # of reusable buffers. A significant number of reusable buffers indicates that either the current DBWR throughput is adequate to keep up with requests for free buffers from server processes or that not too many requests are being made by the server processes due to the database not being heavily used. During media recovery, a high number of reusable buffers generally indicates the former case, since DBWR would be heavily taxed.

Something to remember while looking at these statistics is that some of them are cumulative from the time the database started up. Hence if some of the numbers appear too small, even though you know for a fact that heavy transactions have been occurring or that the last media recovery was very intensive, it's possible that the values presented by these statistics have rolled over. If the values grow beyond the capacity of the data-type holding these statistics, then they roll over starting from a negative value. So if the values are negative or very small, it's an indication of values having rolled over.

Thus, size of the data-block buffer cache and DBWR throughput is critical in determining total recovery time. DML (inserts, updates, and deletes) creating redo during normal database use and redo application during recovery are both enhanced by a larger data-block buffer cache. In fact, redo application is benefited even more, since it does not have to contend with select statements, which use the majority of data-block buffers during normal use (since most applications are read-intensive). With a smaller data-block buffer cache, the number of page faults increases and recovery times are delayed. This is applicable to both stages of recovery: rolling forward, where the redo from archived logs is applied to the data-files, and rolling backward, where the uncommitted transactions applied to the data-files during the first stage are undone. The second stage is necessary because redo information is generated for all changes made to non-temporary (data-files

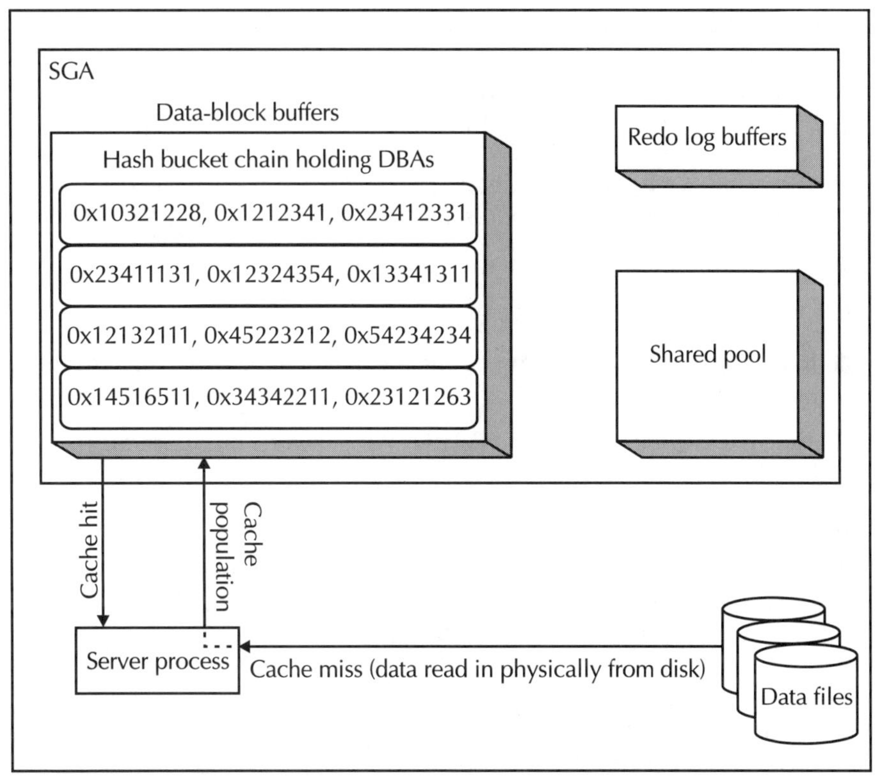

FIGURE 9-10. *Logical miss caused when a required dba is not present in the hash-bucket chain in the data-block buffers*

not belonging to the TEMPORARY tablespace) data-files, including the data-files belonging to the ROLLBACK tablespace.

Ensure that recovery timings are consistent with your SLA MTTR specifications

It is essential that all recovery plans developed consider a variety of outages, in addition to the recovery mechanism used by Oracle. In each outage scenario, the time required to fully recover should be evaluated to ensure that recovery can be achieved within the required MTTR as specified in the SLA. Factors affecting

recovery time (as outlined earlier) need to be well understood. Various elements need to be considered while evaluating each outage scenario, such as

- Time required to detect the outage and notify the administrator to respond
- Time required to decide upon the kind of recovery to perform
- The values for certain critical Oracle parameters, such as the data-block buffer cache, PQO (Parallel Query Option)–related parameters, and so on
- The size of the database and the last backup taken
- Whether a copy of the last backup is available on disk
- If backups are stored only on offline media, the time required to restore the complete backups
- The time to uncompress restored files if they were compressed prior to backing them up
- The number of archived logs to apply
- The time required to apply each archived log (average time is to be considered, since the size of each archived log may vary because redo-log space wastage is not included in the archived log.)
- The time required to open up the database
- The time to restart the listener and all client applications to resume database access
- The time to take a complete backup after recovery (if possible)

While developing the recovery plan, you should be conservative and certainly consider specific (worst-case) scenarios. These worst-case scenarios ought to be developed after a thorough analysis of your environment—historically, what were the worst crashes encountered by your site, or is there a specific crash that has occurred more than once, or what components are most prone to breakage? Once you have estimated the time to perform each step required during recovery, such as restoring the complete backup off tape and applying the archived redo-logs that have been created since the last backup, the next key move is to actually perform each step and ensure that estimated and actual timings match. A subsequent tip provides an example of such a test. Also to verify that the resultant timings of each test satisfy the SLA requirements, all recovery plans have to be tested using actual production hardware/software or in a similarly configured environment (as similar as possible). The tests should absolutely prove that given specific worst-case circumstances, recovery can still be attained within the mandatory recovery times specified in the SLA.

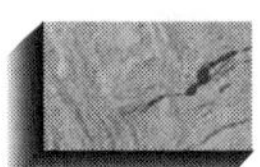

NOTE

Originally, I had used the word "pessimistic" instead of "conservative" in the first sentence of the preceding paragraph. The Technical Editor was quick to respond back with the following comment: "I don't think so. Conservative, yes. I don't think it is realistic to assume that you will get a bad tape, then the tape drive will fail, then you will get a corrupted redo, and during the recovery event your machine will fail". Quite right.

Consider alternative backup/recovery approaches for point-in-time recovery

In order to meet certain stringent recovery timelines, it may be necessary to expand your backup/recovery strategy to include alternate approaches for point-in-time recovery, in addition to using regular hot backups and archived logs. Using hot backups for point-in-time involves high overhead because typically they have to be restored onto a separate machine and rolled forward to a specific point in time. Depending on the partial outage situation (loss of an entire table, loss of a few rows, table corruption, and so on), there are other recovery alternatives available, providing higher recovery flexibility. Some useful approaches include

- Table exports (if exporting the entire database or a specific schema is not feasible).
- Parallel table creation via the CREATE TABLE AS SELECT . . . PARALLEL command (referred to as the "pCTAS" method). This command may be run in UNRECOVERABLE/NOLOGGING mode to increase performance. However, it's advisable to run these commands in RECOVERABLE/LOGGING mode if the resultant creation times are acceptable. An appropriate degree of parallelism needs to be set for both the table and its indexes so that their creation is fast without overly restricting regular production operations.
- Writing the data out from a table to a flat-file (using high-speed OCI or Pro*C routines) and using the flat-file for recovery using SQL*Loader or other data-loading utilities. SQL*Loader supports loading data via direct

path, where the overhead of SQL processing is bypassed and data-loads occur at very high speeds. If the table that is being backed up in this manner is critical but not very large, then a PL/SQL code-block may be used to create the flat-file (starting with Oracle7 v7.3, directly writing to flat-files are supported via the UTL_FILE package). If the table is very large, parallel unload streams may be used, wherein separate threads of the same program or the same program invoked multiple times may read different record ranges and write them to separate flat-files.

- Using Oracle's replication facilities, simple snapshots may be created and refreshed periodically either manually (via an OS scheduler such as *cron* or via Oracle's DBMS_JOB package) or via an Oracle SNP process (by setting the initialization parameters SNAPSHOT_REFRESH_PROCESSES and SNAPSHOT_REFRESH_INTERVAL to appropriate values). Snapshot logs may be created to allow fast refresh times for incremental (delta) changes made to the original table. Snapshots are ideal for maintaining a copy of large tables with little incremental changes (propagation of small changes involves little overhead). Snapshots may be created on the same database (in a different schema, which acts as the staging area for all snapshots), on a separate, smaller database on the same machine, or on different machines. Each option provides the required table-level redundancy. The first option's usefulness in recovery is limited to loss of table-data. It's not useful during database or hardware crashes (since it shares the same database on the same machine with the original table). The second option can be used during database failure, but not during hardware failure. The third option is more versatile, since a different machine is involved. It can be useful during hardware crashes, as well. However, performance is better with the first two options, since there is no network overhead involved (replication does not involve network latency). But again, it is to be borne in mind that snapshots are not meant to replace full-fledged online backups. It is meant to be useful only for point-in-time recovery of certain table data. In case of database or hardware crashes, it's more appropriate to use the online backups to recover. Refer to Chapter 17 for a more detailed coverage of Oracle Replication.
- Using the copy of the table available on the failover instance (if one is maintained). Failover instances can be maintained using a variety of techniques, such as Oracle's Advanced Replication and standby database facilities or other third-party software-based solutions such as Quest Software's SharePlex™ or hardware-based solutions such as EMC's TimeFinder™. Note that there are repercussions to opening the standby database to access a table (when using Oracle's standby database configuration in version 8.0.*x* and below). These repercussions are discussed in Chapter 15.

Remember, these options are not substitutes for a complete hot or cold database backup. Moreover, with some of these approaches, you have to very careful in ensuring that referential integrity is not violated and that all interdependent tables are consistent with each other to the specific point-in-time that recovery is being done.

Ensure that checkpoints occur at sufficient intervals and redo-logs are sized appropriately to prevent recovery delays

This is an example of the classic performance versus availability clash. Setting checkpoints to occur at less frequent intervals enhances performance, since I/O is reduced. However, such delaying checkpoints also set back recovery timings. Setting checkpoints to occur more frequently is advisable for all high-availability sites. Even though checkpoints occur in a variety of situations, to some extent, the size of the online redo-logs and the initialization parameters LOG_CHECKPOINT_INTERVAL and LOG_CHECKPOINT_TIMEOUT primarily decide the frequency of checkpoints. Many sites disable the use of the initialization parameters in determining checkpoint frequency (by setting LOG_CHECKPOINT_TIMEOUT to zero and LOG_CHECKPOINT_INTERVAL to be larger than the largest online redo-log). Accordingly, the onus is often on the size of the online redo-logs to determine checkpoint frequency, as checkpoints are mandatory during log switches (a redo-log group cannot be overwritten unless it has been checkpointed).

So how frequently should a checkpoint actually occur? Once that is decided, how big should the online redo-logs be made so that checkpoints occur at the desired interval? A lot depends on your overall database size and volatility, performance, and recovery timings required by your organization. As a general rule of thumb, checkpoints need to occur at least once every 30 minutes. However, if your database generates a lot of redo every 30 minutes, that could delay recovery times. In such situations, you might need checkpoints to occur more frequently than 30 minutes. Thus, the online redo-logs need to be sized keeping in mind the transactions handled by your database and the redo generated at different times, so that the resultant log switches would force checkpoints at the desired intervals. Also, in such situations, in addition to depending on log switches, either LOG_CHECKPOINT_TIMEOUT or LOG_CHECKPOINT_INTERVAL or both need to be set appropriately to force checkpoints to occur as frequently as required.

The following steps may be performed to evaluate recovery times and use the results as the basis for sizing the online redo-logs.

1. Make a note of the recovery timings that you would like to achieve or those specified in your SLA.
2. If it's a first-time installation, create a test database—10GB or actual size, whichever is smaller (prior to creating the "real" database).

3. If it's an upgrade, then create the same test database on a different machine with similar configurations (so as not to disrupt the original database). If a similar machine is not available for testing, use a less-powered machine for the test. Do not use a machine, which has a higher capacity than the original one (doing so will cause you to overestimate the original machine's recovery capability).
4. Create two online redo-log-files (the size of each file should be the actual size of the redo-logs that you have created or plan to create on the original database).
5. Perform a cold backup of the test database.
6. Create a PL/SQL block (or use Pro*C or SQLJ or your other favorite language/tool) that generates a lot of writes. The writes should be adequate to cause at least four log-switches to occur (thus creating two archived redo-logs to be created and causing both online redo-logs to be overwritten). In order to achieve this, I generally export a reasonably large table (one having a million or so rows) from the original database into the test database (into a non-SYSTEM tablespace), use a PL/SQL block to insert rows off that table into a copy, and then turn around and delete all rows in the copied table. Note that it is imperative to cause the redo-log switches to occur via actual writes and not the ALTER SYSTEM command. The latter would cause smaller archived redo-logs to be created, which won't give a true picture of the time required to roll forward during recovery. Once you get two archived redo-logs, follow your normal process of backing up those archived redo-logs—compress them (if that's your practice), archive them off to tape, and delete them from disk.
7. From the OS, delete a data-file of the tablespace that held the table.
8. Wait for Oracle to crash. Run the same PL/SQL block mentioned in step 6. That will expedite the crash.
9. Restore the deleted data-file to the original directory from the cold backup taken in step 5).
10. Log onto Server Manager and mount the test database.
11. Set auto-recovery off.
12. Attempt to recover the database with the "RECOVER DATABASE" command. It will prompt you for the first archived redo-log.
13. Restore the archived redo-logs from tape (or the actual backup media used to simulate a real recovery scenario). Time the entire restoration process.

14. Apply both the archived redo-logs. Again, time the entire roll-forward process for both logs.
15. Open the database and ensure that all rows in both tables (the original and the copy) are intact.
16. Based on the time it took to roll forward each archived redo-log, note the following:
    - Percentage of time that the roll-forward process takes up in total recovery (for example, roll forward takes up 35 percent of the total recovery time)
    - Maximum number of archived redo-logs permissible to meet your desired recovery times (note that you can afford to apply only a certain number of archived redo-logs, each of a certain size, to meet the required recovery times)

Based on the results of the preceding test, in order to restore availability within the required time, you would need to ensure the following:

- Backups are taken at adequately frequent intervals, so that at any given point in time, not more than a specific number of archived redo-logs files would need to be restored and rolled forward (guaranteeing that recovery occurs within a certain maximum time limit). The more rapidly a tablespace generates redo information, the more useful it is to increase the frequency of backups for that tablespace (so that a fairly current version of the backup can be available during recovery).
- The size of each archived redo-log is set appropriately to prevent total roll-forward times (TRFT) from pushing overall recovery time beyond what is acceptable to the organization. In other words, actual time to roll forward using all archived logs created since the last backup would need to be well within the overall available recovery window. Thus, the following relationship would need to hold true:

```
(Avg. roll-forward time per archived log × maximum # of archived
logs generated since last backup) <= TRFT acceptable
```

The preceding tests would provide you with approximate values for the checkpoint interval and online redo-log sizes—that is, values that would be appropriate for your environment. It might take a few iterations of setting and resetting the values (of LOG_CHECKPOINT_INTERVAL and LOG_CHECKPOINT_TIMEOUT) and dropping and recreating the online redo-logs to arrive at the most appropriate values to ensure that desired recovery timelines are met.

Always consider the lowest unit of recovery

With databases getting bigger and bigger, recovering them completely can take hours, possibly even days. Such high downtime is unthinkable in any 24×7 environment. Accordingly, it is essential for the DBA to evaluate and apply the right unit of recovery, such that overall downtime is minimized.

Oracle allows recovery at different levels: database, tablespace, and data-file. Starting with Oracle8 v8.0.3, even tablespace point-in-time recovery (TSPITR) is supported. (It is to be noted that in v8.0.3, TSPITR was completely manual, making it a complex, error-prone procedure, whereas starting with v8.0.4, scripts have been provided to make it automated, thus increasing its operational reliability.) Each level has varying effects on database availability and MTTR (mean time to recover). For instance, the database has to be shut down in order to perform database recovery, causing zero availability during database recovery. However, the database can be open and only the specific tablespace or data-file needs to be offline and unavailable during tablespace or data-file recovery respectively. Of course, the SYSTEM tablespace and other tablespaces with active rollback segments are exceptions, and the entire database has to be closed while recovering these tablespaces. Depending on the outage situation, each level can expedite or delay the recovery process, thus affecting MTTR. For example, during database recovery, you cannot have multiple sessions applying recovery in parallel, but you can have parallel recovery threads in the same session (if the initialization parameter RECOVERY_PARALLELISM > 1). In the case of tablespace or data-file recovery, you can have multiple sessions with multiple recovery threads for each session, working in parallel on different tablespaces or data-files.

As a general rule-of-thumb, however, it should be noted that the lower the level of recovery, the higher the availability, because lower recovery levels such as for tablespace and data-file recovery allow portions of the database to be open and available to users. Accordingly in any outage situation, always consider data-file recovery first. If that's not appropriate, consider tablespace recovery, and if that's not appropriate either, then try database recovery as the last resort. Also, make it a point not to violate referential integrity or point-in-time consistency across segments, while attempting a lower unit of recovery. This may cause logical corruption with the database. Avoiding such situations requires robust knowledge of the application model from the DBA.

Always examine *v$datafile* prior to recovery

Just prior to performing recovery, always check the status of every data-file, whether they are offline or online. An offline data-file is not recovered by Oracle. In other words, if a data-file is offline while applying archived redo-logs for recovery, that data-file will not be rolled forward. This is convenient in the case of read-only tablespaces, where the data within is not subject to any changes. It's also not an issue if all data-files belonging to a tablespace have been taken offline via the NORMAL option. However, if incomplete recovery has been performed, and a tablespace has been taken offline via the IMMEDIATE or TEMPORARY option, it would need to be rebuilt, potentially causing data-loss within that tablespace. This is because after incomplete recovery, the database would be opened with the RESETLOGS option, thus reinitializing the online redo-logs. When an attempt is made to bring the tablespace online again, it would demand recovery from archived logs that were created prior to using the RESETLOGS option, thus making recovery of that tablespace very difficult.

Data-files can be either online or offline. They are not available for access when they are offline. Data-files may be taken offline individually or at the tablespace level. Generally data-files are not taken offline individually, unless there is a problem, such as read/write errors or file corruption. However, tablespaces may be taken offline either due to problems, for performing maintenance work, or to temporarily prevent access by users. When a tablespace is taken offline, all data-files belonging to that tablespace would be offline. All tablespaces except the SYSTEM tablespace can be taken offline. Tablespaces containing critical data should never be taken offline in a 24×7 environment, unless it's a scheduled outage. A data-file may be taken offline either via the DATAFILE OFFLINE option of the ALTER DATABASE command or via the DATAFILE OFFLINE DROP. The former option may be used only when the database is in ARCHIVELOG mode. A tablespace may also be taken offline in different modes such as NORMAL, IMMEDIATE, and TEMPORARY. When the NORMAL option is used, Oracle performs a checkpoint on all data-files prior to taking them offline, thus ensuring that they are valid and consistent when brought online again. The NORMAL option can be used whether the database is in ARCHIVELOG mode or not and is the recommended way of taking a tablespace offline. However, the NORMAL option cannot be used when one or all of the data-files belonging to the tablespace have problems such as file corruption and it is not possible to checkpoint them. During such situations, it becomes essential to use the TEMPORARY (some data-files unavailable for checkpointing) or IMMEDIATE (all data-files unavailable for checkpointing) options. Those data-files would require recovery to be performed (either data-file recovery or tablespace recovery) prior to making that tablespaces online again. If there is a database crash after the files have been repaired, but prior to making them online again, and the crash requires incomplete media recovery to be performed, the subsequent RESETLOGS option used to recover the database would render that offline tablespace useless. The only way of recovering that tablespace would be to restore a previous backup onto a different machine and use the archived redo-logs to apply recovery until just before the database failure, thus wasting heavy time and resources. Hence, prior to recovery, always make it a point to examine *v$datafile* to ensure all critical tablespaces are online. However, allow data-files of read-only tablespaces (another tip discusses this in detail) or tablespaces taken offline with the NORMAL option to remain that way (because they would already be consistent, and you may not want them to be subjected to recovery operations).

Maintain a special *init.ora file* for recovery operations

Even though recovery occurs rarely during the lifetime of a database, it is essential to ensure that every step is taken to expedite recovery and restore availability. A simple method to achieve high recovery times is to maintain a special *init.ora* file to be used only during recovery. The values of certain Oracle initialization parameters within this file can be set as high as possible, without worrying about concurrent jobs, user-sessions, and so on. Usually during regular operations, values for those initialization parameters cannot be set too high, since the resources are limited and need to be shared among multiple users and processes. However, after the database has crashed, there should be very little (if any, at all) user activity going on in the database server. Accordingly, more resources are available and Oracle should be made to use those resources via a separate "recovery only" *init.ora* file.

Based on the earlier discussion about factors affecting recovery time, the values for the following key parameters should be set differently during recovery (in the special recovery-only *init.ora* file).

DB_BLOCK_BUFFERS

Should be set as high as physical memory will accommodate (that is, excessive paging or swapping should not be caused). Increasing the number of data-block buffers available for recovery will increase cache-hits, since data to be applied to the data-files during both roll-forward and roll-backward can be pre-read and the data-block buffers populated, thus reducing physical disk reads.

SHARED_POOL_SIZE

Should be reduced and set very low. Generally during normal database use, the SHARED_POOL_SIZE should be given precedence and set as high as necessary, even prior to tuning the data-block buffer cache. However, during recovery, the shared-pool plays a minimal role and should be set lower to allow the data-block buffer cache to be increased, instead. Other shared-pool related parameters such as SHARED_POOL_MIN_ALLOC should be tuned down accordingly.

Asynchronous I/O

Enabling asynchronous I/O during recovery allows the server process performing the recovery (or each thread of the server process, in the case of parallel recovery) to obtain higher throughput, since wait-times do not have to be incurred for every system call. The actual parameter name for enabling asynchronous I/O varies with the OS.

DBWR Related Parameters

Another area where asynchronous I/O would help is to increase DBWR thoroughput. If asynchronous I/O does not seem effective for your OS, then try starting up multiple DBWR slaves via the parameters DB_WRITERS (in Oracle7) or DBWR_IO_SLAVES (in Oracle8). In Oracle7, having multiple DBWR processes is mutually exclusive with enabling asynchronous I/O. However, in Oracle8 on certain operating systems, an additional parameter, DB_WRITER_PROCESSES, allows multiple DBWR processes to be started up, even with asynchronous I/O being enabled. In the case of the latter, however, the parameter DB_BLOCK_LRU_LATCHES overrides the DB_WRITER_PROCESSES parameter, and Oracle will only start up as many DBWR processes as specified by DB_BLOCK_LRU_LATCHES (which defaults to 1). Hence, make sure that DB_BLOCK_LRU_LATCHES matches DB_WRITER_PROCESSES. Also, depending on the Oracle version and OS flavor, different initialization parameters such as DB_FILE_SIMULTANEOUS_WRITES, _DB_BLOCK_MAX_SCAN_CNT, _DB_WRITER_SCAN_DEPTH, _DB_WRITER_SCAN_DEPTH_INCREMENT, _DB_WRITER_SCAN_DEPTH_DECREMENT, _DB_BLOCK_WRITE_BATCH, _DB_WRITER_MAX_WRITES, _DB_LARGE_DIRTY_QUEUE, _DB_WRITER_CHUNK_WRITES, _DB_BLOCK_MED_PRIORITY_BATCH_SIZE, _DB_BLOCK_HI_PRIORITY_BATCH_SIZE, _DBWR_ASYNC_IO, and DB_BLOCK_MAX_DIRTY_TARGET can be changed to increase DBWR throughput. (Please refer to Chapter 7 for an explanation of these parameters.) Some of these parameters are undocumented and may not apply to the Oracle version on your platform. You can check whether the Oracle version you use supports these parameters via the following SQL statement:

```
SQL> SELECT ksppinm FROM x$ksppi;
```

Parallel Query Option (PQO)–Related Parameters

PQO should be configured during recovery according to the number of CPUs available, the size and number of data-files to be recovered, the degree of parallelism to be applied during recovery, and so on. Parallel server processes equivalent to the number of CPUs should be pre-started (via the PARALLEL_MIN_PROCESSES). The maximum number of parallel servers should be set to twice the number of CPUs (via PARALLEL_MAX_PROCESSES). RECOVERY_PARALLELISM should be set equivalent to or less than PARALLEL_MAX_PROCESSES, but higher than or equivalent to PARALLEL_MIN_PROCESSES.

As a side note, configuring a large data-block buffer cache is crucial, even more than attempting parallel recovery. Parallel recovery on a non-OPS system still has a single point of input—that is, the archived redo-logs. Accordingly, using parallelism does not substantially enhance the recovery time, because archived logs are the bottleneck. However, configuring a large buffer cache and keeping other recovery-irrelevant memory structures reduced in the recovery-specific initialization parameter file will expedite recovery time.

Multithreaded Server (MTS)–Related Parameters

All MTS parameters should be disabled. Media recovery may not be performed using a dispatcher because, due to memory requirements, this recovery method is not allowed. Even if MTS is enabled, the DBA would need to log on using a dedicated server to perform recovery.

Other important parameters such as SORT_AREA_SIZE, LOG_BUFFERS, and so on may remain untouched, since they do not influence recovery as much. However, if they are set too high, they may be reduced to restrict their resource consumption and instead provide the maximum resources to the data-block buffer cache. It is to be noted that after a certain point, the law of diminishing returns comes into play, and the rate of effectiveness of increasing the data-block buffers or parallelism is reduced and may even prove detrimental. It is desirable that the effectiveness of adding data-block buffers during recovery be tested for each production environment on a similarly configured test box by simulating different recovery scenarios. If this has not been done, then at least ensure that you never cross the limits imposed by physical resources (RAM, number of CPUs, and so on) in allocating data-block buffers, parallelism, and so on. As long as resource limits are never exceeded, increasing values for these parameters may result in diminishing returns; however, they will not prove detrimental. (Only when the values exceed the available resources do they become harmful by increasing inter process/inter-thread communication overheads, paging and swapping, and so on.)

NOTE
All the underscore parameters listed previously are explained purely from an informational perspective—just to aid you understand how Oracle operates internally. Please do not change any undocumented initialization parameters, unless specifically requested to do so by Oracle Support. These parameters are core parameters, directly affecting the way Oracle works. Accordingly, changing them without accurate, in-depth knowledge of their functionality and impact may potentially corrupt your database and render it useless. Also, changing them without Oracle Support's explicit permission violates your Support contract and changes your database into an unsupported one (something every 24×7 site can do without!).

Always use RESETLOGS as the last resort

During recovery, use the RESETLOGS option to open the database as the last option (except when recovering using a hot backup, where using the RESETLOGS option is necessary to recreate the online redo-logs). Always try to open the database with the NORESETLOGS option first. Only if that errors out, use RESETLOGS. As discussed earlier, opening the database with the RESETLOGS option creates a new "incarnation" of the database by reinitializing the online redo-logs (sets the log sequence to 1) and recreating them, if they don't exist. Subsequently, recovery from a different database failure, requiring an older backup and archived redo-logs created prior to the RESETLOGS, is very difficult. In other words, it's very difficult to apply older backups going forward, since Oracle has started a new stream of redo and an older redo stream cannot be easily resolved to mix with the new. Accordingly, after recovery with RESETLOGS, take a hot/cold backup immediately. Another repercussion of using the RESETLOGS option is that if your site uses standby databases, they would need to be rebuilt.

As a side note, starting with Oracle7 v7.3.3, there is a workaround available to recovering past the RESETLOGS option. In versions prior to v7.3.3, recovery beyond RESETLOGS was not possible. Typically, RESETLOGS constituted a one-way trip to a brand new database, making a post-RESETLOGS backup very critical. However, taking a hot backup immediate after RESETLOGS, potentially right in the middle of peak business hours, was not an ideal solution in many cases—since that might cause unacceptable performance during those critical hours. Alternatively, operating without a backup of the database immediately after RESETLOGS jeopardized subsequent changes made to the database. Without backups, recovery only up to the RESETLOGS-SCN was possible. All post-RESETLOGS DML/DDL would have to be manually redone, thus potentially causing large periods of partial or complete downtime (during the time, the batch processes are rerun or data is reentered).

Use RESETLOGS as the Last Resort

Post-RESETLOGS backups are still highly critical. However, in case things go wrong and the backup does not complete successfully, there is still a ray of hope—an option to recover past RESETLOGS in a specific situation. The specific situation involves the following (all conditions must apply) in a v7.3.3 or higher version:

- A valid post-RESETLOGS backup does not exist.
- A valid backup exists that has been taken *just prior* to using the RESETLOGS option (this would be a cold backup).
- A valid control-file of the post-RESETLOGS database incarnation exists.

Also ideally, the alert-log listing the database failure, followed by recovery, use of the RESETLOGS option, and all subsequent operations should be available. Usage of this option is explained in the Oracle documentation set (*Oracle8 Server Backup and Recovery Guide*). However, taking a cold backup just prior to applying the RESETLOGS option may not be realistically viable to 24×7 and/or VLDB sites, due to the extensive downtime involved. There is a workaround for recovery, if an immediate pre-RESETLOGS backup does not exist but an older valid backup exists.

This older valid backup may have been taken any time prior to the RESETLOGS option—it doesn't matter if there is redo generated in the interval between the backup being taken and the RESETLOGS option being used, because the workaround involves rolling forward using the backups up to the point of RESETLOGS. The SCN to roll forward to can be determined either from the alert-log (as outlined in a subsequent paragraph) or by querying for the RESETLOGS_CHANGE# from *v$database* and subtracting one from it. However, this workaround is not endorsed by Oracle Support due to the fact that rolling forward up to RESETLOGS is a delicate and error-prone process. Any errors here may cause the recovery process to be aborted and then restarted, greatly delaying the recovery process. Accordingly, the time invested in taking a backup just prior to using the RESETLOGS option may be more than worth its while. A couple of errors and you are back to square one—having to restart recovery from scratch. In any case, if a standby database is functioning while the primary database is being recovered, there shouldn't be as much pressure to save time by skipping the backup. (Of course, if there isn't a standby database or if the standby database has experienced problems simultaneously or if the standby database server is not capable of handling peak database loads, then there may be enough justification to save every possible second.) The *Oracle8 Backup and Recovery Handbook* from Oracle Press (Osborne/McGraw-Hill Publications) outlines both the supported (where a pre-RESETLOGS backup is taken) and unsupported (where such a backup was not taken or the backup attempt was not successful) versions of recovering past RESETLOGS.

The mechanism that makes recovery beyond RESETLOGS possible works as follows: The control-file (and the appropriate data-file header) maintains the *online SCN* and the *offline SCN* applicable to every online data-file in read/write mode. These online and offline SCNs mark the beginning of the SCN sequence for the current incarnation of the database. In other words, the lifetime of a database is between two successive RESETLOGS points, defined by the online and offline SCNs. Each data-file header also maintains the SCN that was current during the RESETLOGS operation (termed the RESETLOGS SCN). Thus during a RESETLOGS operation, the file header is stamped with a new RESETLOGS SCN and the offline/online SCNs in the control-file are changed accordingly. The online SCN is set equivalent to the RESETLOGS SCN, and the offline SCN is set to RESETLOGS SCN minus one. The offline/online SCN range, is in effect used to make the data-files offline for the duration of the RESETLOGS operation. Thus, the RESETLOGS SCN would not correspond to any genuine transaction within the database. Recovery (while rolling forward) would only be possible up to the SCN just prior to the RESETLOGS SCN. In versions prior to 7.3.3, the offline/online SCN range was not changed after RESETLOGS. The redo sequence was simply reinitialized starting with one, thus making recovery beyond the point of RESETLOGS impossible. In v7.3.3 and above, however, the offline SCN is updated to clearly identify the point of RESETLOGS. The redo is continuous up to and beyond the point of RESETLOGS, so rolling forward using a valid older backup up to that point is physically legal and results in a consistent database. However, to make the database current with DML/DDL changes made after RESETLOGS has been used, a control-file belonging to the post-RESETLOGS incarnation is required. This control-file would have the new offline/online SCNs, indicating the point in the redo stream at which the RESETLOGS occurred. Thus, it is possible for Oracle to "step over" the offline SCN to recover beyond the point of RESETLOGS. A dump of a data-file header would reveal the current offline and online SCNs and other pertinent information such as the checkpoint status, RBA (redo byte address, marking the beginning of a redo-record, explained earlier, within an online or archived redo-log file that would be necessary for rolling forward), and so on. Certain information may also be viewed in the *v$datafile_header* dynamic view (columns such as RESETLOGS_CHANGE# and RESETLOGS_TIME may be useful). The data-file header may be dumped for more detailed information via the following command:

```
SVRMGR> ALTER SESSION SET EVENTS 'IMMEDIATE TRACE NAME FILE_HDRS LEVEL 10';
```

Following is a sample output of the preceding dump command for the first data-file, that is, SYSTEM01.DBF (note that this dump has been produced from a fairly inactive database):

```
DUMP OF DATA FILES: 8 files in database
DATA FILE #1:
  (name #3) D:\ORACLE\ORADATA\ORCL\SYSTEM01.DBF
creation size=25600 block size=4096 status=0xe head=3 tail=3 dup=1
 tablespace 0, index=1 krfil=1 prev_file=0
 unrecoverable scn: 0x0000.00000000 01/01/88 00:00:00
 Checkpoint cnt:590 scn: 0x0000.000e49da 05/25/99 12:58:16
 Stop scn: 0xffff.ffffffff 05/13/99 13:11:19
 Creation Checkpointed at scn:  0x0000.00000003 03/16/99 22:54:09
 thread:1 rba:(0x1.3.10)
 Offline scn: 0x0000.00000000 prev_range: 0
 Online Checkpointed at scn:  0x0000.00000000
 thread:0 rba:(0x0.0.0)
 Hot Backup end marker scn: 0x0000.00000000
FILE HEADER:
       Software vsn=135282688=0x8104000, Compatibility
Vsn=134217728=0x8000000
       Db Id=1351883207=0x509419c7, Db Name='ORC8'
       Control Seq=1681=0x691, File size=51200=0xc800
       File Number=1, Blksiz=4096, File Type=3 DATA
Tablespace #0 - SYSTEM  rel_fn:1
Creation   at   scn: 0x0000.00000003 03/16/99 22:54:09
```

```
Backup taken at scn: 0x0000.00000000 01/01/88 00:00:00 thread:0
reset logs count:0x15797f47 scn: 0x0000.00000001 recovered at 05/25/99
12:58:12
 status:0x4 root dba:0x00400123 chkpt cnt: 590 ctl cnt:589
begin-hot-backup file size: 0
Checkpointed at scn:  0x0000.000e49da 05/25/99 12:58:16
 thread:1 rba:(0x1f4.2.10)
Backup Checkpointed at scn:  0x0000.00000000
External cache id: 0x0 0x0 0x0 0x0
Absolute fuzzy scn: 0x0000.00000000
Recovery fuzzy scn: 0x0000.00000000 01/01/88 00:00:00
```

Also as mentioned earlier, it's advisable to take a backup of the control-file immediately after the RESETLOGS is done, to retain the information regarding the offline ranges for all data-files in the database. When a tablespace status is changed (made online or read/write) after the RESETLOGS, the control-file has new offline ranges for the data-files comprising those tablespaces. In other words, new offline and online SCNs will be maintained. The data-files are not considered as being offline for the SCN generated during the time of RESETLOGS, thus making them useless for recovery beyond RESETLOGS.

To ensure that the correct version of the control-file is being used for recovery beyond RESETLOGS, you can dump the control-file by executing the following command in SQL*Plus:

```
SQL> ALTER SESSION SET EVENTS 'IMMEDIATE TRACE NAME CONTROLF LEVEL 10';
```

When the trace-file containing the control-file dump is opened, search for the line starting with the words "Resetlogs scn." A sample of the control-file dump is shown below:

```
DUMP OF CONTROL FILES, Seq # 1682 = 0x692
 FILE HEADER:
 DB Name "ORC8"
 Database flags = 0x00004000
 Controlfile Creation Timestamp  03/16/99 22:53:00
 Incmplt recovery scn: 0x0000.00000000
Resetlogs scn: 0x0000.00000001 Resetlogs Timestamp  03/16/99 22:52:55
 Prior resetlogs scn: 0x0000.00000000 Prior resetlogs Timestamp  01/01/88
00:00:00
 Redo Version: creation=0x8104000 compatable=0x8103000
 #Data files = 8, #Online files = 8
 Database checkpoint: Thread=1 scn: 0x0000.000e49da
 Max log members = 2, Max data members = 1
 Arch list: Head=0, Tail=0, Force scn: 0x0000.000dad7c
 Controlfile Checkpointed at scn:  0x0000.000e49da
 thread:0 rba:(0x0.0.0)
```

This RESETLOGS SCN must be equivalent to the change # in the database alert-log plus one (the alert-log contains the change # in the RESETLOGS message as "RESETLOGS after complete recovery through change <nnnnnnnnn>" or "RESETLOGS after incomplete recovery until change <nnnnnnnnn>").

Evaluate all UNRECOVERABLE and NOLOGGING operations

Starting with Oracle7 v7.2, the UNRECOVERABLE option is supported for avoiding redo generation during certain DDL operations (such as table/index creations). Oracle8 introduced a new segment attribute called NOLOGGING, where the creation of that segment and all subsequent direct DML activity involving that segment would not generate redo. Evaluate all operations that bypass logging to the online redo-logs. Question the necessity of all such operations. If they are totally needed from a performance perspective, then take a backup as soon as possible to get these operations recorded. Remember, not having transactions logged in the online redo-logs can have other repercussions as well, such as operations not being transferred to the standby database. UNRECOVERABLE/NOLOGGING operations help performance but increase administrative overhead (requiring having to take an additional backup and rebuilding standby databases). As explained in Chapter 1, such operations could also increase downtime. Accordingly, use them only when absolutely necessary. Consider backing up using RMAN's incremental backup facility after all UNRECOVERABLE/NOLOGGING operations to reduce backup time.

Categorize all segments and tablespaces for recovery

Not all segments (tables, indexes, and so on) need to be recovered. In the event of a database crash, applying the backups and rolling forward the archived logs would allow recovery. However, in certain situations (especially DSS systems such as data-warehouses and data-marts), it is easier and faster to rebuild the segments than to apply recovery. If the rebuild time is less than the recovery time, this fact makes the archived logs redundant, since a rational DBA would use the former approach. If it is not feasible to rebuild the segments from scratch, it is desirable to restore the backups and then rerun some of the incremental batch jobs to repopulate the objects and make them current, rather than rolling forward. Let's take a real-life example to illustrate this better.

At one of my client sites, we have a data-mart with a star-schema. The star-schema is composed of four fact tables, six dimensions, and eight summary tables. Each segment type has a different recovery plan, and we have categorized each segment based on its recovery requirements. Table 9-3 outlines the backup/recovery strategy based on each segment category (two tables are provided in each category as an example).

Data-mart: Sales **Used by:** Sales & Marketing Department (S & M Dept.)

Use hours: weekdays 08:00 hrs. to 18:00 hrs.

Availability: Necessary during weekdays during regular use hours. As per SLA, on weekdays, emergency outages consisting of up to 24 hours, once a quarter are tolerable. Downtime is acceptable during weekends and weekdays after hours.

Backup resources available to S & M Dept. during data-mart outages:

- MS-Excel spreadsheets on network file-server
- Printed hard copy of previous days' reports
- Original source of data for the data-mart:
    1. Production database
    2. Manual documents (sales invoices, receipts, and so on)

Archive-log mode: DISABLED

Backup policy:

- OS cold backups during weeknights (run prior to batch jobs that populate data-mart)
- Database exports during weeknights

Reasons for running in NOARCHIVELOG mode:

- Large nightly data-loads cause large number of archived redo-logs to be created and space to hold such large number of archived logs is unavailable
- Recovery policy makes ARCHIVELOG mode unnecessary (time to roll forward using the archived-logs is higher than time to rebuild segments using a combination of OS cold backups and batch-scripts)
- Certain operations involve segments in NOLOGGING mode and those segments need to be rebuilt anyway (even if ARCHIVELOG mode was enabled)

Recovery policy: Database exports are used to recover from table loss. Recovery from disk crashes or file losses (corruptions, deletions, etc.) depends on segment category and is listed under the "Recovery strategy" below.

Segment category I: Restore_and_Rebuild

Segment name	**Segment type**	**Recovery strategy**
Sales_Invoices	Fact table	■ Restore from cold backups to get to previous night's state ■ Rerun previous night's batch jobs (as necessary) to get all latest transactions
Sales_Summaries	Fact/Summary table	

Segment category II: Restore_Only

Segment name	**Segment type**	**Recovery strategy**
Products_Dim	Dimension table	■ Restore from cold backups to get to previous night's state (these tables are static and no batch job needs to be rerun to make these tables current)
Period_Dim	Dimension table	

TABLE 9-3. *Table outlining recovery strategy based on segment categories*

Segment category III: Rebuild_Only

Segment name	Segment type	Recovery strategy
Last_Day_Invoice_Totals Last_Day_Total_Sales	Summary table Summary table	■ These tables are populated based on the previous night's batch jobs. Hence the restore from the cold backup would not populate these with valid values. Hence these tables would need to be truncated and the previous night's batch job to populate them would need to be rerun.

TABLE 9-3. *Table outlining recovery strategy based on segment categories* (continued)

NOTE
Why is an export being done every night, in addition to a cold backup? Both a cold backup and an export may be done nightly to allow more recovery flexibility. An export wouldn't necessarily be of the entire database. It may be done for just a couple of static key tables (depending on the application) to just have a backup of those tables, allowing easy table-recovery (without having to roll forward, and so on). Another useful approach is to export every night certain key dynamic tables, if they need to be pushed across to a DSS environment, where they can be queried without affecting production activity. There are many instances of cold/hot backups and exports being done nightly/weekly at my client sites, mainly to facilitate recovery and/or data migration, with the least impact on the production database (data is quickly exported via direct path to minimize impact).

As mentioned in Table 9-3, some segments in the data-mart are in NOLOGGING mode. Accordingly, certain direct operations (refer to the Oracle8 documentation for a description of these direct operations) would not be logged in the redo-logs. Accordingly, planning merely to apply the archived redo-logs (in the event of a crash prior to a full-fledged backup after the NOLOGGING operation) will not repopulate those segments with all the latest transactions. From this perspective, it is necessary to introduce a "rebuild" strategy for some of these segments into the overall recovery plan to ensure total recovery. In the preceding scenario, cold backups and exports are taken. The cold backup allows the database to be brought to the previous night's state, after which only the "deltas" (changes to the data since last night) need to be captured and propagated into the data-mart via the incremental batch scripts. The exports provide an additional layer of protection and more flexibility for table recovery.

Chapter 6 provides additional examples of segment classifications based on backup/recovery requirements.

Besides classifying segments, it's advisable to categorize all tablespaces/data-files too, based on availability requirements. This helps in determining recovery priority. For instance, if multiple data-files/tablespaces need recovery, it's easier to decide which one to recover and make available first. Another criterion for classifying tablespaces/data-files would be the transactional activity that they undergo. Place tablespaces/data-files undergoing no modifications (read-only), low modifications, and high modifications into separate "recovery groups". Depending on their transaction rate, it can be decided whether recovery for tablespaces/data-files in a certain group needs to be serialized or parallelized. Additionally, physical placement of these tablespaces/data-files (with respect to disks/controllers) should help decide which of these tablespaces/data-files can be recovered simultaneously without impeding each other.

Keep tablespaces without write activity READONLY to expedite backup and recovery

Tablespaces with no write activity do not need recovery. Typically read-only tablespaces contain reference/lookup data (such as dimensions in a data-mart or master tables in an OLTP database) or historical data, and so there are no transactions to roll forward/backward to. Oracle does not try to recover READONLY tablespaces, thus expediting recovery (since there is a lesser number of tablespaces to be recovered). Similarly, this expedites backups, as well. READONLY tablespaces need to be backed up only once (as soon as they are made READONLY). Subsequent backups do not have to back them up. This results in faster backups, since there are fewer tablespaces to be backed up.

When performing incomplete recovery or using a backup control-file, it is essential to take all READONLY tablespaces offline, because otherwise, the RESETLOGS option used during such scenarios will attempt to write to the READONLY data-files. Once recovery is complete, those tablespaces can be made online again. Consider the following when making a tablespace READONLY:

- Ensure that there are no active segments in that tablespace (rollback segments, temporary segments, data-dictionary tables/views owned by SYS, and so on).
- Take a backup (at least of the control-file) as soon as a tablespace is made READONLY. A valid backup can be used for restoring a READONLY tablespace even after opening the database with the RESETLOGS option. Similarly, take a backup when the tablespace is made READ WRITE again.

Once a tablespace is made READONLY, it may be transferred to a read-only medium such as a CD-ROM or an optical WORM drive. With Oracle8*i*, there is an even greater advantage to moving tablespaces to such portable media, since a tablespace may be plugged into any existing database very easily. (Chapter 20 discusses transportable tablespaces in more detail.)

Set AUTORECOVERY on during recovery

When manually recovering an Oracle database via Server Manager or Enterprise Manager, set AUTORECOVERY on (either via the commands SET AUTORECOVERY ON or ALTER DATABASE RECOVER AUTOMATIC or by typing in "AUTO" when prompted for a redo-log filename during media recovery). This expedites recovery, since the names/destination of the archived-logs does not have to be specified in response to frequent prompts. Some DBAs prefer not to use AUTORECOVERY, since it may hamper point-in-time-based recovery or incomplete recovery. However, even in such situations, auto-recovery may be turned on and only the requisite number of archived logs may be kept in the archive-log destination. This way, only the files available in the archive-log destination directory would be applied, subsequently allowing you to open the database with the RESETLOGS option.

Tips for Semi-Technical Managers and Supervisors

The following tips are directed toward semi-technical managers and supervisors:

Always test your backups to ensure valid recovery

No matter how important or obvious this sounds, this is one area that gets ignored more often than one would think. On quite a few occasions, I have visited customer sites where the DBAs were just "too busy" with other tasks to test database backups.

It's absolutely necessary to schedule a recovery "practice run" at periodic intervals. Whenever a new backup strategy is implemented or an existing one is revised, it's essential to test whether recovery is possible within the acceptable windows of time. Accordingly, always make it a priority to test your backups before disaster strikes, and you have to find out the hard way that your database backups are useless.

Ensure that relevant DBA staff are fully trained in recovery operations

Most databases seldom undergo recovery during their lifetimes. In fact, most DBAs hope that their databases never crash and force them to have to perform recovery. While this thought in itself is not condemnable (believe me, you don't wanna have a DBA around who secretly wishes for the database to crash), the reason for it is not! Fear of recovery primarily results from a lack of understanding of the recovery mechanisms used by Oracle, lack of experience in performing recovery, inability to deal with pressure during database outages, or a combination of all of these.

Most times, recovery is delayed and runs into hours due to the DBA staff not being trained in recovery. Add panic and confusion to ignorance and you have a great recipe for high downtime. Oracle recovery options are many, and it requires a deep understand to realize which option to use under what circumstance. Ensure that your DBA staff are fully trained and experienced in recovery. Experience comes with practice. Accordingly, it is necessary to ensure that the DBA staff practice various recovery scenarios in a test environment. Furthermore, make sure that they practice recovery using the tools applicable to your environment (RMAN, EBU, IBM ADSM, Legato Networker, and so on) to expedite and ensure smooth and complete recovery.

Also, in case your organization cannot afford to hire full-time DBAs experienced in recovery, then evaluate purchasing the services of a remote DBA, who can dial in remotely to your systems and perform recovery with adequate support from on-site DBAs or Systems Administration staff. In any case, it's a good idea for any 24×7 site to maintain support contracts with experienced senior DBAs to step in and help whenever necessary. It's like buying life insurance and proves invaluable during emergency database outages.

Create a database recovery team

Create a database recovery team to spring into action during outages and ensure that recovery times specified in the SLA are met. It's advisable to involve key members from different areas such as DBAs, systems administrators, and developers in this team. Doing so will ensure that all recovery options are examined. Ensure that all members are well trained in recovery scenarios to avoid operational delays. During outages, it may become essential to get input from different experts to deduce the quickest possible way to recover. For example, a DBA may be familiar with certain "Oracle-recommended" ways to recover from a table corruption. However, recovering from such a scenario may involve restoring the previous night's backup, rolling forward, and so on. Meanwhile a developer may just know off the top of his head that the particular table in question is a "summary" table, which can be completely repopulated via a quick SQL statement without any loss in data. Restoring from backups and subsequent recovery may be redundant (and time consuming) in such a situation.

Document all database structural changes

Every time any structural changes are made to the database (new tablespaces/data-files are added/dropped, core database parameters such as MAXDATAFILES and MAXLOGFILES are changed), ensure that you take detailed notes (in addition to a backup). In case the database crashes after such a change, but prior to the next backup, it becomes a lot easier to attain complete recovery. For example, if a new data-file is added and, just prior to the next backup, the database crashes, then a restore from the most recent backup would restore all the files, except the newly created one. If someone had documented all details about the new file such as the name/path, size, and which tablespace it belongs to, then it would be possible to recreate an empty file via the ALTER DATABASE command during recovery and populate it from the archived redo-logs. However, if such structural changes are not documented, that would be drastically impede recovery operations, thus greatly increasing MTTR.

Summary

This chapter provided some operational tips regarding some of the most critical maintenance operations: backups and recovery. In addition, the process of archiving was studied in detail, and some good practices that increase availability, performance, and administrative ease were discussed. The next chapter focuses on database startup and shutdown procedures.

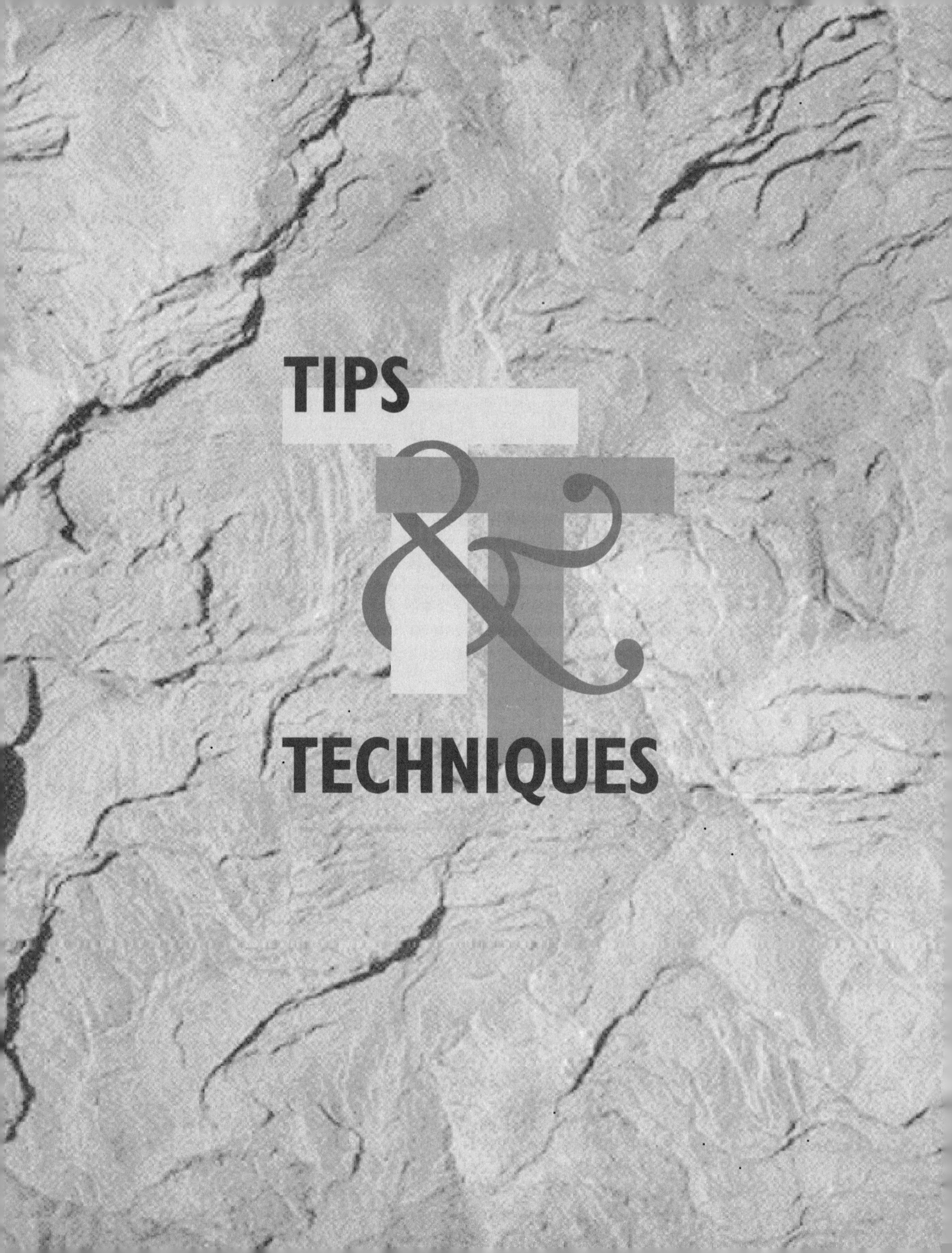
TIPS
&
TECHNIQUES

CHAPTER 10

Startup and Shutdown Procedures

In a 24×7 environment, the terms "startup" and "shutdown" might appear redundant, since a system is theoretically never shut down in such an environment. As any experienced administrator knows, however, these are inevitable events that occur either intentionally or accidentally. Hopefully, in such environments, machines that support mission-critical applications will have adequate failover mechanisms in place to replace the primary systems and reduce the dependence on them when they go down. In the absence of a standby system (I use the term "standby" to refer to a copy of the primary maintained via hardware/software replication techniques, Oracle's standby database feature, etc; these techniques are outlined in Chapters 15–18), however, the speed of restarting a system after it goes down assumes great importance. Even at sites where there are standby systems, albeit less powerful than the primary machines, prolonged periods of operation under the standby systems may not be acceptable to the organization. Accordingly, it becomes critical to restart the primary systems as fast as possible. Additionally, if the time taken to bring up the primary system is lower than or equivalent to the time taken to switch over to a standby system, it may not be worthwhile to resort to using the standby system. Only in situations in which the primary system experiences a serious failure and is expected to remain unavailable for periods longer than the time it takes to switch over to the standby system, is the switch worthwhile. The longer the time taken to restart a system, the higher the MTTR. Having said that, let's take a look at a few tips that affect startup and shutdown procedures, with a view to expediting them, whenever they occur.

NOTE

There are other factors that would influence your decision whether to migrate to the standby database due to the primary database taking a long time to come up. The primary database would need to be resynchronized with the standby database, after it (the primary) finally comes back up. This resynchronizing may take a long time. Furthermore, the standby database may be running on a less powerful system, and once the primary database becomes available, another switchover would need to occur from the secondary to the primary to prevent prolonged periods of running on the less powerful system. This switchback would require another database bounce at the very least, thus adding to the cumulative downtime. Last, the standby would have to be totally rebuilt to match the primary, involving a lot of work.

This chapter offers the following tips and techniques:

- Always automate database startup and shutdown
- Use OEM for starting up/shutting down multiple databases
- Consider a *shutdown abort* during emergencies
- Prior to *shutdown abort*, always do an explicit checkpoint

Startup and Shutdown Procedures

There are certain procedures to expedite startup and shutdown time and make them immune from administrative errors. These are described herein.

Always Automate Database Startup and Shutdown

At times, the systems administrators (see, the DBAs are not the only people causing downtime!) schedule downtime for performing maintenance on a machine. During such times, the database would need to be shut down just prior to taking the box down. When the box is back up and running, the database would need to be restarted. Unless you have a DBA on site *all* the time or your systems administrators are familiar with database startup/shutdown commands, it's necessary that all database startup and shutdown routines be automated, such that the database is shut down and restarted along with the machine. This helps in two ways: a DBA doesn't have to be present during mundane systems maintenance tasks, and it ensures that in case the DBA cannot be reached to restart the database after a scheduled maintenance period, it's not a problem.

Oracle provides different options for automating database startup and shutdown, depending on the platform on which Oracle is being run. Let's take a look at two popular platforms: UNIX and Windows NT.

Database Startup/Shutdown on UNIX

Depending on the version of Oracle installed, either SQL*DBA or Server Manager is primarily used for database startup/shutdown on UNIX. A GUI version of Server Manager is available on Motif/X Window. SQL*DBA had a pseudo-graphical option that worked even in a non-Motif environment. Both SQL*DBA and Server Manager support the line-mode. SQL*DBA can be invoked in line-mode via the commands *sqldba lmode=y* or *sqldba mode=line.* A different executable called *svrmgrl* is provided for invoking Server Manager in line-mode (as compared to *svrmgr,* which is used for invoking Server Manager in graphical mode).

For automatic startup and shutdown on UNIX, Oracle provides two scripts, *dbstart* and *dbshut,* that are present in the *$ORACLE_HOME/bin* directory. A script calling these scripts needs to be placed in the machine boot directories (for example, on Sun Solaris, you would place the calling scripts in the */etc/rc* directories). Both *dbstart* and *dbshut* read the *oratab* configuration file (created by *root.sh* and present in either */etc* or */var/opt/oracle*). All database entries having a "Y" in the last column in *oratab* would be automatically started up or shut down. The *dbstart* script restarts the database even after a hard reboot due to a system crash. Both the *dbstart* and *dbshut* scripts may be modified to perform additional custom tasks such as shutting down the listener (with a non-default name) and other applications prior to shutting down the database, or starting up the listener and other applications after starting up the database (when using the multi-threaded server [MTS] option in Oracle7, it is necessary to start up the listener prior to starting up the database [the reason is explained in a subsequent paragraph]). The precise details of automating database startup/shutdown vary on different UNIX flavors (such as Solaris, HP-UX, AIX, NCR UNIX, etc.). I have attempted to broadly describe them in subsequent paragraphs.

Under System V, all startup/shutdown scripts are placed in the */etc/rc[n].d* directories, where *n* is the script priority level (the higher the number, the higher the priority; this allows critical system processes to be placed in directories with lower priority levels so that they can be shut down last, after all other dependent programs have shut down). Directories with higher values for *n* contain scripts that need to be run during initial stages of system shutdown. Each script is named based on the following convention:

{K|S}{2-digit number} [verbose-name]

The beginning alphabet in the script name needs to be a K or an S, indicating that the script is to be invoked during shutdown or startup, respectively. The scripts within the same directory level (such as */etc/rc2.d*) are invoked in the order of the two-digit number following the K or S. Preference is given to scripts with lower digits. The *verbose-name* is a user-defined name, in most cases, that describes the script functionality. For example, the script to call *dbstart* may be called "S72oracle". Generally, the script that shuts Oracle down is given a lower number (such as "K04oracle"), whereas the script to start up Oracle is given a higher number (such as "S72oracle" in the preceding example). This allows Oracle to be started up after all core dependencies are up and running and allows Oracle to be shut down prior to other core dependencies being shut down.

Under BSD UNIX, all startup scripts can be placed in the */etc/rc* or */etc/rc.local* directories. During shutdown, only the */etc/shutdown* or */etc/rc.shutdown* command is invoked, rather than any system-specific/user-defined scripts. So a script similar to the following would need to be invoked while taking the system down:

```
# !/bin/csh
# to be run as root prior to system shutdown

setenv ORACLE_HOME /oracle/8.0.4
su - oracle -c "$ORACLE_HOME/bin/dbshut"

/etc/shutdown $*
```

The listener also needs to be started up automatically along with the database, so that incoming client requests can be processed. When using the MTS option in Oracle7, it is essential to start up the listener prior to the database, so that the necessary dispatchers and shared servers can be spawned. Otherwise, only the dedicated server(s) get spawned. In Oracle8, this is not an issue; even if the database is started up prior to the listener, the dispatchers and shared servers are still spawned. Nevertheless, in Oracle7, if the listener is not started up prior to the database for some reason, the dispatchers and shared servers can be manually started up via the MTS_DISPATCHERS and MTS_SERVERS options of the ALTER SYSTEM command (these options are invaluable for a 24×7 site, since the listener and the database do not need to be bounced to start up [or even terminate] the requisite number of dispatchers and the shared servers). Similarly, when using MTS, the listener needs to be shut down prior to the database, to prevent new requests from coming in. Starting with SQL*Net v2.x, the *lsnrctl* utility with the *stop <listener-name>* and *start <listener-name>* options may be used to gracefully shut down and start up the listener, respectively (in SQL*Net version 1.x, the protocol-specific tool would need to be used; for example, for TCP/IP, *tcpctl* would be used and for SPX/IPX, *spxctl* would be used). These commands either may be placed in the *dbstart* and *dbshut* scripts (recommended), or they may be placed within separate scripts (with higher or lower priority levels, as necessary). Under BSD UNIX, if the command to shut down the listener(s) is not placed within *dbshut,* then you may place it in the "master" shutdown script described previously. In such a case, the shutdown script would read as follows:

```
# !/bin/csh
# to be run as root prior to system shutdown

setenv ORACLE_HOME /oracle/8.0.4
su - oracle -c "$ORACLE_HOME/bin/lsnrctl stop"
su - oracle -c "$ORACLE_HOME/bin/dbshut"

/etc/shutdown $*
```

Database Startup/Shutdown on Windows NT

On Windows NT, depending on the versions of Oracle installed, there always seem to be a plethora of programs that allow startup and shutdown, such as Oracle

Enterprise Manager, Server Manager, SQL*DBA, Database Manager, and Instance Manager. When to use what is always a puzzle to many DBAs running Oracle on NT. Prior to looking at ways to automate startup/shutdown, let's look at some of these tools and attempt to understand their quirks.

I do not attempt to explain Oracle Enterprise Manager (OEM) here, since it is a rich and multifunctional tool providing far more capabilities than just database startup/shutdown. Moreover, in a subsequent paragraph, I describe Instance Manager, the "component" of OEM (or rather, it is shipped with OEM) that aids in startup/shutdown. Server Manager and SQL*DBA are command-line utilities, very close to their UNIX counterparts (for those who have used them on UNIX). Since they are command-line utilities, they aid in setting up automated scripts, including database startup/shutdown. Unless you are using a version of Oracle prior to 7.2, chances are you won't have to worry about SQL*DBA, since it has been phased out (replaced by Server Manager) and is no longer installed. The executables of SQL*DBA and Server Manager (like other executables on NT) have the tool version number appended to their names. The problem here is, the tool version is not the same as the database version. For example, the version of SQL*DBA for Oracle7 v7.1 is 2.1. Accordingly, the SQL*DBA executable for version 7.1 is called *sqldba21.exe.* Similarly, the version of Server Manager for Oracle7 v7.2 is 2.2, and the executable is named *svrmgr22.exe.* (In Oracle8 v8.0.x, the Server Manager executable on NT is named *svrmgr30.exe.*) This discrepancy seems to have been resolved with Oracle8*i,* where the Server Manager executable is simply *svrmgrl.exe* (like the Server Manager line-mode executable on UNIX). When using either of these tools on an NT box with multiple instances, it's necessary to set the environment variable ORACLE_SID to the instance-name (unless you are connecting to the default instance, set in the Windows registry via the ORACLE_SID registry-key) prior to invoking the tools via the following command:

```
C:\> SET ORACLE_SID=<sid_name>
```

Failure to do so results in the ORA-12203 error ("TNS: Unable to connect to destination"). Figure 10-1 illustrates this.

Another tool that was provided for interactive database startup/shutdown with earlier versions of Oracle is Database Manager. Database Manager is a 16-bit tool intended for Windows version 3.x. However, it can be used on Windows NT under the 16-bit shell (termed as WOW). When used on NT, it needs to be installed on a FAT partition (like all other 16-bit Oracle programs). The executable name for Database Manager is *vsmgr.exe,* and the program is installed under *c:\orawin\bin.* It can be found under the program subgroup *Database Administration Tools.* Database Manager does not refer to the *initSID.ora* file but uses two other files called *vs10.ini* and *vsp10.ini* to store all database parameters (unlike Server Manager or SQL*DBA). It's not advisable to edit these files directly; instead, it's

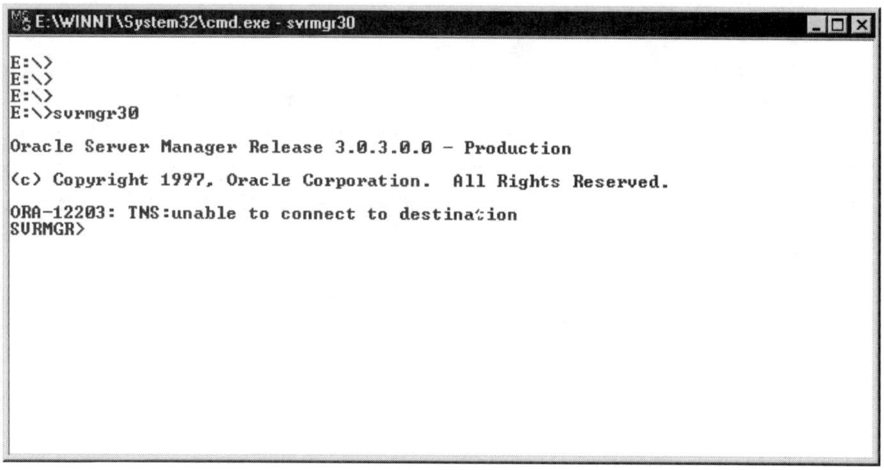

```
E:\WINNT\System32\cmd.exe - svrmgr30

E:\>
E:\>
E:\>
E:\>svrmgr30

Oracle Server Manager Release 3.0.3.0.0 - Production

(c) Copyright 1997, Oracle Corporation.  All Rights Reserved.

ORA-12203: TNS:unable to connect to destination
SVRMGR>
```

FIGURE 10-1. *Invoking Server Manager without setting ORACLE_SID results in an error in multi-instance environments*

advisable to use the tool itself to make changes to the parameters. All changes made via the tool are written to these files. Database Manager handles multiple database instances, since it reads information about each instance from the *oracle.ini* file (this configuration file is also not used anymore, since newer Oracle versions use the NT registry to store configuration information). Database Manager provides a very intuitive GUI interface for database startup/shutdown and displays the database status via a red/yellow/green indicator (similar to a traffic light).

Instance Manager, the portion of OEM that provides database startup/shutdown services, is available in two modes: command-line and interactive. The interactive mode (Figure 10-2) can be invoked via the OEM console or the *Oracle Server for Windows NT* program subgroup along with other OEM tools such as *Backup Manager* and *Schema Manager*. It is a native NT 32-bit application and is named *oradimnn.exe* (where *nn* refers to the actual database version, such as 73 for versions 7.3.x, 80 for versions 8.0.x, and so on). The command-line mode of Instance Manager can be used for scripting database startup and shutdown.

Both the database and the listener can be set for automatic startup in the Services configuration screen (within Control Panel), as shown in Figures 10-3 and 10-4. During shutdown, NT stops all currently running services automatically (including the database and the listener). With some versions of Oracle7, there is a problem during shutdown. Whenever NT goes down, it crashes the Oracle7 instance without shutting it down cleanly. The workaround for this situation is to

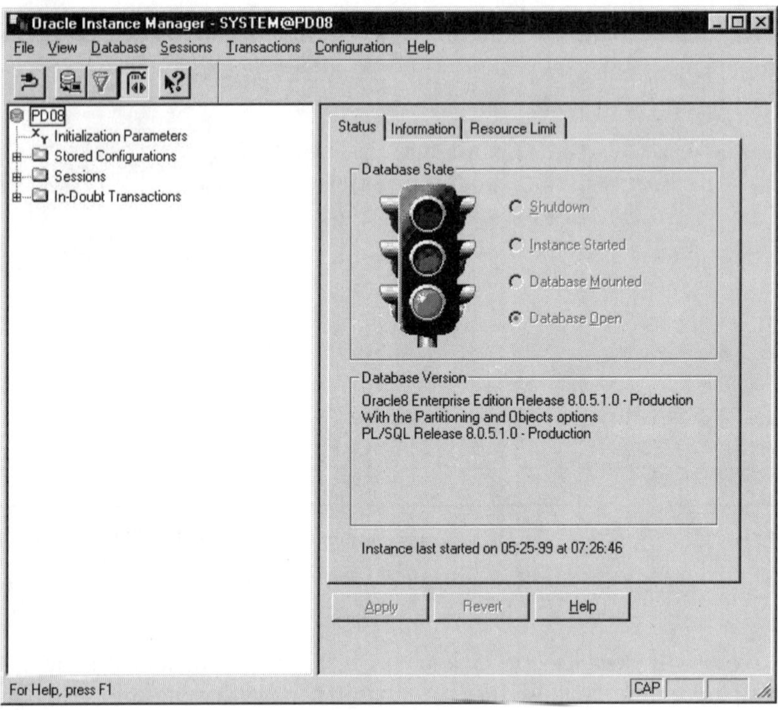

FIGURE 10-2. *Instance Manager in interactive mode*

create a shortcut for the systems administrators to click, prior to rebooting the NT box. This shortcut would run an NT batch file containing the commands to shut down the database and listener gracefully. This can be achieved by invoking Server Manager or Instance Manager in command-line mode within the NT batch file. As a precaution, don't place the shortcut on the NT desktop, since an accidental double-click could cause the database to go down.

Use OEM for Starting Up/Shutting Down Multiple Databases

When managing multiple databases, especially when some of them are on remote machines, it's good to have a single point of control over all the databases. OEM allows such a single point of control via a centralized console that allows you to track different databases either on a single server or spread across different local and

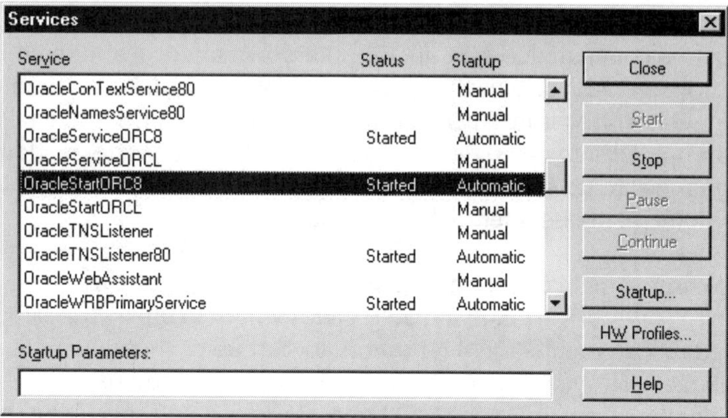

FIGURE 10-3. *The Control Panel Services applet with various Oracle-related services*

remote servers. During an emergency (such as stopping access to a buggy application or applying an urgent patch to all databases), imagine trying to log onto each individual server and shut down the database locally. The process

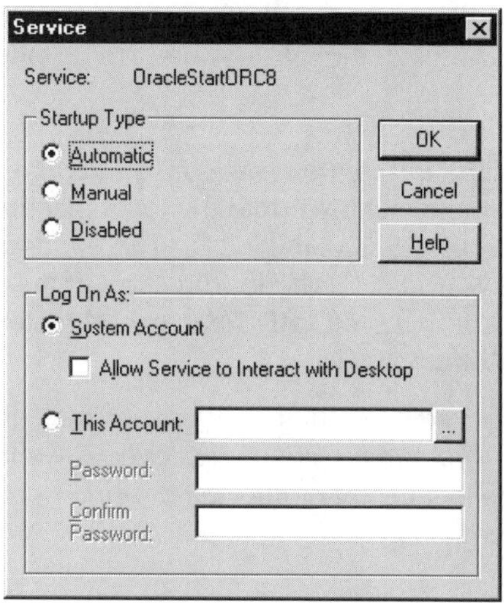

FIGURE 10-4. *The Services applet is used to set the database for automatic startup*

would be susceptible to a number of errors due to the high degree of manual intervention involved.

OEM can be configured to start up and shut down all local and remote databases (from an OEM perspective, local databases are databases on the same machine on which OEM is installed and run). Certain steps need to be taken in order to start up and shut down remote databases. These steps are in addition to the steps required to start up/shut down local databases (for details on controlling local databases via OEM, please refer to the OEM documentation).

- The user ID utilized for starting up or shutting down the database must have the SYSDBA privilege. By default, OEM will try to utilize the same user ID used to log onto the OEM repository to start up or shut down the remote database. This needs to be corrected by selecting the *Preferences* option under the *File* menu of the OEM console screen and specifying the new user ID/password to be utilized for logging onto the remote database. This user ID needs to have the SYSDBA privilege.
- The REMOTE_LOGIN_PASSWORDFILE initialization parameter for the remote database must be set to EXCLUSIVE. Also, the remote server should have an appropriate password file set up via the following command:

```
$ orapwd file=$ORACLE_HOME/dbs/orapw<ORACLE_SID> password=<password>
```

While starting up a remote database via OEM, OEM expects the *init.ora* file for that database to exist locally (that is, on the machine from which OEM is being run). For this reason, the following additional steps need to be taken prior to starting up remote databases:

- Place a copy of the *init<remote-sid>.ora* and *config<remote-sid>.ora* files from the remote machine onto the local machine in the directory *%ORACLE_HOME%\SYSMAN\IFILES. These files are usually present either in the $ORACLE_HOME/dbs* directory (if the source machine runs UNIX) or the *%ORACLE_HOME%/database* directory (if the source machine runs Windows NT).
- Ensure that all nested configuration files specified via the IFILE parameter in the *init<remote-sid>.ora* file are copied over as well and that the IFILE parameter in the local copy of *init<remote-sid>.ora* now points to these local files (rather than continuing to point to the earlier path).

NOTE
Some kind of change-control mechanism needs to be implemented to ensure that all subsequent changes made to the original copies of init.ora *(and other configuration files) are propagated to the local copies used by OEM. Otherwise, the database would be started up with different initialization values depending on where it is started up from (that is, remotely via OEM or locally via Server Manager). Alternatively, starting up the database locally can be prevented (by changing file-access privileges on the Server Manager executables or by renaming them) and the database should only be started up via the OEM console (except during emergencies, such as when the machine running the OEM console is unavailable).*

- Always point to the local copies of the files, whenever starting up the database through OEM either interactively or via a script using the PFILE option.

For Urgent Database Bounce Requirements, Consider a "Shutdown Abort"

Consider this: You need to bounce the database instance real quick—maybe to enable some new initialization parameters or to apply an urgent patch to the OS/database. It's recommended to always perform a normal shutdown. So you log onto Server Manager and type in the command to perform a normal shutdown: *shutdown.* And then you wait . . . and wait . . . and wait . . . The database doesn't seem to want to go down, and in the meantime, all the users are wandering over to your desk asking—"is the database up yet?"

At most sites, especially those dealing with VLDBs, there is always some kind of activity going on in the database that would prevent a normal shutdown. For instance, as the normal shutdown waits for all users to log off, there might be a forgotten user session out there, preventing the shutdown from occurring. During such times a *shutdown immediate* helps. However, even a shutdown immediate may consume a lot of time if a major process is rolling back. During such times, it may be necessary to issue the *shutdown abort* command.

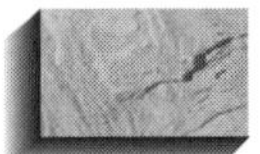

NOTE

This tip does not recommend using the shutdown abort option, unless it's absolutely required. In most cases, the shutdown [normal] or shutdown immediate options should be used. The v$session, v$lock, and v$sqlarea dynamic views can be queried to check the active sessions, the SQL statements they are running, and the objects they have locked (see Chapter 19 for scripts that can be used to query these views to get the requisite information). Based on the results of these queries, a fairly educated decision may be made regarding the mode to be used during the database shutdown. If DML statements, potentially changing a lot of data, are being run, chances are the resultant rollback would consume a lot of time, thus holding up the shutdown process. Hence it would necessitate a shutdown abort. If some small OLTP transactions are being run, however, chances are the rollback won't take a lot of time and the database can safely be shut down in immediate mode.

A shutdown abort terminates all active sessions within the database; prevents new sessions from accessing the database; releases all file-level locks; and, finally, releases the instance-level lock, terminating the instance almost instantaneously. In order to fully comprehend the "shortcut" taken by the shutdown abort command, let's take a look at the steps performed during a normal shutdown:

- Prevent all new sessions from accessing the database (all new attempts to connect would be informed that "database shutdown is currently in progress—new logon denied").
- Take stock of all ongoing database transactions and wait for them to complete their current tasks.
- Release all latches and flush the SGA.
- Wait for all connected users to log out.
- Release all file-level locks.
- Post current SCNs to data-file headers, redo logs, and control files.
- Close the online redo thread for the current instance.
- Release instance-level locks.

Immediately after a shutdown abort, it is advisable to restart the database in restricted mode and then perform a normal shutdown. Then the database is ready for any maintenance activity such as patch applications, initialization parameter changes, cold backups, and so on. After a shutdown abort, when the database is restarted, instance recovery is performed by Oracle, thus causing delays at this point. Many DBAs feel that either way, there is a delay—either you take the hit during shutdown or you take the hit during startup. However, I have observed that instance recovery is usually done a lot faster than the rollback performed during shutdown. The following test serves to illustrate this point:

1. Create a new test database and start up the database.
2. Run any DML statement to perform a lot of writes (a large number of inserts or deletes on a hundred thousand–row table) without any commits. Table *large_test_table* occupies approximately 11MB.

   ```
   SQL> connect appl_user/appl_user

   Connected.

   SQL> DELETE FROM large_test_table;

   120000 rows deleted.
   ```
3. Perform a shutdown immediate.

   ```
   SVRMGR> connect internal

   Connected.

   SVRMGR>shutdown immediate
   ```
4. Record the total time it takes for the database to shut down. In this example situation, it took me a total of 16 minutes for the database to shut down (rolling back the delete of all 120,000 rows or 11MB of data).
5. Restart the database.

   ```
   SVRMGR> startup
   ```
6. Rerun the same large DML statement.

   ```
   SQL> connect appl_user/appl_user

   ERROR: ORA-01041: internal error. hostdef extension doesn't exist


   Connected.
   ```

You get an error (ORA-01041) just prior to the connection being made because the database was shut down while the user "appl_user" was still connected via SQL*Plus.

```
SQL> DELETE FROM large_test_table;

120000 rows deleted.
```

7. Perform a shutdown abort.

```
SVRMGR> connect internal

Connected.

SVRMGR> shutdown abort

ORACLE instance shut down.
```

8. Restart the database.

```
SVRMGR> startup
```

9. Record the total time it takes for the database to start up. In this example, it took a total of *six minutes* for the database to start up.

During the forced rollback caused by a shutdown immediate, PMON cleans up all rollback entries in accordance with the *init.ora* parameter CLEANUP_ROLLBACK_ENTRIES, which defaults to 20 in both Oracle7 and Oracle8. CLEANUP_ROLLBACK_ENTRIES determines the number of undo entries to apply per transaction cleanup. During instance recovery (caused by the subsequent startup after a shutdown abort), depending on the initialization parameter RECOVERY_PARALLELISM, multiple parallel slaves work in tandem to achieve high throughput and fast crash recovery times. By default, parallel recovery is disabled (RECOVERY_PARALLELISM = 0). In the preceding example, RECOVERY_PARALLELISM was set to 4. So there were four parallel processes performing instance recovery.

In the preceding example, it took 6 minutes for instance recovery, compared to the 16 minutes for rollback after a shutdown immediate—a total saving of 10 minutes, or a 62.5 percent improvement. Normally, 10 minutes doesn't sound very impressive or worth doing a shutdown abort. However, in tight situations in which every second is vital with end users breathing down your neck and your company losing revenue, *10 minutes is a lot of time!*

So a shutdown abort may be just the right answer for those genuine *immediate* shutdowns desired by high-availability sites. As long as you immediately perform a restricted startup and a subsequent normal shutdown, you should be just fine.

NOTE
It is absolutely necessary to perform a restricted startup and normal shutdown immediately after a shutdown abort, prior to performing any maintenance tasks such as changing initialization parameters, applying a patch (OS, Oracle, or application), performing cold backups, and so on. There are some known bugs with certain versions of Oracle that could cause database corruption when specific initialization parameters (for instance, the COMPATIBLE parameter) are changed after a shutdown abort (or a startup force). Similarly, a backup (hot or cold) taken immediately after a shutdown abort may be useless.

Just Prior to a SHUTDOWN ABORT do an ALTER SYSTEM CHECKPOINT

Another shutdown-related tip you might find useful is to run the command ALTER SYSTEM CHECKPOINT just prior to a shutdown abort. That will explicitly trigger a checkpoint, after which the shutdown abort may be performed. When you restart the database (to do a normal shutdown), total instance recovery time will be effectively reduced due to a checkpoint having been performed just prior to the shutdown abort. This reduction in crash recovery time is due to the fact that less information in the online redo-logs needs to be applied to the data files after a checkpoint. Let's take a look at the following example (using the same test database mentioned in the previous tip) to see what kind of time savings can be derived:

1. Run a large DML statement without a commit. As mentioned previously, table large_test_table occupies approximately 11MB.

```
SQL> connect appl_user/appl_user

Connected.

SQL> DELETE FROM large_test_table;

120000 rows deleted.
```

2. Trigger an explicit checkpoint and then perform a shutdown abort.

```
SVRMGR> connect internal

Connected.
```

```
SVRMGR> alter system checkpoint;

Statement processed.

SVRMGR> shutdown abort

ORACLE instance shut down.
```

3. Restart the database.

```
SVRMGR> startup
```

4. Record the total time it takes for the database to start up. In this example, it took a total of *40 seconds* for the database to start up, thus translating into a direct time saving of more than 15 minutes or a stunning 2,400 percent improvement over a regular shutdown immediate (as illustrated in the previous tip, the shutdown immediate took 16 minutes).

Summary

This chapter took a brief look at database startup and shutdown procedures with a single objective: to expedite startup and shutdown. Speedy startups are obviously necessary to prevent excessive wait times for users and batch jobs. Shutdown needs to be expedited as well, so that if the situation causing the shutdown is not serious, the database can be restarted immediately (that is, minimizing the time taken by the database bounce). We looked at automating startups and shutdowns, at using OEM for starting up and shutting down remote instances, and also at using the ALTER SYSTEM command to explicitly force a checkpoint, prior to aborting an instance.

The next chapter outlines a variety of general database maintenance tasks and their effects on availability.

PART IV

Database Maintenance

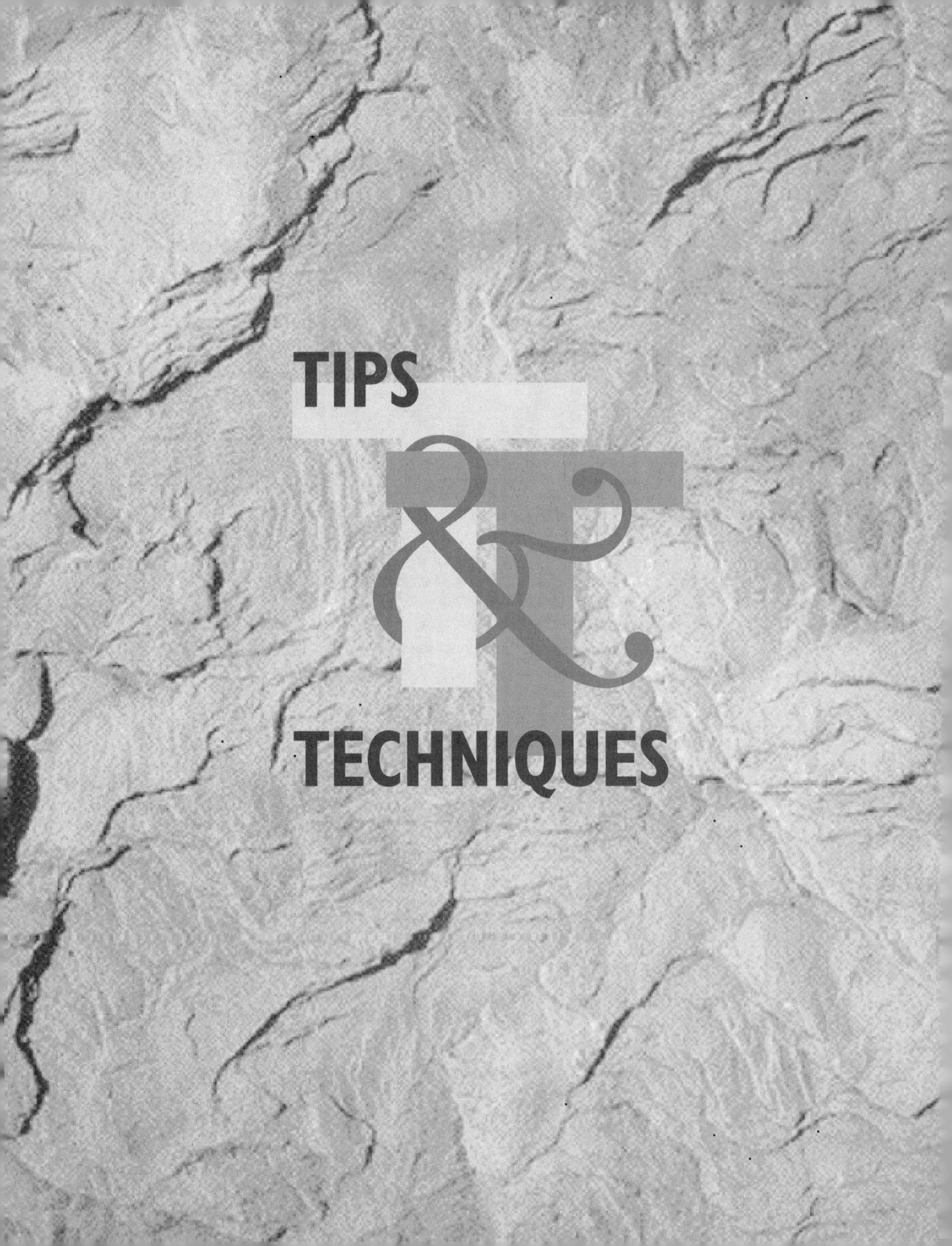
TIPS
&
TECHNIQUES

General Maintenance

Database maintenance is an ongoing effort, undertaken throughout the life of a database. Due to the sophistication of the Oracle RDBMS, it can run without disruption ("lights-out") for certain extended periods. Ironically, the same sophistication involves constant interplay among multiple components, which need to be oiled from time to time to ensure that the system not only runs but also continues to provide acceptable response time and throughput, scaling as necessary to accommodate additional loads. Consider the manifold components involved in the functioning of the database and the ever-increasing data and processing loads driven by enhanced business requirements, and you get an idea about the need for maintenance: patch/version upgrades, initialization parameter changes, defragmentation, index rebuilds, computation of statistics for segments, corruption check/repair, and various other tasks that come under the jurisdiction of maintenance—all become necessary. Many maintenance tasks, especially in versions prior to Oracle8*i*, require downtime. In a 24×7 environment, performing maintenance without violating service level agreements can be a daunting task and requires careful planning and coordination from different administrative personnel.

Note that during certain maintenance tasks, downtime seems to be inevitable. For instance, when applying a patch or repairing table/index corruption or when reorganizing a segment to eliminate fragmentation, access to these segments and at times even the database may have to be disabled, impacting availability adversely. Chapter 15 discusses some strategies that may be used to avoid having to resort to downtime to perform these maintenance tasks. These strategies, such as custom standby databases and standby tables, allow the database and various segments within it to be available for use during the maintenance.

This chapter offers the following tips and techniques:

- Implement robust security at all possible levels
- Understand the "ORA-1555: Snapshot too old" error and take steps to avoid it
- Understand, prevent and resolve latch and enqueue contention
- Be familiar with different wait events and take steps to reduce them
- Periodically watch for and resolve locking conflicts
- Monitor shared-pool effectiveness and tune, if necessary

Proactive and Reactive Maintenance

As mentioned in earlier chapters, maintenance can be proactive or reactive. Reactive maintenance consists of being alerted to (potential) problems and taking corrective actions as soon as possible, often immediately. Proactive maintenance, on the other hand, consists of anticipating common and uncommon problems and taking steps to prevent them from occurring. In any case, constant monitoring is mandatory to ensure that problems that nevertheless occur, get the attention they demand. Generally, reactive maintenance may require immediate downtime to prevent larger periods of downtime in the near future. Proactive maintenance may also require downtime—however, since disaster is not impending, the luxury of planning for and performing such "downtime-requiring" maintenance work during off-peak hours is available. Also, with the appropriate amount of proactiveness and familiarity, one can effectively keep the need for reactive maintenance at bay, preventing potentially large periods of downtime or even sudden outages during peak hours. Realistically, however, one may need to combine proactive and reactive measures to provide end-to-end database maintenance. In any case, one needs to be intimate with the maintenance operations that his or her database requires, carefully evaluate the frequency of such operations, estimate the potential downtime required to perform them, and consider various alternatives/solutions to perform such maintenance work with as little impact on availability as possible.

As I talk of proactive maintenance, a small but sensible rule comes to mind: "If it ain't broke, don't fix it!" What this means is don't go around trying to fix things that are running relatively smoothly in the name of proactive maintenance. By trying to do so, you could possibly cause the component to break down. While locating areas that need proactive maintenance, ensure that you have specific measurable metrics to assist you, such as levels of availability and performance in the SLA. Areas that are having or are likely to have problems if left unattended are candidates for maintenance. Areas that threaten availability and performance currently or in the near future are areas you need to focus on. Most of these areas are easy enough to identify (based on your level of experience). However, there may be some unique components specific to your environment. Ensure that you identify these components via a modeling technique (*Capacity Planning and Performance Modeling* from Prentice Hall is a good source for formulating your models) that allows you to reconcile current processing loads with the capacity and also allows you to predict whether the current capacity will stand up to future anticipated loads. If the current capacity will not, then those components will need to be proactively scaled up.

Maintenance can be scheduled or unscheduled. Generally, proactive maintenance is scheduled, whereas reactive maintenance occurs under urgent circumstances and tends to be unscheduled. Obviously, disruption is greater under the latter scenario. However, even disruptions due to scheduled maintenance may be unacceptable. Accordingly, wherever there is downtime involved, one should schedule it during hours of low database use to minimize impact; and, if 24×7 access is mandatory, then some kind of standby option (standby tables/database) needs to be implemented (Chapters 15 to 18).

Maintenance consists of various tasks that need to occur frequently (regular maintenance), as well as not so frequently (exceptional maintenance). Both regular and exceptional maintenance can be done in a proactive fashion. Examples of regular maintenance tasks include

- Managing database security
- Checking free space and adding data files/tablespaces as necessary; administering segments and space consumption (ensuring that segments do not run out of extents, have adequate free space to extend, and so on)
- Monitoring effectiveness of initialization parameters and altering them, if necessary
- Analyzing segments for CBO use

In other words, steps taken regularly to ensure that availability and performance will not be compromised are geared toward regular maintenance. Examples of exceptional maintenance tasks include

- Database recovery
- Database defragmentation/reorganization
- Corruption repair
- Upgrading versions/applying patches

This chapter focuses on all general maintenance tasks—both regular and exceptional. Also note that there are entire chapters devoted to certain tasks, such as Chapter 8 for handling upgrades, Chapter 9 for performing recovery, Chapter 12 for space management, and Chapter 14 for repairing corruption. Accordingly, this chapter defers these topics and discusses those not mentioned elsewhere. Also, I do not talk about every mundane maintenance task—only certain ones that affect availability. This chapter discusses these tasks—what they involve, why they are required, what would happen if they are not done periodically, their impact on availability, and some ways to perform them with little or no downtime. Also, there are certain important tasks—

such as, say, index rebuilds—that involve downtime in versions 8.0.x and below. To minimize downtime for such tasks, however, would require standby tables (Chapter 15). Accordingly, I do not discuss them here. I also spend time talking about proactively configuring some performance-related areas, so that should you need to use them in the future, you do not have to take the database down (say, to change related initialization parameters), thus avoiding downtime. Finally, I discuss certain critical show-stopping errors that cause application downtime and how to deal with them. I could have placed information on these errors in the troubleshooting section. However, the errors I mention in this chapter need a proactive approach to resolve. Troubleshooting implies a reactive approach (resolving the issue after it has occurred), whereas maintenance, as mentioned earlier, needs to be chiefly proactive. Accordingly, I mention those errors here.

Now, with this background information, let's plunge in and start with the tips!

Implement robust security at all possible levels

One of the most important maintenance tasks has to do with enforcing security within your environment. Robust security is a core requirement at any site supporting a mission-critical application. Lack of security may directly impact availability:

- By fostering user and administrative accidents. For instance, without adequate security in the data center, unauthorized personnel may be tempted to venture in and possibly trip over electric/network cables, putting certain servers (or connectivity to them) out of commission. Similarly, without comprehensive security within the database, new/untrained users could accidentally truncate/drop a table.
- By exposing the database and related components (hardware, software, and network) to malicious attacks.

Remember, user errors typically account for a larger percentage of outages. Accidents could happen even with adequate security in place (for example, a DBA who is an "authorized" superuser could accidentally drop the wrong table). With lax security, however, chances of accidents and attacks are substantially higher. Maintaining a highly secure environment ensures that user errors and accidents are kept to the bare minimum and all hostile attacks are foiled.

Security has to be implemented with regard to the database, as well as external components such as the network and OS (Chapter 1 identifies these components). One of the important maintenance tasks is to watch for signs of security lapses and take steps to correct them. This tip mainly covers database-related security. However, other areas are equally important. For instance, unless robust OS security is in place, critical Oracle files (data-files, control-files, and so on) could be destroyed and the database effectively brought down. There is no overstressing the importance of comprehensive security. Oracle8/8*i* provide various means to define and implement robust database security specifically suited for any environment, without sacrificing application/database functionality and flexibility. Let's explore some of these options.

End-user security is the most effective way to tie a user with specific accountability. Without adequate security, users may be running rampant and performing undesirable tasks they cannot be held responsible for. It is necessary that they be given the privileges to do what they need to do and nothing additional. At the same time, they should not be impeded in the smooth performance of these tasks. End-user identification and authorization is key for implementing such security. The actual implementation is based on one or more of the following aspects:

- **What you know** This is based on a certain unique knowledge that an end user possesses, such as a password to log onto the system.
- **What you have** This is based on a key tangible possession of the end user, such as an identification card or security token with magnetic-encoded stripes that can be read in via a card/token reader or a digital signature that is accepted and compared with an existing predefined one.
- **Who you are** This is biometric security based on verification of an end user's distinct biological traits such as voice, fingerprint, or retinal or facial scans.

There are various Oracle and third-party provisions to implement such end-user authentication. In addition to end-user authentication, client and server machines need to be authenticated as well. Especially if the incoming database requests from clients travel over the Internet, such authentication becomes imperative in the face of high possibilities of system/database abuse. There are various mechanisms for client/server authentication, such as forming a "trust" relationship between specific machines/domains based on host-name/IP addresses (especially if the clients are local). Such trust relationships can be set up on the basis of well-defined rules such as "trust your own self" (that is, trust requests from client processes running directly on the server), "trust other nodes of the cluster," "trust machines belonging to these sub-nets," and so on. If inherent trust relationships cannot be easily formed due to client accesses being from varied remote sources (such as over the Internet), then one or more firewalls (hardware or software based) need to be placed between sensitive in-house servers and the "rest of the world." All client requests need to be routed through this firewall. Additionally, strong cryptography needs to be in place to prevent snooping and altering of potentially sensitive database information exchanged between the servers and the clients. Encryption via 128-bit, 56-bit, or 40-bit public-keys (note that there are export regulations on public-key length and all listed keys may not be available in your geographical area) may be implemented via SSL (Secure Sockets Layer) or IETF TLS (Internet Engineering Task Force Transport Layer Security). Additionally, cryptographic certificates need to be installed on the database server to insulate the clients from possible attacks and allow them to verify that they have indeed contacted the server they need to contact (that is, that their connection requests have not been intercepted and redirected to a rogue server).

Oracle acknowledges the need for the security measures just described and maintains various standardized security schemes both internal and external to the database. Increasingly, advanced security schemes via third-party solutions can be implemented via the Advanced Networking Option (ANO), which is also available with Oracle7. The 24×7 DBA needs to be intimately familiar with these options and be part of any critical team that is responsible for security within the enterprise. Security needs to be enforced via a combination of authentication measures (to establish trust between the database resources and the requesting clients and allow the latter to use the resources in a certain way) and privilege management (to ensure that the resources are not misused).

Password-Based Authentication

Users required to log on need to supply a username and password. Oracle7 allows a relatively simple password-management procedure, where most of the security guidelines (for example, having everybody's password changed at least once in 60 days) may have to be managed manually by the DBA. With Oracle8/8*i*, Password Manager automatically allows a variety of sophisticated password management schemes to be implemented via one or more standard functions. With this, rules such as the following may be easily enforced:

- The password must be at least of a certain length.
- The password must have a combination of alphabetical and numerical characters to ensure they are complex enough not to allow them to be guessed easily (such as actual names of employees) or be deciphered via programs that continuously try words from the dictionary as possible passwords in attempts to break into the database. The password verification function (used by Password Manager) can access a table containing employee first and last names to ensure that these are not used as passwords. Additionally, an account can be set to automatically lock up, after unsuccessful attempts to log on for a certain number of times. This will discourage persistent attempts to try to log on. Also, if the DBA suspects inappropriate user activity, he or she can lock up the account in an ad hoc manner.
- Password changes can be enforced after a certain period, and as they are changed, older passwords should not be repeated indefinitely—or, at least, a new password should not be the same as the five most recent passwords.

Such password management can be enforced globally for all users in the enterprise, a specific subset of users, or even a single user via user profiles. This provides complete flexibility in defining and implementing password-based security.

When passwords move across the network from the client to the server or from server to server, they could potentially be picked up and read by a snooper. Oracle's password-management algorithm recognizes this danger and encrypts the password prior to moving it across the network. This encryption is done at the requesting client or server (via SQL*Net/Net8) via a unique key corresponding to the session. Each subsequent connection attempt uses a different key, so that potential snoopers cannot easily decipher the encrypted stream. After the encrypted password reaches the server, it gets decrypted and reencrypted via a different encryption algorithm, compliant with the Data Encryption Standard. The latter is a one-way encryption process; the final encrypted password is compared with the encrypted passwords maintained within the database for the right match. Such password-based protection can be set up for any local or remote access, including administrative logon attempts (for remote administration).

Note that the Oracle data dictionary is also primarily protected via a password (SYS user ID/INTERNAL/SYSOPER/SYSDBA passwords). Ensure that you always change the default passwords for SYS and SYSTEM and never let them be known to non-DBAs. After a DBA leaves the organization, those passwords are one of the primary things that need to be immediately changed. Other user IDs with DBA privileges cannot directly destroy the data dictionary (by dropping/truncating critical SYS tables), since Oracle enforces complete data-dictionary protection and prevents other user IDs from changing critical metadata.

External User Authentication via the Host

In certain configurations, host-based security can be implemented, where a user is trusted to log onto the database if he or she is already logged on locally to the database server (the host machine on which the database resides). Such configuration is referred to as *external user authentication* or *host-based user authentication.* Here, the OS is responsible for authenticating the user. This security policy is enforced via the IDENTIFIED EXTERNALLY clause of the CREATE USER command. Here, the initialization parameter OS_AUTHENT_PREFIX applies an automatic prefix to every user ID created (by default, this is set to "OPS$"). This prefix allows you to immediately distinguish between regular user IDs and those relying on external identification. A host-dependent scheme may not be appropriate for all mission-critical environments, since it eliminates an important layer of security—between the host and the database.

Advanced Authentication and Encryption

Oracle's Advanced Networking Option (ANO) allows basic password/host-based authentication to be extended according to schemes discussed earlier such as "what you have," "who you are," and so on. It supports a variety of standardized authentication schemes and vendors such as the Data Encryption Standard, biometric authentication technology from *Identix*, security card/tokens from *SecurID*, single sign-on to central services such as *Kerberos* (after which the user can log onto any host/database managed by the service, as required, without having to reauthenticate), and so on. Support for these various vendors and technologies allows database security to be consistent with enterprise-level security.

To mask the data exchanged between server and client or server and server, Net8 (and SQL*Net) allows the data to be encrypted prior to being sent over the network. Here, a random key based on the session is used for the encryption. Additionally, ANO supports RSA Data Security RC4 encryption algorithms and is also compliant with the Data Encryption Standard. Accordingly, using ANO, one can implement more complex encryption algorithms (due to larger public key lengths supported by ANO, such as 128-bit, 56-bit, 40-bit and so on). This prevents snoopers from being able to view the data. Additionally, ANO also allows a cryptographically secure checksum to be included in each packet that traverses the network. On reaching the destination, this checksum is immediately examined by Net8 for possible changes. If a hacker alters the data, the checksum gets altered and the change is detected prior to being processed.

Also, Oracle8 offers certain cryptographic facilities by allowing database applications to create and verify digital signatures, thus allowing users to be validated electronically. Both PL/SQL and OCI support routines to comply with digital signature conventions.

Authentication via Oracle8 Security Server

Oracle8 Security Server permits a site to establish X.509-compliant security certificates that allow clients to authenticate the database resources and vice versa. This is especially useful in e-commerce applications where remote clients and servers can be authenticated prior to accessing the Web server and/or the database, and they, in turn, can feel safe that they are accessing a certified site with the proper credentials. Security Server also provides single sign-on facilities to clients/users. After logging in once, they acquire "global privileges" and can access any database governed under Security Server. Security Server also provides mutual trust across databases in a distributed database environment, where one database needs to access data physically stored in another. In such cases, one specific user ID within each database can be nominated to access the other. This specific user ID is a trusted one and access via any other (un-nominated) user ID is restricted.

Security for Sessions Filtered in via a Middle Tier

Often in n-tier environments, we find an application at the middle tier (such as a Web Application Server or TP Monitor) that is used to route sessions to access the database. Here, each user directly accesses the application and has no direct contact with the database. One of the advantages of using a middle-tier application is that large user populations can be handled. Imagine a situation where users log on from the Web via browsers to access an e-commerce application. If at peak hours there are hundreds and thousands of users concurrently logging on, the database server may not be able to scale up. Accordingly, the middle-tier application may intelligently merge multiple user connections and submit them to the database as a single connection, thus reducing overall connection bandwidth requirements. During such situations, however, Oracle offers features that do not allow security to be compromised. All such connections would use one or more predefined database user IDs to log on. These user IDs should be granted the bare minimum privileges to just perform the requisite tasks and log out. Additionally, OCI8 and above offers a specific feature called *lightweight sessions.* Here, every client process that maps to a specific database session is authenticated by a password to establish trust. Thus, all these client processes that correspond to a single database session are termed as lightweight sessions. This allows the best of both worlds to be combined: Each client process is authenticated, without the database being subjected to a mammoth number of concurrent sessions.

All (custom and/or off-the-shelf) applications and tools on the middle tier need to follow the same basic security norms and guidelines implemented in the database. For example, an application (such as a Web server–based application) may accept a username and password and transmit the password in clear text on the URL to the authentication CGI, which is invoked next. This will easily allow any person standing next to the user to read the password, not to even mention snoopers (even relatively amateur ones) to easily pick up the password without effort. Thus, the application needs to complement the security implemented at the database and related levels and not indulge in reckless manipulation of clear-text passwords.

Direct Privilege Management, Role-Based Security, Auditing, and Profile-Based Security

Here, I refer to the various system and object privileges that may be granted and revoked from individual database user IDs. As mentioned earlier, always follow the "least privilege" path, where the barest minimum privileges are granted to each database user ID. In a bid to ease your overall administration overhead and maintenance time, you may be tempted to grant unwanted privileges to even new users. However, these users may not understand the importance of security and inadvertently reveal their passwords to other users, who could potentially use them for malicious purposes (typical example: the disgruntled employee just about to tender his resignation).

In order to make privilege management easier, Oracle allows use of roles that consolidate privileges and grant them on an as-needed basis. For making management of roles easier in an enterprise environment consisting of multiple applications and databases, the Oracle8 Security Server allows global roles to be defined, which can be centrally defined and interpreted locally within each database. For instance, you may define a global role called MANAGER consisting of various roles within each database. Thus, the MANAGER global role could have the CHANGE_PAY role granted in the Payroll database, whereas it could have the CHECK_INVENTORY role granted in the Inventory database. Thus, a new manager joining the company could be easily assigned this single role, and whenever he or she logs onto the Payroll database, he or she can change people's salaries, whereas if he or she logs onto the Inventory database, he or she can check the current inventory. Ideally, implement privilege management completely as roles. In earlier Oracle7 releases, however, EXECUTE privileges on stored procedures granted via roles do not translate at runtime, thus preventing users from executing them. Accordingly, you may be forced to combine roles and actual privileges in your environment. In any case, understand the scope of database use required by various users (in case they insist on additional privileges beyond what you think is necessary, periodically monitor database use by them to determine their actual needs) and grant/revoke privileges and roles accordingly. Oracle provides a decent audit mechanism to keep track of commands run by various users at various times. This is especially a very useful feature when tracking suspicious activity within the database. (Again if multiple users/applications access the database via a single user ID, the default audit configuration wouldn't help much. In such cases, however, you could write user-defined triggers on various critical tables to log the OSUSER and MACHINE columns from *v$session* into separate administrative tables. However, this approach would only trap DML activity; DDL would still not be traceable.) However, the audit mechanism involves overhead and could impact performance. Accordingly, use it only when necessary.

Finally in mission-critical environments, system resource preservation is essential. Users should not log on, finish their tasks, and tend to leave their connections open for extended periods of time. Even if they have not finished their respective tasks, they should not be allowed to leave their connection unguarded. Besides causing potential locking problems within the database, this could also lead to serious security breaches. As part of a complete security scheme, you need to define profiles and implement them for various users to prevent them from wasting system resources and inducing security hazards. For instance, you may assign a profile to users that will cause their session to disconnect after a certain amount of idle time.

Furthermore, in Oracle8*i*, you can selectively assign higher resources to specific users/applications for timely completion of critical jobs that involve higher complexity than other (mundane) jobs. This is achieved via the Database Resource Manager. This feature assumes great importance for a 24×7 database. If the database is open for extended periods but does not have the capacity to allow critical jobs to complete on

time, then the current availability is not adequate. Oracle, by default, assigns equal priority to all sessions (generally). At times, however, it may be essential to make available a larger pool of resources to certain predetermined sessions. For instance, if the CEO needs to make an important presentation before the Board of Directors next morning in a meeting announced suddenly, he may need access to certain critical information the same evening. If the database cannot provide that, then the availability really needs to be questioned. Database Resource Manager allows resources to be allocated according to a "resource plan." This plan groups various users into specific "resource consumer groups." The plan governs how the groups are allowed to access the resource pool. These plans are very powerful and flexible at the same time. Different plans may be defined and allocated, allowing various groups to acquire different level of resources at different times of the day or night, thus permitting them to meet complex availability needs.

Views, Stored Procedures, and Triggers

Views, stored procedures, and triggers are effective mechanisms to restrict information access. For instance, views can be defined to restrict horizontal (rows) or vertical (columns) visibility via appropriately defined SELECT statements that allow suitable information to be accessible, while camouflaging the rest.

Stored procedures can be written to allow end users to access certain tables via the procedures. Here, the end users executing the stored procedures would not have direct access to the tables. However, they would be given EXECUTE privileges on the stored procedures, thus effectively restricting access to certain tables only via stored procedures. In other words, the stored procedures would act as "wrappers" around specific table accesses permitted by the application. These stored procedures would be written such that they do not perform any inappropriate action. For instance, a stored procedure could be written to delete only certain rows in a table. Thus, the user can delete only those rows via the stored procedure. Since the user does not have direct DELETE privilege on the table(s), that user cannot delete any additional rows. Starting with Oracle8*i*, if necessary, stored procedures can be configured to execute with *invoker's rights,* where the stored procedure gets run according to the existing privileges of the user who invokes it, rather than via the privileges of the user who owns the procedure. This allows the stored procedure execution strategy to be balanced, where, depending on who's executing the stored procedure, it can be executed with the invoker's rights or the owner's rights.

Finally, triggers can be set up on certain critical tables to restrict DML activity on them by certain users or during certain times. For instance, a row-level BEFORE INSERT/UPDATE/DELETE trigger can be written to check the USER and SYSDATE pseudo-columns and raise an exception (RAISE_APPLICATION_ERROR) if either is deemed inappropriate. Prior to using this strategy in your environment, however, ensure that the offending users (or suspected offenders) do not have the privileges to disable the trigger prior to performing DML activity against the corresponding tables.

To summarize, Oracle provides a plethora of mechanisms to implement security at various levels, both internal and external to the database. Ensure that one of the active tasks you perform as part of regular maintenance is to design, implement, evaluate, and if necessary, redesign your database security schemes.

Understand the "ORA-1555: Snapshot too old" error and take steps to avoid it

Almost anyone who has worked with the Oracle server for a while has encountered the "ORA-1555: Snapshot too old" error. This error typically causes the application to fail. For instance, this error may stop a batch job running late at night and subsequently disrupt other jobs that are dependent on the failed one. This typically affects availability, since the jobs do not run successfully and end users do not get the required information in time (reports do not get printed, data-marts do not get loaded, and so on). Note that this error, though more commonly seen with large jobs, can also occur with smaller ones. Obviously, this error needs to be eliminated to prevent application disruption.

ORA-1555 is generally thought of as an intermittent error. At times, after it has occurred, just rerunning the job allows it to complete without reencountering the error. However, a major frustrating factor about this error is that it seldom occurs immediately. Long-running jobs may run for a while (say, a few hours) before they fail due to this error. Merely rerunning the job is not guaranteed to make it succeed, and, after additional hours, the result may very well be the same: failure due to the ORA-1555, thus wasting precious time (machine time, as well as human time). Often, the cause of ORA-1555 is deep rooted in the environment and is a result of multiple factors. If such factors persist, it is possible to reproduce this error consistently and just rerunning the application program does not cause the error to go away. Resolving this error requires a detailed understanding of these various factors, and concrete proactive maintenance steps need to be taken.

Let's start by looking at the root cause of this error. This problem may be categorized under database space management (sub-optimal sizing of rollback segments) or application management/scheduling issues, or even both. More often than not, this problem occurs due to application-related issues. In order to better understand the problem, let's understand some related terminology.

Reads

Reads are operations that cause rows within data blocks to be read, such as during a SELECT statement, SELECT FOR UPDATE statement, WHERE clauses in SELECTs/UPDATEs/DELETEs, or sub-queries within DML and DDL commands. In this context, the processes/threads actually doing the reads are referred to as *readers*.

Writes

Writes are operations that cause rows within data blocks to be written. These are typically INSERTs/UPDATEs/DELETEs. Again, the processes/threads actually doing the writes are called the *writers.* A process/thread can be a reader as well as a writer (for example, an UPDATE statement with a WHERE clause).

Transactions

A transaction combines readers and writers and ends with a commit to make the writes permanent or, alternatively, a rollback to cancel the writes. Thus, a transaction typically begins with one or more reads and then one or more writes, followed by a COMMIT or a ROLLBACK. Once the writes are committed, the changes to data are visible to all transactions that start subsequently.

Read Consistency

Read consistency is one of the primary requirements of any multi-user database server. When there are multiple users making changes to rows within data blocks, such blocks become "dirty" or remain in a state of flux until the time they are committed. Before being committed, they are visible to all statements within the same transaction, but not to other transactions or statements. Once committed, they are made visible to all subsequent transactions and statements. Statements that began prior to the committed transaction cannot see the changes, since those changes weren't present at the time the older statement began. Thus, by default, Oracle uses statement-level read consistency, as opposed to transaction-level read consistency. Refer to the *Oracle8 Server Concepts* manual for a detailed explanation on different options for read consistency. Read consistency is the characteristic where a reader/writer only sees data in the exact state it was in when the read began and only changes made to the data by the current transaction itself are visible. Read consistency is required by all transactions to prevent dirty reads from occurring. For instance, suppose transaction T1 starts at 2200 hrs and transaction T2 starts at 2201 hrs. If T1 is performing a full-table scan of a large table, its read will be time consuming, whereas T2 may be performing a quick index-based update of the same table. Accordingly, T2 may be completed within a few seconds, whereas T1 runs for, say, 20 minutes. As T1 reaches the block where T2 has made changes (it can identify new changes made based on the current SCN/time stamp), it cannot read the changes even though they are committed because it would violate read-consistency rules. It has to be able to access data in the form it was in at exactly 2200 hrs. Changes made at 2201 hrs cannot be/shouldn't be read. Oracle enforces read consistency through a multi-versioning mechanism implemented via rollback segments. In other words, it uses rollback segments to maintain multiple versions of data (the pre-change version or "before-image" is stored in rollback segments, as data blocks are changed). In our example, T1 retrieves the older data from a rollback segment. The "interested transaction list" part of the data block (in the block header) holds details of the rollback segment that was used by T2 to capture the before-image of the rows changed. Accordingly, T1 can acquire the required data from the specific rollback segment and then continue scanning the rest of the table (assuming no more changes have been made to the table). For more details on read consistency, refer to the *Oracle8 Server Concepts* manual.

Snapshots

A *snapshot* is a reference to a consistent result set (not to be confused with snapshots used in Oracle for replication). In order to form a consistent result set, the before-images (the *undo*) held within a rollback segment may have to be accessed. Remember, by default, Oracle uses statement-level read consistency (as opposed to transaction-level read consistency). Accordingly, data has to be consistent with respect to the beginning of the statement. Here the word "snapshot" is used as a generic term to describe the result set with respect to a point in time (the time the statement started executing). If necessary, the data within a rollback segment may be used to construct such a snapshot. For instance, when transaction T2 updates a row, the before-image of the row is retained within a rollback segment. Once the snapshot is held, it may be accessed as necessary by other (earlier) transactions such as T1. The word "snapshot" is not to be confused with the snapshots used for replicating data (with the Distributed Option in Oracle).

Fetch Across Commits

Oracle supports a non-ANSI extension for data retrieval called *fetch across commits,* where data may be retrieved off a cursor, changed, and committed between subsequent fetches. For example, you may have a FOR loop reading a cursor, then making changes to the data retrieved from the cursor, committing those changes and then reading the next row off the cursor. For example, the following piece of PL/SQL code illustrates fetch across commits:

```
DECLARE
    CURSOR tab_row IS
      SELECT name, num_years_worked FROM names;
   My_row tab_row%ROWTYPE;
BEGIN
  FOR my_row IN tab_row LOOP
    IF my_row.num_years_worked > 5 THEN
       UPDATE names SET eligible_for_award = 'Y'
        WHERE CURRENT OF tab_row;
       COMMIT;
    END IF;
    END LOOP;
END;
```

Note that fetch across commits deviates from the ANSI provisions that the cursor gets invalidated after a COMMIT and needs to be closed and reopened subsequently.

Delayed Logging Block Cleanouts

Delayed logging block cleanout, or simply *delayed logging cleanout,* is a mechanism used internally by Oracle to facilitate the response time of writes. When a write occurs, Oracle does not totally "tidy up" the write immediately after it has completed. For instance, let's presume an UPDATE has occurred in a large table holding several million rows. This UPDATE has affected a few thousand rows and so changes several data blocks. The before-images of the changed rows are recorded in a rollback segment, and each data-block header is updated to refer to the specific rollback segment used. Each entry within the rollback segment consists of the before-image of the row and an entry in the appropriate transaction slot in the rollback segment header. When the UPDATE is committed by the transaction, Oracle does not revisit every data block to mark the changes as being made permanent. Instead, it merely updates the transaction slot within the rollback segment header to indicate that the transaction has committed. This allows the write to finish faster and enhances response time. However, every subsequent operation that accesses a data block that has been changed but not made current incurs a penalty by having to make it current, itself. For instance, after the UPDATE, if a SELECT needs to read a block that has been changed, it sees that the block has been changed at a specific time (before or after the SELECT began) and then obtains the identity of the rollback segment that was used to record the change from the data-block header. When it subsequently accesses the rollback segment header (to access the transaction slot pertaining to the change made to the data block), it finds that the transaction has already committed. Accordingly, it updates the data-block header to make the change permanent and revoke the reference to the rollback segment. Hence subsequent operations do not incur the block cleanout penalty. Also, if the change was made by a transaction that started after it (the transaction doing the cleanout) did, it does not include the changed data in its return set—rather, it uses the before-image in the rollback segment.

Familiarity with the preceding terms makes it relatively easier to understand the occurrence of the ORA-1555 error. As may be derived from the preceding text, as a reader scans the blocks for data, a required block may have been changed by a *subsequent* writer. Accordingly, in order to maintain read consistency, the reader needs the previous version of the block, which was current when it started. If the previous version of the block is still present in the buffer cache, it can be easily retrieved from there (via a logical read). However, if the required version is not in the buffer cache, it has to be retrieved from the rollback segment that was used by the writer that changed the block. When the reader tries to acquire the before-image snapshot from the specified rollback segment, the snapshot may no longer be present. This may be evidenced in one of two ways:

- **The actual before-image of the rows may have been overwritten** Once the transactions in a rollback segment have been marked as "committed,"

then the space within the rollback segment is marked free and is available for reuse by other transactions. Considering the preceding example again, an UPDATE may change certain rows. The before-images of these rows are maintained in a rollback segment (selected implicitly by Oracle's rollback segment allocation algorithm or explicitly via the SET TRANSACTION USE ROLLBACK SEGMENT command). Besides using up space within the rollback segment to hold the before-image, a transaction slot is also written with details of the transaction in the rollback segment header. The headers of the blocks in which these rows reside are updated to refer to the appropriate rollback segment that holds the before-image and the appropriate transaction slot within the rollback-segment header.
Once the rows within these blocks are changed and the transaction is committed, Oracle updates the transaction slot to mark the transaction as committed. Once this is done, the space used within the rollback segment is marked as "free" and is available for other transactions. However, this before-image data may still be used by other operations to form read-consistent snapshots and/or during block cleanouts. But once the space is marked as "free," another transaction may overwrite it with before-image data pertaining to other rows/blocks. So the other operations that need the previous before-image result in the ORA-1555 error and crash, causing application failure.

- **The transaction slot within the rollback segment header pertaining to the transaction may have been overwritten** The transaction slots in the rollback segment header are maintained in a circular fashion, wherein the most recent ones are held toward the head of the list. As more transactions use the rollback segment, the older slots get overwritten. Conversely, even though the space used to hold the before-image may be overwritten, the transaction slot may still be retained within the header. During delayed logging block cleanouts, Oracle needs access to only this transaction slot (to check whether the transaction is complete and, if so, to update the data-block header accordingly).

When a reader does not find the required before-image or transaction slot in the specified rollback segment, it cannot produce a read-consistent snapshot of the necessary data and the corresponding transaction fails, giving the "ORA-1555: Snapshot too old" error message. As seen from the preceding explanation, the reason for the snapshot being inaccessible is that the portion of the rollback segment pertaining to that snapshot has been overwritten by newer transactions that have used the rollback segment. What follows are some potential scenarios in which the read-consistent snapshot may be overwritten.

SCENARIO 1: LARGE NUMBER OF TRANSACTIONS, INADEQUATE NUMBER OF ROLLBACK SEGMENTS If a large number of transactions are occurring (such as in a large OLTP environment) and the rollback segments are too few in number, resulting in each of them being used (and reused) frequently by multiple transactions, the chances of ORA-1555 occurring are increased.

SCENARIO 2: INADEQUATE-SIZED ROLLBACK SEGMENTS The rollback segments in use are too small, so previous snapshots held by them are prone to get overwritten fairly quickly by newer transactions. In fact, the actual error message ("ORA-01555: Snapshot too old (rollback segment too small)") always indicates that this is the problem, leading users to believe that this is the *only* problem. The fact is, this is rarely the only cause. The real cause is a result of one or more of the scenarios mentioned here.

SCENARIO 3: INTERMINGLING OF SMALL AND LARGE TRANSACTIONS Large transactions may coexist with small ones. An example of such a scenario is one where large batch operations occur simultaneously with small OLTP transactions. Due to such an arrangement, large reads may occur frequently, involving high periods of read time, increasing the possibility of small writes quickly changing the data being read. This results in the readers having to subsequently access the before-image in the rollback segments to produce read-consistent snapshots. If the writers are abundant and they have overwritten previous snapshots before the readers that need to access them are successfully complete, this prevents the snapshots from being available to the readers. The larger the reads, the more time they take and the higher the chances of data being changed underneath them by small transactions (the higher the period of "vulnerability").

SCENARIO 4: DELAYED LOGGING BLOCK CLEANOUTS Due to the need for various database operations, including readers, having to access rollback segments (since the readers do not change any data, one would automatically assume that access to rollback segments by readers is not required; however, readers "touch" data blocks to retrieve the data and, if the block has not been tidied up yet, the readers are forced to access the rollback segment [header] to perform delayed logging block cleanouts), there is the possibility of even SELECT statements returning the ORA-1555 error, if the required transaction slots in the header have been overwritten. However, note that even if the transaction slots are overwritten, this causes only the reading operation to error out, since it is not able to establish whether the data within the block it is reading has been changed since it started. Data integrity is not violated, since Oracle can use an alternative algorithm to determine the correct SCNs pertaining to the transactions in the blocks not tidied yet. Committed transactions remain committed and do not stay in a state of flux if the reader cannot tidy them up.

SCENARIO 5: FETCH ACROSS COMMITS, ESPECIALLY COMBINED WITH DELAYED LOGGING BLOCK CLEANOUTS Here, rather than another session overwriting the before-image or the transaction slot in the rollback segment, the same session does the overwrite. In other words, a single session allocates the before-image in the rollback segment, commits and frees up the space, and later overwrites the previous before-image by allocating additional before-image data pertaining to other transactions (all generated by the same session) within the same rollback segment. Due to changes being made to the current record set (retrieved by the cursor) being read, Oracle is forced to access the rollback segment each time a reference is made to a row already changed. This increases the possibility of Oracle having to access a before-image for a row that has already been overwritten due to the frequent changes and commits within the loop. The chances of this happening are substantially increased if the same rollback segment is constantly reused by the session performing the fetch across commits (either via the SET TRANSACTION USE ROLLBACK SEGMENT or because only a single non-SYSTEM rollback segment is currently available).

SCENARIO 6: INAPPROPRIATE OPTIMAL CLAUSE Setting the OPTIMAL clause too small for each rollback segment can cause it to shrink often, thereby losing the snapshots required for read consistency by subsequent readers.

SCENARIO 7: BUFFER CACHE TOO SMALL Note that if the previous version of a block required for read consistency is available in the buffer cache, then a reader does not have to go to the rollback segment to acquire it. If the buffer cache is very small, however, then chances of the previous version of the block being present in the buffer cache are very low and the rollback segment will almost always need to be accessed to produce the complete snapshot.

SCENARIO 8: DISCRETE TRANSACTIONS BEING USED If a data block subjected to a discrete transaction operation is subsequently revisited, it may cause the ORA-1555 error.

SCENARIO 9: CORRUPTION The rollback segment that contains the read-consistent snapshot has become corrupt, thereby making it inaccessible.

SCENARIO 10: OS MAC MODE If Trusted Oracle is being used and is configured in OS MAC mode, it may cause ORA-1555.

Now that we have a decent understanding of why the ORA-1555 occurs, let's look at ways to avoid it. The potential solutions are presented in the same sequence of scenarios under which the error occurs.

POTENTIAL SOLUTION TO SCENARIO 1 Increase the number of rollback segments. This will increase the pool of available rollback segments for Oracle to use, thus preventing the same ones from being overused, resulting in previous snapshots being constantly overwritten. Increasing the number of rollback segments increases the possibility of Oracle choosing different rollback segments, allowing each one to retain previous snapshots for longer periods. This will also help delay the circular overwriting of the transaction slots within the rollback segment header, since there will be a larger number of rollback segments (and headers) to share the load and preserve the slots for a longer duration.

POTENTIAL SOLUTION TO SCENARIO 2 Optionally, increase the size of each rollback segment (remember, when transactions are not able to explicitly select rollback segments, it's advisable to configure all of them to be the same size) to accommodate more transactions, thus reducing the chances of different snapshots (old and new) coexisting. This will consequently reduce the chances of older snapshots being overwritten. Also, in situations where the same rollback segment is constantly reused by transactions (via the SET TRANSACTION USE ROLLBACK SEGMENT command), it is necessary to size such rollback segments to be adequately large.

During large operations, you may contemplate reducing the frequency of COMMITs in your programs to reduce the chances of space within rollback segments being overwritten too frequently. Doing so will require larger rollback segments, as well.

POTENTIAL SOLUTION TO SCENARIO 3 Based on my experience, this is the single most common reason for this error. And it is also the toughest and most time-consuming to resolve. An environment where exceptionally large and small transactions concurrently coexist is more often than not the result of a faulty architecture. Such environments ought to be analyzed, and if such concurrence is the result of varied (OLTP and DSS) applications using the same database, then such applications ought to be made to use different databases. For instance, if the production OLTP database is being used (actually "abused" would be a more appropriate word) as a reporting instance as well, then a separate database ought to be created on a different box and the production data needs to be replicated onto the reporting database. All large queries/batch operations can be performed on the new database, and the original database can be exclusively used for small (production) transactions. One of the primary areas of evaluation prior to plugging an application into a specific database is its functionality. Unfortunately, however, functionality is not often considered a major driver. More likely, system resources such as disk space and memory availability tend to be the only drivers. Even though system resources are crucial, they need to be balanced with functional considerations. If the functionality of the new application is different than that of the applications currently using the database, then the application needs to be plugged into a different database/system and a mechanism for replicating data needs to be adopted (Chapters 15 to 18 discuss certain Oracle and third-party replication mechanisms). Such analysis needs to be done fairly early, prior to deployment of the application. Delaying it may result in large amounts of data having to be migrated to the newer database/system and may cause downtime. Under no circumstance should OLTP and DSS be made to live together. However, if the nature of an application is such that it involves large batch transactions, as well as small OLTP transactions, then all batch programs need to be scheduled to run during hours of low use (say, late nights). That way, they will not step on and be stepped on by small transactions. Thus, scheduling plays an important part in preventing ORA-1555. If scheduling cannot be done, however, alternative measures may be required to ensure that data does not get changed during large transactions. Some such alternatives follow. However, note that some of these alternatives have a deep impact on concurrency, and so using them requires careful evaluation.

- Explicitly lock certain key tables in SHARED or EXCLUSIVE mode (via the LOCK TABLE command) prior to running large transactions (even large queries) to prevent other transactions from writing to the table during its execution. Preventing any writes during long operations will reduce the chances of a reader having to refer to the before-image in a rollback segment. And if the need to use the snapshots within rollback segments is reduced, then the snapshots being overwritten shouldn't cause a problem. However, note that this would only eliminate changes to rows after the table has been locked. Changes done prior to the operation may still cause the ORA-1555 error due to delayed logging block cleanouts. Accordingly, the table-locking solution may have to be implemented in combination with another, specifically to address block cleanouts. Solutions toward block cleanouts are outlined in a subsequent paragraph.
- Raise the transaction isolation level from the default READ COMMITTED to SERIALIZABLE or READ-ONLY, as appropriate. Doing so will reduce the level of concurrent changes to data, so that reliance on rollback segments to

acquire a read-consistent snapshot is lowered. For instance, setting the isolation level to SERIALIZABLE allows concurrent transactions to make changes to data only if such changes could have been made while the transactions were run serially. In other words, concurrent transactions likely to change the same data are not permitted. Again, block cleanouts may still require visits to rollback segments. The isolation level can be changed via the SET TRANSACTION or ALTER SESSION command or, alternatively, at the instance level via the SERIALIZABLE and ROW_LOCKING initialization parameters (remember that changing initialization parameters may be inappropriate because it requires downtime and flexibility in using them is lost). Also note that while isolation levels may reduce occurrences of ORA-1555, they may cause other concurrency errors (such as the "ORA-8177: Cannot serialize access for this transaction"). Accordingly, a robust understanding of isolation levels and an evaluation of your database/application environment is required prior to using them. The *Oracle8 Server Concepts* manual discusses transaction isolation levels in detail.

- Reduce the ranges of rows accessed by large operations. For instance, if a query is bound to affect 10,000 rows, then breaking up the query into four queries, each affecting 2,500 rows, may reduce the possibility of the occurrence of the ORA-1555 error. Each query may be written to access a specific (reduced) set of rows based on some qualifying criteria. The following pieces of code illustrate this approach.

```
-- original LARGE query selecting on range of primary-keys
SELECT * FROM names
 WHERE id <= 10000;


-- original LARGE query is broken up into the following four queries
-- SMALL query1
SELECT * FROM names
 WHERE id <= 2500;


-- SMALL query2
SELECT * FROM names
 WHERE id > 2500 id <= 5000;


-- SMALL query3
SELECT * FROM names
 WHERE id > 5000 AND id <= 7500;
```

```
-- SMALL query4
SELECT * FROM names
 WHERE id > 7500 AND id <= 10000;

-- original LARGE query selecting on a date-range
-- to retrieve all rows for people born today or before
SELECT * FROM names
 WHERE date_of_birth <= SYSDATE;


-- original LARGE query is broken up into the following
-- four queries using cut-off dates based on 20-year
-- increments


-- SMALL query1 to get people born prior to 60 years ago
SELECT * FROM names
 WHERE date_of_birth <= SYSDATE - (60 * 365);


-- SMALL query2 to get people born prior to 40 years ago
SELECT * FROM names
 WHERE date_of_birth > (60 * 365) date_of_birth <= (40 * 365);


-- SMALL query3 to get people born prior to 20 years ago
SELECT * FROM names
 WHERE date_of_birth > (40 * 365) AND date_of_birth <= (20 * 365);


-- SMALL query4 to get people born in the last 20 years
SELECT * FROM names
 WHERE date_of_birth > (20 * 365);
```

Explicitly reducing the result set of each query in turn reduces the period of vulnerability of each query to the ORA-1555 error. Since smaller queries have the cursor (implicitly or explicitly) open for a shorter period of time, the chances of snapshots being required are reduced. Even if snapshots are required due to a row in the smaller result set having been changed or a block having to be tidied up, the chances of such snapshots having been overwritten are further reduced. In other words, there are higher chances of a query finding the required row version.

If you have multiple DML statements all accessing/changing the same set of data blocks various times, then if the impact on performance is not too great, try making each statement access the blocks in a sorted fashion (say, via a full-table scan rather than an indexed lookup or via an ORDER BY clause). That would minimize chances of each statement returning to access a block more than once. Assuming that to a certain extent, data within the blocks are sequentially packed, each statement would serially access all rows within each block and then move on to the next block. Generally, returns to a block increase possibility of collisions between readers and writers, where a reader requiring a block has been changed by a subsequent writer. The same concept can be applied to related statements such as sub-queries, too. For instance, if you have an outer cursor and an inner cursor reading the same set of rows with the inner cursor loop changing and committing the rows (fetch across commits), both the inner and outer cursors (especially the outer cursor) are prone to ORA-1555. However, not making the outer cursor access the same block multiple times during the processing would reduce chances of the error.

POTENTIAL SOLUTION TO SCENARIO 4 As we saw earlier, delayed logging block cleanouts, though they help performance, may potentially cause ORA-1555. In order to get the best of both worlds, the trick is to force the block cleanouts to occur prior to a long-running transaction/query. For instance, if transaction T1 will be performing a full-table scan of a large table and then performing certain computations and, subsequently, some UPDATEs, and if you need to ensure that it does not fail after running for a few hours, you can explicitly force a full-table scan on the large table prior to running the actual job. The following piece of code illustrates how:

```
SQL> ALTER SESSION SET OPTIMIZER_GOAL = RULE;

SQL> SELECT COUNT(*) FROM <large_table_name>;
```

Alternatively, if indexes are involved in the operation, the block cleanouts could be occurring on index blocks. You can force index blocks to be cleaned out prior to the actual job via queries similar to the following:

```
SQL> SELECT <columns_in_index> FROM <large_table_name>
     WHERE <leading_index_column> > 0; -- use '' if column is character
```

Instead of a 0 (zero), you can use a '', if the leading index column is a character column. Also, you may make use of hints such as INDEX, INDEX_FFS, and so on to ensure that the correct index is used (always do an EXPLAIN PLAN on the statement to ensure that the index is indeed being used).

Also in Oracle v7.3 and above, delayed logging block cleanouts can be disabled by setting the DELAYED_LOGGING_BLOCK_CLEANOUTS initialization parameter to FALSE (note that doing so may impact response time of certain DML operations).

NOTE
Originally, DELAYED_LOGGING_BLOCK_CLEANOUTS was introduced with the primary intention of aiding Oracle Parallel Server environments, where typically changes made to data blocks by one instance could potentially slow down the other instance, even if the latter merely happens to access those blocks via a SELECT. Thus, in order to reduce the occurrence of situations where the cost of writes by one instance had to be borne by other instances, delayed logging block cleanouts was made tunable. However, this parameter also aids us in reducing the occurrences of ORA-1555.

POTENTIAL SOLUTION TO SCENARIO 5 During a fetch across commits, the cursor is held open throughout multiple cycles of "fetch, change the row fetched, and commit," thereby being highly prone to ORA-1555, since the cursor needs to retain the snapshot right from the time of opening. Also, add delayed logging block cleanouts to the equation and you further increase the chances of ORA-1555 occurring. Change the application code to avoid fetch across commits. Either change the logic such that it no longer is necessary, or alternatively, set the COMMIT to occur after all fetches are completed (after the loop). You may have to configure bigger rollback segments to accommodate this (see "Potential Solution to Scenario 2"), thus trading off disk space for successful job completion. This change to the application code almost instantly eliminates ORA-1555 (if it was being caused by the fetch across commits). If you cannot avoid performing fetch across commits in the application code, the following tips may help:

- As mentioned under "Potential Solution to Scenario 3," if multiple readers (outer and inner cursors) are involved in the fetch across commits operation, make each cursor retrieve the rows in an ordered fashion to prevent revisits to each block, thus avoiding the need for older versions of a block.
- Set the commit interval to be multiples of 'n', where 'n' is the average number of rows per block for that table (computed on the basis of the formula USER_TABLES.NUM_ROWS / USER_TABLES.BLOCKS, done after the table has been analyzed). This increases the chances of every COMMIT covering a specific number of blocks. Accordingly, prior to the COMMIT, the rollback segment space would not be freed and potentially overwritten (that is, the

statement holds on to the rollback segment space). So the statements accessing specific rows within the same blocks would continue to have access to the complete snapshot. Once committed, a specific number of blocks are covered and the queries can move on to the next set of blocks and not have to access the first set again. Of course, this particular strategy only helps prevent the actual before-image in the rollback segment from being overwritten. It does not help much during delayed logging block cleanouts, where the transaction slots in the rollback segment header are overwritten.

POTENTIAL SOLUTION TO SCENARIO 6 Study the growth patterns—shrinks, wraps, extends, and so on of each rollback segment—and adjust the OPTIMAL clause. Set the threshold for shrinking such that shrinks are not too frequent and are well paced out (say, once in two days) to prevent space wastage, to reduce the number of recursive calls, and to allow snapshots to be retained for as long as possible. This requires extensive monitoring of the rollback segments.

POTENTIAL SOLUTION TO SCENARIO 7 Size the buffer cache as high as possible (without straining system resources) to increase the chances of previous data-block versions being acquired via logical hits.

POTENTIAL SOLUTION TO SCENARIO 8 Do not use discrete transactions in such circumstances. If the ORA-1555 error is being returned during a discrete operation, that transaction does not qualify to be a discrete one. In fact, very, very few transactions qualify in most production environments. Make such transactions regular ones.

POTENTIAL SOLUTION TO SCENARIO 9 Please refer to Chapter 14 for information on repairing corrupt rollback segments. Once the repair is successfully performed, subsequent transactions will not incur the ORA-1555 error.

POTENTIAL SOLUTION TO SCENARIO 10 The initialization parameter LOG_CHECKPOINT_INTERVAL may be set to a lower value on the secondary database to avoid the ORA-1555 error.

Note that most of the potential solutions discussed previously are workarounds and are not guaranteed to eliminate the error completely. However, avoiding large and small transactions from intermingling and avoiding fetch across commits definitely go a long way in preventing ORA-1555.

Understand, prevent, and resolve latch and enqueue contention

The Oracle server utilizes several mechanisms, such as latches, enqueues, distributed locks, and global locks (OPS), to control shared access to internal data structures within the SGA (buffer cache, row cache, library cache, redo buffers, and so on). These mechanisms coordinate and control concurrent access by several foreground and background processes. Similar to row- and table-level locks, these internal locking mechanisms may also experience contention at various times, directly affecting performance and limiting throughput and availability. Usage of these locks is dependent on Oracle's internal algorithms, and direct external intervention is not possible. However, Oracle provides certain initialization parameters that may be used to influence their behavior. Having a robust understanding of what these internal locks are and how to detect contention, and, if any is detected, the appropriate actions to take, forms the basis of this tip.

Let's start by taking a look at the two most common internal locking mechanisms.

Latches

Latches are sophisticated fine-grained serialization components used to control access to structures within the SGA. In other words, they are used to serialize access to critical code and memory components, preventing multiple processes from executing the exact same code or writing to the exact same memory structure. They operate at a very low level and as such are highly dependent on the OS. Their implementation may vary across different Oracle ports on diverse platforms in terms of how a process may acquire them—whether it can wait if a latch is not readily accessible and, if so, the duration of the wait. Latches operate at a very quick pace—once acquired, they are used and released almost instantly due to atomic instructions (TEST and SET) used by Oracle. Atomic instructions also ensure that only one process is able to acquire a specific latch at a time. If a process is terminated while it still holds the latch, the PMON cleans up and releases the latch. There is a specific level associated with each latch to prevent deadlock-like situations from arising. Once a process acquires a latch, the very same latch cannot be acquired by another process, and the process itself cannot acquire another latch whose level is equivalent to or lower than the level of the latch currently held by it. Thus, latches are governed by algorithms that guarantee mutual exclusiveness. Latches may be requested in the following modes:

- IMMEDIATE mode, where the process's need for the latch is not susceptible to waiting. If the required latch is not immediately available, then the process skips the request and continues with other processing.

- WILLING TO WAIT mode, where the need for the latch is critical and the process cannot continue without the latch. Accordingly, if the latch is not available, it either sleeps and retries the request (after being woken up by a timer process) or continues spinning on the CPU until the latch becomes available. The duration of the spin is influenced by the SPIN_COUNT initialization parameter or the availability of the latch, whichever is sooner. SPIN_COUNT should be set only on systems with multiple CPUs. We will assume that your 24×7 production database servers have multiple CPUs for the remainder of this discussion.

Latches acquisition is not ordered. In other words, each process may concurrently try, sleep/spin, and retry. Requests are not recorded and catered to on any particular basis such as "first-come, first-served" (that is, no queuing). Accordingly, the process that made the request last may successfully acquire the latch even before the ones that requested the latch earlier. The latter ones, which may be sleeping or waiting to retry, may be relegated and made to continue waiting.

Enqueues

Enqueues, similar to latches, guard specific internal structures. However, they are more advanced in their implementation. Enqueues allow and manage concurrent access by multiple processes to specific memory resources. In other words, rather than relying on a mutual exclusiveness policy, enqueues allow resources to be shared at varying levels. Each process requests an enqueue in a specific mode, and the level of access to the resource is determined by this mode. An OS lock manager process tracks the resources locked. An enqueue may also be requested in IMMEDIATE or WILLING TO WAIT mode; however, all unsatisfied requests are placed in a FIFO-based (first in, first out) queue and the process that made the request first gets the enqueue prior to any other process.

Processes require latches (or enqueues) as they attempt to control/change data structures within the SGA. Only after the latch is successfully acquired are the processes permitted to access the specific data structure. The latch is released immediately after the process has completed accessing the structure. There are different latches based on the specific component of internal data/memory they protect. The *v$latchname* dynamic view lists all these latches. Table 11-1 provides a sample list of certain important latches. Each latch has a version-specific number.

A database, especially with high-volume OLTP transactions, may face the problem of latch contention due to many processes simultaneously seeking latches, more than what is made available. If a latch is not immediately available, then the process must wait, delaying response time and throughput. Additionally, these

Latch Name (from *v$latchname*)	Comments
latch wait list	The *latch wait list* latch needs to be acquired by processes to place an entry in the wait list prior to waiting on other latches.
enqueues	Enqueues are treated as latches for all practical purposes.
cache buffers chains	Foreground server processes acquire this latch as they scan or update the hash bucket chain within the buffer cache (see Chapter 7 for more details).
cache buffers lru chain	Foreground server processes acquire this latch as they scan the LRU list within the buffer cache for free buffers.
multiblock read objects	This latch is used by processes during multiblock reads.
system commit number (SCN)	This latch is acquired by processes prior to generating SCNs.
redo allocation	Processes need this latch as they allocate space within the redo log buffer (see Chapter 7 for more details).
redo copy	The number of *redo copy* latches (is dependent on the initialization parameter LOG_SIMULTANEOUS_ COPIES). This latch is used to alleviate the load on the *redo allocation* latch.
sequence cache	This latch is necessary for allocating space in the SGA for caching sequence entries.
row cache objects	This latch is used as processes access the data-dictionary cache within the shared pool to ensure that object definitions do not inadvertently change.
library cache	This latch is used as processes access the library cache within the shared pool.
virtual circuits	This is used in an MTS architecture as shared servers are allocated to service dispatchers.

TABLE 11-1. *A List of Some Important Latches*

processes take up CPU cycles (as a result of SPIN_COUNT being set to 2000 by default) and may affect overall system performance. As more and more processes join the fray, the resultant waits may become noticeable to end users.

Latch contention needs to be periodically monitored via the *v$latchname, v$latchholder, v$latch, v$latch_misses, v$latch_parent,* and *v$latch_children* dynamic views (please refer to the Oracle8 documentation for information on these views). The *v$latch* view primarily provides various statistics on different latches. Depending on whether the latch was requested in IMMEDIATE or WILLING TO WAIT mode, different columns within *v$latch* need to be viewed. Tables 11-2 and 11-3 list the columns for each mode.

If MISSES and/or SLEEPS seem high compared to the GETS (say, MISSES/SLEEPS are greater than five percent of GETS), then latch contention is a cause for concern.

Similarly, if IMMEDIATE_MISSES seem high compared to IMMEDIATE_GETS, then, again, your database may be experiencing serious latch contention.

The following queries help in identifying latch contention by listing the preceding columns:

```
-- system-wide latch acquisition
SET LINES 240
COLUMN name FORMAT a40
SELECT l.name, l.addr, l.gets, l.misses, l.sleeps,
       l.immediate_gets,  l.immediate_misses, h.pid
  FROM v$latch l, v$latchholder h
 WHERE l.addr = h.laddr(+)
 ORDER BY l.latch#;


-- Specific latch statistics (by latch name)
COLUMN name FORMAT a40
SET LINES 240
SELECT l.name, l.addr, l.gets, l.misses, l.sleeps,
               l.immediate_gets, l.immediate_misses, h.pid
 FROM v$latch l, v$latchholder h
WHERE l.addr = h.laddr(+)
  AND UPPER(l.name) LIKE UPPER('&latch_name_in_upper_case%')
ORDER BY l.latch#;
```

Certain steps can be taken to avoid latch contention. Table 11-4 lists some initialization parameters that influence performance during latch use. Note that some of the parameters in Table 11-4 are underscore (undocumented) parameters and are not to be changed unless one is directed to do so by Oracle Support/Development personnel.

If MISSES or IMMEDIATE_MISSES in *v$latch* seem high, then the number of latches may have to be increased. Note that for certain latches, only GETS/MISSES apply, whereas for others, both GETS/MISSES and IMMEDIATE_GETS/IMMEDIATE_MISSES

Column Name	Description
NAME	Latch name
GETS	Number of times the latch was successfully acquired by processes
MISSES	Number of initial attempts that resulted in failure
SLEEPS	Number of times processes slept (after extinguishing SPIN_COUNT) and re-requested the latch
SPIN_GETS	Number of times processes successfully spun and acquired the latch
WAITERS_WOKEN	Number of times sleeping processes were woken (by timers) to re-request the latch

TABLE 11-2. *The* v$latch *Columns to Be Viewed for Latch Requests in WILLING TO WAIT Mode*

may apply, with the latter usually being more relevant. For instance, only GETS/MISSES apply to the *redo allocation* latch (since there is a single one, processes are forced to wait for it to become available), whereas both GETS/MISSES and IMMEDIATE_GETS/ IMMEDIATE_MISSES (however, the latter deserve more attention) apply to the *redo copy* latches. Similarly, both apply for the *cache buffers lru chain* latch. The best way

Column Name	Description
NAME	Latch name
IMMEDIATE_GETS	Number of successful latch acquisitions
IMMEDIATE_MISSES	Number of failures

TABLE 11-3. *The* v$latch *Columns to Be Viewed for latch Requests in IMMEDIATE Mode*

Initialization Parameter	Description
Oracle7 and Oracle8	
SPIN_COUNT	Duration of each spin while waiting for a latch
ENQUEUE_RESOURCES	The number of enqueue locks available
_MAX_SLEEP_HOLDING_LATCH	Permissible time to sleep while holding a latch
_LATCH_WAIT_POSTING	Helps the timer process determine when to post waiting processes when latch is available
_LATCH_RECOVERY_ALIGNMENT	Used to align necessary structures during latch recovery
_SESSION_IDLE_BIT_LATCHES	Helps to determine whether to use a single latch per session or per group of sessions
_ENQUEUE_HASH_CHAIN_LATCHES	Number of enqueues available to processes for accessing hash chains within the buffer cache
DB_BLOCK_LRU_LATCHES	Number of LRU latches available to processes
_KGL_LATCH_COUNT	Number of library cache latches available to processes
Oracle7 only	
_LATCH_SPIN_COUNT	Number of times to spin while waiting for a latch. After spinning _LATCH_SPIN_COUNT times, the process goes to sleep
_DB_BLOCK_MULTIPLE_HASHCHAIN_ LATCHES	Helps to determine whether to use one latch per hash chain structure, rather than one latch for all hash chains

TABLE 11-4. *Initialization Parameters Governing Latch Use*

to determine which set of columns apply to which latch is to look at both the sets. The ones with the larger values indicate whether the latch is being acquired in WILLING TO WAIT mode or IMMEDIATE mode, or even both. So ensure that you look at both columns, so as not to be misled.

Overall, latches are dependent on the number of CPUs available. If you observe latch contention in spite of reaching the maximum setting applicable for the latch, you may have no option but to upgrade the CPUs on your system.

If a latch is not available, each process spins for a while (depending on the value of SPIN_COUNT and _LATCH_SPIN_COUNT) and then, having extinguished the available spin cycles, it goes to sleeps. Whenever the required latch is available, the sleeping process is posted so that it may retry the acquisition. However, sleeps prove unhealthy for database performance. The higher the number of sleeps, the more degrading is latch contention to database performance. If the SLEEPS column in *v$latch* shows a high value, SPIN_COUNT may be increased to make the processes spin longer. Spinning longer means that there is a higher chance of latches being freed up and being acquired by the spinners. This avoids the need for the spinner having to go to sleep subsequently and thus reduces the occurrences of SLEEPS. Alternatively, you could also increase _LATCH_SPIN_COUNT in Oracle7 to increase the frequency of the spins; however, adjusting SPIN_COUNT to control spins is advisable, rather than _LATCH_SPIN_COUNT, since the latter is an underscore parameter. Note that by increasing SPIN_COUNT, you offset CPU time against latch performance. In a system that already lacks CPU capacity, this obviously is not recommended. In systems where CPUs are being underutilized, however, this may be ideal for reducing SLEEPS and helping performance.

Techniques to resolve latch contention vary, depending on the latch type. Let's look at some specific instances of latch contention and examine ways to resolve them:

- **Redo allocation and redo copy latches** Chapter 7 discusses ways to reduce latch contention for these latches in detail.
- **Row cache objects latch** The row cache (the data-dictionary cache) is part of the shared pool, and reducing latch contention here involves increasing the size of the SHARED_POOL initialization parameter.
- **Cache buffers LRU chain latch** Avoiding contention here includes increasing DB_BLOCK_BUFFERS and increasing DB_BLOCK_LRU_LATCHES to ensure that for every 50 data-block buffers there is at least one latch (DB_BLOCK_LRU_LATCHES defaults to twice the number of CPUs or two percent of the DB_BLOCK_BUFFERS, whichever is less). In Oracle7 (in Oracle8, write-batch units are dynamically computed), _DB_BLOCK_WRITE_BATCH may optionally be increased to allow larger writes to occur, resulting in more LRU latches being available.
- **Cache buffers chain latch** Again, contention here can be resolved by increasing DB_BLOCK_BUFFERS. Optionally, _DB_BLOCK_HASH_BUCKETS may also be increased to alleviate this problem (refer to Chapter 7 for more details).

As a concluding note, it is essential to realize that very often, the preceding steps would only aid in reducing the symptoms (latch contention is a symptom). It is essential to proactively take steps to tackle the problem at the source by tuning all application SQL. Bad SQL can often cause excessive contention. In fact, many DBAs think that by taking certain peripheral steps (such as changing the value for SPIN_COUNT), latch contention can be entirely eliminated. This is not the case.

Even Oracle Corporation recommends a two-pronged approach. In fact, in order to reduce the reliance of many sites (who consider SPIN_COUNT to be a "magic bullet") on SPIN_COUNT and their subsequent disillusionment, future releases of Oracle (or even current releases on certain platforms) will not allow SPIN_COUNT to be tuned. It may be made an underscore parameter or removed altogether.

Be familiar with different wait events and take steps to reduce them

Wait events are events that cause regular processing to stall due to specific delays in actions taken or due to external environmental factors. Oracle tracks different wait events and presents the information for administrative interpretation via the dynamic views *v$session_wait, v$session_event,* and *v$system_event.* The first two views provide information on wait events affecting individual sessions, whereas the third one, *v$system_event,* provides system-wide summary information for all sessions. Figure 11-1 illustrates the level at which the three views provide information.

At the foot of the pyramid in Figure 11-1, *v$session_wait* provides detailed low-level information. It is a straight dump of wait-event data as the Oracle server encounters them. Accordingly, its contents are highly dynamic. You may see information regarding different sessions at different times. Also, at various points in time, the very same session ID may be used by different sessions and may show totally contradictory information due to diverse activity levels in these different

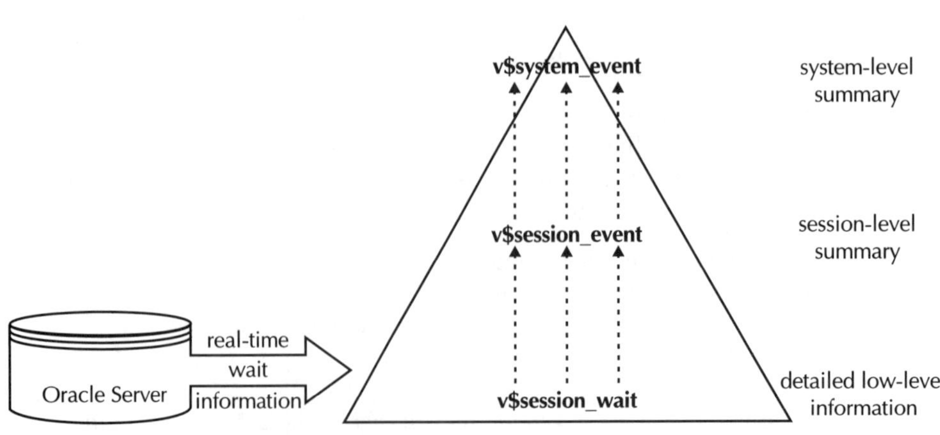

FIGURE 11-1. *A wait-event information pyramid formed by dynamic views*

sessions. Accordingly, constant reference to *v$session* is needed to ensure that you are indeed looking at information for the right session (especially in a dynamic OLTP environment).

At the middle of the pyramid, the *v$session_event* view lists various events and the session IDs of sessions experiencing them. Here, elaborate details such as the *v$session_wait* are not available. However, it gives an idea as to which sessions are experiencing waits most commonly so that one may focus one's tuning efforts on such troubled sessions. Even though both *v$session_event* and *v$session_wait* provide information at the session level, *v$session_wait* is more real-time, and the wait event has to end for it to be reflected in *v$session_event.* Thus, *v$session_event* lists wait-event statistics only after sessions have experienced them (not as they are being experienced).

Finally, at the top of the pyramid, you have *v$system_event,* which provides the same information as *v$session_event,* but without the session-level breakup. It gathers wait-event information from all processes since the instance was started, summarizes the information, and updates its statistics.

Thus, the pyramid structure allows you to drill down from system level to session level for appropriate wait-level information. Also, the *v$event_name* view lists all events applicable to your Oracle release. The *v$waitstat* view provides block-level information on wait events. Accordingly, *v$waitstat* may have to be used in interpreting some of the wait events in *v$session_wait* (such as *buffer busy waits*) to get an insight on the file IDs/block IDs experiencing high waits. Also, the *x$kcbfwait* virtual table provides wait information on a per-file basis, allowing certain wait events to be analyzed more easily. And finally, the *utlbstat/utlestat* report provides a "snapshot" of the wait events over a period of time (this is most useful, allowing you to pinpoint "troublesome" periods). Tables 11-5, 11-6, and 11-7 describe some of the important columns in the *v$session_wait, v$session_event,* and *v$system_event* views.

View: v$session_wait

Column Name	Description
SID	Session ID experiencing the wait from *v$session.*
SEQ#	The order (serial number) of the wait event.
EVENT	The event name from *v$event_name.*

TABLE 11-5. *Important Columns in* v$session_wait

View: v$session_wait

Column Name	**Description**
P1TEXT, P1, P1RAW, P2TEXT, P2, P2RAW, P3TEXT, P3, P3RAW	The parameters associated with the wait event. Each parameter (optionally) provides additional information regarding the event. P1TEXT refers to the name of the first parameter, P1 is the value of the first parameter, and P1RAW is the raw version of the first parameter value. P2 and P3 similarly relate to the second and third parameters. Each set of parameters provides different information depending on the event. For instance, with the *buffer busy waits* event, the P1 set of parameters provides information on the file ID, containing the block pertaining to the data-block buffer, whereas the P2 set of parameters provides the actual block ID and the P3 set provides the point at which the wait event was encountered. With the *checkpoint completed* wait event, however, the parameters do not provide any value.
STATE	The current status of the session incurring the wait event. The status may either be 'WAITING', 'WAITED KNOWN TIME', (with the actual wait time published in the WAIT_TIME column), 'WAITED SHORT TIME' (with the session going to sleep and waking up in the same clock tick), or 'WAITED UNKNOWN TIME' (where WAIT_TIME could not be determined [usually, due to TIMED_STATISTICS being disabled]). Generally, the STATUS starts out as 'WAITING' and then turns to 'WAITED KNOWN TIME' when the waits ends.
WAIT_TIME	The wait time in milliseconds experienced by the session (provided STATE is not 'WAITED UNKNOWN TIME').
SECONDS_IN_WAIT	The clock time at the beginning of the wait listed in seconds (this column, like WAIT_TIME, depends on STATE and needs to be interpreted accordingly).

TABLE 11-5. *Important Columns in* v$session_wait (continued)

View: v$session_event

Column Name	Description
EVENT	The event name from *v$event_name*
SID	The session ID experiencing the wait from *v$session*
TIME_WAITED	The cumulative wait time in milliseconds incurred by the session due to this event
TOTAL_WAITS	The number of times the session incurred this event
AVERAGE_WAIT	The average wait time in milliseconds per occurrence of the event
TOTAL_TIMEOUTS	The number of occurrences of timeouts for this event during this session

TABLE 11-6. *Important columns in* v$session_event

View: v$system_event

Column Name	Description
EVENT	The event name from *v$event_name*
TIME_WAITED	The system-wide cumulative wait time in milliseconds incurred due to this event
TOTAL_WAITS	The number of times this event was incurred since database startup
AVERAGE_WAIT	The average wait time in milliseconds per occurrence of the event
TOTAL_TIMEOUTS	The number of occurrences of timeouts for this event

TABLE 11-7. *Important Columns in* v$system_event

The following query allows you to list the events your database has been waiting on (note that the query output shown is only a sample listing and is not complete):

```
SQL> SELECT SUBSTR(event, 1, 30) "Event",
            ROUND(time_waited/100) "Time (secs)",
            total_waits "Tot waits", total_timeouts "Timeouts",
            ROUND(average_wait/100, 2) "Avg (secs)"
       FROM v$system_event
      ORDER BY 2 DESC

Event                          Time (secs) Tot waits Timeouts Avg (secs)
------------------------------ ----------- --------- -------- ----------
SQL*Net message from client       44532011   7689268      457       5.79
enqueue                              56812     19756      112       2.88
control file sequential read           217     15457        0       0.01
db file scattered read                4378     92381      124       0.05
db file sequential read               9237    296578      875       0.03
process startup                          1        14        0       0.07
```

Let's examine some of the important wait events. Examining all would probably require an entire book by itself. However, the ones listed in the text that follows help you determine how to treat them—whether to try to prevent them from occurring too often or just ignore them. In other words, the ones listed are ones that either need attention or are likely to provoke your curiosity regarding what is to be done with them (they've provoked mine often . . .). Accordingly, I'm elaborating on them. In the following discussion, P1 refers to the first parameter value from *v$session_wait,* and P2 and P3 refer to the second and third parameters, respectively.

SQL*Net Message from Client

This is one of the most prominent wait events (in terms of TIME_WAITED and TOTAL_WAITS in *v$system_event*) that usually show up. This indicates that foreground server processes are waiting for client processes to respond. Here, P1 is the return value of the disconnect routine from the SQL*Net driver currently in use. P2 provides the number of bytes that have been received so far by the foreground process from the client. High occurrences of this wait event (as can be judged from the numbers in *v$system_event*) is usually not a bad sign, since the delay is not due to the database. The database is actually waiting for client responses. However, this may also indicate a possible network clog-up and may merit investigation (please refer to Chapter 5 for more information on tuning networks).

SQL*Net Message to Client

This is the converse of the preceding scenario and indicates foreground processes are sending packets to client processes and are waiting on the packets to reach them. P1 is again the return value of the disconnect routine from the SQL*Net driver currently in use. P2 provides the number of bytes that have been sent so far by the foreground process to the client. Consistent high numbers merit examining the network for possible delays.

WMON Goes to Sleep

WMON is the background process that wakes up sleeping processes during timeouts in UNIX. It can be used to reduce the number of system calls and context switches resulting from constantly setting and resetting timers (timers are used internally to poll sleeping processes). WMON can be made to time out at more frequent intervals if this wait event seems high in *v$system_event*. WMON can be enabled via the initialization parameter REDUCE_ALARM (note that this parameter does not exist on all platforms). An underscore parameter _WAKEUP_TIMEOUT determines how frequently WMON times out and is set in one hundredths of a second. By default, it is set to 100. No parameters show up in *v$session_wait* for this event.

Buffer Busy Waits

This event is caused when sessions are waiting on buffers to become accessible. The required ones are currently busy (possibly being read by another foreground server process). This event is further explained in Chapter 7. Wait times may vary from one to three seconds. The session encountering this wait event has the file ID containing the block pertaining to the buffer in P1. P2 lists the actual block ID within the file, and P3 lists the point in code execution where the wait event was encountered. You may gather more information on the parameters as follows:

- **File ID in P1** The filename can be obtained from *v$datafile* via the following query:

```
SQL> SELECT name FROM v$datafile
      WHERE file# = <file-id from P1>;
```

- **Block ID in P2** The segment name and type causing the wait can be determined based on the block ID in P2.

```
SQL> SELECT segment_name, segment_type FROM dba_extents
      WHERE file_id = <file-id from P1>
        AND <block-id from P2> BETWEEN block_id AND block_id + (blocks-1);
```

Reduce Wait Events

- **Point where event was encountered in P3** There are several points in code execution where the *buffer busy waits* event may be encountered. Table 11-8 lists some of them.

To better understand high *buffer busy waits,* one can examine the block-level wait activity within *v$waitstat.* Also, one may proactively evaluate wait events occurring on every file from *x$kcbfwait.* The following query illustrates how:

```
-- run this query as SYS
 SQL> SELECT df.name, kf.count FROM v$datafile df, x$kcbfwait kf
      WHERE (kf.indx+1) = df.file#;
```

Once you have identified files/blocks and the segments that are prone to high buffer waits (from *v$session_wait*'s parameters and the preceding queries), then you can dig deeper to look at application code to understand DML patterns. If certain segments are prone to high volumes of INSERTs/DELETEs/UPDATEs, then you need to ensure that adequate FREELISTs, FREELIST GROUPS, and INITRANS have been defined for them. Also, PCTUSED and PCTFREE could play a role here, and so could the database block size. If there are a large number of rows within each database block, then that could cause a larger number of processes to access each block, thereby leading to higher *buffer busy waits* due to the additional contention.

Point code present in P3	Description
0 and 1003	Block is currently being read (maybe with undo information in the case of the latter) and is not available.
1007	Waiting to acquire a new block.
1010	Waiting to acquire a buffer in share (S) mode.
1012	Buffer is currently being modified and is not available.
1013 and 1014	Block is currently being read by another session and is not available. This may also be the result of a buffer deadlock (explained later).
1016	Block is currently in incompatible mode. Subsequent waits may result in a buffer deadlock.

TABLE 11-8. *Points Where* buffer busy waits *May Be Encountered*

Buffer Deadlock

This event does not appear too often in the *v$system_event* and *v$session_wait* views, and whenever it does, it occurs very briefly and may be difficult to detect. However, due to its relationship with the *buffer busy waits* event, it is explained here. There are certain points in code execution that cause *buffer busy waits,* and some of these may lead to buffer deadlocks (for example, points 1014 and 1016 in Table 11-8). Buffer deadlocks are not genuine waits and are implied. They only result in the CPU being rescinded. When the buffer cache layer cannot acquire data-block buffers in a certain mode, it waits, leading to *buffer busy waits.* However, subsequent waits causes the buffer cache layer management algorithm to assume that the buffer is in a deadlock. This causes the CPU call to be rescinded, and, generally, the execution point traverses to the end of the processor execution queue.

In the case of *buffer deadlocks,* P1 provides the dba (data-block address) of the block concerned. Chapter 13 provides information on using the dba to pinpoint the segment name and type causing the "deadlock." Alternatively, the other parameters may also be used to derive the information. P2 provides dual information—the class and the mode of the block involved (in the format CLASS*10 + MODE). The following query may be used to reveal the class:

```
SQL> SELECT sid, TRUNC(p2/10) "Block class"
       FROM v$session_wait
      WHERE event = 'buffer deadlock';
```

The class helps to identify the type of block and includes 1 for regular data blocks, 2 for temporary (sort) blocks, 4 for segment header blocks, 6 for free-list blocks, and so on. Certain other class numbers starting with 7 (7 pertains to the SYSTEM rollback segment) are reserved for rollback segment and rollback segment header blocks. The block mode reveals the reason for it not being available. In other words, mode refers to the lock mode held by other processes accessing the block. The following query may be used to obtain the block mode:

```
SQL> SELECT sid, MOD(p2/10, 2) "Block mode"
       FROM v$session_wait
      WHERE event = 'buffer deadlock';
```

The mode includes 0 for NULL, 1 for current share (SCUR), 2 for current exclusive (XCUR), 3 and 4 for consistent read modes (CR or CRX), and 5 for current exclusive new block (NEW). These modes indicate that the block is currently in use.

P3 refers to certain flags set internally by Oracle as it tries to acquire the block. These flags are in hex and indicate whether the block was being used in a sequential scan, in a block cleanout operation, in NOLOGGING mode, and so on.

If *buffer deadlocks* seem prominent, then the same solutions outlined under *buffer busy waits* need to be utilized, that is, identifying which segment is involved, understanding DML patterns, and altering storage characteristics accordingly.

Buffer for Checkpoint

This indicates that certain buffers were not available for checkpointing. This could potentially be due to the buffers being modified. This generally results in a wait of one second, and the buffer cache has to be rescanned, thus delaying checkpoints. Also, this increases shutdown time, if the instance is being shut down at that time (refer to Chapter 10 for a discussion on why shutdown time is critical to a high-availability site).

In this case, P1 contains the buffer number that was unavailable for checkpointing. Details about the buffer can be obtained by querying the *x$bh* table as follows:

```
-- run this query as SYS
SQL> SELECT dbarfil, dbablk, class, state, mode_held, dirty_queue, obj
       FROM x$bh
      WHERE indx = '<buffer # from P1>';
```

P2 contains the dba of the data block corresponding to the buffer. Once the dba is obtained, the segment name and type can be derived (Chapter 13).

P3 contains dual information: state and mode (in the format STATE*10 + MODE). State refers to the buffer status, such as 0 for a free buffer (FREE), 4 for a buffer being read (READ), 6 for a buffer being subjected to instance recovery, and so on. State can be retrieved via the following query:

```
SQL> SELECT sid, TRUNC(p3/10) "Block state"
FROM v$session_wait
      WHERE event = 'buffer for checkpoint';
```

The mode is the lock mode under which the required buffer has been locked (by the process's modifying it and making it unavailable for checkpoint). The actual value for mode is similar to what was discussed under the *buffer deadlock* wait event. Mode can be derived via the following query:

```
SQL> SELECT sid, MOD(p3/10, 2) "Block mode"
       FROM v$session_wait
      WHERE event = 'buffer for checkpoint';
```

If the *buffer for checkpoint* event figures prominently in *v$system_event,* then measures may be taken to resolve it. It is to be borne in mind that generally foreground server processes are not impacted by this event (thus, end-user response time is not affected). Only checkpoints and possibly shutdown operations are delayed. In order to control this problem, it is essential to determine whether this is a popular data block in terms of DML activity incurred. One way of checking that is to find out the number of occurrences (of different versions, possibly) of this block currently in the buffer cache. If the number is high, then it's probably a very popular or "hot" block. Whether a specific number is normal or too high for your database needs to be determined after comparing it with other candidate blocks (of equally popular segments) or studying the same block over a period of time. The following query finds out the number of occurrences within the buffer cache. Prior to running it, you need to find out the file ID and block ID pertaining to the dba of the block (remember the dba is present in P2). Chapter 13 illustrates how to use the dba to find out the file ID/block ID.

```
SQL> SELECT COUNT(*) "# occurrences in buffer cache"
       FROM x$bh
      WHERE dbarfil = <file-id of dba in P2>
        AND dbablk = <block-id of dba in P2>;
```

Once the block has been determined to be hot, DML patterns affecting the block needs to be identified based on the segment it belongs to. Possible areas of contention within the block (inadequate FREELISTS, INITRANS, and so on) that may delay modifications need to be addressed. Also if the block size is too large (causing a large number of rows to be present within the block—the larger the number of rows, the more activity within the block), you need to address that during subsequent reorganizations and upgrades. Also, such internally hot blocks may be subject to I/O bottlenecks, unless specific precautions are taken, such as placing the data-file pertaining to that segment on fast disks/controllers and, if possible, on finely striped disk volumes.

Checkpoint Completed

Here, processes are waiting for the checkpoints to complete. This also delays local checkpoints and instance shutdowns. The wait time here is five seconds—a substantial time for processes to spend waiting. There are no parameters for this wait event in *v$session_wait.* If this wait event figures prominently in *v$system_event,* then you need to take steps to make checkpoints occur less frequently by setting the initialization parameters such as LOG_CHECKPOINT_INTERVAL and LOG_CHECKPOINT_TIMEOUT appropriately. Also, checkpoints (as they happen) should be made to occur faster by increasing the DB_BLOCK_CHECKPOINT_BATCH parameter that influences the units of writes for each checkpoint. Note that checkpoint write sizes (like those for any other writes) are limited by the maximum I/O size imposed by the OS or a quarter portion of the DB_BLOCK_BUFFERS, whichever is smaller. Also, the actual DB_BLOCK_CHECKPOINT_BATCH cannot be higher than the _DB_BLOCK_WRITE_BATCH parameter, which governs the actual write size after considering these parameters and is set dynamically at runtime by Oracle. Only the maximum possible at that juncture is utilized, and larger values are discarded.

Control File–Related Wait Events

There are wait events that show up in *v$system_event* as control-files are being accessed. The following wait events relate to the control-files:

- Control file parallel write
- Control file sequential read
- Control file single write

The first event, *control file parallel write,* occurs when Oracle is writing in parallel to all the control-files, such as when synchronizing control-files with transaction-commit information or changing specific values in the control-files such as name/number of data-files. The wait time is the time it takes for the write to complete on all control files. In this case, P1, P2, and P3 all have the same value—the number of control-files being written to.

The second event, *control file sequential read,* occurs when Oracle reads a specific control-file in cases such as making a copy of the control-file (during backups) or control-file header block, or making other specific block reads. The wait time is the actual time taken to perform the read. In this case, P1 holds the file ID of the control-file being read. The filename of this control-file can be obtained via the following query:

```
SQL> SELECT cfnam FROM x$kcccf

     WHERE indx = <file_id from P1>;
```

P2 holds the starting block number within the control-file being read. Note that this block number is the block offset within the file. The block size here is not the database-block size but the OS physical block size (generally, 512 bytes in UNIX). P3 holds the number of blocks being read.

The third event, *control file single write,* occurs to flush specific control-files (to disk) with shared information. Here, the wait time and the parameters are the same as for the control file sequential read event.

If the control file–related waits seem prominent, then one needs to evaluate the I/O loads on the disks where the control-files are placed and take steps to alleviate I/O hot spots.

Data File–Related Wait Events

The following wait events pertain to data-file access:

- DB file parallel write
- DB file scattered read
- DB file sequential read
- DB file single write

The *db file parallel write* event occurs as files are being written to in parallel by DBWR. The wait time is the time to complete the required I/O calls. Here, P1 is the number of files being written, P2 is the number of blocks being written, and P3 is the total number of parallel I/O requests (usually the same as P2).

The *db file scattered read* event occurs during full-segment scans (full-table scans and fast full index scans) as multiple blocks are being read according to the initialization parameter DB_FILE_MULTIBLOCK_READ_COUNT. Note that multiblock reads need not occur sequentially, since data may be spread across different spindles/volumes due to (intentional and/or unintentional) striping and fragmentation (internal and external to the segment), thus usually requiring multiple scattered reads to obtain all the data required. The wait time is the time required to complete all the I/O calls. Here, P1 provides the file number being read from (the filename can be accessed from *v$datafile* according to the file number), P2 provides the block number from where the read starts, and P3 provides the number of blocks being read.

The *db file sequential read* event occurs during regular reads of data-files by foreground processes, including index lookups and other non-full-segment scans, data-file block dumps, and so on. The wait time is again the time to complete all I/O calls. The parameters are the same as the ones for the *db file scattered read* event.

The *db file single write* event occurs when file headers or other individual blocks are being written. The wait ensues until all I/O calls are completed. The parameters are the same as the ones for the *db file scattered read* event. If the P2 parameter does not contain 1 (indicating the file header) as the value, then the write pertains to a non-header block.

When data file–related events seem high in the *v$system_event* data-file, you need to examine data-file layouts and I/O efficiency in the system. Refer to Chapter 4 for tips on identifying I/O bottlenecks and resolving them.

Enqueue

This wait event indicates that processes are waiting to acquire specific enqueues. The wait time varies based on the enqueue and lasts until it is acquired. P1 here refers to the name of the enqueue and the mode (lock mode) in which it is desired. The enqueue name consists of two characters. Table 11-9 lists some important enqueue names.

The enqueue name can be obtained via the following query:

```
SQL> SELECT CHR(BITAND(<value in P1>, 16777216)/16777215) ||
            CHR(BITAND(<value in P1>, 16711680)/65535) "enqueue name"
       FROM DUAL;
```

Enqueue Name	Description
CF	Control-file transaction lock
DF	Data-file lock
IR	Instance recovery lock
La, where 'a' is another alphabet	Library cache lock
MR	Media recovery lock
PI	Parallel slaves lock
PR	Process startup lock
Qa, where 'a' is another alphabet	Row-cache lock
RT	Redo thread lock
SC	SCN lock
SQ	Sequence lock
ST	Space management transaction lock
TA	Transaction recovery lock
TM	DML lock
TX	Transaction lock
XI	Instance registration enqueue

TABLE 11-9. *List of Enqueue Names*

P1 provides the lock mode within its lower-order bytes. Modes are the same as described under the *buffer deadlock* event. The lock mode can be acquired via the following query:

```
SQL> SELECT BITAND(<value in P1>, 65535)

       FROM DUAL;
```

Values for the P2 and P3 parameters vary according to the actual enqueue. For instance, with an ST (space management transaction) lock, both P2 and P3 are set to 0 (zero), whereas; for an MR (media recovery) lock, both P2 and P3 may be 0, indicating that either recovery is being performed or redo-logs are being reset, or alternatively, P2 could be set to the file number being recovered and P3 remain 0, depending on the status of recovery at the time of the wait.

If high occurrences of enqueue wait events are noticed, then one needs to tune them and make a larger number of enqueues available by increasing the value of the ENQUEUE_RESOURCES initialization parameter, and so on. An earlier tip discusses tuning enqueues and latches.

Free Buffer Waits

These wait events primarily occur when foreground server processes do not find adequate free buffers in the buffer cache. Existing buffers are being either modified or read by other server processes or are dirty due to previous writes. This may occur due to DBWR not keeping up with processing loads and not flushing dirty buffers to disk soon enough. Also, this may occur due to DBWR hitting the *free buffers inspected* limit (Chapter 7) and stopping further scans. This results in free buffers not being made available, and DBWR may be posted to achieve the same. Another reason for this happening is when data-block buffers get invalidated due to specific events such as a file status changing, say, from read-only to read/write, affecting all the blocks within the file. When the status changes, Oracle needs to link each buffer to lock components and then assign each buffer to a specific dba (pertaining to the blocks within the file with the changed status). During this time, foreground server processes that need the buffers may have to wait. The wait time for this event is one second.

In this case, P1 holds the file number pertaining to the file containing the blocks that need to be read into the buffer cache. P2 contains the block ID of the block that needs to be read in.

If this event occurs often in *v$system_event,* then one needs to take appropriate steps to attain the following:

- **Refrain from changing data-file/tablespace status** Avoid changing data-file/tablespace statuses in the middle of peak production hours.

Perform such activities during periods of low use and ensure that the control-file is backed up after any such changes.

- **Increase DBWR throughput** Chapter 7 outlines ways to achieve the same.
- **Tune application SQL** Ensure that unnecessary I/Os are not occurring to read unwanted blocks into the buffer cache (taking up valuable space). Ensure that index scans are occurring wherever appropriate and full-table scans are minimized (in OLTP applications, of course!). Whenever possible, use unique index scans rather than range scans and index-only scans rather than index/table lookups. Verify that application design allows for optimal execution paths to be available. For instance, if queries need to return summarized data and hence use a number of DISTINCT, GROUP BY, and ORDER BY clauses, and so on, make summary tables (materialized views in Oracle8*i*) available with data in a presorted format.
- **Increase DB_BLOCK_BUFFERS** Increase the number of buffers available provided that memory use has not already reached the limit.

Index Block Split

This event occurs as index blocks split (refer to Chapter 6 for a detailed discussion on index block splits). The waiting time here is zero; however, the CPU is rescinded and the point of execution jumps to the end of the CPU execution queue (thus losing its priority in the sequence of execution). Also, this causes additional resource use such as extra CPU cycles—to compute the block-split ratio and actually make the split—and possibly extra I/O. Block splits during peak hours can cause a strain on response time. Here, P1 holds the dba of the block that is currently full and needs to be split. P2 holds the level being split within the index. The leaves are considered to be level zero, whereas the branches (including the root) have a level greater than zero. P3 holds the dba of the new child block that is created as a result of the split. Using the dba in P1, one may determine the indexes causing the split most frequently and rebuild them at the next possible opportunity. Specifying a higher PCTFREE during creation/re-creation will induce block splits to occur during index creation time and not during actual runtime, thus avoiding these events. Refer to Chapters 6 and 12 for further details.

Latch Free

This indicates that latches are not adequately available and processes are waiting to acquire them. Each time a latch wait is encountered, the wait time exponentially increases (without including the spin time). Here, P1/P1RAW contain the address of the latch that is unavailable (*v$latch*.ADDR). P2 contains the latch number (*v$latchname*.LATCH#), and P3 contains the number of attempts made to acquire the latch (including the resultant sleeps). An earlier tip outlines ways to tune latch allocation.

Log Buffer Space

This event occurs as there are waits for log buffer space. The wait time varies, and there are no parameters in *v$session_wait*. Possible solutions include increasing the size of the log buffer via the LOG_BUFFER initialization parameter and increasing the throughput of LGWR by placing the redo-logs on fast disks/controllers. Chapter 7 outlines additional methods to increase LGWR throughput.

Log File–Related Wait Events

The following wait events are related to log-file reads and writes:

- Log file parallel write
- Log file sequential read
- Log file single write

The wait event *log file parallel write* occurs as the multiplexed copies of the CURRENT redo-log group are being written to by LGWR from the log buffer. The wait time includes the time to complete the writes. Here, P1 holds the number of files written, P2 holds the number of blocks written, and P3 holds the number of I/O requests required to accomplish the same.

The wait event *log file sequential read* occurs as redo records within a redo-log file are being read. All files within a log group may be read if the group is being dumped. The wait time consists of the I/O calls required to complete the read. In this case, P1 holds the log-sequence number of the log file being read within the group (note that all files may be read while the group is being dumped). P2 holds the (OS physical block size) block offset within the log file. P3 holds the number of blocks read.

The wait event *log file single write* indicates writes to the log-file headers when log members are being added or control information (SCN, hot backup status, and so on) is being written. Again, wait time varies depending on the time taken for the I/O calls to complete. Here, P1 contains the group number of the log file being written (*v$log*.GROUP#). P2 holds the block offset within the log file being written, and P3 holds the number of blocks being written.

When the number of occurrences of these wait events appears high, then ensure that writes to log files occur as fast as possible. Place the redo-logs on fast disks/controllers and streamline LGWR throughput (Chapter 7).

Log File Space/Switch

This event indicates that Oracle is waiting for the log buffer to be flushed to disk. This wait usually ensues due to lack of adequate space in the CURRENT log file (space is filled up), and a log switch needs to occur to create the necessary space. However, a checkpoint may not have finished on the CURRENT log file, and the log switch needs to wait for the checkpoint to complete. Alternatively, archiving of the CURRENT log file may not be complete, thus causing this wait event. If a user session is associated with this event, then it may be due to inadequate space in the log buffer. Wait time for this event may be as high as ten seconds. There are no parameters for this event. Resolving high occurrences of this event involves understanding DML activity (especially the frequency of COMMITs) in the application(s) and the size of the average redo size. An easier way of approximating the average redo size is to query *v$sysstat* for the total redo size and the number of user commits (WHERE name = 'redo size' AND name = 'user commits'). Once these two figures are obtained, one may divide redo size by user commits to derive the average redo size. One needs to verify that the log buffer is sized adequately to easily accommodate the average redo size (plus some buffer space). Also, increasing the size and number of the online redo-logs may help. Finally, increasing DBWR and ARCH throughputs to expedite checkpoints and archiving, respectively, would also help in reducing the occurrences of this event (Chapter 7 discusses some methods to do that).

Log File Switch (Checkpoint Incomplete)

This event also occurs due to checkpoints not completing on time. There are no parameters to this event, and the actual wait time varies. Solutions to alleviate the occurrences of this event are the same as those discussed under *log file space/switch*.

Log File Switch (Archiving Needed)

This event occurs due to archiving of the CURRENT log file not being complete and thus preventing a log switch. There are no parameters to this event, and, again, actual wait time varies. Solutions include enhancing ARCH throughput (Chapter 7) and increasing the size of online redo-log files (providing ARCH more time to catch up).

Log File Sync

This indicates the time taken to flush the log buffer to the online redo-log files as sessions issue COMMITs. Once LGWR has completed the flush, it posts the user session to continue. The actual wait period consists of the time to flush and then complete the posting; it thus varies. Here, P1 consists of the buffer number within the log buffer. The size of each individual buffer within the log buffer is equivalent to the OS physical block size. If this wait event occurs too frequently, one needs to tune LGWR to ensure that writes and the resultant postings are accomplished quickly. Additionally, one may need to evaluate application code and, possibly, reduce the number of COMMITs.

Parallel Query Create Server

This wait event occurs as Oracle starts up a new parallel query server process. This event may be expensive to incur at runtime, especially during peak hours. The wait time constitutes the time for each parallel query server process to start up and may vary depending on overall system activity. In this case, P1 contains the number of parallel query server processes that are being started up, P2 contains the time spent in getting the processes started, and P3 contains information on the enqueues required to do so. If this event occurs too frequently, then one can prestart the (maximum) required number of parallel query server processes via the PARALLEL_MIN_SERVERS initialization parameter, rather than allow them to be started and terminated dynamically at runtime.

PMON Timer

This indicates the idleness of the PMON background process and can therefore be ignored (since PMON does not have to be active all the time—that would only waste CPU). The wait time is usually three seconds or less. Here, P1 provides the actual duration for which PMON was idle, waiting for the next timeout, when it can be active again.

RDBMS IPC Message and RDBMS IPC Reply

These wait events are incurred due to inter-process communication (ipc) delays between various Oracle processes. The event *rdbms ipc message* indicates waits between subsequent ipc calls sent from one process to another. Here, P1 holds the time in seconds after which the wait will abort. The event *rdbms ipc reply* indicates the waits ensuing for replies from background processes after one or more messages are sent. In this case, P1 holds the process ID (*v$process*.PID) of the process from which the replies are expected. P2 holds the time (in seconds) within which a reply has to arrive; if that is exceeded, a timeout will occur. In both cases, the wait times vary. These wait events are part of normal functioning and can usually be ignored.

SMON Timer

This indicates the idleness of the SMON background process and therefore can usually be ignored. SMON also does not have to be active all the time, since that would only waste CPU. The wait time is usually 300 seconds (five minutes) or less. Here, P1 provides the actual duration in seconds for which SMON has remained idle, waiting for the next timeout, when it can be active again. P2 provides the number of times SMON was posted due to errors in processing requiring SMON's services.

Undo Segment Extension

This event indicates that rollback segments are being subjected to space-management operations (extending, shrinking, and so on). Foreground sessions cannot continue until these operations are complete. The wait time is usually one-hundredth of a second. P1 provides the rollback segment number (*v$rollstat*.USN and *v$rollname*.USN). Solutions include sizing rollback segments appropriately for transaction volumes. OPTIMAL has to be set such that shrinks do not occur too frequently. Chapter 12 outlines various guidelines on sizing rollback segments.

Undo Segment Recovery

This event indicates that dead (aborted) transactions are being recovered by PMON. Typically, one has no choice but to wait for these to be recovered. The wait time is usually around three seconds. P1 provides the rollback segment number where the recovery is being done. P2 contains internal transaction flags in hex specific to the recovery process. A larger number of rollback segments need to be created, so that newer transactions can continue uninterrupted by using other available rollback segments.

Undo Segment TX Slot

This wait occurs due to transaction slots within the rollback segment header being unavailable. This could be due to multiple transactions sharing the same rollback segment. The wait time is usually one second. Here, P1 contains the rollback segment number where the contention is being experienced. This can be alleviated to an extent by making available a larger number of rollback segments and allowing transactions to make use of them.

Write Complete Waits

This wait is incurred by sessions waiting for a specific buffer to be written during the normal course of processing or due to inter-instance pings (in OPS environments). The wait time is usually one second. Here, P1 contains the file number containing the block corresponding to the buffer, P2 contains the actual block ID within the file, and P3 contains a status flag, providing information on where (the execution point at which) the write was required, such as 1034, indicating that the buffer was required due to an inter-instance ping. These waits can be reduced by increasing DBWR throughput.

Periodically watch for and resolve locking conflicts

As common as locking is in any multi-user database, conflicts can easily arise. With Oracle, conflicts are relatively rare, but, nevertheless, they do appear once in a while. And when they occur, they can cause severe blockages to various other production sessions, thus disrupting regular operations—unless locking problems are one of the specific things that the DBA monitors the database for, being alerted so that he or she can jump into action to resolve potential problems. Quite often, a locking conflict is perceived as a "hanging" problem, where specific sessions just seem to be "running" continuously and not finishing. When the right views are examined, however, it becomes clear that the hanging is merely a symptom and the cause is improper use of locks by the application.

Oracle provides a number of utilities to detect locking problems. However, my current favorite is the DBA_WAITERS view. Let's look at some of the utilities available to detect locking conflicts and also look at some possible solutions to resolve the issues once they are detected.

Oracle and Third-Party Utilities

There are various utilities ranging from the good old SQL*DBA/Server Manager to Oracle Enterprise Manager, as well as various third-party tools (seems like a new one is being released almost every month) that allow locks to be monitored and optionally alert the DBA when trouble seems to be brewing. Refer to the appropriate product manual for information on how these specific products work.

Specific SQL Queries

One may use specific SELECT statements to list the locks currently in place by querying *v$lock, v$session,* and so on. The DBA needs to run these queries at frequent intervals (predefined times). That will allow him or her to gauge the kind of locking activity that goes on within the database as part of "normal" processing. So when abnormal situations are observed (too many locks, sudden table-level locks, and so on), the DBA can immediately predict a possible problem and take steps to prevent its escalation. Chapter 19 provides some queries that help in determining lock activity.

catblock.sql

The *catblock.sql* file is a script provided as part of the Oracle installation. This script is present in the *$ORACLE_HOME/rdbms/admin* directory on UNIX (the *%ORACLE_HOME%\rdbmsNN\admin* directory on NT, where *NN* refers to the database version). The *catblock.sql* file provides a set of view definitions that aid in lock interpretation. This script needs to be run as SYS. Once the views are defined, they can be queried directly by the DBA (views such as DBA_LOCKS, DBA_WAITERS, and DBA_BLOCKERS). Alternatively, the *utllockt.sql* script (explained in the text that follows) can be run to query these views. Three of the most important views within *catblock.sql* are

DBA_LOCKS DBA_LOCKS is actually a synonym on top of the DBA_LOCK view. The view gathers various lock statistics from *v$lock* and translates the various lock types and modes into a more easily understandable format.

DBA_WAITERS This view is built on top of the DBA_LOCKS view and provides information on the sessions that are currently waiting for locks (the "waiters") on specific resources and the sessions that currently have those resources locked (the "blockers"). I find DBA_WAITERS to be almost magical in its ability to reveal this information. However, note that it uses a fairly complicated query and may be a little time-consuming (usually, a couple of minutes). One thing I definitely do at every site I visit is to create the DBA_WAITERS view and periodically use it. In certain versions of Oracle, the DBA_WAITERS view causes excessive *recursive calls* and sorts and goes into a "hang." After a while, it consumes all available temporary tablespace and causes genuine application programs to crash—so much for non-disruptive monitoring! However, there is a workaround (produces results, though it is inconvenient): query DBA_WAITERS and after three or so minutes, if there is no response back, then break the query (kill the session, if necessary). Then retrieve the view definition for DBA_WAITERS either from DBA_VIEWS or from *catblock.sql*. Then query *v$session* and make a note of the session_ids (SIDs) that seem to be very slow or even hanging. Change the query from the DBA_WAITERS view definition to refer to those SIDs directly within the query and run it. That will prevent large numbers of recursive calls and stop the sorts from eating up all the temporary tablespace. A response comes back in a few seconds, allowing you to look at information specific to those sessions you hallmarked. Here's an example: The following code provides the actual view definition of DBA_WAITERS.

```
CREATE VIEW dba_waiters AS
 SELECT /*+ all_rows */ w.session_id  waiting_session,
        h.session_id  holding_session,
        w.lock_type,
        h.mode_held,
        w.mode_requested,
        w.lock_id1,
        w.lock_id2
  FROM dba_locks w, dba_locks h
 WHERE h.blocking_others = 'Blocking'
   AND  h.mode_held  !=  'None'
   AND  h.mode_held  !=  'Null'
   AND  w.mode_requested !=  'None'
   AND  w.lock_type  =  h.lock_type
   AND  w.lock_id1   =  h.lock_id1
   AND  w.lock_id2    =  h.lock_id2;
```

Now, let's say you need to find out information pertaining to session IDs 129, 144, and 168. The query from the view definition can be changed (and run) as follows:

```
SELECT /*+ all_rows */ w.session_id  waiting_session,
       h.session_id  holding_session,
       w.lock_type,
       h.mode_held,
       w.mode_requested,
       w.lock_id1,
       w.lock_id2
  FROM dba_locks w, dba_locks h
 WHERE h.blocking_others = 'Blocking'
   AND  h.mode_held   !=   'None'
   AND  h.mode_held   !=   'Null'
   AND  w.mode_requested !=   'None'
   AND  w.lock_type   =   h.lock_type
   AND  w.lock_id1    =   h.lock_id1
   AND  w.lock_id2     =   h.lock_id2
   AND  w.session_id IN (129, 144, 168);
```

There is yet another strategy if the above workaround also seems too slow. Here, a temporary table has to be created to hold a point in time snapshot of the DBA_LOCKS view (the base view for DBA_WAITERS). The table can be created as follows:

```
SQL> CREATE TABLE t_locks
      TABLESPACE TOOLS STORAGE(INITIAL 4K NEXT 4K PCTINCREASE 0)
      AS SELECT * FROM dba_locks
          WHERE session_id IN (129, 144, 168);
```

Now, the DBA_WAITERS query can be duplicated using the T_LOCKS temporary table as follows:

```
SQL> SELECT w.session_id  waiting_session,
       h.session_id  holding_session,
       w.lock_type,
       h.mode_held,
       w.mode_requested,
       w.lock_id1,
       w.lock_id2
  FROM t_locks w, t_locks h
 WHERE h.blocking_others = 'Blocking'
   AND  h.mode_held   !=   'None'
   AND  h.mode_held   !=   'Null'
   AND  w.mode_requested !=   'None'
```

```
AND  w.lock_type  =  h.lock_type
AND  w.lock_id1   =  h.lock_id1
AND  w.lock_id2   =  h.lock_id2;
```

After the requisite information is acquired, the temporary table may be dropped (it cannot be used later, since the information captured within the table is specific to a point in time and would become redundant as the lock statuses change). Using an actual table (T_LOCKS) instead of the DBA_LOCKS view helps greatly by reducing recursive calls, preventing "hanging" situations and returning the required results back instantaneously.

DBA_BLOCKERS This is yet another useful view within *catblock.sql.* This view is built on top of the DBA_WAITERS and DBA_LOCKS views and provides information on which sessions are holding up others, without being held up themselves (by other sessions).

Chapter 19 provides some queries to retrieve information from these views. Also, the view definitions within the *catblock.sql* script are easily readable, and the script itself provides useful comments for detailed interpretation of its usage.

utllockt.sql

Similar to *catblock.sql,* this script is also present in the *$ORACLE_HOME/rdbms/admin* directory. It reads the view definitions created by *catblock.sql* and therefore needs to be run only after the latter has been run. It produces a report on locking statistics in a human-readable "tree-structured" format, properly indenting all the "waiter" sessions. The *utllockt.sql* script also has detailed comments regarding its usage.

Finally, the *utllockt.sql* scripts creates and drops tables in the user's default tablespace. When frequently run as the SYS user ID, it may cause fragmentation within the SYSTEM tablespace. Accordingly, it is advisable to run these scripts as a user that points to a non-SYSTEM tablespace as the default tablespace. Alternatively, change these scripts to create the tables in a specific non-SYSTEM tablespace (such as TOOLS or USERS) where the user running the script has adequate quota.

Debugging Locking Conflicts

Sometimes, locking conflicts cannot be determined by normal methods outlined previously. For example, certain long-running critical jobs may be affected and may not be killed, or many processes may be affected, causing the perception that the entire instance is hanging. Resolving such situations requires use of certain OS and database debugging tools (such as *oradbx* or *oradebug,* and *truss*) to take process-state or system-state dumps, trace SQL calls being issued, and so on. Chapter 13 discusses these methods in more detail.

Once the offending sessions are determined (the ones that hold up other sessions), they need to COMMIT or ROLLBACK to release all locks. In case these sessions are not interactive (such as a batch job) or are running a DDL command (such as an index rebuild) and cannot be explicitly committed or rolled back, then they need to be terminated either via the ALTER SYSTEM KILL SESSION command within Oracle or via an OS equivalent command (such as the *kill* command in UNIX). Note that killing them within Oracle is preferred, especially in an MTS environment. Refer to the Oracle8 documentation set on specific locking guidelines within applications. A few of the important ones are listed here:

- In case users (or administrators) are allowed to perform ad hoc changes to data, ensure that they issue COMMITs or ROLLBACKs explicitly as soon as the statement completes. Omitting COMMITs/ROLLBACKs is one of the most common reasons for locking conflicts. Users may run a statement locking up rows and then venture out for coffee or lunch. Ensure that you implement policy decisions that expressly warn them not to do so under any circumstance. This is absolutely mandatory in a high-availability site.
- As far as possible, do not issue explicit locks (via the LOCK command). Use Oracle's default row-level locking in most/all situations.
- Do not issue commands that affect concurrency, such as certain DDL and DCL commands (CREATE INDEX, ANALYE TABLE VALIDATE STRUCTURE, and so on). Oracle8*i* is more tolerant toward some of these commands, allowing concurrent DML to occur without conflicts.
- Ensure that applications change data in tables in the same order. Mixing the order in which changes are done could potentially lead to deadlocks.
- Create indexes on all foreign keys, especially for larger, popular tables. In certain versions of Oracle, if the foreign key indexes are missing, modifications to the child table cause an implicit SHARE lock to be placed on the parent table, thus greatly impacting concurrency.

Monitor shared pool effectiveness and tune, if necessary

Shared-pool size is one factor that is often not set optimally during initial installation and configuration. Changing shared-pool size requires the database to be bounced. Accordingly, it is imperative that one spends time estimating usage patterns, understands application shared-pool requirements, and uses the formulae in the *Oracle Administrator's Guide* to get the initial sizing right. At times, you won't accurately know the extent of actual use during initial configuration. However, using these sizing tools (application/tool requirements analysis, formulae, and so on) and some educated guesswork, you can get pretty close to reality. That way, at least in the short run, you won't have to announce an emergency, bounce the database, and increase the size. For instance, Oracle Designer v2.1 requires the shared pool to be at least 18MB. So, initially, you need to start off with the shared-pool size being at least 18MB (or equivalent to the results of the formulae, whichever is higher). Being aware of such requirements helps in avoiding unnecessary bounces. However, in order to find out whether the initial size you have set is adequate or not, you will need to monitor shared-pool use extensively. You could include shared-pool monitoring in your bag of "regular maintenance tasks." Additionally, you need to be familiar with the working of the shared pool in order to be able to monitor its effectiveness thoroughly. And that's what constitutes the bulk of this tip. This tip does not repeat the formulae readily available in the Oracle documentation set. However, it attempts to explain the internal working of the shared pool and share some tips in evaluating its post-deployment effectiveness.

The Shared Pool and Components

The shared pool is one of the primary components of the Oracle SGA. As its name indicates, it provides a "common area" for sharing resources such as server code (SQL, PL/SQL statements) and metadata (data dictionary) by various foreground server processes. Such sharing prevents unnecessary duplication—by deferring the need for each server process to separately parse, maintain, and execute its own code. If the required code has already been executed by another server process or even itself earlier, then the code is readily available in the shared pool and can be immediately utilized, thus helping performance and conserving resources. Sizing the shared pool correctly is even more important than sizing other SGA components such as data-block buffers, redo buffers, and so on. This is because a library-cache miss or a data-dictionary cache miss is more expensive than a buffer-cache miss, since the former involves not only I/O but also allocation of certain internal structures at runtime and populating them with the information read in. Accordingly, it is essential for the shared pool to
be sized/configured prior to other SGA components. Also, the shared pool consists of multiple sub-components and structures (as we will see soon). In Oracle7 onward, however, there is only one initialization parameter to set it appropriately. There is no documented finer degree of control to size each individual sub-component separately, making the task of estimating the total shared-pool size easier (just one parameter to deal with) but more prone to inaccuracies (if this single parameter is not set optimally, all sub-components become sub-optimal).

The SGA comprises four primary portions (this information can be viewed in *v$sga*):

- Fixed buffers, consisting of various mandatory Oracle structures, constituting the fixed overhead

- Variable buffers that reside in the "upper SGA heap" (explained later) and account for the shared pool and tertiary structures to hold enqueues, process states, and so on
- The data-block buffer cache, comprising free and dirty data blocks
- Redo log buffers, consisting of the "post image" of changes made to data

Thus, the variable buffers are mainly used to hold the shared pool. Depending on whether information required by foreground server processes is private or public (sharable) and the time frames for which such information is required, it gets stored in the SGA or the PGA. In a dedicated server environment, for instance, memory structures used by the dedicated server are considered private and hence stored in the PGA (specifically, in the UGA, the user global area within the PGA). In MTS and XA configurations, however, the same structures would need to be accessed by multiple foreground server processes (the shared servers) and hence get stored in the variable buffers of the SGA (that is, the user global area would be present in the SGA). Similarly, all code read in and their versions (unparsed, parsed, binded, and so on) that need to be shared are maintained in the shared pool. There are basically four different time frames for which this information will need to be maintained: instance, process, session, and call. These time frames imply that the concerned structures need to be maintained throughout the life of the instance, a foreground server process, a database session, or a call issued within a session by a server process. For instance, memory structures that need to be alive only for the duration of a call are typically placed in the PGA (specifically, into the CGA, the call global area within the PGA). Examples of such structures are local variables, cursor states, and so on. Thus, with some knowledge of the type of information that needs to be stored, how long it needs to be present, and whether it is sharable (public) or not (private), one can get a good feel for what would go into the shared pool.

As may be apparent from the preceding discussion, the shared pool mainly comprises the shared application code, that is, the library cache, and the shared metadata, that is, the data-dictionary cache. The latter is also referred to as the row cache. Besides these two, the shared pool also contains certain overhead information such as enqueues, buffer cache handles, and so on to synchronize access by various processes and to allow recovery when a process holding resources such as enqueue locks is aborted. Just after startup, foreground processes populate the shared pool with various pieces of information. Such information is maintained in the shared pool because it is needed beyond the lifetime of the process that populated it. Accordingly, it is not maintained in the PGA, because then the information would be destroyed when the process exits (the PGA is released to the OS heap when the corresponding process exits or is terminated). The library and data-dictionary caches need to be

maintained for longer time frames than an individual process, so that multiple processes at various times can access them.

The library cache contains various forms of shared code such as shared cursors (private cursors are held in the PGA), packages, procedures, and views, along with their dependencies. The data-dictionary cache contains portions of the data dictionary (ideally, the entire dictionary).

Shared-Pool Management

The shared pool and the PGA use a generic code routine to manage their memory. This code routine is called the KGH heap manager. The heap manager is a built-in Oracle routine and is consistent across platforms. The main function of the heap manager is to allocate memory when requested. In the case of the PGA, it uses *malloc()* calls for allocation (since allocation is dynamic) and frees unused memory via *free()* calls. In the case of the shared pool, however, all required memory is allocated right at the beginning (during the STARTUP NOMOUNT stage). Also, within the shared pool, unused/dormant memory is not freed to the OS but maintained for reuse by other processes. In other words, the shared pool does not shrink. From Oracle's perspective, the shared pool and the rest of the variable buffers constitute the "SGA heap," even though from the OS perspective, the SGA resides in shared memory and not directly in the upper heap area.

The library cache (KGL) internally uses the KGH heap manager to allocate storage for various server code objects (I use the term "object" to refer to various code modules such as SQL statements, packages, and so on). Each object has a specific handle, which is used to locate the actual object and manipulate it, depending on wherever it gets allocated within the library cache. All allocations are made from the top-most portion of the SGA heap. A hashing algorithm is used to determine the handle and its location for quick and efficient access.

The library cache structure as a whole is an array of doubly linked lists consisting of multiple object handles (see Figure 11-2). Each list is referred to as a hash bucket, and the entire series forms a hash table. Initially, 251 hash buckets get allocated. Later as the number of objects that need to be retained within the library cache exceeds 251, additional hash buckets get allocated. The next number that is allocated equals the next higher prime number (251, 509, 1021, and so on). When the hash-table size is increased thus, the table is practically rebuilt; all objects are rehashed to be placed appropriately in the new hash table, and the memory taken up by the earlier table is released. This resizing process takes a few seconds (since everything happens in memory). Since it is a rare phenomenon, it is considered to be relatively inexpensive in the overall scheme of things. Generally, unless your applications rely on an overly high number of distinct SQL statements, procedures, packages, and so on, 251 hash buckets are usually sufficient. However, in case your applications are expected to use a higher number, you could prevent a runtime resizing of the hash table by pre-allocating a higher number of hash buckets during startup. This is accomplished by setting the undocumented initialization parameter _KGL_BUCKET_COUNT to the higher value desired (the next higher prime number). As mentioned earlier, however, the dynamic resizing is not considered to be an expensive operation by Oracle. Accordingly, changing the _KGL_BUCKET_COUNT parameter is not recommended (it is only for your information). Note that the number of buckets does not ever fall lower than 251.

When a hash function is applied to the object handle comprising the object namespace (type such as package, procedure, cursor, and so on), object name, database link (if any), and owner name, it gets hashed to a specific bucket. Note that every object has a name (even anonymous PL/SQL blocks are provided a generated name). Now, this hash bucket is scanned to see whether the object handle exists there. If so, there is a pointer referring to the actual object and its contents. If not, a new entry is allocated for the object in that specific hash bucket (where the hash function maps it), and it gets populated with the object contents. The reason for an object entry not being present is that it is possibly being invoked for the first time or it was present earlier, but since no process was referencing it, it was unpinned from memory to allow another object to reuse its space. The object contents include the following:

- The namespace, indicating whether the object is a procedure, trigger, package, or other. All namespaces are listed in *v$librarycache.*
- Status flags, indicating the current status of the object, such as whether it is existent, being created, being altered, or being dropped.
- A dependency table, listing all objects on which the current object depends (contained in *sys.dependency$* and viewable from *v$object_dependency*).
- A child table, listing the various versions of each object. For instance, if multiple users each issue a SQL statement *DELETE FROM shares_owned,* with a separate SHARES_OWNED table being present under each user ID, then each of these SQL statements gets hashed to the same value (considered the parent statement in this case). However, each invocation, since it refers to a separate table, would be considered a different version of the same statement. The child table would list all such versions corresponding to a parent statement.
- An authorization table, listing the privileges granted on the object to the users and roles within the database.
- KGL data blocks. These are control blocks, each containing a heap descriptor corresponding to a memory heap, storing the object p-code, source code, cursor context area, and other pertinent data. The size of each memory heap is unconstrained and is virtually unlimited. Each KGL data block also stores the heap pin count, which is basically a count of server

processes accessing the heap. Each server process needs to pin a heap prior to accessing (reading, modifying) it. When the pin count is zero, that is an indication that the heap is unused and is a candidate to be freed and replaced by another heap. There are generally eight or less KGL data blocks per object (PL/SQL-based objects use six, whereas shared SQL statements use two). In the case of shared SQL statements, the execution path (revealed via the EXPLAIN PLAN utility) is stored in the KGL data blocks.

Concurrency Control

The library cache utilizes locks, pins, and subsidiary latches to allow concurrent access to objects. Locks are the basic access-control mechanisms. A lock may be acquired in NULL, SHARE, or EXCLUSIVE mode. Both NULL and SHARE locks are acquired for read-only operations, whereas EXCLUSIVE locks are acquired when the object is being created/altered/dropped. The difference between NULL and SHARE is that the former allows the lock to be broken by another process when it needs to

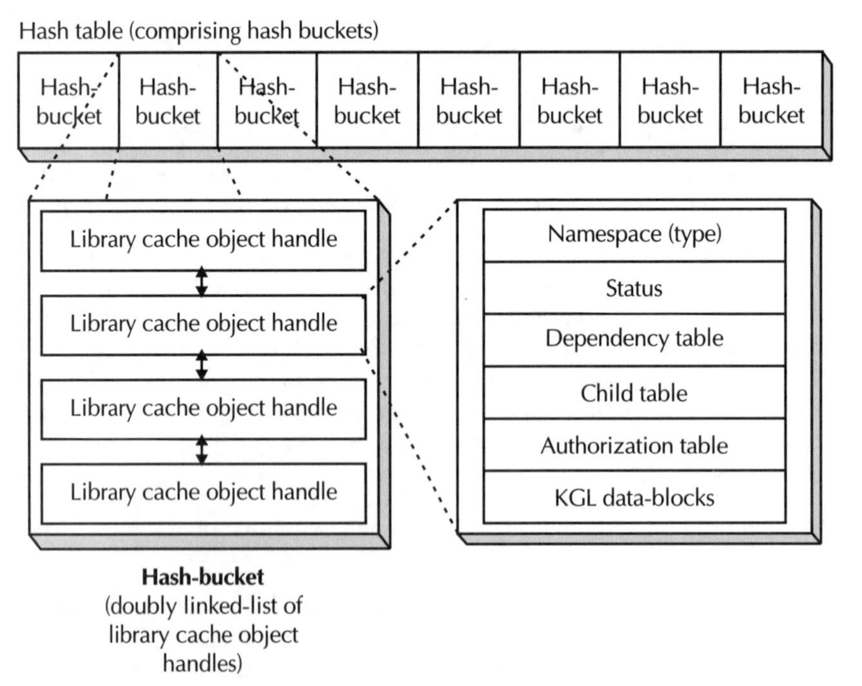

FIGURE 11-2. *Library-cache structures*

pin the object in exclusive mode. Similarly, NULL locks indicate if the current object has become invalid.

Pins are subsidiary access-control mechanisms. Every server process needs to acquire a lock prior to acquiring a pin. A pin allows access to an object to be more finely controlled. Thus, multiple server processes may acquire a lock on the object handle and then acquire a pin (in the required mode) on the object. If a lock or a pin in the desired mode is in use, the process waits for it to become available. A pin may be acquired in SHARE or EXCLUSIVE mode, depending on whether the object is being read or written to.

Finally, latches are acquired on the actual code to prevent it from being executed concurrently by multiple processes. Latches can be acquired at varying levels to prevent locking problems. If a process is terminated while holding a latch, recovery is initiated to free the latch. Library latches and locks/pins go hand in glove. To understand this better, let's look at the kinds of latches used within the library cache:

- The load-lock latch, required to load a new object in the library cache (so that multiple processes cannot simultaneously call and load the object)
- The library cache latch, required by processes prior to acquiring a lock on an object handle
- The pin latch, required by processes prior to pinning the object

The library cache latch needs to be monitored (in *v$latch*) because it is often prone to heavy contention. There are specific steps you can take to reduce this contention. Also, starting with v7.2, multiple library cache latches have been introduced, each corresponding to a range of hash buckets to alleviate the contention.

The Data-Dictionary Cache

The data-dictionary cache or row cache constitutes the other major portion of the shared pool. However, row-cache operations are not as complex as the ones pertaining to the library cache and in fact can be viewed as a subset in terms of functionality. This cache chiefly comprises memory structures corresponding to data-dictionary segments and latches to allow simultaneous access to these structures by server processes (especially during recursive calls to qualify segment names used in SQL statements, check privileges on those segments for the user running the statement, and so on). Furthermore, from a tuning perspective, if problems are observed in the library cache, then there is a high probability of similar problems being observed in the row cache, and likewise, if the library cache is operating smoothly, so will the row cache. Since I have already discussed the library cache in a fairly detailed manner, I will proceed to the next topic, tuning the shared pool.

Evaluating and Tuning Shared-Pool Efficiency

The following steps can be taken to determine the current efficiency of the shared pool:

- Check the cache hit ratios
- Check the number of parses
- Check for library cache latch contention
- Check for fragmentation

Let's look at each in detail and discuss ways to prevent/overcome them.

CACHE HIT RATIOS Cache hit ratios provide excellent insight on the functioning of the library cache and the row cache. If the hit ratios are high (say, > 98 percent), then the caches are set optimally. The following query helps you determine the library-cache hit ratio:

```
SQL> select sum(pins)/(sum(pins)+sum(reloads))*100 from v$librarycache;
```

The following query helps you evaluate the hit ratio for various namespaces (object types) within the library cache:

```
SQL> SELECT namespace, gets, gethitratio, pins, pinhitratio,
            invalidations, reloads
       FROM v$librarycache;
```

Besides the hit ratios just described, you also need to pay attention to the RELOADS and INVALIDATIONS. RELOADS indicate the number of times that objects in the library cache have aged out (that is, not been pinned for a while by any server process) and reacquired shortly after. INVALIDATIONS indicate the number of times these objects became invalid (someone has re-created or recompiled them or a dependency was changed/dropped while these objects were still in memory). Obviously, these are expensive operations that result in reparsing and could lead to higher fragmentation (due to constantly being aged out/invalidated and reloaded on subsequent calls). The following steps need to be taken to prevent them from occurring too frequently:

- Check for developers working in the production environment, who change and recompile procedures, packages, and so forth on the fly, and prevent them from doing that. Ensure that code is well designed, developed, and tested prior to being moved to production. A well-defined process will eliminate the need for on-the-fly recompilation.

- Find out all large code routines (especially packages) and pin them in memory (via DBMS_SHARED_POOL.KEEP). For instance, any code routine over 8KB may be considered large and be a candidate for such pinning). You can determine the actual sizes of large code routines via the following query:

```
SQL> SELECT name, sharable_mem FROM v$db_object_cache
      WHERE sharable_mem > 8192
        AND kept = 'NO'
        AND type IN ('PACKAGE', 'PACKAGE BODY', 'PROCEDURE', 'FUNCTION');
```

- In the case of frequently used large anonymous PL/SQL blocks, convert them into stored procedures or packages and pin them as well.

The following query helps you determine the hit ratio for the row cache:

```
SQL> SELECT SUM(gets)/(SUM(gets)+SUM(getmisses))*100 FROM v$rowcache;
```

If the cache hit ratios seem sub-optimal, then you will need to increase the shared-pool size. Alternatively, if the hit ratios are high and the "free memory" in *v$sgastat* also appears high (> 20 percent of the total shared-pool size) during peak hours, then probably the shared pool is set higher than required and can be made a little smaller, if necessary (especially if you are lacking in memory for other areas such as the buffer cache).

PARSE FREQUENCY You can find out whether certain library-cache objects are being parsed too frequently via the following query:

```
SQL> SELECT name, value FROM v$sysstat

      WHERE name = 'parse count';
```

If the resultant number appears too high or if, during peak hours, the number keeps constantly increasing, then it may indicate a problem. Ensure that you look at the numbers only after the database has been up and running for a while (initially the numbers may be constantly increasing as the library cache is optimally populated with the queries; this does not indicate a problem).

Also, statement executions being less than twice the number of parses is a good indication of excessive parses:

```
SQL> SELECT SUBSTR(sql_text, 1, 30), parse_calls, executions
      FROM v$sqlarea
     WHERE executions < (parse_calls * 2);
```

Additionally, lack of sharing between SQL statements results in constant parsing and increasing the load on the library cache. You can check the portion of statements that are successful in finding earlier versions of the same statements in the library cache already (making sharing possible) via the following query:

```
SQL> SELECT gethitratio FROM v$librarycache

     WHERE namespace = 'SQL AREA';
```

If the GETHITRATIO from the preceding query is low (85 percent or less), then you have reason for worry.

Once you have determined that there are excessive parses, you will need to take the following steps to reduce them:

- Audit application code and ensure consistent standards are in place among the development teams for writing code (code in upper/lowercase, hard carriage returns after the FROM clause, WHERE clause, and so on, indentation).
- Ensure that bind variables are used to prevent each occurrence of the statement from being considered a separate one. For instance, if multiple statements are used throughout the application, such as the following:

  ```
  SELECT name, age FROM names WHERE id = 16;

  SELECT name, age FROM names WHERE id = 120;
  ```

  you could consolidate the preceding statements as follows:

  ```
  SELECT name, age FROM names WHERE id =:id;
  ```

  The value of ":id" could be passed in at runtime as a parameter. Alternatively, in situations where the preceding approach is not convenient, you could declare an explicit cursor and pass in the desired value while opening the cursor as an IN parameter.
- Enable the initialization parameters CURSOR_SPACE_FOR_TIME and SESSION_CACHED_CURSORS (with a TRUE and a higher number of cursors to cache, respectively) so that when users switch between modules that use a high number of cursors (explicit and implicit), those cursors are retained in the library cache. When the parameters are disabled, the cursors are closed every time the module is closed (or not invoked for a while). As soon as a module is called again, the cursors need to be reopened and reparsed. Caching them explicitly can reduce this frequent parsing overhead. However, note that enabling these parameters trades more memory for better performance. Ensure that you have adequate free memory prior to enabling them. Also, SESSION_CACHED_CURSORS can cause higher fragmentation in the shared pool.

LIBRARY CACHE CONTENTION You can check for high latch contention via the following query:

```
SQL> SELECT  COUNT(*) "Waiters for library latch"
       FROM v$latch lt, v$session_wait sw
      WHERE sw.event = 'latch free' AND sw.wait_time = 0
        AND lt.name LIKE 'library%' AND sw.p2 = lt.latch#;
```

If the numbers returned over a period of time seem increasingly large, it is an indication of continuous library cache latch contention. Also, you can get a good feel for hits and misses for the library cache latch via the following query:

```
SQL> SELECT name, gets, misses, immediate_gets, immediate_misses, sleeps
        FROM v$latch
       WHERE name LIKE 'library%';
```

If the number of SLEEPS is high or the ratio of MISSES to GETS and IMMEDIATE_MISSES to IMMEDIATE_GETS seems high (MISSES > 5 percent of GETS), then latch contention may be severe.

Library cache latch contention can be reduced via the following steps:

- Reduce fragmentation within the shared pool (steps to accomplish this are outlined in a subsequent paragraph).
- Reduce parse calls within applications (steps to achieve this have already been discussed).
- In environments where all users log on using their own user IDs, the library cache latch is used more frequently and for longer durations than if the references to segments within application code are not fully qualified. For instance, the following SQL statement is an example of using nonqualified references:

  ```
  SQL> SELECT id, name FROM names;
  ```

The preceding statement relies on runtime synonym translation to figure out the segment owner. The same statement can be rewritten as follows:

```
SQL> SELECT id, name FROM sales.names;
```

Here, the NAMES table is qualified with the owner/schema name, thus avoiding a runtime synonym translation. Qualifying all segments within application code reduces the strain on the library cache latch.

HIGH FRAGMENTATION Fragmentation in the shared pool can be very harmful. Besides affecting performance, it can cause disruption by preventing code modules from loading in the library cache and consequently producing the ORA-4031 error ("unable to allocate N bytes of shared memory"). Some fragmentation is inevitable. However, high fragmentation needs to be identified and rectified as soon as possible.

The easiest (and laziest) way to identify high fragmentation is to look for occurrences of the ORA-4031 error message. This message is produced when there is not adequate contiguous free memory to load a code module. However, note that the occurrence of this error means fragmentation has currently reached an extreme level. This is because this error would not normally occur; starting with v7.2, Oracle does not require contiguous memory equivalent to the size of the code module for the module to load successfully. If there is no contiguous free memory to hold the entire module, the module is broken up into suitable pieces (based on the size of free memory fragments currently available) and loaded. However, if even this reduced size does not result in successful loading of the entire module, then the error will result. Thus, this error would normally occur only when there is extreme fragmentation.

In order to prevent runtime disruptions, you will need to flush the shared pool (via the ALTER SYSTEM command). However, note that this could heavily degrade performance, since the shared pool needs to be explicitly repopulated via disk I/O and the hit ratios will fall. Also, you could trap occurrences of ORA-4031 by setting an event to produce trace-files via the following command issued at the start of the application:

```
SQL> ALTER SESSION SET EVENTS '4031 TRACE NAME ERRORSTACK FOREVER';
```

Then the trace-files could be examined to detect the code module causing the error. You could do so by scanning the trace-files for occurrences of "name=" and "load=" to verify that a code module (of the name indicated by "name=") was being loaded into the shared pool when the error occurred. Once the specific code module is determined, you can pin it in memory.

Pinning objects in the shared pool is one of the most effective mechanisms to combat fragmentation. By identifying (as shown earlier) and pinning all large code modules, you would prevent them from constantly being loaded in, aged out, and then reloaded (when referenced again). This load/reload cycle is one of the root causes of fragmentation, and by limiting the occurrences of this cycle only to small modules (< 8KB), you would be effectively restraining fragmentation. Prime candidates for being pinned in any database are the SYS-owned packages STANDARD and DBMS_STANDARD (in certain versions, only STANDARD may exist), which are especially heavily used in any environment using PL/SQL.

The SYS-owned virtual table *x$ksmlru* can be used to proactively monitor large shared-pool allocations, much prior to the ORA-4031 error occurring. Table 11-10 outlines some important columns in *x$ksmlru,* which are useful toward this end.

Note that the *x$ksmlru* table only stores details regarding the largest allocations that have occurred so far. The contents are erased immediately after they are selected out. This is to allow new statistics to be reflected in the table after the previous ones have been inspected (via the SELECT). Accordingly, rather than merely selecting out the values, create an administrative table called DBA_KSMLRU (in the TOOLS tablespace) and periodically populate it with the contents of *x$ksmlru* (via an INSERT INTO dba_ksmlru SELECT * FROM *x$ksmlru* command). This job may be automated via DBMS_JOB or the UNIX *cron* command. This will prevent the values from being lost, if multiple DBAs are present in your environment and each of them periodically checks the contents. Under such a circumstance, only the first DBA to issue the SELECT will be able to view the contents at a specific point in time.

Reserving a Portion of the Shared Pool

Besides pinning large code modules in memory, Oracle provides another effective mechanism to reduce fragmentation. There are two initialization parameters,

Table: *x$ksmlru*

Column name	Description
KSMLRCOM	Describes the type of allocation. If the columns value is like 'MPCODE%' or 'PLSQL%', then the allocation refers to a PL/SQL code block (which would be a candidate for pinning if the allocation size is large)
KSMLRHON	The name of the object currently being loaded.
KSMLRSIZ	The size of the contiguous shared memory allocated. If this size is greater than 8KB, the code module ought to be pinned.
KSMLRNUM	The number of preexisting objects that were removed from memory to make the current allocation possible. If the current allocation displaces a large number of objects, then this obviously is a problem, since those may have to be reloaded, causing additional I/O, straining latches, and affecting performance.
KSMLRSES	The address of the session that is causing the load to occur.

TABLE 11-10. *Important Columns in* x$ksmlru *to Identify Large Allocations in the Shared Pool*

SHARED_POOL_RESERVED_SIZE and SHARED_POOL_RESERVED_MIN_ALLOC. Using these parameters, you could reserve some space within the shared pool for large code modules. This special area would be used by Oracle only when loading large modules. The size of the reserved area is determined by SHARED_POOL_RESERVED_SIZE, and the size of large modules that would merit being loaded into this reserved area is set via SHARED_POOL_RESERVED_MIN_ALLOC. Any code module smaller than SHARED_POOL_RESERVED_MIN_ALLOC is loaded into the regular library cache area. Creating such a special space allows contiguous space to be assured for large modules. Also, it prevents competition between small and large code modules for space. By setting these parameters, you assure that smaller code modules do not have to pay the price for the higher fragmentation caused by large modules. You can monitor the effectiveness of this reserved space (whether it is large enough or too large) via the *v$shared_pool_reserved* dynamic view (refer to the Oracle documentation for more information on this view and its columns).

Set the size of the reserved shared pool in accordance with your environment. If your environment uses a large number of large packages, stored procedures, and so on, then you could make the reserved size larger (say, 10–30 percent of the total shared pool). Otherwise, the reserved size could be smaller (say, 5–10 percent of the total shared pool) in a conventional environment, where the SYS-owned STANDARD and DBMS_STANDARD are the largest PL/SQL code modules. Typically, SHARED_POOL_RESERVED_MIN_ALLOC needs to be set around 5 to 8KB.

Other Critical Areas That Your General Maintenance Routines Need to Address

Finally, here are some other situations that the DBA needs to monitor as part of his or her general maintenance routine and resolve when necessary (other chapters discuss these situations and their resolution in detail).

- In addition to regular locking conflicts, watch for deadlocks explicitly. Deadlocks can occur for various reasons. Chapter 6 discusses them in more detail.
- Watch for inefficient application SQL code and tune it as necessary.
- Monitor use of system/database resources by various applications and ensure that these resources are not depleted at any stage. Especially with options such as the Parallel Query Option (PQO) and dynamic setting of SORT_AREA_SIZE, users/applications may tend to go overboard and saturate the system, affecting performance and availability adversely.

- Also, be familiar with specific database options utilized by the applications and ensure that these options are optimally configured. For example, if the applications frequently perform hash joins, ensure that HASH_AREA_SIZE and HASH_MULTIBLOCK_IO_COUNT are set adequately. Not doing so could cause system resource use to shoot up. For instance, if these hash join–related parameters are not explicitly set and resort to using the defaults (which are very small), the hash join would consequently occur in small units. This would increase I/O and CPU use, as smaller units of data are repeatedly fetched from disk into memory and merged (these smaller units translate to more trips from disk to memory and vice versa).
- Explicitly code your monitoring scripts to check for certain impending crises (such as MAXEXTENTS reached by segments, adequate free space for segments to extend, and so on) and have yourself paged so that you can take corrective action.

Summary

This chapter expounded the virtues of proactive maintenance. It examined issues related to various database ailments such as fatal errors, problems with locks and latches, and setting certain initialization parameters correctly. The DBA needs to have various routines in place to prevent, monitor and detect, and resolve various factors that make the database sick. Proactively doing so allows the database to remain up and running. Ignoring timely maintenance can literally bring it crashing down.

The next chapter examines database space–related maintenance tasks in detail.

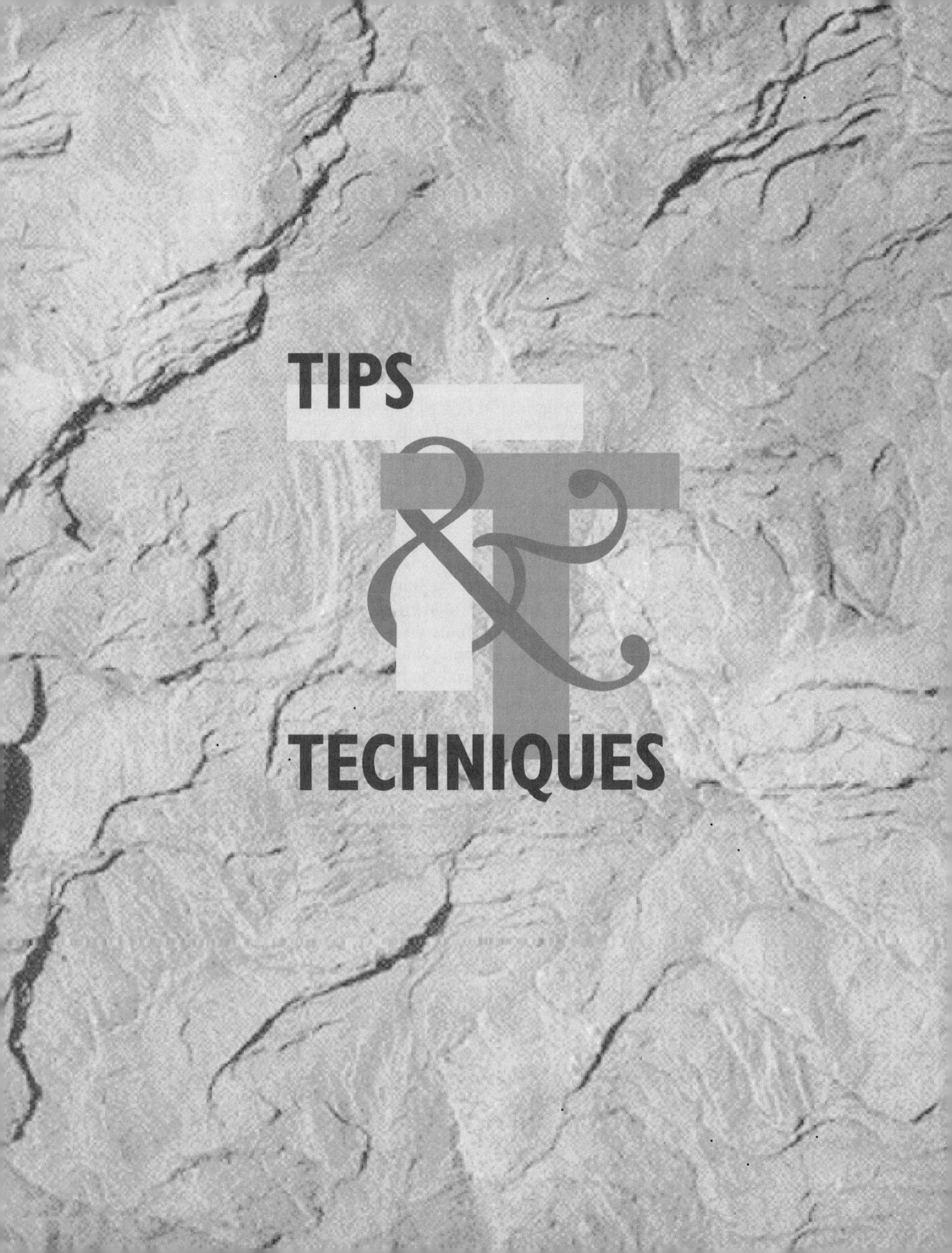
TIPS
&
TECHNIQUES

CHAPTER 12

Space and Growth Management

One of the most common reasons for application failure consists of space- and growth-related errors (such as ORA-1653 due to lack of adequate space for a segment to grow). Though the symptoms of such failure are evidenced via error messages on the application screen and they cause the application to grind to a halt, the causes of these errors do not lie within the application but are a result of inappropriate space and growth management within the database. Space and growth management are two sides of the same coin, requiring in-depth analysis (growth analysis), planning (capacity planning), implementation (space configuration), and monitoring. Not paying adequate attention to either area can easily result in an unmanageable, intermingled quagmire of segments, extents, and blocks with fragments of unusable space between them. Especially as databases get bigger and bigger, the downtime required to repair ineffective physical layouts can be substantial. The good news is that there are certain proactive steps an administrator can take during implementation to prevent irresponsible space allocation and consumption. This chapter looks at some of those methods in detail. Also, the chapter helps to assess the extent of damage that improper space and growth management can cause, the performance degradation that may result, and whether such damage (rather, the performance gain from repairing such damage) justifies a database-reorganization and the downtime that comes with it.

This chapter offers the following tips and techniques:

- Understand the business drivers influencing segment growth
- Understand the units of space-consumption
- Understand the various segments that comprise your database
- Be familiar with the errors and effects that result from inadequate space management
- Enable the AUTOEXTEND feature for all application tablespaces and SYSTEM
- Use standardized file-sizes
- Accommodate the data-file header block in your standardized file-sizes
- Use standardized storage clauses for each segment-type to reduce fragmentation and use space more optimally
- Set INITIAL and NEXT keeping DB_BLOCK_SIZE in mind
- Set PCTINCREASE optimally to reduce fragmentation
- Understand FREELISTS and set them optimally to reduce latch contention
- Periodically coalesce your application tablespaces

- Understand the effect of an erroneous high-water mark
- Periodically deallocate unused blocks
- Avoid dropping data-files explicitly
- Learn the "tablespace shuffle" for emergency unanticipated space requirements
- In a DSS environment, do not blindly accept unrestricted segment growth

Understanding and Managing Space and Growth

Just prior to starting with the tips in this chapter, let's take a moment to ensure that our understanding of space and growth management is the same. The database comprises various segments, each one taking up a certain amount of disk-space. Space management is the administration, manipulation, and control of space-consumption of segments within the database. The rate of growth of a segment has a direct impact on space consumption. Thus, space and growth management consists of estimating the initial size and growth of segments and ensuring that adequate space exists for segments to grow as required by the business.

Understand the business drivers influencing segment growth

Usually I find that there is a lot of ignorance about space consumption within Oracle. A lot of fallacies are perpetuated by ill-informed database "specialists" and publications that have not been made up to date, causing them to be inaccurate. Methodical analysis and planning, mentioned in the opening paragraph, are sadly missing (as usual, the hurry to deploy overcomes the need for systematic analysis). Not paying sufficient attention to growth patterns and not adequately understanding the business drivers that control such growth results in eventual punishment in the form of badly manifested segment growth. It is seldom possible to most accurately predict growth. Accordingly, one can only estimate growth on the basis of broad business parameters and perform the necessary capacity planning to allow a certain degree of growth within a specific time period. Accordingly, the more in-depth understanding of these business drivers, the more accuracy may be derived. In fact, one needs to reconcile the physical model in hand at the time of capacity planning (getting as close to the actual physical model as feasible) with the appropriate business drivers. Getting business analysts (possibly, knowledgeable end-users such as accountants and senior sales personnel) to predict growth is essential. Drawing on discussions with such business folks and the designers of the applications, one needs to reconcile different segments within the database with the business drivers and accordingly comprehend growth patterns. For example, take the case of a simple sales application. Such an application mainly consists of tables such as PRODUCTS, CUSTOMERS, ORDERS, and ORDER_ITEMS. These segments may have varied names in the physical design, depending on the conventions used. However, each of these core tables directly corresponds to a specific business driver such as products currently being manufactured/sold, existing customer-base, orders taken to date, and products making up each order, respectively. Once the business driver is identified, one may use specific business records and goals to introduce a high degree of accuracy in growth analysis. For instance, if the company manufactures or deals in two hundred specific products, there won't be any less than two hundred products in the PRODUCTS table. Additionally, for the current fiscal year, if the company plans to add another two hundred products to the existing product base, that's another two hundred records at the least that would reside in the PRODUCTS table. Considering the average row size and adding some buffer to the predicted segment size and growth, one may be able to estimate segment growth patterns. The same methodology can be adopted to analyze each segment's growth and have a clear picture of the overall growth characteristics. Note that there may be various other peripheral tables. (In addition to the core tables), depending upon the scope and complexity of the application. However, once the primary segments and their growth are identified, it's a matter of mere logistics to put two and two together to make five (the additional one is for the safety "buffer" to allow for unpredicted growth—it's not impossible for the economics of demand and supply in the market to foster unprecedented and unanticipated growth in the business—thus accounting for such growth is always a good idea.)

Note that the sample premise of allowing business drivers to predict segment growth may not always work or may result in gross inaccuracy. However, involving an experienced database architect (with experience in the appropriate industry) will help in reducing such risk. Another fact is, in the world of e-commerce, especially if the company is a startup, it may not always be possible to estimate growth easily. In fact, trying to estimate growth in such environments generally results in either under- or overestimation. Accordingly, the preceding premise is not foolproof. The idea is to use business drivers as much as possible with a provision for reasonable inaccuracy. The buck starts with and stops at the business. In situations, where nothing would help, try to err on the higher side, since a lower estimation may result in the database ceasing to function to process business requirements.

Understand the units of space consumption

The database grows in certain units. It is essential to have a detailed understanding of these units. All these units are well documented in the Oracle documentation set. However, for completeness and to ensure that we start off from the same base, I attempt to quickly describe them.

Logical Storage Units

Logical storage units (see Figure 12-1) pertain to objects within the database (these objects are not visible externally).

TABLESPACES A database comprises of one or more *tablespaces.* The SYSTEM tablespace is the only mandatory tablespace in the database. Generally all databases are segregated into multiple tablespaces for performance, availability, and administrative reasons. An OFA-compliant installation automatically creates different tablespaces. Table 12-1 lists some of the common tablespaces that one will encounter.

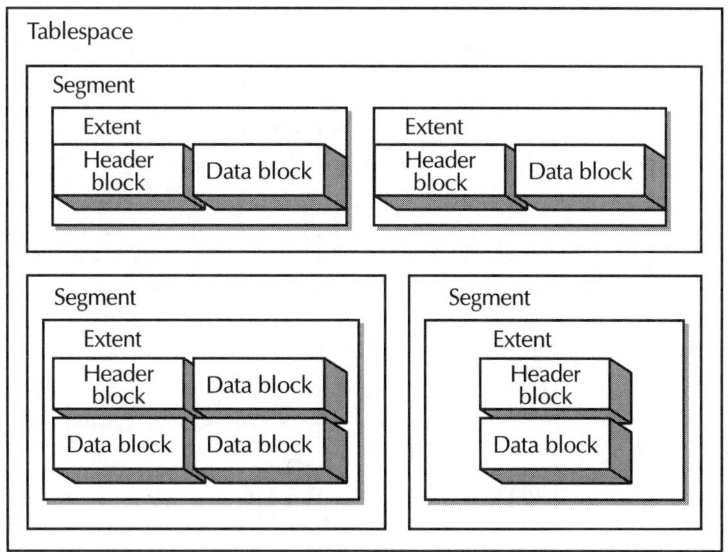

FIGURE 12-1. *View of logical storage units*

Tablespace	Contents and Comments
SYSTEM	Holds segments comprising the data-dictionary (owned by SYS) and the SYSTEM rollback segment. Ideally, shouldn't hold anything else besides these. At times, space is dynamically taken up in SYSTEM for internal Oracle operations. An example is when a tablespace is taken offline with the IMMEDIATE option, Oracle saves rollback information specific to that tablespace to a deferred rollback segment (called SAVEUNDO) in SYSTEM, so that it can be applied when the tablespace is brought online again. Some DBAs advocate editing the *SQL.BSQ* script (run by the CREATE DATABASE command to populate the SYSTEM tablespace with critical data-dictionary segments) to avoid storing the data-dictionary tables holding stored procedures and triggers in the SYSTEM tablespace. Especially if an application uses a lot of these, the SYSTEM tablespace may require additional storage space and may be prone to fragmentation. Ideally, do not edit the SQL.BSQ file, unless you are working with an Oracle Support Analyst. Certain changes to SQL.BSQ may violate your support contract and, worse, corrupt your database. Also, it may be difficult to migrate these changes to newer versions. Accordingly, it's preferable to funnel changes through Oracle Support. Allowed edits to SQL.BSQ include changes to certain storage parameters such as INITIAL, NEXT, PCTINCREASE, MAXEXTENTS, MINEXTENTS, FREELISTS, FREELIST GROUPS, and OPTIMAL. Of these, PCTINCREASE is the only one that can be potentially reduced to a value below the default (others may be increased).
TEMPORARY	Allows temporary segments to be created and dropped during sort operations. Temporary segments are managed automatically by Oracle. No permanent segment should be created here. Once a tablespace is marked as TEMPORARY (v7.3 and upward), Oracle does not allow any permanent segment to be created here.
RBS	Holds all non-SYSTEM rollback segments. The SYSTEM rollback segment is created by the SQL.BSQ script in the SYSTEM tablespace.
TOOLS	Holds SYSTEM-owned segments and segments belonging to certain Oracle and third-party tools (for instance, may be used to store *Oracle Forms* tables).

TABLE 12-1. *Common Tablespaces Present in Most Databases*

Tablespace	Contents and Comments
APPLICATION_DATA	A database may contain one or more tablespaces to hold user/application tables. The actual name of these tablespaces may vary.
APPLICATION_INDEXES	Finally, these are the corresponding tablespace(s) to hold user/application indexes. These tablespaces are primarily created to segregate storage of application tables and indexes and, if possible, spread them across different I/O channels. Again, the actual names of these tablespaces may vary.

TABLE 12-1. *Common Tablespaces Present in Most Databases* (continued)

SEGMENTS *Segments* are the actual entities that reside within a tablespace. Each segment is broken up into one or more extents, each comprising a set of contiguous data-blocks. A subsequent paragraph outlines different segment types.

EXTENTS An *extent* is the unit by which a segment is initially stored and allowed to extend. The size and number of extents that a segment occupies are determined by the STORAGE parameter defined during its creation. In case the STORAGE parameter is not defined, it defaults to the DEFAULT STORAGE parameter specified for the tablespace in which it is being created. However, if the DEFAULT STORAGE parameter has not been specified for that tablespace, the actual extent size defaults to five database blocks. An extent may be considered to be of two types: INITIAL and NEXT. The INITIAL extent is the first extent that is allocated when the segment is created. You can specify the number of extents to be allocated at the time of creation via the MINEXTENTS parameter of the STORAGE clause (when MINEXTENTS is greater than one, the first extent is of the size INITIAL and subsequent extents allocated are of the size NEXT). The NEXT extent refers to every subsequent extent that is dynamically allocated for the segment to accommodate its growth. Note that when using PQO (Parallel Query Option) to create segments, multiple extents (equivalent to the degree of parallelism) of the size INITIAL may be allocated by Oracle (they later get merged). The maximum number of extents that can ever be allocated is determined by the MAXEXTENTS parameter of the STORAGE clause. When a segment needs to allocate an extent beyond MAXEXTENTS, the ORA-1628-32 ("max # of extents reached") error is generated. Prior to v7.3, the MAXEXTENTS value was dependent on the database-block-size (DB_BLOCK_SIZE). The number of allowable extents was limited to the maximum

size of the extent-map that could be held within a single database block. Table 12-2 outlines the maximum allowable value, depending on the database-block size. Starting with v7.3, UNLIMITED is supported as a valid value for MAXEXTENTS, by which the maximum number of extents was made independent of the database-block size. When UNLIMITED is specified, Oracle sets MAXEXTENTS to a very large value (2,147,483,645). It is advisable to set all data-dictionary and application segments to have an UNLIMITED number of extents. This prevents applications from failing due to a segment reaching the default MAXEXTENTS value and failing to extend any further, resulting in downtime. In spite of such an incentive, there are various sites seeking high availability that still continue to use smaller numbers such as 121 or 249. (One of the possible reasons for doing so is that keeping the number for MAXEXTENTS to a smaller number forces the DBAs to be alert and perform proactive monitoring—since the cost of not doing so is downtime! By frequent monitoring, they will also have an insight into segment growth patterns. However, the risk may be too great for many companies, and proactive monitoring in terms of the MAXEXTENTS value is highly advocated). Also keep in mind that it's not a good idea to allow rollback segments and temporary segments to have an UNLIMITED number of extents. This may cause certain berserk jobs to run uncontrollably and cause these segments to grow and fill up entire RBS and TEMPORARY tablespaces. Forcing them to have a limited number of extents causes such jobs to fail when the MAXEXTENTS value is reached (ideally, other mechanisms should be built into each application-module to prevent such occurrences. In the worst case, however, a limited number of MAXEXTENTS for rollback and temporary segments may inevitably stop runaway jobs).

DATA-BLOCKS *Data-blocks,* or simply *blocks,* can be viewed from both logical and physical perspectives. A subsequent paragraph outlines the physical perspective. Logically, a data-block may be of different types (Table 12-3) to accommodate multiple parts of various segment-types.

DB_BLOCK_SIZE	Maximum Allowable Value for MAXEXTENTS
16KB	1,017
8KB	505
4KB	249
2KB	121

TABLE 12-2. *MAXEXTENTS Value for Versions Prior to 7.3*

Block Type	Description
Data segment block	Blocks forming the body of a data-segment (table, index, and so on).
Data segment header block	The first block of each data-segment.
Rollback segment block	Blocks forming the body of a rollback segment.
Rollback segment header block	The first block of a rollback segment
Deferred rollback segment block	Blocks forming the body of a deferred rollback segment. Deferred rollback segments are used by Oracle in specific circumstances such as to hold rollback information pertaining to tablespaces taken offline with the IMMEDIATE option or for data-files taken offline prior to opening the database, until they are brought online again (that is, to hold *save undo* information necessary to change a rollback segment's status from NEEDS RECOVERY to AVAILABLE. A rollback segment's status may change to NEEDS RECOVERY due to a data-file/tablespace being taken offline and made unavailable.) Deferred rollback segments can be identified via the following query: `SELECT * FROM dba_segments WHERE segment_type = 'DEFERRED ROLLBACK';`
Deferred rollback segment header block	The first block of a deferred rollback segment.

TABLE 12-3. *Sample Block Types*

Additionally, in order to accommodate an unlimited number of extents, additional block-types have been introduced in Oracle7 v7.3 (Table 12-4).

Physical Storage Units

Physical storage units (see Figure 12-2) influence the environment outside the database.

FILES All segments are stored within tablespaces. Physically, each tablespace comprises one or more data-files. Thus files, such as data-files, online and archived redo-logs, and control-files, physically make up the database. The data-file number

Block-Type	Description
Extent map block	Blocks to hold the extent map
Unlimited rollback segment header	Rollback segment header to cater to unlimited number of extents
Unlimited deferred rollback segment header	Deferred rollback segment header to cater to unlimited number of extents
Unlimited data-segment header	Data-segment header to cater to unlimited number of extents
Unlimited data-segment header with freelist groups	Data-segment block with freelist groups to cater to unlimited number of extents (OPS environment)

TABLE 12-4. *Block-Types to Support UNLIMITED Extents*

forms part of the row-address (the ROWID) for every row within table and index segments (with some notable exceptions, such as rows in an index-organized table in v8.0.*x*). It is important to realize that a segment can span more than one data-file of a tablespace. However, an individual extent cannot ever span more than more data-file. It has to reside within a contiguous set of blocks, within a single data-file.

Every data-file includes a file-header portion, where internal (kernel-specific) information such as checkpoint data, SCN structures, and backup information are maintained.

BLOCKS From a physical perspective, blocks are literally the building blocks of each file within Oracle. The size of the block is determined at the time of creation according to the value specified by the initialization parameter

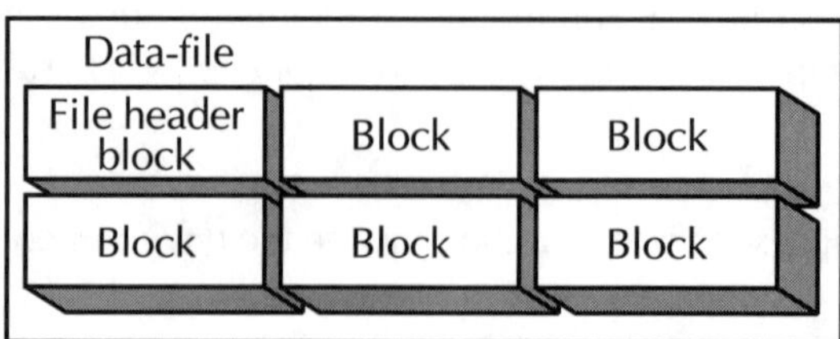

FIGURE 12-2. *View of physical storage units*

DB_BLOCK_SIZE. The ROWID also contains the block-id within the data-file. Every block has a data-block address (dba) that is used in various ways by Oracle internally (such as, to form a linked-list [hash-chained list] within the data-block buffer cache in the SGA).

A block is broken up into various components such as a header-portion containing information such as the dba and segment-type, a table directory that lists the tables that comprise rows in the block, a row directory that maintains row-specific information such as the address of each row-piece and its size, freelist structures, and the high-water mark (see Figure 12-2). Such information constitutes overhead and varies in size between 84 to 107 bytes. The rest of the block is devoted to actual data (the rows) and free-space (governed by the PCTFREE parameter). Part of the free-space may be used to store DML transaction entries (for INSERTs, UPDATEs, DELETEs, and SELECT FOR UPDATE operations). The number of transaction entries are governed by the INITRANS and MAXTRANS parameters and the number of concurrent DML operations. Under most OSs, each transaction entry is approximately 23 bytes in size.

Chapter 19 provides some scripts to derive the physical storage "map" of a tablespace in terms of extents/blocks occupied by various segments within it (a subsequent tip in this chapter also lists a script).

Understand the various segments that comprise your database

An Oracle database comprises of various segment-types. Specific segment-types may be present in high or low numbers in your database. In order to fully comprehend them and their space requirements, it is essential to have a good understanding of the physical database model. The following segments make up your database:

- Tables
- Indexes
- Rollback segments
- Temporary (sort) segments
- Bootstrap (cache) segments

Let's look at some tips in managing space for each of these segments. Note that these tips are explained in more detail in subsequent paragraphs or in other chapters. In case of the latter, a reference is made to the appropriate chapter.

Tables

Tables may be managed as follows:

- Classify each table in your physical data-model based on its size and growth characteristics (see Chapter 6 for details).
- Use standardized storage parameters for each classification (a subsequent tip elaborates on the various physical storage parameters).
- As much as possible, keep INITIAL and NEXT consistent with each other. Older Oracle texts refer to the importance of keeping all table data in a single segment or at least limiting the number of extents as much as possible. In current versions (v7.3 and v8), this is not critical any more, since an UNLIMITED number of extents are supported. This may affect space-management operations a little (during truncation, dropping, and so on). However, regular DML activity does not suffer. Rather than worrying about limiting the number of extents to one, DBAs working with contemporary versions ought to focus on sizing INITIAL and NEXT optimally. As far as possible, enforce the following formula: (INITIAL = NEXT = multiple of the DB_BLOCK_SIZE = multiple of the OS block size = multiple of the stripe-size, in case striping is done, so that an extent can be striped optimally outside the database). Subsequent tips elaborate on how doing so helps performance (such as by optimizing reads and reducing overall I/O during full-table scans).
- Allow extents to grow with time. Rather than allocating one massive INITIAL extent to accommodate all data the segment is ever expected to hold, a more pragmatic approach is for the first extent to hold data for a pre-determined period of time (such as for a month, quarter, or year) and each subsequent extent to hold data for the next similar period. Thus, each extent would correspond to a specific period of time. Determine the size of the data that will get generated during each time period and size INITIAL/NEXT accordingly. Also, introduce some slack in the sizing (for instance, make INITIAL = NEXT = size of data for each time period × 0.2, where 0.2 is the slack). Such slack will accommodate abrupt (unanticipated) growth in data for a time period. When performing exports, ensure that you do not inadvertently clump the entire segment into a single extent by setting *COMPRESS=Y*.

  When queries are apt to access only a specific time period frequently (such as the current time period), as in an OLTP application, then the disk/controller on which that specific extent resides may be subjected to I/O contention. Accordingly, some kind of striping external to the database may be required (such as RAID 0). In case that is not feasible, you may consider breaking up each of these extents (corresponding to specific time periods) into smaller ones and spreading each of these smaller ones across different disks/controllers by pre-allocating such extents.

- Consider partitioning tables that are expected to grow to very large sizes. Partitioning can be done either via the partitioning option in Oracle8 or the partitioned-views feature in Oracle7 v7.3. Note that in case of the latter, you would need to write/change your application code to write to each table (comprising the partitioned-view) individually. In Oracle8, complete partition transparency is provided, so that your application code directly refers to the table name and leaves individual partition management to Oracle. For more information on the advantages of partitioning, refer to the Oracle8 documentation set.
- Periodically monitor space usage and evaluate table growth patterns. If a table seems to seldom grow, you can reduce its NEXT extent-size because having relatively static tables allocate large NEXT extents results in space wastage. For instance, a table with INITIAL 25M and NEXT 25M may have 20M worth of data initially, leaving 5M of free-space within the first extent. Every quarter, the segment may grow by 7M. Thus at the end of the first quarter, this growth will completely fill up the first extent and require another extent to be allocated. However, only 2M of the new extent will be filled up, leaving 22M free-space within it for the rest of the quarter. Such space-wastage will be evidenced in the segment throughout its lifetime, unless you intervene and alter the NEXT value to be a smaller value (such as maybe 10M). In the example, I'm using small values such as 25M and 10M for simplicity. In real life, however, especially in VLDB environments, the sizes and the subsequent space-wastage may be much more substantial. Conversely, such monitoring will help you track segments with high growth rates. If you have (inadvertently) set the NEXT to be rather small for a fast-growing segment, then you may need to intervene to increase the NEXT, so that the number of extents allocated for that segment is not too high (especially if the MAXEXTENTS for that segment is not set to UNLIMITED). A high value for the number of extents allocated may vary for your environment. Generally, however, any segment with more than 100 extents may be regarded to be having a rather large number of extents. Remember, having an exceptionally large number of extents may affect performance of space-management operations and increase the amount of space required to record them in the data-dictionary, thus potentially causing SYS-owned segments in the SYSTEM tablespace to get bigger (causing them to be susceptible to the dangers of reaching MAXEXTENTS or running out of space in the SYSTEM tablespace). As you are probably well

aware, any adverse impact to the SYSTEM tablespace may very well result in database downtime.

In order to know when to intervene, you need to keep track of which segments are extending and when (that is, the frequency of extension). You can do so by having a daily extent report printed out that will state all segments in relevant schemas and the current extents they have allocated. Comparing such reports over different periods (say, daily or specific days of every week or month) will allow you to understand various segment growth patterns. Chapter 19 provides scripts that allow you to monitor segment growth patterns.

- Monitor for signs of harmful fragmentation. If such fragmentation seems quite pervasive, a database rebuild may be required. Alternatively, identifying segments most affected by the fragmentation and repairing only those will also allow most of the fragmentation to be eliminated, with the least impact on availability. A subsequent tip discusses fragmentation in more detail. In any case, following the recommendations on storage parameters will proactively ensure that harmful fragmentation is kept at bay.

Indexes

The tips provided earlier for tables also apply for indexes. However, there are some additional issues regarding indexes that merit discussion. Note that by simply referring to an "index," I mean a B*Tree index, unless explicitly stated otherwise.

- Restrict indexes to columns that are not frequently updated. Also, restrict the number of indexes on tables that are subjected to large inserts and deletes. Indexes on columns that have sequentially increasing values cause the B*Tree to grow gradually toward the right (such as in a primary key index). If you frequently delete the older rows in table on which the index is built, then the B*Tree becomes very sparsely populated toward the left portion (where the older key values are) and densely populated toward the right (due to new rows coming in as the old ones are being deleted). A classic example is a history table where you delete rows belonging to prior periods as rows for current periods are being inserted. Such an index is termed as a "sliding index," which keeps growing in size. Deletes rarely reduce the size of the index. If you need to create indexes on a number of columns in tables prone to high deletes or even columns that are updated quite frequently for performance reasons, consider partitioning the index. Oracle8 allows you to have partitioned indexes on non-partitioned tables, thus giving you the flexibility to consider partitioning sliding or constantly growing indexes, even if partitioning the corresponding table is not feasible. Chapter 6 explains indexes, their growth characteristics, and their reaction to DML in detail.

- Only index certain key columns (primary/unique, foreign, and partitioning keys) and columns most likely to help performance in the initial stage. Later, monitor actual usage and index additional columns as necessary and make it a point to remove the indexes on non-key columns if they are not utilized or do not help performance, as originally expected. Also evaluate the selectivity of each column prior to determining the order of columns within the index; that is, order the columns based on their selectivity.
- Allocate adequate space in memory and disk for index creation and manipulation operations. Some important steps you can take in this direction are
  - Ensure that adequate space in the temporary tablespace (of the user creating the index) is available.
  - Increase SORT_AREA_SIZE as much as possible (without affecting overall system/database performance) up to the size required for the index creation process. In Oracle8, you can increase SORT_AREA_SIZE dynamically (only for the session creating the index) via the ALTER SESSION SET SORT_AREA_SIZE command.
  - In case the index being created is a bitmapped index, then set the CREATE_BITMAP_AREA_SIZE initialization parameter based on the following formula:

```
(column_cardinality × (DB_BLOCK_SIZE × 0.5)) + (column_cardinality ×
(DB_BLOCK_SIZE × 0.5) × 0.15)
```

Here, *column_cardinality* refers to the number of distinct values for the column(s) being indexed. The reason for DB_BLOCK_SIZE being included in the formula is that any single bitmap pattern corresponding to a specific value within the bitmapped index can be up to a maximum of half the database block-size. The first portion of the formula (prior to the plus symbol) ensures that, at the minimum, there is at least enough space in memory to hold a single bitmap pattern for each unique value. However, if the number of rows in the table results in a bitmap pattern greater than half the database block-size, then the bitmap pattern is broken up to adhere to the rule. Thus, you should make an attempt to accommodate at least some of those values in memory (since there may not be enough memory to hold all patterns for all unique values in memory). For this purpose, the latter portion of the formula (after the plus symbol) provides a buffer of 15 percent. You may adjust this variable buffer-portion based on your requirements.

It is to be noted that CREATE_BITMAP_AREA_SIZE is used only during bitmapped index creation. Let's take a closer peek at the bitmapped index creation process to understand how this parameter is utilized. A regular B*Tree index creation process is fairly straightforward and requires little explanation (rows are read and sorted to derive the various key values and form index entries in the B*Tree structure). However, the bitmapped index creation process always has been little understood by DBAs. Figure 12-3 illustrates this process.

1. The entire table is scanned by one or more server processes (depending on whether the index is being created in parallel). In case the table is partitioned, the scan occurs at the partition level (resulting in a local bitmapped index).
2. Each server process feeds the values and ROWIDs of rows read into a bitmap generation engine. This engine accepts the input and prepares an index entry consisting of the value, start and end ROWIDs of rows with that value, and the resultant bitmap pattern of 1's and 0's for the range of rows (specified by the start and end ROWIDs). The CREATE_BITMAP_AREA_SIZE parameter provides the amount of memory that is available to the bitmap generation engine to generate the bitmaps. If inadequate memory is available, it will need to utilize the temporary tablespace, thus delaying the index creation.
3. The bitmaps generated may be split (in case the bitmap is bigger than half the database block-size) or merged. (In case some bitmaps are smaller than half the database block-size, Oracle attempts to combine multiple bitmap patterns [for the same column-value] into a larger one in order to pack the index more efficiently, resulting in space optimization and fewer I/O reads during future index access; the same column-values may initially have multiple bitmap patterns for different row ranges, if those row ranges have been read by different server process during parallel creation or by the same server process during subsequent feeds to the bitmap generation engine).
4. Finally, all the bitmap patterns are sorted and stored in a B*Tree structure. The time taken to perform this final sort depends on the size of the SORT_AREA_SIZE parameter.

A view of the bitmapped index physical structure is provided in Chapter 6. Figure 12-4 reproduces the view to refresh your memory. As may be observed there, the unique structure of bitmapped indexes allows fast retrieval of data in many circumstances. For instance, if a DISTINCT set of the indexed column values is desired, the index need not be scanned—only the key-values need to be returned, thus avoiding the need for a sort to satisfy the DISTINCT clause. Similarly, GROUP BYs can be processed very fast, since only each key-value and a count of rows in

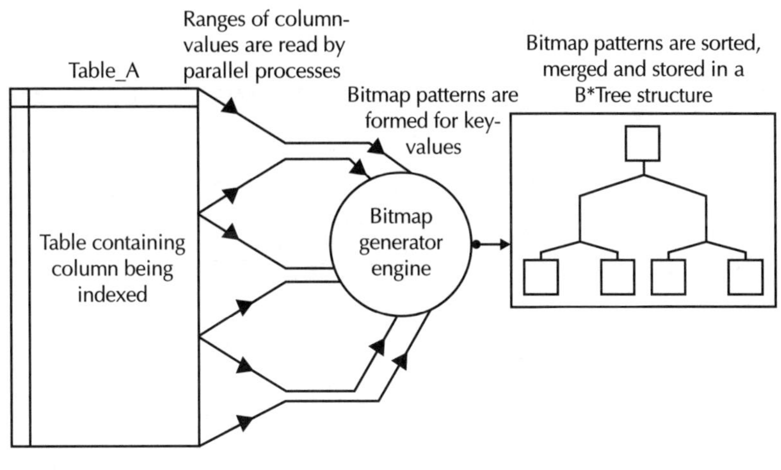
Ranges of column-values are read by parallel processes
Table_A
Bitmap patterns are formed for key-values
Bitmap patterns are sorted, merged and stored in a B*Tree structure
Table containing column being indexed
Bitmap generator engine

FIGURE 12-3. *Bitmapped index creation process*

each bitmap pattern for that key-value has to be returned, thus eliminating a sort normally required to process GROUP BYs.

However, delays may be experienced while processing range-scans via bitmapped indexes, since all bitmap patterns for keys within the required range will have to be merged to return the appropriate result set. The BITMAP_MERGE_AREA_SIZE parameter governs the performance of such merges, since it specifies the size of the memory buffer within which the merge occurs. If the size specified by this parameter is inadequate, then the foreground server process will need to perform several passes to complete the actual merge, resulting in slower performance. It is necessary to understand the size of the largest bitmapped index in your database (not just the current size, but the size the index is expected to reach in the next 3–6 months) and set the parameter to match the index size as nearly as possible. In case you are very familiar with the application code and it is fairly easy to determine the size of the largest range-scan against bitmapped indexes, you can use that information to set the BITMAP_MERGE_AREA_SIZE parameter. For instance, say, Query_A is likely to retrieve 40 percent of ACCOUNTS table, whereas Query_B is likely to process 60 percent of the SALES table. Once you have this kind of information, you can find the BYTES occupied by the largest such table from USER_SEGMENTS and use the percentage to arrive at a good approximation for the required size of the parameter.

- In an Oracle Parallel Server (OPS) environment, you need to be aware of additional issues such as incessant pinging of index-blocks across the different instances. If an application deployed across more than one participating instance requires concurrent access (read and/or write) to index key-values held within the same block, contention may be created on

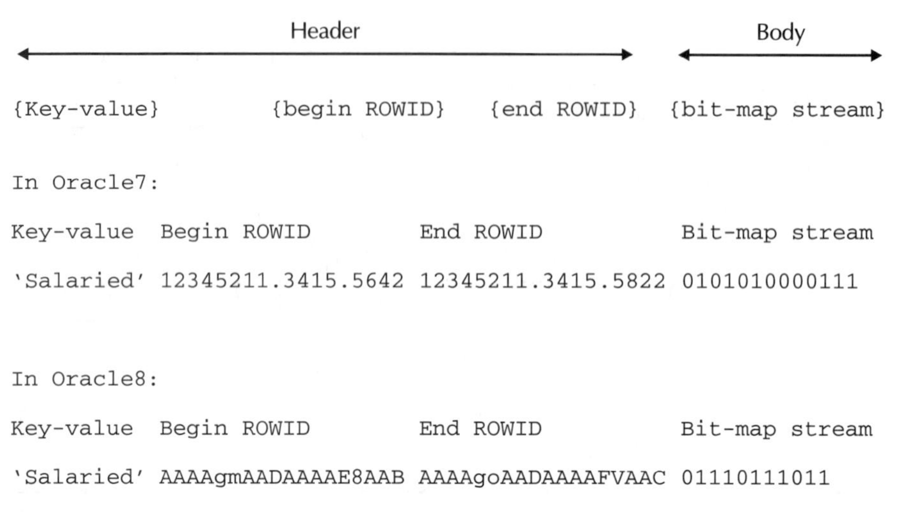

FIGURE 12-4. *Physical view of a bitmapped index*

the disks/controllers holding such "hot" blocks. In such a situation, consider (re)building the index as a reversed key index. Doing so would spread those key-values (across possibly different blocks), thus reducing contention. Sometimes, such contention may be observed in regular (non OPS) configurations, especially when the actual key value is rather small or the DB_BLOCK_SIZE is large (16K for instance), thus causing a large number of key-values to be held in a single block, increasing the chances of contention.

- Quite often, high DML activity on a B*Tree index (note that even keys in bitmapped indexes are eventually stored in a B*Tree structure) results in a non-optimal structure. It is imperative that such "damaged" structures be detected and repaired in a timely fashion before application performance seriously degrades. Quite often you may have noticed that initially when an index is built, certain queries work fine. After a while, the same queries take more and more time to finish. You do an EXPLAIN PLAN on those queries and you find that the execution path has not deviated from the original one—the indexes you had created (a while ago) are still being used. However, the very same indexes, which had a terse structure when they were initially created, now
    - Occupy a much larger number of blocks, most of which are sparsely populated, and/or
    - Have become very tall (remember from Chapter 6, the greater the height of the index, the more I/Os involved in accessing them), and/or
    - Have become "flat" due to a large number of low-cardinality values (in nonunique indexes) being present

It is necessary to monitor all indexes responsible for performance and to detect inefficiencies in their structures. One needs to take certain steps to detect structural deficiencies in indexes.

CONSIDERING AN INDEX-REBUILD This is the million-dollar question that many DBAs and developers face: When should one think about rebuilding an application's indexes? I have noted that in some organizations, there is a fixed schedule: every three months, indexes are recreated on tables undergoing major DML activity. However, some of these frequent index-rebuilds may be unnecessary, or even indexes of less frequently used tables may need to be rebuilt on a more regular basis. How does one determine whether they need to be rebuilt or not? How does one get actual numbers indicating that an index is a candidate for rebuilding? By using the command ANALYZE INDEX...VALIDATE STRUCTURE. There is another old command called VALIDATE INDEX. This is still available in Oracle8 (mainly for backward compatibility). Either of these commands populate the SYS.INDEX_STATS view with meaningful information that helps in determining whether an index should be rebuilt or not. Please refer to Figure 12-5 for a description of the structure of INDEX_STATS view.

As is apparent from the structure, DBAs and developers can use the INDEX_STATS view to glean some useful information. The statistics in INDEX_STATS are different from the ones in DBA_INDEXES. The statistics in DBA_INDEXES are created as a result of using the COMPUTE STATISTICS or ESTIMATE STATISTICS options of the ANALYZE command and are used by the cost-based optimizer (CBO). The statistics in INDEX_STATS are created by the VALIDATE STRUCTURE option of the ANALYZE command. Another important difference is that the ANALYZE STRUCTURE...DELETE STATISTICS command erases statistics in DBA_INDEXES; however, the statistics in INDEX_STATS are not erased. They get erased only when the index is dropped or get recomputed every time the ANALYZE...VALIDATE STRUCTURE command is run. The INDEX_STATS view only contains information about one index at any given point in time. Don't worry about old statistics in the INDEX_STATS misleading CBO. CBO does not use the statistics in INDEX_STATS.

```
SQL> desc sys.index_stats
Name                          Null?    Type              My comments

------------------------- -------- ----              --------------
HEIGHT                                 NUMBER            Height of tree
BLOCKS                                 NUMBER
NAME                                   VARCHAR2(30)
PARTITION_NAME                         VARCHAR2(30)
LF_ROWS                                NUMBER            Leaf rows
LF_BLKS                                NUMBER            Leaf blocks
LF_ROWS_LEN                            NUMBER
LF_BLK_LEN                             NUMBER
BR_ROWS                                NUMBER            Branch rows
BR_BLKS                                NUMBER            Branch blocks
BR_ROWS_LEN                            NUMBER
BR_BLK_LEN                             NUMBER
DEL_LF_ROWS                            NUMBER            Deleted leaves
DEL_LF_ROWS_LEN                        NUMBER
DISTINCT_KEYS                          NUMBER
MOST_REPEATED_KEY                      NUMBER
BTREE_SPACE                            NUMBER
USED_SPACE                             NUMBER
PCT_USED                               NUMBER
ROWS_PER_KEY                           NUMBER          = 1 for UNIQUE keys
BLKS_GETS_PER_ACCESS                   NUMBER
```

FIGURE 12-5. *Description of the INDEX_STATS view in an Oracle8 database*

```
/* Query to determine whether index is to be rebuilt (to be run after
ANALYZE INDEX…VALIDATE STRUCTURE as a DBA user)
*/
COLUMN name FORMAT a25   -- increase if your index-names are > 25 chars
COLUMN "Total leaf rows" FORMAT 999,999,999,999
COLUMN "Deleted leaf rows" FORMAT 999,999,999,999

SELECT name, lf_rows "Total leaf rows", del_lf_rows "Deleted leaf rows"
  FROM SYS.index_stats
 WHERE  name =  UPPER('<indx_name>');
```

The query listed provides the total leaf rows and the deleted leaf rows for a given index. If the deleted leaf rows seem relatively high compared to the total leaf rows, then the index should be rebuilt. This is a good mechanism to detect indexes with a large number of empty slots (sparsely populated blocks), possibly indicating a sliding index. I use 20 percent as a general rule of thumb to classify an index to be a "rogue" index. If the deleted leaf rows are 20 percent or more of the total leaf rows, I recommend rebuilding the index at the next available opportunity (that will least impact availability).

Another criterion for rebuilding an index is if it has grown very tall. You can determine that by looking at the HEIGHT column in INDEX_STATS. If the HEIGHT is equivalent to 4 or more, then it's probably a good candidate for a rebuild. Check the height once again after the rebuild (by reanalyzing it) and ensure that it has indeed gone down. If it hasn't, it might be an indication of some other structural flaw. Maybe such columns are inappropriate for creating an index, in the first place—question whether you need them, because even if they might be used in queries, they may not necessarily result in performance improvements if a relatively high number of I/O calls are required to access such indexes (at times, maybe even more than the I/O calls required to access the table directly).

Yet another criterion for rebuilding an index is to detect whether the number of key-values spread across leaf-blocks is sub-optimal. In order to do so, you will need to dump the index tree-structure.

DUMPING AN INDEX TREE STRUCTURE The command ALTER SESSION SET EVENTS 'IMMEDIATE TRACE NAME TREEDUMP LEVEL <level_number>'; dumps the structure of an index B*tree. It gives useful information such as the number of levels in the index and number of rows per level. Such information helps the DBA to decide whether an index needs to be rebuilt and if so, whether it should be reversed.

The <level_number> mentioned in the preceding command needs to be replaced with an actual number. In Oracle8, the <level-number> is the OBJECT_ID of the index from DBA_OBJECTS. In Oracle7, the <level-number> is the dba (data-block address) of the index header-block. You need to take the following steps to obtain the index header-block's dba:

- Find the index header file-number and block-number:

```
SQL> SELECT header_file, header_block FROM dba_segments
       WHERE segment_type = 'INDEX'
        and segment_name = '<indx_name>;
```

- Use DBMS_UTILITY.MAKE_DATA_BLOCK_ADDRESS to derive the dba using the header file and block numbers derived via the preceding query:

```
SQL> EXEC DBMS_UTILITY.MAKE_DATA_BLOCK_ADDRESS(<header_file>,
<header_block>);
```

Setting the tree-dump event gives a trace-file in the USER_DUMP_DEST directory. The trace-file name usually is of the form "*ora_<SID_NAME>_<PID#>.trc*" where *SID_NAME* is the ORACLE_SID and *PID#* is the process-id number. Immediately after running this command, you can go to the USER_DUMP_DEST directory and use the *ls –lt* command on UNIX to pick up the latest trace file (on Windows NT, use the Windows NT Explorer). A sample trace-file is provided in Figure 12-6. The last lines of the dump-file contain the meat of the output (between "begin tree dump" and "end tree dump"). The trace file size is directly proportional to the size of the index (in other words, the trace file can get pretty large, if the index is large). If your trace-file does not encompass the entire index, check the value of the initialization parameter MAX_DUMP_FILE_SIZE and increase it, if necessary.

The file contents can be interpreted by looking at the number of levels: the branches and the leaves per branch. In the sample file provided in Figure 12-6, there is only one branch (0x40002b) and four leaves (0x4003f0, 0x4003f1, 0x400b0f, and 0x400b10), since the dump was produced for a small index with just 1,819 rows. The rows contained in each leaf are 503, 418, 498, and 400 respectively. This indicates that all the leaves are well balanced (in terms of rows per leaf). So it is a good idea to leave this index alone. However, if the rows in some leaves seem excessively high compared to other leaves, then probably those leaves are hot-spots and could lead to I/O bottlenecks. The leaves with smaller numbers of rows are indicative of sparsely populated leaves (either due to lopsided index-keys or sliding indexes). Also, if the index is large, but the number of leaves is not, then it's probably a "flat" index, where the index-key has a low cardinality (that is, very low degree of uniqueness). Such columns may be better served by not indexing them in the first place or, alternatively, converting such an index to a bitmapped index (since bitmapped indexes desire lower degrees of uniqueness).

Generally, spurts of sequential values or large delete-jobs cause such uneven distribution of keys. If the culprit is merely a huge batch delete job, then probably the situation can be set right by partitioning the table and truncating the partition. If partitioning is a not a feasible solution, then rebuilding the index (without reversing) after such batch-deletes will help. Alternatively, if the imbalance is caused by spurts of sequential values being inserted in the table, then reversing the key(s) will help.

THE REBUILD OPTION With Oracle7 v7.3 and Oracle8, you can use the REBUILD option of the ALTER INDEX command to rebuild indexes. You can even use this option to reverse a regular B*Tree index and vice versa. However, a caveat with REBUILD is that it does not detect and eliminate index corruption, since it bases the rebuild on the existing index (which might be corrupt already).

ANALYZE TABLE...VALIDATE STRUCTURE CASCADE is the best mechanism to detect index corruption. This command matches each row in the table against all indexes and each row in every index against the table. If any corruption is found, an error message is returned. Subsequently the index may be dropped and rebuilt using the regular DROP and CREATE INDEX commands, rather than the REBUILD option of the ALTER INDEX command. However, if no corruption is detected or suspected, you can use the REBUILD option to save time (especially to reduce application downtime due to the corresponding table not being available for concurrent DML in versions 8.0.*x* and earlier).

```
Dump file /opt/app/oracle/admin/dv01/udump/ora_dv01_3157.trc
Oracle8 Enterprise Edition Release 8.0.4.0.0 - Production
PL/SQL Release 8.0.4.0.0 - Production
ORACLE_HOME = /opt/app/oracle/product/8.0.4
System name:    sample
Node name:      sample
Release:        4.0
Version:        3.0
Machine:        3446A
Instance name: dv01
Redo thread mounted by this instance: 1
Oracle process number: 9
Unix process pid: 3157, image: oracledv01

Wed Aug 12 10:48:13 1998
*** SESSION ID:(8.69) 1998.08.12.10.48.13.000
----- begin tree dump
branch: 0x40002b 4194347 (0: nrow: 4, level: 1)
   leaf: 0x4003f0 4195312 (-1: nrow: 503 rrow: 503)
   leaf: 0x4003f1 4195313 (0: nrow: 418 rrow: 417)
   leaf: 0x400b0f 4197135 (1: nrow: 498 rrow: 498)
   leaf: 0x400b10 4197136 (2: nrow: 400 rrow: 400)
----- end tree dump
```

FIGURE 12-6. *Sample trace-file (output of the TREEDUMP trace)*

Rollback segments

Rollback Segments primarily perform two tasks within Oracle:

- They provide the means to undo transactions by holding undo or "before-image" information for all changes made by DML statements. Such information may be required at various stages including recovery from transaction/statement failure, instance failure, and media failure.
- They provide read-consistency for transactions, especially long-running ones, where required blocks may have changed after they were started, thus causing them to use the rollback segments for the correct "before-image" (the one that is consistent with the time they were started).

Managing rollback segment space plays a big role in allowing the required amount of undo to be stored and also providing complete read-consistency as required. Chapter 11 provides detailed information on certain errors that could result if either of these requirements is not met properly (such as "ORA-1555:

snapshot too old" and "ORA-1628: max # of extents reached for rollback segment"). Space management considerations for rollback segments include these:

- Even though logically, rollback segments are unique reusable segments that are used in a circular/round-robin fashion, they are physically similar to other segments such as tables and indexes. Rollback segments grow in extents, and their sizes are governed by the physical STORAGE parameters that indicate the INITIAL and NEXT extent-sizes. PCTINCREASE is always set to zero for rollback segments, and a different value cannot be explicitly mentioned. Ensure that you determine the INITIAL and NEXT values on the basis of transaction volumes and arrive at a consistent set of standard sizes. It is preferable to set the INITIAL and NEXT sizes to be the same for each rollback segment. Due to the nature of allocation and use of rollback segments, it is necessary to have them grow at a predictable and consistent rate. You could set different INITIAL/NEXT sizes for different rollback segments (that is, have different-sized rollback segments), according to application characteristics. Normally in an OLTP database, you would need two sizes to handle regular volumes and exceptional volumes. Smaller or medium-sized rollback segments would be used during regular, day-to-day transactions, whereas larger ones may be required to handle exceptional loads such as batch-jobs. The latter would be kept offline and only be enabled prior to running the exceptional jobs. The exceptional jobs need to be written such that they explicitly point to the larger rollback segments. In situations where that is not possible, all smaller/medium rollback segments need to be disabled and only the larger ones are kept enabled, so that the latter would be used by all exceptional jobs. Once they are complete, the larger rollback segments can be disabled once again and the smaller/medium ones can be re-enabled. The large rollback segments are usually fewer in number to specifically cater to the (generally few) exceptional jobs. Even if at the time of rollback segment creation/configuration, large batch jobs do not exist for your database and larger rollback segments do not seem necessary, it's still a good idea to create a couple of larger ones and keep them offline, so that they are readily available for use in case they are needed in the future. Sometimes, trying to create them later may not be (immediately) convenient, if you have used up most of the space within the tablespace. So it's a good idea to "lock up" the space by pre-creating the larger rollback segments. If the nature of the database is such that large jobs are the norm, rather than the exception (such as in a DSS database), then again, all rollback segments need to be of the same size: large. Maintaining smaller rollback segments or a mixture of smaller and larger rollback segments does not make sense, since a job will fail if it randomly chooses a smaller one.

- Rollback segments generally grow due to rollback information being written to them. Such information needs to be stored for a short time to allow read-consistency for transactions that still might be using that information after the transactions that created the rollback information have ended. After a while, however, the space occupied by such rollback information will only be dead weight, since it is not used anymore and can be overwritten. The real art in managing rollback segments is determining the duration for which the rollback information ought to be retained without being overwritten in your database. Chapter 11 provides some general tips in this area; however, a fine degree of control is seldom possible here; methods have to be determined after a thorough study of transactional characteristics in your database. Oracle provides some facilities so that the space within these rollback segments can be reclaimed and the constant growth of rollback segments limited. One of these methods is the OPTIMAL parameter in the STORAGE clause. OPTIMAL indicates the ideal size of the rollback segment and Oracle automatically shrinks the rollback segment on an as-needed basis to maintain this size. This allows rollback segment growth to be controlled, so that all the space within the tablespace is not used up. However, this parameter needs to be set judiciously. A too-large value would still cause large amounts of space to be wasted within the tablespace, and a too-small value would cause relevant information required for read-consistency to be lost. Also frequent expansion and shrinkage of the rollback segments would require constant space management operations to occur, resulting in high recursive calls. Accordingly, it is necessary to set OPTIMAL such that shrinkage does not occur too often, without resulting in high space wastage. The other way is to shrink rollback segments explicitly via the ALTER ROLLBACK SEGMENT SHRINK command, after monitoring the space consumption by rollback segments. A good space-management approach combines both these methods.
- Ensure that you have a dedicated tablespace (RBS) to hold all rollback segments, other than SYSTEM. Since rollback segments exhibit unique storage requirements, they are better off being stored in a specific tablespace that is sized to accommodate such requirements. In case you have rollback segments of different sizes, they may be stored in the same tablespace or in different tablespaces, especially if you need to segregate them for performance reasons. However, it is always better to have a single tablespace, since a common trap in maintaining different ones is that depending on use, you may run out of space in one, whereas there is still plenty left in the other. However, your transactions may fail due to lack of space in the one that is more commonly used. Maintaining just one tablespace to hold all rollback segments will allow space to used more

optimally, avoiding such situations. As long as you ensure that the INITIAL/NEXT parameters for all these rollback segments are multiples of the DB_BLOCK_SIZE, the space freed up from one rollback segment should be reasonably reused by others.

- If an application cannot explicitly choose rollback segments, ensure that all enabled rollback segments are of the same or larger size. Keeping smaller rollback segments online while running such applications may result in failure, if a smaller one is allocated to a larger transaction. Remember, Oracle allocates rollback segments on a round-robin basis by making passes over the available rollback segments and allocating the first non-SYSTEM one that's not currently being used. If all are being used, the same one may be allocated to more than one transaction (each active transaction uses a different rollback segment block). Oracle finds the one with the least number of active transactions and allocates that to the new transaction. This also applies if the same rollback segment is explicitly chosen by transactions running concurrently.
- Always ensure that there is adequate free space in the RBS tablespace to allow all rollback segments to extend by at least 25 extents. It is preferable to configure rollback segments to have multiple medium/large extents, rather than just two huge extents (MINEXTENTS is always 2 for rollback segments). Some sites try to restrict a rollback segment to have a very large INITIAL and NEXT, hoping to restrict the total number of extents. However, this may not always work due to the way additional extents are allocated for rollback segments. If the next extent that will be written to already has an active transaction, a new extent will be allocated. Thus, configuring a very large INITIAL/NEXT may result in a very large new extent being allocated to cater to a comparatively small transaction that requires a new extent, if the currently existing extents are being accessed by active transactions. Keeping each extent size smaller but allowing a larger number of extents avoids such space wastage and keeps rollback segment growth more balanced throughout the tablespace. One needs to evaluate the number of concurrent transactions (that actively write undo) for your database and configure the necessary number of rollback segments. Ideally, there should be a corresponding rollback segment for every concurrent transaction that generates undo. That will prevent *undo header waits* (contention in accessing the transaction table in the rollback segment header). However, if such concurrent transactions are very high (such as in a high-volume OLTP environment) and/or are expected to grow further, the number of rollback segments to have may not be accurately estimated and you may have to provide for each rollback segment to be able to have the required number of extents (even at the cost of some undo header waits) to accommodate all transactions without excessive space wastage. Generally,

25 extents allow quite a bit of flexibility. However, you may need more, depending on your unique requirements.

As a side note, do not confuse all concurrent transactions with active transactions that generate undo. You may have a large number of concurrent transactions; however, many of these may be running queries rather than changing data. Remember, only changes to data via DML statements (INSERTs/UPDATEs/DELETEs) generate undo. So prior to estimating the number of rollback segments to have, one ought to figure out exactly how many transactions are concurrently generating undo. Chapter 19 provides a query to check that. Typically, you end up getting results as outlined in Table 12-5. As may be seen there, in an environment like this, you don't need 200 or 180 rollback segments—but only around 70 (plus a few additional ones as a buffer to accommodate hike in transactions generating undo). Alternatively, having 35 or 40 rollback segments, each with equi-sized INITIAL/NEXT having the capability to allocate additional extents to accommodate the additional transactions, would also work fine. (The undo header waits shouldn't be too high in such cases, especially if each transaction is very short in nature, as found in a typical OLTP database; these transactions would hold a latch on the undo header for a very short duration. Also considering that a transaction does not place a latch on the undo header for the entire duration of the write operation, there are high chances of at least one rollback segment being without active transactions as a new one comes in and of allowing transactions to be able to use the existing pool of rollback segments without having to wait on each other). Ultimately, you need to monitor the database to detect undo header waits and add more rollback segments, if they appear to be high. Chapter 19 provides a script to query *v$waitstat* to detect undo header waits. Note that in batch-processing or large dedicated write environments (such as databases supporting DSS applications), it is recommended to have at least as many rollback segments as the number of concurrent active transactions generating undo—since the probability of rollback segments being frequently released is less. Even in such environments, however, it is desirable to have medium-sized INITIAL/NEXT extents so that concurrent transactions can grow without allocating huge extents for comparatively smaller writes, resulting in large-scale space wastage. For instance, a transaction may write 202MB of data. If the INITIAL/NEXT of the rollback segments is set high (say 100MB), it may use up the existing two extents (100MB each) and have to allocate another 100MB extent only for the remaining 2MB. This results in 98MB space-wastage. Alternatively, having medium-sized extents (say, 25MB INITIAL/NEXT) causes a total of seven extents to be allocated (excluding the two existing extents) but results in space-wastage of only 23MB. Such medium-sized extents also allow

Type of Sessions	# of Sessions	Comments
Total sessions in the database	200	
Total active sessions	180	
Total sessions running ad-hoc queries	2	Includes DBAs running administrative/monitoring statements.
Total sessions running applications not currently generating undo (reports, other reads, and so on)	108	Though these are queries, they may be using read-consistent views from rollback segments.
Total sessions currently generating undo (UPDATEs, INSERTs, DELETEs)	70	Currently writing to rollback segments.

TABLE 12-5. *Sample Sessions Within the Database To Illustrate What is Typically Encountered*

existing free-space in the tablespace to be used more effectively. For instance, if there are six free-space bubbles throughout the tablespace ranging from 30MB to 60MB, a 100MB extent cannot be allocated, resulting in error. However, multiple 25MB-sized extents can still be allocated, avoiding transaction failure due to the rollback segments not being able to extend.

Temporary (Sort) Segments

Much of the preceding discussion also applies to temporary segments. Let's quickly summarize those points and also look at some new ones, specific to temporary segments.

- Temporary segments are allocated automatically by Oracle on an as-needed basis, when the SORT_AREA_SIZE proves inadequate to perform the sort in memory. In other words, the temporary tablespace is Oracle's implementation of virtual memory within the DBMS. Temporary segments involve I/O, thus delaying the sorts. Ideally, size the SORT_AREA_SIZE such that the entire sort can be accomplished in memory. This will require you to be familiar with applications (or ad hoc queries, in case of a DSS database) that use your database. In case you do not have that knowledge, enlist the help of appropriate application developers/designers. If the entire sort cannot be accommodated in memory due to very large sorting requirements, size SORT_AREA_SIZE to allow as much as possible. That will reduce the need for temporary segments. As mentioned earlier, in Oracle8, SORT_AREA_SIZE can be dynamically changed. This allows exceptional sorting situations (such as index builds or certain unusual queries) to be run after the SORT_AREA_SIZE for that session has been temporarily increased, resulting in low temporary segment allocation.

- Maintain dedicated temporary tablespaces and ensure that all new and existing users use these pre-designated tablespaces for their temporary segment requirements. You can check the current temporary tablespace for each user via the following query:

```
SQL> SELECT username, temporary_tablespace FROM dba_users;
```

- Ensure that no user uses a non-designated tablespace as the temporary tablespace—especially SYSTEM. By default, when a user is created, SYSTEM becomes the temporary tablespace for that user. Ensure that you explicitly specify temporary tablespaces for all users. Users do not require any quotas to allocate temporary segments, since all temporary segments are created under the SYS user-id. Mark all such designated tablespaces as TEMPORARY within Oracle via the CREATE TABLESPACE...TEMPORARY or ALTER TABLESPACE...TEMPORARY commands. This will prevent any permanent segments from being created in the "temporary" tablespaces and also expedite the internal operations required during temporary segment creation and management (Chapter 7 elaborates on this).

- In case your application performs or is expected to perform a lot of sorts, causing the temporary tablespace to be heavily used, it is a good idea to create two temporary tablespaces of equal size. This will give you a lot of flexibility in temporary tablespace maintenance. Due to heavy use, the temporary tablespace may frequently get highly fragmented, requiring you to rebuild it. Having two temporary tablespaces will help you perform the reorganization without any downtime by switching all users to the second temporary tablespace. Whenever new users are added, allocate a specific temporary tablespace to them (say, TEMP1). When you need to reorganize TEMP1 (say, due to large number of unusable bubbles of free-space present within the tablespace, as can be observed in SYS.DBA_FREE_SPACE), you can switch over all users to use TEMP2 as the temporary tablespace. The following steps illustrate how. Note that these steps are to be performed during periods of low (temporary tablespace) use:

    1. Create a script to alter all users to use TEMP2 as their temporary tablespace.

    ```
    SQL> SET ECHO OFF
    SQL> SET PAGE 0
    SQL> SET FEEDBACK OFF
    ```

```
SQL> SELECT 'ALTER USER ' || username || ' TEMPORARY TABLESPACE TEMP2;'
       FROM dba_users
      WHERE temporary_tablespace = 'TEMP1'
SQL> SPOOL alter_temp.sql
SQL>/
SQL> SPOOL OFF
SQL> @alter_temp
```

2. Check and verify that all users have been altered. There shouldn't be any rows returned for the following query.

```
SQL> SELECT username FROM dba_users
      WHERE temporary_tablespace = 'TEMP1';
```

3. Take TEMP1 offline to ensure that none of the active sessions use it anymore.
4. Note down the physical attributes of TEMP1 (number of data-files, their location, names and sizes, default storage parameters, and so on).
5. Drop TEMP1.
6. Re-create TEMP1 with the appropriate data-files and default storage parameters.
7. Now TEMP1 is ready to take over as the temporary tablespace again. You can continue to let users use TEMP2 until the latter gets fragmented and needs to be rebuilt (since TEMP1 and TEMP2 are of the same size, either one can substitute for the other).

   The reason for creating TEMP2 at the same time as TEMP1 (during initial configuration) and not later, when the rebuild is actually required, is that later you may not have the space necessary to create TEMP2. By creating both TEMP1 and TEMP2 at the same time, you virtually lock up the required space, so that you don't inadvertently use it up for other purposes. In case you do not have the necessary space to let two temporary tablespaces coexist, you could temporarily alter users to point to the rollback segment tablespace (RBS) as their temporary tablespace. Once the actual temporary tablespace is rebuilt, you can alter them again to use the original one. Note that this may fragment the RBS tablespace. However, performing the shuffle quickly during low use hours keeps the impact on the "staging" tablespace (RBS) minimal. Also, this allows the temporary tablespace to be rebuilt with no downtime. You may, in fact, use the same method to rebuilt the rollback segment tablespace as well. Do this by marking the temporary tablespace as PERMANENT (in case you have it marked as TEMPORARY), creating a few rollback segments in the temporary tablespace to accommodate user/application requirements (since this whole operation would be done during low use periods, there would be relatively few requirements), making these new rollback segments online, making the existing rollback segments in the RBS tablespace offline and dropping them, and dropping the rollback segment tablespace and rebuilding (recreating) it. Once it's been rebuilt, recreate all necessary rollback segments as they existed originally and make them online. The segments in the temporary tablespace can then be made offline and dropped, and the temporary tablespace can be marked as TEMPORARY again.

- Keep standardized extent sizes for temporary segments. Temporary segment sizes are governed by the DEFAULT STORAGE clause for the appropriate temporary tablespace. Ensure that INITIAL and NEXT are multiples of DB_BLOCK_SIZE (such as 512KB, 1MB, 2MB, 5MB) and PCTINCREASE is set to 0. It is advisable to set INITIAL and NEXT to be equivalent to each other to allow well-balanced segment growth. Another important consideration for temporary segment sizing is the SORT_AREA_SIZE. Remember that temporary tablespace allocations are overflows of what occurs in the SORT_AREA_SIZE. If possible, set the INITIAL and NEXT extent sizes to be equivalent to the SORT_AREA_SIZE plus DB_BLOCK_SIZE (the additional DB_BLOCK_SIZE is to accommodate the header block for the temporary segment). However, if the SORT_AREA_SIZE is relatively too small (example: 64KB or 128KB) due to limited memory and a large user community, then it's desirable to set the INITIAL/NEXT of the temporary tablespace to be multiples of the SORT_AREA_SIZE in order to limit the number of extents allocated and reduce the overall *recursive calls* associated with excessive space management operations. You need to seek a balance between allocating excessive temporary segments and avoiding high space-wastage (that is, a significant portion of the temporary segment should not remain unused once it's allocated by a server process, and such allocation should also not occur too often, since allocation has high overhead. Incidentally, marking a tablespace to be TEMPORARY reduces this overhead, since the temporary segment is not removed and reallocated each time.) If the entire sort cannot be accommodated in memory, make it happen within a single extent of the temporary segment. Also, temporary segments are accessed sequentially. Accordingly, in order to expedite and synchronize large sorting operations resulting from full-segment scans (full-table scans, fast full-index scans), make the INITIAL/NEXT for temporary tablespaces a multiple of the DB_FILE_MULTIBLOCK_READ_COUNT. Also, if temporary segment use is high, it is advisable to stripe the temporary tablespace and/or maintain it on dedicated disks to avoid I/O contention.

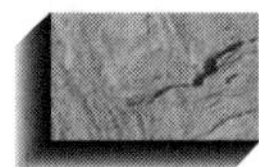

NOTE
This chapter frequently makes reference to recursive calls (as in the preceding paragraph). An explanation is in order. Recursive calls are SQL statements that are generated and executed by Oracle in addition to the regular user/application SQL statements. For instance, a user runs a SQL statement (say, a report). Prior to executing this SQL statement, Oracle parses the original SQL statement and generates other SQL statements to verify whether tables, columns, and such referenced within the query really do exist in the appropriate schema, whether the user has the privileges to access those tables/columns, and so on. Such additional statements are referred to as recursive calls. Other reasons for recursive calls being generated include data-dictionary cache misses; space management operations such as a new extent being allocated, SQL statements within triggers, stored procedures, and such; SQL statements resulting from referential integrity checks; DDL statements; and so on. Excessive recursive calls result in performance degradation, and steps should be taken to prevent them (such as by sizing the shared-pool adequate to prevent data-dictionary cache misses). The recursive calls for your database can be verified in the v$sysstat *dynamic view or in the* utlbstat/utlestat *report.*

- In a mirrored environment, you might consider having temporary tablespaces on non-mirrored volumes (preferably striped). This reduces the costs of writes. Note that if a disk is lost on which a data-file of the temporary tablespace resides, transactions may be lost. However, it is easy to switch all users to the other temporary tablespace (as outlined earlier). This is mostly useful only in DSS environments where there are large sorts (resulting in high use of the temporary tablespace).
- Finally, frequently monitor temporary segment use and adjust temporary tablespace STORAGE parameters accordingly. You need to determine the average size of sorts occurring during peak hours, the size of the biggest sort, how frequently the biggest sort is occurring, whether the DBMS is spending too much time in space-management operations (high recursive calls), and so on. Chapter 19 provides some scripts to monitor temporary segment use.

Bootstrap (Cache) Segments

Bootstrap segments are used internally with Oracle for specific tasks such as tracking the features specific to the current version being used for compatibility purposes. These segments reside in the SYSTEM tablespace, and users/DBAs do not have any control over their creation. They are wholly managed by Oracle. Accordingly, do not worry about them, because Oracle does not provide any documented means for you to change their behavior.

Be familiar with the errors and effects that result from inadequate space management

Space problems often reveal themselves in the form of error messages. As a part of monitoring for space problems, it is essential to be familiar with the errors that are commonly encountered, so that you can specifically watch out for telltale signs that may lead to such errors and take steps to rectify them before they reveal themselves via runtime disruptions. Table 12-6 outlines some of the common errors.

A related problem, or rather, a root cause of common space-related problems is fragmentation. High fragmentation may result in large-scale wastage of space, leading to some of the preceding errors ("ORA-1650-55: Unable to extend"). In other words, controlling fragmentation allows you to restrict the occurrence of space-related errors and use available space more effectively. Since fragmentation may have a major effect on space consumption and possibly performance, it's imperative to develop a deep understanding of the phenomenon, prior to trying to combat resultant space crises.

Fragmentation

Fragmentation, as the name indicates, refers to a single part or component being broken up into two or more pieces. With respect to space management, fragmentation can be encountered within the following components or levels:

- The row level
- The block level
- The segment level
- The tablespace level

From a segment perspective, fragmentation can be internal (within the segment) or external (outside the segment within the tablespace). Row-level, block-level, and segment-level fragmentation are examples of internal fragmentation, whereas tablespace-level fragmentation is external. The causes and effects of fragmentation in each of the preceding components are different and merit a closer look.

Error	Oracle Error Code	Comments
Max # of extents reached	ORA-16[28-32] and ORA-1656	Occurs when the MAXEXTENTS is set to the default value (the default depends on the DB_BLOCK_SIZE) and the number of segments has already reached the MAXEXTENTS and another extent must be allocated. Chapter 19 provides a script to proactively detect this condition. Proactively setting MAXEXTENTS to be UNLIMITED prevents this error. However, bear in mind that you may want to set a lower value for rollback and temporary segments, since this is a useful mechanism to stop runaway processes from filling up the entire tablespace.
Unable to extend	ORA-16[50-55]	Occurs when the tablespace is full or is fragmented such that there is inadequate contiguous free-space to accommodate another extent. A new data-file may have to be added to create more space. Chapter 19 provides a script to monitor this, as well.
Snapshot too old	ORA-1555	This could and generally does happen due to application-related issues. However, rollback segments being improperly sized could also lead to this error. Chapter 11 takes a detailed look at this error.

TABLE 12-6. *Common Space-Related Errors*

ROW-LEVEL FRAGMENTATION Row-level fragmentation manifests itself via the following ways:

- Row chaining, and/or
- Row migration

Each of these causes pieces of a single row or the row and its address to be placed in different data-blocks, thus requiring multiple I/O reads to retrieve the entire row. Besides additional I/O, row chaining and migration also take up additional CPU cycles and memory, since Oracle has to detect the blocks to migrate/chain the row to and actually perform the tasks. In other words, performance suffers due to row fragmentation and needs to be detected and resolved with as little impact on uptime as possible. Let's take a closer look at row chaining and row migration.

Row chaining is caused when a row is physically too large to fit into a single block. For instance, if the database block size is 2KB (2,048 bytes) and the size of the row is 3,012 bytes, then the row cannot be placed within a single block, thus requiring it to be broken into pieces and each piece placed into different blocks. The different pieces are linked via the addresses (the ROWIDs) conforming to the different blocks. However, the primary address (the ROWID pertaining to the first block within which it is placed) is used for all practical purposes, such as within index entries or SELECT statements that retrieve the ROWID. Row chaining can be avoided to an extent by configuring the appropriate database-block size (DB_BLOCK_SIZE) such that it is greater than the size of the biggest row of all tables in your database. In cases, however, where your tables contain LONG/LONG RAW columns or "in-line" LOBs (CLOB/BLOB/NCLOB), it may not always be possible to accommodate all such rows within a single block. Even in the case of "out-of-line" LOBs, where the actual LOB value is stored separately, a LOB locator is used to reference the LOB value (which is akin to chaining). In most cases, however, these occurrences should be relatively rare, being restricted to applications that widely use LONG/LONG RAW or LOB data-types, such as imaging systems and GIS/spatial-data applications. Accordingly, it is necessary to consider row sizes prior to deciding upon the DB_BLOCK_SIZE for your database.

Thus row-chaining is primarily caused during INSERT operations. Row migration occurs primarily during UPDATEs. When a row is updated such that its size increases and the current free-space in the block is not adequate to accommodate the expansion, the entire (expanded) row is taken out and placed into a new block that has the required free-space. (If no blocks have the required free-space, the row may be chained; an error message, "ORA-1650-55: Unable to extend," results if there is no space to accomplish even the chaining.) Thus, the row is reinserted. However, the address of the row is still considered to be the original ROWID pertaining to the block where the row originally lived. All existing index entries still use the original ROWID. This is inefficient because all subsequent reads of the row need to access the original block only to find that the row had been moved, get the forwarding address, and then access the new block (assuming the row has not been migrated any further). Not cleaning up the original block to remove all traces of the row and not making all index entries current should serve to reduce the impact of the UPDATE operation and maximize throughput. However, in addition to delaying subsequent SELECTs (that need to read the row), this also results in wastage of space, albeit this wastage will be relatively small. To understand this better, let's take a closer look to see how space is used by rows within a table.

As may be seen in Figure 12-7, a row consists of two components: a row-header and actual data relating to columns in the row. This is true for both chained and unchained rows. In case of an unchained row, it would be a whole row, and in case of a chained one, it would be a row piece. The row-header takes up at least three bytes and contains meta-data specific to the row, such as ROWID of all row pieces (if the row has been chained/migrated), the number of columns physically present in that row-piece (or the whole row), and the cluster-key (if the table is part of a cluster). The actual data-portion contains a column header and column data. The column header specifies the length of the column-data, following the header. Note that a column (such as a LONG RAW) may span multiple blocks. Accordingly, the column header serves to identify the size of the column-data contained in this block. This is useful also for other variable data-types, such as VARCHAR, VARCHAR2, and RAW, to identify how much column-data is actually contained in the block. For fixed-length columns, the column header specifies the fixed length (such as 7 bytes for a DATE column). The column header portion takes up 1 byte for columns that hold a maximum of 250 bytes and 3 bytes for bigger columns (than 250 bytes). A variable-length column that is smaller than 250 bytes has a 1-byte header. However, if it is updated to a larger size, the column header also expands to 3 bytes. If either of these expansions is not possible due to limited free-space, the row is migrated. Also, if the table contains LOBs and the size of data per LOB is lesser than 4KB, then the actual data is stored in-line (as part of the row) by default. Otherwise, it is stored out-of-line (separately), as specified by the LOB clause of the CREATE/ALTER TABLE commands. It is possible to override the default and force Oracle to store all LOBs out-of-line, irrespective of the data size, via the DISABLE STORAGE IN ROW parameter of the LOB clause in the CREATE/ALTER TABLE commands. It is preferable to store all large LOBs together in a distinct tablespace, so as not to clutter up the other tablespaces and also to help performance and maintenance by allowing a more balanced and controlled spread of different types of data onto specific hallmarked areas (disk/controllers). Note that out-of-line LOB

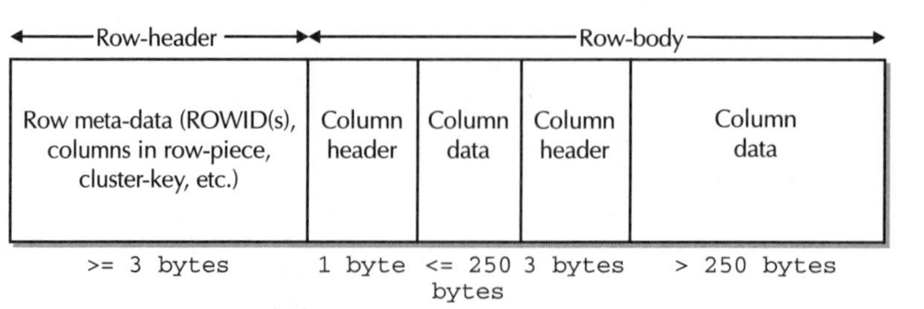

FIGURE 12-7. *Space consumption by a row*

columns also technically result in row fragmentation, since portions of the same row are being stored in separate areas. However, the impact on I/O due to such fragmentation will be restricted to situations when the LOB value needs to be accessed. Generally, non-LOBs columns are likely to be accessed more often than LOBs. Also placing large LOBs in-line increases the chances of row chaining and migration, due to the probability of larger rows being subjected more often to such fragmentation. Storing LOBs in-line will cause even a relatively small row to increase in size and be prone to the faults of a larger row size. Oracle maintains a LOB locator to allow quick access to out-of-line LOBs. LOB locators, which are approximately 24 bytes in size, also serve to identify the location of BFILE columns (which are stored outside the database in a specific directory identified by the CREATE DIRECTORY command). Whenever the size of the data is 4,000 bytes or less, use VARCHAR2, rather than a CLOB (or NVARCHAR2 instead of a NCLOB, if using non-default character sets).

If the column contains a NULL (absence of any value) and it is physically present prior to a NULL or NOT NULL column that actually has a value, then the column header for the preceding NULL column specifies zero as the size of data. Alternatively, if the column containing a NULL value is physically placed at the end of the row, then even the column header is not maintained by Oracle. This is because the start of a new row indicates that the current row has ended and all columns that are not present have NULLs in them. Thus, declaring all mandatory (NOT NULL) columns prior to NULL columns helps to optimize space consumption in the database. Columns are generally stored in the order of declaration, except in specific cases, such as when the table contains a LONG/LONG RAW column, in which case the latter is always stored last. Also, if the table is altered to include a new column, the new column is stored last.

In addition to the foregoing, each row takes up two bytes in the block's header portion (which maintains a "directory" of all rows in the block).

With the preceding explanation, it's easier to picture how rows are stored within a block and how lack of free-space in the block may lead to row chaining and migration. Figures 12-8 and 12-9 depict row chaining and migration respectively.

Row chaining can rarely be controlled (except by choosing a DB_BLOCK_SIZE large enough to accommodate the entire row, which is not always possible). However, row-migration can be effectively restricted via the PCTFREE and PCTUSED parameters of the CREATE/ALTER TABLE commands. The PCTUSED and PCTFREE parameters govern space consumption within each block. Judicious use of these parameters results in an effective mechanism to control row fragmentation. Let's take a look at how these parameters function. Free-lists maintain addresses of blocks that are available for new rows to be inserted. Every INSERT operation only inserts rows into these blocks until the PCTFREE for that block is reached. Once the PCTFREE is reached, these blocks are considered "off-limits" for future INSERTs. In other words, these blocks are evicted from the free-lists, so that future INSERTs

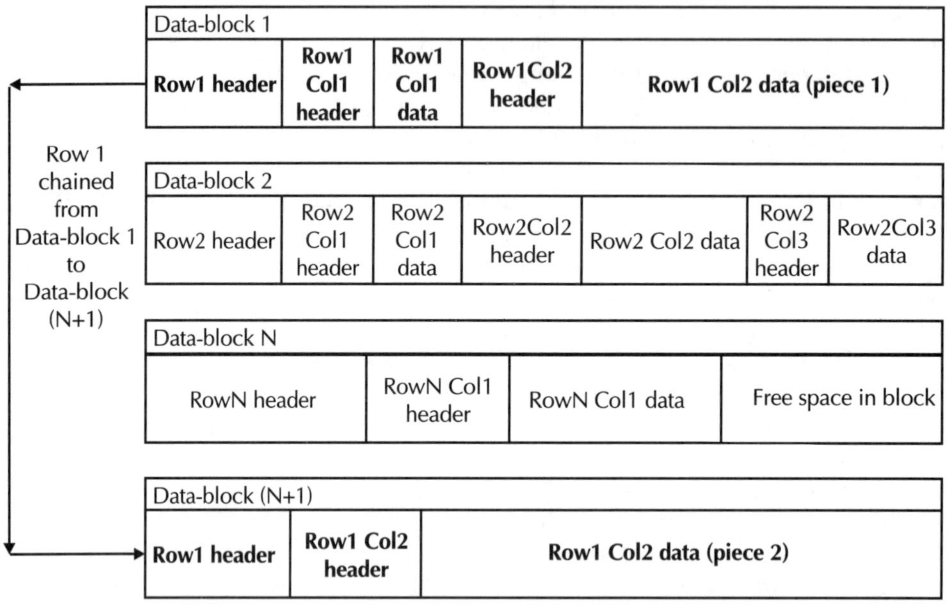

FIGURE 12-8. *Row chaining*

cannot use these blocks. Now the space that is left free in these blocks is available for UPDATEs, since UPDATEs can potentially increase the size of the row. For instance, if the value in a VARCHAR2 column is changed from 'WARDS' to 'BLOOMINGTON EAST COAST', then the size of the row expands. Similarly, if the number 200 is updated to 240000, then again, the row size increases. In other cases, updating a NULL value to a non-NON value will result in row size going up. By using PCTFREE to reserve free-space within each block, you allow the rows to remain in their original block, in spite of such expansion. If PCTFREE were to be zero, then all free-space would be used up by INSERTs and subsequent UPDATEs would cause the row to be migrated to a different block, capable of accommodating the expansion.

Thus, it is necessary (for the DBA or a member in the team) to be familiar with the average and maximum row sizes of tables in the database. Having this knowledge helps in determining the PCTFREE for each table, so that row fragmentation is eliminated. Ideally, set the PCTFREE to cover the difference between the average and maximum row sizes. For instance, if the average row size is estimated to be around 900 bytes and the maximum size possible is 1,250 bytes,

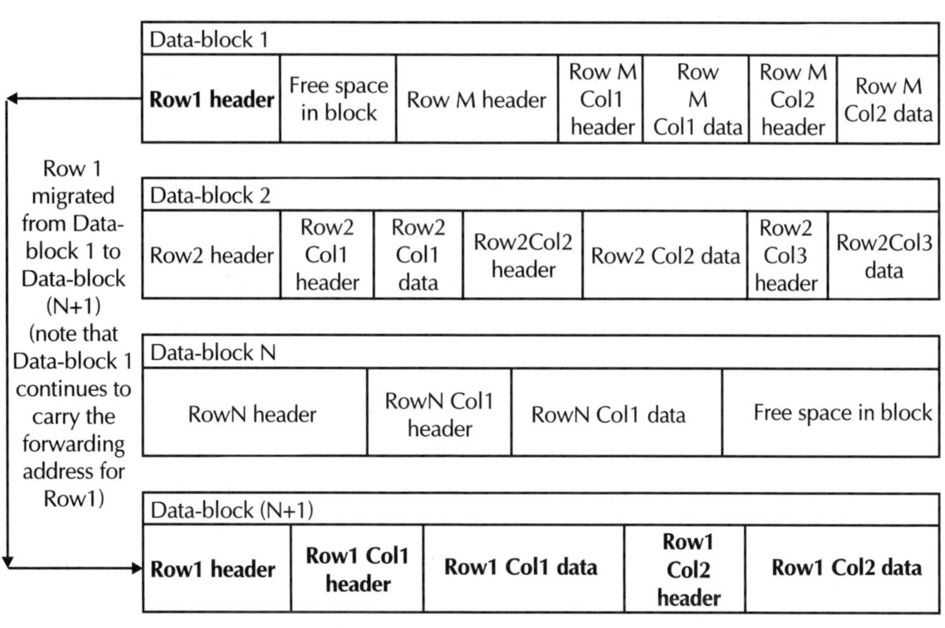

FIGURE 12-9. *Row migration*

then setting PCTFREE somewhere between 10 (the default value) and 30 will help. You may need the help of appropriate application developers and/or designers to understand the average row sizes. The maximum row size can be easily determined by adding the sizes of each individual column. Table 12-7 provides an example of computing maximum row size.

Note that by using this method, you would derive a higher value than would normally be used in most cases. However, by using your familiarity with application INSERT/UPDATE patterns, you can adjust this value accordingly. For instance, if a table is expected to be updated less frequently and such updates will cause only a few columns to increase (not all columns), then you need to take such facts into consideration prior to setting the PCTFREE. Also, for tables that are not subject to UPDATEs, you can choose a very low PCTFREE (such as 5 or even 0). If the table already exists but has a lot of migrated rows and needs to be rebuilt, you can use SQL to compute the average (AVG() function) and maximum (MAX() function) row sizes for each column in the table. For large tables, such SQL statements may be resource-intensive, and it's advisable to run them and calculate the necessary statistics during hours of low use.

Table: NAMES

Column Name	Column Definition (Type and Maximum Size)	Maximum Size of Data the Column Could Ever Hold
NAME_ID	NUMBER(5)	5 bytes
NAME	VARCHAR2(255)	255 bytes
DOB	DATE	7 bytes
ADDRESS	VARCHAR2(2000)	2,000 bytes
Total		2,267 bytes
Maximum row size:		2,267 bytes

TABLE 12-7. *Maximum Row Size Computation*

PCTUSED allows you to optimize space use by preventing too much free-space from lying idle in each block. For instance, a table could be subject to DELETEs, which may cause space previously occupied by the deleted rows within each block to be freed up. Similarly, an UPDATE can cause the values in different columns to shrink (by updating the existing larger-sized values to smaller-sized values), thus freeing up space. Such freed space will add to the free-space already kept reserved through PCTFREE. This may result in space being underutilized. In order to prevent rampant space-wastage under such circumstances, you can set PCTUSED to an appropriate value. PCTUSED determines when a block returns to the free-list. If the deletes cause a certain percentage of the space within a block to be freed up, then future INSERTs can utilize the block to place more rows there. In other words, PCTUSED specifies the threshold of used space below which a block may be reused by subsequent INSERTs. For tables subject to a high volume of DELETEs, you may want to specify an appropriately higher PCTUSED, so that freed-up space does not sit around wasted and is utilized quickly. However, PCTUSED needs to be set relatively lower, to prevent blocks from being pushed into the freelist too quickly and attracting new rows, increasing the chances of row fragmentation. Thus, using the combination of PCTFREE and PCTUSED, you can effectively balance optimal space use with prevention of row fragmentation. Note that for indexes, PCTUSED is not applicable and PCTFREE only determines the extent of block-splitting during index creation. Chapter 6 discusses PCTFREE for indexes in detail.

Examine the "table fetch continued row" statistics in *v$sysstat* (or the *utlbstat/ utlestat* report) to identify occurrences of row fragmentation. Row fragmentation is resolved by rebuilding the affected tables (writing out the data to an export-file or to another temporary table, re-creating the table with more appropriate storage, PCTFREE and PCTUSED parameters and reinserting the data). However, that would involve costly downtime. There is another option to resolve row fragmentation with little (mostly no) impact on availability. The following steps illustrate how:

1. Prepare a list of all tables that are suspected to have chained/migrated rows. You may also include all critical tables that are highly accessed. It's a good idea to routinely analyze all critical tables for row fragmentation, to prevent impact on performance.
2. Create a table to capture the ROWIDs of all chained/migrated rows. A sample table (CHAINED_ROWS) creation script is provided in $*ORACLE_HOME/rdbms/admin/utlchain.sql.* (the actual pathname and filename of this script may vary depending on the OS and Oracle version). A common practice is to have SYSTEM own this table, grant privileges on this table to required administrators, and create the appropriate synonyms. Do not create this table under the SYSTEM tablespace (this, again, is common practice). Instead, specify TOOLS as the tablespace for this table by editing the *utlchain.sql* script. This will prevent fragmentation of the SYSTEM tablespace.
3. Analyze each table in your list as follows:

```
SQL> ANALYZE TABLE <current_table_name> LIST CHAINED ROWS;
```

4. The CHAINED_ROWS.HEAD_ROWID column lists the ROWIDs of all rows that have been chained/migrated. You may then copy all such rows to a different temporary table via a ROWID lookup as follows:

```
SQL> CREATE TABLE <temporary_table_name>
       TABLESPACE users
       STORAGE(<appropriate storage clause>)
       NOLOGGING
       AS SELECT * FROM <current_table_name>
           WHERE ROWID IN (SELECT head_rowid FROM chained_rows
            WHERE table_name = '<current_table_name>');
```

5. Then these rows may be deleted from the original table as follows:

```
SQL> DELETE FROM <current_table_name>
      WHERE ROWID IN
          (SELECT head_rowid FROM chained_rows
            WHERE table_name = '<current_table_name>');
```

6. Then reinsert the deleted rows from the temporary table into the original table as follows:

```
SQL> INSERT INTO <current_table_name>
       SELECT * FROM <temporary_table_name>;
```

7. Then, finally, the temporary table may be dropped and the CHAINED_ROWS table may be deleted to remove all occurrences of the current table:

```
SQL> DROP TABLE <temporary_table_name>;
SQL> DELETE FROM chained_rows
      WHERE table_name = '<current_table_name>';
```

The current table ought to be reanalyzed to check for any further occurrences of row fragmentation. If any are found, then steps 4 to 7 can be repeated. If a significant portion of a critical table is fragmented, then it may still require application downtime (since an application may need to access rows that are being deleted/reinserted). Accordingly, it's advisable to do the repair during low use periods. Also, it may be useful to have standby tables implemented to reduce the impact on uptime. In any case, reset the PCTFREE and PCTUSED parameters via the ALTER TABLE (or CREATE TABLE if the entire table is being rebuilt) command to reduce future occurrences of row fragmentation. While evaluating appropriate values for PCTFREE and PCTUSED, it is highly necessary to ensure that the space calculated as (100% – (PCTUSED + PCTFREE)) within the block be higher than the maximum possible row size in each table.

As may be evident from the preceding discussion, PCTFREE and PCTUSED are powerful means to proactively keep row fragmentation at bay and thus limit the need for maintenance (defragmentation of the rows). This will subsequently limit the occurrences and duration of downtime required to perform such maintenance.

BLOCK-LEVEL FRAGMENTATION A flip-side of row-level fragmentation is block-level fragmentation, which is typically caused due to high influx and removal of rows (see Figure 12-10). As an application inserts rows, free-space within blocks is taken up in an incremental fashion. As these rows get deleted, "holes" get formed in these blocks (due to the rows that once occupied these spots being deleted), causing block fragmentation. These holes are once again filled up by new rows that can fit into these holes. However, new rows cannot come in until the block is referenced within the freelist. The blocks can only be included in the freelist when the percentage of used space falls below PCTUSED. Thus, block-level fragmentation can be effectively controlled by specifying a higher PCTUSED. Similarly, there may be an urge to set a lower PCTFREE to limit free-space within each block. However, as discussed under the paragraphs on row-level fragmentation, one needs to evaluate the frequency and scope of updates and deletes prior to doing so. Especially for tables subject to high deletes, you may want to specify an appropriately high PCTUSED, so that freed-up space is quickly reutilized. However, note that specifying too high a value for PCTUSED may result in a block being referenced in the freelist too soon and then subsequently being taken off, once new rows come in and fill it until PCTFREE is reached. This constant referencing and dereferencing of a block in the freelist may lead to excessive recursive calls, causing overall performance to deteriorate. Also, higher PCTUSED values tend to attract newer rows, potentially increasing the chances of row fragmentation, as newer rows come in and existing rows are updated such that their size increases. Accordingly, PCTUSED needs to be set after considering all such repercussions. The objective should be to maximize space usage within each block, such that all holes from deleted rows are filled up as soon as possible, without causing row fragmentation and performance deterioration.

Eliminating block fragmentation allows a larger number of rows to be packed within each block and subsequently results in a higher number of blocks being read with as few I/O calls as possible. This will help performance tremendously, especially in situations where a large number of rows need to be read as quickly as possible, such as during full-table scans.

Again, a high degree of familiarity with DML activity generated by applications is required to successfully determine the right PCTUSED for different tables. Generally, the default 40 proves useful in most situations. However, the setting for

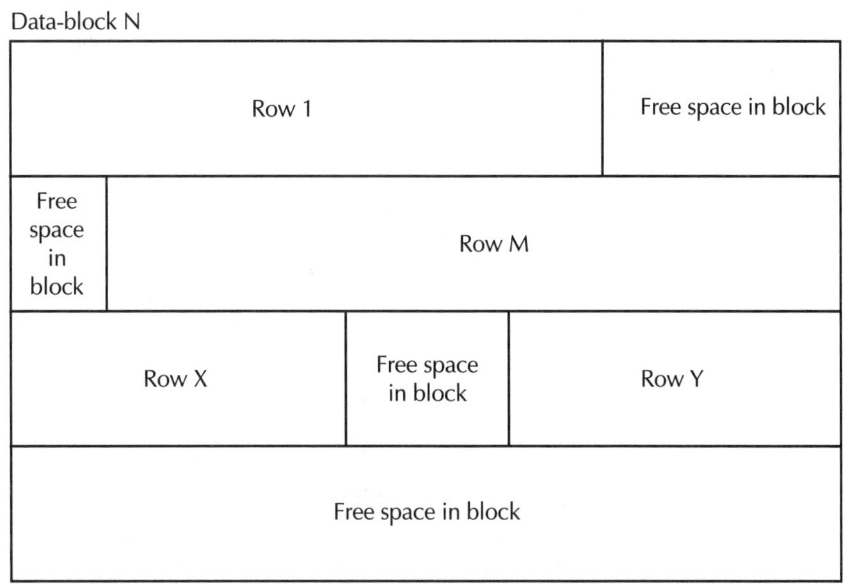

FIGURE 12-10. *Block-level fragmentation*

each critical table needs to be evaluated and determined independently. For instance, PCTUSED does not overly affect a table that is only prone to inserts with few or no updates/deletes. However, such a table needs to have a low PCTFREE, allowing very little space to be wasted within the block. By contrast, a table prone to numerous inserts, deletes, and updates needs to have a higher-than-default PCTFREE accompanied with a higher-than-default PCTUSED. An example would be to set the PCTFREE to 30 and PCTUSED to 60. This will allow new rows to come in as deletes cause the total used space in the block to fall to 59 percent or lower; at the same time, it will restrict newer rows to insert data only up to 70 percent of the total block-size, leaving 30 percent free for future updates. Monitor recursive calls in *v$sysstat* or the *utlbstat/utlestat* report and ensure that they remain low. If they are high, then one of the steps you need to take is to evaluate the PCTUSED of highly used (popular) tables and set it lower, where appropriate.

You can take the following steps to identify block fragmentation:

1. Make a list of popular tables that you suspect to have high block fragmentation. These will generally be the medium and large segments within your database.

2. For each of these tables, compute the average row size (using the AVG() function). If you cannot use SQL to compute the average size due to the size of the tables and the impact on performance, you can estimate the average row size from the row count and the table structure (number of columns, their data-types, whether they are mandatory, and so on) and your familiarity with the application data (the average size of a "name," or the average bytes taken up by the salary column, and so on). You could also use a combination of SQL (to compute the average size of specific columns) and your familiarity with application data to arrive at the approximate average row size. If you use non-SQL methods to determine the average size, add an additional 20 percent to the size as a "safety buffer" against underestimation. Divide the result by the DB_BLOCK_SIZE to estimate the number of blocks required to hold the table data.

3. Find the blocks actually held by the table via the following query:

   ```
   SQL> SELECT blocks FROM dba_segments
          WHERE segment_type = 'TABLE' AND segment_name =
          '<table_name>';
   ```

   Subtract one from the result to discount the segment header block.

4. If there is a substantial difference between the two results (from steps 2 and 3), this may be an indication of high block fragmentation or data for that table being spread across far more blocks than necessary. Note that relatively small differences may not be due to block fragmentation, since

such a difference also commonly arises from the last extent of the segment being relatively unpopulated (having been allocated just recently or the NEXT extent size being very big, thus requiring time to be filled up). Accordingly, consider this fact prior to concluding that there is high block fragmentation.

At times, delayed logging block cleanouts may also play a role in block fragmentation. For instance, a table subject to cycles of large inserts and deletes may experience block fragmentation due to block cleanouts not occurring soon enough. Let's say a table STOCK_TRANSACTIONS has 5,000 rows (just a random number) inserted into it every day. At the same time, say 2,000 older rows are deleted every day. These rows are marked for deletion, but the entries for the rows may still remain in the blocks. Later when the blocks (holding the deleted rows) are "touched" again (say, via a SELECT) by a subsequent transaction, the blocks are "cleaned" out, the rows are physically removed, and the space is freed up. However, between the time the rows are marked for deletion and when they are physically removed, they still continue to use up space, causing dead weight to be held within blocks. Accordingly, new inserts cannot immediately reuse the "available" space. In other words, the "holes" within the blocks caused by the deletions (even though the number of rows deleted may have caused the used space to go below PCTUSED) are not visible due to the blocks not having been cleaned out. They need to wait until the entries for the rows are physically removed. Accordingly, new inserts may trigger off new extent allocations, while the previous blocks remain sub-optimally populated. This will make it seem as if the table is continuously growing, even though rows are being deleted. However, such growth and fragmentation (induced by delayed logging block cleanouts) are temporary in nature, and over a period of time, the space will be freed up and subsequent inserts can reuse the space. Subsequent operations that access such blocks, including indexed lookups, will clean them up. In fact, if the impact on performance is not too high, you may want to do a full-table scan after large deletes to clean out the blocks. Full-table scans, since they access all blocks, will help in forcing block cleanouts. You may place such tables in the RECYCLE pool (in Oracle8) or use the NOCACHE hint to prevent the blocks for these tables from displacing useful blocks in the buffer cache. Also in Oracle v7.3 and above, delayed logging block cleanouts can be disabled by setting the DELAYED_LOGGING_BLOCK_CLEANOUTS initialization parameter to FALSE (note that doing so may impact response time of certain DML operations).

In any case, a full-table scan against tables with highly fragmented blocks may result in slow performance and consume far more system resources than necessary, affecting other processes (even more adversely than necessary). Under such circumstances, a rebuild of the table to exist within a smaller number of blocks may be useful. However, if the table is rarely subjected to full-table scans, then the rebuild may not be too useful (in terms of performance), unless the objective is to optimize space utilization. In any case, setting PCTFREE and PCTUSED appropriately allows block-level fragmentation to minimized proactively.

SEGMENT-LEVEL FRAGMENTATION A segment is said to be fragmented when it encompasses multiple extents. Various Oracle and third-party publications have discussed the pros and cons of having multiple extents versus a single extent, and I won't repeat them here. The general idea is that having multiple extents does not necessarily hurt performance. Subsequent paragraphs summarize a few of the important issues involved in restricting a segment to a single extent versus having multiple extents. Note that in versions prior to 7.3, when the UNLIMITED extents option was not supported, it was certainly advisable to restrict the number of extents to as few as possible, since the consequence of not doing so was potential application downtime (due to segments not being able to extend to accommodate new rows being inserted by applications). With segments capable of having an UNLIMITED number of extents, the utility of restricting the number of extents has certainly gone down on the list of priorities for most DBAs. Also, periodically rebuilding the segment to occupy just one extent potentially causes application downtime—a major deterrent for attempting to do so. Such downtime could be substantial, especially if the segment concerned is large. In today's time, when administrators are willing to try everything possible to keep downtime low and live up to availability clauses in their SLAs, it seems like an oxymoron to periodically try to restrict segments to occupy a single extent. If a segment seems to be growing too fast, one needs to evaluate the rate of growth, ensure adequate free-space is available, and then alter the NEXT extent size and PCTINCREASE clause of the segment to allocate fewer segments, large enough to halt the frequent extent allocation (ideally, every new extent ought to be pre-allocated for performance reasons or allocated based on a pre-determined time-line, say, no sooner than once a month or so, to minimize the impact of space management operations) and small enough to easily fit within the available free-space in the tablespace for months to come. The *Oracle8 Administrator's Guide* provides detailed guidelines and formulas for estimating extent size and space use.

These are common issues regarding extent allocation (one versus many):

- Having multiple extents allows I/O to be spread across different disks/controllers (provided the extent allocations are carefully controlled to occur across the desired I/O channels). Conversely, having a single extent does not guarantee that the data is contiguous within one disk (at the OS/hardware level). Moreover, if the data-file is located on a striped volume (RAID 0, RAID 5, and so on), then there is little chance that the data will be contiguous, since multiple disks/controllers are involved. In fact, preference for contiguous data would violate the premise of striping in many ways, such as by forcing serial data access or potentially introducing I/O hot-spots. Also, contiguous data on a single disk/controller would make use of the Parallel Query Option difficult, since the parallel slaves would step on each other's toes while trying to access the data concurrently, leading to contention among themselves, delaying the parallel operation.

- Segment extension should not occur too frequently, since the resultant dynamic space management operations may cause excessive recursive calls, impacting performance adversely. If the *recursive calls* value in *v$sysstat* appears to be very high, then you may want to configure all popular segments to allocate fewer but larger-sized extents. Ensuring that all data fits within a single extent eliminates this problem. However, in the case of rollback segments, having a larger number of extents is actually beneficial, since having few extents can cause high recursive calls and space wastage. An earlier paragraph provides more details.
- Having a single large extent may expedite full-segment scans (full-table scans and fast full-index scans), since a single read cannot span multiple extents—the maximum number of contiguous blocks prior to the extent border or the number of blocks specified by the parameter DB_FILE_MULTIBLOCK_READ_COUNT, whichever is lower, determines the maximum number of blocks Oracle can read in a single I/O operation (besides other OS/hardware restrictions and multi-user environmental influences, of course). Thus, having a single extent allows each read to progress without being obstructed by the different extent borders. However, if the INITIAL/NEXT sizes (with PCTINCREASE = 0) are determined such that they are multiples of DB_BLOCK_SIZE and consequently DB_FILE_MULTIBLOCK_READ_COUNT, chances of this problem occurring are automatically reduced. Also note that for segments accessed via paths other than full-segment scans, such as indexed lookups, it doesn't matter whether a segment is composed of a single extent or multiple extents, since such reads are small and relatively more random.
- Having too many extents (say, over a few hundred; with the UNLIMITED options—it is fairly easy to do so, before you even realize it) causes the segment extent-map to be spread across multiple database blocks (in versions prior to 7.3, the entire extent-map had to fit within a single database block, causing MAXEXTENTS to be restricted by the database block size), potentially requiring multiple I/O calls to read the entire map. This may cause performance degradation during operations requiring the entire extent-map, such as during full-segment scans and certain DDL operations.

- Remember that even though a segment can span multiple data-files, a single extent cannot. Accordingly, it may be unrealistic to try to fit large segments within a single extent due to file-size and file-system limitations on various mainstream 32-bit OS flavors.
- Allowing segments to have multiple extents in order to grow as required allows investment in disks/controllers to be spread over time, rather than having to buy a lot of disks/controllers right up front, in order to size and accommodate all segments within a single extent each.

As may be evident from the preceding discussion, trying to limit segments to a single extent is a futile operation, potentially requiring downtime and resulting in few or no advantages. On the other hand, having too many extents (say, greater than a hundred) may cause performance degradation. Accordingly, it is essential to control segment fragmentation such that it is based upon certain time (a new extent per month) and performance criteria. In terms of performance, the data-files for appropriate tablespaces need to be laid out such that the additional extents are allocated across the requisite I/O channels. This can be achieved by maintaining each data-file on a distinct disk/controller and sizing each data-file to accommodate a single extent, so that whenever a new extent is allocated (or manually pre-allocated via the ALLOCATE clause of the ALTER/CREATE TABLE/INDEX commands), it goes to the next data-file (on a different disk/controller). This is generally useful only in environments where OS/hardware striping is not in use, since such fine-grained explicit extent management becomes redundant with OS/hardware striping.

TABLESPACE-LEVEL FRAGMENTATION Tablespace fragmentation is fairly common in most databases, and to a certain degree, it is almost inevitable, unless specific steps are taken to prevent it right from the time of initial database configuration and segment creation. Let's take a look at tablespace fragmentation to understand the issues involved and some preventive and ameliorative measures necessary to overcome it.

Tablespace fragmentation can be evidenced either as a contiguous chunk of free-space (termed as a "bubble") or as a series of chunks appearing adjacent to each other (termed as a "honeycomb"). Thus, a bubble comprises one or more blocks that are coalesced, whereas a honeycomb comprises multiple bubbles. A honeycomb can be coalesced to form a single large bubble. Bubbles exist between subsequent extents allocated for segments stored in that tablespace. A small bubble, comprising one or just a few blocks, may result in wastage of space unless it is able to accommodate newer extents of segments within the tablespace. In case of honeycombs, if they comprise a large number of bubbles or even a small number of large bubbles, then chances of space-wastage is minimal, since the honeycomb will be able to accommodate new extent allocations. However, small honeycombs (consisting of say, two or three block bubbles), which are fairly common, are more likely to result in space-wastage, unless the extent sizes of segments that need to expand are small enough to fit within them.

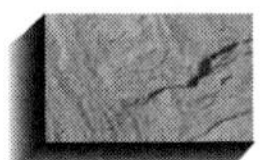

NOTE
Use of the terms "bubble" and "honeycomb" to describe different types of tablespace fragmentation has been originally noted in the Oracle Corporation white paper "Avoiding a Database Reorganization" by Craig A. Shallahamer. This paper, though originally written in 1994, is still a useful source of information for understanding certain critical database reorganization issues.

Both bubbles and honeycombs are remnants of extent deallocations within the tablespace. When a table is dropped or truncated (with the default DROP STORAGE clause), the extents it previously occupied are released. Other reasons for extents being released include use of the ALTER TABLE/INDEX..DEALLOCATE command. Additionally, in the case of rollback segments, extents may be released when the segment is shrunk (either implicitly by Oracle due to the OPTIMAL parameter being set or explicitly via the ALTER ROLLBACK SEGMENT SHRINK command). If the released extents are adjacent to each other, they form a honeycomb. Otherwise, if they are scattered throughout the tablespace, each extent effectively remains as a bubble. Also, if some of these deallocated extents are located next to pre-existing bubbles (created earlier when other segments were dropped/truncated), then they collectively form a honeycomb along with those older bubbles. Note that in the case of honeycombs, by default, the "border" around each bubble remains intact, thus separating them from each other. However, it is possible to coalesce them to bring the borders down and form a contiguous large bubble. Let's take an example to understand this better: If a table with 20 extents of 100K each (assuming DB_BLOCK_SIZE = 4K) is dropped, it releases 20 free-space chunks consisting of 25 data-blocks each. Now, if these chunks are adjacent to each other, they result in a honeycomb and can later be coalesced to form a single (approximately) 2MB bubble. Also, if there are additional neighboring free-space chunks, they can be made part of this large chunk. Whenever a new extent needs to be allocated for a segment and the size of the new extent is lesser than or equivalent to the largest free-space bubble available, the extent can be allocated onto that bubble. If the chunks released from dropping the table are not adjacent to each other nor are there any neighboring chunks of free-space available, each extent remains an independent bubble and a new extent can utilize the bubble only if the new extent requires 25 blocks or less (that is, if the new extent is sized 100KB or less). However, if newer extents (being allocated) require a minimum extent size of say,

1MB, then all of the released 100KB bubbles remain there as islands of free-space, causing wastage of almost 2MB and causing the new allocations to fail. Thus, even though collectively 2MB of free-space is available and is more than adequate to allow the new 1MB extent, each individual 100K bubble is not large enough to be of any value. Thus, each bubble reduces the usability of the tablespace, resulting in sub-optimal space utilization. This example looks at relatively small extents (100KB, 1MB, and so on) and discusses wastage of 2MB of space. However, the same example can be scaled to accommodate complex schemas consisting of tens of tablespaces, hundreds of segments, and manifold extent allocations and deallocations. Considering the larger picture, it's easy to envisage the substantial amount of space that could potentially be wasted due to bubbles being created throughout the tablespace.

Even though tablespace fragmentation clearly results in inefficient space use, it may not cause any perceptible performance problems. This is because once an extent is allocated, the space within the extent is used by regular DML operations. Accordingly, tablespace fragmentation does not impact their performance. However, DDL operations such as CREATE/DROP/TRUNCATE TABLE and dynamic extent allocations (due to segment growth) may be impacted due to multiple scans (of SYS.FET$) required to obtain the necessary free-space. This performance impact may be perceptible, especially if the bubbles are tiny, since it may take time to coalesce these fragments into usable space. SMON may be set to periodically coalesce this space automatically, or you may do it manually (a later tip provides more details). But even the performance impact on DDL and space-management operations is not scary, since such operations are not as commonplace and frequent as DML. If your segments are sized appropriately, space-management operations (performed during extent allocations) ought to be minimal. Frequent segment extension is an indication of bad physical design (or the lack of one). The real fear here is that high fragmentation may result in application downtime. If a segment cannot extend whenever it needs to, the application freezes due to inability to insert new rows. Let's take a quick look at the series of steps that occur when a row is being inserted into a table from an application:

1. The table's free-list is consulted about where the new rows can be placed. If no free blocks are available, a new extent needs to be allocated.
2. Oracle scans the SYS.FET$ table to locate free-space for the new extent within the tablespace.
3. This first scan tries to spot bubbles that can accommodate the new extent. The size of the new extent is computed after rounding up the number of blocks required for that extent to the next number divisible by 5. For instance, if an extent consists of 23 blocks, the number is rounded up to 25 blocks. However, if the request is for 5 blocks or less, then the rounding

does not occur. Once the number of blocks is thus determined, the first scan searches for bubbles that comprise the exact number of blocks required.

4. If an exact match is not found, then Oracle scans for a larger bubble. If the larger bubble comprises 5 blocks or more over the number of blocks required (after the rounding, of course), then the free-space in the bubble is split into the sizes necessary to accommodate the extent and free-space. The new (smaller) free-space bubble will consist of the surplus (5 or more) blocks over the required number. For instance, if the number of blocks required is 25 and a 32-block bubble is found, then Oracle takes up 25 of those blocks to allocate the extent and the remaining 7 blocks form a separate bubble that remains there. Alternatively, if a 28-block bubble is found, then the extent is merely allocated onto that larger bubble. In other words, no breakup occurs if the number of surplus blocks is less than 5.
5. If all existing bubbles are too small to cater to the extent (that is, if neither an equivalent size nor a larger bubble is found), then a third scan occurs to see if there are honeycombs that can be coalesced to acquire the necessary free-space. After the coalescing, steps 3 and 4 occur once again.
6. If none of the preceding steps succeed in procuring a bubble capable of accommodating the extent allocation, Oracle checks to see whether the AUTOEXTEND feature has been enabled (more about this option later) and if so, whether the data-file can be enlarged.
7. If AUTOEXTEND has not been enabled or if there is not adequate room on the disk (where the data-file resides) to enlarge the data-file, Oracle returns the "ORA-1650-55: Unable to extend" error message, causing application failure.

From the preceding steps, it is easy to see that due to miniscule bubbles being present, besides the cumulative space wastage, performance of space-management operations is impacted due to the additional scans required to make the extent allocation succeed. Also, if none of the subsequent scans succeed, then application failure is a real possibility. As you may have noted from the preceding steps, Oracle inherently tries to prevent bubbles or small honeycombs from proliferating by initially rounding off all extent sizes and then allocating a larger extent than requested, if a free bubble comprises less than 5 blocks over the required number. Such a small number of surplus blocks, if left alone, will most probably result in space wastage.

Now that we understand the symptoms of tablespace fragmentation, let's evaluate the causes. As stated earlier, bubbles and honeycombs are caused due to extents being deallocated. However, why should they result in fragmentation? How do minute bubbles get created? The answers lies in the storage parameters in effect for segments sharing a tablespace. If the storage parameters are incompatible with each other (that is, if they are not multiples of each other), then the space released by a segment being dropped either will be partially used or cannot be used by other segments. In the former case, being partially used may leave behind totally unusable fragments of free-space. In one of the preceding examples, if a segment with 20 extents is dropped, it leaves behind bubbles comprising 25 blocks each. If other segments that extend take up 20 blocks from many of these bubbles, then several 5-block bubbles are left behind. Now, when the other segments need to extend again, they only have 5 block bubbles, not 20 block bubbles. If the same segment that originally released those bubbles needs to extend, it also needs 25 blocks. If these five-block bubbles are adjacent, then they can be coalesced. If not, however, then they just waste free-space. Some of the following precautions may help prevent such scenarios. Note that other tips in this chapter elaborate on each of these. Accordingly, I do not elaborate here.

- Segregate all segments based on size and growth rates (as outlined in Chapter 6). Different-sized segments that grow at different rates ought to be maintained in separate tablespaces. Conversely, segments of the same size growing at similar rates should be kept in the same set of tablespaces. Allowing segments of the same size to be placed together ensures that freed bubbles can be effectively reused by other segments without the bubbles remaining underused. As we saw earlier, underusing bubbles results in smaller-sized fragments being created, increasing the chances of their not being usable.
- Ideally, all segments within a tablespace ought to have the same storage parameters (same INITIAL/NEXT for each segment). If this is not possible, ensure that the storage parameters of different segments are multiples of each other. That will at least reduce the chances of large-scale fragmentation by allowing new extents to step into the shoes of deallocated ones. Other tips in this chapter elaborate further in this area.
- Specify DEFAULT STORAGE parameters for all tablespaces. Additionally, specify the DEFAULT STORAGE only after giving adequate thought to the segments that will reside there. For instance, if large segments are expected to reside in a tablespace, specify appropriately large DEFAULT STORAGE parameters.
- Wherever possible, specify PCTINCREASE = 0. When that is not possible due to undefined growth patterns, use 100 as a potential value for PCTINCREASE. In any case, do not use random values such as 1, 5, and so on. This will prevent creation of odd-sized extents.

- Periodically coalesce your application tablespaces explicitly. Do not configure SMON to automatically coalesce your tablespaces for you, since that entails specifying the PCTINCREASE value to be greater than zero in the DEFAULT STORAGE clause of the tablespaces.
- Use PQO (Parallel Query Option) judiciously for creating indexes and tables (via CREATE TABLE AS SELECT), since it may result in odd-sized extents being created. Each parallel slave allocates an extent of the size INITIAL during creation. Also, each slave initially allocates extents as specified by the MINEXTENTS parameter. In the end, these extents may be merged (by the query coordinator) leading to the odd-sized extents and the additional unused space, if any is released. Such odd-sized extents can be observed in USER_EXTENTS when using parallelism, irrespective of the actual tool used, whether it be SQL*Plus, SQL*Loader (direct or conventional path), or what have you. These odd-sized extents can blow away a carefully thought-out strategy to keep fragmentation at bay. Often, however, the number of such odd-sized extents can be controlled by adjusting the degree of parallelism.
- Avoid specifying a higher degree of parallelism than the number of data-files available to the tablespace. Doing so while a segment is being created potentially causes space-wastage within all extents but the last (for each data-file) and releases less space after the final merge of all extents allocated by the parallel slaves. Oracle allocates parallel slaves on a round-robin basis to each data-file. For instance, if a tablespace has two data-files and an index is being created with a parallel degree of four, then two slaves are allocated onto each data-file and each of these slaves allocate an extent of size INITIAL, thus causing each data-file to have two extents. Finally, as the extents are being merged, only the free-space in the last extent in each data-file can be released onto the tablespace and coalesced with adjacent pre-existing free-space (if possible). The extents allocated prior to the last extent retain their free-space (thus, causing *internal* fragmentation within segments) for future inserts. This free-space may be wasted depending on the probability and frequency of future inserts. Thus, in the example just given, assuming that there was no need for any further extents, the INITIAL extents created by the first two query slaves will retain free-space, whereas the free-space in the extents created by the other query slaves may be released. This problem would be further intensified if there were only one data-file. In this case, three of the extents would retain free-space and only the free-space in the fourth extent would be released. Figure 12-11 illustrates this process. Besides specifying a degree of parallelism smaller than or equivalent to the number of data-files, another step you can take to reduce space wastage is to specify a smaller

INITIAL and larger NEXT. That will cause all parallel slaves to allocate a small INITIAL extent (the smaller the extent, the less the wastage), and then additional extents on as as-needed basis can be incrementally allocated by each slave. In order to prevent segment fragmentation for certain tables where large amounts of data are being written in parallel (by causing too many extents to be allocated), you can specify a much larger NEXT extent-size for such tables to limit the overall number of extents allocated. Note that you can take these steps even when using SQL*Loader in parallel.

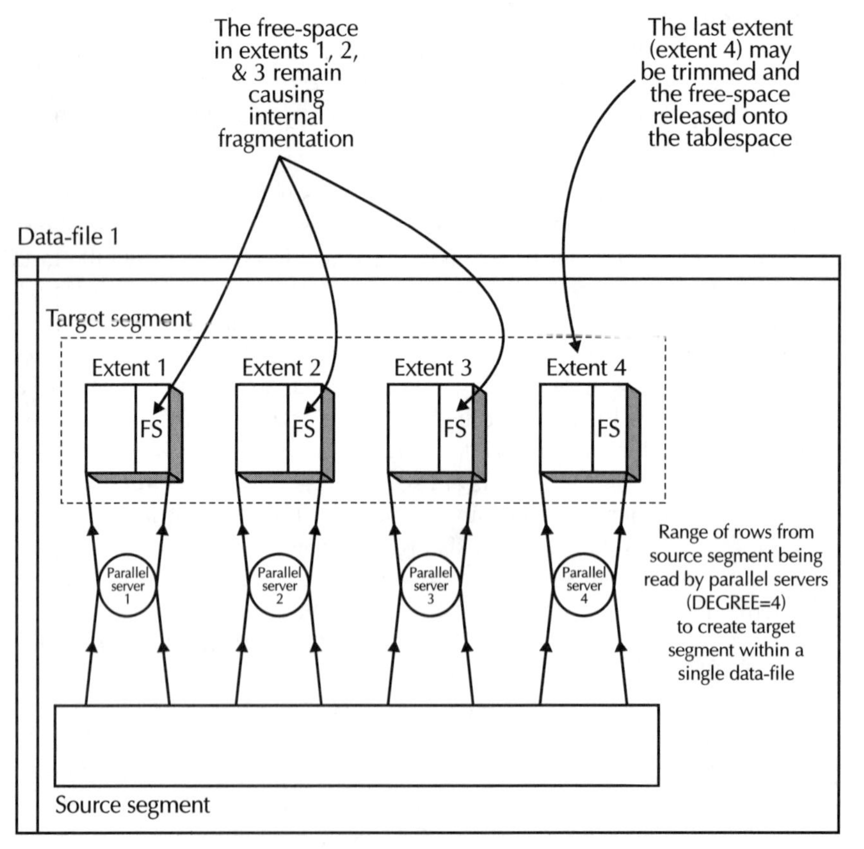

FIGURE 12-11. *Potential wastage of space within all extents except the last one for each data-file while using PQO*

The preceding steps suggest some proactive things that can be done to avoid fragmentation. However, if your tablespace is already fragmented, you may have to rebuild the entire tablespace to eliminate fragmentation. If that is not feasible due to the potential downtime required, then you can at least alter the storage parameters of all segments in that tablespace to allocate reasonable-sized extents henceforth. Also, if your applications are about to fail due to rampant fragmentation, you may have to add more data-files to prevent such failure in the short run. Then optionally identify the data-files (pertaining to that tablespace) that are most fragmented and rebuild only those data-files during periods of low use. If you have taken advantage of Oracle8's partitioning features and carefully thought out your partitioning strategy, then such maintenance may not cause you any downtime, since you can pinpoint the partitions that have rows in such fragmented data-files and only rebuild the ones pertaining to inactive partitions.

The following steps can be taken to identify fragmentation in tablespaces and reorganize only specific data-files:

- Identify bubbles and honeycombs within each application tablespace. The following query lists actual extents, bubbles, and honeycombs within a tablespace:

```
SET LINES 132
SET PAGES 500
COLUMN "Fil_ID" FORMAT 999 HEADING "Fil|ID"
COLUMN "Fil" FORMAT A55 HEADING "Fil-name"
COLUMN "Segment" FORMAT A55
COLUMN "Start blk" FORMAT 999999 HEADING "Strt|blk"
COLUMN "# blocks" FORMAT 999,999 HEADING "#|blks"
SELECT d.file_id "Fil_ID", d.file_name "Fil", segment_type || ' ' ||
       owner || '.' || segment_name "Segment",
       e.block_id "Start blk", e.blocks "# blocks"
  FROM dba_extents e, dba_data_files d
 WHERE e.tablespace_name = UPPER('&&tblspc_name')
   AND d.tablespace_name = e.tablespace_name
   AND d.file_id = e.file_id
UNION
SELECT s.file_id "Fil_ID", d.file_name "Fil", 'Free chunk' "Segment",
       s.block_id "Start blk", s.blocks "# blocks"
  FROM  dba_free_space s, dba_data_files d
 WHERE s.tablespace_name = UPPER('&&tblspc_name')
   AND d.tablespace_name = s.tablespace_name
   AND d.file_id = s.file_id
 ORDER BY 1, 4, 5
/
```

  The preceding query produces output as in Figure 12-12.

- If a large number of bubbles are scattered throughout the tablespace, especially small ones that cannot accommodate any extents, it may be necessary to rebuild that data-file. For instance, in Figure 12-12, data-file

```
Fil Fil-name                        Segment              Strt     #
 ID                                                       blk    blks
--- ------------------------------ -------------------- ----   ----
  1 C:\ORANT\DATABASE\SYS1ORC8.ORA ROLLBACK SYS.SYSTEM     2      25  -- extent
  1 C:\ORANT\DATABASE\SYS1ORC8.ORA ROLLBACK SYS.SYSTEM    27      25  -- extent
  1 C:\ORANT\DATABASE\SYS1ORC8.ORA CLUSTER SYS.C_OBJ#     52      65
  1 C:\ORANT\DATABASE\SYS1ORC8.ORA INDEX SYS.I_OBJ#      117       5
  1 C:\ORANT\DATABASE\SYS1ORC8.ORA Free chunk            122       5  -- bubble
  1 C:\ORANT\DATABASE\SYS1ORC8.ORA INDEX SYS.I_TS#       127       5
  1 C:\ORANT\DATABASE\SYS1ORC8.ORA Free chunk            142       5  -- bubble
  1 C:\ORANT\DATABASE\SYS1ORC8.ORA CLUSTER SYS.C_USER#   147       5
  1 C:\ORANT\DATABASE\SYS1ORC8.ORA INDEX SYS.I_USER#     152       5
  1 C:\ORANT\DATABASE\SYS1ORC8.ORA TABLE SYS.UNDO$       157       5
  1 C:\ORANT\DATABASE\SYS1ORC8.ORA Free chunk            162       5  -- honeycomb
  1 C:\ORANT\DATABASE\SYS1ORC8.ORA Free chunk            167       5
  1 C:\ORANT\DATABASE\SYS1ORC8.ORA Free chunk            172       5
  1 C:\ORANT\DATABASE\SYS1ORC8.ORA Free chunk            177      25
  1 C:\ORANT\DATABASE\SYS1ORC8.ORA INDEX SYS.I_COBJ#     202       5
  1 C:\ORANT\DATABASE\SYS1ORC8.ORA Free chunk            207  11,455  – bubble
  2 C:\ORANT\DATABASE\SYS2ORC8.ORA INDEX SYS.I_OBJ#        2      10  – 2nd data-file
  2 C:\ORANT\DATABASE\SYS2ORC8.ORA Free chunk             12  12,789  – bubble
```

FIGURE 12-12. *Output of query listing extents, bubbles, and honeycombs within the SYSTEM tablespace (honeycombs are highlighted in bold)*

1 (*c:\orant\database\sys1orc8.ora*) displays a higher degree of fragmentation than data-file 2 (*c:\orant\database\sys2orc8.ora*), which is scarcely populated. In this sample scenario, data-file 1 is a better candidate for being rebuilt. Note that Figure 12-12 provides a listing of objects within the SYSTEM tablespace merely as an example of how the preceding query works. Rebuilding SYSTEM is not recommended, since it involves mandatory downtime. The same illustration may be applied to any application tablespace (DATA, INDEXES, and so on) to detect fragmentation and rebuild the appropriate data-file.

- Once the appropriate data-files are identified, a list of segments need to be made that are present within those data-files (again, the preceding query supplies that information). You need to consider each segment and evaluate the downtime associated with it. If any of the segments are popular ones and would required substantial downtime due to their size, it may not be feasible to rebuild that data-file. However, if the segments are fairly inactive (such as inactive partitions or history tables/indexes) or are reasonably small in size, you may wish to rebuild the data-files holding them during low use hours. Also, with standby tables implemented, you can defragment data-files holding popular (active, highly used) segments with very little downtime.

Once the decision has been made to rebuild certain data-files, you need to take the following steps:

1. Save the data within such segments (use export or the CREATE TABLE AS SELECT command to save the table-data; in the case of indexes, keep the necessary CREATE INDEX scripts ready for rebuilding them).
2. Drop the segments within the data-files.
3. Coalesce the tablespaces that belong to the data-files via the ALTER TABLESPACE COALESCE command. That will make the space within the data-files contiguous.
4. Recreate the segments within the tablespace.
5. Rerun the query to check for fragmentation to ensure that all segments are tightly packed in and large-scale fragmentation has been eliminated.

In case there are a large number of data-files that may affect availability drastically, then you may want to break up the task into smaller units and defragment only a few data-files at any given time. You can defragment the others during other periods, thus deferring the impact on availability to more convenient and acceptable time frames. Even with standby tables present, you may wish to break up the entire task into smaller units to keep the overall impact low. In any case, if any downtime is not acceptable, you can always ignore the existing fragmentation and alter the storage parameters of the "culprit" segments within the fragmented tablespaces to allocate appropriately sized extents in the future to optimize space use and if necessary, add data-files to avert space shortages in the short to medium term.

Enable the AUTOEXTEND feature for all application tablespaces and SYSTEM

As mentioned earlier, one of the most common errors is "ORA-1650-55: Unable to extend." This error occurs due to lack of adequate free space, when a segment within the tablespace needs to extend (that is, to allocate another extent), and may cause downtime. Rectifying the error usually requires the DBA to add another data-file to the tablespace, so that segments within can grow. Generally, one may use a script to check each tablespace for lack of free space and have it page the DBA to alert him or her to potential disasters, if any. Chapter 19 provides a script to check whether any segment would fail to allocate another extent in a tablespace. However, this precaution is basically reactive in nature, since it requires the DBA to respond to the alert and add a new data-file or resize the current data-file(s) to accommodate the additional growth. Starting with v7.2, it is possible to allow a

data-file to extend automatically if there is inadequate free-space and a segment needs to extend. This may be achieved by setting the AUTOEXTEND option of the CREATE/ALTER TABLESPACE command. Using this option, you may request Oracle to enlarge the data-file if necessary and specify units for enlargement (the incremental size to enlarge each time). Additionally, you can specify a maximum size beyond which the data-file will not enlarge via the MAXSIZE parameter. Thus, you can set your tablespaces to be resized up to available disk-space (in case of raw disks, set the maximum size to be at least 1MB less than the disk-size to prevent overwriting disk-control information on cylinder 0).

Proactively enabling AUTOEXTEND will allow Oracle to operate without disruptions even if the DBAs are unreachable during periods of sudden critical growth. Such Oracle features help greatly in meeting your service level expectations. You may use the AUTOEXTEND feature for all application tablespaces and the SYSTEM tablespace due to their intrinsically critical nature. However, for tablespaces holding temporary and rollback segments, it's not advisable to use this feature for the same reason that you shouldn't set MAXEXTENTS to be UNLIMITED for such segments: Setting AUTOEXTEND on would enable them to grow without inhibitions, fostering runaway transactions. Keeping AUTOEXTEND disabled would at least, in worst-case scenarios, stop runaway transactions via brute force by not providing adequate space to grow.

Use standardized file-sizes

Standardizing the file-sizes in your database eases both system and database administration. Using standardized file-sizes allows your database to exist in a specific pre-determined number of well-sized chunks and also allows well-controlled incremental growth—rather than dealing with a random number of haphazardly sized files. This increases your tuning options and also allows smooth migration to other systems and versions. Additionally, if you are on raw devices or plan to migrate to raw-devices or back to file-systems either partially or fully, this is of the utmost importance.

Generally, you will have your file-system configured in specific chunks such as 1GB, 2GB, or 4GB. Based on these sizes, you can arrive at a set of standard file-sizes such as 500MB, 1GB, 2GB, and so on. (Keep the 2GB file-size barrier in mind if your OS is a 32-bit OS not supporting large files). You may have different standard file-sizes to accommodate data-files and redo-logs. The sizes of control-files and archived redo-logs are controlled by Oracle. Ensure that each standard file-size is a multiple of DB_BLOCK_SIZE and also a multiple of the OS stripe size. The range of standard file-sizes should be such that the largest of tablespaces (example: APPLICATION_DATA) can be accommodated in conjunction with the smallest ones (typically, SYSTEM) with minimal wastage of space and without having to allocate too many data-files. In Oracle7, there is a constant fear of reaching MAXDATAFILES by allocating a high number of data-files. Also, you may have to adjust the initialization parameter DB_FILES to allow a large number of files (less than MAXDATAFILES). Having to adjust either of these requires downtime, since adjusting OPEN_FILES requires a database bounce and increasing MAXDATAFILES (provided the upper limit is not already reached) requires the control-file to be re-created. Thus, given the situation, it's more practical to endure some space wastage by choosing large file-sizes, rather than having to endure downtime.

Accommodate the data-file header block in your standardized file-sizes

Include data-file header in your sizing

The first block of every data-file contains the file-header, used for storing internal information used by Oracle, including current SCNs, checkpoint structures, and so on. Accordingly, the first block is never used to store actual (application) data. Many DBAs create data-files in "rounded up" sizes such as 1,024MB (a gig) or even 1,000MB, and so on. (Note that as of v8.0.*x*, you still need to allocate space in either bytes, kilobytes. or megabytes only; gigabytes and higher are not yet supported.) This makes allocating files relatively convenient. However, such rounded-up sizes cause extents to be uneven. For instance, a 1,000MB data-file holds 128,000 8KB blocks (assuming DB_BLOCK_SIZE = 8K)—a nice, well-rounded number. However, one block is taken up by the file-header, leaving 127,999 blocks for extents of various segments to use. If your standard extent-sizes for this particular tablespace are, say, 1MB, 10MB, and 100MB (to keep the illustration simple), then each extent will take up either 128, 1,280, or 12,800 blocks respectively (assuming that PCTINCREASE = 0). In other words, these even-sized extents will not use the available 127,999 blocks optimally, resulting in space-wastage. Some DBAs may create some uneven (non-standard) extents to avoid any space wastage and use up this remaining odd number of blocks. Other DBAs will just prefer the space-wastage, rather than incur the risk of fragmentation by introducing non-standard extent sizes. However, during crunch-times, sometimes it may be necessary to use up all available space and so use non-standard extent sizes. For instance, to buy additional time to determine the best disk-area and allocate a new data-file before an application fails due to a segment not being able to extend, the DBA may have to alter the segment to make the next extent fit within the available contiguous free-space with the existing data-files. Generally, the initial perception is, disk-space is relatively inexpensive, so why bother with such minute details? However, when your monitoring script suddenly pages you, screaming that a segment-extension is about to fail due to insufficient free-space, you immediately diverge from that line of thinking—every KB becomes important. In order to prevent such scenarios that may force you to deviate from using non-standard extent sizes, it is advisable to try to accommodate the file-header block in your standard extent

sizes. Rather than creating a 1,000MB or 1,024MB data-file, you might want to create a 1,001MB or 1,025MB data-file. Using such relatively complicated file-sizes allow you to use regular, standard extent sizes for each segment (for instance, using well-rounded extent sizes such as 1MB, 10MB, and so on still allows optimal space consumption, without the file header-block being an impediment). A point worth noting here is, when it comes to 2GB data-files on platforms that do not support large file sizes (that is, files greater than 2GB), you might want to use standard data-file sizes such as 2,048,008KB (2,000MB + 8KB) rather than 2,097,152KB (2,048MB, or exactly 2GB) for the obvious reason that you cannot go higher than 2,097,152KB on a 2GB file-system. So accommodating the additional file-header block will not be possible. Also, making it a rule to use standard file-sizes, which are smaller than the file-system, also makes using raw devices less complicated—in case you are already using them or plan to use them in the future (since, when using raw-devices, you need to ensure that the data-file is smaller than the actual raw device size; refer to Chapter 4 for more details).

Use standardized storage clauses for each segment-type to reduce fragmentation and use space more optimally

Now that the importance of standardizing data-file sizes has been discussed, let's take a step further and examine the importance of standardizing the use of space within a data-file. No matter how standardized and well thought-out the external file-size may be, if the space within is not used optimally, then little advantage will be derived. Such environments will still be susceptible to all the drawbacks of improper space management. Accordingly, it is highly necessary to analyze and arrive at optimal storage clauses. While determining such standard storage clauses, you need to consider segment type, size, and growth patterns, in terms of application functionality and usage. Such standardized clauses should allow each segment to grow as required without hindrance to application scalability and with as little fragmentation as possible. Chapter 6 provides some sample STORAGE clauses, based on size and growth considerations. Table 12-8 looks at the different clauses affecting physical storage characteristics and how they determine space consumption. These allow space to be used more optimally and help in reducing fragmentation.

Also keep in mind while determining your standardized storage clauses that Oracle uses certain algorithms internally, while allocating extents to reduce wastage of space such as the following:

- If the size of a subsequent extent determined after considering NEXT and PCTINCREASE results in a number that is not a multiple of

STORAGE Clause	Description
INITIAL	Influences the size of the original extent (the reason I use the word "influences" rather than "determines" is explained in a subsequent paragraph).
NEXT	This, along with PCTINCREASE, influences the size of every subsequent extent.
PCTINCREASE	This determines the growth rate of every subsequent extent. This is explained in more detail in a subsequent tip.
PCTFREE	The percentage of free space to leave in a block during inserts. It is necessary to specify a larger PCTFREE for tables that are expected to be updated frequently. Conversely, a lower PCTFREE (even zero) may be specified for tables not expected to be updated. This will reduce dead weight within a block and allow space to be used more optimally. Also, it is necessary to specify a larger PCTFREE for indexes to induce higher block-splitting at creation time (reducing the need for block-splitting at runtime). If faster index creation is desired, then PCTFREE is to be set to a higher value, so that block-splitting is deferred to occur during runtime (speeding up index creation, but affecting runtime performance). Chapter 6 elaborates on PCTFREE for indexes.
PCTUSED	PCTUSED determines the percentage of used space that will that place a block in the freelist. Note that you cannot specify PCTUSED for indexes.
FREELISTS	The number of structures maintaining information on blocks with free-space. Insert operations refer to freelists. Note that a block is represented in the freelist only when the free-space in it falls below PCTUSED. If there is only one freelist defined (the default value is 1) and there are multiple insert statements affecting the same segment, the first insert operation acquires a latch on the freelist, causing the others to wait, resulting in latch contention. Accordingly, if concurrent insert operations are anticipated, increase the number of freelists for such segments to match the maximum number of concurrent inserts to prevent contention. If concurrent inserts are too high (say, greater than 10), then concurrent inserts divided by 2 may be sufficient. If concurrent inserts across instances are expected in an OPS environment, set up an appropriate number of freelist groups, each group matching the maximum number of concurrent inserts within an instance. A subsequent paragraph elaborates further on freelists.

TABLE 12-8. *Parameters Determining Space Consumption*

STORAGE Clause	Description
INITRANS	The number of 23-byte slots (for entries) per block allocated at creation time for transactions. If INITRANS is set to 1 (the default value) and there are multiple concurrent transactions that affect the rows in a block, the required number of transaction slots will be allocated by Oracle at runtime, thus affecting runtime performance. Pre-allocating a larger number of slots by setting INITRANS to a value greater than one will prevent the runtime overhead. Set INITRANS *at least* equivalent to FREELISTS. Also, Oracle documentation recommends that the value for INITRANS not be set greater than 10.
MAXTRANS	The maximum number of 23-byte slots that can be allocated per block for transactions.
MINEXTENTS	The number of extents that are pre-allocated for the segment during creation. The first extent has a size specified by INITIAL, and the others have a size equivalent to NEXT.
MAXEXTENTS	The maximum number of extents permissible for the segment. Proactively, set this to UNLIMITED for all application segments and tablespaces that will have application segments reside in them.
OPTIMAL	This is specific to rollback segments. It specifies the optimal size of a rollback segment, causing Oracle to automatically shrink it, if it grows beyond the optimal size. Once the rollback segment grows due to a specific transaction, a subsequent transaction that uses the rollback segment will detect whether the rollback segment has extended and the oldest extents will be deallocated (the oldest extents go first, so that read consistency for other transactions is affected as little as possible). Every time the "head" of the transaction wraps to "current – extent + 1," it checks to see whether "current – extent + 2" already exists and if so, whether it is a candidate for deallocation (it can be deallocated if no active transactions are using it). Please refer to the *Oracle8 Backup and Recovery Handbook* (Oracle Press) for more details on this operation.

TABLE 12-8. *Parameters Determining Space Consumption* (continued)

DB_BLOCK_SIZE, then the resultant size is rounded up to the nearest multiple of DB_BLOCK_SIZE. For instance, if you have your DB_BLOCK_SIZE set to 8K and the segment that requires a new extent has a NEXT of 15K and a PCTINCREASE of 0, then Oracle will round up the size of the new extent to 16K (two blocks), rather than 15K. This also works the same way for the very first extent (INITIAL). Similarly, if you specify a fractional value (such as 12.5K) for INITIAL or NEXT, the value is again rounded up (to 13K).

- As explained earlier, if less than five blocks reside between two subsequent extents, such space is more or less wasted, since chances of so few blocks being used to accommodate an entire extent are relatively rare. Oracle's extent-allocation algorithm aims to prevent such wastage by detecting and using up blocks that are unlikely to be used up later. For instance, let's say the extent size is determined to be 1MB (that is, 128 8K blocks). However, while actually allocating the extent, if Oracle finds that there is a free one hundred twenty-ninth block, after which another extent begins, it will make the size of the current extent to be 129 blocks, rather than 128 blocks, to prevent the free one hundred twenty-ninth block from being wasted. Figure 12-13 illustrates this algorithm.

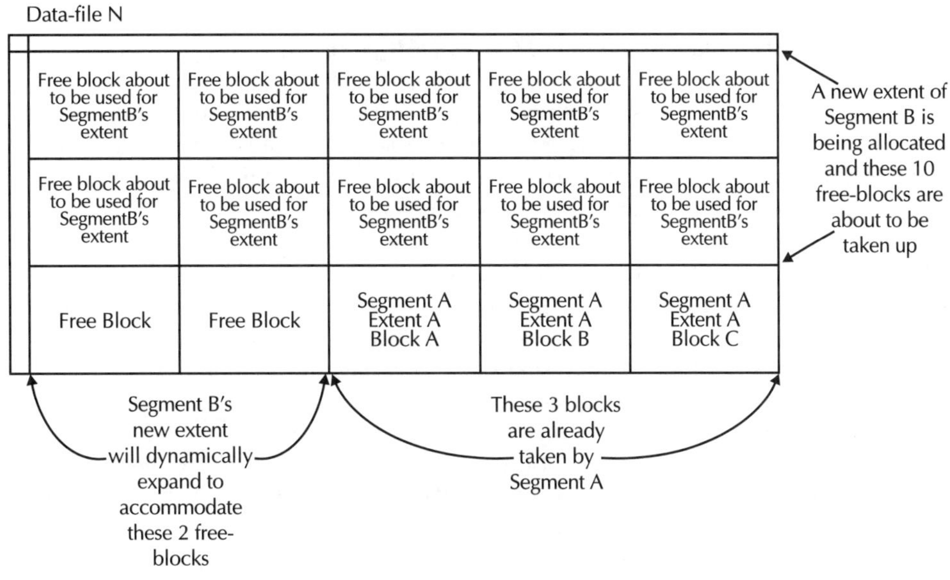

FIGURE 12-13. *Oracle's extent allocation algorithm expands the current extent to accommodate free blocks that may be wasted otherwise*

Due to the dynamic nature of the extent allocation algorithm, one may safely say that the INITIAL, NEXT, and PCTINCREASE values only influence the actual extent size and do not determine it. The final size is a result of these parameters and other environmental events.

Set INITIAL and NEXT keeping DB_BLOCK_SIZE in mind

When arriving at your standardized storage clauses, ensure that the INITIAL and NEXT for each storage clause are multiples of the DB_BLOCK_SIZE. Once this criterion is met, other requirements should automatically fall in line. By "other requirements," I imply that the INITIAL/NEXT values should be multiples of the OS block size and, in case you are using RAID 0 or some kind of hardware/software striping, the INITIAL/NEXT should be a multiple of the stripe-size or vice versa (depending on the segment and stripe sizes). As explained in Chapter 4, it is imperative to consider these while arriving at the DB_BLOCK_SIZE. Thus, taking DB_BLOCK_SIZE into consideration while deriving INITIAL/NEXT, you should automatically be cognizant of the others. For instance, if your DB_BLOCK_SIZE is 8K, use INITIAL/NEXT values such as 8K, 1M, 10M, 100M, and so on. Furthermore, set the INITIAL/NEXT for various segments such that they are multiples of each other.

Keeping INITIAL/NEXT values and DB_BLOCK_SIZE synchronized reduces the chances of free-space fragmentation in the tablespace. For instance, disparate INITIAL/NEXT values for various segments such as 12M, 115M, 256M, and so on (they might get that way especially if PCTINCREASE is set to a non-zero value) may result in unusable chunks of free-space being created. For instance, deletes in one segment may result in odd-sized free-space chunks. However, when another segment with different storage parameters requires another extent, it may not be able to optimally use that free-space chunk—either the free-space chunk may not be adequate for it to allocate a new extent or part of that free-space chunk will be used by the new allocation, leaving bubbles of tiny free-space chunks, that no segment can ever use (thus resulting in large-scale space-wastage over a period of time).

Another importance reason for ensuring that INITIAL/NEXT are multiples of DB_BLOCK_SIZE is the fact that doing so aids multi-block reads during full-table scans and fast full-index scans (v7.3 onward). Multi-block reads are influenced by the initialization parameter DB_FILE_MULTIBLOCK_READ_COUNT. For instance, if this parameter specifies a value of 8 and the DB_BLOCK_SIZE is 8K, then up to 64K of data will be read in during each I/O operation, thus assisting in pre-reading of data and reducing the overall number of I/O operations to read the entire segment. Since DB_FILE_MULTIBLOCK_READ_COUNT already depends on DB_BLOCK_SIZE, configuring INITIAL/NEXT to be a multiple of the latter allows relatively more optimal reads to occur. The reason for this is, multi-block reads cannot span extents. For instance, as long as the entire 64K of data belongs to a single extent, it will be read in one I/O operation. However, if the 64KB of data is spread across multiple extents, the data in each extent will be read via a different I/O call, thus potentially increasing the number of I/O calls required to read the entire segment. In other words, multi-block reads gather the lesser of the two in a single I/O operation:

- DB_FILE_MULTIBLOCK_READ_COUNT × DB_BLOCK_SIZE
- Remaining blocks to be read in the current extent being accessed

Thus, ensuring that DB_BLOCK_SIZE and the extent-sizes (INITIAL/NEXT) are synchronized enhances the chances of each I/O call retrieving the maximum data possible (DB_FILE_MULTIBLOCK_READ_COUNT × DB_BLOCK_SIZE), rather than being restricted by reaching the end-of-extent and thus reading only the blocks left in that extent. Let's take an example to understand this better: If a table consists of 5 extents, each consisting of 128 8K data-blocks (that is, INITIAL & NEXT = 1MB), then 5MB or 5,120KB will need to be read during a full-table scan. If the DB_FILE_MULTIBLOCK_READ_COUNT is 8 (the DB_BLOCK_SIZE being 8K), then a theoretical maximum of 80 (5,120K / (8K × 8)) I/O calls will be required to read the entire table. Thus, each extent will be read in 16 I/O calls. Alternatively, if a different INITIAL/NEXT size is used, then the number of calls may vary. For instance, if the same segment consists of 5 extents, with each extent comprising 65 8K data-blocks (that is, INITIAL & NEXT = 520KB), then 2.54MB or 2,600KB will need to be read during a full-table scan. Assuming that DB_FILE_MULTIBLOCK_READ_COUNT is still 8, a theoretical maximum of 45 I/O calls will be required to access the entire table. Since the second table (2,600KB) is around half the size of the first (5,120KB), one would assume that the resultant theoretical maximum for the smaller table will be approximately half the number of I/O calls (give or take one or two calls) required for the entire table to be read. However, there's a total of five I/O calls made, which are in addition to the 50 percent assumption. Let's take a deeper look at what exactly happens while the second table is being accessed. Each extent in the second table consists of 520K (2,600K / 5) or 65 data-blocks. Now given the value for DB_FILE_MULTIBLOCK_READ_COUNT, up to 64K can be read in a single I/O call. Thus, it will require 9 I/O calls to access each extent (8 I/O calls to read more than 98 percent of each extent, or 64 blocks and the ninth call to read the last block). Since the ninth call reads a mere 8K (the last block), it is not optimal. Each of the five extents requires a ninth call merely to read the last block in each extent, resulting in 5 additional I/O calls. If the INITIAL/NEXT were better sized to be a multiple of the (DB_BLOCK_SIZE × DB_FILE_MULTIBLOCK_READ_COUNT), the additional 5 blocks could have been read with a single additional call. For instance, if INITIAL/NEXT = 512K, then merely 41 I/O calls will be required to scan the entire table, saving 4 additional calls. Here we are looking at a segment with 5 extents. However, as databases get bigger and bigger, the number of extents may be considerably higher, thus correspondingly increasing the I/O calls. Accordingly, it is essential to ensure that INITIAL/NEXT sizes are specified keeping the DB_BLOCK_SIZE in mind. The other important parameter, DB_FILE_MULTBLOCK_READ_COUNT, is usually specified as 8, 16, 32, and so on to reach the OS maximum value per I/O call. Thus, usually it is automatically synchronized with DB_BLOCK_SIZE to provide optimal I/O.

As a final note, it is important to bear in mind that the preceding examples use theoretical numbers. In real life, for instance, 64K is not guaranteed to be read in a single I/O call, even with DB_FILE_MULTIBLOCK_READ_COUNT being 8 and DB_BLOCK_SIZE being 8K. This is because a lot depends on the other concurrent activity going on within the system. Such concurrent activity may include other database as well as non-database (OS housekeeping, backups, and so forth) I/O requests. Depending on how the OS processes I/O requests (list, async, and so forth), data pertaining to other I/O calls may interrupt a smooth continuous flow of reads pertaining to a specific full-segment scan. However, the preceding examples serve to illustrate how chances of getting more data with less I/O operations are enhanced with optimal INITIAL/NEXT extent sizes.

Set PCTINCREASE optimally to reduce fragmentation

First, let's understand how PCTINCREASE works in detail. The following pseudo-code illustrates how Oracle allocates the next extent:

```
if another extent is required then
   if NEXT is a fraction then
      round it up;
   end-if;

   if NEXT is not a multiple of DB_BLOCK_SIZE then
      round it up to the nearest multiple of DB_BLOCK_SIZE;
   end if;

   if this new extent is the 2nd one then
      allocate extent of size NEXT;
   else
      allocate extent of size PREVIOUS_EXTENT_SIZE * (1 + PCTINCREASE/100);
   end-if;

  if free potentially unusable blocks are encountered while allocating extent then
     expand the actual extent-size to accommodate such potentially unusable blocks;
  end-if;
end-if;
```

Based on the preceding pseudo-code, Tables 12-9 and 12-10 plot out the various sizes of extents in a database with a database block-size equivalent to 8K. Note that the actual final extent-size will depend on whether there are neighboring free blocks (that may increase the actual final extent-size).

As seen from the preceding pseudo-code and explanation, PCTINCREASE plays an important role in influencing the size of every subsequent extent. Set haphazardly, it can easily result in an inconsistent set of varying extent-sizes that result in high fragmentation throughout the tablespace in a relatively short time span. However, PCTINCREASE is also a powerful weapon to restrict the number of extents in scenarios where the growth rate is not known (that is, where the person responsible for physical database design is not aware of application growth characteristics). This feature is especially useful in versions prior to 7.3 (the UNLIMITED option is supported in v7.3, thus allowing an unrestricted number of extents to be present) and environments where application scalability cannot be accurately predicted, such as in e-commerce applications. Thus, setting PCTINCREASE to 100 (for example) would allow a segment to start off with

SEGMENT STORAGE(INITIAL 8K NEXT 8K PCTINCREASE 50 MAXEXTENTS 5)

Extent Seq. #	**Formulae Used To Compute Extent Size**	**Nascent Extent Size**	**# of Blocks for Extent**	**Final Extent Size**	**Cumulative Segment Size**
1	INITIAL	8K	1	8K	8K
2	NEXT	8K	1	8K	16K
3	Sizeof(previous_extent) × (1 + PCTINCREASE/100) = 8K × (1 + 50 / 100)	12K	2	16K	32K
4	16K × (1 + 50 / 100)	24K	3	24K	56K
5	24K × (1 + 50 / 100)	36K	5	40K	96K
6	Will result in error "ORA-1631: max # of extents reached in table"				

TABLE 12-9. *Extents Sizes with STORAGE(INITIAL: 8K NEXT 8K PCTINCREASE 50 MAXEXTENTS 5)*

SEGMENT STORAGE(INITIAL 10M NEXT 10M PCTINCREASE 20 MAXEXTENTS 5)					
Extent Seq. #	**Formulae Used to Compute Extent Size**	**Nascent Extent Size**	**# of Blocks for Extent**	**Final Extent Size**	**Cumulative Segment Size**
1	INITIAL	10M	1,280	10M	10M
2	NEXT	10M	1,280	10M	20M
3	Sizeof(previous_extent) × (1 + PCTINCREASE/100) = 10M × (1 + 20 / 100)	12M	1,536	12M	32M
4	12M × (1 + 20 / 100)	14.4M	1,844	14.4M	46.4M
5	14.4M × (1 + 20 / 100)	17.28M	2,212	17.28M	63.68M
6	Will result in error "ORA-1631: max # extents reached in table"				

TABLE 12-10. *Extents Sizes with STORAGE(INITIAL: 10M NEXT 10M PCTINCREASE 20 MAXEXTENTS 5)*

relatively small extents and dynamically scale to accommodate high application growth. If there is no growth, then an additional extent won't be allocated and the segment can remain small. If growth occurs, however, then every subsequent extent size will exponentially grow and the overall segment can easily accommodate this growth without having to allocate a large number of small extents, thus reducing high fragmentation. PCTINCREASE can be suitably adjusted to any value between 0 and 100, depending on the familiarity with segment growth characteristics and how much dynamism is desired in influencing the size of subsequent extents.

Whenever possible, set PCTINCREASE to zero. This will cause the next-extent size to be influenced purely via the NEXT parameter, rather than via PCTINCREASE. Also, it will allow the size of each subsequent extent to (relatively) be more easily predictable, thus making administration simpler. Alternatively, if this is not possible, set it to 100. Generally, non-zero PCTINCREASE values cause irregular-sized extents to be allocated. These extents may be hard to fill up once they are deallocated (due to large deletes and such), resulting in high fragmentation. Even periodically coalescing such tablespaces may not be too useful if parts of those deallocated extents are used up by other (smaller) extents (of other segments). Similarly, set the PCTINCREASE to zero or 100, even for the DEFAULT STORAGE clause of tablespaces, for the same reason—to avoid fragmentation. Remember, the DEFAULT STORAGE clause applies to segments for which you don't explicitly specify STORAGE clauses.

Understand FREELISTS and set them optimally to reduce latch contention

It is necessary to have a detailed understanding of Oracle's data-segment free-space maintenance procedure in order to influence better space use by choosing the right parameters during segment creation, and to be familiar with potential areas of contention to optimize performance. For each table and index, Oracle tracks the amount of free-space available in each block currently allocated via a freelist structure. As a new extent is created, blocks with free-space more than PCTFREE have an entry in the freelist. Later as the blocks get populated with rows and the free-space falls below PCTFREE, they are taken off the freelist. However, as rows get deleted or updated (such that it shrinks their size) and the used-space goes below PCTUSED, they are considered to have the requisite free-space to have an entry in the freelist again. This includes partially as well as totally unused blocks below the high-water mark and all blocks above the high-water mark. A freelist structure consists of the following:

- A used-status flag, indicating whether the freelist is used or not
- The dba (data-block address) of the block at the beginning of the freelist chain
- The dba of the block at the end of the freelist chain

The freelist forms a chain of free blocks in each segment. Each block in the chain has a flag to indicate whether it has an entry in the freelist. If so, it has a reference to the dba of the next block in the chain. This logical chain-like structure continues until the reference becomes a "zero" value, indicating that the current block is the last one in the chain. Whenever a new block is added to the freelist, its dba is reflected at the beginning of the chain. Each block is represented only once in the freelist.

There are different types of freelists. Furthermore, in an OPS environment, freelist groups may be created, each comprising the different freelist types.

- **Master freelist** Every table and index has, by default, a single freelist tracking free-space within the segment. This freelist structure is referred to as the master freelist or the segment master freelist; it provides a common pool of free-blocks for all processes inserting rows into the segment. Processes concurrently inserting rows into a single segment results in contention for the master freelist, especially in the case of OLTP applications with large number of concurrent DML activity.

- **Process freelist** In order to alleviate contention on the master freelist, you can explicitly use the FREELISTS clause of the CREATE/ALTER TABLE/INDEX commands to specify additional freelists. In such a situation, a single master freelist still remains, but additional process freelists are created. The free-blocks are partitioned across all the process freelists, thus allowing different processes to use different blocks, and so minimizing contention. Each process is directed to a specific freelist according to its process-id (*v$process.pid*), as per the formulae (PID % (# of freelists)) + 1, where (# of freelists) is determined by the FREELISTS clause of the CREATE/ALTER TABLE/INDEX commands.
- **Transaction freelist** When a transaction frees up space in a block (due to an UPDATE or DELETE), it needs to allocate a transaction freelist entry to reflect the free space. This entry is later reconciled with the master freelist (or process freelists, if they have been created and the master freelist is updated subsequently). Transaction freelists are dynamically allocated by Oracle as needed. Each transaction freelist is bound to a specific transaction. There are a minimum of 16 transaction freelists per segment, and this number grows as necessary until there is no more room in the segment header block. Note that only those transactions that impact free-space have a transaction freelist allocated (not all transactions do).

  When a transaction needs to allocate a transaction freelist entry, it first checks whether one has been allocated to it already, and if not, it scans the segment header block to see whether any existing transaction freelists are free (that is, have not been allocated to any transaction yet or have just been released due to transactions just having committed). If transaction freelists are available, one is selected based on the formula (PID % (# of available transaction freelists)), where PID is the process-id (PID) of the transaction from *v$process.* Once obtained, the transaction places a *TX enqueue* on the freelist. If a transaction freelist is not readily available, Oracle allocates one dynamically, provided there is room in the segment header block. If not, the transaction has to wait for a transaction freelist to be released from the existing transactions. As an existing transaction releases a freelist, it can reuse it immediately if necessary. However, other transactions (the ones waiting) can use the freelist only after the original transaction has committed. A wait for a transaction freelist is initiated by requesting a *TX enqueue* in shared-mode on the transaction freelist selected via the preceding formula. Once the transaction that currently holds the *TX enqueue* on the freelist commits, the wait ends and the freelist is obtained by the waiting transaction.

> Now let's understand the interaction between the master freelist, the process freelists (assuming that they have been created via the FREELISTS clause), and the transaction freelists. The master freelist can be looked upon as a superset of the other freelist types. This is the case even in an OPS environment, where multiple freelist groups are defined. In environments where freelist groups exist, the FREELISTS clause defines the number of process freelists within each freelist group. Thus each freelist group has a master freelist, and one of the freelists among these is nominated as the "segment master" freelist. Thus, a hierarchy of freelist structures may be formed as depicted in Figure 12-14.

As mentioned earlier, the freelist entries are spread across (partitioned among) the various process freelists. Whenever a transaction requires free-space (say, to insert a bunch of rows), it checks the process freelist allocated to the process running the transaction. The process freelist is scanned starting at the beginning. If it

Data-block N (if multiple FREELIST GROUPS are not defined, these would be part of the segment header block)

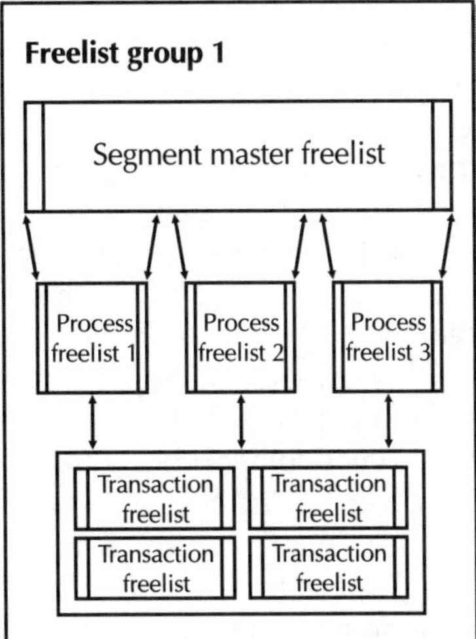

Data-block M

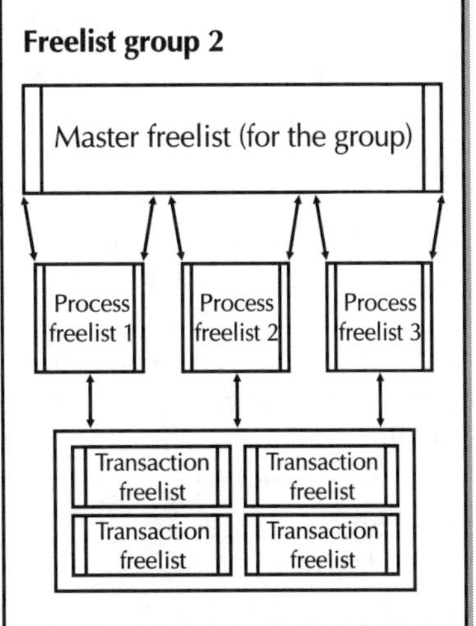

FIGURE 12-14. *A logical "hierarchy" among freelist structures*

encounters blocks at the beginning that do not have the requisite free-space, they are unlinked from the freelist (if the number of blocks that fail the scan for adequate free-space is above a certain threshold, by default, 5) and optionally moved toward the end. The *unlink* operation is done only if the failed blocks are at the head of the freelist. This increases the chances of subsequent scans being able to find blocks with a higher free-space at the beginning of the freelist, and thus it expedites the scans. Finally, as the process runs through the process freelist, it eventually finds blocks that have the requisite free-space to accommodate the INSERT operation. If no such blocks are found, a new extent may have to be allocated. Either way, assuming that free blocks have been found, the transaction inserts the necessary rows and takes up room in the block. If that causes the free-space within the block to go beyond PCTFREE or if the total used space goes above PCTUSED, then the block has to be unlinked from the process freelist. However, the transaction does not directly change the process freelist. Instead a transaction freelist is allocated by Oracle and the transaction posts an entry to unlink the block there. Likewise, if the transaction frees up space by deleting/updating rows, then the blocks with the free-space are linked into the transaction freelist. If the transaction rolls back, the transaction freelist is released and the process freelist is not updated. However, if the transaction commits, the transaction freelist entries are reflected in the process freelist. Thus, these changes to the process freelist may cause it to get out of sync with the master freelist (at a given point in time—eventually they are synchronized). Thus, different process freelists may coexist with different chains of free-blocks.

In the preceding example, we noted a potential scenario where blocks with the adequate free-space may not be available in the process free-list, requiring a new extent. However, a new extent is an extreme step (the last resort), and prior to using that option, Oracle refreshes the process freelist with another chain of free blocks from the master freelist. This operation is termed as *freelists merge*. The process continues to scan this new batch of blocks for adequate free-space, and this refresh/scan cycle continues until either the requisite free-space is obtained or there are no more blocks in the master freelist. Note that at the same time, other process freelists may have access to additional free-blocks that the master freelist does not (due to space having been recently freed up by the corresponding processes). However, these process freelists are not referred to at this time. This is primarily to avoid suddenly resynchronizing the master freelist with other process freelists and offloading the newer chains onto the current process freelist, thus avoiding sudden performance surges. The resynchronization is spread out to minimize impact on performance. However, this may cause some free-space to be left unused at the time, even though it is available. Once there are no more unscanned blocks in the master freelist, all available transaction freelists from recently committed transactions are scanned to potentially find any blocks with the requisite free-space. If any are found, a portion of the blocks (in units of 5) are moved to the master freelist and these are offloaded to the current process freelist. The scan of the current process freelist continues until a block with the required free-space is found. If none are found, Oracle tries to allocate blocks above the high-water mark (if they have not been already used up). If any unused blocks above the high-water mark are found, the high-water mark is incremented based on the formulae in Table 12-11.

Finally if none of the earlier attempts result in the required free-space, a new extent is allocated (another tip outlines the algorithm used to allocate an extent) and the master freelist is updated with the free-blocks in the new extent. Once this is accomplished, the current process freelist is refreshed again and the scan continues for blocks with the required free-space. However, due to the new extent being allocated, the scan will result in success.

Note that usually, all the transaction entries for the segment are present within a single block (the segment header block). However, in an OPS environment, when multiple freelist groups are allocated, an additional block is dedicated to each freelist group. These blocks exist right after the segment header block and consist of a master freelist and process freelists as defined by FREELISTS. The remaining space within each block is used for allocating transaction freelists. As mentioned earlier, of all the master freelists, one is nominated as the segment master. Spreading freelist groups onto separate blocks reduces inter-instance pinging, since each instance can use a different freelist group (the INSTANCE_NUMBER initialization parameter influences the freelist allocation to every process accessing a specific instance).

# of Blocks to increase High-Water Mark by	Condition for Use of Specified Number/Algorithm
1	If the current extent is the INITIAL one and the table is a small table, currently occupying less than five blocks (that is, the current high-water mark is less than five blocks) OR If the new block allocated would not need an entry in the freelist (initially the process freelist and subsequently the master freelist)
5 blocks or number of unused blocks left in the current extent, whichever is less	Versions prior to Oracle 7.2
5 blocks × (# of FREELISTS + 1) or the number of unused blocks left in the current extent, whichever is less	Versions 7.2 and above

TABLE 12-11. *Formulae for Incrementing the Segment High-Water Mark*

Periodically coalesce your application tablespaces

Coalescing refers to the process of combining adjoining smaller chunks of free-space (honeycombs) to form a single large free-space area (a bubble). As discussed earlier, extents get deallocated when segments get truncated/dropped or as unused space is explicitly deallocated. Depending on the sizes of the extents, various chunks of free-space result from the deallocations. Whenever another segment needs to extend, Oracle scans for a chunk with adequate free-space to accommodate the new extent. There may be a high percentage of free-space in the tablespace. However, such free-space may be scattered across the tablespace in uneven chunks. If a single contiguous chunk of free-space large enough to accommodate the new extent is not available, Oracle needs to perform the coalescing at runtime (this entire algorithm is outlined in an earlier tip), thus impacting performance. Also by not proactively coalescing tablespaces periodically, opportunities for wider/denser coalescing may be lost due to portions of adjacent space being consumed (as bubbles from a honeycomb are used up to accommodate other smaller extents). Finally only uneven far-spread bubbles will remain, eventually causing the "ORA-1650-55: Unable to extend" error. Combining all adjoining free chunks to form a large chunk relatively early on (before different bubbles get consumed) increases the success rate of scans for adequately sized free chunks. In fact, chances of success become higher in the first few passes itself, avoiding the need for multiple diverse passes, thus enhancing the performance of space management operations.

Coalescing of a tablespace is performed by SMON and can be achieved in multiple ways:

- Starting with v7.3, the ALTER TABLESPACE COALESCE command is supported to coalesce specific tablespaces.
- In previous versions where the command is not supported, the ALTER SESSION SET EVENTS command may be utilized as follows:

  ```
  SQL> ALTER SESSION SET EVENTS 'IMMEDIATE TRACE NAME COALESCE LEVEL
  &<tblspc_num>';
  ```

  Here, <tblspc_num> is the tablespace-number from SYS.TS$.
- In all versions, setting the PCTINCREASE to a non-zero value in the DEFAULT STORAGE clauses of all tablespaces causes SMON to periodically coalesce the tablespace. Certain third-party texts recommend setting PCTINCREASE for such tablespaces to 1, so that they will get coalesced periodically. This is not advisable, because then all segments with no explicit STORAGE parameters will acquire a PCTINCREASE of 1, thus causing them to grow unevenly and increasing the chances of

fragmentation in the tablespace. Thus, I recommend using the ALTER TABLESPACE or ALTER SESSION SET EVENTS command to perform the coalescence, rather than playing around with PCTINCREASE. However, in case you prefer to use the latter approach, then set PCTINCREASE to 100, rather than some arbitrary value such as 1. This will increase the chances of free chunks (due to extent deallocation) being reused.

Finally, do not attempt to coalesce ROLLBACK and TEMPORARY tablespaces, because they contain rollback and sort segments, which are highly dynamic in nature. Attempting to coalesce them will not result in any space optimization and it is best to manage space within these tablespaces by setting appropriate STORAGE parameters at the segment level for rollback segments (appropriate INITIAL, NEXT, and OPTIMAL values) and at the tablespace level for temporary segments (appropriate INITIAL and NEXT with a PCTINCREASE of zero).

Understand the effect of an erroneous high-water mark

The high-water mark for tables is the level at which the table was the most populated during its current lifetime. The lifetime of a table, in this context, is the period between two successive DDL statements. For instance, the table comes into existence via a CREATE TABLE statement, and the data within lives until a DROP TABLE or TRUNCATE TABLE command is executed. In other words, the high-water mark indicates the highest sequence in the blocks occupied by a table. High-water marks are maintained for individual tables and indexes, as well as clusters.

A table can be created in the following ways:

- As an empty table via the CREATE TABLE command
- With data via the CREATE TABLE AS SELECT command

With the first method, the high-water mark is set to "zero" (extent 0/block 0 for tables and 1 for indexes), since the table has never held any data. With the second method, the high-water mark is computed from the number of blocks that get filled up with data. During regular use, insert statements that cause more blocks to be populated continue to increment the high-water mark. A table grows in extents. However, not all the blocks in an extent are populated, causing certain blocks to remain allocated, but empty. Such empty blocks do not contribute to the high-water mark. Only blocks with data are considered. For instance, in a table with an INITIAL of 1MB and a database block-size of 8K, 128 database blocks are allocated to the table. However, only the first 5 blocks may hold data. Here, the high-water mark will be composed of only those 5 blocks. Oracle generally computes the high-water

mark in units of 5 blocks (there are some exceptions to this rule, as outlined in the discussion on freelists). Accordingly, if 7 blocks were populated in the preceding example, the high-water mark would be computed on the basis of 10 blocks (rather than 7).

The high-water mark is used by Oracle during full-segment scans to determine up to which block to read, thus saving time. Considering the preceding example, Oracle has to read only the first five blocks, not all the 128 database blocks that make up the extent, to complete the full-table scan. Thus the high-water mark is designed to help performance. At times, however, this can have an adverse impact on performance, as well. As mentioned earlier, the high-water mark is never reset between two successive DDL commands. Consider a table with a lot of data populated via bulk inserts. Every insert operation that causes an additional block to be taken up sets the high-water mark higher and higher. So if the table constitutes 25,600 blocks of 8K each (twenty extents of 10MB each), a full-table scan needs to read and process all 25,600 blocks (note that even though multiple blocks may be picked up in a single read operation, a significant number of reads will be required to pick up all 25,600 blocks). Now, let's say the table is subjected to a large delete operation deleting a major portion of the table (leaving just a few records). This has various effects; for instance, multiple blocks within the twenty extents are freed up, unused extents are deallocated, and the freed blocks are reflected in the freelist (assuming that the delete operation caused used-space to go down to a lower value than specified by PCTUSED). Unfortunately, however, the high-water mark does not get decremented to reflect the current fewer number of populated blocks. It remains constant, still pointing to the original large value. Subsequent full-table scans take this high-water mark to be the correct indicator of the table's size and continue to scan up to the blocks mentioned in the high-water mark. Thus, these redundant scans cause additional I/O and consume system resources, without any real necessity. You may have noticed this various times in real life, when performing a full-table scan or a row-count on a small table (that used to be large). The result may be a very small number, or even zero. However, the time taken to return that result may be extraordinarily high. Thus, an incorrect high-water mark may cause delays during certain circumstances.

The only way to reset the high-water mark without dropping and recreating it is to use the TRUNCATE command. Even the ALTER TABLE DEALLOCATE UNUSED command only frees unused space above the high-water mark, keeping the high-water mark intact. Use of the TRUNCATE command on a table involves the following phases:

- Obtain an exclusive lock on the segment (to have exclusive access to the segment header block). If another transaction is currently writing to the table (row-level or table-level lock), then the truncate process has to wait by requesting a TX lock in shared mode.

- Flush all blocks of this table from the buffer cache to disk.
- Release all extents beyond MINEXTENTS.
- Update all freelists in the table header block to reflect this release. If multiple freelist groups are defined, update all blocks corresponding to each freelist group.
- Reset the high-water mark.
- If multiple instances are configured (OPS environment), flush the segment header and blocks holding freelist groups to disk.

The obvious effect of the TRUNCATE command is that all rows are removed. However, in order to eliminate the performance drawbacks associated with an erroneous high-water mark, one may perform the following steps to reset it (assuming that there are valid rows in the table and that the TRUNCATE command cannot directly be used to prevent those valid rows from being removed):

1. Save the data in the table via an export or via pCTAS (parallel CREATE TABLE AS SELECT).

```
SQL> CREATE TABLE names_backup
     TABLESPACE user_data
     STORAGE(INITIAL 10M NEXT 10M PCTINCREASE 0)
     PARALLEL(DEGREE 4)
     NOLOGGING
     AS SELECT * FROM names_backup;
```

   Note that all methods (including export and the pCTAS command shown previously) will still scan all blocks indicated in the high-water mark during the backup of the valid rows. If the number of blocks indicated is very high and very few rows actually remain in the table, you may use an index-scan to prevent all bocks from being accessed. The following piece of code illustrates how (assuming that there is an index on NAME_ID):

```
SQL> CREATE TABLE names_backup
     TABLESPACE user_data
     STORAGE(INITIAL 10M NEXT 10M PCTINCREASE 0)
     PARALLEL(DEGREE 4)
     NOLOGGING
     AS SELECT * FROM names_backup
         WHERE name_id > 0;
```

2. If the NAME_ID column is a CHAR/VARCHAR2 column, you may use '' (empty quotes) to force the index to be used. Alternatively, for a DATE

column, you may use a clause such as WHERE date_of_birth < SYSDATE to fetch all required rows.Now, truncate the table.

```
SQL> TRUNCATE TABLE names;
```

3. Now, reenter the saved rows:

```
SQL> INSERT INTO names
     SELECT * FROM names_backup;
SQL> COMMIT;
SQL> DROP TABLE names_backup;
```

If the NAMES_BACKUP table contains a large number of rows, then a PL/SQL procedure may be written to commit once every 5,000 or so rows, while inserting the data.

Note that the procedure described may require application downtime. Accordingly, it is a good idea to do this during periods of low use and have some kind of standby option implemented (standby database/tables) to prevent/reduce downtime. Since downtime is involved, it is necessary to detect which tables have erroneous high-water marks, evaluate whether the performance impact associated with each of these tables is acceptable or not, and reset the high-water marks of only those tables where the performance gain justifies the cost of downtime. The following steps can be taken to identify candidate tables for the reset operation (note that analyzing the tables is a prerequisite for the steps below; it is advisable to compute the statistics; if that's not feasible, at least specify 20 percent or higher as the sample percentage while estimating statistics). Perform these steps only for tables that are prone to high delete activity (since those are the ones most likely to have erroneous high-water marks). If such tables cannot be easily determined (due to unfamiliarity with the applications), prepare a list of tables that have large INITIAL/NEXT allocated to them. You may find out which tables have large INITIAL/NEXT via the following query:

```
SQL> SELECT table_name, initial_extent/1024/1024 "Initial_MB",
            next_extent/1024/1024 "Next_MB"
       FROM user_tables
      WHERE initial_extent >= <size_you_would_consider_large>
         OR next_extent >= <size_you_would_consider_large>;
```

Once you have a list of such tables, check with the application developers/designers whether these tables have high delete activity or else are fairly static (not prone to any further growth). You may also spend time observing the behavior of these tables. That will help you narrow down the list. Then you may perform the following steps to confirm that those tables indeed have erroneous high-water marks:

1. Find out the total number of blocks occupied by each of the preceding tables (let's term the result TOT_BLOCKS). Note that TOT_BLOCKS will include the segment header-block (one block).

```
SQL> SELECT blocks FROM user_segments
      WHERE segment_type = 'TABLE'
       AND segment_name = '<tbl_name>';
```

2. Find out the total number of unused blocks above the high-water mark (let's term the result UNUSED_BLOCKS). Note that UNUSED_BLOCKS will not comprise unused blocks below the high-water mark.

```
SQL> SELECT empty_blocks FROM user_tables
      WHERE table_name = '<tbl_name>';
```

3. The blocks currently composing the high-water mark can be determined as (let's term the result HIGHWTMK_BLOCKS):

```
HIGHWTMK_BLOCKS  = (TOT_BLOCKS - UNUSED_BLOCKS) - 1.
```

   The final subtraction by 1 allows the segment header-block to be removed from the final result.

   Alternatively, starting with version 7.3, the blocks currently composing the high-water mark can also be determined via the DBMS_SPACE.UNUSED_SPACE procedure. A subsequent paragraph illustrates usage of this procedure.

4. Now, find out the number of blocks actually containing data (let's term the result REALDATA_BLOCKS):

```
SQL> SELECT blocks FROM user_tables
      WHERE table_name = '<tbl_name>';
```

   The following queries provide an alternative way of finding out the number of blocks actually containing data. This latter method may be used when the objective is merely to find out the number of blocks taken up when the table has not been analyzed (such as in a environment using RBO).

```
-- in Oracle7
SQL> SELECT COUNT(DISTINCT SUBSTR(ROWID, 1, 8) || SUBSTR(ROWID, 15, 4))
       FROM <tbl_name>;

-- in Oracle8
SQL> SELECT COUNT(DISTINCT
              SUBSTR(DBMS_ROWID.ROWID_TO_RESTRICTED(ROWID, 0), 1, 8) ||
              SUBSTR(DBMS_ROWID.ROWID_TO_RESTRICTED(ROWID, 0), 15, 4))
       FROM <tbl_name>;
```

   The preceding statements may cause a full-table scan on the table, which may take a long time (depending on the size of the table). Verify whether this is indeed the case via an EXPLAIN PLAN. You may avoid the full-table scan if a B*Tree index is present on a mandatory column in the table. You may also do an index-only lookup to get the required information (since only the file and block components of the ROWID are being counted—ROWIDs are present in all B*Tree indexes). You may use the INDEX hint or use a WHERE clause such as WHERE leading_indexed_number_column > 0 or WHERE leading_indexed_char_column >. The index has to be on a mandatory column (such as a primary-key index), so that all rows in the table will be counted (indexes on nullable columns will not have a key-entry for NULL values, thus causing such rows not to be counted).

If the difference between HIGHWTMK_BLOCKS and REALDATA_BLOCKS is substantial, then the table has an erroneous high-water mark and may benefit from the high-water mark being reset. The following formula may be utilized to compute the degree of difference:

```
((HIGHWTMK_BLOCKS - REALDATA_BLOCKS) / HIGHWTMK_BLOCKS) x 100
```

If the degree of difference is 40 percent or more, then performing the rebuild to reset the high-water mark may be worthwhile. However, consider the overall database size in terms of the number of rows in the tables, the total blocks held by the table, and the frequency of full-table scans being performed (on that table), prior to deciding whether the difference between HIGHWTMK_BLOCKS and REALDATA_BLOCKS is substantial and whether the table is indeed a candidate for resetting the high-water mark. For instance, there may be a relatively high degree of difference between HIGHWTMK_BLOCKS and REALDATA_BLOCKS for a table. However, if the TOT_BLOCKS is relatively small (just a few blocks), then it may not be worthwhile to make the effort to reset the high-water mark. For instance, suppose the degree of difference is 75 percent (HIGHWTMK_BLOCKS = 4 and REALDATA_BLOCKS = 1); however, TOT_BLOCKS is 6, which makes reorganization impractical. Also, even given that TOT_BLOCKS is high, if the table is accessed infrequently, there may not be adequate motivation to reset the segment high-water mark.

Note that in the case of a partitioned table, you would be dealing with high-water marks at the partition level. You may take the same steps as listed previously to detect and eliminate erroneous high-water marks for specific partitions.

Periodically deallocate unused blocks

In the preceding tip, we discussed identifying the unused (empty) blocks. Unused blocks may exist above as well as below the high-water mark. As discussed earlier, unused blocks may be present below the high-water mark due to deletions having occurred in the table. Also, the high-water mark generally gets incremented in units of 5 blocks. Accordingly, even when a single additional block is used up due to one or more inserts, the high-water mark goes up by 5 blocks, thus leaving 4 unused blocks below the high-water mark.

There could also be unused space above the high-water mark, due to the INITIAL and/or NEXT extents specifying a much larger number of blocks than what is actually used. Let's study a few examples to understand this better:

- A table could have allocated an INITIAL extent of 10MB, thus occupying 1,280 blocks (in a database with block-size = 8KB), whereas the data present in the table only takes up 45 blocks.
- A table could have allocated both an INITIAL extent of 10MB and a NEXT extent of 10MB, thus occupying a total of 2,560 blocks, whereas the data present in the table only takes up 1,282 blocks (the entire INITIAL extent and two blocks from the NEXT extent).
- You could pre-allocate four extents across four disks/controllers, with the INITIAL and NEXT extents being 10MB (assuming PCTINCREASE = 0). Thus, you would be pre-allocating a total of 5,120 blocks, in anticipation of data in the near future. After a few months, however, you discover that there are only a handful of rows in the table, taking up a mere one block.

These situations may be a result of zealous overestimation of table sizes during the physical database design. Once their sizes are monitored after a few months, you may find that there is not very much data in these tables and by allocating all those blocks, you are only wasting space. Accordingly, you may wish to free up the space by deallocating as many blocks as possible. In any case, from a space-optimization perspective, it is a good idea to periodically scan for unused/empty blocks and deallocate them, if they are not expected to be used in the short to medium term.

Similar to the high-water mark, these empty blocks do not get released until you TRUNCATE the table with the DROP STORAGE clause. However, starting with Oracle7.3, you may use the ALTER TABLE DEALLOCATE UNUSED command to explicitly deallocate unused blocks. However, only those empty blocks that are above the high-water mark can be deallocated. (This is probably so because Oracle believes that blocks up to the high-water mark have been populated in the past; so there are chances of their being repopulated in the future; accordingly, deallocating them would not be optimal.) The ALTER TABLE DEALLOCATE UNUSED command supports a KEEP clause that allows you to retain a certain number of bytes above the high-water mark, in case you would like to retain some space as a precautionary measure (in case more data is expected), thus preventing the entire space from being deallocated. Doing so will only cause the new data to be stored elsewhere (resulting in fragmentation) if such new data is inserted in the future (and the previously freed space has already been taken up by another segment), causing the table to grow beyond the current high-water mark. By default, without the KEEP clause, unused space within the MINEXTENTS is retained (including the INITIAL extent). However, by specifying a smaller number of bytes in the KEEP clause, you can cause even space within MINEXTENTS to be released. If such deallocation results in the current number of extents being smaller than MINEXTENTS, then MINEXTENTS (within the data-dictionary) is reset to the number of extents existing currently (after the deallocation). Similarly, if the deallocation results in the first extent being smaller than INITIAL, then INITIAL is reset to the current size of the initial extent.

Note that besides tables, you can also deallocate unused space for indexes, overflow data-segments (where overflow occurs for index-organized tables), and LOB segments (where LOBs are stored out of line). Note that certain direct/PDML operations (bulk inserts) use the high-water mark to determine the block where rows can be speedily inserted (that is, such operations do not refer to the freelists to determine available blocks below the high-water mark). However, that is no reason to retain unused space above the high-water mark if such space would remain stagnant for a while (causing wastage), and anyway, direct/PDML operations can allocate additional extents after the high-water mark if no unused blocks are already present—so such operations won't be obstructed due to the space being released. After these operations complete, the high-water mark is reset to the new level.

You can identify whether a segment is a candidate for deallocating unused blocks via the DBMS_SPACE.UNUSED_SPACE procedure. The procedure accepts three INPUT parameters (four in Oracle8) and seven OUTPUT parameters. The INPUT parameters specify the schema-name, segment-name, and segment-type. In Oracle8, an additional parameter is accepted specifying the partition-name (for information specific to a single partition). The seven OUTPUT parameters allow the following information to be retrieved:

- Total number of block allocated for the segment/partition
- Total bytes allocated for the segment/partition (previous information in bytes)
- Unused blocks above the current high-water mark of the segment/partition
- Unused bytes above the current high-water mark of the segment/partition (previous information in bytes)
- File-id of the last extent that contains data
- Block-id of the last extent that contains data
- Last used block within the last extent containing data

The following piece of code illustrates usage of the procedure:

```
SET SERVEROUTPUT ON SIZE 5000
DECLARE
  tot_blks       NUMBER;
  tot_byts       NUMBER;
  unused_blks    NUMBER;
  unused_byts    NUMBER;
  last_file_id   NUMBER;
  last_blk_id    NUMBER;
  last_used_blk  NUMBER;
BEGIN
  DBMS_SPACE.UNUSED_SPACE('SCOTT', 'NAMES', 'TABLE',
                          tot_blks, tot_byts, unused_blks,
                          unused_byts, last_file_id,
                          last_blk_id, last_used_blk);
  DBMS_OUTPUT.PUT_LINE('Space information for table SCOTT.NAMES : ')
  DBMS_OUTPUT.PUT_LINE('Total blocks allocated : ' ||
TO_CHAR(tot_blks));
  DBMS_OUTPUT.PUT_LINE('Total bytes allocated  : ' ||
TO_CHAR(tot_byts));
  DBMS_OUTPUT.PUT_LINE('Unused blocks : ' || TO_CHAR(unused_blks));
  DBMS_OUTPUT.PUT_LINE('Unused bytes  : ' || TO_CHAR(unused_byts));
  DBMS_OUTPUT.PUT_LINE('File-id of last used extent   : ' ||
TO_CHAR(last_file_id));
  DBMS_OUTPUT.PUT_LINE('Block-id of last used extent : ' ||
TO_CHAR(last_blk_id));
  DBMS_OUTPUT.PUT_LINE('Last used block : ' ||
TO_CHAR(last_used_blk));
  DBMS_OUTPUT.PUT_LINE('** end of information **');
END;
/
```

Note that DBMS_SPACE.UNUSED_SPACE provides an alternative method to determine the high-water mark. From the preceding code, the number of unused blocks may be subtracted from the total number of blocks to find the number of blocks composing the high-water mark.

Avoid dropping data-files explicitly

Try not to OFFLINE DROP any data-files, especially in a production instance. Doing so would require you to rebuild the tablespace subsequently, potentially causing downtime. If forced to OFFLINE DROP a data-file (due to hardware or software based data-file write errors or other reasons), ensure that you proactively schedule a tablespace rebuild as soon as possible (during off-peak periods), not waiting until Oracle forces you to do so at a more critical time. If you don't rebuild the

tablespace after the OFFLINE DROP option is used, Oracle will still try to use the space in that data-file whenever it needs to grow beyond the previous data-file (prior to the data-file that has been subjected to the OFFLINE DROP operation) in that tablespace. Even if you add another data-file after you have done an OFFLINE DROP on the previous datafile, Oracle will still try to use the previous data-file and not the new one you just added, whenever it needs to grow. This is because the SYS.FET$ table (which stores information about free extents for each data-file) is referred to as additional space needs to be allocated to accommodate segment growth within that tablespace. The FET$ does not maintain file-status information (whether a file is online, offline, and so on), and so it comes up with free space in the offline-dropped file. Another unit of code attempts to allocate the additional extent in the "free space" in that data-file and reports an error when it is unable to do so (due to the file being unavailable). Accordingly, to avoid such problems that may potentially occur during critical peak hours, ensure that you schedule some time as early as possible to repair the data-file offline-drop by rebuilding the tablespace.

Note that if you are running the database in ARCHIVELOG mode, you can use the OFFLINE option (of the ALTER DATABASE command) to make a data-file offline, rather than having to use the OFFLINE DROP option—another reason to run the database in ARCHIVELOG mode in a high-availability environment (such as a data-warehouse where you initially may not be inclined to run the database in ARCHIVELOG mode if the data-volume is large and you are not interested in taking hot backups, since data-rebuilds may be faster than taking backups and subsequently applying recovery in your situation).

Learn the "tablespace shuffle" for emergency unanticipated space requirements

One of the things I have learned from experience is that no matter how prepared you are—you are never fully prepared! There is always a sudden emergency that will come along one day when you are least expecting it and shoot down all your pre-calculations and smug assumptions about your proactiveness. This is especially so in e-commerce environments where growth and scalability cannot be easily regulated. So unpleasant surprises are relatively more common. One day you could be having just a couple of thousand users on your site, whereas in a few weeks you could be having several thousand. A frequently scarce commodity is disk-space. Though it is relatively inexpensive, you can never seem to have enough of it. Look at the PC on your desktop as an example. A few years ago, having 10GB of hard-disk space on your PC was unheard of. And today, it's the norm, and as you would guess—even that's proving insufficient. If you scale this example to a high-end UNIX or NT box, you know what I mean.

Sometimes your production box has to support an application temporarily (since the original box on which it was placed has crashed) or you need to expand an actively used tablespace immediately and you don't have the necessary space available (the new disks won't come in until after two days). In such circumstances, you may have to shuffle your tablespaces, such that inactive or dormant tablespaces can be temporarily removed and a new one or a currently active one can be created/expanded onto the space made available due to the removal. For instance, if your APPL_DATA tablespace needs to expand immediately and your new disks will come in only after a day, you can take the USERS tablespace offline (if it's not being actively used) or reduce the size of the TEMPORARY tablespace. If you choose the latter option, you can simply point the users to use a different tablespace as their temporary tablespace for a short while as you drop the original temporary tablespace and rebuild it as a smaller one (just enough to meet all productions requirements for a day until the new disks come in). Then you can alter the users again to use the new smaller temporary tablespace. Then you can expand the active tablespace or build the new tablespace on the space made available. Once the new disks come in, you can drop and rebuild the new tablespace on the new disks and also rebuild the temporary tablespace to use its original disks, or you can let the new tablespace exist on the current disks and enlarge the currently smaller temporary tablespace to use the new disks, so that it can go back to its original larger size. Letting the temporary tablespace expand onto the new disks is least disruptive, since tablespaces with genuine application data do not have to be rebuilt. In case you decide to use a dormant tablespace (such as USERS) to accommodate the new tablespace (or the expansion of an existing tablespace), then you would need to back up the dormant tablespace (say, by making an export and transferring the export dump-file off to tape) and drop the tablespace. Once this is done and space is released, the new tablespace can be created (or a data-file added to the existing active tablespace) in its place. Then when the new disks come in or the need to support the temporary application goes away (the original box supporting the application is up and running again), the new tablespace can be backed up and dropped and the original dormant tablespace can be restored from the backup (by re-creating the original USERS tablespace and restoring all segments within that tablespace via an import). If the dormant tablespace was taken away to accommodate the expansion of an active tablespace, then the active tablespace could be left alone on the disks (to prevent disruption by having to rebuild it) and the dormant tablespace could be restored onto the new disks that come in.

Learn the "tablespace shuffle"

If the period for which you are evicting a dormant tablespace is very small (say, a day or two), you can even take that tablespace offline and perform the shuffle, rather than having to drop and re-create it. If you choose to take the tablespace offline, then you can merely do an OS backup of the data-files of the dormant tablespace (rather than having to identify all segments within that tablespace and exporting them) and delete its data-files from the OS. Using the offline and rebuild method compared to a drop and rebuild method is also useful when the dormant tablespace is quite large in size (making exports inconvenient).

Certain important precautions need to be taken prior to performing the shuffle:

- Ensure that removal of the dormant tablespace (or space released by reduction of the temporary tablespace) will provide the space that is required in the first place (or the purpose of the whole shuffle operation is defeated). Similarly, if the temporary tablespace is indeed being reduced, ensure that the new smaller size of the temporary tablespace will be adequate to handle production operations prior to reducing its size.
- While choosing a dormant tablespace for dropping or taking offline, ensure that it is indeed not being utilized by users currently. A tablespace may appear to be "dormant" currently (say, during day hours). However, it may be utilized by batch jobs running at night. Alternatively, it may be used by the CFO, who is absent today. Accordingly, evaluate all such usage possibilities before concluding that a tablespace is dormant and evicting it.
- Ensure that no referential integrity violations will occur due to certain pertinent tables being present in the dormant tablespace being dropped/made offline.
- Ensure that indexes for certain active tables are not present in the dormant tablespace.
- Ensure that no data-dictionary segments (due to the SQL.BSQ file being edited) are present in the dormant tablespace.
- Ensure that online rollback segments are not present in the dormant tablespace.
- Provide adequate advance notice to all users regarding the temporary unavailability of such "dormant" tablespaces, so that objections, if any, can be brought to your notice prior to your removing it.
- In any case, ensure that you back up the control-file before *and* after any shuffle operation.

Taking such important precautions is very necessary to ensure that you do not inadvertently cause any service disruptions.

Also note that with Oracle8*i*, the need for complex shuffling is reduced, since *transportable tablespaces* are supported. Chapter 20 provides more details on transportable tablespaces.

In a DSS environment, do not blindly accept unrestricted segment growth

One important fact that often gets left out in the physical database design is the purge frequency of various segments. Ironically, such omission is more frequent in DSS environments such as data-warehouses and data-marts, where the data is voluminous and requires to be periodically purged. Data is often considered to be moving in a single direction, i.e., into the warehouse. However, there has to be a point where part of the data is considered "old" or irrelevant for any business analysis and needs to be purged. This cutoff point may differ for different applications within the organization. For instance, a data-mart may consider all data older than five years to be irrelevant, whereas the corporate data-warehouse may require data as old as ten years. In any case, it is necessary to find out this point, beyond which data can be purged after archiving it, if necessary. For instance, a company may require five years of financial data to be compliant with certain statutory requirements. However, the last ten years of data may have to be available on an as-needed basis (during exceptional audits to resolve forgery, or similar circumstances). Here, data older than five years will not be needed on a regular basis and hence can be kept offline on tape. Only relevant, regularly used data will be kept online.

Keeping online only the bare minimum data allows the database to retain its leanness, thus making data management and database administration easier. The smaller the data, the higher the administrative flexibility. Also, as the size of data increases (unless specific steps are taken otherwise), performance may deteriorate. For instance, compare the response times when doing a full-table scan on a million-row table versus a 50-million row table. And relatively less resources are required to maintain smaller data-volumes, reducing the overall cost. Thus there are manifold advantages to restricting data size.

However, users generally clamor for more data. A user performing trend-analysis would like the option to spread the analysis over the last ten years, if necessary, rather than restricting himself or herself to just five years. In certain cases it may make genuine business sense to have such data available online. In other cases, it may not be worthwhile to attempt to do so. You need to consider the overall business requirements and the higher cost involved. Reconciling both will generally provide the answer. In any case, the correct cutoff point has to be determined that will allow the cost to remain as low as possible with the least impact on business.

Once the cutoff point is determined, you can take advantage of Oracle's partitioning options to manage the data-loads and purges effectively. You can implement a "rolling window" scheme to truncate older partitions after optionally exporting the older data off those partitions. Then the export dump-files can be

saved onto one or more tapes. However, the cutoff point has to be determined as part of the initial analysis (while defining the business rules for the application). Only then can you formulate and blend the partitioning and the purge strategy into the overall design. Introducing partitioning at a later stage may make the integration rougher, especially after the application has gone live. At such later stages, large volumes of data may be involved, making the conversion from regular tables to partitions more challenging.

Summary

This chapter talked about some basic maintenance tasks—space and growth management. Ideally, these tasks should form an important part of the overall physical database design, thus reducing the need to perform periodic database reorganizations or to perform reactive maintenance on an ongoing basis throughout the lifetime of the database. The basic issues surrounding space management, including fragmentation, were examined, so that defensive measures to react correctly to serious space errors, with as little impact on uptime as possible, can be taken.

The next section provides a close look at some troubleshooting techniques within Oracle.

PART V

Troubleshooting

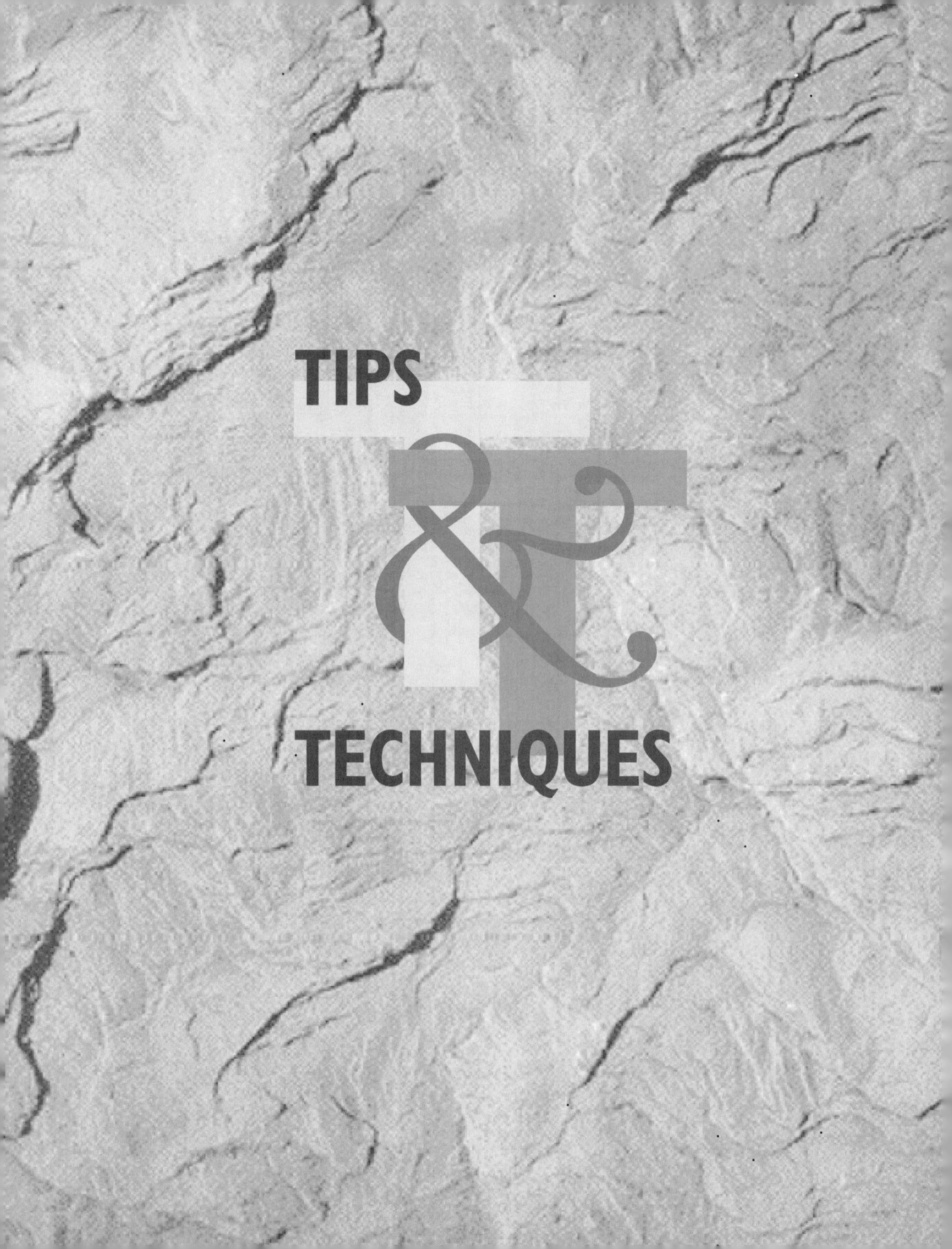
TIPS
&
TECHNIQUES

CHAPTER 13

Interpreting the Alert-Log and Trace-Files

A database running smoothly without disruptions and providing peak performance is a result of various factors such as hiring capable and talented administrative personnel; detailed requirements analysis and capacity planning; careful selection of the hardware and software architecture; optimal installation, configuration, and tuning; and, finally, proactive monitoring. From time to time, however, the database gets sick and provides indications of such sickness by writing warning and/or error messages in the database alert-log or trace-files. Part of such proactive monitoring involves parsing the alert-log and trace-files, extracting the relevant information, and resolving the problem, such that Oracle can continue working uninterrupted. Even if it's a problem that's occurred and is interrupting Oracle from operating smoothly, then quickly detecting the problem allows fast action to be taken to resolve the problem. In other words, the alert-log and trace-files are critical mechanisms for Oracle to alert the user/administrator to current or future problems. They provide some of the earliest warnings of poor performance and downtime. In spite of their importance, there's very little documentation on interpreting the information in these files. Let's take a detailed look at both these mechanisms and understand how to monitor them for errors, how to interpret the messages correctly, and how to react to the symptoms of some common errors found there.

This chapter contains the following tips and techniques:

- Whenever possible, continually tail the alert-log
- Be familiar with events/messages in the alert-log
- Edit repetitive error-messages to be listed just once
- Archive and trim the alert-log once every two weeks to three months
- Know what to look for in a trace-file
- Know how to identify trace-files belonging to a specific event/session
- Know what causes trace-files to be generated
- Whenever necessary, make your trace-files readable by developers

The Alert-Log

The alert-log, as the name indicates, is one of the primary alert mechanisms used by Oracle to bring the administrator's attention to errors and abnormal situations, as well as certain permanent actions such as DDL causing structural changes to the database. In other words, the alert-log provides a record of intrinsic events within the database. Each event potentially affects performance and availability. The date and time of each event is listed. There are entries indicating the start and end times for certain events. The alert-log is one of the first places to look for information while investigating a database issue/problem. Information logged in the alert-log includes the following:

- Redo-log switches
- Checkpoints (optional)
- Critical errors and warnings (including internal or ORA-600 errors). Such errors may also cause trace-files to be produced, during which process the names of the trace-files related to the error would be present in the alert-log.
- Important events such as the following:
    - Database startup and shutdown
    - Structural changes to the database such as tablespaces/data-files being added/dropped, being taken offline/online, or being made read-only/read/write; redo-logs being created or dropped; control-file being re-created; or database being placed in ARCHIVELOG/ NOARCHIVELOG modes
    - Changes to segment status such as rollback segments being added/ dropped or taken offline/online
    - Instance and media recoveries performed and their outcome

The alert-log is physically a text file, created by Oracle in the directory specified by the initialization parameter BACKGROUND_DUMP_DEST. One may use the SHOW PARAMETER BACKGROUND_DUMP_DEST command in Server Manager or use the following query to determine the directory path:

```
SQL> SELECT name, value
      FROM v$parameter WHERE name = 'background_dump_dest';
```

The default location of BACKGROUND_DUMP_DEST is *$ORACLE_HOME/ rdbms/log*. On Windows NT, it is *%ORACLE_HOME%\rdbms80\log* (the version

number is appended to the *rdbms* directory name). The alert-log filename is usually in the following format: *alert_<SID>.log,* where *<SID>* is the value specified by the ORACLE_SID environment variable (registry entry in the case of Windows NT).

Whenever possible, continually tail the alert-log

As mentioned earlier, all critical events are highlighted in the alert-log by Oracle in the way of errors, warnings, and informatory messages. The listed information follows the actual sequence of occurrence with the actual date/time stamp. Thus, looking at the alert-log, you can determine which events occurred and when. The alert-log accordingly helps to gauge the history of the database and allows tracing of specific events through its lifetime. Many DBAs have a custom of looking at the alert-log first thing in the morning (as they get into work). Some also look at the alert-log at the end of the day, prior to leaving work. However, information is written out to the alert-log by Oracle throughout the day. It may contain certain error messages or warning messages about potentially disruptive events about to occur in the very near future. However, if the DBA does not look at the messages as soon as they are written, chances are, he or she may not have sufficient time to react as necessary to avert the situation. For instance, errors about a remote transaction failing or a potential deadlock in an application can be detected and resolved in a timely fashion, before these erroneous situations remain unresolved and escalate into disruptive problems, and then have to be resolved. A potential solution to prevent such scenarios is to have a window running a command to view the tail-end of the alert-log. This view needs to be (automatically) continuously refreshed to list out the latest writes to the log. For instance, in a UNIX environment, one may dedicate a window to run the *tail* command with the *-f* switch on the alert-log as follows:

```
zurich:/opt/apps/oracle/admin/DT08/bdump#DT08> tail -f alert_TST4.log
Completed: drop rollback segment rbs7
Thu Jul  1 17:05:11 1999
alter database backup controlfile to trace
Completed: alter database backup controlfile to trace
Thu Jul  1 22:23:35 1999
alter database backup controlfile to trace
Completed: alter database backup controlfile to trace
Thu Jul  1 22:30:12 1999
alter database backup controlfile to trace
Completed: alter database backup controlfile to trace
```

This shows the most recent writes to the alert-log. As soon as any errors/warnings are noted, the DBA can promptly act to resolve the situation as best as possible. Note that tailing the alert-log does not guarantee that errors would be spotted immediately by the DBA. It is merely an approach to alert the DBA as early as possible. It needs to augmented by complimentary mechanisms such as a timer-based script to periodically parse the alert-log and page the DBA, in the event of an error. Such mechanisms will also provide for situations where the DBA is too engrossed to notice errors being written to the alert-log or the DBA is not present at his or her desk (which is a fair assumption, since DBAs need to run around frequently).

It is advisable for the DBA to tail the alert-logs of all production instances. However, if there are a high number of production instances, it may not be practical to tail and continuously monitor all of them. The DBA needs to judiciously monitor only the "primary" instances or ones that require 24x7 uptime. Once the file is tailed, the output written to the file ought to be read and interpreted in the right fashion. All informatory messages need to be noted, whereas error messages may require the DBA to take immediate remedial action, depending on the nature and severity of the error. In any case, one needs to be aware of the common (routine) messages and be trained to spot any new abnormal messages.

Be familiar with events/messages in the alert-log

As you scan the alert-log, you may see error messages relating to various database events. Your ability to quickly resolve critical errors without impacting availability directly depends on your knowledge and experience with the message and the error. Be familiar with the routine/non-routine informative messages that get listed in the alert-log. Identify all non-critical errors, so no panic is caused when they are observed. Keep your eyes open for critical disruptive errors. Have actions/responses well-documented in order to react to specific critical error situations logged in the alert-log. Thus, listings in the alert-log may be classified as follows:

- Routine informative messages
- Non-routine informative messages
- Non-critical errors or warnings
- Critical errors

The online Oracle error facility can be invoked to get more information on the errors that show up, such as *oerr ora 1578* (where the error code is ORA-1578). Examples of some commonly encountered messages (classified according to previously mentioned criteria) in the alert-log are shown below. Note that they are not comprehensive but are just samples to aid in reading and interpretation of the alert-log. Any errors regarding which you lack information should be reported to Oracle Support, so that appropriate remedial action can be taken, as soon as possible.

Following are some routine and non-routine informative messages.

Database Startup

```
Starting ORACLE instance (normal)
LICENSE_MAX_SESSION = 0
LICENSE_SESSIONS_WARNING = 0
LICENSE_MAX_USERS = 0
Starting up ORACLE RDBMS Version: 8.0.5.1.0.
System parameters with non-default values:
  processes              = 200
  shared_pool_size       = 18000000
  control_files          = /opt/apps/oracle/ORAKRNL/DT08/cntrl01DT08.ctl,

/opt/apps/oracle/odata1/DT08/ORAKRNL/cntrl02DT08.ctl,

/opt/apps/oracle/odata2/DT08/ORAKRNL/cntrl03DT08.ctl
----------------- other parameters with non-default values -----------------
PMON started with pid=2
DBW0 started with pid=3
LGWR started with pid=4
CKPT started with pid=5
SMON started with pid=6
RECO started with pid=7
SNP0 started with pid=8
Mon May 24 11:17:04 1999
alter database  mount
Mon May 24 11:17:08 1999
Successful mount of redo thread 1, with mount id 3682681652.
Mon May 24 11:17:08 1999
Database mounted in Exclusive Mode.
Completed: alter database  mount
Mon May 24 11:17:08 1999
alter database open
Mon May 24 11:17:08 1999
Thread 1 opened at log sequence 1882
  Current log# 1 seq# 1882 mem# 0: /opt/apps/oracle/ORAKRNL/DT08/log01DT08.log
  Current log# 1 seq# 1882 mem# 1:
/opt/apps/oracle/odata1/DT08/ORAKRNL/log01DT08.log
Successful open of redo thread 1.
Mon May 24 11:17:08 1999
SMON: enabling cache recovery
SMON: enabling tx recovery
Mon May 24 11:17:09 1999
Completed: alter database open
```

FIGURE 13-1. *Database startup message*

Database Shutdown

```
Sat Mar 20 07:59:12 1999
Shutting down instance (immediate)
License high water mark = 78
Sat Mar 20 07:59:13 1999
ALTER DATABASE CLOSE NORMAL
Sat Mar 20 07:59:13 1999
SMON: disabling tx recovery
SMON: disabling cache recovery
Sat Mar 20 07:59:16 1999
Thread 1 closed at log sequence 1084
Sat Mar 20 07:59:17 1999
Completed: ALTER DATABASE CLOSE NORMAL
Sat Mar 20 07:59:17 1999
ALTER DATABASE DISMOUNT
Completed: ALTER DATABASE DISMOUNT
```

FIGURE 13-2. *Database shutdown message*

Log Switches

```
Sun May 23 11:52:52 1999
Thread 1 advanced to log sequence 1836
  Current log# 3 seq# 1836 mem# 0: /opt/apps/oracle/ORAKRNL/DT08/log03DT08.log
  Current log# 3 seq# 1836 mem# 1: /opt/apps/oracle/odata1/DT08/ORAKRNL/log03DT08.log
Sun May 23 11:54:04 1999
Thread 1 advanced to log sequence 1837
  Current log# 1 seq# 1837 mem# 0: /opt/apps/oracle/ORAKRNL/DT08/log01DT08.log
  Current log# 1 seq# 1837 mem# 1: /opt/apps/oracle/odata1/DT08/ORAKRNL/log01DT08.log
```

FIGURE 13-3. *Message indicating log switches*

Checkpoints (When Initialization Parameter LOG_CHECKPOINTS_TO_ALERT Is Enabled)

```
Thu Jul  1 16:32:11 1999
Beginning log switch checkpoint up to RBA [0x762.2.10], SCN: 0x0000.076683b5
Thread 1 advanced to log sequence 1890
  Current log# 3 seq# 1890 mem# 0: /opt/apps/oracle/ORAKRNL/DT08/log03DT08.log
  Current log# 3 seq# 1890 mem# 1: /opt/apps/oracle/odata1/DT08/ORAKRNL/log03DT08.log
Thu Jul  1 16:32:11 1999
Completed checkpoint up to RBA [0x762.2.10], SCN: 0x0000.076683b5
Thu Jul  1 16:34:24 1999
Beginning log switch checkpoint up to RBA [0x763.2.10], SCN: 0x0000.076684d5
Thread 1 advanced to log sequence 1891
  Current log# 1 seq# 1891 mem# 0: /opt/apps/oracle/ORAKRNL/DT08/log01DT08.log
  Current log# 1 seq# 1891 mem# 1: /opt/apps/oracle/odata1/DT08/ORAKRNL/log01DT08.log
Thu Jul  1 16:34:24 1999
Completed checkpoint up to RBA [0x763.2.10], SCN: 0x0000.076684d5
```

FIGURE 13-4. *Checkpoint messages*

Rollback Segment Being Created, Being Taken Online/Offline, and Being Dropped

```
Thu Jul  1 16:37:46 1999
create rollback segment rbs7 tablespace rbs storage(initial 1m next 1m optimal 5m maxextents 249)
Thu Jul  1 16:37:46 1999
Completed: create rollback segment rbs7 tablespace rbs storag
Thu Jul  1 16:37:55 1999
alter rollback segment rbs7 online
Completed: alter rollback segment rbs7 online
Thu Jul  1 16:38:00 1999
alter rollback segment rbs7 offline
Completed: alter rollback segment rbs7 offline
Thu Jul  1 16:38:06 1999
drop rollback segment rbs7
Completed: drop rollback segment rbs7
```

FIGURE 13-5. *Rollback segment activity*

Tablespace Being Created, Being Taken Offline/Online, Being Made Read-Only/Read/Write, Data-File Being Added, and Tablespace Being Dropped

```
Thu Jul  1 16:55:27 1999
create tablespace DES2K_DATA datafile
'/opt/apps/oracle/odata5/DT08/usr_dbf/des2_data01.dbf' size 10m
  default storage(initial 16k next 16k pctincrease 0)
Thu Jul  1 16:55:31 1999
Completed: create tablespace DES2K_DATA datafile '/opt/apps/o
Thu Jul  1 16:59:26 1999
alter tablespace DES2K_DATA offline
Thu Jul  1 16:59:26 1999
Completed: alter tablespace DES2K_DATA offline
Thu Jul  1 16:59:34 1999
alter tablespace DES2K_DATA online
Completed: alter tablespace DES2K_DATA online
Thu Jul  1 17:00:32 1999
alter tablespace DES2K_DATA read only
Thu Jul  1 17:00:32 1999
Completed: alter tablespace DES2K_DATA read only
Thu Jul  1 17:00:42 1999
alter tablespace DES2K_DATA read write
Completed: alter tablespace DES2K_DATA read write
Thu Jul  1 17:01:29 1999
alter tablespace DES2K_DATA add datafile
'/opt/apps/oracle/odata5/DT08/usr_dbf/des2_data02.dbf' size 10m
Thu Jul  1 17:01:34 1999
Completed: alter tablespace DES2K_DATA add datafile '/opt/app
Thu Jul  1 17:01:50 1999
drop tablespace DES2K_DATA including contents
Thu Jul  1 17:01:54 1999
Completed: drop tablespace DES2K_DATA including contents
```

FIGURE 13-6. *Tablespace/data-file activity*

Control-File Backup Acknowledgment

```
Thu Jul  1 17:05:11 1999
alter database backup controlfile to trace
Completed: alter database backup controlfile to trace
```

FIGURE 13-7. *Control-file backup*

Instance (Crash) Recovery Message

```
Thu Mar 13 19:42:34 1997
alter database open
Beginning crash recovery of 1 threads
Thu Mar 13 19:44:01 1997
Crash recovery completed successfully
Thu Mar 13 19:44:02 1997
Thread 1 advanced to log sequence 1943
  Current log# 2 seq# 1943 mem# 0: /opt/apps/oracle/ORAKRNL/DT08/log02DT08.log
  Current log# 2 seq# 1943 mem# 1: /opt/apps/oracle/odata9/DT08/ORAKRNL/log02DT08.log
Successful open of redo thread 1.
Thu Mar 13 19:44:04 1997
SMON: enabling cache recovery
SMON: enabling tx recovery
Thu Mar 13 19:44:07 1997
Completed: alter database open
```

FIGURE 13-8. *Instance (crash) recovery*

Media Recovery (Roll-Forward) Messages

```
Sun Jul 04 21:32:58 1999
alter database open
Sun Jul 04 21:32:58 1999
Errors in file C:\ORANT\RDBMS73\trace\orclDBWR.TRC:
ORA-01157: cannot identify data file 2 - file not found
ORA-01110: data file 2: 'E:\ORADATA\ORCL\TOOLS01.DBF'
ORA-09202: sfifi: error identifying file
OSD-04002: unable to open file
O/S-Error: (OS 2) The system cannot find the file specified.
ORA-1157 signalled during: alter database open...
Sun Jul 04 21:33:32 1999
ALTER DATABASE RECOVER   database
Sun Jul 04 21:33:32 1999
Media Recovery Start
Media Recovery Log
ORA-279 signalled during: ALTER DATABASE RECOVER   database  ...
Sun Jul 04 21:33:56 1999
ALTER DATABASE RECOVER    CONTINUE DEFAULT
Media Recovery Log e:\oradata\orcl\%ORACLE_SID%01030.001
Media Recovery Complete
```

FIGURE 13-9. *Media recovery*

Redo Log Group Being Created, New Member Being Added/Dropped, Group Being Dropped

```
Thu Jul  1 21:54:04 1999
alter database add logfile group 4 ('/opt/apps/oracle/ORAKRNL/DT08/redog4f1.log') size 2m
Thu Jul  1 21:54:05 1999
Completed: alter database add logfile group 4 ('/opt/apps/ora
Thu Jul  1 21:59:02 1999
alter database add logfile member '/opt/apps/oracle/odata5/DT08/ORAKRNL/redog4f2.log' to group 4
Thu Jul  1 21:59:03 1999
Completed: alter database add logfile member '/opt/apps/oracl
Thu Jul  1 22:01:05 1999
alter database drop logfile member '/opt/apps/oracle/odata5/DT08/ORAKRNL/redog4f2.log'
Thu Jul  1 22:01:05 1999
Completed: alter database drop logfile member '/opt/apps/orac
Thu Jul  1 22:01:16 1999
alter database drop logfile group 4
Thu Jul  1 22:01:16 1999
Completed: alter database drop logfile group 4
```

FIGURE 13-10. *Redo-log activity*

Data-File/Redo-Log Being Renamed

```
Thu Jul  1 22:14:50 1999
alter database  mount
Thu Jul  1 22:14:55 1999
Successful mount of redo thread 1, with mount id 3686055391.
Thu Jul  1 22:14:55 1999
Database mounted in Exclusive Mode.
Completed: alter database  mount
Thu Jul  1 22:16:30 1999
alter database rename file '/opt/apps/oracle/odata2/DT08/sys_dbf/tools01.dbf' to
'/opt/apps/oracle/odata2/DT08/sys_dbf/tools_01.dbf'
Thu Jul  1 22:16:30 1999
Completed: alter database rename file '/opt/apps/oracle/odata
Thu Jul  1 22:17:51 1999
alter database rename file '/opt/apps/oracle/ORAKRNL/DT08/redog4f1.log' to
    '/opt/apps/oracle/ORAKRNL/DT08/redog4f1.dbf'
Thu Jul  1 22:17:51 1999
Completed: alter database rename file '/opt/apps/oracle/ORAKR
Thu Jul  1 22:17:56 1999
alter database open
Thu Jul  1 22:17:57 1999
Thread 1 opened at log sequence 1891
  Current log# 1 seq# 1891 mem# 0: /opt/apps/oracle/ORAKRNL/DT08/log01DT08.log
  Current log# 1 seq# 1891 mem# 1: /opt/apps/oracle/odata1/DT08/ORAKRNL/log01DT08.log
Successful open of redo thread 1.
```

FIGURE 13-11. *Database file renaming*

Database Being Altered to Enable ARCHIVELOG Mode (All ALTER DATABASE Commands Are Reflected in the Alert-Log)

```
Thu Jul  1 22:26:45 1999
Alter database  mount
Thu Jul  1 22:26:50 1999
Successful mount of redo thread 1, with mount id 3686048170.
Thu Jul  1 22:26:50 1999
Database mounted in Exclusive Mode.
Completed: alter database  mount
Thu Jul  1 22:26:59 1999
alter database archivelog
Completed: alter database archivelog
```

FIGURE 13-12. *Database alteration*

Non-critical and critical, normal and abnormal error messages and warnings may optionally produce one or more trace-files. These errors generally require you to take action (reactive maintenance) immediately to resolve them.

Segments Unable to Extend Due to Inadequate Space

- **Symptom(s)** Error messages on user screen and/or alert-log
- **Possible reason(s)**
  - Genuine lack of space
  - Available space is fragmented and unusable
- **Possible solution(s)**
  - Proactively setting segment physical storage parameters to reduce fragmentation (discussed in Chapter 12)
  - Adding another data-file, usually the most effective solution in the immediate term
  - Periodically reorganizing fragmented segments/tablespaces to optimize space usage


```
Thu Mar 13 13:37:49 1997
OER-1653: unable to extend table/cluster MIKI.MIKI_ACCTS by 25600 in            tablespace
MIKI_DATA

Sun Jan 26 18:29:35 1997
OER-1654: unable to extend index MIKI.MIKI_ACCTS_IDX02 by 3200 in tablespace            MIKI_INDX


Sat Mar 29 04:34:22 1997
ORA-1652: unable to extend temp segment by 1280 in tablespace          TEMP
Sat Mar 29 05:24:39 1997
ORA-1652: unable to extend temp segment by 1280 in tablespace          TEMP


Mon Aug 10 13:44:52 1998
ORA-1650: unable to extend rollback segment RBS1 by 640 in        tablespace RBS1
Failure to extend rollback segment 2 because of 1650 condition
ORA-1650: unable to extend rollback segment RBS1 by 640 in        tablespace RBS1
Failure to extend rollback segment 2 because of 1650 condition
```

FIGURE 13-13 *Lack of space for segment to extend*

Lack of Adequate User Licenses

- **Symptom(s)**
  - Users unable to log onto the database
  - Error messages on user screens and/or alert-log
- **Possible reason**
  - Allowable number of users/sessions exceeded (check in *v$license* for maximum allowable number for your site). This could either be because the number of users (or sessions required per user) have grown due to genuine scaling over time, or, alternatively, it could just be that users/sessions remain connected to the database even after they have obtained the data they need (due to sheer negligence, lack of instructions to the contrary, or other reasons).
- **Possible solution(s)**
  - If it's a genuine scalability issue and you need provision for additional users/sessions, procure the necessary licenses from Oracle Corporation.
  - If this problem is evidenced due to users not logging off after they are done, provide guidelines to help them do so. If that does not work, set up profiles to disconnect the session after a certain idle-time threshold is reached and allocate such profiles to each user.

```
Mon Jan  6 16:54:22 1997
LICENSE_MAX_USERS = 16
Tue Jan  7 09:58:46 1997
LICENSE_MAX_SESSION = 8
LICENSE_SESSIONS_WARNING = 7
Non-DBA logon denied; current logons equal maximum (8)
Tue Jan  7 10:52:56 1997
License warning limit (7) exceeded
Tue Jan  7 11:07:22 1997
Non-DBA logon denied; current logons equal maximum (8)
```

FIGURE 13-14. *License problems*

```
Thu Dec 3 13:13:28 1998
Errors in file /opt/apps/oracle/admin/DT08/bdump/smon_dt08_11196.trc:
ORA-01575: timeout waiting for space management resource
Thu Dec  3 13:13:34 1998
Errors in file /opt/apps/oracle/admin/DT08/bdump/smon_dt08_11196.trc:
ORA-01575: timeout waiting for space management resource
```

FIGURE 13-15. *Space-management resource timeouts*

Timeout Waiting for Space Management Resources

- **Symptom(s)** Described under section on "Trace-Files"
- **Possible reason(s)** Described under section on "Trace-Files"
- **Possible solution(s)** Described under section on "Trace-Files" (under "Database/Session Hanging")

Cannot Allocate New Log (Checkpoint Not Complete)

- **Symptom** Messages in the alert-log
- **Possible reason(s)**
  - Online redo-logs too small
  - Inadequate number of online redo-log groups
  - DBWR throughput inadequate
  - ARCH not keeping up (if archiving is enabled)
- **Possible solution** Please refer to Chapter 7.

```
Thu Mar 13 10:29:40 1997
Thread 1 advanced to log sequence 1880
  Current log# 2 seq# 1880 mem# 0: /opt/apps/oracle/ORAKRNL/DT08/log02DT08.log
  Current log# 2 seq# 1880 mem# 1: /opt/apps/oracle/odata9/DT08/ORAKRNL/log02DT08.log
Thu Mar 13 10:33:57 1997
Thread 1 cannot allocate new log, sequence 1881
Checkpoint not complete
  Current log# 2 seq# 1880 mem# 0: /opt/apps/oracle/ORAKRNL/DT08/log02DT08.log
Current log# 2 seq# 1880 mem# 1: /opt/apps/oracle/odata9/DT08/ORAKRNL/log02DT08.log
```

FIGURE 13-16. *Unable to switch redo-logs*

Archiver Stuck

- **Symptom(s)**
  - Database is hung (frozen)
  - Error messages in the alert-log
- **Possible reason(s)**
  - Archive log directory full
  - Oracle bug (ARCH process failure)
- **Possible solution(s)**
  - Make free space available in archive-log destination. Chapter 9 discusses this in more detail.
  - Contact Oracle Support if an Oracle bug is suspected.

```
Sat Dec 12 16:21:07 1998
ARCH: Archival stopped, error occurred. Will continue retrying
Sat Dec 12 16:21:07 1998
ORACLE Instance DT08 - Archival Error
Sat Dec 12 16:21:07 1998
ORA-00255: error archiving log 2 of thread 1, sequence # 57582
ORA-00312: online log 2 thread 1: '/opt/apps/oracle/odata7/DT08/ORAKRNL/log02DT08.log'
ORA-00312: online log 2 thread 1: '/opt/apps/oracle/odata8/DT08/ORAKRNL/log02DT08.log'
ORA-00272: error writing archive log
ARCH:
 ORA-00255: error archiving log 2 of thread 1, sequence # 57582
ORA-00312: online log 2 thread 1: '/opt/apps/oracle/odata7/DT08/ORAKRNL/log02DT08.log'
ORA-00312: online log 2 thread 1: '/opt/apps/oracle/odata8/DT08/ORAKRNL/log02DT08.log'
ORA-00272: error writing archive log
Sat Dec 12 16:22:07 1998
Thread 1 advanced to log sequence 57584
  Current log# 4 seq# 57584 mem# 0: /opt/apps/oracle/odata7/DT08/ORAKRNL/log04DT08.log
  Current log# 4 seq# 57584 mem# 1: /opt/apps/oracle/odata8/DT08/ORAKRNL/log04DT08.log
Sat Dec 12 16:23:49 1998
ORACLE Instance DT08 - Can not allocate log, archival required
Sat Dec 12 16:23:49 1998
Thread 1 cannot allocate new log, sequence 57586
All online logs needed archiving
  Current log# 1 seq# 57585 mem# 0: /opt/apps/oracle/ORAKRNL/DT08/log01DT08.log
  Current log# 1 seq# 57585 mem# 1: /opt/apps/oracle/odata5/DT08/ORAKRNL/log01DT08.log
Sat Dec 12 17:09:17 1998
Archiver process freed from errors. No longer stopped.
```

FIGURE 13-17. *Archiver stuck*

```
Mon Jul  7 23:18:48 1997
Errors in file /opt/apps/oracle/admin/DT08/bdump/pmon_DT08_16593.trc:
ORA-00600: internal error code, arguments: [6856], [0], [0], [], [], [], [], []
Mon Jul  7 23:18:57 1997
Errors in file /opt/apps/oracle/admin/DT08/bdump/pmon_DT08_16593.trc:
ORA-01578: ORACLE data block corrupted (file # 10, block # 32379)
ORA-01110: data file 10: '/opt/apps/oracle/odata8/DT08/usr_dbf/miki_data01.dbf'
ORA-00600: internal error code, arguments: [6856], [0], [0], [], [], [], [], []
Errors in file /opt/apps/oracle/admin/DT08/bdump/pmon_DT08_16593.trc:
ORA-00600: internal error code, arguments: [6856], [0], [0], [], [], [], [], []
Mon Jul  7 23:38:08 1997
ORACLE Instance DT08 (pid = 6) - Error 600 encountered while recovering
transaction (4, 94) on object 14151.
Mon Jul  7 23:38:08 1997
Errors in file /opt/apps/oracle/admin/DT08/bdump/smon_DT08_16601.trc:
ORA-00600: internal error code, arguments: [6856], [0], [0], [], [], [], [], []
```

FIGURE 13-18. *Block corruption*

Database Corruption

- **Symptom(s)** Please refer to Chapter 14.
- **Possible reason(s)** Please refer to Chapter 14.
- **Possible solution(s)** Please refer to Chapter 14.

Application Deadlock Detected

- **Symptom(s)**
  - Error messages in the alert-log
  - Transaction failures in applications (such transactions are rolled back by Oracle)

- **Possible reason(s)**
  - Application issues involving non-default locking mechanisms such as randomly issuing explicit table-level locks or improper locking order for different code routines (where Module_A first locks Row_1/Table_1 and then Row_1/Table_2, whereas Module_B first locks Row_1/Table_2 and then Row_1/Table_1. When both Module_A and Module_B are run concurrently, deadlocks may be caused). Further explained in Chapter 6.
  - Oracle bugs.
- **Possible solution(s)**
  - Detect and resolve application issues. Refer to the Oracle documentation for details on resolving application-related deadlocks. Chapter 6 also provides some tips in this area.
  - Contact Oracle Support, if a bug is suspected.

```
Tue Jun  22 00:02:27 1999
Errors in file /opt/apps/oracle/admin/DT08/udump/ora_DT08_9949.trc:
ORA-00600: internal error code, arguments: [4406], [2306963552],
[2306961104], [], [], [], [], []
ORA-00060: deadlock detected while waiting for resource
```

FIGURE 13-19. *Deadlock detected*

```
Dump file /opt/apps/oracle/admin/DT08/udump/ora_DT08_9949.trc
Oracle8 Enterprise Edition Release 8.0.5.1.0 - Production
With the Partitioning and Objects options
PL/SQL Release 8.0.5.1.0 - Production
ORACLE_HOME = /opt/apps/oracle/product/8.0.5
System name:    hercules
Instance name: DT08
Redo thread mounted by this instance: 1
Oracle process number: 24
Unix process pid: 9949, image: oracleDT08

*** 1999.06.22.00.02.27.000
*** SESSION ID:(38.35615) 1999.06.22.00.02.27.000
ksqded1:  deadlock detected via did
DEADLOCK DETECTED
Current SQL statement for this session:
UPDATE PRODUCT_ACCOUNTS SET BUSINESS_LINE_ID = :1, MIRF_BUSINESS_LINE_CODE = :2,
UPDATE_DATE = :3 WHERE PRODUCT_ACCOUNT_ID = :4
The following deadlock is not an ORACLE error. It is a
deadlock due to user error in the design of an application
or from issuing incorrect ad-hoc SQL. The following
information may aid in determining the deadlock:
Deadlock graph:
                         ---------Blocker(s)--------  ---------Waiter(s)---------
Resource Name            process session holds waits  process session holds waits
TX-00020028-00002e32          24      38     X             28       9          S
TX-00090004-00003eba          28       9     X             24      38          S
session 38: DID 0001-0018-00000001       session 9: DID 0001-001C-00000001
session 9: DID 0001-001C-00000001        session 38: DID 0001-0018-00000001
Rows waited on:
Session 9: no row
Session 38: no row
=========================================================
PROCESS STATE
-------------
Process global information:
     process: 219a6be8, call: 21c27b04, xact: 21b9fd28, curses: 219da588, usrses: 219da588
  ----------------------------------------
  SO: 219a6be8, type: 1, owner: 0, flag: INIT/-/-/0x00
```

FIGURE 13-20. *Corresponding deadlock information from trace-file (relevant portions of trace-file ora_DT08_9949.trc listed in the error message in the alert-log in Figure 13-19; note that the trace-file includes a process dump of the errant process)*

```
  (process) Oracle pid=24, calls cur/top: 21c27b04/21c27b04, flag: (0) -
           int error: 0, call error: 0, sess error: 0, txn error 0
  (post info) last post received: 0 0 1
             last post received-location: kslfre
             last process to post me: 219a573c 66 0
DATA BLOCKS:
        data#      heap  pointer status pins change
        ----- -------- -------- ------ ---- ------
            0 2271acf0 22c29870 I/P/A     0 NONE
            6 22c29820 22830ec0 I/-/A     0 NONE
      ---------------------------------------
      SO: 21c1d164, type: 23, owner: 219da588, flag: INIT/-/-/0x00
      LIBRARY OBJECT LOCK: lock=21c1d164 handle=2288d300 mode=N
      call pin=21c1df94 session pin=0
      user=219da588 session=219da588 count=1 flags=[00] savepoint=105
      LIBRARY OBJECT HANDLE: handle=2288d300
      name=
UPDATE OPB_SRVR_RECOVERY SET I_HIGH_TID = :1, I_LOW_TID = :2, LAST_TIMESTAMP = :3 WHERE
SESSION_ID = :4 AND TARGET_ID = :5
      hash=1951996 timestamp=05-25-1999 08:25:14
      namespace=CRSR flags=RON/TIM/PN0/MED/[50010000]
LIBRARY OBJECT: object=2288d18c
        type=CRSR flags=EXS[0001] pflags= [00] status=VALD load=0
        CHILDREN: size=16
DATA BLOCKS:
        data#      heap  pointer status pins change
        ----- -------- -------- ------ ---- ------
            0 224e37b0 224e368c I/P/A     0 NONE
            6 224e363c 22668008 I/P/A     1 NONE
      ---------------------------------------
      SO: 21c1b00c, type: 23, owner: 219da588, flag: INIT/-/-/0x00
UPDATE PRODUCT_ACCOUNTS SET BUSINESS_LINE_ID = :1, MIRF_BUSINESS_LINE_CODE = :2,
UPDATE_DATE = :3 WHERE PRODUCT_ACCOUNT_ID = :4
      hash=7d4e2557 timestamp=06-21-1999 23:58:41
      namespace=CRSR flags=RON/TIM/PN0/MED/[50010000]
LIBRARY OBJECT: object=2211b600
        type=CRSR flags=EXS[0001] pflags= [00] status=VALD load=0
****************************************************
END OF PROCESS STATE
```

FIGURE 13-20. *Corresponding deadlock information from trace-file (relevant portions of trace-file ora_DT08_9949.trc listed in the error message in the alert-log in Figure 13-19; note that the trace-file includes a process dump of the errant process)* (continued)

```
Wed Jan  8 08:26:15 1997
Errors in file /opt/apps/oracle/admin/DT08/udump/ora_DT08_23604.trc:
ORA-00600: internal error code, arguments: [729], [1593252], [space leak], [], [], [], [], []
Wed Jan  8 08:37:01 1997
```

FIGURE 13-21. *Space-leak problem*

Memory Leak

- **Symptom** Error messages in the alert-log
- **Possible reason** Oracle bug
- **Possible solution** Contact Oracle Support for a patch or a higher release that fixes the problem.

Background Processes Being Terminated

- **Symptom(s)**
  - Oracle crashes
  - Error messages in alert-log and trace-files
- **Possible reason(s)**
  - Oracle bugs
  - Process being explicitly killed by administrator (an "accident")
- **Possible solution(s)**
  - If the process has been explicitly killed, the Oracle instance just needs to be restarted. Instance (crash) recovery is performed during startup.
  - If this is an intermittent problem and cannot be easily explained, contact Oracle Support immediately.

```
Thu Jun  5 14:58:14 1997
Errors in file /opt/apps/oracle/admin/DT08/udump/ora_DT08_10384.trc:
ORA-00603: ORACLE server session terminated by fatal error
ORA-00449: background process 'LGWR' unexpectedly terminated with error 7497
ORA-07497: sdpri: cannot create trace file ''; errno = .
ORA-01092: ORACLE instance terminated. Disconnection forced
```

FIGURE 13-22. *Background process (LGWR) being abruptly terminated*

Internal Errors

- **Symptom(s)** ORA-600 error messages in alert-log and trace-files
- **Possible reason(s)**
  - Oracle bugs.
  - Abnormal critical errors in internal Oracle structures (that the end user wouldn't be able to diagnose) requiring intervention from Oracle Support/Development.
- **Possible solution(s)** Contact Oracle Support to further diagnose the issue. ORA-600s are described in detail following Figure 13-23.

```
Mon Jan  4 00:05:08 1999
Errors in file /opt/apps/oracle/admin/DT08/udump/ora_DT08_27313.trc:
ORA-00600: internal error code, arguments: [4414], [0], [0], [12221], [2], [], [], []
ORA-01092: ORACLE instance terminated. Disconnection forced
ORA-06512: at line 47

Thu Feb 11 15:22:09 1999
Errors in file /opt/apps/oracle/product/7.1.6/rdbms/log/ora_DT08_4130.trc:
ORA-00600: internal error code, arguments: [15785], [0], [], [], [], [], [], []

Fri Nov 13 09:23:27 1998
Errors in file /opt/apps/oracle/admin/DT08/bdump/p000_DT08_3321.trc:
ORA-07445: exception encountered: core dump [SIGSEGV] [Address not mapped to object]
[2147741720] [] [] []
ORA-00600: internal error code, arguments: [9999], [], [], [], [], [], [], []
```

FIGURE 13-23. *Samples of ORA-600 errors*

ORA-600 is an internal error that is generated by the Oracle kernel whenever basic sanity checks fail (for instance, when an extent is attempted to be read, that does not exist in SYS.FET$). Unlike other Oracle errors, any two ORA-600 errors may not refer to the same error condition. ORA-600s denote various internal errors. Additionally, ORA-600 errors may accompany any of the other ORA errors (for example, ORA-600 occurring along with ORA-1578 when corrupt blocks are encountered).

ORA-600s errors are usually displayed with a set of arguments in square parentheses. These arguments mean different things, depending on the actual internal error. Additionally, these arguments may mean different things for different Oracle versions. They are not documented and usually require a qualified Oracle Support analyst to decipher. Generally, the first argument provides information about the actual error (such as 1578 in the case of block corruption). The other arguments provide related relevant information (such as the block number Oracle was expecting to read and the block number actually read, in the case of block corruption). Since these errors refer to core internal structures that the end user/administrator does not have a clear understanding of, they appear as ORA-600 errors with diverse arguments to prevent the user from panicking or being confused. An example of the ORA-600 follows:

```
ORA-00600   [102344][2202][4718][][][]
```

In case the ORA-600 error does not have any arguments, that itself may be another bug and may require the following events to be set via the EVENT initialization parameter to dump the error stack and process state at the time of the error:

```
EVENT = "600 TRACE NAME ERRORSTACK, LEVEL 10"
EVENT = "600 TRACE NAME PROCESSSTATE, LEVEL 10"
```

These events may not be set dynamically at the session level, due to lack of sufficient information about which session may be causing them.

ORA-600 arguments are split across various (Oracle) kernel layers. These splits may differ between releases. Table 13-1 provides a sample list of how the error codes are bifurcated to refer to different components of the Oracle kernel. Note that these error codes often appear as the first argument for the ORA-600 errors. Accordingly, being familiar with these codes gives you a fair idea as to which component the ORA-600 is referring to, thus allowing you to examine those areas in detail. Thus, you can focus on such areas and gather as much information as possible to give a head start to Oracle Support/Development in resolving the issue. Such lists are used internally by Oracle Support/Development personnel to debug problems evidenced by various ORA-600 errors.

Layer	Code	Description
Service layer: 0000		
Layer	Code	Description
KIESCBAS	1	Notifier component
KIESDBAS	100	Debug component
KIESEBAS	300	Error component
KIESLBAS	500	Lock component
KIESMBAS	700	Memory component
KIESSBAS	1100	System state object component
KIESQBAS	1150	Enqueue component
KIESABAS	1400	Async-messages component
KIESKBAS	1700	License key component
Cache layer (Component base internal error values): 2000		
Layer	Code	Description
KIECCBAS	2100	Control-file management component
KIECMBAS	2200	Miscellaneous (SCN, etc.)
KIECHBAS	2400	Buffer hash table
KIECRBAS	2600	Redo file component
KIECFBAS	2800	Data-file component
KIECABAS	3000	Redo application component
KIECZBAS	3400	Archival/media-recovery component base
KIECLBAS	3500	Direct-path loader component base
KIECVBAS	3600	Recovery component base
KIECKBAS	3800	Compatibility segment (DBA_SEGMENTS.SEGMENT_TYPE = 'CACHE') component base
Transaction layer: 4000		
Layer	Code	Description
KIETUBAS	4000, 4100 to 4199	Transaction undo component
KIETABAS	4600	Transaction table component
KIETEBAS	5000	Transaction extent

TABLE 13-1. *The ORA-600 Error Code "Splits" Across Various Kernel Layers (Note that this list is just a sample to give you an idea of how the codes are split and may not be consistent across Oracle releases.)*

Data layer: 6000

Access layer: 8000

Control layer: 10000

User interface layer: 12000

System/platform dependent layer: 14000 (Note that different Oracle ports [across different platforms] may reuse internal error codes/arguments.)

Layer	Code	Description
KIESFBAS	14000	File component
KIESCBAS	14100	Concurrency component
KIESPBAS	14200	Process component
KIESMBAS	14500	Memory component

Security layer: 15000

Code ranges	Description
15600–15619, 15670–15679, 15700–15799, etc.	Reserved for certain components of the Parallel Query Option
15660–15669	Reserved for certain components of the job queuing facility

Loader layer: 16000

Code ranges	Description
16000–16199	Reserved for direct path

Generic: 17000

Code ranges	Description
17990–17999	Reserved for PL/SQL

Two-phase commit: 18000

Object layer: 19000 (up to 19999)

TABLE 13-1. *The ORA-600 Error Code "Splits" Across Various Kernel Layers (Note that this list is just a sample to give you an idea of how the codes are split and may not be consistent across Oracle releases)* (continued)

ORA-600 errors generally produce one or more trace-files, which provide important diagnostic information.

Prior to calling Oracle Support, it's advisable to have as much information about the error as possible, such as

- When the error occurred.
- How often does the error occur.
- What are the exact error messages/arguments (especially the first argument), each time the error occurs.
- Whether the database freezes during the error.
- Whether performance (response time/throughput) is adversely impacted during the error (if database has not frozen altogether).
- How many active jobs were running at the time of error (active sessions/ processes).
- What kind of DML/DDL statements were these jobs running.
- Whether any background/foreground process died during the error.
- Whether there is any known hardware/OS problem (a record of all OS patches may be required).
- How many trace-files were created (the trace-files may have to be sent to the Oracle Support Analyst).
- The initialization parameters in use (the *init<SID>.ora* and *config<SID>.ora* files may have to be sent, as well).

Edit repetitive error messages to be listed just once

At times, Oracle repeats the same error and subsequently continuously writes out the same error message tens and hundreds of times. These may accompany failures of certain core events such as attempts to connect to a remote database by an SNP process for refreshing a snapshot. Such failures will result in retries. Every time the SNP process retries and fails, an error message is logged in the alert-log, thus producing a series of the same error message, resulting in the size of the alert-log shooting up, possibly taking up substantial disk space and, more important, making it cumbersome to open the alert-log in the future. During such occurrences, the DBA

needs to resolve the issue and, once the issue is resolved, remove all occurrences of the error message, save a couple, so that the space wastage is avoided, and the one or two occurrences act as a placeholder to indicate that there were multiple occurrences of that specific error message at that date/time. Additionally, the DBA needs to doctor the alert-log only during periods of low activity or when nothing is expected to be written to the alert-log during the time he or she has the file open and is making the changes. In case Oracle also writes to the alert-log while the manual doctoring is being done, the most recent changes by Oracle will be overwritten and lost when the DBA saves the changes he or she has made. To reduce the possibility of this happening, the DBA may open the file and make a mental note of the line numbers that need to be truncated (for example, in the *vi* editor, the *set nu* command may be used to set line numbers on). Later when the database is undergoing low activity, the file may be edited to remove the necessary lines, noted before.

Archive and trim the alert-log once every two weeks to three months

Oracle continuously appends to the existing alert-log. However, with the passage of time and/or a high level of database activity, the alert-log may grow to a large size. Accordingly, it needs to be archived and trimmed periodically. If necessary, keep the latest archive on disk. However, the main alert-log needs to be lean while preserving an entire month's data. Excessively bulky alert-logs are cumbersome, not to mention time-consuming, to open and read. However, do not just trim off the alert-log. Always archive the previous contents. Ideally, the entire alert-log for all production instances needs to be maintained from the time of database creation to the current day, including all version upgrades and patch installations. You never know when you might need to access old database information again. Remember, the alert-log may very well be the only source of database history and provides important diagnostic information regarding the past and current health of the database. When it is required to find out the cause of a specific error or bug, either you or Oracle Support analysts may require specific portions of the alert-log. Thus, archiving it prior to trimming may allow such relevant portions to be accessible. Also, try not to trim the alert-log too frequently. Retain at least two weeks' worth of log info on disk. This will prevent excessive delays when having to access recent log information. Since the information is available online, the time to restore from offline media and uncompress it (if it was compressed prior to storing) can be avoided. One month is a fairly good period for most databases. For low-to-medium activity databases, up to three months of log info can be maintained online.

Also, alert-log trimming may be accomplished by cutting off the lines in the top portion of the file and leaving just the bottom 1,000 (or so) lines in the file (Chapter 19 provides a script to do that periodically). This file can be trimmed while the database is up and running. However, it is not recommended to directly delete this file, expecting Oracle to re-create it. Generally, Oracle tends to write to it via a pointer to that specific file. This pointer is obtained at startup via the following algorithm:

```
if <BACKGROUND_DUMP_DEST>/alert<SID>.log is present
then
   get pointer to existing <BACKGROUND_DUMP_DEST>/alert<SID>.log;
else
   create new <BACKGROUND_DUMP_DEST>/alert<SID>.log
   get pointer to new <BACKGROUND_DUMP_DEST>/alert<SID>.log;
endif
```

When the file is removed while Oracle is still up and running, Oracle continues to write to that file pointer. I have seen situations in the past (on more than one platform) where I have removed the file, due to the file size being too big. I would then do a *"df -k ."* on the BACKGROUND_DUMP_DEST directory to see whether space has been released. I would find that it had. Then after a few minutes, I would check to see whether Oracle had created a new alert-log. I observed that it hadn't. I would then do a *"df -k ."* again only to see that the space freed up previously had been taken up again (it seemed that, once Oracle started writing to the file pointer representing the alert-log and flushed the output, the freed-up space was occupied again). Subsequent iterations of this command after a few hours would show that space was being used up in that directory and the file was not even visible or accessible to me any more. The Oracle Support analyst I called up offered the solution that I would need to bounce the database to force a new alert-log to be created, which I could (once again) access. He also suggested that henceforth, rather than deleting the file, I use commands such as *cut* (in UNIX) or open the file in an editor and trim it manually. That will still keep the file intact and allow Oracle to access it without problems. Also, the file will be visible and accessible without Oracle continuing to write to a phantom file and taking up disk space. Thus, the only option I had was to bounce the database, an operation I scheduled for that night. The space was freed up once again at that point, and a brand new alert-log was created in that directory. In 24×7 sites, bouncing the database is a rare occurrence (if it is ever done). Accordingly, taking small precautions such as not deleting the alert-log directory go a long way in maintaining availability.

In the case of trace-files also, ensure that you delete unwanted ones, back up the required ones (prior to deleting them), and keep the trace directories as clean as possible. Also, keep on disk all the trace-files that are currently being debugged/diagnosed.

Trace-Files

Trace-files are created by Oracle whenever an abnormal event is encountered. Trace-files often accompany error messages in the alert-log. The general idea is that the alert-log would contain a summary (a few lines) of the erroneous event and the accompanying trace-file(s) would have detailed information about the event (if the event is significant enough to merit detailed information).

Know what to look for in a trace-file

A trace-file contains the following:

- Memory dumps optionally consisting of the SGA, PGA, and/or upper-stack contents
- A call stack trace
- Addresses of data blocks (dbas) affected by the error

One of the first things to look for is the dba of any blocks that are suspected to be affected by the error resulting in the trace-file. The dbas referred to within the trace-files can be decoded to point to a specific data-file and a block within the data-file. This block may encompass a table, an index, a rollback, or a temporary or bootstrap segment. Alternatively, besides data-files, it may also point to an online redo-log or control-file. Look for the redo thread number and the rba (redo byte address) mentioned in the trace-file (rbas are explained in Chapter 9). Prima facie, you may attempt to use the dbas provided in the trace-files to try to identify the afflicted areas and, once they are identified, to pinpoint the segments afflicted. The following steps allow you to identify whether the error refers to a data-file and, if so, to detect the segment that caused the error.

1. Locate the dbas listed in the trace-file. Figure 13-24 highlights certain dbas in a sample trace-file.

```
oradbx

oradbx: Release 7.1.6.2.1 - Production on Fri Jul  2 17:21:11 1999
Copyright (c) Oracle Corporation 1979, 1994.  All rights reserved.
Type 'help' for help.

(oradbx) help
help                    - print help information
show                    - show status
debug <pid>             - debug process
dump SGA                - dump SGA
dump PGA                - dump PGA
dump stack              - dump call stack
dump core               - dump core without crashing process
dump level 0            - dump error buffer
dump level 1            - level 0 + call stack
dump level 2            - level 1 + process state objects
dump level 3            - level 2 + context area
dump system 1           - brief system states dump
dump system 2           - full system states dump
dump ipc                - dump ipc information
dump controlfile #      - dump control file at level #
dump datafile #         - dump data file header at level #
dump procstat           - dump process statistics
event <event-trace>     - turn on event trace
unlimit trace           - unlimit the size of trace file
exit                    - exit this program
!                       - shell escape
```

FIGURE 13-24. *Sample trace-file highlighting dbas*

2. Use DBMS_UTILITY.DATA_BLOCK_ADDRESS_FILE and DBMS_UTILITY.DATA_BLOCK_ADDRESS_BLOCK to resolve each dba and detect the data-file and block to which it belongs. An example of their usage is provided here:

```
SQL> EXEC DBMS_UTILITY.DATA_BLOCK_ADDRESS_FILE(<dba>);
SQL> EXEC DBMS_UTILITY.DATA_BLOCK_ADDRESS_BLOCK(<dba>);
```

3. Identify which segment the dba belongs to via the following query (<fil-number> and <blk-number> are the file and block numbers identified previously):

```
SQL> SELECT segment_name, segment_type FROM dba_extents
      WHERE file_id = <fil-number>
        AND <blk-number> BETWEEN block_id AND block_id + (blocks-1);
```

4. If the query does not retrieve any rows, then the error may possibly be elsewhere and may require intervention from Oracle Support for a speedy and effective resolution.

5. Alternatively, if any of the dbas do not prove very helpful, then one may also scan for the object ID of the afflicted segment. The object ID is usually listed in the trace-files in hexadecimal. The sample trace-file that follows provides the object ID (object ID specific details are printed in bold):

```
buffer dba: 0x32005ed0 inc: 0x00000024 seq: 0x0000004d
       ver: 1 type: 6=trans data
Block header dump: dba: 0x46002db0
Object id on Block? Y
seg/obj: 0x4430  csc: 0x1c0.4c604f0  itc: 2  flg: -  typ: 1 - DATA
     fsl: 0  fnx: 0x0
 Itl           Xid                  Uba              Flag  Lck         Scn/Fsc
0x01   0x0003.03e.00004787  0x08500fdc.0078.3d  C-U-    0  scn 0x01c0.03c5f055
0x02   0x0003.05b.000088c1  0x08500fdb.0078.15  C U     0  scn 0x01c0.03c5f055
```

Once converted to decimal (via a scientific calculator), the actual segment name may be obtained via the following query:

```
SQL> SELECT object_type, object_name FROM dba_objects
     WHERE object_id = <obj_ID_in_decimal>;
```

Such segments (the ones identified via the preceding steps) may be corrupt and may require repair. Alternatively, there could be corruption in the file header or in memory causing an internal sanity-check failure, resulting in the error. If it is determined that the erroneous dba does not refer to any data-file and there are other block addresses and/or error messages that point to other files such as redo-logs or control-files or any file headers (including data-files), then these files may need to be examined more closely. That can be achieved by dumping them to other (new) trace-files via the ALTER SESSION SET EVENTS IMMEDIATE command. Chapter 6 in the *Oracle8 Backup and Recovery Handbook* from Oracle Press provides instructions on dumping suspect blocks, file headers, control-files, and redo-logs. Again, do not set any events within the database without the explicit recommendation of an Oracle Support analyst. Certain events are known to crash the instance, if set inappropriately.

Know how to identify trace-files belonging to a specific event/session

Trace-file names follow a consistent pattern so that they can be easily reconciled with the OS process/Oracle session that generated them. The trace-file name for background processes usually has the following format on UNIX: *<BGP_Name>_<SID>_<UNIX_PID>,* where *<BGP_Name>* is the name of the background process such as DBWR or SMON, *<SID>* is the value of the ORACLE_SID environment variable, and *<UNIX_PID>* is the OS process ID for that background process. Foreground processes on UNIX cause trace-files with the following filename format to be generated: *ora_<SID>_<UNIX_PID>.trc.* The *<UNIX_PID>* can be verified by checking the output of the *ps -ef* command. On Windows NT, the trace-file names for threads constituting background processes have the following format: *<SID><BGP_Name>.trc,* where *<SID>* is the value of ORACLE_SID (can be obtained from the ORACLE_SID Registry entry) and *<BGP_Name>* is the actual name of the thread constituting the background process (this name can be determined from the NAME column in the *v$bgprocess* dynamic view). On Windows NT, names of trace-files for foreground processes have the following form: *ORA00<nnn>.trc,* where *<nnn>* refers to the decimal value in the SPID column in the *v$process* dynamic view. The SPID can be derived in hex as follows:

```
SQL> SELECT spid FROM v$process
      WHERE username = '<Oracle username generating the trace-file>';
```

Once the hex value of the SPID is obtained, it can be converted to decimal using a scientific calculator (such as the one on your Windows desktop). This decimal value can be used to figure out the trace-file name generated. Usually, more than one trace-file gets generated referring to a specific event. These trace-files are considered to be within "a set". Each trace-file within a set provides additional information on the event causing the error, allowing better diagnosis of the issue. The trace-files composing a set can be identified by performing an *ls -lt* (which orders the directory listing based on the date/time stamp on each file). All the files having the same date/time stamp are considered to be part of the same set.

Know what causes trace-files to be generated

Trace-files are written by a special background process called TRWR (the trace writer). Its existence can be verified via the following query:

```
SQL> SELECT name, description FROM v$bgprocess;
NAME  DESCRIPTION
----- ------------------------------------------------------------
PMON  process cleanup
. . .
TRWR  trace writer process
DBWR  db writer process
ARCH  Archival
LGWR  Redo etc.
. . .
```

Trace-files can be produced for background (DBWR, SMON, PMON) as well as foreground server processes. Background server processes generally cause a trace-file to be produced only when exceptions are encountered. Sometimes, trace-files may be incomplete, so they may not have necessary information, thus requiring you to re-create the error-generating situation, with the intention of generating more complete trace-files. Specific events at different levels can be set within the database (via the initialization parameter EVENT) or via the ALTER SESSION command to produce detailed trace-files. A foreground process could cause a trace-file to be produced when certain exceptions are encountered, as well as when tracing is enabled explicitly (either at the session level or the database level). Tracing for a specific session can be enabled via the ALTER SESSION SET SQL_TRACE TRUE command, whereas it can be enabled at the database level by setting the initialization parameter SQL_TRACE to TRUE. Different tools/languages may require different commands to be used for enabling SQL_TRACE at the session level. TIMED_STATISTICS may have to be enabled to produce a meaningful trace (TIMED_STATISTICS is a dynamic initialization parameter, meaning it can be enabled either by setting it to TRUE in the initialization parameter file or via the ALTER SYSTEM command). Trace-files are produced for background processes in the directory specified by the BACKGROUND_DUMP_DEST initialization parameter, whereas they are produced for foreground processes in the directory specified by the initialization parameter USER_DUMP_DEST.

Let's examine a few of the commonly encountered errors that cause trace-files to be produced. Again, this list is not comprehensive and only provides a sample of trace-files as an exercise in interpreting them and trying to debug the problem. Such exercises should be undertaken purely from a diagnostic perspective to resolve the issue, whenever possible. It's highly advisable to involve Oracle Support personnel, when in doubt (definitely prior to making any changes to your production environment).

Timeout Waiting for Space Management Resource

- **Symptom(s)** Errors in the alert-log and related trace-file sets (ORA-1575: timeout waiting for space management resource)
- **Possible reason(s)**
  - Oracle bug.
  - SMON being excessively busy due to space management activity. This is more pronounced in OPS environments, when SMON has to simultaneously keep up with space management in all participating nodes.
- **Possible solution(s)** Outlined under "Database/Session Hanging"

Memory/Space Leaks

- **Symptom(s)**
  - Error messages in the alert-log and related trace-file sets (ORA-600s with arguments of [SPACE LEAK]).
  - Per-process memory (as monitored from the OS) constantly growing and not being released. Swapping/excessive paging observed. At times, the machine may panic and shut down due to all available swap space being used up.
- **Possible reason(s)** Oracle bug.
- **Possible solution(s)**
  - Identification of problem-causing component and application of necessary Oracle patches.

- Downgrading to a stable version may be necessary, if patches are not readily available.

Database/Session Crashes

- **Symptom(s)**
  - Instance crashes
  - Session aborts consistently for no apparent reason
- **Possible reason(s)**
  - Oracle bug.
  - Hardware/OS faults.
  - Oracle utilities linked in single-task being run in two-task environment, inadvertently poking Oracle kernel code.
  - Inappropriate events set via the EVENT initialization parameter or setting certain underscore (undocumented) parameters incorrectly.
  - User/administrative accidents (a DBA accidentally killing a background process or deleting a control-file).
  - Database corruption.
  - Could happen during recovery if bad redo is being used during roll-forward. Bad redo from the primary database could also cause the standby database instance to crash.
- **Possible solution(s)** Varies depending on reason. This and other chapters in this book address each of the preceding reasons except the last. In case the standby database instance crashes due to bad redo from the primary database, the redo generated at the primary site needs to be examined. This can be achieved by dumping the online redo-log files. The ALTER SYSTEM command can be used to achieve this. The following pieces of code illustrate its usage:

```
SQL> ALTER SYSTEM DUMP LOGFILE <log_file_to_be_dumped>;
```

This command supports multiple options such as starting and ending dba values, starting and ending rba values, and starting and ending redo-write time stamp. These options allow more flexibility during the redo dump. For instance, if a related trace-file in the set reveals a dba of a segment suspected of causing the instance crash (for example, due to a data-dictionary segment being corrupt), this dba may be used to specify the start and end dba (the same value) while performing a redo dump concerning only changes made to this dba. The following code sample illustrates how:

```
/* first get the file and block numbers for that dba */
SQL> EXEC DBMS_UTILITY.DATA_BLOCK_ADDRESS_FILE(<dba_value_in_decimal>);
SQL> EXEC DBMS_UTILITY.DATA_BLOCK_ADDRESS_BLOCK(<dba_value_in_decimal>);

/* dump each online redo-log specifying the file/block numbers for that dba */
SQL> ALTER SYSTEM DUMP LOGFILE '/u1/oradata/TST4/redog1f1.ora'
    DBA MIN <fil_number>.<blk_number>
    DBA MAX <fil_number>.<blk_number>;
```

Database Corruption

- **Symptom(s)**
  - Oracle errors in the alert-log and accompanying trace-files (ORA-1578: ORACLE data block corrupted (file # 7, block # 59882); ORA-600s with first argument being [1578], etc.)
  - Oracle errors on user screen while issuing DML statements
- **Possible reason(s)** Please refer to Chapter 14.
- **Possible solution(s)** Please refer to Chapter 14.

Database/Session Hanging

- **Symptom(s)**
  - The database appears to be frozen or hanging (that is, there is no response from the database or any active sessions connected). Database hangs seem to be more frequent in OPS environments, where one or more instances seem to be frozen, while others seem operational.
  - One (or more) specific session(s) seems to be stuck.
- **Possible reason(s)**

- Oracle bug.
- Internal error (such as timeouts while waiting for space-management resources).
- The archive-log destination directory is full (no free space).
- Sometimes, certain resource-intensive tasks can cause poor performance and make the database appear to be frozen (such as an excessive number of locks or having the DELETE CASCADE option enabled and deleting a master row in a schema with many child tables or child tables with a large number of dependent rows). It is very important to ensure that it is genuinely a database hang and not just slow performance.
- Oracle process priorities have been changed at the OS level (via *nice, renice,* etc.).
- Oracle files have been created under unsupported configurations such as on NFS-mounted volumes.
- Certain OS/hardware errors.

- **Possible solution(s)**
  - It is possible that a *shutdown abort* followed by a *startup* may resolve this in the short term. However, the root cause responsible for the hanging needs to be identified and addressed. Otherwise, it may recur, causing downtime each time.
  - Resolution of database hanging issues generally requires intervention from Oracle Support. Gather as much information as possible, prior to calling them. For instance, collect all error messages generated (ORA-600s with all arguments, ORA-1575, etc.) in the alert-log and all related trace-file sets. Get system-state dumps (at least two) and examine the dumps. A system-state dump provides information on the various memory structures present during the freeze. A system-state dump may be taken as follows:

```
SQL> ALTER SESSION SET EVENTS 'IMMEDIATE TRACE NAME SYSTEMSTATE LEVEL 10';
```

```
Dump file /opt/apps/oracle/admin/DT08/udump/ora_DT08_5126.trc
Oracle8 Enterprise Edition Release 8.0.5.1.0 - Production
PL/SQL Release 8.0.5.1.0 - Production
ORACLE_HOME = /opt/apps/oracle/product/8.0.5
System name:    zurich
Node name:      zurich
Release:        4.0
Instance name: DT08
Redo thread mounted by this instance: 1
Oracle process number: 9
Unix process pid: 5126, image: oracleDT08

*** 1999.07.01.23.43.00.000
*** SESSION ID:(8.22) 1999.07.01.23.43.00.000
==================================================
SYSTEM STATE
------------
System global information:
     Processes: base 23f22508, size 200, cleanup 23f22af0
     Allocation: free sessions 23f4c0b8, free calls 23fbab7c
     Control alloc errors: 0 (process), 0 (session), 0 (call)
     System statistics:
          0         49 logons cumulative
          0          8 logons current
          0        556 opened cursors cumulative
          0          1 opened cursors current
          0          0 user commits
          0          0 user rollbacks
          0      11312 recursive calls
0          0 DBWR skip hot writes
0          0 DBWR checkpoint buffers written
0          0 DBWR transaction table writes
0          0 DBWR undo block writes
0          0 DBWR checkpoint write requests
0          0 DBWR incr. ckpt. write requests
0          0 DBWR revisited being-written buffer
0          0 DBWR timeouts
```

FIGURE 13-25. *Sample portions of a system-state dump*

The dump files created are usually large in size, and it may be time-consuming to spot and extract necessary error information. Figure 13-25 provides a sample listing of a system-state dump.

```
0          0 DBWR make free requests
0          0 DBWR free buffers found
0          0 DBWR lru scans
0          0 DBWR summed scan depth
0          0 DBWR buffers scanned
0          0 DBWR checkpoints
0          0 DBWR Flush object cross instance calls
        0          0 DBWR Flush object call found no dirty buffers
0 DBWR cross instance writes
------------ other statistics ------------
PROCESS 1:
----------------------------------------
  SO: 23f227fc, type: 1, owner: 0, flag: INIT/-/-/0x00
  (process) Oracle pid=1, calls cur/top: 0/0, flag: (10) PSEUDO
            int error: 0, call error: 0, sess error: 0, txn error 0
  (post info) last post received: 0 0 0
              last post received-location: No post
              last process to post me: none
(latch info) wait_event=0 bits=0
    O/S info: user: , term: , ospid:
    OSD pid info: Unix process pid: 0, image:
PROCESS 2:
----------------------------------------
(latch info) wait_event=0 bits=0
    O/S info: user: oracle, term: ?, ospid: 1980
    OSD pid info: Unix process pid: 1980, image: ora_pmon_DT08
    ----------------------------------------
waiting for 'pmon timer' seq=1526 wait_time=0
                duration=12c, =0, =0
    ----------------------------------------
    SO: 23fba624, type: 2, owner: 23f22af0, flag: INIT/-/-/0x00
    (call) sess: cur 23f4772c, rec 0, usr 23f4772c; depth: 0
----------- other process info -----------
NO DETACHED BRANCHES.END OF SYSTEM STATE
```

FIGURE 13-25. *Sample portions of a system-state dump* (continued)

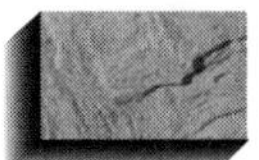

NOTE
Do not take system-state dumps based on a specific event code set in the initialization parameter file, such as forcing a system-state dump to occur during a specific error. For example, setting the following EVENT in the initialization parameter file during database startup will cause Oracle to generate a system-state dump, whenever the error ORA-1575 occurs:

EVENT = "1575 TRACE NAME SYSTEMSTATE FOREVER, LEVEL 10"

However, this may cause the instance to crash while generating the system-state dump during the error. System-state dumps are only to be taken when a problem is evidenced (such as the database hanging) via the ALTER SESSION SET EVENTS IMMEDIATE command, unless otherwise specified by Oracle Support.

If operating in OPS mode, gather system-state dumps of all instances (since any node may be causing the database to hang). Also for OPS, get the lock-manager dump for all instances at the time of the hang. A lock-manager dump may be produced as follows:

```
SQL> ALTER SESSION SET EVENTS 'IMMEDIATE TRACE NAME LOCKS LEVEL 5';
```

The LEVEL may be kept small initially to limit the size of the dumps produced. If no useful information is extracted, however, the LEVEL may be progressively increased until some meaningful data is observed.

Once the information is gathered, you may also make an attempt to diagnose the erroneous situation. For instance, compare the system-state and lock-manager dumps to see whether internal processes/threads seem to be deadlocking against each other or, in the case of OPS, one instance is perpetually waiting for a resource held by another instance, rather than timing out (possibly due to a bug). Also in OPS, see whether excessive space-management routines are being performed by SMON. A dump of the row cache (the memory structure holding information regarding the data dictionary in the SGA) for all instances may reveal some useful information. A row-cache dump can be attained as follows:

```
SQL> ALTER SESSION SET EVENTS 'IMMEDIATE TRACE NAME ROW_CACHE LEVEL 5';
```

If excessive space management seems suspect (ORA-1575 errors observed just prior to the hangs), it may be useful to disable SMON on all nodes, except one (the primary node). Check with your Oracle Support analyst for details on achieving this.

When a session appears to be hanging, use your OS-specific tool to trace the system calls that are currently being made by the session. For instance, tools such as *truss, glance, trace,* and *par.* help in diagnosing whether the session is waiting on an I/O-related call or just sleeping. The following example uses *truss* on an NCR UNIX platform (the <UNIX_PID> is the OS process ID obtained via *ps -ef*):

```
$ truss -o <output_file> -p <UNIX_PID>
```

The following example uses *par* on a Silicon Graphics UNIX environment to produce output similar to the one produced by *truss:*

```
% par -s -i -SS -o <output_file> <executable>
```

The *truss* command produces output similar to Figure 13-26.

```
zurich:/opt/apps/oracle/admin/DT03/#DT03> truss -p 9014
semop(16385, 0x08046BF8, 1)      (sleeping...)
    Received signal #14, SIGALRM, in semop() [caught]
semop(16385, 0x08046BF8, 1)                         Err#91 ERESTART
sigprocmask(SIG_UNBLOCK, 0x080469A8, 0x08046998) = 0
setcontext(0x085C7050)
times(0x08046550)                                   = 891845623
poll(0x00000000, 0, 10)                             = 0
times(0x080466E0)                                   = 891845626
getcontext(0x085C7050)
times(0x080461D8)                                   = 891845640
lseek(7, 9617408, 0)                                = 9617408
read(7, "0601\0\09604\001 i m\0\0".., 40960)        = 40960
times(0x080461D8)                                   = 891845676
getcontext(0x085C7050)
setitimer(0, 134507512, 0)                          = 0
semop(16385, 0x08046BF8, 1)      (sleeping...)
```

FIGURE 13-26. *Sample* truss output

Note that in order to *truss* a process, you need to be the owner of the process or to have superuser privileges at the OS level.

Also, run a *ps -ef* command on UNIX to check whether the process has somehow become an orphan or a zombie process, due to its parent or the process itself getting killed. On Windows NT, you could use the TASK-LIST to check the status of the program (whether it's *not responding*). Also, a process dump on the errant session may be useful. A process dump provides information on the memory structures controlled by the session. A process dump may be taken via *oradebug* (or *oradbx* in versions prior to 7.3.*x*) or via the following command:

```
SQL> ALTER SESSION SET EVENTS 'IMMEDIATE TRACE NAME
     PROCESSSTATE LEVEL <pid_from_v$process>';
```

Process dumps are created in the directory specified by the USER_DUMP_DEST initialization parameter.

If the database has been frozen due to lack of adequate space in the archive-log destination directory, make free space available in that directory (see Chapter 9 for considerations while freeing the space and methods available to do so).

If the database merely appears to be hanging due to slow performance, the reason for such an effect needs to be determined and eliminated (such as terminating the offending session that is causing the locking problem or disabling the DELETE CASCADE clauses on tables with a large number of dependent rows and deleting the children first with optimized SQL statements, or, alternatively, creating all necessary foreign keys to allow efficient DELETE CASCADEs without the entire parent tables being locked). In other words, adequate performance tuning needs to be done to prevent database performance from being misunderstood as "hanging." The following issues ought to be well-understood, prior to resolving the problem:

- What is the capacity of the existing hardware and software components?
- Are more resources than available being gobbled up by existing users and jobs?
- Can the hanging be reproduced—during certain hours of the day, with a certain number of users, certain jobs, or ad hoc statements running? Or is it intermittent or totally random?
- What is the scope of the hanging? Do only the large jobs appear to be hanging or do even the tiniest statements appear not to be responding?
- How long does the hanging last?
- Can the hanging be traced to a lack of a specific resource? Check I/O, memory, and CPU utilization (in that order) via OS commands.
- Does the hanging occur only when a specific option is used (parallel query, remote database access/use of snapshots, and so on)?

- Is there any data-dictionary corruption (corruption in a SYS-owned cluster such as C_TS# or a table such as FET$)?
- Are you using non-default locking mechanisms, such as specifying different values for the initialization parameters ROW_LOCKING and SERIALIZABLE?

The following v$ dynamic views need to be queried to determine the cause of the waits: *v$session_wait, v$waitstat, v$system_event, v$sysstat, v$sesstat, v$latch, v$latchholder*, etc. Chapter 19 provides scripts using these views to narrow down the cause of the problem. UTLBSTAT/UTLESTAT and SQL_TRACE/TKPROF (with the EXPLAIN PLAN option) ought to be used to understand the state of the database and specific application statements at the time of the hanging.

If certain Oracle process priorities have been changed, they need to be reset back. It is highly advisable not to tamper with Oracle process priorities or with any process on the database server (both Oracle and non-Oracle processes).

Do not place any Oracle files (especially data-files, redo-logs, and control-files) on NFS-mounted partitions. If that has already been done, move all such files to non-NFS file systems (raw, UFS, VxFS, xFS, and so on).

Tracing

A fact worth mentioning here is that the preceding discussion of trace-files refers either to trace-files generated automatically by background and foreground processes during exceptions encountered or to ones generated by foreground processes due to SQL_TRACE being enabled. Other situations may call for explicit tracing, such as to debug a specific problem. Tracing allows the internal sequence of operations followed in the execution of a product to be written out to a flat file. This flat file can then be examined for possible causes of errors and subsequently rectified.

Let's take a look at how certain critical Oracle products support tracing. Also, a provision for tracing needs to be created in all in-house application programs developed (possibly based on a parameter requesting trace to be enabled).

SQL*Net and Net8 Tracing

With Oracle's emphasis on the Network Computing Architecture, there are at least three tiers involved (client tier, application (middle) tier, and database (back-end) tier. While connecting to the database either from a middle tier or directly from a client, there may be network-related errors. Resolving them may require SQL*Net/Net8 tracing. Tracing within SQL*Net/Net8 can be initiated for different components. Henceforth, this chapter will refer to tracing that can be done via both SQL*Net and Net8 as SQL*Net tracing, whereas new tracing features provided within Net8 will be referred to as Net8 tracing.

SQL*Net tracing can be set at different levels, depending on the verbosity required. As a rule of thumb, start with the lowest level. Look at the trace data generated. If it's not detailed enough, you may set tracing at a higher level. Alternatively, if you are looking for specific trace data generated only by higher trace levels or an Oracle Support Analyst has required you to specify a higher level, then you may start with that level. Following are the levels supported:

- 0 or no tracing (can also be specified as OFF)
- 4 or basic tracing (can also be specified as USER)
- 10 or administrative tracing (can also be specified as ADMIN)
- 16 or detailed tracing required by Oracle Support for debugging problems (can also be specified as SUPPORT)

Note that tracing has to be enabled with caution, since it may result in performance degradation. The reason for the performance degradation is the additional work the component has to perform to generate and write out the trace information resulting in additional resource consumption (CPU, I/O). If the I/O channels and CPUs are already being taxed heavily or even saturated, tracing may result in substantial performance degradation, especially with higher tracing levels (such as 16) due to data regarding many low-level calls having to be written to the trace-file. The higher the tracing level, the higher the chances of performance being impacted. Additionally, setting tracing on for certain components would mean having to reset (bounce) the component, thus causing a disruption (albeit, a very short one) in service. Moreover, this disruption would need to occur at least twice—once to enable tracing and then to disable it; sometimes, you may have to experiment with different levels, thus causing at least two disruptions for each level. This problem wouldn't necessarily be resolved by proactively setting the highest level either, because, in addition to the higher performance overhead mentioned earlier, a higher trace level may produce very big trace-files—files that are sometimes unusable due to the vast amount of data captured (it becomes difficult to spot the needle in the haystack of data). Hence, it is desirable to start with a lower level and then move up the levels, if necessary. So how do you minimize impact to availability? A possible solution is to refrain from enabling tracing for components that require a bounce. Instead, always evaluate whether tracing can be enabled for components that don't have to be bounced. For instance, if your Support Analyst wants you to set a trace level for the database listener to debug some network-related problems, ask him or her whether you could instead enable client-level tracing (for a few of the clients that connect to the database). If the listener indeed needs tracing, then consider enabling tracing via the TRACE command of the listener-control utility (*lsnrctl*), rather than bouncing it. In other words, tracing should be enabled with a lot of forethought and for only as much time as necessary to gain information about a specific problem.

Now, let's take a peek at the SQL*Net and newer Net8 components that support tracing.

Listener Tracing

Listener tracing is initiated via the parameter TRACE_LEVEL_<listener-name> in the listener configuration file (*listener.ora*). This parameter sets the verbosity required (0, 16, and so forth). The default value for <listener-name> is LISTENER. The listener trace information is written to a log file specified by the *listener.ora* parameters TRACE_DIRECTORY_<listener-name> and TRACE_FILE_<listener-name>, which default to *$ORACLE_HOME/net80/trace* (or *$ORACLE_HOME/network/trace,* if SQL*Net is being used) and *<listener-name>.TRC,* respectively. However, these parameters won't take effect until the listener has been bounced. As mentioned earlier, in case the listener cannot be bounced, then tracing needs to be initiated via the TRACE command within the *lsnrctl* utility.

Also note that in addition to tracing, a regular log file is maintained by the listener. The location for this log file is determined by LOG_DIRECTORY_<listener-name> and LOG_ FILE_<listener-name> parameters, defaulting to *$ORACLE_HOME/net80/log* and *<listener-name>.LOG,* respectively.) The log file itself contains quite a bit of information and may provide useful diagnostic information in case a network problem is suspected. In case the information in the log file is not adequate, however, then tracing may be turned on. And once the problem is resolved, tracing needs to be disabled. Figures 13-27 and 13-28 provide a sample output of listener logging and tracing.

```
TNSLSNR for Intel SVR4 UNIX: Version 8.0.5.0.0 - Production on 23-MAY-99 12:11:26

(c) Copyright 1997 Oracle Corporation.  All rights reserved.

System parameter file is /var/opt/oracle/listener.ora
Log messages written to /opt/apps/oracle/product/8.0.5.0/network/log/listener.log

Listening on: (ADDRESS=(PROTOCOL=ipc)(DEV=6)(KEY=DT08))
Listening on: (ADDRESS=(PROTOCOL=ipc)(DEV=10)(KEY=PNPKEY))
Listening on: (ADDRESS=(PROTOCOL=tcp)(DEV=11)(HOST=10.212.56.225)(PORT=1527))
TIMESTAMP * CONNECT DATA [* PROTOCOL INFO] * EVENT [* SID] * RETURN CODE
23-MAY-99 12:11:25 * (CONNECT_DATA=(SID=DT08)(GLOBAL_NAME=DT08.world)(CID=(PROGRAM=)(HOST=zurich)
(USER=oracle))) * (ADDRESS=(PROTOCOL=tcp)(HOST=10.212.56.225)(PORT=1706))
* establish * DT08 * 0
23-MAY-99 12:11:27 *
(CONNECT_DATA=(CID=(PROGRAM=)(HOST=zurich)(USER=oracle))(COMMAND=status)(ARGUMENTS=64)
(SERVICE=LISTENER)(VERSION=134238208)) * status * 0
23-MAY-99 12:11:34 *
(CONNECT_DATA=(CID=(PROGRAM=)(HOST=zurich)(USER=oracle))(COMMAND=stop)(ARGUMENTS=64)
(SERVICE=LISTENER)(VERSION=134238208)) * stop * 0
```

FIGURE 13-27. *Listener log file sample output*

```
TNSLSNR for Intel SVR4 UNIX: Version 8.0.5.0.0 - Production on 02-JUL-99 15:17:16

(c) Copyright 1997 Oracle Corporation.  All rights reserved.

--- TRACE CONFIGURATION INFORMATION FOLLOWS ---
New trace stream is "/opt/apps/oracle/product/8.0.5.0/network/trace/listener.trc"
New trace level is 10
--- TRACE CONFIGURATION INFORMATION ENDS ---
tnslsnr: Resolved "CONNECT_TIMEOUT_LISTENER" to: 0
tnslsnr: Resolved "STARTUP_WAIT_TIME_LISTENER" to: 0
nsdo: cid=5, opcode=67, *bl=45, *what=10, uflgs=0x0, cflgs=0x3
nscon: sending NSPTRF packet
nspsend: 57 bytes to transport
nsevwait: 3 registered connection(s)
nsevwait: 1 added to NT list for 0x8
nttcnr: waiting to accept a connection.
nttvlser: entry
nttvlser: valid node check on incoming node 10.200.4.227
nttvlser: Accepted Entry: 10.200.4.227
nscon: doing connect handshake...
nscon: recving a packet
nsprecv: 231 bytes from leftover
nscon: got 173 bytes connect data
nsevwait: 1 newly-posted event(s)
nsevfnt: cxd: 0x83f1300 stage 4: NT events set:
        WRITE
nsevfnt: cxd: 0x83f1300 stage 4: NS events set:
       OUTGOING CALL COMPLETE
nsevdansw: at STAGE 4
nsevdansw: exit
```

FIGURE 13-28. *Listener trace-file sample output (trace level = 10)*

Usually, depending on the number of connection requests that come in, both the log file and the trace-file (if tracing is enabled) grow very fast. There is always a potential threat that the drive on which these files reside may get full quite fast. Accordingly, these files may have to be truncated periodically (after backing up the log and trace information, if necessary; usually, it's not necessary to back up the listener log or trace information. However, if a recurring problem is suspected, then backing up these files prior to truncation would be advisable). Do not physically remove these files. For instance, commands similar to the ones that follow need to be utilized (the commands provided run under UNIX):

```
$ cat /dev/null > $ORACLE_HOME/net80/log/listener.log
$ cat /dev/null > $ORACLE_HOME/net80/trace/listener.trc
```

Removing either of these files physically would cause the listener to continue writing to these files (thus filling up the destination drive), since it still holds the file pointers, in spite of their being removed externally. And, since you have already removed the files, you do not see an external entry for them and cannot delete them again. Accordingly, you can only stand by and watch helplessly as the directories get full. The only way this can be resolved is by bouncing the listener (causing a service disruption). Once the listener is bounced, it will re-create those files again and they will be visible externally, as usual.

Server or Client Packet Tracing

SQL*Net/Net8 packet tracing may be initiated either on the server (for all clients) or on a specific client that's connecting to the server (if a problem is noticed only for that client). Setting packet tracing on at the server level can be achieved via the parameters TRACE_LEVEL_SERVER to set the trace level, TRACE_DIRECTORY_SERVER to set the destination directory for the trace-file, and TRACE_FILE_SERVER to set the trace-file name in the *sqlnet.ora* configuration file (you may have to create this file, if it doesn't already exist on the server). The trace level needs to be set to 16 to produce packet traces (lower levels provide trace information; however, packet contents are not written to the trace-files). Similarly, the parameters TRACE_LEVEL_CLIENT, TRACE_DIRECTORY_CLIENT, and TRACE_FILE_CLIENT within *sqlnet.ora* on the client may be set to control tracing on the client. Also, the parameter TRACE_UNIQUE_CLIENT can be used to generate trace-files with distinct names on the client for every new process, preventing the existing files from being overwritten. Distinct trace-file names are created either by appending a two-digit hexadecimal number or the process ID (depending on the platform) to the end of the trace-file name specified by TRACE_FILE_CLIENT. When TRACE_UNIQUE_CLIENT needs to be enabled, it's advisable to keep TRACE_FILE_CLIENT to four characters or less (by default, it's six ["CLIENT"] on certain platforms) to allow unique files to be created without problems (since the maximum filename size for client trace-files is six, on certain platforms).

These parameters allow tracing of connections initiated via both dedicated server processes and dispatcher (MTS) processes. If your site happens to be using a version of Oracle7 prior to v7.1.3, then an event in the initialization parameter file needs to be set to perform tracing of MTS connections:

```
EVENT = "10248 TRACE NAME CONTEXT FOREVER, LEVEL 10"
```

Since trace-files can be large in size, it may be necessary to slice them up (via *cut* in UNIX) to easily open and read them. Alternatively, you may search for and write out specific patterns of information to a different file (via the redirection operator) and read the new files.

Oracle Names

Oracle Names supports the following parameters to control tracing: NAMES.TRACE_FILE to set the trace-file name (by default, it is set to NAMES.TRC), NAMES.TRACE_DIRECTORY to set the name of the directory where the trace-file is to be created, NAMES.TRACE_LEVEL to set the trace level (supports values of 0/OFF, 4/USER, 10/ADMIN; by default it is OFF), and NAMES.TRACE_UNIQUE to allow distinct trace-files to coexist each time a new process is initiated. Each of these parameters needs to be set within the NAMES.ORA configuration file and will require the names server to be bounced. Alternatively, for high-availability environments, the *namesctl* utility may be used for trace levels to be set dynamically while the names server is up and running via the TRACE_FILE, TRACE_DIRECTORY, TRACE_LEVEL, and TRACE_UNIQUE commands.

- **Connection Manager** Tracing may be enabled within Net8 Connection Manager by setting the TRACING parameter to YES in the Connection Manager configuration file (*cman.ora*).
- **Enterprise Manager Daemon** Tracing for the Enterprise Manager daemon can be enabled via the DAEMON.TRACE_DIRECTORY (to set the directory where the trace-files are to be created), DAEMON.TRACE_LEVEL (can be set to 0, 4, 10, or 16), and DAEMON.TRACE_MASK (to mask the trace output to control what is captured in the trace-files) parameters in the *sqlnet.ora* file on the Enterprise Manager console.

Now, let's look at some tools to manage tracing.

Trace Assistant

Starting with SQL*Net v2.3.3, a tool called Trace Assistant allows SQL*Net/Net8 trace-files to be interpreted and diagnosed with more ease, thus allowing network-related problems to be resolved faster. Trace Assistant was formerly known as *Trace Evaluator.* The Trace Assistant shipped with Net8 supports advanced capabilities of Net8 Connection Manager, such as Connection Pooling and Connection Concentration (multiplexing), and also trace-files produced via Oracle Trace (explained in the text that follows). Thus, troubleshooting of problems (if any) associated with these features is possible via the corresponding trace files. Trace Assistant provides a utility to quickly decipher error messages that appear in the trace-file (without having to check the Error Codes Manual). Trace Assistant can be invoked as *trcasst.* Figures 13-29 and 13-30 illustrate Trace Assistant usage and output (in Figure 13-29, TTC stands for "Two-Task Common"). Trace Assistant is to be used only when tracing is set to level 16 (SUPPORT). Please refer to the *SQL*Net/Net8 Administrator's Guide* for more details on Trace Assistant.

```
$ trcasst
Trace Assistant Utility for Intel SVR4 UNIX: Version 8.0.5.0.0 - Production on 02-JUL-99 15:36:45
(c) Copyright 1997 Oracle Corporation.  All rights reserved.
TNS-04202: Trace Assistant Usage ERROR: Not enough arguments

Usage: trcasst [options] <filename>
              [options]  default values are: -odt -e -s
              <filename> is always the last argument
   Options can be zero or more of the following:
   -o   Enables display of SQL*Net and TTC information
        After the -o the following options can be used:
         c or d for summary or detailed SQL*Net information respectively
         u or t for summary or detailed TTC information respectively
         q displays SQL commands (used together with u)
   -p   Enables application perfomance measurement
   -s   Enables display of statistical information
   -e   Enables display of error information
        After the -e, zero or one error decoding level may follow:
         0 or nothing, translates NS error numbers
1 displays NS error translation plus all other errors
         2 displays error number without translation
```

FIGURE 13-29. *Trace Assistant usage*

```
$ trcasst -s listener.trc
Trace Assistant Utility for Intel SVR4 UNIX: Version 8.0.5.0.0 - Production on 02-JUL-99 15:43:00
(c) Copyright 1997 Oracle Corporation.  All rights reserved.
    ************************************************************************
    *                       Trace  Assistant  Tool                         *
    *                              TRCASST                                 *
    ************************************************************************
    =====================================================================
     Trace File Statistics:
    ---------------------------------------------------------------------
    SQL*Net:
 Total Calls:         5 sent,          3 received,          0 upi
 Total Bytes:       779 sent,        718 received
       Average Bytes:        155 sent,        239 received
       Maximum Bytes:        410 sent,        256 received

    GRAND TOTAL PACKETS  sent:       5       received:       3
    ************************************************************************
    *                    Trace Assistant has completed                     *
    *                              TRCASST                                 *
    ************************************************************************
```

FIGURE 13-30. *Trace Assistant output*

Oracle Trace

Oracle Trace is a tool to track tracing within various components of Oracle (not restricted to just SQL*Net/Net8) and can be accessed as part of the Oracle Enterprise Manager Performance Pack suite. It provides a GUI interface to manage the whole tracing process, such as by enabling tracing, setting appropriate trace levels, disabling tracing, and formatting and interpreting trace-file output. Figure 13-31 provides a screen snapshot of Oracle Trace. Oracle Trace uses the Enterprise Manager repository and produces binary files with the *.DAT* and *.CDF* extensions. These binary files may be converted into readable text files (.TXT) via the *trcfmt* utility. These text files may be further formatted for easier interpretation with Trace Assistant.

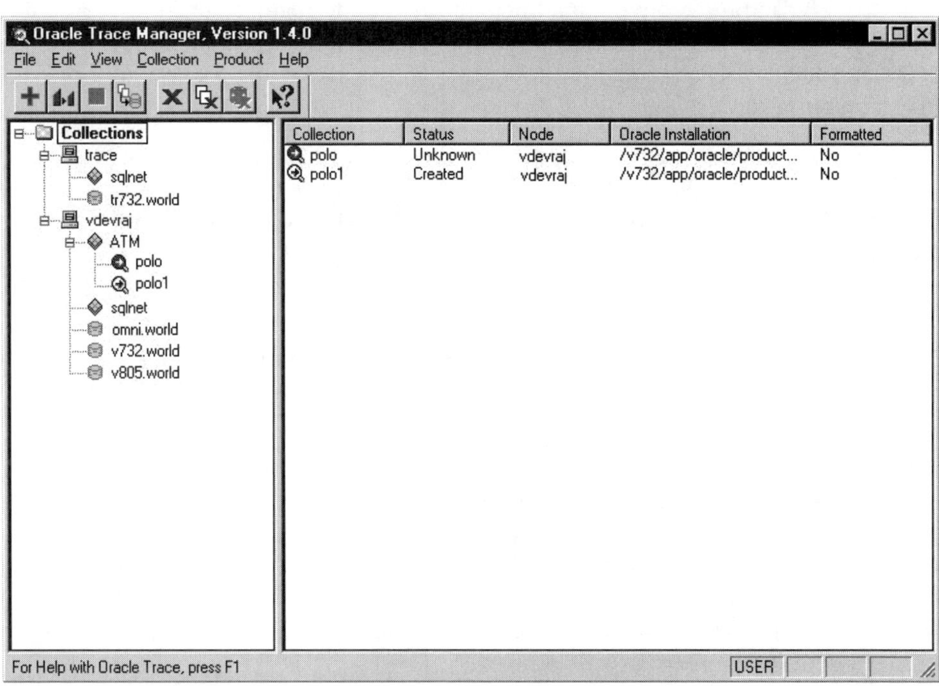

FIGURE 13-31. *Oracle Trace Manager screen*

PL/SQL Tracing

Robust tracing features are provided in Oracle to trace PL/SQL, starting with v2.3.*x* (database version 7.3.*x*). PL/SQL tracing can be initiated in two ways:

- Via regular trace-files
- By dumping a buffer that contains PL/SQL runtime information. This buffer may be dumped in response to certain events that occur at runtime.

Let's examine both methods in detail.

PL/SQL Tracing via Regular Trace-Files

Event 10928 can be set to write out trace information to regular trace-files. This event can be set at the session level or at the instance level. The following command sets PL/SQL tracing for a specific session (invoke this command prior to calling any PL/SQL code):

```
SQL> ALTER SESSION SET EVENTS '10928 TRACE NAME CONTEXT LEVEL 1'
```

The EVENT initialization parameter needs to be set to allow PL/SQL tracing at the instance level (this requires the database to be bounced):

```
EVENT = "10928 TRACE NAME CONTEXT LEVEL 1"
```

Setting these events creates trace-files outlining the PL/SQL calls made in the USER_DUMP_DEST directory. Figure 13-32 provides sample output of such a trace-file.

```
Dump file /opt/apps/oracle/admin/DT08/udump/ora_DT08_17336.trc
Oracle8 Enterprise Edition Release 8.0.5.1.0 - Production
PL/SQL Release 8.0.5.1.0 - Production
ORACLE_HOME = /opt/apps/oracle/product/8.0.5
System name:    zurich
Node name:      zurich
Instance name: DT08
Redo thread mounted by this instance: 1
Oracle process number: 9
Unix process pid: 17336, image: oracleDT08
*** 1999.07.02.16.40.19.000
```

FIGURE 13-32. *A sample portion of a regular PL/SQL trace-file*

```
*** SESSION ID:(8.252) 1999.07.02.16.40.19.000
Entry #1
00001: ENTER     64, 0, 1, 1
00009: INFR      DS[0]+84
  Frame Desc Version = 1, Size = 31
    # of locals = 3
    TC_SSCALAR: FP+8, d=FP+32, n=FP+40
    TC_CURSREF: FP+16, d=FP+44, n=FP+48
    TC_SSCALAR: FP+24, d=FP+52, n=FP+60
<source not available>
00014: INSTC2    GF[0], DS[0]+32, FP+16
00024: DEFINE    FP+16, 0, SQLT_DAT(12), FP+24
00033: EXECC     FP+16, 0x82e0
00038: CVTEI     FP+24, FP+8
<source not available>
Entry #0
SYS.DBMS_OUTPUT: 00001: ENTER     4, 0, 1, 1
SYS.DBMS_OUTPUT: 00009: INFR      DS[0]+488
  Frame Desc Version = 1, Size = 85
    # of locals = 10
    TC_SSCALAR: GF[0], d=GF[40], n=GF[44]
```

FIGURE 13-32. *A sample portion of a regular PL/SQL trace-file* (continued)

PL/SQL Tracing by Dumping Buffer Contents

When this option is enabled, the PL/SQL runtime engine allocates a buffer to store relevant runtime information. This buffer is of fixed size. In Oracle7 v7.3.4, you may explicitly set the 10940 event to determine the buffer size either at the session level or at the instance level. For instance, you may use the following command, prior to making any PL/SQL calls, to set the buffer size to 512KB (the LEVEL specifies the buffer size in KB).

```
SQL> ALTER SESSION SET EVENTS '10940 TRACE NAME CONTEXT LEVEL 512';
```

Alternatively, the EVENT initialization parameter may be set to accomplish the same for all PL/SQL calls:

```
EVENT = "10940 TRACE NAME CONTEXT LEVEL 512"
```

In Oracle8, this event need not be set, since the buffer is managed by the PL/SQL runtime engine. The buffer is reusable—that is, when the buffer gets full, it is automatically overwritten with new contents, thus making it a "circular" or reusable buffer. Occurrence of specific pre-determined events would cause the buffer contents to be dumped out to trace-files prior to being overwritten. You can enable dumping of this PL/SQL runtime buffer by setting the 10938 event (in both Oracle7 7.3.x and Oracle8 8.0.*x*). Again, this event can be set at the session level or at the instance level (within the *init.ora*). The following code samples illustrate its usage at both levels:

```
SQL> ALTER SESSION SET EVENTS '10938 TRACE NAME CONTEXT LEVEL <level>'

EVENT = "10938 TRACE NAME CONTEXT LEVEL <level>"
```

The <level> here is an output mask that controls what is dumped out of the buffer. As noted in Table 13-2, LEVEL 16 sets the contents of the buffer to be dumped out.

Multiple levels may be indicated by specifying a cumulative number (that combines two or more levels). An example follows:

```
SQL> EVENT = "10938 TRACE NAME CONTEXT LEVEL 17"
```

Here, the level 17 means use both levels 1 and 16. Thus, the buffer will be used and all PL/SQL calls will be traced. When level 16 is not set, all traced calls are written to the trace-files directly (not via the buffer, making the method akin to event 10928, described earlier). If the buffer is used, an underscore (undocumented) parameter _PLSQL_DUMP_BUFFER_EVENTS may be used to specifically determine the events that would cause the buffer to be dumped out. Different events may be specified for this parameter. These events can be PL/SQL-related Oracle error codes (that is, ORA runtime errors; PLS errors may not be specified, since they do not

<level> Value	**Description**
1	Trace every PL/SQL call.
2	Trace only procedures/functions/packages compiled with the DEBUG option.
4	Trace every exception encountered.
8	Trace only exceptions in procedures/functions/packages compiled with the DEBUG option.
16	Use the PL/SQL buffer.
32	Trace only bind variables.

TABLE 13-2. *Event 10938 Levels and Their Descriptions*

occur at runtime) or specific reserved words to indicate certain events. All events need to be within double quotes, in uppercase, and comma-delimited with no spaces in between. The reserved words to indicate events are the following:

- ALL_EXCEPTIONS, indicating that the buffer contents will be dumped out to a trace-file whenever an exception is encountered in the PL/SQL code
- ON_EXIT, indicating that the buffer contents will be dumped out when the PL/SQL engine exits, thus allowing the contents of the buffer to be captured during the exit

Here is an example of setting the _PLSQL_DUMP_BUFFER_EVENTS parameter:

```
_PLSQL_DUMP_BUFFER_EVENTS = "6052,ALL_EXCEPTIONS"
```

Figure 13-33 provides a sample output of the buffer contents.

```
Dump file /opt/app/oracle/admin/DT08/udump/ora_dt08_1505.trc
Oracle8 Enterprise Edition Release 8.0.5.1.0 - Production
PL/SQL Release 8.0.5.1.0 - Production
ORACLE_HOME = /opt/app/oracle/product/8.0.5
System name:    oasis
Instance name: DT08
Redo thread mounted by this instance: 1
Oracle process number: 13
Unix process pid: 1505, image: oracleDT08

*** 1999.07.06.17.01.01.000
*** SESSION ID:(10.4) 1999.07.06.17.01.01.000
------------ PL/SQL TRACE INFORMATION -----------
Levels set :  1    16
*** 1999.07.06.17.03.50.000
------------ PL/SQL TRACE INFORMATION -----------
Levels set :  1    16
<<<<START PLSQL TRACING DUMP<<<<<<<
***Got ORA-1422 while running PLSQL***
>>>>>>CIRCULAR BUFFER DUMP>>>>>>>>
Current end is: 1561
Trace:  ANONYMOUS BLOCK: Stack depth = 1
Trace:   PACKAGE BODY SYS.STANDARD: Call to entry at line 472 Stack depth = 2
Trace:   PACKAGE BODY SYS.STANDARD: ICD vector index = 21 Stack depth = 2
Trace:   PACKAGE BODY SYS.STANDARD: Call to entry at line 472 Stack depth = 2
Trace:   PACKAGE BODY SYS.STANDARD: ICD vector index = 21 Stack depth = 2
```

FIGURE 13-33. *Sample output of buffer contents dumped out to a trace-file*

```
||END
>>>>>>END PLSQL TRACING DUMP>>>>>>>
<<<<START PLSQL TRACING DUMP<<<<<<<
***Got ORA-20001 while running PLSQL***
>>>>>>CIRCULAR BUFFER DUMP>>>>>>>>
Current end is: 62
Trace:  ANONYMOUS BLOCK: ICD vector index = 0 Stack depth = 1
||END
>>>>>>END PLSQL TRACING DUMP>>>>>>>
<<<<START PLSQL TRACING DUMP<<<<<<<
***Got ORA-20001 while running PLSQL***
>>>>>>CIRCULAR BUFFER DUMP>>>>>>>>
Current end is: 62
Trace:  ANONYMOUS BLOCK: ICD vector index = 0 Stack depth = 1
||END
>>>>>>END PLSQL TRACING DUMP>>>>>>>
```

FIGURE 13-33. *Sample output of buffer contents dumped out to a trace-file* (continued)

ODBC Tracing

Quite often, ODBC is utilized from Windows/Windows NT clients to connect to a database server. In-house or third-party code written using certain front-end tools such as *Visual Basic* or *Visual C++* may utilize ODBC. Also, off-the-shelf data-load tools such as *Informatica PowerMart* use ODBC for performing certain functions. The following steps can be taken to enable tracing for database connections initiated via ODBC:

1. Go to the 32-bit ODBC Data-Source Administrator v3 (usually, via Control Panel on the client machine); select the TRACING tab, and set appropriate parameters as necessary, such as "When to trace" (select "all the time" or "one time only") and "Log file Path."
2. Set the TRACE_LEVEL_CLIENT in the SQLNET.ORA file to 16 on the client machine.
3. Run the necessary application code. Once it is run, tracing from ODBC may be disabled (to prevent trace-files from getting too large and unwieldy). Disabling consists of setting TRACE_LEVEL_CLIENT within SQLNET.ORA to OFF and setting "When to trace" to "Don't trace" in the TRACING tab of the 32-bit ODBC Data-Source Administrator.

Core Dumps

Core dumps are files containing the process state of a crashed process at the time of crash. Core dumps are produced as a result of segmentation faults, or when a program attempts an illegal operation such as accessing memory allocated to another process, writing to or reading from invalid media, and so on. Core dumps may also be produced when an attempt is made to run an improperly linked program (that is, one in which all object references are not fully resolved). Core dumps are generally named *core*. You may have to manually rename them, so that previous core dumps do not get overwritten with new ones. Core dumps in Oracle are produced in the directory specified by the initialization parameter CORE_DUMP_DEST. A core dump provides diagnostic information that may be useful in resolving the error that led to the crash.

A core dump contains a call stack trace that provides the sequence of commands that were being executed at the time of crash. However, a core file may be huge and is often not very legible (the use of the UNIX command *strings core* may help in reading the core dump, if your platform supports the *strings* command). At times, Oracle produces a trace-file that automatically contains the call stack trace. You may check in the *USER/BACKGROUND_DUMP_DEST* directories for such trace-files. In case Oracle has not generated a call stack trace, then you may have to create one manually. Oracle Support has a document entitled "How to Generate a Stack Trace from a Core File" that has detailed instructions on manually creating a call stack trace in UNIX. Note that doing so requires familiarity with an OS debugger such as *dbx, adb,* or *gdb* (whichever one is available on your platform).

Oracle Debugging Tools

Oracle provides a few debugging tools that can be used to diagnose specific problems, such as database corruption or internal errors. These tools are not documented and are meant to be used by Oracle Support analysts (unless an Oracle Support analyst provides instructions on using them, so that you can provide certain necessary information via these tools). Let's take a look at some of these tools.

Oradbx

Oradbx has been available since Oracle6 v6.0.29 for debugging. Oradbx allows you to debug Oracle processes that are currently running. This is accomplished via asynchronous messaging between the currently running Oracle and the debugger. Messages are sent to the process to provide necessary debugging information, such as memory dumps, process state dumps, core dumps containing stack traces, event-based dumps, inter-process communication, and (IPC) dumps. Other than IPC dumps (which are dumped out to the screen from which the debugger is being run), all other dumps are created in the *USER/BACKGROUND_DUMP_DEST* directories.

One of the most powerful capabilities of the tool is taking an event-based dump from a running Oracle process (explained in a subsequent section). When help is typed in at the Oradbx prompt, a listing of all allowable commands is provided. Figure 13-34 shows the help screen.

Oradebug

Starting with Oracle 7.3.2, Oradbx has been replaced with Oradebug, which is an enhanced version of Oradbx. Oradebug is accessed via Server Manager. Typing in "HELP" as the argument when invoking Oradebug provides a list of all options available with the tool. Figure 13-35 provides a view of the Oradebug help screen.

```
oradbx

oradbx: Release 7.1.6.2.1 - Production on Fri Jul  2 17:21:11 1999
Copyright (c) Oracle Corporation 1979, 1994.  All rights reserved.
Type 'help' for help.

(oradbx) help
help                  - print help information
show                  - show status
debug <pid>           - debug process
dump SGA              - dump SGA
dump PGA              - dump PGA
dump stack            - dump call stack
dump core             - dump core without crashing process
dump level 0          - dump error buffer
dump level 1          - level 0 + call stack
dump level 2          - level 1 + process state objects
dump level 3          - level 2 + context area
dump system 1         - brief system states dump
dump system 2         - full system states dump
dump ipc              - dump ipc information
dump controlfile #    - dump control file at level #
dump datafile #       - dump data file header at level #
dump procstat         - dump process statistics
event <event-trace>   - turn on event trace
unlimit trace         - unlimit the size of trace file
exit                  - exit this program
!                     - shell escape
(oradbx)
```

FIGURE 13-34. *Oradbx help screen output*

```
%svrmgrl

Oracle Server Manager Release 3.0.5.0.0 - Production
(c) Copyright 1997, Oracle Corporation.  All Rights Reserved.
Oracle8 Enterprise Edition Release 8.0.5.1.0 - Production
PL/SQL Release 8.0.5.1.0 - Production

SVRMGR> connect internal
Connected.
SVRMGR> oradebug help
HELP           [command]                Describe one or all commands
SETMYPID                                Debug current process
SETOSPID       <ospid>                  Set OS pid of process to debug
SETORAPID      <orapid> ['force']       Set Oracle pid of process to debug
DUMP           <dump_name> <level>      Invoke named dump
DUMPSGA        [bytes]                  Dump fixed SGA
DUMPLIST                                Print a list of available dumps
EVENT          <text>                   Set trace event in process
SESSION_EVENT  <text>                   Set trace event in session
DUMPVAR        <p|s|uga> <name> [level] Print/dump a fixed PGA/SGA/UGA variable
SETVAR         <p|s|uga> <name> <value> Modify a fixed PGA/SGA/UGA variable
PEEK           <addr> <len> [level]     Print/Dump memory
POKE           <addr> <len> <value>     Modify memory
WAKEUP         <orapid>                 Wake up Oracle process
SUSPEND                                 Suspend execution
RESUME                                  Resume execution
FLUSH                                   Flush pending writes to trace file
TRACEFILE_NAME                          Get name of trace file
LKDEBUG                                 Invoke lock manager debugger
CORE                                    Dump core without crashing process
IPC                                     Dump ipc information
UNLIMIT                                 Unlimit the size of the trace file
PROCSTAT                                Dump process statistics
CALL           <func> [arg1] ... [argn] Invoke function with arguments
SVRMGR>
```

FIGURE 13-35. *Oradebug help screen output*

Some of the useful tasks that Oradebug allows are the following:

- Regular debugging of a user session, such as changing memory contents, suspending/resuming operations, dumping program statistics, or producing a core dump

- Dumping the fixed portion of the SGA
- Dumping the PGA of a specific session
- Enabling trace externally for a user session, including process-diagnostic tracing and SQL tracing

In order to understand how the tool works, let's take a small example: let's say we need to enable SQL_TRACE for a specific user session. We would need to take the following steps to achieve that:

1. Obtain the Oracle process ID for that user session via the following query:

```
SQL> SELECT pid FROM v$process
       WHERE username = '<Oracle_Username>';
```

2. Attach to that session using Oradebug within Server Manager:

```
SVRMGR> ORADEBUG SETORAPID <PID_FROM_PREVIOUS_QUERY>
```

3. Enable SQL_Trace for that session:

```
SVRMGR> ORADEBUG EVENT 10046 TRACE NAME CONTEXT FOREVER, LEVEL 12
```

4. After the necessary trace-files have been produced off that session, SQL_Trace may be disabled:

```
SVRMGR> ORADEBUG EVENT 10046 TRACE NAME CONTEXT OFF
```

5. Now, the appropriate trace-files may be located and formatted via TKPROF.

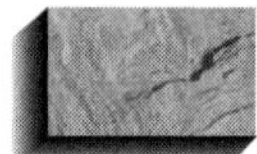

NOTE

You can also enable SQL_TRACE for a specific user session via the DBMS_SYSTEM.SET_SQL_TRACE_IN_SESSION procedure. This procedure accepts the SID and SERIAL# (from v$session) of the session in which you want to enable SQL_TRACE and a Boolean value of TRUE or FALSE (to enable/disable SQL_TRACE). The DBMS_SYSTEM package is defined in $ORACLE_HOME/rdbms/admin/dbmsutil.sql in v7.3; whereas in Oracle8, it has been moved to $ORACLE_HOME/rdbms/admin/prvtutil.plb (since prvtutil.plb is wrapped, it helps to discourage end users from using DBMS_SYSTEM).

Usage of Oradebug is provided merely for information. As a cautionary note, do not use debugging utilities (such as *oradbx, oradebug, dbx,* or DBMS_SYSTEM) on production instances without Oracle Support's intervention (if you do, please don't blame me). If a problem is suspected that requires these tools to be used, ensure that

Oracle Support personnel are involved in the operation. Using debugging utilities (even with good knowledge of the Oracle kernel) may cause a background or foreground process to die (if the wrong memory structure is "poked") and cause the entire instance to crash.

In fact, so that customers do not accidentally play with the tool and cause problems, a default Oracle installation does not link the debuggers to make the executable available. For instance, the executable for Oradbx needs to be explicitly created by manual linking as follows (in versions prior to Oracle7 v7.3.2):

```
$ cd $ORACLE_HOME/rdbms/lib
$ make -f oracle.mk oradbx
```

The assumption is that these tools are not ordinarily required by the day-to-day administrative personnel and, if necessary, an Oracle Support analyst can guide them on how to use it.

Events and Setting Events Using a Debugger

At times, it becomes necessary to get more information from a process that's currently running without killing it. For instance, if a batch job that's been running for half a day or so needs to be debugged without having to kill and restart it, debuggers such as Oradebug and Oradbx may be very useful. Using these debuggers, you can set an event such that the process will produce a trace-file whenever that event occurs. These trace-files allow detailed diagnosis of the event, to check for possible errors and bugs. Again, these tasks need to be done in conjunction with Oracle Support personnel. Besides producing trace and diagnostic information, in order to debug a problem, Oracle Support and Development personnel may need to even change the default behavior of Oracle in certain respects. Events make all this possible. Let's take the time to understand events better.

Events

Setting events allows the following:

- Dumping out event-based diagnostic information (when an event occurs)
- Dumping out unconditional diagnostic information (immediate dumps, without waiting for any specific event to occur)
- Changing the default behavior of Oracle

One of the primary issues in event-based debugging is determining the correct event code, the resultant action to be taken, and the parameter(s) to be supplied for that action. These codes are not documented and may potentially change from version to version. Based on my experience, I have seen old event codes go away in

newer releases or new event codes get created; however, I have not observed any existing events getting a new code (or codes being swapped across events) in newer releases. Existing events, if they are still supported in the newer release, seem to retain the event code from the previous release. Oracle maintains an event-code table, listing all the supported events. The current event codes for your release are available in the file *$ORACLE_HOME/rdbms/mesg/oraus.msg.* They currently range from 10000 to 10999. Table 13-3 provides a sample of some useful events (some are listed throughout the chapter to explain certain points). Remember, Oracle does warn us that these event codes may not be static across releases.

Event Code	**Description**
10000	Control-file debug event
10010	Begin transaction
10011	End transaction
10012	Abort transaction
10013	Instance recovery
10014	Rollback to savepoint
10015	Undo segment recovery
10016	Undo segment extend
10017	Undo segment wrap
10018	Data segment create
10019	Data segment recovery
10021	Latch cleanup for state objects (KSS)
10027	Latch cleanup for enqueue locks (KSQ)
10028	Latch cleanup for enqueue resources (KSQ)
10029	Session logon (KSU)
10030	Session logoff (KSU)
10034	Access path analysis (APA*)
10035	Parse SQL statement (OPIPRS)
10039	Type checking (OPITCA)

TABLE 13-3. *A Sample List of Event Codes and Their Description (Note that these event codes are not guaranteed to remain the same across releases.)*

Event Code	Description
10040	Dirty cache list
10042	Trap error during undo application
10045	Free list update operations—ktsrsp
10046	Enable SQL statement timing
10101	Atomic redo write recovery
10200	Block cleanout
10201	Consistent read undo application
10202	Consistent read block header
10203	Consistent read buffer status
10204	Signal recursive extend
10205	Row cache latch clean up
10206	Transaction table consistent read
10210	Check data block integrity
10211	Check index block integrity
10212	Check cluster integrity
10213	Crash during control-file header write
10214	Dump control-file header sequence numbers
10216	Dump control-file header
10217	Debug sequence numbers
10219	Monitor multi-pass row locking
10220	Show updates to the transaction table
10221	Show changes done with undo
10222	Row cache
10224	Index block split/delete trace
10227	Verify (multi-piece) row structure
10229	Simulate I/O error against data-files
10230	Check redo generation by copying before applying

TABLE 13-3. *A Sample List of Event Codes and Their Description (Note that these event codes are not guaranteed to remain the same across releases.)* (continued)

Event Code	Description
10231	Skip corrupted blocks on table scans
10233	Trace allocation/extend/deallocation of context area
10235	Check consistency of transaction table and undo block
10237	Simulate ^C (for testing purposes)
10240	Dump dbas of blocks that we wait for
10246	Print trace of PMON actions to trace file

TABLE 13-3 *A Sample List of Event Codes and Their Description (Note that these event codes are not guaranteed to remain the same across releases.)* (continued)

Events can be set in the following ways:

- At the session level via the ALTER SESSION command
- At the instance level via the EVENT initialization parameter
- Via the DBMS_SYSTEM.SET_EV procedure
- From the debuggers Oradbx and Oradebug via the EVENT command

Note that not all events are dynamic (that is, can be enabled via ALTER SESSION or DBMS_SYSTEM.SET_EV or from a debugger). Other events can only be enabled via the EVENT initialization parameter (requiring a database bounce). Conversely, it does not make sense to set certain events at the instance level. For example, if a specific block has to be dumped, it needs to happen immediately via the ALTER SESSION SET EVENTS IMMEDIATE command, rather than via the EVENT initialization parameter. When the IMMEDIATE clause is used, Oracle does not look up the event from the event-code table, because IMMEDIATE is not a real event, but just a symbolic name requesting immediate action.

Setting an event basically means requesting a specific action when the event is encountered. Thus, the event syntax may be translated to mean

```
ON EVENT <event_number_or_symbolic_name>, TAKE AN ACTION WITH
THE PARAMETERS <parameter-list>
```

A parameter list can be used to specify the level (of tracing required) or the address of the block to be dumped. For instance, the event 604 can be set either as

ALTER SESSION SET EVENTS '604 TRACE NAME ERRORSTACK FOREVER' or

EVENT = "604 TRACE NAME ERRORSTACK FOREVER"

These commands may be translated as follows: "ON EVENT 604, DUMP THE ERRORSTACK TO A TRACE FILE AND CONTINUE DOING THIS FOREVER (throughout the life of the session)." The syntax is further explained in the *Oracle8 Backup and Recovery Handbook* from Oracle Press.

In the preceding example, the action refers to dumping out a trace-file. However, an action could mean any of the following:

- Dump out a trace-file
- Crash the process
- Invoke the debugger

Let's look at these in detail.

DUMPING OUT TRACE-FILES Dumping out a trace-file is specified via "TRACE" (example: "604 **TRACE** NAME ERRORSTACK FOREVER"). The name (after TRACE) refers to a symbolic name that links the trace to a specific dump/debug operation. Examples of names supported are provided in Table 13-4.

Trace Name	**Purpose**
BUFFERS	To dump buffers from the buffer cache
CONTROLF	To dump control-file contents
FILE_HDRS	To dump data-file headers
PROCESSSTATE	To dump process state of a session
SYSTEMSTATE	To dump the system state
CONTEXT	To determine how detailed the dump should be
ERRORSTACK	To dump the process call stack during an error

TABLE 13-4. *Symbolic Trace Names and Their Descriptions*

Trace Name	Purpose
BLOCKDUMP	To dump a block
LATCHES	To dump latches
ENQUEUES	To dump enqueues
SAVEPOINTS	To dump savepoints currently defined
REDOHDR	To dump the redo header
CONTEXTAREA	To dump the cursor context areas
ALL	Refers to all the preceding

TABLE 13-4. *Symbolic Trace Names and Their Descriptions* (continued)

The <parameter-list> allows a bunch of parameters to be submitted to the action (in this case, TRACE). Some such parameters are listed in Table 13-5.

Parameter Name	Description
LEVEL N	The LEVEL keyword is supported by more than one of the previously listed names. However, it may have a different purpose for each name. For instance, with CONTEXT, N determines how detailed the trace should be, whereas with BLOCKDUMP, it specifies the address of the block to be dumped.
AFTER N TIMES	Specifies that a trace should be started after N times the event has occurred.
LIFETIME N	Perform the trace only for N occurrences of the event. Disable the trace after that.
FOREVER	Perform the trace each time the event occurs.
TYPE INCREMENT	Set trace level to maximum.
TYPE DECREMENT	Set trace level to zero (disable).
OFF	Disable tracing.

TABLE 13-5. *Parameter List for Trace Names*

CRASHING THE PROCESS Setting the action of an event to be "crashing the process" causes the process to be terminated whenever the event occurs. This may be necessary if the process happens to start looping uncontrollably (goes into a "spin"), taking up all CPU resources, thus requiring it to crash immediately when the error occurs. Only Oracle Support and Oracle Development personnel would need to use this option during debugging operations. A production DBA should not have any reason to use this option, unless asked to do so by Oracle Support personnel. This information is being provided here only for your knowledge.

Table 13-6 lists some of the parameters supported for CRASH.

Parameter Name	Description
AFTER N TIMES	Crash after N times.
OFF	Disable crashing.

TABLE 13-6. *Parameter List for the CRASH Action*

INVOKING THE DEBUGGER Again, this option would only be required by Oracle Support/Development personnel during debugging operations, and this information is being provided here only for your knowledge. With this action, on the occurrence of the event, the debugger (Oradbx or Oradebug) would be invoked. Table 13-7 provides the parameters supported by this action.

Parameter Name	Description
AFTER N TIMES	Invoke the debugger after N times the event occurs.
LIFETIME N	Invoke the debugger for N times the event occurs. Don't invoke it after that.
FOREVER	Invoke the debugger every time the event occurs.
OFF	Don't invoke the debugger anymore, next time the event occurs.

TABLE 13-7. *Parameter List for Invoking the Debugger*

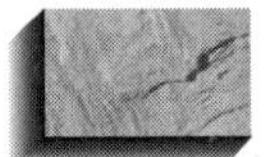

NOTE
Examples for usage of the "crash" and "invoke the debugger" actions are not provided because these options are not intended to be used in a production environment. They are mentioned here so that a 24x7 DBA can understand what are the various events, how to enable/disable them, and what kind of events and actions are supported. Such information should help him or her in providing capable assistance (when necessary) to Oracle Support personnel in using these options.

Whenever necessary, make your trace-files readable by developers

On UNIX, by default, all trace-files created by Oracle have the privileges set to 640 (user: READ/WRITE, group: READ and others: NO ACCESS). Thus, administrators in the *dba* group can read the files, but others (developers, for instance) cannot. Generally, these trace-files can be very complex to read (a lot of hexadecimal values and internal addresses), and there is a need to keep unauthorized prying eyes away from these files. At times, however, it is essential for developers to be able to read the trace-files (such as PL/SQL trace dumps or SQL_TRACE outputs), so that they may have more information while debugging specific application errors. This can be achieved by setting the underscore initialization parameter _TRACE_FILES_PUBLIC to TRUE. This makes Oracle create trace-files that are readable by all.

Summary

This chapter dealt with some of the most important weapons in your arsenal for figuring out which are the ailments currently afflicting your database: the alert-log and trace-files. Besides helping you to troubleshoot current problems, they will often provide valuable advance warning regarding serious ailments that might strike in the near future, causing performance nosedives or, even more important, service outages. Learning how to interpret the information in the alert-log and trace-files can be very valuable to help you proactively react to warnings to resolve issues before they turn into ugly problems. Being familiar with these processes also helps reduce the time needed in working with Oracle Support. The chapter also discussed how to deal with segmentation faults and core dumps, so that they can be diagnosed for errors and treated accordingly either before they result in an outage or, if an outage is already imminent, to limit its duration. Some important debugging and diagnostic tools, Oradbx and Oradebug, were discussed. Finally, the process of setting events, even for active processes, was studied.

The following chapter provides information on another critical but "under-documented" area: database corruption and how to resolve it.

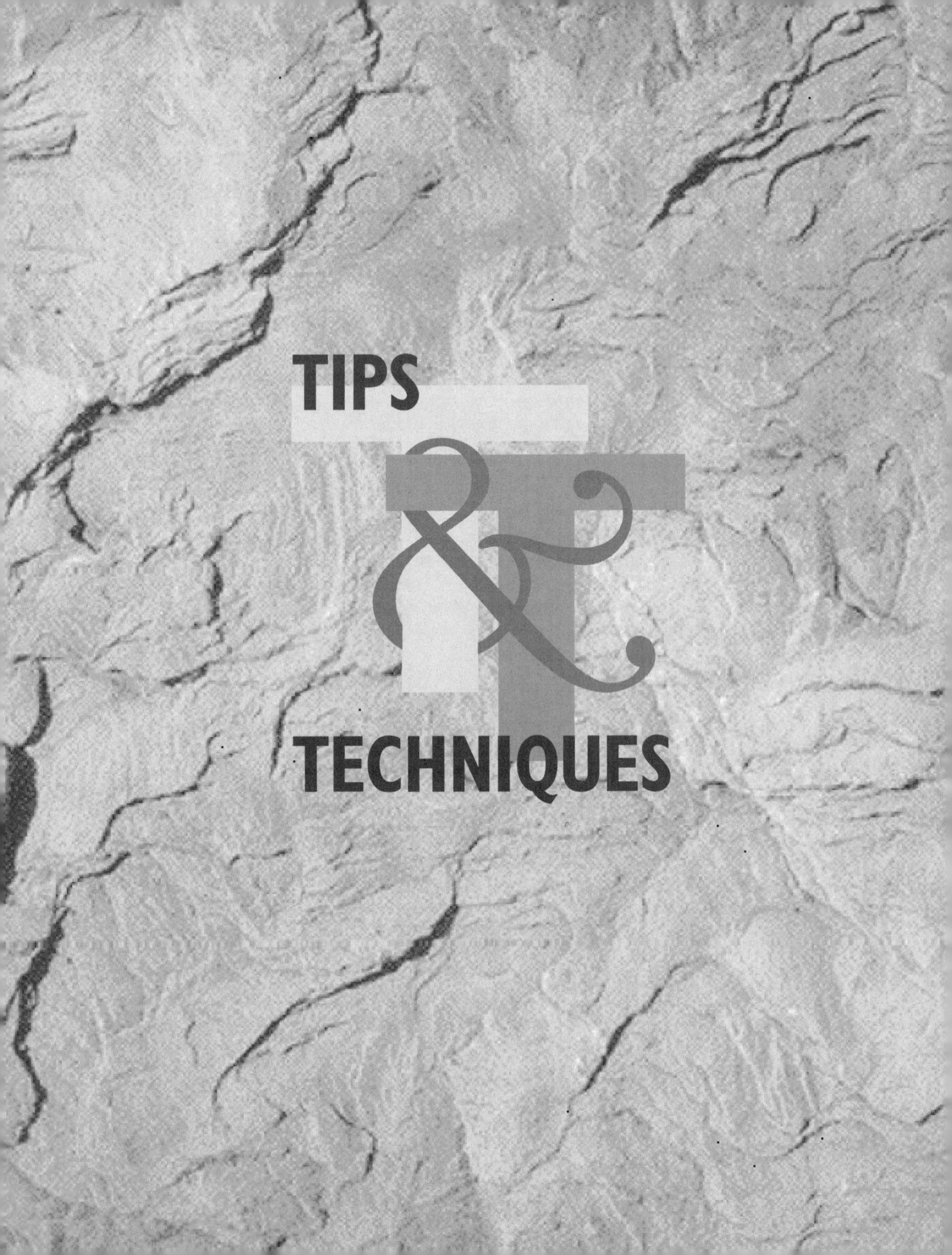
TIPS
&
TECHNIQUES

CHAPTER 14

Identifying and Repairing Database Corruption

Corruption is the bane of any database. In addition to the data that is potentially lost, corruption may also cause high downtime to detect and repair the corruption and restore the corrupt data. Corruption may adversely impact availability either completely or partially. The scope of such an impact depends on the extent and type of corruption that the database is afflicted with. Most of the time, the data can be retrieved either by reentering it or rerunning required batch jobs to regenerate it, or else by using the most current backups to restore and perform recovery, if necessary, either on the original machine or on a different one (especially if point-in-time recovery is desired). At times, however, the data may be irreplaceably lost, if adequate, valid backups do not exist or the backups also are corrupt (which happens more often than one would believe).

Both detection and repair can be quite challenging. Accordingly, this chapter discusses procedures that can be used to combat corruption, identify it, and rectify it in a timely fashion with as little impact to availability as possible. At times, however, avoiding impact to availability is very difficult (if not impossible). Accordingly, during such times, the presence of a standby database will significantly help in reducing the pressure on administrative personnel working to repair the corruption. Furthermore, this chapter also discusses proactive measures to avoid corruption and the monitoring that will help in unearthing corruption.

This chapter offers the following tips and techniques:

- Understand corruption and the ways it can manifest itself
- Understand what you can do to prevent media corruption
- Proactively check for and detect media corruption
- Identify all components susceptible to corruption
- Identify measures to prevent, detect, and repair corruption totally
- Retain relevant information regarding the corruption
- Train your administrators to handle corruption

Understanding, Preventing, and Repairing Corruption

Corruption, as with any serious threat to availability, requires a good understanding of the issues involved, so that proactive steps can be taken to restrict corruption. Additionally, a deep understanding of the issues involved will allow timely detection, repair, and data restoration in case it does occur.

Understand corruption and the ways it can manifest itself

There are various types and classifications of corruption depending on the extent and areas of affliction. Corruption can manifest itself either at the hardware level or the software level and is generally caused by a bug. In case the bug is a salient one, which occurs only during a specific circumstance such as a specific level of high use or a specific level of capacity is reached, it can be very difficult to detect. If the bug is active and occurs all the time, it is relatively easier to detect. However, it may or may not be easy to fix, especially with the intent of keeping impact on availability low. In the case of hardware, it may occur within various components such as the I/O subsystem, memory, or network equipment. Hardware corruption generally requires that the faulty component be replaced. Also, various good practices suggested in earlier chapters will help in restricting and combating corruption via techniques such as mirroring (especially triple mirroring, where one mirror lags behind the others by at least half an hour) and other RAID subsystems involving parity check and reconstruction, redundant hardware components, and so on. In the case of software, corruption may occur at the OS kernel level; at the database layer, within middle-layer components such as a Web Server, application servers, transaction processing (TP) monitors; or even at the client level, in individual applications, end-user tools, and so on. In any case, a detailed test environment, where hardware and software is well tested for bugs; and other problems prior to deployment, will be very useful in dealing with corruption arising from such bugs. This chapter deals primarily with detecting and repairing corruption within the database, even though such corruption may be caused by any of the diverse sources mentioned previously.

Corruption within the database may be broadly classified as the following:

- Physical corruption
    - Media or data-block corruption
    - Memory corruption

- Logical or data corruption

Let's take a detailed look at each.

Physical Corruption

Physical corruption is, simply stated, damage to the data block(s) or memory structures, such that data cannot be reliably retrieved and/or processed. Physical corruption generally occurs due to a hardware fault, such as a disk-controller read/write error, or due to a software/OS bug, or even due to user/administrative errors such an accidental removal of a data-file. Physical corruption renders database blocks (either on disk or in memory) unable to be read or written to by Oracle, thus resulting in error messages.

Media Corruption

Media or data-block corruption is generally caused by faults or bugs in the hardware, such as disks/controllers, or software, such as the OS, volume managers, RAID managers, or even Oracle itself. Media corruption affects portions of a disk and is experienced at the data-block level within Oracle. In other words, one or more Oracle data blocks are deemed to be corrupt, thus making the rows within such blocks irretrievable.

Depending on which data blocks are affected, any component of the database can become corrupt. Thus, corruption can be experienced within any of the following:

- Data-files
- Online redo-logs
- Archived redo-logs
- Control-file

Let's take a close look at each of these areas.

MEDIA CORRUPTION IN DATA-FILES

Media corruption in data-files causes data to be unreadable. The severity of such corruption depends on the area of affliction: blocks in the file header or the file body. The file header is the first block of the data-file; it maintains key information on various internal structures and makes access of blocks in the file body possible. Such key information includes SCN information, backup/recovery status, block version/sequence number, checkpoint information, resetlogs status, and so on. If the information in the file-header block is not accessible, the entire data-file may be inaccessible. On the other hand, even if certain blocks within the file body are inaccessible, only the segments within such blocks will be partially (or fully, depending on the size of the segments, the number of blocks they encompass, and whether such blocks are affected by the corruption or not) inaccessible. In most cases, restoring from the latest backup and performing recovery is the only realistic means of recovering from corruption in the file header. Figure 14-1 illustrates the file header, some of the key structures it contains, and the file body.

Diverse segments can be held within the blocks forming the file body. Thus, depending on the data-file blocks that have become corrupt, any of the following segments (or portions of such segments) may be inaccessible:

- Table (including tables in clusters)
- Index
- Temporary segment
- Rollback segment

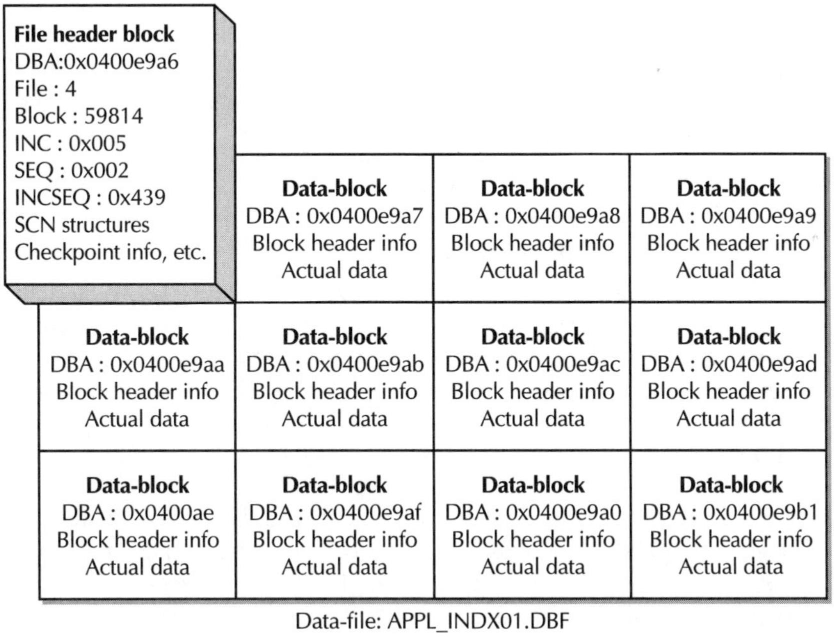

FIGURE 14-1. *Data-file structure*

Additionally, the headers of each of the preceding segments can be affected, thus causing the entire segment to be unavailable. Any of the segments just listed can either belong to the Oracle data-dictionary owner SYS (that is, a data-dictionary segment in the SYSTEM tablespace) or an application owner. A single corrupt segment within the SYSTEM tablespace can potentially cause serious downtime by crashing the entire database. A corrupt segment in the SYSTEM tablespace always has serious repercussions. Let's take a peek at the types of segments that will typically be found in the SYSTEM tablespace and could potentially become corrupt (user/application segments should not be present in SYSTEM):

- Data-dictionary clusters (example: c_ts#), tables (example: FET$), and indexes (example: cluster key and table indexes on aforementioned segments). The *sql.bsq* script (run by the CREATE DATABASE command) provides the DDL to create these segments. However, the DDL cannot be used to re-create these segments, in case they get corrupt. This is because many of these segments form the *bootstrap* set of segments, used by Oracle in starting up the instance and keeping it up. Oracle will crash if an attempt is made to rebuild some of these segments. Additionally, the relationship between the core segments forming the Oracle data dictionary is not well-documented, and so trying to rebuild some of them may result in the database sinking even deeper in the quagmire of corruption. There are various static (DBA_USERS, ALL_USERS, DBA_SEGMENTS, and so on) and dynamic (*v$session, v$process, x$ksppi,* and so on) tables/views built on top of these segments.
- The SYSTEM rollback segment (always present and created prior to any of the other rollback segments).
- The *compatibility* segment (listed as SEGMENT_TYPE = 'CACHE' in SYS.DBA_SEGMENTS). This segment keeps track of features being used in the database, which are specific to the current Oracle version. This "current-version" feature list proves helpful when downgrading to an earlier version of Oracle, since these features will need to be disabled. This segment is built dynamically by Oracle when the instance is started up.

Repairing corruption to the segments forming the data dictionary and the SYSTEM rollback segment always involves restoring the most recent backup and performing recovery. Such recovery may not always be complete and may be point-in-time based, if recovery prior to the time of corruption is necessary. If the compatibility segment becomes corrupt, it generally requires a database bounce to be repaired.

Thus, each of the preceding segment types (tables, indexes, clusters, and so on) may cause different levels of downtime. Now, let's take a closer look at what repairing corruption in each of the preceding segment types involves.

Segment corruption (tables, indexes, and so on) is usually highlighted via the ORA-1578 error. The text for this error is of the following form: "ORACLE data block corrupted (file # <fil>, block # <blk>)". A sample error message is given here:

```
ORA-00604: error occurred at recursive SQL level 1
ORA-01578: ORACLE data block corrupted (file # 7, block # 59882)
ORA-01110: data file 7: '/u1/oradata/TST5/userdata01.dbf'
```

In Oracle8, this "file #" is the absolute file number. The first thing to do is to figure out which segments are contained in that file/block combination to determine the extent of corruption. Either of the following queries may be run to make the determination (where <fil> and <blk> are the file and block numbers mentioned in the ORA-1578 error-message text):

```
SQL> SELECT segment_name, segment_type FROM dba_extents
      WHERE file_id = <fil>
        AND <blk> BETWEEN block_id AND block_id + (blocks-1);

/* run this query as SYS */
SQL> SELECT s.* FROM dba_segments s, uet$ u
      WHERE s.header_file = <fil>
        AND <blk> BETWEEN u.block# AND u.block# + (u.length-1)
        AND u.segfile# = s.header_file
        AND u.segblock# = s.header_block;
```

Sometimes, accompanying trace-files or error messages may provide additional information regarding the corruption, such as the dba (data block address) of the corrupt block. The dba is a 48-bit integer that refers to the data-file number and the block number within the file. Upon reading a block, Oracle expects a specific dba. If the dba in the block header does not match the expected one, then the inconsistency is reported via an ORA-600 (with the first argument being 3339, the second one being the dba found in the block header, and the third being the dba that Oracle was expecting). Such information can be reconciled with the ORA-1578 error-message text to ensure that you do not accidentally consider a valid block to be corrupt or, conversely, you consider all relevant information regarding the corrupt block. The following sample lists relevant portions of a trace-file for a database running on Windows NT (please refer to Chapter 13 on decoding a dba to reveal the correct data-file and block):

```
Dump file C:\ORANT\RDBMS80\trace\ORA00185.TRC
Fri May 15 12:24:42 1999
ORACLE V8.0.4.0.1 - Production Release vsnsta=0
vsnsql=a vsnxtr=3
Fri May 15 12:24:42 1999
Corrupt block dba: 0x0400e9a6 file=4. blocknum=59814. found during buffer read
on disk type:6. ver:1. dba: 0x0400e9a6 inc:0x00000439 seq:0x00000002 incseq:0x0
incseq:0x04390002
```

Once the dba is obtained, one may dump the block to examine the contents via the following command:

```
/* here, 67168678 is the decimal representation of the dba value */
SQL> ALTER SESSION SET EVENTS
         'IMMEDIATE TRACE NAME BLOCKDUMP LEVEL 67168678';
```

Also, the header portion and blocks of different Oracle files (even entire files, themselves) such as redo-logs, control-files, and data-files can be dumped out via the ALTER SESSION SET EVENTS command for detailed diagnosis. Chapter 6 of the *Oracle8 Backup & Recovery Handbook* (Oracle Press) provides information on performing such dumps. At times, performing an OS-level raw dump of the corrupt blocks using OS utilities (such as *dd*) may provide some insight on the corruption.

Based on which segment types are affected, the methods to repair vary. However, the source of the problem should be determined and repaired prior to repairing the corruption within the database. For instance, if the corruption occurs due to a bad disk, the disk ought to be replaced. Then database corruption repair can be performed using the methods described in the text that follows. If you will be using a backup to restore and recover, you need to restore onto the new disk, rename the data-file on the bad disk, and then open the database (the database will need to be in mounted mode, while renaming a data-file).

REPAIRING TABLE CORRUPTION When a block comprising rows from one or more tables is corrupt, such rows are generally irrevocable. Accordingly, repairing table corruption consists of the following steps, as shown in Figure 14-2:

1. Retrieve as much data as possible (i.e., retrieve the rows in the blocks that are not corrupt).
2. Identify the lost rows.
3. Re-create the lost rows.

Alternatively, the affected tables may be recovered by using the latest backup. Furthermore, if you have implemented mirrors (RAID 1 and so on) to have an online backup, it is possible to bring the mirrored disks up as a separate database and export the corrupted tables out (after setting event 10231—explained in the text that follows). The database can be brought up by creating a new control-file pointing to the underlying volumes in the mirror. For instance, if the mirror is, say, */dev/rdsk/dafatfile01,* then the volumes may be set up as

/dev/rdsk/vola01	active
/dev/rdsk/volb01	active
/dev/rdsk/vold01	inactive

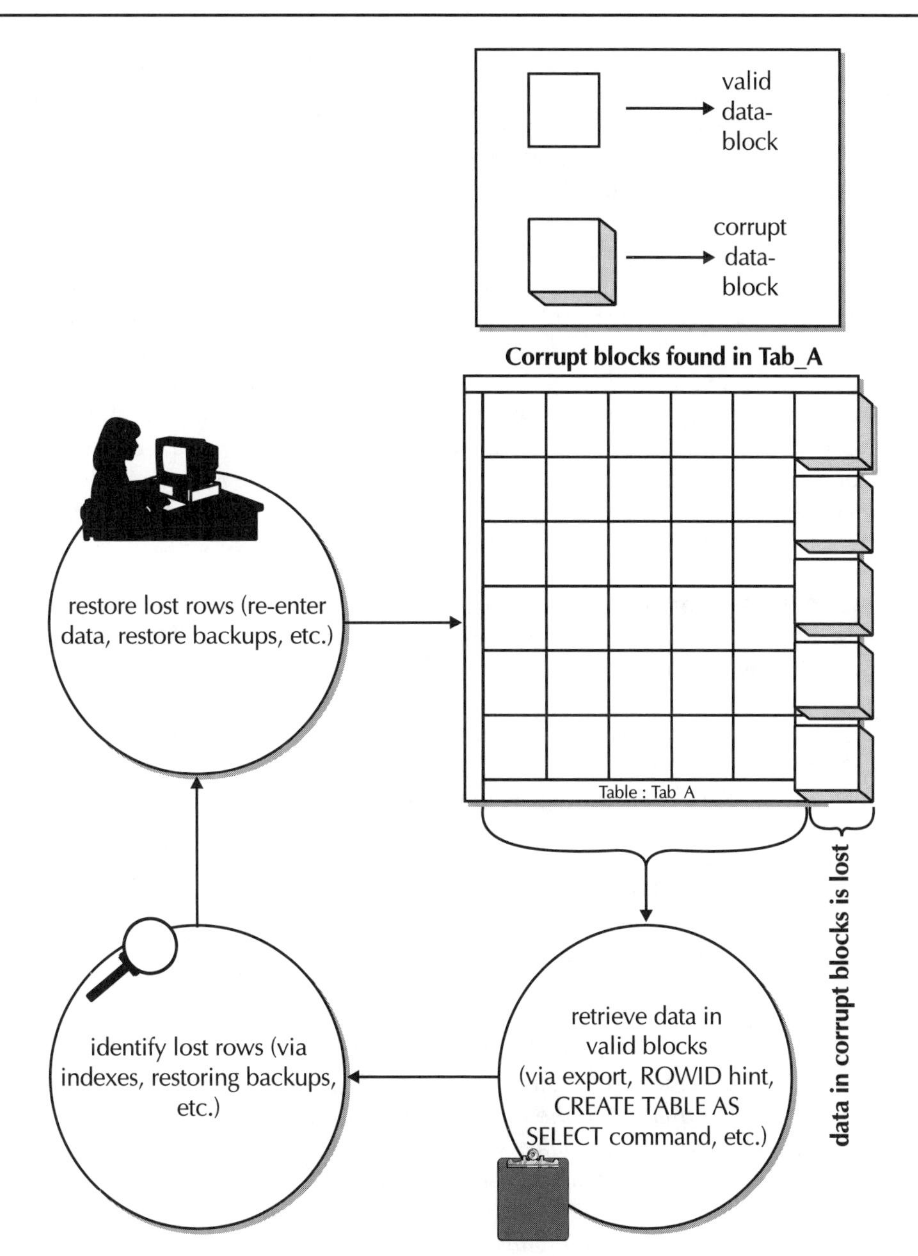

FIGURE 14-2. *Table corruption repair "life cycle"*

If you make the control-file point to */dev/rdsk/vold01* and rename the necessary data-files after mounting, you can bring up that database to do an export.

The decision to use the backup or perform the steps listed previously (manually retrieving as much data as possible, and so on) should be driven by the duration of downtime caused by the two methods, and the one with the least impact on availability ought to be selected. Let's understand the previously mentioned steps further.

Retrieval may be done by working around the corrupt rows to read only the good rows and writing them out (either to a separate table or an export dump-file). Once that is accomplished, the original table with the corrupt blocks needs to be dropped. Then the new table (if a separate table is used) may be renamed to refer to the original name and all privileges may be restored. Similarly, if an export dump-file is utilized, the data needs to be imported back. A normal full-table scan will only retrieve rows stored in blocks prior to the corrupt blocks. The corrupt blocks and any valid blocks after the corrupt blocks will not be accessible. The only way to access the rows in blocks after the corrupt blocks is to retrieve them via their ROWID. Following are some ways to retrieve the unaffected rows.

VIA THE 10231 DATABASE EVENT The 10231 event may be set within the database, via the EVENT initialization parameter. Setting this event skips blocks, which are already marked as corrupt by Oracle (that is, blocks that have the sequence number [SEQ] reset to zero in the block header) and allows the good rows to be read. The problem with this method is that it does not always work. If a corrupt block has not already been identified by Oracle (a subsequent tip outlines how this can be achieved by setting event number 10210), reading such blocks will not succeed. Accordingly, this method may have to be used in conjunction with other events (such as 10210). The 10231 event may be set as follows in the initialization parameter file:

```
event = "10231 trace name context forever, level 10"
```

NOTE
A database event either helps in diagnosis and debugging of specific situations by writing out more information in the form of trace-files, or helps to alter the default behavior of Oracle to overcome undesired/buggy characteristics. Most events can be set via any of the following ways (please refer to Chapter 13 for more details):

- Methods not requiring a database bounce:
  - SET EVENTS clause of the ALTER SESSION command
  - OraDBX or OraDebug
  - The new DBMS_SYSTEM.SET_EV procedure
- Methods requiring a database bounce:
  - EVENT initialization parameter

VIA EXISTING INDEXES If an index is present on the table (which is a very reasonable assumption in Oracle7 and Oracle8, since every table will ideally have at least a unique index for its primary key, albeit this assumption is not valid in Oracle8*i* because an index is not mandatory to enforce unique constraints), it may be used to read rows present in blocks prior to and after each corrupt block (thus skipping the rows in the corrupt blocks). The following example illustrates this better.

Let's say column PERSON_ID is the primary key for table NAMES and there is a unique index on PERSON_ID. In a unique index, there is a one-to-one correspondence between a key value and a ROWID. A ROWID in Oracle7 is in hexadecimal and comprises the file number, the block number (within the file), and the row offset (within the block), each separated by a period: BBBBBBBB.NNNN.FFFF (where BBBBBBBB is the block number, FFFF is the file number, and NNNN is the block offset).

The same ROWID can be derived in Oracle8 as well, via the DBMS_ROWID. ROWID_TO_RESTRICTED procedure (present within *$ORACLE_HOME/rdbms/admin/dbmsutil.sql*). The external representation of the ROWID is 18 bytes in size. Using the file number (<fil>) and the block number (<blk>) displayed in the ORA-1578 error, one can use the following query to retrieve all rows present in blocks prior to the corrupted block. Let's assume that <fil> is 4 and <blk> is 6 and that NAMES_IDX01 is the name of the unique index:

```
SQL> SELECT /*+ INDEX(names names_idx01) */ MAX(person_id)
     FROM names WHERE ROWIDTOCHAR(ROWID) LIKE '00000006.%.0004';
```

Here, the maximum key value of the rows within the corrupt block is to be noted from the output of the preceding statement.

```
SQL> SELECT /*+ INDEX(names names_pk) */ MIN(person_id)
     FROM names WHERE ROWIDTOCHAR(ROWID) LIKE '00000006.%.0004';
```

Then, the minimum key value of the rows within the corrupt block should be noted from the output of the preceding statement.

An EXPLAIN PLAN needs to be done prior to running the statements to ensure that an index-only lookup is indeed performed (that is, the table is not accessed).

Finally, a query similar to the following may be used to save the rows present in blocks that are prior to the corrupt block onto a different table via the CREATE TABLE AS command (that is, specifying the query in the AS portion). In Oracle8*i*, the same query may be specified in the export process to export these rows.

```
SQL> SELECT * FROM names WHERE person_id < <minimum-value-in-corrupt-blk>;
```

The following statement will fetch the rows in blocks after the corrupt one. These rows may be inserted into the table created previously (via the CREATE TABLE AS command) or to another export process to create a second export dump-file.

```
SQL> SELECT * FROM names WHERE person_id > <maximum-value-in-corrupt-blk>;
```

Also, variations of the preceding statements may be utilized. For instance, the following approach retrieves all the primary keys of all rows in non-corrupt blocks and places them in a temporary table. Once that is achieved, a join is performed between the two tables (the original table with the corrupt blocks and the temporary table) to create a third table containing only the rows in non-corrupt blocks (if these tables are large, you could also create them in UNRECOVERABLE/NOLOGGING mode with an appropriate parallel degree). Then the original corrupt table can be dropped and the third table can be renamed to refer to the original table name (privileges will need to be regranted).

```
SQL> CREATE TABLE t_names AS
     SELECT  /*+ INDEX(names names_pk) */ person_id FROM names
      WHERE ROWID NOT LIKE '00000006.%.0004';

SQL> CREATE TABLE names_new AS
     SELECT n.* FROM names n, t_names t
      WHERE t.person_id = n.person_id;
```

Even if the unique key consists of a column with the VARCHAR2 data type, these techniques will work. And if the unique index consists of a compound key (multiple columns in the index), one may convert them all to character (via the TO_CHAR function) and concatenate them together to treat all columns as a single unit.

The next step is to identify all the rows in the corrupt blocks (the irrecoverable rows). If an index is present (as mentioned previously), the key value for all such rows can be obtained via the following statement:

```
SQL> CREATE TABLE lost_row_keys AS
     SELECT /*+ INDEX(names names_pk) */ person_id
       FROM names WHERE ROWIDTOCHAR(ROWID) LIKE '00000006.%.0004';
```

Once the keys are obtained, one may reenter/re-create all such rows from the original source of record. Alternatively, one may use a backup to retrieve and recover all such rows. The backups may even help in recovery, even when there is no unique index on the table, by restoring the entire table onto the primary database, tracing the rows that are lost (via a SQL statement such as a MINUS or an outer join between the original table from the backup and the table from which the corrupt rows were eliminated).

VIA THE ROWID HINT If you need to recover corrupt blocks in a table without any indexes (something that should be relatively rare in Oracle7/Oracle8 environments) and the table concerned is not clustered, you could use the ROWID hint in conjunction with an appropriate parallel degree (greater than 1, thus invoking the Oracle Parallel Query Option). That would cause a range scan to occur, rather than a full-table scan (even though there are no indexes, the range scan would occur on the ROWID), thus reading around the corrupt blocks. Without PQO or the ROWID hint, this would result in a regular full-table scan. For instance, the following statement will be necessary to recover the PERSON_IDs from corrupt blocks if there are no indexes.

```
SQL> CREATE TABLE lost_row_keys
     PARALLEL(DEGREE 2) AS
     SELECT /*+ ROWID(names) PARALLEL(names, 2) */ MIN(person_id)
       FROM names WHERE ROWIDTOCHAR(ROWID) LIKE '00000006.%.0004';
```

Once that is accomplished, the steps mentioned earlier can be followed to recover rows with PERSON_IDs not present in the LOST_ROW_KEYS table. In Oracle8, the ROWID hint is not necessary, since a range scan (rather than a full-table scan) is automatically enforced due to the ROWID check being present in the WHERE clause.

Also, in case you are using Oracle8 and do not wish to use the DBMS_ROWID. ROWID_TO_RESTRICTED procedure to recover blocks in an Oracle7-compliant fashion (to eliminate reliance on an earlier version), you need to understand the changes to the ROWID in Oracle8 and the procedures necessary to recover from corruption. In Oracle8, the ROWID is termed to be "extended" and is structured as follows: OOOOOOFFFBBBBBBSSS, where "OOOOOO" is the base-64 representation of the object number, "FFF" is the base-64 representation of the relative file number, "BBBBBB" is the base-64 representation of the block number within the file, and "SSS" is the base-64 representation of the slot number (the row offset within the block). The object number helps in maintaining multiple segment versions, since certain operations can cause a ROWID (and the redo) to become stale, generating different versions. Thus, the ROWID contains the relative file number, whereas the ORA-1578 error message contains the absolute file number. An absolute file number is unique within the database, whereas a relative file number is relative to the tablespace, thus potentially causing two files to have the same relative file number (in tablespaces with 1,024 data-files or less, the absolute file number always matches the relative file number).

In order to accomplish the repair routines outlined earlier, you need to construct the Oracle8 ROWID, on the basis of the absolute file number and the block number in the ORA-1578 error message. That can be accomplished via the following steps:

1. Get the object number (<obj#>) for the corrupt segment via the following query (you must be connected as SYS or INTERNAL to run this query). In the case of a partitioned table, each partition should be treated as a distinct segment, since each will have its own distinct object number.

```
SQL> SELECT obj# FROM SYS.tabpart$ WHERE file# = <fil> AND block# = <blk>;
```

2. Find the relative file number (<rfil>), based on the absolute file number (<fil>) in the ORA-1578 error message.

```
SQL> SELECT relative_fno rfil FROM dba_data_files
      WHERE file_id = <fil>;
```

3. Now the DBMS_ROWID.ROWID_CREATE function may be used to create the rowid of rows before and after the corrupt block. The ROWID_CREATE function accepts the following input parameters: ROWID_TYPE, where '0' is restricted (Oracle7 format) and '1' is extended (Oracle8 format), OBJECT_NUMBER (needs to be NULL for restricted ROWID formats), the relative file number (<rfil>), the block number (<blk>), and the slot/row number (can be zero, indicating the first row in the block). The ROWID of rows in blocks prior to and after the corrupt block helps us retrieve and save such rows in a different table (via the CREATE TABLE AS SELECT command). The following statements may be used to retrieve the rows prior to the corrupt block (substitute <obj#>, <rfil>, <blk> with the appropriate object numbers, relative file numbers, and block numbers; note that <blk> is the block number displayed in the ORA-1578 error message):

```
/* retrieve the start-ROWID, prior to the corrupt block; note that <blk>-1 is
specified to refer to the block, prior to the corrupt block; let's call this
"Query-A" */
SELECT DBMS_ROWID.ROWID_CREATE(1, <obj#>, <rfil>, <blk>-1, 0)
  FROM names;

/* now, retrieve the start-ROWID, after the corrupt block; note that <blk>+1
is specified to refer to the block, after the corrupt block; let's call this
"Query-B" */
SELECT DBMS_ROWID.ROWID_CREATE(1, <obj#>, <rfil>, <blk>+1, 0)
  FROM names;

/* now, create a table with rows in blocks, prior to the corrupt block */
```

```
CREATE TABLE names_new
    AS SELECT *
         FROM names
        WHERE ROWID <= <result from Query-A>;

/* now, insert into the table with rows in blocks, after the corrupt block */
INSERT INTO names_new
  SELECT * FROM names
   WHERE ROWID >= <result from Query-B>;
```

4. Now, we can retrieve the key values of rows in the corrupt block by reconstructing the ROWID of such rows. The ROWID of rows in the corrupt block helps us identify which rows are corrupt by allowing the key value to be fetched via either an index lookup or a range scan (in the absence of an index), as mentioned earlier.

```
/* Retrieve the ROWID of rows in the corrupt block; note that <blk> is
specified to refer to the corrupt block, from the ORA-1578 error-message;
let's call this "Query-C" */
SELECT DBMS_ROWID.ROWID_CREATE(1, <obj#>, <rfil>, <blk>, 0)
  FROM names;

/* now, save the key-values for such rows in a different table; for the
<result from Query-C>, specify the result as follows 'BBBhB2BAFABBAAC%',
where "BBBhB2" is the <obj#> from Query-C, "BAF" is the <rfil> from Query-C,
"ABBAAC" is the <blk> from Query-C and "%" refers to the slot/row number
within the block */
CREATE TABLE lost_row_keys
PARALLEL(DEGREE 2) AS
SELECT person_id FROM names
WHERE ROWIDTOCHAR(ROWID) LIKE '<result from Query-C>';
```

As far as possible, try to re-create the corrupt rows from the source of record. Generally, rows in such corrupt blocks will be relatively few (depending on the size of the database block and the size of segments involved) and will be fairly easy to re-create. However, their capability to cause downtime depends on their importance to the application. As a general rule of thumb, using backups to recover corrupted rows is to be used as a last resort, since it would take far more resources. Also, if there is a standby database/table or a replicated table in a distributed database environment, one could consider using the copy of the table to restore normalcy.

In case the table is part of a cluster, potentially all the tables that make up the cluster may be corrupt. In such cases, all tables that make up the cluster may be considered as a single "super table" and the same techniques (except the ROWID with PQO technique) discussed previously may be followed to repair them. Again, it is necessary to bear in mind that such methods may not be effective against tables with LONG or LONG RAW columns (due to the inherent restrictions of LONGs/LONG RAWs).

REPAIRING INDEX CORRUPTION When only an index block is determined to be corrupt, it will require the index to be dropped and re-created. Since the source data for the index (that is, the table) is still available, index corruption does not lead to data loss. The index could be dropped immediately, so that application behavior and functionality are not impacted. The index does not have to be re-created immediately, if the subsequent performance delay is tolerable. Then at the earliest possible opportunity, the index could be rebuilt, thus deferring downtime to a less critical time. True 24×7 sites could resort to standby tables/databases to achieve uptime during the rebuild.

REPAIRING TEMPORARY SEGMENT CORRUPTION Temporary segment corruption may cause the transaction (using those segments) to fail. If the corruption is caused by an intermittent hardware problem, restarting such transactions will generally overcome such corruption. If it's a persistent problem (such as an Oracle/OS bug), then the cause of corruption needs to be repaired prior to restarting them. In any case, the cause of corruption needs to be analyzed and repaired as soon as possible (not necessarily prior to restarting the transaction), to prevent future incidences of corruption. In case the corruption is persistent due to a specific problem (such as the disk going bad, on which the temporary tablespace resides), then the temporary tablespace may have to be relocated in order to minimize the impact on database operations. The following steps can be taken to perform the relocation:

1. Create a new temporary tablespace.
2. Alter all users to use the new temporary tablespace (rather than the existing one). The following commands may be used to achieve the same (let's assume the new temporary tablespace is named TEMP2).

```
SQL> SELECT 'ALTER USER ' || username ||
            ' TEMPORARY TABLESPACE temp2;'
      FROM dba_users;
SQL> SPOOL chg_temp.sql
SQL> /
SQL> SPOOL OFF
/* edit the chg_temp.sql script to remove all unnecessary command output
(such as echoes, prompts, etc.). Alternatively you can disable echo,
feedback, etc., prior to running the command. */

-- now execute the chg_temp.sql script
SQL> @chg_temp
```

Now, the cause of corruption can be repaired while transactions continue, thus keeping database disruption to the minimum.

REPAIRING ROLLBACK SEGMENT CORRUPTION Repairing corruption in online rollback segments is always a challenge. If the rollback segment is being used by active transactions, then transaction consistency is destroyed for all such active transactions. Even if the rollback segment is not currently held by active transactions, it could still be implicitly used by readers (SELECT statements, UPDATEs and DELETEs with WHERE clauses, and so on) for read consistency due to current changes to rows being read (changes being made by other active transactions) or delayed block cleanout (where prior transactions have made changes). Accordingly, corruption to rollback segments causes these (multiple) transactions to break down, affecting availability for users/applications running these transactions. Corruption to offline rollback segments is not a major issue. If an offline rollback segment has experienced corruption, it will give error messages when one attempts to make it online. Subsequently, it can be dropped and re-created. Thus, neither availability nor transaction consistency is affected.

The first and foremost thing that needs to be done when rollback segment corruption is detected is to try to take it offline. Once that has been accomplished, it may be dropped and re-created. Sometimes, however, this may not be possible, due to active transactions being "trapped" in the corrupt rollback segment blocks. Rollback segment corruption can be experienced either by the blocks forming the header (undo header blocks) or the segment body (undo blocks). Strategies to repair rollback segment corruption may vary accordingly. Following are some such strategies:

- **Perform recovery using the latest backup** Point-in-time recovery may be needed, such that the corruption is not introduced again. However, if the cause/time of corruption is not known, such recovery may not necessarily succeed. If the corruption was caused by an intermittent hardware problem, then recovery may eliminate the corruption. However, if the redo-log blocks also contain the corruption (assuming no initialization parameters have been enabled to detect/prevent such corruption), then the recovery performed may be useless. Also, if recovery cannot be performed within acceptable MTTR, then other methods to recover need to be explored.
- **Recovery using initialization parameters** When rollback segments are corrupt, the trapped (active) transactions may need to be manually resolved. Such manual resolution may be complicated; the success of such resolution depends on the following:
  - Application knowledge possessed by the DBA (or the "recovery team") performing the recovery

- Amount of information at hand regarding segments affected by the corruption. Such information may be derived by setting an event in the database initialization parameter file:

```
event = "10015 trace name context forever, level 10"
```

This event examines rollback segment recovery during instance startup and produces a trace-file if corruption is detected. In versions prior to 7.3.x, the corrupt rollback segment causes database startup to fail due to failure in recovery of the trapped transactions. In version 7.3 and upward, transaction recovery is deferred, allowing the database to be started up. Once the trace-file is created, one can search the file to identify the segments participating in the trapped transactions. This can be achieved by looking up the dba (data block address) of the affected blocks and arriving at the segment name (see Chapter 13 on how to identify segments, based on their dba). Alternatively, the object ID of the affected segments can be obtained from the trace-file (again, Chapter 13 explains identifying a segment based on its object ID). Once the segment(s) are identified, the transactions need to be manually resolved. Examples of such resolution include:

- Drop and re-create the segment(s) and regrant the appropriate privileges to other schemas/user IDs (public or private synonyms under such schemas do not have to be re-created). Point-in-time recovery may have to be performed to restore these segments. If the segments are fairly small (dimension tables, reference tables, and so on), they may be re-created via manual means (having the data reentered, restoring the data from postal department media [such as for zip-code reference tables], and so on). All referential integrity and inter-segment consistency has to be manually managed.
- Examining the impact of the transactions (how many rows were inserted/updated/deleted and in which segments) and manually reissuing the statements to make the incomplete (trapped) transactions consistent.

Some of the dbas obtained in the trace-file may refer to certain rollback segments (the source of corruption). In order to resolve the corruption, one needs to drop and re-create the affected rollback segments. If the ALTER ROLLBACK SEGMENT (if the database is open) does not work (results in error messages) or the database fails to open, then the _OFFLINE_ROLLBACK_SEGMENTS (underscore) initialization parameter may be used to refer to the rollback segments that need to be taken offline. This will force the database to be opened up, in spite of transaction inconsistencies. Once the database is open, these inconsistencies need to be manually resolved (as mentioned previously). Only after these transactions are resolved can these offline rollback segments be dropped (dropping them prior to resolution would cause those transactions to be forcibly saved, since Oracle would commit them). The _OFFLINE_ROLLBACK_SEGMENTS initialization parameter may be set as follows:

```
_OFFLINE_ROLLBACK_SEGMENTS = (RBS4, RBS6)
```

If the rollback segment header is corrupt and/or critical blocks in the rollback segment body are corrupt, such that Oracle cannot take them offline (even forcibly), then such segments may be marked corrupt via another initialization parameter: _CORRUPTED_ROLLBACK_SEGMENTS. Usage of this parameter is similar to _OFFLINE_ROLLBACK_SEGMENTS. When _CORRUPTED_ROLLBACK_SEGMENTS is set, Oracle bypasses the resolution of active transactions in those rollback segments and opens up the database, nevertheless. When using the _CORRUPTED_ROLLBACK_SEGMENTS parameter, it's advisable to rebuild the database as soon as possible (to eliminate inconsistencies and chances of logical corruption). Having a standby database will allow operations to continue as the primary database is being rebuilt.

One important fact to bear in mind, prior to using these parameters, is that they are not documented and hence not supported. Using them without Oracle Support's intervention may cause irreparable damage. Once these parameters have served their purpose, they need to be unset (removed from the initialization parameter file). Also, always attempt using the _OFFLINE_ROLLBACK_SEGMENTS prior to using the _CORRUPTED_ROLLBACK_SEGMENTS, since the latter involves a potential database rebuild (as compared to manual transaction resolution) and, hence, more downtime.

MEDIA CORRUPTION IN ONLINE REDO-LOGS

Online redo-logs are used only during recovery scenarios. Media recovery may require the online redo-logs. If the archived redo-logs comprise all relevant information, the online redo-logs may not be used at all (thus allowing the database to be opened with the RESETLOGS option, without any loss in data). The current online redo-log is always used during instance recovery. If all members in an online redo-log group become corrupt, the instance could potentially crash, especially if the current redo-log group is involved in the corruption. If all the members in a log group are not corrupt, then Oracle can access the mirrored log members that are still available and continue working. If a non-current unarchived online redo-log is corrupt (such that ARCH cannot read it), then the database could crash. Thus, redo-log corruption may be highly dangerous, potentially causing immediate disruption of services and additionally impeding both instance and media recovery.

Redo-log corruption could occur due to reasons such as the following:

- Hardware/OS faults in reading from/writing to them
- User/administrative errors, such as a file being accidentally overwritten

- It is also to be noted that logical corruption within the database can be inadvertently caused by incorrectly applying the online redo-logs while rolling forward. Such improper backup/recovery procedures, causing the "end-of-backup" marker in the online redo-logs (this mark is stamped via the ALTER TABLESPACE END BACKUP command) to be applied, makes the recovery process terminate prematurely.

The following steps may be taken to recover from online redo-log corruption (note that prior to making an attempt to recover, the cause of corruption needs to be well understood and repaired. Failure to do so may make the recovery process futile by merely reintroducing the corruption):

- If the online redo-log group is mirrored (this is highly critical in a 24×7 environment) and one of the members in each group is not corrupt and accessible, then it will allow Oracle to continue working. Usually, if all members in a mirrored online redo-log group are corrupt and that group happens to be the current group, then Oracle will fail. However, in case all members are corrupt and this group is not the current redo-log group, then the group may be reset via the ALTER DATABASE CLEAR LOGFILE command. This command is especially invaluable when the redo-log group becomes corrupt before it has been archived. Since it is not accessible for archiving, the group cannot be overwritten, thus causing the database to freeze when the redo goes around a full circle and comes back to the corrupt redo-log group. During such situations, to prevent ARCH from hanging, the corrupt redo-log group can be reset via the ALTER DATABASE CLEAR LOGFILE command. When the group to be reset has not been archived, the UNARCHIVED clause becomes necessary. The syntax of the command is as follows:

  ```
  SQL> ALTER DATABASE CLEAR [UNARCHIVED] LOGFILE GROUP <grp#>;
  ```

  Note that in case you have an Oracle standby database implemented, resetting the online redo-logs thus may require the standby to be rebuilt, since the redo stream gets interrupted.

- The other method to recover may cause substantial downtime and needs to be used in conjunction with a standby database, so that a major outage does not result. This method would be necessary when the preceding method (resetting the logs) does not work or all members in the current redo-log group are corrupt. This method involves restoring the latest backups to recover to a point in time prior to the corruption, resulting in valid redo-log groups.

- Finally, when all the preceding measures fail (the backups are not valid or an archived redo-log is missing, preventing acceptable recovery) and the database is down due to corruption in the online redo-logs, the underscore (undocumented) initialization parameter _ALLOW_RESETLOGS_CORRUPTION may be used to open the database. This parameter forces the database open without fully resolving redo-log corruption and without applying the contents of the online redo-logs to take the database to a consistent state. It bypasses some of the core checks that would normally occur, such as consistency checks of critical structures (checkpoint structures, incarnation, and sequence) in the data-file headers. Accordingly, it places the onus for making the database consistent upon the DBA. The DBA will have to manually traverse through and understand the latest transactions that may have occurred and the extent to which they may have been committed (completely or partially, violating parent/child relationships, and so on). Thus, the DBA will need to perform the tasks that Oracle would normally do, when the online redo-logs are available. The problem here is, manual reconciliation of the transactions is hardly reliable, and the errors introduced may not be immediately obvious or traceable. Accordingly, it is highly recommended that the database be rebuilt as soon as possible using valid data within the database. Such a rebuild will also remove logical corruption within the data dictionary, due to the usage of _ALLOW_RESETLOGS_CORRUPTION. This parameter takes a value of TRUE or FALSE. It is vital that it be used only after gaining a through understanding of all pertinent issues and again, only under the guidance of Oracle Support. It is to be borne in mind that this parameter is not guaranteed to always work and hence is not the magic bullet against redo-log corruption. Whenever possible, the methods described earlier ought to be given precedence to ensure complete repair and lower downtime.

MEDIA CORRUPTION IN ARCHIVED REDO-LOGS

Issues surrounding corruption in the archived redo-logs are similar to the ones described previously, while discussing online redo-log corruption. The database, however, will not crash if an archived redo-log becomes corrupt. The archived redo-logs are required by Oracle only during media recovery. But, if an archived redo-log becomes corrupt and is inaccessible, then it creates a hole in the archived redo-log sequence, thus making complete recovery impossible. Recovery cannot proceed beyond the corrupt archived redo-log. Oracle will give an error similar to the following:

```
ORA-00283: Recovery session canceled due to errors
ORA-00354: corrupt redo log block header
ORA-00353: log corruption near block 1255 time stamp 01/06/98 00:00:00
ORA-00334: archived log: '/u11/oracle/arch_logs/TST9/arch_0000040888_TST9'
```

Accordingly, it is highly desirable to perform a backup as soon as possible to create a new starting point for the archived redo-log sequence and making the corrupt archived redo-log file unnecessary during recovery.

Corruption of the archived redo-logs is caused (in addition to reasons discussed previously) primarily by incorrect backup procedures such as the following:

- Backing up incompletely archived redo-log files (while they are still being created). An example would be running a *cron* job to copy/move archived logs, without checking the archived status.
- Improperly reading/copying the archived redo-log file to the backup media (such as by FTPing it in ASCII mode).

In Oracle8, using the new initialization parameter LOG_ARCHIVE_DUPLEX_DEST to write to multiple archive-log destinations simultaneously reduces the chances of corruption in one destination from crippling database recoverability.

MEDIA CORRUPTION IN CONTROL-FILES

The control-file is a relatively small file that maintains key database structural and consistency information. It is highly advisable for any site to maintain at least three copies of the control-file via the CONTROL_FILES initialization parameter on separate disks/controller, so that hardware faults do not affect all copies. The fact to be remembered is that even if one control-file copy is corrupt, the database crashes. Accordingly, it is necessary to maintain current backups of the control-file in various forms, such as

- A binary backup via the following command:

  ```
  SQL> ALTER DATABASE BACKUP CONTROLFILE TO '<filename>';
  ```

- An ASCII version, containing the CREATE CONTROLFILE command. This can be generated in the USER_DUMP_DEST directory via the following command:

  ```
  SQL> ALTER DATABASE BACKUP CONTROLFILE TO TRACE;
  ```

- In the form of an ASCII dump via the following command:

  ```
  SQL> ALTER SESSION SET EVENTS 'IMMEDIATE TRACE NAME CONTROLF LEVEL 10';
  ```

- By meticulously documenting all structural changes to the database (such as adding or dropping tablespaces/data-files, and so on) in both computer and paper files.

The following methods can be used to recover from control-file corruption:

- Edit the CONTROL_FILES initialization parameter (usually present in the *config<SID>.ora* file, rather than *init<SID>.ora*) to eliminate the suspected corrupt file. If one is unsure about which of the control-file copies is corrupt, then the reference to the first control-file may be removed from the CONTROL_FILES parameter and the database may be started up. If that does not work, one may progressively remove each successive reference, until the database is successfully started up. Then, at the next earliest available opportunity, one needs to copy the valid control-file over the others and restore all references (as they were prior to the corruption) in the CONTROL_FILES parameter (thus pointing to the multiple copies once again).
- If all control-file copies have become corrupt, use a script containing the current CREATE CONTROLFILE command (by current, I refer to a script containing references to all data-files and their correct path-names, file sizes, and so on) to re-create the control-file, after the instance is brought up in NOMOUNT mode. In case a current script does not exist, use computer/paper records to make the script up-to-date (thus, it is very critical to maintain up-to-date information on the database structure).

Remember that recovering from a control-file crash may be quick. In most cases, a switchover to a standby instance may not be necessary (since the switchover may take up more time than recovering from the control-file crash). In order to minimize downtime, however, it is recommended to retain copies of the CREATE CONTROLFILE command (with both RESETLOGS and NORESETLOGS options in separate scripts) to be used as necessary.

Proactively check for and detect media corruption

When left undetected, media corruption is experienced via a runtime error message (ORA-1578, ORA-1545, and sometimes ORA-600) on the screen, while the corrupt blocks are being accessed for read/write. Media corruption may be detected in a more proactive fashion in the following ways:

- Running *db_verify* (*dbv*) regularly to detect irregularities in the actual data-files or the backups (see Chapter 4 for details on running db_verify against data-files on raw devices without corruption being incorrectly reported).

- Running the following SQL command (as a DBA user):

  ```
  SQL> ALTER SYSTEM CHECK DATAFILES GLOBAL;
  ```

  This command verifies that all online data-files can be accessed by all open instances. In case this is not so, an error is written to the database alert-log. In case of an OPS configuration, if you want to verify access to data-files only for the current instance, you may use the keyword LOCAL instead of GLOBAL in the preceding command (by default, GLOBAL is used, when none are specified).

- Analyzing segments periodically with the VALIDATE STRUCTURE option, with the additional CASCADE option to detect corruption (more about this is mentioned in the paragraph on logical corruption).

- Use of specific initialization parameters such as DB_BLOCK_CHECKSUM and LOG_BLOCK_CHECKSUM. These parameters are explained in a subsequent paragraph on memory corruption (since they aid in determining inconsistencies between data blocks in the data-files and data blocks in the buffer cache, as well).

- Periodically querying data-file–related dynamic views such as *v$datafile* and *v$recover_file* to check the status of each data-file and its header. If any data-file that is supposed to be online and available has been taken offline by Oracle, then that file may be corrupt/inaccessible. Oracle takes a data-file offline if the file header is inaccessible due to corruption, deletion, or the like. Also, check the STATUS column in *v$rollstat* for a value of 'NEEDS RECOVERY' to detect corrupt rollback segments.

- Periodically checking the database alert-log and the trace-files in the USER_DUMP_DEST directory for corruption-related errors (such as ORA-1578 for corrupted data segments and ORA-1545 for corrupted online rollback segments; ORA-1578 may also be generated while a corrupt rollback segment is being utilized for read consistency) or errors that might potentially be due to/lead to corruption (such as ORA-600 with the first parameter between 4000 and 5000). These errors also provide an "address" of the suspected corruption in terms of the data-file number and the corrupted block number within the data-file, making it easier to trace the segment(s) affected by the corruption.

- By setting specific events such as 10210 (tables), 10211 (indexes), and 10212 (clusters) in the initialization parameter file (if corruption is suspected). Setting these events causes Oracle to perform certain integrity checks on blocks read. If these checks reveal inconsistency, then the blocks are marked as corrupt by setting the sequence number (SEQ) in the block header to zero, thus alerting any subsequent read of such blocks. Normally, reads of rows in that block may not result in errors, unless these events are set (on the other hand, writes to such blocks will always report errors, irrespective of the events). The events can be set as follows (substitute <event #> with the actual event number mentioned previously):

```
event = "<event #> trace name context forever, level 10"
```

Understand what you can do to prevent media corruption

Media corruption can often be prevented from crippling database services by following the steps below:

- **Hardware evaluation and redundancy** By careful evaluation of all hardware components, prior to use. Appropriate redundancy either via mirroring or parity-based solutions should be achieved to guard against corruption caused by errant hardware operations. Furthermore, hot-swappable hardware should be used, so that in case corruption does occur in certain non-critical components, they can be swapped out and new ones put in their place. Critical components (such as disks with Oracle data-files) may not be easily swapped out (even though they may be hot-swappable physically), since that may cause the system/database to crash. Corruption in such critical components would require switchover to a standby server to minimize downtime.
- **Redundancy within Oracle** Besides plain hardware redundancy, one should also introduce a required level of redundancy within Oracle to prevent corruption in one copy of the component from disrupting operations. Such redundancy allows for higher administrative flexibility during corruption. All online redo-logs and control-files need to be mirrored. If possible, one may also mirror the archived redo-logs (in Oracle8) by writing to multiple destinations simultaneously.
- **Robust test environment** By extensively testing all software (OS, volume managers, Oracle, and so on) installations and upgrades (new releases and patches) in a test environment that is configured in a manner similar to production, prior to actual deployment. In case potentially corruption-causing bugs are found, then the install/upgrade should not be undertaken.
- **Security** Maintaining a secure environment, where an operational system cannot be accidentally pushed or moved, causing the read/write head to be hit on impact or allow an Oracle file to be accidentally deleted, will help greatly in reducing chances of media corruption due to user/administrative accidents.

- **Valid backups** Valid backups are key to prevent corruption from being introduced after a restore/recovery has been performed. Accordingly, all backups need to be periodically checked for corruption. It is to be borne in mind that corruption may be introduced even after backups are successfully done, if they are stored in online/offline media, prone to corruption. Hence, all backup media need to be verified periodically to ensure there is no corruption.

The preceding steps are only precautions and are not guaranteed to prevent media corruption from all possible sources. Accordingly, when it does occur, it needs to be detected as soon as possible, so that appropriate action may be taken to repair the damage and safely restore the data. If the extent of damage is large, then operations may switch over to the standby database, so that the resultant repair will not cause high downtime.

Be Familiar with techniques to deal with memory corruption

Besides media corruption, physical corruption also manifests itself in the Oracle memory structures.

Memory Corruption

Memory corruption may have various reasons, such as hardware/OS faults, a buggy Oracle release, application code, or specific user actions. Application code can potentially cause memory corruption, especially in a single-task environment, if it attaches itself to the same memory space as Oracle. Similarly, specific user actions such as using certain Oracle tools/utilities (example: import/export) in single-task mode may potentially cause memory corruption.

Memory corruption may occur within any of the SGA (shared or system global area) and/or PGA (program global area) structures. However, corruption within the SGA, rather than within the PGA, is what causes concern. PGA corruption may cause the corresponding (individual) user process to be aborted. PMON and other background processes will perform the necessary block recovery to clean up (return the changed blocks to a consistent state) by rolling back all pending transactions and releasing resources such as locks and latches held by the process. Accordingly, there is no serious threat of data loss or loss of availability. The end user may see error messages due to the sudden disconnect. However, manually reconnecting (if it's an application and does not have the code for automatic connection-termination detection and reconnection, the application may have to be manually restarted) should resolve the situation. However, in case the corruption is present in the SGA, then potentially data may be lost, in addition to the impact on availability. To be more specific, data loss may occur if contents of the data-block buffer cache are lost (termed as "buffer cache corruption"). Corruption in other areas of the SGA such as the shared pool (data dictionary cache, library cache) or session information (in MTS configuration) will not result in data loss. However, there are very high chances of the instance crashing from SGA corruption. Corruption in the redo-log buffer during recovery may cause the recovery attempt to fail. Manually restarting the instance may resolve the memory corruption (unless there is a more permanent physical hardware problem, such as memory board damage). Even then, a sudden intermittent database bounce, potentially during peak hours, will hurt availability and may violate the uptime clauses specified within the SLA.

Buffer cache corruption usually originates in memory itself. It is not caused by a corrupt data block being read into the buffer cache by foreground server processes. As a foreground server process populates the buffer, inherent checks are performed by Oracle to guard against media corruption creeping into memory. For instance, the block version/sequence numbers maintained in the block header are matched against those maintained in the footer of the block to verify its validity. If the match results in a failure, then there may be corruption in the block header and/or the footer. Such a situation will result in error and not cause the block to be loaded into the buffer cache.

DETECTING MEMORY CORRUPTION Buffer cache corruption may be detected by either a foreground or background process during any of the following circumstances:

- While a foreground server process is reading/changing the block to satisfy a user request
- While PMON is trying to clean up an aborted session
- While DBWR is trying to write dirty data-block buffers to disk either during a checkpoint or while trying to free up space in the buffer cache, as requested by a foreground server process

In environments where memory corruption is suspected, certain initialization parameters may be enabled to detect them. The initialization parameters are the following:

- **DB_BLOCK_CHECKSUM** By setting DB_BLOCK_CHECKSUM to TRUE, diagnostics are performed by Oracle for every block read and written. This includes blocks already present in the buffer cache (blocks, once read/changed, remain in the cache until they are phased out via the LRU algorithm). The parameter causes DBWR to compute/recompute a checksum value for every block written/changed and store this checksum in the block header. This checksum is also calculated for blocks when DBWR is bypassed during certain direct operations (such as direct-path loads using SQL*Loader). Subsequently, when the block is read (physical or logical read; a logical read is satisfied by a block already in memory), Oracle computes the checksum and compares it against the checksum contained in the block header. If this does not result in a match, then the block is marked as corrupt. This check is performed only if a checksum has been written for that block in a previous write operation. DB_BLOCK_CHECKSUM is a dynamic parameter. In other words, its value can be set dynamically via the ALTER SYSTEM command (thus restricting downtime by saving a database bounce). On certain (older) Oracle versions, there was another initialization parameter, DB_BLOCK_COMPUTE_CHECKSUMS, that when set to TRUE computed a checksum and placed it in the block prior to writing it to disk. Whenever the block was read, Oracle would always authenticate the checksum, even if DB_BLOCK_COMPUTE_CHECKSUMS was set to FALSE. The block incarnation number (INC) and the sequence number (SEQ) are written to the tail portion of the block. This cannot be read if the middle portion of the block is corrupt. Accordingly, writing the checksum to the block header and authenticating it during every read will help detect corruption. DB_BLOCK_COMPUTE_CHECKSUMS existed as an underscore (undocumented) parameter in certain versions of Oracle.

- **_DB_BLOCK_CACHE_PROTECT** This parameter is available only on specific Oracle ports (mostly non-UNIX, such as VAX/VMS and certain mainframe platforms) that allow the necessary memory management. Enabling it makes Oracle trace and detect writes made to the buffer cache by foreground server processes. If a process writes to a buffer without locking it first or to a buffer pinned by another process, then this is treated as a violation and disallowed, producing a trace-dump for diagnosis.

- **LOG_BLOCK_CHECKSUM** Setting this parameter to TRUE causes Oracle to compute and write a checksum value in each redo block header. Later during recovery, Oracle computes the checksum for that block and compares it with the one contained in the redo block header. If they do not match, Oracle flags that as an error. Again, this check is performed only if the checksum had been computed and stored in that block earlier. LOG_BLOCK_CHECKSUM is not a dynamic parameter.

It is to be borne in mind that these parameters, when enabled, take up additional resources such as CPU and memory, usually causing an adverse impact on performance. Accordingly, enabling these parameters is only suggested where corruption is suspected or when recommended by Oracle Support personnel.

Furthermore, enabling LOG_BLOCK_CHECKSUM without a genuine reason only causes downtime (since the instance will have to be bounced initially to enable LOG_BLOCK_CHECKSUM, and then again later to disable it). In short, don't enable these diagnostic parameters without reason, especially in production environments, due to the overhead involved.

PREVENTING/REPAIRING MEMORY CORRUPTION Unfortunately, in the case of memory corruption there is seldom scope for immediate repair. Once buffer cache corruption is detected, Oracle causes an error message to be generated in the alert-log and at times causes one or more trace-files to be written out to the directory specified by the USER_DUMP_DEST initialization parameter. Additionally, if the corruption is severe, the Oracle instance crashes (DBWR would abort the instance, giving an ORA-600 error with a first argument of [3398], so that corrupt blocks are not written to disk). If the cause of memory corruption is determined to be a specific hardware fault or software release, then it needs to be corrected prior to restarting the instance, lest it crash again. The error message written out to the alert-log is an ORA-600 with the first argument being in the range 2000 to 8000 or between 17000 and 17999 (as mentioned in Chapter 13, ORA-600 is used to imply various internal errors—not just corruption; the first argument usually provides insight into the nature of the error).

Steps to proactively prevent memory corruption include

- Extensively testing all application code prior to deployment.
- Avoiding linking and using Oracle tools/utilities in single-task mode in a two-task environment (such as UNIX), unless expressly allowed by Oracle. Note that I recommend not using single-task only in production environments, where the Oracle instance is up and running. I do recommend using single-task during upgrades and migrations, while the instance is not up or alternatively is up on a standby server.
- Extensively testing all new Oracle releases and patches on a test server, prior to upgrading your production instance.

Be Familiar with techniques to deal with logical corruption

Unlike physical corruption that is mostly structural in nature, logical corruption manifests itself within the data. As such, it may be deadlier and more difficult to detect and repair, especially if it is dormant afflicting only certain scenarios (data-sets). Let's take a closer look at it.

Logical Corruption

Logical or data corruption is inconsistency within the data, resulting in inaccuracy and violation of critical business rules. For instance, there may be phantom or orphaned rows (that is, child rows without parents, causing them to violate referential integrity) within the database. Interestingly, logical corruption may not necessarily be flagged as an Oracle error (for instance, when orphaned rows exist, Oracle may not reject such rows due to referential integrity being defined, but disabled). However, it is still considered a form of corruption due to basic business rules and application dependencies being violated and queries potentially returning incorrect results. Such corruption may have reasons such as the following:

- Application bugs (data-load programs allowing corrupt data to be loaded or loading valid data in a wrong fashion, introducing logical corruption). Such bugs may result from flawed design, as well as erratic coding.
- User/administrative errors (accidental table deletions/truncations, and so on).
- Incomplete recovery (inconsistent point-in-time recovery mechanisms such as segment point-in-time recovery (where the recovered segment is out of sync with the other segments in the schema), tablespace point-in-time recovery (where the segments in the recovered tablespace are out of sync with the segments in other tablespaces), incomplete recovery of tablespaces with active rollback segments, and so on).
- Corrupt segments, such as indexes, that don't have a corresponding entry for all rows in the table.
- Infrequently, Oracle bugs (allowing duplicate rows to creep in, due to a corrupt unique index or errors noticed when using a specific Oracle option, such as the Parallel Query Option or the cost-based optimizer).

DETECTING LOGICAL CORRUPTION Detecting and resolving logical errors may require good knowledge of the application. One needs to look at the various schemas and the inter-relationships among them, the status of database constraints during batch runs, database options being utilized, frequency of segments being analyzed, hints used in SQL statements (for instance, the INDEX_DESC hint in v7.3.3 returns incorrect rows), view definitions, privileges, and the SQL statements themselves (for verifying functional accuracy). Also in case data is being acquired externally for loading via batch operations, then the source data and the sequence of segments being loaded need to be examined. If the source data is very large, then the large file may be sliced and examined individually, either entirely or by random sampling. The sequence of tables being loaded may be important, such that tables required to satisfy referential integrity may have to be loaded first.

PREVENTING/REPAIRING LOGICAL CORRUPTION Similar to the causes, steps for preventing and repairing logical corruption are diverse:

- Extensive testing of the application required, prior to deployment. A robust test environment is the single most effective way to prevent corruption in production environments due to application bugs. Robust application design and development practices help in achieving this goal.
- Security in production environments needs to be robust, so that unauthorized changes in segment structures, chances of accidental deletes/truncates, and so on, are minimized.
- The database may need to be re-created (either completely or in specific sub-sets, based on application schemas and the inter-relationships) after incomplete recovery is performed to prevent logical corruption. Having a standby database will limit downtime during the rebuild. Also, points of contact in the application user/developer community are needed so that the DBA will have knowledgeable help in determining what is missing.
- Periodically analyzing the segments with the VALIDATE STRUCTURE option will help detect segment corruption. Using this option with the CASCADE clause on tables reconciles all index entries with the table and vice versa. Any inconsistencies are reported. The following piece of code illustrates its usage:

```
SQL> ANALYZE TABLE orders VALIDATE STRUCTURE CASCADE;
```

If corruption is detected in a segment, it will have to be rebuilt. Also, it's advisable to analyze the segment at least twice, prior to deciding to rebuild it. The error(s) initially encountered (during actual use by DML statements or during the first ANALYZE) should be reconciled against the error(s) generated during subsequent analyzes. If the errors are the same each time (such as ORA-1498), they may refer to internal corruption within the segment. If the errors are different or have different arguments (different file #s, block #s within ORA-1578) each time, then they may represent a serious media error (bad disk, controller, SCSI channel, or the like).

Prior to running the VALIDATE STRUCTURE command (since it is time-consuming), one should run an EXPLAIN PLAN on the SQL statement that seems to be producing incorrect output and find out what segments are actually being utilized by the SQL statement (for instance, the access path may read only an index in an index-only scan or a fast full index scan, rather than the table). Accordingly, an initial idea may be derived that the index may potentially be corrupt. Similarly, in a join of two tables, the driving table (or index) may be corrupt, leading to incorrect results. Thus, doing an EXPLAIN PLAN provides a good understanding of the segments that may possibly be corrupt. Only such segments will require the VALIDATE STRUCTURE command to be run on them (rather than all segments used by the statement). Alternatively, the EXPLAIN PLAN output provides a view of the access path utilized by the statement. A detailed observation of the access path may provide an insight into potential Oracle bugs in the access path.

At a client site, we had planned an outage to re-create a fragmented index. So at 1:00 in the morning on a Sunday, another DBA and I got together to perform the task. All the applications were taken down (since the table was a popular one, used by all the applications). The database used Oracle7 v7.3, and we re-created the index using the REBUILD option, hoping to keep downtime to the minimum. The table had around 12 million rows, and the task was completed in around 45 minutes (even though we had scheduled an hour's outage). All the applications were then brought back up, and we were live again. As we were patting ourselves on the back and heading out, my phone rang. It was the CTO of the company. He had tried to log onto one of the Web-based applications to ensure that things were OK. His logon attempt was being rejected by the application. Logon information was part of the data in the table, whose index we had just rebuilt. What could go wrong with a simple index rebuild, we had thought. Well, surprise, surprise! My colleague and I started looking at various views such as DBA_SEGMENTS, DBA_OBJECTS, DBA_TABLES, DBA_INDEXES, and so on, to ensure that everything was existing and valid (DBA_OBJECTS.STATUS = 'VALID'). Finally, one of the developers also working on the problem remotely (from home) called up and said that the new index might be corrupt. How could that be, we asked ourselves; we had just rebuilt it! He e-mailed us the EXPLAIN PLAN output for the SQL statement responsible for allowing a user to log on (the developer clearly was a very knowledgeable one, with access to the application source code). The plan showed that the statement was using an index-only lookup of the index we had just rebuilt to verify that the user ID and password (that the user was using to log on) were valid. There was no doubt left in our minds that the index might somehow have become corrupt. I ran an ANALYZE command with the VALIDATE STRUCTURE CASCADE option on the table and got a confirmation that the index was indeed missing some keys. It seemed that since we had used the REBUILD option of the ALTER INDEX command (rather than using the CREATE INDEX command), the existing index, rather than the actual table, had been the source of input to the new index. The original index may have been corrupt already. However, we never detected it (the CTO and other users, who may have been afflicted by the corruption, never logged on at that time, causing the corruption to remain undetected). Now the corruption had cascaded to the new index. Immediately we dropped the index and re-created it via the CREATE INDEX command. This time, it took a little more than an hour to create it (since the actual table was used as the source by the CREATE INDEX command). The total outage lasted for around three hours. Hardly enough reason to pat each other on the back, anymore! This period included the time taken to run the ANALYZE VALIDATE STRUCTURE CASCADE command. During the running of this command, the applications had to be taken down for an extended period as well, due to the table lock acquired by this command and due to the inability of this command to support the parallel query option in v7.3, thus running in serial mode. These make its use very unrealistic in mission-critical environments with large tables and stringent availability requirements. This has been rectified to a major extent in Oracle8*i* by allowing the command to run in parallel mode. In prior versions, the time taken to run this command makes a standby database or standby/mirrored tables almost mandatory to limit downtime while debugging corruption-related issues (please refer to Chapter 15 for a discussion of standby/mirrored tables).

Another time, at a different client site, it was brought to my attention by a developer that a join being run in a development environment was returning an incorrect number of rows. After running an EXPLAIN PLAN on the statement, we found that the optimizer (CBO in v7.2.1) was using a hash join to evaluate the results. All the segments seemed valid. Analyzing them with the VALIDATE STRUCTURE option did not disclose any errors. Finally, we reported the matter to Oracle Support, who confirmed that there was a bug in hash joins in that release; we were shipped a patch.

Thus, running an EXPLAIN PLAN on the erroneous statement may greatly help in pinpointing the exact source of the error and so reduce the time to repair the corruption.

If the cause of logical corruption cannot be determined or it seems to be the symptom of a bug, the situation needs to be reported to Oracle Support for a solution. The instance may have to be upgraded with the appropriate patch/newer release, if one is available. If the situation is serious and no patch is currently available (in spite of a reproducible test case), the issue may have to be escalated, until a patch is made available as promptly as possible.

Identify and list all components susceptible to corruption

All components, external and internal to the database, that are susceptible to corruption need to be identified and listed. Such a list needs to be developed on the basis of input from various administrative groups such as systems administrators, network administrators, database administrators, application designers/developers (a few representatives from the designer/developer team are essential to provide input on detailed application-related issues), and systems/database operators (the operators' input is key, because they are usually the ones to spot the error messages before anyone else). Each component needs to be classified as hardware/OS, network, database, and so on, so that the right administrative group can address them and formulate ways to prevent, detect, and repair corruption and restore normalcy. Again, such a list needs to consider history and the corruption that has been experienced by the company (and, if possible, other companies operating in a similar fashion—peer relationships and user/special interest groups should greatly help in garnering knowledge about experiences and strategies at other companies). Detailed documentation needs to be maintained about each corruption scenario as it occurs and is resolved, so that regardless of individuals actually dealing with it, other personnel, including their successors, can have an insight about the kinds of afflictions suffered so far and the solutions applied. This would be a splendid means of anticipating corruption from diverse sources and ways to prevent and combat each possible source.

Such a list will also help each group to decide what, when, and how to monitor each component, what kind of preventive steps to take for each component, the correct reaction when corruption is encountered nevertheless, and the fastest ways to overcome the corruption and restore normalcy. The time to restore normalcy depends on the scope of corruption and how well prepared the administrative groups are that deal with the corruption. Preparing such a list will help each group understand its "enemy" and arm itself sufficiently, so that the battle will be short and result in victory.

Table 14-1 provides a sample format to list database components that are susceptible to corruption. This list may be used to outline all components that have failed or are likely to fail in your environment. It may be easily expanded to accommodate any number of components or corruption scenarios. A similar format may be utilized to document corruption in hardware/OS, applications, and middle-tier and client-tier areas.

Identify and list measures to prevent, detect, and repair corruption in your environment

As stated earlier, the response of administrative personnel while dealing with corruption is crucial in keeping downtime to a minimum. Such responses may depend on a variety of subjective factors, such as knowledge level, skill level, confidence, and mood of the administrator(s) currently in place to deal with the situation, the nature and scope of the corruption (as interpreted by the administrator), the urgency of the situation (corruption surfacing during peak hours or non-peak hours), and so on. Certain urgent situations may almost require "nerves of steel" to methodically analyze the situation and take action promptly to restrict downtime to clauses mentioned in the SLA. A less-experienced administrator may easily crumble and make errors, thus worsening the already grim situation. Accordingly, an attempt should be made to reduce subjectivity as much as possible. By clearly listing ways to prevent, detect, and repair the corruption (at least, the more common ones), a sense of confidence is built up in the administrator(s) handling the issue. He or she knows that potential solutions are clearly listed—all that is required is good analysis of the nature and scope of

Component	Reason for Corruption (as Determined)	Potential Solutions (List in order of preference and state expected downtime.)	Preventive Steps
Classification: Physical (MEDIA)			
Online current redo-log group (one member)			
Online current redo-log group (all members)			
Online non-current unarchived redo-log group (one member)			
Online non-current unarchived redo-log group (all members)			
Online non-current archived redo-log group (one member)			
Online non-current archived redo-log group (all members)			
Archived redo-log (not backed up to tape)			
Control-file (one copy)			
Control-file (all copies)			
Data-file belonging to SYSTEM tablespace			
Data-file belonging to APPL_DATA tablespace			
Data-file belonging to APPL_INDX tablespace			
Classification: Physical (memory)			

TABLE 14-1. *A Sample List of Database Components Susceptible to Corruption*

Component	Reason for Corruption (as Determined)	Potential Solutions (List in order of preference and state expected downtime.)	Preventive Steps
SGA (buffer cache)			
SGA (shared pool)			
SGA (log buffer)			
PGA			
Classification: logical			
Primary-key violation			
Referential integrity violation			
CHECK constraint violation			
Incorrect number of rows returned by query			

TABLE 14-1. *A Sample List of Database Components Susceptible to Corruption* (continued)

corruption, and the rest is merely a selection of the best possible method to resolve the corruption. Having said that, let's summarize some of the techniques discussed in the preceding paragraphs, list some new ones, and place them in perspective.

Proactive Measures to Prevent Corruption

Following are some measures to prevent corruption from creeping in:

- Robust application design and development practices.
- Application-code version control and strict deployment procedures.
- Robust test environment testing hardware/software functionality and capacity.
- Security.
- Keeping all data-files restricted to 2GB or less, unless necessary. All 64-bit OSs (Digital UNIX, Solaris 7) and some 32-bit OSs (Solaris 2.6) support large files (that is, files greater than 2GB in size). Also, 32-bit OSs can support such file sizes via a method called "62on32" implementation, wherein a 64-bit integer is used for file addressing. However, all Oracle ports do not support large files (especially in the older versions, since the dba was a 32-bit integer [rather than

the current 48-bit or higher], preventing address of files over 2GB in size). Moreover, the OS may have bugs in addressing large files and may need specific patches. Creating files within Oracle without proper knowledge and installation of these OS patches may cause reads/writes to be wayward, since the block offset within a file may be interpreted incorrectly, thus introducing media corruption. Hence, as a safety precaution, do not create data-files greater than 2GB, unless you are managing a VLDB. I have at times observed sites with a small database (less than 50GB) and a handful of tablespaces creating 4GB data-files, unnecessarily incurring the risk of corruption. Bear in mind that when you have smaller files, you may need to specify a large value for the MAXDATAFILES parameter at the time of database creation (to allow a large number of files). Also, the DB_FILES initialization parameter needs to be set high (which will increase the size of the PGA/SGA and thus increase memory consumption). In a VLDB environment, you may be forced to create large files to stay within the limit imposed for MAXDATAFILES in Oracle (note that this limit has substantially increased in Oracle8 to a theoretical maximum of 256 million, thus reducing the danger of hitting the maximum limit).

Methods for Early Corruption Detection

A combination of methods ought to be followed to detect the corruption, as early as possible, after it has occurred. Accordingly, measures need to be taken on a regular basis to periodically check for corruption at various levels—both external and internal to the database. External checking aids in detecting hardware/system-level corruption and certain varieties of database physical corruption. Internal checking aids in detecting other varieties of database physical corruption and logical corruption. The objective is to check for errors within all components determined to be susceptible to corruption.

- System and database monitoring
- Monitoring system logs, database alert-logs and trace-logs, audit trails (if auditing is enabled), and application-related log files (if any exist). Relevant files can be periodically parsed (using *grep* or similar tools) for errors (and the DBA can be paged, if an error is found).
- Periodic analyzing of segments (tables, indexes, and clusters) with the VALIDATE STRUCTURE [CASCADE] option.
- Periodically using DB_VERIFY to verify block integrity within Oracle. DB_VERIFY is Oracle's utility (available starting with v7.3.2) to check for corruption. It may be used to validate backups and ensure that they are consistent with the original data-files. DB_VERIFY can also be run directly against a data-file (on certain OSs, such as Windows NT, there may be an

access violation, since the database is open and is accessing all data-files; the workaround is to copy the data-file and run DB_VERIFY against the copy). DB_VERIFY does not check for most logical corruption errors. The actual (executable) name for DB_VERIFY is OS-dependent. On most UNIX platforms, it is called *dbv,* whereas on NT, it is called *dbverf73, dbverf80,* and so on (that is, the Oracle version is appended to the name).

The basic syntax for using DB_VERIFY is as follows:

```
C:\> dbverf80 file=<file-name> [blocksize=<DB_BLOCK_SIZE>]
```

Specifying the block size becomes necessary if the Oracle block size (DB_BLOCK_SIZE) is different from the default (2,048 bytes, or 2KB). Not doing so would result in misleading corruption-related error messages.

A sample output of DB_VERIFY follows:

```
C:\> dbverf80 file= c:\orant\database\usr4orc8.ora
DBVERIFY: Release 8.0.3.0.0 - Production on Thu Jun 10 1:32:1 1999
(c) Copyright 1997 Oracle Corporation.  All rights reserved.
DBVERIFY - Verification starting : FILE = c:\orant\database\usr4orc8.ora
DBVERIFY - Verification complete

Total Pages Examined         : 2560
Total Pages Processed (Data) :  832
Total Pages Failing   (Data) :    0
Total Pages Processed (Index):  730
Total Pages Failing   (Index):    0
Total Pages Empty            :  424
Total Pages Marked Corrupt   :    0
Total Pages Influx           :    0
```

In the preceding output, "Total Pages Examined" refers to the total number of Oracle blocks read (that the file is made up of). "Total Pages Influx" refers to blocks currently being accessed (hence they are in a state of flux). If DB_VERIFY shows that certain blocks are corrupt, then it is advisable to run DB_VERIFY once again to check whether the messages are repeated. Sometimes, a high number of "influx" blocks may result in misleading messages. Other information in the output is self-explanatory.

Table 14-2 provides a sample list of return values from DB_VERIFY.

Refer to the Oracle documentation for further detailed instructions on use of this utility. Also, Chapter 4 provides instructions to use DB_VERIFY against raw devices.

- Initialization parameters such as DB_BLOCK_CHECKSUM, LOG_BLOCK_CHECKSUM, DB_BLOCK_COMPUTE_CHECKSUMS, and _DB_BLOCK_CACHE_PROTECT.

Value	Description
0	Block OK
1	Row locked by non-existent transaction
2	Row begins beyond end of block
7	There are free slots not on free list
23	Row length inconsistency
25	Row count in table index incorrect

TABLE 14-2. *A Sample List of Values Returned by DB_VERIFY (Note that this list is not comprehensive.)*

- Database events (set via ALTER SYSTEM/SESSION commands or via the initialization parameter EVENT) such as 10015 (to detect rollback segment corruption), 10210 (to detect table block corruption), 10211 (to detect index block corruption), and 10212 (to detect cluster block corruption).
- OS tools and utilities such as the following:
  - ***sum*** Available on various UNIX platforms (for example, Solaris and HP-UX), *sum* allows a checksum (generally 16-bit) to be calculated for a specified file. It returns the checksum value computed and the size of the file (in bytes or physical blocks, that is, 512-byte blocks) and, optionally, the name of the file. It may be used to calculate a checksum for any regular file. The *sum* command may be used to validate database backups by performing a checksum on the original Oracle files (data-files, redo-logs, and so on) and their backups and comparing the results. If the checksum between the two does not match, then there is a possibility of corruption.
  - ***cksum*** This command is similar to *sum;* however, it uses a CRC (cyclical redundancy check) mechanism to compute a checksum value. This CRC value can be computed for both the original Oracle file and its backup, which can then be reconciled. Any resulting discrepancy may refer to corruption in the file. Unlike *sum,* which has different variations implemented under various UNIX flavors (sometimes even under different versions of the same flavor), *cksum* is implemented in most flavors in a consistent fashion. Accordingly, it may be used to compare files across different machines (such as comparing a data-file on a test instance versus a data-file on the production instance). However, it is to be borne in mind that the behavior of *cksum* may be influenced via the

CMD_ENV environment variable. Based on the setting of this variable, *cksum* may compute checksums based on different implementations of the Ethernet standard frame check (X/Open or IEEE 1003.2). As long as a specific standard is consistently adopted across all machines, then the resultant checksums for a file will be consistent, as well.

Please refer to the UNIX *man* pages for more details on the use of *sum* and *cksum.*

Indications of Corruption

The following symptoms tend to highlight corruption:

- Error messages such as ORA-1578 or ORA-600 on the users' screens or in the alert-log
- Inconsistent results from DML/DDL statements
- Core dumps and trace-file generation

Measures to Prevent Corruption from Affecting Availability

The following measures would prevent any major service disruptions, in case corruption does strike in your environment:

- Hardware redundancy
- Hot-swappable hardware components
- Standby tables/databases
- Fast detection and repair of corruption and data restore
- Applications designed and programmed to handle corruption, in terms of connecting to a standby database or to a mirrored segment (replicated segment), when a critical segment is not accessible or when certain corruption-related errors are encountered.

Methods and Tools to Repair Corruption

Repairing corruption involves using available means to restore normalcy and may consist of steps to fix/replace the bad component (replace the bad hardware component, downgrade the current software release, and so on) and re-create lost data. Repair eliminates corruption, treats the afflicted segments, and restores consistency within the database. The methods available for such repair depend upon the nature and scope of the corruption. The following are some of the common methods available to combat database corruption:

- Database events such as 10231 (to skip corrupt blocks during segment scans)
- Row retrieval based on existing indexes
- Row retrieval via range scans of ROWIDs
- Reentry of data and/or rerunning batch jobs

Retain relevant information regarding the corruption

If corruption is detected or suspected, retain all information pointing to this fact. This information may be useful in providing the required insight to Oracle Support/Development personnel, so that they may debug the situation and pinpoint the possible causes. Such information may include

- The alert-log with the ORA-600 and other errors (if the alert-log is large and the required portions are relatively tiny, such portions may be copied and pasted into a separate file to ease handling).
- Trace-files created in the USER_DUMP_DEST directory.
- The heap dump-file created (as a trace-file in the USER_DUMP_DEST directory) via the command

  ```
  SQL> ALTER SESSION SET EVENTS 'IMMEDIATE TRACE NAME HEAPDUMP, LEVEL 10';
  ```

  The heap dump helps in providing information on the contents of the heap section of physical memory. This may be required by Oracle Support to diagnose memory corruption.
- Documentation of events that were current at the time of the error (as best as possible)—new patches, programs running, ad hoc statements, non-database activities on the machine, specific database events set, and so on.
- The initialization parameter file that was current at the time of the error.
- A reproducible test case, if possible.

Table 14-3 provides an example of documenting and collecting information on each occurrence of data-block corruption. It can easily be expanded to accommodate other types of media, memory, and logical corruption.

Train your administrators to handle corruption

The best confidence booster is knowledge. Accordingly, training to deal with corruption will tremendously increase confidence in the administrator, regarding his

Date & time of occurrence	04-APR-1999 23:01:00
Database & server name	TST4 on ZEUS (service name: TST4)
Error code & complete message	ORA-01578: ORACLE data block corrupted (file #7, block #59882)
Corrupt file number	7
Corrupt block number	59882
Segments affected (list along with segment type and schema owner)	NAMES (TABLE, APPL_OWNR)
Latest backup taken on	04-APR-1999 03:00:00
Latest backup available online	04-APR-1999 03:00:00
Error occurred during peak/non-peak hours	Non-peak
Symptoms of corruption	Error message on SELECT statements performing full-table scans on NAMES
Suspected/actual reason of corruption	Actual—bad disk sectors
Downtime (if any) caused	None
Number of active sessions at the time of corruption	26 (15 batch, 6 ad hoc, 5 administrative)
Active DML at the time of corruption	SQLAREA dump in file *zeus:/u1/oracle/admin/TST4/doc/corruption/dml_0404.lst*
Any non-database problems/issues noted	Bad disk sectors
File containing portion of alert-log just prior to, during, and just after the corruption incidence	*zeus:/u1/oracle/admin/TST4/doc/corruption/alrt_0404.lst*
Name of file containing block dump	*zeus:/u1/oracle/admin/TST4/doc/corruption/blkdump_0404.lst*
Names of relevant trace-files	*zeus:/u1/oracle/admin/TST4/bdump/102213_TST4.trc*
Summary of possible solutions and possible time to recover via each one	Documented in *zeus:/u1/oracle/admin/TST4/doc/corruption/resolution_0404.lst*

TABLE 14-3. *A Convenient Method for Documenting All Occurrences of Corruption*

Resolution adopted	Used mirror to let database remain operational, while bad disk was replaced with a new one. Then the new disk was resilvered with the mirror.
Time to resolve	0 hours, 26 minutes (approx.)
Total time taken to restore normalcy (from the time of detection to repair and restore of data)	2 hours, 0 minutes (approx.)
Recommended steps to prevent such corruption	Refer to *artemis:c:\db_doc\corruption\prevention\hardware_corruption.doc*

TABLE 14-3. *A Convenient Method for Documenting All Occurrences of Corruption* (continued)

or her ability to deal with the situation and successfully overcome it. Besides theoretical knowledge (derived from books and the lists mentioned in previous tips), practical knowledge ought to be derived by simulating various corruption scenarios and ways to recover from each of them on a test environment. Ideally, such test environment should mirror the production instance as closely as possible. In this specific case, however, even if the test environment is different from the actual production, it will still give the administrator an insider's look at database corruption and ways to recover from it. So during "peace time," when there is no corruption and things are normal, administrative personnel should be trained in recovering from corruption.

Summary

This chapter took a detailed look at dealing with database corruption. The term "corruption" was explained, and different types of corruption were listed. Some proactive measures to prevent corruption were outlined. However, totally eliminating corruption is very difficult, and so steps for early detection of corruption, whenever it strikes, were discussed. Some tools to repair corruption and restore normalcy as early as possible were also discussed. This concludes the section on troubleshooting in a 24x7 environment. Of course, there are various other problems, besides those mentioned in this section, that could seriously threaten availability. However, many of them are discussed in the previous chapters under earlier sections (since other implications, such as proactive maintenance, also govern such issues, besides mere troubleshooting).

Starting with the next section, we take a look at various Oracle and third-party solutions to attain higher availability.

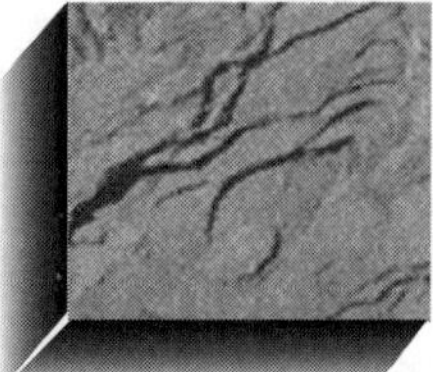

PART VI

High Availability Solutions

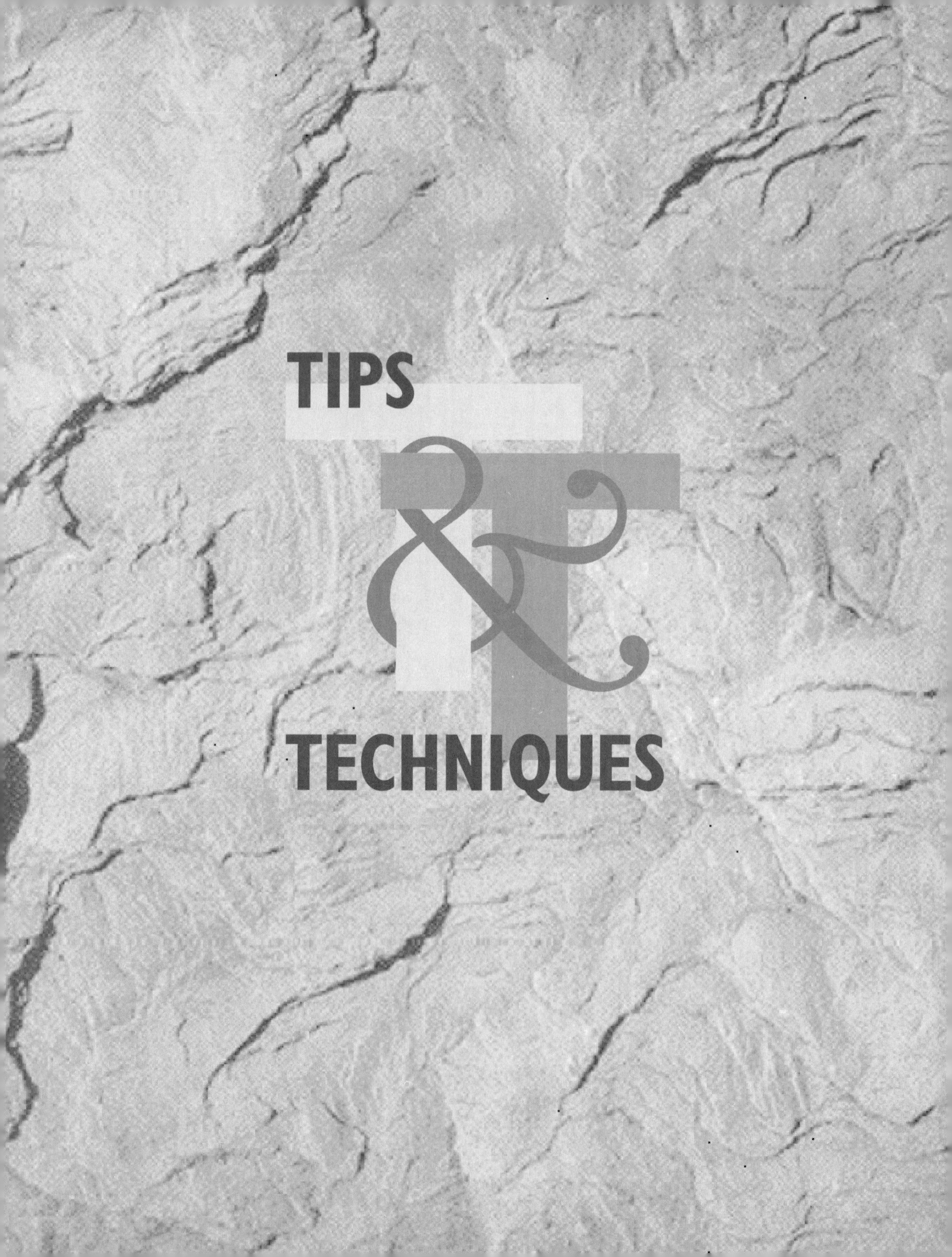
TIPS
&
TECHNIQUES

CHAPTER 15

Standby Options

Redundant standby resources have been traditionally used to reduce downtime during system failures and disasters. In this chapter, we look at the standby options available within Oracle. Additionally, we explore certain custom standby options, such as triggers and journal tables, that can be implemented using Oracle's standard functionality. These custom strategies allow availability during various routine maintenance procedures, migrations, version upgrades, and emergencies.

This chapter offers the following tips and techniques:

- Consider using a standby database for disaster recovery
- Consider using standby instances in environments where true 24x7 uptime is not mandatory
- Consider combining multiple solutions to form a comprehensive one
- Evaluate using a Custom Standby Database (CSD)
- Consider using standby tables to cater to segment-level failures
- Be aware of caveats with the custom solutions described here

Standby Options from Oracle

This section focuses on standby options available from Oracle. Two standby options are discussed : standby databases and standby instances.

Consider using a standby database for disaster recovery

A standby database, as the name implies, is a copy of a functioning database, kept ready to be used in lieu of the latter for availability during disasters and system/database failures (when the functioning primary database has crashed and is unavailable). Figure 15-1 illustrates a standby database. Generally, only the production database is cloned; it is referred to as the *primary* or the *source* database, and the standby database is referred to as the *secondary* or the *target* database. The mechanics for implementing a standby database have been officially available within Oracle since v7.3. However, with every release (especially with Oracle8*i*), the standby database feature has been made more robust and automatic. Irrespective of the version, every standby database implementation follows certain well-defined steps. I have referred to this standby database implementation provided within Oracle as the "regular" or "conventional" standby implementation (as opposed to a "custom" approach outlined subsequently). Based on the version, the actual method/command for performing certain steps may differ. However, the overall objectives remain the same. Refer to your version-specific Oracle documentation set for complete details on configuring standby databases in your environment. Here, the objective is not to reproduce the information in the Oracle documentation set, but to give you an insight into standby databases, how they work, how they enhance availability, and what pertinent issues you need to be aware of prior to deciding to implement standby databases. Also, I have elaborated on some new standby database features available in the latest Oracle release: Oracle8*i*. Now, let's look at how standby databases operate.

NOTE
The standby database feature has been provided within Oracle only starting with v7.3, because prior versions do not store data-file statuses and control-file changes in the online and archived redo-logs and lack the inherent integrity checks required for a standby implementation. However, it is possible to maintain a standby database in earlier versions via manual methods to create a clone, refresh it periodically via the archived logs, and switch over when necessary by wrapping up recovery via the RECOVER USING BACKUP CONTROLFILE command. However, all means to maintain database structural integrity and control are manual. In such environments, automation of all tasks via pre-written scripts and stringent monitoring is highly essential to prevent errors and corruption.

The transactions occurring in the primary database are applied to the standby database via the former's archived redo-logs. As transactions get written to the online redo-logs, the logs get full, switch, and are archived by ARCH prior to being overwritten. Thus, both the primary and standby databases need to be in ARCHIVELOG mode. The archived logs are copied across the network to the remote standby server (note that in Oracle8*i*, the archived logs can be directly written to a remote standby location). The standby database is continuously in a state of recovery (mounted, not open). All archived logs copied over are applied to the standby database to allow it to catch up with the primary database. The standby database is always behind the primary database. Even if all the archived logs generated thus far have been already applied, it still lags behind because transactions are currently being written to the primary's online redo-logs and these can be applied only after they are archived and copied over. Note that backups of both the primary and secondary databases need to occur, in addition to the standby implementation. In other words, the standby implementation is not a substitute for taking backups.

When the primary database experiences failure, switchover may occur, wherein the standby database is taken out of recovery mode, all remaining archived redo-logs are applied (whenever possible, the current online redo-logs of the primary are archived and applied, as well, to ensure that there is no transaction loss), and the standby database is made the primary. After the original primary database has been repaired/restored, it becomes the standby database. Thus, it is kept in mounted mode, and all archived redo-logs (from the current primary) are applied to it. Thus, whenever the current primary database experiences a failure, the current standby takes over as the primary with very little downtime (during the switchover). Once the switchover is complete, the applications and user sessions need to be switched over to access the new primary database.

Note that the switchover from primary to secondary occurs whenever there is a failure. However, switchback (from the original secondary to original primary) may occur even when there is no failure. If the original secondary server has lower resources than the original primary, then performance and throughput are impacted. Also if the original secondary lacks the desired capacity to fully support the site, some non-mission critical applications may have to be disabled, so that only core applications requiring high-availability run. Once the original primary is available again, rather than retaining it as standby, switchback needs to be scheduled as soon as possible (preferably during low-use hours) to make it primary once again (and make the current primary the standby again) to reverse the impact on performance. Keep in mind that immediately after switchover and before the other server is put back in place as a standby, there is a window of exposure where only the primary server will be functioning. There won't be a standby (since the other server is being repaired/restored). During such times, if another database failure occurs, then there won't be any means to limit downtime, unless multiple standby servers are utilized.

As you have seen, the standby database is in a state of constant recovery. That means the database cannot be used (for reporting, ad hoc queries, and so on) by end-users. This may be perceived to be a waste of resources by management. Thus in Oracle*8i*, the standby database can be kept open for certain periods in read-only mode. However, when the database is open, archived redo-logs from the primary database cannot be applied to it, since recovery and open access are mutually exclusive (at least, in current releases). But once access is complete, the database can be put back in recovery mode and the process of applying archived logs can continue. This is a very useful feature for certain environments where maintaining dual environments is necessary. Thus, during the day-time when users need to issue ad hoc queries, the standby database can be kept open in read-only mode. The archived logs from the primary that need to be applied can be accumulated on the standby server. After the day ends, the standby database can be closed and placed in recovery mode again. Then the accumulated archived logs can be applied. For example, in the eight hours of regular business-hours, there may be 20–25 archived logs that get accumulated, which could be applied in the evening. In case the primary database fails during business hours, the MTTR will be higher as the remaining archived logs are applied to make the standby relatively current and switchover occurs. However, the higher MTTR needs to be reconciled with organizational availability requirements to see whether that is acceptable.

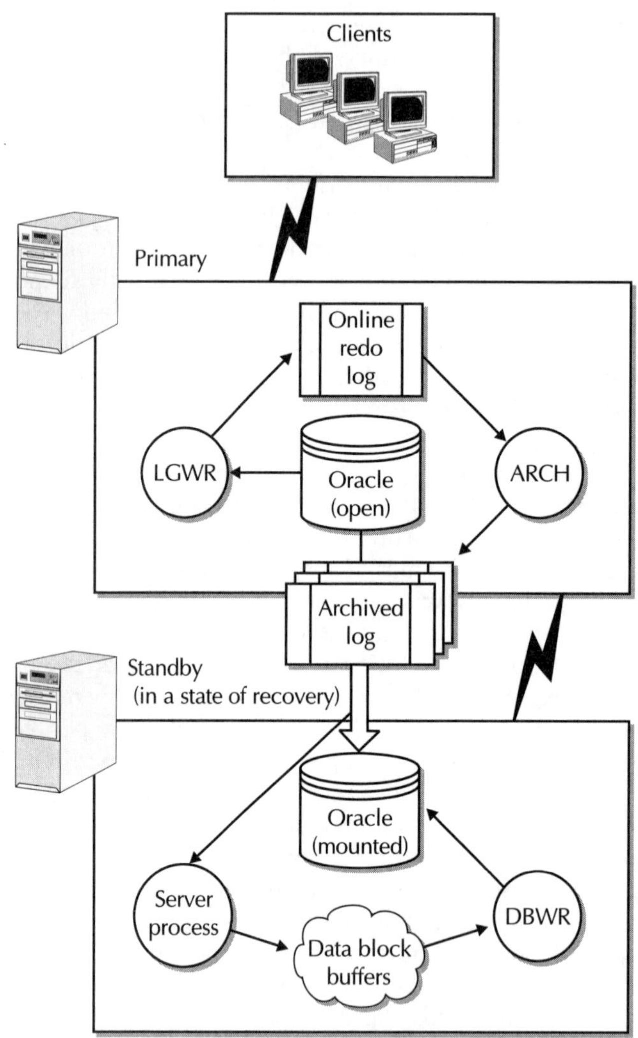

FIGURE 15-1. *Regular standby database implementation*

Obviously, in a true 24x7 environment, that wouldn't be an acceptable alternative (trading potential downtime for better usage of dormant resources).

In theory, the process sounds simple enough; however, obviously complex issues need to be addressed prior to and during the implementation. Let's look at the steps involved in a standby database implementation.

Choosing the Standby Server

A standby database can be maintained on the same server (machine) as the primary. However, this scenario is not recommended, since it does not allow disaster recovery (floods, tornadoes, and so on) or even availability during system failures (the server becomes a single point of failure). Additionally, the sharing of system resources could impact the primary database adversely (since less resources would be available for the primary database). Accordingly, it is necessary to invest in a separate server, similar in configuration to (ideally, exactly the same) the primary server. It is highly recommended that the standby server be maintained in a remote location (again, for disaster recovery). It is necessary that the primary and standby servers have identical resources (disk-space, memory, CPUs, and so on). This ensures that performance does not degrade after switchover and that switchback (from original secondary to original primary) does not become very urgent. Of all the resources, disk-space on the standby server needs to match that on the primary server because as the primary database expands, the secondary database should also be able to expand correspondingly. Otherwise, the redo from the primary specific to the new data-file(s) cannot be applied to the standby, resulting in the standby getting out-of-sync. Also, the primary and standby servers should have the same OS version and patch levels (any major or jumbo patches should be applied on both machines).

Setting Up the Network

The next logical step is ensuring that a network with adequate bandwidth exists between the primary and standby servers. Absence of adequate bandwidth would prove to be a bottleneck in keeping the standby database in-sync. Also the network should allow reliable transfer of files. If the archived redo-logs being copied over (via FTP, rcp, or the like) are interrupted mid-stream or time-out or encounter errors due to excessive traffic, then the redo-application will be interrupted. Checks should be put in place (such as OS checksums on the source and target servers to ensure that the complete archived files have reached the target) to detect network-related errors. Another area that needs some thinking is performing online backups of the primary database. If you use the older hot backups method to perform online backups, additional redo will get generated during the backups (while the tablespaces are in hot backup mode). This will increase the traffic between the primary and the standby. Ensure that the network has adequate bandwidth to support the transfer of the additional traffic. If the database is a VLDB, then your backup plan needs to accommodate partial backups (for example, one tablespace a day) to prevent the network traffic from being overwhelming.

Creating the Standby Database

The Oracle versions on both the primary and standby servers should be the same (same release number, such as Oracle8 or Oracle8*i*; minor version differences are acceptable but not recommended). The COMPATIBLE initialization parameters on both databases need to match. Certain other initialization parameters need to match (such as DB_NAME, DB_FILES, and DB_BLOCK_SIZE). If the resources on the standby server are fewer, then corresponding initialization parameters need to be toned down on the standby (such as DB_BLOCK_BUFFERS, SHARED_POOL, and SORT_AREA_SIZE). The init.ora file on the primary needs to have specific initialization parameters defined, such as LOG_ARCHIVE_DEST_<N> (specifies mandatory/optional, local/remote archive-log destinations), LOG_ARCHIVE_DEST_STATE_<N> (to dynamically or statically disable/enable some of these archive-log destinations), and LOG_ARCHIVE_TRACE (to dynamically trace writes to archived logs). Note that these example parameters are specific to Oracle8*i*. Additionally, the standby init.ora file needs to have other specific parameters defined, such as STANDBY_ARCHIVE_DEST (specifies a path for the recovery process on the standby database to look for archived redo-logs) and DB_FILE_STANDBY_NAME_CONVERT (specifies that the file-paths for data-files are different on the primary and standby servers and provides the source and target values for path-substitution). Some of these parameters are optional, and the exact number and names of these parameters differ across versions (refer to your documentation on what they are). The standby database needs to have the exact same physical structure as the primary in terms of number of tablespaces, number of data-files, and so on. However, the physical file-path (as mentioned earlier) and the status of the tablespaces and data-files could vary (online versus offline, read-only versus read/write, and so on), especially if you want to restrict application of redo to certain non-mission critical tablespaces. However, it is recommended that the status of every tablespace/data-file match its primary counterpart to avoid complexities during switchover.

Implementing the Standby Configuration

A special standby control-file is created off the primary database, and the latest backups (hot backups, Recovery Manager online backup groups, and so on) are used to create the secondary database. There should be an automated smooth flow of archived redo-logs from the primary to the secondary. All the archived logs from the time of the latest backups need to be applied. If there is an interruption in the redo-stream (wherein the online redo-logs at the primary are cleared or the remote copy mechanism skips some archived logs), the standby database becomes invalid. Accordingly, in order to prevent manual errors, the entire implementation, including switchover, should be automated via scripts. Thus, the script needs to check whether the archival of a redo-log is complete (via the ARCHIVED column in *v$log*) prior to copying it over. Copying over an incomplete archived log-file and applying it to the standby database may result in corruption of the standby database, requiring it to be subsequently rebuilt. In versions prior to Oracle8*i*, sites had to rely on methods external to the database (such as FTP or copying it over an NFS-mounted partition).

However, with Oracle8*i*, remote archive-log destinations are supported, wherein for every ARCH process on the primary database, a corresponding remote file server (RFS) process is created on the standby database. The RFS process shares I/O with ARCH and directly writes out the entire archived log to the remote standby server, eliminating the need for external intervention. Furthermore, it keeps the standby control-file in-sync with every new archived redo-log written. However, for this process to work efficiently, the network needs to provide adequate throughput; otherwise, the performance of the primary database would be impacted (since the online redo-logs cannot be overwritten unless they are archived). This is made possible via the new initialization parameters LOG_ARCHIVE_DEST_<N> and LOG_ARCHIVE_DEST_STATE_<N> in Oracle8*i*. These can be enabled/disabled dynamically (while the primary database is up and running), without impact to availability. Additionally, Oracle8*i* introduces a new feature called "managed" recovery that further automates the standby implementation. Rather than manually setting up the standby database to be in continuous recovery-mode, the standby database is mounted and placed in managed recovery mode. Here, the recovery process will automatically check the standby control-file and apply new archived redo-logs, as necessary.

Transaction Resolution and Maintenance

Most activities that occur in the primary are recorded in the redo-logs and hence get propagated automatically to the standby. However, certain activities do not. For instance, all DDL and DML activity occurring in UNRECOVERABLE/NOLOGGING mode (such as a SQL*Loader process using DIRECT path and NOLOGGING mode or an index or table being built in NOLOGGING mode) or certain structural changes to the database (such as a new data-file being added) are not reflected in the redo-logs. Accordingly, these transactions do not appear in the standby database. In order to reflect them, you will need to rebuild the standby database or perform those steps manually when the standby database is opened (during switchover). Accordingly, in a standby database implementation, you need to question the usage of any command that does not propagate automatically, record such commands after use, and ensure that they are played back in the right order in the standby database. For instance, when a new data-file is added on the primary, the continuous recovery on the secondary database needs to be cancelled, and the corresponding data-file also needs to be added via the ALTER DATABASE ADD DATAFILE command. Then recovery can continue as before. Alternatively, the standby database can be completely rebuilt using a new backup control-file (which reflects the new data-file) and the latest backups.

Monitoring scripts need to be put in-place to check for UNRECOVERABLE/ NOLOGGING operations and database structural changes and page the DBA to synchronize the standby database (if necessary). Structural changes can be detected by parsing the alert-log (CREATE/ALTER DATABASE/TABLESPACE commands show

up in the alert-log). For detecting UNRECOVERABLE/NOLOGGING operations, the script can run the following query:

```
SQL> SELECT unrecoverable_change#, unrecoverable_time FROM v$datafile;
```

This query reveals the latest SCN and time-stamp corresponding to the UNRECOVERABLE/NOLOGGING operation specific to a data-file. If the SCN and/or time-stamp are different from what is previously recorded (in a special journal table perhaps), then the DBA needs to be intimated so that the changes can be manually propagated.

Error Propagation

At times, when certain user-errors occur (such as a table being truncated/dropped), you don't want such errors to be propagated to the standby because that would prevent switchover if the errors are propagated across both the primary and standby databases. Similarly, certain kinds of corruption (for example, where the index and table keys do not match) would also get propagated through normal means. Switchover is not possible if both the primary and secondary databases are afflicted with the same failure. It is essential to introduce some delays in propagation so that some time is available for error-detection and breaking the redo stream, preventing the archived logs that contain the user-errors/corruption from being applied to the standby. Thus, the standby database needs to be kept at least a half-hour to an hour (say, two to five archived redo-logs) behind the primary database. As soon as the error is detected (via alerts by systems operators, application errors, pages from administrative scripts that are monitoring for errors, or the like), the archive-log stream needs to be broken by aborting the automated process that copies the archived redo-logs to the remote standby server or dynamically disabling the automatic archival to the remote server by disabling the value for LOG_ARCHIVE_DEST_STATE_<N> (where <N> refers to the remote archive-destination) via the ALTER SYSTEM command (the latter option is applicable to Oracle8*i* only). If the suspect archived redo-logs have already been copied over to the remote standby server, then one needs to cancel recovery on the standby database to prevent the erroneous changes from being applied. As may be apparent, the standby database is susceptible to errors being propagated. Even if the standby trails behind by a few hours, there is no guarantee that the errors will not be propagated. If the errors remain undetected for those hours, it's just a matter of time before they reach the standby. Also keep in mind that the more the standby database trails behind the primary database, the higher will be the MTTR during normal switchovers (where there are no user-errors or the like but the primary system/database has crashed), since the unapplied archived logs will need to be applied prior to activating the standby database. Accordingly, rather than mere reliance on delays in archived-log propagation, extensive monitoring needs to be in place to spot errors before they are applied to the standby database. All monitoring needs to be implemented via automated scripts to page the DBA when (potential) errors are observed. Errors specific to your environment need to be explicitly coded and checked for via DBMS_JOB or cron on UNIX. Some of the common things to check for in a standby database implementation are as follows (when these errors are observed, it is necessary to page the DBA):

- Ensure that the primary server and database are up and running.
- The number of data-files and redo-logs need to be periodically recorded (in a journal table), and if they are different from what was previously recorded, then an alert needs to be raised.
- Ensure that the online redo-log status in *v$log* is not 'STALE' or 'INVALID'.
- Make a list of all critical application tables and periodically verify their existence. It is necessary to check for the existence of the table structures and data within those tables. For instance, you can periodically perform a script to run a "SELECT COUNT(*) FROM <appl_table_1> WHERE ROWNUM < 11." If the table structure does not exist (it has been dropped accidentally) or the COUNT(*) is equivalent to zero (it has been deleted or truncated), there is an error.
- Ensure that the directories holding the archived logs (on both the primary and standby systems) do not ever get full.
- Ensure that the network is up and throughput has not reduced and that the archived logs can always be transferred (directly written or copied over) to the standby system.

Testing

The standby configuration needs to be extensively tested to ensure that no unanticipated (unpleasant) surprises crop up. Both switchover and switchback need to be tested. Furthermore, it needs to be seen whether user-errors and the like are detected in time before being applied to the standby. Also, propagation of scenarios such as tablespace/data-file changes or NOLOGGING operations needs to be tested.

Switchover

When it becomes necessary for the switchover to occur, you need to consider the following issues:

- The DBAs and other administrative personnel performing the switch need to be well-trained (with lots of practice) to prevent panic-oriented responses.

- The entire switchover needs to be well-scripted to prevent human errors from inadvertently corrupting the standby database during switchover.
- As many archived logs as possible should be applied to the standby database prior to activating it, so that there is minimal transaction loss during the switchover. If the primary database is still functioning (maybe in a limited capacity), the online redo-logs may be archived and applied to the standby to ensure there is absolutely no transaction loss. However, if errors or corruption are involved, then you may choose not to apply the latest archived logs. In any case, ensure that you do not lose more transactions than you have to.
- It is pertinent to implement a mechanism to track writes to the database (for example, via audit columns such as CREATE_DATE or UPDATE_DATE to each table and possibly a trigger to write all DELETE information, such as the entire old row, to a journal table). Such a mechanism allows you to find out which transactions have not been applied during switchover from primary to standby and prevent them from being irretrievably lost. The primary database may have crashed at the time of switchover. However, once it is repaired/restored, you can use these audit mechanisms to track the newest writes and carry them over to the standby database (currently functioning as the primary database). Also, in Oracle8*i*, the *LogMiner* utility will help in analyzing the transactions contained in the archived logs.
- After switchover, the original primary database has to be rebuilt as soon as possible and then made the standby database to prevent extended exposure to potential failure (especially since there may not be another standby database to cover the current primary database).
- Note that during switchover, the ALTER DATABASE ACTIVATE STANDBY DATABASE command implicitly issues a RESETLOGS, thus clearing/resetting the online redo-logs of the standby database, which is being made primary. Due to this RESETLOGS, the original primary database (which is now unavailable) cannot be reinstated as the standby quickly. Once the original primary database is repaired, it cannot be made the standby, because the current primary has undergone a RESETLOGS operation and its archived redo-logs cannot be applied anymore to the original primary. Accordingly, you can only use the original backups to recover any lost transactions (that were lost during the switchover) and then use the latest backups of the current primary to rebuild the standby database. It is not always reasonable to take a backup of the current primary immediately after switchover, especially if the switchover occurs during peak use hours. During the time the backups are taken, the original primary is repaired, the lost transactions are recovered, and the standby database is rebuild, the current primary is

vulnerable to various dangers (without a standby database covering it). Accordingly, it is imperative to avoid the RESETLOGS operation, if possible. There is a relatively safe but undocumented (read, currently unsupported by Oracle Support) way to achieve switchover without the ACTIVE STANDBY DATABASE command and a corresponding RESETLOGS. This method is called "graceful switchover and switchback" and is explained in detail in an Oracle Corporation white-paper, "Graceful Switch Over and Switch Back using Oracle Standby Databases" by Lawrence To. This method is useful during planned outages (such as initialization parameter changes or OS patch application) and requires both that the primary and standby databases be available (thus, this method cannot be used for disaster recovery) and that RESETLOGS version be the same (that is, no RESETLOGS operation should have been performed on the primary recently without the standby having been rebuilt). It requires all archived logs prior to the outage to be applied to the standby database (no online redo-logs, just archived ones). Then both databases need to be shut down and the online redo-logs and control-file from the primary need to be copied over to the standby (rename the standby's old control-files and online redo-logs prior to copying the new ones to prevent overwriting them). Then the online redo-logs at the standby can be renamed (if necessary), recovery can be performed (to recover from online redo-logs), and the standby can be restarted as the primary. Thus, this method basically fools the standby database into thinking that it's the primary. Then, the client applications can be switched-over to connect to the standby. Finally after the planned outage is complete, the original primary needs to be made the standby by creating a standby control-file at the current primary (via the ALTER DATABASE CREATE STANDBY CONTROLFILE command) and using it to mount the original primary database and apply the archived logs generated at the current primary. Obviously, the steps can be reversed to switch back the current primary to become the standby and the current standby to become the primary later, when necessary. This method is relatively straight-forward. However, be sure that you understand all the prerequisites and pros and cons of the method, prior to attempting it. If done right and under the right circumstances, it could save you a lot of time and prevent the primary database from being exposed to danger for an extended period. However, done wrong, it could cause grief by corrupting the primary and/or standby database. Even though Oracle Support does not endorse this method, you should solicit the support of a knowledgeable Oracle Support Analyst prior to attempting this operation (and as always, ensure that the latest backups and all archived redo-logs subsequent to them are in mint condition. Since you are not attempting a RESETLOGS, the backups should be usable).

Application Failover

Finally, applications need to be rerouted to use the standby database, instead of the original primary. Chapter 6 discusses some Oracle-based and custom methods to do this. Alternatively, this switchover can occur at the hardware/OS level or via special software with network switching capabilities such as IP-address takeover or host-name takeover, wherein all requests to the original primary (which is unavailable now) are routed to the new primary (which was originally the standby) in a fashion that is transparent to the client processes.

Read-Only Access

As mentioned earlier, Oracle8*i* allows the standby database to be opened in read-only mode without invalidating it. Only queries (no writes) are permitted on the standby database, allowing it to be used as a temporary reporting instance. The reason it can only be kept open temporarily is that while it is open, the archived redo-logs from the primary cannot be applied to it. Thus, depending on how much time it is kept open, it may lag behind the primary database quite a bit. Then if the primary database fails, the standby will be very far behind. Rolling forward all the accumulated archived logs will increase MTTR. Accordingly, it is necessary to keep it in mounted mode most of the time. In case a permanent reporting database is needed, then a third database needs to be explicitly configured. A burning question you may want to ask is, "What about writes caused by sort/temporary segments within the read only database, when running queries on large tables with clauses such as DISTINCT or ORDER BY?." Yes, temporary segments created in the temporary tablespace do cause writes to occur to the data-dictionary tables (SYS.FET$, SYS.UET$, and so on) to record the temporary segments, and these are allowed as well. Accordingly, in order to run such (complex) queries on the read-only standby, you need to create a LOCALLY MANAGED temporary tablespace comprising tempfiles. LOCALLY MANAGED temporary tablespaces do not use the data-dictionary to allocate space. Instead, they use bitmaps within the tablespace for tracking space allocation and tempfiles for sort segments. Tempfiles are not recorded in the data-dictionary. However, their creation also does not get recorded in the redo-logs (and hence they do not get propagated to the standby). Accordingly, the tempfiles will need to be added once again to the temporary tablespace once the standby database is opened to allow sort segments to be created there. The following steps are necessary to allow a standby database to be opened in read-only mode for running complex queries:

1. Create a LOCALLY MANAGED temporary tablespace in the primary database.

```
SQL> CREATE TEMPORARY TABLESPACE <temp_tblspc_name>
TEMPFILE '<file-name>' SIZE 500M
       EXTENT MANAGEMENT LOCAL
       UNIFORM SIZE 5M;
```

2. Create a new user to perform all queries in the primary database (this command cannot be directly run in the standby database, since it would cause a write to the data-dictionary tables).

```
SQL> CREATE USER <qryusr> IDENTIFIED BY <passwd>
DEFAULT TABLESPACE users
     TEMPORARY TABLESPACE <temp_tblspc_name>;
```

3. Grant necessary privileges to the user to perform the required queries.
4. Archive the current redo-logs that recorded the preceding commands and apply them to the standby database.
5. Start up the standby database in read-only mode (after canceling the current recovery mode and verifying that all required data-files are online).

```
SVRMGR> RECOVER MANAGED STANDBY DATABASE CANCEL;
SVRMGR> SELECT * FROM v$datafile;
SVRMGR> SELECT * FROM v$recover_file;
SVRMGR> ALTER DATABASE OPEN READ ONLY;
```

6. Add the tempfile to the LOCALLY MANAGED temporary tablespace (since the tempfile creation was not previously recorded in the redo-logs, only the tablespace creation was recorded in SYS.TS$). The following command to add the tempfile does not cause a write in the standby database (in the data-dictionary) and is permitted.

```
SVRMGR> ALTER TABLESPACE <temp_tblspc_name>
          ADD TEMPFILE '<file-name> SIZE 500M;
```

7. Now log on as the new query user in the standby database and run the required queries.
8. When you are ready to switch-back and continue applying archived logs to the standby database, you can shut down the standby, mount it, and re-commence recovery.

```
SVRMGR> SHUTDOWN
SVRMGR> STARTUP PFILE=<initstndby.ora> NOMOUNT
SVRMGR> ALTER DATABASE MOUNT STANDBY DATABASE;
SVRMGR> SELECT * FROM v$datafile;
SVRMGR> RECOVER MANAGED STANDBY DATABASE;
```

Consider using standby instances in environments where true 24x7 uptime is not mandatory

A standby instance is basically a second instance that allows failover during specific database/system failures. A standby instance is an HA (high availability) option available on cluster-based architectures such as IBM's HACMP/6000, NCR's

LifeKeeper, and Sun's Sun Clusters. Many vendors providing cluster solutions have an "Oracle configuration pack" that pre-configures a standby instance on a non-primary node to take over during disasters. For Windows NT, Oracle provides Fail Safe®, which can be implemented on Microsoft Cluster Server (formerly code-named Wolfpack). Additionally, third-party software such as VERITAS FirstWatch® and VERITAS Cluster Server® is available for monitoring and managing failover.

A standby instance is not to be confused with OPS (Oracle Parallel Server), which is an alternative HA solution that can be implemented on clusters. With OPS, multiple (parallel) instances concurrently mount a single database resident on the cluster's shared disks. Thus with OPS, concurrent access to the database is possible via any node that houses an instance. In the case of a standby instance, there is only one instance mounting a database at any given point in time. This instance is referred to as the *primary instance.* The database is still resident on the cluster's shared disks (so that any node can access it). When the node on which the primary instance resides fails, another pre-designated node takes over control of the shared disks and immediately starts up another instance to mount the database, performs crash recovery, and re-opens the database. All client processes that were connected to the database via the earlier instance experience a service disruption. Any new incoming client connections that come in during the failover will get an error-message that the connection request has failed (unless a middle-tier TP Monitor or an Application Server is configured to insulate the client from the error and, if necessary, connect instead to a remote geo-mirrored database; also OCI applications can utilize transparent application failover features in Oracle8/8*i*). However, as soon as the failover completes and the new instance is up and running, they can all re-connect and continue processing. The re-connection is seamless; they do not need to have any major application-code changes implemented (other than putting in messages asking users to reconnect after three or so minutes if the database connection is broken or cannot be established) or SQL*Net/Net8 failover features enabled. They attempt to re-connect as they normally would, and their connection requests are routed to the new node. As expected, uncommitted transactions will be lost during the brief service disruption. The duration of the disruption is generally a few minutes during failover (especially dependent on the time required to perform crash recovery). Chapter 3 describes architectural details of clusters with regards to standby instances and Figure 3-5 (in Chapter 3) illustrates cluster-operation.

Standby instances are sometimes looked at as a "poor man's OPS." However, this is not entirely correct. It is true that in the case of OPS due to another parallel instance already being up and available, failover is instantaneous (the connected client sessions will still experience a disruption; however, they can immediately re-connect and continue without having to wait for the standby instance to come up). Additionally, OPS offer higher scalability than standby instances, since in the case of the latter, the scalability is limited to a single node's maximum capacity.

However, standby instances have other advantages. The most important advantage is the lowered cost and maintenance/administrative overhead. With standby instances, your site does not need to purchase an OPS license. Additionally, no raw-devices are required, whereas raw-devices are mandatory in an OPS configuration (refer to Chapter 4 for a discussion on the disadvantages of raw-devices). There is only a single instance to be monitored and tuned (the very same tuning changes will apply to the standby instance, as well). There is no need to worry about appropriate application partitioning. Considering the very few occasions that failures occur and depending on the overall availability requirements of your organization (as determined by your SLA), standby instances may very well be the answer to your availability needs. An important point to keep in mind is that, generally, cluster-based solutions such as standby instances (and even OPS, for that matter) are not capable of providing disaster recovery due to the close proximity of the nodes in the cluster. A remote solution will still need to be configured, if your availability requirements are stringent enough to warrant one.

Let's examine two examples of standby instances: on the IBM HACMP/6000 and Oracle Fail Safe on Microsoft Cluster Server (on Windows NT). Even though the examples refer to specific platforms, the basic concepts remain the same and, once understood, can be utilized on any cluster-based solution (since nowadays, most cluster-based solutions offer comparable features). The following discussions presume that the cluster configurations described in the text that follows have two nodes (one for the primary instance and the other for the standby instance).

Standby Instance Configuration on IBM HACMP/6000

The HACMP/6000 cluster, comprising loosely coupled RS/6000 systems (nodes), was introduced by IBM in 1991. The cluster architecture focuses on HA and can handle different types of failures, such as network, node, disk, and adapter, with little downtime (up to a few minutes). Currently, multiple nodes can be connected using either Ethernet, a high-speed Optical Link, or Token Ring. Each machine has access to local disks, as well as shared disks. Local disks are primarily used to maintain OS (AIX) and certain node-specific or non-critical data. Data that needs to be accessible by different nodes, such as Oracle data-files, are kept on the shared disks. Typically Oracle software is installed on the local disks on the primary and standby nodes. Furthermore, each of the disks (local and shared) can be mirrored via AIX's Logical Volume Manager. If a disk fails, access can continue uninterrupted via the mirror. The architecture is flexible and supports various node configurations. Here I describe a configuration especially suited for standby instances, as shown in Figure 15-2.

A HACMP daemon called the *cluster manager* runs on each node and monitors cluster topology and network status. When a status changes, specific shell-scripts called *events* are run. These shell-scripts are complex and are responsible for various cluster activities such as introduction of new nodes in the cluster,

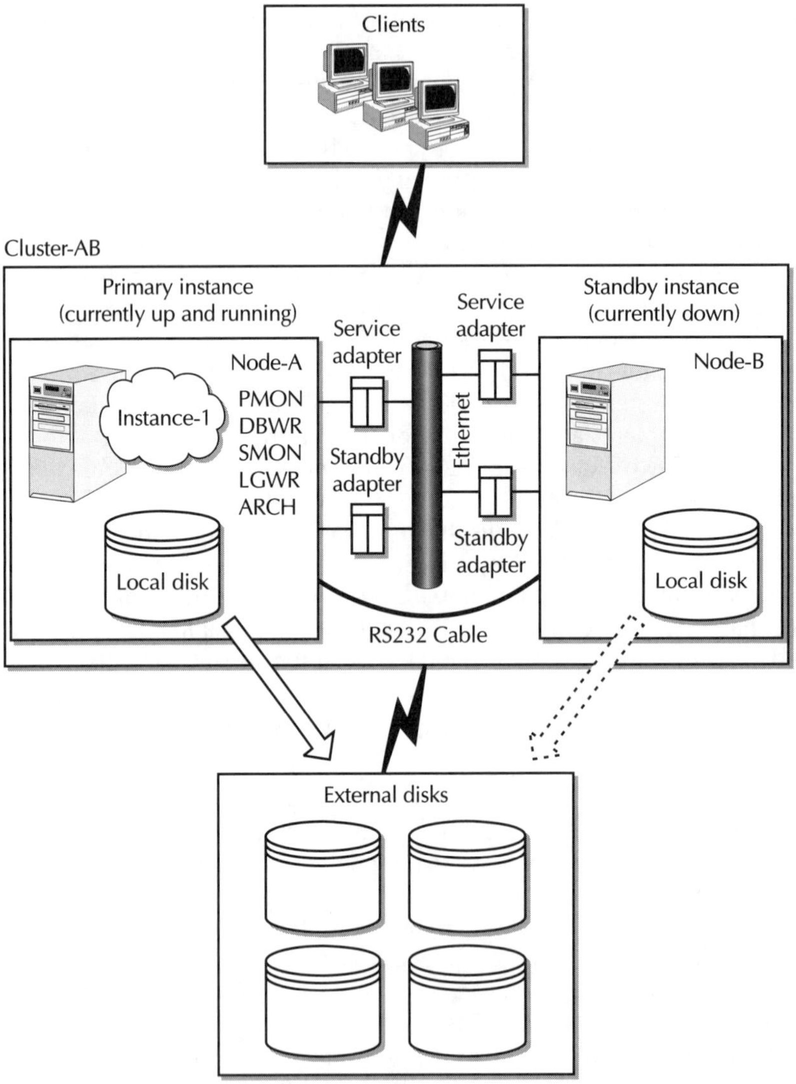

FIGURE 15-2. *Standby instance configuration on IBM HACMP/6000*

failure/removal of existing nodes from the cluster, and adapter swapping. Each event can call a customized shell-script either as a pre or post event job. Each node has dual network adapters: the primary service adapter and the standby adapter. The node communicates with the network via the service adapter. Both are connected to the network (for instance, via twisted pair connections). The standby adapter takes over when the service adapter fails (however, at this point, the network adapter is a single point of failure and if the standby adapter also fails, failover to another node must be initiated). There are different IP addresses corresponding to the service and standby adapters. These are referred to as the *service address* and the *standby address* respectively and can operate on different subnets. Additionally, host-names can be configured for each node. At startup, each node acquires a specific IP address called the *boot address.* When the cluster manager is started up, the node address will revert to its service address.

Each node periodically sends the other "keep alive" packets. By default this ping is exchanged every 0.5 seconds. In addition to the regular connection to the network, the nodes within the cluster are also connected via a serial cable (RS232). This cable provides a fallback path for the "keep alive" packets, should the primary path (the network) fail. When there is a node failure, the ping does not return successfully. Each node, by default, allows 12 unsuccessful pings, after which the destination node is assumed to be down and IP address takeover occurs, where the service address of the failed node (primary node) is taken over by the node that detected the failure. The service address of the failed node now migrates to the standby address of the node performing the takeover (the standby node). Thus, the service addresses of both nodes (the failed node and the standby node) are now functional. Any access requests to the failed node or the standby node will be routed to the standby node. Additionally, the shared disks that are mounted by the failed node are unmounted and the standby node mounts them. After the failed node has been repaired and as it boots up, its service adapter should be configured to boot from an alternate IP address on the same subnet as the original service address. This prevents two nodes on the network from ending up with the same IP address (the standby node that took over the original service address and the primary node that failed and is now restarted). Once the original node is back, the primary instance can be re-started on this original node either automatically or via planned downtime. For the failover to occur automatically, the *smit clstop* command may be used on the standby and the *takeover* option may be selected in response to *Stop cluster manager graceful, takeover or forced.* This option stops HA, releasing all pertinent resources, which are then acquired by the other (primary) node. This may not work at all times, especially if user-activity is still being written to the shared disks. If so, HA may have to be forcibly shut down and restarted with all nodes intact.

The takeover activates an event. After the primary node's service address is taken over by the standby node and the shared disks are re-mounted, a user-defined shell-script needs to be run to start up the database as a post-event task. The standby node needs access to the *init.ora* and *config.ora* files. In case the primary node stored these on its local disks (assuming ORACLE_HOME for both were on local disks), the standby node needs to have them on its own local disks, as well. Alternatively, the entire ORACLE_HOME and the configuration files can be maintained on the shared disk (provided there are adequate disks/controllers on the shared disk sub-system to prevent contention between the data-files and the Oracle software). In any case, the user-defined shell-script starts up the instance. Crash recovery is automatically performed as the database opens. Note that during failover, the only delay consists of the time to complete the takeover and start up the standby instance. The standby node is already up and running, so there is no time wasted to start up the standby node. The shell-script to start up the database needs to account for specific situations such as the database being in hot backup mode during the node failure. If so, the script needs to either explicitly apply recovery or, in v7.2 and above, an ALTER DATABASE END BACKUP command may be used to end the backup and open the database.

From a client application's perspective, users need to be provided an error-message stating that failover is occurring and asking them to re-connect after a few minutes (the exact number of minutes to be specified in the error-message needs to be determined after conducting tests indicating the minimum, maximum, and average time to failover). Then, they could just re-try their connection and (re-)start their activity upon successful connection to the standby instance on the standby node.

Standby Instance Configuration via Oracle Fail Safe on Microsoft Cluster Server

Oracle Fail Safe (OFS) is primarily designed to cater to departmental and workgroup users, who need ease-of-use, without compromising on database availability. OFS adds a layer of protection for single-instance Oracle databases on Microsoft Cluster Server (MSCS) by tightly integrating with the cluster management software to detect node failure and migrate to another node in the cluster group, start up a new instance, perform crash recovery, and allow clients to re-connect and continue processing (see Figure 15-3).

Windows NT and MSCS support cluster-based solutions via *cluster groups*. A cluster group is logical collection of cluster resources (nodes, shared disks, disk-mirrors, interconnect, and so on). All resources in a group are considered to be a single unit of failover. Only one node can actively access the resources within a group at a given point in time. There cannot be any inter-dependency across different groups. Each group is given a unique (host) name and an IP address. All client applications connect to the cluster group (via this unique name/IP address), rather than to an individual node. Thus, each group consisting of more than one node can be considered to be a single logical server, with each node providing failover capability for the other. A "heartbeat" message is exchanged between the nodes to detect node failure. When node failure is detected, the surviving node starts up a new instance, performs crash recovery, and allows database access to resume. Clients do not need to do anything other than re-connect (after waiting for

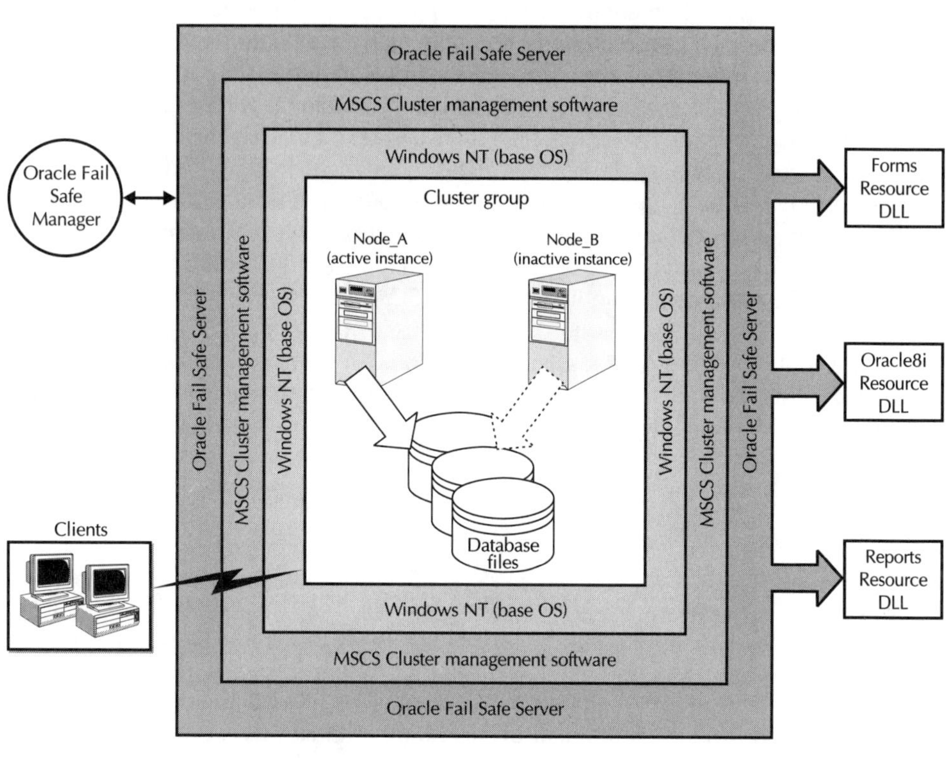

FIGURE 15-3. *Standby instance configuration via Oracle Fail Safe*

failover to complete) and continue their work. Users need to be given adequate training to recognize failover symptoms and wait for a few minutes (the actual time depends on the time taken to perform failover and database crash recovery) before attempting to re-connect. Also, user-friendly messages need to be coded in the applications to alert users about the failover. All uncommitted transactions will be lost and will need to be re-issued.

OFS consists of two primary components: Oracle Fail Safe Server (OFSS) and the Oracle Fail Safe Manager (OFSM). OFSS is the component that actually interacts with MSCS to track inter-node communication, overall node-activity, and failures on a regular basis. OFSM allows the Oracle database to be configured to utilize HA features on MSCS. In addition, OFSM provides management, trouble-shooting, and static load-balancing for an Oracle database. The database is managed via Oracle Resource DLLs installed on each node within the cluster. With Oracle Fail Safe 8*i*, additional Resource DLLs are provided to make many applications (at the middle or database-tier) fail-safe compliant. These applications include Web application servers and the Forms Server and Reports Server in Oracle Developer 6. OFSM can be used in multiple ways, including via a GUI-based screen that makes the overall OFS configuration very easy. It provides a variety of wizards, drag-and-drop features, property sheets, and extensive online help (in addition to a tutorial). This approach allows default configuration parameters to be used in many cases, optimized for quick failover. These parameters may be easily overwritten, if necessary. It also has a command-line interface (FSCMD) for scripting cluster-dependent database jobs to be run. Furthermore, it can be used with *Oracle Enterprise Manager* (OEM) for easier database administration. An *Oracle Intelligent Agent* needs to be installed and configured on each cluster node that allows discovery of the Oracle services by OEM.

Architectural Alternatives for Standby Instances

Following are some architectural alternatives for standby instances.

THE PRIMARY/STANDBY CONFIGURATION Under this configuration, one or more databases are configured on a single node in the cluster (see Figure 15-4). This node forms the primary node. Another node is pre-designated as the standby node. The standby node issues "keep-alive" heartbeats to ensure that the primary is up and running. If the heartbeats fail, then it takes over as the primary node. Here, the standby node is totally idle and only provides node-redundancy. There are no applications that run on it. Accordingly, organizations that seek a higher return on investment and would like to utilize the standby node, as well need to evaluate the other configuration.

THE PRIMARY-STANDBY/PRIMARY-STANDBY CONFIGURATION This is ideal for sites that have more than one large database or use an N-tier architecture (see Figure 15-5). Here, one or more databases are created on both nodes (the primary and the standby) in a mutually exclusive manner. For instance, database_A may be created on node_A, and database_B may be created on node_B. When node_A fails, node_B takes over, restarts database_A, and runs both database_A and database_B. Alternatively, node_A does the same for node_B. Thus, each node acts as a primary, as well as a standby node. This example uses databases to illustrate the primary-standby relationship between the two nodes. However, the same scenario can be adopted in a multi-tier environment. For example, the database can

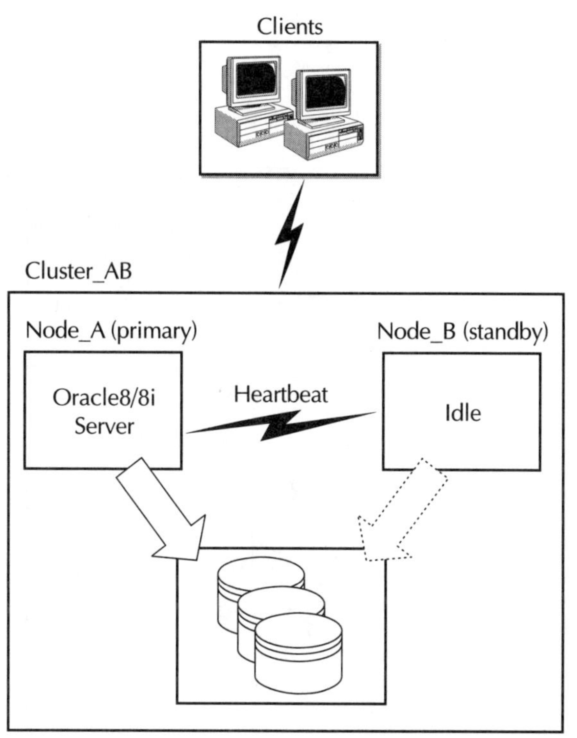

FIGURE 15-4. *The primary/standby configuration*

reside on node_A, whereas application servers (Web Application Server, Forms Server, Reports Server, and so on) can reside on node_B. When node_A fails, node_B can take over the database services, whereas when node_B fails, node_A can take over the application servers.

Note that under these scenarios, performance problems could arise after failover. Each node could already be performing at peak capacity prior to the failover. However, after failover, when each node takes on additional responsibilities, performance will begin to degrade, since peak capacity was already reached earlier. In order to alleviate the load on performance, one may need to temporarily stop some of the application related jobs on the surviving node or reduce client access to 50 percent of the normal load after failover. Once the failed node is restored, the

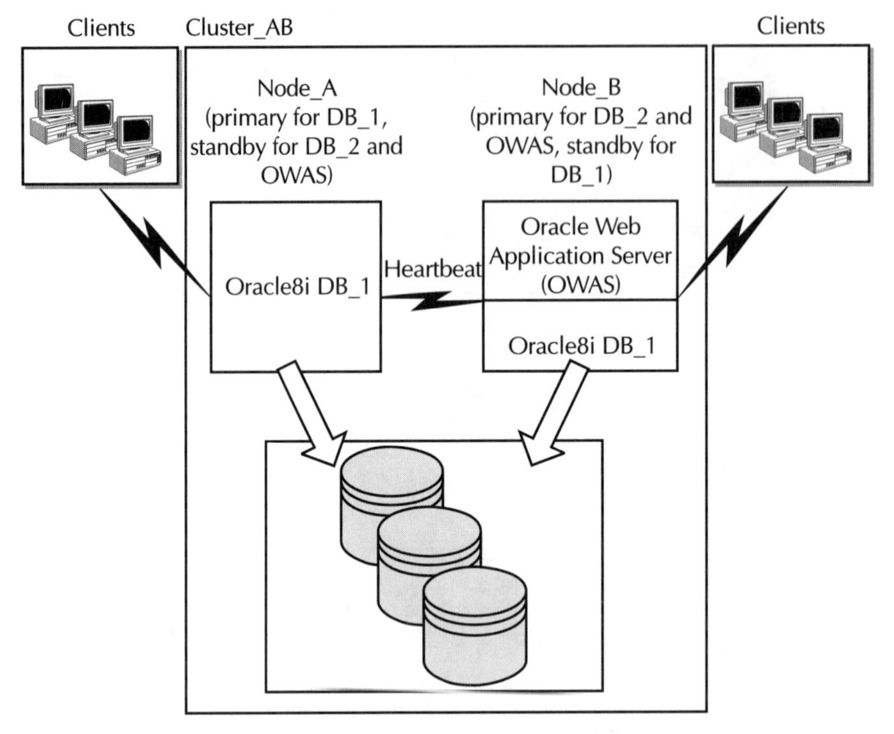

FIGURE 15-5. *The primary-standby/primary-standby configuration*

application jobs and normal client access may be restored. However, this affects availability adversely (if the database cannot handle 100 percent of client requests after being failed over, then the availability is questionable). Alternatively, the nodes may be run at non-peak capacity during normal use. For instance, on a regular basis, each node will be 50 percent utilized (the system capacity plan needs to be able to accommodate this). After failover, the surviving node will be 100 percent utilized. However, the 50 percent utilization of nodes again raises the original issue of inadequate return on investment for the organization. In fact, the 50 percent utilization option is merely a derivative of the Primary/Standby architecture (since the equivalent of one entire node is idle). However, it does provide better load-balancing, since two nodes are being used, as opposed to just one. You could also evaluate other options such as running one node (the primary database node) at 60 percent and the other node (the primary middle-tier applications node) at 40 percent capacity. Again, you and the architectural team in your organization need to decide what is best for you, based on overall availability, response-time and throughput requirements, and, of course, the hardware resource availability. Also keep in mind that it is recommended to always run a system at much less-than 100 percent capacity in order to accommodate future scalability. Capacity figures need to be derived based on current and future peak-hour use. The "100 percent capacity" figures I refer to earlier need to be viewed in a logical fashion, rather than based on the physical numbers pertaining to system capacity observed via system monitoring tools such as *vmstat, iostat,* and *sar.* For instance, more than 60 percent utilization of the I/O resources on a continuous basis may lead to I/O bottlenecks in your environment. Accordingly, the 60 percent physical I/O utilization should correspond to 100 percent logical utilization for your system. Anything additional should be considered beyond capacity.

Consider combining multiple solutions to form a comprehensive one

Note that besides standby instances and databases, various high-availability solutions are available from Oracle and third-party vendors to reduce overall downtime. These are discussed in subsequent chapters. Some such solutions are

- Oracle Parallel Server configuration.
- Oracle Advanced Replication option.
- Certain third-party hardware-based and/or software-based solutions. Examples of such solutions are EMC's SRDF (Symmetrix Remote Data Facility) (hardware-based) and Quest Software's SharePlex (software-based).

Very often, it becomes necessary to combine more than one HA solution to achieve higher uptime. For instance, having multiple standby databases or combining OPS and a remote standby database implementation will allow high availability during a variety of failures. With multiple standby databases, one standby (the first standby) could be kept almost current with the primary, in terms of all archived redo-logs being applied (only the current online redo-logs being written to at the primary site would not have been applied). A second standby database can be maintained, which is say, four hours behind the primary database. In other words, this standby would be eight or ten archived redo-logs behind the primary. Each of these standby databases could be maintained separately at remote sites to allow disaster recovery. Whenever there is a disaster/failure, the standby that is almost current with the primary database (the first standby) will be used to switch

over. If possible, the transactions in the current online redo-logs (at the primary) could be archived and applied to the first standby prior to making it the primary. In case the online redo-logs are lost due to the disaster, then the transactions in those logs will be lost. However, the first standby database can be immediately made the primary (within a few minutes), and those transactions can be rerun in many cases. Now, the second standby would be made as current as possible to the current primary (that is, all archived redo-logs would be applied immediately). In other words, the second standby is promoted to being the first standby, and when the original primary database is repaired/restored, it becomes the new second standby and is kept eight to ten redo-logs behind the current primary.

Now, instead of a disaster, let's say a user drops an important table accidentally. Let's presume that by the time this problem is discovered, an hour has already passed and the error has been propagated to the first standby database. In such situations, the first standby cannot be used for failover. However, the error has not been propagated to the second standby (which is four hours behind). Now the second standby database can be made almost current by applying as many archived logs as possible (up to the one containing the error). Stringent error-detection procedures need to be adopted to detect the exact archive log that contains the error that occurred an hour ago (the *v$log* and *v$log_history* dynamic views can be used for this process; additionally, Oracle8*i*'s *LogMiner* utility will greatly simplify this process) and prevent it from being applied to the second standby. Now, the second standby can be made the primary. The MTTR in such a case may be longer (applying all the remaining archived logs up to the log containing the error to get as current as possible). However, it certainly beats recovering the primary database from a backup. Also here, the second standby (that has been made primary) will not have transactions pertaining to the last one hour since the time the error occurred. However, they could be reapplied via manual methods from the original primary database (which is still up and running, albeit without that critical table that was dropped), or the transactions could simply be rerun. Then the original primary database and the first standby can be rebuilt to become the first and second standby databases respectively. This solution of maintaining multiple standby databases proves useful in a variety of situations but is highly expensive due to the additional number of servers (machines) and software licenses required. Additionally, maintenance requirements increase, requiring more administrative personnel to be hired.

The second combination mentioned earlier, OPS and a standby database, also proves useful in a variety of situations (OPS is discussed in detail in Chapter 16). For instance, if a node fails, crashing an instance, the other instances will still allow the database to be accessed. The other instances are already up and running. Accordingly, failover can be immediate, resulting in very low MTTR. However, this wouldn't help much during disaster recovery. Typically, all nodes across which OPS is configured are physically placed at close proximity and connected via a LAN (cluster-based solutions do not function very well over a WAN). Accordingly, a disaster could wipe out all nodes (and the instances on them). To counter such situations, a standby database can be maintained remotely and kept a few hours behind the primary database. During disaster recovery and even user-errors (provided these errors are detected within a few hours, prior to being propagated to the standby), the standby database can be made the primary after applying the remaining archived redo-logs (including the online redo-logs from the primary, if possible). Here again, the cost factor would be substantial in acquiring and maintaining a multi-node primary server (for OPS) and a secondary server to host the standby database.

Strategies for Availability During Routine Maintenance and Emergencies

In earlier chapters, we examined various issues pertaining to 24×7 availability. The importance of getting things correct right from the start was emphasized. Techniques to expedite downtime-causing maintenance procedures and quickly troubleshoot/repair certain critical failures were discussed. In spite of intricate knowledge in these areas, there is always some amount of downtime involved. For instance, say your table is suddenly afflicted with severe block-corruption. You may possess very deep technical knowledge of corruption and be able to quickly repair it, allowing the table to be accessed again within a few hours. However, during those hours, all applications using that table are down and not available, and users are not able to get to the data. Similarly, in the migration case-study provided in Chapter 8, up to four hours of downtime on a Saturday night/Sunday morning was acceptable to the client, provided their customers were informed in advance of the outage and stringent SLA clauses were not violated (that is, the four hours didn't stretch into more). However, for some organizations, even four hours of downtime may be unacceptable. Overall downtime may be reduced by following certain steps, as illustrated in the case-study. Even then some downtime may still be inevitable. Only when downtime is controlled do you have a reasonable chance of adhering to your SLA requirements. Downtime needs to be somehow averted during all maintenance operations, migrations, and emergencies. Any complete 24×7 strategy needs to seriously address these issues.

So far in this chapter, we looked at regular standby solutions available in Oracle. Standby databases are especially beneficial for disaster recovery. However, they do not address certain issues very well, for example, availability during essential maintenance operations such as patch application/version upgrades, sudden segment-level emergencies such as corruption problems, or user errors where one or more tables are accidentally dropped. Certain patches that do not

result in significant changes to the release can still be applied in a regular standby scenario; however, major patches and version upgrades will invalidate the standby. For instance, if a company has implemented Oracle's standby database configuration and needs to upgrade the database version (say, from Oracle7 to Oracle8*i*), how can it prevent downtime during and after the upgrade? It may be able to switch over to the standby database to prevent immediate downtime during the upgrade. However, once the original primary database is upgraded to the new version, the current primary (the original standby) continues to use an earlier version. Now re-synchronizing the two via the redo-logs will not be possible, since the two redo streams will be incompatible. The current primary and original primary will pertain to different versions and different points in time. Alternatively, in a scenario where the switchover to the standby does not occur prior to the upgrade, downtime is caused, and furthermore, the standby database ceases to be a true standby and is reduced to being a previous point-in-time backup. If the primary database fails after the upgrade, there is no standby to revert to. Also, these solutions tend to propagate user-accidents such as a table being truncated to the secondary database. Besides regular standby databases, this is also the case with certain other mirroring schemes such as, say, local or geo-mirroring. Granted, it is possible to set an explicit delay prior to propagation. Usually such a delay varies from 20 to 60 minutes (to prevent the standby database from lagging too much behind the primary). Unless extensive error-detection routines are in place to detect the error during this lag-time, the propagation nevertheless takes place (gradually), afflicting the standby database with the same erroneous symptoms as the primary database.

Availability during certain scenarios is challenging to achieve even with solutions such as standby instances and OPS. In both these solutions, multiple database instances are involved (either standby or parallel). However, the physical database is shared between the instances and becomes a single point of failure. If a table is accidentally dropped or there is block corruption, then either of the instances cannot be used to access it, thus causing downtime. Also, as mentioned earlier, multi-node solutions such as standby instances and OPS, in their basic implementation, are not very well suited for disaster recovery.

In other words, addressing a combination of the downtime-causing scenarios just described poses a daunting challenge to most high-availability solutions in the market. Accordingly, there is a strong need to combine multiple off-the-shelf HA solutions (such as by configuring standby databases to co-exist with OPS) or to devise custom HA strategies to complement an off-the-shelf solution to make the overall HA strategy more watertight.

In this section we examine custom standby solutions to possibly provide higher availability during certain maintenance (migrations, version upgrades, and so on) and troubleshooting scenarios (such as corruption repair), where any specific HA solution such as OPS or a regular standby implementation may be inadequate. These custom solutions need to be built after extensive evaluation of the existing environment (number of users and peak transactions, required throughput, and so on). Two custom solutions are presented here. These custom solutions use basic replication techniques to build a standby database/table. These basic techniques such as triggers and journal tables help in avoiding the higher overhead normally associated with Oracle's Advanced Replication Option (ARO), which also uses triggers to achieve the replication (starting with Oracle8/8*i*, many of these triggers have been integrated via C code into the Oracle kernel). Consequently, our custom solution does not provide many of the sophisticated features that ARO provides, such as guaranteeing transaction propagation in the original sequence, a master/master (multi-way writes) relationship between the primary and secondary databases, and multiple conflict resolution methods. The relationship configured via these custom solutions is basically master/slave (single-way writes). Compared to ARO, these custom solutions are less complex in nature. They are effective during situations such as version upgrades, where most ready-made solutions are not usable. Obviously, since these custom solutions use triggers, they may adversely impact performance for sites with heavy transaction rates. If the performance strain is unacceptable, then these custom solutions can be used temporarily during specific situations, such as to avert downtime during version upgrades. Other HA solutions, such as OPS, automated standby databases, and Advanced Replication, ought to be utilized on a more permanent basis. However, if the performance strain is tolerable, retaining some kind of a custom solution on a permanent basis will be beneficial from an availability perspective (a subsequent paragraph discusses this in more detail).

With this background information, let's look at the custom solutions.

Evaluate using a Custom Standby Database (CSD)

Maintaining a CSD primarily allows major downtime to be averted during patch application/version upgrades. Implementing a CSD involves maintaining a separate copy of the database on a different (secondary) system and introducing certain triggers and a journal table in both the primary and secondary databases (Figure 15-6 illustrates a CSD). CSDs use a combination of *push* and *pull* methods (mainly *pull*) to keep the standby database synchronized with the primary database. Note that certain third-party hardware/software solutions also allow a variation of CSDs via mirroring techniques (such as local mirroring or geo-mirroring), wherein every write is transferred to a separate system/database maintained at a local or remote location (geo-mirroring is discussed in Chapter 18). However, CSDs are not similar to such mirroring, since the latter generally functions at the hardware/OS level, totally external to the database. CSDs employ triggers and tables to record all writes in the primary database and play them back to the secondary database. Thus, they are also different from regular standby databases supported by Oracle, since they do not use the redo-logs in any way to copy writes to the standby. As a result, reliance

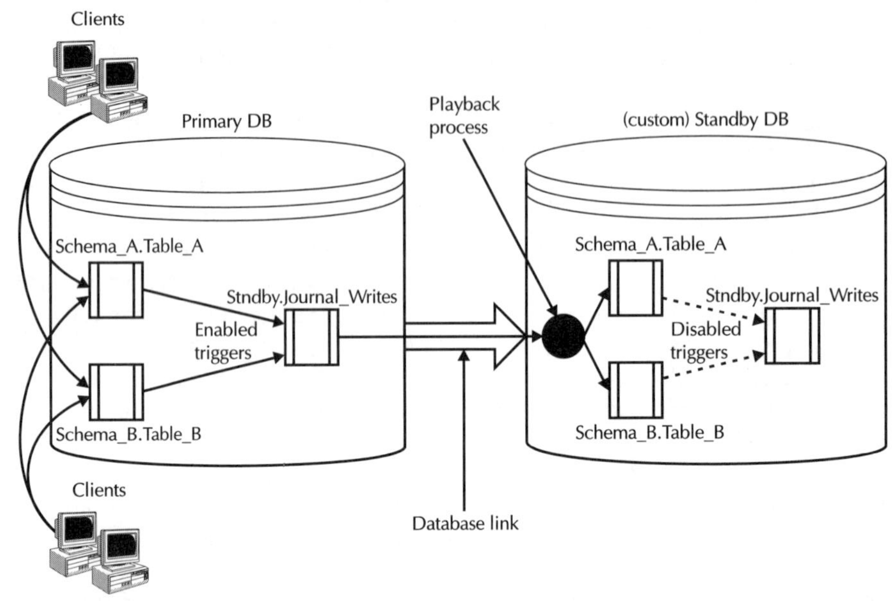

FIGURE 15-6. *Illustration of a CSD implementation*

on the database physical structures is totally eliminated in the case of CSDs. For all practical purposes, even the primary and standby database versions can be different, and the physical attributes (such as the number of online redo-logs, tablespaces, data-files, and file-paths) can differ, as well.

Let's take an example to understand CSDs better. Let's say, we have four important application-schemas (in addition to the SYSTEM schema). Note that the SYSTEM schema does not have to be duplicated (unlike the conventional standby database feature in Oracle). The SYSTEM schema, along with the TEMPORARY and RBS (rollback segment) tablespaces are already present on the secondary database. As mentioned earlier, the secondary database doesn't have to exactly match the primary database in terms of physical or external (to the database) characteristics. As long as the application-specific schemas and the segments within are duplicated, that is more than enough. The details of the four schemas are mentioned in Table 15-1 (note that each table and its indexes within each schema are considered as a single unit; in other words, the indexes are counted as part of the table itself).

For each of the tables in all the application schemas, all writes need to be recorded, such that they can be played back onto any target system/database,

Schema-Name	Approximate # of Tables	24×7 Access Required
FINANCE	255	Y
SALES	85	Y
COST_ACCT	14	N
INVENTORY	35	Y

TABLE 15-1. *Schema Details in a Sample CSD Implementation*

irrespective of version/release-number. Thus, CSDs do not rely on version-specific features to record and play back writes. This mandatory requirement rules out any direct use of redo-logs and/or data-files. This is because the contents of redo-logs and data-files are stored in an undocumented format and are not easily available or known to most administrative personnel (albeit this scenario is changing with the advent of LogMiner™ in Oracle8*i;* also certain third-party HA solutions such as Quest Software's SharePlex™ read and interpret the redo-logs directly). Accordingly, this leaves us with two ways to record (or journal) all writes:

- Code the journalizing within the application (thus, design and code each application module to record all INSERTs/UPDATEs/DELETEs in the journal table), or
- Employ triggers on each table to record all writes made to the table in the journal table. This method is especially useful when dealing with applications that have already been written in the past and are functioning as desired (thus, introducing a reluctance in management to alter functional code). Also, this method is the only option during situations where one does not have access to or any control over application code, such as when dealing with "canned" third-party applications.

As one of the initial steps, all the segments (tables, indexes, and rollback segments) on the primary database are pre-created on the secondary (standby) database. Also, all the data is copied over (using various mechanisms discussed earlier). Now, only the data that is written on an ongoing basis needs to be copied over regularly. Note that all schemas and segments from the primary database do not have to be copied over to the CSD—only the segments that need to be available 24×7 need to be present on the secondary database. This is yet another advantage of CSDs, since this allows just the critical segments to be identified and duplicated, unlike a conventional standby database method, where the entire primary database has to be duplicated—irrespective of whether all schemas are mission-critical or not. In our example, only the tables in the FINANCE, SALES, and INVENTORY schemas need to be present in the secondary database. If we decide to implement the CSD on Sunday at 2:00 in the morning (just about any low use hour will work), then the logical delta is determined to be that time (logical deltas are discussed at length in the case-study in Chapter 8). To enforce the logical delta cleanly, a small outage (say, a few minutes) needs to be taken to create the journal table and the necessary triggers to record all writes in the journal table. Then the data prior to the delta can be easily copied over to the secondary database. The data that comes in after the marked delta (Sunday 2:00 A.M.) needs to be copied over to the secondary database on a periodic basis (say, every half-hour). Based on the contents of the journal table, the new writes can be copied over to the secondary database on an incremental basis. It is necessary to let the secondary database lag behind the primary database at least by half an hour, so that chances of user-errors (such as data within a table being accidentally deleted) being propagated to the secondary database can be kept low. That way, you can safely switch over to the standby database during such user errors to limit total downtime. Note that all DDL changes (ALTER/TRUNCATE) are not propagated automatically under any circumstance. They need to be propagated manually to the secondary database. Furthermore, if any of the critical tables are dropped (if the applications don't need them any more) or new ones are created, then this fact needs to be reflected manually in the secondary database, and the triggers that populate the journal table need to undergo corresponding changes. For instance, if new tables need to be journalized, then triggers need to be created on those, and if existing tables are deemed to be no longer critical, then the journalizing triggers on those need to be dropped. This reliance on manual intervention to propagate permanent (DDL) changes prevents them from being inadvertently propagated to the secondary. Thus, the necessity of every DDL change made to the primary database needs to evaluated, and then the change must be manually propagated (if necessary) to ensure that accidents are not automatically carried forward. This is another area where CSDs differ from regular standby database configurations (where the redo application would propagate even DDL changes; conversely UNRECOVERABLE/NOLOGGING operations would not be propagated in regular standby database configurations, whereas in CSDs, since every DDL statement is manually propagated, usage of UNRECOVERABLE/ NOLOGGING would not really matter). Note that physical/structural changes to the primary database (such as data-files being added/dropped or redo-logs being added/dropped) need not be propagated to the secondary (yet another advantage!).

A separate journal table can be created in every critical schema, or alternatively, a single one may be created in a common administrative schema to record writes to all tables in all critical schemas. This journal table needs to be accessible (via read and write privileges and necessary synonyms) by all critical schemas. Ideally, in order to keep the implementation fairly simple and clean, create the journal table in a separate administrative schema and grant all necessary privileges to this administrative schema to refer to all the tables on which the writes are taking place. Also, grant all the schemas owning the tables permission to access the journal table in the administrative schema (so that their triggers can write to the journal table). The CSD strategy outlined here assumes that the journal table is present in such an administrative schema, accessible by all other schemas. In case you wish to implement a separate journal table in each critical schema, you may have to make some changes to the implementation procedures described here (these changes are fairly straight-forward, and as you read through, you should be able to understand them better). The structure of the journal table is outlined in Table 15-2.

Once the journal table has been created, triggers need to be created on all tables in schemas supporting mission-critical applications. The overall format of all these triggers will be the same. For instance, the trigger on SALES.SALES_ORDERS

Table-Name: JOURNAL_WRITES

Column-Name	Data-Type(Length)	Comments
SCHEMA_NAME	VARCHAR2(32)	Schema, where the critical table resides
TABLE_NAME	VARCHAR2(32)	Name of the critical table, whose writes need to be recorded
DML_OPERATION	VARCHAR2(2)	'AI' => INSERT, 'AU' => UPDATE, 'ZD' => DELETE Here, I'm not simply using 'I' for inserts, 'U' for updates, and 'D' for deletes; I've adopted these alternative terms so that they can be sorted later (during retrieval for playback), such that inserts are retrieved first, then updates, and finally deletes.
PRMRY_TBL_ROWID	VARCHAR2(18)	ROWID of row in primary database that has been inserted/updated/deleted (as a point of reference to the source row in the primary database)
UPDDEL_WHERE_ CLAUSE	VARCHAR2(2000)	The WHERE clause that is applicable to the UPDATE and DELETE. This will typically be of the form: 'WHERE <primary-key-col1> = <value> AND <primary-key-col2> = <value>'
RECORD_TIME	DATE	Time the DML operation took place

TABLE 15-2. *JOURNAL_WRITES Table Structure*

table will resemble the following code. All these triggers should be considered as "part of the application" and should be subject to the same mechanisms adopted for managing regular application-code, such as strict version-control and passing test/QA cycles. Note that these routines can be run in any Oracle version, starting with 7.*x*. Also, these routines assume that all tables in all critical schemas have a primary key defined. If this assumption is not correct (in your environment), the routines need to be modified to accommodate logical keys (unique columns in such tables that have primary key characteristics but have not been explicitly declared as the primary key).

```
/* Module    : t_sales_ord01 [trigger on SALES_ORDERS table]
**             01 after the trigger name indicates the trigger-number
**             on the SALES_ORDERS table
** Functionality : used to record all writes to SALES_ORDERS table.
**                 All INSERTs/UPDATEs/DELETEs are saved in JOURNAL_WRITES
**                 table. Later these rows are read from the secondary
**                 database and the DML is applied to the corresponding
**                 tables there.
** Notes    : a) This trigger assumes that the current schema (where the
**              trigger is present) has appropriate privileges to the
**              JOURNAL_WRITES table and the right synonym has
**              been created to point to the table (in case it is
**              different schema)
** Author   : Venkat S. Devraj
** History :
** 08/97VSD      Written
*/

CREATE TRIGGER t_sales_ord01
AFTER INSERT OR UPDATE OR DELETE ON sales_orders
FOR EACH ROW
DECLARE
  -- this variable is used to construct and insert a WHERE
  -- clause for UPDATE/DELETE statements in the JOURNAL_WRITES table
  -- to be run on the secondary database during playback
  cWHEREclause VARCHAR2(2000);

BEGIN
   IF INSERTING THEN
      INSERT INTO journal_writes(schema_name, table_name,
                                 dml_operation, prmry_tbl_rowid,
                                 upddel_where_clause, record_time)
        VALUES ('SALES', 'SALES_ORDERS', 'AI',
                 ROWIDTOCHAR(:NEW.ROWID), NULL, SYSDATE);
   ELSIF UPDATING THEN
        -- for updates, it is necessary to be able to change ALL columns
        -- in the secondary database to match the change in the primary
        -- database. Tracking down changes to each individual column would
```

```
    -- be expensive. As such, the entire row is treated as a single unit
    -- and all columns are updated, regardless of whether they have been
    -- actually changed in the primary database or not. Thus, even an
    -- UPDATE in the primary database to a single column would cause all
    -- columns of the corresponding table in the secondary database to
    -- be updated. As such to track the exact same row in the secondary
    -- database, the primary key will have to be saved (the ROWID won't
    -- suffice, since the ROWID for the row would differ across
    -- databases. The primary key for each updated row is saved in
    -- JOURNAL_WRITES in the form of a WHERE clause that can be directly
    -- run during playback.

    -- in the case of SALES_ORDERS table, the primary key consists
    -- of two columns : ORDER_ID (NUMBER) and SALES_TAG (VARCHAR2)

    cWHEREclause := ' WHERE order_id = '  || :OLD.order_id
            ' AND sales_tag = ''' || :OLD.sales_tag || '''';

   INSERT INTO journal_writes(schema_name, table_name,
                              dml_operation, prmry_tbl_rowid,
                              upddel_where_clause,record_time)
     VALUES ('SALES', 'SALES_ORDERS', 'AU',
             ROWIDTOCHAR(:OLD.ROWID), cWHEREclause, SYSDATE);

ELSIF DELETING THEN
    -- for deletes, merely saving the old ROWID also won't help
    -- because the original row has been deleted and cannot be
    -- referenced anymore. As such, the primary key will have to
    -- be saved for each table in JOURNAL_WRITES in the form of
    -- a WHERE clause that can be directly run during playback


   cWHEREclause := ' WHERE order_id = '  || :OLD.order_id
            ' AND sales_tag = ''' || :OLD.sales_tag || '''';

   INSERT INTO journal_writes(schema_name, table_name,
                              dml_operation, prmry_tbl_rowid,
                              upddel_where_clause,record_time)
     VALUES ('SALES', 'SALES_ORDERS', 'ZD',
             ROWIDTOCHAR(:OLD.ROWID), cWHEREclause, SYSDATE);
END IF;
EXCEPTION
  WHEN OTHERS THEN
    RAISE_APPLICATION_ERROR(-20101,
           'Error during CSD journal writes on SALES_ORDERS');
END;
/
```

Next, a DBMS_JOB routine needs to be set-up on the secondary database to run periodically (every half-hour or each hour) a stored procedure to play back all recorded transactions. The stored procedure and all other related procedures can be placed in a package. The code within the package will look as follows:

```
/* Module        : playback_from_primary
** Module type : PACKAGE
** Functionality : used to playback all writes to tables in the primary.
**                 database. This package uses a database link to
**                 read the JOURNAL_WRITES table in the primary
**                 database. The package assumes that the
**                 appropriate database link has already been created
**                 to refer to the right schema on the primary database.
**
** Author   : Venkat S. Devraj
** History :
** 08/97       VSD     Written
*/

CREATE OR REPLACE PACKAGE playback_from_primary AS
  PROCEDURE playback;
END playback_from_primary;
/
CREATE OR REPLACE PACKAGE BODY playback_from_primary AS
  -- define local procedures within package

  -- procedure to construct the entire DELETE statement to
  -- be run via DBMS_SQL
  PROCEDURE PrepareDelStmt(pStmt IN OUT VARCHAR2
                          ,pSchema IN VARCHAR2
                          ,pTable  IN VARCHAR2
                          ,pWHERE  IN VARCHAR2) IS
  BEGIN
    pStmt := 'DELETE FROM ' || pSchema || '.'
               || pTable || pWHERE;
  END PrepareDelStmt;

  -- procedure to construct the entire UPDATE statement
  -- to be run via DBMS_SQL
  PROCEDURE PrepareUpdStmt(pStmt IN OUT VARCHAR2
                          ,pSchema IN VARCHAR2
                          ,pTable  IN VARCHAR2
                          ,pROWID  IN VARCHAR2
                          ,pWHERE  IN VARCHAR2) IS

    -- get all non primary key columns (they are the ones
    -- to be updated)
    CURSOR c_nonPKcols IS
      SELECT column_name FROM all_tab_columns@primary_db
       WHERE owner = pSchema
        AND table_name = pTable
        AND column_name NOT IN (SELECT column_name
               FROM all_cons_columns@primary_db
```

```
            WHERE constraint_name = (SELECT constraint_name
             FROM all_constraints@primary_db
            WHERE owner = pSchema
              AND table_name = pTable
              AND constraint_type = 'P'));

  r_nonPKcols c_nonPKcols%ROWTYPE;
  TYPE ColTab IS TABLE OF VARCHAR2(32) INDEX BY BINARY_INTEGER;
  nonPKcols ColTab;
  nIndex BINARY_INTEGER := 0;
  nCtr BINARY_INTEGER;
BEGIN
  -- start with the leading portion of the statement
  pStmt := 'UPDATE ' || pSchema || '.'
           || pTable || ' SET (';

  -- get and place all columns to be updated (non-PK cols)
  -- and place them in a PL/SQL table (array) for later usage
  FOR r_nonPKcols IN c_nonPKcols LOOP
    nIndex := nIndex + 1;
    nonPKcols(nIndex) := r_nonPKcols.column_name;
  END LOOP;

  -- now, append all columns to the statement as per
  -- correct UPDATE syntax
  FOR nCtr IN 1..nIndex LOOP
      IF nCtr = 1 THEN
        pStmt := pStmt || nonPKcols(nCtr);
    ELSE
        pStmt := pStmt || ', ' || nonPKcols(nCtr);
    END IF;
  END LOOP;

  -- now, append sub-query to get values to update columns
  -- from primary database table based on ROWID of the row
  -- and then finally append the final WHERE clause to the
  -- UPDATE statement
  pStmt := pStmt || ')' || ' = (SELECT ';
  FOR nCtr IN 1..nIndex LOOP
    IF nCtr = 1 THEN
       pStmt := pStmt || nonPKcols(nCtr);
    ELSE
       pStmt := pStmt || ', ' || nonPKcols(nCtr);
    END IF;
  END LOOP;

  pStmt := pStmt || ' FROM ' || pSchema || '.' || pTable
          '@primary_db WHERE ROWID = CHARTOROWID(''' ||
          pROWID || '''))' || pWHERE;
END PrepareUpdStmt;

-- define global procedure within package
```

```
  PROCEDURE playback IS
    -- this cursor uses a database link to grab the recordings off the
    -- JOURNAL_WRITES table in the primary database
    -- the output is sorted by DML_OPERATION (so that inserts are
    -- retrieved first, then updates and finally, deletes)
    CURSOR c_writes IS SELECT schema_name, table_name, dml_operation,
                              prmry_tbl_rowid, upddel_where_clause,
                              record_time
                         FROM journal_writes@primary_db
                       ORDER BY dml_operation;

    r_writes c_writes%ROWTYPE;
    max_time DATE;
    cStmt VARCHAR2(2000);
    cursor_id INTEGER;
    ret_val INTEGER;
BEGIN
    FOR r_writes IN c_writes LOOP
    -- capture the maximum date/time in JOURNAL_WRITES table
    -- for that period
    IF max_time IS NOT NULL THEN
       IF r_writes.record_time > max_time THEN
          max_time := r_writes.record_time;
       END IF;
    ELSE
       max_time := r_writes.record_time;
    END IF;

    -- reproduce the necessary DML statements
    -- process INSERTs first, then UPDATEs, then DELETEs
    cStmt :=  ' ';
    IF r_writes.dml_operation = 'AI' THEN
       -- the statements assume that the schema-name across
       -- the primary and secondary databases are the same
       -- (note that this is a mandatory requirement for CSDs)

       -- Also, the statements assume that the schema on the
       -- primary database pointed to by the database link
       -- have appropriate privileges and synonyms to access
       -- all the tables to which these DML statements have earlier
       -- been run (on the primary database)

       cStmt := 'INSERT INTO ' || r_writes.schema_name || '.'
                || r_writes.table_name ||
                ' SELECT * FROM ' || r_writes.table_name ||
                '@primary_db WHERE ROWID = CHARTOROWID(''' ||
                r_writes.prmry_tbl_rowid || ''')';

    ELSIF r_writes.dml_operation = 'AU' THEN
      PrepareUpdStmt(cStmt, r_writes.schema_name,
                     r_writes.table_name, r_writes.prmry_tbl_rowid,
                     r_writes.upddel_where_clause);
```

```
    ELSIF r_writes.dml_operation = 'ZD' THEN
      PrepareDelStmt(cStmt, r_writes.schema_name,
                     r_writes.table_name,
                     r_writes.upddel_where_clause);
    ELSE
      RAISE_APPLICATION_ERROR(-20141,
           'Invalid DML operator found in JOURNAL_WRITES table');
    END IF;

    BEGIN
      cursor_id := DBMS_SQL.OPEN_CURSOR;
      DBMS_SQL.PARSE(cursor_id, cStmt, DBMS_SQL.NATIVE);
      ret_val := DBMS_SQL.EXECUTE(cursor_id);
      DBMS_SQL.CLOSE_CURSOR(cursor_id);
    EXCEPTION
      -- this exception will allow certain valid discrepancies
      -- from aborting this routine. For instance, if a row that
      -- has been previously inserted/updated, is deleted from the
      -- primary database, then during playback there will be no row
      -- to refer back to. We don't want such situations to abort the
      -- entire playback process.
      WHEN OTHERS THEN
         IF DBMS_SQL.IS_OPEN(cursor_id) THEN
             DBMS_SQL.CLOSE_CURSOR(cursor_id);
         END IF;
         RAISE;
    END;

    COMMIT;
  END LOOP;

  -- use the maximum date/time captured earlier off both
  -- tables to delete off those rows that have already been
  -- played back (so that they do not get played back once again
  -- in the future causing duplicate writes). Also, the maximum
  -- date/time is used as the DELETE criteria so that new rows
  -- that have come into these tables (since the time this procedure
  -- started running) are not inadvertently deleted
  DELETE FROM journal_writes@primary_db
   WHERE record_time <= max_time;

  COMMIT;
 END playback;  /*EOF Playback */
END playback_from_primary;   /* EOF Package Body */
/
```

The DBMS_JOB routine can be defined on the secondary database within the same administrative schema (same schema-name) as defined on the primary database as follows. Prior to setting up the job, ensure that the database has been configured to use DBMS_JOB by setting the necessary initialization parameters and so on. Refer to the *Oracle8 Administrator's Guide* for information on configuring the DBMS_JOB package.

```
DECLARE
nRetVal BINARY_INTEGER;
BEGIN
    -- playback all writes from primary database every half-hour
    DBMS_JOB.SUBMIT(nRetVal, 'playback_from_primary.playback',
                    SYSDATE, 'SYSDATE + 1/48');
    COMMIT;
END;
/
```

Now, things are recorded and played back on a periodic basis, and the secondary database is kept in-sync with the primary. Since the secondary database is open and accessible, it can even be used as a reporting database to allow users to issue DSS-type queries on the data, without impacting the primary database (provided the primary and secondary databases are maintained on different systems). Now, whenever a patch is being applied on the primary database or it is being upgraded or some internal re-organization/maintenance is being done there, the secondary database can be used in its stead. The following steps need to occur during switchover to the secondary database. Ensure that the switchover is scheduled (as far as possible) to occur during periods of very low use.

1. Disable (break) the DBMS_JOB in the secondary database.
2. Manually apply the final transactions in the journal table to the secondary database to make it current. This can be done by explicitly running the DBMS_JOB one more time (just prior to the switchover). (In case, the primary database crashes during this time, the final transactions in the journal table cannot be applied during that time [temporarily resulting in some data loss]. Later after the primary database is recovered/repaired, the final transactions can be applied. Alternatively, if a parallel HA solution such as a conventional standby database is configured, then it can be utilized in case the primary database crashes at the critical juncture of applying the transactions in the journal table to the secondary database.)
3. Route all client sessions to the secondary database (which has now become primary) and make the previous primary database inaccessible to end-users. Chapter 6 discusses some methods for implementing such automatic client/application failover. Note that such switchover needs to consider client sessions that are already connected to the database and are actively running transactions, sessions that are connected but are currently inactive (not running any transactions), and also sessions that are initiating a new database session (in-flux sessions). Typically, the ones that are already connected and are active are the most difficult to fail over, and these may

be abruptly disconnected, causing the corresponding users/applications to see error-messages. A simple way to avoid this unpleasant scenario is to monitor the primary database for active sessions. Possibly there may be a lull in incoming sessions, and that's the best time to commence switchover, so that active sessions are not terminated.

4. Between steps (2) and (3), it is possible that some additional "last-second" user transactions may sneak in to the previous primary database that get recorded in the journal table. Accordingly the journal table needs to be checked for such "last-second" transactions. If there are none, then that's very good. However, if there are some, then these transactions won't have made it to the secondary database (that is about to be made primary) and need to be played back as one of the final stages in the switchover to make the secondary database completely current. Playing back these final transactions shouldn't normally take more than a few seconds, or at most minutes, due to the switchover being scheduled during low-use periods (unless the transaction load during switchover is still high). These final transactions can either

    - Be played back after the switchover is complete and client sessions have started accessing the secondary database (which has now become primary), or
    - Take a small outage (for a few minutes) and make both the primary and secondary databases unavailable to users. During the outage the final transactions can be replayed onto the secondary, and the switchover can occur after the secondary is fully up-to-date.

While the secondary database is being made current with these "last-second" transactions, it ideally needs to be inaccessible to end-users. Thus, a small outage may need to take place to synchronize the secondary with the primary. This will ensure that the users see only the most current data. However, if even such small periods of downtime are not acceptable, then the secondary database may be made accessible to users immediately. Now the playback can occur, even as the users are accessing the secondary database (which has now become the primary). Note that certain users may not be able to access the latest transactions. For instance, if a user has posted a financial entry into the ledger within the last half-hour, that may not be accessible to him/her as the playback is still going on. Similarly, a previously deleted row may still be accessible, or a user may have updated his or her password on the system a few minutes previously, and suddenly the new password doesn't seem to work. Thus, playing back the latest transactions as end-users are concurrently accessing the database could induce partial logical corruption, and the ill-effects of such a scenario may be confusing to end-users (at the very least). The extent of such confusion may be varied, depending on the extent of use. Furthermore, such a scenario may extend the logical corruption and expose the database to undesirable actions such as allowing rows to be inserted twice with different values each time or allowing a previously deleted row to be updated. However, if you have already provided advance warning to users of possible problems for a short while (during the playback), then it may help to alleviate the confusion. Also in cases where the primary database has crashed, switchover to the secondary database has to be immediate without waiting for the playback to occur. Playback can be done after the primary database has been recovered. During disasters where the primary database is completely destroyed, the latest transactions in the journal table will be lost. To summarize, whenever possible, take a small outage and complete the playback (only if there are any "last-second" transactions in the journal table) and then make the database accessible to users. Especially if the switchover is scheduled to occur during low-use hours, the few minutes of downtime necessary for the synchronization should generally be acceptable. Only if absolutely necessary, make the final playback and usage concurrent (or if the primary database is destroyed or has failed, skip the playback).

Conversely, if the primary database needs to go down only for a few minutes (a typical patch application does not take longer than 10–15 minutes), then the need to switch over to the secondary database must be evaluated, especially if you are going to allow user access only after the final playback is complete. Considering that the final playback may take up to a few minutes as well, evaluating whether the switchover is worth it or not will take careful analysis of the specific situation in your environment. However, in case no downtime is permissible, then CSDs do allow you to remain accessible even with the final playback currently being run. Also, in situations where the latest information (the rows that get into the primary database just prior to/during the switchover) is not expected to be accessed by end-users in most cases, then immediate switchover makes complete sense and may be implemented without hesitation.

Note that the CSD mechanisms need to be implemented on both the primary and secondary databases. In other words, the journal table, the triggers, and the stored procedure for DBMS_JOB need to be created and kept ready on the primary and secondary databases. However, recording needs to be dormant on the secondary database, whereas playback needs to be dormant on the primary database (so that the recording and playback of all transactions is mutually exclusive between the two databases). Once the secondary database is functioning as the primary, the original database becomes the secondary one. Now it may be made the CSD, and the same mechanisms may be used to record and playback all transactions that are currently occurring. So recording transactions in the (current) primary database needs to commence (the DBMS_JOB needs to be "un-broken"), and playback in the current CSD needs to be started, as well. For instance, say database_A is being upgraded from Oracle7 to Oracle8*i*, so the current CSD database_B is made primary. All transactions remaining in the journal table in database_A are played back to make database_B current, and database_A is shut down. The upgrade is done and then database_A is reopened and made the CSD. All transactions off the journals tables in database_B are now periodically played back onto database_A (this time, database_A lags behind by half-an-hour or so). During the next available opportunity when use is low, another switchover needs to occur, and the newly upgraded database_A needs to become the primary once again after all the latest transactions from database_B are incorporated into database_A. Now database_B can be upgraded to Oracle8*i* and made the CSD once again. Thus, the switchover cycle between the two databases can continue to prevent any downtime (of course, if both databases are maintained on the same location, then disasters could potentially wipe both out, causing downtime—however, that's when solutions such as geo-mirroring and remote standby databases should be considered).

As may be apparent, CSDs have an impact on performance (typically 5 to 10 percent) due to the constant recording of transactions on the primary database. The impact may be higher or lower for your site, depending on your transaction volume. The playback shouldn't impact performance, since it is done on the secondary database, unless both databases are maintained on the same system, defeating the purpose of the standby to an extent (the system becomes a single point of failure). Also for performance reasons, the CSD strategy outlined here does not use database links to perform the playback (since potentially a large number of rows may need to be played back and using database links will be highly inefficient in such a scenario). In order to avoid any long-term impacts, CSDs can be temporary/transitional in nature. For instance, they can be implemented just prior to a major migration effort. This implementation may involve a very small period of downtime to create the necessary triggers and the journal table (as mentioned earlier, a smaller hit may help to avoid a bigger hit). However, such small downtime periods can be planned and scheduled well in advance to occur during relatively low-use periods (such as late Saturday night). Bear in mind, though, that implementing CSDs to occur temporarily would not help during sudden emergencies, such as block corruption on a large table/index. A permanent CSD implementation gives you a fair chance to overcome unanticipated problems without downtime. Again, this is an example of the classic conflict between availability and performance (Chapter 1 elaborates on this), and you and your organization's technical management team need to decide whether your organization is willing to compromise on (a little bit of) performance to make higher availability possible. Moreover, note that this impact on performance can be highly reduced (almost made negligible) by carefully planning the physical database layout to accommodate the additional writes. The journal table needs to be physically placed on disks different from the primary tables, such that concurrent writes are spread out on different I/O channels, preventing bottlenecks. In fact, these additional writes should not be regarded as overhead but be considered critical for availability and treated as such by planning for them right from the start. Also, you could resort to a combination of CSDs, standby tables (discussed next) and the conventional Oracle standby database feature. During normal circumstances, you would have implemented only standby tables and the conventional Oracle standby database. That way, your impact on performance is not as much as from implementing CSDs continuously (full-time). Only critical tables are made standby (allowing you to handle sudden emergencies concerning them with little or no downtime), and the redo-logs need to be transferred over and applied to the standby database (allowing you to overcome scenarios where the entire primary database is affected). However, just prior to a major upgrade effort, you can implement CSDs, since conventional standby databases would not operate across the current version and the upgraded version, forcing you to come up with a custom solution to prevent downtime.

Another issue with CSDs (as with any standby solution) is the high financial cost incurred to maintain a duplicate system/database. The nature of CSD allows it to be implemented even on a less powerful system (the primary system can have higher capacity than the secondary). However, during/after switchover, the performance provided by the secondary system/database may not be acceptable. Especially if the primary database is expected to be down for a long time, this may be a serious issue to consider, and ensuring that the primary and secondary databases are hosted on identical systems (with equal capacity) may be necessary. This should ideally be the case for every standby scenario—the primary and secondary systems should be clones. An advantage with CSDs is that the secondary database is continuously open. So it may be used as a reporting instance to reduce the load on the primary database. This will allow better return on investment and may allow better justification to senior management for investing in the secondary resources.

Case-Study in Implementing CSDs

This section presents a case-study to fully illustrate the deployment of a CSD.

THE SCENARIO ABC, Inc., has six Oracle8 v8.0.5 databases, out of which one (let's call it PT05) needs very high availability. Tables belonging to an e-commerce application reside on three different schemas within PT05. The application allows customers around the world to send personalized electronic greeting cards to friends, family, and other acquaintances. The availability requirements (based on extensive monitoring of application usage patterns) are listed in Table 15-3.

THE PROBLEM In order to ensure that there are no outages during the hours when availability is critical, ABC, Inc., decided to invest in a standby system/database configuration. Their IT department listed possible reasons for downtime in their database environment (disk failure; segment corruption; user-errors/accidents; and routine maintenance such as index rebuilds, defragmentation, version upgrades, and patch application), and it was apparent that the conventional standby database approach exposed them to potentially high downtime during certain critical tasks

Period	Availability Required/Downtime Allowed
Fifteen days before any holiday (ABC, Inc. has a list of holidays celebrated around the world). Additionally, between Oct. 1 and Jan. 31 (Christmas & New Year holiday season)	*True* 24×7
Between Feb. 1 and Sep. 30 (not counting holiday periods)	Up to 1 hour of downtime allowed between the hours of 2:00 A.M. and 5:00 A.M. EST on week-nights and up to 3 hours of downtime permissible on Saturday night/Sunday morning between 2:00 A.M. and 5:00 A.M. However, such downtime is allowable only during emergencies. Ideally, 24×7 access is required, even during these hours.

TABLE 15-3. *Table Listing Availability Requirements for the PT05 Instance at ABC, Inc.*

such as patch application and corruption repair. Furthermore, during version upgrades they could not even directly switch over to the standby database due to different database versions being involved and Oracle's inability to use redo from a previous version during roll forward. Also, many user errors (incorrect DDL statements accidentally issued) seemed to get propagated across to the standby prior to being detected by administrative personnel, thus making the standby susceptible to the same problems plaguing the primary database. Thus, ABC, Inc., needed a solution that would allow them to be open both during major emergencies such as rampant corruption and segment reorganization (to recover from I/O bottlenecks) and during routine maintenance such as defragmentation and patch application. Furthermore, the solution should allow them to remain online, even as the database was being upgraded from Oracle8 to Oracle8*i* (which they planned to do in the very near future). This solution was obviously not the conventional standby database configuration.

INTERMEDIATE SOLUTION(S) EXAMINED/APPLIED AND THE NEED FOR A BETTER SOLUTION The IT personnel evaluated some hardware-based solutions; however, those either failed to meet one or more of their requirements or were too expensive for a company of their size (they were a startup with limited venture capital funds). Thus, there was a strong need for a solution that didn't compromise on availability and didn't require them to stretch too much on their IT budget (they had, after all, just managed to get the approval from the senior management for the new standby system and additional database licenses).

THE CUSTOM STANDBY DATABASE SOLUTION A technical team was called in from a consulting company (I had the privilege to be part of the team) to evaluate their requirements and the overall scenario and recommend the best solution, keeping their "limited funds" situation in mind. Based on all the input, we recommended a CSD-based solution to them. Having obtained permission to go ahead and implement it, we designed and deployed it as follows:

- A secondary database was created on the standby server. The latest (online) backups of the primary database were used to create the secondary database. We had the option of duplicating only the three relevant schemas that required high availability (in addition to the SYSTEM, TEMPORARY, and RBS tablespaces). However, that would mean initially only duplicating the segment structures (tables, indexes, triggers, stored procedures, and so on) and then manually populating them. Since the data retrieval from the primary (to subsequently populate the secondary) would affect the normal functioning of the primary, we decide to use the backups instead to keep the impact on the primary nil. Then the online redo-logs on the primary were used to keep the standby database in-sync (similar to a regular standby database configuration).
- Next we identified a logical delta (logical deltas are discussed in Chapter 8) on the primary and decided to implement the journal table and the required triggers on the tables within the three primary schemas (to populate the journal table) during the interval (the small outage taken) to implement the logical delta. The logical delta was determined to be next Sunday at 2:30 A.M. We were allowed downtime up to three hours to implement the logical delta. However, all we needed was 15 minutes to stop all applications accessing the schemas, archive all unarchived online redo-logs, bounce the database (to disconnect any lingering user connection), create the journal table, and then finally create the necessary trigger on each table. We had developed and kept ready (well-tested) scripts to perform the entire work to allow fast creation and to prevent human errors. By the time we were actually done on Sunday morning, we had taken up less than 12 minutes. All the archived redo-logs generated thus far were copied over to the standby server to be applied one last time to the secondary database. Then all the applications were re-started and tested to ensure there were no unwanted side-effects due to the new triggers. All the archived redo-logs copied over were applied to the secondary, and it was made completely current up to the logical delta defined by us. Finally, the script to create the triggers and the journal table was run on the secondary database as well (in case it ever had to become the primary, those would be needed). However, the triggers were kept disabled.

- Then the DBMS_JOB routine was created on the secondary database to periodically poll the journal table on the primary database and play back all the transactions recorded there. The routine was set to run once every 30 minutes.
- Things seemed to be running fairly smoothly, and we got a chance to test the CSD configuration relatively early. After a couple of dozen weeks or so, on a lazy Wednesday afternoon, the pagers of the administrative personnel went berserk: The database had crashed and all the applications could not access it anymore. Users on the Web could no longer use the applications and the site was down! On quickly checking the alert-log of the database, it became apparent that the database could not access some of the data-files. Further checks revealed that these data-files were not present on the system any more: They had been deleted (accidentally, we later discovered, by a new systems administrator). Immediately we decided to switch over to the CSD. We broke the DBMS_JOB on the secondary database and enabled the triggers to populate the journal table (again, these steps were well-scripted and tested). All applications were re-routed via Net8 (Chapter 6 talks about application failover and re-routing) to use the CSD. Now, the applications could operate as before. All new transactions generated were written to the journal table (ready to be applied to the original primary database, after it was repaired and brought back up). Total downtime under the circumstance was slightly under six minutes. Later the original primary database was recovered using the latest hot backups and made the CSD. The triggers on the tables to write to the journal table were disabled, and the DBMS_JOB was created to play back all writes from the journal table on the current primary database.

RESULT OF THE CUSTOM STANDBY DATABASE SOLUTION Needless to say, the CSD implementation was an outstanding success! Overall downtime was kept very low under dire circumstances, and the CSD proved to be a great savior. Lots of practice and pre-written scripts helped to avert panic among the administrative personnel and any unnecessary complications during the switchover. As expected, performance is slighted impacted. Most of the impact seems to be due to excessive I/O and sub-optimal physical database layout. However, with the inflow of additional funds down the line, they have been able to invest in more disks/ controllers to resolve burning I/O bottlenecks. Additionally, tuning of all SQL used within the application has greatly helped in keeping I/O to the minimum. Overall, the current small impact (we observe around 5 percent during non-peak hours and around 8–10 percent during peak hours) on performance is a small price to pay for the extended availability in a wide variety of downtime-causing situations.

Consider using standby tables to cater to segment-level failures

The architecture just described (CSD) is useful for providing availability during external (to the database) problems encountered such as during upgrades, downgrades, or patch applications. Thus, the entire database is prevented from being a single point of failure during these scenarios. However, during certain emergencies, you may be forced to perform internal re-organizations, where the availability of the entire database is not at stake, but only a component thereof, such as a table or a group of tables. For example, when a table or its index is deemed to be corrupt or a table has a very high degree of row-chaining and needs to be rebuilt, these specific segments would need to be made unavailable during the maintenance, thus affecting overall database availability. Especially if these segments are popular (used very often by one or more applications), then any maintenance work or re-organization performed on them poses a serious problem. During such times, standby databases have limited utility, since you do not want the entire database to be rolled-over to the standby. You just need certain tables to be available while maintenance work is being performed on them or they have been afflicted with a problem that requires immediate attention and causes them to be unavailable to applications. Note that Oracle8*i* brings a number of key advantages to the table by allowing tables to remain online while maintenance work is being done on them via features such as non-blocking index rebuilds and enhanced partitioning options. Chapter 20 elaborates on some of these features. However, even with Oracle8*i*, segments cannot be kept available during specific emergencies such as data-block or index/table corruption or user accidents (say, a table being dropped/truncated). Partitioning does bring some advantages in some of these scenarios. For example, if a table is broken into multiple partitions, certain partitions can be taken offline (some restrictions do apply, such as that they must be on different tablespaces and no global indexes should exist on these tables, to make such partial availability possible), and maintenance work can be done on them, while users continue to access the remaining partitions. However, if a partition that a user is interested in is afflicted with corruption or is inadvertently dropped/truncated, then availability is impacted. These situations do need to be addressed in any complete, end-to-end availability solution. Accordingly, in order to completely insulate the database against these kind of segment-specific problems and retain availability even during such crises, I recommend a strategy called standby tables, illustrated in Figure 15-7.

Standby tables, as the name itself indicates, are implemented by keeping one or more copies of *critical* tables within the same database. Note the emphasis on the word "critical." Use of standby tables does not involve replicating all tables in every schema, or even all tables in a specific schema. This is one important area where standby tables differ from other conventional Oracle and third-party replication methods. Theoretically, you could still go ahead and have a standby table for every table used by your applications. However, in case all tables within a schema or

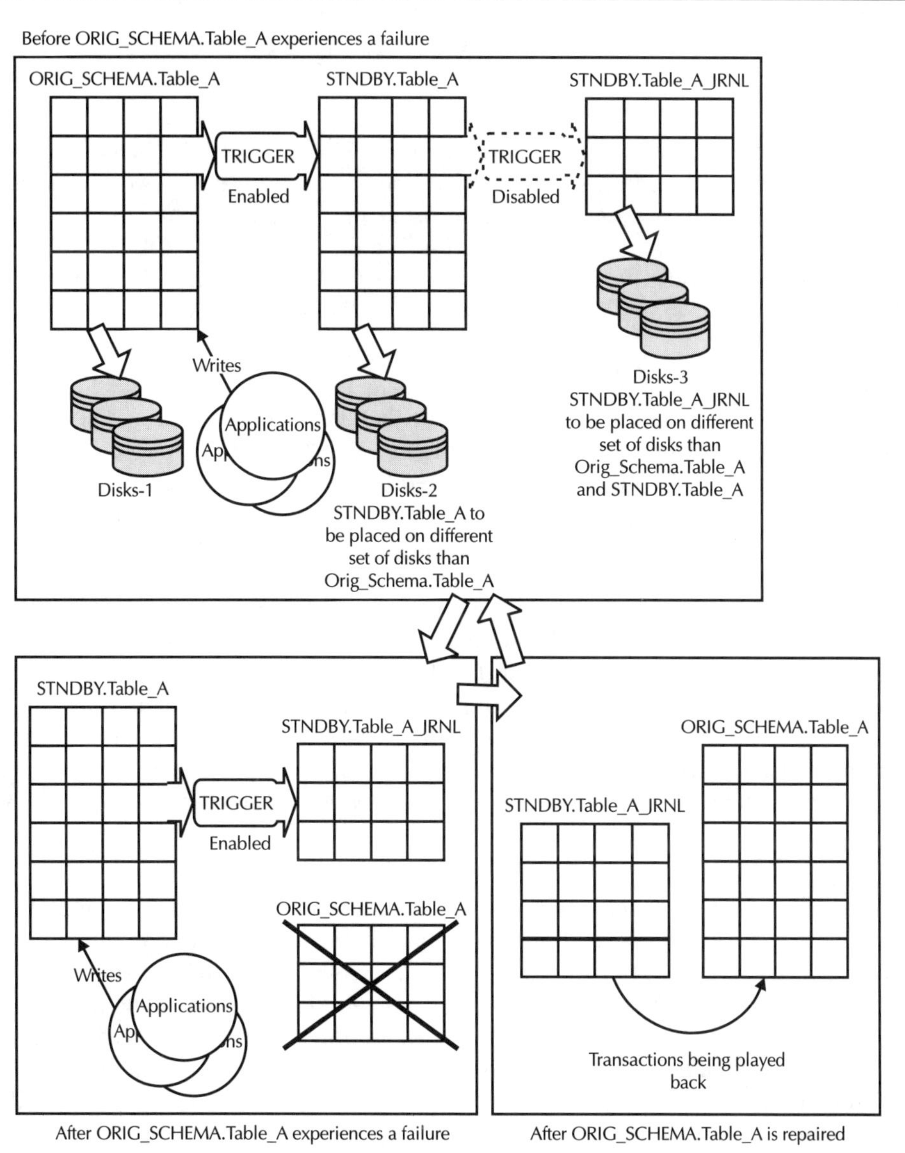

FIGURE 15-7. *Illustration of a standby table implementation*

even the entire database need to be replicated, you ought to look at other solutions that operate at a broader level, such as standby databases (regular or custom), Advanced Replication, or geo-mirroring (some of which at any rate need to be implemented at any site seeking 24×7 availability in addition to segment-level

replication to overcome global database failures). Some key criteria help in determining which tables to replicate via the standby tables method:

Criticality

In every application, irrespective of whether it is a DSS-type or OLTP-type application, there are certain key tables that dominate it. These tables corner most of the application reads and/or writes. For instance, in a star-schema based data-mart or data-warehouse, these would be the fact tables. In an OLTP sales order processing system, these would be tables such as ORDERS and ORDER_ITEMS. These are the "core" tables that need to be made standby.

Size

Even among these core tables, there are some that are quite tiny. For example, in a star-schema based design, besides the fact tables, the dimension tables can also be very critical (depending on how denormalized the fact tables are). Some of these dimension tables are quite large (say, a few hundred thousand rows), whereas some are quite tiny, comprising of a few thousand rows or less (example: the TIME_DIMENSION table, which holds days in a year). Generally, the ones that are tiny are held within a few Oracle blocks and are generally not prone to too many problems (such as rampant fragmentation or requiring frequent index rebuilds). Even if certain problems arise (such as block corruption), these tables can be quickly rebuilt/restored from a backup or from the standby database (if one is available) with little impact on downtime (usually, the amount of downtime in such cases would not be a lot more than the downtime incurred during a standby table switchover). Accordingly, due to their small size, they do not really merit having standby tables.

Activity

Some of these core tables can be highly volatile, whereas some may be pretty static. Static tables can be fairly easily restored/re-built in most cases. Accordingly, they generally do not deserve to be made standby. However, tables with medium to high level activity do need to be made standby, since rebuilding/restoring them would require point-in-time recovery, thus causing more downtime than needs to occur.

Again, these "rules" only provide general guidelines in helping you determine which tables to make standby. They should be used with discretion in your specific environment.

How Standby Tables Work

Standby tables focus on individual tables that are critical for an application to function. Here's how standby tables work:

IDENTIFY CORE SEGMENTS Identify your core tables, on which all applications requiring 24×7 access depend.

CREATE ADMINISTRATIVE SCHEMA Create a new administrative schema to hold all the mirror tables. This schema's default tablespace should rest on separate disks/controllers than where the original core tables are present to prevent I/O contention during simultaneous writes to the original tables and the mirrors.

CREATE TABLE MIRRORS Create mirrors of these tables (throughout this chapter, we will be talking about implementing a single mirror to keep the impact on performance and maintenance low) in the administrative schema. The mirror for each table would be the exact same table-name (since the original/primary table and its mirror/standby are present in different schemas, that shouldn't pose a problem). Each mirrored table would have the same indexes and constraints as the original one. In the case of triggers, you need to do some analysis and see whether a similar trigger on the mirrored table makes sense. For each specific table, your evaluations may differ (depending on what the trigger is doing).

CREATE JOURNAL TABLES For each mirrored/standby table, create a corresponding journal table. This journal table will record all writes made to the standby table. Later these writes will be played back to the original table (after the emergency/maintenance work on the original table is complete and it is available again). The structure of the journal table is described in a later paragraph. If appropriate, the journal table can be created in the very same administrative schema where the standby tables are created. While doing so, if the source tables are large, ensure that the journal table is created on data-files that are on separate disks/controllers than the standby tables to eliminate I/O contention between them (actually, between all three: the source tables, the standby mirrors, and the journal table).

GRANT PRIVILEGES Grant ALL privileges to the schemas (that own the primary tables) on the mirrored tables in the administrative schema. Ensure that you grant the privileges only to schemas that own the primary tables corresponding to the mirrors. In other words, do not grant privileges on specific mirrored tables to schemas that do not own the original counterparts. For instance, if schema SALES owns the SALES_ORDERS table, then grant privileges to SALES only on that and other tables owned by it. Do not grant privileges to SALES on the INCOMING_MATERIALS table, which is owned by the INVENTORY schema. Following this guideline will prevent security hazards. Additionally, grant privileges as needed (SELECT, INSERT, and so on) to other end-user schemas and/or roles that need to access these tables. Such end-user schemas should have equal access to the original tables and their mirrors (no extra privileges should be given). Ideally, place all these additional table-creation and privilege-grant commands in scripts that can be re-run as needed, and source-control these scripts.

CREATE PUBLIC SYNONYMS Create public synonyms on each of the mirrored tables. Public synonyms are necessary to allow the mirrored tables to be present as a standby to the original tables. Thus, the primary tables co-exist with the standby tables via the public synonyms. Thus, whenever the SALES schema refers to the SALES_ORDERS table, it will refer to the primary SALES_ORDERS table (owned by it). When the primary SALES_ORDERS table has a problem, it can be made unavailable and the public synonym will take over. All subsequent references to the SALES_ORDERS table will point to the standby SALES_ORDERS table in the administrative schema. Note that this step may or may not require a substantial change to your environment. Let's look at some possible scenarios for your current application-implementation:

1. **All end-users access the primary tables directly via the owning schema** Here, all end-users directly log-on as the owning schema and access the tables. For example, end-users accessing the SALES application log-on via the SALES schema-id. Here, there is a single point of access. Either all the end-users know the password of the owning schema or they are provided with custom screens that log-in internally for them, without their having to know the password. This scenario is not a totally unlikely assumption and is prevalent in many e-commerce applications or any application, for that matter, where the end-users are not identifiable and are routed through a third-tier (a Web-application server, for instance). Thus, every user logs on as the original table owner (with an end-user community comprising a million-plus users in the case of many e-commerce applications, it is seldom possible to assign a distinct Oracle user-id to each end-user).

2. **All end-users access the primary tables via private synonyms** Here, each end-user schema has a private synonym pointing to the primary table in the owning schema. Typically, the private synonyms are named the same as the primary table. Thus, each end-user references the primary table by name without the qualifying schema-name prefix. The private synonym translates the reference and points to the primary table.

3. **All end-users access the primary tables by direct reference** Here, instead of a private synonym, end-users directly refer to the primary table via a qualified reference, where the actual owning schema-name is prefixed to each primary table. For instance, SALES_ORDERS is referenced as SALES.SALES_ORDERS.

4. **All end-users access the primary tables via public synonyms** Here, public synonyms are created for each primary table and all end-users access the primary tables via these public synonyms. Typically, the public synonym names are the same as the actual primary table names.

With scenarios 1 and 2, you don't have a problem implementing standby tables. However, with scenarios 3 and 4, there are impending issues due to interference with the access via the public synonyms referring to the standby tables that would become active after switchover. In scenario 3, the users bypass all public synonyms by directing referencing each table in the owning schema with qualified names. At times, even with method 2, you may find application code referencing tables with the schema name prefixed (thus bypassing even the private synonyms created). Accordingly, you may need to change application code to cease such direct access and instead create private synonyms to enforce referencing via the private synonyms. In case the tables are accessed in an ad hoc fashion by end-users (such as in a DSS environment), then the end-users need to be trained to use the private synonyms rather than direct reference.

Additionally, if the applications are canned third-party applications, where you cannot change the application-code, then you need to make a slight change to the standby tables implementation strategy. Instead of naming the standby table the same as the primary table and placing the former in a separate administrative schema, you will need to place it in the same schema as the primary table and name it something different (than the primary) such as *table_name*_STNDBY. That way, when the primary table has problems and goes down, you can rename it to something else such as *table_name*_OLD and rename the standby table to the original primary table-name to allow applications/end-users to access it. By doing so, you won't need a public synonym to point to the standby table. Here, switchover is not automatic (since it involves manually renaming the standby table); however, it still allows standby tables to be implemented in sites that use third-party applications and limits downtime.

In the case of scenario 4, the existing public synonyms would conflict with the new public synonyms that are necessary for the standby database. In other words, Oracle wouldn't allow you create two public synonyms with the same name. Scenario 4 is pretty prevalent in many companies where the end-users are limited (say, a few hundred) and each can be assigned a distinct user-id. However, you would need to drop all public synonyms on the primary tables that the end-users use and replace them with private synonyms in each end-user's schema. That would allow public synonyms to be created for the standby table (with the same name as the primary table). That's the only change in the implementation that you would need to make for scenario 4. For instance, if user-id SAMG accesses the SALES.SALES_ORDERS table via a public synonym, that needs to be dropped so that the public synonym can be recreated to point to the standby SALES_ORDERS table in the administrative schema. Then a private synonym pointing to SALES.SALES_ORDERS can be created for SAMG and the rest of the users. Thus, whenever the standby table needs to be used, the original SALES.SALES_ORDERS can be made unavailable and the users will still refer to SALES.SALES_ORDERS via the private synonym. However, the private synonym will now also be re-directed to the public synonym via the SALES schema (since the original SALES.SALES_ORDERS table is unavailable/not present and SALES.SALES_ORDERS now refers to the public synonym SALES_ORDERS that the SALES schema uses).

SEGMENT FAILOVER In the previous paragraph, we often refer to the original table being made unavailable. Whenever the original table has critical problems such as, say, block corruption, it can be instantly renamed to table_name_OLD (as soon as the DBA detects/is alerted to the problem). For instance, when SALES.SALES_ORDERS has a problem, it can be renamed to SALES.SALES_ORDERS_OLD. Thus, the original table becomes unavailable, and all references are re-directed to the mirrored table via the public synonym. Similarly, if the SALES.SALES_ORDERS table is accidentally truncated, it can be renamed as well. However, if the SALES.SALES_ORDERS table is accidentally dropped, then the renaming does not have to occur, since it is automatically unavailable. Thus, the mirror allows the table to be available even when it is afflicted with a problem. Note that this strategy still does not prevent downtime during the time taken to detect the problem and make the problematic table unavailable. For instance, if the DBA is alerted to block corruption only after 20 minutes or so, he or she can respond and switch over to the standby table. However, during the last 20 or so minutes, the problem has prevented applications/users from properly accessing the table. This problem is reduced to an extent if extensive monitoring is put in place to periodically check for database and/or application errors and immediately alert the DBA, if any are spotted. In any case, standby tables prevent excessive downtime. For instance, if there were no standby tables, then the 20 minutes of downtime could escalate to much higher downtime as the extent of corruption is determined and the problem is fixed. Of course, you could switch over to a standby database (regular or custom). However, switching over to a standby table (as the preceding paragraphs allude) is much faster than switching over to a standby database.

KEEPING THE ORIGINAL AND STANDBY TABLES SYNCHRONIZED

Finally, we come to the issue of keeping the original table and the standby table in-sync. This is attained via triggers on both the original and standby tables. The trigger on the original table copies all writes to the standby table. The trigger on the standby table ought to be kept dormant (disabled) and enabled only when the standby table takes over as the primary table (whenever the original table becomes unavailable). The trigger on the original table copies all writes to the standby table, and the trigger on the standby table copies all writes made to it to a third journal table. The writes to the standby table (as it is made primary) need to be copied over to the journal table and not the original table, because the original table may be unavailable for extended periods of time (as it is being repaired/restored) and there needs to be a mechanism to track all (new) writes made to the standby table. These new writes can be easily transferred from the journal table to the original table once again, as the original table is later restored to being the primary (after it is repaired/restored).

HANDLING DDL CHANGES TO ORIGINAL TABLE Any DDL changes to the original and/or standby will need to be manually applied to both the original and the standby tables. For instance, if the original table is truncated or altered to add a new column, the same change will need to be explicitly applied to the standby table. Thus, automatic application of DDL activity to the standby tables is not allowed (unlike regular standby databases). Such manual propagation of DDL activity is performed explicitly by administrative personnel only when the original DDL statement is deemed appropriate (that is, it was not an accident in the first place). Since the secondary database holding the standby tables will be open, there shouldn't be a problem propagating the DDL changes.

Example in Using Standby Tables

Now, let's take an example to understand the standby table implementation better. Let's use the same table SALES.SALES_ORDERS (used earlier to illustrate CSDs) in our example. The structure of the SALES_ORDERS table is listed in Table 15-4.

The structure listed in Table 15-4 will pertain to both the original table and the standby. As mentioned earlier, both the original table and the standby table will match each in terms of indexes and constraints. Implementing foreign key relationships for the standby table is explained in Table 15-4. The SALES schema owns the original SALES_ORDERS table, and the STANDBY schema owns the

Table: SALES_ORDERS

Column-Name	Data-Type(Length)	Constraint
ORDER_ID	NUMBER(5)	Primary-key
SALES_TAG	VARCHAR2(5)	Primary-key
ORDER_DATE	DATE	NOT NULL
SALESPERSON_ID	NUMBER(5)	Foreign-key referring to SALES.SALESPERSONS table. If the SALESPERSONS table is also made standby, the standby SALES_ORDERS table will refer to the standby SALESPERSONS table; otherwise, it will directly refer to the SALES.SALESPERSONS table.
CUSTOMER_ID	NUMBER(5)	Foreign-key referring to SALES.CUSTOMERS table. Again as in the preceding situation, if the CUSTOMERS table has also been made standby, then the standby SALES_ORDERS table will refer to the standby CUSTOMERS table; otherwise, it will refer directly to the SALES.CUSTOMERS table to implement this particular foreign key relationship
CREATE_DATE	DATE	

TABLE 15-4. *SALES_ORDERS Structure*

standby SALES_ORDERS table. The SALES schema needs to have INSERT, UPDATE, DELETE, and SELECT privileges on the STANDBY.SALES_ORDERS table, and there needs to be a PUBLIC SYNONYM on STANDBY.SALES_ORDERS table. Additionally, the STANDBY schema also owns a journal table, SALES_ORDERS_JRNL. The structure of the journal table is listed in Table 15-5.

The structure listed in Table 15-4 will pertain to both the original table and the standby. As mentioned earlier, both the original table and the standby table will match each in terms of indexes and constraints. Implementing foreign key relationships for the standby table is explained in Table 15-4. The SALES schema owns the original SALES_ORDERS table, and the STANDBY schema owns the standby SALES_ORDERS table. The SALES schema needs to have INSERT, UPDATE, DELETE, and SELECT privileges on the STANDBY.SALES_ORDERS table. And there needs to be a PUBLIC SYNONYM on STANDBY.SALES_ORDERS table. Additionally, the STANDBY schema also owns a journal table, SALES_ORDERS_JRNL. The structure of the journal table is listed in Table 15-5.

Table: SALES_ORDERS_JRNL

Column-Name	**Data-Type(Length)**	**Comments**
STANDBY_ROWID	VARCHAR2(18)	ROWID of the row in the standby SALES_ORDERS table that has been inserted/updated/deleted
DML_OPERATION	VARCHAR2(2)	'AI' => INSERTs / 'AU' => UPDATEs / 'ZD' => DELETEs
PK_ORDER_ID	NUMBER(5)	Portion of the primary-key of the row in the standby SALES_ORDERS table that has been updated/deleted
PK_SALES_TAG	VARCHAR2(5)	(Remaining) portion of the primary-key. Journal tables corresponding to other tables may have less or more primary-key related columns, depending on whether the primary-key is a single-column key or a compound key for those tables.

TABLE 15-5. *Journal Table SALES_ORDERS_JRNL Structure*

A trigger needs to be defined on the original table to copy all writes to the standby table. The trigger on the original SALES.SALES_ORDERS will be as follows:

```
/* Module     : t_sales_ord02 [trigger on SALES_ORDERS table]
**              02 after the trigger name just indicates the current
**              trigger-number on the SALES_ORDERS table
** Functionality : used to copy all writes to STANDBY.SALES_ORDERS
** Notes    : 1) To be run as the primary table schema-owner

** Author   : Venkat S. Devraj
** History  :
** 08/97      VSD    Written
*/

CREATE TRIGGER t_sales_ord02
AFTER INSERT OR UPDATE OR DELETE ON sales_orders
FOR EACH ROW
BEGIN
   IF INSERTING THEN
      INSERT INTO standby.sales_orders(order_id, sales_tag,
                       order_date, salesperson_id,
                       customer_id, create_date)
        VALUES(:NEW.order_id, :NEW.sales_tag, :NEW.order_date,
            :NEW.salesperson_id, :NEW.customer_id, :NEW.create_date);
   ELSIF UPDATING THEN
      UPDATE standby.sales_orders
         SET order_date = :NEW.order_date,
             salesperson_id = :NEW.salesperson_id,
             customer_id = :NEW.customer_id,
             create_date = :NEW.create_date
       WHERE order_id = :OLD.order_id
          AND sales_tag = :OLD.sales_tag;
   ELSIF DELETING THEN
     DELETE standby.sales_orders
      WHERE order_id = :OLD.order_id
        AND sales_tag = :OLD.sales_tag;
   END IF;
END;
/
```

Now, every INSERT/UPDATE/DELETE that occurs on the primary table will be copied to the standby table. As mentioned earlier, in order to keep the impact on performance low, it is necessary to maintain the standby table on a separate set of disks/controllers than the primary table.

Whenever the primary table has problems and needs to be made unavailable, the standby table takes over and is written to, instead of the original primary table. Now, there has to be a way to track the writes and later transfer them to the original primary table as it becomes available once again. That's where the journal table plays its role and allows all writes to the standby table to be recorded. This trigger is normally disabled and is enabled only when the switchover to the standby table occurs (the enabling has to be done manually as part of the switchover process). The trigger on the STANDBY.SALES_ORDERS table (which has now become the primary table) is as follows:

```
/* Module    : t_stndby_sales_ord01 [trigger on STANDBY.SALES_ORDERS
table]
**             01 after the trigger name merely indicates the current
**             trigger-number on the STANDBY.SALES_ORDERS table
** Functionality : used to record all writes to the standby table,
that
**                 can be played back onto the original primary table
later
** Notes   : 1) To be run as the STANDBY schema owner
** Author  : Venkat S. Devraj
** History :
** 08/97      VSD    Written
*/

CREATE TRIGGER t_stndby_sales_ord01
AFTER INSERT OR UPDATE OR DELETE ON standby.sales_orders
FOR EACH ROW
BEGIN
   IF INSERTING THEN
      INSERT INTO standby.sales_orders_jrnl(standby_rowid,
                    dml_operation, pk_order_id, pk_sales_tag)
        VALUES(ROWIDTOCHAR(:NEW.ROWID), 'AI', :NEW.ORDER_ID,
               :NEW.SALES_TAG);

   ELSIF UPDATING THEN
     INSERT INTO standby.sales_orders_jrnl(standby_rowid,
                    dml_operation, pk_order_id, pk_sales_tag)
        VALUES(ROWIDTOCHAR(:OLD.ROWID), 'AU', :OLD.ORDER_ID,
               :OLD.SALES_TAG);

   ELSIF DELETING THEN
     INSERT INTO standby.sales_orders_jrnl(standby_rowid,
                    dml_operation, pk_order_id, pk_sales_tag)
        VALUES(ROWIDTOCHAR(:OLD.ROWID), 'ZD', :OLD.ORDER_ID,
               :OLD.SALES_TAG);

   END IF;
END;
/
```

Later, as problems (such as block corruption) on the original primary table are resolved and it is ready to become online again, all the writes recorded in the journal need to be played back to make it current. However, as it is being made current, other transactions may get written to the standby table, thus inserting additional rows into the journal table. Accordingly, the switchover to the original primary needs to occur during very low use periods. Thus, there will be few (if any, at all) new records that get written to the journal table during playback. In any case, if there are any new records, those need to be applied as well. Now, there are two ways this can be done:

- Take a small outage (disable only those applications that access this table), apply the latest set of rows in the journal table, and then make the original primary table available again after disabling the standby table.
- Make the standby table unavailable and immediately make the original primary table available without taking an outage (other than to perform the actual switchover) and then apply the latest rows in the journal table to the primary table as it is being accessed by applications/users.

There are pros and cons to each scenario. For instance, with the first scenario, the switchover is "clean" without any chances of logical corruption. However, in the second scenario, logical corruption could creep in (as explained earlier in the section on CSDs). However, in the first scenario, the outage is comparatively larger than in the second. In the second scenario, the outage would be a few minutes to accomplish the switchover, whereas in the first, the switchover has to occur, and then the final playback has to complete. Note that the final playback may not take more than a few more minutes, since the task is being done during low use hours. However, this assumption may not be true for your environment. Also, scenario 2 may not be entirely bad for your environment, if users/applications are not expected to access the latest rows during that time-frame. So scenario 2 can be safely accomplished. In any case, you know your environment best. Evaluate the pros and cons, keeping data integrity uppermost in your mind (there is no sense being *totally* available, if the data is not valid anymore), and decide on the method that suits your company best. Also, be sure to provide advance intimation of the switchover to your users, so that they expect the downtime (however little it may be) and plan their work (possibly) around it.

Once the final playback is complete, you need to disable the trigger (T_STNDBY_SALES_ORD01) on the standby table and truncate the journal table (since those records have already been played back and are useless). Ensure that the trigger (T_SALES_ORD02) on the primary table is enabled and all writes made to the primary table continue to be copied over to the standby table.

For DSS applications such as data-warehouses and data-marts, you may not need the triggers and the journal table, if your tables are not subjected to any interactive writes. If the only writes for your tables occur as data is being loaded in the form of bulk-inserts, then you can merely maintain the primary table and the standby table. Instead of keeping them in-sync via triggers, you can write the data-load routines such that both tables are populated. Also this will eliminate the issue of the final playback from the journal table during switchover from standby to primary, since the switchover ought to be scheduled to occur during periods when data-loads are not simultaneously occurring.

Note that implementing standby tables involves making some routine policy enhancements:

- Robust security should be in-place so that nobody other than the DBAs responsible for the switchover should have administrative access to the standby tables (so that they cannot be dropped, altered, and so on).
- The backup plan/procedure needs to back up the administrative schema that holds the standby tables, as well.
- During recovery, the standby tables can be recovered last. Accordingly, the DBA performing the recovery needs to be able to identify which tablespace(s)/data-file(s) hold the standby tables. This will be common knowledge if the DBA works in-house. However, if an external consultant has been brought in to perform the recovery, he/she may not know this fact. Accordingly, the standby schema and its tables need to be well-documented.
- From a performance perspective, the physical database layout may have to be changed to accommodate the standby tables and the journal tables. I/O contention needs to be monitored for specifically between these tables, and steps need to be taken proactively to prevent them (such as spreading them across different I/O channels).

Case-Study in Implementing Standby Tables

This section discusses a case-study to drive home the concept of standby tables.

THE SCENARIO XYZ Corporation has four Oracle8 databases. Two of these databases primarily run DSS-type applications, whereas the third one runs an OLTP application-suite consisting of three schemas (details in Table 15-6). The fourth database is a standby database and is a clone of the third one. The standby database is kept synchronized by copying the online redo-logs to the standby database server and applying them once every 15 minutes (in a regular standby database configuration supported by Oracle). The application modules in the third database pertaining to ORDER_ENTRY are accessed around the clock by end-users at various levels (field salespersons, tele-marketing personnel, sales managers) and require 24×7 access.

THE PROBLEM The ORDER_ENTRY schema has 24 tables, out of which six tables are very large (each more than a million rows) and are very volatile. These

Schema-Name	# of Tables	24×7 Access Required
ORDER_ENTRY	24	Y
HRD	55	N
MATERIALS_MGMT	40	N

TABLE 15-6. *Three Schemas Used by Applications in XYZ Corporation*

tables are heavily accessed by various modules within the application. The rest of the tables are master, reference, or code tables that are fairly static and are much smaller in size (50,000 rows or less). The six tables in question have been afflicted with certain problems in the past, such as fragmentation and index corruption (due to the high influx of rows). Furthermore, one of the tables got accidentally truncated a few weeks ago when an application patch was being applied by some senior developers (the actual patch was fairly small and was not expected to cause any problems, hence they ran it during off-peak late evening hours when usage was relatively low; however, an incorrect version of the patch was run, leading to the truncation). This was not noticed by the administrative personnel immediately. The alarm was raised by the end-users, and by the time the DBAs noticed what was happening, 20 minutes had already elapsed since the truncation. As a result, the redo-logs that had the truncation recorded had been copied over to the standby server and were applied, causing the table to be truncated in the standby database, as well.

The only option to recover for the DBAs was to use the latest backup and perform point-in-time recovery. However, this caused a total of six hours of application downtime as the table was recovered and restored. The downtime resulted in substantial loss of revenue for the company. XYZ Corporation's senior management issued a stern warning to the IT department: Take steps to rectify the situation and prevent such incidents in the future AT ANY COST.

INTERMEDIATE SOLUTION(S) APPLIED AND THE NEED FOR A BETTER SOLUTION The administrative personnel immediately changed the frequency of redo-log copying to the standby server to occur every 30 minutes rather than 15 to allow themselves more time to understand the problem and, if need be, switch over to the standby database, thus restricting total downtime. However, they agreed that this would only extend the time to respond and not really address the root of the problem. If the problem was a different one and it took more than 30 minutes to be alerted (in spite of extensive monitoring), then they would still face the same problem and there would be heavy revenue loss once again. What was needed was an effective way to replicate the six large tables and their indexes, with complete manual control over permanent actions such as truncation of data and dropping of tables. Automatic propagation of such irreversible actions to the standby database had to be finely controlled. Additionally, switchover to the standby had to be very fast, with very little or no downtime.

THE STANDBY TABLES SOLUTION Here, we (our consulting "SWAT" team, consisting of one senior DBA and a technical architect [yours truly, again!]) had the opportunity to implement standby tables. We identified the six tables, created a new administrative schema to hold their standby counterparts, and granted INSERT/UPDATE/DELETE/SELECT privileges to the ORDER_ENTRY schema on these standby tables. All other end-users accessed these tables via the application that resorted to database-level security. Each end-user had a specific user-id within the database and accessed the tables via public synonyms. We had the public synonyms dropped and replaced them with private synonyms within each end-user's schema. Then, we re-created the public synonyms to refer to the standby tables. Finally we created six journal tables corresponding to each of the standby tables and put the triggers in place to keep the standby tables in-sync and also populate the journal table, after switchover.

The switchover (both ways) was fully tested after manually re-creating problems for each of six tables (we truncated the data, dropped a few of the tables, and so forth). Switchover was smoothly accomplished each time (with manual intervention, of course) with very limited downtime. Downtime in each case was never more than four minutes. The only potential factor causing delay was the problem of detecting the failure as soon as it occurred. In order to achieve that, we changed the application-code (it was an Oracle Forms 4.5 application) to raise the exceptions whenever there was an error accessing the data in any critical table and have the entire DBA team paged immediately. As soon as the DBAs got the page, the on-call DBA addressing the issue would send out an e-mail message to the others saying that he or she was on top of the situation. If no such e-mail message was received within five minutes of receiving the page, another DBA would own the issue and send out the e-mail (this was to prevent multiple administrative personnel from trying to attempt table switchover).

The following steps would be taken by the responding DBA to cause the switchover:

- Check the problem and see whether the situation merits a switchover (if the error-message does not persist, then maybe it was a false alarm caused by an intermittent error).
- If so, then find out exactly which table is experiencing problems and run a switchover script targeted toward that table (each critical table for which standby was implemented had a corresponding script, where the entire switchover was scripted to occur smoothly without human errors). The script performed the following tasks:

- Enable the trigger on the standby table to populate the journal table.
- Rename the afflicted table to *table_name*_OLD.
- Disable the trigger on *table_name*_OLD that populates the standby table.

- Ensure that the application is functioning smoothly now without errors.
- Diagnose the cause and effect of the problem and determine the extent of damage to the original primary table.
- Repair the damage, as needed.
- Test the table to ensure that there are no more problems to the table (that all data prior to the problem is intact without any kind of corruption).
- During the next available opportunity (say, late night when use is minimal), switch back to the original primary table. This switchback is done partly manually. (This is because it requires application of human intelligence and also this time, there is no pressure since the database is functioning. Accordingly, the switchback can be done without silly errors. In any case, two DBAs join hands to perform the switchback to ensure that no typing errors and the like creep in). The following steps are taken to switch back to the original primary table:

1. Replay the transactions in the journal table and delete the ones replayed (so that they don't get replayed again).
2. Stop the ORDER_ENTRY application for a few minutes and then run a script (again, each table has a switchback script to prevent unnecessary human error) to perform the following:

   a. Apply the rest of the transactions in the journal table (the ones that may have come in while step 1 was being done). If no transactions are currently left in the journal table, then do not perform this step.

   b. Rename the standby (currently the primary) table to *table_name*_STNDBY.

   c. Disable the trigger to write to the journal table (since future writes to the standby table from the primary table should not cause the journal table to be written).

   d. Re-enable the trigger on the original primary table to copy all writes to the standby table.

   e. Rename the original primary table from *table_name*_OLD to *table_name.*

3. Re-start the ORDER_ENTRY application.
4. Test the application to ensure that things are working smoothly and there are no new problems.

As a side-note, the standby tables were implemented in both the primary and secondary databases (remember, XYZ Corporation had a regular standby database, as well).

RESULT OF THE STANDBY TABLES SOLUTION As of the time of writing of this book, XYZ Corporation has been using standby tables for more than two years now. Needless to say, the standby tables have highly enhanced their availability and prevented some serious mishaps (and prevented a few heads from rolling in the IT department). There was initially a 10 percent impact on performance of the ORDER_ENTRY application due to the additional I/O involved. However, after analyzing their hardware and performance characteristics, we were able to substantially reduce the impact on performance until it became almost imperceptible (except during peak hours). They have extended the use of standby tables to other applications requiring high-availability.

Even though both CSDs and standby databases involve a downtime of a few minutes during switchover, if properly implemented, they still allow you to maintain 99.999 percent availability from the database perspective (since the database does not have to go down for you to perform any maintenance work or during sudden emergencies). This should hopefully far exceed your SLA requirements.

The custom strategies discussed previously or a variation (of your own choice) can be utilized under any of the following scenarios:

- To allow the database to be available during tasks normally requiring downtime, such as corruption-repair (steps to quickly detect and repair corruption are discussed in Chapter 14) and patch application
- To migrate from one database version to another, such as from Oracle7 to Oracle8/8*i*
- To re-engineer the database physical architecture to aid performance (breaking up a single VLDB into multiple smaller databases onto different machines or vice versa, breaking up a table functionally into different smaller tables or vice versa, partitioning large tables into different tablespaces/data-files, separating large segments that are concurrently accessed into different disk locations, and so on)
- To enhance the database design to implement changes in the application (application scope/functionality changes)
- To change the ownership of data (move large segments across schemas)
- To change physical storage characteristics (as part of maintenance to perform defragmentation/rebuilds and so forth)

Be aware of caveats with the custom solutions described here

The following caveats need to be borne in mind prior to implementing any of the custom standby solutions described earlier:

- There is a high reliance on the journal table. If the journal table itself becomes corrupt or experiences failure (cannot extend due to lack of free-space, MAXEXTENTS reached, or the like), then the entire standby strategy fails. Accordingly, it is necessary to take steps to prevent the journal table from being a single point of failure. Such steps could include transaction splitting (writing each transaction directly to multiple copies of the journal table), ensuring the table will always have adequate space to extend, and so on.
- Certain constraints (such as foreign key constraints) may have to be relaxed on the secondary database, since pieces of each transaction are transferred to the secondary database in independent units. For instance, a child row could be successfully transferred. However, the parent table (in the secondary database) may not be able to extend, and as a result, the parent row will not successfully go through. Alternatively, the primary database could crash before the parent row is successfully transferred. In such situations, a child row could exist without a parent, causing logical corruption within the database. Accordingly, well-tested manual measures need to be in place to detect and resolve all such conflicts during incomplete propagation of data from the primary to the secondary.
- This piece of advice especially applies if you intend to use your own variation of any of the custom standby solutions outlined earlier. When the primary database/table becomes unavailable, switchover occurs to the standby database/table. After the original database/table is repaired, it sometimes is necessary to switch back to the original database/table. This fact needs to be kept in mind while implementing any custom standby solution. Ensure that you include provisions to make switchback occur as smoothly as possible. Earlier paragraphs explain switchback for the custom standby solutions illustrated here.

Summary

In this chapter we examined some standby solutions for enhancing availability during both routine maintenance and emergencies. In order to make these strategies more robust overall (and instantaneous), they may need to be augmented with other high-availability solutions such as the Oracle Parallel Server, Advanced Replication, or other third-party hardware/software based solutions. These solutions are discussed in subsequent chapters.

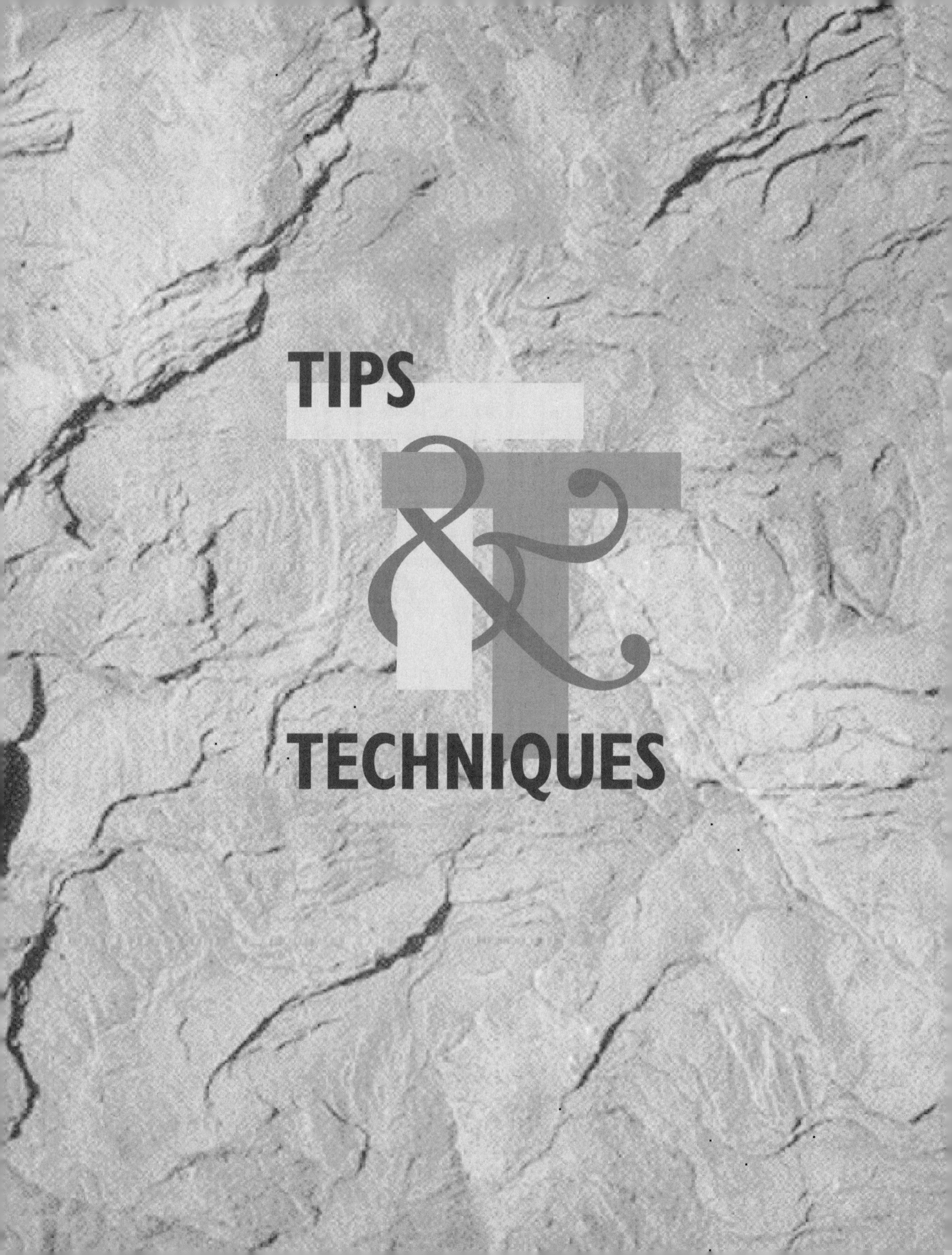
TIPS
&
TECHNIQUES

CHAPTER 16

Oracle Parallel Server

Oracle Parallel Server (OPS) offers various features to boost performance and scalability, and many sites, regardless of whether they are interested in high-availability, use OPS to utilize these features. However, from a high-availability perspective, OPS also provides numerous features to take advantage of different cluster and MPP-based architectures. In this chapter, we will primarily focus on OPS as a high-availability solution. The performance and scalability features will be evident as we discuss OPS in detail. OPS, like any single-instance scenario, requires detailed analysis and pre-implementation planning. Earlier chapters have covered these in detail. However, OPS has certain additional quirks and options, where it differs from a regular configuration and needs extra attention. For instance, OPS requires raw devices to function. Unless raw devices are configured and used with a lot of forethought, they can easily lock your site into a non-uniform environment consisting of Oracle-files of various shapes and sizes, impeding smooth growth, performance, and even availability. Thus, the core features that OPS boasts of can very well be smothered due to improper configuration. Accordingly, it is highly essential to ensure that you take adequate time to define proper procedures and thoroughly implement them. Chapter 4 discusses implementing raw devices in detail. The OPS architecture and components that differ from a regular non-OPS configuration are briefly described here, from a high-availability perspective. It is recommended that the reader refer to the Oracle documentation set for a detailed explanation of the overall OPS architecture prior to reading this chapter.

This chapter is structured to cover the following areas:

- What is OPS? How does it enhance availability?
- How do the OPS components work together?
- What are the prominent caveats in an OPS environment and how to overcome them?

Based on the above structure, the following tips and techniques are presented:

- Know what OPS is and how it enhances availability
- Understand, detect, and eliminate false pinging
- Partitioning applications prior to deploying them on OPS

Understanding and Managing an OPS Environment

An OPS environment is more complex than a regular (single instance) Oracle environment. Let us attempt to understand it better.

Know what OPS is and how it enhances availability

Simply described, OPS is a database configuration where multiple instances can be up and running simultaneously, with each instance referring to the same physical set of data-files (see Figure 16-1). OPS is configured on specific environments that support such a configuration in terms of multiple systems (nodes), all sharing the disks on which the files reside—namely, clusters and MPP-based systems. These architectures are described in Chapter 3. The OPS implementation on each architecture differs slightly. For example, on MPP, different nodes can be simultaneously utilized to distribute query processing and increase throughput due to fast data movement via the high-speed interconnect. This may not be the case on certain cluster platforms. Refer to your platform-specific documentation for more details. Each node that supports an instance is referred to as a "participating" node, and they all access the shared disks. Each instance shares a sibling relationship with the other, rather than a parent/child association. As such, failure of one or more (the "parent" instances) does not cause the entire database to be inaccessible. Theoretically, as long as there is at least one surviving instance, database availability should not be impacted. From a unilateral perspective, each participating node's instance can be viewed as a regular (non-OPS) instance. Thus, two or more of these instances make up an OPS configuration. Each instance's access to the shared disks is synchronized and controlled via a specialized piece of software called the DLM (Distributed Lock Manager).

Under OPS, if one node crashes (due to component malfunctions or network failures), the database is still accessible via the other nodes. This prevents the entire node from being a single point of failure. When single node failure occurs and the instance on that node crashes, a surviving node (the one that detected the instance failure) performs the necessary instance recovery. If the failure is not automatically detected yet, the instance recovery occurs as the crashed instance is manually re-started.

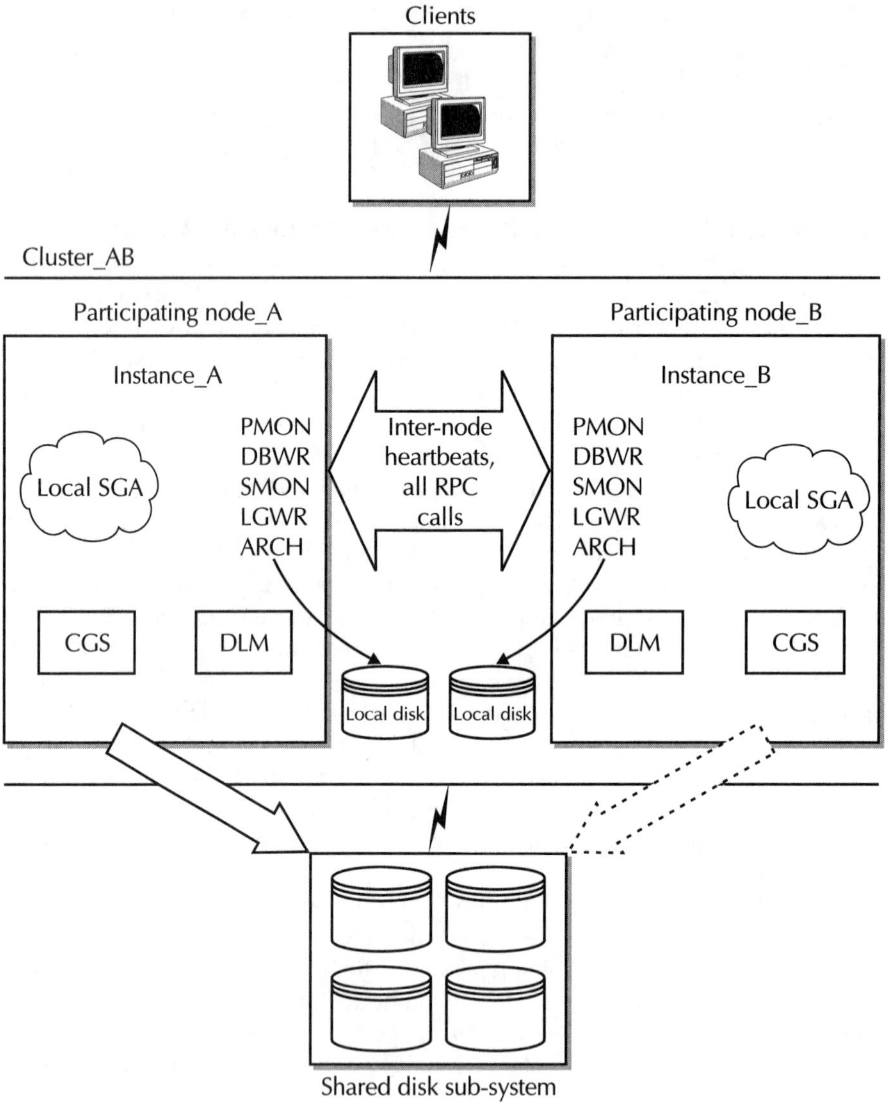

Clients

Cluster_AB

Participating node_A

Participating node_B

Instance_A

Local SGA

PMON
DBWR
SMON
LGWR
ARCH

CGS

DLM

Inter-node heartbeats, all RPC calls

Instance_B

PMON
DBWR
SMON
LGWR
ARCH

Local SGA

DLM

CGS

Local disk

Local disk

Shared disk sub-system

FIGURE 16-1. *OPS architecture*

OPS provides the following primary advantages:

- It provides availability during node failure. It automates instance recovery after intermittent node failures, thus enhancing MTTR.
- It enhances performance via load-balancing (access being distributed across instances, allowing memory and CPUs from different nodes to be used concurrently).
- It provides higher capacity and scalability, especially in MPP configurations, by allowing a large number of nodes to be utilized (a new node can be incrementally "plugged in" as necessary).

Note that it requires an appropriate design and explicit manual configuration for these features to be utilized (that is, concurrent multi-node access is not automatic in an OPS environment). An OPS configuration may be prone to the following caveats:

- Note that since all participating nodes share disk sub-systems, the configuration is still prone to disk failures, unless specific steps are taken to prevent them, such as OS and/or hardware mirroring (RAID 1, 0+1, and so on). Also, other single points of failure (CPUs, memory, I/O channels) depend on your specific hardware platform and what resources are shared across nodes. It is necessary to identify all such components and provide adequate redundancy.
- Availability and performance may be affected if applications are not explicitly designed to be "OPS-aware." Availability is affected if in-flight transactions already connected to the database are abruptly terminated when the node through which they are accessing the database fails. However, specific steps can be taken by using TAF features in OCI8/8*i* and SQL*Net/Net8 failover capabilities, to alleviate this problem and allow smoother application failover. Again, if the application is not partitioned to perform adequately across multiple nodes, it could cause high contention among different instances for various database resources and adversely impact performance.
- Maintenance requirements increase. With the increase in the number of nodes and corresponding instances, more software and hardware components are introduced to allow multiple instances to co-exist. The

greater the number of components, the more tuning and servicing is required to ensure smooth running.

- System complexity rises. As the number of core components go up, so does the need to be intricately familiar with them to correctly configure them and monitor them for signs of failure.
- Last, system cost goes up. But as mentioned in the opening chapter, if the cost of downtime is higher than the system cost, the investment toward OPS-capable architecture ought to be easily justifiable. Additionally, OPS, when compared to certain other high-availability solutions, is not overly expensive.

OPS Architectural Components and Operations

Each instance in an OPS configuration opens the database in shared/parallel mode (as opposed to EXCLUSIVE mode in regular non-OPS configurations). Each instance uses its own *init.ora* file, which lists all instance-specific parameters. Additionally, each instance uses certain parameters that need to have the same values across instances (these parameters are typically placed in the *config.ora* file). As mentioned earlier, these parameters are used by the DLM to synchronize all instances with the database files. Let's look at some core OPS components that make it unique as compared to regular (non-OPS) environments.

THE DLM The DLM has traditionally been a vendor-specific component that Oracle processes would communicate and work with. However, starting with Oracle8, the DLM is provided by Oracle itself, thus reducing the reliance on factors external to Oracle and also moving in the direction of predictable, uniform behavior across platforms. The new DLM is referred to as Integrated DLM or IDLM. However, the remainder of the chapter refers to it simply as DLM, since only the implementation mechanics have changed and the functionality that was originally supported externally is still present internally as part of the Oracle instance (additionally, by referring to it as DLM, Oracle7-specific configuration details can also be explained). The DLM-specific initialization parameters allocate necessary structures in each instance's SGA to handle messaging, locks, and instance-specific cache management for manipulation by the various Oracle processes. These structures are logical and are referred to as DLM resource structures (not to be confused with system resources such as CPU and physical memory or OS resources such as semaphores and shared memory). DLM resources are objects that multiple nodes are likely to request and, accordingly, access of the resources by each node requires coordination. Examples of DLM resources are blocks within the data-files, control-file structures, and objects in the shared-pool. Every process that needs to access certain resources that are protected by the DLM must acquire a lock on the resource, which translates to an entry in the appropriate DLM structures. Depending on the version of Oracle, the DLM structures could be present in kernel memory or shared/user memory (the latter generally being more efficient due to processes being directly able to access the structures, without the intervention of the Lock Daemon when allocating non-converting locks [more about the Lock Daemon and non-converting locks later]). Instance-specific cache management pertains to the coordination of these resources that are commonly used by all instances. Active coordination is required due to these resources being in the memory of different participating nodes at various points in time. Resources that are being used by a certain node in specific modes cannot be concurrently used by other nodes.

The DLM enforces this mutually exclusive relationship for resource usage between nodes without the effect being felt by the end-user in terms of excessive waits and performance degradation (as much as possible). The services provided by the DLM include

- Maintenance of information on system resource availability and enforcement of locking mechanisms to control shared (inter-instance) access to these resources.
- Remote and local inter-process communication across foreground and background processes.
- Inherent failure detection mechanisms, such as for detecting deadlocks and application of recovery, where appropriate. Resources are cleaned up and returned to the available resource pool when processes that use them terminate abruptly.

As outlined previously, the DLM coordinates resource-usage via locks. Different processes that need to access a resource make a request to lock the resource in a specific mode (similar to row/table locking). For instance, process_A on instance_A may request a lock on a specific resource in EX (exclusive) mode and obtain it. Immediately after, process_B on instance_B may also request the same resource in EX mode. Obviously, process_B needs to wait until Process_A has completed and notified the DLM of its completion. Once notified, the DLM allows process_B (assuming no other processes of equal or higher priority are waiting) to obtain the lock. The DLM also allows process_A to be informed that process_B is waiting for a lock on the resource in a contradictory mode. Note that locks are not necessarily allocated on a "first-come, first-served" basis; rather, they are based on optimization algorithms that make a decision based on process priority (how urgent it is for a specific process to acquire a lock). However, no locks are made to wait indefinitely either. So timing/duration is also a factor that influences the decision. Resources can also be locked in complementary modes (example, S [shared] mode), where different processes can simultaneously access the resource, provided they do not seek to intercede with each other (via lock converts). There are two primary lock-related queues: GRANTED and CONVERT. Once locks are acquired, they are listed in the GRANTED queue, whereas the ones that are waiting to be acquired are listed in the CONVERT queue. Once acquired, the latter are shifted to the GRANTED queue as well. Different lock types are requested for different purposes such as coordinating access to various files, rollback segments, and segment headers by processes across participating nodes. A subsequent paragraph discusses locks in more detail.

The information on locks and other structures maintained by the DLM is referred to as the DLM database. The DLM distributes its database redundantly across all participating instances, thus preventing critical meta-data from being lost during node failure. This also allows lock rebuilds during failures to be expedited and generally enhances performance by allowing demands on DLM structures to be balanced across nodes.

The DLM mainly comprises three sub-components:

- **Lock Daemon (LD)** The LD is the "keeper" of the DLM database. It controls the various lock requests (the GRANTED and CONVERT queues), notifies waiting processes of lock availability, manages time-outs, and performs deadlock detection. When a process requests a lock in a specific mode, the LD checks whether it can be granted. If so, it notifies the client process via an *acquisition asynchronous system trap* (AAST). If the lock cannot be granted due to another process (the blocker) holding an incompatible lock, the blocker is signaled via a *blocking asynchronous system trap* (BAST). The blocker may be on the same node (local) or on a different one (remote). When the blocker is intimated, it releases the lock whenever possible. If not, it attempts to downgrade the lock-mode, so that the new process can acquire the lock it desires. If neither scenario is possible, then the new process has to wait for the lock to become available (that is, to be in the CONVERT queue). This "lock convert" operation is described in more detail in the *Oracle8 Parallel Server Concepts and Administration* manual. When two processes attempt to acquire incompatible locks and neither are ready to backtrack/wait, a deadlock may ensue. A deadlock is relatively a rare phenomenon and occurs only for non-PCM locks (non-PCM locks are explained later). It does not occur for PCM locks

(BL). LD periodically checks for deadlocks on each node, on a round-robin basis. Deadlock detection is initiated by looking for blockers that are also waiters and placing them in a "search list." If a process is determined to be in a deadlock situation, the process is notified. If the deadlock resolution times out before getting completely resolved, then the entry pertaining to that process is moved to the end of the search list, so that other processes can be given attention as well, and other potential deadlocks can be detected (rather than focusing on just one deadlock resolution).

- **Lock Monitor (LM)** The LM is responsible for creation of the DLM database and recovering dead processes that were using the DLM (to free up resources that were held by the dead processes). It allocates the memory to hold the structures forming the DLM database and lays down the channels for inter-process communication, allowing the participating nodes to exchange lock and other resource information. The LM also works in conjunction with the Connection Manager to perform recovery, as necessary. When the LM has allocated the space for the DLM database, it sleeps most of the time (unless it is explicitly called upon to perform recovery) and periodically wakes up to proactively search the DLM process table for dead processes. On special occasions, it re-distributes DLM resources across nodes. Such occasions include new nodes being plugged into the cluster configuration, existing nodes being unplugged, and LCK background process failures.
- **Connection Manager (CM)** Whenever a new node is added to the configuration or an existing one is rolled off, it needs to be registered with the CM component of the DLM. The CM interacts with the Cluster Group Services (CGS) to track node-status and keep the database aware of all participating nodes (the CGS is a vendor-supplied component working closely with the hardware/OS). The CM is responsible for facilitating communications between different member nodes via virtual circuits that ensure that all nodes respond to each other. The communication is based on a *heartbeat* message exchanged between nodes on the virtual circuits. This message ensures that the node is up and running. If a node does not respond within a pre-determined time-out period, system reconfiguration is attempted to leave out the unresponsive node. Manual resolution by the systems administrators may be (and is generally) required to ensure smooth node roll-off.

The scope of functionality of these sub-components may change depending on the DLM implementation utilized (Oracle-specific or hardware-vendor specific). For

instance, if the DLM structures are maintained in kernel memory, each process has to route all lock requests through the LD; whereas in shared memory implementations, processes having the *dlmlib* library routines (the actual library name may vary) linked in have direct access to the DLM structures for certain operations such as lock-mode lookups and requesting non-converting locks. Thus, the scope of functionality of the LD, in this example, is dependent on the location of the DLM structures.

THE DLM DATABASE As stated earlier, the DLM needs to monitor locks on resources, modes in which they are currently granted, which processes are waiting for those locks to be released, and what lock-modes do the waiting processes seek. All this information is maintained by the DLM in a "database" comprising specific DLM resource structures such as the ones required to hold information on allocation/release/conversion of locks and the directory tree information (the directory tree is explained subsequently) maintained by all participating nodes. This repository of information is referred to as the *DLM lock database*. The exact location of the lock database varies depending on the node that requests a specific lock most often. The DLM attempts to establish node affinity (to reduce inter-node traffic across the interconnect) by duplicating the lock database on the node that often requests locks. Initially, when a node requests a lock for the first time, the necessary DLM structures are created on this node. If another node requests a different lock, the necessary structures are duplicated on the new node to prevent frequent lock-related messages from traveling back and forth across nodes. These lock-related messages would pertain to lock-acknowledgment, mode-changes, lock releases, and so on. The original structures (on the first node) would be refreshed periodically. Finally, as more and more nodes start requesting locks, the resources would be migrated to the node requesting locks most often. In reality, the number of nodes would be very finite (most HA sites have between two and four participating nodes). As such, the migration of the lock database would not be too frequent.

Besides establishing node affinity, the migration/duplication of the lock database also allows load-balancing and quick re-creation of the lock database if the node that holds the original structure crashes, causing portions of the lock database to be destroyed. The primary objective is that the DLM lock database should not be exposed to any single points of failure.

DIRECTORY TREE The directory tree is a portion within the DLM process memory that maintains information on various DLM resources and the nodes that currently hold them. When a node requests a lock on a specific resource, the directory tree determines whether the resource is already held by the node and, if not, which other node owns it. Since the directory tree is part of the DLM database, portions of it may be spread across all the nodes. A hashing algorithm is applied to the resource-name to detect which node would possess the relevant portion of the directory tree that would allow the requested resource to be tracked. Once the node is identified, the lock request is allocated to the node. And then the normal lock allocation algorithms take over (to see whether another node holds a conflicting lock on the resource and, if so, whether the lock can be downgraded, and so on).

BACKGROUND PROCESSES: LCKN, LMON, AND LMD0 In addition to the regular background processes such as PMON, DBWR, SMON, LGWR, and ARCH, OPS configurations also have at least one lock process: the LCKn process. The LCKn process is primarily responsible for managing locks on the current node/instance (including allocations, conversions, and releases). Most lock requests pertaining to the current instance are handled by LCKn processes. Certain lock requests are handled by the foreground server processes (such as transaction locks and certain session-level locks) and background processes (such as the media recovery lock required by DBWR or the SCN instance lock required by LGWR) themselves. By default, a single lock process, LCK0, starts up. However, in case of sites accommodating an exceptionally high number of lock requests, a single LCK0 process proves inadequate, and additional lock processes (up to nine more, from LCK1 to LCK9) can be started up, as necessary (via the GC_LCK_PROCS initialization parameter). Multiple LCKn processes enhance recovery and startup time in environments where LCK0 is the bottleneck. All instances must be set to use the same number of lock processes. Note that LCK0 can handle PCM, as well as non-PCM locks, whereas the other LCKn processes (LCK1 to LCK9) can handle only PCM locks (PCM/non-PCM locks are explained in a subsequent paragraph).

Also, with the inception of the Integrated DLM in Oracle8, two new background processes have been introduced to coordinate global lock-management: LMON and LMD0. LMON reconfigures and reallocates the global locks as new instances are started (on previously non-participating nodes) or existing ones are shut down. Also, it cleans up and invalidates global locks after server processes (or instances) that utilize these locks are terminated abruptly. LMD0 is primarily responsible for managing re-directed remote global lock requests. After the IDLM checks the directory tree and re-routes the lock request to a remote node, the node initiating the request coordinates with LMD0 on the remote node to acquire the lock.

DLM LOCKS As soon as an instance starts up on a node, various DLM locks are acquired. These locks are primarily classified as PCM (Parallel Cache Management) locks and non-PCM locks. Parallel Cache Management is the technology that allows concurrent access of shared resources by multiple instances. It allows one node to access data residing in the buffer cache of another node. PCM locks are used for locking the database blocks, whereas non-PCM locks (also referred to as Global Enqueues) are used for locking all other shared DLM resources (such as data-files and objects in the shared-pool).

PCM LOCKS During startup, all PCM locks are requested in NULL mode. Since NULL mode does not conflict with any other mode, these requests are granted. The DLM then records the lock structures in local memory. The DLM lock database is built on the node that starts up its instance first. This node is referred to as having "mastered" the DLM resources. Re-mastering may occur as the lock database is migrated to other nodes that start up their respective instances. The number of locks to be acquired during instance-startup by each node is specified via various GC_* initialization parameters, such as GC_FILES_TO_LOCKS, GC_LCK_PROCS, GC_LATCHES, GC_RELEASABLE_LOCKS, GC_ROLLBACK_LOCKS, etc. Note that certain GC_* parameters such as GC_DB_LOCKS and GC_SEGMENTS are obsolete in Oracle8 and higher versions, since they are managed internally within Oracle.

During startup, Oracle rounds up the values specified for the GC_* initialization parameters to the next highest prime number. GC_SEGMENTS (in versions prior to Oracle8) is computed via the following formula: GC_SEGMENTS = PRIME(GC_SEGMENTS specified in *init.ora* × 1.5). This warrants an adequate number of locks for segment header-blocks. Blocks for freelist groups (adjacent to the segment header) for all segments are then derived via the following formula: (GC_SEGMENTS value derived earlier for segment header-blocks × 5). The actual number of locks acquired for each of these initialization parameters can be verified via the SYS.X$LE virtual table. As mentioned earlier, in Oracle8/8*i*, several of the GC_* initialization parameters have been made obsolete. Oracle determines their values dynamically (based on various run-time criteria). You can use the following query to find out the actual number of locks allocated by Oracle:

```
SQL> SELECT le_class, COUNT(*) FROM SYS.x$le
      GROUP BY le_class;
```

The LE_CLASS column in SYS.X$LE provides the different block classes. These block classes correspond to the various GC_* initialization parameters. However, the LE_CLASS column contains a number that needs to be translated prior to interpretation. Table 16-1 maps some of the GC_* initialization parameters and the LE_CLASS (block-class) values.

A hash algorithm is utilized to find out which DLM lock corresponds to a given database block. Based on the value derived for GC_DB_LOCKS, the total number of locks are divided into multiple hash-buckets as per the mapping of files to locks specified by GC_FILES_TO_LOCKS. A single hash-bucket is assigned to at least one file, and each file is assigned to a single hash-bucket. Each hash-bucket stores meta-data on the number of locks it contains, the beginning offset, and whether the mapping of data-blocks to locks is contiguous or round-robin based. When the former method is utilized, only contiguous data-blocks (multiple data-blocks placed next to each other) are assigned PCM locks. In the case of the round-robin method, all blocks are mapped to a PCM lock. If Oracle runs out of locks, then multiple

Initialization Parameter (check your version-specific documentation to determine which ones are obsolete and not applicable)	X$LE.LE_CLASS value
GC_DB_LOCKS	1
GC_FILES_TO_LOCKS	1
GC_SAVE_ROLLBACK_LOCKS	3
GC_SEGMENTS	4
GC_TABLESPACES	5
GC_ROLLBACK_LOCKS	8
GC_ROLLBACK_SEGMENTS	7

TABLE 16-1. *Sample GC_* Initialization Parameters and the Block-Classes They Are Mapped To*

blocks are assigned to each lock. When a data-block needs to be read into the buffer cache by a server process, the block's file-number is used to locate the appropriate hash-bucket; and, based on the starting offset, the total number of locks in the bucket, and the mapping method used (contiguous or round-robin), the corresponding lock is found.

NON-PCM LOCKS In a non-OPS environment, various latches and enqueues are utilized (Chapter 11 discusses these). In an OPS environment, latches and enqueues are still utilized. However, most of them acquire a global perspective due to synchronization between multiple instances being mandatory. Thus, these enqueues are referred to as Global Enqueues. However, their basic characteristics (such as the modes in which they are acquired) do not change. Global Enqueues make up the primary composition of non-PCM locks. Non-PCM locks include Library Cache Locks (N[A-Z]), Dictionary Cache Locks (Q[A-Z]), Table Locks (TM), Transaction Locks (TX), System Change Number (SC), Database Mount Lock (DM), and so on. PCM locks are relatively static (basically determined during the physical design stage and allocated via the GC_* parameters). However, non-PCM locks are dynamic, and their number and memory requirements are dependent on the values of various initialization parameters.

Please refer to the *OPS Concepts and Administrator's Guide* for a detailed description of the various OPS components, their descriptions and functionality, and guidelines on how to configure them.

Automatic Failure Recovery

Now that we have a basic understanding of various OPS architectural components, we can attempt to understand how instance recovery is automatically initiated after node failure. Failure could be due to a variety of reasons—such as node component failure, network failure, or instance failure. After a node fails, recovery needs to occur at the hardware/OS-level, as well as within Oracle at the instance-level. If only the instance has crashed, no hardware/OS level recovery is necessary. Let's look at the overall failure recovery in a sequential manner.

NODE (COMPONENT) FAILURE AND CLUSTER RE-ORGANIZATION

The CM (Connection Manager) ensures that each node in the cluster is alive by periodically exchanging heartbeat messages. Node failure is detected via persistent timeouts of consecutive heartbeat messages. These consecutive timeouts ascertain that the node is indeed down and not just too busy to respond to the heartbeat messages. Once node failure is determined, the connection is marked as broken and cluster re-organization needs to occur to exclude the broken node. At the end of the re-organization, only healthy nodes are attached to the current cluster configuration. Later, as the node is repaired/replaced, CM would detect the new node. Cluster re-organization would occur again to induct the new node in the overall configuration.

REBUILDING THE DLM DATABASE The DLM lock database has to be rebuilt immediately following the cluster re-organization. The LM (Lock Monitor) initiates the rebuild. The DLM database is primarily in the cache of each instance. One or more instance failures cause a portion of the database to be lost. The surviving instances help in re-constructing the lost information. Initially, all lock activity is frozen. No new locks can be acquired by any instance. Then, all persistent PCM locks are invalidated and released, including the locks pertaining to the failed instance. Then each surviving instance re-acquires all its local locks. Non-local locks pertaining to remote processes are discarded. The DLM directory tree is cleaned out and rebuilt based on the new lock structure.

INSTANCE RECOVERY Now, instance recovery is initiated. Instance recovery is very similar to crash recovery that is performed on startup in non-OPS configurations. The only difference is that instance recovery is performed by another (surviving) instance. Instance recovery involves two primary operations: restoring the cache integrity (cache recovery) and restoring the transaction state (transaction recovery). This basically involves writing dirty buffers to disk such that all committed transactions are reflected in the data-files, whereas uncommitted transactions are removed. Any user/application process connected to the failed instance would need to be switched over to a surviving instance either automatically or via re-connection. (Some techniques for automatic switchover are discussed in Chapter 6.) The end-users/applications may see an Oracle error-message (ORA-3113, ORA-3114, and so on) regarding the instance failure. One of the surviving instances is notified about the failure when it tries to lock a row that was previously locked by a (dead) transaction in the failed instance or when it tries to acquire a PCM lock on buffer resources that were previously locked by a dead transaction. Such PCM locks would have been declared dubious during the DLM database rebuild. The SMON process belonging to the node that detects the failure is posted to perform instance recovery on the failed node. The time to detect the instance failure primarily depends on the extent of data-sharing across the various nodes. In environments where the applications are cleanly partitioned and there is little or no data-sharing, detection of instance failure may take longer. In any case, SMON periodically wakes up (every five minutes) and makes various consistency checks, one of which is for any sign of instance failure (such as dead redo threads). Once SMON is activated, it initiates both cache and transaction recovery to clean up all resources pertaining to the failed instance and bring the database to a consistent state.

During cache recovery, the statuses of all PCM locks are checked. All PCM locks that were marked dubious (during DLM database rebuild) correspond to certain data-blocks. These are locks at lower modes than Concurrent Read mode, allowing these blocks to have been (potentially) written to by the failed instance. Now, the writes may not have been entirely successful. Accordingly, recovery is performed on all such data-blocks beginning from the last checkpoint of the redo-thread pertaining to the failed instance. During the instance roll-forward stage, all the dubious locks are validated and cleaned. Evidence of cache recovery can be observed via instance recovery messages in the *alert-log*.

As cache recovery completes, all dirty buffers pertaining to the failed instance are applied to the corresponding data-files. This includes fully committed and uncommitted writes. During transaction recovery, all uncommitted writes are rolled back. This transaction rollback can be performed by multiple SMON processes (of each surviving instance). Each SMON process acquires a specific rollback segment and performs rollback as necessary. Each SMON process can only work on a single rollback segment at a time. Once all undo records in a rollback segment are completely rolled back, the SMON process moves on to the next rollback segment in a round-robin fashion until all the rollback segments are collectively covered. With each pass, SMON reads and applies a specific number of undo records. The number is influenced by the CLEANUP_ROLLBACK_ENTRIES initialization parameter. SMON does not attempt to apply the entire rollback segment contents in a single batch. This allows smaller transactions to be marked as consistent without having to wait for all the larger transactions to be completely rolled back. This also prevents other instances that are interested in accessing data-blocks involved in such transactions from being held up excessively. In order to alleviate the sudden load on SMON processes, server processes of surviving instances can also roll back failed transactions if they come across dubious locks pertaining to transactions initiated by a failed instance. Once transaction recovery is complete, instance recovery is considered complete.

DATABASE AVAILABILITY DURING AUTOMATIC FAILURE RECOVERY
During automatic instance recovery, database access via the surviving instances remains largely unaffected except during certain critical junctures. Following are some instances of availability being affected during the failure recovery:

- During the DLM database rebuild, all PCM lock operations are frozen. Any activity, including buffer cache reads, can continue, as long as it does not need a new lock or has to use an existing lock.
- During cache recovery, requests made by any of the surviving instances to lock or write to the data-block buffers being recovered would be held up until cache recovery pertaining to those buffers is complete.
- Locks on rows already locked by transactions pertaining to the failed instance cannot be allocated, unless those failed transactions have been completely recovered (rolled back). The server processes discovering the lock remnants can themselves roll back the transactions (rather than waiting for SMON to do it). However, if the failed transactions are part of a distributed transaction, the locks cannot be immediately revoked, unless the remote transactions are resolved and the outcomes of the transactions are known. This may require manual intervention from the DBA. However, in most cases, as long as the remote database is reachable, the external *Transaction Manager* resolves the outcome of the distributed transaction, allowing the changes to the rows to be rolled back or committed and the locks to be released.

Understand, detect, and eliminate false pinging

Oracle's Parallel Cache Management algorithm focuses on maintaining node-affinity during data-access. When a node needs to update certain data-blocks, the server process pertaining to that node reads the data-blocks into its local buffer cache (presuming those data-blocks are not already present in the buffer cache of that or other nodes). The server process posts the LCKn background process to acquire DLM locks on the data-block buffers. Even after the update and subsequent commit are complete, the node continues to hold the locks and the data-blocks remain in the local cache of the node. The locks are not released until another node makes a request via the DLM for the same blocks. Even though this involves inter-node traffic, the rationale for retaining the blocks in the local buffers is that the probability of a node reusing a recently accessed block is much higher than that of another node using the same block. Especially if the applications are well-partitioned and separated across nodes, then this would indeed be the case. However, in real-life, applications are not cleanly partitioned and chances are high of other nodes seeking the same set of blocks, albeit not as frequently as the same node reusing them. When another node needs to write to the same data-blocks, it submits a request to the DLM, which coordinates access to the blocks in the remote buffer cache. The node holding the blocks is notified about the remote need, the DLM locks are released, and the blocks are flushed back to disk by DBWR. The DLM then notifies the remote node, whose server processes then proceed to read the blocks into its local buffer cache. The writing out of the blocks from one node so that they can be accessed by another is termed as "inter-instance pinging" or merely "pinging" (see Figure 16-2). Apparently, high I/O overhead is incurred during pinging.

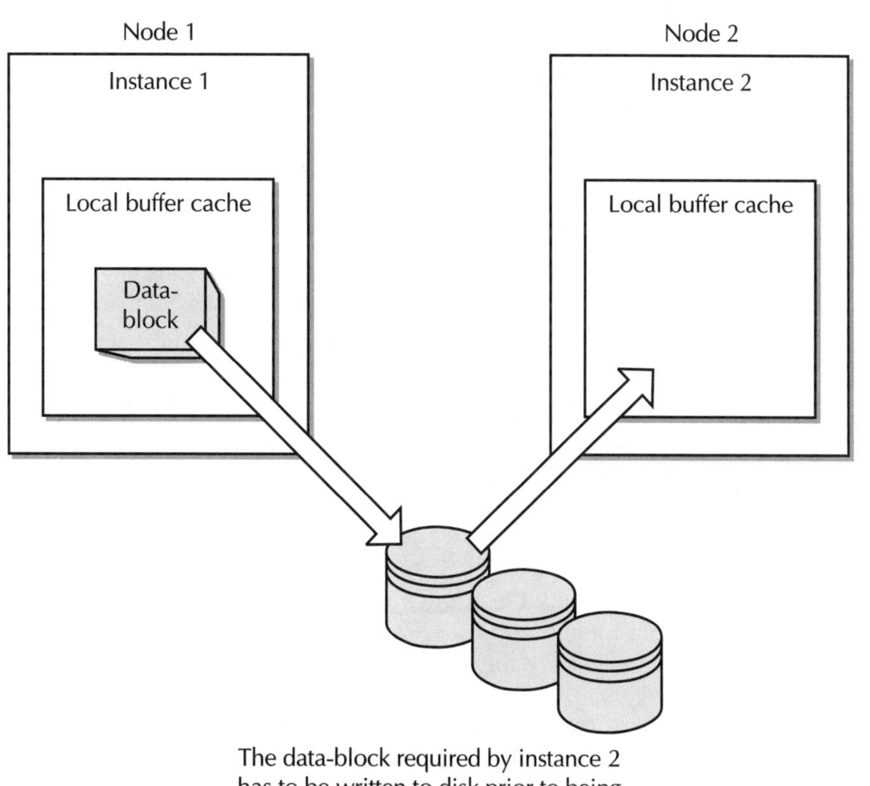
Node 1
Instance 1
Local buffer cache
Data-
block
Node 2
Instance 2
Local buffer cache
The data-block required by instance 2
has to be written to disk prior to being
loaded into instance 2's cache, if the
data-block has been changed by
instance 1

FIGURE 16-2. *Pinging in an OPS environment*

NOTE
Oracle8i's Cache-Fusion helps to alleviate some of the overhead incurred during block-pings (see Figure 16-3). Pings in pre-Cache Fusion scenarios incur I/O as well as CPU and memory utilization for context switching. Cache Fusion, on the other hand, dramatically helps to reduce the overhead by enabling data-blocks to be shipped directly from the buffer cache of one node to another via the interconnect in certain scenarios (where both nodes are not interested in writing to the blocks). The overhead doesn't entirely go away, but still is relatively much smaller, equivalent to normal RPC (remote process communication) calls. As long as the requesting node does not seek to update blocks that have been just updated by the earlier node (that is, a Write/Write conflict between the two nodes), disk I/O is avoided. Wherever Cache Fusion is possible, there is no I/O and the CPU utilization is reduced, as well. Future versions of Cache Fusion are expected to avoid disk I/O even when both nodes are interested in writing to the blocks.

In any case, if the need for access by the remote node is genuine, then the overhead (conventional buffer-to-disk overhead or Cache Fusion buffer-to-buffer overhead) incurred due to the pinging is worthwhile. However, if the need is false (false pinging), then the overhead is in vain. Let's examine some scenarios that lead to pinging, which among these are genuine (need to be reduced), and which are false (need to be eliminated). Obviously, some genuine pinging is a necessity and cannot be avoided, whereas false pinging needs to be eliminated altogether.

- **Read/Read** Here, both the original node and the requesting node intend to read the data-blocks (via plain SELECTs, without the FOR UPDATE clause). Both nodes have the resources pertaining to the required data-block buffers locked in SHARED mode. Accordingly, there is no pinging involved. The first node acquires the data-blocks and places SHARED locks on the resources. When another node needs to read them as well, it requests SHARED locks as well, via the LCKn process, which intimates the DLM. The DLM performs the necessary directory tree lookup to find out which node has currently mastered the required resources. Once the DLM knows that the resources pertaining to the blocks are currently locked in SHARED mode, it notifies the LCKn process (of the requesting node) via an AAST and the requesting node proceeds to acquire SHARED locks, as well. Thus, no pinging or I/O is involved during Read/Read conflicts.

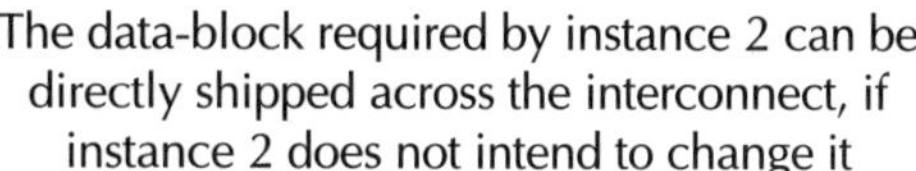

The data-block required by instance 2 can be
directly shipped across the interconnect, if
instance 2 does not intend to change it

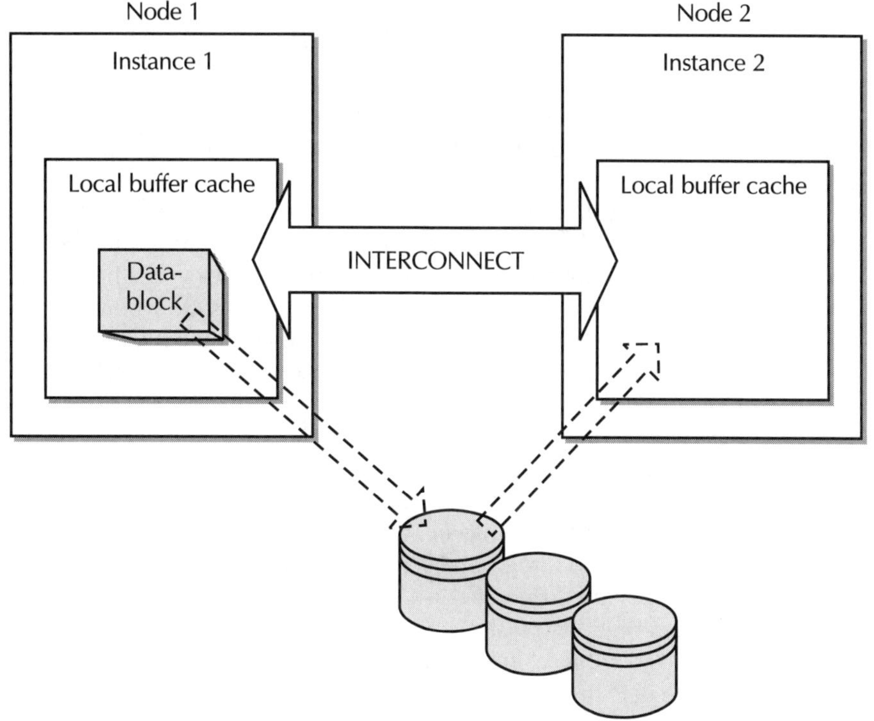

loaded into instance 2's cache, only if the data-block has been
changed by instance 1 and instance 2 intends to
change it, as well

FIGURE 16-3. *Cache fusion in Oracle8*i *Parallel Server*

- **Read/Write and Write/Write** These are incompatible situations that incur pings. Here, the requesting node needs to read or write certain data-blocks. Again, its LCKn process communicates with the DLM and the latter checks the directory tree to find the owner (if any) who has mastered the resources pertaining to those blocks. This time, it finds that a remote node has the resources locked in EXCLUSIVE mode (since it has updated the data-blocks). The DLM notifies the remote node via a BAST of the conflicting request for the data-blocks. The LCKn process on the node currently holding the locks posts the local DBWR to write the required data-blocks to disk. Once flushed, the LCKn notifies the local DLM to downgrade the lock-mode from EXCLUSIVE to SHARED. The local DLM does so and notifies the remote requesting node via an AAST. The requesting node now acquires the necessary locks, and its foreground server processes begin to read the data-blocks off disk. Here, pinging is involved.

So far, so good! The previously mentioned scenarios illustrate when pings are necessary and when they are not. Now, let's understand the circumstances that lead to false pings.

As seen before, DLM locks are acquired on the resources corresponding to the data-blocks prior to loading them in the local buffer cache and accessing them. Now, the set of locks may correspond to a larger group of blocks. In other words, an individual lock may be responsible for locking multiple blocks. So when a specific block among the set is requested by another node in an incompatible mode, the current lock has to be downgraded/released. Prior to doing so, all the blocks that are covered by the corresponding lock have to be written to disk, as well, along with the block that is actually required. No doubt, the block that is actually required needs to be written to disk—that would be a genuine ping. However, the other blocks that are forced to go with it result in additional I/O (than what is required). These pings are referred to as false pings or soft pings. Besides additional I/O, false pings also cause the LCKn and foreground server processes to wait until all blocks (not just the one required) are flushed to disk by DBWR. The actually required block may already have been written to disk. However, it cannot be remastered and accessed until all blocks in the set are written.

False pings can be detected via periodic monitoring. The following query measures the amount of pinging occurring currently (note that *v$lock_activity* needs to be explicitly created prior to running this query; the *catparr.sql* script in the $ORACLE_HOME/rdbms/admin directory creates *v$lock_activity*):

```
SQL> SELECT (s.value/(la1.counter + la2.counter + la3.counter))*100 "% Pings"
       FROM v$sysstat s, v$lock_activity la1,
            v$lock_activity la2, v$lock_activity la3
      WHERE s.name = 'DBWR cross instance writes'
        AND la1.from_val = 'X'
        AND la1.to_val = 'NULL'
        AND la2.from_val = 'X'
        AND la2.to_val = 'S'
        AND la3.from_val = 'X'
        AND la3.to_val = 'SSX';
```

Interpretation of the "% Pings" determined via the above query is provided in Table 16-2.

"% Pings" Value	Interpretation
< 100%	False pinging may be occurring. However, it is not excessive, since, overall, lock operations are more than the pings.
= 100%	There is a one-to-one correspondence between a lock operation and a write. In such a scenario, false pinging is inevitable; however, may not be excessive.
> 100%	False pinging is occurring, since the writes are more than the number of lock operations. Typically, this indicates excessive false pinging.

TABLE 16-2. *"% Pings" Interpretation*

The following query may be used to check the number of false pings compared to total writes:

```
SQL> SELECT s1.value "All Writes", s2.value "Ping Writes",
        (s2.value * p.Ping_Prcntg) "False Pings"
       FROM v$sysstat s1, v$sysstat s2,
           (SELECT
      (s.value/(la1.counter + la2.counter + la3.counter))*100 Ping_Prcntg
               FROM v$sysstat s, v$lock_activity la1,
                    v$lock_activity la2, v$lock_activity la3
              WHERE s.name = 'DBWR cross instance writes'
                AND la1.from_val = 'X'
                AND la1.to_val = 'NULL'
                AND la2.from_val = 'X'
                AND la2.to_val = 'S'
                AND la3.from_val = 'X'
                AND la3.to_val = 'SSX') p
      WHERE s1.name = 'physical writes'
        AND s2.name = 'DBWR cross instance writes';
```

If false pings are high, certain steps need to be taken to eliminate them. The following are the two most effective ways to counter false pinging.

- Generally, the main reason for high false pinging is an inadequate number of PCM locks. Note that even an unlimited number of PCM locks will not serve to eliminate genuine pings, since they are mandatory for maintaining cache coherency across all nodes. However, having inadequate locks would result in each lock corresponding to a large number of blocks. Accordingly, when any of these blocks are required, the entire set would need to be written out to disk (if they are in memory). Such situations can be reduced, if not eliminated, by allocating as many PCM locks as the number of *dirty* data-block buffers (this is possible, especially with DBA or fine-grained locking, introduced in v7.3). Note that it may not be realistic to allocate as many locks as the total number of data-block buffers. However, clean buffers do not cause pinging—only the dirty ones that need to be shared across instances do. Accordingly, configuring a sufficient number of locks to provide granular control over these dirty blocks is usually adequate. Generally, it requires a combination of familiarity with application usage patterns and monitoring of the buffer cache to determine the percentage of such dirty blocks. Also, this advice comes with a caveat: Locks consume system resources. Excessive locks can result in less (and possibly inadequate) resources being made available to the core database and OS kernels. Additionally, all the PCM locks are acquired during instance startup. Therefore, a large number of locks can delay database startup (refer to Chapter 10 for the importance of fast startup in a high-availability environment). And there is also a platform-specific limitation on the total number of DLM locks available. Accordingly, one needs to attain some balance here. PCM locks are allocated via the GC_* initialization parameters. The *OPS Concepts and Administrator's Guide* provides guidelines on setting these parameters effectively (based on total SGA size and per-lock memory requirements).

- Reckless configuration of an application that fosters inter-instance sharing of the same tables in conflicting modes leads to high pinging (both genuine and false pings). Applications need to be carefully partitioned with a lot of pre-implementation analysis. Partitioning will reduce the need for data-sharing across nodes, thus reducing the need for pinging. The next tip elaborates further.

Partitioning applications prior to deploying them on OPS

OPS application partitioning (not to be confused with the Oracle8 partitioning option) refers to the process of segregating like-usage of segments to different instances to prevent Read/Write and Write/Write collisions between the instances. As seen earlier, such collisions result in excessive pinging. For instance, when the transaction rate is high, all applications/users writing to a specific table or a table partition should be bound to a single instance, rather than being allowed to be scattered across instances. The latter option would result in higher collisions. The primary objective of any application partitioning strategy should be twofold:

- Eliminate false pinging
- Reduce genuine pinging

Multiple applications with little or no data-sharing deployed on the same database can be cleanly partitioned across different instances. But not all scenarios and applications lend themselves to totally clean partitioning. For instance, partitioning a single large application to prevent Read/Write and Write/Write conflicts may be challenging, especially if the user-population is large and one also wishes to make use of the scalability that OPS offers. Note that in the case of DSS-type applications such as data-warehouses and data-marts, partitioning becomes less significant, since such applications primarily consist of reads only. Different schemes exist for effective application partitioning, such as

- Partitioning by application or application module (different applications/modules access different instances to enforce segment locality)
- Partitioning by users (users accessing different segments/applications are connected to different instances)
- Partitioning by hours of usage (applications/users accessing same segments via different instances can be made to work during different hours of day/night, preventing concurrent access)

Furthermore, here are a few "ground rules" and techniques for partitioning applications and their segments:

- Have a large number of tablespaces to allow flexibility in maneuvering for lock allocations.
- Segments subject to both heavy reads and writes should not be kept on the same tablespace, unless they are accessed from a single instance (also, if they are concurrently accessed, they should be spread out to prevent I/O bottlenecks).
- Group all segments accessed by the same instance together and keep them physically separate from other groups, accessed via other instances.
- Stripe and spread out large segments concurrently accessed by multiple instances into different tablespaces/data-files. Oracle8's partitioning option proves tremendously useful for achieving this.
- Application partitioning can be implemented either horizontally or vertically. Horizontal partitioning refers to the scenario where, based on ranges of rows in specific core tables, users and applications are routed to a specific instance. These row-ranges need to be pre-determined and based on these row-ranges, and the core tables need to be partitioned and maintained across different tablespaces/data-files physically, thus triggering distinct lock allocations. Alternatively, if the table structure does not lend itself to being partitioned easily (no proper partition-key is available), it may

be broken up into multiple extents, each pertaining to a specific instance (via the ALLOCATE EXTENT . . . INSTANCE clause of the ALTER TABLE command). Vertical partitioning refers to the scenario where, based on the tables (or even columns in the case of highly denormalized tables) being accessed, users and applications are routed to different instances. As mentioned earlier, all related tables can be grouped and each group can be explicitly made available to a specific instance only. The application and SQL*Net/Net8 can be configured to control which instance could access which tables/groups. For instance, "group_A" (a logical group comprising Table_A and Table_B) can be accessed only by users/applications connected to instance_A. So all users/applications that need to access "group_A" would connect to a Net8 service-name that corresponds to instance_A.

- All read-only data should be stored together (separate from other segments). Since pinging does not occur for blocks subject to read-only operations, a few PCM locks (or even one) can cover the entire data-file. By allowing read-only data-blocks to mingle with read/write data-blocks, you may cause even the read-only data-blocks to be locked along with the blocks that are being written (if they happen to be adjacent and the PCM lock is configured to lock resources pertaining to multiple blocks). Also, read-only data-blocks typically get populated in batches. Accordingly, having few PCM locks for the entire data-file would be effective in locking resources pertaining to multiple data-blocks as they get written together (during bulk inserts, updates, and so on).
- In the case of tables that need to be shared by different applications spread across different instances (such as a table storing postal zip-codes), major contention could result. Each instance needs to access the table. The table may or may not have a large number of rows; however, each individual row-size would be typically smaller than a data-block. Thus, multiple rows required by different instances could reside in the same block, thus causing high pinging for such "popular" blocks. As a solution, you could define physical storage parameters for these tables such that only one or a very few rows exist in a single block. Thus, the data for such tables are spread out over a number of blocks, avoiding (not preventing) contention and pinging. For instance, you could set the physical storage attributes of the zip-codes table to be STORAGE(INITIAL 8K NEXT 8K PCTINCREASE 0) PCTFREE 99 PCTUSED 1. This would cause each block pertaining to this table to be 99 percent empty. Thus, very few rows would be stored in each block. This may result in space-wastage; however, it would definitely reduce contention. Also, if these tables are small, then the space-wastage would be minimal. The same technique can also be applied to some of the data-dictionary tables. The data-dictionary tables, though relatively small, are highly referenced by all instances. Mostly the access is read-only, but

writes can frequently occur, too. For instance, the free-extents table SYS.FET$ is constantly updated by all instances as new data is inserted and existing tables are truncated/dropped (unless the instance caters specifically to read-only data). The problem here is that the data-dictionary tables already exist if your database is currently operational. However, in case you are planning a new OPS database implementation, then you could edit the *SQL.BSQ* file to change the storage parameters for certain data-dictionary tables. It is necessary that you work with an Oracle Support Analyst to edit the *SQL.BSQ* file, so that potentially destructive changes are not inadvertently made.

- Certain Oracle features such as the Oracle8 partitioning option may be used to reduce contention for data-blocks (thus reducing the need for pinging). Some of these features are
  - Reversing indexes that are prone to have progressively rising key-values (Chapter 6).
  - Creating multiple free-list groups to avoid contention for the segment-header blocks (Chapter 12).
  - Using different sequences for different instances. In case the values need to be unique, then each sequence may be configured to use a different range of values (each range should be sufficient to serve an application for as long a period as necessary).

Finally, ensure that all application-partitioning strategies are thoroughly tested prior to going live.

Summary

This chapter took a look at OPS as a possible high-availability solution. The basic architecture and its various components were studied. OPS configurations corresponding to both v7.3.*x* and v8/8*i* were explored. Furthermore, two critical issues impacting OPS implementations—false pinging and application partitioning—were discussed.

Here, we looked at OPS from a server-centric view. Instance recovery in the event of node-failures via surviving nodes was explained. However, instance recovery is meaningless, unless it goes hand-in-glove with smooth application failover. Chapter 6 discusses application failover strategies. For this reason, the information presented in this chapter needs to be consolidated with the application failover techniques in Chapter 6, prior to your designing any comprehensive availability solution for your environment. The next chapter examines another high-availability solution: Oracle Advanced Replication.

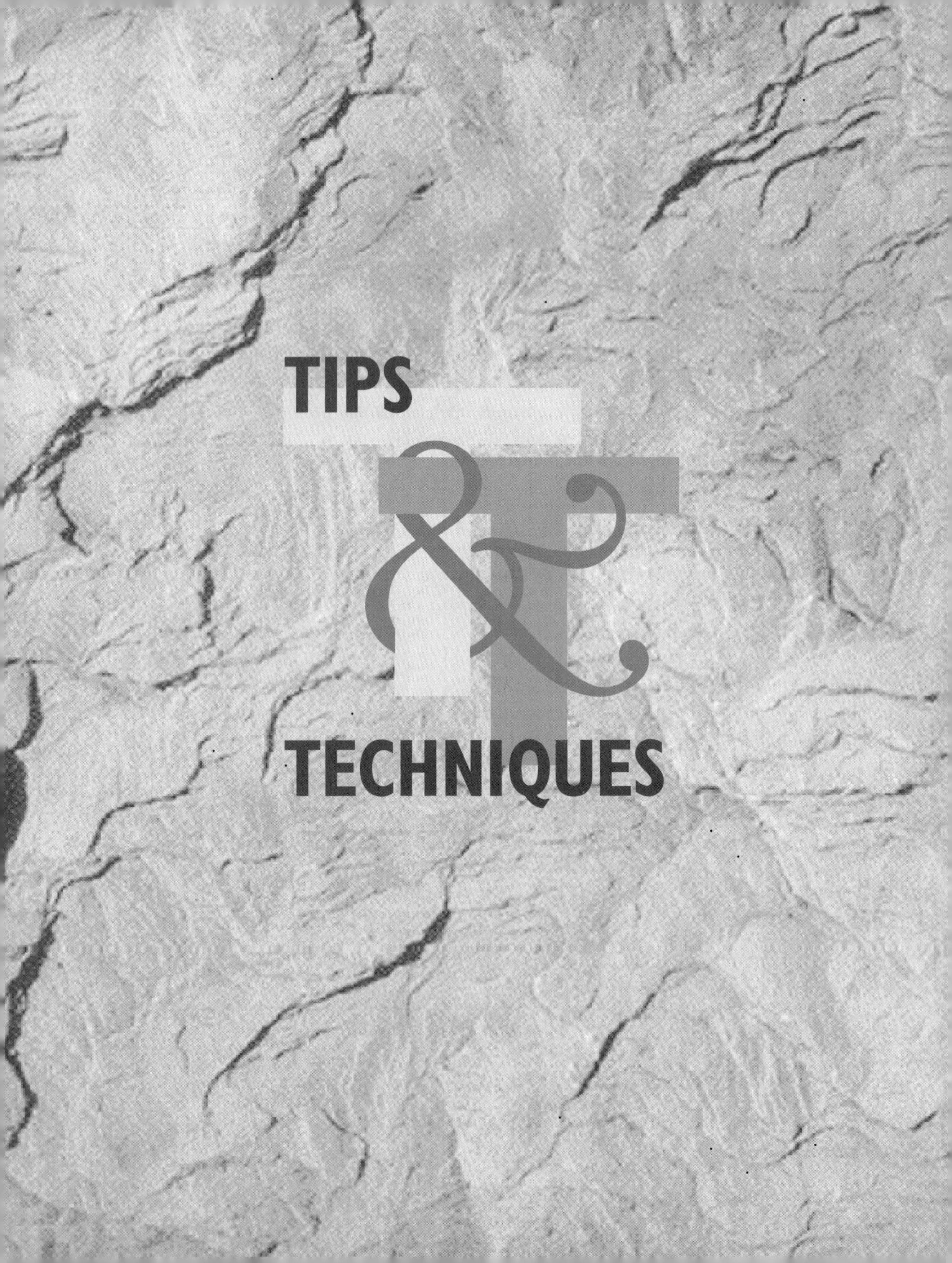
TIPS
&
TECHNIQUES

CHAPTER 17

Advanced Replication

Advanced Replication (AR) is a sophisticated replication mechanism available in Oracle. AR allows one or more source databases, certain pre-determined schemas, or even specific segments within each database to be replicated to one or more target database in a one-way or multi-way replication scheme. Thus, both the source and target databases can concurrently handle reads and writes. All databases involved in the replication scheme form a distributed database environment. AR was originally introduced in Oracle7 v7.1.6 and was called Symmetric Replication. However, in Oracle7, it suffered from various drawbacks, mainly performance and configuration related (described below). It was often perceived to be overly complicated and "slow as a slug." However, with later releases, it has been re-christened Advanced Replication and has slowly been gaining maturity, industrial strength, and acceptance due to powerful new features and ease-of-use. Starting with v7.3, AR has been integrated into the Oracle7 database. However, only with the releases of Oracle8 and 8*i* has it finally taken shape as a solution that needs to be seriously considered by any site seeking failover capabilities, load-balancing features, and higher scalability, or purely as a separate database copy for reporting purposes. Each of these reasons is legitimate and merits investment in an AR environment. This chapter discusses AR purely from a high-availability (HA) standpoint. It does not outline steps required to implement AR. These steps are already documented in detail in the Oracle Server documentation set. This chapter rather focuses on AR core functionality and features available in Oracle8/8*i* and elaborates why AR is a viable HA solution.

This chapter offers the following tips and techniques:

- Be familiar with AR operations and basic functioning
- Understand your options for highly available ar implementations
- Be aware of possible ar architectural alternatives

Understanding AR

From a logical perspective, AR provides a "hot" standby database. Unlike in a conventional standby database scenario, the target database is open and available for immediate failover if the source database were to crash (see Figure 17-1). Ideally, the target should be maintained on a separate machine at a remote location for disaster recovery purposes. Due to the target being continuously open, it can be utilized as a reporting instance, allowing end-users or DSS-type applications to use it for issuing complex queries that cannot normally be issued in the production OLTP database (for fear of hurting production performance).

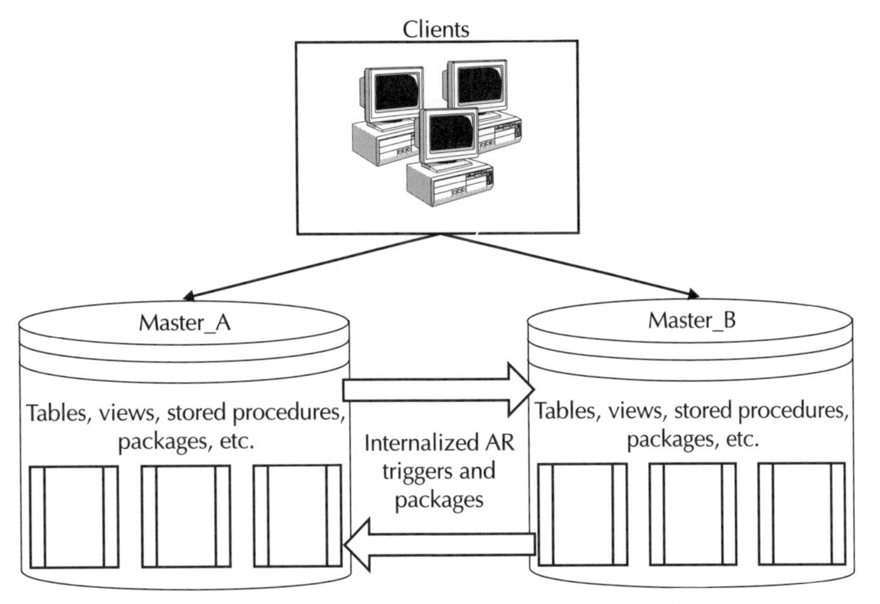

FIGURE 17-1. *Advanced Replication configuration*

Be familiar with AR operations and basic functioning

Under AR, multiple copies of the database (the entire database or specific subsets) can be concurrently written to and they can be kept synchronized in near real-time fashion. Such a configuration is termed as a multi-master configuration (since there are multiple master copies). If immediate synchronization is not desired, then an event-based approach may be taken to propagate the transactions in each master to the others. For instance, the propagation can be time-based, where the propagation occurs during specific low-usage hours. However, if replication is being done for failover purposes, synchronization would typically be immediate. Thus, each database copy can be maintained in a "peer-to-peer" manner. All writes are initially stored locally and then forwarded to each target database via the "push" mechanism (as opposed to simple replication snapshots, which "pull" the data from the source database).

Each transaction is propagated in a consistent fashion to prevent data-integrity violations. If there are integrity violations or conflicts, specific conflict-resolution schemes can be set. Conflicts could occur for a variety of reasons. For instance, if the same copy of the row has been changed differently in each database by different users, then that would be a conflict. A unique-key violation is another example of such conflicts. Conflicts need to be detected and resolved amicably. AR provides powerful algorithms for conflict detection and resolution. Conflict resolution can be consistent across the database or vary at the segment or even column level. Following are some useful conflict resolution techniques:

- Use the most current change (latest timestamp).
- Use the earliest change (oldest timestamp).
- Use changes specific to a certain site/database (site priority).
- Use changes specific to a certain snapshot group (group priority).
- Use the maximum value.
- Use the minimum value.
- Use the average value.
- Append the site name to the new record to enforce uniqueness.
- Append a sequence value to enforce uniqueness.
- Use a user-defined function to resolve specific conflicts.

As transactions are being forwarded, if a specific target database is unavailable, the transactions are retained in the local deferred queue (at the source). When the target database is available again, the transactions are applied. Non-availability of one or more target databases will not prevent the transactions being propagated to the remaining database copies.

Both DML and DDL statements are propagated across all the masters. Let's look at typical user-activity and how it gets propagated in a sequential manner. The following example assumes that three masters are involved in the replication group.

1. A user connects to one of the master databases (let's call it the first master) and updates a row in a table and issues a COMMIT.
2. The transaction is applied to the table and related indexes and then gets stored in the deferred queue. Both the before-image and the after-image of the transaction get stored in the queue (depending on the Oracle version, the actual contents and size of the images would differ). The after-image is required to apply the change, and the before-image is required to detect conflicts, if any.

3. Based on the configuration (immediate or event-based), the transactions in the deferred queue get "pushed" to the other master databases. The push occurs via remote procedure calls (RPC) issued by the SNP job process and uses the two-phase commit protocol to ensure transaction consistency.
4. The transactions are successfully applied to the second master.
5. However, there is a conflict at the third master. The before-images do not match, as another user process has already updated the row in question. This causes an error-log entry to be generated. A pre-defined conflict-resolution algorithm is used to resolve this conflict and the new row is accepted or over-written. If the new row in the third master is accepted, the same changes have to be applied to the other masters to keep them all consistent. This additional change will be placed in the third master's deferred queue. If the third master were to be unavailable, the transactions would be retained in the first master's deferred queue to be applied later to the third master.
6. If the transaction was successfully applied to the second and third masters, then the transactions are removed from the local queue of the first master.

AR has traditionally used triggers and various journal tables to implement different replication schemes. Internal routines were used to propagate DDL changes. Trigger-based replication is effective under certain scenarios. However, in environments with large-scale concurrent DML, overall response-time and throughput are adversely affected due to high trigger activity (and the resultant recursive SQL). In addition to basic triggers, in Oracle7 AR, the mechanisms used to allow replication suffer from certain inherent drawbacks, such as these:

- Propagation of transactions from the source to the target occurs serially (non-parallel mode).
- Modification of even a single column within a table prompts the entire row's before-image and after-image to be placed in the deferred queue. Thus, the before-images of all columns are compared with the current row in the target to ensure data-integrity and consistency prior to application of the after-image. However, all columns are not really necessary—only the primary-keys and the actual changed columns are. This "feature" requires the excess baggage of all columns to be transferred over the network for applying changes to the target databases. This is especially bad for an HA site, where the target database is maintained purely for failover and hence does not incur writes. Comparing each column would be highly redundant during such a scenario.

- In an environment consisting of multiple replication groups (of related segments), it is not possible to pause the execution of just one or more groups without affecting the others.
- Creating an updatable snapshot based on multiple master (base) tables is not possible. Furthermore, updatable snapshots cannot have constraints declared on them. Once they are defined, the DBA cannot detect the snapshots currently defined from a master site. He or she can only figure out the corresponding master site from the snapshot site.
- LONG (and LONG RAW) columns are not replicated. There is no other provision or workaround for replication of large column-types inside the database.
- Replication configuration is a highly complicated task.

As may be apparent, the various flaws described here affect functionality, performance, and manageability. So the reluctance of DBAs and architects to adopt AR as a high-availability solution was understandable. Given the state of technology, these measures were necessary to enforce global data-integrity, in addition to the replication. However, AR in Oracle8/8*i* overcomes many of these flaws. The primary focus is on enhancing performance and manageability, both of which are critical to a smoothly functioning HA site. Performance, especially, is absolutely necessary for the near real-time replication required to keep the failover site (almost) current with the production database. The following objectives are addressed to derive higher performance:

- Implementing a mechanism to copy all writes at the source with as little overhead as possible
- Minimizing the number and size of data-elements to be transferred over to the target database (reducing these to the bare minimum without compromising data-integrity)
- Minimizing the time to actually transfer the data-elements over to the target
- Efficiently applying the data-elements to the target

These objectives make (real-world) AR implementation a practical reality. As we look at some of the following core options and features within AR, the implementation of these objectives becomes apparent.

Internalization of Triggers and Packages

As mentioned earlier, AR in Oracle8/8*i* uses internalized triggers and packages (Oracle8*i* provides a higher degree of code internalization than Oracle8). Regular segment-level triggers are inefficient for high-volume long-term replication.

Especially prior to Oracle7 v7.3, trigger p-code was not stored in a readily compiled fashion in the database (like stored procedures, functions, and so on). They were only compiled upon invocation. In any case, the triggers and packages used to store transactions in the deferred queue prior to being applied to the target have been internalized. Internal triggers and packages are *C* code modules linked right into the Oracle kernel. This makes the code relatively more tamper-proof (higher security) and also very lightweight and efficient, allowing the implementation to be speedy and scalable. There are no external components to configure and maintain. Since packages and triggers are not generated, they can be instantiated faster.

Reduced Data-Element Propagation

AR stores and forwards the bare minimum data required to apply all changes in a consistent fashion. Rather than storing the entire row, it only stores the following:

- Key columns values required to identify the target rows and propagate the changes
- The new columns values (for example, in an UPDATE, these would only be changed columns values, whereas in an INSERT, this would be the entire new row)
- Column values required for conflict detection at the target database (such as the old column value or the timestamp)

For instance, say the AR configuration has been set to use a higher timestamp-based conflict resolution algorithm. The following table includes a column to store the timestamp during which new data-elements or changes to existing ones are recorded.

```
SQL> desc SALES_ORDERS
Name                         Null?                  Type
---------------------------- ---------------------- ----
ORDER_ID                     NOT NULL               NUMBER(5,0)
NUM_ITEMS                    NOT NULL               NUMBER(11,0)
SALESPERSON_CODE             VARCHAR2(5)
TIMESTAMP                    NOT NULL               DATE
```

Whenever NUM_ITEMS is updated, the new NUM_ITEMS value, the key ORDER_ID, and the TIMESTAMP column are stored and forwarded. The ORDER_ID is used to locate the corresponding order-record in the target database. If the existing TIMESTAMP column at the target database is lower than the current TIMESTAMP column (in-hand), then the existing NUM_ITEMS gets overwritten. By being selective about propagating only new data-elements, overall overhead is reduced. For instance, consider the case of rows with a big VARCHAR2 column (4,000 bytes) or even a LOB column. If these columns are rarely changed, it makes absolutely no sense to store and forward these column values. They only end up increasing the network traffic.

The MIN_COMMUNICATION parameter (specified in procedures such as CREATE_SNAPSHOT_REPOBJECT, GENERATE_REPLICATION_TRIGGER, GENERATE_REPLICATION_SUPPORT, and GENERATE_SNAPSHOT_SUPPORT in the DBMS_REPCAT package) enforces reduced data propagation.

Parallel Data-Element Propagation

During propagation of the stored data-elements to the target database, AR utilizes parallelism to push them over faster (see Figure 17-2). Multiple parallel streams are started up to increase the data transfer throughput. Inter-dependencies between the parallel streams are kept intact to ensure overall transaction integrity. The query coordinator process determines inter-transactional dependencies prior to propagating them. Each transaction stream is ordered in the original sequence that they were applied at the source. This preserves inter-transactional dependencies, albeit at the cost of serializing the actual application process, which, in turn, reduces the overall transaction volume that can be concurrently applied. However, this is necessary to enforce data-integrity and consistency. Note that multiple transactions that have no dependencies can be applied in parallel. However, realistically, in a relational environment, this is more often an exception than the norm. However, even with this limiting requirement, the parallel propagation allows vast increase in AR throughput, especially compared to the serial propagation mechanisms in versions prior to Oracle8.

Parallel propagation, for the most part, utilizes the same underlying mechanisms of regular PQO (parallel query option) used during a parallel CREATE TABLE AS SELECT or a parallel index creation. The existing pool of parallel query servers determined by the initialization parameters PARALLEL_MIN_SERVERS and PARALLEL_MAX_SERVERS is utilized by setting an explicit degree of parallelism for each scheduled job. The coordinator process allocates work to each parallel server

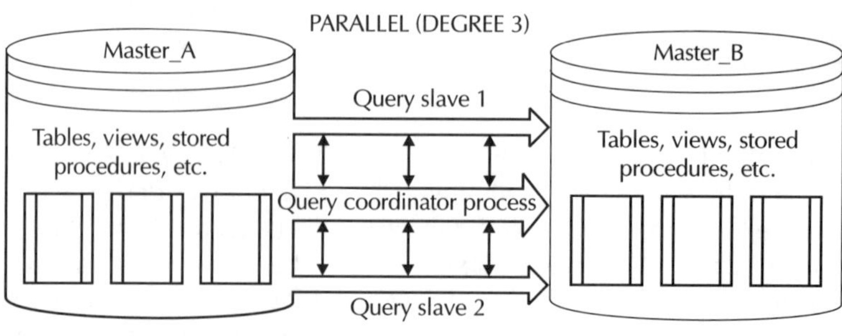

FIGURE 17-2. *Parallel propagation of replicated data*

process based on overall transactional dependencies and tracks progress. No transaction is propagated until the transactions it depends on are already sent, preventing it from being applied ahead of the dependencies. Prior to heavily adopting the parallel propagation methods, follow all precautions you would normally follow when using PQO, such as overall resources available, the degree of parallelism utilized by all concurrently running jobs, and network throughput.

Fine-Grained Replication Group Quiescing

AR in Oracle8/8*i* supports a finer degree of control over replication groups. In previous versions, if a specific group had to be paused for incorporating changes, tuning, and so on, other groups could not continue with their replication activity. However, AR now supports fine-grained quiescing, where a single group can be taken offline. For instance, say half-a-dozen replication groups, each pertaining to a different schema/application and comprising different objects, are deployed. If a specific table in one of the groups needs to have a new column added to it, then only the group to which that table belongs needs to be quiesced. Other groups can function uninterrupted.

To allow maximum flexibility in fine-grained quiescing, the physical architect needs to indulge in a good amount of forethought prior to defining replication groups. For instance, objects with a high degree of inter-dependence (often used together) need to be placed in the same group. For achieving an optimal configuration, one needs to have a high degree of familiarity with the applications; otherwise, multiple replication groups may still be affected to implement changes to one or more objects within the groups.

Replication of Partitioned Segments

AR supports Oracle8 partitioned segments, albeit with certain restrictions, such as

- Currently, replicating a partitioned subset (that is, only certain partitions) is not directly supported. All partitions defined at the source are replicated at the target. If the tablespaces on which the partitions reside at the source do not exist at the target, the partitions get created in the default tablespace of the schema at the target. If a new partition is added at the source, corresponding partitions need to be added at the target. The workaround for this is to define updatable snapshots on the target, rather than a regular Master/Master configuration (these configurations are described in a subsequent paragraph).
- Global indexes or local non-prefixed indexes on the partitioned tables are not supported.

LOB Support

Even though LONGs are still not supported (and not recommended either), the new Oracle8 LOBs are (except BFILEs). LOBs are capable of holding twice the amount of data held by LONGs and allow easier manipulation via the DBMS_LOB package. Existing LONGs can also be converted to LOBs via this package. When replicating tables with LOBs, ensure that you use reduced data-propagation techniques (by using the MIN_COMMUNICATION parameter) to allow them to be propagated only when necessary.

Replication Manager

Newer AR versions provide Replication Manager (RM), an easy-to-use GUI-based tool, to configure and customize the replication environment. RM can be invoked from the central Oracle Enterprise Manager (OEM) console. RM introduces wizards, simple dialog boxes, and drag-and-drop features, allowing quick and easy setup. Multiple replication groups, each consisting of tables and related objects, such as indexes, views, and stored procedures, can be easily set up (and managed) as a single unit. Instances of various groups can be easily dragged into different databases to add the replication groups there. If new objects are added or existing objects are removed from any of these groups, they are reflected across all instances of the group in a consistent fashion. Setting up the refresh interval (when the transactions ought to be applied to the target database) is as easy as setting up a regular alarm clock via the graphical calendar/clock tool within RM. Rather than requiring a bunch of manual SQL scripts to be run, RM takes most of the complexity away and makes replication much easier to deploy via innovative and intuitive features. The troubleshooting features allow manual intervention to resolve error-conditions. Pre-defined events have been included in OEM to monitor errors and failed snapshot refreshes. Note that the Replication Wizard in RM can be used in Oracle8 and higher versions only. Replication Manager can be run almost from anywhere in the network—editions are available to run on non-Windows platforms.

Security

AR allows security at all target databases to be consistent with the source database, preventing any weak links in security globally. Also, since Net8 is the underlying mechanism used during propagation of the replication data, all its security and encryption features can be utilized to prevent any unauthorized viewing or tampering of the replication data.

Either a single global user-id or separate user-ids can be registered at the source and target databases for the pushing and receiving of the deferred queue (the *propagator* and the *receiver*), respectively. In an HA configuration, a single global user-id (such as REPADMIN) is recommended to enforce uniformity across databases. The DEFPROPAGATOR table can be queried to check which user-id has been designated. During error-resolution, a DBA may need to connect and manually push the transactions in the queue. The EXECUTE_AS_USER parameter of the DBMS_DEFER_SYS.EXECUTE procedure determines whether the currently connected user performs the push or the user does who originally set up the refresh. By setting this parameter to TRUE, the connected user can perform the push (typically achieved as REPADMIN).

Understand your options for highly available AR implementations

From an HA perspective, AR can be implemented based on either of two strategies.

- **Active/Passive strategy** Here, the source database would be the active instance, whereas the copy would be passive. The active instance would allow normal processing, including both reads and writes, whereas the passive instance would allow only read-only access (enforced via database security—by granting users and roles only read privileges on various application segments). All writes occurring at the active instance are propagated to the passive instance via AR routines. When the active instance is unavailable due to planned or unplanned downtime, failover would occur and the passive instance would become active. All client sessions would access it, instead of the original production instance. All transactions occurring in the current active instance would be held in the deferred queue, until the original production database comes up again. Then the latter can be made the passive instance and all transactions in the deferred queue of the active instance can be applied. When necessary, the original production can be made the active instance once again (especially if the original production database resides on a more powerful machine) and the currently active database can switch back to being the passive one. Under this strategy, all client sessions access only one database. The other merely keeps itself up-to-date and takes over when the active one fails. However, it has the same AR routines defined to allow transactions occurring there (after failover) to be applied to the original production database. Thus, this would be a multi-way replication scenario, with only one-way being active at any given point in time.

- **Active/Active strategy** Here, both databases are normally active and accept client connections. This is also a multi-way replication scenario with AR configured on both databases. Both databases are exact copies of each other and any changes to application segments are synchronized across each other in a near real-time fashion. This option also proves to be effective for failover. Moreover, this allows better scalability and load-balancing features, since the resources of multiple systems/databases are concurrently utilized, whereas in the Active/Passive strategy, there is no load-balancing and scalability would be limited to the maximum capacity of any one machine. However, the near real-time replication required here may cause performance to be impeded (even with additional resources), due to constant high remote process communication (RPC) overhead. Also, if both systems are normally run at peak capacity, after failover, the single machine currently running may be loaded beyond capacity, causing performance to be poor. Accordingly, you may want to utilize each system at less than 100 percent capacity on a normal basis, so that adequate capacity is left in each system for handling the required loads (normally handled by two systems) after failover. Otherwise, you may have to lower the load after failover (only mission-critical loads would be run), until both systems are online again.

Be aware of possible AR architectural alternatives

AR can be configured in different ways, as listed below.

Master/Master Configuration

The Master/Master (or multi-master) configuration basically involves real-time or deferred replication of two or more servers or sub-components thereof. These can be in Active/Active or Active/Passive mode, as described earlier. Either entire databases or specific mission-critical schemas within a database can be replicated. Alternatively, specific tables, in their entirety, could be replicated in a Master/Master configuration. Each replicated site would be considered a master-site, since changes to data could be made at any site and propagated to the others. All changes are stored in local deferred queues and propagated either in near real-time or at specific intervals (every three hours, at the end of the day, and so on). All earlier discussions regarding transaction consistency, parallel propagation, and conflict resolution can be applied in this context. Note that the more masters involved, the higher the overhead. Accordingly, in high-transaction environments, I do not recommended more than two masters.

Updatable snapshots

Updatable snapshots are useful in scenarios where only certain tables or subsets thereof need to be replicated, not an entire schema or database. Updatable snapshots are similar in concept to a regular (read-only) snapshot. However, one can be updated at either site—the source (master) site or the target site. Prior to Oracle8, updatable snapshots could only be simple snapshots based on a single base (master) table. However, AR in Oracle8/8*i* has done away with many of these restrictions. Thus, updatable snapshots can now be based on multiple tables (joins), use of sub-queries, and so on.

Updatable snapshots (in Oracle8/8*i*) offer various useful and powerful features, such as those listed in the text that follows.

DATA PARTITIONING VIA SNAPSHOTS Snapshots reflect partitioned data at two levels: horizontal partitioning and vertical partitioning (not to be confused with the Oracle8 Partitioning Option). Both allow certain sub-sets of the data from the master table to be reflected in the snapshot. Such partitioning is highly necessary for security purposes, faster refreshes, and reduction in system and network resource consumption (since less data is involved, the refreshes are faster and consume fewer resources).

Horizontal partitioning allows only certain rows to be acquired based on specific query conditions (determined by the WHERE clause in the snapshot definition). For instance, the following snapshot condition limits the rows retrieved to only pertain to those students that have taken BIOLOGY as a subject.

```
SQL> CREATE SNAPSHOT biology_students FOR FAST REFRESH
        AS SELECT * FROM students_subjects@college.world
           WHERE subject_taken = 'BIOLOGY';
```

Vertical partitioning, on the other hand, limits the snapshot to specific columns of the master table. For instance, in the preceding example, one could define the snapshot BIOLOGY_STUDENTS to retrieve only the STUDENT_ID from the STUDENTS_SUBJECTS master table, rather than all the columns ("*"). Vertical partitioning helps protect the snapshot from structural changes to the master table. Thus, a new column could be added to the master table without the snapshot being affected. Similarly, an existing column could be dropped (Oracle8*i* only) without affecting the snapshot, provided the snapshot does not reference the column. This is especially useful when creating snapshots on tables with LOBs. If the LOB columns do not need to be replicated, then they can be left out via vertical partitioning, thus avoiding large amounts of data from traversing the network during each refresh.

Vertical partitioning is possible only in Oracle8*i* AR via usage of deployment templates. It is only available when you add a snapshot object to a deployment template using Oracle Replication Manager and is not available when using the Replication Management API. Deployment templates are described in a subsequent paragraph.

SUBQUERY SUBSETTING Subqueries for updatable snapshots are supported by AR in Oracle8/8*i*. As mentioned earlier, prior to Oracle8, updatable snapshots could only be simple snapshots (that is, complex snapshots could not be made updatable). This prevented any complex SQL criteria such as table-joins or

sub-queries from being used in the definition of updatable snapshots. The new subquery subsetting feature allows specific pre-defined data sub-sets to be copied over from the master tables based on complex conditions. Subquery subsetting can be used with fast refreshes. Subsetting allows various advantages, especially in mass snapshot deployments (such as in a "mobile agent" application with hundreds of field service personnel or in an environment with branch offices all over the world using snapshots defined off master tables in the data-center in the corporate headquarters). Via subsetting, you can insulate the master tables at the source from unwanted structural changes. For instance, as part of an example used previously, let's say an HR application is used at the corporate headquarters, which has an EMPL_SALARY table used as the master for snapshots defined at the remote branches. Initially, code similar to the following would have been used to create a simple (updatable) snapshot at each branch:

```
SQL> CREATE SNAPSHOT empl_salary FOR FAST REFRESH
        AS SELECT * FROM empl_salary@hr.world;
```

However, this would give access to the salary information of all employees worldwide to each branch. Subsequently, the company senior management may decide to rectify this flaw by allowing each branch to access only salary information pertinent to that branch. In order to enforce this, a new column (say, BRANCH_CODE) would typically have to be added to the EMPL_SALARY table (in an updatable snapshot scenario prior to subquery subsetting). This would cause various effects; for instance, it would

- Unnecessarily denormalize the master table (more than what is actually required).
- Invalidate all the snapshots at the remote sites.
- Require a script to be written and run at the master-site to selectively update the rows in the master table with the appropriate branch-code information.
- Potentially cause downtime at the master-site as other code-modules in the HR and related applications referring to the EMPL_SALARY table are modified as appropriate to include/exclude the new BRANCH_CODE column.
- Cause downtime for the HR application at the remote sites by requiring the snapshots to be rebuilt. For instance, the branch in Mumbai would need to rebuild their snapshot as follows:

```
SQL> CREATE SNAPSHOT empl_salary FOR FAST REFRESH
        AS SELECT * FROM empl_salary@hr.world
            WHERE branch_code = 'MUMBAI';
```

This rebuild could take a long time if the master table is large.

- Such structural changes may require certain values to be hard-coded in the snapshot definition (such as BRANCH_CODE = 'MUMBAI'), making the snapshot further vulnerable to changes in data-values. For instance, the 'MUMBAI' branch-code may have to be changed if multiple branches are started in Mumbai. Each time the BRANCH_CODE changes, corresponding snapshots have to be rebuilt, and availability at the remote site is affected.

Subquery subsetting provides solutions to eliminate all the preceding scenarios, except 5 (even the downtime caused in scenario 5 can be effectively reduced to a few minutes by making a local [temporary] copy of the required data in the EMPL_SALARY table via the CREATE TABLE AS SELECT method prior to rebuilding the snapshot, and having all applications refer to this local copy, rather than the snapshot, as the latter is being rebuilt. References can be changed to point to this local table via synonyms. Once the redefined snapshot is back again, all references can be restored to use the snapshot, instead of the local table). These solutions help to

- Insulate the master table from structural changes
- Avoid the need for hard-coding data-values

In the preceding situation, rather than introducing the new BRANCH_CODE column in the EMPL_SALARY table, one could create a new BRANCH_CODES table at the master site. This branch-code table would hold branch-codes and names. Then a local table called the BRANCH_EMPL table would be created to list all employees currently working in the branch. This table would hold the EMPL_ID from the master EMPL_SALARY table for all employees in the current branch.

Then, finally, the snapshot at each branch can be rebuilt as follows:

```
SQL> CREATE SNAPSHOT empl_salary FOR FAST REFRESH
       AS SELECT * FROM empl_salary@hr.world es
            WHERE EXISTS (SELECT empl_id FROM branch_empl
                               WHERE empl_id = es.empl_id);
```

The BRANCH_EMPL table would be maintained by each individual branch as new employees come in or existing ones leave. Thus, via this approach using subquery subsetting, one can avoid structural changes to the master table and also prevent the view-definition from having to be hard-coded. Any time the branch-code (or any other pertinent data) changes, the snapshot can remain as it is, enhancing availability. Thus, it has to be rebuilt just once, as compared to the conventional approach of changing the master table structure, where the snapshot may have to be rebuilt multiple times to accommodate structural and data-changes, enforced by changes in the business model. As you may have noticed in the preceding example (in the final snapshot rebuild), subquery subsetting allows complex conditions such as foreign key lookups, usage of varied SQL clauses (such as EXISTS), and so on, providing great flexibility in its definition.

PRIMARY KEY SNAPSHOTS AR creates snapshots based on the master table's primary-key values, rather than the ROWIDs (only ROWID-based snapshots are available in Oracle7). This, in conjunction with the fast snapshot refresh functionality, avoids reliance on the physical structure of the master table and enhances snapshot availability. For instance, if the master table or its partitions need to be reorganized (for defragmentation, to move specific partitions to a different tablespace, and so on), the corresponding snapshots can still work with the snapshot log and do not have to be dropped and re-created, thus preserving snapshot availability during the reorganization. This is especially important if the master tables are large, causing the reorganization to be very time-consuming.

This reliance on the logical primary key, rather than the physical ROWID, may slightly affect performance, since, during fast refreshes, it may take an additional (primary-key) index lookup to locate the actual ROWID of the master table. However, due to enhanced availability, that small performance hit is often acceptable.

AUTOMATIC SNAPSHOT REGISTRATION When snapshots are created off a master table or subsequently dropped, the events are registered with the master database, allowing DBAs to be familiar with all snapshots currently existing without having to query the target databases. Note that in Oracle7, automatic registration is not available and the DBA cannot estimate the number of snapshots currently defined off a master table (from within the master database). Automatic registration is especially useful for sites where a large number of snapshots are deployed (for example, a Sales application, where product information snapshots are held by a large number of field personnel on their laptop/palm-top via Oracle8*i* Lite). The daunting task of tracking all snapshots currently defined is greatly simplified.

CONSTRAINTS ON SNAPSHOTS AR allows constraints to be defined on snapshots. All or some constraints declared on the master table can also be declared on each individual snapshot. Furthermore, using the Oracle8 deferred constraint functionality, AR can be configured to avoid constraint checks during snapshot refreshes, allowing the refreshes to occur faster. However, note that in Oracle7 AR constraints cannot be declared on snapshots; if necessary, they can be enforced via triggers.

Hybrid Configuration

In a distributed database environment, the Master/Master and updatable snapshot approaches can be combined to provide a complete customized AR solution. For instance, the production database A can be replicated at a different site for disaster recovery purposes. In addition to the preceding, a specific schema can be replicated onto another site for application load-balancing purposes. Then, updatable snapshots can be utilized for replicating certain tables or portions of these tables for "standby table" scenarios (as described in Chapter 15) or for usage in other databases. All of these factors together illustrate a hybrid approach to replication.

Synchronous Replication

Synchronous replication provides real-time replication and is comparable to hardware/OS based replication facilities such as geo-mirroring. When writes occur in a synchronous replication environment, Oracle ensures that the local copy of the table is written and all replicated copies are written as well. Thus, writes to all the copies of the table would form a single unit of work. If the write to any copy fails, the transaction can be rolled back. As may be obvious, here the writes are not placed in a deferred queue for forward. Instead they are applied immediately.

Synchronous replication sounds ideal for HA. However, practical constraints make it very difficult to implement. For instance, network connections capable of handling large loads (especially during peak hours) would be mandatory. Lack of network bandwidth or any resource, for that matter, would make performance horrendous. Additionally, if writes to all the replicated copies are made mandatory and the network or any of the remote databases goes down, it would cause the writes to fail, affecting application availability. Of course, writes to the local site could be configured to be mandatory, whereas the writes to the remote copies could be made optional. However, these mandatory/optional scenarios may be better served in a regular Master/Master configuration, which provides for partial failures via the deferred queue functionality.

Synchronous replication is best suited to sites with substantial network capacity, where geographical distance between sites (partaking in the replication) is not too great. Wherever possible, a LAN implementation is recommended to avoid unacceptable performance and also to allow reliable writes to occur across the network. However, note that a LAN implementation would not be helpful for disaster recovery (due to close proximity of replicated machines). A WAN implementation could be used alternatively, provided not more than a few hundred kilometers separate each site (again, if the disaster is a large one, such as an earthquake, all the sites may be wiped out). In any case, to ensure transactional reliability, do not implement synchronous replication to occur over the Internet (a write-call may not return over the Internet). Private networks are highly desirable to ensure reliability and quality of writes occurring over the network. Abundant architectural analysis needs to be done prior to adopting and implementing synchronous replication.

Procedural Replication

At certain times, a bulk batch process may be run on the master database. Replicating a large number of individual rows during such massive jobs may not be prudent. Rather, it may be more efficient to run the actual job at the remote sites to duplicate the same writes that occur at the master site. This replication strategy that focuses on duplicating the original writes, rather than copying them over to other sites once they are complete, is referred to as *procedural replication*. In a procedural replication setup, a procedure called at the master site would also be invoked at the remote sites. Procedural replication also uses deferred RPC calls to achieve the desired replication effect. It may be combined with regular Master/Master configurations. For example, you could set up a replication scheme to use Master/Master for routine processing. However, during the year-end, when you would need to run massive year-end jobs, you could utilize procedural replication only during that specific period.

Mass Deployment

One of the primary architectural concerns when deploying AR is the audiences to whom the replicated information would be made available and their locations. If the number of users is immense and they are geographically spread out, the usual manual snapshot deployment schemes would be very cumbersome and not effective at all. For instance, the replicated information may have to be made available to hundreds or thousands of field sales-personnel, who typically use a laptop or a palm-top with, say, Oracle8*i* Lite™, to access the information and refresh the information at the beginning of each day. Instead of having the DBA manually deploy each replicated group to each salesperson, AR in Oracle8*i* provides a *deployment template* to automate most of the work.

Deployment templates allow a DBA to configure a "template" consisting of required replication groups (each group would comprise certain snapshots, stored procedures, packages, triggers, views, and so on). Each template would contain the necessary DDL to create all the required groups. The objects within the template can utilize performance-oriented features such as fast refreshes. Then a template can be installed by the DBA or by the users themselves. Thus, deployment templates work on the concept of "configure once, install many times." Each template can be linked to security information in the master database and also use parameters to customize each template. Multiple templates allow different replicated groups to be provided to different classes of users (such as field personnel, retail shops, and wholesalers). Once installed, the template can be instantiated on the end-user's machine and refreshed. Templates can utilize either online or offline instantiation mechanisms, where the user can refresh his or her groups directly from the master database (online instantiation) or, to reduce high concurrent loads, from pre-designated offline media, such as a CD-ROM (offline instantiation).

Of the preceding configurations, typically a Master/Master configuration is more pertinent for high-availability. This is because, during failover, in most cases the complete copy of the database (or certain mission-critical segments) would be required so that applications can continue to use them, as required. However, once the failed database/segments have been repaired and restored, the transactions running in the current primary need to be played back to the restored one. Thus, if a Master/Master scenario is not utilized, then new transactions would not be posted to the deferred queue to be applied to the restored database/segments (after they are made available).

Summary

This chapter examined the Advanced Replication option in Oracle, another effective mechanism for enhancing availability. Certain core AR defects in Oracle7 were discussed, along with how the new AR features in Oracle8/8*i* address these defects. Some options for implementing replication effectively in an HA environment were discussed. In the next chapter, we take a peek at certain HA-based third-party solutions available on the market.

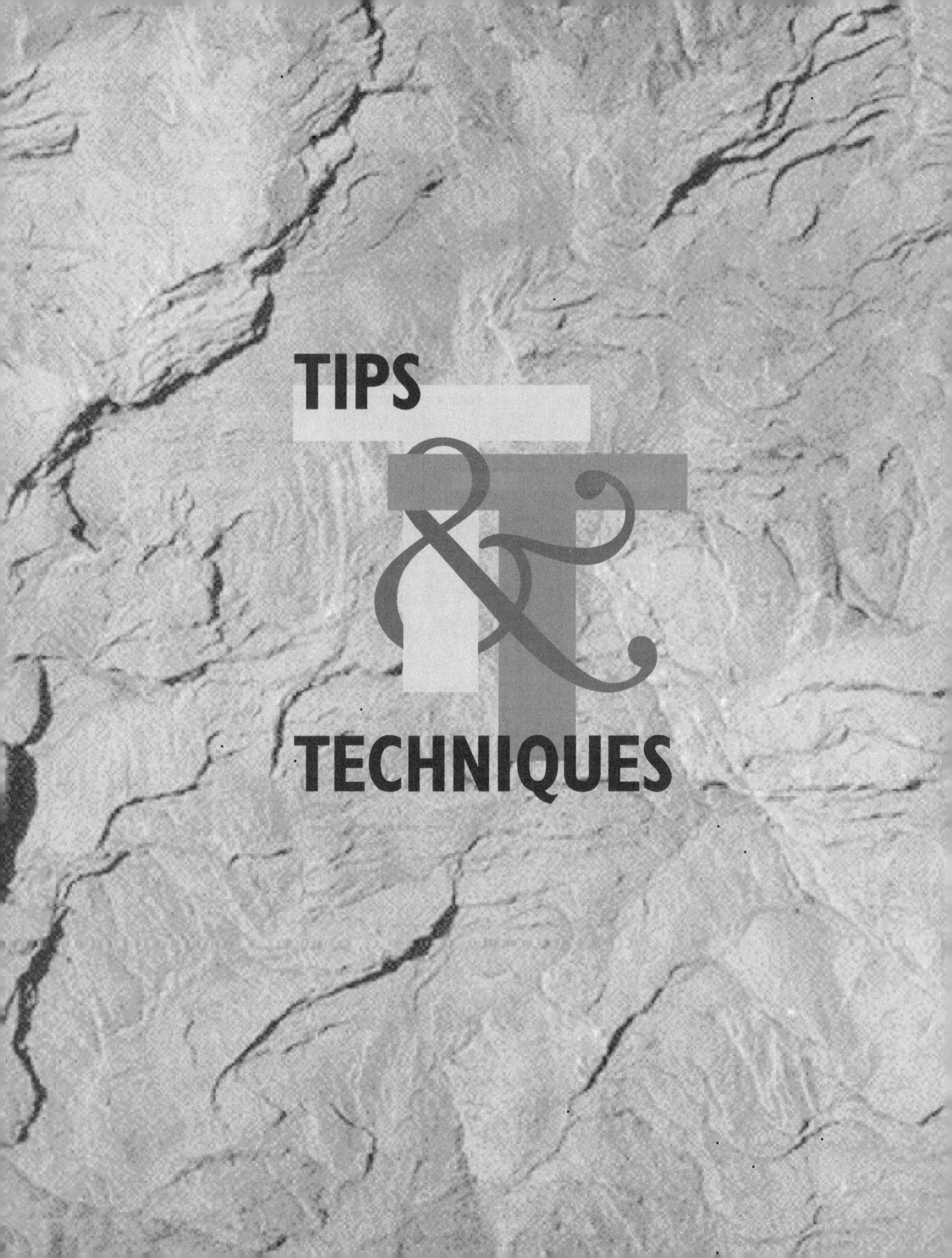
TIPS
&
TECHNIQUES

CHAPTER 18

Third-Party HA Solutions

Previous chapters in this section outlined various HA solutions available within Oracle. In addition to such solutions, various third-party HA-oriented solutions are also available in the market. In this chapter, I list some of the popular ones that I often come across at client-sites. I do not attempt to endorse or denounce any particular product. The inclusion or exclusion of any specific product in this chapter is not a reflection of its capability or lack of it. Rather, my objective is to choose among the popular third-party HA solutions that *I have specifically worked with* and provide a high-level description to illustrate how these products work. Please note the information that I provide here may not be the most current. Also, I describe features and flaws of these products, as per my experiences with them. As experience (in anything) is always limited, these pages may not adequately describe the product's capabilities, or at times, inaccuracies may creep in due to incorrect use of the product. Also, I focus only on product capabilities that enhance database uptime. For the latest and most complete information on each of the listed products, please visit the Web-site of the respective companies that manufacture them (listed in Appendix A). Finally, prior to deciding to deploy any third-party product, ensure that you perform the necessary analysis to determine whether it's suitable to your specific environment.

This chapter illustrates products at two levels:

- Hardware/OS based (tightly integrated with the hardware and/or OS)
- Database-based (tightly integrated with the Oracle server)

Based on this overall structure, this chapter offers the following tips and techniques:

- Consider EMC SRDF™ for disaster-recovery purposes
- Evaluate using EMC TIMEFINDER™ for higher return on investment
- Consider Quest Software's Shareplex™ for Oracle for higher standby flexibility and concurrent reporting access

Note that the products listed here may not be the only ones that offer the corresponding functionality. Other products in the same market-space may offer similar features and functionality. The products listed here are representative of solutions in a specific category. Also note that products examined in all of the preceding categories may not have specific knowledge of Oracle configurations. In fact, you may be able to deploy them in non-Oracle environments, as well. However, due to Oracle's sheer market penetration, many third-party vendors do offer products catering specifically to Oracle environments in the form of an "Oracle Database Pack," an "Oracle Server Pack," and so on. The actual names of these product-suites may vary. They typically consist of a wide variety of tools that can be used in Oracle installation, configuration, routine maintenance, event monitoring and alerts, and so forth. However, I do not specifically cover such utilities/tools here. Instead I focus on HA-oriented solutions, rather than tools for various purposes that enhance availability along the way.

Hardware/OS Based

The products listed here are representative of hardware-based solutions available in the market today.

Consider EMC SRDF™ for disaster-recovery purposes

SRDF (Symmetrix Remote Data Facility) is a geo-mirroring solution from EMC Corporation. It provides online real-time data replication across sites situated in geographically disparate locations (WAN-based replication). As such, it is effective for many disaster recovery scenarios. SRDF operates at the physical hardware (disk) level. It is totally external to Oracle. It consists of two or more duplicate storage systems, of which one is considered to be the primary system. Each system is placed at a separate location and is completely independent. Typically, LGWR and DBWR write the contents of the log-buffer and buffer cache to the online redo-logs and data-files, respectively (with some periodic writes to the control-files). These writes are made to the primary system. Every write made to the primary system is propagated to the secondary system.

Ideally, two exact same EMC storage systems (the EMC Symmetrix 3000 or 5000 series) are set up in an SRDF configuration (see Figure 18-1). Additional storage systems can be added for higher redundancy, if necessary. The primary storage system would exist at the primary data-center, whereas the second system could exist at a local off-site location (across the street or somewhere in the same city) and a third system could potentially exist across the globe. Standard SRDF configurations allow replication across remote systems residing from 10 feet to 66 kilometers from the primary. High-speed ESCON-compliant fiber-optic connections are utilized for such configurations. If replication across greater distances is required, then the SRDF FarPoint™ software can be utilized, which supports various industry-standard communication links, such as ATM, T1/E1, and T3/E3.

The primary disks are kept in read/write mode, whereas the secondary disks operate in read-only mode. In other words, users/applications can read and write only to the primary. The secondary disk-sectors are protected by EMC and only written to by SRDF internal routines to keep the secondary synchronized with the primary. If necessary, the secondary disks can be taken out of read-only mode and used for application/user failover or simply as a separate DSS system by plugging the disks into another host. However, this may cause the consistency between primary and secondary to be broken.

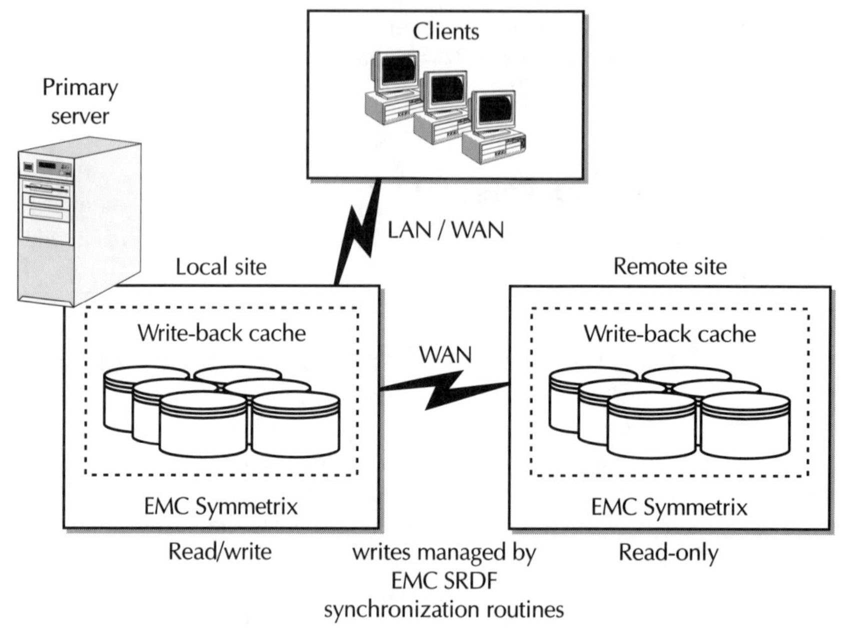

FIGURE 18-1. *EMC SRDF architecture*

EMC SRDF Characteristics

Following are some of the characteristics of EMC SRDF.

NO IMPACT TO HOST SYSTEM SRDF utilizes the EMC storage system itself to implement the replication. For this reason, the primary host system (the database server) is not impacted, since its resources are not used (the mirroring occurs at the hardware level and not at the OS level). The database server's resources (CPU and memory) are left dedicated to Oracle and other software that may be running.

UTILIZATION OF WRITE-BACK CACHES Rather than direct I/O to the storage system physical disks, all writes to both the primary and secondary storage systems occur via *write-back caches*. Since the caches are memory-based, writes occur very fast. The slower mechanical speed of actual disk-based I/O is avoided by writing to this cache. This write-back cache is also managed by the storage system.

REPLICATION OPTIONS The replication can occur under any of the following modes or a combination thereof:

- **Synchronous mode** In this mode, concurrent I/O calls are issued to both the primary and secondary storage systems. Thus, both primary and secondary are kept in-sync at the same time. An I/O operation is not considered complete until both the primary and secondary systems register it and issue back an acknowledgment. Thus, an atomic I/O unit consists of writes to both the primary and secondary each time. The main advantage here is, the secondary system is fully kept current in real-time. Any time the primary fails, failover to the secondary system can be done instantly. If the secondary system fails while the primary is still intact, only the propagation is aborted, with users/applications continuing to access the primary system without disruption. Synchronous mode provides the most optimal replication strategy, with no data-loss during failures. During failover (as the primary fails), the secondary becomes the primary without any synchronization necessary. This option impacts availability the least by keeping MTTR as low as possible during failures. Accordingly, synchronous mode is the preferred mode in an Oracle environment requiring high-availability.
- **Synchronous mode with domino attribute enabled** The *domino attribute* enforces continuous concurrent writes to both the primary and the secondary. Acknowledgments of every I/O operation have to be returned from both the primary and the secondary systems at all times. Synchronous mode, when used in conjunction with the domino attribute, is prone to what is termed the *domino effect.* Here, if the secondary fails (instead of the primary), subsequent I/O calls will freeze, since acknowledgment of the previous call has not returned from the secondary. It would require manual intervention to let subsequent database operations proceed without the secondary or to repair/replace the secondary and let the normal processing finish. This manual intervention typically causes a service disruption. Thus, the domino effect involves downtime during secondary system failures. Obviously, this configuration is not desirable in most Oracle environments requiring high-availability. This configuration is only useful in scenarios where the secondary system is expected to be totally in-sync with the primary, such as for real-time query-intensive access of OLTP data. Under this latter scenario, the primary and the secondary are kept completely current. When the users need to issue heavy DSS-type queries, the replication between the primary and the secondary is manually broken by running SRDF routines. This allows the primary system access to continue without

disruption. However, the secondary ceases to be a true standby and merely becomes a point-in-time online backup. Then it may be plugged into a separate host and users may start accessing the database in the secondary system directly to issue their queries. Breaking the replication is necessary; otherwise, queries cannot be directly issued against the secondary, since no writes are possible (even queries could generate writes by causing temporary/sort segments to be created in the temporary tablespace). Once the queries are complete, the secondary system can be re-synched with the primary once again without user disruption.

- **Semi-synchronous mode** Under this mode, writes to the primary are completed first. Then writes to the secondary are done (rather than simultaneously). Thus, since I/O to the primary is allowed to complete before issuance of I/O calls to the secondary, performance of the primary is enhanced, when compared with synchronous mode. Even under this mode, subsequent writes to the primary are not made until an acknowledgment is received from the secondary regarding successful completion of the previous write. However, if the secondary system is determined to have failed, then access of the primary continues without disruption.
- **Adaptive copy** Under this mode, every I/O unit applied to the primary storage system is propagated to the secondary system. However, any subsequent write to the primary does not wait for an acknowledgment from the secondary system (pertaining to the previous write). Thus, writes to the primary and the propagation to the secondary occur in asynchronous mode. This approach aims at best possible performance, tolerating a high degree of independence between the primary and secondary systems. The propagation is not in sequential order as determined by the application/user process generating the writes. Thus, from an Oracle perspective, a specific INSERT may occur prior to another INSERT. However, units of the second INSERT may be propagated before the first in adaptive copy mode. This is normally not a problem, as long as all writes get propagated sooner or later. However, if the primary system fails abruptly during the propagation, then the secondary system may not be logically consistent and may not be suitable for failover. Thus, adaptive copy mode is not usually suitable in an Oracle environment, since logical consistency and data-integrity are key issues (in fact, Oracle does not recommend operating in adaptive mode; synchronous mode is the only certified mode). However, adaptive copy mode may be utilized temporarily during bulk writes, where high performance is desired and the writes are reproducible (even if the primary system fails, leaving the secondary in a fuzzy state). Adaptive mode may also be utilized when SRDF replication is configured to occur across more than two systems (this option is elaborated subsequently).

A combination of the preceding modes can also be utilized. For example, for sites with long-distance replication as a serious requirement, a third replication site can be set up. Since long-distance replication is always time-consuming (due to the higher distance data has to travel), the primary and secondary systems can be placed reasonably close to each other (within a few kilometers). The primary and secondary can operate in synchronous mode. Since the distance between the two is shorter, performance normally will not deteriorate. However, if the third site also uses synchronous mode, chances are greater of performance deteriorating due to long-distance data travel. Every transaction will incur this long-distance overhead. Accordingly, the third site can operate in adaptive mode, where each subsequent write to the primary and secondary does not have to wait for previous writes to the third system to complete. If the primary fails, failover will normally occur onto the secondary system. The third system will be utilized only when both the primary and secondary fail. In these latter cases, there need to be well-defined methods in place to resolve logical inconsistencies, if any, in the third system.

NOTE
In addition to adaptive mode, for long-distance scenarios, SRDF provides a feature called multi-hop mirroring, where only incremental writes are queued up and applied to a third system during potentially low-use hours. This feature propagates only disk-tracks that have new data written to them. These new writes can be propagated via lower-cost long-distance communication lines. Although such lines will have relatively less network bandwidth, it shouldn't be a problem since only incremental changes will be sent across and the writes propagated will be less mission-critical. (Normally, the primary and secondary systems will already hold all writes, including the incremental ones—thus, the writes to the third system will be less mission-critical, since it only provides additional redundancy over longer distances.)

Based on my experience, synchronous mode is the most optimal SRDF mode for Oracle sites. The only time it can cause high MTTR is when the writes to the secondary are failing and the primary also fails at the same time or shortly after. There are two possible reasons for writes to the secondary storage system failing: either the secondary storage system itself has failed, or the connectivity from the host to the secondary storage system is lost. When failure is due to the connectivity being lost, the secondary will cease to be a true standby anymore. Instead, it will

just be an online database copy, current as of the time the failure occurred. If the primary system fails subsequently, failover to the secondary cannot be done immediately. Instead, the secondary must be brought up to speed using the online or archived redo-logs generated at the primary. If these logs are not available, data-loss may be incurred. After the secondary is made current (after roll-forward), it can be made the primary (until the original primary is repaired and is made available again). Thus, MTTR will include the time taken to roll-forward the secondary, since the database will be unavailable for immediate use. Alternatively, if the actual secondary system fails (rather than the connectivity) and the primary also subsequently fails before the secondary has been repaired and re-synchronized, this situation will also cause high MTTR, since both the primary and the secondary are unavailable. However, do bear in mind that concurrent failure of both primary and secondary resources is always fatal to availability under any disaster-recovery solution. Accordingly, keeping the low probability of concurrent failure in mind, I recommend synchronous mode (with the domino attribute disabled). However, my recommendation may not be applicable to your specific environment. Accordingly, I would strongly suggest that you evaluate all available SRDF modes and, after adequate analysis, determine what is best for your site. Select the mode that will allow you to restrict MTTR to be within your SLA specifications under all circumstances. Subsequent paragraphs in this section assume that SRDF has been configured in synchronous mode.

FAILOVER DURING DISASTER RECOVERY With local and remote storage systems providing redundancy, retaining availability during almost any disaster is possible. There are usually at least two communication links (remote link directors) connecting the primary and secondary for redundancy. Accordingly, even if one communication link is lost, the other is still able to sustain the synchronization. Also, disks within each storage system can be locally made redundant via RAID 1 or RAID S. Thus, if only one of the local disks is lost, the mirrored disk can be utilized or parity information can be used to reconstruct the failed disk. The only time the synchronization between primary and secondary would be lost or terminated, leaving the secondary in an incomplete state (causing some data loss), would be if sudden disaster occurs at the primary site, either destroying the primary system or all communication links between the two.

If the primary system still fails in spite of these precautions, failover to the secondary system can be initiated. During host failures, a host other than the primary (a standby host) can be plugged into the configuration and used for failover. Failover is fairly instantaneous with little or no impact on uptime, and there is no need for performing Oracle-based recovery (which would add to the MTTR), such as rolling forward or applying undo. However, application/user switchover may have to be handled externally to EMC via methods prescribed in Chapter 6.

FALLBACK AFTER NORMALCY IS RESTORED After failover has occurred, the original secondary storage system will become the primary and allow application/user access to continue. However, the original primary will not be the secondary because either it has been destroyed completely or partially or communication links between the two have been severed (with the fault being at the original primary). In any case, the original primary or the communication links need to be repaired/replaced. Hot disk switchover is possible, allowing faulty disks to be replaced without shutting the system down. After the original primary and/or the communication links are restored, the original primary is not in-sync with the current primary system anymore. This exposes the current primary to potential disasters without any scope for failover. Accordingly, the original primary has to be made the secondary almost immediately after it is restored. However, there is no automatic method to achieve this. This is done by re-synchronizing the original primary with the current primary via SRDF routines. Such re-synchronization occurs in a series of "snapshots." For instance, immediately after the original primary is made available again, it will be totally different from the current primary. The disk-tracks across the original primary and the current primary will have different information. All "dirty" tracks at the current primary will need to be applied to the original primary to synchronize both again. SRDF maintains information on such dirty tracks via internal track tables, where changes to tracks on the current primary are recorded. When the first round of re-synchronization starts, there may be 500,000 dirty tracks that will need to be applied. So the current "snapshot" will consist of 500,000 tracks. As these are being applied to the original primary, the current primary is up and being accessed by users/applications. Accordingly, additional tracks may become dirty. These additional tracks will not be applied in the first round. A subsequent round will have to be initiated to apply the new dirty tracks. The incremental number of dirty tracks depends on the extent of on-going activity at the time of re-synchronization. If this occurs during low-use hours, then chances of the original primary catching up fairly quickly are high. Once all the dirty tracks have been propagated, the re-synchronization completes and the original primary becomes the secondary and is made read-only, with only the SRDF routines writing to it. Thus, if the current primary fails after re-synchronization, failover to the original primary is possible. Thus, exposure to downtime is reduced once again.

During the process of re-synchronization, the original primary may fail yet again. This is called a "rolling disaster." If this occurs, the re-synchronization will fail and the original primary will remain in an unusable state until it is repaired/replaced and re-synchronization is re-initiated.

However, things do not end here. In reality, after failover, fallback is usually desired. Fallback becomes necessary even when the primary and secondary systems are exactly the same. This is because, typically, the primary system is maintained at the primary data-center, with the secondary at a remote site. The remote site may not have as many administrators as the primary site. Also, every user/application access will need to travel longer distances (to the remote system) each time. When the primary fails, operating via the remote system would be acceptable. However, once the original primary is up and running again, fallback to the original primary may be re-initiated so that complete normalcy is restored (with all users/applications accessing the primary system at the primary data-center).

Fallback may require some downtime. After re-synchronization of the original primary with the current primary is complete, all user/application access will have to be disabled for a short while, as SRDF routines are run to make the original primary the current primary and the current primary the secondary. This will cause the original primary to be made read/write again and the current primary to be made read-only. It is recommended that all SRDF routines be scripted and run to prevent administrative errors from delaying the operation. Fallback needs to be scheduled during hours of low use. Theoretically, there shouldn't be too much hurry to implement the fallback, since both a primary and a secondary (the original primary) will be operational prior to the fallback, protecting the site from any disaster during the window of time between the original primary being repaired/replaced and the fallback. Accordingly, the recommendation of scheduling the fallback to occur during low-use hours to minimize overall disruption is not impractical. Additionally, scheduling the re-synchronization and fallback to occur during low-use hours reduces the possibility of rolling disasters, since re-synchronization will occur very fast (due to very few or no incremental dirty tracks being generated during each round of re-synchronization).

CONCURRENT SUPPORT FOR MULTIPLE PLATFORMS In a large IT shop, typically multiple systems across a vast number of platforms run mission-critical databases. EMC SRDF supports UNIX, Windows NT, mainframe, and AS/400 platforms. If required, it is possible to implement parallel SRDF configurations for these platforms.

Caveats in Using SRDF

A drawback when using hardware-based mirroring solutions is that all user-errors (such as a table being accidentally dropped/truncated) and administrative errors (such as a data-file being physically deleted) at the source are also propagated across to the target. SRDF is no exception. Similarly, certain corruption scenarios (such as where keys in an index do not match keys in the corresponding table) are also propagated. Accordingly, one may have to implement a custom standby database or standby table solution in addition to SRDF for complete protection against any potential failure.

SRDF may impose a performance overhead on the source system. This overhead is proportional to the number of transactions occurring (that is, the higher the number of transactions, the higher the overhead). Accordingly, this overhead is more evident at sites with high transaction rates (especially during peak hours). On a system with fairly low I/O, the overhead was negligible. In a fairly robust OLTP system, I have observed a 2 to 10 percent overhead (in synchronous mode with the remote system being around 50 meters away), whereas with heavy batch jobs that did a lot of writing, the overhead went up by as much as 15 to 20 percent.

Evaluate using EMC TIMEFINDER™ for higher return on investment

Another availability-enhancing product from EMC Corporation is EMC TimeFinder. Here, a Business Continuance Volume (BCV) device is created as a mirror to an existing disk configuration (see Figure 18-2). The existing disk configuration may already be mirrored (via RAID 1) or may be using parity-based redundancy (RAID S). It may even be remotely mirrored via SRDF. In such configurations, the BCV device may be regarded as an additional mirror. The main purpose of this additional redundancy is to expedite various maintenance operations without disrupting the primary system. Additionally, it serves to offload DSS operations and testing from the production database server to other databases/host machines. For instance, if a BCV device is established at a primary system, all writes made to the physical disk at the primary are propagated to the BCV device. When backups need to be taken or DSS-type queries need to be run on real-time data, the BCV device may be split from the configuration and used for the previously mentioned purposes. This would avoid the need for the primary system to participate in such time- and resource-consuming operations and would permit it to function without interruption. Since redundancy would already be built into the primary system (via RAID 1, RAID S, or the like), sudden failures can be effectively countered. Thus, the primary objective of TimeFinder is not to act as a basic mirror (though it can do so), but to allow the primary system to function without routine disruptions typically enforced by concurrent maintenance operations. Since dedicated BCV devices are utilized for performing maintenance, throughput of such operations greatly improves, as well. Thus, in addition to enhancing availability, a TimeFinder configuration can be used for tertiary functions such as building test systems, building DSS/reporting instances, and so on. This added functionality helps derive higher return on investment (ROI), when compared with HA solutions that merely provide redundancy and do not allow the standby resources to be used for any purpose other than failover.

In a typical TimeFinder configuration, a disk within the primary storage system (EMC Symmetrix configurations) is associated with a BCV disk to form a "BCV pair." This process is referred to as establishing the BCV device. The source system disk is considered to be the "standard" device, whereas the target is the BCV device. Initially, all writes that have occurred at the standard device are completely established at the BCV device. Then, on an ongoing basis, only new writes can be incrementally

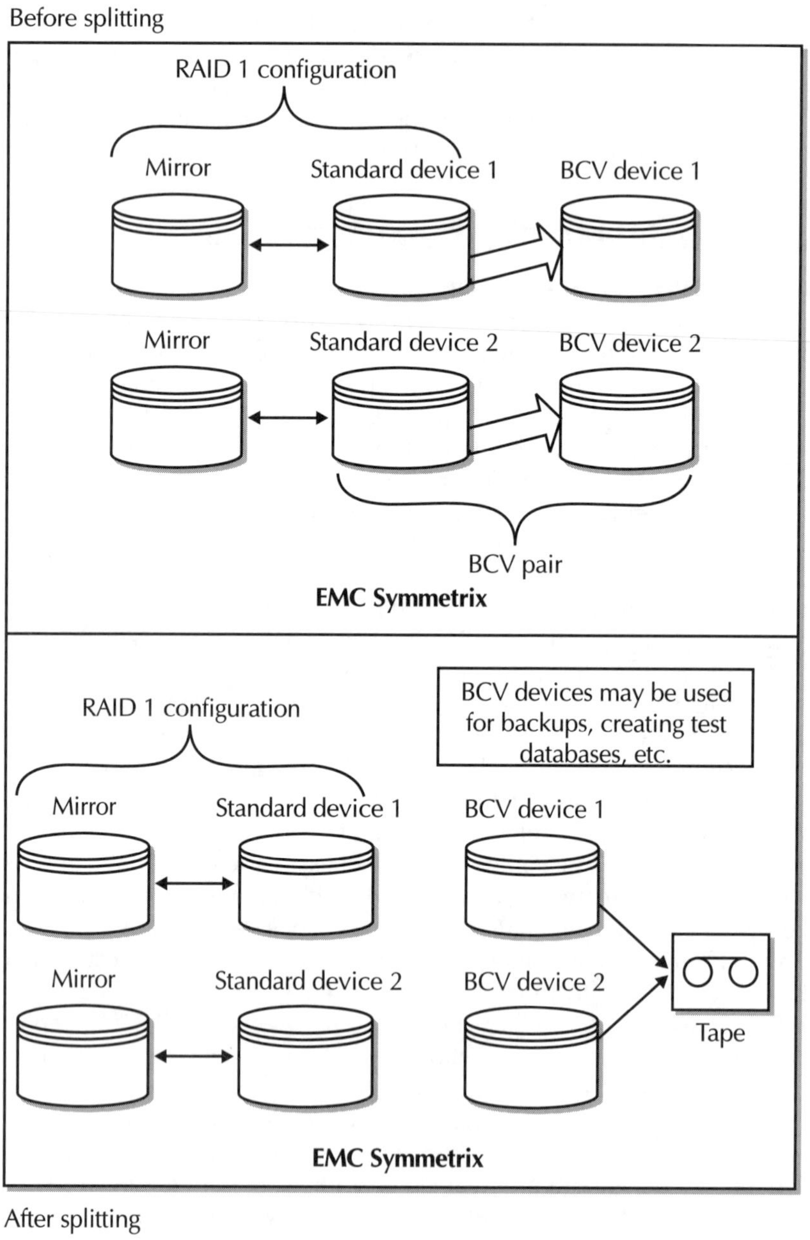

FIGURE 18-2. *EMC TimeFinder™ configuration*

propagated. During both complete and incremental synchronization, the standard device does not suffer any downtime, since synchronization occurs in the background. Whenever necessary, the BCV device can be split from the standard device and be directly accessed by the same host (that is writing to the standard device) or via another host. A split BCV device may be used for just about any concurrent operation that needs to be performed without any impact on regular production access and business continuance. Examples of such operations are as follows:

- **For issuing real-time DSS-type queries on production data** Another host may be plugged in and the BCV devices may be accessed via a database on the new host. Ideally, access via the same host (that is writing to the standard device) should be avoided, since that would cause its valuable system resources to be shared between production and DSS use. Note that such DSS-type use of the BCV devices may cause it to lose its synchronization with the standard devices. However, once all the queries are complete, the BCV devices may be re-established at the standard devices. Such re-establishing may be configured to occur incrementally (with only changed tracks being re-written).
- **For performing database backups off the BCV devices** Once split, the BCV device becomes a point-in-time backup of the database. It may be used as the source to write the backups to tape. Also, in case the standard devices fail (in spite of inherent RAID 1/S redundancy), the BCV devices may be used to quickly restore the point-in-time database copy.
- **Loading data-warehouses and data-marts from production data** The production data may be massaged to denormalize it and then used to populate data-warehouses and data-marts.
- **As a test system** The BCV devices can be used to completely re-construct the production database for testing the most recent data.

The preceding examples serve to give an idea of the utility of BCV devices. One of the most important advantages of using TimeFinder is the rapid synchronization/re-synchronization of the BCV devices with the standard devices. All writes are propagated at the physical disk level (all bits and bytes changed on every disk track). Track tables are maintained internally by TimeFinder for comparing changes within the standard device and propagating those changes to the BCV device. Track tables are basically bit vectors, consisting of 0's and 1's, corresponding to physical tracks of disk-volumes. Each track is 32KB in size. Thus, a disk-volume would comprise a group of 32KB tracks. Whenever new information is written to a track or existing information is changed, a bit is set in the corresponding track table, allowing all changes to be identified immediately. Track tables are maintained for both standard and BCV devices. These tables are maintained even after they are split. This is necessary so that reconciliation of tracks is possible during re-establishes or restores. During both complete and incremental establishes (or re-establishes) of a BCV device, the track tables of the standard device are considered the master source in bringing the BCV device up to speed.

When using TimeFinder in an SRDF configuration, BCV devices can be established either at the primary system, at the secondary system, or both. EMC TimeFinder is available for a variety of platforms, including multiple UNIX flavors, Windows NT, certain mainframe configurations, and IBM AS/400.

Caveats in Using TimeFinder

Following are the caveats that one needs to be aware of prior to using TimeFinder:

- The BCV device needs to be established during low use hours. This is because the standard device is taxed heavily during the initial (complete) establishing. Incremental establishes do not impact the standard device as heavily. If the policy of allowing a complete establish (or re-establish) only during non-peak hours is enforced, then this is not a major reason for worry, since only an incremental establish would occur on a regular basis (a complete establish would be more of an exception).
- BCV devices aid external maintenance (such as taking backups or disk-reorganizations). However, certain maintenance operations, such as index rebuilds or table defragmentation, are internal to the database. BCV devices cannot be used for such operations. This is a logical restriction. Theoretically, once split, BCV devices may be used for anything, including internal maintenance operations. However, while these operations are occurring on the BCV devices, the standard devices are being subjected to regular production use. Accordingly, both the standard and BCV devices will reflect different parallel points in time. During a re-establish, one has to be over-written with changes from the other. Since new production data cannot be discarded, obviously, internal maintenance done within the BCV devices will have to be discarded as dirty tracks from the standard devices are propagated across.
- When using BCV devices for restoring the database (when the primary database on the standard devices has been destroyed), ensure that they are a consistent point-in-time copy of the original database. In case they have been changed (for example, due to explicit denormalization for optimal DSS use), the changed data will be restored.

Additional information on EMC SRDF and EMC TimeFinder is available at http://www.emc.com.

Database-Based

The product listed here is representative of HA solutions that primarily work with the database.

Consider Quest Software's Shareplex™ for Oracle for higher standby flexibility and concurrent reporting access

Quest Software's SharePlex for Oracle is a log-based replication solution. Once configured, it uses the online redo-logs to interpret the changes that have occurred in the primary database, reconstructs the corresponding SQL statements, and applies them to the secondary database(s). The writes are propagated in a sequential manner, with the original order of writes to the source database being kept intact during writes to the target database. SharePlex is capable of replicating data across databases on the same system, across databases on systems connected via a LAN, as well as across databases on systems connected via a WAN. Both the primary (source) and secondary (target) databases can remain open and accessible, allowing quick failover in case the primary database/system goes down, concurrent load-balancing during regular processing (especially during peak-hours), and concurrent ad hoc reporting needs (off the secondary databases). From a disaster recovery perspective, the primary and secondary databases would need to be placed on systems in geographically disparate areas connected via a WAN.

Shareplex Architecture and Operations

The SharePlex architecture primarily consists of a controller process, multiple daemons, and a set of "queue" files on the source and target systems. In addition, a set of tables are used within the Oracle databases. Figure 18-3 illustrates the interaction between the primary components. The controller process is typically started up during system boot-time. It monitors and administers the entire replication operation. If for some reason (say, administrative "accidents") any of the daemons die, replication will stop. The controller process detects this and restarts them to commence replication again.

- A *capture* process and a *reader* process (daemons) run on the source system, closely interacting with the database to continuously capture all writes to the online redo logs and record them. This change-capture occurs in incremental units as new changes get written to the online redo-logs. This allows the capture process to be relatively well-paced (on a normal basis), rather than occurring in periodic bursts of activity. This scenario prevents any sudden (excessive) impact to the source system/database. Of course, if a large number of writes to the source system occur in a sudden burst (such as during the nightly batch run), then the capture process will also have to keep up.

- A set of files on the source system (external to the database) implement a queuing mechanism on the source system. DML changes captured from the online redo-logs are recorded in these files by the daemons running on the primary system. Upon reading the online redo-logs, the contents are filtered to capture only those pertaining to the replicated tables and sequences. Then the corresponding SQL syntax is written to the files in a compressed fashion. This compression helps in reducing network traffic as these writes are propagated across the network to the target database(s). On a normal basis when both the source and target systems are up and running, the writes recorded in these files will be minimal (determined by the current database activity). However, if the target system and/or database is unavailable due to planned or unplanned outages, then the writes will be queued up in these files for later propagation (when the target system/database is up and running again).
- The contents of these files on the source system are then transferred to the target system via SharePlex export/import processes (not to be confused with the Oracle export/import utilities). SharePlex does not use SQL*Net/Net8 for the propagation. Instead it uses a proprietary stream protocol-based high-speed transport layer. This reduces the dependence on Oracle and totally eliminates the reliance on SQL*Net/Net8. So, in case the Oracle software on the target system is unstable due to disk-errors or administrative accidents, the propagation of writes from the source can still continue unabated (and get queued on the target system, until the Oracle software and the database on the target system are stabilized). Also, in case the network is unavailable, the writes will not get transferred to the target system. Instead, they will accumulate in the files on the source system. SharePlex periodically polls the network to check its availability; once the network is available, the writes continue to be propagated. Accordingly, when the target system is unavailable, the size of the files can increase to accommodate all writes occurring until the target system is available again.
- The compressed SQL information sent in from the source is written to a set of files on the target system. These files act as a queuing mechanism on the target. During normal processing, when the target system is up and running, the queue size will be limited (again, the actual size will depend on the current database activity at the source), since the contents are immediately applied to the target database. However, if the target database is unavailable, then the writes will get queued up, increasing the size of the queue files (obviously, this will require higher disk-space on the target system).
- Finally, a *post* process reads the files and applies the writes to the target database, thus synchronizing the target with the source.

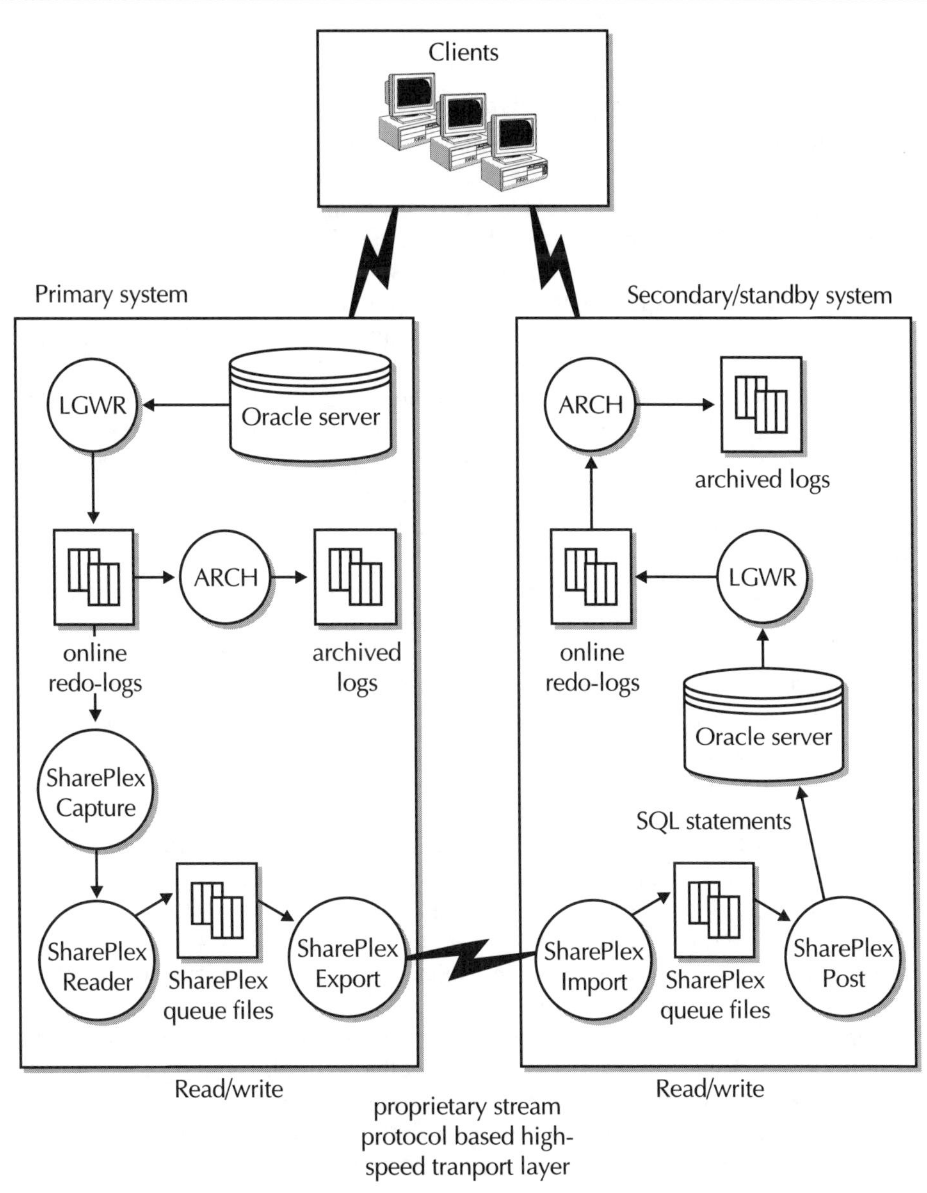

FIGURE 18-3. *Replication via SharePlex for Oracle*

Shareplex Characteristics

SharePlex has the following characteristics.

SECONDARY DATABASE CONCURRENTLY AVAILABLE Since SharePlex reconstructs SQL statements at the source database and applies them to the target database, the target database is always open and available for access. Thus, the target database can be used for load-balancing, or simply real-time ad hoc reporting requirements. Using a tool such as Oracle Discoverer, end-users can directly query the production data without adversely impacting the production system/database. Since there are no restrictions on temporary segment creation during complex queries (temporary segment creation causes writes to a database, violating the "read-only" requirement), the queries can directly be issued. (This is unlike the Oracle8*i* standby database option where locally managed tablespaces are required for temporary segment creation during read operations; also in the Oracle8*i* standby database option, opening the database for queries does not allow it to be continuously synchronized with the primary database, since it is not in mounted mode anymore.) Furthermore, if the reporting instance needs to have a higher degree of denormalization than the production database, then custom routines can be used at the target database to read the source (production) data in the normalized structures, convert them into denormalized form, and write those records to the denormalized tables. Again, the entire operation can be accomplished in the target database without any adverse impact on the source production database. This ensures a higher ROI than a regular Oracle standby scenario, where the secondary database is in mounted mode and not open for access (since recovery is continuously being done).

SUPPORT FOR MULTIPLE CONCURRENT OS/ORACLE VERSIONS SharePlex allows the secondary database to be used during migrations across versions (upgrades, downgrades, and so on). In other words, the Oracle version at the primary site can be different than the version at the secondary site(s). For instance, SharePlex can be used to retain availability when upgrading from Oracle7 to Oracle8/8*i*. Initially, the primary and secondary databases may be on Oracle7. Later, when you are upgrading the primary database to Oracle8, applications/users can continue to use the secondary database directly. SharePlex will need to be directed to treat the original secondary database as the current primary. The writes occurring at the current primary can be replicated across other existing databases (secondary databases; not the one being upgraded) to prevent exposure to downtime if the current primary experiences a failure (since the original primary is being upgraded and is not available for failover). Also, the SharePlex post process on the original primary system will need to be disabled, so that SharePlex does not attempt to apply current writes to the database being upgraded. After the primary database is upgraded to Oracle8, the writes that occurred in the current primary (the Oracle7 database) will be available in the queue files on the original primary system (because only the post process was suspended, not the export/import processes that transferred all writes since the switchover to the original primary system). These writes can then be applied to the original primary (the Oracle8 database), and the Oracle8 database can continue to function as the secondary database. During the next available window of opportunity (say, late at night when use is relatively low), swichover can again occur to make the Oracle7 database (the current primary) the secondary database, and the Oracle8 database can become the primary.

This rule also applies to the OS. SharePlex is available for Sun Solaris, HP-UX, and IBM AIX. The source and target systems do not have to have matching hardware and OSs (though it is recommended that they match each other in terms of resources to prevent performance from being impacted after switchover). In other words, the primary database can be on a Sun machine, whereas the secondary database(s) can be on other systems.

This, and the fact that the secondary database can continuously remain open, are the two most attractive options about SharePlex for any 24×7 site.

SUPPORT FOR MULTIPLE REPLICATION SCENARIOS SharePlex supports multiple replication scenarios, including

- **Peer-to-peer replication** This is the conventional and simplest replication mode. Here, typically, writes from a single primary database are propagated to a single secondary database. The secondary database will be in "read-only" mode (queries can be directly issued, without the DBA having to worry about temporary segment creation). Either the entire primary database or only a sub-set of the tables and sequences (those used by mission-critical applications) can be replicated. No explicit writes to any of the replicated segments are allowed. However, such writes are not physically prevented (that is, SharePlex does not incorporate any mechanism to guard against explicit writes). If writes do occur, then the secondary database will not remain consistent with the primary anymore. Further propagation from SharePlex may not be successful (for instance, propagation of a row deletion that has been manually made in the secondary database may fail), resulting in a conflict. Such conflicts will be logged in the SharePlex event-log for manual resolution by the DBA.
- **Broadcast replication** Here, a single primary database or sub-set is replicated to multiple databases. A different set of tables and sequences can be replicated across each target database. Thus, you could have a bunch of smaller systems supporting smaller databases, with a specific sub-set of the primary database replicated on it.

- **Consolidation replication** Here, you can have multiple primary databases, each replicating to a single (bigger) secondary database. Thus, different sub-sets of data from each primary database can be replicated to a common target. Whenever any of the primary databases fail, switchover can be initiated to a single secondary database.
- **Multi-tier replication** An N-tier approach is allowed in this mode, where data from a primary database can be replicated to one or more secondary databases via a middle-tier. The middle-tier does not require a database. It simply allows SharePlex daemons and queue files to be placed on the middle-tier, which propagate the writes across to pre-defined target systems. This architecture allows writes to be propagated to a large number of target systems (say, from the company's main data-center to hundreds of branch locations), without causing heavy strain on the system and network resources of the primary. The primary merely replicates to the single middle-tier system, and the onus for further replication to multiple target systems is placed on the middle-tier system (which can be dedicated to the task).
- **Master/Master replication** Here, both the databases are considered to be "primary." In other words, both databases can be directly accessed for reads and writes. All writes to the replicated objects in either database are propagated to the other database. Conflict-resolution routines need to be defined within SharePlex to achieve Master/Master replication. (For instance, if the same row is deleted in one database and updated in the other, which write should be considered "correct" and which should be rolled back?) A separate product from Quest Software called I/Watch can be used to detect conflicts in a SharePlex environment and immediately alert the DBA.
- **Hierarchical replication** Here, a sub-set of the primary database is replicated onto a "secondary" database. This secondary database may have other tables in addition to the replicated segments from the primary, which may be written to directly by applications/users. These other tables may become the "primary" and be replicated across other downstream target systems. Thus, multiple levels of replication across different databases can be achieved in a "grandfather-father-grandson" fashion.

INSTANTANEOUS FAILOVER Since the target system is open and available, immediate failover can be initiated during disasters and other failures at the source system/database. Failover will chiefly consist of application/user failover, where the applications and user processes will have to be redirected to connect to the target system, rather than the source (Chapter 6 discusses application failover in more detail). Even with instantaneous database failover, a key question needs to be asked: How much of the "latest" data is your site willing to lose during failover? Prior to your initiating failover, there may be some "trapped" writes that have not been fully propagated. Especially, at times, if the source system/database fails during peak traffic, a relatively high number of writes may not have been fully propagated. There are three main scenarios you need to consider:

- The writes to the online redo logs at the source have not been fully captured and written to the queue files at the source.
- The writes to the online redo logs have been captured and written to the queue files, but they have not been propagated successfully to the target system.
- The writes have been successfully propagated to the target system queue files, but they have not been completely applied to the target database.

In case of the third scenario, the writes will automatically get applied to the target database in a short period of time (say, a few minutes or so). No manual intervention is required. However, in the case of the first two scenarios, the latest writes are not immediately available/transferable into the target. These writes will be captured and transferred once the primary system/database is fully restored and recovered. However, they are not available for immediate failover purposes. In case your applications/users do not need the latest writes, then the latest writes not being available will be acceptable and failover can be truly immediate. However, if your applications/users need all writes, including the latest that are missing, then you need a mechanism to manually identify the ones that are lost and re-create them prior to failing over to the secondary database. Such mechanisms may include re-running certain portions of the application and re-entering the missing rows directly into the secondary database. In case it is not possible to re-create the writes, then you can evaluate whether the applications/users can function without the latest writes. In most cases, re-producing the writes shouldn't take up too much time, since the number of writes during the failure should be relatively small. Accordingly, failover can be accomplished with very little or no downtime. In case the writes are manually re-created at the secondary, they need to be manually prevented from being propagated to the secondary database after the primary database is restored/recovered to prevent the writes from being applied twice to the secondary.

PLANNED OUTAGES In the case of planned outages (defragmenting/re-organizing the database, migrating to a different version, applying an OS or database patch, and so on), smooth switchover to the secondary is possible without losing any writes. This can be achieved by re-directing all application/user

processes to access the secondary database. All pending writes at the primary will be applied to the secondary database in the normal course of processing, thus making the latter consistent with the primary. Once this is completed, the secondary database will become the current primary. All new writes done at the current primary will be placed in the queue files to be applied to the original primary after the planned outage is complete and the original primary becomes available again. Once it becomes available, it can be made the secondary database. If necessary, at an opportune time, switchover can occur and it can be made the primary once again, whereupon the current primary will revert to its role as the secondary.

OTHER USEFUL FEATURES

- SharePlex can be configured to replicate data from a certain table in the source database to a different table in a separate schema in the target database, provided the structures of both are similar.
- SharePlex supports LONG and LONG RAW data-types, as well as Oracle8 LOBs.
- SharePlex allows referential integrity to remain enabled on replicated tables.
- SharePlex allows newer segments to be added to the replication process in a dynamic fashion without having to stop and restart replication.

Caveats in Using Shareplex For Oracle

The following are some of the caveats you need to be aware of prior to deciding to use SharePlex in your environment.

"READYMADE" SECONDARY DATABASE REQUIRED DURING INITIAL CONFIGURATION While setting up replication via SharePlex, the secondary database needs to be made consistent with the primary prior to initiating the replication process. Normally, in order to create a consistent copy, you would need to use a data-copying routine such as export/import. However, such methods can result in high downtime to configure SharePlex. In order to prevent such downtime, the SharePlex *reconciliation utility* needs to be used in conjunction with the latest hot backup of the primary database. Once the files (composing the hot backup) are copied over to the target system, all archived redo-logs (since the backup) need to be applied to make the target database (reasonably) current with the primary. At this point, only the online redo-logs from the primary will not have been applied to the secondary database. Then the target database can be opened and the SharePlex reconciliation utility can be run. After this, the post process can be started and replication initiated. From this point on, all writes in the online redo-logs at the primary are propagated to the secondary. Initial configuration needs to be achieved during low-use hours to minimize impact to the source database (explained later).

An alternative way of creating a "readymade" database to be used as the secondary for SharePlex configuration without downtime is to use mirrored disks at the hardware level. For instance, using EMC TimeFinder™, you can replicate the entire production database on the secondary system via TimeFinder BCV devices. Once this is accomplished, SharePlex processes can be initiated to continue the replication and keep the secondary synchronized with the primary. SharePlex provides a specific configuration called SharePlex Overdrive™ to set up replication in conjunction with EMC mirroring mechanisms.

TABLE LOCKS DURING INITIAL CONFIGURATION When a new table is added to SharePlex to be replicated, SharePlex runs an ANALYZE command on the table to validate its structure and acquire row-chaining information. The ANALYZE command places a lock on the table, thus affecting concurrent DML/DDL operations. This impact to the source database is an important reason for configuring SharePlex during low-use hours. However, analyzing of each table occurs only once as the table is included for replication.

Also, SharePlex needs to be kept current regarding all structural changes made to replicated segments in the source database. For instance, if a new column is added to a table or an existing column is modified, SharePlex rereads the entire segment structure definition and adapts its expectation of data pertaining to the segment.

INABILITY TO READ ARCHIVED REDO-LOGS SharePlex currently lacks the capability to read the archived redo-logs. It can only capture writes to the online redo-logs. However, if for some reason the SharePlex (controller) process is not running or has died, replication will abort. During this time, new writes may fill up the online redo-logs and log-switches will occur. Once archived, these redo-logs may be over-written with new data. At this point, if SharePlex is restarted, the replication will not comprise the data that was written to the redo-logs prior to their being over-written. These writes will be contained in the archived redo-logs and will need to be manually applied to the secondary database to make it current with the primary.

A flip side to this limitation is that your online redo-logs need to be adequately sized to accommodate log switches during peak-hour traffic. The number and size of the online redo-logs need to be at least enough to give SharePlex processes reasonable time to read the contents prior to being over-written. Determine the optimal size after analyzing and testing the redo generation volume and replication throughput at your site.

NOLOGGING/UNRECOVERABLE OPERATIONS As with any standby database solution that relies on the Oracle redo-logs, SharePlex does not propagate NOLOGGING/UNRECOVERABLE operations on the source database to the target database. Accordingly, use of any NOLOGGING/UNRECOVERABLE operation needs to be carefully evaluated. If such operations are absolutely required, then the exact same operation needs to be manually run in the target database.

In the case of direct-path operations (such as via SQL*Loader or direct bulk inserts), data is written to the redo-logs if ARCHIVELOG mode is enabled. Since in a 24×7 environment that will be the case, direct-path operations do not have to be manually propagated.

DISABLE TRIGGERS ON TARGET DATABASE Triggers that modify data in the target database should be disabled to prevent duplicate writes from occurring (if the triggers are already defined on the primary database). SharePlex provides a script to automatically make each trigger ignore changes coming in from the SharePlex post process.

DISABLE DATA-DICTIONARY REPLICATION While configuring SharePlex, ensure that data-dictionary contents are not replicated from the source database. Only replicate application-related segments. Since writes to the application segments would generate data-dictionary writes automatically on the source and target databases, replicating such information would be redundant and possibly cause dictionary corruption and inconsistencies due to duplicate data.

PERFORMANCE REPERCUSSIONS Normally, SharePlex's replication mechanisms are non-intrusive to the database and do not impose any substantial overhead. However, during peak hours, the additional system resource consumption by the multiple SharePlex processes is noticeable as performance begins to drag. Hence, it is essential to benchmark and ensure that your systems have adequate capacity to support the SharePlex functionality prior to deploying it.

Additional information on SharePlex is available on Quest Software's Web-site at http://www.quests.com.

PART VII

Building a Real-World Arsenal

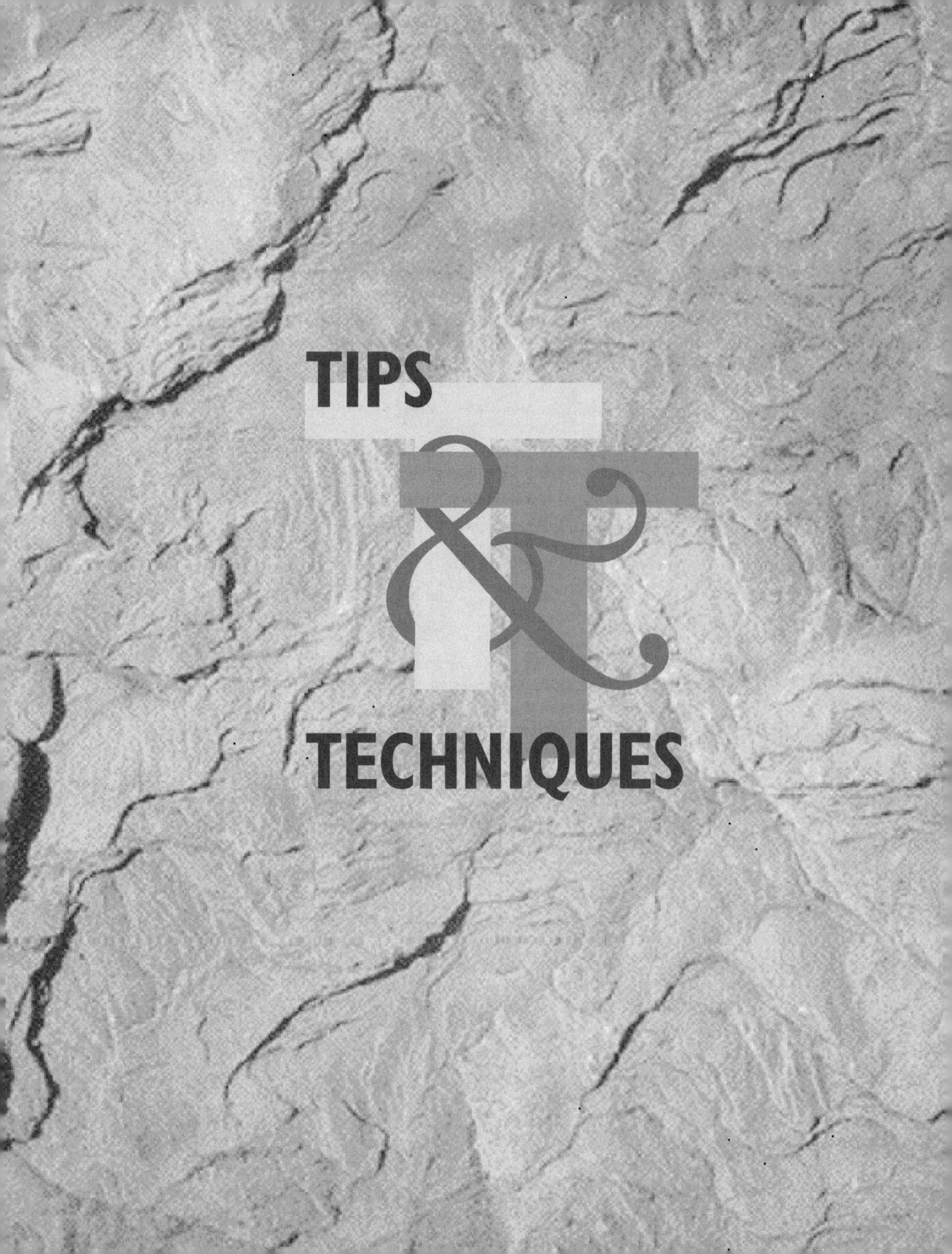
TIPS
&
TECHNIQUES

CHAPTER 19

The 24×7 Toolkit

Previous chapters discuss various scenarios in which certain critical information is extracted from the database to help alert administrative personnel to impending and/or existing database and application/user process failures. For instance, an important segment inside the database may not have the contiguous space necessary to allocate another extent. Alternatively, an application process may be continuously consuming large amounts of space from the temporary tablespace, causing it and other processes to run out of space. By periodically querying the database for certain irregularities, you can detect them and take preventive action in time. For instance, a script may be deployed to check the database for potential problems every half-hour and page the DBAs if any are detected. This helps greatly in avoiding certain major service disruptions. If some of the scripts are resource consuming, then they can be run less frequently (say, every two hours). The objective is to be alerted to potential problems as early as possible with minimal impact on the production database.

This chapter offers the following tips and techniques:

- Monitor for specific failures by running poll-scripts periodically
- Be familiar with techniques for application failover when calling PL/SQL

Using Scripts to Be Alerted to Disruptive Problems

This chapter presents a series of scripts that may be used to poll the database and report problems. A master shell-script is provided at the very onset that can call a bunch of SQL and PL/SQL (if necessary) scripts. Each of the latter can check for occurrences of a specific error-condition. Note that this chapter does not present a comprehensive set of scripts to check every possible error. Rather, it serves to provide an example of checking for certain commonly encountered "show-stopping" errors and paging the DBAs. Prior to adopting these scripts in your environment, you would need to spend a fair amount of time analyzing the potential problems specific to your site and, if necessary, plug-in additional scripts to specifically check for those. The current set of scripts may not be a complete solution for your site.

Finally, this chapter also presents a shell-script to illustrate application failover when calling PL/SQL code blocks.

Now, let's look at the various scripts that may be utilized as part of your "24x7 toolkit." Note that the shell-scripts provided are meant to be used in a UNIX environment. In case your OS is different (Windows NT, VAX VMS, or what have you), then you will need to use the same algorithm illustrated here to code scripts specific to your environment. The SQL and PL/SQL scripts provided here can still be invoked via the new scripts (specific to your OS) that you create.

Monitor for specific failures by running poll-scripts periodically

The Korn shell-script that follows allows specific SQL statements to be run to poll the database and report specific errors. The shell-script may be run every half-hour or so via an OS scheduling utility such as *cron* or any third-party scheduling program.

```
#!/bin/ksh
# Script : ChkErr.ksh
# Functionality : Template to check for errors and page DBAs, if necessary
# Author : Venkat S. Devraj
# Modification history
# 07/1997              VSD             Written
# 07/1997              VSD             Added check for MAXEXTENTS
#

if [[ $# -lt 3 ]]; then
  echo "Usage: $0 <READONLY_MONITORING_USERID> <PASSWORD> <LOGFILE>"
  exit 1
fi

USR_ID=$1
USR_PASS=$2
LOGFIL=$3
NOTIFY_LIST=oncall_dba_pager@att.net

# check 1) verify that no critical segments are reaching
#          MAXEXTENTS. If so, page the DBA
sqlplus -s <<EOF >$LOGFIL 2>/dev/null
$USR_ID/$USR_PASS
    SET PAGES 0
    SELECT DISTINCT 'YES' FROM dba_segments
     WHERE extents >= (max_extents-5);
EOF
grep -i '^ORA-' $LOGFIL >/dev/null
if [ $? -eq 0 ]
then
   mailx -s "${ORACLE_SID} : Script failed" $NOTIFY_LIST <<EOF
      Monitoring script $0 failed.
      Please check $LOGFIL for more details.
EOF
   exit 1
fi

MAXEXTENTS_REACHED=`awk '{ print $1 }' $LOGFIL`
if [ "$MAXEXTENTS_REACHED" = "YES" ]
```

```
then
    mailx -s "${ORACLE_SID} : MAXEXTENTS reached" $NOTIFY_LIST <<EOF
      MAXEXTENTS has been reached for a segment.
      Please run willfail_maxextents.sql in $ORACLE_SID for more details.
EOF
   exit 1
fi

# check 2) Check for "Unable to Allocate Next Extent"
sqlplus -s <<EOF >$LOGFIL 2>/dev/null
$USR_ID/$USR_PASS
    SET PAGES 0
    SELECT DISTINCT 'YES' FROM dba_segments ds
     WHERE next_extent >
       (SELECT MAX(bytes) FROM dba_free_space
         WHERE tablespace_name = ds.tablespace_name);
EOF
grep -i '^ORA-' $LOGFIL >/dev/null
if [ $? -eq 0 ]
then
   mailx -s "${ORACLE_SID} : Script failed" $NOTIFY_LIST <<EOF
      Monitoring script $0 failed.
      Please check $LOGFIL for more details.
EOF
   exit 1
fi

POSSIBLE_NEXTEXT_FAIL=`awk '{ print $1 }' $LOGFIL`
if [ "$POSSIBLE_NEXTEXT_FAIL" = "YES" ]
then
    mailx -s "${ORACLE_SID} : Impending next extent failure" $NOTIFY_LIST <<EOF
      Next extent allocation will fail for a segment.
      Please run willfail_nextextent.sql in $ORACLE_SID for more details.
EOF
   exit 1
fi

# other checks, as necessary
echo "Successful completion of $0 " `date`
```

Now, the preceding script may be invoked via *cron* from an administrative user-account, so that the Oracle user-name and password are not visible to non-administrative users. Also, the output from the script needs to be redirected (appended via >>) to a log-file, which can be scanned on a daily basis for errors from the execution of this shell-script. This log-file is a permanent one (storing results of multiple runs) and is different from the temporary log-file specified via $LOGFIL (which stores results of only the current run).

Note that the preceding script template only checks for two specific failure scenarios: impending failure due to MAXEXTENTS being reached or nearly reached (five more extents to go) and inability to allocate the next extent due to lack of adequate free-space in the tablespace. These two failure scenarios are provided as an example for checking potentially disruptive events. You will need to add all possible disruptive events specific to your environment prior to using this script. Following are some additional failure scenarios that need to be checked. The check for each scenario is provided as a separate script to allow them to be run independently, as well as be called from the preceding shell-script (in fact, the preceding shell-script makes references to the names of the following SQL scripts in the alerts [pages] sent to the administrative personnel). The names are something I use as a handy reference for these scripts (they can be named just about anything). Prior to your calling these scripts from the preceding shell script, they may have to be changed to return a single flag (such as 'YES') rather than the multiple columns they currently retrieve. The scripts that follow are ones that I use most frequently at various client sites. Some of them have been originally written by me. Some have been adapted from the source-code for the DBA_* and *v$* views in *SQL.BSQ* and *catalog.sql*. Yet others have been collected over the years from various Oracle and third-party books, magazines, articles, white-papers, and so on.

- MAXEXTENTS being reached (*willfail_maxextents.sql*)

```
COLUMN segment_name FORMAT a30
SELECT owner, segment_name, segment_type, extents
      ,max_extents, tablespace_name
  FROM dba_segments
 WHERE extents >= (max_extents-5);
```

- Unable to allocate next extent (*willfail_nextextent.sql*)

```
COLUMN segment_name FORMAT a30
SELECT owner, tablespace_name, segment_name, next_extent
  FROM dba_segments ds
 WHERE next_extent > (SELECT MAX(bytes)
                        FROM dba_free_space
                       WHERE tablespace_name = ds.tablespace_name);
```

- Lack of space in the temporary tablespace (*willfail_tempextent.sql*). This script needs to have the name of the temporary tablespace hard-coded. You could alternatively check the TEMPORARY column to find whether any of the tablespaces are explicitly marked as temporary to avoid the hard-coding. However, in case you do not explicitly mark a tablespace as temporary, that strategy will fail. For this reason, here I'm playing it safe and requesting you to include the temporary tablespace name in the script itself.

```
SELECT 'Inadequate space in temporary tablespace to allocate INITIAL/NEXT'
  FROM dba_tablespaces dt, (SELECT MAX(bytes) max_size, tablespace_name
                             FROM dba_free_space
                            WHERE tablespace_name = 'TEMP'
                            GROUP BY tablespace_name) fs
 WHERE dt.tablespace_name = fs.tablespace_name
   AND (dt.initial_extent > fs.max_size OR dt.next_extent > fs.max_size);
```

- Detect locking problems and deadlocks (*lock_problem.sql*). In some Oracle versions, you may have problems querying DBA_WAITERS and DBA_BLOCKERS directly. Chapter 11 discusses some workarounds.

```
SELECT * FROM dba_waiters;
```

or

```
SELECT * FROM dba_blockers;
```

- Supplementary script to check current locks in the database (*what_locks.sql*):

```
SELECT SUBSTR(v$lock.sid,1,4) "SID",
  SUBSTR(username, 1, 12) "UserName",
  SUBSTR(object_name, 1, 25) "ObjectName",
  v$lock.type "LockType",
  DECODE(RTRIM(SUBSTR(lmode,1,4)),
         '2', 'Row-S (SS)', '3', 'Row-X (SX)',
         '4', 'Share',      '5', 'S/Row-X (SSX)',
         '6', 'Exclusive',  'Other' ) "LockMode",
  SUBSTR(v$session.program, 1, 25) "ProgramName"
  FROM v$lock, sys.dba_objects, v$session
 WHERE (object_id = v$lock.id1
   AND v$lock.sid = v$session.sid
   AND username IS NOT NULL
   AND username NOT IN ('SYS', 'SYSTEM')
   AND serial# != 1);
```

Other Useful Scripts

Following are some other scripts that provide useful information on the functioning of the database. They draw upon our discussions in the earlier chapters.

- Find total allocated size for each tablespace/data-file (*find_alloc_space.sql*).

```
SELECT tablespace_name "Tablespace Name",
       file_name "DataFile Name",
```

```
       SUM(bytes)/1024/1024 "Allocated Space (MB)"
   FROM dba_data_files
 GROUP BY tablespace_name, file_name;
```

- Find current free-space in all tablespaces (*find_free_space.sql*).

```
SELECT tablespace_name "Tablespace Name",
       SUM(bytes)/1024/1024 "Free Space (MB)",
       MAX(bytes)/1024/1024 "Largest chunk (MB)"
  FROM dba_free_space
 GROUP BY tablespace_name;
```

- Find current sessions logged on (*find_sessions.sql*). When run over a period of time, this script provides a good feel for the overall database activity occurring at various times. This may be used in conjunction with *find_curr_sql.sql* (listed next) to drill down on the SQL statements actually being executed by an ACTIVE session.

```
SELECT username, osuser, server, status, count(*)
  FROM v$session
 WHERE username IS NOT NULL
   AND username NOT IN ('SYS', 'SYSTEM')
 GROUP BY username, osuser, server, status;
```

- Find the SQL statements being executed by a particular session (*find_curr_sql.sql*).

```
SELECT sql_text FROM v$sqltext_with_newlines
 WHERE (hash_value, address) IN
  (SELECT sql_hash_value, sql_address FROM v$session
    WHERE username = UPPER('&Oracle_username'))
  ORDER by address, piece;
```

- Detect badly written SQL preventing sharing of SQL statements in the library cache (*SQL_high_loads.sql*).

```
SELECT sql_text, loaded_versions, version_count, sharable_mem
  FROM v$sqlarea
 WHERE loaded_versions > 5
 ORDER by sharable_mem;
```

- Detect high SQL statement parses occurring in the database (*find_parses.sql*). If the value here continuously increases, especially during peak-hours, at a fast rate (say more than ten per second), then it may be indicative of a SQL problem in the library cache.

```
SELECT name, value FROM v$sysstat
 WHERE name LIKE 'parse count%';
```

- Find which process is using which rollback segment (*find_which_rbs.sql*).

```
COLUMN "Oracle UserName" FORMAT a15
COLUMN "RBS Name" FORMAT a15
SELECT r.name "RBS Name", p.spid, l.sid "ORACLE PID",
       s.username "Oracle UserName"
  FROM v$lock l, v$process p, v$rollname r, v$session s
 WHERE s.sid = l.sid AND l.sid = p.pid(+)
   AND r.usn = TRUNC(l.id1(+)/65536)
   AND l.type(+) = 'TX' AND l.lmode(+) = 6
 ORDER BY r.name;
```

- Map of the contents of a tablespace (*tlbspc_map.sql*, original source [to the best of my knowledge]: *DBA Handbook* by Kevin Loney, Oracle Press/Osborne/McGraw Hill). Given the name of a (highly used) tablespace, this script prints out the map indicating used-space, free-space, and fragmentation within the tablespace. A sample output of this script is provided in Chapter 12.

```
SET LINES 132 PAGES 1000
COLUMN "Fil_ID" FORMAT 999 HEADING "Fil|ID"
COLUMN "Fil" FORMAT A55 HEADING "Fil-name"
COLUMN "Segment" FORMAT A55
COLUMN "Start blk" FORMAT 999999 HEADING "Strt|blk"
COLUMN "# blocks" FORMAT 999,999 HEADING "#|blks"
SELECT d.file_id "Fil_ID", d.file_name "Fil", segment_type || ' ' ||
       owner || '.' || segment_name "Segment",
       e.block_id "Start blk", e.blocks "# blocks"
  FROM dba_extents e, dba_data_files d
 WHERE e.tablespace_name = UPPER('&&tblspc_name')
   AND d.tablespace_name = e.tablespace_name
   AND d.file_id = e.file_id
UNION
SELECT s.file_id "Fil_ID", d.file_name "Fil", 'Free chunk' "Segment",
       s.block_id "Start blk", s.blocks "# blocks"
  FROM  dba_free_space s, dba_data_files d
 WHERE s.tablespace_name = UPPER('&&tblspc_name')
   AND d.tablespace_name = s.tablespace_name
   AND d.file_id = s.file_id
 ORDER BY 1, 4, 5;
```

- Current waits being encountered by all sessions (*find_sess_waits.sql*). If necessary, you can filter out certain harmless waits (normally) such as "SQL*Net message from client," "SQL*Net message to client," and so forth.

```
COLUMN event FORMAT a25
SELECT event,
```

```
       SUM(DECODE(wait_time, 0, 1, 0)) "Currently Waiting",
       COUNT(*) "Total Waits"
  FROM v$session_wait
 GROUP BY event
 ORDER BY 3;
```

- Current waits being encountered by a specific session (*find_user_waits.sql*).

```
COLUMN event FORMAT a25
SELECT event,
       SUM(DECODE(wait_time, 0, 1, 0)) "Currently Waiting",
       COUNT(*) "Total Waits"
  FROM v$session_wait
 WHERE sid IN (SELECT sid FROM v$session
               WHERE username = '&OracleUsrName'
                 AND osuser = '&OSUsrName')
 GROUP BY event
 ORDER BY 3;
```

- Waits encountered so far in the database (*find_db_waits.sql*).

```
SELECT event, total_waits FROM v$system_event
 ORDER BY 2;
```

- Monitor temporary segment usage (*monitor_sorts.sql*).

```
SELECT tablespace_name, added_extents, free_extents
  FROM v$sort_segment;
```

- Detect waits for rollback segment header blocks.

```
SELECT class, count FROM v$waitstat
 WHERE class IN ('undo header', 'system undo header');
```

- Track segment-growth in relevant schemas by examining the number of extents they have allocated. This script should be run daily. Examining the results over a period of time will give good insight into segment growth patterns and appropriate proactive action can be taken prior to the segments facing growth problems (such as running out of free space in the tablespace or reaching MAXEXTENTS).

```
SET LINESIZE 132
COLUMN owner FORMAT a15
COLUMN segment_name FORMAT a30
COLUMN segment_type FORMAT a5 HEADING "Type"
SELECT owner, segment_name, segment_type,
       initial_extent/1024 "Initial (KB)",
       next_extent/1024 "Next (KB)", extents "# extents"
  FROM dba_segments
```

```
WHERE segment_type IN ('TABLE', 'INDEX')
  AND owner IN ('relevant-schema1', 'relevant-schema2')
ORDER BY owner, segment_type, extents DESC;
```

- Acquire inter-table relationship information (somewhat of an ERD of the physical database model). These scripts assume that all referential integrity is declared within the database.
  - Find all parent tables for a given table. Run this script as the owner of the tables. If not the owner, use ALL_CONSTRAINTS or DBA_CONSTRAINTS views, instead of USER_CONSTRAINTS.

```
SELECT prnt.table_name "Parent tables"
  FROM user_constraints prnt, user_constraints chld
 WHERE chld.table_name = UPPER('&child_tbl_nm')
   AND prnt.constraint_type = 'P'
   AND chld.r_constraint_name = prnt.constraint_name;
```

  - Find all child tables for a given table.

```
SELECT table_name "Child tables" FROM user_constraints
 WHERE r_constraint_name IN
    (SELECT constraint_name
       FROM user_constraints
      WHERE table_name = UPPER('&parent_tab_nm')
        AND constraint_type = 'P');
```

- Delete all core-dumps and trace-files older than 14 days via *cron*. Note that the commands that follow do not archive the files prior to removing them. If you need to save the old trace-files to tape, you can do so by adding the *tar* or *cpio* commands here or in a separate script that can be called via *cron*.

```
# cron entries in the "oracle" user-account
# Remove all old core-dumps for PT05 database
0 3 * * *   /usr/bin/find /opt/app/oracle/admin/PT05/cdump -name core\?
-mtime +14 -exec rm -f {} \;
# Remove all old background dumps for PT05 database
0 3 * * *   /usr/bin/find /opt/app/oracle/admin/PT05/bdump -name \*.trc
-mtime +14 -exec rm -f {} \;
# Remove all old user dumps for PT05 database
0 3 * * *   /usr/bin/find /opt/app/oracle/admin/PT05/udump -name \*.trc
-mtime +14 -exec rm -f {} \;
# if necessary, other files (such as audit-files) can be added here
```

- Trim the *alert-log* and *listener-log* files, leaving just the 1,000 most recent lines within the files. This is to control growth of these files (in particular, the *listener-log* can grow very fast in an environment with a large number of database connections, in which case this script can be broken up to trim the *alert-log* and *listener-log* separately and the script to trim the *listener-log* can be run more frequently). Note that the older alert-log is not being archived to tape prior to being trimmed. If the database against which you are deploying this script is a production database, you should add the commands to archive the alert-log prior to trimming it.

```
#!/bin/ksh
# Functionality:        To trim alert-log and listener-log
#

echo "start time `date`" >
/opt/app/oracle/admin/PT05/admin_logs/trim_logs.lst

exec 3< /var/opt/oracle/oratab    #open oratab as file-descriptor 3

while read -r -u3 LINE
do
    case $LINE in
        \#*)            ;;                #Ignore comments in oratab
        *)
            ORACLE_SID=$(print $LINE | awk -F: '{print $1}' -)
            ORACLE_HOME=$(print $LINE | awk -F: '{print $2}' -)

         ALERTLOG=\
/opt/app/oracle/admin/$ORACLE_SID/bdump/alert_$ORACLE_SID.log
          tail -1000 $ALERTLOG > /tmp/$ORACLE_SID.log
        # if necessary, archive $ALERTLOG, prior to overwriting
          cp /tmp/$ORACLE_SID.log $ALERTLOG
          rm /tmp/$ORACLE_SID.log
        ;;
    esac
done

LISTENERLOG=$ORACLE_HOME/network/log/listener.log
if [[ -f $LISTENERLOG ]]; then
    tail -1000 $LISTENERLOG > /tmp/listener.log
    # archive $LISTENERLOG if necessary, prior to being overwritten
    cp /tmp/listener.log $LISTENERLOG
    rm /tmp/listener.log
fi
```

- Compress all archived logs except the most current. Here, the older archived logs are being transferred to tape prior to being removed. If necessary, you can modify this script to avoid removing them (if your ARCHIVE_LOG_DEST directory is large enough to accommodate the archived logs). Then a *cron* entry can be set up to remove them once every two days or so (after they have been backed up). You can also change the script to avoid compressing the older archived logs but just copy them directly to tape. Here, it is assumed that no ARCH slaves are configured. However, if multiple ARCH I/O slaves are configured (via the initialization parameter ARCH_IO_SLAVES available from Oracle8 onward), then compress all the archived logs, except the N+1 most current (where, N is equivalent to the number of ARCH I/O slaves configured). This script can be called via *cron* every couple of hours or so.

```
echo "`date` Compressing older archived logs" >
/opt/app/oracle/admin/PT05/admin_logs/compress_archs.lst

# check to see whether process is running already
if [ -f /opt/app/oracle/admin/PT05/arch/proc_currently_running* ]; then
   exit
fi

/bin/touch /opt/app/oracle/admin/PT05/arch/proc_currently_running

# if your ARCH file-names are different, then change below command to
# reflect proper names. Also, if multiple ARCH I/O slaves are configured,
# then change "head -1" to "head -[N+1]", where [N+1] is number of ARCH
# slaves plus one.
/bin/compress -f `ls -t /opt/app/oracle/admin/PT05/arch/*.arch | grep -v
\`ls -t /opt/app/oracle/admin/PT05/arch/*.arch | head -1\``

# ensure that your tape-device name is set properly
tar cvf /dev/rmt0 /opt/app/oracle/admin/PT05/arch/*Z

# Next step is optional. If your ARCHIVE_LOG_DEST is large
# enough to accommodate at least 2 days worth of archived logs,
# then don't do this. Instead, set up a cron job to remove all
# compressed archived logs older than 2 days. Keeping required
# archived logs on disk will enhance recovery time (if recovery is required).
rm -f /opt/app/oracle/admin/PT05/arch/*Z

rm /opt/app/oracle/admin/PT05/arch/proc_currently_running*
```

- Script to run an export off a named-pipe and simultaneously compress the export dump-file. This script can be extremely useful when the data being exported is large and disk-space is scarce. This script can be modified to directly write the compressed dump-file to tape (if there is not sufficient disk-space to even accommodate the compressed dump-file). Note that this export script uses a parameter (*.par*) file defining all the export options to be utilized (do not define the LOG option; this is defined separately along with the EXP command). The script pages the DBAs if errors are encountered during the export.

```
#!/bin/ksh
# Functionality : to export the data via a named-pipe and
#                 compress the resultant dump-file.

EXPDIR=/opt/app/oracle/admin/PT05/backs
DUMPFILE=Full_PT05.dmp
LOGDIR=/opt/app/oracle/admin/PT05/admin_logs
LOGFILE=${LOGDIR}/Full_PT05.log
EXPLOG=${EXPDIR}/Full_PT05.log
PARAMFILE=${EXPDIR}/Full_PT05.par
PAGEDBA_FILE=/tmp/pagefile
EXITSTATCODE=0
NOTIFY_LIST=oncall_dba_pager@att.net

# preserve existing dump-files (rather than overwriting them)
if [ -f ${EXPDIR}/${DUMPFILE}.Z ]; then
   mv -f ${EXPDIR}/${DUMPFILE}.Z ${EXPDIR}/${DUMPFILE}.old.Z
fi

# create a named pipe and begin the compress
/sbin/mknod ${EXPDIR}/${DUMPFILE} p
compress < ${EXPDIR}/${DUMPFILE} > ${EXPDIR}/${DUMPFILE}.Z &

# start the export
cd $EXPDIR
echo "Export/compress started at `date`" > $PAGEDBA_FILE > $LOGFILE
$ORACLE_HOME/bin/exp log=$EXPLOG parfile=$PARAMFILE

# check for errors during the export
if egrep 'ORA-|EXP-' ${EXPLOG}   >> $PAGEDBA_FILE >> $LOGFILE
then
   EXITSTATCODE=1
   echo "Export failed at `date`"     >> $PAGEDBA_FILE >> $LOGFILE
fi
echo "============================" >> $PAGEDBA_FILE >> $LOGFILE

tail ${EXPLOG} >> $PAGEDBA_FILE
ls -lt ${EXPDIR}/${DUMPFILE}*   >> $PAGEDBA_FILE >> $LOGFILE
echo "Export/compress ended at `date`" >> $PAGEDBA_FILE >> $LOGFILE

# remove the named pipe
```

```
rm -f ${EXPDIR}/${DUMPFILE}
ls -lt ${EXPDIR}/${DUMPILE}*   >> $PAGEDBA_FILE >> $LOGFILE

mailx -s "Full export of PT05" $NOTIFY_LIST < $PAGEDBA_FILE
exit $EXITSTATCODE
```

- Script to run an import off a compressed dump-file via a named-pipe. This script is a companion script of the previous one (where the export and compress were done via a named pipe). Note that this import script uses a parameter (*.par*) file defining all the import options to be utilized (do not define the LOG option; this is defined separately along with the IMP command). The script pages the DBAs if errors are encountered during the import.

```
#!/bin/ksh
# Functionality : to import data off a compressed dump-file
#                 via a named-pipe.

IMPDIR=/opt/app/oracle/admin/PT05/backs
DUMPFILE=Full_PT05.dmp
LOGDIR=/opt/app/oracle/admin/PT05/admin_logs
LOGFILE=${LOGDIR}/Full_PT05.log
IMPLOG=${IMPDIR}/Full_PT05.log
PARAMFILE=${IMPDIR}/Full_PT05.par
PAGEDBA_FILE=/tmp/pagefile
EXITSTATCODE=0
NOTIFY_LIST=oncall_dba_pager@att.net

# create the named pipe and start the uncompress of the compressed
# dump-file
/sbin/mknod ${IMPDIR}/${DUMPFILE} p
uncompress < ${IMPDIR}/${DUMPFILE}.Z > ${IMPDIR}/${DUMPFILE} &

# start the import
echo "Uncompress/import started at `date`" > $PAGEDBA_FILE > $LOGFILE
cd $IMPDIR
$ORACLE_HOME/bin/imp log=$IMPLOG parfile=$PARAMFILE

# check for errors during the import
if egrep 'ORA-|IMP-' ${IMPLOG}   >> $PAGEDBA_FILE >> $LOGFILE
then
   EXITSTATCODE=1
   echo "Import failed at `date`"     >> $PAGEDBA_FILE >> $LOGFILE
fi
echo "============================" >> $PAGEDBA_FILE >> $LOGFILE
```

```
tail ${IMPLOG} >> $PAGEDBA_FILE
ls -lt ${IMPDIR}/${DUMPFILE}*    >> $PAGEDBA_FILE >> $LOGFILE
echo "Uncompress/import ended at `date`" >> $PAGEDBA_FILE >> $LOGFILE

# remove the named pipe
rm -f ${IMPDIR}/${DUMPFILE}
ls -lt ${IMPDIR}/${DUMPILE}*    >> $PAGEDBA_FILE >> $LOGFILE

mailx -s "Import of PT05" $NOTIFY_LIST < $PAGEDBA_FILE
exit $EXITSTATCODE
```

Be familiar with techniques for application failover when calling PL/SQL

Besides checking for error-conditions and possible service disruptions, you also need application failover capabilities built into all mission-critical programs. Chapters 15 to 18 describe database failover and in Chapter 6, a piece of pseudo-code illustrates failover after checking for certain Oracle errors at runtime (such as ORA-1092 and ORA-3113). Such a strategy can be directly applied when using 3GLs such as Pro*C and C/OCI. However, this may be challenging to achieve in 4GL scenarios, such as in PL/SQL. In PL/SQL, direct reconnection cannot be obtained within a code block. Therefore, you need to plug-in the failover code within the external calling routines (that call the code block). Sample code for achieving this is provided in this chapter. Here, a PL/SQL script is called via a Korn shell-script with the failover code embedded within the shell-script. This strategy or a suitable variation needs to be adopted in conjunction with other application failover features (via SQL*Net/Net8, TAF, and so on) to allow seamless reconnection to the standby/parallel database/instance when the current connection is aborted (and retrying the current connection does not result in success).

```
#!/bin/ksh
# Script : Call_SQL.ksh
# Functionality : Sample script to call PL/SQL code-block and illustrate failover
# Author : Venkat S. Devraj
# Modification history
# 07/1997              VSD              Written
#

if [ $# -ne 5 ]
then
   echo "Usage: $0 <script_name> <username> <password> <primary_db> <stndby_db>"
   echo "Where: script_name is the name of the PLSQL script to run"
   echo "Where: username is the Oracle user-id"
   echo "Where: password is the Oracle password"
```

```
   echo "Where: primary_db is the connect-string for the primary database"
   echo "Where: stndby_db is the connect-string for the standby database"
   exit 1
fi

PLSCRIPT=$1
USR=$2
PASSWD=$3
PRIM_DB=$4
STND_DB=$5

echo "Start date and time: " date

# connect to primary db to run script
sqlplus -s $USR/$PASSWD@PRIM_DB @$PLSCRIPT
RETVAL=$?
echo "Exit-code from primary database" $RETVAL

# check exit-code returned from script
if  [ $RETVAL -eq -1033 ] || [ $RETVAL -eq -1034 ] || [ $RETVAL -eq -1089 ] ||
    [ $RETVAL -eq -9352 ]
then
     echo "Failure to connect to the primary database " $PRIM_DB
     echo "Now trying to connect to standby" $STND_DB
     sqlplus -s $USR/$PASSWD@STND_DB @$PLSCRIPT
     RETVAL=$?
     echo "Exit-code from secondary database " $RETVAL
     if  [ $RETVAL -eq -1033 ] || [ $RETVAL -eq -1034 ] || [ $RETVAL -eq -1089 ] ||
          [ $RETVAL -eq -9352 ]
     then
        echo "Cannot connect to either primary or secondary database. Aborting"
        exit $RETVAL
     elif  [ $RETVAL -eq -1092 ] || [ $RETVAL -eq -3113 ] || [ $RETVAL -eq -3114 ]
     then
      echo "Script was abruptly terminated from secondary database" $RETVAL
       exit $RETVAL
     fi

elif  [ $RETVAL -eq -1092 ] || [ $RETVAL -eq -3113 ] || [ $RETVAL -eq -3114 ]
then
   echo "Script aborted due to abrupt session termination in primary"
   echo "Now trying to connect to standby (to rerun script) " $STND_DB
   sqlplus -s $USR/$PASSWD@STND_DB @$PLSCRIPT
   RETVAL=$?
   echo "Exit-code from secondary database " $RETVAL
   if  [ $RETVAL -eq -1033 ] || [ $RETVAL -eq -1034 ] || [ $RETVAL -eq -1089 ] ||
      [ $RETVAL -eq -9352 ]
   then
     echo "Cannot connect to secondary database. Aborting"
     exit $RETVAL
   elif  [ $RETVAL -eq -1092 ] || [ $RETVAL -eq -3113 ] || [ $RETVAL -eq -3114 ]
```

```
   then
    echo "Script was abruptly terminated from secondary database too" $RETVAL
    exit $RETVAL
   elif [ $RETVAL -ne 0 ]
   then
     echo "Some other error in script" $RETVAL
     exit $RETVAL
   fi

elif [$RETVAL -ne 0 ]
   echo "Some other error in script" $RETVAL
   exit $RETVAL
fi

# No errors.
# Successful completion of script either in primary or secondary db
echo "End date and time: " `date`
```

Now the following sample PL/SQL code may be used with the preceding shell-script:

```
$ cat upd_sal.sql
/* Name : upd_sal.sql
** Functionality : Update salary, give everyone a raise!
** History :
** 06/99Written  VSD
**
*/
SET SERVEROUTPUT ON
SPOOL upd_sal.log
WHENEVER SQLERROR EXIT SQL.SQLCODE ROLLBACK
WHENEVER OSERROR EXIT SQL.OSCODE ROLLBACK

BEGIN
  DBMS_OUTPUT.PUT_LINE('Start time : ' || TO_CHAR(SYSDATE, 'mm/dd/yyyy hh24:mi:ss');
  UPDATE empl SET sal = sal * 1.1;
  COMMIT;
  DBMS_OUTPUT.PUT_LINE('End time : ' || TO_CHAR(SYSDATE, 'mm/dd/yyyy hh24:mi:ss');
EXCEPTION
  WHEN OTHERS THEN
    DBMS_OUTPUT.PUT_LINE('Error encountered : ' || SQLCODE || ' : ' ||
                         SQLERRM);
    RETURN SQLCODE;
END;
/
SPOOL OFF
EXIT
```

Now the *Call_SQL.ksh* script can be invoked as follows:

```
$ Call_SQL.ksh  upd_sal.sql  HRD_User  HRD_UsrPasswd  Prim_DB  Stnd_DB
```

Summary

This chapter provided some critical SQL scripts to detect current or impending service disruptions. Common causes of disruption, such as lack of space or locking conflicts, are monitored. The chapter also provided a sample template to use these SQL scripts within a shell-script that can be run via a scheduler at pre-determined intervals. Finally, a shell script to illustrate failover in a PL/SQL environment was provided. These scripts and strategies should help you build your own 24×7 toolkit and, if you already have one, should help you reinforce your arsenal.

The next chapter looks at new high-availability features in Oracle8*i*.

PART VIII

New Features

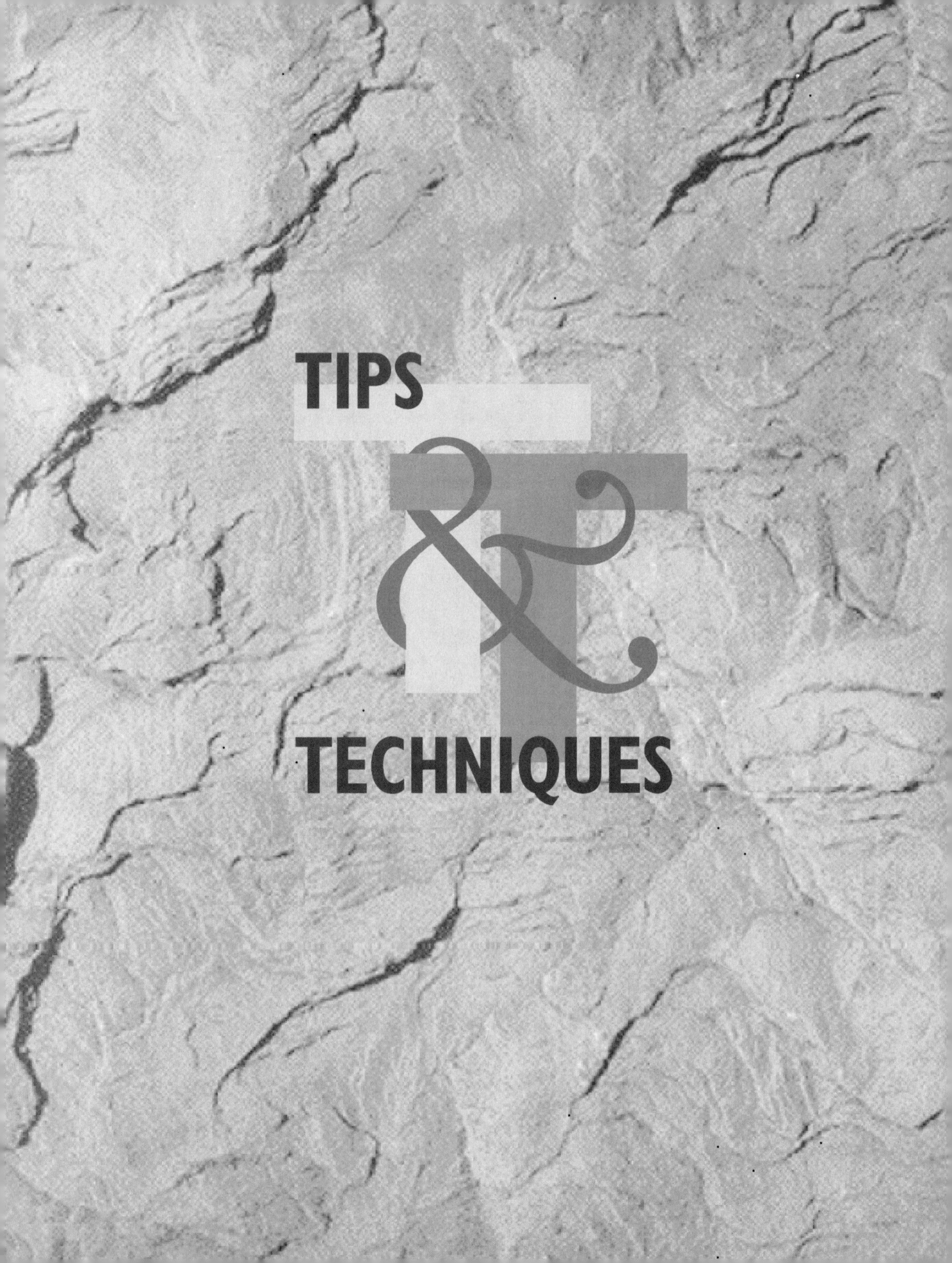
TIPS
&
TECHNIQUES

CHAPTER 20

New HA Features in Oracle8*i*

The latest version of the Oracle Server—Oracle8*i*—has introduced enhancements to the core kernel in various areas, including high availability (HA). Having been heavily touted as the database for e-business, HA occupies center-stage in the Oracle8*i* scheme of things. This concluding chapter lists some of the newer HA-oriented features. Each of the features listed here addresses issues already raised and discussed in the previous chapters. Accordingly, here I only focus on the specific features themselves, rather than the underlying concepts. Moreover, the concepts are covered in-depth in the Oracle8*i* documentation set. Hence, the list here is intended to be a quick new-feature reference (so that you know what is available in Oracle8*i*, prior to attempting to acquire more information on it).

Certain HA-oriented features in Oracle8*i*, such as OPS Cache Fusion; automated standby databases allowing managed recovery; and enhancements in Advanced Replication, Transparent Application Failover (TAF), and such have been covered in earlier chapters. For this reason, I do not list them here. Also note that certain features listed here require the Oracle8*i* Enterprise Edition. Check your configuration and license details regarding which edition you have, prior to deciding to use any of these features.

This chapter offers the following tips and techniques:

- consider transportable tablespaces for quick movement of data subsets
- consider locally managed tablespaces to prevent fragmentation
- be familiar with new change management features
- create, rebuild, and defragment indexes online
- be familiar with non-partitioned table reorganization features
- drop columns, when necessary, with greater ease
- be aware of partitioning enhancements that promote uptime
- be familiar with new techniques to repair corruption
- utilize methods to facilitate and expedite RMAN backups
- control and expedite recovery time
- use newer listener failover and load-balancing services
- be familiar with LogMiner functionality
- be aware of an option to eliminate "fat" os overhead

Maintenance-Oriented Features

Following are some of the facilities to make various database management tasks such as migrations, troubleshooting, and segment-rebuilds faster and easier with little or no downtime.

Consider transportable tablespaces for quick movement of data subsets

The transportable tablespace feature allows you to move/copy a subset of an Oracle database from one Oracle database to another. Transportable tablespaces aid in any situations requiring bulk data to be transferred such as during the following scenarios:

- Archival of pertinent data prior to purging it without significant impact to the source database
- Migration of the source data from an OLTP database to a reporting database or transfer of data from operational data sources (ODSs) to the data-warehouse
- Transfer of production data to a test platform
- Copying data from the enterprise data-warehouse to temporary staging databases for massaging/converting data prior to loading down-stream data-marts

Moving data via transportable tablespaces is much faster than conventional unload/load utilities, such as export/import and SQL*Loader. The reason for this is that, transporting a tablespace only requires the datafiles to be copied across from the source to the target database and integrating meta-data pertaining to the tablespace structure. Index data can also be copied/moved without them having to be rebuilt.

When a tablespace is to be transported, it is placed in read-only mode to ensure that a consistent image of the data is captured. Then only specific dictionary information is exported from the source data-dictionary. Next, the tablespace data-files are copied across to the target database via any OS utilities/commands (*cp, ftp,* and so on). Then the meta-data describing the tablespace is imported into the target database. This is very fast because the size of the import is miniscule. Optionally, the transferred tablespace can then be placed in read/write mode. The actual implementation includes using the *exp/imp* utilities. The *exp* utility has a new option, TRANSPORT_TABLESPACE, whereas *imp* has three new options,

TRANSPORT_TABLESPACE (mandatory), DATAFILES (mandatory), and TTS_OWNERS (optional), to support this feature.

In the current release, you can transport tablespaces only between Oracle databases that use the same data block size and character set. Also, the source and target platforms should be compatible and, if possible, from the same hardware vendor. Also, to prevent violation of functional and physical dependencies and referential integrity, another limitation allows only "self-contained" tablespaces to be transported. "Self-contained" means that there should be no references within the tablespace pointing to segments outside the tablespace. For example, if the tablespace set being transported comprises indexes whose corresponding tables are in different tablespaces, then the source tablespace set is not self-contained. The tablespace set you wish to copy must contain either all or none of the partitions of a partitioned table. The procedure DBMS_TTS.TRANSPORT_SET_CHECK can be used to determine whether or not the tablespaces in question are self-contained. All violations reported by this procedure can be seen within the TRANSPORT_SET_VIOLATIONS view (which will be empty when there are no violations). In order to determine which of the tablespaces in the current database have been transported, the PLUGGED_IN column in DBA_TABLESPACES can be checked.

Additionally, TSPITR can now be used with transportable tablespaces, thereby providing more flexibility over the TSPITR available in Oracle8.

Consider locally managed tablespaces to prevent fragmentation

With an aim of proactively preventing fragmentation, Oracle8*i* now provides two types of tablespaces:

- Dictionary-managed tablespaces, where extent management is done via the data-dictionary. This is the conventional and default tablespace type.
- Locally managed tablespaces, where extent management is done by the tablespace itself.

An important fact to keep in mind is, once a specific type is chosen, it cannot be altered. A locally managed tablespace manages its own extents via a bitmap in each data-file to keep track of the free/used data-blocks. Each bit in the bitmap corresponds to one or more blocks. When an extent is allocated or freed, Oracle changes the bitmap values to reflect the new block-status. No rollback information is generated in this case, because the data-dictionary tables are not typically updated (that is, no inserts or updates are made to SYS.UET$, SYS.FET$, and so on). This helps in reducing recursive SQL. However, during certain occasions, certain data-dictionary information does have to be changed, such as when it is required to update tablespace quota information pertaining to various database users. Locally managed tablespaces also do automatic tracking of adjacent free-space, eliminating the need to coalesce free extents.

The sizes of extents that are managed locally can be determined automatically by Oracle8*i*. Alternatively, all extents can have the same size (that is, uniform extents). Allowing all extents to have the same size eliminates bubble fragments, since all new extents can easily fit into the existing bubbles. It's only when you have diverse extent sizes that unusable bubbles get created, resulting in space wastage. The extent-management clause is specified as part of the segment CREATE commands via the EXTENT MANAGEMENT LOCAL [AUTOALLOCATE | UNIFORM] clause. AUTOALLOCATE implies that the size of the initial extent is explicitly specified, and Oracle determines the optimal size of additional extents, with a minimum extent-size of 64KB. This is the default for permanent tablespaces. With UNIFORM, you can specify a custom extent-size or use the default size, which is 1MB. Temporary tablespaces that manage their extents locally can only use this type of allocation.

Storage parameters such as DEFAULT STORAGE, NEXT, PCTINCREASE, MINEXTENTS, and MAXEXTENTS are not valid for extents in locally managed tablespaces. Even the SYSTEM tablespace can be locally managed. However, rollback segments for such a database must also be created in UNIFORM locally managed tablespaces. The new columns EXTENT_MANAGEMENT (domain: Local or Dictionary) and ALLOCATION_TYPE have been added to the DBA_TABLESPACES view to support this feature.

Be familiar with new change management features

Oracle8*i* provides two new features that prevent changing of a SQL statement execution-plan during specific scenarios, such as after a version upgrade or new index builds. First, the capability to store existing execution-plans and insulate an application from upgrades is provided. A second feature, *extensible optimization,* allows DBAs and developers to control the three main components that cost-based optimization uses to select an execution plan: statistics, selectivity, and cost evaluation.

Plans can remain consistent across re-issue of ANALYZE COMPUTE/ESTIMATE STATISTICS commands, new indexes, newer Oracle releases, initialization parameter changes, and so on. This is known as *plan stability.* Plan stability preserves execution plans via specific stored outlines. A stored outline can be created for one or more SQL statements. The optimizer can then generate corresponding execution-plans from these outlines. Outlines are maintained in the OL$ table, and explicit hints used are kept in the OL$HINTS table. Unless these are removed, the outlines remain and are used indefinitely. The execution-plans are retained in the cache and Oracle only re-creates them if they become invalid or if the cache is too small to hold all of them.

Stored outlines are automatically created if the initialization parameter CREATE_STORED_OUTLINES is enabled. When activated, outlines are created for all executed SQL statements. Stored outlines for specific statements can also be created via the new CREATE OUTLINE statement. Enabling the parameter USE_STORED_OUTLINES causes the stored outlines to be used during SQL statement compilation. Additionally, the OUTLN_PKG package is available for managing stored outlines. Once optimal execution-paths are derived for all application SQL, they can be guaranteed not to change. This fact allows application performance to be predictable across versions, without the need for any downtime to further tune the new version database with an intention of deriving more consistent performance.

Other Statistics-Related Enhancements

The process of CBO statistics collection has been enhanced. Statistics can be generated automatically as part of regular index-creation with very little overhead. The CREATE INDEX command supports a new COMPUTE_STATISTICS clause for this purpose. Also, statistics can now be collected in parallel mode. Statistics may be retrieved from the data-dictionary and stored in a user-defined table. This allows the statistics to be manually modified and re-inserted into the data-dictionary (since the data-dictionary tables should not be modified directly). This method allows the statistics to be copied across databases. Thus, application performance can be made predictable across development, test, and production databases due to the consistency of the transferable statistics.

Create, rebuild and defragment indexes online

In versions prior to Oracle8*i,* index creation or rebuilds placed a SHARE table-level lock on the corresponding table, preventing concurrent DML writes. This would cause application downtime. In the case of large tables, this downtime can run into several hours. Oracle8*i* supports the *online* creation or rebuilding of an index that works for both partitioned and non-partitioned B*Tree indexes, including index-organized tables (IOTs). Since the table is not locked in a conflicting mode, operations and queries can concurrently access the base table (while the index is being built). Oracle uses a journal-table to record changes made to the base table during the online build. Note, however, that DDL operations are not permitted during an online index build. The ONLINE keyword has been added to the CREATE/ALTER INDEX commands to implement this feature. Parallel DML (PDML) is not supported during online index builds. If you specify ONLINE and then issue parallel DML statements, an error is returned.

As discussed in Chapter 6, fragmentation is the bane of indexes in OLTP environments. Oracle8*i* provides two facilities to defragment an existing index:

online rebuilds and in-place coalesces. Via the online rebuild mechanism discussed previously, the index can be completely rebuilt to recover space and relocate it, if necessary. However, you don't have to rebuild it every time. If there is a high amount of internal fragmentation (within the index structure), you can use the COALESCE option. There are certain pros and cons to each approach. Evaluate these prior to choosing a specific approach:

- REBUILD can relocate an index to another tablespace, while COALESCE cannot.
- REBUILD requires higher amount of free disk-space, since it uses the existing index to build an entirely new tree and then shrinks the tree, if possible. Alternatively, COALESCE does not require higher disk space, because it operates within the same index. It basically coalesces blocks holding leaf-nodes within the same branch. In other words, it combines leaf-nodes blocks that have split in the past (during creation via PCTFREE or at run-time). It frees up leaf-node blocks for future use. For instance, if two leaf-node blocks are 40 percent and 60 percent full, respectively, then after the coalescing, one of the blocks is completely filled up, freeing up the second.

Be familiar with non-partitioned table reorganization features

A new MOVE clause in the ALTER TABLE command allows easy reorganization of a non-partitioned table by moving data into a new segment while keeping all views, privileges, and so forth defined on the table intact. Thus, the command may be used to relocate data of a non-partitioned table into a new segment, optionally in a different tablespace with different storage characteristics.

IOTs, which are prone to high fragmentation due to their unique structure, are prime candidates for using the MOVE clause. You can move IOTs with no overflow data-segment via the ONLINE option. As mentioned earlier, ONLINE allows concurrent DML writes on the index-organized table during the rebuild. Again, note that the current Oracle8*i* release does not support PDML during an online MOVE.

The introduction of logical ROWIDs for IOTs makes the rebuild possible. Logical ROWIDs contain the primary key of the referenced row, instead of a physical location within the database. This means that if a row is moved to a new location, the logical ROWID would still contain a valid reference to the row and would not need to be updated. To retain the speed of conventional ROWIDs, logical ROWIDs also contain a physical location hint, which can be used to optimize performance. If an index is created on a field other than the primary key (note that IOTs now support secondary indexes), Oracle8*i* will create a logical index using logical ROWIDs to reference the table rows.

Drop columns, when necessary, with greater ease

Previous versions of Oracle required DBAs to perform various downtime-involving acrobatics to change column-names. (There is an easier undocumented method I have seen, which involves changing data in certain data-dictionary tables owned by SYS. However, that is highly risky and does not warrant mention in a book on high-availability.) A new drop column capability allows the DBA to easily remove unused columns in the database with little or no downtime. Now it is no longer necessary to use utilities such as export/import. New syntax for the ALTER TABLE statement allows a column to be marked as unusable (via the SET UNUSED clause), without freeing up space in the table, or to be dropped from the table with the data deleted (via the DROP UNUSED clause).

Note that specifying the SET UNUSED clause does not actually remove the target columns from each row in the table (that is, it does not restore the disk space used by these columns). Therefore, the response time is faster than it would be if you execute the DROP UNUSED clause, which reclaims the extra disk space from unused columns in the table. Due to this being an ALTER TABLE command, the table would be locked for a specific duration (depending on whether SET UNUSED or DROP UNUSED is used).

Be aware of partitioning enhancements that promote uptime

The following partitioning enhancements have been introduced in Oracle8*i*:

Merging Partitions

With Oracle8, combining partitions is time-consuming. Since there is no explicit MERGE statement, either the DROP PARTITION or EXCHANGE PARTITION clauses need to be used to perform the merge. The first option involves using the export/import utilities. The second option consists of exchanging the partition with an intermediate regular table, dropping the exchanged partition and inserting the rows from the intermediate table into the partition with the next higher value of the partitioning key. These operations can impose high downtime since, during these operations, the involved partitions and their corresponding index partitions are unusable.

Oracle8*i* vastly simplifies the merge and makes it quicker by providing the new MERGE PARTITIONS clause to the ALTER TABLE command. This clause may be used against tables partitioned via the range partitioning method to merge two adjoining partitions into a single one.

Updateable Partition Keys

The CREATE/ALTER TABLE commands support another new clause, ENABLE ROW MOVEMENT, that allows row-migrations across partitions. This allows partition-keys to be updated, even though this may cause a row to move into a different partition. The default option (DISABLE ROW MOVEMENT) disables such row-movement. Any updates that would result in partition-migration are disallowed, with errors being returned to the user. The ENABLE ROW MOVEMENT option needs to be used with caution and after adequate analysis, since this could potentially result in high implicit I/O.

Composite Partitioning

Oracle8*i* introduces the hash and composite (hash/range) partitioning strategies. From an HA standpoint, composite partitioning provides the availability and manageability benefits of pure range partitioning, with the data distribution advantages of pure hash partitioning. Here, the user specifies ranges of values for the primary partitions of the segment, in addition to the number of hash sub-partitions. Sub-partitions can be added/dropped to maintain even distribution of data across all partitions. Rolling-window partitioning schemes can be easily maintained at the primary partition level, without any effect on sub-partitions.

Sub-partitions can be identified and stored in distinct tablespaces. Local indexing is available with both hash and composite partitioning. All existing SQL statements work with both new partitioning methods, and new/extended DDL statements are also provided.

Partitioning IOTs and Tables with LOBs

IOTs can now be partitioned. Also, partitioned IOTs can be bulk-loaded via SQL*Loader DIRECT path.

Additionally, tables that contain LOBs can now be partitioned. However, a partitioning key cannot comprise a LOB. The LOB data and LOB index segments of a LOB column are equi-partitioned with the base table. All LOB types including BFILEs are supported. Various operations such as ADD, DROP, EXCHANGE, IMPORT/EXPORT, LOAD, MODIFY, MOVE, SPLIT, and TRUNCATE work on partitioned tables with LOB columns, as well.

Troubleshooting Features

The following feature is oriented toward problem detection and troubleshooting.

Be familiar with new techniques to repair corruption

Many times, DBAs encountering corrupt blocks have to drop and re-create the object. Dropping and re-creating large segments can be extremely time-consuming and involves heavy downtime (unless some kind of failover strategy is utilized). Oracle8*i* gives an additional way to resolve block corruption with downtime being effectively controlled via DBMS_REPAIR. This is a new package that helps detection and repair of data-block corruption on segments.

DBMS_REPAIR provides a procedure called CHECK_OBJECT to check and report data-block corruption. In addition to detecting corruption, CHECK_OBJECT also identifies possible fixes that would occur if DBMS_REPAIR.FIX_CORRUPT_BLOCKS is subsequently run on the segment. This information is made available by populating a repair table, which must first be created via DBMS_REPAIR.ADMIN_TABLES. After DBMS_REPAIR.CHECK_OBJECT is run, the repair table may be queried to display corruption and repair-directives. Using this information, you can decide the best method to address and resolve the problems reported.

If the current corruption is likely to cause data-loss, all blocks prone to such loss are explicitly marked corrupt by DBMS_REPAIR.FIX_CORRUPT_BLOCKS. Then, DBMS_REPAIR.SKIP_CORRUPT_BLOCKS may be run to skip all blocks marked corrupt. This basically makes all unaffected portions of the segment accessible. Finally, DBMS_REPAIR.DUMP_ORPHAN_KEYS and DBMS_REPAIR.REBUILD_FREELISTS procedures can be run as a step toward restoring lost data. DBMS_REPAIR.DUMP_ORPHAN_KEYS reveals index entries that point to rows in corrupt data blocks. The index-key values and corresponding ROWIDs are inserted into an orphan key table. DBMS_REPAIR.REBUILD_FREELISTS can be used to reinitialize the corrupt segment's freelists. The data-blocks pertaining to the segment are scanned and verified, and all non-corrupt blocks are added to the master freelist. All corrupt blocks are ignored. Depending on the extent of corruption and the recovery options available, the lost rows in the afflicted segments have to be restored eventually.

Note that, currently, DBMS_REPAIR cannot be used to detect/repair corruption in data-blocks pertaining to clustered segments, LOBS, bitmap indexes, or function-based indexes.

Backup and Recovery-Oriented Features

The following tips are geared toward enhancing backup and recovery operations in an Oracle8*i* environment.

Utilize methods to facilitate and expedite RMAN backups

Recovery Manager, introduced in Oracle8, has been enhanced in Oracle8*i*. Following are the HA-oriented enhancements.

Proxy Copy

Proxy copy is an Oracle8*i* extension to basic media management API that allows the media manager to directly control backups and restores from disk to the backup media (typically tape). Third-party vendors can utilize the API to coordinate database backups and restores via RMAN. Proxy copy allows the backups/restores to be driven directly via the Oracle database management console (the administrative client PC, for example). This prevents the host system and network from being bogged down by backup/restore and reduces the impact on the database. When used with a media manager that supports proxy copy (such as *EMC Data Manager*), RMAN can be directed to perform database backups using proxy copy. In case your media manager does not currently support proxy copy, then RMAN can be made to either revert to conventional backups or error out. The *v$proxy_datafile* and *v$proxy_archivedlog* virtual views can be used to monitor backups taken with proxy copy.

Database Cloning

RMAN in Oracle8*i* allows an entire (production) database to be cloned via the DUPLICATE command using the database backups. By default, the DUPLICATE command creates the database copy using the most recent backups of the target database and then performs recovery to the most recent consistent point contained in the incremental and archived redo-log backups. This duplicated database can be given a different DBNAME or have the same DBNAME as the original one. Cloned databases can be utilized for failover or as a query-only database in a HA environment.

Duplexed Backup Sets

RMAN in Oracle8*i* allows redundant backup sets of data-files and archived logs to be created via duplexing. There are two related terms here—multiplexing and duplexing—and they are not to be confused with each other. *Multiplexing* means that the various file-types are interspersed with each other in a single backup set. *Duplexing,* on the other hand, means producing up to four exact copies of each backup set. Both can be consolidated to have multiple copies of multiplexed backup sets. The new SET DUPLEX command is used to specify how many copies of output files to create. The BACKUP_TAPE_IO_SLAVES initialization parameter must be enabled in order to create duplexed backup sets.

Control and expedite recovery time

The following new features allow you to have fine-grained control over recovery time.

Fast-Start Fault Recovery

Fast-Start fault recovery allows the Oracle Server to quickly recover from system faults and minimize the impact on users. It consists of multiple facets, which are explained below.

Fast-Start Checkpointing

This feature controls the time required by the roll-forward phase of recovery, by allowing the DBA to specify an upper limit on the number of I/O operations that Oracle will need to perform during roll-forward. Using this feature causes checkpoints to occur more often and posts DBWR to write out additional buffers during normal processing. This limits the number of dirty buffers in the buffer cache at any given point in time. During failure as well, the number of dirty buffers would be small, expediting roll-forward during recovery, allowing the database to be re-opened quicker. Statistics are collected and are available to the DBA through dynamic performance views to allow judicious balance between regular runtime performance and recovery speed.

A new dynamic parameter FAST_START_IO_TARGET is introduced to control Fast-Start checkpointing. The number of buffers that DBWR should process during recovery is provided as the parameter value. FAST_START_IO_TARGET allows a high degree of control over total recovery time, since the recovery time is directly related to the number of I/O operations required. Setting FAST_START_IO_TARGET to smaller values enhances recovery time, but there is an implicit tradeoff of higher overhead imposed during normal processing.

Fast-Start On-Demand Rollback

Fast-Start on-demand rollback or non-blocking rollback defers the rollback phase during recovery. It allows aborted transactions to be recovered on demand. In earlier Oracle versions, users were blocked until the entire aborted transaction was resolved. As a result, it was not possible to access any objects that were involved in these transactions until all uncommitted changes were rolled back completely. This resulted in frustration in the case of large transactions. With this feature, however, the user-session immediately recovers only the blocks that the new transaction needs, thereby allowing the session to proceed, leaving the rest of the dead transaction to be recovered in the background.

Fast-Start Parallel Rollback

Fast-Start parallel rollback allows transaction recovery to be done in parallel mode. Transaction recovery in earlier versions exploited parallelism in the roll-forward phase; however, the subsequent rollback occurred serially. This tended to impact the availability of the portion of the database involved in the failed transactions. The parallel rollback enhances overall recovery throughput.

SMON initiates Fast-Start parallel rollback only if it is beneficial (that is, if the cost of serial rollback is higher than parallel rollback). SMON makes this decision based on the value of the initialization parameter FAST_START_PARALLEL_ROLLBACK (previously known as PARALLEL_TRANSACTION_RECOVERY). This parameter indicates the number of slaves that SMON will start to enable parallel recovery. Use of this feature can be monitored via the virtual views *v$fast_start_servers* and *v$fast_start_transactions.*

Miscellaneous HA Features

This section covers features that do not fall in the above categories.

Use newer listener failover and load-balancing services

The Net8*i* listener provides sophisticated failover and load-balancing features in environments with multiple (replicated) databases or OPS configurations with multiple instances. The service-names corresponding to the databases/instances are used to configure the failover/load-balancing functionality. Both explicit and automatic load-balancing are possible (Chapters 6 and 7 outline some of these strategies). Here, the multiple database instances corresponding to a single service-name are registered with the listener. A client program explicitly specifies the name of the service it would like to connect to. The listener finds the least burdened instance in the service and the least busy dispatcher in the instance. The listener then routes the client to that specific dispatcher. In cases where a specific instance/database in the service has failed, the listener routes the request to the surviving instance/database.

Be familiar with LogMiner functionality

Prior to Oracle8*i*, an easy-to-use tool for reading and interpretation of the redo logs had been much longed for but never made available by Oracle. Reading the redo logs allows you to know almost everything that's occurring inside your database. LogMiner, available with Oracle8*i*, is a fully relational tool that allows redo logs to be read, analyzed, and interpreted via SQL commands. LogMiner can view any valid redo log file (online or archived) from Oracle8 onward. LogMiner is very useful for detecting and eliminating logical corruption. Additionally, redo can be interpreted, and the original SQL statements can be reconstructed and played back

on an open standby database, allowing a robust custom strategy for implementing standby databases (in fact, certain third-party HA products, such as *Quest Software's SharePlex,* utilize this technique to implement custom replication).

The SQL_REDO column in *v$logmnr_contents* lists the reconstructed SQL statements pertaining to the original operations, and the SQL_UNDO column lists the corresponding SQL statement to undo the operations. Thus, original SQL statements can be undone via SQL_UNDO and played-back via SQL_REDO. If used with caution, this information can save a lot of time and effort involved in figuring out and repairing the damage caused by user-errors and accidents. Other pertinent data in *v$logmnr_contents* can be utilized to detect the point-in-time when logical corruption might have actually begun. (The exact SCN or time can be determined so as to allow the DBA to perform incomplete recovery.) Furthermore, changes can be tracked on a per-segment or per-user basis. Additionally, the information reveals database access patterns, which aid extensively in capacity planning.

The *v$logmnr_parameters* (current parameter settings for LogMiner), *v$logmnr_dictionary* (the dictionary file in use), and *v$logmnr_logs* (the redo-logs being currently analyzed) are additional LogMiner views. LogMiner can be used to read redo-logs while the database is open, mounted, or even unmounted. An optional (but recommended) dictionary file is used to mark the database that created the redo-log being read. Without the dictionary file, reading the contents becomes very cumbersome, since an internal object-id is used to represent every segment occurring in the SQL statement, and hex values are used to indicate column-values. In order to better understand the contents of the redo-logs, create a dictionary file by mounting a database (the same database that generated the redo-logs being analyzed) and then extracting dictionary information into an external file. In an HA environment, you do not ordinarily have the luxury of keeping the production database mounted (for any length of time). However, during planned downtime (when the site is running on a standby database) or in an OPS configuration, you can create the dictionary file.

Application support for using this tool is provided in the form of the following PL/SQL packages:

- DBMS_LOGMNR_D, primarily containing the BUILD procedure to create the LogMiner dictionary file. This procedure queries the dictionary tables of the current database and creates a text-based file containing their contents.
- DBMS_LOGMNR, the package supplying LogMiner with the list of filenames and SCNs required during initialization. After initialization, the server is ready to process SELECT statements against the *v$logmnr_contents* view. It is important to note here that no additional collection overhead is incurred to obtain data for LogMiner.

Be aware of an option to eliminate "fat" OS overhead

Previously code-named Raw Iron, the Oracle8*i* Appliance is Oracle's pre-configured, ready-to-run Oracle8*i* solution typically geared toward small- and medium-sized companies wanting to deploy databases in a seamless manner. The Appliance attempts to cut down on overhead, especially "fat" operating systems, replacing them instead with a thin "micro-kernel." The Appliance is typically a complete Oracle system running on Intel hardware (typically, one to four processors) and a completely scaled down version of a UNIX-based OS, one that is both network and Internet ready, aided by Oracle Enterprise Manager (OEM), management packs, and a robust RAID sub-system for disk-redundancy. The scaled-down OS is a very interesting feature, since it incorporates only the bare-bones functionality that's absolutely necessary to run an Oracle8*i* database (just core services such as process scheduling and memory management). There are no bells and whistles, and so unnecessary overhead is considerably reduced. Oracle is partnering with certain hardware vendors, including Dell, HP, Siemens, and Compaq, to manufacture this system. The scaled-down OS is typically a micro-kernel from Sun.

Oracle states that the system is exceptionally simple to install (taking less than an hour) and is easily manageable (compliant with the original vision of "just plug it in and turn it on"). The manageability comes from the fact that each appliance comes with an integrated OEM Pack. This OEM Pack provides several predefined events and jobs (like the "index rebuild" event and an associated rebuild job). These jobs take certain actions based on the event. For instance, the job for a "disk full" event may send an alert to administrative personnel when adequate space is lacking.

From a recovery standpoint, it is heartening to know that in the event of a complete system failure, the entire system can be recovered by using the Oracle8*i* Appliance CD-ROM and local or remote backups. The data-files, redo-logs, and control-files reside on a RAID sub-system, which means they are subject to the advantages and disadvantages of the particular RAID sub-system deployed. Another interesting feature being promoted about this architecture is *adaptive configuration.* What this means is that the Appliance will automatically reconfigure itself when additional hardware is added as the number of users on the system grow. For instance, if additional CPUs or RAM chips are added to the system, the appliance will automatically set the initialization parameter values to effectively use the new hardware additions.

Overall, this technology is very new and unproven. Most availability issues and solutions discussed in the previous pages for regular SMP, NUMA, cluster-based, and MPP architectures would also apply here. However, realistically, strategies for

continuous availability, database and client failover, and so on, may have to be custom-designed (and extensively tested) for such a platform.

Summary

The newest release of the Oracle Server, Oracle8*i*, introduces various HA-oriented features. These features help in various scenarios, such as database backup and recovery, space management and other routine maintenance, corruption repair, and miscellaneous troubleshooting. Additionally, it provides enhanced disaster-recovery schemes, such as automated standby databases, faster replication, and less I/O-intensive OPS configurations. This chapter listed some of these HA-oriented features. With this tour of the newest, fastest, and best version (so far) of the Oracle Server, we conclude our journey into the challenging but exciting world of database availability.

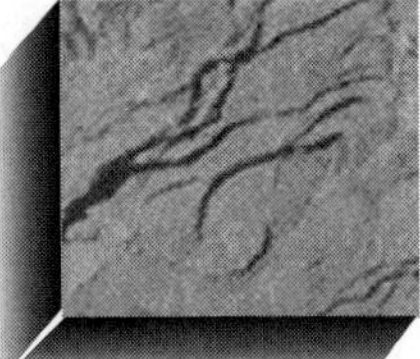

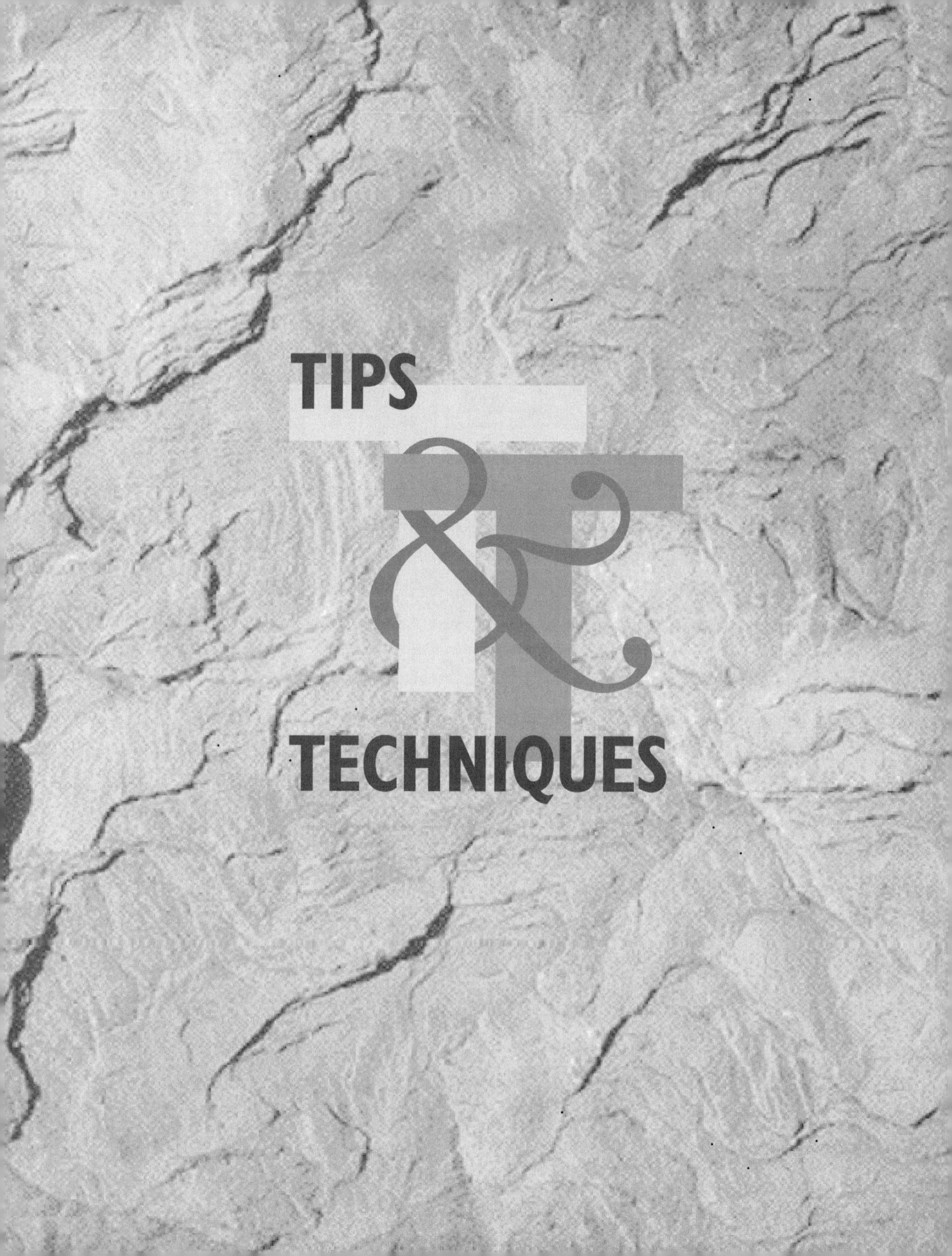
TIPS
&
TECHNIQUES

APPENDIX A

References

In this appendix I list all the publications I have used as references throughout the book. Many of the listed documents are references for more than one chapter (hence the reason for listing them all in a separate References section, rather than listing them at the end of each chapter and repeating some each time or alternatively, missing some in a specific chapter). Note that some of these documents may be internal documents (belonging to their respective companies) and as such, may be available only to personnel working for that company. Nevertheless, many of the documents are available on the Web (for example, on *Oracle MetaLink*, www.orapub.com, and so on). All these publications make for excellent further reading.

- Boar, Bernard H. *The Art of Strategic Planning for Information Technology*. New York: John Wiley & Sons, 1993.
- Gray, Jim, and Andreas Reuter. *Transaction Processing: Concepts and Techniques*. New York: Morgan Kaufmann, 1992.
- Menascé, Daniel A., Virgilio A. F. Almeida, and Larry W. Dowdy. *Capacity Planning and Performance Modeling*. Englewood Cliffs, NJ: Prentice Hall, 1994.
- Jain, Raj. *The Art of Computer Systems Performance Analysis*. New York: John Wiley & Sons, 1991.
- Kern, Harris, and Randy Johnson. *Rightsizing the New Enterprise*. Upper Saddle River, NJ: Prentice Hall, 1997.
- McClain, Gary R. *OLTP Handbook*. New York: McGraw-Hill, 1993.
- Chen, Peter M., Edward K. Lee, Garth A. Gibson, Randy H. Katz, and David A. Patterson. *"RAID: High-Performance, Reliable Secondary Storage." ACM Computing Surveys,* ACM, Inc. Vol. 26, No. 2, June, 1994.
- Loukides, Mike. *System Performance Tuning*. Sebastopol, CA: O'Reilly & Associates, 1990.
- Nemeth, Evi, Garth Snyder, Scott Seebass, and Trent H. Hein. *UNIX System Administration Handbook,* 2nd Edition. Upper Saddle River, NJ: Prentice Hall, 1995.
- Cockcroft, Adrian, and Richard Pettit. *Sun Performance and Tuning,* 2nd Edition. Palo Alto, CA: Sun Microsystems Press, Prentice Hall, 1998.
- Siyan, Karanjit S. *Inside TCP/IP*, 3rd Edition. Indianapolis, IN: New Riders, 1997.

- Alomari, Ahmed. *Oracle8 and UNIX Performance Tuning.* Upper Saddle River, NJ: Prentice Hall, 1999.
- Velpuri, Rama, and Anand Adkoli. *Oracle8 Backup and Recovery Handbook.* Berkeley, CA: Oracle Press/Osborne/McGraw-Hill, 1998.
- Loney, Kevin. *Oracle8 DBA Handbook.* Berkeley, CA: Oracle Press/Osborne/McGraw-Hill, 1998.
- Dodge, Gary, and Tim Gorman. *Oracle8 Data Warehousing.* New York: John Wiley & Sons, 1998.
- Arnoff, Eyal, Kevin Loney, and Noorali Sonawalla. *Oracle8 Advanced Tuning and Administration.* Berkeley, CA: Oracle Press/Osborne/McGraw-Hill, 1998.
- Millsap, Cary. *"Making the Decision to Use UNIX Raw Devices."* Oracle Support document.
- Holmer, Deana, *"Diagnosing Database Hanging Issues."* Oracle Support document.
- *"How to Handle Core Dumps on UNIX."* Oracle Support document.
- *"How to Enable SQL Trace for Another Session Using Oradebug."* Oracle Support document.
- *"ORA-600 Internal Error Code Described."* Oracle Support Bulletin #105787.757.
- Millsap, Cary. *"Configuring Oracle for VLDB."* Oracle Corporation white paper, March, 1996.
- Millsap, Cary. *"Designing Your System to Meet Your Requirements."* Oracle Corporation white paper, January, 1996.
- Millsap, Cary. *"Optimal Flexible Architecture."* Oracle Corporation white paper, September, 1995.
- Shallahamer, Craig. *"Avoiding A Database Reorganization"*, v2.2. Oracle Corporation white paper, November, 1994.
- Shallahamer, Craig. *"Direct Contention Identification Using Oracle's Session Wait Virtual Tables"*, version 4a. Orapub, Inc., January, 1999.
- To, Lawrence. *"List of Database Outages."* Oracle Corporation paper, December, 1995.

- To, Lawrence. *"Outage Prevention, Detection, And Repair."* Oracle Corporation white paper, October, 1995.
- Millsap, Cary. *"Oracle7 Server Space Management, An Oracle Services Advanced Technologies Research Paper",* Oracle Corporation.
- Ozbutun, Cetin. *"Bitmap Indexes, Oracle 7.3 and 8.0."* Oracle Corporation white paper, June, 1997.
- Shrivastava, Rajesh. *"Transparent Application Failover with Oracle8 Parallel Server."* Oracle Corporation white paper, August, 1997.
- To, Lawrence. *"Oracle8i Standby Database."* Oracle Support Services, Oracle Corporation, June, 1999.
- To, Lawrence. *"Graceful Switch Over and Switch Back using Oracle Standby Databases."* Oracle Corporation white paper, 1998.
- *"PL/SQL Tracing Features."* Oracle Support document, Document ID: 210161.
- McCay, Bruce. *"Identifying Corrupt Oracle Files and Blocks."* CMSI Presentation, RMOUG Training Days '99, February, 1999.
- Clarke, Laurence. *"Oracle Fail Safe Solutions for Windows NT Clusters."* Oracle New England Development Center, Oracle Corporation white paper, September, 1998.
- Cheng, Robert. *"Highly Available Forms and Reports Applications with Oracle® Fail Safe 8i."* Oracle Corporation white paper.
- Carwin, Daniel, Edward Griffin, Michael Leone, Anand Thiagarajan. *"Oracle Parallel Server on Windows NT Clusters: Implementing Client Failover."* Oracle Corporation white paper, February, 1998.
- *"Oracle Parallel Server, Solutions for Mission Critical Computing."* Oracle Corporation white paper, February, 1999.
- Jain, Pavana. *"Make the Best of Oracle8 Advanced Replication."* Oracle World Wide Customer Support, Oracle Corporation white paper.
- *"Prevention, Detection, and Repair of Database Corruption."* Oracle Corporation white paper.
- Nobel, Nigel. *"Techniques for Fast Database Reorganization."* Churchill Insurance.

- Koppelaars, Toon. *"Solving Oracle Data Block Corruption, Easy Solutions for a Startling Problem." Oracle Magazine* Technical Support section, January/February, 1996.
- Kyte, Tom. *"Digging-in to Oracle8i—Digging-in to Function-Based Indexes." Internet Developer* magazine, July, 1999.
- *"Database Security in Oracle8, An Oracle Technical White Paper."* Oracle Corporation, February, 1998.
- *"Oracle8 Advanced Replication - Subquery Subsetting."* Oracle Corporation white paper, June, 1997.
- Chan, Vincent. *"Oracle 8i Replication Migration and New Features."* Oracle Corporation white paper. June, 1999.
- Hayes, Tasman. *"Techniques for Achieving High Availability with the Oracle Database."* Oracle South-Asia, Oracle Corporation presentation.
- Pratt, Lyn. "Fault-Tolerant Architecture." Oracle Corporation presentation.
- *"Oracle8i Advanced Replication."* Oracle Corporation white paper, February, 1999.
- *"Oracle8i High Availability Enhancements Features Overview."* Oracle Corporation white paper, 1999.
- *"Oracle8i Online Data Reorganization and Defragmentation Features Overview."* Oracle Corporation white paper, 1999.
- *"Oracle8i Recovery Manager Features Overview."* Oracle Corporation white paper, 1999.
- Gorman, Tim. *"Oracle8 Dumps and Crashes."* IOUG-A '99 Mini-lesson from Oracle Corporation, April, 1999.
- Ensor, Dave. *"Oracle Performance Acceptable to Users? No Problem."* BMC Software, Inc.
- Devraj, Venkat S. *"24x7 : Possible Solutions to Real-world Problems."* Raymond James Consulting white paper. November, 1998.
- Aronoff, Eyal. *"ORACLE Database Block Size—Larger Is Better."* Quest Software white paper, 1999.
- Ganeshan, Ramaswami. *"Defragmenting Large Tablespaces."* Tip of the Week from Oracle Magazine Interactive (www.oramag.com), July 29, 1996.

- *"The Quest for an Efficient Oracle Replication Solution."* Quest Software white paper on SharePlex™ for Oracle. January, 1999.
- Devraj, Venkat S. *"Art of Indexing."* Oracle OpenWorld '98 conference proceedings, November, 1998.
- Khare, Rohit, and Adam Rifkin. *"Weaving a Web of Trust." World Wide Web Journal,* Volume 2, Number 3, Summer 1997.
- *"Requirements and Performance of Enterprise Computer Solutions: SMP, Clustered SMP, and MPP."* Sequent Computer Systems, Inc. white paper, 1999.
- *"SMP Systems or MPP Systems: What's the best choice?"*. Siemens Nixdorf white paper, PartnerChip No2, February, 1996.
- Kirkpatrick, Keith. *"The Move to NUMA." ZDNet's Computer Shopper Magazine.* Ziff Davis, Inc., June, 1997.
- Stern, Hal. *"Caches, Thrashes, and Smashes."* SysAdmin column appearing in *SunWorld Online,* August, 1996.
- SCO Performance Guide; online version at http://www.med2000.com:457/PERFORM/CONTENTS.html. Santa Cruz Operations, Inc., 1995.
- "A RAID Taxonomy." Intelligent Solutions, Inc. white paper from www.intel-sol.com.
- Sun Microsystems white papers from www.sun.com.
- EMC Corporation white papers from www.emc.com.
- VERITAS Software Corporation white papers from www.veritas.com.
- Quantum Corporation white papers from www.quantum.com.
- Quest Software, Inc. white papers from www.quests.com.
- http://www.whatis.com/ (online information service provided by whatis.com Inc.).
- Oracle7 v7.1 documentation set.
- Oracle7 v7.2 documentation set.
- Oracle7 v7.3 documentation set.
- Oracle8 v8.0.5 documentation set.
- Oracle8 v8.1.5 (Oracle8*i*) documentation set.

- Bug/problem descriptions and papers from the Oracle Corporate Support Problem Repository, available at the Oracle Support Web site (http://www.oracle.com/support), accessible via *MetaLink*.
- Other Oracle Corporation and Oracle Support white papers and bulletins. (Authors include Nitin Vengurlekar, Hasan Rizvi, Anjo Kolk, Sameer Patkar, Lawrence To, Basab Maulik, Carol Colrain, Prabhakar Gongloor, Roderick Manalac, J. Diet, Stefan Pommerenk, Shari Yamaguchi, Brian Quigley, Deepak Gupta, Erik Peterson, B. Klots, Rama Velpuri, Satish Mahajan, Cristina Añonuevo, Betty Wu, and various others.)

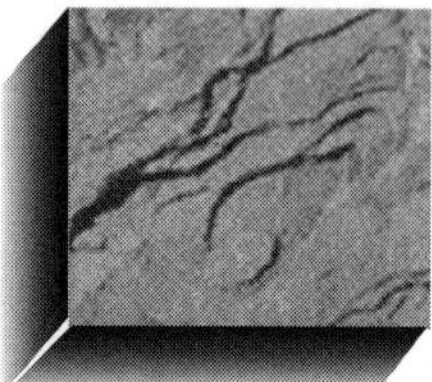

Index

A

B

C

D

E

F

G

H

I

J

K

L

M

P

Q

R

S

T

U

V

W

X

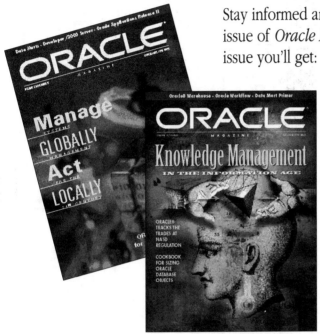